BEHAVIOR SCIENCE BIBLIOGRAPHIES

ETHNOGRAPHIC BIBLIOGRAPHY OF NORTH AMERICA

4th EDITION

Volume 5: Plains and Southwest

GEORGE PETER MURDOCK
and
TIMOTHY J. O'LEARY

with the assistance of

JOHN BEIERLE   ALLISON BUTLER MATTHEWS
SARAH T. BRIDGES   JOHN MUSGRAVE
DONALD HORTON   JOAN STEFFENS
JOHN B. KIRBY, JR.   FREDERICK W. VOGET
            BARBARA A. YANCHEK

HUMAN RELATIONS AREA FILES PRESS
NEW HAVEN
1975

Compilation of this volume has been
financed in part by grant GN35418 from
the National Science Foundation.

CONTENTS

SCHEMATIC TABLE OF CONTENTS
FOR
COMPLETE BIBLIOGRAPHY

Preface to the Fourth Edition

This, the fourth edition of the *Ethnographic Bibliography of North America*, is intended to provide a basic coverage of the published literature on the Native Peoples of North America through the end of the year 1972. This edition differs in a number of ways from the third edition, which was published in 1960. The most obvious change is that the bibliography is now appearing in five volumes. As with every other discipline in the last twenty years, Native American studies has had to cope with an information explosion. Some idea of the magnitude of this explosion can be gained from the fact that while the third edition contained approximately 17,300 bibliographic entries in one volume, the present edition contains close to 40,000 entries in five volumes, most of this increase pertaining to the fourteen-year period 1959-1972, inclusive. Part of the increase, however, also comes from the increased span of coverage of the present edition, which includes a number of subject areas not covered previously.

Another obvious change is in the format of presentation. With one major exception, full bibliographic information has been given for each citation in the bibliography where it has been available. Each citation gives the author's full name, the full title and subtitle, place of publication, publisher, date of publication, etc. If the citation be from a journal, the name of the journal is given in full. This is a major change from previous editions, where such information was compressed as much as possible, using abbreviations for journal names and using short or abbreviated titles wherever possible, all with the idea of saving space so as to be able to include the whole bibliography in one volume. This compression was not necessary in the present edition, since we realized before we started the compilation of citations that there would have to be more than one volume. The major exception noted above is that whereas we have expanded the citations listed in the third edition whenever we could (giving full titles of books, the names of journals in full, etc.) we found it impossible to do a full and thorough job on this expansion, since it would have meant verifying each and every citation in the original. This could not be done with the time and funds allotted to us for the preparation of this edition of the bibliography. As a result, there are some inconsistencies in citation format in the bibliography that follows. It is hoped that for the next edition, all of the pre-

1959 citations will have been verified and full information given for each.

The number of ethnic groups covered by the bibliography has been expanded somewhat, especially in the North Mexican area, in order to have the ethnic groups covered in the bibliography correspond more closely to the groups covered in the forthcoming *Handbook of North American Indians*. Also, we have dropped the general use of the word "tribal" when referring to ethnic groups, since many of the groups named in the bibliography are not "tribes" in the traditional sense.

Another major change from the third edition is that this is a computerized bibliography, based on a variation of the Human Relations Area Files Automated Bibliographic System (HABS), which has been developed over the past ten years (see Koh 1973). This computerization will make the preparation of future editions much less expensive, less time-consuming, and far easier to accomplish. Once the bibliographic information has been correctly put into machine-readable form, this inputting should never have to be done again. In addition, with a change in the programming of the computer, new formats can be used and special bibliographies can be printed without the laborious compilation process that was previously necessary. Several people were involved in the adaptation of the HABS for the purposes of this bibliography. HABS programming development has been by John Dow. Programming and computer operations were accomplished by Richard Hart and Joan Steffens. The computer used for the arrangement and printing of the citations was the IBM 370/158 at the Yale University Computer Center. The actual printing was performed with the use of a special IBM print train (developed with the aid of the American Library Association), which carries most of the pertinent diacritics used in a bibliography of this type.

Since the publication of the third edition of this bibliography, a number of individuals have written to us, offering suggestions, additions, and corrections. Such contributions are essential to an undertaking like this, since one individual or organization can neither hope to comprehend all of the requirements of the anticipated users of the bibliography nor control the diversity of the published materials relevant to the purpose of the bibliography. Therefore, we are very pleased to acknowledge the assistance of Lowell John Bean, David M. Brugge,

Harold C. Conklin, Alan Cooke, Gordon M. Day, Alan Dundes, May Ebihara (and her class), James L. Fidelholtz, Don D. Fowler, Stanley A. Freed, Robert F. Heizer, James H. Howard, Dell Hymes, Ira S. Jacknis, Janet Jordan, Luis S. Kemnitzer, Herbert Landar, William S. Lyon, John Moore, Vernon H. Nelson, Wendell Oswalt, Nancy J. Pollock, Bert Salwen, Claude E. Schaeffer, Samuel L. Stanley, Omer C. Stewart, Willard Walker, Margaret Wheat, and Richard B. Woodbury.

Special notes of thanks must go to two people. William C. Sturtevant has been a constant source of encouragement from the beginning of the project, taking time out from his very strenuous duties (among others of editing the forthcoming *Handbook of North American Indians*) to note new books and sources of information, errors in the previous editions, people to contact, etc. June Helm has been of great help in the preparation of the Northern Athabascan bibliographies (Area 2), sending on new versions of her own ongoing computerized bibliography as they became available. They, and the other scholars noted above, receive our most grateful thanks for their assistance. Naturally, they are in no way responsible for whatever deficiencies may remain in the bibliography, but they are very definitely responsible in part for whatever merit it may have for the user.

Most of the actual compilation of this bibliography was accomplished at various libraries within the Yale University system. Our particular thanks go to Harry P. Harrison and the staff of the Circulation Department at the Sterling Memorial Library at Yale, to Robert E. Balay and the staff of the Reference Department at Sterling Memorial Library, and to the staff of the Yale Anthropology Library for courteous and efficient assistance and many kindnesses throughout the period of research.

The compilation of this bibliography was financed in part by a grant (GN-35418) from the National Science Foundation to Frank W. Moore and Timothy J. O'Leary as co-principal investigators. Moore provided institutional coordination and general supervision of the project. O'Leary was responsible for the overall compilation and supervision of the project and for the final printed bibliography. He was very fortunate to be assisted in the compilation by John Beierle, Sarah T. Bridges, John B. Kirby, Jr., Joan Steffens, and Barbara A. Yanchek, all trained researchers with an interest in Native American studies. The data processing of the citations, i.e. the keypunching, proofreading, and editing, which for this bibliography proved to be a far more intellectually demanding task than had originally been envisioned, was very ably carried out by a team under the supervision of Joan Steffens, consisting of Ella Gibson and Lillian Ljungquist, with the assistance of Mary Elizabeth Johnson and Victoria Alexander. Frank W. Moore, who prepared and drew the maps for the 1960 edition, revised them where necessary for this edition.

Our very special thanks, finally, go to George Peter Murdock, who, while not actively engaged in the preparation of this edition of "his" bibliography, has constantly made his influence felt through the guidelines and the general level of excellence he established in the previous editions. While the current set of volumes may present a considerably altered face to the world, in its essentials it has followed the basic pattern of search, selection, and classification that was so ably established by him forty years ago. We certainly hope that he will look with favor on this edition of the bibliography.

Timothy J. O'Leary
New Haven, June 1975

Koh, Hesung C. HABS: a research tool for social science and area studies. Behavior Science Notes, 8(1973):169-199.

Preface to the Third Edition

[This preface is reprinted unchanged from the third edition (1960) in order to give the reader a brief historical background to the compilation of this bibliography. The reader should note that a number of basic changes have been made in the format of the bibliography, and therefore should not take as a guide to the new edition the statements contained in this Preface. The new format is described in the Introduction beginning on p. xi.   TOL]

Some thirty years ago the author began systematically to assemble bibliographical references on primitive and historical cultures with the object, partly of directing distributional and other studies in the classroom, partly of recommending library purchases, and partly of preparing for a projected study which later materialized as the Cross-Cultural Survey at the Institute of Human Relations.[1] By utilizing odd moments of time between appointments, useless for consistent research, to verify references in the Yale University Library, he was able over a period of years to prepare a classified worldwide ethnographic bibliography of considerable size.

This bibliography proved exceedingly useful, to the author and to others, in directing dissertations, making classroom assignments, surveying the existing literature preparatory to field work, and providing ready access to the relevant sources for topical and regional studies of all kinds. A considerable demand was expressed that at least the portion on aboriginal North America be made generally available by publication. The present work in its several editions represents a response to that demand.

The principle of classification by tribal groups having been adopted as the most serviceable to modern anthropologists, the first task was to determine the groups to be used. As a compromise between the segregation of all tribes bearing traditional names, which would have increased the bulk and cost of the work by necessitating frequent repetition of the same references for adjacent peoples, and a classification into a few large areal groups, which would have reduced the usefulness of the volume, it was decided to adopt as a norm the nationally self-conscious tribes of regions with some measure of political development, e.g., those of the Plains. For regions with less extensive political integration, groups of approximately the same degree of linguistic and cultural homogeneity were formed by arbitrarily uniting a number of tribelets or local groups, usually under the name of one of them. Thus under Snuqualmi were lumped the Salishan Dwamish, Nisqualli, Puyallup, Samamish, Skagit, Snohomish, Snuqualmi, and Squaxon of Puget Sound; under Massachuset, the Algonkian Massachuset, Nauset, Nipmuc, and Wampanoag of southeastern New England; and under Wailaki the Athapaskan Kato, Lassik, Mattole, Nongatl, Sinkyone, and Wailaki of Northwestern California. In this way, all of North America as far south as Tehuantepec was divided into 277 tribal groups, a manageable number.

The second task was to prepare a map showing the location of these groups. This was done in 1937 with the cooperation of the students in a graduate class in Systematic Ethnography. The map, which is appended to the present volume, shows, with approximate boundaries, the location of the various tribal groups as of the period of their first extensive contacts with Europeans.[2] It is thus not valid for any single period but represents a shifting date-line, which becomes later as one moves from south to north, from east to west, and from coast to interior. Since the locations of many tribes did not remain constant over three centuries, the shifting date-line made necessary a number of compromises in the fixing of boundaries. Careful mapping by a series of predecessors, notably Kroeber on California, Spier on the Plateau, Osgood on the Mackenzie-Yukon, and Sauer on Mexico, proved of invaluable assistance. Probably the least satisfactory area, because of severe early territorial dislocations, is the Midwest, despite aid generously given by the late Truman Michelson. It is gratifying to note the very high degree of correspondence between our map of North America and those prepared independently by Kroeber and by Driver, et al.[3]

In the selection of names for our 277 groups, established usage was followed in most instances. A few adjectival tribal names, e.g., Costanoan and Salinan, were changed to their nominal forms. Diacritical marks were eliminated. Where several well-known tribes were grouped together, the name of the most important or most familiar was usually given to the cluster. The only radical decision was with regard to names like Apache, Paiute, Shoshoni, and Sioux, which are ambiguous because applied, although commonly with qualifying adjectives, to several different tribal groups. Except in the case of the Eskimo, where it seemed impracticable, such names were either eliminated entirely or confined to a single group. In a few instances this has resulted in a certain arbitrariness in naming. Thus the traditional Coast Miwok have been called Olamentke, the Eastern Dakota are termed Santee, the Owens Valley Paiute of Steward have been grouped with their western congeners as Mono, the Western Apache are dubbed Coyotero, and the Western Shoshoni are named Panamint from their best known sub-group.

The preparation of the map prevented subsequent changes in our groupings, even when clearly advisable. Thus the Eyak, discovered by Birket-Smith and de Laguna, have been classed arbitrarily with the Ahtena (II-1) even though they deserve an independent classification.

The map does not divide the tribal groups into culture areas, but this has been done for the presentation of the bibliography. We have distinguished sixteen areas, adding Oregon Seaboard, Peninsula, Basin, Midwest, Eastern Canada, and Gulf to the ten proposed by Wissler.[4] The decision as to allocation has been close in several instances. Thus the Caddo might well have been placed in the Southeast instead of the Plains, the Klamath in the Plateau instead of in California, the Nanticoke in the Southeast rather than in the Northeast, the Sarsi in the Plains on the basis of culture instead of in the Mackenzie-Yukon on the basis of language, and the Seri in the Southwest rather than in the Peninsula. Mexico, an area embracing 24 tribal groups, though shown on the map, has not been included in the bibliography for the sole reason that pressure of other research has prevented the author from bringing this section of North America to a sufficient degree of completeness to justify publication at the present time. The bibliography therefore covers only 253 of the total of 277 tribal groups distinguished.

The work is organized by areas and within each area by tribal groups arranged in alphabetical order. Under the areal headings are included regional studies, geographical and historical sources, travel accounts, and other works presenting little specific original information on individual tribes. Under the tribal headings are included works pertaining directly to the particular group or its sub-groups. The order of arrangement of items under each heading is alphabetical by author's surname and thereunder by title. One exception is to be noted: standard monographs covering large segments of a tribal culture, or, in default thereof, other general works of considerable scope, are placed ahead of the alphabetical list of other sources. An appendix includes references to works on North America in general or on a number of areas; this list is very incomplete since no special effort was made to assemble such items.

To compress a classified bibliography on a whole continent into a single volume requires selectivity and compactness. The former has been achieved by including only such references as seemed likely to prove of value to an anthropologist desirous of discovering what is known about a particular culture. Works in which the tribe is barely mentioned or in which no new information of value is given have in general been excluded. Compactness has been sought through a standard system of abbreviating references. Space is saved by giving initials rather than full names of authors, by omitting unimportant information such as name of publisher, by using abbreviations for journals, series, and collections which recur frequently,[5] by omitting subtitles except when necessary to indicate the content of a work, and by shortening titles themselves wherever words or phrases could be deleted at the end of a title without loss of meaning or obscuring of content.

Pages have been indicated for all periodical items as a rough indication of quantity of material. For books, similarly, the number of volumes or of pages has been noted in most instances, although frequently the particular pages on which the most relevant information occurs are indicated instead. Diacritical marks are omitted except for a few standard accents. Within a serial volume, the number is noted only when it is separately paginated. Where the indicated date of a volume differs from its actual published date, the former is usually given preference. A few inconsistencies have arisen as a result of changes in the procedure of notation over a period of years. In the earlier years of compilation, for instance, the number of pages of single books was not noted, and the date of actual publication was preferred to the indicated date of a volume in a series. Since these inconsistencies did not seem serious, it was decided to ignore them rather than undertake the vast labor of checking back over all previous work.

Approximately seventy per cent of the works cited have been personally examined by the author, and most of the rest have similarly been seen by his assistants in the course of amassing the references. Perhaps five per cent of the references, including all those that are incomplete, have not been personally assessed—most of them works listed in other bibliographical sources but not available in the Yale University Library.

Effort has been exerted to make the tribal bibliographies as complete as possible on all ethnographical subjects. Works on physical anthropology and linguistics, and on archeology where pertinent to a known historical culture, have been listed whenever obtained in the search for ethnographic items, but no extended canvass for them has been made and the coverage of these subjects, particularly in regard to earlier works, remains incomplete. Complete runs of most of the serials listed in the Key to Abbreviations have been searched for pertinent materials. No consistent search, however, has been made of United States Congressional documents and series, and references to these appear in the Bibliography only when they were obtained incidentally in the search for ethnographic materials. The Bibliography is restricted to published materials, and no reference is made to unpublished manuscripts, dissertations, etc. For such materials, researchers should consult the standard reference works.[6]

In general, fugitive materials and items appearing in popular journals have not been included in this Bibliography, except in cases where they seemed to be of some importance. The cut-off date of this third edition was originally intended to be December, 1958, and the Bibliography is reasonably complete as of that date. However, an effort was made to include materials in the major anthropological journals and important books which have appeared since that time. Coverage of materials appearing in 1959 and early 1960 is, therefore, very incomplete.

Mistakes are inevitable in a work such as this. The frequent recopying incidental to compilation introduces typographical errors which escape even careful proofreading. Important references are overlooked, lost, or misjudged and excluded, and errors of allocation occur in areas with which the author is not especially familiar. The present volume pretends to be only so accurate as reasonable care and effort can make it.

Fortunately there is a remedy for errors and omissions. In future editions, corrections can be made, newly published titles added, overlooked sources noted, the Mexican area included, the general North American appendix expanded, and the archeological, linguistic, and physical anthropological literature covered as exhaustively as the ethnographical. To accomplish really satisfactory revisions, the author must have the cooperation of his anthropological colleagues. He, therefore, requests that users of this work call his attention to errors and omissions in areas familiar to them.

The first edition of this Bibliography appeared in 1941 as Volume 1 of the Yale Anthropological Series. The second edition appeared in 1953 as a Behavior Science Bibliography published by the Human Relations Area Files. In terms of number of entries, the first edition had approximately 9,400 and the second edition about 12,700. The present edition contains more than 17,300 entries.

The author received valuable assistance from Donald Horton and Frederick W. Voget in the preparation of the first edition, and from Mrs. Allison Butler Matthews and John Musgrave in the preparation of the second edition. In regard to the present or third edition, he is indebted to many colleagues who have supplied new references, and especially to William C. Sturtevant of the Smithsonsian Institution for generous advice and assistance. Its actual compilation is almost exclusively the product of the devoted effort of Timothy J. O'Leary.

Yale University
June, 1960

George Peter Murdock

NOTES

1   See G.P. Murdock, "The Cross-Cultural Survey," *American Sociological Review*, V (1940), 361-70.

2   Only 276 groups are actually located. The Seminole of the Southeast, having originated subsequent to intensive white contact, do not appear on the map.

3   See A.L. Kroeber, "Cultural and Natural Areas of Native North America," *University of California Publications in American Archaeology and Ethnology*, XXXVIII (1939), Map 1A; H.E. Driver, et al., "Indian Tribes of North America," *Memoirs of the International Journal of American Linguistics*, IX (1953), end map.

4   C. Wissler, *The American Indian* (2d edit., New York, 1931), p. 219.

5   A key to abbreviations, which precedes the text, presents the full titles and places of publication of these serial works.

6   E.G., F.J. Dockstader, "The American Indian in Graduate Studies; A Bibliography of Theses and Dissertations," CMAI, XV (1957), and W.N. Fenton et al., American Indian and White Relations to 1830, Chapel Hill, 1957.

General Introduction

Background

During the thirty-five years since the publication of the first edition in 1941, this bibliography has served as a standard reference work on the Native Peoples of North America — for the anthropologist in particular and, in general, for all those with a factual interest in learning about the ways of life of these peoples. The bibliography has continuously been expanded in its various editions, both in the types of information included and in the number of works cited, until this fourth edition is more than four times the size of the original. This growth reflects both an expansion of interest by writers and scholars in these peoples and an increase in the efficiency of the reference tools that attempt to control the literature on them.

This bibliography is a selected bibliography of published factual books and articles describing the cultures of the Native Peoples of North America. These peoples are considered to be the Eskimo of Greenland, northern Canada, Alaska, and eastern Siberia; and the Indians of Alaska, Canada, the United States, and Mexico north of the northern boundary of Mesoamerica (the area of "high cultures" in Mexico and Central America). It does not include citations to publications on immigrant ethnic groups settled in this area. For this reason, the title of the bibliography might more properly be reworded as an "Ethnographic Bibliography of the Native North Americans." However, as the present work has been known under its title for so many years, it will remain so in this edition.

The primary focus of the bibliography is on the ethnography of these peoples, i.e. on the description of their cultures and ways of life. The bibliography is restricted to citations of published books and articles. It does not contain references to unpublished manuscripts, to maps, or to sound recordings, films, or other audiovisual materials. An attempt will be made later on in this introduction to provide guidance for those who are interested in locating such materials. In spite of the extent of these volumes, this is a *selected* bibliography, more stringently so for the earlier materials. Many more citations were examined than are listed. Most of those dropped from consideration were peripheral to the scope of the bibliography or were ephemeral in nature (e.g. newspaper articles, broadsides, articles published in commercial house organs, etc.). The bibliography is limited to factual accounts; no fiction about these groups is knowingly listed, except in the very rare cases where experts have agreed that the fictionalized account was in accord with ethnographic fact. These few cases should be obvious on examination.

While the primary focus of the bibliography has remained ethnographic, other subject areas have gradually been added through the various editions until the present one tries to include references to published materials on all subjects relevant to the study of the Native Americans, such as history, psychology, and human biology and medicine, among others. Because of this expansion through the years, not all fields of interest are covered equally thoroughly. Basic ethnographic description remains the most completely covered field, followed by linguistics, by archeology, and then by history, relations of the ethnic groups with the federal governments, education, medicine, human geography, urbanism, and Pan-Indianism. It is to be hoped that eventually all of these subject fields will be covered to the same extent. However, the primary focus will still remain ethnographic description.

In the remainder of this introduction, we will discuss more extensively the subject, area, and ethnic group coverage of this edition; the new format of the bibliography; and the search plan used for its compilation. We will also attempt to provide introductory guides to the location of the types of materials not included in the bibliography, such as most government publications, manuscripts, maps, and audiovisual materials, and also to the use of the Educational Resources Information Center (ERIC). The ERIC will be discussed because of its function in making generally available the results of much research on the Native Americans. Finally, we will provide a brief general discussion of some of the tools used in keeping up with the new literature as it is published, and of going beyond this bibliography in search of older published works.

Coverage

The citations in this edition of the bibliography are restricted to published materials on the Native Peoples of North America issued up to and including the year 1972. It is intended that the bibliography be as exhaustive as possible of those materials which are considered to be of professional quality or which contain valuable data not otherwise available. An effort has been made to have the individual ethnic group bibliographies as complete as possible on the traditional ethnographic subjects. Works on physical anthropology, linguistics, and on archeology where pertinent to a known historical culture have been listed wherever possible. In the earlier editions, no special effort was made to include materials on ethnic history, psychology, education, and other fields peripheral to ethnography. However, for the compilation of this edition we have tried to include everything published during the period 1959-1972 that relates to Native American studies. This broadening of coverage helps to account for the radical increase in the size of the bibliography.

An attempt was made to cover publications in all Western languages, including the Slavic languages. Publications in non-Western languages, however, are covered very sparsely. On the whole, the literature in these latter languages is not very large, although there is a growing body of good ethnographic material in Japanese which has been almost completely missed, since there was no easy way for us to get at it. There may also be material of equal value in other literatures whose languages the compilers were not capable of handling. It is to be hoped that such materials can be included in future editions of this bibliography.

The total number of individual ethnic group bibliographies presented is now 269, compared to the 253 in the earlier editions. The new bibliographies are included so as to make the coverage of the total bibliography more congruent to that of the forthcoming *Handbook of North American Indians* (which will be discussed briefly at the end of the introduction). The additional bibliographies are on the Northern Métis, Red River Métis, Sioux (as a whole), Oklahoma Indians, Middle Atlantic States Mestizos, Lumbee, Southeastern Mestizos, Acaxee, Cazcan, Tepehaun, Totorame, Zacatec, Chichimec, Pame, Cora, and Huichol. They are not as full as those for other ethnic groups in the bibliography, for we did not have the time to make a thorough search of the earlier literature. However, we hope that we have included enough citations to make at least some research on these groups possible.

As in previous editions, no consistent search was made of United States, Canadian or Mexican government publications, and such materials are generally included only when they were obtained incidentally in the search for ethnographic materials. An exception was made for the various publications of the Smithsonian Institution, the Bureau of American Ethnology, and the National Museum of Canada. The field of government publication is the great gap in both this and other bibliographies on the Native Americans. From the sampling we have made during the compilation of this edition, we estimate that the size of this bibliography would have been nearly doubled if a search of all relevant government publications could have been made and the citations included. However, these publications are generally poorly controlled bibliographically, and very difficult to locate in toto. For the convenience of the users of this bibliography who may want to do research in this field, a brief introduction to locating such publications is given later in the introduction.

It was hoped that citations to films, sound recordings, and maps relating to the Native Americans could be included in this edition, but because of the unexpectedly large amount of printed literature encountered, this part of the compilation process had to be abandoned—with reluctance. We have, however, included a brief discussion of sources of these types of materials.

Neither fugitive materials nor items appearing in popular journals have been included, except in cases where they seemed to be of some special importance. As far as possible, all materials listed in the bibliography have been seen by the compilers. In the case of those not seen, an effort was made to verify the citations by locating them in at least two independent indexing tools. For books and monographs not seen, the standard source for verification was the *National Union Catalog* in its various cumulations. (Unless noted otherwise, titles given in italics will be discussed later in this Introduction.)

Search Pattern

In compiling this edition of the bibliography, a standard search pattern was evolved and followed. Using as a base the list of periodicals in the 1960 edition, as well as lists found in several other bibliographical tools, such as the *International Bibliography of Social and Cultural Anthropology* and the *Social Sciences and Humanities Index*, a search was made of the holdings of periodicals, as well as books, contained in the Yale University library system. Yale University has one of the largest libraries in North America, and it possesses strong holdings in fields related to Native American studies. Searches were also made of several printed library catalogs for materials not encountered in the search of the Yale University Library. These included, among others, the *Library of Congress Catalog. Books: Subjects* for the period 1958-1973, the Harvard Peabody Museum Library catalog, the research catalog of the American Geographical Society, the catalog of the Edward E. Ayer collection of the Newberry Library in Chicago, and the catalog of the History of the Americas Collection of the New York Public Library. Also checked as sources of citations were continuing bibliographical serials, such as the *Arctic*

Bibliography, the *International Bibliography of Social and Cultural Anthropology*, the *Bibliographie Américaniste*, and the *Index to Literature on the American Indian*. A search for relevant citations in *Research in Education, Dissertation Abstracts International*, and the current indexes discussed later in this introduction was also made. Also used as sources of citations to be verified were bibliographies and references contributed by individual correspondents and bibliographies on specific groups, areas, or subjects that had been published during the period 1959-1972.

The citations found during the search were transferred to individual worksheets, verified where necessary, edited, and transferred to keypunched cards for computer manipulation. Approximately 14,000 worksheets were completed during the course of compilation, of which approximately 11,000 were finally utilized. The remainder were withheld for a number of reasons, the two basic ones being a lack of real relevance to the purpose of the bibliography and the presence of obvious inaccuracies that could not be rectified in time for inclusion. These additional worksheets will remain on file at the Human Relations Area Files for further reference and analysis, should this prove necessary. It is estimated that each of the citations included on the worksheets appears twice on the average as an entry in the bibliography (some of the citations contain material on more than twenty groups). This total, when added to the more than 17,000 entries in the 1960 edition, gives the estimated total of 40,000 entries in the present edition that is referred to in the Preface. (It should be noted that the general bibliographies for each of the fifteen culture areas appear twice, once in the general volume and once in a regional volume.) Thus, the present edition is more than twice the size of the 1960 edition.

Format

General Discussion

When preliminary estimates gave the figure of approximately 2,000 pages for the bibliographic entries alone, without introductory materials, maps, or ethnic group lists, it became obvious that the bibliography would have to appear as a multivolume publication. We decided that, while no specific division is ideal, a five-volume format should meet the requirements of most users. The first volume is a general volume, covering all of North America, while the others divide North America into four regional volumes that are approximately equal in size in terms of the number of bibliographical entries—except for the larger final volume, which includes entries on Areas 9 (Plains), 14 (Gulf), and 15 (Southwest).

The first volume includes the general sections from each of the fifteen major areas in the bibliography, which are equivalent to culture areas (e.g. Southwest, Plateau). Into each of these major area bibliographies we have integrated the individual monographs and articles that we feel give the best cultural descriptions of the individual ethnic groups covered in each of the areas. Also included as Area 16 is the bibliography on General North America, which appeared as an appendix in previous editions. This general bibliography now also includes individual bibliographies on Pan-Indianism, Urban Indians, United States Government Relations with the Native Peoples, Canadian Indians in General, and Canadian Government Relations with the Native Peoples. Since these bibliographies are new to this edition, they are not as complete retrospectively as the other bibliographies in the volume. Also included in the first volume are ethnic group maps for each of the areas and the general ethnic group listing that was used in compiling and classifying the bibliography. We hope that this volume can serve as a general introductory bibliography on North American Native Peoples for users who do not feel the need for the finer classifications and more exhaustive listings found in the regional volumes.

Within each of the other four regional volumes is a set of area bibliographies, including detailed bibliographies on individual ethnic groups within the areas, corresponding to the fifteen culture areas established by Murdock (see the Preface to the Third Edition, p. vii). Each of the regional volumes contains bibliographies on a set of contiguous culture areas, which combine to form a major area of North America. Thus, Volume 2, on the Arctic and Subarctic, contains bibliographies covering Area 1 (Arctic Coast), Area 2 (Mackenzie-Yukon), and Area 11 (Eastern Canada). Together, these cover a block of land which forms the northern part of North America. In similar fashion, Volume 3 covers the Far West and Pacific Coast; Volume 4, the eastern part of the United States; and Volume 5, the Plains and Southwest. (See the frontispiece maps and the schematic table of contents for more detailed contents of each volume.) As a result of this regional grouping of bibliographies, the order in which the bibliographies are presented in this edition does not always correspond to the way in which they were presented in earlier editions, but we do not believe that this arrangement will present any grave problems to the user.

The general culture classification closely follows that devised by Murdock for the previous editions. The major difference is that several ethnic group bibliographies have been added for groups or conglomerates of peoples not previously distinguished (e.g. Sioux, Oklahoma Indians, Southeastern Mestizos). In addition, several ethnic group bibliographies have been added to Area 15 (Southwest), so as to have the southern boundary of that area correspond more closely to that used in the *Handbook of North American Indians*. There is a sketch map for each of the fifteen areas, showing the general boundaries and location of groups for which bibliographies have been compiled. As in the previous editions, these maps show the location of the ethnic groups as of the period of their first extensive contacts with Europeans. Since, in addition to the Seminole listed in previous editions, a number of the groups added for this edition of the bibliography originated subsequent to the period of extensive European contact, they are not included on these maps. These ethnic groups are the Northern Métis, the Red River Métis, the Middle Atlantic States Mestizos, Lumbee, Southeastern Mestizos, and the general inclusive category of Oklahoma Indians. The Sioux and the Chichimec also are not located on the ethnic group maps, since the materials included in their respective bibliographies refer to a number of component groups scattered over a large area. An indication of their location is given in the relevant area introductions, however. These latter introductions provide a brief sketch of each area and some information on each of the peoples covered in the individual ethnic group bibliographies, including location, linguistic affiliations, and important monographs and bibliographies which have appeared since 1972, as they are known to the compilers.

In these regional volumes, each areal set of bibliographies contains first a general bibliography pertaining to the culture area as a whole. This general bibliography includes regional studies, general geographical and historical sources, travel accounts, and other materials not specific to any group within the area. The individual ethnic group bibliographies follow in alphabetical order by name of unit, except where new bibliographies have been added (e.g. Lumbee follows Yuchi in Area 13, Southeast). Within each individual bibliography, the entries are arranged in alphabetical order by author's name (surname first). Where an author has more than one entry following his name, they are arranged alphabetically by the first word in the title (*not* by date). Where there is more than one entry for an author, the author's full name is repeated for each entry. Within each individual ethnic group bibliography, any cited bibliography which pertains to that ethnic group has been placed at the beginning of the listing, separated from the main body of entries. In addition, a limited number of works which have been considered by Murdock and/or O'Leary to give a good, basic description of the culture have been asterisked.

This separation of bibliographies from the main listing and asterisking of basic cultural descriptions represent major changes in format from previous editions. Formerly, works presenting basic cultural descriptions were placed at the head of each bibliography, and bibliographies as such were not given any special treatment. We have made these changes in the present edition because we felt that bibliographies are important resources, which warrant further checking, since they generally represent viewpoints and present materials not always agreed with or used by the present compilers. We admit that this viewpoint may be debatable, but feel that no essential information is lost, since the basic cultural descriptions are tagged by the asterisks.

So far as the basic cultural descriptions (now asterisked) are concerned, we should note that some reviewers of the previous editions misunderstood the reason for the separate placement, usually noting that "important" works have been separated from the remainder of the listing. That was not the point. While "standard monographs covering large segments of a tribal culture" are certainly important, there are numerous other works in the bibliography not so designated that are certainly "important" as well, but perhaps for different reasons. Examples of these would be Casagrande's "Comanche linguistic acculturation," Lounsbury's "A semantic analysis of the Pawnee kinship usage," and Mead's "The changing culture of an Indian tribe."

Each regional volume concludes with an ethnic group synonymy (or ethnonymy), which pertains to the groups covered in that volume. This ethnonymy is derived from the complete ethnonymy used in the compilation of the bibliography, which may be found in Volume 1. No attempt has been made to list the numerous variant and obsolete spellings for the names that are included. For fuller listings, see Hodge (1910) and Swanton (1952). At the end of each volume is a map of North America, showing the total ethnic group coverage of the complete bibliography.

Formats for Individual Citations

There is a considerable difference between the citation formats used for the third edition of the bibliography and those used for the present edition. In the third edition, because it was desirable to keep the bibliography to one volume, compactness of citation form was a great desideratum. Therefore, a standard system of abbreviating references was followed. Authors' given names were represented by initials; the names of book publishers were omitted; abbreviations were used for the titles of journals, series, and collections that recurred frequently; subtitles were generally omitted; and titles themselves were often shortened.

In this edition, both because it was obvious that it would be impossible to issue the bibliography as a single volume and also because of the impracticability of using the old system for a computerized bibliography, it was decided to present the citations with as full bibliographical information as it was possible to obtain. This meant that the citations in the third edition had to be expanded as fully as possible to correspond to the new citation formats. Since resources were not available for rechecking each of the 17,000 entries in the third edition and thereby making their formats completely consistent with that of the new citations, it was decided to make use only of the information already available. As a result, of the three major citation types in the third edition—i.e. book, book chapter, and journal article—the book citation format is almost identical in the third and fourth editions, while the others show varying amounts of expansion. The expansion has been accomplished mainly by replacing the abbreviations used in the third editon with fuller information. For instance, MA is now given as Minnesota Archaeologist, and MAH as Magazine of American History, etc. This simple replacement procedure does not, of course, take into account the name changes that many of the journals have gone through. However, library catalogs generally cross-reference these varying titles to each other, so we feel the user will not be greatly inconvenienced by this transformation.

As an illustration of the types of format changes that were involved for these citations from the third edition, we will give some examples of the same citations in the two formats. The third edition format will be presented first, then the expanded format for the same citation, as used in this edition.

Book.

> Dobbs, A. An Account of the Countries Adjoining to Hudson's Bay. 211 pp. London, 1744.

> Dobbs, A. An account of the countries adjoining to Hudson's Bay. London, 1744. 211 p.

Note how little the book citation format changed. The differences lie in the capitalization of words within the title, the use of the abbreviation 'p.' to indicate pages, and the moving of the page count to the end of the citation.

Journal article.

> Sapir, E. The Na-dene Languages. AA, n.s., XVII, 535-58. 1915.

> Sapir, Edward. The Na-dene languages. American Anthropologist, n.s., 17 (1915): 535-558.

Note how this citation format changes. Where we knew the first name of the author, it is now generally given in full. Only the first word and proper nouns are capitalized in the title. The name of the journal is written out in full; Roman numerals are changed to Arabic; pagination is given in full; and the year is enclosed within parentheses.

Chapter in a book.

> Service, E. R. The Canadian Eskimo. PPC, 64-85. 1958.

> Service, Elman R. The Canadian Eskimo. <u>In</u> his A Profile of Primitive Culture. New York, 1958: 64-85.

Again the author's full name is given. The title of the book from which the chapter is taken is spelled out, with all significant words having initial capitals, and being preceded by the underlined words "<u>In his</u>," which indicate that the author of the book was Service. The inclusive pagination is moved to the end of the citation.

Within the present volumes, two types of citation format are used in addition to the above. The first is restricted to this introduction. We have used this format, which includes the use of italics, because it provides a visual emphasis of the various titles that are being discussed in the introduction. This emphasis is not needed in the main body of new bibliographic citations in the remainder of the volumes, and, therefore, a different format has been used for these citations. While still fairly compact compared to many other citation styles, these latter formats are much expanded over those used in previous editions of the bibliography. In addition, a fourth citation format type, that for an article in the proceedings of a conference or a congress, has been added. These new individual formats are discussed in order below.

Citation format for books.

> Smith, G. Hubert. Like-a-Fishhook Village and Fort Berthold, Garrison Reservoir, North Dakota. Washington, D.C., National Park Service, 1972. 12, 196 p. illus., maps. (U.S., National Park Service, Anthropological Papers, 2)

This is an example of a monograph which was published as part of a series. The author's name comes first, with the surname and given names reveresed to facilitate alphabetizing. Following the name is the title, which ends with a period. After the title comes the imprint, which consists of the place of publication, the publisher, and the date of publication. Following the imprint comes the collation, which in our format includes the pagination (in this case including both introductory pages and the main body of text), the fact that the monograph is illustrated, and that it contains maps. The phrase within parentheses is the series statement. This indicates that the monograph was the second in the series called Anthropological Papers, which are issued by the U.S. National Park Service. Where applicable, the format may also contain information on the edition cited (if not the first edition by the publisher), on multiple authors, on editors, and on translators. Some other examples of this format are:

Moziño, Jose Mariano. Noticias de Nutka; an account of Nootka Sound in 1792. Translated and edited by Iris Higbie Wilson. Seattle, University of Washington Press, 1970. 54, 142 p. (American Ethnological Society, Monograph, 50)

Waddell, Jack O., ed. The American Indian in urban society. Edited by Jack O. Waddell and O. Michael Watson. Boston, Little, Brown, 1971. 14, 414 p.

Harkins, Arthur M., et al., comps. Modern Native Americans: a selective bibliography. Minneapolis, University of Minnesota, Training Center for Community Programs, 1971. 131 p. ERIC ED054890.

Note that in this last citation, three or more individuals were responsible for the compilation of the bibliography. Only the name of the first compiler (or author) is given, however, together with the phrase "et al." The example previous to this one shows the format for a case where there are two authors, editors, or compilers. Note that the name of the second individual is given, along with the first individual, in a statement following the title. The note ERIC ED054890 in the third citation indicates that the bibliography is also available from the Educational Resources Information Center (ERIC). This organization is discussed later in the introduction.

Citation format for journal articles.

Oswalt, Wendell H. The future of the Caribou Eskimo. By Wendell H. Oswalt and James W. VanStone. Anthropologica, n.s., 2 (1960): 154-176.

The author and title sections here are similar to those in the book citation format. However, in this example there are two authors. This is indicated by the statement following the title. Following this author

statement is the journal citation. It includes the name of the journal; the abbreviation "n.s.," which indicates that it is the new series of the journal which is being referred to; the volume number; the year, enclosed within parentheses, to which the volume number refers (1960), followed by a colon; and the inclusive pagination of the article in full (154-176), followed by a period. Another example of the format is:

Amoss, Pamela Thorsen. The persistence of aboriginal beliefs and practices among the Nooksack Coast Salish. Dissertation Abstracts International, 32 (1971/1972): 6174B. UM 72-15, 064.

The latter citation shows two variations. When the date to which a journal volume refers extends over two or more years, that fact is indicated by listing the beginning year and the ending year and placing a slash (/) between the two years. The note UM 72-15,064 indicates that this citation refers to a dissertation which is available from Xerox University Microfilms. These dissertations are discussed later in the introduction.

Citation format for chapters in books.

Stanton, Max E. A remnant Indian community: the Houma of southern Louisiana. In J. Kenneth Morland, ed. The Not So Solid South. Athens, Ga., Southern Anthropological Society, 1971: 82-92.

The author and title sections here are as in previous examples. Following the title is the name of the book in which the chapter may be found. This section begins with the word "In," underlined, followed by the name of the author(s) or editor(s) of the book, and the title of the book. Then comes the imprint information for the book (place of publication, publisher, and date of publication), followed by a colon, and then the inclusive pagination for the article within the book.

Citation format for articles in the proceedings of conferences or congresses.

Spicer, Edward H. Apuntes sobre el tipo de religión de los Yuto-Aztecas centrales. In Congreso Internacional de Americanistas, 35th. 1962, México. Actas y Memorias, 2. México, D. F., 1964: 27-38.

Rose, A. P. Can religion be treated as a branch of anthropology? In Pacific Science Congress of the Pacific Science Association, 9th. 1957, Bangkok. Proceedings, 3, Anthropology and Social Sciences. Bangkok, The Secretariat, Ninth Pacific Science Congress, 1963: 230-232.

Again, the author and the title are handled like those in the book citation format. Following the title here is the underlined word "In." After this comes the name of the conference or congress as it appears on the title page, and the number of the conference, if it occur regularly. Then comes the date on which the conference was held and the place where it was held. This is followed by the particular title of the volume (if it have one) and the volume number if applicable. Then comes the imprint for that volume, including the place of publication (which may be different from the place where the conference was held), the publisher (if different from the conference), and the date of publication. The date of publication is followed by a colon and then by the inclusive pagination of the article, and is closed by a period.

The preceding examples cover the basic types of the citation formats for the items included in this bibliography. There may be minor additions to the format which include further information, but these will not change the basic form. We believe that these formats are clear and easy to use. The major variation from the bibliographic style with which most researchers are probably familiar lies in the duplication of the author's name in a case where there are two authors. This is done in order to accord with the usual procedure librarians follow in making catalog cards. The book citation format closely follows that of the Library of Congress catalog cards, in order that users may quickly locate books in library catalogs.

Government Publications

As mentioned previously, no specific effort was made to locate and cite government publications. While it had been hoped at the beginning of the compilation process that we would be able to make a thorough search for materials of this type, it proved to be impossible to accomplish with the limited amount of time and other resources we had available. We certainly did not realize at the time the magnitude of the task, the general inaccessibility of these materials, and the great amount of specialized knowledge necessary to locate the materials. However, such publications have been included whenever we encountered them during the course of the compilation. We did, of course, include the standard publications and series relevant to the study of Native American peoples, such as the publications of the Bureau of American Ethnology. Because of their importance, however, we do want to indicate to the user of this bibliography at least how to start doing a bibliographic search for government materials on the Native Americans. Accordingly, we have prepared a brief listing and explanation of the major

reference tools for locating these publications. We will discuss the United States federal, state, and municipal publications first, and then the Canadian. We do not know enough about Mexican government publications to be able to include a discussion of them in this introduction.

The major reference tools for locating United States federal government publications are government publications themselves. They cover the period from 1774 to the present. Until the establishment of the Government Printing Office in 1861, government publications were printed by private contractors. There is still no complete listing of these publications. The closest one can get to such a complete listing is Poore's catalog, referenced as follows:

Poore, Benjamin Perley
    1885 *A descriptive catalogue of the government publications of the United States, September 5, 1775—March 4, 1881, compiled by order of Congress.* Washington, D.C., Government Printing Office. (U.S., 48th Congress, 2d Session, Senate, Miscellaneous Document, 67) [reprint edition available]

The citations in Poore are arranged chronologically by Congress (covering the 1st through the 46th Congresses), and within each Congress by title of the publication (not in any discernible order). There is a large index, with publications on Indians being listed on pages 1302-1304, and individual Indian tribes being listed alphabetically on pages 1303-1304. However, there is no listing on the Eskimo. References in the index are to pages in the body of the bibliography, and not to a specific citation. The approximately fifty items on each page must be scanned until the particular item wanted is found.

John G. Ames compiled an index to United States Government publications for the period 1881-1893, thereby taking up the task where Poore left off. The full citation is:

U.S. Superintendent of Documents
    1905 *Comprehensive index to the publications of the United States Government, 1881-1893.* By John G. Ames. Washington, D.C., Government Printing Office. 2v. (U.S., 58th Congress, 2d Session, House of Representatives, Document, 754) [reprint edition available]

This tool is a combined catalog and index. The index is a list of the documents arranged alphabetically by the key word in the title, e.g. "Indian women marrying white men, legislation prescribing citizenship in U.S. as effect of, recommended"/vol. 1, p. 677/. Eskimos are indexed on page 445 of vol. 1. Indians are indexed on pages 665-677 of vol. 1. An alphabetical list of tribal names appears on page 673 of vol. 1.

For most of the period from 1893 to the present, there are two reference tools that can be used. The first is the permanent and complete catalog of all United States government publications, usually known as the *Document Catalog*, from the binder's title on the spine of each volume. The full citation is:

U.S. Superintendent of Documents
1896- *Catalogue of the public documents of*
1945 *Congress and of all departments of the Government of the United States for the period March 4, 1893-[Dec. 31, 1940].* Washington, D.C., Government Printing Office. 25 v. (SuDocs no. GP3.6:) [reprint edition available]

This catalog provides approximately one volume for each Congress, from the 53d Congress to the 76th Congress, inclusive. It is a dictionary catalog, with the same document appearing under the author, the subject, and the title when necessary. The serial numbers for the documents themselves are usually included only with the main (author) entry. Superintendent of Documents classification numbers are sometimes given. An explanation of these numbers is given later in this section. The major key terms to be checked in each volume are Eskimo, Indian, Indians, and the names of individual tribes.

The second tool to be used for this period is the *Monthly Catalog of United States Government Publications*, which covers the period from 1895 to the present. The full citation is:

U.S. Superintendent of Documents
1895- *Monthly catalog of United States Government publications.* Washington, D.C., Government Printing Office. (SuDocs no. GP3.8:)

This catalog is supposed to be a current bibliography of all publications issued by all branches of the federal government. However, in practice it is essentially a list of all publications printed by the Government Printing Office, in addition to whatever materials the various government agencies send to the Superintendent of Documents. Since most agencies are not compelled to send their publications to the Superintendent of Documents (although they are supposed to), there are large gaps in the listing—one of the reasons why working with government publications can be so difficult. Publications are listed in each monthly issue, alphabetically by the name of the issuing office. Since 1945, there has been a monthly index, and there is an annual index. In 1974 a three-part index, consisting of author, title, and subject indexes, was begun. Again the

most used key terms are Eskimo, Indian, Indians, and the names of individual tribes. A major problem for most users of the index is that the indexing has been very erratic, and it is easy to miss key items. There is now available a cumulated subject index to the *Monthly Catalog* for the period 1900-1971. This is a great time-saver in making retrospective searches through the *Catalog*. The full citation is:

U.S. Superintendent of Documents
1974- *Cumulative subject index to the monthly*
1975 *catalog of United States Government publications, 1900-1971.* Compiled by William W. Buchanan and Edna M. Kanely. Washington, D.C., Carrollton Press. 14 v.

By using the above tools, one can get at least an idea of what has been issued on the Native Peoples in United States government publications. However, the hardest part of the search is actually locating copies of the needed publications. Since, so far as we know, there is no complete set of United States government publications existing anywhere, locating a needed publication can be a very long job for the individual researcher and for the government publications librarian who will have to assist him. A recent directory is certain to be of great assistance in this type of search since it lists more than 1,900 libraries in the United States with government document collections. The citation is:

American Library Association. Government Documents Round Table
1974 *Directory of government document collections & librarians.* Washington, D.C., Congressional Information Service.

For general information concerning the publications of the United States federal government, a good guide is:

Schmeckebier, Laurence F., and Roy B. Eastin
1969 *Government publications and their use.* 2d rev. ed. Washington, D.C., Brookings Institution.

While this is a very useful volume, it can only begin to give the researcher an idea of the complexity and volume of federal government publications. As noted above, most researchers in this field will become highly dependent on their local government publications librarian.

We mentioned Superintendent of Documents classification numbers previously. These refer to the codes of the Superintendent of Documents classification system, which is used in the Public Documents Library of the Government Printing Office. It is an unusual classification, in that its basis is the issuing agency for the individual publications, and not the subjects of the individual publications. An individual code consists of a combination of letters and numbers, which, taken together, are unique to a specific document. The letters, which precede the numbers, designate the issuing agency of the document. The numbers indicate the issuing office within the agency, the particular series of documents issued by that office, and the particular number of the document within that series. Thus GS stands for General Services Administration; HE for the Department of Health, Education, and Welfare; LC for Library of Congress; and Y for the publications of Congress. The SuDocs (the usual abbreviation for Superintendent of Documents) number S12.3:78, for example, is the number for *Bureau of American Ethnology Bulletin* 78 (Kroeber's *Handbook of the Indians of California*). The SI stands for Smithsonian Institution, and the 2 stands for the Bureau of American Ethnology within the Smithsonian Institution, or, alternatively, SI2 stands for Bureau of American Ethnology. The .3 indicates the third type of publication issued by the Bureau of American Ethnology, in this case the *Bulletin* (.1 would indicate the series *Annual Reports*). The colon indicates that the document represented by the number (or sometimes by a combination of letters and numbers) following is issued as part of the preceding series. In the SuDocs numbers given in this bibliography, where a reference is given to a complete series of publications, we have not indicated any number or code after the colon. since by including such a number or code we would be specifying a particular volume in the series. Thus, in the citation in the next paragraph, the SuDocs no. LC30.9: refers to the complete series titled *Monthly checklist of state publications*. If we do include a number or code after the colon, we are specifying a single publication; thus, SuDocs no. CR1.10:33 refers to the *American Indian civil rights handbook*, published in 1972. This is the general form that SuDocs numbers follow, with variations. Many collections of government publications are arranged according to this classification, and the numbers must be used when ordering publications from the Government Printing Office.

Moving from the federal level to the state and municipal levels, the situation immediately becomes much more difficult. There is only one general listing of state publications, which is issued by the Library of Congress. The full citation is:

U.S. Library of Congress. Exchange and Gift Division
    1910- *Monthly checklist of state publications.* Washington, D.C., Government Printing Office. (SuDocs no. LC 30.9:)

This listing is limited to publications received by the Library of Congress. While the Library makes every effort to ensure that they receive everything, in the course of events this does not happen. Each monthly checklist is arranged alphabetically by states, territories, and insular possessions, with individual publications listed under each category. Each title is accompanied by the necessary cataloging information. The table of contents of an individual publication is sometimes listed, if it is a composite report. There is no monthly index, but there is an annual index published separately. The key terms again are Eskimo, Indian, Indians of North America, and the names of individual tribes.

This is the only recurrent general listing of state publications, and it is incomplete. There is also one general guide to state publications, which is now quite out of date. It may be of some use in the search of the earlier literature, however. The citation is:

Wilcox, Jerome Kear
    1940 *Manual on the use of state publications.* Chicago, American Library Association.

When we turn to municipal publications, the situation is almost hopeless so far as having any bibliographical control is concerned. There is only one recent general index or listing available, and it is, comparatively, quite limited in scope. The citation is:

Index to current Urban Documents
    1972- Westport, Conn., Greewood Press.

This index tries to make available complete and detailed descriptions of the majority of the known official documents issued annually by the largest cities and counties in the United States and Canada. In the 1974 volume, the publications of 173 cities and 26 counties of one million or more inhabitants in the United States (as determined from the 1970 Census), and 23 Canadian cities were surveyed. The two headings to be checked are Indians and Minority Groups. So far, very little has been indexed on the Native Americans.

Aside from the above, there is no general index or listing. Therefore, for each municipality one would have to check with the local library and the city or town hall and go through their holdings. Such a procedure could be very profitable in particular municipalities. Here, the individual researcher is completely on his own so far as this bibliography is concerned. concerned.

When we turn to Canada, we find most of the same problems as with United States government publications. The general bibliographical control of earlier publications is probably not quite as good. The one general guide that discusses publications issued between 1668 and 1935 contains a good index. The citation is:

Higgins, Marion Villiers
    1935 *Canadian government publications; a
         manual for librarians*. Chicago, Ameri-
         can Library Association.

There is one official catalog series, which covers
the period 1928 to the present. The citation is:

Canada. Department of Public Printing and Sta-
         tionery
    1928- *Canadian Government publications:
         catalogue*. Ottawa. (formerly titled:
         *Catalogue of official publications of
         the Parliament and Government of
         Canada*)

The series is bilingual in English and French, and
is now a monthly. It covers parliamentary publications and publications of federal agencies and
departments. Key terms to check in the index are
Eskimo, Esquimau, Indians, Indiens, and the names
of various tribes.

Two other series also cover government publications and offer somewhat better indexing for our
purposes. These are:

*The Canadian Catalogue of Books Published in
         Canada, Books about Canada, as Well as
         Those Written by Canadians*
    1921-Toronto, Department of Education of
    1951 Ontario, Public Libraries Branch.

*Canadiana. Publications of Canadian Interest Re-
         ceived by the National Library of Can-
         ada.*
    1950-Ottawa, Information Canada.

These are also bilingual publications, in French and
English, and do a somewhat better job of indexing
than the *Canadian Government Publications: Catalogue. Canadiana* has two sections which index
federal and provincial publications. Part VII indexes
publications of the government of Canada, and Part
VIII indexes publications of the provincial governments of Canada. However, it indexes only those
publications received by the National Library and
is therefore incomplete.

There are a few catalogs which cover the publications of some of the Canadian provinces. These
are:

Bishop, Olga Bernice
    1957 *Publications of the governments of
         Nova Scotia, Prince Edward Island,
         New Brunswick, 1758-1852*. Ottawa,
         National Library of Canada.

Holmes, Marjorie C.
    1950 *Publications of the government of
         British Columbia, 1871-1947*. Victoria,
         Provincial Library.

MacDonald, Christine
    1952 *Publications of the governments of the
         Northwest Territories, 1876-1905 and
         of the Province of Saskatchewan, 1905-
         1952*. Regina, Legislative Library.

Unfortunately, however, none of these guides is very
helpful for obtaining citations about the Native Peoples of Canada. Beyond these listings, both on the
provincial and on the municipal level, there is very
little to consult, aside from the *Index to Current
Urban Documents*, noted previously.

From the preceding discussion, it can be seen that
a great need in the field of Native American studies
is a comprehensive, well-indexed bibliography and
guide to the government publications of the United
States, Canada, and Mexico. To compile such a guide
and bibliography would take a great deal in time,
money, personnel, and dedication, but the result
would well repay the effort involved. We do not
see any possibility of such a guide's being published
in the near future, however.

Finally, a recent publication provides an extensive
sampling of various types of U.S. federal government
documents relating to the North American Indian,
including Reports of the U.S. Commissioner of Indian
Affairs, congressional debates on Indian affairs, treaties, etc. This should give the researcher a good idea
of the kind of information contained in these various
types of publication. The citation is:

Washburn, Wilcomb E., comp.
    1973 *The American Indian and the United
         States; a documentary history*. New
         York, Random House. 4 v.

Indian Claims

Closely related to the preceding is a group of
publications partly governmental and partly non-
governmental in origin. These relate to the United
States Indian Claims Commission and comprise its
decisions, the reports of expert testimony before it,
and the General Accounting Office reports on its
awards. The Indian Claims Commission hears and
determines claims against the United States on behalf
of any Indian tribe, band, or other identifiable group
of American Indians residing within the United States.
The Commission was established by Act of Congress
of August 13, 1946, and is independent of all other
agencies of the U.S. government. A large number of
claims has been adjudicated by the Commission
since that time. In the course of adjudication, claims
have been brought, the testimony of Indians and
academic experts (e.g. anthropologists, historians,
lawyers) heard, and decisions rendered. Naturally,
since these claims involve American Indian groups,
all of the information contained in these cases is
properly the subject of this bibliography. Unfor-

tunately, until very recently, this information has not been generally available. However, two private companies, both based in New York City, are now in the process of publishing most, if not all, of these data.

Garland Publishing, Inc. has organized reports of expert testimony and findings by tribe into 118 volumes, with the series entitled "American Indian Ethnohistory," being edited by David Agee Horr of Brandeis University. The Clearwater Publishing Company is making available on microfiche the decisions of the Commission and also the reports of expert testimony. Index volumes to each of the series are available in hard copy or on microfiche. The publishers also plan to make available on microfiche the General Accounting Office reports on awards. In additon, individual reports of expert testimony on hard copy (i.e. paper, not microfiche) are available on demand. In general, for information on the availability of all these material, it is a good idea to check the current *Subject Guide to Books in Print* under the heading Indians of North American—Indian Claims, or write the publishers. It might be noted that the total number of pages involved in these cases will probably exceed 150,000 (the equivalent of approximately 500 volumes containing 300 pages each). Having this vast amount of data available should have a great effect on studies of the North American Indian.

ERIC

ERIC (Educational Resources Information Center) is a nationwide, comprehensive information system under the jurisdiction of the Department of Health, Education, and Welfare, which is concerned with the transmittal of the results of research in education and related fields to the government, the public, the education profession, and to commercial and industrial organizations. A network of clearinghouses in different parts of the country under the general supervision of central ERIC in Washington gathers, organizes, indexes, and disseminates the most significant educational research or research-related documents that fall within their specialized subject areas. As part of its function, ERIC publishes the abstract journal *Resources in Education* (formerly *Research in Education*). This journal catalogs, abstracts, and indexes a large number of reports, both published and unpublished, every year. Many of these reports relate directly or indirectly to Native American studies. A very valuable feature of this journal is that nearly all of the items abstracted are available in a reproduced form on microfiche and/or paper copy. For the user, this means that many papers and fugitive documents, which would otherwise be extremely difficult to locate and ac-

quire, are now easily available. In the following bibliography, where it is known that ERIC has made the document available, we have included the ERIC accession number—which is needed for ordering the document—as part of the citation. This accession number appears at the end of the citation as a six-digit number, preceded by the acronym ERIC and the letters ED, e.g. ERIC ED045687. To order an ERIC document, follow the directions given below, which are taken from the May 1975 issue of *Resources in Education*. Since ERIC prices have changed in the past, it is best to check the most recent issue of *Resources in Education* to be certain of the price schedule, but the essentials are listed here. We have tried to be as accurate as possible in transferring the ERIC accession numbers in *Resources in Education* to the citations in this bibliography. However, it is probable that some errors in transcription have crept in during the process. Therefore, it would probably be safest if the user were to check the original abstracts in *Resources in Education* before ordering. The abstracts are listed in accession number order in the journal from 1966 on.

ORDERING ERIC DOCUMENTS

Mail orders to:
ERIC Document Reproduction Service
P.O. Box 190,
Arlington, Virginia 22210

Order by accession number (ED Number)
Specify microfiche (MF) or paper copy (HC)
Use the price schedule below.
Enclose check or money order PAYABLE TO EDRS
Official institution, State, Federal government purchase
 orders accepted.

MICROFICHE (MF)

Number of microfiche	Price
1 to 5	$ .75
6	.90
7	1.05
8	1.20
Each additional microfiche	.15

Postage: $.18 for up to 60 microfiche
 $.08 for each additional 60 fiche

PAPER COPY (HC)

Number of pages	Price
1 to 25	$1.50
26 to 50	1.85
51 to 75	3.15
76 to 100	4.20
Each additional 25 pages	1.20

Postage: $.18 for first 100 pages
$.08 for each additional 100 pages

Note
1. Postage for first class airmail or foreign is extra.
2. Paper copy (HC) will be full page reproductions with heavy paper covers.

Theses and Dissertations

This bibliography classifies and lists published printed materials on Native American studies, but does not attempt to do the same for the many unpublished documents that are available. This is not to say, however, that such materials do not form an important adjunct to Native American studies — in fact, in the case of theses and dissertations, a vitally important one. Fortunately, we have two very useful aids for locating and making available theses and dissertations relating to our subject field. These are the two-volume bibliography compiled by the Dockstaders and the publications of Xerox University Microfilms.

The full citations for the Dockstader volumes are:

Dockstader, Frederick J., comp.
1973 *The American Indian in graduate studies; a bibliography of theses and dissertations.* 2d ed. New York, Museum of the American Indian, Heye Foundation. (Museum of the American Indian, Heye Foundation, Contributions, v. 25, pt. 1)

Dockstader, Frederick J., and Alice W. Dockstader, comps.
1974 *The American Indian in graduate studies; a bibliography of theses and dissertations.* New York, Museum of the American Indian, Heye Foundation. (Museum of the American Indian, Heye Foundation, Contributions, v. 25, pt. 2)

In spite of the title, theses and dissertations on the Eskimos are also included in this bibliography. The two volumes list 7,446 items, covering the period between 1890 and 1970, inclusive. It is well indexed (in part 2) and easy to use, and includes the addresses of the relevant institutions for borrowing purposes. This is the only reference tool that contains a comprehensive listing of master's theses relating to our subject. The listing of dissertations overlaps considerably that in the tools discussed immediately below, but it has the advantages of being specific to our subject and of being available in an easily usable, compact form.

Xerox University Microfilms (XUM) publishes two important aids, which together control the vast number of dissertations issued in the United States and Canada and several other countries as well. These are:

Dissertation Abstracts International
1935- Ann Arbor, Mich., Xerox University Microfilms. (formerly called *Microfilm Abstracts* and *Dissertation Abstracts*)

Comprehensive Dissertation Index, 1861-1972
1973- Ann Arbor, Mich., Xerox University Microfilms. 37 v. (annual cumulations are also issued)

Dissertation Abstracts International is a monthly compilation of abstracts of the doctoral dissertations that have been submitted to XUM by cooperating educational institutions, principally in the United States and Canada. It is, therefore, an incomplete listing, since some institutions do not require that dissertations be sent to XUM, and some institutions make copies of the dissertations available on their own. However, a tremendous number are abstracted and indexed. The journal is issued in two sections: Humanities (A) and Sciences (B), which are paginated separately. Key-word title indexes and author indexes are published in each issue. These monthly indexes are cumulated annually. Each of the sections (A) and (B) is divided into subsections by major academic discipline. Most of the dissertations relevant to Native American studies will be found in the subsections devoted to Anthropology, Education, Geography, and History. However, they are also found scattered through a range of other subsections as disparate as Home Economics and Geology.

A major problem in using *Dissertation Abstracts International* is that what must be used as a subject index is the key-word title index, in which the bibliographic entries are classified and arranged alphabetically by key words contained in the title only. In other words, if a title does not contain the key words Indian, Eskimo, Native American, or the name of a tribal group, the dissertation will not be found under any of these headings in the index. Thus it could be very easy to miss what might be a very important dissertation relating to a particular research subject. The same caution applies to the *Comprehensive Dissertation Index*, which will be discussed below. Because of this problem, the compilers of this edition of the bibliography, in addition to using the various indexes, also checked the abstracts on every page of the most relevant discipline subsections (Anthropology, History, Education, Geography, Geology, Home Economics, Psychology, Social Psychology, Sociology) for the years 1955 to 1972 inclusive in *Dissertation Abstracts International*. Through this procedure, we hope that we have been able to list most of the dissertations relevant to Native American studies. We have been so thorough because we believe that such dissertations contain much of the most important recent work in this field. The citations listed in our bibliography refer to the abstracts in the journal only, and not to the original dissertations. Our citations also include the XUM publication number, which will be found at the end of the citation, e.g. UM 61-23, 609. We have included the publication number, because each dissertation so designated is available from XUM either on microfilm or in Xerographic paper copy. The ordering information for such copies is as follows (information taken from the April 1975 issue of *Dissertation Abstracts International*):

1. Order by publication number and author's name and specify whether a positive microfilm copy or a bound Xerographic paper copy is wanted.

2. Send the order to Xerox University Microfilms, Dissertation Copies, Post Office Box 1764, Ann Arbor, Michigan 48106. The standard charge for any microfilmed dissertation is $5.00; for a Xerographic paper copy, $11.00. Shipping and handling charges and any applicable taxes are additional. Individuals must send checks or money orders with their orders.

While we have made every effort in the compilation of this bibliography to make sure that we have copied the XUM publication numbers correctly, ordinary caution dictates that the abstract itself be rechecked before ordering from XUM.

The *Comprehensive Dissertation Index 1861-1972* covers about 417,000 doctoral dissertations accepted by United States educational institutions and by some foreign universities. It is based both on entries from *Dissertation Abstracts International* and on local school handlists. The indexing system is similar to that in *Dissertation Abstracts International* and has the same inherent problem of the title key-word index. Under each key word, the titles are listed first by the date of the dissertation, with the most recent first, followed alphabetically by the name of the school, and then by the name of the author. This is the most comprehensive listing of dissertations available and is quite useful for that reason. The *Index* is supplemented by annual cumulations.

Manuscripts and Archives

Research with manuscripts and archives is a very special and complicated field, which is outside the scope of this bibliography. However, there is a great fund of information available in these resources, which can be very useful in some specialized studies. Since these types of materials cannot be discussed adequately in the space available here, we will simply list first a general work discussing research in archives, and then a few publications relating to archives and manuscript collections which contain material relevant to Native American studies.

Brooks, Philip Coolidge
    1969 *Research in archives; the use of unpublished primary sources.* Chicago, University of Chicago Press.

This is an introduction for the beginner, which concentrates on research procedures, with emphasis on American archives.

Beers, Henry Putney
    1957 *The French in North America; a bibliographical guide to French archives, reproductions, and research missions.* Baton Rouge, Louisiana State University Press.

    1964 *The French & British in the Old Northwest; a bibliographical guide to archive and manuscript sources.* Detroit, Wayne State University Press.

California. University. Bancroft Library
    1963 *A guide to the manuscript collections.* Edited by Dale L. Morgan and George P. Hammond. Berkeley, Published for the Bancroft Library by the University of California Press. v. 1.

Carnegie Institution, Washington
    1906- *[Guides to manuscript materials for the*
    1943 *history of the United States.]* Washington, D.C., The Institution. 23 v. (Reprinted in 1965. The title is a collective one, with individual titles varying considerably.)

Canada. Public Archives
    1968 *Union list of manuscripts in Canadian repositories.* Ottawa, Public Archives of Canada.

Fenton, William N., et al.
    1957 *American Indian and White relations to 1830: needs and opportunities for study.* Chapel Hill, University of North Carolina Press.

Fliegel, Carl John
    1970 *Index to the records of the Moravian Mission among the Indians of North America.* New Haven, Research Publications.

Freeman, John Frederick
    1966 *A guide to the manuscripts relating to the American Indian in the library of the American Philosophical Society.* Philadelphia, The Society. (American Philosophical Society, Memoir, 65)

National Union Catalog of Manuscript Collections
    1959- Hamden, Conn., Shoe String Press; Washington, D.C., Library of Congress. (SuDocs no. LC9.8:) (Still in progress; lists a very large number of collections, many relevant to Native American studies.)

Newberry Library, Chicago. Edward E. Ayer Collection
    1937 *A check list of manuscripts in the Edward E. Ayer collection.* Compiled by Ruth Lapham Butler. Chicago, The Library.

U.S. National Archives
    1972 *The American Indian. Select catalog of National Archives microfilm publications.* Washington, D.C., National Archives and Records Service. (U.S. National Archives, Publication 72-27) (SuDocs no. GS4. 2: In 2)

    1974 *Guide to the National Archives of the United States.* Washington, D.C., National Archives and Records Service. (SuDocs no. GS4.6/2:N21)

U.S National Historical Publications Commission
    1961 *A guide to archives and manuscripts in the United States.* Philip M. Hamer, ed. New Haven, Yale University Press. (A basic listing. Look under Indians, American.)

Yale University. Library. Yale University Collection of Western Americana
    1952 *A catalogue of the manuscripts in the Collection of Western Americana founded by William Robertson Coe, Yale University Library.* Compiled by Mary C. Withington. New Haven, Yale University Press.

In addition to the above, the archives catalog of numbered manuscripts of the National Anthropological Archives at the Smithsonian Institution in Washington is scheduled for publication by G. K. Hall in Boston in 1975. The catalog will cover about a quarter of the total collection and will obviously be of great importance to researchers on the Native Americans.

Nonprint Materials and Maps

As noted previously, nonprint materials and maps have not been included in this bibliography. Because of their growing importance and widespread use, however, we will try to indicate in the following section the principal resources to use in locating relevant materials of these types. A general introductory work on reference tools in the audiovisual field is that by Limbacher, which annotates a number of the basic sources. Also basic is the Brigham Young University bibliography, which lists about 1,400 items, covering all types of nonprint instructional materials. The citations are:

Limbacher, James
    1972 *A reference guide to audiovisual information.* New York, R. R. Bowker.

Brigham Young University, Provo, Utah. Instructional Development Program
    1972 *Bibliography of nonprint instructional materials on the American Indian.* Provo, Institute of Indian Services and Research. ERIC ED070310.

The most complete general tools in this field are the *Library of Congress Catalog* and its continuation, the *National Union Catalog*, cited as:

U.S. Library of Congress
    1947-
    1955 *Library of Congress catalog; a cumulative list of works represented by Library of Congress printed cards. Books: authors.* Washington, D.C., The Library. (SuDocs no. LC30.8:)

National Union Catalog: A Cumulative Author List Representing Library of Congress Printed Cards and Some Titles Reported by Other American Libraries.
    1956- Washington, D.C., The Library. (SuDocs no. LC30.8:)

These two publications list a large number of sound recordings, films, and maps. Beginning in 1953, entries for *Maps and Atlases, Films and Filmstrips,* and *Music and Phonorecords* formed separate parts of the *Library of Congress Catalog.* In the *National Union Catalog, Films and Other Materials for Projection* (formerly *Motion Pictures and Filmstrips*) and *Music and Phonorecords* form separate parts of the catalog, but the section on maps and atlases does not. The *National Union Catalog* is issued monthly, with nine monthly issues and three quarterly cumulations each year, four annual cumulations, and a general cumulation every five years. These latter quinquennial cumulations have been issued for the years 1953-1957, 1958-1962, 1963-1967, and 1968-1972. The sections cited within these cumulations, with their individual subject indexes, form a great bibliographical resource for nonprint materials. The Library of Congress publishes a listing of the subject headings used in its dictionary catalogs and publications. Users of these publications should become familiar with these headings, since they facilitate use of the catalogs and indexes. These headings are discussed more fully on p. xxviii.

Since the above catalogs list only those materials received *and* cataloged by the Library of Congress and the cooperating libraries, the researcher must necessarily use other tools as well, if he wants his search to be as complete as possible. Therefore, we will go on to discuss other reference tools for locating relevant information on sound recordings, films, and maps, in that order.

Sound Recordings

As a brief introduction to the field, the user might want to consult the article by Highwater, which mentions some of the problems involved and the general types of recordings available:

Highwater, Jamake Mamake (J. Marks)
    1973 American Indian music; a brief guide
        to the (recorded) real thing. *Stereo*
        Review, 30, no. 3: 134-135.

Two major reference tools may be used to keep up with sound recordings generally. The first is:

U.S. Library of Congress
    1973- *Music, books on music and sound*
        recordings. Washington, D.C., The
        Library. (SuDocs no. LC30.8/6:)

This is a continuing and cumulative list of works that have been cataloged by the Library of Congress and by several North American libraries selected by the Music Library Association as representing a broad spectrum of music collections. It appears semiannually and is cumulated annually, and in the quinquennial cumulations of the *National Union Catalog* (noted above). Check the subject index under the usual Library of Congress subject headings.

The journal *Ethnomusicology*, published by the Society for Ethnomusicology, includes in each issue a current bibliography and discography of ethnic music, as well as reviews of selected sound recordings. Native American materials are listed in the

bibliography under "Americas-recordings."

The National Information Center for Educational Media (NICEM) publishes irregularly two indexes which indicate the availability of a number of specialized sound recordings. These are the *Index to Educational Audio Tapes* and the *Index to Educational Records*. The subject index in each should be checked under the headings Social Science-Indians of North America, Sociology-Anthropology, and History-U.S. The index entries refer back to the main listings, which include information on availability and contents.

For current information on commercially available phonograph recordings, check the semiannual *Schwann-2 Guide* under the heading Indian, American, in the section headed International Popular & Folk Music. The full citation is:

Schwann-2 Record & Tape Guide
    1965- Boston, W. Schwann.

Three sources taken together list many of the earlier sound recordings relating to the Native Americans. These are:

International Folk Music Council
    1954 *International catalogue of recorded*
        folk music. Edited by Norman Fraser.
        London, Published for UNESCO by
        Oxford University Press. (Archives de
        la Musique Enregistrée, Série C: Musique Ethnographique et Folklorique,
        4)

Kunst, Jaap
    1959, *Ethnomusicology, a study of its na-*
    1960 *ture, its problems, methods and repre-*
        sentative personalities to which is
        added a bibliography. 3d enlarged
        edition, and supplement. The Hague,
        Martinus Nijhoff.

U.S. Library of Congress. Music Division
    1964 *Folk music; a catalog of folk songs,*
        ballads, dances, instrumental pieces,
        and folk tales of United States and
        Latin America on phonograph records.
        Washington, D.C., The Library (SuDocs no. LC12.2:F71/3/964)

While the above tools will help the researcher locate information on particular recordings, he still has to find the recordings themselves. The Archive of Folk Song at the Library of Congress has quite a large collection of recordings of Native American music. In addition, the researcher should turn to the following publication, which lists 124 collections in the United States and Canada, most of which have holdings in the music of the Native Americans:

Society for Ethnomusicology
1971 *Directory of ethnomusicological and sound recording collections in the U.S. and Canada*. Edited by Ann Briegleb. Ann Arbor, Mich., Society for Ethnomusicology. (Society for Ethnomusicology, Special Series, 2)

Films

A basic source of information on films is the Library of Congress publication, *Films and Other Materials for Projection*, whose subject index should be consulted under the usual Library of Congress subject headings. This continuing list of works cataloged by the Library of Congress appears quarterly and is cumulated annually and quinquennially, the latter as part of the *National Union Catalog*. The full citation is:

U.S. Library of Congress
1953- *Films and other materials for projection*. Washington, D.C., The Library. (SuDocs no. LC30.8/4:) formerly titled *Motion Pictures and Filmstrips*)

There is quite a good listing of 251 "Educational films on the American Indian" compiled by George Hunt and Frank Lobo, on pages 718-744 of Owen et al.'s source book. This title list with annotations presents films available in 1965-1966 and is a good place to begin a search. The full citation is:

Owen, Roger C., et al.
1967 *The North American Indians: a source book*. New York, Macmillan.

The National Information Center for Educational Media at the University of Southern California in Pasadena has published since 1969 a series of educational film indexes, which include much material relating to the Native Americans. These NICEM Media Indexes, which are revised at irregular intervals, are:

Index to 16mm. educational films;
Index to 35mm. educational filmstrips;
Index to 8mm. motion cartridges;
Index to educational overhead transparencies;
Index to educational video tapes.

In the subject indexes, the primary heading to investigate is Social Sciences-Indians of North America. Other headings which should be checked are History-U.S. and Sociology-Anthropology.

In addition to the above, the American Anthropological Association publishes a selected catalog of ethnographic films for teaching purposes. The films are listed alphabetically by title. The listings include technical data, rental and purchase fees, a directory of distributors, a brief description of each film, and bibliographical and review data. Relevant films can be located under North America in the geographical index. The citation is:

Heider, Karl G.
1972 *Films for anthropological teaching*. 5th ed. Washington, D.C., American Anthropological Association.

Maps

It is not easy to locate relevant maps for research purposes. Maps are included in the printed catalog of the Library of Congress, but except for a few years in the 1950s, they are not listed separately from books. As a result, trying to locate a map in the various card catalogs issued by the Library is a long and tedious process, and is not recommended. Among the many reference tools available, the following would probably be the more helpful to users of this bibliography.

The American Geographical Society has two publications, a retrospective catalog and a current list, which are good places to check for maps in this field. These are:

American Geographical Society of New York
1938- *Current geographical publications; additions to the research catalogue of the American Geographical Society*. New York, The Society.

1968, *Index to maps in books and period-*
1971 *icals*. Boston, G. K. Hall. 10 v. plus one supplement.

The first lists selected maps received by the Society in a separate section in each issue, and is arranged by region and then by subject. Look under the human (cultural) geography numbers (5-57). The second is a bibliography of maps that have appeared in books or articles, not as separate publications. Check under Eskimos, Ethnography, Ethnology, Indians, and the names of various tribes.

Another general retrospective source is the card catalog of the Map Division of the New York Public Library, which has a very large collection. Check under Eskimos, Ethnology (with the names of tribes), and Indians. The citation is:

New York (City) Public Library. Research Libraries
1971 *Dictionary catalog of the Map Division*. Boston, G. K. Hall. 10 v.

In additon to these American publications, there are two foreign-language current and comprehensive indexes available. These are the *Bibliographie Cartographique Internationale* (French) and *Referativnyi Zhurnal: Geografiia* (Russian), with the former probably being more accessible to American users. The citations are:

Bibliographie Cartographique Internationale
1938- Paris, Armand Colin.

Referativnyi Zhurnal: Geografiia
1954- Moskva, Akademiia Nauk SSSR, Institut Nauchnoi Informatsii.

In addition to the above, two other bibliographies may be useful for special purposes. These are:

Wheat, Carl Irving
1957- *Mapping the Transmississippi West,*
1963 *1540-1861.* San Francisco, Institute of Historical Cartography. 5 v. in 6.

Wheat, James Clements, and Christian F. Brun
1969 *Maps and charts published in America before 1800; a bibliography.* New Haven, Yale University Press.

Beyond these, there are several lists and catalogs of individual collections which can be very helpful in locating individual maps. Especially to be noted are those in the National Archives, which contain basic data on Native American groups over a 200-year period.

California. University. Bancroft Library
1964 *Index to printed maps.* Boston, G. K. Hall.

Newberry Library, Chicago. Edward E. Ayer Collection
1927 *List of manuscript maps in the Edward E. Ayer collection.* Compiled by Clara A. Smith. Chicago, The Library.

U.S. Library of Congress. Map Division
1909- *A list of geographical atlases in the*
1973 *Library of Congress with bibliographical notes.* Compiled by Philip Lee Phillips and Clara Egli LeGear. Washington, D.C., Government Printing Office. 7 v. (in progress) (SuDocs no. LC5.2:G291/)

1950- *United States atlases; a catalog of*
1953 *national, state, county, city, and regional atlases in the Library of Congress and cooperating libraries.* Compiled by Clara Egli LeGear. Washington, D.C., Government Printing Office. 2 v. (SuDocs no. LC5.2:Un351/)

U.S. National Archives
1954 *List of cartographic records of the Bureau of Indian Affairs (Record group 75).* Compiled by Laura E. Kelsay. Washington, D.C., National Archives. (U.S., National Archives, Publications, 55-1; Special Lists, 13) (SuDocs no. GS4.7:13)
1971 *Guide to cartographic records in the National Archives.* Washington, D.C., National Archives and Records Service. (U.S., National Archives, Publications, 71-16) (SuDocs no. GS4.6/2:C24)
1974 *Cartographic records in the National Archives of the United States relating to American Indians.* Washington, D.C., National Archives and Records Service. (SuDocs no. GS4.15:71)

In addition to the publications listed above, the reference tools listed in the section on government publications should also be checked, since the United States and Canadian governments publish many maps.

Going Beyond This Bibliography

While this bibliography is certainly a large one, it is still a *selected* bibliography, and it does not pretend to approach completeness on its subject, particularly for the earlier materials. Therefore, if completeness on a particular group or subject is desired, recourse must be made to a large variety of bibliographical reference tools, those used depending upon whether the researcher intend to make a complete retrospective search for all relevant published materials, or whether he/she be interested only in recently published items. If it be the latter, he/she will use recent issues of recurrent periodical and book indexes. If he/she be interested in a complete search, he/she will use these as well as numerous retrospective bibliographies and catalogs. The general approach to library research and use of these bibliographical tools is examined in a number of works. Reference can be made to those listed immediately below, and to the volumes by Freides and Katz listed later in this section.

Cook, Margaret G.
1963 *The new library key.* 2d ed. New York, H. W. Wilson.

Downs, Robert B.
1966 *How to do library research.* Urbana, University of Illinois Press.

Frantz, Charles
1972 *The student anthropologist's handbook; a guide to research, training, and career.* Cambridge, Mass., Schenkman Publishing Company.

Fried, Morton H.

1972 *The study of anthropology.* New York, Thomas Y. Crowell Company.

Hook, Lucyle, and Mary V. Gaver

1969 *The research paper; gathering library material, organizing and preparing the manuscript.* 4th ed. Englewood Cliffs, N.J., Prentice-Hall.

Current Bibliographical Tools

Because this is a retrospective bibliography through the year 1972, and because a new edition is not scheduled to be compiled for several years, we have decided that a brief commentary on what we have found to be the more useful of the recurrent bibliographical tools for obtaining information about the Native Americans might be of benefit to the researcher. The following list of bibliographies and indexes is only a small part of the large number of reference tools that can be used for this type of search. All of those listed, except for the *Current Index to Journals on Education*, the *Social Sciences Index*, the *National Indian Law Library Catalogue*, and the *Internationale Bibliographie des Zeitschriftenliteratur aus allen Gebieten des Wissens*, were utilized in the preparation of the present bibliography. Perhaps the basic tools for anyone doing a bibliographic search of current materials on the Native Americans would be, in order of currentness: *American Book Publishing Record*; *Public Affairs Information Service Bulletin*; *Anthropological Index to Current Periodicals Received in the Library of the Royal Anthropological Institute; America: History and Life; Library of Congress Catalog. Books: Subjects; Subject Guide to Books in Print; Index to Literature on the American Indian; International Bibliography of Social and Cultural Anthropology;* and the *Bibliographie Américaniste.* Many of the indexes and bibliographies listed below are discussed in the general reference works, particularly those by Freides and Katz, to be mentioned later.

The indexes and bibliographies discussed below are subject indexed or classified in some way. The most commonly used subject headings are based on the system used by the Library of Congress. However, many indexes follow an arrangement based on the Dewey Decimal Classification. *Resources in Education* and *Current Index to Journals in Education* use a special set of descriptors listed in the *Thesaurus of ERIC Descriptors.* Those not using any of the above usually have their own special classifications and headings, with which the researcher should become familiar before using the indexes and bibliographies. The numerous indexes published by the

H. W. Wilson Company and the R. R. Bowker Company use subject headings based primarily on the Library of Congress list and on the Sears list (see below).

We list below the most relevant headings in each of the three major systems for ease in using the reference tools based on these systems.

Library of Congress Subject Headings:

Aleut
Beadwork
Eskimos
Folk-lore, Eskimo
Folk-lore, Indian
Hymns, [plus tribal name]
Indian Ponies
Indian Warfare
Indians
Indians of North America
Indians of North America as Soldiers
Indians, Civilization of
Moccasins
Numeration, Indian
Picture-writing, Indian
Wampum, Indian
Yuit Language

Dewey Decimal Classification:

016.9701 (bibliography on the American Indian)
497 (American aboriginal languages)
722.91 (architecture, ancient American)
784.751 (songs of Amerindians)
789.91364751 (recordings of Amerindian songs)
897 (literatures in American aboriginal languages)
917.1-917.98 (geography of North America)
970.1 (Indians of North America)
970.3 (specific Indian tribes)
970.4 (Indians in specific places in North America)
970.5 (government relations with Indians)

The terms "Amerindian" and "Indian" used here also include Eskimo.

ERIC Descriptors:
American Indian
American Indians
Bureau of Indian Affairs
Canadian Indians
Canadian Eskimos
Eskimo
Eskimos

The citations for the base documents for these headings are:

Dewey, Melvil
    1971 *Decimal classification and relative index*. 18th ed. Lake Placid Club, N.Y., Forest Press, Inc., of Lake Placid Club Education Foundation. 3 v.

Sears, Minnie E.
    1972 *Sears list of subject headings*. 10th ed. Edited by Barbara M. Westby. New York, H. W. Wilson.

U.S. Educational Resources Information Center
    1974 *Thesaurus of ERIC descriptors*. 5th ed. New York, Macmillan Information.

U.S. Library of Congress. Subject Cataloging Division
    1966 *Subject headings used in the dictionary catalogs of the Library of Congress*. 7th ed. Edited by Marguerite V. Quattlebaum. Washington, D.C., The Library. (SuDocs no. LC26.7:7)

The following list of recurrent indexes and bibliographies is divided into several sections, with comments on general reference tools being followed by comments on reference tools in several subject fields. We have indicated in these listings whether the reference tool uses the Library of Congress subject headings (alone or in conjunction with the Sears headings), the Dewey Decimal Classification, or the ERIC Descriptors, by placing the label [LC], [DDC], or [ERIC], respectively, after the title.

Books.

American Book Publishing Record [DDC]
    1961- New York, R. R. Bowker.

Canadiana [DDC]
    1951- Ottawa, Information Canada.

Bibliografía Mexicana
    1967- México, D. F., Biblioteca Nacional de México, Instituto de Investgaciones Bibliográficas.

U.S. Library of Congress [LC]
    1950- *Library of Congress catalog. Books: subjects. A cumulated list of works represented by Library of Congress printed cards*. Washington, D.C., The Library. (SuDocs no. LC30.8/3:)

Cumulative Book Index [LC]
    1898- New York, H. W. Wilson.

Subject Guide to Forthcoming Books
    1967- New York, R. R. Bowker.

These six tools are grouped together because they appear a varying number of times each year. The *American Book Publishing Record* appears monthly, and is cumulated annually and quinquennially in *BPR Cumulative* (not discussed here). It lists books by United States publishers only, but includes some foreign works handled by these publishers. Book titles are classified by subject, with an author and title index. *Canadiana* appears monthly, with annual cumulations. It is concerned with books, pamphlets, and periodicals (but not articles) of Canadian interest. It is a classified list of catalog cards, and has French- and English-language indexes. *Bibliografía Mexicana* appears bimonthly in a classified arrangement with an author-title subject index in the individual issues. It is not cumulated, and refers only to Mexican book publications. Basic headings to check are etnología, costumbres, folclore, and arqueología. The *Library of Congress Catalog. Books: Subjects* appears in three quarterly issues, with annual and quinquennial cumulations. It is international in scope and covers books cataloged during a specified period. Thus it is a retrospective tool as well. The *Cumulative Book Index* is a monthly, with quarterly and annual cumulations. It includes most books published in the English language and is not limited to American publications. The *Subject Guide to Forthcoming Books* appears bimonthly and lists books by American publishers due to appear in the near future. Headings to check are History-U.S. and Sociology, Anthropology, and Archeology-Anthropology.

Subject Guide to Books in Print [LC]
    1957- New York, R. R. Bowker.

Subject Guide to Microforms in Print
    1962/63- Washington, D.C., Microcard Editions.

These two annual guides provide subject approaches for determining the availability for purchase of in-print books and microforms, respectively. The first is based on *Books in Print*, which provides an author-title approach to currently available United States publications. The *Books in Print Supplement*, an annual that was first issued in 1973, provides an author-title-subject approach to the books published since the last annual issue of *Books in Print*. Thus it also supplements the *Subject Guide to Books in Print*. The *Subject Guide to Microforms in Print* is a classified list of available microfilm, microcards, and microfiche books. Relevant items can be located under 440 (America-General) and 970 (Languages and Literatures-Non-European). These guides are restricted to publications available in the United States.

Articles.

    Reader's Guide to Periodical Literature [LC]
        1905- New York, H. W. Wilson.

    Canadian Periodical Index
        1948- Ottawa, Canadian Library Association.

    Essay and General Literature Index [LC]
        1900- New York, H. W. Wilson.

    Internationale Bibliographie des Zeitschriften-
        literatur aus allen Gebieten des Wissens
        1965- Osnabrück, Felix Dietrich.

These four tools are concerned with indexing journal articles, together with essays and book chapters forming parts of collected works. The *Reader's Guide to Periodical Literature* appears semimonthly, with quarterly, annual, and biennial cumulations. It covers about 160 magazines of broad, general, and popular interest published in the United States. The *Canadian Periodical Index* is a monthly subject index to about 90 general magazines published in Canada and is approximately equivalent in aims and type of coverage to the *Reader's Guide to Periodical Literature.* The *Essay and General Literature Index* analyzes essays and articles in volumes of English-language collections of essays and miscellaneous works written by individual authors in all fields of the humanities and the social sciences. Individual chapters are listed by author and subject. Since very few indexes cover the contents of such collections, this is the only relatively easy way to get at this type of material. The *Internationale Bibliographie . . .* is an attempt at a world periodical index, with more than 7,500 periodicals being consulted. Headings to check in the "Schlagwort" index are Eskimo, Eskimo-ische, Indianer, and Indianische.

Books and articles combined.

    Arctic Institute of North America
        1953- *Arctic bibliography.* Washington, D.C.,
            and Montreal. (SuDocs no. D1.22:)

    Bibliographie Américaniste
        1914/19- Paris, Société des Américanistes.

    Vertical File Index [LC]
        1932/34- New York, H. W. Wilson.

    Index to Literature on the American Indian
        1972- San Francisco, Indian Historian Press.
            (Covers the literature from 1970 on.)

These four tools index a combination of materials. The *Arctic Bibliography* appears irregularly and apparently will cease publication in the near future. It covers and abstracts published materials in all lan-

guages relating to the Arctic, and thus contains citations relating to Alaska, Greenland, and most of Canada and eastern Siberia. It is one of the best available bibliographies in terms of completeness, coverage, and indexing. The index should be consulted under Aleuts, Eskimos, and Indians. The *Bibliographie Américaniste* appeared annually as part of the *Journal de la Société des Américanistes* through vol. 53 (1964), and as a separate publication thereafter. It is classified by major subjects (archéologie, ethnologie, etc.) and within the major subjects by major areas (Amérique du Nord, etc.). It is very good for non-English-language materials, but lags greatly in publication. The *Vertical File Index* covers separate publications that are fewer that 49 pages in length and not usually picked up by the book and article indexes. It occasionally includes publications of much greater length. It appears monthly, with annual cumulations. The *Index to Literature on the American Indian* is an annual compilation by a group of Native American scholars which covers both Eskimo and Indian English-language materials. About 150 periodicals are searched and relevant books listed, usually under a variety of subject categories. This index, while not pretending to completeness, is a good place to begin a bibliographic search, because of its indexing and the completeness of its citations. Special features of its 1970 and 1971 volumes were long lists of Native American periodicals, with ordering information. This is a good place to see what was happening in this special field at that time.

Social Sciences.

    Public Affairs Information Service
        1915- *Bulletin.* New York, The Service.

    Social Sciences Index [LC]
        1974- New York, H. W. Wilson.

Both of these items are general social science indexes, with the first probably being the more useful at present. The *Public Affairs Information Service Bulletin*, usually known as *PAIS*, is a weekly index which is cumulated five times a year and annually. It is a selected subject index to more than 1,000 periodicals, as well as to some of the books and U.S. government publications that fall within this very broad field. Limited to works written in the English language, its coverage is international. Headings to check are Eskimos, Indians, and United States-Indian Affairs Bureau. The Service also publishes a bulletin surveying foreign-language materials, but it rarely includes any material on Native Americans in it. The *Social Sciences Index* replaced the *Social Sciences and Humanities Index* in 1974. A quarterly, with annual cumulations, it indexes 263 of the more scholarly English and American journals in the social sciences.

Anthropology.

Royal Anthropological Institute of Great Britain and Ireland. Library

1963- *Anthropological index to current periodicals received in the library of the Royal Anthropological Institute.* London, The Institute.

International Bibliography of Social and Cultural Anthropology

1955- London, Tavistock; Chicago, Aldine.

These tools cover the general anthropological literature. The *Anthropological Index* appears quarterly, has a worldwide coverage, and indexes about 500 periodicals in all fields of anthropology. Each issue classifies the articles listed by major world areas, and then by broad subject categories (archeology, cultural anthropology, etc.). The key section to check is America. The *International Bibliography of Social and Cultural Anthropology* appears annually and covers the anthropological publications issued during the listed year. Each volume appears two to three years after the listed date, which is understandable, considering its extensive coverage of books and articles in all languages. The citations are arranged in a unique classification scheme, with an author index and subject indexes in English and in French. Subject entry is therefore possible, and at times necessary, in three ways, through the classification and through both indexes, since the latter do not always jibe with each other.

History.

America: History and Life

1964- Santa Barbara, Calif., American Bibliographic Center-Clio Press.

Writings on American History

1906- New York, etc.

Revue d'Histoire de l'Amérique Française

1947- *Bibliographie d'histoire de l'Amérique française.* Montréal, Institut d'Histoire de l'Amérique Française.

Each of these tools contains numerous citations on the Native Peoples. *America: History and Life* is a quarterly abstract journal of United States and Canadian publications. Originally indexing only periodical literature, it began in 1974 to appear in three parts, A—article abstracts and citations; B—Index to book reviews; and C—American history index (books, articles, and dissertations). Subject headings to check are Eskimos, Indians, and the names of tribes. A cumulation of annotated entries on the

American Indian for the period 1954-1972, totaling 1,687 items, was issued in 1974. The citation is:

Smith, Dwight L., ed.

1974 *Indians of the United States and Canada; a bibliography.* Santa Barbara, Calif., ABC-Clio.

Writings on American History is an annual that has appeared irregularly and has ceased publication at various times in the past. The time lag between date of coverage and publication is now about fifteen years, but efforts are being made to catch up. Attempting a complete listing, it has a very thorough coverage of American publications. Check under Indians in the index. The *Bibliographie d'Histoire de l'Amérique Française* appears quarterly in the *Revue. . . .* Publications on Native America are covered in Section A. 1 ("Les civilisations amérindiennes et les premières découvertes"). The area coverage is limited to French America, but includes many books, articles, and theses that are hard to locate elsewhere.

Other Subjects.

Ethnomusicology

1953- *Current bibliography and discography.* Ann Arbor, Mich., Society for Ethnomusicology.

Music Index

1949- Detroit, Information Coordinators.

These list publications on Native American music. The *Current Bibliography . . .* appears three times a year in the journal *Ethnomusicology.* See the section labeled "Americas." The *Music Index* is a monthly, cumulated annually, giving subject and author entry to about 180 periodicals on music. Check the headings Eskimo Music; Indian, American; Indian Music, American; and Indian Music, North American.

American Geographical Society of New York

1938- *Current geographical publications.* New York, The Society.

This monthly is a classified listing of books, periodical articles, and maps received in the library of the Society. It is arranged by region, then by the Society's subject classification. Check North America and then the codes 5-57 for human (cultural) geography.

Art Index [LC]

1929- New York, H. W. Wilson.

This is a quarterly, with annual cumulations. It has a dictionary catalog arrangement and lists materials on many subjects related to the field of art, including, among others, archeology, arts and crafts, art history, and fine arts.

Current Index to Journals in Education [ERIC]
    1969- New York, Macmillan Information.

Education Index [LC]
    1929- New York, H. W. Wilson.

Resources in Education [ERIC]
    1966- Washington, D.C., U.S. Office of Education. (SuDocs no. HE18.10:)

The *Current Index to Journals in Education* (known also as *CIJE*) is a monthly index, cumulated annually, of about 700 United States and foreign education journals, which are scanned, briefly abstracted, and indexed by ERIC descriptors. The *Education Index* is a monthly, cumulated annually, subject index to 200 English-language education journals. There is some, but not a great deal of, overlap with *CIJE*. *Resources in Education* (formerly *Research in Education*) is a monthly listing of abstracts of research reports selected by ERIC clearinghouses and is indexed by ERIC descriptors.

Index Medicus
    1960- Washington, D.C., National Library of Medicine. (SuDocs no. HE20.3612:)

Biological Abstracts
    1926- Philadelphia.

Psychological Abstracts
    1927- Washington, D.C., American Psychological Association.

The *Index Medicus* (cumulated annually by the *Cumulated Index Medicus*, which is not discussed here) is a monthly subject index to the world's medical and medical-related periodical literature. It surveys several thousand periodicals in all languages, with over 200,000 articles being indexed each year. It is a basic index for human biology. It has its own list of subject headings, which is printed as part of each January issue. The two headings to check are Eskimos and Indians, North American. *Biological Abstracts* is a semimonthly abstract journal, covering more than 5,000 periodicals, which has a computer-produced index based on all significant words in the titles and the abstracts. It complements *Index Medicus* for human biology and related fields. *Psychological Abstracts* is a monthly abstract journal of periodical articles and books, with semiannual and annual subject indexes. Relevant citations will generally be found under Ethnology in the index, although this has varied in the past.

Business Periodicals Index [LC]
    1958- New York, H. W. Wilson.

Index to Legal Periodicals [LC]
    1909- New York, H. W. Wilson.

National Indian Law Library
    1973/74- *Catalogue.* Boulder, Colo.

Modern Language Association of America
    1921- *MLA international bibliography of books and articles on the modern languages and literatures.* New York, The Association.
Bibliographie Linguistique de l'Année . . .
    1949- Utrecht, Spectrum, for Comité International Permanent de Linguistique.

Business Periodicals Index is a monthly, cumulated annually, subject index to about 120 business periodicals, most of them not covered by other indexes. The *Index to Legal Periodicals* is a quarterly subject index to about 300 English-language legal periodicals, mainly university law reviews and bar association journals. Many articles are listed on Indian claims and general government relations. The *National Indian Law Library Catalogue* is a new annual index to Indian legal materials and resources. It has not yet been seen by the compilers. The *MLA International Bibliography . . .* is an annual bibliography in four volumes, which are bound together in the library edition. Volume 1 covers folklore, and Volume 3, linguistics. Each contains materials relating to the Native Americans in a classified arrangement, but the indexes are difficult to use. The *Bibliographie Linguistique . . .* is an annual bibliography containing a section on American languages [Langues américaines], with an author index. In spite of the publication lag of about three years, it is probably the first choice for information on Native American languages.

Retrospective Bibliographical Tools

Since this bibliography itself is a retrospective bibliography, and since the major tools for making retrospective searches are to be discussed comprehensively in the forthcoming introductory volume of the *Handbook of North American Indians*, the use of these tools will not be further dicussed here. However, we will list some references which will enable the researcher to make a beginning in this direction. In addition, the bibliographies listed in the area and ethnic bibliographies in the present set of volumes should be perused for additional materials, since not all of the citations contained in them have been utilized in the present bibliography.

Freides, Thelma K.
    1973 *Literature and bibliography of the social sciences.* Los Angeles, Melville Publishing Company.

Katz, William A.
    1974 *Introduction to reference work.* 2d ed. New York, McGraw-Hill Book Company. 2 v.

McInnis, Raymond G., and James W. Scott
    1975   *Social science research handbook.*
        New York, Harper and Row, Barnes
        and Noble Books.

Walford, Arthur J., ed.
    1973   *Guide to reference materials.* 3d ed.
        London, Library Association. 3 v.

White, Carl M., and associates
    1973   *Sources of information in the social
        sciences; a guide to the literature.* 2d
        ed. Chicago, American Library Associ-
        ation.

Winchell, Constance M., ed.
    1967   *Guide to reference books.* 8th ed.
        Chicago, American Library Associ-
        ation. (Three supplements compiled by
        Eugene P. Sheehy covering the years
        1965 through 1970 have also been is-
        sued.)

Winchell and Walford are standard general guides to the reference literature, Winchell with an American and Walford with a European slant. The annotations of reference works in Winchell are more descriptive, while those in Walford are more critical. White and associates discuss social science materials in general and include separate chapters on history, geography, economics and business administration, sociology, anthropology, psychology, education, and political science. Each chapter contains two sections, one a bibliographical essay concentrating on the history of the subject, trends, areas of concern, and important works; the other a guide to the literature, annotating various types of information sources, such as abstracts and summaries, current and retrospective bibliographies, directories and biographical information, and sources of current information. The McInnis and Scott handbook is a bibliographical guide for students and others engaged in social science research. It is in two parts, one devoted to studies by discipline (anthropology, sociology, etc.), the other to area studies. Its orientation is toward the immediate assistance of students engaged in research, while that of White and associates is toward the scrutiny of the general social science information system and the evaluation of its major products. These four works together provide a general characterization of the tools available for bibliographical research, from which the researcher wishing to proceed further in his search for materials on the Native Americans may select the particular tools relevant to his needs. The remaining two works, by Katz and Freides, contain assessments of the general reference and social science literature and information from the librarian's point of view on how to proceed in library research. They form quite a useful adjunct to the detailed guides listed previously.

There remains the problem of actually locating copies of the chosen books and articles, once citations to them have been found. Procedures for doing this at the local library level are given in the guides cited at the beginning of this section (e.g. Cook 1963, Hook and Gaver 1969). If the materials not be in the local library, recourse may be made to the interlibrary loan system, the use of which can be arranged for by the librarian. Locations of library holdings of individual books in the United States and Canada are given in the *National Union Catalog,* while the locations of libraries that contain holdings of particular periodicals are given in the *Union List of Serials* and in *New Serial Titles,* cited below. A good aid for locating libraries with substantial holdings in the field is Ash's guide to subject collections, which lists numerous collections under the two headings: Eskimos and Indians of North America.

Ash, Lee, with the assistance of William Miller and
        Alfred Waltermire, Jr.
    1974   *Subject collections; a guide to special
        book collections and subject emphases
        as reported by university, college, pub-
        lic, and special libraries and museums
        in the United States and Canada.* 4th
        ed. New York, R. R. Bowker.

New Serial Titles
    1950- Washington, D.C., Library of Con-
        gress. (8 issues a year, cumulated
        quarterly and annually) (SuDocs no.
        LC1.23/5:)

New Serial Titles 1950-1970
    1972   New York, R. R. Bowker. 5 v. (cum-
        ulates the preceding)

*Union List of Serials in Libraries of the United
        States and Canada*
    1965   3d ed. Edited by Edna Brown Titus.
        New York, H. W. Wilson. 5 v.

Handbook of North American Indians

Mention has been made a number of times in this introduction of the forthcoming *Handbook of North American Indians.* The *Handbook,* which is under the general editorship of William C. Sturtevant, is scheduled to be issued in 20 large volumes by the Smithsonian Institution Press beginning in 1976. This mammoth enterprise will summarize what is known of the anthropology and history of the Native Americans north of Mesoamerica. It should remain the standard reference work in the field for many years. As of this date, there has been only one generally available published description concerning the *Handbook,* its structure and contents. This is:

Sturtevant, William C.
    1971   Smithsonian plans new Native American handbook. *Indian Historian 4, no. 4:* 5-8.

As noted previously, this edition of the bibliography has been enlarged and generally organized to cover as much as possible the same groups as are discussed in the *Handbook*. However, the fit between them is not particularly close at times, because of the different classificatory systems and emphases of the two works. We should point out that the articles in the *Handbook* will complement this bibliography very directly, in that much of the literature is given a critical discussion in these articles. In addition, the articles themselves will provide extensive bibliographies on the ethnic groups and subject fields discussed. Since the individual bibliographies will have been prepared by experts on these groups and fields, it is inevitable that there will be much in them which is not to be found in this bibliography. Of course, the converse will also be the case. Therefore, it will behoove the conscientious investigator to peruse both the present bibliography and those in the *Handbook* articles, in order to be certain that he/she has defined the general bibliographical parameters of the ethnic groups and subjects that he/she is studying.

Timothy J. O'Leary
June 1975

REFERENCES

Hodge, Frederick Webb, ed.
    1910   *Handbook of American Indians north of Mexico. Pt. 2.* Washington, D.C., Government Printing Office. (U.S., Bureau of American Ethnology, Bulletin, 30, pt. 2) (SuDocs no. SI2.3:30/pt.2)

Swanton, John R.
    1952   *The Indian tribes of North America.* Washington, D.C., Government Printing Office. (U.S., Bureau of American Ethnology, Bulletin, 145) (SuDocs no. SI2.3:145)

Abbreviations

A.D.	Anno Domini	n.p.	no place of publication
Alta.	Alberta	n.s.	new series
app.	appendix	N.Y.	New York
Apr.	April	no.	number
assoc.	association	Nov.	November
B.C.	British Columbia; Before Christ	Nr.	Nummer (number, in German)
Bd.	Band (volume in German)	o.s.	old series
ca.	circum, circa	Oct.	October
Calif.	California	Ont.	Ontario
Co.	Company	Or.	Oregon
col.	column(s)	p.	page, pages
Colo.	Colorado	pt.	part
comp.	compiler(s)	rev.	revised
Conn.	Connecticut	S.D.	South Dakota
D.C.	District of Columbia	Sask.	Saskatchewan
D.F.	Distrito Federal	sec.	section
Dec.	December	Sept.	September
dept.	department	SSSR	Soiuz Sovetskikh Sotsialisticheskikh
ed.	editor; edited; edition		Respublik (Union of Soviet Socialist Republics)
enl.	enlarged	SuDocs	Superintendent of Documents (see
ERIC	Educational Resources Information Center (see discussion on pp. xxi-xxii)		discussion on pp. xii-xix)
		suppl.	supplement
et al.	et alii (and others)	t.	tome (volume, in French)
fasc.	fascicle	tr.	translator; translated; translations
Feb.	February	UM	University Microfilms (see discussion
illus.	illustration(s); illustrated		on p. xxii-xxiii)
Jan.	January	U.S.	United States
Jr.	Junior	v.	volume, volumes
jt.	joint	Vt.	Vermont
Ky.	Kentucky	1st	first
l.	leaves (i.e. pages printed on one side only)	2d	second
		3d	third
Mar.	March	4th	fourth
Mass.	Massachusetts		
Me.	Maine		
mimeo.	mimeographed		
ms., mss.	manuscript, manuscripts		
n.d.	no date of publication		
n.F.	neue Folge (new series, in German)		

It should also be noted that underlining has been used in the citations to indicate that letters or numbers are superscript letters or numbers. Thus, "blood group antigen Di^{a}" is given as "blood group antigen Di$\underline{a}$" in the listing.

09 Plains

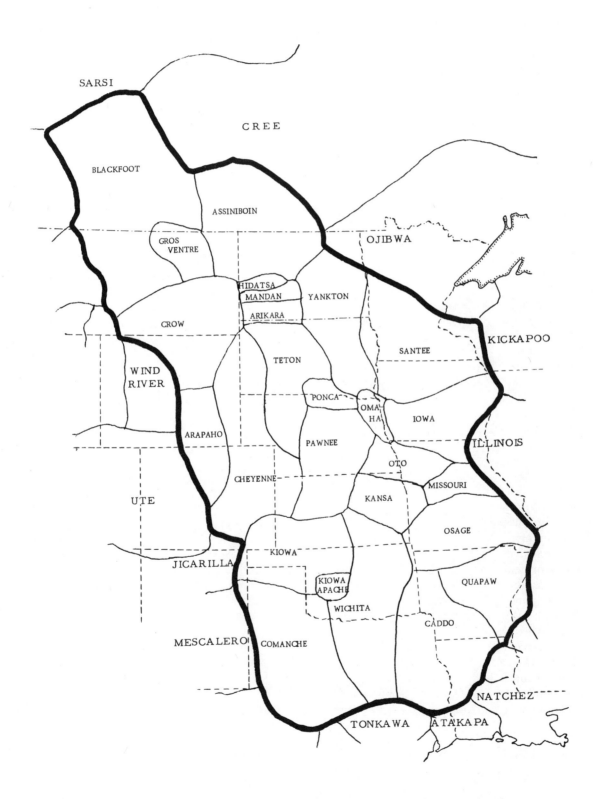

09 Plains

This large area stretches from central Alberta to southern Texas and from the eastern foothills of the Rocky Mountains to the western Mississippi River region. From east to west the Plains can be divided into three major environmental provinces: the tall-grass prairies, the short-grass plains, and the Rocky Mountain foothills. The inhabitants of the prairies were basically sedentary farmers, while the dwellers in the short-grass plains and the foothills were nomadic hunters. Bison meat was the basis of subsistence throughout most of the area, with maize, beans, and squash supplanting it in the east, although bison meat formed an important part of the diet here as well. After 1600 A.D. the horse was available for hunting and warfare, which in the western part of the area provoked a cultural florescence culminating in the nineteenth century in a way of life familiar as a stereotype to most readers. Some of the highlights of this culture were bison hunting on horseback, a nomadic life with definite territories, the skin tipi, the Sun Dance, war bonnets, coup counting, and constant warfare with other groups and with the United States government. This contrasted greatly with the life of the sedentary farmers in the eastern sections, who had permanent villages, horticulture, and a relatively more peaceful life.

Most of these groups had an advanced socio-political organization, but a few, such as the Comanche, Kiowa Apache, and Teton Dakota, never passed the level of band organization. They generally occupied fairly well-defined territories which were defended against enemies. The nomads often assembled for communal bison hunts and religious rituals, and representatives from many different groups would gather for the Sun Dance ceremonial. Most groups were led by chiefs and councils, with military and other societies enforcing regulations during war, travel, and the communal hunts. They generally distinguished between civil and war leaders, the offices being mutually exclusive.

As with the Northeast and the Southeast, there was extensive migration of individual Plains groups during the historic period. For instance, the Comanche moved from the Wyoming area to southwestern Texas and into Mexico; the Arikara had a long tradition of successive movements up the Missouri River; the Teton Dakota probably did not cross the Missouri River until about 1750; and most of the others had similar records of population movements. The Plains was also an area of great dislocation of population with the advent of European settlement. The wars fought by most of the Plains groups with the Federal government are famous in United States history, the last major wars occurring in the 1880s. As a result of these, the Plains groups were resettled on reservations scattered throughout the area.

American Indian Research Project. Oyate iyechinka woglakapi; an oral history collection. Vermillion, University of South Dakota, Institute of Indian Studies, 1970-1973. 4 v.

South Dakota, State Library Commission. South Dakota Indian bibliography. Pierre, 1972. 34p. ERIC ED072915.

09-01. Arapaho. The Arapaho (Inunaina) lived principally in eastern Wyoming and north-central Colorado. The Northern Arapaho live on the Wind River Indian Reservation in Wyoming with the Wind River Shoshone, while the Southern Arapaho live in a Federal trust area in west-central Oklahoma. They speak an Algonquian language and numbered 2,993 in 1970.

09-02. Arikara. The Arikara (Padani, Panimaha, Ree, Ricari, Ricaree, Sanish, Starrahhe) in historic times lived along the Missouri River between the Cheyenne River in northern South Dakota and Fort Berthold in west-central North Dakota. They now live with the Mandan and the Hidatsa on the Fort Berthold Indian Reservation in the latter area. They speak a Caddoan language closely related to Pawnee and numbered 928 in 1970.

09-03. Assiniboin. The Assiniboin (Stoney, Stonies) lived in the basins of the Saskatchewan and Assiniboine Rivers in Alberta and Saskatchewan, and in Montana and North Dakota north of the Milk and Missouri Rivers. They now live principally on the Fort Peck and Fort Belknap Indian Reservations in northeastern Montana and on several reserves in Alberta and Saskatchewan. They speak a Siouan language closely related to Dakota and numbered 3,110 in Canada in 1967 and 2,219 in the United States in 1970, a total of 5,329.

09-04. Blackfoot. The Blackfoot (Siksika), including the Blood (Kainah), Northern Blackfoot, and Piegan (Peigan), lived in Alberta and north-central Montana from the North Saskatchewan River south to the southern affluents of the Missouri River. They now live on the Blackfoot, Blood, and Peigan Reserves in Alberta and on the Blackfeet Indian Reservation in Montana. They speak an Algonquian language and numbered 7,310 in Canada in 1967 and 9,921 in the United States in 1970, a total of 17,231, with 6,216 being on the Blackfeet Indian Reservation in 1972.

09-05. Caddo. The Caddo (Ceni, Caddoquis, Teja), with the Adai, Natchitoches, Eyeish (Aays, Aix, Aliche, Haish), Hasinai (Assinay, Asinai), and Hainai, lived in northwestern Louisiana and northeastern Texas, as well as in southeastern Arkansas and southeastern Oklahoma. They now live in a Federal trust area in west-central Oklahoma. They speak Caddoan languages and numbered 1,207 in 1970, with 800 in the trust area in 1972.

09-06. Cheyenne. The Cheyenne (Dzitsistas), including the Sutaio, lived in the west-central Plains in the border area of Wyoming, South Dakota, Nebraska, eastern Colorado, and northwestern Kansas. They separated into two groups in the first half of the nineteenth century, the Northern Cheyenne and the Southern Cheyenne. The Northern Cheyenne now live on the Northern Cheyenne Indian Reservation in southeastern Montana, while the Southern Cheyenne live in a Federal trust area in western Oklahoma. They speak an Algonquian language and numbered 6,872 in 1970.

09-07. Comanche. The Comanche (Nemene, Nimenim, Padouca, Yampah, Paduca) lived in a number of areas in the western and southwestern Plains, from Wyoming into Mexico. They now live in a Federal trust area in southwestern Oklahoma. They speak a Shoshonean language and numbered 4,250 in 1970, with 3,300 in the trust area in 1972.

09-08. Crow. The Crow (Absaroke, Apsaroke) lived in southeastern Montana and north-central Wyoming in the basin of the Yellowstone River and its branches particularly the Powder River, the Wind River, and the Big Horn River. They now live on the Crow Indian Reservation in Montana in the same area. They speak a Siouan language related to Hidatsa and numbered 3,799 in 1970, with 4,208 on the reservation in 1972.

09-09. Gros Ventre. The Gros Ventre (Atsina, Gros Ventres of the Plains, Fall Indians, Haaninin, Minnetarees of the Plains) lived in north-central Montana and northward to the South Saskatchewan River in Alberta. They now live on the Fort Belknap Indian Reservation in north-central Montana. They speak an Algonquian language closely related to Arapaho and numbered 1,519 in 1970.

09-10. Hidatsa. The Hidatsa (Minitari, Minnetaree, Gros Ventres of the Missouri, Minnetarees of the Prairies) lived in North Dakota along the Missouri River between the Heart River and the Little Missouri River. They now live on the Fort Berthold Indian Reservation in west-central North Dakota with the Arikara and Mandan. They speak a Siouan language closely related to Crow and probably number around 1,100.

09-11. Iowa. The Iowa (Pahodja) lived throughout much of the present state of Iowa and in adjoining parts of Minnesota and Missouri. They now live principally on the Iowa Indian Reservation, which straddles the Kansas-Nebraska state boundary along the Missouri River and in a Federal trust area in central Oklahoma. They speak a Chiwere Siouan language and in 1972, numbered 903 of whom 133 were in Oklahoma and 772 in Kansas.

09-12. Kansa. The Kansa (Kaw, Hutanga) lived in the general area of the Kansas River in northeastern Kansas and in the adjoining part of Missouri. They now live in a Federal trust area in north-central Oklahoma. They speak a Dhegiha Siouan language and numbered 130 in 1972.

09-13. Kiowa. The Kiowa (Tepkinägo) lived in the general area of the Oklahoma Panhandle and adjoining parts of the states of Kansas, Colorado, New Mexico, and Texas. They now live in a Federal trust area in southwestern Oklahoma. They speak a Tanoan language related to Tewa and Tiwa of the Southwest and numbered 4,337 in 1970 (a total which may include the Kiowa Apache) with 3,300 located in the trust area in 1972.

09-14. Kiowa Apache. The Kiowa Apache (Prairie Apache, Semat) lived in the same general area of the Oklahoma Panhandle as the Kiowa, with whom they have long been associated. They now live in a Federal trust area with the Kiowa in southwestern Oklahoma. They speak an Athabascan language closely related to Jicarilla Apache and Lipan Apache and numbered 500 in 1972.

09-15. Mandan. The Mandan (Mantanne, Numakaki) lived on the Missouri River in North Dakota between the Heart River and the Little Missouri River. They now live on the Fort Berthold Indian Reservation in west-central North Dakota with the Arikara and the Hidatsa. They speak a Siouan language and numbered 705 in 1970.

09-16. Missouri. The Missouri (Niutachi) lived in north-central Missouri along the Missouri River, including one probable village in Saline County. Their descendants now live with the Oto in a Federal trust area in north-central Oklahoma. They spoke a Chiwere Siouan language and together with the Oto numbered 980 in 1972.

09-17. Omaha. The Omaha (Maha) lived in northeastern Nebraska along the Missouri River. They now live on the Omaha Indian Reservation in the same area. They speak a Dhegiha Siouan language and numbered 1,367 in 1972.

09-18. Osage. The Osage (Wazhazhe) lived in southern Missouri and adjacent northwestern Arkansas. They now live in a Federal trust area in north-central Oklahoma. They speak a Dhegiha Siouan language and numbered 4,923 in 1970, with 3,368 in the trust area in 1972.

> Bailey, Garrick Alan. Changes in Osage social organization 1673-1960. Eugene, University of Oregon Press, 1973. 6, 122 p. illus., maps. (Oregon, University, Anthropological Papers, 5)

09-19. Oto. The Oto (Chewaere, Hoctatas, Octotatas) lived in eastern Nebraska on the lower course of the Platte River and on the Missouri River. They now live in a Federal trust area in north-central Oklahoma with the Missouri. They speak a Chiwere Siouan language and together with the Missouri numbered 980 in 1972.

09-20. Pawnee. The Pawnee (Padana, Panana, Pani) lived in central Nebraska and central Kansas in the central basin of the Platte River and the basin of the Republican River. They now live in a Federal trust area in north-central Oklahoma. They speak a Caddoan language and numbered 1,928 in 1970, with 1,010 in the trust area in 1972.

09-21. Ponca. The Ponca lived in northern Nebraska and southern South Dakota in the Niobrara River region. Some of them still live in the same region, while the remainder live in a Federal trust area in north-central Oklahoma. They speak a Dhegiha Siouan language and numbered 926 in 1970, with 1,560 in the trust area in 1972.

09-22. Quapaw. The Quapaw (Kwapa, Akansa, Arkansas) lived at or near the mouth of the Arkansas River where it meets the Mississippi River in southeastern Arkansas. They now live in a Federal trust area in northeastern Oklahoma. They speak a Dhegiha Siouan language and numbered 1,285 in 1972.

09-23. Santee. The Santee (Eastern Dakota, Isanyati), including the Mdewakanton, Santee, Sisseton, Wahpekute, and Wahpeton, lived principally in southern Minnesota, northern Iowa, and eastern South Dakota. They now live on a number of reservations, including the Flandreau Indian Reservation and the Sisseton Indian Reservation in South Dakota, the Santee Indian Reservation in Nebraska, the Lower Sioux River Indian Reservation, the Upper Sioux River Indian Reservation, the Prairie Island Indian Reservation and the Prior Lake Indian Reservation in Minnesota, and several Canadian reserves. They speak Siouan languages and probably number about 5,500.

09-24. Teton. The Teton (Western Dakota, Lakota), including the Brule (Sicangu), Hunkpapa (Uncpapa), Kuluwitcatca, Minneconju (Miniconjou), Oglala, Sans Arc, Sihasapa (Blackfoot Sioux), Teton, Two Kettle, and Wazhazha, lived in western South Dakota and western Nebraska. They now live on a number of reservations in the same area, including the Cheyenne River Indian Reservation, the Lower Brule Indian Reservation, the Pine Ridge Indian Reservation, the Rosebud Indian Reservation, and the Standing Rock Indian Reservation, all in South Dakota, and on several reserves in Manitoba and Saskatchewan, Canada. They speak Siouan languages and probably number around 30,000.

09-25. Wichita. The Wichita (Black Pawnee, Panis Noirs, Panis Piques, Picks, Quivira, Speckled Pawnee), with the Kichai (Kitsei, Quichais, Kitsai), Waco, Tawekoni, Tawehash, and Yscani (Ascani, Hyscani, Ixcani), lived in an area running from southeastern Kansas, through central Oklahoma, into north-central Texas. They now live in a Federal trust area in west-central Oklahoma. They speak Caddoan languages and numbered 485 in 1970, with 470 located in the trust area in 1972.

09-26. Yankton. The Yankton (Nakota, Wiciyela), plus the Yanktonnai and Pabaksa (Cutheads), lived in eastern North Dakota and eastern South Dakota. They now live on the Crow Creek Indian Reservation and the Yankton Indian Reservation in South Dakota, and on several reserves in Canada. They speak Siouan languages and probably number about 4,500.

09-27. Siouans. This bibliographical division includes citations to Siouan-speaking groups which are not otherwise identified, to modern Plains Sioux living on reservations which are known to include more than one Siouan group, and to the Siouan-speakers as a whole, including the Eastern Siouans. However, there are very few citations to the latter in this bibliographical division. Since this division refers to more than one ethnic group, it is not distinguished on the maps.

09-28. Oklahoma Indians. This bibliographical division includes citations to the Native Americans living in Oklahoma which are not identified as to specific ethnic group, and to the general culture of the Native Americans living in this state. This bibliographical division is not indicated on the maps.

09-00 Plains Area Bibliography

Beidleman, R. G. A partial, annotated bibliography of Colorado ethnology. Colorado College Studies, 2 (1958): 1-55.

Ewers, J. C. Selected references on the Plains Indians. Smithsonian Anthropological Bibliographies, 1. Washington, D.C., 1960. 36 p.

Hurt, Wesley R. Bibliography of theses done on South Dakota Indians. South Dakota, State University, W. H. Over Museum, Museum News, 22, no. 10 (1961): 2-6.

Petersen, William J. Bibliography on Iowa Indians. Palimpsest, 50 (1969): 271-272.

Pilling, J. C. Bibliography of the Siouan languages. U.S. Bureau of American Ethnology, Bulletin, 5 (1887): 1-87.

Rittenhouse, Jack D. The Santa Fe Trail; a historical bibliography. Albuquerque, University of New Mexico Press, 1971. 271 p. illus., map.

Abel, A. H. Indian reservations in Kansas. Kansas State Historical Society, Collections, 8 (1902): 72-109.

Abel, A. H. The history of events that resulted in Indian consolidation west of the Mississippi River. American Historical Association, Annual Report, 1 (1908): 233-450.

Albers, Patricia. The Plains vision experience: a study of power and privilege. By Patricia Albers and Seymour Parker. Southwestern Journal of Anthropology, 27 (1971): 203-233.

Alcorn, Rowena L. Aged Nez Perce recalls the 1877 tragedy. By Rowena L. and Gordon D. Alcorn. Montana, the Magazine of Western History, 15, no. 4 (1965): 54-67.

Alexander, H. B. The horse in American Indian culture. In D. D. Brand and F. E. Harvey, eds. So Live the Works of Men. Albuquerque, 1939: 65-74.

Alexander, Ralph W., Jr. The hybrid origin of the Arikara Indians of the Great Plains. Dissertation Abstracts International, 32 (1971/1972): 4988B. UM 72-9961.

Allen, L. Siouan and Iroquoian. International Journal of American Linguistics, 6 (1931): 185-193.

American Indian Research Project. Oyate iyechinka woglakapi; an oral history collection. Vermillion, S.D., 1970.

Anderson, Harry H. Cheyennes at the Little Big Horn--a study of statistics. North Dakota History, 27 (1960): 81-93.

Anderson, Harry H. Stand at the Arikaree. Colorado Magazine, 41 (1964): 336-342.

Anderson, Harry H. The Fort Lookout trading post sites--a reexamination. Plains Anthropologist, 6 (1961): 221-229.

Anderson, Irving W. J. B. Charbonneau, son of Sacajawea. Oregon Historical Quarterly, 71 (1970): 247-264.

Anderson, John A. The Sioux of the Rosebud; a history in pictures. Photographs by John A. Anderson. Text by Henry W. Hamilton and Jean Tyree Hamilton. Norman, University of Oklahoma Press, 1971. 32, 320 p. illus., maps.

Anderson, R. Reduction of variants as a measure of cultural integration. In Essays in the Science of Culture in Honor of Leslie A. White. New York, 1960: 50-62.

Andrist, Ralph K. The long death; the last days of the Plains Indians. New York, Macmillan, 1964. 9, 371 p. illus., maps.

Andrist, Ralph K. The long death: the last days of the Plains Indians. New York, Collier Books, 1969. 11, 371 p. illus.

Anonymous. Indians on Federal Reservations in the United States. U.S. Public Health Service, Publication, 615, no. 2 (1958): 1-17; no. 3 (1959): 1-73.

Anonymous. Trading on the Missouri and Upper Mississippi--1831. Museum of the Fur Trade Quarterly, 2, no. 2 (1966): 7-10.

Anonymous. Two Teton Dakota winter count texts. Edited by James H. Howard. North Dakota History, 27 (1960): 67-79.

Antrei, Albert. Father Pierre Jean DeSmet. Montana, the Magazine of Western History, 13, no. 2 (1963): 24-43.

Appleman, Roy E. Lewis and Clark: the route 160 years after. Pacific Northwest Quarterly, 57 (1965): 8-12.

Artichoker, J. Indians of South Dakota. South Dakota, Department of Public

Instruction, Bulletin, 67A. Pierre, 1956.

Aumann, F. R. Dispossession of the tribes. Palimpsest, 50 (1969): 234-239.

Averkieva, ÍUlia P. Indeĭskie plemena severoamerikanskikh stepeĭ i plato. In A. V. Efimov and S. A. Tokarev, eds. Narody Ameriki. Vol. 1. Moskva, Izdatel'stvo Akademiĭa Nauk SSSR, 1959: 243-265.

Averkieva, ÍUlia P. On the role of military democracy in the history of society. In International Congress of Anthropological and Ethnological Sciences, 8th. 1968, Tokyo and Kyoto. Proceedings. Vol. 2. Tokyo, Science Council of Japan, 1969: 194-196.

Averkieva, J. P. and I. A. Zolotorevskaĭa. Indejcy Prerij. Akademiĭa Nauk SSSR, Institut Etnografiĭ imeni N. N. Miklukho-Maklaĭa, Trudy, 25 (1955): 98-110.

Bannon, John F. Missouri, a borderland. Missouri Historical Review, 63 (1968/1969): 227-240.

Barbeau, M. and G. Melvin. The Indian speaks. Toronto, 1943. 117 p.

Barber, B. A socio-cultural interpretation of the peyote cult. American Anthropologist, n.s., 43 (1941): 673-675.

Barlow, Earl J. Indian education; Johnson-O'Malley activities: annual report, 1969-1970. By Earl J. Barlow and Dwight A. Billedeaux. Helena, Montana State Department of Public Instruction, 1970. 84 p. tables. ERIC ED051922.

Barry, David F. David F. Barry: catalog of photographs. Denver, Denver Public Library, 1962. 24 p.

Barry, Louise. Kansas before 1850: a revised annals. Kansas Historical Quarterly, 27 (1961): 67-93, 201-219, 353-382, 497-543; 28 (1962): 25-59, 167-204, 317-369, 497-514; 29 (1963): 41-81, 143-189, 324-359, 429-487; 30 (1964): 62-91, 209-244, 339-412, 492-559; 31 (1965): 138-199, 256-339; 32 (1966): 33-112, 210-282, 426-503; 33 (1967): 13-64, 377-405.

Barry, Louise. The ranch at Cow Creek Crossing (Beach Valley, P.O.). Kansas Historical Quarterly, 38 (1972): 416-444.

Barry, Louise. The ranch at Little Arkansas Crossing. Kansas Historical Quarterly, 38 (1972): 287-294.

Barry, Louise. The ranch at Walnut Creek Crossing. Kansas Historical Quarterly, 37 (1971): 121-147.

Barsness, John. The Sully expedition of 1864. By John Barsness and William Dickinson. Montana, the Magazine of Western History, 16, no. 3 (1966): 23-29.

Bass, William Marvin, III. The variation in physical type of the prehistoric Plains Indians. Dissertation Abstracts, 22 (1961/1962): 967-968. UM 61-3485.

Baydo, Gerald. Overland from Missouri to Washington Territory in 1854. Nebraska History, 52 (1971): 65-87.

Bean, Geraldine. General Alfred Sully and the Northwest Indian Expedition. North Dakota History, 33 (1966): 241-259.

Beckwourth, James P. The life and adventures of James P. Beckwourth. Edited by T. D. Bonner. New York, Arno Press, 1969. 8, 537 p. illus.

Beckwourth, James P. The life and adventures of James P. Beckwourth. As told to Thomas D. Bonner. Lincoln, University of Nebraska Press, 1972. 13, 649 p.

Bell, Gordon L. General Custer in North Dakota. North Dakota History, 31 (1964): 101-113.

Belous, Russell E. Will Soule; Indian photographer at Fort Sill, Oklahoma, 1869-74. By Russell E. Belous and Robert A. Weinstein. Los Angeles, Ward Ritchie Press, 1969. 7, 120 p. illus., map.

Benedict, R. F. The vision in Plains culture. American Anthropologist, n.s., 24 (1922): 1-23.

Berlandier, Luis. The Indians of Texas in 1830. By Jean Louis Berlandier. Translated by Patricia Reading Leclercq. Edited by John C. Ewers. Washington, D.C., Smithsonian Institution Press, 1969. 11, 209 p. illus., maps.

Biasutti, R. Le razzi e i popoli della terra, 2d ed., Vol. 4: 402-424. Torino, 1957.

Blankinship, J. W. Native economic plants of Montana. Montana, State Agricultural Experiment Station, Bulletin, 56 (1905): 1-38.

Boller, H. A. Among the Indians. Philadelphia, 1868. 428 p.

Boller, Henry A. Among the Indians; eight years in the Far West, 1858-1866. Edited by Milo M. Quaife. Chicago, Lakeside Press, 1959. 39, 461 p. illus., map.

Boller, Henry A. Among the Indians: four years on the Upper Missouri, 1858-1862. Edited by Milo M. Quaife. Lincoln, University of Nebraska Press, 1972. 15, 370 p.

Boller, Henry A. Henry A. Boller: Upper Missouri River fur trader. Edited by R. H. Mattison. North Dakota History, 33 (1966): 107-219.

Boller, Henry A. Journal of a trip to, and residence in, the Indian country. Introd. and notes by Ray H. Mattison. North Dakota History, 33 (1966): 261-315.

Bolton, H. E., ed. Spanish exploration in the Southwest, 1542-1706. New York, 1916. 487 p.

Bonnell, George W. Topographical description of Texas. To which is added an account of the Indian tribes. Waco, Texian Press, 1964. 150 p.

Bourke, J. G. MacKenzie's last fight with the Cheyennes. Military Service Institution of the United States, Journal, 11 (1890): 29-49, 198-221.

Braasch, W. F., et al. Survey of medical care among the Upper Midwest Indians. American Medical Association, Journal, 139 (1949): 220-225.

Brackenridge, H. M. Views of Louisiana. Pittsburgh, 1814. 304 p.

Brackenridge, Henry M. Views of Louisiana. Ann Arbor, University Microfilms, 1966. 268 p. (March of America Facsimile Series, 60)

Brackenridge, Henry M. Views of Louisiana. Together with a Journal of a voyage up the Missouri River, in 1811. Chicago, Quadrangle Books, 1962. 302 p.

Bradbury, John. Travels in the interior of America. Ann Arbor, University Microfilms, 1966. 12, 364 p.

Bray, Robert T. The Missouri Indian tribe in archaeology and history. Missouri Historical Review, 55 (1960/1961): 213-225.

Briggs, Jerome Robert. A steppe-oasis association in native North America. Dissertation Abstracts, 29 (1968/1969): 1911B-1912B. UM 68-16,898.

Brooklyn Institute of Arts and Sciences, Museum. Art of the eastern Plains Indians; the Nathan Sturges Jarvis collection. Catalogue by Norman Feder. Brooklyn, N.Y., Brooklyn Museum, 1964. 67 p. illus., map.

Broughton, Paul L. Pipes and smoking customs of the Plains Amerindians. Anthropological Journal of Canada, 10, no. 4 (1972): 11-25.

Brown, Joseph Epes. The spiritual legacy of the American Indian. Wallingford, Pa., Pendle Hill Publications, 1964. 32 p. illus.

Bucca, Salvador. Kitsai phonology and morphophonemics. By Salvador Bucca and Alexander Lesser. International Journal of American Linguistics, 35 (1969): 7-19.

Burgess, Charles E. The De Soto myth in Missouri. Missouri Historical Society, Bulletin, 24 (1967/1968): 303-325.

Burnet, William E. The removal of the Texas Indians and the founding of Fort Cobb. Oklahoma City, 1961. 95 p.

Bushnell, D. I. Ethnographical material from North America in Swiss collections. American Anthropologist, n.s., 10 (1908): 1-15.

Bushnell, D. I. The various uses of buffalo hair by the North American Indians. American Anthropologist, n.s., 11 (1909): 401-425.

Butcher, Thomas. Touring the Southeast Kansas area in 1896: from the diary of Thomas Butcher. Edited by Betty Littleton. Kansas Historical Quarterly, 35 (1969): 143-154.

Butterfly. Butterfly's Mandan winter count: 1833-1876. Edited by James H. Howard. Ethnohistory, 7 (1960): 28-43.

Caldwell, Warren W. Fortified villages in the Northern Plains. Plains Anthropologist, 9 (1964): 1-7.

Caldwell, Warren W., ed. The Northwestern Plains: a symposium. Billings, 1968. 95 p. map. (Rocky Mountain College, Center for Indian Studies, Occasional Papers, 1)

Cameron, W. B. Costumes of the Plains Indians. Beaver, 274, no. 3 (1943): 33-37.

Campbell, T. N. Origin of the mescal bean cult. American Anthropologist, 60 (1958): 156-160.

Carey, Raymond. The puzzle of Sand Creek. Colorado Magazine, 41 (1964): 279-298.

Carriker, Robert C. Fort Supply, Indian
    Territory; frontier outpost on the
    Plains. Norman, University of Oklahoma
    Press, 1970. 241 p.

Carroll, H. B. The Texan Santa Fe Trail.
    Panhandle-Plains Historical Review, 24
    (1954): 1-201.

Carter, R. G. On the border with
    MacKenzie, 253-300. Washington, D.C.,
    1935.

Catlin, G. North American portfolio. New
    York, 1845. 16 p.

Catlin, George. Les Indiens de la
    prairie. Paris, Club des Librairies de
    France, 1959. 11, 250 p. illus., map.

Catlin, George. Letters and notes on the
    manners, customs, and condition of the
    North American Indians. Minneapolis,
    Ross and Haines, 1965. 2 v. illus.,
    maps.

Catlin, George. North American Indian
    portfolio. Chicago, Sage Books, 1970.

Catlin, George. Self-torture and wild
    horses. In Milton A. Rugoff, ed. The
    Great Travelers. Vol. 2. New York,
    Simon and Schuster, 1960: 828-834.

Chalmers, John W. Myself the wanderer
    . . . Canada's literate artist, Paul
    Kane. Montana, the Magazine of Western
    History, 20, no. 4 (1970): 36-49.

Chardon, Francis A. Chardon's journal at
    Fort Clark, 1834-1839. Freeport, N.Y.,
    Books for Libraries Press, 1970. 46,
    458 p. illus.

Childears, L. Montana place-names from
    Indian myth and legend. Western
    Folklore, 9 (1950): 263-264.

Chipp, H. B. Art styles of primitive
    cultures: the Plains Indians of North
    America. Journal of Aesthetics, 19,
    no. 2 (1960): 161-165.

Chittenden, H. M. The American fur trade
    of the Far West, Vol. 2: 841-881. New
    York, 1902.

Chittenden, H. M. and A. T. Richardson,
    eds. Life, letters and travels of
    Father Pierre-Jean De Smet. New York,
    1905. 4 v.

Chivington, John M. To the people of
    Colorado. Synopsis of the Sand Creek
    investigation. Denver, Colorado, June
    1865. [n.p.] 186-? 17 p.

Clark, Ella E. Indian legends from the
    northern Rockies. Norman, University of

Oklahoma Press, 1966. 25, 350 p.
    illus., map.

Clark, W. P. The Indian sign language.
    Philadelphia, 1885. 443 p.

Clements, F. Plains Indian tribal
    correlations with sun dance data.
    American Anthropologist, n.s., 33
    (1931): 216-227.

Coleman, John Melton. The Missouri Valley
    of South Dakota, its human geography at
    Euroamerican contact. Dissertation
    Abstracts, 29 (1968/1969): 1399B-1400B.
    UM 68-13,681.

Collier, D. The sun dance of the Plains
    Indians. América Indígena, 3 (1943):
    359-364.

Colorado State Historical Society. The
    Indians of Colorado. Denver, 1957.
    52 p.

Conn, Richard G. The pony bead period: a
    cultural problem of western North
    America. Society for Historical
    Archaeology, Newsletter, 5, no. 4
    (1972): 7-13.

Conner, Stuart W. The Fish Creek, Owl
    Canyon and Grinnvoll Rock Shelter
    pictographic sites in Montana. Plains
    Anthropologist, 7 (1962): 24-35.

Conner, Suart. Rock art of the Montana
    high plains. By Suart and Betty Lu
    Conner. Santa Barbara, University of
    California, 1971. 67 p. illus., map.

Corrigan, Samuel W. The Plains Indian
    powwow: cultural integration in Manitoba
    and Saskatchewan. Anthropologica, n.s.,
    12 (1970): 253-277.

Covington, James W., ed. Correspondence
    between Mexican officials at Santa Fe
    and officials in Missouri: 1823-1825.
    Missouri Historical Society, Bulletin,
    16 (1959/1960): 20-32.

Crockett, B. N. Health conditions in
    Indian Territory. Chronicles of
    Oklahoma, 35 (1957): 80-90; 36 (1958):
    21-39.

Cunningham, William D. Anto Wicharti.
    Library Journal, 94 (1969): 4496-4499.

Custer, Elizabeth B. Following the
    guidon. New ed. Norman, University of
    Oklahoma Press, 1966. 37, 341 p.
    illus.

Custer, George A. My life on the Plains.
    New ed. Norman, University of Oklahoma
    Press, 1962. 418 p. illus.

Cutler, J. A topographical description of the State of Ohio, Indiana Territory, and Louisiana. Boston, 1812. 219 p.

Cutright, Paul Russell. Lewis and Clark begin a journey. Missouri Historical Society, Bulletin, 24 (1967/1968): 20-35.

Cutright, Paul Russell. Lewis and Clark Indian peace medals. Missouri Historical Society, Bulletin, 24 (1967/1968): 160-167.

Cutright, Paul Russell. The odyssey of the magpie and the prairie dog. Missouri Historical Society, Bulletin, 23 (1966/1967): 215-228.

Dale, H. C., ed. The Ashley-Smith explorations and the discovery of a central route to the Pacific. Cleveland, 1918.

Danker, Donald F. The North brothers and the Pawnee scouts. Nebraska History, 42 (1961): 161-179.

Danziger, Edmund J., Jr. Civil War problems in the Central and Dakota Superintendencies: a case study. Nebraska History, 51 (1970): 411-424.

Danziger, Edmund J., Jr. The Crow Creek experiment: an aftermath of the Sioux War of 1862. North Dakota History, 37 (1970): 105-123.

DeBarthe, J. Life and adventures of Frank Grouard. Norman, 1958. 296 p.

Deissler, Kenneth L. A study of South Dakota Indian achievement problems. Journal of American Indian Education, 1, no. 3 (1961/1962): 19-21.

Delano, Alonzo. Life on the Plains and among the diggings. Ann Arbor, University Microfilms, 1966. 384 p. illus.

Dempsey, Hugh A. Jerry Potts: plainsman. Montana, the Magazine of Western History, 17, no. 4 (1967): 2-17.

Dempsey, Hugh A. Western Plains trade ceremonies. Western Canadian Journal of Anthropology, 3, no. 1 (1972): 29-33.

Devoto, B. Across the wide Missouri. Boston, 1947. 511 p.

Dillon, Richard H. Meriwether Lewis, Manuel Lisa, and the tantalizing Santa Fe trade. Montana, the Magazine of Western History, 17, no. 2 (1967): 46-52.

Dillon, Richard H. Stephen Long's great American desert. American Philosophical Society, Proceedings, 111 (1967): 93-108.

Dippie, Brian W. "What will Congress do about it?" the Congressional reaction to the Little Big Horn disaster. North Dakota History, 37 (1970): 161-189.

Dobie, J. F. Indian horses and horsemanship. Southwest Review, 35 (1950): 265-275.

Dodge, H. Report on the expedition of dragoons. American State Papers, Military Affairs, 6 (1861): 130-146.

Dodge, R. I. The Plains of the Great West and their inhabitants. New York, 1877. 448 p.

Dodge, Richard I. Our wild Indians. New York, Archer House, 1960. 657 p. illus.

Dodge, Richard I. The Plains of the great West and their inhabitants. New York, Archer House, 1959. 4, 452 p. illus., map.

Domenech, E. Seven years residence in the great deserts of North America. London, 1860. 2 v. (1) 469 p. (2) 477 p.

Donaldson, T. The George Catlin Indian Gallery in the U.S. National Museum. United States National Museum, Reports (1885): 1-939.

Dorsey, J. O. Camping circles of Siouan tribes. American Anthropologist, 2 (1889): 175-177.

Dorsey, J. O. Migrations of Siouan tribes. American Naturalist, 20 (1886): 211-222.

Dorsey, J. O. Nanibozhu in Siouan mythology. Journal of American Folklore, 5 (1892): 293-304.

Dorsey, J. O. Siouan onomatopes. American Anthropologist, 5 (1892): 1-8.

Dorsey, J. O. The place of gentes in Siouan camping circles. American Anthropologist, 2 (1889): 375-379.

Douglas, F. H. An incised bison rawhide parfleche. Denver Art Museum, Material Culture Notes, 6 (1938): 23-25.

Douglas, F. H. Plains beads and beadwork designs. Denver Art Museum, Indian Leaflet Series, 73/74 (1936): 90-96.

Douglas, F. H. Plains Indian clothing.
Denver Art Museum, Indian Leaflet
Series, 24 (1931): 1-4.

Douglas, F. H. Plains Indian tribes.
Denver Art Museum, Indian Leaflet
Series, 23 (1931): 1-4.

Douglas, F. H. The buffalo and the
Indian. Denver Art Museum, Indian
Leaflet Series, 7 (1930): 1-4.

Douglas, F. H. The Plains Indian earth
lodge. Denver Art Museum, Indian Leaflet
Series, 20 (1931): 1-4.

Douglas, F. H. The Plains Indian tipi.
Denver Art Museum, Indian Leaflet
Series, 19 (1931): 1-4.

Douglas, F. H. Two Plains bison hair
ropes. Denver Art Museum, Material
Culture Notes, 5 (1938): 19-22.

Douglas, F. H. and A. Marriott. Metal
jewelry of the peyote cult. Denver Art
Museum, Material Culture Notes, 17
(1942): 17-82.

Downey, Fairfax D. The Buffalo Soldiers
in the Indian wars. New York, McGraw-
Hill, 1969. 127 p. illus.

Dräger, Lothar. Indianer der Prärie.
Leipzig, Museum für Völkerkunde,
Staatliche Forschungsstelle, 1968.
46 p. illus.

Driver, H. E. The measurement of
geographical distribution form. American
Anthropologist, n.s., 41 (1939): 583-
588.

Driver, H. E. and A. L. Kroeber.
Quantitative expression of cultural
relationships. California, University,
Publications in American Archaeology and
Ethnology, 31 (1932): 226-236.

Dunn, Adrian R. A history of old Fort
Berthold. North Dakota History, 30
(1963): 157-240.

Dunn, D. Oscar Howe: Sioux artist. El
Palacio, 64 (1957): 167-173.

Dunn, D. The development of modern
American Indian painting in the
Southwest and Plains areas. El Palacio,
58 (1951): 331-353.

Dunn, Dorothy. American Indian painting
of the Southwest and Plains areas.
Santa Fe, University of New Mexico
Press, 1968. 27, 429 p. illus.

Edwards, Philip S. The Medicine Lodge
Indian peace treaty and a brief
narrative history of the Indian wars on

the Southern Plains. Kechi, Kan., Mid-
America Publications, 1961. 46 p.
illus.

Eisenstadt, S. N. Plains Indian age
groups. Man, 54 (1954): 6-8.

Ellis, Everett L. To take a scalp. Annals
of Wyoming, 31 (1959): 140-143.

Ellis, Richard N. After Bull Run: the
later career of General John Pope.
Montana, the Magazine of Western
History, 19, no. 3 (1969): 46-57.

Ellis, Richard N. General John Pope and
the Southern Plains Indians, 1875-1883.
Southwestern Historical Quarterly, 72
(1968/1969): 152-169.

Ellis, Richard N. General Pope and the
old "hand-to-mouth" way. In Richard N.
Ellis, ed. The Western American Indian.
Lincoln, University of Nebraska Press,
1972: 63-75.

Ellis, Richard N. Political pressures and
Army policies on the Northern Plains,
1862-1865. Minnesota History, 42
(1970/1971): 43-53.

Ellis, Richard N., ed. Bent, Carson, and
the Indians, 1865. Colorado Magazine, 46
(1969): 55-68.

Ellison, Rosemary. Contemporary Southern
Plains Indian painting. Edited by Myles
Libhart. Anadarko, Oklahoma Indian Arts
and Crafts Cooperative, 1972. 80 p.
illus.

Erdoes, Richard. The Sun Dance people;
the Plains Indians, their past and
present. New York, Knopf, 1972.
218 p. illus.

Essin, Emmett M., III. Mules, packs, and
packtrains. Southwestern Historical
Quarterly, 74 (1970/1971): 52-63.

Essin, Emmett M., III. The cavalry and
the horse. Dissertation Abstracts, 29
(1968/1969): 2621A. UM 69-737.

Ewers, J. C. Hair pipes in Plains Indian
adornment. U.S. Bureau of American
Ethnology, Bulletin, 164 (1957): 29-86.

Ewers, J. C. Plains Indian painting.
Palo Alto, 1939. 84 p.

Ewers, J. C. Plains Indian war medicine.
Tomorrow, 4, no. 3 (1956): 85-90.

Ewers, J. C. The Indian trade of the
Upper Missouri before Lewis and Clark.
Missouri Historical Society, Bulletin,
10 (1954): 429-446.

Ewers, John C. Contraceptive charms among the Plains Indians. Plains Anthropologist, 15 (1970): 216-218.

Ewers, John C. Indian life on the Upper Missouri. Norman, University of Oklahoma Press, 1968. 18, 222 p. illus., map.

Ewers, John C. Not quite Redmen: the Plains Indian illustrations of Felix O. C. Darley. American Art Journal, 3, no. 2 (1971): 88-98.

Ewers, John C. Plains Indian painting: the history and development of American art form. American West, 5, no. 2 (1968): 4-15, 74-76.

Ewers, John C. Plains Indian reaction to the Lewis and Clark Expedition. Montana, the Magazine of Western History, 16, no. 1 (1966): 2-12.

Ewers, John C. The emergence of the Plains Indian as the symbol of the North American Indian. Smithsonian Institution, Annual Report of the Board of Regents (1963/1964): 531-544.

Ewers, John C. The horse in Blackfoot Indian culture, with comparative material from other Western tribes. Washington, D.C., Smithsonian Institution Press, 1969. 15, 374 p. illus., maps.

Ewers, John C. The White Man's strongest medicine. Missouri Historical Society, Bulletin, 24 (1967/1968): 36-46.

Ewers, John C. Thomas M. Easterly's pioneer daguerreotypes of Plains Indians. Missouri Historical Society, Bulletin, 24 (1967/1968): 329-339.

Farabee, W. C. Dress among the Plains Indian women. Museum Journal, 12 (1921): 239-251.

Farb, Peter. Rise and fall of the Indian of the Wild West. Natural History, 77, no. 8 (1968): 32-41.

Farber, W. O., et al. Indians, law enforcement, and local government. South Dakota, State University, Government Research Bureau, Report, 37 (1951): 1-92.

Farnham, T. J. Travels in the great western prairies. Early Western Travels, 28, 29 (1906).

Fay, George E., ed. Charters, constitutions and by-laws of the Indian tribes of North America. Part IIa: The Northern Plains. Greeley, 1967. 6, 141 l. maps. (University of Northern

Colorado, Museum of Anthropology, Occasional Publications in Anthropology, Ethnology Series, 3) ERIC ED051923.

Fay, George E., ed. Military engagements between United States troops and Plains Indians; documentary inquiry by the U.S. Congress. Part I: 1854-1867. Greeley, 1972. 2 v. (236 l.). (University of Northern Colorado, Museum of Anthropology, Occasional Publications in Anthropology, Ethnology Series, 26)

Feder, Norman. North American Indian painting. New York, Museum of Primitive Art, 1967. illus.

Fellows, Fred R. The people's pillion: a study of western saddles. Montana, the Magazine of Western History, 16, no. 1 (1966): 57-83.

Filipiak, Jack D. The battle of Summit Springs. Colorado Magazine, 41 (1964): 343-354.

Finerty, John F. War-path and bivouac. Norman, University of Oklahoma Press, 1961. 358 p. illus.

Fisher, Anthony D. The Algonquian Plains? Anthropologica, n.s., 10 (1968): 219-234.

Fisher, John R. The Royall and Duncan pursuits: aftermath of the Battle of Summit Springs, 1869. Nebraska History, 50 (1969): 293-308.

Flanagan, Vincent J. Gouverneur Kemble Warren, explorer of the Nebraska Territory. Nebraska History, 51 (1970): 171-198.

Fletcher, A. C. The emblematic use of the tree in the Dakotan group. American Association for the Advancement of Science, Proceedings, 45 (1896): 191-209.

Forbes, Allan, Jr. The Plains agon--a gross typology. Plains Anthropologist, 17 (1972): 144-155.

Forbes, Jack D. The Indian in the West: a challenge for historians. Arizona and the West, 1 (1959): 206-215.

Forbis, Richard G. The direct historical approach in the Prairie Provinces of Canada. Great Plains Journal, 3 (1963/1964): 9-16.

Forbis, Richard G. The Old Women's Buffalo Jump, Alberta. In Contributions to Anthropology 1960. Part I. Ottawa, Queen's Printer, 1962: 57-123. (Canada, National Museum, Bulletin, 180)

Forsyth, T. Thomas Forsyth to Lewis Cass, October 29, 1831. Ethnohistory, 4 (1957): 198-210.

Foster, James Monroe, Jr. Fort Bascom, New Mexico. New Mexico Historical Review, 35 (1960): 30-62.

Fowke, G. Antiquities of central and southeastern Missouri. U.S. Bureau of American Ethnology, Bulletin, 37 (1910): 1-116.

Fowler, J. The journal of Jacob Fowler. New York, 1898. 183 p.

Frederikson, O. F. The liquor question among the Indian tribes in Kansas, 1804-1881. Kansas University, Bulletin, Humanistic Studies, 4, no. 4 (1932): 1-103.

Frémont, D. Les aborigènes du Nord-Ouest Canadien au temps de La Vérendrye. Société Royale du Canada, Mémoires, 43, 3e sér., Sect. 1 (1949): 7-21.

Fremont, J. C. Narrative of the exploring expedition to the Rocky Mountains. New York, 1846. 186 p.

Friesen, John W. The Plains Indians and educational theory. By John W. Friesen and Linda Moseson. Journal of American Indian Education, 11, no. 1 (1971/1972): 19-26.

Fuller, H. M. and L. R. Hafen, ed. The journal of Captain John R. Bell. The Far West and the Rockies Historical Series 1820-1875, 6 (1957): 1-349.

Gallagher, O. R. and L. H. Powell. Time perspective in Plains Indian beaded art. American Anthropologist, 55 (1953): 609-613.

Galpin, Charles. The Galpin journal: dramatic record of an odyssey of peace. Edited by Louis Pfaller. Montana, the Magazine of Western History, 18, no. 2 (1968): 2-23.

Garcia, Andrew. Tough trip through paradise, 1878-1879. Edited by Bennett H. Stein. Boston, Houghton Mifflin, 1967. 18, 446 p. illus., maps.

Garth, T. R. A comparison of the intelligence of Mexican and mixed and full blood Indian children. Psychological Review, 30 (1923): 388-401.

Garth, T. R. The intelligence of full blood Indians. Journal of Applied Psychology, 9 (1925): 382-389.

Gass, P. A journal of the voyages and travels of a corps of discovery. Pittsburgh, 1807.

Gaston, Edwin W., Jr. Travel accounts of the Southern Plains, 1800-1850. Texas Journal of Science, 4 (1959): 3-16.

Gates, Paul Wallace. Land and credit problems in underdeveloped Kansas. Kansas Historical Quarterly, 31 (1965): 41-61.

Gebhard, David. The shield motif in Plains rock art. American Antiquity, 31 (1965/1966): 721-732.

Gerber, Rudolph J. Old Woman River. Missouri Historical Review, 56 (1961/1962): 328-346.

Gibson, Arrell M. Ranching on the southern Great Plains. Journal of the West, 6 (1967): 135-153.

Gilbert, B. Miles. Sacajawea: a problem in Plains anthropology. Plains Anthropologist, 17 (1972): 156-160.

Gilmore, M. R. Some Indian ideas of property. Indian Notes, 5 (1928): 137-144.

Gilmore, M. R. The aboriginal geography of the Nebraska country. Mississippi Valley Historical Association, Proceedings, 6 (1913): 317-331.

Gladwin, T. Personality structure in the Plains. Anthropological Quarterly, 30 (1957): 111-124.

Goldman, Henry H. A survey of federal escorts of the Santa Fe trade, 1829-1843. Journal of the West, 5 (1966): 504-516.

Goodale, Ephriam. A civilian at Fort Leavenworth and Fort Hays, 1878-1879; extracts from a diary of Ephriam Goodale. Edited by Roy Goodale. Kansas Historical Quarterly, 33 (1967): 138-155.

Gray, John S. Arikara scouts with Custer. North Dakota History, 35 (1968): 443-478.

Gray, John S. The Northern Overland pony express. Montana, the Magazine of Western History, 16, no. 4 (1966): 58-73.

Gray, John S. Trials of a trailblazer . . . P. W. Norris and Yellowstone. Montana, the Magazine of Western History, 22, no. 3 (1972): 54-63.

Green, Jerome A. The Hayfield Fight; a
reappraisal of a neglected action.
Montana, the Magazine of Western
History, 22, no. 4 (1972): 30-43.

Gregg, J. Commerce of the prairies. New
York, 1844. 2 v.

Grey, Don. Big Horn Medicine Wheel Site,
48BH302. Plains Anthropologist, 8
(1963): 27-40.

Grinnell, G. B. The story of the Indian.
New York, 1895. 268 p.

Grinnell, George B. The passing of the
great West. Selected papers of George
Bird Grinnell. Edited by John F. Reiger.
New York, Winchester Press, 1972.
182 p. illus.

Grinnell, George B. When buffalo ran.
Norman, University of Oklahoma Press,
1966. 114 p. illus.

Grinnell, George Bird. Coup and scalp
among the Plains Indians. In Frederica
de Laguna, ed. Selected Papers from the
American Anthropologist 1888-1920.
Evanston, Row, Peterson, 1960: 650-664.

Guidieri, Remo. L'archéologie et les
problèmes ethnologiques en Amérique du
Nord. Homme, 9, no. 1 (1969): 66-73.

Gunnerson, Dolores A. An unusual method
of flint chipping. Plains
Anthropologist, 14 (1969): 71-72.

Gunnerson, Dolores A. Man and bison on
the Plains in the protohistoric period.
Plains Anthropologist, 17 (1972): 1-10.

Gunnerson, James H. An introduction to
Plains Apache archeology--the Dismal
River Aspect. Washington, D.C.,
Government Printing Office, 1960. 131-
260 p. illus., map. (U.S., Bureau of
American Ethnology, Anthropological
Papers, 58. U.S., Bureau of American
Ethnology, Bulletin, 173)

Gunther, E. The westward movement of some
Plains traits. American Anthropologist,
52 (1950): 174-180.

Haekel, J. Totemismus und Zweiklassen-
System bei den Sioux-Indianern.
Anthropos, 32 (1937): 210-238, 450-501,
795-848.

Haekel, J. Zum ethnologischen Aussagewert
von Kulturparallelen. Wiener
Völkerkundliche Mitteilungen, 3 (1955):
176-190.

Hafen, L. R. and A. W. Hafen, eds. Rufus
B. Sage, his letters and papers, 1836-
1847. The Far West and the Rockies

Historical Series 1820-1875, 4 (1956):
1-354; 5 (1956): 1-360.

Hafen, L. R. and A. W. Hafen, eds. The
Utah Expedition, 1857-1858. The Far West
and the Rockies Historical Series 1820-
1875, 7 (1958): 1-375.

Hafen, L. R. and A. W. Hafen, eds. To the
Rockies and Oregon, 1839-1842. The Far
West and the Rockies Historical Series
1820-1875, 3 (1955): 1-315.

Hafen, Le Roy R. Fort Vasquez. Colorado
Magazine, 41 (1964): 198-212.

Hafen, Le Roy R., ed. Powder River
campaigns and Sawyers Expedition of
1865. Edited by Le Roy R. Hafen and Ann
W. Hafen. Glendale, Calif., A. H.
Clark, 1961. 386 p. illus., maps.
(The Far West and Rockies Historical
Sketches, 1820-1875, 12)

Hagan, William T. Kiowas, Comanches, and
cattlemen, 1867-1906: a case study of
the failure of U.S. Reservation policy.
Pacific Historical Review, 40 (1971):
333-355.

Haines, F. The northward spread of horses
among the Plains Indians. American
Anthropologist, n.s., 40 (1938): 429-
437.

Haines, F. Where did the Plains Indians
get their horses? American
Anthropologist, n.s., 40 (1938): 112-
117.

Hall, H. U. A buffalo robe biography.
Museum Journal, 17 (1926): 5-35.

Hall, H. U. Some shields of the Plains
and Southwest. Museum Journal, 17
(1926): 37-61.

Hamilton, Henry W. Remington Schuyler,
artist and writer. By Henry W. Hamilton
and Jean Tyree Hamilton. Missouri
Historical Society, Bulletin, 25
(1968/1969): 118-122.

Hamilton, W. T. My sixty years on the
Plains. New York, 1905. 244 p.

Hamilton, William T. My sixty years on
the Plains. Norman, University of
Oklahoma Press, 1960. 184 p. illus.

Hammond, G. P. and A. Rey, eds.
Narratives of the Coronado Expedition,
1540-1542. Albuquerque, 1940. 413 p.

Hampton, H. D. The Powder River
Expedition; 1865. Montana, the Magazine
of Western History, 14, no. 4 (1964): 2-
15.

Hanson, Charles E., Jr. The Indian garden
project. Museum of the Fur Trade
Quarterly, 2, no. 3 (1966): 3-6.

Hanson, Charles E., Jr. The post-war
Indian gun trade. Museum of the Fur
Trade Quarterly, 4, no. 3 (1968): 1-11.

Hanson, Marshall Roy. Plains Indians and
urbanization. Dissertation Abstracts, 21
(1960/1961): 23. UM 60-2392.

Harcourt, R. d'. Arts de l'Amérique, 35-
42. Paris, 1948.

Harrington, M. R. Indian tribes of the
Plains. Masterkey, 15 (1941): 116-128,
168-177, 213-220; 16 (1942): 5-15, 86-
93.

Haskell, M. L. Rubi's inspection of the
frontier presidios of New Spain, 1766-
1768. Southern California Historical
Society, Publications, 5 (1917): 33-43.

Heald, Weldon F. The Yellowstone story;
genesis of the National Park idea. Utah
Historical Quarterly, 28 (1960): 98-110.

Helper, Malcolm M. Use of the semantic
differential to study acculturation in
American Indian adolescents. By Malcolm
M. Helper and Sol L. Garfield. Journal
of Personality and Social Psychology, 2
(1965): 817-822.

Hermant, P. Évolution économique et
sociale de certaines peuplades de
l'Amérique du Nord. Société Royale Belge
de Géographie, Bulletin, 29 (1905): 5-
30.

Herrington, Henry E. Indian and White
attitudes relating to Indian
assimilation: a comparison of Indian and
White pupils of Montana with respect to
goals and attitudes toward each other.
By Henry E. Herrington and George V.
Douglas. Bozeman, 1968. 25 p.
(Montana, Agricultural Experiment
Station, Bulletin, 623)

Herzog, G. Plains ghost dance and Great
Basin music. American Anthropologist,
n.s., 37 (1935): 403-419.

Hewitt, J. N. B., ed. Journal of Rudolph
Friederich Kurz. U.S. Bureau of American
Ethnology, Bulletin, 115 (1937): 1-382.

Hickman, Russell. The Reeder
Administration inaugurated; part 2--the
census of early 1855. Kansas Historical
Quarterly, 36 (1970): 424-455.

Hill, Burton S. The great Indian treaty
council of 1851. Nebraska History, 47
(1966): 85-110.

Hillyer, Edwin. From Waupun to Sacramento
in 1849: the Gold Rush journal of Edwin
Hillyer. Edited by John O. Holzhueter.
Wisconsin Magazine of History, 49
(1965/1966): 210-244.

Hjelmseth, Donald E. A study of attitudes
of selected elementary school teachers
toward American Indian students in the
state of Montana. Dissertation Abstracts
International, 33 (1972/1973): 1551A-
1552A. UM 72-25,075.

Hoffhaus, Charles E. Fort de Cavagnail;
Imperial France in Kansas, 1744-1764.
Kansas Historical Quarterly, 30 (1964):
425-454.

Hoffman, Dean Kay. Relationship of self-
concept and academic self-assessment to
the educational aspirations of
underprivileged adolescent Indians.
Dissertation Abstracts International, 30
(1969/1970): 1226B-1227B. UM 69-11,302.

Hoffman, J. J. Molstad Village. Lincoln,
Smithsonian Institution, River Basin
Surveys, 1967. 6, 123 p. illus., maps.
(Smithsonian Institution, River Basin
Surveys, Publications in Salvage
Archeology, 4)

Holder, Preston. The hoe and the horse on
the Plains; a study of cultural
development among North American
Indians. Lincoln, University of
Nebraska Press, 1970. 12, 176 p.
illus., map.

Holling, H. C. The book of Indians, 45-
72. New York, 1935.

Holmer, N. M. Lexical and morphological
contacts between Siouan and Algonquian.
Lunds Universitets Arsskrift, n.s., 45
(1949): 1-36.

Holmes, Kenneth L. The Benjamin Cooper
expeditions to Santa Fe in 1822 and
1823. New Mexico Historical Review, 38
(1963): 139-150.

Holmes, Louis A. Fort McPherson,
Nebraska, Fort Cottonwood, N.T.,
guardian of the tracks and trails.
Lincoln, Johnson, 1963. 108 p. illus.,
maps.

Holstein, Friedrich von. Friedrich von
Holstein's hunting trips, 1865-1866.
Edited by Ralph H. Pickett. Kansas
Historical Quarterly, 32 (1966): 314-
324.

Holt, Roy D. Heap many Texas chiefs. San
Antonio, Naylor, 1966. 15, 350 p.

Holtz, Milton E. Old Fort Kearny--1846-
1848: symbol of a changing frontier.

Montana, the Magazine of Western History, 22, no. 4 (1972): 44-55.

Honnell, William R. Candles of yesteryear . . . Kansas lived and relived. Kansas City, Kan., 1970. 37 p. illus.

Hornaday, W. T. The extermination of the American bison. United States National Museum, Reports (1887): 369-548.

Hotz, Gottfried. Indianische Ledermalereien; Figurenreiche Darstellungen von Grenzkonflikten zwischen Mexiko und dem Missouri um 1720. Berlin, Reimer, 1960. 384 p. illus., maps.

Houck, L., ed. The Spanish régime in Missouri. Chicago, 1909. 2 v.

Hough, W. Ceremonial and other practices on the human body among the Indians. International Congress of Americanists, Proceedings, 19 (1915): 283-285.

Howard, J. H. Pan-Indian culture of Oklahoma. Scientific Monthly, 81 (1955): 215-220.

Howard, J. H. Plains Indian feathered bonnets. Plains Anthropologist, 2 (1954): 23-26.

Howard, J. H. The mescal bean cult of the Central and Southern Plains. American Anthropologist, 59 (1957): 75-87.

Howard, James H. Dakota winter counts as a source of Plains history. Washington, D.C., Government Printing Office, 1960. 335-416 p. illus. (U.S., Bureau of American Ethnology, Anthropological Papers, 61. U.S., Bureau of American Ethnology, Bulletin, 173)

Howard, James H. Mescalism and peyotism once again. Plains Anthropologist, 5 (1960): 84-85.

Howard, James H. Northern Plains Grass Dance costume. American Indian Hobbyist, 7, no. 1 (1960): 18-27.

Howard, James H. The northern style grass dance costume. American Indian Hobbyist, 7, no. 1 (1960): 18-27.

Howell, Edgar M. A special artist in the Indian wars; Theodore R. Davis and the Hancock Campaign of 1867. Montana, the Magazine of Western History, 15, no. 2 (1965): 2-23.

Hrdlička, A. Catalogue of human crania in the United States National Museum Collections. United States National Museum, Proceedings, 69, no. 5 (1927): 1-127.

Hudson's Bay Company. Saskatchewan journals and correspondence: Edmonton House 1795-1800; Chesterfield House 1800-1802. Edited by Alice M. Johnson. London, 1967. 102, 368, 14 p. map. (Hudson's Bay Record Society, Publications, 26)

Hultkrantz, Åke. Shoshoni Indians on the Plains: an appraisal of the documentary evidence. Zeitschrift für Ethnologie, 93 (1968): 49-72.

Hultkrantz, Åke. The structure of theistic beliefs among North American Plains Indians. Temenos, 7 (1971): 66-74.

Humphrey, N. D. A characterization of certain Plains associations. American Anthropologist, n.s., 43 (1941): 428-436.

Hunter, J. O. Manners and customs of the several Indian tribes. Minneapolis, 1957. 407 p.

Hurlbut, William J. Beyond the border: a thousand mile tramp in Dakota on a government survey, 1874. Edited by Dayton W. Canaday. South Dakota History, 1 (1970/1971): 1-32.

Hurt, Wesley R. Factors in the persistence of peyote in the Northern Plains. Plains Anthropologist, 5 (1960): 16-27.

Huscher, Harold A. Deer Raiser and Corn Mother: the corn origin myth of the Upper Missouri and the Athapaskan Southwest. Plains Anthropologist, 10 (1965): 56.

Huscher, Harold A. Salt traders of Cibola. Great Plains Journal, 5 (1965/1966): 73-83.

Hyde, G. E. Indians of the High Plains. Norman, 1959. 231 p.

Ingenthron, Elmo. Indians of the Ozark Plateau. Point Lookout, Mo., School of the Ozarks Press, 1970. 3, 182 p. illus., maps.

Innis, H. A. Peter Pond, fur trader and adventurer. Toronto, Irwin and Gordon, 1930. 153 p. map.

Institute of Texan Cultures. The Indian Texans. San Antonio, 1970.

Irving, W. The adventures of Captain Bonneville. New York, 1851. 428 p.

Isinger, Bryan J. Saskatchewan catlinite tablets. Na'páo, 3, no. 1 (1971): 5-11.

Jackson, Donald.   Journey to the Mandans, 1809; the lost narrative of Dr. Thomas. Missouri Historical Society Bulletin, 20 (1963/1964): 179-192.

Jackson, Donald.   Lewis and Clark among the Oto. Nebraska History, 41 (1960): 237-248.

Jackson, Donald.   Zebulon Pike and Nebraska. Nebraska History, 47 (1966): 355-369.

Jackson, Donald D.   Some books carried by Lewis and Clark. Missouri Historical Society, Bulletin, 16 (1959/1960): 3-13.

Jennings, J. D.   Plainsmen of the past. Washington, D.C., 1948.

Jennings, J. D.   The archeology of the Plains: an assessment.   Salt Lake City, 1955.   180 p.

Johnson, Dorothy M.   The hanging of the chiefs. Montana, the Magazine of Western History, 20, no. 3 (1970): 60-69.

Johnson, J. R.   Colonel John Miller Stotsenburg: a man of valor. Nebraska History, 50 (1969): 339-357.

Johnson, Sally A.   The Sixth's Elysian Fields--Fort Atkinson on the Council Bluffs. Nebraska History, 40 (1959): 1-38.

Jones, Dorothy V.   A preface to the settlement of Kansas. Kansas Historical Quarterly, 29 (1963): 122-136.

Jones, Dorothy V.   John Dougherty and the Pawnee rite of human sacrifice: April, 1827. Missouri Historical Review, 63 (1968/1969): 293-316.

Jones, Robert Huhn.   The Northwestern Frontier and the impact on the Sioux War, 1862. Mid-America, 41 (1959): 131-153.

Jorgensen, Joseph G.   The sun dance religion; power for the powerless. Chicago, University of Chicago Press, 1972.   448 p.

Kaiser, Leo M.   Flood of silver, flood of gold: oratory in St. Louis. Missouri Historical Society, Bulletin, 16 (1959/1960): 303-321.

Kane, P.   Wanderings of an artist among the Indians.   London, 1859.   455 p.

Karnes, Thomas L.   Gilpin's volunteers on the Santa Fe Trail. Kansas Historical Quarterly, 30 (1964): 1-14.

Keenan, Gerald.   The seventeenth of June. North Dakota History, 26 (1959): 25-31.

Keenan, Jerry.   Exploring the Black Hills: an account of the Custer Expedition. Journal of the West, 6 (1967): 248-261.

Kehoe, Alice B.   Ceramic affiliations in the northwestern Plains. American Antiquity, 25 (1959/1960): 237-246.

Kehoe, Thomas F.   Stone tipi rings in North-Central Montana and the adjacent portion of Alberta, Canada: their historical ethnological, and archeological aspects.   Washington, D.C., Government Printing Office, 1960. 417-474 p.   illus., map.   (U.S., Bureau of American Ethnology, Anthropological Papers, 62. U.S., Bureau of American Ethnology, Bulletin, 173)

Keim, De Benneville Randolph.   Sheridan's troopers on the borders: a winter campaign on the Plains.   Freeport, N.Y., Books for Libraries Press, 1970. 308 p.   illus.

Kelsey.   Background to Sand Creek. Colorado Magazine, 45 (1968): 279-300.

Kenner, Charles L.   A history of New Mexican-Plains Indian relations. Norman, University of Oklahoma Press, 1969.   9, 250 p.   illus., maps.

Kenner, Charles Leroy.   A history of New Mexican-Plains Indian relations. Dissertation Abstracts, 28 (1967/1968): 595A.   UM 66-12,762.

King, C. Richard.   James Clinton Neill. Texana, 2 (1964): 231-252.

King, James T.   Forgotten pageant--the Indian Wars in western Nebraska. Nebraska History, 46 (1965): 177-192.

King, James T.   General Crook at Camp Cloud Peak: "I am at a loss what to do". Journal of the West, 11 (1972): 114-127.

King, James T.   Needed: a re-evaluation of General George Crook. Nebraska History, 45 (1964): 223-235.

Krause, F.   Zur Besiedelungsgeschichte der nordamerikanischen Prärie. Deutsche Gesellschaft für Anthropologie, Ethnologie und Urgeschichte, Korrespondenz-Blatt, 44 (1913): 66-70.

Krieg, Frederick C.   Chief Plenty Coups; the final dignity. Montana, the Magazine of Western History, 16, no. 4 (1966): 28-39.

Kroeber, A. L.   The ceremonial organization of the Plains Indians.

International Congress of Americanists, Proceedings, 15, vol. 2 (1906): 53-63.

Kroeber, Alfred L. Sign language inquiry. International Journal of American Linguistics, 24 (1958): 1-19.

Krusche, R. Soziale Gruppierungen und politische Autorität bei indianischen Stämmen im Zentral-Plains-Gebiet und ihr historischer Wandel. Leipzig, Museum für Völkerkunde, Jahrbuch, 28 (1972): 373-398.

Krush, Thaddeus P., et al. Some thoughts on the formation of personality disorder: study of an Indian boarding school population. American Journal of Psychiatry, 122 (1966): 868-876.

Kurath, Gertrude P. A comparison of Plains and Pueblo songs. Ethnomusicology, 13 (1969): 512-517.

La Barre, Weston. The peyote cult. New Haven, Yale University, Department of Anthropology, 1938. 188 p. illus. (Yale University Publications in Anthropology, 19)

Lange, C. H. A reappraisal of evidence of Plains influences among the Rio Grande Pueblos. Southwestern Journal of Anthropology, 9 (1953): 212-230.

Lange, C. H. Plains-Southwestern inter-cultural relations during the historic period. Ethnohistory, 4 (1957): 150-173.

Larpenteur, C. Forty years a fur trader on the Upper Missouri. Ed. by E. Coues. New York, 1898. 2 v.

Larson, Wayne L. A comparative analysis of Indian and non-Indian parents' influence on educational aspirations, expectations, preferences and behavior of Indian and non-Indian high school students in four high schools. Bozeman, 1971. 26, 3 p. illus. (Montana, State Agricultural Experiment Station, Bulletin, 660)

Larson, Wayne L. A comparison of the differential effect of ethnicity and perception of family income on educational aspirations, preparation, and parental influence-attempts of Indian and non-Indian students in four rural high schools in Montana. Bozeman, 1971. 19, 4 p. illus. (Montana, State Agricultural Experiment Station, Bulletin, 659)

Lass, William E. Steamboating on the Missouri: its significance on the northern Great Plains. Journal of the West, 6 (1967): 53-67.

Lavender, David. Ramsay Crooks's early ventures on the Missouri River: a series of conjectures. Missouri Historical Society, Bulletin, 20 (1963/1964): 91-106.

Laviolette, G. Notes on the aborigines of the prairie provinces. Anthropologica, 2 (1956): 107-130.

Laxson, Joan Dorothy. Aspects of acculturation among American Indians: emphasis on contemporary Pan-Indianism. Dissertation Abstracts International, 32 (1971/1972): 6796B-6797B. UM 72-18,638.

Leckie, William H. The military conquest of the Southern Plains. Norman, University of Oklahoma Press, 1963. 269 p. illus.

Lecompte, Janet. Don Benito Vasquez in early Saint Louis. Missouri Historical Society, Bulletin, 26 (1969/1970): 285-305.

Lecompte, Janet. Gantt's Fort and Bent's picket post. Colorado Magazine, 41 (1964): 111-125.

Lecompte, Janet. Sand Creek. Colorado Magazine, 41 (1964): 314-335.

Lee, John D. Diary of the Mormon Battalion Mission. Edited by Juanita Brooks. New Mexico Historical Review, 42 (1967): 165-209, 281-332.

Lehmer, Donald J. Introduction to Middle Missouri archeology. Washington, D.C., Government Printing Office, 1971. 10, 206 p. illus. (U.S., National Park Service, Anthropological Papers, 1)

Lehmer, Donald J. The Plains bison hunt--prehistoric and historic. Plains Anthropologist, 8 (1963): 211-217.

Leland, J. A. C. Indian names in Missouri. Names, 1 (1953): 266-273.

Lesser, A. Some aspects of Siouan kinship. International Congress of Americanists, Proceedings, 23 (1928): 563-571.

Lester, Gurdon P. A round trip to the Montana mines: the 1866 travel journal of Gurdon P. Lester. Edited by Charles W. Martin. Nebraska History, 46 (1965): 273-313.

Levy, Jerrold E. Ecology of the South Plains. In Viola E. Garfield, ed. Symposium: Patterns of Land Utilization and Other Papers. Seattle, University of Washington Press, 1961: 18-25. (American Ethnological Society,

Proceedings of the Annual Spring
Meeting, 1961)

Lewis, M. and W. Clark. Travels. London,
1815. 3 v.

Linton, R. The origin of the Plains earth
lodge. American Anthropologist, n.s., 26
(1924): 247-257.

Livingston-Little, D. E. An economic
history of North Idaho, 1800-1900.
Journal of the West, 2 (1963): 121-132,
459-467; 3 (1964): 47-74, 175-198, 318-
354.

Ljung, Magnus. Principles of a
stratificational analysis of the Plains
Indian sign language. International
Journal of American Linguistics, 31
(1965): 119-127.

Llewellyn, Karl N. Emergence of law on
the Plains. By Karl N. Llewellyn and E.
Adamson Hoebel. In Walter R.
Goldschmidt, ed. Exploring the Ways of
Mankind. New York, Holt, 1960: 391-395.

Long, J. Journal, 1768-1782. Early
Western Travels, 2 (1904): 1-329.

Lowie, R. H. Indians of the Plains. New
York, 1954. 222 p.

Lowie, R. H. Marriage and family life
among the Plains Indians. Scientific
Monthly, 34 (1932): 462-464.

Lowie, R. H. Plains Indian age-societies.
American Museum of Natural History,
Anthropological Papers, 11 (1916): 877-
992.

Lowie, R. H. Reflections on the Plains
Indians. Anthropological Quarterly, 3
(1955): 63-86.

Lowie, R. H. Some problems in Plains
Indian folklore. Journal of American
Folklore, 60 (1947): 401-403.

Lowie, R. H. Studies in Plains Indian
folklore. California, University,
Publications in American Archaeology and
Ethnology, 40 (1942): 1-28.

Macgregor, Gordon. Community development
and social adaptation. Human
Organization, 20 (1961/1962): 238-242.

MacKenzie, A. Voyages. Toronto, 1927.
498 p.

MacLean, J. Canadian savage folk.
Toronto, 1897. 641 p.

Madigan, La Verne. Indian survival on the
Great Plains; a field report. New York,

Association on American Indian Affairs,
1957. 10 p. (Indian Affairs, 22)

Madigan, La Verne. We shake hands: an
action to encourage neighborly relations
between Indians and their fellow
citizens on the Great Plains. New York,
Association on American Indian Affairs,
1958. 44 p.

Magnaghi, Russell Mario. The Indian slave
trader: the Comanche, a case study.
Dissertation Abstracts International, 32
(1971/1972): 4531A. UM 72-5301.

Mahan, Bruce E. Indian affairs and
treaties. Palimpsest, 42 (1961): 472-
488.

Mahan, Bruce E. Indian amusements.
Palimpsest, 50 (1969): 247-252.

Mails, Thomas E. The mystic warriors of
the Plains. Garden City, Doubleday,
1972. 17, 618 p. illus., maps.

Mallery, G. Sign language among North
American Indians. U.S. Bureau of
American Ethnology, Annual Reports, 1
(1880): 263-552.

Mallery, G. The sign language of the
Indians of the Upper Missouri. American
Antiquarian and Oriental Journal, 2
(1880): 218-228.

Malouf, Carling. The tipi rings of the
High Plains. American Antiquity, 26
(1960/1961): 381-389.

Marcy, R. B. Adventure on Red River.
Norman, 1937. 199 p.

Mardock, Robert W. The Plains frontier
and the Indian peace policy, 1865-1880.
Nebraska History, 49 (1968): 187-201.

Margry, P. Découvertes et établissements
des Français, parts 1-60. Paris, 1875-
1886.

Marshall, Samuel L. A. Crimsoned prairie;
the wars between the United States and
the Plains Indians during the winning of
the West. New York, Scribner, 1972.
14, 256 p. illus., maps.

Mattes, Merrill J. Indians, infants and
infantry; Andrew and Elizabeth Burt on
the frontier. Denver, Old West
Publishing, 1960. 304 p. illus.

Matthews, G. H. Proto-Siouan kinship
terminology. American Anthropologist, 61
(1959): 252-278.

Matthews, W. The earth lodge in art.
American Anthropologist, n.s., 4 (1902):
1-12.

Mattison, R. H. The Indian reservation system on the Upper Missouri, 1865-1890. Nebraska History, 36 (1955): 141-172.

Mattison, Ray H. Fort Union: its role in the Upper Missouri fur trade. North Dakota History, 29 (1962): 181-208.

Mattison, Ray H. Indian missions and missionaries on the Upper Missouri to 1900. Nebraska History, 38 (1957): 127-154.

Mattison, Ray H. The Upper Missouri fur trade: its methods of operation. Nebraska History, 42 (1961): 1-28.

Mauck, Genevieve Powlison. Kanesville. Palimpsest, 42 (1961): 385-398.

Mayhall, Mildred P. Camp Cooper--first federal fort in Texas to fall, 1861, and events preceding its fall. Texana, 5 (1967): 317-342.

Mayhall, Mildred P. Indian wars of Texas. Waco, Texian Press, 1965. 21, 270 p. illus., map.

McAllister, J. Gilbert. The four quartz rocks medicine bundle of the Kiowa-Apache. Ethnology, 4 (1965): 210-224.

McCone, R. Clyde. Cultural factors in crime among the Dakota Indians. Plains Anthropologist, 11 (1966): 144-151.

McCracken, H. George Catlin and the old frontier. New York, 1959. 216 p.

McDermott, Louis M. The primary role of the military on the Dakota frontier. South Dakota History, 2 (1971/1972): 1-22.

McFadden, Thompson. Thompson MacFadden's diary of an Indian campaign, 1874. Edited by Robert C. Carriker. Southwestern Historical Quarterly, 75 (1971/1972): 198-232.

McFarling, L. Exploring the Northern Plains, 1804-1878. Caldwell, 1955. 452 p.

Meline, James F. Two thousand miles on horseback, Santa Fé and back. Altuquerque, Horn and Wallace, 1966. 10, 317 p. map.

Melvin, Dorothy M. Parasitologic surveys on Indian reservations in Montana, South Dakota, New Mexico, Arizona, and Wisconsin. By Dorothy M. Melvin and M. M. Brooke. American Journal of Tropical Medicine and Hygiene, 11 (1962): 765-772.

Meyer, Roy W. Fort Berthold and the Garrison Dam. North Dakota History, 35 (1968): 217-355.

Meyer, Roy W. The Iowa Indians, 1836-1885. Kansas Historical Quarterly, 28 (1962): 273-300.

Michelson, T. Algonquian notes. International Journal of American Linguistics, 9 (1939): 103-112.

Michon, Jean-Louis. Une visite chez les Indien des Plaines. Société Suisse des Américanistes, Bulletin, 17 (1959): 16-17.

Miller, Carl F. The excavation and investigation of Fort Lookout Trading Post II (39LM57) in the Fort Randall Reservoir, South Dakota. Washington, D.C., Government Printing Office, 1960. 49-82 p. illus., map. (U.S., Bureau of American Ethnology, River Basin Surveys Papers, 17. U.S., Bureau of American Ethnology, Bulletin, 176)

Miller, Harold J. The effects of integration on rural Indian pupils. Final report. Grand Forks, University of North Dakota, 1968. 163 p. ERIC ED022864.

Mishkin, B. Rank and warfare among the Plains Indians. American Ethnological Society, Monographs, 3 (1940): 1-65.

Miya, Ann. Plains Indians: the new native; a study of the Indian community in Parshall, North Dakota. Brooklyn, N.Y., 1964. 22 p. (Brooklyn Children's Museum, Occasional Papers in Cultural History, 7)

Möllhausen, B. Diary of a journey from the Mississippi to the coasts of the Pacific. London, 1858. 2 v.

Monahan, Forrest D., Jr. The Kiowas and New Mexico, 1800-1845. Journal of the West, 8 (1969): 67-75.

Monahan, Forrest Dewey, Jr. Trade goods on the Prairie, the Kiowa tribe and White trade goods, 1794-1875. Dissertation Abstracts, 26 (1965/1966): 3886-3887. UM 65-12,999.

Montana, Office of the State Co-ordinator of Indian Affairs. Tribal governments and law and order. Helena, Department of Indian Affairs, 1966. 37 p.

Montana Study. The Montana Study, a program of community education in the humanities sponsored by the Rockefeller Foundation and the University of Montana, 1944-1947. Helena, 1947. 3 v. illus., maps.

Mooney, J. The ghost-dance religion. U.S. Bureau of American Ethnology, Annual Reports, 14 (1896): 640-1136.

Mooney, James. The ghost-dance religion and the Sioux outbreak of 1890. Edited and abridged with an introduction by Anthony F. C. Wallace. Chicago, University of Chicago Press, 1965. 23, 359 p. illus.

Moret, Aimé. Le symbolisme et l'art pictographique chez les Indiens des Plaines. Société Suisse des Américanistes, Bulletin, 19 (1960): 42-43.

Morgan, Dale L., ed. The West of William H. Ashley. Denver, Old West Publishing, 1964. 54, 341 p. illus., maps.

Morgan, Lewis H. The stone and bone implements of the Arickarees. North Dakota History, 30 (1963): 115-135.

Morris, A. The treaties of Canada with the Indians of Manitoba, the North-West Territories, and Kee-wa-tin. Toronto, 1880.

Morse, J. Report to the Secretary of War. New Haven, 1822. 400 p.

Mulloy, W. A preliminary historical outline for the Northwestern Plains. Wyoming, University, Publications, 22, nos. 1/2 (1958): 1-235.

Mulloy, W. The Northern Plains. In J. B. Griffin, ed. Archeology of Eastern United States. Chicago, 1952: 124-138.

Mulvaney, C. P. The history of the North-West Rebellion of 1885. Toronto, 1885. 424 p.

Munkres, Robert L. Indian-White contact before 1870: cultural factors in conflict. Journal of the West, 10 (1971): 439-473.

Munkres, Robert L. The Plains Indian threat on the Oregon Trail before 1860. Annals of Wyoming, 40 (1968): 193-221.

Munn, Fred M. Fred Munn, veteran of frontier experiences, remembered the days he rode with Miles, Howard and Terry. As told to Robert A. Griffen. Montana, the Magazine of Western History, 16, no. 2 (1966): 50-64.

Muntsch, A. The relations between religion and morality among the Plains Indians. Primitive Man, 4 (1931): 22-29.

Murdock, George Peter. Ethnographic atlas. By George Peter Murdock et al. Ethnology, 3 (1964): 329-334.

Murray, Robert A. The Hazen inspection of 1866. Montana, the Magazine of Western History, 18, no. 1 (1968): 24-33.

Murray, William G. Louisiana Purchase to 1838. Palimpsest, 48 (1967): 441-443.

Nasatir, A. P. Before Lewis and Clark. St. Louis, 1952. 2 v. (882 p.).

Neuman, Robert W. Check-stamped pottery on the northern and central Great Plains. American Antiquity, 29 (1963/1964): 17-26.

Neumann, G. The origin of the Prairie physical type of American Indian. Michigan Academy of Science, Arts and Letters, Papers, 27 (1941): 539-542.

Newcomb, W. W. A re-examination of the causes of Plains warfare. American Anthropologist, 52 (1950): 317-330.

Newcomb, William W., Jr. The Indians of Texas, from prehistoric to modern times. Austin, University of Texas Press, 1961. 404 p. illus.

Newcomb, William W., Jr. The rock art of Texas Indians. Paintings by Forrest Kirkland. Austin, University of Texas Press, 1967. 14, 239 p. illus., maps.

Newell, Robert. Memoranda. Edited by Dorothy O. Johansen. Portland, Or., Champoeg Press, 1959. 159 p. illus., maps.

Newman, T. M. Documentary sources on the manufacture of pottery by the Indians of the Central Plains and Middle Missouri. Plains Anthropologist, 4 (1955): 13-20.

Nichols, Roger L. General Henry Atkinson, a Western military career. Norman, University of Oklahoma Press, 1965. 14, 243 p. illus., maps.

Nichols, Roger L. The army and the Indians 1800-1830--a reappraisal: the Missouri Valley example. Pacific Historical Review, 41 (1972): 151-168.

Noyes, Lee. Major Marcus A. Reno at the Little Big Horn. North Dakota History, 28 (1961): 5-11.

Nunis, Doyce B., Jr. The Sublettes of Kentucky and the Far West, 1830-1857. Kentucky Historical Society, Register, 58 (1960): 129-144.

Nydahl, T. L. The pipestone quarry and the Indians. Minnesota History, 31 (1950): 193-208.

Nye, Wilbur S. Carbine and lance; the story of old Fort Sill. Norman,

University of Oklahoma Press, 1969. 21, 361 p. illus., maps.

Nye, Wilbur S. Plains Indian raiders. Norman, University of Oklahoma Press, 1968. 20, 418 p. illus., maps.

Oglesby, Richard E. Pierre Menard, reluctant mountain man. Missouri Historical Society, Bulletin, 24 (1967/1968): 3-19.

Oglesby, Richard Edward. Vision of empire: Manuel Lisa and the opening of the Missouri fur trade. Dissertation Abstracts, 23 (1962/1963): 3335-3336. UM 63-1327.

Oliver, Symmes C. Ecology and cultural continuity as contributing factors in the social organization of the Plains Indians. Berkeley, 1962. 90 p. map. (California, University, Publications in American Archaeology and Ethnology, 48, no. 1)

Ortiz, Francisco Xavier. Razón de la visita a las misiones de la Provincia de Texas: 2. México, Vargas Rea, 1955. 38 p.

Osgood, Ernest S. Clark on the Yellowstone, 1806. Montana, the Magazine of Western History, 18, no. 3 (1968): 8-29.

Over, W. H. Indian picture writing in South Dakota. South Dakota, University, Archaeological Studies, 4 (1941): 1-59.

Ozee, D. W. An historic Indian cache in Clay County. Texas Archeological and Paleontological Society, Bulletin, 26 (1955): 256-258.

Paget, A. M. The people of the Plains. Toronto, 1909.

Parker, John. The fur trader and the emerging geography of North America. Museum of the Fur Trade Quarterly, 2, no. 3 (1966): 6-10; 2, no. 4 (1966): 7-11.

Parker, Watson. The majors and the miners: the role of the U.S. Army in the Black Hills gold rush. Journal of the West, 11 (1972): 99-113.

Parsons, Joseph A., Jr. Civilizing the Indians of the Old Northwest, 1800-1810. Indiana Magazine of History, 56 (1960): 195-216.

Paul Wilhelm, Duke of Wuerttemburg. First journey to North America. South Dakota Historical Collections, 19 (1938): 7-473.

Perrin du Lac, M. Travels through the two Louisianas. London, 1807. 106 p.

Perrin du Lac, M. Voyage dans les deux Louisianes. Lyon, 1805. 472 p.

Petersen, Karen Daniels. Howling Wolf; a Cheyenne warrior's graphic interpretation of his people. Palo Alto, American West Publishing, 1968. 63 p. illus.

Petersen, Karen Daniels. Plains Indian art from Fort Marion. Norman, University of Oklahoma Press, 1971. 20, 340 p. illus.

Petersen, William J. Stephen Watts Kearny. Palimpsest, 43 (1962): 1-9.

Petersen, William J. The Northwest Passage to Iowa. Palimpsest, 49 (1968): 401-415.

Petersen, William J. Up the Missouri with Atkinson. Palimpsest, 44 (1963): 28-38.

Pfaller, Louis. Charles Larpenteur. North Dakota History, 32 (1965): 5-17.

Pfaller, Louis. Indian scare of 1890. North Dakota History, 39, no. 1 (1972): 4-17.

Pfaller, Louis. Mystery martyr in Badlands baffles historians. North Dakota History, 29 (1962): 267-272.

Pfaller, Louis. Sully's expedition of 1864 featuring the Killdeer Mountain and Badland's Battles. North Dakota History, 31 (1964): 25-77.

Pfaller, Louis. The Brave Bear murder case. North Dakota History, 36 (1969): 121-139.

Pike, Z. M. Account of expeditions to the sources of the Mississippi. Philadelphia, 1810. 2 v.

Pike, Zebulon Montgomery. Pike's Mississippi expedition. Edited by William J. Petersen. Palimpsest, 49 (1968): 47-80.

Point, Nicolas. Wilderness kingdom: Indian life in the Rocky Mountains: 1840-1847; the journals and paintings of Nicolas Point, S.J. Translated and introduced by Joseph P. Donnelly. New York, Holt, Rinehart and Winston, 1967. 13, 274 p. illus., maps.

Pope, John. General Pope's report on the West, 1866. Edited by Richard N. Ellis. Kansas Historical Quarterly, 35 (1969): 345-372.

Pope, Polly. Trade in the Plains:
affluence and its effects. Kroeber
Anthropological Society Papers, 34
(1966): 53-61.

Powell, L. H. A study of Indian beadwork
of the North Central Plains. St. Paul
Science Museum, Indian Leaflets, 5-7
(1953): 1-8.

Provinse, J. H. The underlying sanctions
of Plains Indian culture. In F. Eggan,
ed. Social Anthropology of North
American Tribes. 2d ed. Chicago, 1955:
341-376.

Raemsch, Bruce Ellenwood. The
Indianization of the mountain men.
Dissertation Abstracts, 27 (1966/1967):
4225B. UM 67-7871.

Rathjen, Frederick William. The Texas
Panhandle frontier. Dissertation
Abstracts International, 31 (1970/1971):
5994A-5995A. UM 71-11,597.

Rauch, J. W. Report [on the medical and
economical botany of Iowa]. Iowa State
Medical and Chirurgical Society,
Proceedings, 2 (1851): 11-52.

Ray, V. F. Historic backgrounds of the
conjuring complex in the Plateau and the
Plains. In Essays in Memory of E. Sapir.
Menasha, 1941: 204-216.

Reading, Robert S. Arrows over Texas. 3d
ed. San Antonio, Naylor, 1967. 19,
270 p. illus.

Reese, Calvin Lee. The United States Army
and the Indian, Low Plains area 1815-
1864. Dissertation Abstracts, 24
(1963/1964): 5365. UM 64-5163.

Reid, Russell. Sakakawea. North Dakota
History, 30 (1963): 101-113.

Reid, Russell. Verendrye's journal to
North Dakota in 1738. North Dakota
History, 32 (1965): 117-129.

Renaud, E. B. Indian petroglyphs of the
Plains. In D. D. Brand and F. E. Harvey,
eds. So Live the Works of Men.
Albuquerque, 1939: 295-310.

Reynolds, Sam. A Dakota tipi. North
Dakota History, 40, no. 4 (1973): 20-29.

Rickett, H. W. John Bradbury's
explorations in Missouri Territory.
American Philosophical Society,
Proceedings, 94 (1950): 59-90.

Rickey, Don, Jr. The establishment of
Custer Battlefield National Monument.
Journal of the West, 7 (1968): 203-216.

Ridley, F. Cultural contacts of Iroquoian
and Plains. Pennsylvania Archaeologist,
27 (1957): 33-38.

Roberts, R. Jay. The history of Agate
Springs. Nebraska History, 47 (1966):
265-293.

Robinson, Charles. Charles Robinson--
Yankee '49er: his journey to California.
Edited by Louise Barry. Kansas
Historical Quarterly, 34 (1968): 179-
188.

Rodee, Howard D. The stylistic
development of Plains Indian painting
and its relationship to ledger drawings.
Plains Anthropologist, 10 (1965): 218-
232.

Röder, J. Der wissenschaftliche Nachlass
von Maximilian, Prinz zu Wied.
International Congress of Americanists,
Proceedings, 30 (1955): 187-192.

Roe, F. G. From dogs to horses among the
Western Indian tribes. Royal Society of
Canada, Proceedings and Transactions,
ser. 3, 33, pt. 2 (1939): 209-275.

Roe, F. G. White buffalo. Royal Society
of Canada, Proceedings and Transactions,
ser. 3, 38, pt. 2 (1944): 155-173.

Rogers, Edward S. Indians of the Plains.
Toronto, Royal Ontario Museum, 1970.
16 p. illus., maps.

Rollins, P. A., ed. The discovery of the
Oregon Trail. New York, 1935. 391 p.

Rowe, David C. Government relations with
the fur trappers of the Upper Missouri:
1820-1840. North Dakota History, 35
(1968): 481-505.

Rydjord, John. Indian place-names; their
origin, evolution, and meanings,
collected in Kansas from the Siouan,
Algonquian, Shoshonean, Caddoan,
Iroquoian, and other tongues. Norman,
University of Oklahoma Press, 1968. 11,
380 p. illus., maps.

Sandoz, M. The look of the West--1854.
Nebraska History, 35 (1954): 243-254.

Sandoz, Mari. The Battle of the Little
Bighorn. New York, J. F. Carr, 1966.
206 p. illus., map.

Schlesier, Karl H. Rethinking the Dismal
River Aspect and the Plains Athapaskans,
A.D. 1692-1768. Plains Anthropologist,
17 (1972): 101-133.

Schlesier, Karl-Heinz. Migration und
Kulturwandel am Mittleren Missouri,

1550-1850. Zeitschrift für Ethnologie, 93 (1968): 23-48.

Schroeder, Albert H.   A re-analysis of the routes of Coronado and Oñate into the Plains in 1541 and 1601. Plains Anthropologist, 7 (1962): 2-23.

Schuck, Cecilia.   Indian children of the Dakotas: boarding school diets, growth and development of adolescent girls. By Cecilia Schuck, Burness G. Wenberg, and Margaret Talcott Boedeker.   Brookings, 1964.   25 p.   illus.   (South Dakota, Agricultural Experiment Station, Brookings, Bulletin, 514)

Schusky, Ernest L.   The Upper Missouri Indian Agency, 1819-1868. Missouri Historical Review, 65 (1970/1971): 249-269.

Schusky, Mary Sue.   A center of primary sources for Plains Indian history? By Mary Sue and Ernest L. Schusky. Plains Anthropologist, 15 (1970): 104-108.

Scott, H. L.   The sign language of the Plains Indians. International Folk-Lore Association, Archives, 1 (1893): 1-206.

Secoy, F. R.   Changing military patterns on the Great Plains. American Ethnological Society, Monographs, 21 (1953): 1-120.

Selinger, Alphonse D.   The American Indian graduate: after high school, what? Portland, Or., Northwest Regional Educational Laboratory, 1968.   123 p. ERIC ED026165.

Selinger, Alphonse D.   The American Indian high school dropout: the magnitude of the problem.   Portland, Or., Northwest Regional Educational Laboratory, 1968. 176 p.   ERIC ED026164.

Settle, Raymond W.   A problem in identity: two Nathaniel Pryors. By Raymond W. and Mary Lund Settle. Nebraska History, 46 (1965): 139-155.

Shane, Ralph M.   A short history of the Fort Berthold Indian Reservation. North Dakota History, 26 (1959): 181-214.

Sheehan, John F.   Carcinoma of the cervix in Indian women. By John F. Sheehan, George J. Basque, and Harle V. Barrett. Nebraska State Medical Journal, 50 (1965): 553-558.

Shelby, C. C.   St. Denis's declaration concerning Texas in 1717. Southwestern Historical Quarterly, 26 (1923): 165-183.

Shelby, C. C.   St. Denis's second expedition to the Rio Grande, 1716-1719. Southwestern Historical Quarterly, 27 (1924): 190-216.

Ship, Irwin I.   Nutrition and dental caries: effects of phosphate supplements. In Environmental Variables in Oral Disease.   Washington, D.C., 1966: 129-151.   (American Associaton for the Advancement of Science, Publication, 81)

Shonle, R.   Peyote. American Anthropologist, n.s., 27 (1925): 53-75.

Sibley, George C.   George C. Sibley's plea for the "Garden of Missouri" in 1824. Edited by William E. Unrau. Missouri Historical Society, Bulletin, 27 (1970/1971): 3-13.

Sievers, Michael A.   The administration of Indian affairs on the Upper Missouri, 1858-1865. North Dakota History, 38 (1971): 366-394.

Siiger, H.   Indianerne og bisonen. Geografisk Tidsskrift, 47 (1945): 155-174.

Siiger, H.   Praerieindianerne og piben. Kobenhavn, Fra Nationalmuseets Arbejdsmark (1946): 24-29.

Sizemore, Mamie, et al.   Colorado Indian Education Workshop papers.   Alamosa, Colo., Adams State College, 1964.   81 p. ERIC ED012193.

Skinner, A. E.   Forgotten guardians; the activities of Company C, Frontier Forces, 1870-1871. Texana, 6 (1968): 107-121.

Slotkin, J. S.   Early eighteenth century documents on peyotism north of the Rio Grande. American Anthropologist, 53 (1951): 420-427.

Smet, P. J. de.   Letters and sketches. Philadelphia, 1843.

Smet, P. J. de.   Voyages aux Montagnes Rocheuses. New ed.   Paris, 1873.

Smet, Pierre Jean de.   Father DeSmet in North Dakota. Edited by James B. Connolly. North Dakota History, 27 (1960): 5-24.

Smet, Pierre Jean de.   Western missions and missionaries: a series of letters. Shannon, Irish University Press, 1972. 13, 532 p.

Smith, Carlyle S.   Time perspective within the Coalescent tradition in South

Dakota. American Antiquity, 28 (1962/1963): 489-495.

Smith, Cornelius C., Jr. Crook and Crazy Horse. Montana, the Magazine of Western History, 16, no. 2 (1966): 14-26.

Smith, G. Hubert. Archeological investigations at the site of Fort Stevenson (32ML1), Garrison Reservoir, North Dakota. Appendix by Carlyle S. Smith. Washington, D.C., Government Printing Office, 1960. 159-238 p. illus., maps. (U.S., Bureau of American Ethnology, River Basin Surveys Papers, 19. U.S., Bureau of American Ethnology, Bulletin, 176)

Smith, G. Hubert. Fort Pierre II (39ST217), a historic trading post in the Oahe Dam area, South Dakota. Washington, D.C., Government Printing Office, 1960. 83-158 p. illus., maps. (U.S., Bureau of American Ethnology, River Basin Surveys Papers, 18. U.S., Bureau of American Ethnology, Bulletin, 176)

Smith, M. G. Political organization of the Plains Indians. Nebraska, University, Studies, 24 (1925): 1-84.

Smith, M. W. The war complex of the Plains Indians. American Philosophical Society, Proceedings, 78 (1938): 425-464.

Smith, Marian. Mandan "history" as reflected in Bufferfly's winter count. Ethnohistory, 7 (1960): 199-205.

Smith, Marian W. The war complex of the Plains Indians. In Roger L. Nichols and George R. Adams, eds. The American Indian: Past and Present. Waltham, Xerox College Publishing, 1971: 146-155.

Snell, Joseph W. When the Union and Kansas Pacific built through Kansas. By Joseph W. Snell and Robert W. Richmond. Kansas Historical Quarterly, 32 (1966): 334-352.

South Dakota, Department of Public Instruction. Indians of South Dakota. Pierre, 1954. 63 p.

Spencer, Milton. The letters of Private Milton Spencer, 1862-1865: a soldier's view of military life on the Northern Plains. Edited by Carol G. Goodwin. North Dakota History, 37 (1970): 233-269.

Spier, L. An analysis of Plains Indian parfleche decoration. Washington, University, Publications in Anthropology, 1 (1925): 89-112.

Spier, L. Plains Indian parfleche designs. Washington, University, Publications in Anthropology, 4 (1931): 293-322.

Spier, L. The sun dance of the Plains Indians. American Museum of Natural History, Anthropological Papers, 16 (1921): 451-527.

Spindler, Will H. Tragedy strikes at Wounded Knee, and other essays on Indian life in South Dakota and Nebraska. Vermillion, University of South Dakota, 1972. 138 p. illus.

Stanley, Henry M. A British journalist reports the Medicine Lodge peace councils of 1867. Kansas Historical Quarterly, 33 (1967): 249-320.

Stanley, Henry M. Henry M. Stanley's letters to the Missouri Democrat. Edited by Douglas L. Wheeler. Missouri Historical Society, Bulletin, 17 (1960/1961): 269-286.

Steckler, Gerard G. North Dakota versus Frederick Jackson Turner. North Dakota History, 28 (1961): 33-45.

Steege, L. C. The sequence in Northern Plains prehistory. Annals of Wyoming, 31 (1959): 101-108.

Steinmetz, Paul B. The relationship between Plains Indian religion and Christianity: a priest's viewpoint. Plains Anthropologist, 15 (1970): 83-86.

Stenberg, M. P. The peyote culture among Wyoming Indians. Wyoming, University, Publications, 12 (1946): 85-156.

Stevens, Harry R. A company of hands and traders: origins of the Glenn-Fowler Expedition of 1821-1822. New Mexico Historical Review, 46 (1971): 181-221.

Stevens, O. A. Plants used by Indians in the Missouri River area. North Dakota History, 32 (1965): 101-106.

Stewart, E. I. Custer's luck. Norman, 1955. 538 p.

Stewart, Omer C. Ute Indians: before and after White contact. Utah Historical Quarterly, 34 (1966): 40-61.

Stirling, M. W. Indians of our Western Plains. National Geographic Magazine, 86 (1944): 73-108.

Stockman, Wallace Henry. Historical perspectives of federal educational promises and performance among the Fort Berthold Indians. Dissertation Abstracts

International, 33 (1972/1973): 1475A-
1476A. UM 72-25,221.

Stoller, Marianne L. A sacred bundle of
the Arapaho Indians. Pittsburgh,
Carnegie Museum, Annals, 35 (1957/1960):
11-25.

Strate, David K. Sentinel to the
Cimarron: the frontier experience of
Fort Dodge, Kansas. Dodge City,
Cultural Heritage and Arts Center, 1970.
148 p. illus.

Strong, W. D. An introduction to Nebraska
archeology. Smithsonian Miscellaneous
Collections, 93, no. 10 (1935): 1-323.

Strong, W. D. From history to prehistory
in the northern Great Plains.
Smithsonian Miscellaneous Collections,
100 (1940): 353-394.

Strong, W. D. The Plains culture area in
the light of archaeology. American
Anthropologist, n.s., 35 (1933): 271-
287.

Strong, William Duncan. From history to
prehistory in the northern Great Plains.
Plains Anthropologist, 17 (1972): 353-
394 [sic].

Stroud, Harry A. Conquest of the
prairies. Waco, Texian Press, 1968.
12, 281 p. illus.

Sturgis, William. A cattleman views
Indian policy--1875. Edited by Gene M.
Gressley. Montana, the Magazine of
Western History, 17, no. 1 (1967): 2-11.

Sullivan, L. R. Anthropometry of the
Siouan tribes. National Academy of
Sciences, Proceedings, 6 (1920): 131-
134.

Taylor, Allan R. The classification of
the Caddoan languages. American
Philosophical Society, Proceedings, 107
(1963): 51-59.

Taylor, Colin. Early Plains Indian quill
techniques in European museum
collections. Plains Anthropologist, 7
(1962): 58-69.

Taylor, Joe F., ed. The Indian campaign
on the Staked Plains, 1874-1875.
Panhandle-Plains Historical Review, 34
(1961): 1-216; 35 (1962): 215-368.

Taylor, Morris F. Capt. William Craig and
the Vigil and St. Vrain grant. Colorado
Magazine, 45 (1968): 301-321.

Taylor, Morris F. Kicking Bird: a chief
of the Kiowas. Kansas Historical
Quarterly, 38 (1972): 295-319.

Taylor, Morris F. Plains Indians on the
New Mexico-Colorado border: the last
phase, 1870-1876. New Mexico Historical
Review, 46 (1971): 315-336.

Taylor, Morris F. The mail station and
the military at camp on Pawnee Fork,
1859-1860. Kansas Historical Quarterly,
36 (1970): 27-39.

Taylor, V. H. and J. Hammons. The letters
of Antonio Martinez. Austin, 1957.
379 p.

Tefft, Stanton K. From band to tribe on
the Plains. Plains Anthropologist, 10
(1965): 166-170.

Tefft, Stanton K. From band to tribe on
the Plains. Plains Anthropologist, 10
(1965): 57.

Texas, State Library, Austin, Archives
Division. Texas Indian papers. Edited
by Dorman H. Winfrey, et al. Austin,
1959-1966. 5 v. illus., maps.

Thomas, A. B. The Plains Indians and New
Mexico, 1751-1778. Albuquerque, 1940.
232 p.

Thomas, A. B., ed. After Coronado.
Albuquerque, 1935. 307 p.

Tibbles, T. H. Buckskin and blanket days.
Garden City, 1957. 336 p.

Tilghman, Z. A. Source of the buffalo
origin legend. American Anthropologist,
n.s., 43 (1941): 487-488.

Tomkins, W. Universal sign language of
the Plains Indians. San Diego, 1926.
77 p.

Tretsven, Venus E. Incidence of cleft lip
and palate in Montana Indians. Journal
of Speech and Hearing Disorders, 28
(1963): 52-57.

Troike, Rudolph C. A Pawnee visit to San
Antonio in 1795. Ethnohistory, 11
(1964): 380-393.

Troike, Rudolph C. The origins of Plains
mescalism. American Anthropologist, 64
(1962): 946-963.

Truteau, J. B. Journal. American
Historical Review, 19 (1914): 299-333.

Unrau, William E. A prelude to war.
Colorado Magazine, 41 (1964): 299-313.

Unrau, William E. Indian agents vs. the
Army: some background notes on the
Kiowa-Comanche Treaty of 1865. Kansas
Historical Quarterly, 30 (1964): 129-
152.

U.S., Bureau of Indian Affairs. Indians
of the Central Plains. Washington,
D.C., Government Printing Office, 1968.
24 p. ERIC ED028869.

U.S., Bureau of Indian Affairs. Indians
of the Dakotas. Washington, D.C.,
Government Printing Office, 1968. 24 p.
ERIC ED028868.

U.S., Congress, Senate, Committee on
Interior and Insular Affairs. Fort
Belknap Indian Reservation and the Fort
Belknap Builders, Inc.; staff report.
Washington, D.C., Government Printing
Office, 1972. 5, 45 p.

U.S., Indian Arts and Crafts Board.
Contemporary Indian artists, Montana,
Wyoming, Idaho. Edited by Dorothy Jean
Ray. Rapid City, S.D., Tipi Shop, 1972.
80 p. illus.

Utley, Robert M. Fort Union and the Santa
Fe Trail. New Mexico Historical Review,
36 (1961): 36-48.

Vanmeter, Abel J. Abel J. Vanmeter, his
park and his diary. Edited by Jean Tyree
Hamilton. Missouri Historical Society,
Bulletin, 28 (1971/1972): 3-37.

Various. Leadership and development in a
bi-cultural setting. Bozeman, 1971.
22 p. (Montana, Agricultural Experiment
Station, Bulletin, 657)

Vatter, E. Historienmalerei und
heraldische Bilderschrift der
nordamerikanischen Präriestämme. Ipek
(1927): 46-81.

Vestal, S. Warpath and council fire. New
York, 1948. 338 p.

Voegelin, C. F. A problem in morpheme
alternants and their distribution.
Language, 23 (1947): 245-254.

Voegelin, C. F. Internal relationships of
Siouan languages. American
Anthropologist, n.s., 43 (1941): 246-
249.

Voegelin, Carl F. Selection in Hopi
ethics, linguistics, and translation. By
C. F. Voegelin and F. M. Voegelin.
Anthropological Linguistics, 2, no. 2
(1960): 48-78.

Voegelin, Carl F. Sign language analysis
on one level or two? International
Journal of American Linguistics, 24
(1958): 71-77.

Vogdes, Ada A. The journal of Ada A.
Vogdes, 1868-71. Edited by Donald K.
Adams. Montana, the Magazine of Western
History, 13, no. 3 (1963): 2-18.

Vogel, Virgil J. The origin and meaning
of "Missouri". Missouri Historical
Society, Bulletin, 16 (1959/1960): 213-
222.

Voget, Fred W. American Indian
reformations and acculturation. In
Contributions to Anthropology 1960. Part
II. Ottawa, Queen's Printer, 1963: 1-
13. (Canada, National Museum, Bulletin,
190)

Wagner, G. Entwicklung und Verbreitung
des Peyote-Kultes. Baessler-Archiv, 15
(1932): 59-144.

Wagner, H. R. The Plains and the Rockies.
3d ed. Columbus, 1953. 601 p.

Wagner, Oswald F. Lutheran zealots among
the Crows. Montana, the Magazine of
Western History, 22, no. 2 (1972): 2-19.

Wake, C. S. Mythology of the Plains
Indians. American Antiquarian and
Oriental Journal, 27 (1905): 9-16, 73-80
323-328; 28 (1906): 205-212.

Walker, Deward E., Jr. New light on the
Prophet Dance controversy. Ethnohistory,
16 (1969): 245-255.

Walker, J. R. Sign language of the Plains
Indians. Chronicles of Oklahoma, 31
(1953): 168-177.

Ward, Allen T. Letters of Allen T. Ward,
1842-1851, from the Shawnee and Kaw
(Methodist) Missions. Edited by Lela
Barnes. Kansas Historical Quarterly, 33
(1967): 321-376.

Ware, Eugene F. The Indian War of 1864.
With an introduction and notes by Clyde
C. Walton. New York, St. Martin's
Press, 1960. 483 p. illus.

Webb, W. P. The Great Plains, 47-84.
Boston, 1931.

Wedel, Mildred Mott. Corn horticulture.
Palimpsest, 42 (1961): 561-569.

Wedel, W. R. An introduction to Kansas
archeology. U.S. Bureau of American
Ethnology, Bulletin, 174, (1959): 1-723.

Wedel, W. R. Environment and native
subsistence economies in the Central
Great Plains. Smithsonian Miscellaneous
Collections, 101, no. 3 (1941): 1-30.

Wedel, W. R. Prehistory and environment
in the Central Great Plains. Kansas
Academy of Science, Transactions, 50
(1947): 1-18.

Wedel, W. R. Some aspects of human ecology in the Central Plains. American Anthropologist, 55 (1953): 499-514.

Wedel, Waldo R. After Coronado in Quivira. Kansas Historical Quarterly, 34 (1968): 369-385.

Wedel, Waldo R. Coronado's route to Quivira 1541. Plains Anthropologist, 15 (1970): 161-168.

Wedel, Waldo R. The High Plains and their utilization by the Indian. American Antiquity, 29 (1963/1964): 1-16.

Weer, P. Preliminary notes on the Caddoan family. Indiana Historical Society, Prehistory Research Series, 1, no. 4 (1938): 111-130.

Weer, P. Preliminary notes on the Siouan family. Indiana History Bulletin, 14 (1937): 99-120.

Wells, Robin F. Plains Indian political structure: a comparative study. Kroeber Anthropological Society Papers, 24 (1961): 1-16.

Welskopf, Elisabeth Charlotte. Akkulturationsprobleme der Prärie-Indianer in Canada. Ethnographisch-Archäologische Zeitschrift, 5 (1964): 97-110.

Weltfish, G. The question of ethnic identity. Ethnohistory, 6 (1959): 321-346.

Weltfish, Gene. The Plains Indians: their continuity in history and their Indian identity. In Eleanor Burke Leacock and Nancy Oestreich Lurie, eds. North American Indians in Historical Perspective. New York, Random House, 1971: 200-227.

Wemett, W. M. Making a path to the Pacific; the story of the Steven's survey. North Dakota History, 29 (1962): 303-319.

West, G. Derek. The Battle of Adobe Walls (1874). Panhandle-Plains Historical Review, 36 (1963): 1-36.

West, G. Derek. The Battle of Sappa Creek (1875). Kansas Historical Quarterly, 34 (1968): 150-178.

Whipple, A. W. Lieutenant A. W. Whipple's railroad reconnaissance across the Panhandle of Texas in 1853. Edited by Ernest R. Archambeau. Panhandle-Plains Historical Review, 44 (1971): 1-128.

White, Douglas Richie. Decision making in equestrian Indian societies: an essay in comparative pragmatics. Dissertation Abstracts International, 30 (1969/1970): 3002B. UM 69-20,070.

White, Lonnie J. From bloodless to bloody: the Third Colorado Cavalry and the Sand Creek Massacre. Journal of the West, 6 (1967): 535-581.

White, Lonnie J. General Sully's expedition to the North Canadian, 1868. Journal of the West, 11 (1972): 75-98.

White, Lonnie J. Indian raids on the Kansas frontier, 1869. Kansas Historical Quarterly, 38 (1972): 369-388.

White, Lonnie J. The Battle of Beecher Island: the scouts hold fast on the Arickaree. Journal of the West, 5 (1966): 1-24.

White, Lonnie J. The Hancock and Custer Expeditions of 1867. Journal of the West, 5 (1966): 355-378.

White, Lonnie J. Warpaths on the Southern Plains: the battles of the Saline River and Prairie Dog Creek. Journal of the West, 4 (1965): 485-503.

White, Lonnie J. White women captives of Southern Plains Indians, 1866-1875. Journal of the West, 8 (1969): 327-354.

White, M. C. David Thompson's journals relating to Montana and adjacent regions, 1808-1812. Missoula, 1950. 507 p.

Wilbarger, J. W. Indian depradations in Texas. Austin, Pemberton Press, 1867. 14, 672 p. illus.

Will, George F. Corn among the Indians of the Upper Missouri. By George F. Will and George E. Hyde. Lincoln, University of Nebraska Press, 1964. 323 p. illus.

Williamson, A. W. The Dakotan languages. American Antiquarian and Oriental Journal, 4 (1882): 110-128.

Wilson, H. Clyde. An inquiry into the nature of Plains Indian cultural development. American Anthropologist, 65 (1963): 355-369.

Wilson, Peter. The letters of Peter Wilson, first resident agent among the Teton Sioux. Edited by Harry H. Anderson. Nebraska History, 42 (1961): 237-264.

Wilson, Wesley. The U.S. Army and the Piegans--the Baker Massacre of 1870. North Dakota History, 32 (1965): 40-58.

Wind River Reservation Curriculum
Development Workshop. The Wind River
Reservation: yesterday and today. Fort
Washakie, Wyo., 1972. 58 p.

Winfrey, Dorman H., et al. Indian tribes
of Texas. Waco, Texian Press, 1971. 7,
178 p. illus.

Wishart, David John. An historical
geography of the fur trade of the Upper
Missouri, 1807-1843. Dissertation
Abstracts International, 32 (1971/1972):
2790B. UM 71-28,656.

Wissler, C. Changes in population
profiles among the Northern Plains
Indians. American Museum of Natural
History, Anthropological Papers, 36
(1936): 1-67.

Wissler, C. Costumes of the Plains
Indians. American Museum of Natural
History, Anthropological Papers, 17
(1915): 39-91.

Wissler, C. Diffusion of culture in the
Plains. International Congress of
Americanists, Proceedings, 15, vol. 2
(1906): 39-52.

Wissler, C. Distribution of moccasin
decorations among the Plains tribes.
American Museum of Natural History,
Anthropological Papers, 29 (1927): 1-23.

Wissler, C. Ethnographical problems of
the Missouri Saskatchewan area. American
Anthropologist, n.s., 10 (1908): 197-
207.

Wissler, C. General discussion of
shamanistic and dancing societies.
American Museum of Natural History,
Anthropological Papers, 11 (1916): 853-
876.

Wissler, C. North American Indians of the
Plains. New York, 1912. 147 p.

Wissler, C. Population changes among the
Northern Plains Indians. Yale University
Publications in Anthropology, 1 (1936):
1-20.

Wissler, C. Riding gear of the North
American Indians. American Museum of
Natural History, Anthropological Papers,
17 (1915): 1-38.

Wissler, C. Structural basis to the
decoration of costumes among the Plains
Indians. American Museum of Natural
History, Anthropological Papers, 17
(1916): 93-114.

Wissler, C. The distribution and
functions of tribal societies among the
Plains Indians. National Academy of
Sciences, Proceedings, 1 (1915): 401-
403.

Wissler, C. The influence of the horse in
the development of Plains culture.
American Anthropologist, n.s., 16
(1914): 1-25.

Wissler, C. Types of dwellings and their
distribution in Central North America.
International Congress of Americanists,
Proceedings, 16 (1908): 477-487.

Wolff, H. Comparative Siouan.
International Journal of American
Linguistics, 16 (1950): 61-66.

Wood, W. Raymond. Notes on Ponca
ethnohistory, 1785-1804. Ethnohistory, 6
(1959): 1-27.

Woolworth, Alan R. Excavations at Kipp's
Post. By Alan R. Woolworth and W.
Raymond Wood. North Dakota History, 29
(1962): 237-252.

Woolworth, Nancy L. Captain Edwin V.
Sumner's expedition to Devil's Lake in
the summer of 1845. North Dakota
History, 28 (1961): 79-98.

Wright, M. H. A guide to the Indian
tribes of Oklahoma. Norman, 1951.
300 p.

Wyoming Archaeological Society. A report
on the medicine wheel investigation.
Annals of Wyoming, 31 (1959): 94-100.

Zo-Tom. 1877: Plains Indian sketch books
of Zo-Tom and Howling Wolf. By Zo-Tom
and Howling Wolf. Flagstaff, Northland
Press, 1969. 25 p. illus.

09-01 Arapaho

Salzmann, Zdeněk. Bibliography of works
on the Arapaho division of Algonquian.
International Journal of American
Linguistics, 27 (1961): 183-187.

Anonymous. Arapaho and Cheyenne Indians.
H.R. 11359, 70th Congress, 1st Session,
March 1 and 15, 1928. Washington, D.C.,
1928.

Anonymous. Sioux treaty of 1868. Indian
Historian, 3, no. 1 (1970): 13-17.

Beals, R. L. Ethnology of Rocky Mountain
Park: the Ute and Arapaho. Berkeley,
1935. 27 p.

Benjamin, Peggy H.   The last of Captain
Jack. Montana, the Magazine of Western
History, 10, no. 2 (1960): 22-31.

Berthrong, D. J.   Federal Indian policy
and the Southern Cheyennes and
Arapahoes, 1887-1907. Ethnohistory, 3
(1956): 138-153.

Berthrong, Donald J.   Cattlemen on the
Cheyenne-Arapaho Reservation, 1883-1885.
Arizona and the West, 13 (1971): 5-32.

Berthrong, Donald J.   Federal Indian
policy and the Southern Cheyennes and
Araphoes, 1887-1907. In Richard N.
Ellis, ed. The Western American Indian.
Lincoln, University of Nebraska Press,
1972: 133-143.

Boas, F.   Zur Anthropologie der
nordamerikanischen Indianer. Berliner
Gesellschaft für Anthropologie,
Ethnologie und Urgeschichte,
Verhandlungen (1895): 367-411.

Bushnell, D. I.   Villages of the
Algonquian, Siouan and Caddoan tribes.
U.S. Bureau of American Ethnology,
Bulletin, 77 (1922): 33-37.

Byron, Elsa Spear.   The Fetterman fight.
Annals of Wyoming, 36 (1964): 63-66.

Callahan, Charles J.   Historical sketch of
Two Babies, Arapaho Indian. Chronicles
of Oklahoma, 45 (1967): 217-220.

Cardenal, Ernesto, tr.   Poesía de los
indios de Norteamérica. América
Indígena, 21 (1961): 355-362.

Carriker, Robert Charles.   Fort Supply,
Indian Territory: frontier outpost on
the Southern Plains, 1868-1894.
Dissertation Abstracts, 28 (1967/1968):
2158A.   UM 67-15,910.

Carter, J. G.   The Northern Arapaho flat
pipe and the ceremony of covering the
pipe. U.S. Bureau of American Ethnology,
Bulletin, 119 (1938): 69-102.

Cocking, Rodney R.   Fantasy confession
among Arapaho Indian children. Journal
of Genetic Psychology, 114 (1969): 229-
235.

Collings, Ellsworth.   Roman Nose: chief of
the Southern Cheyenne. Chronicles of
Oklahoma, 42 (1964): 429-457.

Corbusier, William T.   Camp Sheridan,
Nebraska. Nebraska History, 42 (1961):
29-51.

Curtis, E. S.   The North American Indian,
Vol. 6: 138-150, 159-164, 167-173.
Norwood, 1911.

Curtis, N., ed.   The Indians' book, 197-
217.   New York, 1907.

Dangberg, G. M.   Letters to Jack Wilson,
the Paiute prophet. U.S. Bureau of
American Ethnology, Bulletin, 164
(1957): 279-296.

Densmore, F.   Cheyenne and Arapaho music.
Southwest Museum Papers, 10 (1936): 9-
111.

Dodge, R. I.   Our wild Indians.   Hartford,
1882.   650 p.

*Dorsey, G. A.   The Arapaho sun dance.
Field Museum, Anthropological Series, 4
(1903): 1-228.

*Dorsey, G. A. and A. L. Kroeber.
Traditions of the Arapaho. Field Museum,
Anthropological Series, 5 (1903): 1-475.

Douglas, F. H.   A Northern Arapaho quilled
cradle. Denver Art Museum, Material
Culture Notes, 13 (1941): 53-59.

Dyer, D. B.   Fort Reno or picturesque
Cheyenne-Arapaho army life before the
opening of Oklahoma.   New York, 1896.
216 p.

Edwards, T. A.   Early days in the C and A.
Chronicles of Oklahoma, 27 (1949): 148-
161.

Eggan, F.   The Cheyenne and Arapaho
kinship system. In F. Eggan, ed. Social
Anthropology of North American Tribes.
2d ed.   Chicago, 1955: 35-98.

Elkin, H.   The Northern Arapaho of
Wyoming. In R. Linton, ed. Acculturation
in Seven American Indian Tribes.   New
York, 1940: 207-258.

Ellis, Richard N., ed.   The Western
American Indian: case studies in tribal
history.   Lincoln, University of
Nebraska Press, 1972.   203 p.

Fay, George E., ed.   Charters,
constitutions and by-laws of the Indian
tribes of North America. Part V: The
Indian tribes of Oklahoma.   Greeley,
1968.   14, 104 l.   map.   (University of
Northern Colorado, Museum of
Anthropology, Occasional Publications in
Anthropology, Ethnology Series, 6)   ERIC
ED046555.

Fay, George E., ed.   Military engagements
between United States troops and Plains
Indians; documentary inquiry by the U.S.
Congress. Part I: 1854-1867.   Greeley,
1972.   2 v. (236 l.).   (University of
Northern Colorado, Museum of
Anthropology, Occasional Publications in
Anthropology, Ethnology Series, 26)

Fendall, Lon W.   Medorem Crawford and the Protective Corps. Oregon Historical Quarterly, 72 (1971): 55-77.

Fisher, M. C.   On the Arapahoes, Kiowas, and Comanches. Ethnological Society (London), Journal, n.s., 1 (1869): 274-287.

Fletcher, A. C.   Indian story and song from North America. Boston, 1907. 126 p.

Foreman, G.   The last trek of the Indians, 296-302. Chicago, 1946.

Fowler, Loretta Kay.   Political process and socio-cultural change among the Arapahoe Indians. Dissertation Abstracts International, 31 (1970/1971): 5130B-5131B. UM 71-5097.

Fritz, Henry E.   The making of Grant's "peace policy". Chronicles of Oklahoma, 37 (1959): 411-432.

Githens, John H.   Prevalence of abnormal hemoglobins in American Indian children. Survey in the Rocky Mountain area. By John H. Githens, Henry K. Knock, and William E. Hathaway. Journal of Laboratory and Clinical Medicine, 57 (1961): 755-758.

Goddard, Ives.   Notes on the genetic classification of the Algonquian languages. In Contributions to Anthropology: Linguistics I. Ottawa, Queen's Printer, 1967: 7-12. (Canada, National Museum, Bulletin, 214)

Gross, F.   Language and value changes among the Arapaho. International Journal of American Linguistics, 17 (1951): 10-17.

Gross, F.   Nomadism of the Arapaho Indians of Wyoming. Wyoming, University, Publications, 15, no. 3 (1950): 35-55.

Haine, J. J. F.   A Belgian in the gold rush: California Indians. A memoir by J. J. F. Haine. Translated, with an introduction by Jan Albert Goris. California Historical Society Quarterly, 38 (1959): 141-155.

Hampton, James E.   Pernicious anemia in American Indians. Oklahoma State Medical Association, Journal, 53 (1960): 503-509.

Harmon, E. M.   The story of the Indian fort near Granby, Colorado. Colorado Magazine, 22 (1945): 167-171.

Harrison, Lowell H.   Damage suits for Indian depredations in the Adobe Walls area, 1874. Panhandle-Plains Historical Review, 36 (1963): 37-60.

Hayden, F. V.   Contributions to the ethnography and philology of the Indian tribes of the Missouri Valley. American Philosophical Society, Transactions, n.s., 12 (1863): 321-339.

*Hilger, M. I.   Arapaho child life and its cultural background. U.S. Bureau of American Ethnology, Bulletin, 148 (1952): 1-269.

Hockett, C. F.   Sapir on Arapaho. International Journal of American Linguistics, 12 (1946): 243-245.

Hodge, Patt.   The history of Hammon and the Red Moon School. Chronicles of Oklahoma, 44 (1966): 130-139.

Howbert, Irving.   Memories of a lifetime in the Pike's Peak region. Glorieta, N.M., Rio Grande Press, 1970. 298 p. illus., map.

Howbert, Irving.   The Indians of the Pike's Peak region. Glorieta, N.M., Rio Grande Press, 1970. 10, 230 p. illus., map.

Hudson's Bay Company.   Saskatchewan journals and correspondence: Edmonton House 1795-1800; Chesterfield House 1800-1802. Edited by Alice M. Johnson. London, 1967. 102, 368, 14 p. map. (Hudson's Bay Record Society, Publications, 26)

Hultkrantz, A.   Some notes on the Arapaho sun dance. Ethnos, 17 (1952): 24-38.

Hurst, C. T.   Colorado's old-timers. Southwestern Lore, 12 (1946): 19-26.

Jones, Douglas C.   Medicine Lodge revisited. Kansas Historical Quarterly, 35 (1969): 130-142.

Kate, H. F. C. ten.   Reizen en onderzoekingen in Noord-Amerika. Leiden, 1885. 464 p.

Kaufman, Edmund G.   Mennonite missions among the Oklahoma Indians. Chronicles of Oklahoma, 40 (1962): 41-54.

Kehoe, Alice B.   The function of ceremonial sexual intercourse among the Northern Plains Indians. Plains Anthropologist, 15 (1970): 99-103.

Kroeber, A. L.   Arapaho dialects. California, University, Publications in American Archaeology and Ethnology, 12 (1916): 71-138.

Kroeber, A. L. Decorative symbolism of the Arapaho. American Anthropologist, n.s., 3 (1901): 308-336.

Kroeber, A. L. Symbolism of the Arapaho Indians. American Museum of Natural History, Bulletin, 13 (1900): 69-86.

*Kroeber, A. L. The Arapaho. American Museum of Natural History, Bulletin, 18 (1902-1907): 1-229, 279-454.

Kroeber, A. L. The symbolism of the Arapaho Indians. Scientific American Supplement, 1297 (1900).

Kroeker, Marvin. Colonel W. B. Hazen in the Indian Territory. Chronicles of Oklahoma, 42 (1964): 53-73.

Larned, William L. The Fisk Expedition of 1864: the diary of William L. Larned. Edited by Ray H. Mattison. North Dakota History, 36 (1969): 209-274.

Law, Howard. Rank fused person morphemes and matrix methodology in Arapaho (Algonkin). Linguistics, 75 (1971): 5-30.

McKinley, J. W. J. W. McKinley's narrative. Panhandle-Plains Historical Review, 36 (1963): 61-69.

Meserve, C. F. The first allotment of lands in severalty among the Oklahoma Cheyenne and Arapaho Indians. Chronicles of Oklahoma, 11 (1933): 1040-1043.

Michelson, T. Narrative of an Arapaho woman. American Anthropologist, n.s., 35 (1933): 595-610.

Michelson, T. Phonetic shifts in Algonquian languages. International Journal of American Linguistics, 8 (1935): 131-171.

Michelson, T. Some Arapaho kinship terms and social usages. American Anthropologist, n.s., 36 (1934): 137-139.

Mooney, J. Arapaho. U.S. Bureau of American Ethnology, Bulletin, 30, vol. 1 (1907): 72-74.

Mooney, J. The ghost-dance religion. U.S. Bureau of American Ethnology, Annual Reports, 14, vol. 2 (1893): 953-1023.

Moran, P. Shoshone Agency. In United States Department of the Interior, Census Office, Eleventh Census, Report on Indians Taxed and Indians not Taxed. Washington, D.C., 1890: 629-634.

Munkres, Robert L. The Plains Indian threat on the Oregon Trail before 1860. Annals of Wyoming, 40 (1968): 193-221.

Muntsch, A. Notes on age-classes among the Northern Arapaho. Primitive Man, 5 (1932): 49-52.

Murphy, James C. The place of the Northern Arapahoes in the relations between the United States and the Indians of the Plains 1851-1879. Annals of Wyoming, 41 (1969): 33-61, 203-259.

Nettl, B. Musical culture of the Arapaho. Musical Quarterly, 41 (1955): 325-331.

Nettl, B. Text-music relationships in Arapaho songs. Southwestern Journal of Anthropology, 10 (1954): 192-199.

Nettl, Bruno. Zur Kompositionstechnik der Arapaho. Jahrbuch für Musikalische Volks- und Völkerkunde, 2 (1966): 114-118.

Neuman, Robert W. Porcupine quill flatteners from central United States. American Antiquity, 26 (1960/1961): 99-102.

Painter, C. C. G. Cheyenne and Arapaho revisited. Philadelphia, 1893. 62 p.

Pajeken, F. J. Religion und religiöse Vorstellungen der Arrapahoë-Indianer. Ausland, 63 (1890): 1011-1015.

Peery, D. W. The Indians' friend, John H. Seger. Chronicles of Oklahoma, 10 (1933): 348-368, 570-591; 11 (1933): 709-732, 845-868, 967-994.

Perkins, Georgia B. Report of pediatric evaluations of a sample of Indian children--Wind River Indian Reservation, 1957. By Georgia B. Perkins and Gertrude M. Church. American Journal of Public Health, 50 (1960): 181-194.

Poteet, Chrystabel Berrong. The ending of a Cheyenne legend. Chronicles of Oklahoma, 41 (1963): 9-14.

Radin, P. Jessie Clay's account of the Arapaho manner of giving the peyote ceremony. U.S. Bureau of American Ethnology, Annual Reports, 37 (1923): 415-419.

Rawlings, Charles. General Connor's Tongue River battle. Annals of Wyoming, 36 (1964): 73-77.

Rawlings, Charles. The Sawyer expedition. Annals of Wyoming, 36 (1964): 69-73.

Roberts, J., tr. Hethadence waunauyaunee
vadan Luke vanenana. New York, 1903.
102 p.

Robinett, Paul M. The military career of
James Craig. By Paul M. Robinett and
Howard V. Canan. Missouri Historical
Review, 66 (1971/1972): 49-75.

Rogers, Bess. Big Jake's crossing.
Chronicles of Oklahoma, 38 (1960): 50-
54.

Ruiz, José Francisco. Report on the
Indian tribes of Texas in 1828.
Translated by Georgette Dorn. Edited by
John C. Ewers. New Haven, Yale
University Library, 1972. 18 p.

Salzmann, Z. An Arapaho version of the
star husband tale. Hoosier Folklore, 9
(1950): 50-58.

Salzmann, Z. Arapaho tales III. Midwest
Folklore, 7 (1957): 27-37.

Salzmann, Z. Contrastive field experience
with language and values of the Arapaho.
International Journal of American
Linguistics, 17 (1951): 98-101.

Salzmann, Z. and J. Salzmann. Arapaho
tales I. Hoosier Folklore, 9 (1950): 80-
96.

Salzmann, Z. and J. Salzmann. Arapaho
tales II. Midwest Folklore, 2 (1952):
21-42.

Salzmann, Zdeněk. A sketch of Arapaho
grammar. Dissertation Abstracts, 24
(1963/1964): 3742. UM 64-509.

Salzmann, Zdeněk. Arapaho. International
Journal of American Linguistics, 22
(1956): 49-56, 151-158, 266-272; 27
(1961): 151-155; 31 (1965): 39-49, 136-
151; 33 (1967): 209-223.

Salzmann, Zdeněk. Arapaho kinship terms
and two related ethnolinguistic
observations. Anthropological
Linguistics, 1, no. 9 (1959): 6-10.

Salzmann, Zdeněk. Concerning the assumed
L-sound in Arapaho. Plains
Anthropologist, 6 (1961): 270-271.

Salzmann, Zdeněk. On the inflection of
transitive animate verbs in Arapaho. In
Contributions to Anthropology:
Linguistics I. Ottawa, Queen's Printer,
1967: 135-139. (Canada, National
Museum, Bulletin, 214)

Salzmann, Zdeněk. Salvage phonology of
Gros Ventre (Atsina). International
Journal of American Linguistics, 35
(1969): 307-314.

Salzmann, Zdeněk. Some aspects of Arapaho
morphology. In Contributions to
Anthropology: Linguistics I. Ottawa,
Queen's Printer, 1967: 128-134.
(Canada, National Museum, Bulletin, 214)

Salzmann, Zdeněk. Two brief contributions
toward Arapaho linguistic history.
Anthropological Linguistics, 2, no. 7
(1960): 39-48.

Schmidt, W. Die Arapaho. In his Die
Ursprung der Göttesidee. Bd. 2. Münster
i. W., 1929: 680-756.

Schmidt, W. Die Arapaho. In his Die
Ursprung der Göttesidee. Bd. 5. Münster
i. W., 1934: 664-676.

Schutz, W. D., et al. Indian ranching on
the Wind River Reservation, Wyoming.
Laramie, 1960. 36 p. illus., map.
(Wyoming, Agricultural Experiment
Station, Bulletin, 366)

Scott, H. L. The early history and names
of the Arapaho. American Anthropologist,
n.s., 9 (1907): 545-560.

Seger, J. H. Early days among the
Cheyenne and Arapahoe Indians. Ed. by S.
Vestal. Norman, 1956. 164 p.

Shakespeare, Tom. The sky people. New
York, Vantage Press, 1971. 117 p.

Smith, J. S. Arapahoes. In H. R.
Schoolcraft, ed. Information respecting
the History, Condition, and Prospects of
the Indian Tribes of the United States.
Vol. 3. Philadelphia, 1853: 446-459.

Starkloff, C. F. American Indian religion
and Christianity; confrontation and
dialogue. Journal of Ecumenical Studies,
8 (1971): 317-340.

Stewart, D. D. Cheyenne-Arapaho
assimilation. Phylon, 13 (1952): 120-
126.

Stoller, Marianne L. A sacred bundle of
the Arapaho Indians. Pittsburgh,
Carnegie Museum, Annals, 35 (1957/1960):
11-25.

Sweezy, Carl. The Arapaho way; a memoir
of an Indian boyhood. New York, C. N.
Potter, 1966. 80 p. illus.

Taylor, Allan R. Some observations on a
comparative Arapaho-Atsina lexicon. In
Contributions to Anthropology:
Linguistics I. Ottawa, Queen's Printer,
1967: 113-127. (Canada, National
Museum, Bulletin, 214)

Tefft, Stanton K. Anomy, values and
culture change among teen-age Indians:

an exploratory study. Sociology of
Education, 40 (1967): 145-157.

Tefft, Stanton K. Task experience and
intertribal value differences on the
Wind River Reservation. Social Forces,
49 (1970/1971): 604-614.

Thayer, B. H. Additional Arapaho moccasin
characteristics. Minnesota
Archaeologist, 8 (1942): 30-40.

Thompson, David. David Thompson's
narrative 1784-1812. Edited by Richard
Glover. Toronto, 1962. 102, 410 p.
map. (Champlain Society, Publications,
40)

Toll, Oliver W. Arapaho names and trails;
a report of a 1914 pack trip. [n.p.]
1962. 43 p. illus.

Trenholm, Virginia C. Arapahoes in
council. Annals of Wyoming, 44 (1972):
234-240.

Trenholm, Virginia C. The Arapahoes, our
people. Norman, University of Oklahoma
Press, 1970. 18, 372 p. illus., maps.

Uhlenbeck, C. C. Additional Blackfoot-
Arapaho comparisons. International
Journal of American Linguistics, 4
(1927): 227-228.

Underhill, R. M. Peyote. International
Congress of Americanists, Proceedings,
30 (1955): 143-148.

Underhill, R. M., et al. Modern Arapaho.
Southwestern Lore, 17 (1951): 38-42.

Unrau, William Errol. The role of the
Indian agent in the settlement of the
South-Central Plains, 1861-1868.
Dissertation Abstracts, 25 (1964/1965):
1884. UM 64-4389.

Vaughn, J. W. Sergeant Custard's wagon
train fight. Annals of Wyoming, 32
(1960): 227-234.

Voegelin, Carl F. Sign language analysis
on one level or two? International
Journal of American Linguistics, 24
(1958): 71-77.

Vogdes, Ada A. The journal of Ada A.
Vogdes, 1868-71. Edited by Donald K.
Adams. Montana, the Magazine of Western
History, 13, no. 3 (1963): 2-18.

Voth, H. R. Arapaho tales. Journal of
American Folklore, 25 (1912): 43-50.

Voth, H. R. Funeral customs among the
Cheyenne and Arapaho Indians.
Folklorist, 1 (1893).

Wake, C. S. Nihacan, the White man.
American Antiquarian and Oriental
Journal, 26 (1904): 225-231.

Webb, Frances Seely. The Indian version
of the Platte Bridge fight. Annals of
Wyoming, 32 (1960): 234-236.

Wedel, W. R. The Arapaho and Cheyenne.
U.S. Bureau of American Ethnology,
Bulletin, 174 (1959): 80-81.

White, Lonnie J. Indian battles in the
Texas Panhandle, 1874. Journal of the
West, 6 (1967): 278-309.

White, Lonnie J. The Cheyenne barrier on
the Kansas frontier, 1868-1869. Arizona
and the West, 4 (1962): 51-64.

White, Lonnie J. Winter campaigning with
Sheridan and Custer: the expedition of
the Nineteenth Kansas Volunteer Cavalry.
Journal of the West, 6 (1967): 68-98.

White, Lonnie J., ed. Kansas newspaper
items relating to the Red River War of
1874-1875. Panhandle-Plains Historical
Review, 36 (1963): 71-88.

Wildschut, W. Arapaho medicine bundle.
Indian Notes, 4 (1927): 83-88.

Wildschut, W. Arapaho medicine-mirror.
Indian Notes, 4 (1927): 252-257.

Wilson, Paul Burns. Farming and ranching
on the Wind River Indian Reservation,
Wyoming. Dissertation Abstracts
International, 34 (1973/1974): 272B-
273B. UM 73-15,406.

Woodward, George A. The Northern Cheyenne
at Fort Fetterman; Colonel Woodward
describes some experiences of 1871.
Edited by John E. Parsons. Montana, the
Magazine of Western History, 9, no. 2
(1959): 16-27.

Wright, Bessie L., ed. Diary of a member
of the first mule pack train to leave
Fort Smith for California in 1849.
Panhandle-Plains Historical Review, 42
(1969): 61-119.

09-02 Arikara

*Abel, A. H., ed. Tabeau's Narrative of
Loisel's Expedition to the Upper
Missouri. Norman, 1939. 272 p.

Agogino, George A. Osteology of the Four
Bear burials; 1958-59 excavation season.
By George A. Agogino and Eugene
Galloway. Plains Anthropologist, 8
(1963): 57-60.

Alexander, Ralph W., Jr. The hybrid
  origin of the Arikara Indians of the
  Great Plains. Dissertation Abstracts
  International, 32 (1971/1972): 4988B.
  UM 72-9961.

Anonymous. Arikara creation myth. Journal
  of American Folklore, 22 (1909): 90-92.

Anonymous. Senor Don Manuel Lisa.
  Missouri Historical Society, Bulletin,
  23 (1966/1967): 52-58.

Anonymous. South Dakota physical types.
  South Dakota, University, William H.
  Over Museum, Museum News, 12, no. 5
  (1952): 1.

Archaeological Project, South Dakota Works
  Project Administration. Arikara Indians
  of South Dakota. Vermillion, 1941.
  62 p.

Bass, William M. The excavation of
  Arikara burials from the Leavenworth
  Site, 39CO9, Corson County, South
  Dakota. Plains Anthropologist, 11
  (1966): 162.

Bass, William M. Two human skeletons from
  39LM227, a mound near the Stricker Site,
  Lyman County, South Dakota. By William
  M. Bass and Richard L. Jantz. Plains
  Anthropologist, 10 (1965): 20-30.

Bass, William M., et al. The Leavenworth
  Site cemetery: archaeology and physical
  anthropology. Lawrence, 1971. 200 p.
  illus. (Kansas, University,
  Publications in Anthropology, 2)

Bass, William M., III. The variation in
  physical types of the prehistoric Plains
  Indians. Lincoln, Plains Conference,
  1964. 65-145 p. illus. (Plains
  Anthropologist, Memoir, 1)

Bass, William Marvin, III. The variation
  in physical type of the prehistoric
  Plains Indians. Dissertation Abstracts,
  22 (1961/1962): 967-968. UM 61-3485.

Becker, David A. Enteric parasites of
  Indians and Anglo-Americans, chiefly on
  the Winnebago and Omaha Reservations in
  Nebraska. Nebraska State Medical
  Journal, 53 (1968): 293-296, 347-349,
  380-383, 421-423.

Boas, F. Zur Anthropologie der
  nordamerikanischen Indianer. Berliner
  Gesellschaft für Anthropologie,
  Ethnologie und Urgeschichte,
  Verhandlungen (1895): 367-411.

Boller, Henry A. Henry A. Boller: Upper
  Missouri River fur trader. Edited by R.
  H. Mattison. North Dakota History, 33
  (1966): 107-219.

Brackenridge, H. M. Views of Louisiana,
  245-258. Pittsburgh, 1814.

Brackenridge, Henry M. Views of
  Louisiana. Ann Arbor, University
  Microfilms, 1966. 268 p. (March of
  America Facsimile Series, 60)

Brackenridge, Henry M. Views of
  Louisiana. Together with a Journal of a
  voyage up the Missouri River, in 1811.
  Chicago, Quadrangle Books, 1962. 302 p.

Bradbury, J. Travels in the Interior of
  America. Liverpool, 1817.

Bradbury, John. Travels in the interior
  of America. Ann Arbor, University
  Microfilms, 1966. 12, 364 p.

Brown, Margaret Kimball. Native made
  glass pendants from east of the
  Mississippi. American Antiquity, 37
  (1972): 432-439.

Bruner, E. M. Assimilation among Fort
  Berthold Indians. American Indian, 6,
  no. 4 (1953): 21-29.

Buckles, William G. The 1959 excavation
  of the Four Bear Site cemetery. South
  Dakota, State University, W. H. Over
  Museum, Museum News, 20, no. 7 (1959):
  1-4.

Bushnell, D. I. Villages of the
  Algonquian, Siouan and Caddoan tribes.
  U.S. Bureau of American Ethnology,
  Bulletin, 77 (1922): 167-179.

Butler, Ronald Jerome. The helicoidal
  pattern of dental attrition in a
  protohistoric Arikara population from
  the Northern Plains. Dissertation
  Abstracts International, 30 (1969/1970):
  2513B. UM 69-21,500.

Chardon, Francis A. Chardon's journal at
  Fort Clark, 1834-1839. Freeport, N.Y.,
  Books for Libraries Press, 1970. 46,
  458 p. illus.

Culbertson, T. A. Journal of an
  expedition to the Mauvaises Terres and
  the Upper Missouri in 1850. U.S. Bureau
  of American Ethnology, Bulletin, 147
  (1952): 1-172.

Curtis, E. S. The North American Indian,
  Vol. 5: 59-100, 148-152, 155-163, 169-
  180. Cambridge, 1909.

Cutler, Hugh. Analysis of maize from the
  Four Bear Site and two other Arikara
  locations in South Dakota. By Hugh
  Cutler and George A. Agogino.
  Southwestern Journal of Anthropology, 16
  (1960): 312-316.

Deetz, James J. F. The dynamics of stylistic change in Arikara ceramics. Urbana, University of Illinois Press, 1965. 111 p. illus., maps. (Illinois Studies in Anthropology, 4)

*Deland, C. E. The aborigines of South Dakota. South Dakota Historical Collections, 3 (1906): 269-586.

Denig, Edwin T. Five Indian tribes of the Upper Missouri: Sioux, Arickaras, Assiniboines, Crees, Crows. Edited by John C. Ewers. Norman, University of Oklahoma Press, 1961. 217 p. illus.

Dorsey, G. A. An Arikara story-telling contest. American Anthropologist, n.s., 6 (1904): 240-243.

Dorsey, G. A. Traditions of the Arikara. Washington, D.C., 1904. 202 p.

Evans, David R. A preliminary report of the artifacts from the burial area of the Leavenworth Site, 39CO9, Corson County, South Dakota. Plains Anthropologist, 11 (1966): 172.

*Ewers, J. C. Edwin T. Denig's "Of the Arickaras". Missouri Historical Society, Bulletin, 6 (1950): 189-215.

Ewers, John C. Mothers of the mixed-bloods. El Palacio, 69 (1962): 20-29.

Fay, George E., ed. Charters, constitutions and by-laws of the Indian tribes of North America. Part IIa: The Northern Plains. Greeley, 1967. 6, 141 l. maps. (University of Northern Colorado, Museum of Anthropology, Occasional Publications in Anthropology, Ethnology Series, 3) ERIC ED051923.

Fenenga, F. The interdependence of archaeology and ethnology as illustrated by the ice-glider game of the Northern Plains. Plains Anthropologist, 1 (1954): 31-38.

Fletcher, A. C. Arikara. U.S. Bureau of American Ethnology, Bulletin, 30, vol. 1 (1907): 83-86.

Fort Berthold Mission, ed. A few Bible translations and hymns. Fort Berthold, 1900. 27 p.

Gerber, Max E. The Custer Expedition of 1874: a new look. North Dakota History, 40, no. 1 (1973): 4-23.

Gilbert, Robert M. Seasonal dating of burials at the Leavenworth Site (39CO9), with the use of fly pupae. Plains Anthropologist, 11 (1966): 172.

Gilmore, M. R. Arikara account of the origin of tobacco and catching of eagles. Indian Notes, 6 (1929): 26-33.

Gilmore, M. R. Arikara basketry. Indian Notes, 2 (1925): 89-95.

Gilmore, M. R. Arikara commerce. Indian Notes, 3 (1926): 13-18.

Gilmore, M. R. Arikara consolation ceremony. Indian Notes, 3 (1926): 256-274.

Gilmore, M. R. Arikara fish-trap. Indian Notes, 1 (1924): 120-134.

Gilmore, M. R. Arikara genesis and its teachings. Indian Notes, 3 (1926): 188-193.

Gilmore, M. R. Arikara household shrine to Mother Corn. Indian Notes, 2 (1925): 31-34.

Gilmore, M. R. Arikara units of measure. Indian Notes, 2 (1925): 64-66.

Gilmore, M. R. Arikara uses of clay and of other earth products. Indian Notes, 2 (1925): 283-289.

Gilmore, M. R. Buffalo-skull from the Arikara. Indian Notes, 3 (1926): 75-79.

Gilmore, M. R. Glass bead making by the Arikara. Indian Notes, 1 (1924): 20-21.

Gilmore, M. R. Months and seasons of the Arikara calendar. Indian Notes, 6 (1929): 246-250.

Gilmore, M. R. Notes on Arikara tribal organization. Indian Notes, 4 (1927): 332-350.

Gilmore, M. R. Notes on gynecology and obstetrics of the Arikara tribe. Michigan Academy of Science, Arts and Letters, Papers, 14 (1930): 71-81.

Gilmore, M. R. Origin of the Arikara silverberry drink. Indian Notes, 4 (1927): 125-127.

Gilmore, M. R. Some games of Arikara children. Indian Notes, 3 (1926): 9-12.

Gilmore, M. R. The Arikara book of genesis. Michigan Academy of Science, Arts and Letters, Papers, 12 (1929): 95-120.

Gilmore, M. R. The Arikara method of preparing a dog for a feast. Michigan Academy of Science, Arts and Letters, Papers, 19 (1933): 37-38.

Gilmore, M. R. The Arikara tribal temple. Michigan Academy of Science, Arts and Letters, Papers, 14 (1930): 47-70.

Gilmore, M. R. The cattail game of Arikara children. Indian Notes, 5 (1928): 316-318.

Gilmore, M. R. The coyote's boxelder knife. Indian Notes, 4 (1927): 214-216.

Gilmore, M. R. The making of a new head chief by the Arikara. Indian Notes, 5 (1928): 411-418.

Gilmore, M. R. The plight of living scalped Indians. Michigan Academy of Science, Arts and Letters, Papers, 19 (1933): 39-45.

Gilmore, M. R. The sacred bundles of the Arikara. Michigan Academy of Science, Arts and Letters, Papers, 16 (1931): 33-50.

Gilmore, M. R. Use of cat-tails by Arikara. El Palacio, 24 (1928): 114, 116.

Glatfelter, Noah M. Letters from Dakota Territory, 1865. Missouri Historical Society, Bulletin, 18 (1961/1962): 104-134.

Goddard, P. E. Indian ceremonies of the long ago. Natural History, 22 (1922): 559-564.

Gray, John S. Arikara scouts with Custer. North Dakota History, 35 (1968): 443-478.

Gregg, John B. Ear disease in skulls from the Sully burial site. By John B. Gregg, James P. Steel, and Sylvester Clifford. Plains Anthropologist, 10 (1965): 233-239.

Gregg, John B. Ear disease in the Indian skulls at the Museum of the State Historical Society of North Dakota. North Dakota History, 32 (1965): 233-242.

Gregg, John B. Exostoses in the external auditory canals. By John B. Gregg and William M. Bass. Annals of Otology, Rhinology and Laryngology, 79 (1970): 834-839.

Gregg, John B. Hrdlicka revisited (external auditory canal exostoses). By John B. Gregg and Robert N. McGrew. American Journal of Physical Anthropology, n.s., 33 (1970): 37-40.

Gregg, John B. Roentgenographic evaluation of temporal bones from South Dakota Indian burials. By John B. Gregg, James P. Steele, and Ann Holzhueter. American Journal of Physical Anthropology, n.s., 23 (1965): 51-61.

Hanson, Charles E., Jr. The Indian garden project. Museum of the Fur Trade Quarterly, 2, no. 3 (1966): 3-6.

Hayden, F. V. Contributions to the ethnography and philology of the Indian tribes of the Missouri Valley. American Philosophical Society, Transactions, n.s., 12 (1863): 351-363.

Herrala, Elizabeth Ann. The incidence of dental caries of pre-historic and historic Indian groups. Indiana Academy of Science, Proceedings, 71 (1961): 57-60.

Hilger, M. I. Some customs related to Arikara Indian child life. Primitive Man, 24 (1951): 67-71.

Hoffman, C. The water babies, an Arickaree story. American Antiquarian and Oriental Journal, 14 (1892): 167-169.

Hoffman, J. J. An unusual pottery object from South Dakota. Plains Anthropologist, 13 (1968): 29-30.

Hoffman, J. J. Molstad Village. Lincoln, Smithsonian Institution, River Basin Surveys, 1967. 6, 123 p. illus., maps. (Smithsonian Institution, River Basin Surveys, Publications in Salvage Archeology, 4)

Hoffman, J. J. The Bad River Phase. By J. J. Hoffman and Lionel A. Brown. Plains Anthropologist, 12 (1967): 323-343.

Hoffman, W.-J. La fête annuelle des Indiens Arikaris. Société d'Anthropologie (Paris), Bulletin, sér. 3, 7 (1884): 526-532.

Hoffman, W.-J. Remarks on Indian tribal names. American Philosophical Society, Proceedings, 23 (1886): 294-296.

*Holder, P. Social stratification among the Arikara. Ethnohistory, 5 (1958): 210-218.

Holzhueter, Ann M. A search for stapes footplate fixation in an Indian population, prehistoric and historic. By A. M. Holzhueter, J. B. Gregg, and S. Clifford. American Journal of Physical Anthropology, n.s., 23 (1965): 35-40.

Howard, James H. An Arikara Bear Society initiation ceremony. North Dakota History, 21, no. 4 (1954): 168-179.

Howard, James H. Arikara native-made
   glass pendants: their probable function.
   American Antiquity, 37 (1972): 93-97.

Howard, James H. Notes on the
   ethnogeography of the Yankton Dakota.
   Plains Anthropologist, 17 (1972): 281-
   307.

Hughes, Jack Thomas. Prehistory of the
   Caddoan-speaking tribes. Dissertation
   Abstracts International, 30 (1969/1970):
   950B. UM 69-9198.

Hurt, Wesley R. Seasonal economic and
   settlement patterns of the Arikara.
   Plains Anthropologist, 14 (1969): 32-37.

Hurt, Wesley R., Jr., et al. Report of
   the investigations of the Four Bear
   Site, 39DW2, Dewey County, South Dakota,
   1958-1959. Vermillion, 1962. 6, 97 p.
   illus., maps. (South Dakota, State
   University, W. H. Over Museum,
   Archaeological Studies, Circular, 10)

Hyde, G. E. The mystery of the Arikaras.
   North Dakota History, 18 (1951): 187-
   218; 19 (1952): 25-58.

Jackson, Donald. Journey to the Mandans,
   1809; the lost narrative of Dr. Thomas.
   Missouri Historical Society Bulletin, 20
   (1963/1964): 179-192.

Jantz, Richard L. Cranial variation and
   microevolution in Arikara skeletal
   populations. Plains Anthropologist, 17
   (1972): 20-35.

Jantz, Richard Lynn. Change and variation
   in skeletal populations of Arikara
   Indians. Dissertation Abstracts
   International, 31 (1970/1971): 3126B.
   UM 70-25,353.

Jaques. Notes of a tourist through the
   Upper Missouri region. Missouri
   Historical Society, Bulletin, 22
   (1965/1966): 393-409.

Kohlepp, H. W. A missionary trip to the
   land of the Arikara. Minnesota
   Archaeologist, 3 (1937): 90-93.

Krause, Richard A., Jr. Arikara ceramic
   change: a study of the factors affecting
   stylistic change in late 18th and early
   19th century Arikara pottery.
   Dissertation Abstracts, 28 (1967/1968):
   3979B-3980B. UM 68-5172.

Krause, Richard A., Jr. Nordvold I: a
   preliminary evaluation. Plains
   Anthropologist, 7 (1962): 94.

Lehmer, Donald J. Arikara archeology: the
   Bad River phase. By Donald J. Lehmer and
   David T. Jones. Lincoln, 1968. 3,

170 p. illus., maps. (Smithsonian
   Institution, River Basin Surveys,
   Publications in Salvage Archeology, 7)

Lehmer, Donald J. The Fire Heart Creek
   Site. Lincoln, Smithsonian Institution,
   River Basin Surveys, 1966. 5, 114 p.
   illus., maps. (Smithsonian Institution,
   River Basin Surveys, Publications in
   Salvage Archeology, 1)

Leigh, R. W. Dental pathology of Indian
   tribes. American Journal of Physical
   Anthropology, 8 (1925): 179-199.

Libby, O. G. Typical villages of the
   Mandan, Arikara and Hidatsa. North
   Dakota, State Historical Society,
   Collections, 2 (1908): 498-508.

Libby, O. G., ed. The Arikara narrative
   of the campaign against the hostile
   Dakotas. South Dakota Historical
   Collections, 6 (1920): 1-276.

*Lowie, R. H. Societies of the Arikara
   Indians. American Museum of Natural
   History, Anthropological Papers, 11
   (1915): 645-678.

Lowie, R. H. Some problems in the
   ethnology of the Crow and village
   Indians. American Anthropologist, n.s.,
   14 (1912): 60-71.

Lyon, William Sherman, III. A
   multivariate statistical analysis of
   Arikara crania from the Northern Plains.
   Dissertation Abstracts International, 31
   (1970/1971): 3126B-3127B. UM 70-25,372.

*Macgowan, E. S. The Arikara Indians.
   Minnesota Archaeologist, 8 (1942): 83-
   122.

Metcalf, George. Small sites on and about
   Fort Berthold Indian Reservation,
   Garrison Reservoir, North Dakota.
   Washington, D.C., Government Printing
   Office, 1963. 1-56 p. illus., map.
   (U.S., Bureau of American Ethnology,
   River Basin Surveys Papers, 26. U.S.,
   Bureau of American Ethnology, Bulletin,
   185)

Metcalf, George. Star Village: a
   fortified historic Arikara site in
   Mercer County, North Dakota.
   Washington, D.C., Government Printing
   Office, 1963. 57-122 p. illus., maps.
   (U.S., Bureau of American Ethnology,
   River Basin Surveys Papers, 27. U.S.,
   Bureau of American Ethnology, Bulletin,
   185)

Mitchell, D. D. Indian feats of
   legerdemain. Missouri Historical
   Society, Bulletin, 18 (1961/1962): 310-
   312.

Morgan, L. H. Systems of consanguinity
and affinity. Smithsonian Contributions
to Knowledge, 17 (1871): 291-382.

Morgan, L. H. The Indian journals, 1859-
62, 146, 161-164. Ann Arbor, 1959.

Morgan, L. H. The stone and bone
implements of the Arickarees. University
of the State of New York, Annual Report
of the Regents, 21 (1871): 25-46.

Morgan, Lewis H. The stone and bone
implements of the Arickarees. North
Dakota History, 30 (1963): 115-135.

Mulloy, W. The Northern Plains. In J. B.
Griffin, ed. Archeology of Eastern
United States. Chicago, 1952: 124-138.

Nasatir, A. P. Before Lewis and Clark.
St. Louis, 1952. 2 v. (882 p.).

Neal, Bigelow. The last of the thundering
herd. New York, Dodd, Mead, 1960.
287 p. illus.

Neuman, Robert W. Porcupine quill
flatteners from central United States.
American Antiquity, 26 (1960/1961): 99-
102.

Nunis, Doyce B., Jr. The Sublettes of
Kentucky: their early contribution to
the opening of the West. Kentucky
Historical Society, Register, 57 (1959):
20-34.

Over, W. H. Lewis and Clark Site. South
Dakota, University, William H. Over
Museum, Newsletter, 16, no. 1 (1955): 1-
4.

Read, Catherine E. Predicting
acculturative behavior of the Mandan,
Hidatsa, and Arickara Indians.
Anthropology UCLA, 2, no. 2 (1970): 1-5.

Reid, R. The earth lodge. North Dakota
Historical Quarterly, 4 (1930): 174-185.

Russell, Don. Custer's last or, The
battle of the Little Big Horn. Fort
Worth, Amon Carter Museum of Western
Art, 1968. 5, 67 p. illus.

Smith, Carlyle S. Time perspective within
the Coalescent tradition in South
Dakota. American Antiquity, 28
(1962/1963): 489-495.

Smith, G. H. J. B. Trudeau's remarks on
the Indians of the Upper Missouri.
American Anthropologist, n.s., 38
(1936): 565-568.

Smith, G. Hubert. Historical archeology
in Missouri Basin reservoir areas:

current investigations. Plains
Anthropologist, 5 (1960): 58-64.

Snow, Fred S. Fred Snow's account of the
Custer Expedition of 1874. Edited by
Ernest J. Moyne. North Dakota History,
27 (1960): 143-151.

Sperry, James E. 1961 summer excavations
at the Leavenworth Site, 39CO9. By James
E. Sperry and Richard A. Krause. Plains
Anthropologist, 7 (1962): 80.

Steele, James P., et al. Paleopathology
in the Dakotas. South Dakota Journal of
Medicine, 18, no. 10 (1965): 17-29.

Stephenson, Robert L. Blue Blanket Island
(39WW9) an historic contact site in the
Oahe Reservoir near Mobridge, South
Dakota. Plains Anthropologist, 14
(1969): 1-31.

Stewart, T. Dale. Lesions of the frontal
bone in American Indians. By T. D.
Stewart and Lawrence G. Quade. American
Journal of Physical Anthropology, n.s.,
30 (1969): 89-109.

Stewart, T. Dale. The effects of
pathology on skeletal populations.
American Journal of Physical
Anthropology, n.s., 30 (1969): 333-449.

Stirling, M. W. Archaeological
investigations in South Dakota.
Smithsonian Institution, Explorations
and Field-Work (1924): 66-71.

Stirling, M. W. Arikara glassworking.
Washington Academy of Sciences, Journal,
37 (1947): 257-263.

Stockman, Wallace Henry. Historical
perspectives of federal educational
promises and performance among the Fort
Berthold Indians. Dissertation Abstracts
International, 33 (1972/1973): 1475A-
1476A. UM 72-25,221.

Strong, W. D. Studying the Arikara and
their neighbors. Smithsonian
Institution, Explorations and Field-Work
(1932): 73-76.

Swanton, J. R. Arikara pottery making.
American Antiquity, 10 (1944): 100-101.

Taylor, Allan R. The classification of
the Caddoan languages. American
Philosophical Society, Proceedings, 107
(1963): 51-59.

Taylor, Colin. Early Plains Indian quill
techniques in European museum
collections. Plains Anthropologist, 7
(1962): 58-69.

Thompson, Ralph Stanton. The final story of the Deapolis Mandan Indian village site. North Dakota History, 28 (1961): 143-153.

Troike, Rudolph C. The Caddo word for "water". International Journal of American Linguistics, 30 (1964): 96-98.

Trudeau, J. B. Description of the Upper Missouri. Mississippi Valley Historical Review, 8 (1921): 149-179.

Trudeau, J. B. Journal. South Dakota Historical Collections, 7 (1914): 453-462.

Ubelaker, Douglas. Arikara-made glass pendants. Plains Anthropologist, 11 (1966): 172-173.

Ubelaker, Douglas H. Arikara glassworking techniques at Leavenworth and Sully Sites. By Douglas H. Ubelaker and William M. Bass. American Antiquity, 35 (1970): 467-475.

Ubelaker, Douglas H. Artificial interproximal grooving of the teeth in American Indians. By Douglas H. Ubelaker, T. W. Phenice, and William M. Bass. American Journal of Physical Anthropology, n.s., 30 (1969): 145-149.

Weakly, Ward J. 1960 summer excavations at the Leavenworth Site, 39CO9. Plains Anthropologist, 6 (1961): 58.

Wedel, W. R. Archeological materials from the vicinity of Mobridge, South Dakota. U.S. Bureau of American Ethnology, Bulletin, 157 (1955): 69-188.

Wedel, W. R. Observations on some nineteenth-century pottery vessels from the Upper Missouri. U.S. Bureau of American Ethnology, Bulletin, 164 (1957): 87-114.

Wetmore, Alphonso, ed. Biographical notice of Genl. William H. Ashley. Edited by Alphonso Wetmore and Charles Keemle. Missouri Historical Society, Bulletin, 24 (1967/1968): 348-354.

Whitehouse, Joseph. The journal of Private Joseph Whitehouse, a soldier with Lewis and Clark. Edited by Paul Russell Cutright. Missouri Historical Society, Bulletin, 28 (1971/1972): 143-161.

Wied-Neuwied, M. zu. Reise in das innere Nordamerika. Coblenz, 1839-1841. 2 v.

Wied-Neuwied, M. zu. Travels in the interior of North America. Early Western Travels, 22 (1906): 335-336; 23 (1906): 386-395; 24 (1906): 210-214.

Will, G. F. Archaeology of the Missouri Valley. American Museum of Natural History, Anthropological Papers, 22 (1924): 285-344.

Will, G. F. Arikara ceremonials. North Dakota Historical Quarterly, 4 (1930): 247-265.

Will, G. F. Indian agriculture at its northern limits. International Congress of Americanists, Proceedings, 20, vol. 1 (1922): 203-205.

Will, G. F. Notes on the Arikara Indians and their ceremonies. Old West Series, 3 (1934): 5-48.

Will, G. F. and G. E. Hyde. Corn among the Indians of the Upper Missouri. St. Louis, 1917. 317 p.

Wood, W. R. Historical and archaeological evidence for Arikara visits to the Central Plains. Plains Anthropologist, 4 (1955): 27-39.

Wood, W. Raymond. A stylistic and historical analysis of shoulder patterns on Plains Indian pottery. American Antiquity, 28 (1962/1963): 25-40.

Woolworth, Alan R. Excavations at Kipp's Post. By Alan R. Woolworth and W. Raymond Wood. North Dakota History, 29 (1962): 237-252.

Woolworth, Alan R. The archeology of a small trading post (Kipp's Post, 32MN1) in the Garrison Reservoir, North Dakota. By Alan R. Woolworth and W. Raymond Wood. Washington, D.C., Government Printing Office, 1960. 239-306 p. illus., map. (U.S., Bureau of American Ethnology, River Basin Surveys Papers, 20. U.S., Bureau of American Ethnology, Bulletin, 176)

Works Progress Administration. Arikara Indians. South Dakota, State University, W. H. Over Museum, Museum News, 22, nos. 2/3 (1961): 1-6; 24, no. 6 (1963): 1-5; 24, no. 7 (1963): 1-10; 24, no. 8 (1963): 1-7; 24, no. 9 (1963): 1-8; 24, no. 10 (1963): 1-7.

09-03 Assiniboin

Andersen, Raoul. Agricultural development of the Alexis Stoney. Alberta Historical Review, 20, no. 4 (1972): 16-20.

Andersen, Raoul R. Alberta Stoney (Assiniboin) origins and adaptations: a case for reappraisal. Ethnohistory, 17 (1970): 49-61.

Andersen, Raoul R. An inquiry into the
political and economic structures of the
Alexis Band of Wood Stoney Indians,
1880-1964. Dissertation Abstracts, 29
(1968/1969): 852B-853B. UM 68-12,480.

Anonymous. Smallpox epidemic of 1869-70.
Alberta Historical Review, 11, no. 2
(1963): 13-19.

Barbeau, C. Marius. Indian days on the
western prairies. Ottawa, Queen's
Printer, 1960. 6, 234 p. illus., end
maps. (Canada, National Museum,
Bulletin, 163)

Barbeau, M. Indian days in the Canadian
Rockies. Toronto, 1923. 208 p.

Bowen, P. Serum protein polymorphisms in
Indians of Western Canada: gene
frequencies and data on the Gc/albumin
linkage. By P. Bowen, F. O'Callaghan and
Catherine S. N. Lee. Human Heredity, 21
(1971): 242-253.

Breton, A. C. The Stoney Indians. Man, 20
(1920): 65-67.

Brown, L. A. Arikara Indian ceramics.
Ceramics Monthly, 17, no. 3 (1969): 16-
19.

Buchler, Ira R. The distinctive features
of pronominal systems. By Ira R. Buchler
and R. Freeze. Anthropological
Linguistics, 8, no. 8 (1966): 78-105.

Burpee, L. J., ed. Journals and letters
of Pierre Gaultier de Varennes de la
Vérendrye and his sons. Champlain
Society, Publications, 16 (1927): 1-548.

Bushnell, D. I. Burials of the
Algonquian, Siouan and Caddoan tribes.
U.S. Bureau of American Ethnology,
Bulletin, 83 (1927): 42-49.

Bushnell, D. I. Sketches by Paul Kane in
the Indian country, 1845-1848.
Smithsonian Miscellaneous Collections,
99, no. 1 (1940): 1-25.

Bushnell, D. I. Villages of the
Algonquian, Siouan and Caddoan tribes.
U.S. Bureau of American Ethnology,
Bulletin, 77 (1922): 71-77.

Campbell, Robert. The private journal of
Robert Campbell. Edited by George R.
Brooks. Missouri Historical Society,
Bulletin, 20 (1963/1964): 3-24, 107-118.

Capes, Katherine H. The W. B. Nickerson
survey and excavations, 1912-15, of the
southern Manitoba mounds region.
Ottawa, Queen's Printer, 1963. 3,
178 p. illus., maps. (Canada, National
Museum, Anthropology Papers, 4)

Chown, B. and M. Lewis. The blood group
and secretor genes of the Stony and
Sarcee Indians of Alberta, Canada.
American Journal of Physical
Anthropology, n.s., 13 (1955): 181-189.

Cocking, M. An adventurer from Hudson
Bay. Ed. by L. J. Burpee. Royal Society
of Canada, Proceedings and Transactions,
ser. 3, 2, pt. 2 (1908): 89-121.

Coues, E., ed. Manuscript journals of
Alexander Henry and of David Thompson.
New York, 1897. 3 v.

Culbertson, T. A. Journal of an
expedition to the Mauvaises Terres and
the Upper Missouri in 1850. U.S. Bureau
of American Ethnology, Bulletin, 147
(1952): 1-172.

Curtis, E. S. The North American Indian,
Vol. 18: 163-176, 214-218. Norwood,
1928.

Curtis, E. S. The North American Indian,
Vol. 3: 125-133, 152-159. Cambridge,
1908.

Dangberg, G. M. Letters to Jack Wilson,
the Paiute prophet. U.S. Bureau of
American Ethnology, Bulletin, 164
(1957): 279-296.

Dempsey, Hugh A., ed. Final treaty of
peace. Alberta Historical Review, 10,
no. 1 (1962): 8-16.

Denig, E. T. Assiniboine. In H. R.
Schoolcraft, ed. Information respecting
the History, Condition, and Prospects of
the Indian Tribes of the United States.
Vol. 4. Philadelphia, 1854: 416-431.

*Denig, E. T. Indian tribes of the Upper
Missouri. Ed. by J. N. B. Hewitt. U.S.
Bureau of American Ethnology, Annual
Reports, 46 (1930): 375-628.

Denig, Edwin T. Five Indian tribes of the
Upper Missouri: Sioux, Arickaras,
Assiniboines, Crees, Crows. Edited by
John C. Ewers. Norman, University of
Oklahoma Press, 1961. 217 p. illus.

Dorsey, J. O. Preface. Contributions to
North American Ethnology, 9 (1893): xi-
xxxii.

Dorsey, J. O. Siouan sociology. U.S.
Bureau of American Ethnology, Annual
Reports, 15 (1894): 222-226.

Doughty, A. G. and C. Martin, eds. The
Kelsey papers. Ottawa, 1929.

Dusenberry, Verne. Notes on the material
culture of the Assiniboine Indians.
Ethnos, 25 (1960): 44-62.

Eggleston, Edward. George W. Northrup:
the Kit Carson of the Northwest; the-
man-that-draws-the-handcart. Edited by
Louis Pfaller. North Dakota History, 33
(1966): 4-21.

Evans, G. Edward. Prehistoric Blackduck-
historic Assiniboine: a reassessment.
Plains Anthropologist, 6 (1961): 271-
275.

*Ewers, J. C. Edwin T. Denig's "Of the
Assiniboine". Missouri Historical
Society, Bulletin, 8 (1952): 121-150.

Ewers, J. C. The Assiniboin horse
medicine cult. Primitive Man, 29 (1956):
57-68.

Ewers, J. C. The bear cult among the
Assiniboin and their neighbors of the
Northern Plains. Southwestern Journal of
Anthropology, 11 (1955): 1-14.

Ewers, John C. Bodily proportions as
guides to lineal measurements among the
Blackfoot Indians. American
Anthropologist, 72 (1970): 561-562.

Ewers, John C. Mothers of the mixed-
bloods. El Palacio, 69 (1962): 20-29.

Ewers, John C. Was there a Northwestern
Plains sub-culture? An ethnographic
appraisal. Plains Anthropologist, 12
(1967): 167-174.

Fay, George E., ed. Charters,
constitutions and by-laws of the Indian
tribes of North America. Part IIa: The
Northern Plains. Greeley, 1967. 6,
141 l. maps. (University of Northern
Colorado, Museum of Anthropology,
Occasional Publications in Anthropology,
Ethnology Series, 3) ERIC ED051923.

Fenenga, F. An early nineteenth century
account of Assiniboine quillwork. Plains
Anthropologist, 3 (1955): 19-22.

Gilmore, M. R. Old Assiniboin buffalo-
drive in North Dakota. Indian Notes, 1
(1924): 204-211.

Graham, Andrew. Andrew Graham's
observations on Hudson's Bay, 1767-91.
Edited by Glyndwr Williams. London,
1969. 72, 423 p. illus., maps.
(Hudson's Bay Record Society,
Publications, 27)

Hady, Walter M. Indian migrations in
Manitoba and the West. Historical and
Scientific Society of Manitoba, Papers,
ser. 3, 17 (1960/1961): 24-53.

Hainline, Jane. Genetic exchange: model
construction and a practical

application. Human Biology, 35 (1963):
167-191.

Hassrick, R. B. Assiniboin succession.
North Dakota History, 14 (1947): 146-
167.

Hayden, F. V. Contributions to the
ethnography and philology of the Indian
tribes of the Missouri Valley. American
Philosophical Society, Transactions,
n.s., 12 (1863): 379-391.

Hector, J. and W. S. W. Vaux. Notice of
Indians seen by the exploring expedition
under the command of Captain Palliser.
Ethnological Society (London),
Transactions, n.s., 1 (1861): 245-261.

Henry, A. Travels and adventures: 266-
297. Ed. by M. M. Quaife. Chicago,
1921.

Henry, Alexander. New light on the early
history of the greater Northwest. Edited
by Elliott Coues. Minneapolis, Ross and
Haines, 1965. 2 v. (28, 1,027 p.)
maps.

Henry, Alexander. Travels and adventures
in Canada and the Indian territories,
between the years 1760 and 1776. New ed.
New York, B. Franklin, 1969. 33,
347 p. illus., maps.

Henry, Alexander. Travels and adventures
in Canada and the Indian territories,
between the years 1760 and 1776. Edited
by James Bain. Edmonton, M. C. Hurtig,
1969. 46, 347 p. illus., maps.

Hollow, Robert C., Jr. A note on
Assiniboine phonology. International
Journal of American Linguistics, 36
(1970): 296-298.

Hudson's Bay Company. Saskatchewan
journals and correspondence: Edmonton
House 1795-1800; Chesterfield House
1800-1802. Edited by Alice M. Johnson.
London, 1967. 102, 368, 14 p. map.
(Hudson's Bay Record Society,
Publications, 26)

Jenks, A. E. The wild rice gatherers of
the Upper Lakes. U.S. Bureau of American
Ethnology, Annual Reports, 19, vol. 2
(1898): 1013-1137.

Johnson, Roy P. Fur trader Chaboillez at
Pembina. North Dakota History, 32
(1965): 83-99.

Kehoe, Alice B. The Ghost Dance religion
in Saskatchewan, Canada. Plains
Anthropologist, 13 (1968): 296-304.

Kennedy, Dan. Recollections of an
Assiniboine chief. Edited by James R.

Stevens. Toronto, McClelland and
Stewart, 1972. 160 p. illus.

Larner, John William, Jr. The Kootenay
Plains (Alberta) land question and
Canadian Indian policy, 1799-1947.
Dissertation Abstracts International, 33
(1972/1973): 3545A-3546A. UM 73-842.

Leechman, D. The trappers. Beaver, 288,
no. 3 (1957): 24-31.

Levin, Norman Balfour. Classification of
three syntactic types of languages: a
reality? Linguistics, 24 (1966): 38-42.

Levin, Norman Balfour. The Assiniboine
language. Bloomington, Indiana
University, 1964. 7, 166 p. (Indiana,
University, Research Center in
Anthropology, Folklore, and Linguistics,
Publication 32)

Levin, Norman Balfour. The Assiniboine
language. Dissertation Abstracts, 22
(1961/1962): 1168. UM 61-3532.

Levin, Norman Balfour. The inflection of
Assiniboine nominal theme. In
International Congress of Linguists,
9th. 1962, Cambridge, Mass. Proceedings.
The Hague, Mouton, 1964: 604. (Janua
Linguarum, Series Maior, 12)

Lind, Robert William. Familistic
attitudes and marriage role expectations
of American Indian and White
adolescents. Dissertation Abstracts
International, 32 (1971/1972): 5288B.
UM 72-10,035.

Long, J. L. Land of Nakoda. Helena,
1942. 296 p.

*Lowie, R. H. The Assiniboine. American
Museum of Natural History,
Anthropological Papers, 4 (1910): 1-270.

Lowie, Robert H. A few Assiniboine texts.
Preface by Luella Cole Lowie.
Anthropological Linguistics, 2, no. 8
(1960): 1-30.

MacEwan, John W. G. Portraits from the
Plains. Toronto, McGraw-Hill of Canada,
1971. 287 p. illus., map.

MacEwan, John W. G. Tatanga Mani: Walking
Buffalo of the Stonies. By Grant
MacEwan. Edmonton, M. G. Hurtig, 1969.
208 p. illus., map.

Matson, G. A. Blood groups and ageusia in
Indians of Montana and Alberta. American
Journal of Physical Anthropology, 24
(1938): 81-89.

Mattison, Ray H. Fort Union: its role in
the Upper Missouri fur trade. North
Dakota History, 29 (1962): 181-208.

McDonnell, J. Some account of the Red
River. In L. F. R. Masson, ed. Les
Bourgeois de la Compagnie du Nord-Ouest.
Vol. 1. Quebec, 1889: 265-295.

McDougall, John (Mrs.). Incidents of
mission life, 1874. Alberta Historical
Review, 14, no. 1 (1966): 26-29.

McGee, W J. The Siouan Indians. U.S.
Bureau of American Ethnology, Annual
Reports, 15 (1894): 157-204.

Mooney, J. and C. Thomas. Assiniboin.
U.S. Bureau of American Ethnology,
Bulletin, 30, vol. 1 (1907): 102-105.

Morgan, L. H. Systems of consanguinity
and affinity. Smithsonian Contributions
to Knowledge, 17 (1871): 291-382.

Morgan, L. H. The Indian journals, 1859-
62: p. 166. Ann Arbor, 1959.

Morton, Desmond, ed. Telegrams of the
North-West Campaign 1885. Edited by
Desmond Morton and Reginald H. Roy.
Toronto, 1972. 103, 431 p. illus.,
maps. (Champlain Society, Publications,
47)

Nasatir, A. P. Before Lewis and Clark.
St. Louis, 1952. 2 v. (882 p.).

Orchard, W. C. Porcupine quill
ornamentation. Indian Notes, 3 (1926):
59-68.

Paget, A. M. The people of the Plains.
Toronto, 1909. 199 p.

Palliser, J. Further papers. London,
1860. 325 p.

Parker, John. The fur trader and the
emerging geography of North America.
Museum of the Fur Trade Quarterly, 2,
no. 3 (1966): 6-10; 2, no. 4 (1966): 7-
11.

Pierce, Joe E. Possible electronic
computation of typological indices for
linguistic structures. International
Journal of American Linguistics, 28
(1962): 215-226.

Pocaterra, George W. Among the nomadic
Stoneys. Alberta Historical Review, 11,
no. 3 (1963): 12-19.

Potts, W. J. Creation myth of the
Assinaboines. Journal of American
Folklore, 5 (1892): 72-73.

Ray, Arthur Joseph, Jr. Indian exploitation of the forest-grassland transition zone in Western Canada, 1650-1860: a geographical view of two centuries of change. Dissertation Abstracts International, 32 (1971/1972): 3432B. UM 71-28,359.

Riggs, S. R. Dakota grammar, texts and ethnography. Contributions to North American Ethnology, 9 (1893): 1-232.

Rodnick, D. An Assiniboine horse-raiding expedition. American Anthropologist, n.s., 41 (1939): 611-616.

Rodnick, D. Political structure and status among the Assiniboine Indians. American Anthropologist, n.s., 39 (1937): 408-416.

*Rodnick, D. The Fort Belknap Assiniboine of Montana. New Haven, 1938. 125 p.

Rogers, Edward S. The Assiniboine. Beaver, 302, no. 2 (1971/1972): 40-43.

Rolland, Walpole. My Alberta notebook. Alberta Historical Review, 18, no. 1 (1970): 21-30.

Shera, John W. Poundmaker's capture of a wagon train. Pioneer West, 1 (1969): 7-9.

Sibbald, Andrew. West with the MacDougalls. Alberta Historical Review, 19, no. 1 (1971): 1-4.

Smet, P. J. de. Western missions and missionaries, 130-205. New York, 1863.

Somogyi-Csizmazia, W. Three-rooted mandibular first permanent molars in Alberta Indian children. By W. Somogyi-Csizmazia and A. J. Simons. Canadian Dental Association, Journal, 37 (1971): 105-106.

Spry, Irene M., ed. The papers of the Palliser Expedition 1857-1860. Toronto, 1968. 138, 694 p. illus., map. (Champlain Society, Publications, 44)

Sullivan, L. R. Anthropometry of the Siouan tribes. American Museum of Natural History, Anthropological Papers, 23 (1920): 81-174.

Weekes, M. An Indian's description of the making of a buffalo pound. Saskatchewan History, 1 (1948): 14-17.

Wenzel, Johanna. Walking Buffalo, wise man of the West. Beaver, 298, no. 4 (1967/1968): 19-23.

Wied-Neuwied, M. zu. Reise in das innere Nordamerika. Coblenz, 1839-1841. 2 v.

Wied-Neuwied, M. zu. Travels in the interior of North America. Early Western Travels, 22 (1906): 370-371; 23 (1906): 14-24; 24 (1906): 215-217.

Wissler, Clark. Population changes among the Northern Plains Indians. New Haven, Yale University Press, 1936. 20 p. (Yale University Publications in Anthropology, 1)

Wissler, Clark. Population changes among the Northern Plains Indians. New Haven, Human Relations Area Files Press, 1970. 20 p. (Yale University Publications in Anthropology, 1)

Woolworth, Nancy L. The Grand Portage Mission: 1731-1965. Minnesota History, 39 (1964/1965): 301-310.

Writers' Program, Montana. The Assiniboine: from the accounts of the Old Ones told to First Boy (James Larpenteur Long). New ed. Edited by Michael S. Kennedy. Norman, University of Oklahoma Press, 1961. 75, 209 p. illus., maps.

09-04   Blackfoot

Allen, Terry, ed. The whispering wind; poetry by young American Indians. Garden City, Doubleday, 1972. 16, 128 p.

Anonymous. Naming of Medicine Hat. Alberta Historical Review, 9, no. 1 (1961): 7.

Anonymous. Religious significance of Blackfoot quillwork. Plains Anthropologist, 8 (1963): 52-53.

Anonymous. Smallpox epidemic of 1869-70. Alberta Historical Review, 11, no. 2 (1963): 13-19.

Barbeau, C. Marius. Indian days on the western prairies. Ottawa, Queen's Printer, 1960. 6, 234 p. illus., end maps. (Canada, National Museum, Bulletin, 163)

Barrett, S. A. The Blackfoot Iniskim or buffalo bundle. Public Museum of the City of Milwaukee, Yearbook, 1 (1921): 80-84.

Barrett, S. A. The Blackfoot sweat lodge. Public Museum of the City of Milwaukee, Yearbook, 1 (1921): 73-80.

Barrett, S. A. The painted lodge or ceremonial tipi of the Blackfoot. Public Museum of the City of Milwaukee, Yearbook, 1 (1921): 85-88.

Berry, Gerald L. Fort Whoop-up and the whiskey traders. Pioneer West, 1 (1969): 21-25.

Berry, Gerald L. The Whoop-Up Trail (Alberta-Montana relationships). Edmonton, Applied Art Products, 1953. 143 p. illus., maps.

Boas, F. Zur Anthropologie der nordamerikanischen Indianer. Berliner Gesellschaft für Anthropologie, Ethnologie und Urgeschichte, Verhandlungen (1895): 367-411.

Boller, Henry A. Henry A. Boller: Upper Missouri River fur trader. Edited by R. H. Mattison. North Dakota History, 33 (1966): 107-219.

Bradley, J. H. Characteristics, habits, and customs of the Blackfeet Indians. Historical Society of Montana, Contributions, 9 (1923): 255-287.

Brown, A. Prairie totems. Canadian Geographical Journal, 23 (1941): 148-151.

Browne, J. M. Indian medicine. In W. W. Beach, ed. Indian Miscellany. Albany, 1877: 74-85.

Bryan, Alan L. An alternative hypothesis for the origin of the name Blackfoot. Plains Anthropologist, 15 (1970): 305-306.

Bull Plume. Blackfoot legends. Masterkey, 7 (1933): 41-46, 70-73.

Burch, Thomas A. Epidemiological studies on rheumatic diseases. Military Medicine, 131 (1966): 507-511.

Burch, Thomas A. Occurrence of rheumatoid arthritis and rheumatoid factor in families of Blackfeet Indians. By Thomas A. Burch, William M. O'Brien, and Joseph J. Bunim. Arthritis and Rheumatism, 5 (1962): 640.

Burpee, L. J. Henday discovers the Blackfoot. Canadian Geographical Journal, 33 (1946): 188-189.

Burpee, L. J., ed. An adventurer from Hudson Bay. Royal Society of Canada, Proceedings and Transactions, ser. 3, 2, pt. 2 (1908): 109-112.

Burpee, L. J., ed. York Factory to the Blackfeet country. Royal Society of Canada, Proceedings and Transactions, ser. 3, 1, pt. 2 (1907): 307-354.

Bushnell, D. I. Burials of the Algonquian, Siouan and Caddoan tribes. U.S. Bureau of American Ethnology, Bulletin, 83 (1927): 10-13.

Bushnell, D. I. Sketches by Paul Kane in the Indian country, 1845-1848. Smithsonian Miscellaneous Collections, 99, no. 1 (1940): 1-25.

Bushnell, D. I. Villages of the Algonquian, Siouan and Caddoan tribes. U.S. Bureau of American Ethnology, Bulletin, 77 (1922): 25-33.

Byrne, William John. The archaeology and prehistory of southern Alberta as reflected by ceramics: late prehistoric and protohistoric cultural developments. Dissertation Abstracts International, 34 (1973/1974): 32B. UM 73-16,766.

Canada, Department of Mines and Resources, Indian Affairs Branch. Census of Indians in Canada, 1939. Ottawa, 1940.

Canada, Department of Mines and Resources, Indian Affairs Branch. Census of Indians in Canada, 1944. Ottawa, 1944.

Catlin, G. Illustrations of the manners, customs and condition of the North American Indians, Vol. 1: 29-43, 51-53. New York, 1841.

Chown, B. and M. Lewis. The ABO, MNSs, P, Rh, Lutheran, Kell, Lewis, Duffy and Kidd blood groups and the secretor status of the Blackfoot Indians of Alberta, Canada. American Journal of Physical Anthropology, n.s., 11 (1953): 369-383.

Cocking, M. An adventurer from Hudson Bay. Ed. by L. J. Burpee. Royal Society of Canada, Proceedings and Transactions, ser. 3, 2, pt. 2 (1908): 89-121.

Conn, R. Blackfeet Soumak necklaces. Davidson Journal of Anthropology, 1 (1955): 99-112.

Conner, Stuart W. The Fish Creek, Owl Canyon and Grinnvoll Rock Shelter pictographic sites in Montana. Plains Anthropologist, 7 (1962): 24-35.

Cooper, J. M. The shaking tent rite among Plains and Forest Algonquians. Primitive Man, 17 (1944): 60-84.

Coues, E., ed. Manuscript journals of Alexander Henry and of David Thompson. New York, 1897. 3 v.

Cramer, Joseph L. The Lian site, an historic log shelter in Yellowstone County, Montana. Plains Anthropologist, 6 (1961): 267-270.

Culbertson, T. A. Journal of an expedition to the Mauvaises Terres and the Upper Missouri in 1850. U.S. Bureau of American Ethnology, Bulletin, 147 (1952): 1-172.

Curtis, E. S. The North American Indian, Vol. 18: 176-198. Norwood, 1928.

Curtis, E. S. The North American Indian, Vol. 6: 3-83, 153-155, 167-173. Norwood, 1911.

Cutright, Paul Russell. Lewis and Clark and Cottonwood. Missouri Historical Society, Bulletin, 21 (1965/1966): 35-44.

Cutright, Paul Russell. Lewis on the Marias, 1806. Montana, the Magazine of Western History, 18, no. 3 (1968): 30-43.

Dempsey, H. A. Social dances of the Blood Indians. Journal of American Folklore, 69 (1956): 47-52.

Dempsey, H. A. Stone "medicine wheels". Washington Academy of Sciences, Journal, 46 (1956): 177-182.

Dempsey, H. A. The amazing death of Calf Shirt. Montana Magazine of History, 3, pt. 1 (1953): 65-72.

Dempsey, Hugh A. A Blackfoot winter count. Calgary, 1965. 20 p. illus. (Glenbow-Alberta Institute, Occasional Paper, 1)

Dempsey, Hugh A. An unwilling diary. Alberta Historical Review, 7, no. 3 (1959): 7-10.

Dempsey, Hugh A. Crowfoot, chief of the Blackfeet. Norman, University of Oklahoma Press, 1972. 19, 226 p.

Dempsey, Hugh A. David Thompson under scrutiny. Alberta Historical Review, 12, no. 1 (1964): 22-28.

Dempsey, Hugh A. Western Plains trade ceremonies. Western Canadian Journal of Anthropology, 3, no. 1 (1972): 29-33.

Dempsey, Hugh A., ed. Alexander Culbertson's journey to Bow River. Alberta Historical Review, 19, no. 4 (1971): 8-20.

Dempsey, Hugh A., ed. Final treaty of peace. Alberta Historical Review, 10, no. 1 (1962): 8-16.

Dempsey, Hugh A., ed. Robertson--Ross' diary; Fort Edmonton to Wildhorse, B.C., 1872. Alberta Historical Review, 9, no. 3 (1961): 5-22.

Dempsey, Hugh A., ed. Thompson's journey to the Red Deer River. Alberta Historical Review, 13, no. 1 (1965): 1-8; 13, no. 2 (1965): 7-15.

Denman, Clayton Charlton. Cultural change among the Blackfeet Indians of Montana. Dissertation Abstracts, 29 (1968/1969): 1244B-1245B. UM 68-13,897.

Denny, C. Blackfoot magic. Beaver, 275, no. 2 (1944): 14-15.

*Devereux, G. Reality and dream. New York, 1951. 464 p.

Devereux, G. Three technical problems in the psychotherapy of Plains Indian patients. American Journal of Psychotherapy, 5 (1951): 411-423.

*Devereux, George. Reality and dream; psychotherapy of a Plains Indian. 2d ed. Garden City, N.Y., Anchor Books, 1969. 48, 615 p. illus.

Dodge, Grenville M. Biographical sketch of James Bridger. Annals of Wyoming, 33 (1961): 159-177.

Donaldson, T. The George Catlin Indian Gallery. United States National Museum, Reports (1885): 101-106.

Doty, James. A visit to the Blackfoot camp. Edited by Hugh A. Dempsey. Alberta Historical Review, 14, no. 3 (1966): 17-26.

Douglas, F. H. The Blackfoot Indians. Denver Art Museum, Indian Leaflet Series, 37/38 (1931): 1-8.

Edmonson, Munro S. A measurement of relative racial difference. Current Anthropology, 6 (1965): 167-198. [With comments].

Ege, Robert J. Tell Baker to strike them hard; incident on the Marias, 23 Jan. 1870. Bellevue, Neb., Old Army Press, 1970. 9, 146 p. illus., maps.

Ellison, W. H. Adventures of George Nidever. In C. W. Hackett, G. P. Hammond, et al. New Spain and the Anglo-American West. Vol. 2. Los Angeles, 1932: 21-45.

Evans, G. Edward. Prehistoric Blackduck-historic Assiniboine: a reassessment. Plains Anthropologist, 6 (1961): 271-275.

Ewers, J. C. Blackfeet crafts. Indian Handcrafts, 9 (1945): 1-66.

Ewers, J. C. Identification and history of the Small Robes Band of Piegan

Indians. Washington Academy of Sciences, Journal, 36 (1946): 397-401.

Ewers, J. C. Self-torture in the Blood Indian sun dance. Washington Academy of Sciences, Journal, 38 (1948): 166-173.

*Ewers, J. C. The Blackfeet. Norman, 1958. 366 p.

Ewers, J. C. The Blackfoot war lodge: its construction and use. American Anthropologist, n.s., 46 (1944): 182-192.

Ewers, J. C. The case for Blackfoot pottery. American Anthropologist, n.s., 47 (1945): 289-299.

*Ewers, J. C. The horse in Blackfoot Indian culture. U.S. Bureau of American Ethnology, Bulletin, 159 (1955): 1-390.

Ewers, J. C. The last bison drives of the Blackfoot Indians. Washington Academy of Sciences, Journal, 39 (1949): 355-360.

Ewers, J. C. The medicine rock of the Marias. Montana Magazine of History, 2, no. 3 (1952): 51-55.

Ewers, J. C. The story of the Blackfeet. Indian Life and Customs Pamphlets, 6 (1944): 1-66.

Ewers, J. C. Were the Blackfoot rich in horses? American Anthropologist, n.s., 45 (1943): 602-610.

Ewers, John C. A unique pictorial interpretation of Blackfoot Indian religion in 1846-1847. Ethnohistory, 18 (1971): 231-238.

Ewers, John C. Blackfoot Indian pipes and pipemaking. Washington, D.C., Government Printing Office, 1963. 29-60 p. illus. (U.S., Bureau of American Ethnology, Anthropological Papers, 64. U.S., Bureau of American Ethnology, Bulletin, 186)

Ewers, John C. Bodily proportions as guides to lineal measurements among the Blackfoot Indians. American Anthropologist, 72 (1970): 561-562.

Ewers, John C. Contraceptive charms among the Plains Indians. Plains Anthropologist, 15 (1970): 216-218.

Ewers, John C. Mothers of the mixed-bloods. El Palacio, 69 (1962): 20-29.

Ewers, John C. Primitive American commandos. Masterkey, 17 (1943): 117-125.

*Ewers, John C. The horse in Blackfoot Indian culture, with comparative material from other Western tribes. Washington, D.C., Smithsonian Institution Press, 1969. 15, 374 p. illus., maps.

Ewers, John C. The influence of the horse on Blackfoot culture. In Deward E. Walker, Jr., ed. The Emergent Native Americans. Boston, Little, Brown, 1972: 252-270.

Ewers, John C. Was there a Northwestern Plains sub-culture? An ethnographic appraisal. Plains Anthropologist, 12 (1967): 167-174.

Fay, George E., ed. Charters, constitutions and by-laws of the Indian tribes of North America. Part IIa: The Northern Plains. Greeley, 1967. 6, 141 l. maps. (University of Northern Colorado, Museum of Anthropology, Occasional Publications in Anthropology, Ethnology Series, 3) ERIC ED051923.

Fellows, Fred R. The people's pillion: a study of western saddles. Montana, the Magazine of Western History, 16, no. 1 (1966): 57-83.

Fieldsteel, A. Howard. An epidemiologic and immunologic study of poliomyelitis on an Indian reservation. By A. Howard Fieldsteel and Tom D. Y. Chin. American Journal of Hygiene, 76 (1962): 1-14.

Fisher, Anthony Dwight. The perception of instrumental values among the young Blood Indians of Alberta. Dissertation Abstracts, 27 (1966/1967): 2231B. UM 66-14,660.

Forbis, R. G. Some late sites in the Oldman River region, Alberta. National Museum of Canada, Bulletin, 162 (1960): 119-164.

Forbis, Richard G. The Old Women's Buffalo Jump, Alberta. In Contributions to Anthropology 1960. Part I. Ottawa, Queen's Printer, 1962: 57-123. (Canada, National Museum, Bulletin, 180)

Fowler, Don D., ed. Notes on the early life of Chief Washakie. Annals of Wyoming, 36 (1964): 35-42.

Frantz, Donald G. Blackfoot paradigms and matrices. In Contributions to Anthropology: Linguistics I. Ottawa, Queen's Printer, 1967: 140-146. (Canada, National Museum, Bulletin, 214)

Frantz, Donald G. Correspondence on Blackfoot. International Journal of American Linguistics, 32 (1966): 212-213.

Frantz, Donald G. Person indexing in Blackfoot. International Journal of American Linguistics, 32 (1966): 50-58.

Frantz, Donald G. The reciprocal in Blackfoot (and English). Glossa, 2 (1968): 185-190.

Fraser, Frances. The wind along the river. New York, Macmillan, 1968. 83 p.

Friesen, John W. Progress of southern Alberta native peoples. By John W. Friesen and Louise C. Lyon. Journal of American Indian Education, 9, no. 3 (1969/1970): 15-23.

Gates, Merrill E. A visit to the northern reservations in Oregon and Montana. In Lake Mohonk Conference on the Indian and Other Dependent Peoples, 17th. 1899, Boston. Proceedings. [Boston?] 1900: 57-66.

Gaudst, V. Au pays des Peaux-rouges. Lille, 1911. 238 p.

Geers, G. J. The adverbial and prepositional prefix in Blackfoot. Leiden, 1917.

Githens, John H. Prevalence of abnormal hemoglobins in American Indian children. Survey in the Rocky Mountain area. By John H. Githens, Henry K. Knock, and William E. Hathaway. Journal of Laboratory and Clinical Medicine, 57 (1961): 755-758.

Gofton, J. P., et al. Sacro-iliitis in eight populations. Annals of the Rheumatic Diseases, 25 (1966): 528-533.

Gold, Douglas. A schoolmaster with the Blackfeet Indians. Caldwell, Caxton Printers, 1963. 287 p.

Goldfrank, E. S. Administrative programs and changes in Blood society during the reserve period. Human Organization, 2, no. 2 (1943): 18-23.

Goldfrank, E. S. Changing configurations in the social organization of a Blackfoot tribe during the reserve period. American Ethnological Society, Monographs, 8 (1945): 1-73.

Goldfrank, E. S. Observations on sexuality among the Blood Indians of Alberta. Psychoanalysis and the Social Sciences, 3 (1951): 71-98.

Goldfrank, E. S. "Old Man" and the father image in Blood (Blackfoot) society. In G. B. Wilbur and W. Muensterberger, eds. Psychoanalysis and Culture. New York, 1951: 132-141.

Goldfrank, E. S. The different patterns of Blackfoot and Pueblo adaptation to White authority. International Congress of Americanists, Proceedings, 29, vol. 2 (1952): 74-79.

Greenfield, Charles D. Little Dog, once-fierce Piegan warrior, was wise and just beyond his time. Montana, the Magazine of Western History, 14, no. 2 (1964): 23-33.

Grinnell, G. B. A Blackfoot sun and moon myth. Journal of American Folklore, 6 (1893): 44-47.

Grinnell, G. B. Blackfeet Indian stories. New York, 1913. 214 p.

Grinnell, G. B. Blackfoot lodge tales. New York, 1892.

Grinnell, G. B. Childbirth among the Blackfeet. American Anthropologist, 9 (1896): 286-287.

Grinnell, G. B. Early Blackfoot history. American Anthropologist, 5 (1892): 153-174, 582-583.

Grinnell, G. B. The butterfly and the spider among the Blackfeet. American Anthropologist, n.s., 1 (1899): 194-196.

Grinnell, G. B. The lodges of the Blackfeet. American Anthropologist, n.s., 3 (1901): 650-668.

Grinnell, G. B. The punishment of the stingy, 127-235. New York, 1901.

Grinnell, George B. A White Blackfoot. Masterkey, 46 (1972): 142-151.

Grinnell, George B. Blackfoot lodge tales; the story of a prairie people. Lincoln, University of Nebraska Press, 1962. 310 p. illus. (Bison Book, BB129)

Grinnell, George B. Pawnee, Blackfoot, and Cheyenne: history and folklore of the Plains. New York, Scribner, 1961. 301 p.

Habgood, Thelma E. A hide painting from the Blood Reserve, Alberta. Archaeological Society of Alberta, Newsletter, 11 (1966): 1-5, 7-8.

Hady, Walter M. Indian migrations in Manitoba and the West. Historical and Scientific Society of Manitoba, Papers, ser. 3, 17 (1960/1961): 24-53.

Hainline, Jane. Genetic exchange: model construction and a practical application. Human Biology, 35 (1963): 167-191.

Hale, H. Report on the Blackfoot tribes.
British Association for the Advancement
of Science, Annual Meeting, Report, 55
(1885): 696-708.

Hamperl, H. Osteological consequences of
scalping. By H. Hamperl and W. S.
Laughlin. Human Biology, 31 (1959): 80-
89.

Hanks, L. M. A psychological exploration
in the Blackfoot language. International
Journal of American Linguistics, 20
(1954): 195-205.

*Hanks, L. M. and J. R. Hanks. Tribe under
trust. Toronto, 1950. 220 p.

Hanks, L. M. and J. Richardson.
Observations on Northern Blackfoot
kinship. American Ethnological Society,
Monographs, 9 (1945): 1-31.

Harrod, Howard L. Early Protestant
missions among the Blackfeet Indians.
Methodist History, 5, no. 4 (1967): 15-
24.

Harrod, Howard L. Mission among the
Blackfeet. Norman, University of
Oklahoma Press, 1971. 21, 218 p.
illus., maps.

Harrod, Howard L. The Blackfeet and the
divine "establishment". Montana, the
Magazine of Western History, 22, no. 1
(1972): 42-51.

Hayden, F. V. Contributions to the
ethnography and philology of the Indian
tribes of the Missouri Valley. American
Philosophical Society, Transactions,
n.s., 12 (1863): 248-273.

Hendry, A. York Factory to the Blackfoot
country. Ed. by L. J. Burpee. Royal
Society of Canada, Proceedings and
Transactions, ser. 3, 1, pt. 2 (1907):
307-360.

Henry, Alexander. New light on the early
history of the greater Northwest. Edited
by Elliott Coues. Minneapolis, Ross and
Haines, 1965. 2 v. (28, 1,027 p.)
maps.

Hertzog, Keith P. Shortened fifth medial
phalanges. American Journal of Physical
Anthropology, n.s., 27 (1967): 113-117.

Holterman, Jack. Seven Blackfeet stories.
Indian Historian, 3, no. 4 (1970): 39-
43.

Hudson's Bay Company. Saskatchewan
journals and correspondence: Edmonton
House 1795-1800; Chesterfield House
1800-1802. Edited by Alice M. Johnson.
London, 1967. 102, 368, 14 p. map.

(Hudson's Bay Record Society,
Publications, 26)

Hultkrantz, Åke. The Indians in
Yellowstone Park. Annals of Wyoming, 29
(1957): 125-149.

Hyde, G. E. The early Blackfeet and their
neighbors. Old West Series, 2 (1933): 5-
45.

Jackson, Donald. Journey to the Mandans,
1809; the lost narrative of Dr. Thomas.
Missouri Historical Society Bulletin, 20
(1963/1964): 179-192.

Johnson, Olga W. Thriving in the loop of
the Kootenai: Libby and Troy. Montana,
the Magazine of Western History, 16,
no. 3 (1966): 44-55.

Johnston, Alex. Blackfoot Indian
utilization of the flora of the
northwestern Great Plains. Economic
Botany, 24 (1971): 301-324.

Johnston, Alex. Uses of native plants by
the Blackfoot Indians. Alberta
Historical Review, 8 (1960): 8-13.

Johnston, Alexander. Chenopodium album as
a food plant in Blackfoot Indian
prehistory. Ecology, 43 (1962): 129-130.

Johnston, Alexander, comp. The battle of
Belly River; stories of the last great
Indian battle. Lethbridge, Historical
Society of Alberta, Lethbridge Branch,
1966. 22 p. illus., maps.

Jones, Rosalie May. The Blackfeet
medicine lodge ceremony: ritual and
dance-drama. Salt Lake City, 1968. 11,
163 l. illus.

Josselin de Jong, J. P. B. de. Blackfoot
texts. Amsterdam, Koninklijke Akademie
van Wetenschappen, Afdeeling
Letterkunde, Verhandelingen, n.s., 14,
no. 4 (1914): 1-154.

Josselin de Jong, J. P. B. de. Prof. C.
C. Uhlenbeck's latest contribution to
Blackfoot ethnology. Internationales
Archiv für Ethnographie, 21 (1913): 105-
115.

Josselin de Jong, J. P. B. de. Social
organization of the Southern Peigans.
Internationales Archiv für Ethnographie,
20 (1912): 191-197.

Kaklamani, E. Secretor and Lewis gene
frequencies in Blackfeet Indians. By E.
Kaklamani and E. J. Holborow. Vox
Sanguinis, 8 (1963): 231-234.

Kane, P. Wanderings of an artist among the Indians of North America. London, 1859. 329 p.

Kehoe, Alice B. The function of ceremonial sexual intercourse among the Northern Plains Indians. Plains Anthropologist, 15 (1970): 99-103.

Kehoe, T. F. Stone "medicine wheels" in southern Alberta and the adjacent portion of Montana. Washington Academy of Sciences, Journal, 44 (1954): 133-137.

Kehoe, T. F. Tipi rings. American Anthropologist, 60 (1958): 861-873.

Kehoe, T. F. and A. B. Kehoe. A historical marker, Indian style. Alberta Historical Review, 5, no. 4 (1957): 6-10.

Kehoe, T. F. and A. B. Kehoe. Boulder effigy monuments in the Northern Plains. Journal of American Folklore, 72 (1959): 115-127.

Kehoe, Thomas F. A probable late Blackfoot clay vessel. By Thomas F. and Alice B. Kehoe. Plains Anthropologist, 6 (1961): 43-45.

Kehoe, Thomas F. Stone tipi rings in North-Central Montana and the adjacent portion of Alberta, Canada: their historical ethnological, and archeological aspects. Washington, D.C., Government Printing Office, 1960. 417-474 p. illus., map. (U.S., Bureau of American Ethnology, Anthropological Papers, 62. U.S., Bureau of American Ethnology, Bulletin, 173)

Kehoe, Thomas F. The Boarding School Bison Drive Site. Plains Anthropologist, 12 (1967): 1-165.

Kelkar, Ashok R. Participant placement in Algonquian and Georgian. International Journal of American Linguistics, 31 (1965): 195-205.

Kennedy, G. A. The last battle. Alberta Folklore Quarterly, 1 (1945): 57-60.

Knox, R. H. A Blackfoot version of the magic flight. Journal of American Folklore, 36 (1923): 401-403.

Laidlaw, G. E. The sun dance among the Blackfeet. American Antiquarian and Oriental Journal, 8 (1886): 169-170.

Lancaster, Richard. Piegan; a look from within at the life, times, and legacy of an American Indian tribe. Garden City, Doubleday, 1966. 359 p. illus.

Lancaster, Richard. Piegan; chronique de la mort lente. La réserve indienne des Pieds-Noirs. Paris, Plon, 1970. 394 p.

Lanning, C. M. A grammar and vocabulary of the Blackfoot language. Fort Benton, 1882. 143 p.

Lawrence, H. Frank. Early days in the Chinook belt. Alberta Historical Review, 13, no. 1 (1965): 9-19.

Lee, Lawrence B. The Mormons come to Canada, 1887-1902. Pacific Northwest Quarterly, 59 (1968): 11-22.

Legal, E. J. Au nord-ouest canadien: les Pieds-Noirs. Société de Géographie (Paris), Bulletin, sér. 7, 20 (1899): 450-461.

Lepley, John G. The prince and the artist on the Upper Missouri. Montana, the Magazine of Western History, 20, no. 3 (1970): 42-54.

Levine, P. Distribution of blood groups and agglutinogen M among "Blackfeet" and "Blood" Indians. Society for Experimental Biology and Medicine, Proceedings, 33 (1935): 287-299.

Lewis, O. Manly-hearted women among the North Piegan. American Anthropologist, n.s., 43 (1941): 173-187.

Lewis, O. The effects of White contact upon Blackfoot culture with special reference to the role of the fur trade. American Ethnological Society, Monographs, 6 (1942): 1-73.

Lewis, Oscar. Manly-hearted women among the North Piegan. In his Anthropological Essays. New York, Random House, 1970: 213-228.

Lewis, Oscar. The effects of White contact upon Blackfoot culture. In his Anthropological Essays. New York, Random House, 1970: 137-212.

L'Heureux, J. Ethnological notes on the astronomical customs and religious ideas of the Chokitapia or Blackfeet Indians. Royal Anthropological Institute of Great Britain and Ireland, Journal, 15 (1885): 301-304.

L'Heureux, J. The Kekip-Sesoators, or ancient sacrificial stone, of the northwest tribes of Canada. Royal Anthropological Institute of Great Britain and Ireland, Journal, 15 (1885): 161-164.

L'Heureux, Jean. The Kelip-Sesoators or ancient sacrificial stone of the N.W.T.,

Canada. Alberta Historical Review, 7, no. 4 (1959): 12-15.

Lincoln, J. S. The dream in primitive cultures. London, 1935. 359 p.

Linderman, F. B. American. New York, 1930. 324 p.

Linderman, F. B. Blackfeet Indians. St. Paul, 1935. 65 p.

Linderman, F. B. Indian why stories. New York, 1915. 236 p.

Livingston-Little, D. E. An economic history of North Idaho, 1800-1900. Journal of the West, 2 (1963): 121-132, 459-467; 3 (1964): 47-74, 175-198, 318-354.

Long Lance, Buffalo Child. Long Lance. New York, 1928. 278 p.

Lothrop, Gloria Ricci. Father Gregory Mengarini, an Italian Jesuit missionary in the transmontane West: his life and memoirs. Dissertation Abstracts International, 31 (1970/1971): 2286A. UM 70-23,170.

MacEwan, John W. G. Portraits from the Plains. Toronto, McGraw-Hill of Canada, 1971. 287 p. illus., map.

MacGregor, James. Lord Lorne in Alberta. Alberta Historical Review, 12, no. 2 (1964): 1-14.

Maclean, John. Blackfoot medical priesthood. Alberta Historical Review, 9, no. 2 (1961): 1-7.

Martin, John. Prairie reminiscences. Alberta Historical Review, 10, no. 2 (1962): 5-19.

Matson, G. A. Blood groups and ageusia in Indians of Montana and Alberta. American Journal of Physical Anthropology, 24 (1938): 81-89.

Matson, G. A. Unexpected differences in distribution of blood groups among American Indians. Society for Experimental Biology and Medicine, Proceedings, 30 (1933): 1380-1382.

Matson, G. A. and H. F. Schrader. Blood grouping among the "Blackfeet" and "Blood" tribes. Journal of Immunology, 25 (1933): 155-163.

Matson, G. A., et al. Distribution of the sub-groups of A and agglutinogens among the Blackfeet Indians. Society for Experimental Biology and Medicine, Proceedings, 33 (1936): 25, 46-47.

Mattison, Ray H. Fort Union: its role in the Upper Missouri fur trade. North Dakota History, 29 (1962): 181-208.

McAllester, D. Water as a disciplinary agent among the Crow and Blackfoot. American Anthropologist, n.s., 43 (1941): 593-604.

McBride, Dorothy McFatridge. Hoosier schoolmaster among the Sioux. Montana, the Magazine of Western History, 20, no. 4 (1970): 78-97.

McClintock, W. A Blackfoot circle-camp. Masterkey, 1 (1927): 5-12.

McClintock, W. Blackfoot legends. Masterkey, 6 (1933): 41-46, 70-73.

McClintock, W. Blackfoot medicine-pipe ceremony. Southwest Museum Leaflets, 21 (1948): 1-9.

McClintock, W. Blackfoot warrior societies. Masterkey, 11 (1937): 148-158, 198-204; 12 (1938): 11-23.

McClintock, W. Bräuche und Legenden der Schwarzfuss-Indianer. Zeitschrift für Ethnologie, 40 (1908): 606-614.

McClintock, W. Dances of the Blackfoot Indians. Masterkey, 11 (1937): 77-86, 111-121.

McClintock, W. Medizinal- und Nutzpflanzen der Schwarzfuss-Indianer. Zeitschrift für Ethnologie, 41 (1909): 273-279.

McClintock, W. Old Indian trails. London, 1923. 336 p.

McClintock, W. Painted tipis and picture-writing of the Blackfoot Indians. Masterkey, 10 (1936): 121-133, 169-179.

McClintock, W. Saitsiko, the Blackfoot doctor. Masterkey, 15 (1941): 80-86.

McClintock, W. The Blackfoot beaver bundle. Masterkey, 9 (1935): 77-84, 108-117.

McClintock, W. The Blackfoot. Masterkey, 10 (1936): 85-96.

McClintock, W. The Blackfoot tipi. Masterkey, 10 (1936): 85-96.

*McClintock, W. The old North trail. London, 1910. 532 p.

McClintock, W. The thunderbird motive in Blackfoot art. Masterkey, 15 (1941): 129-134.

McClintock, W. The thunderbird myth. Masterkey, 15 (1941): 164-168, 224-227; 16 (1942): 16-18.

McClintock, W. The tragedy of the Blackfoot. Masterkey, 4 (1930): 22-26.

McClintock, W. The tragedy of the Blackfoot. Southwest Museum Papers, 3 (1930): 1-53.

*McClintock, Walter. The old north trail; or, Life, legends and religion of the Blackfeet Indians. Lincoln, University of Nebraska Press, 1968. 26, 539 p. illus., map.

McCracken, Harold. A heritage of the Blackfeet. By Harold McCracken and Paul Dyck. Cody, Wyo., Buffalo Bill Historical Center, 1972. 22 p. illus.

McDougall, John (Mrs.). Incidents of mission life, 1874. Alberta Historical Review, 14, no. 1 (1966): 26-29.

McFee, Malcolm. Modern Blackfeet: contrasting patterns of differential acculturation. Dissertation Abstracts, 23 (1962/1963): 4066-4067. UM 63-2729.

McFee, Malcolm. Modern Blackfeet; Montanans on a reservation. New York, Holt, Rinehart and Winston, 1972. 10, 134 p. illus.

McFee, Malcolm. The 150 percent man, a product of Blackfeet acculturation. American Anthropologist, 70 (1968): 1096-1107.

McGusty, H. A. An English man in Alberta. Alberta Historical Review, 14, no. 1 (1966): 11-21.

McLean, J. Blackfoot amusements. American Antiquarian and Oriental Journal, 23 (1901): 163-169.

McLean, J. Blackfoot Indian legends. Journal of American Folklore, 3 (1890): 296-298.

McLean, J. Blackfoot mythology. Journal of American Folklore, 6 (1893): 165-172.

McLean, J. Canadian savage folk. Toronto, 1896.

McLean, J. Picture-writing of the Blackfeet. Canadian Institute, Transactions, 5 (1898): 114-120.

McLean, J. Social organization of the Blackfoot Indians. Canadian Institute, Transactions, 4 (1895): 249-260.

McLean, J. The Blackfoot language. Canadian Institute, Transactions, 5 (1898): 128-165.

McLean, J. The Blackfoot sun-dance. Canadian Institute, Proceedings, ser. 3, 6 (1888): 231-237.

McLean, J. The gesture language of the Blackfeet. Canadian Institute, Transactions, 5 (1898): 44-48.

McLean, J. The Indians of Canada. 3d ed. London, 1892. 351 p.

McLean, J. The mortuary customs of the Blackfeet Indians. Canadian Institute, Proceedings, ser. 3, 5 (1887): 20-24.

McQuesten, C. The sun dance of the Blackfoot. Rod and Gun in Canada, 13 (1912): 1169-1177.

Meeker, L. L. Piegan fortune-telling. American Anthropologist, 9 (1896): 368.

Meeussen, A. E. Correspondence on Blackfoot. International Journal of American Linguistics, 32 (1966): 212.

Michelson, T. A Piegan tale. Journal of American Folklore, 29 (1916): 408-409.

Michelson, T. Notes on some word-comparisons between Blackfoot and other Algonquian languages. International Journal of American Linguistics, 3 (1925): 233-235.

Michelson, T. Notes on the Piegan system of consanguinity. In Holmes Anniversary Volume. Washington, D.C., 1916: 320-333.

Michelson, T. Phonetic shifts in Algonquian languages. International Journal of American Linguistics, 8 (1935): 131-171.

Michelson, T. Piegan tales. Journal of American Folklore, 24 (1911): 238-248.

Middleton, S. H. Kainai chieftainship. Lethbridge, 1951. 179 p.

Middleton, S. H. The story of the Blood Indians. Alberta Folklore Quarterly, 1 (1945): 85-88.

Miller, Anthony G. Cooperation and competition among Blackfoot Indian and urban Canadian children. By Anthony G. Miller and Ron Thomas. Child Development, 43 (1972): 1104-1110.

Mitchell, Jessie Lincoln. A portal to the past: the Blackfeet and their white friends. Montana, the Magazine of

Western History, 14, no. 2 (1964): 75-81.

Mooney, J. Siksika. U.S. Bureau of American Ethnology, Bulletin, 30, vol. 2 (1910): 570-571.

Morgan, L. H. Systems of consanguinity and affinity. Smithsonian Contributions to Knowledge, 17 (1871): 291-382.

Morgan, L. H. The Indian journals, 1859-62: p. 98, 128-129, 144-145, 200. Ann Arbor, 1959.

Morton, Desmond. Des canadiens errants: French Canadian troops in the North-West Campaign of 1885. Journal of Canadian Studies, 5, no. 3 (1970): 28-39.

Morton, Desmond, ed. Telegrams of the North-West Campaign 1885. Edited by Desmond Morton and Reginald H. Roy. Toronto, 1972. 103, 431 p. illus., maps. (Champlain Society, Publications, 47)

Nettl, Bruno. Biography of a Blackfoot Indian singer. Musical Quarterly, 54 (1968): 199-207.

Nettl, Bruno. Blackfoot music in Browning, 1965. Functions and attitudes. In Ludwig Finscher and Christoph-Hellmut Mahling, eds. Festschrift für Walter Wiora. Kassel, Bärenreiter, 1967: 593-598.

Nettl, Bruno. Studies in Blackfoot Indian musical culture. Ethnomusicology, 11 (1967): 141-160, 293-309; 12 (1968): 11-48, 192-207.

Neuman, Robert W. Check-stamped pottery on the northern and central Great Plains. American Antiquity, 29 (1963/1964): 17-26.

Neuman, Robert W. Porcupine quill flatteners from central United States. American Antiquity, 26 (1960/1961): 99-102.

Nuttall, Sue. The ghost house: acculturation in Blackfoot burial patterns. Philadelphia Anthropological Society, Bulletin, 13, no. 2 (1960): 23-28.

O'Brien, William M. Genetics of hyperuricaemia in Blackfeet and Pima Indians. By William M. O'Brien, Thomas A. Burch, and Joseph J. Bunim. Annals of the Rheumatic Diseases, 25 (1966): 117-119.

O'Brien, William M., et al. A genetic study of rheumatoid arthritis and rheumatoid factor in Blackfeet and Pima

Indians. Arthritis and Rheumatism, 10 (1967): 163-179.

Ogden, Peter Skene. Ogden's Snake Country journals. London, 1950-1971. 3 v. illus., maps. (Hudson's Bay Record Society, Publications, 13, 23, 28)

Old Person, Earl. Blackfeet leader on "Peigan". Indian Historian, 1, no. 1 (1967/1968): 26.

Owen, J. Journals and letters. Ed. by S. Dunbar and P. C. Phillips. New York, 1927.

Palliser, J. Further papers. London, 1860. 325 p.

Parry, Keith William John. "To raise these people up": an examination of a Mormon mission to an Indian community as an agent of social change. Dissertation Abstracts International, 33 (1972/1973): 1906B. UM 72-28,785.

Pepin, David. 'Grandma was an Indian'. Recorded by Harriet D. Munnick. Pacific Historian, 12, no. 1 (1968): 45-53.

Petitot, E. F. S. Traditions indiennes du Canada nordouest. Littératures Populaires de Toutes les Nations, 23 (1886): 489-507.

Petitot, E. F. S. Vocabulaire piéganie. Société Philologique, Actes, 14 (1885): 170-198.

Point, Nicolas. Religion and superstition: vignettes of a wilderness mission. Translated by Joseph P. Donnelly. American West, 4, no. 4 (1967): 34-43, 70-73.

Point, Nicolas. Wilderness kingdom: Indian life in the Rocky Mountains: 1840-1847; the journals and paintings of Nicolas Point, S.J. Translated and introduced by Joseph P. Donnelly. New York, Holt, Rinehart and Winston, 1967. 13, 274 p. illus., maps.

Post, Peter W. Histological and histochemical examination of American Indian scalps, mummies, and a shrunken head. By Peter W. Post and Farrington Daniels, Jr. American Journal of Physical Anthropology, n.s., 30 (1969): 269-293.

Ray, Arthur Joseph, Jr. Indian exploitation of the forest-grassland transition zone in Western Canada, 1650-1860: a geographical view of two centuries of change. Dissertation Abstracts International, 32 (1971/1972): 3432B. UM 71-28,359.

Richardson, J. and L. M. Hanks. Water discipline and water imagery among the Blackfoot. American Anthropologist, n.s., 44 (1942): 331-333.

Robbins, Lynn A. Economics, household composition, and the family cycle: the Blackfeet case. In June Helm, ed. Spanish-Speaking People in the United States. Seattle, University of Washington Press, 1968: 196-215. (American Ethnological Society, Proceedings of the Annual Spring Meeting, 1968)

Robbins, Lynn Arnold. Blackfeet families and households. Dissertation Abstracts International, 32 (1971/1972): 6177B-6178B. UM 72-14,755.

Rolland, Walpole. My Alberta notebook. Alberta Historical Review, 18, no. 1 (1970): 21-30.

Ronan, Peter. History of the Flathead Indians. Minneapolis, Ross and Haines, 1965. 85 p. illus.

Rowand, John. A letter from Fort Edmonton. Alberta Historical Review, 11, no. 1 (1963): 1-6.

Sanders, H. F. The white quiver. New York, 1913. 344 p.

Sanderson, James F. Indian tales of the Canadian prairies. Calgary, Historical Society of Alberta, 1965. 15 p. illus.

Sanderson, James F. Indian tales of the Canadian prairies. Alberta Historical Review, 13, no. 3 (1965): 7-21.

Schaeffer, C. E. Bird nomenclature and principles of avian taxonomy of the Blackfeet Indians. Washington Academy of Sciences, Journal, 40 (1950): 37-46.

Schaeffer, C. E. Was the California condor known to the Blackfoot Indians? Washington Academy of Sciences, Journal, 41 (1951): 181-191.

Schaeffer, Claude E. Blackfoot shaking tent. Calgary, 1969. 38 p. illus. (Glenbow-Alberta Institute, Occasional Paper, 5)

Schemm, M. W. The major's lady: Natawista. Montana Magazine of History, 2, no. 1 (1952): 5-16.

Schmidt, W. Die Blackfeet. In his Die Ursprung der Göttesidee. Bd. 2. Münster i. W., 1929: 659-670.

Schoenberg, Wilfred P. Historic St. Peter's Mission: landmark of the Jesuits and the Ursulines among the Blackfeet.

Montana, the Magazine of Western History, 11, no. 1 (1961): 68-85.

Schultz, Hart Merriam (Lone Wolf). Lone Wolf returns . . . to that long ago time. Edited by Paul Dyck. Montana, the Magazine of Western History, 22, no. 1 (1972): 18-41.

Schultz, J. W. Apauk, caller of buffalo. Boston, 1916. 226 p.

Schultz, J. W. Blackfeet tales. Boston, 1916. 241 p.

Schultz, J. W. Friends of my life as an Indian. Boston, 1923. 299 p.

Schultz, J. W. My life as an Indian. New York, 1907. 426 p.

Schultz, J. W. Signposts of adventure. Boston, 1926. 225 p.

Schultz, J. W. and J. L. Donaldson. The sun god's children. Boston, 1930. 255 p.

Schultz, James Willard. Blackfeet and buffalo; memories of life among the Indians. Norman, University of Oklahoma Press, 1962. 384 p. illus.

Schultz, James Willard. My life as an Indian. Greenwich, Conn., Fawcett Publications, 1968. 204 p.

Sharp, Paul F. Blackfeet of the border . . . one people divided. Montana, the Magazine of Western History, 20, no. 1 (1970): 2-15.

Sheire, James W. Glacier National Park; historic resources study. Washington, D.C., Office of History and Historic Architecture, Eastern Service Center, 1970. 8, 228 p. map.

Smet, P. J. de. Western missions and missionaries. New York, 1863.

Smith, DeC. Indian experiences. Caldwell, 1943. 387 p.

Somogyi-Csizmazia, W. Three-rooted mandibular first permanent molars in Alberta Indian children. By W. Somogyi-Csizmazia and A. J. Simons. Canadian Dental Association, Journal, 37 (1971): 105-106.

Spier, L. Blackfoot relationship terms. American Anthropologist, n.s., 17 (1915): 603-607.

Spindler, George D. The instrumental activities inventory: a technique for the study of the psychology of acculturation. By George Spindler and

Louise Spindler. Southwestern Journal of Anthropology, 21 (1965): 1-23.

Spitzer, Allen. Social disorganization among the Montana Blackfeet. American Catholic Sociological Review, 11 (1950): 218-233.

Spry, Irene M., ed. The papers of the Palliser Expedition 1857-1860. Toronto, 1968. 138, 694 p. illus., map. (Champlain Society, Publications, 44)

Stanley, J. M. Visit to the Piegan camp. In Reports of Explorations and Surveys to Ascertain the Most Practicable and Economical Route for a Railroad from the Mississippi River to the Pacific Ocean (33d Congress, 2d Session, H.R. Ex. Doc. 91). Vol. 1. Washington, D.C., 1855: 447-449.

Steward, J. H. The Blackfoot. Berkeley, 1934. 92 p.

Taylor, Allan R. Initial change in Blackfoot. In Contributions to Anthropology: Linguistics I. Ottawa, Queen's Printer, 1967: 147-156. (Canada, National Museum, Bulletin, 214)

Taylor, Allen Ross. A grammar of Blackfoot. Dissertation Abstracts International, 31 (1970/1971): 748A. UM 70-13,183.

Thompson, David. David Thompson's narrative 1784-1812. Edited by Richard Glover. Toronto, 1962. 102, 410 p. map. (Champlain Society, Publications, 40)

Tietema, Sidney J. Indians in agriculture. II. Cattle ranching on the Blackfeet Reservation. By Sidney J. Tietema, Ralph E. Ward, and C. B. Baker. Bozeman, 1957. (Montana, Agricultural Experiment Station, Bulletin, 532)

Tietema, Sidney J. Indians in agriculture. III. Alternatives in irrigation farming for the Blackfeet and Crow Indian Reservations. Bozeman, 1958. 59 p. map. (Montana, Agricultural Experiment Station, Bulletin, 542)

Tims, J. W. Grammar and dictionary of the Blackfoot language. London, 1889. 191 p.

Tyrrell, J. B., ed. David Thompson's narrative of his explorations in Western America. Champlain Society, Publications, 12 (1916): 345-371.

Uhlenbeck, C. C. A concise Blackfoot grammar. Amsterdam, Koninklijke Akademie van Wetenschappen, Afdeeling

Letterkunde, Verhandelingen, n.s., 41 (1938): 1-240.

Uhlenbeck, C. C. A new series of Blackfoot texts. Amsterdam, Koninklijke Akademie van Wetenschappen, Afdeeling Letterkunde, Verhandelingen, n.s., 13, no. 1 (1912): 1-264.

Uhlenbeck, C. C. A survey of the non-pronominal and non-formative affixes of the Blackfoot verb. Amsterdam, Koninklijke Akademie van Wetenschappen, Afdeeling Letterkunde, Verhandelingen, 20, no. 2 (1920): 1-130.

Uhlenbeck, C. C. Additional Blackfoot-Arapaho comparisons. International Journal of American Linguistics, 4 (1927): 227-228.

Uhlenbeck, C. C. Blackfoot imità(ua), dog. International Journal of American Linguistics, 3 (1925): 236.

Uhlenbeck, C. C. Blackfoot kimmat. In Scriti in onore de Alfredo Trombetti. Milano, 1936: xiv.

Uhlenbeck, C. C. Blackfoot notes. International Journal of American Linguistics, 2 (1923): 181; 5 (1929): 119-120; 9 (1939): 76, 119.

Uhlenbeck, C. C. Flexion of substantives in Blackfoot. Amsterdam, Koninklijke Akademie van Wetenschappen, Afdeeling Letterkunde, Verhandelingen, n.s., 14, no. 1 (1913): 1-40.

Uhlenbeck, C. C. Geslachts- en persoonsnamen der Peigans. Koninklijke Akademie van Wetenschappen, Afdeeling Letterkunde, Mededeelingen, ser. 4, 11 (1912): 4-29.

Uhlenbeck, C. C. Het emphatisch gebruik van relatief-promominale uitgangen in het Blackfoot. In W. Koppers, ed. Festschrift Publication d'Hommage Offerte au P. W. Schmidt. Wien, 1928: 148-156.

Uhlenbeck, C. C. Ontwerp van eene vergelijkende vormleer van eenige Algonkin-talen. Amsterdam, Koninklijke Akademie van Wetenschappen, Afdeeling Letterkunde, Verhandelingen, n.s., 11, no. 3 (1910): 1-67.

Uhlenbeck, C. C. Original Blackfoot texts. Amsterdam, Koninklijke Akademie van Wetenschappen, Afdeeling Letterkunde, Verhandelingen, n.s., 12, no. 1 (1911): 1-106.

Uhlenbeck, C. C. Philological notes to Dr. J. P. B. de Josselin de Jong's Blackfoot texts. Amsterdam, Koninklijke

Akademie van Wetenschappen, Afdeeling Letterkunde, Verhandelingen, n.s., 16, no. 1 (1915): 1-43.

Uhlenbeck, C. C. Some Blackfoot song texts. Internationales Archiv für Ethnographie, 23 (1916): 241-242.

Uhlenbeck, C. C. Some general aspects of Blackfoot morphology. Amsterdam, Koninklijke Akademie van Wetenschappen, Afdeeling Letterkunde, Verhandelingen, n.s., 14, no. 5 (1914): 1-61.

Uhlenbeck, C. C. Some word-comparisons between Blackfoot and other Algonquian languages. International Journal of American Linguistics, 3 (1924): 103-108.

Uhlenbeck, C. C. The origin of the otter-lodge. In Festschrift Vilhelm Thomsen. Leipzig, 1912: 74-77.

Uhlenbeck, C. C. and R. H. van Gulick. A Blackfoot-English vocabulary. Amsterdam, Koninklijke Akademie van Wetenschappen, Afdeeling Letterkunde, Verhandelingen, n.s., 33, no. 2 (1934): 1-380.

Uhlenbeck, C. C. and R. H. van Gulick. An English-Blackfoot vocabulary. Amsterdam, Koninklijke Akademie van Wetenschappen, Afdeeling Letterkunde, Verhandelingen, n.s., 29, no. 4 (1930): 1-261.

Uhlenbeck, Christianus C. A survey of the non-pronomial and non-formative affixes of the Blackfoot verb. Wiesbaden, M. Sändig, 1969. 130 p.

U.S., Bureau of Indian Affairs, Missouri River Basin Investigations Project. The Blackfeet Reservation area--its resources and development potential. Billings, Mont., 1972. 8, 139 p. (U.S., Bureau of Indian Affairs, Report, 199)

U.S., Museum of the Plains Indian, Browning, Mont., Archives Division. Blackfeet Agency archives; correspondence relating to affairs at Blackfeet Agency, Montana, 1873-1910. Browning, 1962. 14 l.

Voegelin, C. F. The position of Blackfoot among the Algonquian languages. Michigan Academy of Science, Arts and Letters, Papers, 24 (1941): 505-512.

Wallace, James Nevin. Early explorations along the Bow and Saskatchewan Rivers. Alberta Historical Review, 9, no. 2 (1961): 12-21.

Walton, E. L. Dawn boy; Blackfoot and Navaho songs. New York, 1926. 82 p.

Watt, Ellen. Transferral of a bundle. Beaver, 298, no. 1 (1967/1968): 22-25.

Weber, Francis J., ed. Grant's peace policy: a Catholic dissenter. Montana, the Magazine of Western History, 19, no. 1 (1969): 56-63.

Wedel, Waldo R. Culture sequence in the Central Great Plains. Plains Anthropologist, 17 (1972): 291-352 [sic].

Wells, Donald N. Farmers forgotten: Nez Perce suppliers of the North Idaho gold rush days. Journal of the West, 11 (1972): 488-494.

Welskopf, Elisabeth Charlotte. Akkulturationsprobleme der Prärie-Indianer in Canada. Ethnographisch-Archäologische Zeitschrift, 5 (1964): 97-110.

West, Helen B. Blackfoot country. Montana, the Magazine of Western History, 10, no. 4 (1960): 34-44.

West, Helen B. Flood; the story of the 1964 Blackfeet disaster. Browning, Mont., Blackfeet Tribal Council, 1970. 47 p. illus., map.

West, Helen B. Robare: elusive outpost in Blackfeet country. Montana, the Magazine of Western History, 15, no. 3 (1965): 44-57.

West, Helen B. Starvation winter of the Blackfeet. Montana, the Magazine of Western History, 9, no. 1 (1959): 2-19.

Wetmore, Alphonso, ed. Biographical notice of Genl. William H. Ashley. Edited by Alphonso Wetmore and Charles Keemle. Missouri Historical Society, Bulletin, 24 (1967/1968): 348-354.

Wied-Neuwied, M. zu. Reise in das innere Nordamerika. Coblenz, 1839-1841. 2 v.

Wied-Neuwied, M. zu. Travels in the interior of North America. Early Western Travels, 23 (1906): 86-164; 24 (1906): 217-220.

Wildschut, W. Blackfoot beaver bundle. Indian Notes, 1 (1924): 138-141.

Wildschut, W. Blackfoot pipe bundles. Indian Notes, 5 (1928): 419-433.

Willcomb, Roland H. Bird Rattle and the medicine prayer. Montana, the Magazine of Western History, 20, no. 2 (1970): 42-49.

Wilson, E. F. Report on the Blackfoot tribes. British Association for the

Advancement of Science, Annual Meeting, Report, 57 (1887): 183-200.

Wilson, R. N. Blackfoot star myths. American Antiquarian and Oriental Journal, 15 (1893): 149-150, 200-203.

Wilson, R. N. The sacrificial rite of the Blackfoot. Royal Society of Canada, Proceedings and Transactions, ser. 3, 3, pt. 2 (1909): 3-21.

Wilson, Wesley. The U.S. Army and the Piegans--the Baker Massacre of 1870. North Dakota History, 32 (1965): 40-58.

*Wissler, C. Ceremonial bundles of the Blackfoot Indians. American Museum of Natural History, Anthropological Papers, 7 (1912): 65-289.

Wissler, C. Comparative study of Pawnee and Blackfoot rituals. International Congress of Americanists, Proceedings, 29 (1915): 335-339.

Wissler, C. Decorative art of the Sioux Indians. American Museum of Natural History, Bulletin, 18 (1904): 276-277.

*Wissler, C. Material culture of the Blackfoot Indians. American Museum of Natural History, Anthropological Papers, 5 (1910): 1-175.

Wissler, C. Smoking Star, a Blackfoot shaman. In E. C. Parsons, ed. American Indian Life. New York, 1925: 45-62.

*Wissler, C. Societies and dance associations of the Blackfoot Indians. American Museum of Natural History, Anthropological Papers, 11 (1913): 359-460.

Wissler, C. The Blackfoot Indians. Annual Archaeological Report, being Part of Appendix to the Report of the Minister of Education, Ontario (1905): 162-178.

*Wissler, C. The social life of the Blackfoot Indians. American Museum of Natural History, Anthropological Papers, 7 (1912): 1-64.

*Wissler, C. The sun dance of the Blackfoot Indians. American Museum of Natural History, Anthropological Papers, 16 (1918): 223-270.

Wissler, C. and D. C. Duvall. Mythology of the Blackfoot Indians. American Museum of Natural History, Anthropological Papers, 2 (1908): 1-163.

Wissler, Clark. Population changes among the Northern Plains Indians. New Haven, Human Relations Area Files Press, 1970.

20 p. (Yale University Publications in Anthropology, 1)

Wissler, Clark. Population changes among the Northern Plains Indians. New Haven, Yale University Press, 1936. 20 p. (Yale University Publications in Anthropology, 1)

Wissler, Clark. Population changes among the Northern Plains Indians. New Haven, Human Relations Area Files Press, 1970. 20 p. (Yale University Publications in Anthropology, 1)

Young, Harrison S. Impressions of Fort Edmonton. Alberta Historical Review, 14, no. 1 (1966): 22-25.

Zo-Tom. 1877: Plains Indian sketch books of Zo-Tom and Howling Wolf. By Zo-Tom and Howling Wolf. Flagstaff, Northland Press, 1969. 25 p. illus.

09-05 Caddo

Antle, H. R. Excavation of a Caddoan earth lodge. Chronicles of Oklahoma, 12 (1934): 444-446.

Bell, R. E. Caddoan prehistory. Texas Archeological and Paleontological Society, Bulletin, 19 (1948): 148-154.

Bennett, Kenneth A. Artificial cranial deformation among the Caddo Indians. Texas Journal of Science, 13 (1961): 377-390.

Boas, F. Zur Anthropologie der nordamerikanischen Indianer. Berliner Gesellschaft für Anthropologie, Ethnologie und Urgeschichte, Verhandlungen (1895): 367-411.

Bolton, H. E. Athanase de Mesières and the Louisiana-Texas frontier. Cleveland, 1914. 2 v.

Bolton, H. E. Nabedache. U.S. Bureau of American Ethnology, Bulletin, 30, vol. 2 (1910): 1-4.

Bolton, H. E. Nacogdoche. U.S. Bureau of American Ethnology, Bulletin, 30, vol. 2 (1910): 6-8.

Bolton, H. E. Neche. U.S. Bureau of American Ethnology, Bulletin, 30, vol. 2 (1910): 49-50.

Bolton, H. E. Texas in the middle eighteenth century. California, University, Publications in History, 4 (1915): 1-501.

Bolton, H. E. The native tribes about the East Texas missions. Texas State Historical Association Quarterly, 11 (1908): 249-276.

Bolton, H. E. Xinesi. U.S. Bureau of American Ethnology, Bulletin, 30, vol. 2 (1910): 981.

Brugge, David M. Some Plains Indians in the church records of New Mexico. Plains Anthropologist, 10 (1965): 181-189.

Castaneda, C. Myths and customs of the Tejas Indians. Texas Folk-Lore Society, Publications, 9 (1931): 167-174.

Chafe, Wallace L. The ordering of phonological rules. International Journal of American Linguistics, 34 (1968): 115-137.

Clark, R. C. The beginnings of Texas. Texas State Historical Quarterly, 1, no. 3 (1902): 171-205.

Connelley, W. E. Notes on the early Indian occupancy of the Great Plains. Kansas State Historical Society, Collections, 14 (1918): 438-470.

Davis, William Robert. The Spanish borderlands of Texas and Chihuahua. Texana, 9 (1971): 142-155.

Derbanne, François Dion Deprez. Natchitoches and the trail to the Rio Grande: two early eighteenth-century accounts by the Sieur Derbanne. Translated and edited by Katherine Briggs and Winston De Ville. Louisiana History, 8 (1967): 239-259.

DeRosier, Arthur H., Jr. William Dunbar, explorer. Journal of Mississippi History, 25 (1963): 165-185.

Dickinson, S. D. Notes on the decoration and form of Arkansas Caddo pottery. Texas Archeological and Paleontological Society, Bulletin, 15 (1943): 9-29.

Dormon, C. Caddo pottery. Art and Archaeology, 35 (1934): 59-68.

Dorsey, G. A. Caddo customs of childhood. Journal of American Folklore, 18 (1905): 226-228.

Dorsey, G. A. Traditions of the Caddo. Washington, D.C., 1905. 136 p.

Douglas, F. H. The grass house of the Wichita and Caddo. Denver Art Museum, Indian Leaflet Series, 1, no. 42 (1932): 1-4.

Estep, Raymond. Lieutenant William E. Burnet letters: removal of the Texas Indians and the founding of Fort Cobb. Chronicles of Oklahoma, 38 (1960): 369-396.

Estep, Raymond. Lieutenant William E. Burnet letters: removal of the Texas Indians and the founding of Fort Cobb. Chronicles of Oklahoma, 39 (1961): 15-41.

Estep, Raymond. Lieutenant Wm. E. Burnet: notes on removal of Indians from Texas to Indian Territory. Chronicles of Oklahoma, 38 (1960): 274-309.

Ethridge, A. N. Indians of Grant Parish. Louisiana Historical Quarterly, 23 (1940): 1108-1131.

Fay, George E., ed. Charters, constitutions and by-laws of the Indian tribes of North America. Part V: The Indian tribes of Oklahoma. Greeley, 1968. 14, 104 l. map. (University of Northern Colorado, Museum of Anthropology, Occasional Publications in Anthropology, Ethnology Series, 6) ERIC ED046555.

Fletcher, A. C. Adai. U.S. Bureau of American Ethnology, Bulletin, 30, vol. 1 (1907): 12-13.

Fletcher, A. C. Bidai. U.S. Bureau of American Ethnology, Bulletin, 30, vol. 1 (1907): 145-146.

Fletcher, A. C. Caddo. U.S. Bureau of American Ethnology, Bulletin, 30, vol. 1 (1907): 179-182.

Fletcher, A. C. Kadohadacho. U.S. Bureau of American Ethnology, Bulletin, 30, vol. 1 (1907): 638-639.

Ford, J. A. Analysis of Indian village site collections from Louisiana and Mississippi. Louisiana, Department of Conservation, Anthropological Studies, 2 (1936): 1-285.

Foreman, G. The last trek of the Indians, 282-286, 291-295. Chicago, 1946.

Gibson, A. M. An Indian Territory United Nations: the Creek Council of 1845. Chronicles of Oklahoma, 39 (1961): 398-413.

Gilmore, Kathleen K. A documentary and archeological investigation of Presidio San Luis de las Amarillas and Mission Santa Cruz de San Sabá. Austin, Tex., State Building Commission, 1967. 1, 72 p. illus., map. (Texas, State Building Commission Archeological Program, 9)

Glover, W. B. A history of the Caddo
Indians. Louisiana Historical Quarterly,
18 (1935): 872-946.

Gray, Margery P. Blood groups of Caddoan
Indians of Oklahoma. By Margery P. Gray
and William S. Laughlin. American
Journal of Human Genetics, 12 (1960):
86-94.

*Griffith, W. J. The Hasinai Indians of
East Texas as seen by Europeans, 1687-
1772. Middle American Research
Institute, Philological and Documentary
Studies, 2 (1954): 43-165.

Griffith, W. J. The Spanish occupation of
the Hasinai country, 1690 to 1737.
Middle American Research Institute,
Studies, 3 (1954): 1-147.

Hammack, Laurens C. Archaeology of the
Ute dam and reservoir. Santa Fe, 1965.
69 p. illus., maps. (Museum of New
Mexico, Papers in Anthropology, 14)

Harby, Mrs. L. C. The Tejas. American
Historical Association, Annual Report
(1894): 63-82.

Harrington, M. R. Certain Caddo sites in
Arkansas. Indian Notes and Monographs,
n.s., 10 (1920): 1-349.

Hatcher, M. A. Descriptions of the Tejas
or Asinai Indians. Southwestern
Historical Quarterly, 30 (1927): 206-
218, 283-304; 31 (1927): 50-62, 150-180.

Hatcher, M. A. Myths of the Tejas
Indians. Texas Folk-Lore Society,
Publications, 6 (1927): 107-118.

Havins, T. R. Noah T. Byars at Torrey's
Trading Post. Texana, 8 (1970): 328-340.

Heflin, E. The Oashuns or dances of the
Caddo. Oklahoma Anthropological Society,
Bulletin, 1 (1953): 39-42.

Hilder, F. F. A Texas Indian myth.
American Anthropologist, n.s., 1 (1899):
592-594.

Hodges, T. L. Suggestion for
identification of certain mid-Ouachita
pottery as Cahinnio Caddo. Texas
Archeological and Paleontological
Society, Bulletin, 16 (1945): 98-116.

Hodges, T. L. The Cahinnio-Caddo. Texas
Archeological and Paleontological
Society, Bulletin, 28 (1957): 190-197.

Hughes, Jack Thomas. Prehistory of the
Caddoan-speaking tribes. Dissertation
Abstracts International, 30 (1969/1970):
950B. UM 69-9198.

Humble, S. L. The Ouachita Valley
expedition of DeSoto. Louisiana
Historical Quarterly, 25 (1942): 611-
643.

Hungate, M. Religious beliefs of the
Nebraska Indian. Nebraska History, 14,
no. 3 (1938): 207-226.

Hyde, G. E. The Pawnee Indians. Old West
Series, 4 (1934): 5-54; 5 (1934): 3-50.

Jackson, A. T. Fire in East Texas burial
rites. Texas Archeological and
Paleontological Society, Bulletin, 10
(1938): 77-113.

Jennings, J. D. Prehistory of the Lower
Mississippi Valley. In J. B. Griffin,
ed. Archeology of Eastern United States.
Chicago, 1952: 256-271.

Joutel, H. Journal of La Salle's last
voyage. New ed. Albany, 1906. 258 p.

Joutel, H. Relation. In P. Margry, ed.
Découvertes et Établissements des
Français dans l'Ouest et dans le Sud de
l'Amérique Septentrionale. Vol. 3.
Paris, 1879: 91-534.

Kunkel, P. A. The Indians of Louisiana
about 1700. Louisiana Historical
Quarterly, 34 (1951): 175-204.

La Barre, Weston. The peyote cult. New
Haven, Yale University, Department of
Anthropology, 1938. 188 p. illus.
(Yale University Publications in
Anthropology, 19)

Lesser, A. and G. Weltfish. Composition
of the Caddoan linguistic stock.
Smithsonian Miscellaneous Collections,
87, no. 6 (1932): 1-15.

Lyon, O. The trail of the Caddo. Arkansas
Historical Quarterly, 11 (1952): 124-
130.

Mansanet, D. Carta. Texas State
Historical Association Quarterly, 2
(1899): 254-312.

McGimsey, Charles R., III. Indians of
Arkansas. Fayetteville, Arkansas
Archeological Survey, 1969. 7, 1-47 p.
illus., maps. (Arkansas Archeological
Survey, Publications on Archeology,
Popular Series, 1)

McLean, Malcolm D. Tenoxtitlan, dream
capital of Texas. Southwestern
Historical Quarterly, 70 (1966/1967):
23-43.

Mooney, J. The ghost-dance religion. U.S.
Bureau of American Ethnology, Annual
Reports, 14, vol. 2 (1893): 1092-1102.

Morfi, J. H. de. Memorias for the history of the Province of Texas. Ed. by F. M. Chabot. San Antonio, 1932. 85 p.

Morris, Wayne. Traders and factories on the Arkansas frontier, 1805-1822. Arkansas Historical Quarterly, 28 (1969): 28-48.

Nasatir, A. P. Before Lewis and Clark. St. Louis, 1952. 2 v. (882 p.).

Neighbours, Kenneth F. Jose Maria: Anadarko chief. Chronicles of Oklahoma, 44 (1966): 254-274.

Newell, H. P. and A. D. Krieger. The George C. Davis Site, Cherokee County, Texas. Society for American Archaeology, Memoirs, 5 (1949): 1-271.

Oklahoma, University, Bureau of Business Research. The utilization of property of specified Wichita, Caddo, and Delaware Indian tribes' land in Caddo County, Oklahoma. Norman, 1964. 9, 108 p. map.

Orr, K. G. Survey of Caddoan area archeology. In J. B. Griffin, ed. Archeology of Eastern United States. Chicago, 1952: 239-254.

Padilla, J. A. Texas in 1820. Tr. by M. A. Hatcher. Southwestern Historical Quarterly, 23 (1919): 47-68.

*Parsons, E. C. Notes on the Caddo. American Anthropological Association, Memoirs, 57 (1941): 1-76.

Peck, W. M. Caddolina. Denison, 1917. 45 p.

Sayles, E. B. An archaeological survey of Texas. Medallion Papers, 17 (1935): 1-164.

Shea, J. G., ed. Early voyages up and down the Mississippi. Albany, 1861. 191 p.

Sibley, J. A report from Natchitoches. Indian Notes and Monographs, n.s., 25 (1922): 5-102.

Sibley, J. Vocabulary of the Caddoquis or Caddo language. American Naturalist (1879): 787-790.

Smith, R. A. Account of the journey of Bénard de la Harpe. Southwestern Historical Quarterly, 62 (1958/1959): 75-86, 246-259, 371-385, 525-541.

Spier, L. Wichita and Caddo relationship terms. American Anthropologist, n.s., 26 (1924): 258-263.

Swanton, J. R. Indians of the Southeastern United States. U.S. Bureau of American Ethnology, Bulletin, 137 (1946): 11-832.

*Swanton, J. R. Source material on the history and ethnology of the Caddo Indians. U.S. Bureau of American Ethnology, Bulletin, 132 (1942): 1-332.

Swanton, J. R. The Caddo social organization and its possible historical significance. Washington Academy of Sciences, Journal, 21 (1931): 203-206.

Taylor, Allan R. The classification of the Caddoan languages. American Philosophical Society, Proceedings, 107 (1963): 51-59.

Troike, Rudolph C. The Caddo word for "water". International Journal of American Linguistics, 30 (1964): 96-98.

Vigness, David M. Don Hugo Oconor and New Spain's northeastern frontier, 1764-1776. Journal of the West, 6 (1967): 27-40.

Vila Vilar, Luisa. Aculturacion de los grupos indigenas de Texas segun la documentacion española del siglo XVIII. In Congreso Internacional de Americanistas, 36th. 1964, España. Actas y Memorias. Tomo 2. Sevilla, 1966: 161-165.

Walker, W. M. A Caddo burial site at Natchitoches. Smithsonian Miscellaneous Collections, 94, no. 14 (1935): 1-15.

Walker, W. M. A variety of Caddo pottery from Louisiana. Washington Academy of Sciences, Journal, 24 (1934): 99-104.

Webb, C. H. A second historic Caddo site at Natchitoches. Texas Archeological and Paleontological Society, Bulletin, 16 (1945): 52-83.

Webb, C. H. House types among the Caddo Indians. Texas Archeological and Paleontological Society, Bulletin, 12 (1940): 49-75.

Webb, C. H. The Belcher Mound. Society for American Archaeology, Memoirs, 16 (1959): 1-285.

Webb, Murl L. Religious and educational efforts among Texas Indians in the 1850's. Southwestern Historical Quarterly, 69 (1965/1966): 22-37.

Weddle, Robert S. La Salle's survivors. Southwestern Historical Quarterly, 75 (1971/1972): 413-433.

Weer, P. Preliminary notes on the Caddoan
family. Indiana Historical Society,
Prehistory Research Series, 1 (1938):
111-130.

Williams, J. W. Coronado; from the Rio
Grande to the Concho. Southwestern
Historical Quarterly, 63 (1959/1960):
190-220.

Winfrey, Dorman H., ed. The Indian papers
of Texas and the Southwest, 1825-1916.
Edited by Dorman H. Winfrey and James M.
Day. Austin, Pemberton Press, 1966.
412 p.

Woodall, Joe Ned. Cultural ecology of the
Caddo. Dissertation Abstracts
International, 31 (1970/1971): 1675B.
UM 70-19,260.

Zavala, A. de. Religious beliefs of the
Tejas or Hasanias Indians. Texas Folk-
Lore Society, Publications, 1 (1916):
39-43.

09-06 Cheyenne

Abel, A. H., ed. Tabeau's narrative of
Loisel's expedition to the Upper
Missouri. Norman, 1939. 272 p.

Alexander, T. and R. Anderson. Children
in a society under stress. Behavioral
Science, 2 (1957): 46-55.

Anderson, Harry H. Cheyennes at the
Little Big Horn--a study of statistics.
North Dakota History, 27 (1960): 81-93.

Anderson, Harry H. Indian peace-talkers
and the conclusion of the Sioux War of
1876. Nebraska History, 44 (1963): 233-
254.

Anderson, R. The buffalo men.
Southwestern Journal of Anthropology, 12
(1956): 92-104.

Anderson, R. The Northern Cheyenne war
mothers. Anthropological Quarterly, 4
(1956): 82-90.

Anderson, Robert. Notes on Northern
Cheyenne corn ceremonialism. Masterkey,
32 (1958): 57-63.

Anonymous. Arapaho and Cheyenne Indians.
H.R. 11359, 70th Congress, 1st Session,
March 1 and 15, 1928. Washington, D.C.,
1928.

Anonymous. Custer's first massacre: the
battle of the Washita. Amarillo, Tex.,
Humbug Gulch Press, 1968. 40 p.
illus., map.

Anonymous. Mormon girl stopped Indian
attack. Annals of Iowa, 35 (1959): 35.

Anonymous. Senor Don Manuel Lisa.
Missouri Historical Society, Bulletin,
23 (1966/1967): 52-58.

Askin-Edgar, Sylvia. Die Cheyennes und
der letzte Hüter der heiligen Pfeile;
eine Studie der Cheyennes im 20.
Jahrhundert. Zeitschrift für Ethnologie,
96 (1971): 205-216.

Askin-Edgar, Sylvia. Die heilige Pfeile
der Cheyennes und ihr Hüter. Zeitschrift
für Ethnologie, 96 (1971): 202-204.

Barde, Fred S. Edmund Gasseau Choteau
Guerrier: French trader. Chronicles of
Oklahoma, 47 (1969/1970): 360-376.

Barrett, S. M. Hoistah, an Indian girl.
New York, 1913. 136 p.

Bate, Walter N. Eyewitness reports of the
Wagon Box fight. Annals of Wyoming, 41
(1969): 193-202.

Bent, George. Life of George Bent written
from his letters, by George E. Hyde.
Edited by Savoie Lottinville. Norman,
University of Oklahoma Press, 1968. 25,
389 p. illus., maps.

Berthrong, D. J. Federal Indian policy
and the Southern Cheyennes and
Arapahoes, 1887-1907. Ethnohistory, 3
(1956): 138-153.

Berthrong, Donald J. Cattlemen on the
Cheyenne-Arapaho Reservation, 1883-1885.
Arizona and the West, 13 (1971): 5-32.

Berthrong, Donald J. Federal Indian
policy and the Southern Cheyennes and
Araphoes, 1887-1907. In Richard N.
Ellis, ed. The Western American Indian.
Lincoln, University of Nebraska Press,
1972: 133-143.

Boas, F. Zur Anthropologie der
nordamerikanischen Indianer. Berliner
Gesellschaft für Anthropologie,
Ethnologie und Urgeschichte,
Verhandlungen (1895): 367-411.

Bonnerjea, B. Reminiscences of a Cheyenne
Indian. Société des Américanistes,
Journal, n.s., 27 (1935): 129-143.

Bourke, J. G. MacKenzie's last fight with
the Cheyennes. Military Service
Institution of the United States,
Journal, 11 (1890): 29-49, 198-221.

Brant, C. S. Peyotism among the Kiowa-
Apache and neighboring tribes.
Southwestern Journal of Anthropology, 6
(1950): 212-222.

Brown, D. N. The ghost dance religion among the Oklahoma Cheyenne. Chronicles of Oklahoma, 30 (1952): 408-416.

Buck, Royal. Red Willow County letters of Royal Buck, 1872-1873. Edited by Paul D. Riley. Nebraska History, 47 (1966): 371-397.

Burbank, E. A. and E. Caldwell. Burbank among the Indians, 164-174. Caldwell, 1946.

Bushnell, D. I. Burials of the Algonquian, Siouan and Caddoan tribes. U.S. Bureau of American Ethnology, Bulletin, 83 (1927): 7-10.

Bushnell, D. I. Villages of the Algonquian, Siouan and Caddoan tribes. U.S. Bureau of American Ethnology, Bulletin, 77 (1922): 21-25.

Byron, Elsa Spear. The Fetterman fight. Annals of Wyoming, 36 (1964): 63-66.

Campbell, S. The Cheyenne tipi. American Anthropologist, n.s., 17 (1915): 685-694.

Campbell, S. Two Cheyenne stories. Journal of American Folklore, 29 (1916): 406-408.

Carriker, Robert Charles. Fort Supply, Indian Territory: frontier outpost on the Southern Plains, 1868-1894. Dissertation Abstracts, 28 (1967/1968): 2158A. UM 67-15,910.

Cohoe, William. A Cheyenne sketchbook. Norman, University of Oklahoma Press, 1964. 15, 96 p.

Collings, Ellsworth. Roman Nose: chief of the Southern Cheyenne. Chronicles of Oklahoma, 42 (1964): 429-457.

Collins, Dennis. The Indians' last fight; or, the Dull Knife raid. New York, AMS Press, 1972. 326 p.

Corbusier, William T. Camp Sheridan, Nebraska. Nebraska History, 42 (1961): 29-51.

Costo, Rupert. "Seven Arrows" desecrates Cheyenne. Indian Historian, 5, no. 2 (1972): 41-42.

Cowles, Calvin Duvall. A soldier's life on the Indian frontier, 1876-1878: letters of 2Lt. C. D. Cowles. Edited by Weymouth T. Jourdan, Jr. Kansas Historical Quarterly, 38 (1972): 144-155.

Curtis, E. S. The North American Indian, Vol. 19: 107-148, 224-226, 230-238. Norwood, 1930.

Curtis, E. S. The North American Indian, Vol. 6: 89-134, 155-158, 167-173. Norwood, 1911.

Curtis, N., ed. The Indians' book, 147-193. New York, 1907.

Custer, George A. In memoriam: Louis McLane Hamilton, Captain 7th U.S. Cavalry. Chronicles of Oklahoma, 46 (1968): 362-386.

Davis, Irvine. Phonological function in Cheyenne. International Journal of American Linguistics, 28 (1962): 36-42.

Deloria, Vine, Jr. The Cheyenne experience. Natural History, 81, no. 9 (1972): 96-100.

Densmore, F. Cheyenne and Arapaho music. Southwest Museum Papers, 10 (1936): 9-111.

Devereux, G. Cultural factors in psychoanalytic therapy. American Psychoanalytic Association, Journal, 1 (1953): 629-655.

Dizmang, Larry H. Suicide among the Cheyenne Indians. Bulletin of Suicidology, 7 (1967): 8-11.

Dodge, R. I. Our wild Indians. Hartford, 1882. 650 p.

Donaldson, T. The George Catlin Indian Gallery. United States National Museum, Reports (1885): 88-94.

Dorsey, G. A. The Cheyenne. Field Museum, Anthropological Series, 9 (1905): 1-186.

Dorsey, George A. The Cheyenne. Glorieta, N.M., Rio Grande Press, 1971. 186 p. illus.

Douglas, F. H. A Cheyenne peyote fan. Denver Art Museum, Material Culture Notes, 12 (1939): 47-52.

Dyer, D. B. Fort Reno or picturesque Cheyenne-Arapaho army life before the opening of Oklahoma. New York, 1896. 216 p.

Eggan, F. The Cheyenne and Arapaho kinship system. In F. Eggan, ed. Social Anthropology of North American Tribes. 2d ed. Chicago, 1955: 35-98.

Ellis, Everett L. To take a scalp. Annals of Wyoming, 31 (1959): 140-143.

Ellis, Richard N., ed. The Western American Indian: case studies in tribal history. Lincoln, University of Nebraska Press, 1972. 203 p.

Ellis, Richard Nathaniel. General John Pope and the development of federal Indian policy, 1862-1886. Dissertation Abstracts, 29 (1968/1969): 528A. UM 68-10,609.

Everett, Mark Allen, et al. Light-sensitive eruptions in American Indians. Archives of Dermatology, 83 (1961): 243-248.

Ewers, John C. Primitive American commandos. Masterkey, 17 (1943): 117-125.

Fay, George E., ed. Charters, constitutions and by-laws of the Indian tribes of North America. Part V: The Indian tribes of Oklahoma. Greeley, 1968. 14, 104 l. map. (University of Northern Colorado, Museum of Anthropology, Occasional Publications in Anthropology, Ethnology Series, 6) ERIC ED046555.

Fay, George E., ed. Charters, constitutions and by-laws of the Indian tribes of North America. Part IIa: The Northern Plains. Greeley, 1967. 6, 141 l. maps. (University of Northern Colorado, Museum of Anthropology, Occasional Publications in Anthropology, Ethnology Series, 3) ERIC ED051923.

Fay, George E., ed. Military engagements between United States troops and Plains Indians; documentary inquiry by the U.S. Congress. Part I: 1854-1867. Greeley, 1972. 2 v. (236 l.). (University of Northern Colorado, Museum of Anthropology, Occasional Publications in Anthropology, Ethnology Series, 26)

Fendall, Lon W. Medorem Crawford and the Protective Corps. Oregon Historical Quarterly, 72 (1971): 55-77.

Finerty, John F. War-path and bivouac. Norman, University of Oklahoma Press, 1961. 358 p. illus.

Flying Eagle Goodbear, P. Southern Cheyenne ghost narratives. Primitive Man, 24 (1951): 10-20.

Foreman, G. The last trek of the Indians: 296-302. Chicago, 1946.

Fowler, Don D., ed. Notes on the early life of Chief Washakie. Annals of Wyoming, 36 (1964): 35-42.

Franck, Lavina M. Cheyenne dress: a functional analysis. Indian Historian, 4, no. 4 (1971): 25-29.

Frantz, Donald G. Cheyenne distinctive features and phonological rules. International Journal of American Linguistics, 38 (1972): 6-13.

Frantz, Donald G. The origin of Cheyenne pitch accent. International Journal of American Linguistics, 38 (1972): 223-225.

Fraser, Douglas. Village planning in the primitive world. New York, George Braziller, 1968. 128 p. illus.

Fritz, Henry E. The making of Grant's "peace policy". Chronicles of Oklahoma, 37 (1959): 411-432.

Gage, Duane. Black Kettle: a noble savage? Chronicles of Oklahoma, 45 (1967): 244-251.

Garrard, L. H. Wa-to-yah and the Taos trail. Norman, 1955.

Goddard, Ives. More on the nasalization of PA *a in Eastern Algonquian. International Journal of American Linguistics, 37 (1971): 139-145.

Goggin, J. M. A note on Cheyenne peyote. New Mexico Anthropologist, 3 (1939): 26-30.

Grange, Roger T., Jr. Treating the wounded at Fort Robinson. Nebraska History, 45 (1964): 273-294.

Grinnell, G. B. A buffalo sweatlodge. American Anthropologist, n.s., 21 (1919): 361-375.

Grinnell, G. B. A Cheyenne obstacle myth. Journal of American Folklore, 16 (1903): 108-115.

Grinnell, G. B. Account of the Northern Cheyennes concerning the messiah superstition. Journal of American Folklore, 4 (1891): 61-69.

Grinnell, G. B. By Cheyenne campfires. New Haven, 1926. 305 p.

Grinnell, G. B. Cheyenne stream names. American Anthropologist, n.s., 8 (1906): 15-22.

Grinnell, G. B. Cheyenne woman customs. American Anthropologist, n.s., 4 (1902): 13-16.

Grinnell, G. B. Coup and scalp among the Plains Indians. American Anthropologist, n.s., 12 (1910): 296-310.

Grinnell, G. B. Early Cheyenne villages.
American Anthropologist, n.s., 20
(1918): 359-380.

Grinnell, G. B. Falling-Star. Journal of
American Folklore, 34 (1921): 308-315.

Grinnell, G. B. Lone Wolf's last war
trip. Masterkey, 17 (1943): 162-167,
219-224.

Grinnell, G. B. Notes on some Cheyenne
songs. American Anthropologist, n.s., 5
(1903): 312-322.

Grinnell, G. B. Social organization of
the Cheyennes. International Congress of
Americanists, Proceedings, 13 (1902):
135-146.

Grinnell, G. B. Some Cheyenne plant
medicines. American Anthropologist,
n.s., 7 (1905): 37-43.

Grinnell, G. B. Some early Cheyenne
tales. Journal of American Folklore, 20
(1907): 169-194; 21 (1908): 269-320.

*Grinnell, G. B. The Cheyenne Indians.
New Haven, 1923. 2 v.

Grinnell, G. B. The Cheyenne medicine
lodge. American Anthropologist, n.s., 16
(1914): 245-256.

*Grinnell, G. B. The fighting Cheyennes.
2d ed. Norman, 1956. 470 p.

Grinnell, G. B. The great mysteries of
the Cheyenne. American Anthropologist,
n.s., 12 (1910): 542-575.

Grinnell, G. B. When buffalo ran. New
Haven, 1920. 114 p.

Grinnell, George B. By Cheyenne
campfires. Lincoln, University of
Nebraska Press, 1971. 24, 305 p.
illus.

*Grinnell, George B. The Cheyenne Indians:
their history and ways of life.
Lincoln, University of Nebraska Press,
1972. 2 v. illus.

Grinnell, George Bird. The Battle of the
Washita, 1868. In Richard N. Ellis, ed.
The Western American Indian. Lincoln,
University of Nebraska Press, 1972: 37-
47.

Habegger, Lois R. Cheyenne trails; a
history of Mennonites and Cheyennes in
Montana. Newton, Kan., Mennonite
Publication Office, 1959. 65 p.
illus., map.

Hafen, L. R. A report from the first
Indian agent of the Upper Platte and

Arkansas. In C. W. Hackett, G. P.
Hammond, et al. New Spain and the Anglo-
American West. Vol. 2. Los Angeles,
1932: 121-137.

Haine, J. J. F. A Belgian in the gold
rush: California Indians. A memoir by J.
J. F. Haine. Translated, with an
introduction by Jan Albert Goris.
California Historical Society Quarterly,
38 (1959): 141-155.

Hampton, James E. Pernicious anemia in
American Indians. Oklahoma State Medical
Association, Journal, 53 (1960): 503-
509.

Hanson, Marshall Roy. Plains Indians and
urbanization. Dissertation Abstracts, 21
(1960/1961): 23. UM 60-2392.

Harmon, E. M. The story of the Indian
fort near Granby, Colorado. Colorado
Magazine, 22 (1945): 167-171.

Harrison, Lowell H. Damage suits for
Indian depredations in the Adobe Walls
area, 1874. Panhandle-Plains Historical
Review, 36 (1963): 37-60.

Hayden, F. V. Contributions to the
ethnography and philology of the Indian
tribes of the Missouri Valley. American
Philosophical Society, Transactions,
n.s., 12 (1863): 274-320.

Hilger, M. I. Notes on Cheyenne child
life. American Anthropologist, n.s., 48
(1946): 60-69.

Hill, Burton S. Bozeman and the Bozeman
Trail. Annals of Wyoming, 36 (1964):
204-233.

Hodge, Patt. The history of Hammon and
the Red Moon School. Chronicles of
Oklahoma, 44 (1966): 130-139.

Hoebel, E. A. Associations and the state
in the Plains. American Anthropologist,
n.s., 38 (1936): 433-438.

Hoebel, E. A. The Cheyennes. New York,
1960. 103 p.

Howard, James H. Arikara native-made
glass pendants: their probable function.
American Antiquity, 37 (1972): 93-97.

Howbert, Irving. Memories of a lifetime
in the Pike's Peak region. Glorieta,
N.M., Rio Grande Press, 1970. 298 p.
illus., map.

Howbert, Irving. The Indians of the
Pike's Peak region. Glorieta, N.M., Rio
Grande Press, 1970. 10, 230 p. illus.,
map.

Hurst, C. T. Colorado's old-timers. Southwestern Lore, 12 (1946): 19-26.

*Jablow, J. The Cheyenne in Plains Indian trade relations, 1795-1840. American Ethnological Society, Monographs, 19 (1951): 1-110.

Jones, Douglas C. Medicine Lodge revisited. Kansas Historical Quarterly, 35 (1969): 130-142.

Kate, H. F. C. ten. Reizen en onderzoekingen in Noord-Amerika. Leiden, 1885. 464 p.

Kaufman, Edmund G. Mennonite missions among the Oklahoma Indians. Chronicles of Oklahoma, 40 (1962): 41-54.

Keenan, Jerry. The Wagon Box Fight. Journal of the West, 11 (1972): 51-74.

Kennedy, Thomas G. Crow-Northern Cheyenne selected for study. Journal of American Indian Education, 11, no. 1 (1971/1972): 27-31.

King, James T. The Republican River Expedition, June-July, 1869. Nebraska History, 41 (1960): 165-199, 281-297.

Kirkus, Peggy Dickey. Fort David A. Russell: a study of its history from 1867 to 1890; with a brief summary of events from 1890 to the present. Annals of Wyoming, 41 (1969): 83-111.

Kroeber, A. L. Cheyenne tales. Journal of American Folklore, 13 (1900): 161-190.

Kroeker, Marvin. Colonel W. B. Hazen in the Indian Territory. Chronicles of Oklahoma, 42 (1964): 53-73.

Krusche, Rolf. "Custer's massacre". Leipzig, Museum für Völkerkunde, Mitteilungen, 35 (1971): 13-20.

Larned, William L. The Fisk Expedition of 1864: the diary of William L. Larned. Edited by Ray H. Mattison. North Dakota History, 36 (1969): 209-274.

Lee, John D. Diary of the Mormon Battalion Mission. Edited by Juanita Brooks. New Mexico Historical Review, 42 (1967): 165-209, 281-332.

Liberty, Margot. A priest's account of the Cheyenne Sun Dance. South Dakota, University, Museum, Museum News, 29, nos. 1/2 (1968): 1-25.

Liberty, Margot. Fights with the Shoshone, 1855-1870; a Northern Cheyenne Indian narrative. By Margot Liberty in cooperation with John Stands-in-Timber.

Missoula, 1961. 23 p. (Montana State University, Occasional Papers, 2)

Liberty, Margot. Suppression and survival of the Northern Cheyenne Sun Dance. Minnesota Archaeologist, 27 (1965): 121-143.

Liberty, Margot P. Priest and shaman on the Plains: a false dichotomy? Plains Anthropologist, 15 (1970): 73-79.

Liberty, Margot P. The Northern Cheyenne Sun Dance and the opening of the Sacred Medicine Hat 1959. Plains Anthropologist, 12 (1967): 367-385.

Lind, Robert William. Familistic attitudes and marriage role expectations of American Indian and White adolescents. Dissertation Abstracts International, 32 (1971/1972): 5288B. UM 72-10,035.

*Llewellyn, K. N. and E. A. Hoebel. The Cheyenne way. Norman, 1941. 360 p.

Malm, Einar. De kämpade förgäves. Stockholm, Rabén and Sjögren, 1967. 213 p. illus.

Mardock, Robert W. The Plains frontier and the Indian peace policy, 1865-1880. Nebraska History, 49 (1968): 187-201.

Marquis, T. B. A warrior who fought Custer. Minneapolis, 1931. 384 p.

Maxwell, Linda Lee. Satanta: last of the Kiowa war chiefs. Texana, 7 (1969): 117-135.

McCracken, H. The sacred white buffalo. Natural History, 55 (1946): 304-309.

McKinley, J. W. J. W. McKinley's narrative. Panhandle-Plains Historical Review, 36 (1963): 61-69.

Meeussen, A. E. The independent order in Cheyenne. Orbis, 11 (1962): 260-288.

Meserve, C. F. The first allotment of lands in severalty among the Oklahoma Cheyenne and Arapaho Indians. Chronicles of Oklahoma, 11 (1933): 1040-1043.

Michelson, T. Field-work among the Catawba, Fox, Sutaio and Sauk Indians. Smithsonian Miscellaneous Collections, 63, no. 8 (1914): 836.

Michelson, T. The narrative of a Southern Cheyenne woman. Smithsonian Miscellaneous Collections, 87, no. 5 (1932): 1-13.

Mitchell, Michael Dan. Acculturation problems among the Plains tribes of the

government agencies in Western Indian
Territory. Chronicles of Oklahoma, 44
(1966): 281-289.

Mooney, J. A Cheyenne tree burial.
Southern Workman, 36 (1907): 95-97.

Mooney, J. The Cheyenne Indians. American
Anthropological Association, Memoirs, 1
(1907): 357-442.

Mooney, J. The ghost-dance religion. U.S.
Bureau of American Ethnology, Annual
Reports, 14, vol. 2 (1893): 1023-1042.

Moore, John H. Review of "Seven Arrows"
by Hyemoyohsts Storm. American
Anthropologist, 75 (1973): 1040-1042.

Morgan, L. H. Systems of consanguinity
and affinity. Smithsonian Contributions
to Knowledge, 17 (1871): 291-382.

Morgan, L. H. The Indian journals, 1859-
62: p. 95-97, 110. Ann Arbor, 1959.

Mulloy, W. The Northern Plains. In J. B.
Griffin, ed. Archeology of Eastern
United States. Chicago, 1952: 124-138.

Munkres, Robert L. The Plains Indian
threat on the Oregon Trail before 1860.
Annals of Wyoming, 40 (1968): 193-221.

Munn, Fred M. Fred Munn, veteran of
frontier experiences, remembered the
days he rode with Miles, Howard and
Terry. As told to Robert A. Griffen.
Montana, the Magazine of Western
History, 16, no. 2 (1966): 50-64.

Murphy, James C. The place of the
Northern Arapahoes in the relations
between the United States and the
Indians of the Plains 1851-1879. Annals
of Wyoming, 41 (1969): 33-61, 203-259.

Murray, Robert A. The Wagon Box fight: a
centennial appraisal. Annals of Wyoming,
39 (1967): 104-107.

Nasatir, A. P. Before Lewis and Clark.
St. Louis, 1952. 2 v. (882 p.).

Oswald, James M. History of Fort Elliott.
Panhandle-Plains Historical Review, 32
(1959): 1-59.

Ottaway, Harold N. A possible origin for
the Cheyenne Sacred Arrow complex.
Plains Anthropologist, 15 (1970): 94-98.

Painter, C. C. G. Cheyennes and Arapahoes
revisited. Philadelphia, 1893. 62 p.

Peery, D. W. The Indians' friend, John H.
Seger. Chronicles of Oklahoma, 10
(1933): 348-368, 570-591; 11 (1933):
709-732, 845-868, 967-994.

Petersen, Karen Daniels. Cheyenne soldier
societies. Plains Anthropologist, 9
(1964): 146-172.

Petersen, Karen Daniels. Howling Wolf; a
Cheyenne warrior's graphic
interpretation of his people. Palo
Alto, American West Publishing, 1968.
63 p. illus.

Petersen, Karen Daniels. On Hayden's list
of Cheyenne military societies. American
Anthropologist, 67 (1965): 469-472.

Petersen, Karen Daniels. The writings of
Henry Roman Nose. Chronicles of
Oklahoma, 42 (1964): 458-478.

Petter, Bertha K. Cheyenne mission
souvenir. By Bertha E. Kinsinger.
[n.p.] 1911. 51 p. illus.

Petter, R. C. Cheyenne grammar. Newton,
Kansas, 1952. 196 p.

Petter, R. C. English-Cheyenne dictonary.
Kettle Falls, 1913-1915.

Petter, R. C. Sketch of the Cheyenne
grammar. American Anthropological
Association, Memoirs, 1 (1907): 443-478.

Petter, R. C., tr. Nivova-pavhosto. Lame
Deer, Montana, 1928. 273 p.

Petter, R. C., tr. The Kingdom of God.
Lame Deer, Montana, 1926. 282 p.

Petter, Rodolphe C. Reminiscences of past
years in mission service among the
Cheyenne. [and] Two life sketches of
Vxzeta and Vohokass. By Mrs. Bertha K.
Petter. Newton, Kan., Herald
Publishing, 1936. 79 p. illus.

Petter, Rodolphe C., tr. Pavosto, the
gospels of Luke and John translated in
the Cheyenne language and printed for
the interest of the Mennonite Mission
among the Cheyenne Indians. Berne,
Ind., Witness Printing, 1902. 240 p.

Poteet, Chrystabel Berrong. The ending of
a Cheyenne legend. Chronicles of
Oklahoma, 41 (1963): 9-14.

Powell, P. J. Issiwun: sacred buffalo hat
of the Northern Cheyenne. Montana, 10,
no. 1 (1960): 24-40.

Powell, Peter J. Journey to Se'han.
Montana, the Magazine of Western
History, 18, no. 1 (1968): 71-75.

Powell, Peter J. Ox'zem: Box Elder and
his sacred wheel lance. Montana, the
Magazine of Western History, 20, no. 2
(1970): 30-41.

*Powell, Peter J. Sweet medicine. Norman, University of Oklahoma Press, 1969. 2 v. (37, 935 p.) illus.

Powell, Peter John. Issiwun: sacred buffalo hat of the Northern Cheyenne. Montana, the Magazine of Western History, 10, no. 1 (1960): 24-40.

Randolph, R. W. Sweet medicine. Caldwell, 1937. 196 p.

Robertson, G. G. Psychiatric consultation on two Indian reservations. By G. G. Robertson and Michael Baizerman. Hospital and Community Psychiatry, 20 (1969): 186.

Robinett, Paul M. The military career of James Craig. By Paul M. Robinett and Howard V. Canan. Missouri Historical Review, 66 (1971/1972): 49-75.

Rodee, Howard D. The stylistic development of Plains Indian painting and its relationship to ledger drawings. Plains Anthropologist, 10 (1965): 218-232.

Rogers, Bess. Big Jake's crossing. Chronicles of Oklahoma, 38 (1960): 50-54.

Rolston, Alan. The Yellowstone Expedition of 1873. Montana, the Magazine of Western History, 20, no. 2 (1970): 20-29.

Sandoz, Mari. Cheyenne autumn. London, Eyre and Spottiswoode, 1966. 17, 283 p. illus., maps.

Sapir, E. Algonkin p and s in Cheyenne. American Anthropologist, n.s., 15 (1913): 538-539.

Schmidt, M. F. and D. Brown. Fighting Indians of the West, 41-62, 113-228. New York, 1948.

Schmidt, W. Die Cheyenne. In his Die Ursprung der Göttesidee. Bd. 2. Münster i. W., 1929: 757-774.

Schmidt, W. Die Cheyenne. In his Die Ursprung der Göttesidee. Bd. 5. Münster i. W., 1934: 677-715.

Scudder, Ralph E. Custer country. Portland, Or., Binfords and Mort, 1963. 63 p. illus., maps.

Scully, B. The Cheyenne and peyote. In Mission Almanac of the Seraphic Mass Association. Ashland, Mont., May, 1941: 6-14.

Seger, J. H. Cheyenne marriage customs. Journal of American Folklore, 11 (1898): 298-301.

Seger, J. H. Early days among the Cheyenne and Arapahoe Indians. Ed. by S. Vestal. Norman, 1956. 164 p.

Service, E. R. The Cheyenne of the North American Plains. In his A Profile of Primitive Culture. New York, 1958: 110-135.

Shirk, George H. Campaigning with Sheridan: a farrier's diary. Chronicles of Oklahoma, 37 (1959): 68-105.

Shirk, George H. The case of the plagiarized journal. Chronicles of Oklahoma, 36 (1958/1959): 371-410.

Smith, J. S. Cheyennes. In H. R. Schoolcraft, ed. Information respecting the History, Condition, and Prospects of the Indian Tribes of the United States. Vol. 3. Philadelphia, 1853: 446-459.

Smith, W. B. S. Some Cheyenne forms. Studies in Linguistics, 7 (1949): 77-85.

Spence, L. Cheyenne. In J. Hastings, ed. Encyclopaedia of Religion and Ethics. Vol. 3. New York, 1911: 513-514.

Springer, Charles H. Soldiering in Sioux country: 1865. Edited by Benjamin Franklin Cooling, III. San Diego, Frontier Heritage Press, 1971. 82 p. illus., maps.

Stage, Thomas B. A psychiatric service for Plains Indians. By Thomas B. Stage and Thomas J. Keast. Hospital and Community Psychiatry, 17 (1966): 74-76.

Stands In Timber, John. Cheyenne memories. By John Stands In Timber and Margot Liberty, with the assistance of Robert M. Utley. New Haven, Yale University Press, 1967. 15, 330 p. illus., maps.

Stands In Timber, John. I bid you farewell. Indian Historian, 1, no. 1 (1967/1968): 10-11.

Stewart, D. D. Cheyenne-Arapaho assimilation. Phylon, 13 (1952): 120-126.

Storm, Hyemoyohsts. Seven arrows. New York, Harper and Row, 1972. 371 p. illus.

Swanton, J. R. Some neglected data bearing on Cheyenne, Chippewa, and Dakota history. American Anthropologist, n.s., 32 (1930): 156-160.

Thetford, Francis. Battle of the Washita Centennial, 1968. Chronicles of Oklahoma, 46 (1968): 358-361.

Thompson, David. David Thompson's narrative 1784-1812. Edited by Richard Glover. Toronto, 1962. 102, 410 p. map. (Champlain Society, Publications, 40)

Thornburgh, Luella. Paul "Flying Eagle" Goodbear. New Mexico Historical Review, 36 (1961): 256-262.

Thunderbird, Chief. Cheyenne ceremony for girls. Masterkey, 23 (1949): 178-179.

Todd, John B. S. The Harney expedition against the Sioux: the journal of Capt. John B. S. Todd. Edited by Ray H. Mattison. Nebraska History, 43 (1962): 89-130.

Tomkins, W. Universal Indian sign language. San Diego, 1927. 96 p.

Turner, Charles W., ed. Reuben Knox letters. North Carolina Historical Review, 37 (1960): 66-93.

Unrau, William Errol. The role of the Indian agent in the settlement of the South-Central Plains, 1861-1868. Dissertation Abstracts, 25 (1964/1965): 1884. UM 64-4389.

Vaughn, J. W. Sergeant Custard's wagon train fight. Annals of Wyoming, 32 (1960): 227-234.

Vogdes, Ada A. The journal of Ada A. Vogdes, 1868-71. Edited by Donald K. Adams. Montana, the Magazine of Western History, 13, no. 3 (1963): 2-18.

Voth, H. R. Funeral customs among the Cheyenne and Arapaho Indians. Folklorist, 1 (1893).

Webb, Frances Seely. The Indian version of the Platte Bridge fight. Annals of Wyoming, 32 (1960): 234-236.

Wedel, W. R. The Arapaho and Cheyenne. U.S. Bureau of American Ethnology, Bulletin, 174 (1959): 80-81.

Weist, Katherine Morrett. The Northern Cheyennes: diversity in a loosely structured society. Dissertation Abstracts International, 32 (1971/1972): 687B-688B. UM 71-20,924.

White, Lonnie J. Indian battles in the Texas Panhandle, 1874. Journal of the West, 6 (1967): 278-309.

White, Lonnie J. The Cheyenne barrier on the Kansas frontier, 1868-1869. Arizona and the West, 4 (1962): 51-64.

White, Lonnie J. Winter campaigning with Sheridan and Custer: the expedition of the Nineteenth Kansas Volunteer Cavalry. Journal of the West, 6 (1967): 68-98.

White, Lonnie J., ed. Kansas newspaper items relating to the Red River War of 1874-1875. Panhandle-Plains Historical Review, 36 (1963): 71-88.

Wildschut, W. Cheyenne medicine blanket. Indian Notes, 3 (1926): 33-36.

Will, G. F. and G. E. Hyde. Corn among the Indians of the Upper Missouri. St. Louis, 1917. 317 p.

Wilson, H. Clyde. An inquiry into the nature of Plains Indian cultural development. American Anthropologist, 65 (1963): 355-369.

Wood, W. Raymond. A stylistic and historical analysis of shoulder patterns on Plains Indian pottery. American Antiquity, 28 (1962/1963): 25-40.

Wood, W. Raymond. Biesterfeldt: a post-contact coalescent site on the northeastern Plains. Washington, D.C., Smithsonian Institution Press, 1971. 15, 108 p. illus., maps. (Smithsonian Contributions to Anthropology, 15)

Wooden Leg. Wooden Leg, a warrior who fought Custer. Interpreted by Thomas E. Marquis. Lincoln, University of Nebraska Press, 1962. 384 p. illus. (Bison Book, BB126)

Woodward, George A. The Northern Cheyenne at Fort Fetterman; Colonel Woodward describes some experiences of 1871. Edited by John E. Parsons. Montana, the Magazine of Western History, 9, no. 2 (1959): 16-27.

Wright, Bessie L., ed. Diary of a member of the first mule pack train to leave Fort Smith for California in 1849. Panhandle-Plains Historical Review, 42 (1969): 61-119.

Wright, Peter M. The pursuit of Dull Knife from Fort Reno in 1878-1879. Chronicles of Oklahoma, 46 (1968): 141-154.

Wynkoop, E. The battle of the Washita: an Indian agent's view. Chronicles of Oklahoma, 36 (1958/1959): 474-475.

Zimmerman, Jean L. Colonel Ranald S. Mackenzie at Fort Sill. Chronicles of Oklahoma, 44 (1966): 12-21.

09-07   Comanche

Agnew, Brad.   The 1858 war against the
Comanches. Chronicles of Oklahoma, 49
(1971/1972): 211-229.

Armbruster, Henry C.   Torrey's trading
post. Texana, 2 (1964): 112-131.

Atkinson, M. J.   The Texas Indians, 227-
332.   San Antonio, 1935.

Bailey, Minnie Elizabeth Thomas.
Reconstruction in Indian Territory,
1865-1877. Dissertation Abstracts, 29
(1968/1969): 198A.   UM 68-8362.

Bancroft, H. H.   The native races of the
Pacific States, Vol. 1: 473-525.   New
York, 1875.

Becker, D. M.   The Comanches, their
philosophy and religion. Smoke Signals,
6, no. 4 (1954): 4-5.

Bell, Thomas W.   Thomas W. Bell letters.
Edited by Llerena Friend. Southwestern
Historical Quarterly, 63 (1959/1960):
299-310.

Boas, F.   Zur Anthropologie der
nordamerikanischen Indianer. Berliner
Gesellschaft für Anthropologie,
Ethnologie und Urgeschichte,
Verhandlungen (1895): 367-411.

Bollaert, W.   Observations on the Indian
tribes in Texas. Ethnological Society
(London), Journal, 2 (1850): 262-283.

Bolton, H. E.   Athanase de Mézières and
the Louisiana-Texas frontier.
Cleveland, 1914.   2 v.

Brant, C. S.   Peyotism among the Kiowa-
Apache and neighboring tribes.
Southwestern Journal of Anthropology, 6
(1950): 212-222.

Brugge, David M.   Navajos in the Catholic
Church records of New Mexico, 1694-1785.
Window Rock, Navajo Tribe, 1968.   16,
160 p.   (Research Reports, 1)

Burbank, E. A. and E. Royce.   Burbank
among the Indians, 185-191.   Caldwell,
1946.

Burnet, D. G.   The Comanches and other
tribes of Texas. In H. R. Schoolcraft,
ed. Information respecting the History,
Condition, and Prospects of the Indian
Tribes of the United States. Vol. 1.
Philadelphia, 1851: 229-241.

Calleja, Félix.   Nuevo Santander in 1795:
a provincial inspection by Félix
Calleja. Translated and edited by David

M. Vigness. Southwestern Historical
Quarterly, 75 (1971/1972): 461-506.

Canonge, E. D.   Voiceless vowels in
Comanche. International Journal of
American Linguistics, 23 (1957): 63-67.

Canonge, Elliot.   Comanche texts.
Introduction by Morris Swadesh.   Norman,
University of Oklahoma, Summer Institute
of Linguistics, 1958.   13, 156 p.
(Summer Institute of Linguistics,
Publications in Linguistics and Related
Fields, 1)

Carlson, G. A. and V. H. Jones.   Some
notes on uses of plants by the Comanche
Indians. Michigan Academy of Science,
Arts and Letters, Papers, 25 (1939):
517-542.

Carriker, Robert Charles.   Fort Supply,
Indian Territory: frontier outpost on
the Southern Plains, 1868-1894.
Dissertation Abstracts, 28 (1967/1968):
2158A.   UM 67-15,910.

Carroll, H. B. and J. V. Haggard, eds.
Three New Mexico chronicles.
Albuquerque, 1942.   342 p.

Carter, James D.   Background of Anglo-
American colonization of Texas. Texana,
4 (1966): 75-92.

Carter, Robert G.   On the border with
Mackenzie; or, Winning West Texas from
the Comanches.   New York, Antiquarian
Press, 1961.   580 p.   illus.

Casagrande, J. B.   Comanche baby language.
International Journal of American
Linguistics, 14 (1948): 11-14.

Casagrande, J. B.   Comanche linguistic
acculturation. International Journal of
American Linguistics, 20 (1954): 140-
151, 217-237; 21 (1955): 8-25.

Catlin, G.   Illustrations of the manners,
customs and condition of the North
American Indians, Vol. 2: 64-69.   New
York, 1841.

Cavazos Garza, Israel.   Las incursiones de
los bárbaros en el noreste de México,
durante el siglo XIX. Humanitas
(Monterrey), 5 (1964): 343-356.

Cessac, L. de.   Renseignements
ethnographiques sur les Comanches. Revue
d'Ethnographie, 1 (1882): 94-118.

Chapman, Berlin B.   The day in court for
the Kiowa, Comanche and Apache tribes.
Great Plains Journal, 2 (1962/1963): 1-
21.

Chiodo, Beverly Ann. Real County.
  Southwestern Historical Quarterly, 65
  (1961/1962): 348-365.

Clark, C. U. Excerpts from the journals
  of Prince Paul of Wurtemberg, year 1850.
  Southwestern Journal of Anthropology, 15
  (1959): 291-299.

Concha, Fernando de la. Colonel Don
  Fernando de la Concha diary, 1788.
  Edited by Adlai Feather. New Mexico
  Historical Review, 34 (1959): 285-304.

Conrad, David E. The Whipple Expedition
  on the Great Plains. Great Plains
  Journal, 2 (1962/1963): 42-66.

Conroy, William. The Llano Estacado in
  1541: Spanish perception of a
  distinctive physical setting. Journal of
  the West, 11 (1972): 573-581.

Corwin, Hugh D. Comanche and Kiowa
  captives in Oklahoma and Texas.
  Guthrie, Okla., Printed by Cooperative
  Publishing, 1959. 237 p. illus.

Coult, Allan D. A simplified method for
  the transformational analysis of kinship
  terms. American Anthropologist, 68
  (1966): 1476-1483.

Crocchiola, Stanley F. L. Fort Bascom,
  Comanche-Kiowa barrier. By F. Stanley.
  Pampa, Tex., 1961. 224 p.

Culton, Don Henry. The early Panhandle
  surveys. Panhandle-Plains Historical
  Review, 46 (1973): 1-16.

Cummins, H. and M. S. Goldstein.
  Dermatoglyphics in Comanche Indians.
  American Journal of Physical
  Anthropology, 17 (1932): 229-235.

Curtis, E. S. The North American Indian,
  Vol. 19: 181-196, 228-238. Norwood,
  1930.

Dacus, J. A. The Comanches: an
  ethnological sketch. Missouri Historical
  Society, Bulletin, 16 (1959/1960): 333-
  341.

Daniel, James M. The Spanish frontier in
  West Texas and northern Mexico.
  Southwestern Historical Quarterly, 71
  (1967/1968): 481-495.

Day, James M. Two Quanah Parker letters.
  Chronicles of Oklahoma, 44 (1966): 313-
  318.

Dixon, Ford. Cayton Erhard's
  reminiscences of the Texan Santa Fe
  expedition, 1841. Southwestern
  Historical Quarterly, 66 (1962/1963):
  424-456.

Dodge, Henry. Journal of Colonel Dodge's
  expedition from Fort Gibson to the
  Pawnee Pict village. American State
  Papers, Military Affairs, 5 (1860): 373-
  382.

Eagleton, N. E. An historic Indian cache
  in Pecos County. Texas Archeological and
  Paleontological Society, Bulletin, 26
  (1955): 200-217.

Eastman, E. Seven and nine years among
  the Camanches and Apaches. Jersey City,
  1874. 309 p.

Ellis, Richard Nathaniel. General John
  Pope and the development of federal
  Indian policy, 1862-1886. Dissertation
  Abstracts, 29 (1968/1969): 528A. UM 68-
  10,609.

Espinosa, A. M., ed. Los Comanches. New
  Mexico, University, Bulletin, Language
  Series, 1 no. 1 (1907): 1-46.

Estep, Raymond. Lieutenant William E.
  Burnet letters: removal of the Texas
  Indians and the founding of Fort Cobb.
  Chronicles of Oklahoma, 39 (1961): 15-
  41.

Estep, Raymond. Lieutenant William E.
  Burnet letters: removal of the Texas
  Indians and the founding of Fort Cobb.
  Chronicles of Oklahoma, 38 (1960): 369-
  396.

Estep, Raymond. Lieutenant Wm. E. Burnet:
  notes on removal of Indians from Texas
  to Indian Territory. Chronicles of
  Oklahoma, 38 (1960): 274-309.

Fallwell, Gene. The Comanche trail of
  thunder and the massacre at Parker's
  Fort. [n.p.] 1960. 26 p. illus., map.
  (Historic Trails Society, Bulletin, 1)

Farrar, Horatio Russ. Tales of New Mexico
  Territory. Edited by Harold R. Farrar.
  New Mexico Historical Review, 43 (1968):
  137-152.

Faulk, Odie B. Spanish-Comanche relations
  and the Treaty of 1785. Texana, 2
  (1964): 44-53.

Faulk, Odie B. The Comanche invasion of
  Texas, 1743-1836. Great Plains Journal,
  9 (1969/1970): 10-50.

Fay, George E., ed. Charters,
  constitutions and by-laws of the Indian
  tribes of North America. Part V: The
  Indian tribes of Oklahoma. Greeley,
  1968. 14, 104 l. map. (University of
  Northern Colorado, Museum of
  Anthropology, Occasional Publications in
  Anthropology, Ethnology Series, 6) ERIC
  ED046555.

Field, William T.   Fort Colorado: a Texas
ranger frontier outpost in Travis
County, Texas. Southwestern Historical
Quarterly, 72 (1968/1969): 183-199.

Fisher, M. C.   On the Arapahoes, Kiowas,
and Comanches. Ethnological Society
(London), Journal, n.s., 1 (1869): 274-
287.

Fleming, Elvis Eugene.   Captain Nicholas
Nolan; lost on the Staked Plains.
Texana, 4 (1966): 1-13.

Ford, Richard I.   Barter, gift, or
violence: an analysis of Tewa
intertribal exchange. In Edwin N.
Wilmsen, ed. Social Exchange and
Interaction. Ann Arbor, University of
Michigan, 1972: 24-45. (Michigan,
University, Musuem of Anthropology,
Anthropological Papers, 46)

Foreman, G., ed.   Adventure on Red River.
Norman, 1937. 199 p.

Garcia Rejon, M.   Vocabulario del idioma
comanche. Mexico, 1866. 29 p.

Gatschet, A. S.   Zwölf Sprachen aus dem
Südwesten Nordamerikas. Weimar, 1876.
150 p.

Gibson, A. M.   An Indian Territory United
Nations: the Creek Council of 1845.
Chronicles of Oklahoma, 39 (1961): 398-
413.

Giles, Albert S., Sr.   Ca-Vo-Yo, giver of
names. Southwest Review, 53 (1968): 56-
62.

Gladwin, T.   Comanche kin behavior.
American Anthropologist, n.s., 50
(1948): 73-94.

Goldstein, M. S.   Anthropometry of the
Comanches. American Journal of Physical
Anthropology, 19 (1934): 289-321.

Gordon, B. L.   Heroes and ethos of the
Jicarilla Apache. Masterkey, 44 (1970):
54-62.

Greene, A. C.   The last captive. Austin,
Encino Press, 1972. 21, 161 p. illus.

Greenleaf, Richard E.   The Nueva Vizcaya
frontier, 1787-1789. Journal of the
West, 8 (1969): 56-66.

Gregg, J.   Commerce of the Prairies. Early
Western Travels, 20 (1905): 342-352.

Grinnell, G. B.   Who were the Padouca?
American Anthropologist, n.s., 22
(1920): 248-260.

Griswold, G.   Old Fort Sill. Chronicles of
Oklahoma, 36 (1958): 2-15.

Gunnerson, James H.   Plateau Shoshonean
prehistory: a suggested reconstruction.
American Antiquity, 28 (1962/1963): 41-
45.

Hagan, William T.   Kiowas, Comanches, and
cattlemen, 1867-1906: a case study of
the failure of U.S. Reservation policy.
Pacific Historical Review, 40 (1971):
333-355.

Hagan, William T.   Quanah Parker, Indian
judge. El Palacio, 69 (1962): 30-39.

Haine, J. J. F.   A Belgian in the gold
rush: California Indians. A memoir by J.
J. F. Haine. Translated, with an
introduction by Jan Albert Goris.
California Historical Society Quarterly,
38 (1959): 141-155.

Haley, J. E.   The Comanchero trade.
Southwestern Historical Quarterly, 38
(1936): 157-176.

Haley, J. E.   The great Comanche war
trail. Panhandle-Plains Historical
Review, 23 (1950): 11-21.

Hammack, Laurens C.   Archaeology of the
Ute dam and reservoir. Santa Fe, 1965.
69 p. illus., maps. (Museum of New
Mexico, Papers in Anthropology, 14)

Hammel, Eugene A.   A simplified method for
the transformational analysis of kinship
terms: a rejoinder to Coult. American
Anthropologist, 68 (1966): 1483-1488.

Hamp, Eric P.   Prosodic notes.
International Journal of American
Linguistics, 24 (1958): 321-322.

Harrison, Lowell H.   Damage suits for
Indian depredations in the Adobe Walls
area, 1874. Panhandle-Plains Historical
Review, 36 (1963): 37-60.

Harston, J. Emmor.   Comanche land. San
Antonio, Naylor, 1963. 206 p. illus.

Hasdorff, James Curtis.   Four Indian
tribes of Texas 1758-1858: a
reevaluation of historical sources.
Dissertation Abstracts International, 32
(1971/1972): 4512A. UM 72-4805.

Hasskarl, R. A.   An unusual historic
Indian house in Washington County,
Texas. Texas Archeological and
Paleontological Society, Bulletin, 28
(1957): 232-239.

Havins, T. R.   Noah T. Byars at Torrey's
Trading Post. Texana, 8 (1970): 328-340.

Havins, Thomas R. Beyond the Cimarron; Major Earl Van Dorn in Comanche land. Brownwood, Tex., Brown Press, 1968. 8, 113 p. illus.

Havins, Thomas R. Camp Colorado, a decade of frontier defense. Brownwood, Tex., Brown Press, 1964. 9, 199 p. map.

Hoebel, E. A. Comanche and Hekandika Shoshone relationship systems. American Anthropologist, n.s., 41 (1939): 440-457.

Hoebel, E. A. The Comanche sun dance and messianic outbreak of 1873. American Anthropologist, n.s., 43 (1941): 301-303.

*Hoebel, E. A. The political organization and law-ways of the Comanche Indians. American Anthropological Association, Memoirs, 54 (1940): 1-149.

Hoebel, E. Adamson. Plains Indian law in development: the Comanche. In Donald Ray Cressey and David A. Ward, eds. Delinquency, Crime, and Social Process. New York, Harper and Row, 1969: 67-78.

Hoffman, W. J. Remarks on Indian tribal names. American Philosophical Society, Proceedings, 23 (1886): 299-301.

Howard, J. H. A Comanche spear point used in a Kiowa-Comanche peyote ceremonial. South Dakota, University, Museum, Museum Notes, 7 (1950): 3-6.

Howard, James H. Half Moon Way: the Peyote Ritual of Chief White Bear. South Dakota, University, Museum, Museum News, 28, nos. 1/2 (1967): 1-24.

Hultkrantz, Åke. Shoshoni Indians on the Plains: an appraisal of the documentary evidence. Zeitschrift für Ethnologie, 93 (1968): 49-72.

Humfreville, J. L. Twenty years among our savage Indians. Hartford, 1897. 674 p.

Jackson, J. Brantley. The Jared Site: a Comanche burial at Fort Sill, Oklahoma. Plains Anthropologist, 17 (1972): 316-325.

Jelinek, Arthur J. Environment and aboriginal population seen through the historical record. In A Prehistoric Sequence in the Middle Pecos Valley, New Mexico. Ann Arbor, University of Michigan, 1967: 18-40. (Michigan, University, Museum of Anthropology, Anthropological Papers, 31)

Jenkins, J. H., ed. Recollections of early Texas. Austin, 1958. 333 p.

Jenkins, Myra Ellen. Taos Pueblo and its neighbors; 1540-1847. New Mexico Historical Review, 41 (1966): 85-114.

Jones, David E. Sanapia, Comanche medicine woman. New York, Holt, Rinehart and Winston, 1972. 17, 107 p. illus.

Jones, Douglas C. Medicine Lodge revisited. Kansas Historical Quarterly, 35 (1969): 130-142.

Jones, J. H. A condensed history of the Apache and Comanche Indian tribes. San Antonio, 1899.

Jones, William K. Three Kwahari Comanche weapons. Great Plains Journal, 8 (1968/1969): 31-47.

Kate, H. F. C. ten. Notes ethnographiques sur les Comanches. Revue d'Ethnographie, 4 (1885): 120-136.

Kate, H. F. C. ten. Reizen en onderzoekingen in Noord-Amerika, 377-394. Leiden, 1885.

Kenner, Charles L. The great New Mexico cattle raid--1872. New Mexico Historical Review, 37 (1962): 243-259.

Kenner, Charles Leroy. A history of New Mexican-Plains Indian relations. Dissertation Abstracts, 28 (1967/1968): 595A. UM 66-12,762.

Kroeker, Marvin. Colonel W. B. Hazen in the Indian Territory. Chronicles of Oklahoma, 42 (1964): 53-73.

La Barre, Weston. The peyote cult. New Haven, Yale University, Department of Anthropology, 1938. 188 p. illus. (Yale University Publications in Anthropology, 19)

Leathers, Frances Jane, ed. Christopher Columbus Goodman: soldier, Indian fighter, farmer, 1818-1861. Southwestern Historical Quarterly, 69 (1965/1966): 353-376.

Lecompte, Janet. Bent, St. Vrain and company among the Comanche and Kiowa. Colorado Magazine, 49 (1972): 273-293.

Lee, John D. Diary of the Mormon Battalion Mission. Edited by Juanita Brooks. New Mexico Historical Review, 42 (1967): 165-209, 281-332.

Lee, N. Three years among the Camanches. Norman, 1957. 179 p.

Lehmann, H. Nine years among the Indians. Austin, 1927. 235 p.

Leutenegger, Benedict, tr. and ed. New documents on Father José Mariano Reyes. Southwestern Historical Quarterly, 71 (1967/1968): 583-602.

Levy, J. E. Kiowa and Comanche: report from the field. Anthropology Tomorrow, 6, no. 2 (1958): 30-44.

Linton, R. The Comanche sun dance. American Anthropologist, n.s., 37 (1935): 420-428.

Linton, R. The study of man. New York, 1936. 497 p.

Lowie, R. H. Dances and societies of the Plains Shoshone. American Museum of Natural History, Anthropological Papers, 11 (1915): 809-812.

Lowie, R. H. The Comanche, a sample of acculturation. Sociologus, n.s., 3 (1953): 122-127.

Lyman, Wyllys. The Battle of Lyman's Wagon Train. Edited by Ernest R. Archambeau. Panhandle-Plains Historical Review, 36 (1963): 89-101.

Magnaghi, Russell Mario. The Indian slave trader: the Comanche, a case study. Dissertation Abstracts International, 32 (1971/1972): 4531A. UM 72-5301.

Marcy, R. B. Exploration of the Red River of Louisiana. Washington, D.C., 1853. 320 p.

Marcy, R. B. Thirty years of army life on the border. New York, 1866. 442 p.

Maxwell, Linda Lee. Satanta: last of the Kiowa war chiefs. Texana, 7 (1969): 117-135.

McKinley, J. W. J. W. McKinley's narrative. Panhandle-Plains Historical Review, 36 (1963): 61-69.

McLane, William. William McLane's narrative of the Magee-Gutierrez expedition, 1812-1813. Edited by Henry P. Walker. Southwestern Historical Quarterly, 66 (1962/1963): 457-479, 569-588.

Middlebrooks, Audy J. Holland Coffee of Red River. By Audy J. and Glenna Middlebrooks. Southwestern Historical Quarterly, 69 (1965/1966): 145-162.

Miller, Wick R. Uto-Aztecan cognate sets. Berkeley and Los Angeles, University of California Press, 1967. 5, 83 p. map. (California, University, Publications in Linguistics, 48)

Mitchell, Michael Dan. Acculturation problems among the Plains tribes of the government agencies in Western Indian Territory. Chronicles of Oklahoma, 44 (1966): 281-289.

Monahan, Forrest D., Jr. The Kiowa-Comanche Reservation in the 1890's. Chronicles of Oklahoma, 45 (1967): 451-463.

Monahan, Forrest D., Jr. The Kiowas and New Mexico, 1800-1845. Journal of the West, 8 (1969): 67-75.

Mooney, J. Comanche. U.S. Bureau of American Ethnology, Bulletin, 30, vol. 1 (1907): 327-329.

Morfi, J. A. de. Memorias for the history of the Province of Texas. Ed. by F. M. Chabot. San Antonio, 1932. 85 p.

Nasatir, A. P. Before Lewis and Clark. St. Louis, 1952. 2 v. (882 p.).

Neighbors, K. F. The Marcy-Neighbors exploration of the headwaters of the Brazos and Wichita Rivers in 1854. Panhandle-Plains Historical Review, 27 (1954): 27-46.

Neighbors, R. S. The Na-ü-ni or Comanches of Texas. In H. R. Schoolcraft, ed. Information respecting the History, Condition, and Prospects of the Indian Tribes of the United States. Vol. 2. Philadelphia, 1852: 125-134.

Neighbours, Kenneth F. Jose Maria: Anadarko chief. Chronicles of Oklahoma, 44 (1966): 254-274.

Neighbours, Kenneth F. The German-Comanche Treaty. Texana, 2 (1964): 311-322.

Newcomb, W. W. An historic burial from Yellowhouse Canyon, Lubbock County. Texas Archeological and Paleontological Society, Bulletin, 26 (1955): 186-199.

Nye, W. S. Carbine and lance. Norman, 1937. 441 p.

Opler, M. K. The origins of Comanche and Ute. American Anthropologist, n.s., 45 (1943): 155-163.

Osborn, H. and W. A. Smalley. Formulae for Comanche stem and word formation. International Journal of American Linguistics, 15 (1949): 93-99.

Oswald, James M. History of Fort Elliott. Panhandle-Plains Historical Review, 32 (1959): 1-59.

Park, Joseph F. Spanish Indian policy in northern Mexico, 1765-1810. Arizona and the West, 4 (1962): 325-344.

Parker, W. B. Manners, customs, and history of the Indians of south-western Texas. In H. R. Schoolcraft, ed. Information respecting the History, Condition, and Prospects of the Indian Tribes of the United States. Vol. 5. Philadelphia, 1855: 682-685.

Parker, W. B. Notes taken during the expedition commanded by Capt. R. B. Marcy, 188-203, 230-241. Philadelphia, 1856.

Parsons, Mark L. Archeological investigations in Crosby and Dickens counties, Texas during the winter, 1966-1967. Austin, Texas State Building Commission, 1967. 108 p. illus., maps. (Texas, State Building Commission, Archeological Program, 7)

Patten, Roderick E., tr. and ed. Miranda's inspection of Los Almagres: his journal, report, and petition. Southwestern Historical Quarterly, 74 (1970/1971): 223-254.

Pennington, William David. Government policy and farming on the Kiowa Reservation: 1869-1901. Dissertation Abstracts International, 33 (1972/1973): 1123A. UM 72-23,107.

Peters, J. H. Dyeing, spinning and weaving by the Comanches, Navajoes, and other Indians of New Mexico. In W. W. Beach, ed. Indian Miscellany. Albany, 1877: 352-360.

Pike, Albert. Albert Pike's journeys in the prairie, 1831-1832. Edited by J. Evetts Haley. Panhandle-Plains Historical Review, 41 (1968): 1-84.

Plato, Chris C. Polymorphism of the C line of palmar dermatoglyphics with a new classification of the C line terminations. American Journal of Physical Anthropology, n.s., 33 (1970): 413-419.

Porter, K. W. Negroes and Indians on the Texas Frontier, 1831-1876. Journal of Negro History, 41 (1956): 185-214, 285-310.

Radzyminski, Stanley F. Charles Radziminski: patriot, exile, pioneer. Chronicles of Oklahoma, 38 (1960): 354-368.

Rasch, Philip J. Alias "Whiskey Jim". Panhandle-Plains Historical Review, 36 (1963): 103-114.

Rice, Josiah M. A cannoneer in Navajo country; journal of Private Josiah M. Rice, 1851. Edited by Richard H. Dillon. Denver, Published for the Denver Public Library by the Old West Publishing, 1970. 123 p. illus., map.

Richardson, R. N. The Comanche barrier to South Plains settlement. Glendale, 1933. 424 p.

Richardson, R. N. The culture of the Comanche Indians. Texas Archeological and Paleontological Society, Bulletin, 1 (1929): 58-73.

Riggs, V. Alternate phonemic analyses of Comanche. International Journal of American Linguistics, 15 (1949): 229-231.

Rister, C. C. Comanche bondage. Glendale, 1955. 210 p.

Ruiz, José Francisco. Report on the Indian tribes of Texas in 1828. Translated by Georgette Dorn. Edited by John C. Ewers. New Haven, Yale University Library, 1972. 18 p.

Schlesier, Karl H. Rethinking the Dismal River Aspect and the Plains Athapaskans, A.D. 1692-1768. Plains Anthropologist, 17 (1972): 101-133.

Schmidt, M. F. and D. Brown. Fighting Indians of the west, 63-88. New York, 1948.

Secoy, F. R. The identity of the "Paduca". American Anthropologist, 53 (1951): 525-542.

Shimkin, D. B. Shoshone-Comanche origins and migrations. Pacific Science Congress, Proceedings, 6, vol. 4 (1940): 17-25.

Shirk, G. H. Peace on the Plains. Chronicles of Oklahoma, 28 (1950): 2-41.

Sibley, George C. George C. Sibley's journal of a trip to the Salines in 1811. Edited by George R. Brooks. Missouri Historical Society, Bulletin, 21 (1964/1965): 167-207.

Simmons, Marc, ed. Border Comanches; seven Spanish colonial documents, 1785-1819. Santa Fe, Stagecoach Press, 1967. 41 p.

Smalley, W. A. Phonemic rhythm in Comanche. International Journal of American Linguistics, 19 (1953): 297-301.

Smith, C. L. and D. Jeff. The boy
   captives. Ed. by J. M. Hunter. Bandera,
   1927.

Smith, R. A. Account of the journey of
   Bénard de la Harpe. Southwestern
   Historical Quarterly, 62 (1958/1959):
   75-86, 246-259, 371-385, 525-541.

Smith, Ralph A. The Comanche bridge
   between Oklahoma and Mexico, 1843-1844.
   Chronicles of Oklahoma, 39 (1961): 54-
   69.

Smith, Ralph A. The scalp hunt in
   Chihuahua--1849. New Mexico Historical
   Review, 40 (1965): 116-140.

Smith, Ralph A. The scalp hunter in the
   borderlands 1835-1850. Arizona and the
   West, 6 (1964): 5-22.

Smith, Ralph A. The scalp hunter in the
   borderlands 1835-1850. In Roger L.
   Nichols and George R. Adams, eds. The
   American Indian: Past and Present.
   Waltham, Xerox College Publishing, 1971:
   156-167.

Sowell, Andrew J. Early settlers and
   Indian fighters of Southwest Texas. New
   York, Argosy-Antiquarian, 1964. 2 v.
   (8, 844 p.) illus.

St. Clair, H. H. and R. H. Lowie.
   Shoshone and Comanche tales. Journal of
   American Folklore, 22 (1909): 273-282.

Stacey, Joseph. The consummate artistry
   of Diane O'Leary--"Opeche". Arizona
   Highways, 48, no. 9 (1972): 44-47.

Stephens, A. Ray. The Killough Massacre.
   Texana, 7 (1969): 322-327.

Tate, Michael L. Frontier defense on the
   Comanche ranges of Northwest Texas,
   1846-1860. Great Plains Journal, 11
   (1971/1972): 41-56.

Taylor, Morris F. Some aspects of
   historical Indian occupation of
   southeastern Colorado. Great Plains
   Journal, 4 (1964/1965): 17-28.

Tefft, Stanton K. The Comanche kinship
   system in historical perspective. Plains
   Anthropologist, 6 (1961): 252-263.

Tefft, Stanton Knight. Cultural
   adaptation: the case of the Comanche
   Indians. Dissertation Abstracts, 21
   (1960/1961): 2075. UM 60-5176.

Thomas, A. B. After Coronado. Norman,
   1935. 307 p.

Thomas, A. B. An eighteenth century
   Comanche document. American
   Anthropologist, n.s., 31 (1929): 289-
   298.

Thompson, Erwin N. The Negro soldier on
   the frontier: a Fort Davis case study.
   Journal of the West, 7 (1968): 217-235.

Tilghman, Z. A. Quanah, the eagle of the
   Comanches. Oklahoma City, 1938. 196 p.

Tyler, Ronnie. Quanah Parker's narrow
   escape. Chronicles of Oklahoma, 46
   (1968): 182-188.

Underhill, R. M. Peyote. International
   Congress of Americanists, Proceedings,
   30 (1955): 143-148.

Unrau, William E. Indian agents vs. the
   Army: some background notes on the
   Kiowa-Comanche Treaty of 1865. Kansas
   Historical Quarterly, 30 (1964): 129-
   152.

Unrau, William E. Investigation or
   probity? Investigations into the affairs
   of the Kiowa-Comanche Indian Agency,
   1867. Chronicles of Oklahoma, 42 (1964):
   300-319.

Unrau, William Errol. The role of the
   Indian agent in the settlement of the
   South-Central Plains, 1861-1868.
   Dissertation Abstracts, 25 (1964/1965):
   1884. UM 64-4389.

Utley, Robert M. Fort Davis National
   Historic Site, Texas. Washington, D.C.,
   1965. 62 p. illus., maps. (National
   Park Service Historical Handbook Series,
   38)

Utley, Robert M. The range cattle
   industry in the Big Bend of Texas.
   Southwestern Historical Quarterly, 69
   (1965/1966): 419-441.

Utley, Robert M., ed. Captain John Pope's
   plan of 1853 for the frontier defense of
   New Mexico. Arizona and the West, 5
   (1963): 149-163.

Vigness, D. M. Indian raids on the lower
   Rio Grande, 1836-1837. Southwestern
   Historical Quarterly, 59 (1955): 14-23.

Vigness, David M. Don Hugo Oconor and New
   Spain's northeastern frontier, 1764-
   1776. Journal of the West, 6 (1967): 27-
   40.

Vila Vilar, Luisa. Aculturacion de los
   grupos indigenas de Texas segun la
   documentacion española del siglo XVIII.
   In Congreso Internacional de
   Americanistas, 36th. 1964, España. Actas
   y Memorias. Tomo 2. Sevilla, 1966: 161-
   165.

Vizcaya Canales, Isidro. La invasión de los indios bárbaros al noreste de México, en los años de 1840 y 1841. Monterrey, N.L., 1968. 296 p. (Monterrey, Instituto Tecnologico y de Estudios Superiores de Monterrey, Publicaciones, Serie: Historia, 7)

Wallace, E. David G. Burnett's letters describing the Comanche Indians. West Texas Historical Association Yearbook, 30 (1954): 115-140.

Wallace, E. The Comanche eagle dance. Texas Archeological and Paleontological Society, Bulletin, 18 (1947): 83-86.

Wallace, E. The Comanches on the White Man's road. West Texas Historical Association Yearbook, 29 (1953): 3-32.

*Wallace, E. and E. A. Hoebel. The Comanches. Norman, 1952. 400 p.

Wallace, Ernest. Ranald S. Mackenzie on the Texas frontier. Lubbock, West Texas Museum Association, 1964. 10, 214 p. maps.

Webb, Murl L. Religious and educational efforts among Texas Indians in the 1850's. Southwestern Historical Quarterly, 69 (1965/1966): 22-37.

Weddle, Robert S. San Juan Bautista: mother of Texas missions. Southwestern Historical Quarterly, 71 (1967/1968): 542-563.

Weddle, Robert S. The San Sabá Mission: approach to the Great Plains. Great Plains Journal, 4 (1964/1965): 29-38.

Weddle, Robert S. The San Sabá Mission, Spanish pivot in Texas. Austin, University of Texas Press, 1964. 13, 238 p. illus., maps.

Wedel, W. R. The Comanche. U.S. Bureau of American Ethnology, Bulletin, 174 (1959): 75-77.

Whilden, Charles E. Letters from a Santa Fe Army clerk, 1855-1856. Edited by John Hammond Moore. New Mexico Historical Review, 40 (1965): 141-164.

White, Lonnie J. Disturbances on the Arkansas-Texas border, 1827-1831. Arkansas Historical Quarterly, 19 (1960): 95-110.

White, Lonnie J. Indian battles in the Texas Panhandle, 1874. Journal of the West, 6 (1967): 278-309.

White, Lonnie J. Winter campaigning with Sheridan and Custer: the expedition of the Nineteenth Kansas Volunteer Cavalry. Journal of the West, 6 (1967): 68-98.

White, Lonnie J., ed. Kansas newspaper items relating to the Red River War of 1874-1875. Panhandle-Plains Historical Review, 36 (1963): 71-88.

Williams, Lyle Wayne. Struggle for survival: the hostile frontier of New Spain, 1750-1800. Dissertation Abstracts International, 31 (1970/1971): 2820A. UM 70-25,179.

Winfrey, Dorman H., ed. The Indian papers of Texas and the Southwest, 1825-1916. Edited by Dorman H. Winfrey and James M. Day. Austin, Pemberton Press, 1966. 412 p.

Wright, Bessie L., ed. Diary of a member of the first mule pack train to leave Fort Smith for California in 1849. Panhandle-Plains Historical Review, 42 (1969): 61-119.

Zimmerman, Jean L. Colonel Ranald S. Mackenzie at Fort Sill. Chronicles of Oklahoma, 44 (1966): 12-21.

09-08   Crow

Anderson, Harry H. The war club of Sitting Bull, the Oglala. Nebraska History, 42 (1961): 55-61.

Anonymous. Crows. U.S. Bureau of American Ethnology, Bulletin, 30, vol. 1 (1907): 367-369.

Anonymous. Native America today. Indian Historian, 4, no. 1 (1971): 55-56, 66.

Bad Heart Bull, Amos. A pictographic history of the Oglala Sioux. Text by Helen H. Blish. Lincoln, University of Nebraska Press, 1967. 22, 530 p. illus.

Bass, William M. A human skeleton from the Pryor Creek burial, 24YL404, Yellowstone County, Montana. By William M. Bass and Jon C. Barlow. Plains Anthropologist, 9 (1964): 29-36.

Bearss, Edwin C. Bighorn Canyon National Recreation Area, Montana-Wyoming: history basic data. Washington, D.C., U.S. Office of History and Historic Architecture, Eastern Service Center, 1970. 2 v. (23, 687, 88 p.) illus.

Beckwourth, J. P. Life and adventures. Ed. by T. D. Bonner. New York, 1931. 405 p.

Beckwourth, James P.   Mountain man, Indian chief.   New York, Harcourt, Brace and World, 1968.   8, 184 p.   illus., maps.

Beckwourth, James P.   The life and adventures of James P. Beckwourth. As told to Thomas D. Bonner.   Lincoln, University of Nebraska Press, 1972.   13, 649 p.

Beckwourth, James P.   The life and adventures of James P. Beckwourth. Edited by T. D. Bonner.   New York, Arno Press, 1969.   8, 537 p.   illus.

Befu, Harumi.   Political complexity and village community: test of an hypothesis.   Anthropological Quarterly, 39 (1966): 43-52.

Berrien, Joseph Waring.   Overland from St. Louis to the California gold field in 1849: the diary of Joseph Waring Berrien.   Edited by Ted and Caryl Hinckley.   Indiana Magazine of History, 56 (1960): 273-351.

Boas, F.   Zur Anthropologie der nordamerikanischen Indianer. Berliner Gesellschaft für Anthropologie, Ethnologie und Urgeschichte, Verhandlungen (1895): 367-411.

Bradley, J. H.   Indian traditions. Historical Society of Montana, Contributions, 9 (1923): 288-299.

Bradley, James H.   The march of the Montana Column; a prelude to the Custer disaster.   Edited by Edgar I. Stewart. Norman, University of Oklahoma Press, 1961.   182 p.   illus.

Brown, Lionel A.   A Crow lodge frame. Plains Anthropologist, 8 (1963): 273-274.

Burbank, E. A. and E. Royce.   Burbank among the Indians, 147-163.   Caldwell, 1946.

Bushnell, D. I.   Villages of the Algonquian, Siouan and Caddoan tribes. U.S. Bureau of American Ethnology, Bulletin, 77 (1922): 150-155.

Campbell, Robert.   The private journal of Robert Campbell. Edited by George R. Brooks. Missouri Historical Society, Bulletin, 20 (1963/1964): 3-24, 107-118.

Campbell, W. S.   The tipis of the Crow Indians. American Anthropologist, n.s., 29 (1927): 87-104.

Catlin, G.   Illustrations of the manners, customs and condition of the North American Indians, Vol. 1: 42-51.   New York, 1841.

Corson, E. F.   Long Hair, chief of the Crows. Archives of Dermatology and Syphilology, 56 (1947): 443-447.

Cortesi, Lawrence.   Jim Beckwourth; explorer-patriot of the Rockies.   New York, Criterion Books, 1971.   224 p.

Cramer, Joseph L.   The Lian site, an historic log shelter in Yellowstone County, Montana. Plains Anthropologist, 6 (1961): 267-270.

Culbertson, T. A.   Journal of an expedition to the mauvaises terres and the Upper Missouri in 1850. U.S. Bureau of American Ethnology, Bulletin, 147 (1952): 1-172.

Curtis, E. S.   The North American Indian, Vol. 4: 3-126, 175-180, 189-210. Cambridge, 1909.

DeHoyos, Genevieve.   The Crow Indian Reservation of Montana. By Genevieve DeHoyos and Arturo DeHoyos.   Provo, Utah, Brigham Young University, Institute of American Indian Research and Services, 1969.   22 p.   ERIC ED043406.

Denig, Edwin T.   Five Indian tribes of the Upper Missouri: Sioux, Arickaras, Assiniboines, Crees, Crows. Edited by John C. Ewers.   Norman, University of Oklahoma Press, 1961.   217 p.   illus.

Dodge, Grenville M.   Biographical sketch of James Bridger. Annals of Wyoming, 33 (1961): 159-177.

Donaldson, T.   The George Catlin Indian Gallery. United States National Museum, Reports (1885): 106-115.

Douglas, F. H.   A Crow beaded horse collar. Denver Art Museum, Material Culture Notes, 2 (1937): 5-8.

Douglas, Frederic H.   An incised bison rawhide parfleche. Denver, Art Museum, Department of Indian Art, Material Culture Notes, 6 (1938): 23-25.

Dunraven, W. T. W., Earl.   The great divide, 59-128.   London, 1876.

Ehrlich, C.   Tribal culture in Crow mythology. Journal of American Folklore, 50 (1937): 307-408.

*Ewers, J. C.   "Of the Crow Nation". By Edwin Thompson Denig. U.S. Bureau of American Ethnology, Bulletin, 151 (1953): 1-74.

Ewers, J. C.   Three ornaments worn by Upper Missouri Indians a century and a quarter ago. New York Historical Society Quarterly, 41 (1957): 24-33.

Ewers, John C. Was there a Northwestern Plains sub-culture? An ethnographic appraisal. Plains Anthropologist, 12 (1967): 167-174.

Fay, George E., ed. Charters, constitutions and by-laws of the Indian tribes of North America. Part IIa: The Northern Plains. Greeley, 1967. 6, 141 l. maps. (University of Northern Colorado, Museum of Anthropology, Occasional Publications in Anthropology, Ethnology Series, 3) ERIC ED051923.

Frison, George. Daugherty Cave, Wyoming. Plains Anthropologist, 13 (1968): 253-295.

Frison, George Carr. Archaeological evidence of the Crow Indians in northern Wyoming: a study of a late prehistoric period buffalo economy. Dissertation Abstracts, 28 (1967/1968): 2701B. UM 67-17,761.

Gilmore, Kathleen K. A documentary and archeological investigation of Presidio San Luis de las Amarillas and Mission Santa Cruz de San Sabá. Austin, Tex., State Building Commission, 1967. 1, 72 p. illus., map. (Texas, State Building Commission Archeological Program, 9)

Goldenweiser, A. A. Remarks on the social organization of the Crow Indians. American Anthropologist, n.s., 15 (1913): 281-294.

Gordon, Raymond G., Jr. Pitch accent in Crow. International Journal of American Linguistics, 38 (1972): 191-200.

Hamp, Eric P. Prosodic notes. International Journal of American Linguistics, 24 (1958): 321-322.

Hanson, Charles E., Jr. The battle of Crow Butte. Museum of the Fur Trade Quarterly, 5, no. 3 (1969): 2-4.

Hanson, Marshall Roy. Plains Indians and urbanization. Dissertation Abstracts, 21 (1960/1961): 23. UM 60-2392.

Hayden, F. V. Contributions to the ethnography and philology of the Indian tribes of the Missouri Valley. American Philosophical Society, Transactions, n.s., 12 (1863): 391-420.

Heidenreich, Charles Adrian. Ethno-documentary of the Crow Indians of Montana, 1824-1862. Dissertation Abstracts International, 32 (1971/1972): 3125B-3126B. UM 72-934.

Hilger, M. Inez. Notes on Crow culture. Baessler-Archiv, n.F., 18 (1970): 253-294.

Hoffman, W. J. An Absaroka myth. Royal Anthropological Institute of Great Britain and Ireland, Journal, 10 (1880): 239-240.

Hultkrantz, Åke. The Indians in Yellowstone Park. Annals of Wyoming, 29 (1957): 125-149.

Jaques. Notes of a tourist through the Upper Missouri region. Missouri Historical Society, Bulletin, 22 (1965/1966): 393-409.

Kaschube, D. Examples of tone in Crow. International Journal of American Linguistics, 20 (1954): 34-36.

Kaschube, Dorothea V. Structural elements of the language of the Crow Indians of Montana. Boulder, 1967. 6, 106 p. (Colorado, University, University of Colorado Studies, Series in Anthropology, 14)

Kaschube, Dorothea Vedral. Structural elements of Crow. Dissertation Abstracts, 21 (1960/1961): 425. UM 60-2825.

Kehoe, T. F. and A. B. Kehoe. Boulder effigy monuments in the northern Plains. Journal of American Folklore, 72 (1959): 115-127.

Kennedy, Thomas G. Crow-Northern Cheyenne selected for study. Journal of American Indian Education, 11, no. 1 (1971/1972): 27-31.

Koch, P. A trading expedition among the Crow Indians, 1873-1874. Mississippi Valley Historical Review, 31 (1944): 407-430.

Krieg, Frederick C. Chief Plenty Coups; the final dignity. Montana, the Magazine of Western History, 16, no. 4 (1966): 28-39.

Laroque, F. A. Journal. Canadian Archives, Publications, 3 (1910): 55-70.

Leonard, Z. Adventures of Zenas Leonard. Norman, 1959. 189 p.

Liberty, Margot P. Priest and shaman on the Plains: a false dichotomy? Plains Anthropologist, 15 (1970): 73-79.

Lincoln, J. S. The dream in primitive cultures. London, 1935. 359 p.

Lind, Robert William. Familistic attitudes and marriage role expectations of American Indian and White adolescents. Dissertation Abstracts International, 32 (1971/1972): 5288B. UM 72-10,035.

Linderman, F. B. American. New York, 1930. 313 p.

Linderman, F. B. Old Man Coyote. New York, 1931. 254 p.

Linderman, F. B. Red mother. New York, 1932. 256 p.

Linderman, Frank B. Pretty-shield, medicine woman of the Crows. New York, John Day, 1972. 256 p. illus.

Lowie, R. H. A Crow tale. Anthropological Quarterly, 2 (1954): 1-22.

Lowie, R. H. A Crow text. California, University, Publications in American Archaeology and Ethnology, 29 (1930): 155-175.

Lowie, R. H. A Crow woman's tale. In E. C. Parsons, ed. American Indian Life. New York, 1925: 35-40.

Lowie, R. H. A trial of shamans. In E. C. Parsons, ed. American Indian Life. New York, 1925: 41-43.

Lowie, R. H. Alleged Kiowa-Crow affinities. Southwestern Journal of Anthropology, 9 (1953): 357-368.

Lowie, R. H. Crow curses. Journal of American Folklore, 72 (1959): 105.

Lowie, R. H. Crow Indian art. American Museum of Natural History, Anthropological Papers, 21 (1922): 271-322.

Lowie, R. H. Crow Indian clowns. American Museum Journal, 12 (1912): 74.

Lowie, R. H. Crow prayers. American Anthropologist, n.s., 35 (1933): 433-442.

Lowie, R. H. Indian theologians. El Palacio, 35 (1933): 217-231.

Lowie, R. H. Marriage and society among the Crow Indians. In A. L. Kroeber and T. T. Waterman, eds. Source Book in Anthropology. Rev. ed. New York, 1931: 304-309.

*Lowie, R. H. Military societies of the Crow Indians. American Museum of Natural History, Anthropological Papers, 11 (1913): 143-217.

Lowie, R. H. Minor ceremonies of the Crow Indians. American Museum of Natural History, Anthropological Papers, 21 (1924): 323-365.

Lowie, R. H. Myths and traditions of the Crow Indians. American Museum of Natural History, Anthropological Papers, 25 (1918): 1-308.

Lowie, R. H. Observations on the literary style of the Crow Indians. In Beiträge zur Gesellungs- und Völkerwissenschaft. Berlin, 1950: 271-283.

Lowie, R. H. Primitive religion, 2-32. New York, 1925.

Lowie, R. H. Proverbial expressions among the Crow Indians. American Anthropologist, n.s., 34 (1932): 739-740.

*Lowie, R. H. Social life of the Crow Indians. American Museum of Natural History, Anthropological Papers, 9 (1912): 179-248.

Lowie, R. H. Some problems in the ethnology of the Crow and village Indians. American Anthropologist, n.s., 14 (1912): 60-71.

Lowie, R. H. Studies in Plains Indian folklore. California, University, Publications in American Archaeology and Ethnology, 40 (1942): 1-28.

Lowie, R. H. Takes-the-Pipe, a Crow warrior. In E. C. Parsons, ed. American Indian Life. New York, 1925: 17-33.

*Lowie, R. H. The Crow Indians. New York, 1956. 350 p.

Lowie, R. H. The Crow language. California, University, Publications in American Archaeology and Ethnology, 39 (1941): 1-142.

Lowie, R. H. The Crow sun dance. Journal of American Folklore, 27 (1914): 94-96.

Lowie, R. H. The kinship systems of the Crow and Hidatsa. International Congress of Americanists, Proceedings, 19 (1915): 340-343.

*Lowie, R. H. The material culture of the Crow Indians. American Museum of Natural History, Anthropological Papers, 21 (1922): 201-270.

Lowie, R. H. The Omaha and Crow kinship terminologies. International Congress of Americanists, Proceedings, 24 (1934): 102-108.

Lowie, R. H. The oral literature of the Crow Indians. Journal of American Folklore, 72 (1959): 97-104.

Lowie, R. H. The relations between the Kiowa and the Crow Indians. Société Suisse des Américanistes, Bulletin, 7 (1953): 1-5.

*Lowie, R. H. The religion of the Crow Indians. American Museum of Natural History, Anthropological Papers, 25 (1922): 309-444.

Lowie, R. H. The sun dance of the Crow Indians. American Museum of Natural History, Anthropological Papers, 16 (1915): 1-50.

Lowie, R. H. The Tobacco Society of the Crow Indians. American Museum of Natural History, Anthropological Papers, 21 (1919): 101-200.

Lowie, Robert H. Bemerkungen über die Rolle der Religion im Alltagsleben der Crow-Indianer. Zeitschrift für Ethnologie, 84 (1959): 1-4.

Lowie, Robert H. Crow texts. Preface by Luella Cole Lowie. Berkeley and Los Angeles, University of California Press, 1960. 13, 550 p.

Lowie, Robert H. Crow word lists; Crow-English and English-Crow vocabularies. Berkeley, University of California Press, 1960. 10, 411 p.

Lowie, Robert H. Notes on the social organization and customs of the Mandan, Hidatsa, and Crow Indians. New York, 1917. 1-99 p. (American Museum of Natural History, Anthropological Papers, 21, pt. 1)

Marquis, T. B. Memoirs of a White Crow Indian. New York, 1928. 356 p.

Mason, J. A. A collection from the Crow Indians. Museum Journal, 17 (1926): 393-413.

Matthews, G. H. Morphophonemic changes in Crow and Hidatsa. MIT Research Laboratory of Electronics, Quarterly Progress Report, 59 (1960): 165-168.

Matthews, G. H. On tone in Crow. International Journal of American Linguistics, 25 (1959): 135-136.

Matthews, G. H. Syntactic change in Crow and Hidatsa. MIT Research Laboratory of Electronics, Quarterly Progress Report, 58 (1960): 281-284.

Mattison, Ray H. Fort Union: its role in the Upper Missouri fur trade. North Dakota History, 29 (1962): 181-208.

McAllester, D. Water as a disciplinary agent among the Crow and Blackfoot. American Anthropologist, n.s., 43 (1941): 593-604.

McGee, W J. The Siouan Indians. U.S. Bureau of American Ethnology, Annual Reports, 15 (1894): 157-204.

McGinnis, Dale K. The Crow people. By Dale K. McGinnis and Floyd W. Sharrock. Phoenix, Indian Tribal Series, 1972. 5, 106 p. illus.

Merwin, W. S. Crow versions. Alcheringa, 1 (1970): 29-31.

Morgan, L. H. Systems of consanguinity and affinity. Smithsonian Contributions to Knowledge, 17 (1871): 291-382.

Morgan, L. H. The Indian journals, 1859-62: p. 167-176, 183-190, 197. Ann Arbor, 1959.

Morton, Desmond, ed. Telegrams of the North-West Campaign 1885. Edited by Desmond Morton and Reginald H. Roy. Toronto, 1972. 103, 431 p. illus., maps. (Champlain Society, Publications, 47)

Mulloy, W. The Northern Plains. In J. B. Griffin, ed. Archeology of Eastern United States. Chicago, 1952: 124-138.

Munkres, Robert L. The Plains Indian threat on the Oregon Trail before 1860. Annals of Wyoming, 40 (1968): 193-221.

Munn, Fred M. Fred Munn, veteran of frontier experiences, remembered the days he rode with Miles, Howard and Terry. As told to Robert A. Griffen. Montana, the Magazine of Western History, 16, no. 2 (1966): 50-64.

Murdock, G. P. Our primitive contemporaries, 264-290. New York, 1934.

Nasatir, A. P. Before Lewis and Clark. St. Louis, 1952. 2 v. (882 p.).

Nash, Philleo. Nash and Crow Tribe delegates on U.S. Indians today. Americas, 14, no. 9 (1962): 6-11.

Nevins, A., ed. Narratives of exploration and adventure by John Charles Frémont. New York, 1956. 542 p.

New, Lloyd. Institute of American Indian Arts. Arizona Highways, 48, no. 1 (1972): 5, 12-15, 44-45.

O'Neil, Floyd A. An anguished odyssey: the flight of the Utes, 1906-1908. Utah Historical Quarterly, 36 (1968): 315-327.

Oswalt, Wendell H. Other peoples, other customs; world ethnography and its history. New York, Holt, Rinehart and Winston, 1972. 15, 430 p. illus., maps.

Partridge, William L. An analysis of Crow enculturation (as compared to Sioux enculturation) 1868 to 1880. Florida Anthropologist, 18 (1965): 225-234.

Pierce, J. E. Crow vs. Hidatsa in dialect distance and glottochronology. International Journal of American Linguistics, 20 (1954): 134-136.

Plenty-Coups. Plenty-Coups, chief of the Crows. By Frank B. Linderman. New York, John Day, 1972. 9, 312 p. illus.

Plenty-Coups. Plenty-Coups, chief of the Crows. By Frank B. Linderman. Lincoln, University of Nebraska Press, 1962. 324 p. illus. (Bison Book, BB128)

Plummer, Rachel P. Narrative of the capture and subsequent sufferings of Mrs. Rachel Plummer. Waco, Texian Press, 1968. 28 p.

Powell, Peter J. Journey to Se´han. Montana, the Magazine of Western History, 18, no. 1 (1968): 71-75.

Quaife, M. M., ed. Narrative of the adventures of Zenas Leonard, 227-252. Chicago, 1934.

Quivey, A. M., ed. Bradley manuscript, book "F". Historical Society of Montana, Contributions, 8 (1917): 197-250.

Robertson, G. G. Psychiatric consultation on two Indian reservations. By G. G. Robertson and Michael Baizerman. Hospital and Community Psychiatry, 20 (1969): 186.

Russell, Don. Custer's last or, The battle of the Little Big Horn. Fort Worth, Amon Carter Museum of Western Art, 1968. 5, 67 p. illus.

Schultz, Hart Merriam (Lone Wolf). Lone Wolf returns . . . to that long ago time. Edited by Paul Dyck. Montana, the Magazine of Western History, 22, no. 1 (1972): 18-41.

Sievers, Michael A. The administration of Indian affairs on the Upper Missouri, 1858-1865. North Dakota History, 38 (1971): 366-394.

Simms, S. C. A Crow monument to shame. American Anthropologist, n.s., 5 (1903): 374-375.

Simms, S. C. Crow Indian hermaphrodites. American Anthropologist, n.s., 5 (1903): 580-581.

Simms, S. C. Cultivation of "medicine tobacco" by the Crows. American Anthropologist, n.s., 6 (1904): 331-335.

Simms, S. C. Traditions of the Crows. Field Museum, Anthropological Series, 2 (1903): 281-324.

Simms, S. C. Water transportation by the early Crows. American Anthropologist, n.s., 6 (1904): 191-192.

Smith, DeC. Indian experiences. Caldwell, 1943.

Stafford, John Wade. Crow culture change: a geographical analysis. Dissertation Abstracts International, 33 (1972/1973): 783B-784B. UM 72-22,289.

Stage, Thomas B. A psychiatric service for Plains Indians. By Thomas B. Stage and Thomas J. Keast. Hospital and Community Psychiatry, 17 (1966): 74-76.

Stephenson, Robert L. The Mouat Cliff burials (24TE401). Plains Anthropologist, 7 (1962): 94.

Taylor, Colin. Early Plains Indian quill techniques in European museum collections. Plains Anthropologist, 7 (1962): 58-69.

Tietema, Sidney J. Indians in agriculture. III. Alternatives in irrigation farming for the Blackfeet and Crow Indian Reservations. Bozeman, 1958. 59 p. map. (Montana, Agricultural Experiment Station, Bulletin, 542)

Two Leggings. Two Leggings; the making of a Crow warrior. Edited by Peter Nabokov. New York, Crowell, 1967. 25, 226 p.

Voegelin, C. F. Historical results of Crow-Hidatsa comparisons. Indiana Academy of Science, Proceedings, 50 (1941): 39-42.

Voegelin, C. F. Kiowa-Crow mythological affiliations. American Anthropologist, n.s., 35 (1933): 470-474.

Voget, F. Crow socio-cultural groups. International Congress of Americanists, Proceedings, 29, vol. 2 (1952): 88-93.

Voget, F. Individual motivation in the diffusion of the Wind River Shoshone sundance to the Crow Indians. American Anthropologist, n.s., 50 (1948): 634-645.

Wagner, G. D. and W. A. Allen. Blankets and moccasins. Caldwell, 1933. 304 p.

Wagner, Oswald F. Lutheran zealots among the Crows. Montana, the Magazine of Western History, 22, no. 2 (1972): 2-19.

Ward, R. E., et al. Indians in agriculture. Montana, State Agricultural Experiment Station, Bulletin, 522 (1956): 1-52.

Ward, Ralph E., et al. Indians in agriculture. I. Cattle ranching on the Crow Reservation. Bozeman, 1956. (Montana, Agricultural Experiment Station, Bulletin, 522)

Wied-Neuwied, M. zu. Reise in das innere Nordamerika. Coblenz, 1839-1841. 2 v.

Wied-Neuwied, M. zu. Travels in the interior of North America. Early Western Travels, 22 (1906): 346-355.

Wildschut, W. A Crow pictographic robe. Indian Notes, 3 (1926): 28-32.

Wildschut, W. A Crow shield. Indian Notes, 2 (1925): 315-320.

Wildschut, W. Crow love medicine. Indian Notes, 2 (1925): 211-214.

Wildschut, W. Crow sun-dance bundle. Indian Notes, 3 (1926): 99-107.

Wildschut, W. Crow war bundle of Two-Leggings. Indian Notes, 3 (1926): 284-288.

Wildschut, W. Moccasin-bundle of the Crows. Indian Notes, 3 (1926): 201-205.

Wildschut, W. The Crow skull medicine bundle. Indian Notes, 2 (1925): 119-122.

Wildschut, W. and J. C. Ewers. Crow Indian beadwork. Museum of the American Indian, Heye Foundation, Contributions, 16 (1959): 1-55.

Wildschut, William. Crow Indian medicine bundles. Edited by John C. Ewers. New York, 1960. 9, 178 p. illus. (Museum of the American Indian, Heye Foundation, Contributions, 17)

Wilson, H. Clyde. An inquiry into the nature of Plains Indian cultural development. American Anthropologist, 65 (1963): 355-369.

Wiltsey, Norman B. Plenty Coups: statesman chief of the Crows. Montana, the Magazine of Western History, 13, no. 4 (1963): 28-39.

Wood, W. Raymond. A stylistic and historical analysis of shoulder patterns on Plains Indian pottery. American Antiquity, 28 (1962/1963): 25-40.

Woodruff, J. Indian oasis, 21-157. Caldwell, 1939.

Yeast, William E. The presidential Indian peace medal. Annals of Iowa, 37 (1964): 318-320.

Yellowtail, Robert. Fine horses--pride of the Crows. Indians at Work, 4, no. 17 (1937): 37-39.

09-09 Gros Ventre

Barry, L. With the First U.S. Cavalry in Indian country, 1859-1861. Kansas Historical Quarterly, 24 (1958): 257-284.

Boas, F. Zur Anthropologie der nordamerikanischen Indianer. Berliner Gesellschaft für Anthropologie, Ethnologie und Urgeschichte, Verhandlungen (1895): 367-411.

*Cooper, J. M. The Gros Ventres of Montana. II. Religion and ritual. Catholic University of America, Anthropological Series, 16 (1956): 1-500.

Cooper, J. M. The shaking tent rite among Plains and Forest Algonquians. Primitive Man, 17 (1944): 60-84.

Curtis, E. S. The North American Indian, Vol. 5: 103-139, 152-154, 164-177, 180-184. Cambridge, 1909.

Dempsey, Hugh A., ed. Final treaty of peace. Alberta Historical Review, 10, no. 1 (1962): 8-16.

Dodge, Grenville M. Biographical sketch of James Bridger. Annals of Wyoming, 33 (1961): 159-177.

Dusenberry, Verne. Ceremonial sweat lodges of the Gros Ventre Indians. Ethnos, 28 (1963): 46-62.

Dusenberry, Verne. The significance of the Sacred Pipes to the Gros Ventre of Montana. Ethnos, 26 (1961): 12-29.

Ewers, John C. Was there a Northwestern Plains sub-culture? An ethnographic appraisal. Plains Anthropologist, 12 (1967): 167-174.

Flannery, R. Individual variation in culture. International Congress of the

Anthropological and Ethnological
Sciences, Acts, 5 (1960): 87-92.

Flannery, R. Men's and women's speech in
Gros Ventre. International Journal of
American Linguistics, 12 (1946): 133-
135.

Flannery, R. The changing form and
functions of the Gros Ventre grass
dance. Primitive Man, 20 (1947): 39-70.

Flannery, R. The dearly-loved child among
the Gros Ventres of Montana. Primitive
Man, 14 (1941): 33-38.

Flannery, R. The Gros Ventre shaking
tent. Primitive Man, 17 (1944): 54-59.

*Flannery, R. The Gros Ventres of Montana.
I: Social life. Catholic University of
America, Anthropological Series, 15
(1953): 1-234.

Flannery, R. and J. M. Cooper. Social
mechanisms in Gros Ventre gambling.
Southwestern Journal of Anthropology, 2
(1946): 391-419.

Graham, Andrew. Andrew Graham's
observations on Hudson's Bay, 1767-91.
Edited by Glyndwr Williams. London,
1969. 72, 423 p. illus., maps.
(Hudson's Bay Record Society,
Publications, 27)

Haas, Mary R. Historical linguistics and
the genetic relationship of languages.
In Theoretical Foundations. The Hague,
Mouton, 1966: 113-153. (Current Trends
in Linguistics, 3)

Hady, Walter M. Indian migrations in
Manitoba and the West. Historical and
Scientific Society of Manitoba, Papers,
ser. 3, 17 (1960/1961): 24-53.

Hartmann, Horst. Die Gros Ventres und ihr
Hochgott. Zeitschrift für Ethnologie, 93
(1968): 73-83.

Hayden, F. V. Contributions to the
ethnography and philology of the Indian
tribes of the Missouri Valley. American
Philosophical Society, Transactions,
n.s., 12 (1863): 340-345.

Hayden, Willard C. The battle of Pierre's
Hole. Idaho Yesterdays, 16, no. 2
(1972): 2-11.

Hudson's Bay Company. Saskatchewan
journals and correspondence: Edmonton
House 1795-1800; Chesterfield House
1800-1802. Edited by Alice M. Johnson.
London, 1967. 102, 368, 14 p. map.
(Hudson's Bay Record Society,
Publications, 26)

Kehoe, Alice B. The function of
ceremonial sexual intercourse among the
Northern Plains Indians. Plains
Anthropologist, 15 (1970): 99-103.

Kroeber, A. L. Arapaho dialects.
California, University, Publications in
American Archaeology and Ethnology, 12
(1916): 71-138.

*Kroeber, A. L. Ethnology of the Gros
Ventre. American Museum of Natural
History, Anthropological Papers, 1
(1907): 145-281.

Kroeber, A. L. Gros Ventre myths and
tales. American Museum of Natural
History, Anthropological Papers, 1
(1907): 55-139.

Lepley, John G. The prince and the artist
on the Upper Missouri. Montana, the
Magazine of Western History, 20, no. 3
(1970): 42-54.

Mooney, J. Atsina. U.S. Bureau of
American Ethnology, Bulletin, 30, vol. 1
(1907): 113.

Morgan, L. H. Systems of consanguinity
and affinity. Smithsonian Contributions
to Knowledge, 17 (1871): 291-382.

Morgan, L. H. The Indian journal, 1859-
62: p. 165-166, 169. Ann Arbor, 1959.

Morrill, Allen. "Old church made new". By
Allen and Eleanor Morrill. Idaho
Yesterdays, 16, no. 2 (1972): 16-23.

Morton, Desmond, ed. Telegrams of the
North-West Campaign 1885. Edited by
Desmond Morton and Reginald H. Roy.
Toronto, 1972. 103, 431 p. illus.,
maps. (Champlain Society, Publications,
47)

Ray, Arthur Joseph, Jr. Indian
exploitation of the forest-grassland
transition zone in Western Canada, 1650-
1860: a geographical view of two
centuries of change. Dissertation
Abstracts International, 32 (1971/1972):
3432B. UM 71-28,359.

Rowand, John. A letter from Fort
Edmonton. Alberta Historical Review, 11,
no. 1 (1963): 1-6.

Salzmann, Zdeněk. Arapaho. International
Journal of American Linguistics, 22
(1956): 49-56, 151-158, 266-272; 27
(1961): 151-155; 31 (1965): 39-49, 136-
151; 33 (1967): 209-223.

Salzmann, Zdeněk. Arapaho kinship terms
and two related ethnolinguistic
observations. Anthropological
Linguistics, 1, no. 9 (1959): 6-10.

Salzmann, Zdeněk. Salvage phonology of
    Gros Ventre (Atsina). International
    Journal of American Linguistics, 35
    (1969): 307-314.

Salzmann, Zdeněk. Two brief contributions
    toward Arapaho linguistic history.
    Anthropological Linguistics, 2, no. 7
    (1960): 39-48.

Sanderson, James F. Indian tales of the
    Canadian prairies. Calgary, Historical
    Society of Alberta, 1965. 15 p. illus.

Sanderson, James F. Indian tales of the
    Canadian prairies. Alberta Historical
    Review, 13, no. 3 (1965): 7-21.

Schmidt, W. Die Gros Ventres. In his Die
    Ursprung der Göttesidee. Bd. 2. Münster
    i. W., 1929: 671-679.

Scott, H. L. The early history and names
    of the Arapaho. American Anthropologist,
    n.s., 9 (1907): 545-560.

Stallcop, Emmett A. The Gros Ventre
    ceremony of supplication for long life.
    Plains Anthropologist, 15 (1970): 307-
    308.

Stallcop, Emmett A. The so-called Sun
    Dance of the Gros Ventre. Plains
    Anthropologist, 13 (1968): 148-151.

Taylor, Allan R. Some observations on a
    comparative Arapaho-Atsina lexicon. In
    Contributions to Anthropology:
    Linguistics I. Ottawa, Queen's Printer,
    1967: 113-127. (Canada, National
    Museum, Bulletin, 214)

Wied-Neuwied, M. zu. Reise in das innere
    Nordamerika. Coblenz, 1839-1841. 2 v.

Wied-Neuwied, M. zu. Travels in the
    interior of North America. Early Western
    Travels, 23 (1906): 70-77; 24 (1906):
    226-227.

Wissler, Clark. Population changes among
    the Northern Plains Indians. New Haven,
    Human Relations Area Files Press, 1970.
    20 p. (Yale University Publications in
    Anthropology, 1)

Wissler, Clark. Population changes among
    the Northern Plains Indians. New Haven,
    Yale University Press, 1936. 20 p.
    (Yale University Publications in
    Anthropology, 1)

09-10 Hidatsa

Beckwith, M. W. Mandan and Hidatsa tales.
    Folk-Lore Foundation, Publications, 14
    (1934): 269-320.

Beckwith, M. W. Mandan-Hidatsa myths and
    ceremonies. American Folk-Lore Society,
    Memoirs, 32 (1938): 1-320.

Beckwith, M. W. Myths and ceremonies of
    the Mandan and Hidatsa. Folk-Lore
    Foundation, Publications, 12 (1932):
    117-267.

Beckwith, M. W. Myths and hunting stories
    of the Mandan and Hidatsa Sioux. Folk-
    Lore Foundation, Publications, 10
    (1930): 1-116.

*Bowers, Alfred W. Hidatsa social and
    ceremonial organization. Washington,
    D.C., Government Printing Office, 1965.
    12, 528 p. illus., maps. (U.S., Bureau
    of American Ethnology, Bulletin, 194)

Bruner, E. M. Assimilation among Fort
    Berthold Indians. American Indian, 6,
    no. 4 (1953): 21-29.

Bruner, E. M. Cultural transmission and
    cultural change. Southwestern Journal of
    Anthropology, 12 (1956): 191-199.

Bruner, E. M. Primary group experience
    and the processes of acculturation.
    American Anthropologist, 58 (1956): 605-
    623.

Bruner, E. M. Two processes of change in
    Mandan-Hidatsa kinship terminology.
    American Anthropologist, 57 (1955): 840-
    850.

Bruner, Edward M. Cultural transmission
    and cultural change. In Deward E.
    Walker, Jr., ed. The Emergent Native
    Americans. Boston, Little, Brown, 1972:
    69-75.

Bushnell, D. I. Burials of the
    Algonquian, Siouan and Caddoan tribes.
    U.S. Bureau of American Ethnology,
    Bulletin, 83 (1927): 73-78.

Bushnell, D. I. Villages of the
    Algonquian, Siouan, and Caddoan tribes.
    U.S. Bureau of American Ethnology,
    Bulletin, 77 (1922): 140-150.

Byrne, William John. The archaeology and
    prehistory of southern Alberta as
    reflected by ceramics: late prehistoric
    and protohistoric cultural developments.
    Dissertation Abstracts International, 34
    (1973/1974): 32B. UM 73-16,766.

Catlin, G. Illustrations of the manners,
    customs, and condition of the North
    American Indians, Vol. 1: 185-202. New
    York, 1841.

Chardon, Francis A. Chardon's journal at
    Fort Clark, 1834-1839. Freeport, N.Y.,

Books for Libraries Press, 1970. 46,
458 p. illus.

Culbertson, T. A. Journal of an
expedition to the mauvaises terres and
the Upper Missouri in 1850. U.S. Bureau
of American Ethnology, Bulletin, 147
(1852): 1-172.

Curtis, E. S. The North American Indian,
Vol. 4: 129-172, 180-196, 210-211.
Cambridge, 1909.

Cutright, Paul Russell. Lewis and Clark
and Cottonwood. Missouri Historical
Society, Bulletin, 21 (1965/1966): 35-
44.

DeLand, C. E. The aborigines of South
Dakota. South Dakota Historical
Collections, 3 (1906): 269-586.

Densmore, F. Mandan and Hidatsa music.
U.S. Bureau of American Ethnology,
Bulletin, 80 (1923): 1-186.

Densmore, Frances. Mandan and Hidatsa
music. New York, Da Capo Press, 1972.
20, 192 p. illus.

Dorsey, J. O. A study of Siouan cults.
U.S. Bureau of American Ethnology,
Annual Reports, 11 (1890): 513-518.

Dorsey, J. O. Preface. Contributions to
North American Ethnology, 9 (1893):
xviii-xxx.

Dorsey, J. O. Siouan sociology. U.S.
Bureau of American Ethnology, Annual
Reports, 15 (1894): 242-243.

Douglas, Frederic H. An Hidatsa burden
basket. Denver, Art Museum, Department
of Indian Art, Material Culture Notes,
14 (1941): 60-65.

Ewers, John C. Mothers of the mixed-
bloods. El Palacio, 69 (1962): 20-29.

Fay, George E., ed. Charters,
constitutions and by-laws of the Indian
tribes of North America. Part IIa: The
Northern Plains. Greeley, 1967. 6,
141 l. maps. (University of Northern
Colorado, Museum of Anthropology,
Occasional Publications in Anthropology,
Ethnology Series, 3) ERIC ED051923.

Gilmore, M. R. Being an account of an
Hidatsa shrine and the beliefs
respecting it. American Anthropologist,
n.s., 28 (1926): 572-573.

Hady, Walter M. Indian migrations in
Manitoba and the West. Historical and
Scientific Society of Manitoba, Papers,
ser. 3, 17 (1960/1961): 24-53.

Hanson, Charles E., Jr. The Indian garden
project. Museum of the Fur Trade
Quarterly, 2, no. 3 (1966): 3-6.

Harris, Z. S. Culture and style in
extended discourse. International
Congress of Americanists, Proceedings,
29, vol. 3 (1951): 210-215.

Hartle, Donald D. The dance hall of the
Santee Bottoms on the Fort Berthold
Reservation, Garrison Reservoir, North
Dakota. Washington, D.C., Government
Printing Office, 1963. 123-132 p.
illus. (U.S., Bureau of American
Ethnology, River Basin Surveys Papers,
28. U.S., Bureau of American Ethnology,
Bulletin, 185)

Hartle, Donald Dean. Rock Village, an
ethnohistorical approach to Hidatsa
archaeology. Dissertation Abstracts, 21
(1960/1961): 2431-2432. UM 60-5091.

Hayden, F. V. Contributions to the
ethnography and philology of the Indian
tribes of the Missouri Valley. American
Philosophical Society, Transactions,
n.s., 12 (1863): 420-426.

Howard, James H. A Mandan-Hidatsa
headdress and its origin legend. South
Dakota, University, Museum, Museum News,
13, no. 2 (1952): 1-5.

kehoe, Alice B. The function of
ceremonial sexual intercourse among the
Northern Plains Indians. Plains
Anthropologist, 15 (1970): 99-103.

Kehoe, T. F. and A. B. Kehoe. Boulder
effigy monuments in the northern Plains.
Journal of American Folklore, 72 (1959):
115-127.

Lévi-Strauss, Claude. Rapports de
symétrie entre rites et mythes de
peuples voisins. In Thomas O. Beidelman,
ed. The Translation of Culture. London,
Tavistock, 1971: 161-178.

Libby, O. G. Typical villages of the
Mandans, Arikara, and Hidatsa. North
Dakota, State Historical Society,
Collections, 2 (1908): 498-508.

Lowie, R. H. Hidatsa texts. Indiana
Historical Society, Prehistory Research
Series, 1 (1939): 173-239.

*Lowie, R. H. Societies of the Hidatsa and
Mandan Indians. American Museum of
Natural History, Anthropological Papers,
11 (1913): 221-293, 323-354.

Lowie, R. H. Some problems in the
ethnology of the Crow and village
Indians. American Anthropologist, n.s.,
14 (1912): 60-71.

Lowie, R. H. Studies in Plains Indian folklore. California, University, Publications in American Archaeology and Ethnology, 40 (1942): 1-28.

Lowie, R. H. The Hidatsa sun dance. American Museum of Natural History, Anthropological Papers, 16 (1919): 411-431.

Lowie, R. H. The kinship systems of the Crow and Hidatsa. International Congress of Americanists, Proceedings, 19 (1915): 340-343.

Lowie, Robert H. Notes on the social organization and customs of the Mandan, Hidatsa, and Crow Indians. New York, 1917. 1-99 p. (American Museum of Natural History, Anthropological Papers, 21, pt. 1)

Malouf, Carling. Crow-Flies-High (32MZ1), a historic Hidatsa village in the Garrison Reservoir area, North Dakota. Washington, D.C., Government Printing Office, 1963. 133-166 p. illus., maps. (U.S., Bureau of American Ethnology, River Basin Surveys Papers, 29. U.S., Bureau of American Ethnology, Bulletin, 185)

Matthews, G. H. Morphophonemic changes in Crow and Hidatsa. MIT Research Laboratory of Electronics, Quarterly Progress Report, 59 (1960): 165-168.

Matthews, G. H. Syntactic change in Crow and Hidatsa. MIT Research Laboratory of Electronics, Quarterly Progress Report, 58 (1960): 281-284.

Matthews, G. H. The ergative relation in Hidatsa. MIT Research Laboratory of Electronics, Quarterly Progress Report, 56 (1960): 184-186.

Matthews, George H. Hidatsa syntax. The Hague, Mouton, 1965. 299 p. illus. (Papers on Formal Linguistics, 3)

*Matthews, W. Ethnography and philology of the Hidatsa Indians. U.S. Geological and Geographical Survey, Miscellaneous Publications, 7 (1877): 1-239.

Matthews, W. Grammar and dictionary of the language of the Hidatsa. New York, 1873-1874. 169 p.

*Matthews, Washington. Ethnography and philology of the Hidatsa Indians. New York, Johnson Reprint, 1971. 26, 6, 239 p.

*Matthews, Washington. Ethnography and philology of the Hidatsa Indians. Topeka, Plains Anthropologist

Corporation, 1969. 173-252 p. (Plains Anthropologist, 14, no. 45)

McGee, W J. The Siouan Indians. U.S. Bureau of American Ethnology, Annual Reports, 15 (1894): 157-204.

Metcalf, George. Small sites on and about Fort Berthold Indian Reservation, Garrison Reservoir, North Dakota. Washington, D.C., Government Printing Office, 1963. 1-56 p. illus., map. (U.S., Bureau of American Ethnology, River Basin Surveys Papers, 26. U.S., Bureau of American Ethnology, Bulletin, 185)

Mooney, J. Hidatsa. U.S. Bureau of American Ethnology, Bulletin, 30, vol. 1 (1907): 547-549.

Morgan, L. H. Systems of consanguinity and affinity. Smithsonian Contributions to Knowledge, 17 (1871): 291-382.

Morgan, L. H. The Indian journals, 1859-62: p. 155-160, 163, 169, 189-190, 195-196, 200. Ann Arbor, 1959.

Muller, Jon. The Harmon Site (39MO42). Plains Anthropologist, 7 (1962): 94.

Muller, Jon D. The Harmon Site, 32MO42. Plains Anthropologist, 7 (1962): 119-124.

Nasatir, A. P. Before Lewis and Clark. St. Louis, 1952. 2 v. (882 p.).

Neuman, Robert W. Check-stamped pottery on the northern and central Great Plains. American Antiquity, 29 (1963/1964): 17-26.

Pepper, G. H. and G. L. Wilson. An Hidatsa shrine and the beliefs respecting it. American Anthropological Association, Memoirs, 2 (1908): 275-328.

Pierce, J. E. Crow vs. Hidatsa in dialect distance and glottochronology. International Journal of American Linguistics, 20 (1954): 134-136.

Read, Catherine E. Predicting acculturative behavior of the Mandan, Hidatsa, and Arickara Indians. Anthropology UCLA, 2, no. 2 (1970): 1-5.

Riggs, S. R. Dakota grammar, texts, and ethnography. Contributions to North American Ethnology, 9 (1893): xviii-xxix.

Robinett, F. M. Hidatsa. International Journal of American Linguistics, 21 (1955): 1-7, 160-177, 210-216.

Romney, A. K. and D. Metzger. On the
processes of change in kinship
terminology [with rejoinder by E. M.
Bruner]. American Anthropologist, 58
(1956): 551-556.

Smith, C. S. An analysis of the firearms
and related specimens from Like-A-
Fishhook Village and Fort Berthold I.
Plains Anthropologist, 4 (1955): 3-12.

Stetson, R. H. An experimentalist's view
of Hidatsa phonology. International
Journal of American Linguistics, 12
(1946): 136-138.

Stockman, Wallace Henry. Historical
perspectives of federal educational
promises and performance among the Fort
Berthold Indians. Dissertation Abstracts
International, 33 (1972/1973): 1475A-
1476A. UM 72-25,221.

Taylor, Colin. Early Plains Indian quill
techniques in European museum
collections. Plains Anthropologist, 7
(1962): 58-69.

Thompson, David. David Thompson's
narrative 1784-1812. Edited by Richard
Glover. Toronto, 1962. 102, 410 p.
map. (Champlain Society, Publications,
40)

Thompson, Ralph Stanton. The final story
of the Deapolis Mandan Indian village
site. North Dakota History, 28 (1961):
143-153.

Voegelin, C. F. Historical results of
Crow-Hidatsa comparisons. Indiana
Academy of Science, Proceedings, 50
(1941): 39-42.

Voegelin, C. F. and F. M. Robinett.
'Mother language' in Hidatsa.
International Journal of American
Linguistics, 20 (1954): 65-70.

Wedel, Waldo R. Two house sites in the
Central Plains: an experiment in
archaeology. Nebraska History, 51
(1970): 225-252.

Wied-Neuwied, M. zu. Reise in das innere
Nordamerika. Coblenz, 1839-1841. 2 v.

Wied-Neuwied, M. zu. Travels in the
interior of North America. Early Western
Travels, 22 (1906): 357-366; 23 (1906):
252-385; 24 (1906): 24-35, 67-68, 261-
276.

Will, G. F. Archaeology of the Missouri
Valley. American Museum of Natural
History, Anthropological Papers, 22
(1924): 285-344.

Will, G. F. Some Hidatsa and Mandan
tales. Journal of American Folklore, 25
(1912): 93-94.

Will, G. F. and G. E. Hyde. Corn among
the Indians of the Upper Missouri. St.
Louis, 1917. 317 p.

Wilson, G. L. Agriculture of the Hidatsa
Indians. Minnesota, University, Studies
in the Social Sciences, 4 (1917): 1-129.

Wilson, G. L. Goodbird the Indian. New
York, 1914. 80 p.

Wilson, G. L. Hidatsa eagle trapping.
American Museum of Natural History,
Anthropological Papers, 30 (1928): 99-
245.

Wilson, G. L. The Hidatsa earthlodge. Ed.
by B. Weitzner. American Museum of
Natural History, Anthropological Papers,
33 (1934): 341-420.

Wilson, G. L. The horse and the dog in
Hidatsa culture. American Museum of
Natural History, Anthropological Papers,
15 (1924): 127-311.

Wilson, G. L. Waheenee. St. Paul, 1921.
189 p.

Wilson, Gilbert L. Waheenee: an Indian
girl's story told by herself to Gilbert
L. Wilson. North Dakota History, 38,
no. 1-2 (1971): i-vi, 1-189.

Wood, W. Raymond. A stylistic and
historical analysis of shoulder patterns
on Plains Indian pottery. American
Antiquity, 28 (1962/1963): 25-40.

Woolworth, Alan R. Excavations at Kipp's
Post. By Alan R. Woolworth and W.
Raymond Wood. North Dakota History, 29
(1962): 237-252.

09-11   Iowa

Ashby, D. Anecdotes. Glimpses of the
Past, 8 (1941): 105-112.

Aumann, F. R. The Ioway. Palimpsest, 50
(1969): 215-218.

Caldwell, Dorothy J. The Big Neck affair:
tragedy and farce on the Missouri
frontier. Missouri Historical Review, 64
(1969/1970): 391-412.

Carman, J. N. and K. S. Pond. The
replacement of the Indian languages of
Kansas by English. Kansas Academy of
Science, Transactions, 58 (1955): 137-
150.

Catlin, G. Notice sur les Indiens Ioways. Paris, 1845. 24 p.

Donaldson, T. The George Catlin Indian Gallery. United States National Museum, Reports (1885): 142-153.

Dorsey, J. O. A study of Siouan cults. U.S. Bureau of American Ethnology, Annual Reports, 11 (1890): 423-430.

Dorsey, J. O. On the comparative phonology of four Siouan languages. Smithsonian Institution, Annual Reports of the Board of Regents (1881): 919-929.

Dorsey, J. O. Preface. Contributions to North American Ethnology, 9 (1893): xviii-xxx.

Dorsey, J. O. Siouan sociology. U.S. Bureau of American Ethnology, Annual Reports, 15 (1894): 238-240.

Dorsey, J. O. The sister and brother: an Iowa tradition. American Antiquarian and Oriental Journal, 4 (1882): 286-288.

Dorsey, J. O. The social organization of the Siouan tribes. Journal of American Folklore, 4 (1891): 336-340.

Dorsey, J. O. and C. Thomas. Iowa. U.S. Bureau of American Ethnology, Bulletin, 30, vol. 1 (1907): 612-614.

Fay, George E., ed. Charters, constitutions and by-laws of the Indian tribes of North America. Part XIII: Midwestern tribes. Greeley, 1972. 3, 101 l. map. (University of Northern Colorado, Museum of Anthropology, Occasional Publications in Anthropology, Ethnology Series, 14)

Fay, George E., ed. Charters, constitutions and by-laws of the Indian tribes of North America. Part V: The Indian tribes of Oklahoma. Greeley, 1968. 14, 104 l. map. (University of Northern Colorado, Museum of Anthropology, Occasional Publications in Anthropology, Ethnology Series, 6) ERIC ED046555.

Fay, George E., ed. Treaties, and land cessions, between the bands of the Sioux and the United States of America, 1805-1906. Greeley, 1972. 7, 139 l. (University of Northern Colorado, Museum of Anthropology, Occasional Publications in Anthropology, Ethnology Series, 24)

Field, Gabriel. The Camp Missouri-Chariton Road, 1819: the journal of Lt. Gabriel Field. Edited by Roger L. Nichols. Missouri Historical Society, Bulletin, 24 (1967/1968): 139-152.

Foster, Thomas. The Iowa; a reprint from The Indian Record. As originally published and edited by Thomas Foster. With introduction, and elucidations through the text by William Harvey Miner. Cedar Rapids, The Torch Press, 1911. 35, 100 p. illus., map. (Little Histories of North American Indians, 2)

Gallaher, Ruth A. Rantchewaime. Palimpsest, 41 (1960): 277-283.

Griffin, J. B. The archaeological remains of the Chiwere Sioux. American Antiquity, 2 (1937): 180-181.

Hamilton, W. Remarks on the Iowa language. In H. R. Schoolcraft, ed. Information respecting the History, Condition, and Prospects of the Indian Tribes of the United States. Vol. 4. Philadelphia, 1854: 387-406.

Hamilton, W. and S. M. Irvin. An Ioway grammar. 1848. 152 p.

Harkins, Arthur M. Indian Americans in Omaha and Lincoln. By Arthur M. Harkins, Mary L. Zemyan, and Richard G. Woods. Minneapolis, University of Minnesota, Training Center for Community Programs, 1970. 42, 24 p. ERIC ED047860.

Harrington, M. R. An archaic Iowa tomahawk. Indian Notes and Monographs, 10 (1920): 55-58.

Hayden, F. V. Contributions to the ethnography and philology of the Indian tribes of the Missouri Valley. American Philosophical Society, Transactions, n.s., 12 (1863): 444-456.

Irvin, S. M. The Waw-ru-haw-a: the decline and fall of Indian superstitions. Philadelphia, 1871.

Irvin, S. M. and W. Hamilton. Iowa and Sac tribes. In H. R. Schoolcraft, ed. Information respecting the History, Condition, and Prospects of the Indian Tribes of the United States. Vol. 3. Philadelphia, 1853: 259-277.

Jackson, Donald. Trading with the Indians. Palimpsest, 47 (1966): 42-46.

Lesser, Alexander. Siouan kinship. Dissertation Abstracts, 19 (1958/1959): 208. UM 58-2596.

McGee, W J. The Siouan Indians. U.S. Bureau of American Ethnology, Annual Reports, 15 (1894): 157-204.

Meyer, Roy W. The Iowa Indians, 1836-1885. Kansas Historical Quarterly, 28 (1962): 273-300.

Morgan, L. H. Systems of consanguinity
    and affinity. Smithsonian Contributions
    to Knowledge, 17 (1871): 291-382.

Morgan, L. H. The Indian journals, 1859-
    62: p. 67-70, 99, 137-138. Ann Arbor,
    1959.

Nasatir, A. P. Before Lewis and Clark.
    St. Louis, 1952. 2 v. (882 p.).

Petersen, William. The Ioways.
    Palimpsest, 41 (1960): 261-267.

Petersen, William J. Ancient Indians of
    Iowa. Palimpsest, 45 (1964): 465-472.

Petersen, William J. The Ioways bid
    farewell. Palimpsest, 50 (1969): 264-
    267.

Plank, P. The Iowa, Sac and Fox Indian
    mission. Kansas State Historical
    Society, Transactions, 10 (1908): 312-
    325.

Schmidt, W. Die Iowa. In his Die Ursprung
    der Göttesidee. Bd. 2. Münster i. W.,
    1929: 648-653.

Sibley, George C. George C. Sibley's
    journal of a trip to the Salines in
    1811. Edited by George R. Brooks.
    Missouri Historical Society, Bulletin,
    21 (1964/1965): 167-207.

Skinner, A. A summer among the Sauk and
    Ioway Indians. Public Museum of the City
    of Milwaukee, Yearbook, 2 (1922): 16-22.

*Skinner, A. Ethnology of the Ioway
    Indians. Public Museum of the City of
    Milwaukee, Bulletin, 5 (1926): 181-354.

Skinner, A. Medicine ceremony of the
    Menomini, Iowa and Wahpeton Dakota.
    Indian Notes and Monographs, 4 (1920):
    189-261.

*Skinner, A. Societies of the Iowa.
    American Museum of Natural History,
    Anthropological Papers, 11 (1915): 679-
    740.

Skinner, A. Some unusual ethnological
    specimens. Public Museum of the City of
    Milwaukee, Yearbook, 3 (1925): 103-109.

Skinner, A. Traditions of the Iowa
    Indians. Journal of American Folklore,
    38 (1925): 425-506.

Vincent, John R. Midwest Indians and
    frontier photography. Annals of Iowa, 38
    (1965): 26-35.

Whitman, W. Descriptive grammar of Ioway-
    Oto. International Journal of American
    Linguistics, 13 (1947): 233-248.

Will, G. F. and G. E. Hyde. Corn among
    the Indians of the Upper Missouri. St.
    Louis, 1917. 317 p.

Wyatt, P. J. Iowas, Sacs and Foxes of
    Kansas. Emporia, Kansas State Teachers
    College, 1962. 25 p. illus. (Heritage
    of Kansas, 6, no. 4)

Wylie, Helen. On the warpath. Palimpsest,
    50 (1969): 253-257.

09-12   Kansa

Adams, F. G. Reminiscences of Frederick
    Chouteau. Kansas State Historical
    Society, Transactions, 8 (1904): 423-
    434.

Anonymous. Extracts from the diary of
    Major Sibley. Chronicles of Oklahoma, 5
    (1927): 196-218.

Anonymous. Kansa. U.S. Bureau of American
    Ethnology, Bulletin, 30, vol. 1 (1907):
    653-656.

Anonymous. Senor Don Manuel Lisa.
    Missouri Historical Society, Bulletin,
    23 (1966/1967): 52-58.

Barry, L. With the First U.S. Cavalry in
    Indian country, 1859-1861. Kansas
    Historical Quarterly, 24 (1958): 257-
    284.

Bushnell, D. I. Villages of the
    Algonquian, Siouan and Caddoan tribes.
    U.S. Bureau of American Ethnology,
    Bulletin, 77 (1922): 89-97.

Chapman, B. B. Charles Curtis and the Kaw
    Reservation. Kansas Historical
    Quarterly, 15 (1947): 337-351.

Connelley, W. E. Notes on the early
    Indian occupancy of the Great Plains.
    Kansas State Historical Society,
    Collections, 14 (1918): 438-470.

Dorsey, J. O. A study of Siouan cults.
    U.S. Bureau of American Ethnology,
    Annual Reports, 11 (1890): 361-422.

Dorsey, J. O. Mourning and war customs of
    the Kansas. American Naturalist, 10
    (1885): 671-680.

Dorsey, J. O. On the comparative
    phonology of four Siouan languages.
    Smithsonian Institution, Annual Reports
    of the Board of Regents (1893): 919-929.

Dorsey, J. O. Preface. Contributions to
    North American Ethnology, 9 (1893):
    xviii-xxx.

Dorsey, J. O. Siouan sociology. U.S.
Bureau of American Ethnology, Annual
Reports, 15 (1894): 230-233.

Dorsey, J. O. The social organization of
the Siouan tribes. Journal of American
Folklore, 4 (1891): 333-334.

Fay, George E., ed. Charters,
constitutions and by-laws of the Indian
tribes of North America. Part V: The
Indian tribes of Oklahoma. Greeley,
1968. 14, 104 l. map. (University of
Northern Colorado, Museum of
Anthropology, Occasional Publications in
Anthropology, Ethnology Series, 6) ERIC
ED046555.

Finney, F. F. The Kaw Indians and their
Indian Territory agency. Chronicles of
Oklahoma, 35 (1957): 416-424.

Foreman, G. The last trek of the Indians,
277-282. Chicago, 1946.

Goodrich, James W. In the earnest pursuit
of wealth: David Waldo in Missouri and
the Southwest, 1820-1878. Missouri
Historical Review, 66 (1971/1972): 155-
184.

Harkins, Arthur M. Indian Americans in
Omaha and Lincoln. By Arthur M. Harkins,
Mary L. Zemyan, and Richard G. Woods.
Minneapolis, University of Minnesota,
Training Center for Community Programs,
1970. 42, 24 p. ERIC ED047860.

Howard, James H. The persistence of
Southern Cult gorgets among the historic
Kansa. American Antiquity, 21
(1955/1956): 301-303.

Hunter, J. D. Manners and customs of
several Indian tribes. Philadelphia,
1823.

James, E. Account of an expedition from
Pittsburgh to the Rocky Mountains. Early
Western Travels, 14 (1905): 186-209; 17
(1905): 290-298.

James, Edwin. Account of an expedition
from Pittsburgh to the Rocky Mountains.
Ann Arbor, University Microfilms, 1966.
2 v. illus., maps.

Lane, William Carr. William Carr Lane,
diary. Edited by Wm. G. B. Carson. New
Mexico Historical Review, 39 (1964):
181-234, 274-332.

Lesser, Alexander. Siouan kinship.
Dissertation Abstracts, 19 (1958/1959):
208. UM 58-2596.

Long, S. H. The Kansas Indians. Kansas
State Historical Society, Transactions,
1/2 (1881): 280-301.

McGee, W J. The Siouan Indians. U.S.
Bureau of American Ethnology, Annual
Reports, 15 (1894): 157-204.

Morehouse, G. P. History of the Kansa or
Kaw Indians. Kansas State Historical
Society, Transactions, 10 (1908): 327-
368.

Morgan, L. H. Systems of consanguinity
and affinity. Smithsonian Contributions
to Knowledge, 17 (1871): 291-382.

Morgan, L. H. The Indian journals, 1859-
62: p. 29, 34-35, 82-83. Ann Arbor,
1959.

Nasatir, A. P. Before Lewis and Clark.
St. Louis, 1952. 2 v. (882 p.).

Neuman, Robert W. Check-stamped pottery
on the northern and central Great
Plains. American Antiquity, 29
(1963/1964): 17-26.

Nichols, Roger L. Martin Cantonment and
American expansion in the Missouri
Valley. Missouri Historical Review, 64
(1969/1970): 1-17.

Remsburg, G. J. An old Kansas Indian town
on the Missouri. Plymouth, Iowa, 1919.
11 p.

Riggs, S. R. Dakota grammar, texts and
ethnography. Contributions to North
American Ethnology, 9 (1893): xviii-
xxix.

Sibley, George C. George C. Sibley's
journal of a trip to the Salines in
1811. Edited by George R. Brooks.
Missouri Historical Society, Bulletin,
21 (1964/1965): 167-207.

Skinner, A. Kansa organizations. American
Museum of Natural History,
Anthropological Papers, 11 (1915): 741-
775.

Spencer, J. The Kaw or Kansas Indians.
Kansas State Historical Society,
Transactions, 10 (1908): 373-382.

Sunder, John E. British Army officers on
the Santa Fe Trail. Missouri Historical
Society, Bulletin, 23 (1966/1967): 147-
157.

Unrau, William E. The Council Grove
merchants and Kansa Indians, 1855-1870.
Kansas Historical Quarterly, 34 (1968):
266-281.

Unrau, William E. The Kansa Indians; a
history of the Wind People, 1673-1873.
Norman, University of Oklahoma Press,
1971. 244 p.

Voe, C. de. Legends of the Kaw. Kansas
City, 1904. 215 p.

Ward, Allen T. Letters of Allen T. Ward,
1842-1851, from the Shawnee and Kaw
(Methodist) Missions. Edited by Lela
Barnes. Kansas Historical Quarterly, 33
(1967): 321-376.

Wedel, W. R. The Kansa Indians. Kansas
State Historical Society, Transactions,
49 (1946): 1-35.

Wedel, W. R. The Kansa. U.S. Bureau of
American Ethnology, Bulletin, 174
(1959): 50-54.

White, Lonnie J. Winter campaigning with
Sheridan and Custer: the expedition of
the Nineteenth Kansas Volunteer Cavalry.
Journal of the West, 6 (1967): 68-98.

Wilmeth, Roscoe. Kansa village locations
in the light of McCoy's 1828 journal.
Kansas Historical Quarterly, 26 (1960):
152-157.

09-13   Kiowa

Anonymous. "Chief Stumbling Bear Pass";
historical marker honoring a great Kiowa
chief and peacemaker. Chronicles of
Oklahoma, 45 (1967): 472-476.

Asplin, Ray. A history of Council Grove
in Oklahoma. Chronicles of Oklahoma, 45
(1967): 433-450.

Barry, L. With the First U.S. Cavalry in
Indian country, 1859-1861. Kansas
Historical Quarterly, 24 (1958): 257-
284.

Battey, T. C. The life and adventures of
a Quaker among the Indians. Boston,
1875. 339 p.

Battey, Thomas C. The life and adventures
of a Quaker among the Indians. Norman,
University of Oklahoma Press, 1968. 26,
355 p. illus.

Boas, F. Zur Anthropologie der
nordamerikanischen Indianer. Berliner
Gesellschaft für Anthropologie,
Ethnologie und Urgeschichte,
Verhandlungen (1895): 367-411.

Brant, C. S. Peyotism among the Kiowa-
Apache and neighboring tribes.
Southwestern Journal of Anthropology, 6
(1950): 212-222.

Brant, Charles S. Indian-White cultural
relations in southwestern Oklahoma.
Chronicles of Oklahoma, 37 (1959): 433-
439.

Brugge, David M. Some Plains Indians in
the church records of New Mexico. Plains
Anthropologist, 10 (1965): 181-189.

Burbank, E. A. and E. Caldwell. Burbank
among the Indians, 185-191. Caldwell,
1946.

Cardenal, Ernesto, tr. Poesía de los
indios de Norteamérica. América
Indígena, 21 (1961): 355-362.

Carriker, Robert Charles. Fort Supply,
Indian Territory: frontier outpost on
the Southern Plains, 1868-1894.
Dissertation Abstracts, 28 (1967/1968):
2158A. UM 67-15,910.

Cavazos Garza, Israel. Las incursiones de
los bárbaros en el noreste de México,
durante el siglo XIX. Humanitas
(Monterrey), 5 (1964): 343-356.

Chapman, Berlin B. The day in court for
the Kiowa, Comanche and Apache tribes.
Great Plains Journal, 2 (1962/1963): 1-
21.

Collier, D. Conjuring among the Kiowa.
Primitive Man, 17 (1944): 45-49.

Conrad, David E. The Whipple Expedition
on the Great Plains. Great Plains
Journal, 2 (1962/1963): 42-66.

Corwin, Hugh D. Comanche and Kiowa
captives in Oklahoma and Texas.
Guthrie, Okla., Printed by Cooperative
Publishing, 1959. 237 p. illus.

Corwin, Hugh D. Delos K. Lone Wolf,
Kiowa. Chronicles of Oklahoma, 39
(1961): 433-436.

Corwin, Hugh D. Protestant missionary
work among the Comanches and Kiowas.
Chronicles of Oklahoma, 46 (1968): 41-
57.

Crocchiola, Stanley F. L. Fort Bascom,
Comanche-kiowa barrier. By F. Stanley.
Pampa, Tex., 1961. 224 p.

Crocchiola, Stanley F. L. Satanta and the
Kiowas. By F. Stanley. Borger, Tex.,
Jim Hess Printers, 1968. 4, 391 p.

Crowell, E. E. A preliminary report on
Kiowa structure. International Journal
of American Linguistics, 15 (1949): 163-
167.

Curtis, N., ed. The Indians' book, 221-
240. New York, 1907.

Cutler, Lee. Lawrie Tatum and the Kiowa
Agency 1869-1873. Arizona and the West,
13 (1971): 221-244.

Dennis, William W. Fort Richardson, Texas, 1867-1878, and the Mackenzie Trail. Jacksboro, Tex., 1964. 40 p. illus., map.

Dodge, Henry. Journal of Colonel Dodge's expedition from Fort Gibson to the Pawnee Pict village. American State Papers, Military Affairs, 5 (1860): 373-382.

Ellis, Richard Nathaniel. General John Pope and the development of federal Indian policy, 1862-1886. Dissertation Abstracts, 29 (1968/1969): 528A. UM 68-10,609.

Estep, Raymond. Lieutenant William E. Burnet letters: removal of the Texas Indians and the founding of Fort Cobb. Chronicles of Oklahoma, 39 (1961): 15-41.

Everett, Mark Allen, et al. Light-sensitive eruptions in American Indians. Archives of Dermatology, 83 (1961): 243-248.

Fintzelberg, Nicholas M. Peyote paraphernalia. San Diego, 1969. 9 l. illus. (San Diego Museum of Man, Ethnic Technology Notes, 4)

Fisher, M. C. On the Arapahoes, Kiowas, and Comanches. Ethnological Society (London), Journal, n.s., 1 (1869): 274-287.

Fleming, Elvis Eugene. Captain Nicholas Nolan; lost on the Staked Plains. Texana, 4 (1966): 1-13.

Gamble, J. I. Changing patterns in Kiowa Indian dances. International Congress of Americanists, Proceedings, 29, vol. 2 (1952): 94-104.

Garrett, Roland. The notion of language in some Kiowa folktales. Indian Historian, 5, no. 2 (1972): 32-37, 42.

Gatschet, A. S. Phonetics of the Kayowe language. American Antiquarian and Oriental Journal, 4 (1882): 280-285.

Gatschet, A. S. Sinti, der erste Mensch. Ausland, 63 (1890): 901-904.

Gatschet, A. S. Zwölf Sprachen aus dem Südwesten Nordamerikas. Weimar, 1876. 150 p.

Griswold, G. Old Fort Sill. Chronicles of Oklahoma, 36 (1958): 2-15.

Hagan, William T. Kiowas, Comanches, and cattlemen, 1867-1906: a case study of the failure of U.S. Reservation policy.

Pacific Historical Review, 40 (1971): 333-355.

Haine, J. J. F. A Belgian in the gold rush: California Indians. A memoir by J. J. F. Haine. Translated, with an introduction by Jan Albert Goris. California Historical Society Quarterly, 38 (1959): 141-155.

Hale, Kenneth. Jemez and Kiowa correspondences in reference to Kiowa-Tanoan. International Journal of American Linguistics, 28 (1962): 1-5.

Hale, Kenneth. Toward a reconstruction of Kiowa-Tanoan phonology. International Journal of American Linguistics, 33 (1967): 112-120.

Hammack, Laurens C. Archaeology of the Ute dam and reservoir. Santa Fe, 1965. 69 p. illus., maps. (Museum of New Mexico, Papers in Anthropology, 14)

Harrington, J. P. Kiowa memories of the Northland. In D. D. Brand and F. E. Harvey, eds. So Live the Works of Men. Albuquerque, 1939: 162-176.

Harrington, J. P. On phonetic and lexical resemblances between Kiowa and Tanoan. American Anthropologist, n.s., 12 (1910): 119-123.

Harrington, J. P. Three Kiowa texts. International Journal of American Linguistics, 12 (1946): 237-242.

Harrington, J. P. Vocabulary of the Kiowa language. U.S. Bureau of American Ethnology, Bulletin, 84 (1928): 1-255.

Harrington, M. R. Peyote outfit. Masterkey, 18 (1944): 143-144.

Harrison, Lowell H. Damage suits for Indian depredations in the Adobe Walls area, 1874. Panhandle-Plains Historical Review, 36 (1963): 37-60.

Howard, J. H. A Comanche spear point used in a Kiowa-Comanche peyote ceremonial. South Dakota, University, Museum, Museum Notes, 7 (1950): 3-6.

Howard, James H. Half Moon Way: the Peyote Ritual of Chief White Bear. South Dakota, University, Museum, Museum News, 28, nos. 1/2 (1967): 1-24.

Hultkrantz, Åke. The Indians in Yellowstone Park. Annals of Wyoming, 29 (1957): 125-149.

Jacobsen, O. B. Kiowa Indian art. Nice, 1929.

Jensen, D. O. Wo-haw: Kiowa warrior. Missouri Historical Society, Bulletin, 7 (1950): 76-88.

Jones, Douglas C. Medicine Lodge revisited. Kansas Historical Quarterly, 35 (1969): 130-142.

Jones, William M. Origin of the place-name Taos. Anthropological Linguistics, 2, no. 3 (1960): 2-4.

Kroeker, Marvin. Colonel W. B. Hazen in the Indian Territory. Chronicles of Oklahoma, 42 (1964): 53-73.

La Barre, W. Kiowa folk sciences. Journal of American Folklore, 60 (1947): 105-114.

La Barre, Weston. The peyote cult. New Haven, Yale University, Department of Anthropology, 1938. 188 p. illus. (Yale University Publications in Anthropology, 19)

Leathers, Frances Jane, ed. Christopher Columbus Goodman: soldier, Indian fighter, farmer, 1818-1861. Southwestern Historical Quarterly, 69 (1965/1966): 353-376.

Lecompte, Janet. Bent, St. Vrain and company among the Comanche and Kiowa. Colorado Magazine, 49 (1972): 273-293.

Levy, J. E. Kiowa and Comanche: report from the field. Anthropology Tomorrow, 6, no. 2 (1958): 30-44.

Lowie, R. H. A note on Kiowa kinship terms and usages. American Anthropologist, n.s., 25 (1923): 279-281.

Lowie, R. H. Alleged Kiowa-Crow affinities. Southwestern Journal of Anthropology, 9 (1953): 357-368.

Lowie, R. H. Notes on the Kiowa Indians. Tribus, 4/5 (1956): 131-138.

Lowie, R. H. Societies of the Kiowa. American Museum of Natural History, Anthropological Papers, 11 (1916): 837-851.

Lowie, R. H. The relations between the Kiowa and the Crow Indians. Société Suisse des Américanistes, Bulletin, 7 (1953): 1-5.

Lyman, Wyllys. The Battle of Lyman's Wagon Train. Edited by Ernest R. Archambeau. Panhandle-Plains Historical Review, 36 (1963): 89-101.

Marriott, A. Greener fields. New York, 1953. 274 p.

Marriott, A. The ten grandmothers. Norman, 1945. 306 p.

Marriott, A. Winter-telling stories. New York, 1947. 84 p.

Marriott, Alice L. Greener fields. New York, Greenwood Press, 1968. 232 p.

Marriott, Alice L. Kiowa years, a study in culture impact. New York, Macmillan, 1968. 13, 173 p. illus., map.

Marriott, Alice L. Saynday's people; the Kiowa Indians and the stories they told. Lincoln, University of Nebraska Press, 1963. 226 p. illus.

Marriott, Alice L., comp. Winter-telling stories. New York, Crowell, 1969. 82 p. illus.

Maxwell, Linda Lee. Satanta: last of the Kiowa war chiefs. Texana, 7 (1969): 117-135.

Mayhall, Mildred P. The Kiowas. 2d ed. Norman, University of Oklahoma Press, 1971. 18, 364 p. illus.

McKenzie, P. and J. P. Harrington. Popular account of the Kiowa language. Archaeological Institute of America, School of American Research, Santa Fe, Monographs, 12 (1948): 1-21.

McKinley, J. W. J. W. McKinley's narrative. Panhandle-Plains Historical Review, 36 (1963): 61-69.

Merill, James M. General Sherman's letter to his son: a visit to Fort Sill. Chronicles of Oklahoma, 47 (1969): 126-131.

Merrifield, William R. Classification of Kiowa nouns. International Journal of American Linguistics, 25 (1959): 269-270.

Merrifield, William R. The Kiowa verb prefix. International Journal of American Linguistics, 25 (1959): 168-176.

Metcalf, George. Some notes on an old Kiowa shield and its history. Great Plains Journal, 8 (1968/1969): 16-30.

Methvin, J. J. Andele, or the Mexican-Kiowa captive. Louisville, 1899.

Miller, W. R. A note on Kiowa linguistic affiliations. American Anthropologist, 61 (1959): 102-105.

Mishkin, B. Rank and warfare among the Plains Indians. American Ethnological Society, Monographs, 3 (1940): 1-65.

Mitchell, Michael Dan. Acculturation problems among the Plains tribes of the government agencies in Western Indian Territory. Chronicles of Oklahoma, 44 (1966): 281-289.

Momaday, Natachee Scott. The journey of Tai-me. Santa Barbara, Printed at the University of California, 1967. illus.

Momaday, Natachee Scott. The way to rainy mountain. Albuquerque, University of New Mexico Press, 1969. 88 p. illus.

Monahan, Forrest D., Jr. Kiowa--Federal relations in Kansas, 1865-1868. Chronicles of Oklahoma, 49 (1971/1972): 477-491.

Monahan, Forrest D., Jr. The Kiowa-Comanche Reservation in the 1890's. Chronicles of Oklahoma, 45 (1967): 451-463.

Monahan, Forrest D., Jr. The Kiowas and New Mexico, 1800-1845. Journal of the West, 8 (1969): 67-75.

Monahan, Forrest Dewey, Jr. Trade goods on the Prairie, the Kiowa tribe and White trade goods, 1794-1875. Dissertation Abstracts, 26 (1965/1966): 3886-3887. UM 65-12,999.

Mooney, J. A Kiowa mescal rattle. American Anthropologist, 5 (1892): 64-65.

Mooney, J. Calendar history of the Kiowa Indians. U.S. Bureau of American Ethnology, Annual Reports, 17, vol. 1 (1896): 141-447.

Mooney, J. Field-work among the Kiowa. Smithsonian Miscellaneous Collections, 70, no. 2 (1919): 99-103.

Mooney, J. Indian shield heraldry. Southern Workman, 30 (1901): 500-504.

Mooney, J. Kiowa. U.S. Bureau of American Ethnology, Bulletin, 30, vol. 1 (1907): 699-701.

Mooney, J. The ghost-dance religion. U.S. Bureau of American Ethnology, Annual Reports, 14, no. 2 (1893): 1078-1091.

Nye, W. S. Carbine and lance. Norman, 1937. 441 p.

Nye, Wilbur S. Bad medicine and good; tales of the Kiowas. Norman, University of Oklahoma Press, 1962. 291 p. illus.

Nye, Wilbur S. Carbine and lance; the story of old Fort Sill. Norman, University of Oklahoma Press, 1969. 21, 361 p. illus., maps.

Olmsted, O. On the linguistic classification of Kiowa. Southwestern Lore, 17 (1951): 15-17.

Parsons, E. C. Kiowa tales. American Folk-Lore Society, Memoirs, 22 (1929): 1-151.

Pennington, William David. Government policy and farming on the Kiowa Reservation: 1869-1901. Dissertation Abstracts International, 33 (1972/1973): 1123A. UM 72-23,107.

Pike, Albert. Albert Pike's journeys in the prairie, 1831-1832. Edited by J. Evetts Haley. Panhandle-Plains Historical Review, 41 (1968): 1-84.

Prentice, R. A. Pictograph story of Koñate. El Palacio, 58 (1951): 90-96.

Rachlin, Carol K. The Native American Church in Oklahoma. Chronicles of Oklahoma, 42 (1964): 262-272.

Richardson, J. Law and status among the Kiowa Indians. American Ethnological Society, Monographs, 1 (1940): 1-136.

Schmidt, M. F. and D. Brown. Fighting Indians of the West, 63-88. New York, 1948.

Schmitt, K. Wichita-Kiowa relations and the 1874 outbreak. Chronicles of Oklahoma, 28 (1950): 154-160.

Scott, H. L. Notes on the Kado, or sun dance of the Kiowa. American Anthropologist, n.s., 13 (1911): 345-379.

Shirk, G. H. Peace on the Plains. Chronicles of Oklahoma, 28 (1950): 2-41.

Sivertsen, E. Pitch problems in Kiowa. International Journal of American Linguistics, 22 (1956): 117-130.

Smith, Ralph A. The scalp hunt in Chihuahua--1849. New Mexico Historical Review, 40 (1965): 116-140.

Speirs, Randall H. Number in Tewa. In M. Estellie Smith, ed. Studies in Linguistics in Honor of George L. Trager. The Hague, Mouton, 1972: 479-486. (Janua Linguarum, Series Maior, 52)

Spier, L. Notes on the Kiowa sun dance. American Museum of Natural History, Anthropological Papers, 16 (1921): 433-450.

Taylor, Morris F. Kicking Bird: a chief of the Kiowas. Kansas Historical Quarterly, 38 (1972): 295-319.

Trager, Edith Crowell. The Kiowa
     language: a grammatical study.
     Dissertation Abstracts, 21 (1960/1961):
     886. UM 60-3619.

Trager, George L. Taos IV: morphemics,
     syntax, semology in nouns and in
     pronomial reference. International
     Journal of American Linguistics, 27
     (1961): 211-222.

Trager, George L. The name of Taos, New
     Mexico. Anthropological Linguistics, 2,
     no. 3 (1960): 5-6.

Trager, George L. The Tanoan settlement
     of the Rio Grande area: a possible
     chronology. In Dell H. Hymes and William
     E. Bittle, eds. Studies in Southwestern
     Ethnolinguistics. The Hague, Mouton,
     1967: 335-350. (Studies in General
     Anthropology, 3)

Tsa Toke, M., et al. The peyote ritual.
     San Francisco, 1957. 84 p.

Unrau, William E. Indian agents vs. the
     Army: some background notes on the
     Kiowa-Comanche Treaty of 1865. Kansas
     Historical Quarterly, 30 (1964): 129-
     152.

Unrau, William E. Investigation or
     probity? Investigations into the affairs
     of the Kiowa-Comanche Indian Agency,
     1867. Chronicles of Oklahoma, 42 (1964):
     300-319.

Unrau, William Errol. The role of the
     Indian agent in the settlement of the
     South-Central Plains, 1861-1868.
     Dissertation Abstracts, 25 (1964/1965):
     1884. UM 64-4389.

Vestal, P. A. and R. E. Schultes. The
     economic botany of the Kiowa Indians.
     Cambridge, 1939. 110 p.

Vigness, D. M. Indian raids on the lower
     Rio Grande, 1836-1837. Southwestern
     Historical Quarterly, 59 (1955): 14-23.

Vizcaya Canales, Isidro. La invasión de
     los indios bárbaros al noreste de
     México, en los años de 1840 y 1841.
     Monterrey, N.L., 1968. 296 p.
     (Monterrey, Instituto Tecnologico y de
     Estudios Superiores de Monterrey,
     Publicaciones, Serie: Historia, 7)

Voegelin, Carl F. Methods for
     typologizing directly and by distinctive
     features (in reference to Uto-Aztecan
     and Kiowa-Tanoan vowel systems). Lingua,
     11 (1962): 469-487.

Voegelin, E. W. Kiowa-Crow mythological
     affiliations. American Anthropologist,
     n.s., 35 (1933): 470-474.

Wallace, Ernest. Ranald S. Mackenzie on
     the Texas frontier. Lubbock, West Texas
     Museum Association, 1964. 10, 214 p.
     maps.

Wedel, W. R. The Kiowa and Kiowa Apache.
     U.S. Bureau of American Ethnology,
     Bulletin, 174 (1959): 78-80.

Wharton, C. Satanta, the great chief of
     the Kiowas and his people. Dallas,
     1935. 239 p.

Whilden, Charles E. Letters from a Santa
     Fe Army clerk, 1855-1856. Edited by John
     Hammond Moore. New Mexico Historical
     Review, 40 (1965): 141-164.

White, Lonnie J. Indian battles in the
     Texas Panhandle, 1874. Journal of the
     West, 6 (1967): 278-309.

White, Lonnie J. Winter campaigning with
     Sheridan and Custer: the expedition of
     the Nineteenth Kansas Volunteer Cavalry.
     Journal of the West, 6 (1967): 68-98.

White, Lonnie J., ed. Kansas newspaper
     items relating to the Red River War of
     1874-1875. Panhandle-Plains Historical
     Review, 36 (1963): 71-88.

Winfrey, Dorman H., ed. The Indian papers
     of Texas and the Southwest, 1825-1916.
     Edited by Dorman H. Winfrey and James M.
     Day. Austin, Pemberton Press, 1966.
     412 p.

Wonderly, W. L., et al. Number in Kiowa.
     International Journal of American
     Linguistics, 20 (1954): 1-7.

Wright, Bessie L., ed. Diary of a member
     of the first mule pack train to leave
     Fort Smith for California in 1849.
     Panhandle-Plains Historical Review, 42
     (1969): 61-119.

Zbinden, Ernst A. Nördliche und südliche
     Elemente im Kulturheroenmythus der
     Südathapasken. Anthropos, 55 (1960):
     689-733.

Zimmerman, Jean L. Colonel Ranald S.
     Mackenzie at Fort Sill. Chronicles of
     Oklahoma, 44 (1966): 12-21.

Zo-Tom. 1877: Plains Indian sketch books
     of Zo-Tom and Howling Wolf. By Zo-Tom
     and Howling Wolf. Flagstaff, Northland
     Press, 1969. 25 p. illus.

09-14   Kiowa Apache

Battey, T. C. The life and adventures of
     a Quaker among the Indians. Boston,
     1875. 339 p.

Beals, Kenneth. The dynamics of Kowa Apache peyotism. Papers in Anthropology, 12, no. 1 (1971): 35-89.

Bittle, William E. A brief history of the Kiowa Apache. Papers in Anthropology, 12, no. 1 (1971): 1-34.

Bittle, William E. Kiowa-Apache. In Harry Hoijer, et al., eds. Studies in the Athapaskan Languages. Berkeley and Los Angeles, University of California Press, 1963: 76-101. (California, University, Publications in Linguistics, 29)

Bittle, William E. The Manatidie: a focus for Kiowa Apache tribal identity. Plains Anthropologist, 7 (1962): 152-163.

Blackbear, Joe. Joe Blackbear's story of the origin of the peyote religion. Recorded by Charles S. Brant. Plains Anthropologist, 8 (1963): 180-181.

Boatright, M. C., ed. The sky is my tipi. Texas Folklore Society, 22 (1949): 1-243.

Boatright, Mody C., ed. The sky is my tipi. Dallas, Southern Methodist University Press, 1966. 9, 243 p. (Texas Folklore Society, Publications, 22)

Brant, C. S. Kiowa Apache culture history. Southwestern Journal of Anthropology, 9 (1953): 195-202.

Brant, C. S. Peyotism among the Kiowa-Apache and neighboring tribes. Southwestern Journal of Anthropology, 6 (1950): 212-222.

Brant, C. S. The cultural position of the Kiowa-Apache. Southwestern Journal of Anthropology, 5 (1949): 56-61.

Brant, Charles S. White contact and cultural disintegration among the Kiowa Apache. Plains Anthropologist, 9 (1964): 8-13.

Bross, Michael Grantham. The Kiowa Apache body concept in relation to health. Papers in Anthropology, 12, no. 2 (1971): 1-80.

Chapman, Berlin B. The day in court for the Kiowa, Comanche and Apache tribes. Great Plains Journal, 2 (1962/1963): 1-21.

Edgerton, Faye E. The tagmemic analysis of sentence structure in Western Apache. In Harry Hoijer, et al., eds. Studies in the Athapaskan Languages. Berkeley and Los Angeles, University of California Press, 1963: 102-148. (California,

University, Publications in Linguistics, 29)

Freeman, Patricia Anne. Kiowa Apache concepts and attitudes toward the child. Papers in Anthropology, 12, no. 1 (1971): 90-160.

Hoijer, H. Phonetic and phonemic change in the Athapaskan languages. Language, 18 (1942): 218-220.

Hoijer, H. Pitch accent in the Apachean languages. Language, 19 (1943): 38-41.

Hoijer, H. The Apachean verb. International Journal of American Linguistics, 11 (1945): 193-203; 12 (1946): 1-13, 51-59; 14 (1948): 247-259; 15 (1949): 12-22.

James, E. Account of an expedition from Pittsburgh to the Rocky Mountains. Early Western Travels, 16 (1905): 109-119, 194-212.

James, Edwin. Account of an expedition from Pittsburgh to the Rocky Mountains. Ann Arbor, University Microfilms, 1966. 2 v. illus., maps.

Kroeker, Marvin. Colonel W. B. Hazen in the Indian Territory. Chronicles of Oklahoma, 42 (1964): 53-73.

McAllister, J. G. Kiowa-Apache social organization. In F. Eggan, ed. Social Anthropology of North American Tribes. 2d ed. Chicago, 1955: 99-172.

McAllister, J. Gilbert. Dävéko; Kiowa-Apache medicine man. Austin, 1970. 61 p. illus. (Texas Memorial Museum, Bulletin, 17)

McAllister, J. Gilbert. The four quartz rocks medicine bundle of the Kiowa-Apache. Ethnology, 4 (1965): 210-224.

Monahan, Forrest D., Jr. The Kiowa-Comanche Reservation in the 1890's. Chronicles of Oklahoma, 45 (1967): 451-463.

Mooney, J. Calendar history of the Kiowa Indians. U.S. Bureau of American Ethnology, Annual Reports, 17, vol. 1 (1896): 245-253.

Mooney, J. Kiowa Apache. U.S. Bureau of American Ethnology, Bulletin, 30, vol. 1 (1907): 701-703.

Nye, W. S. Carbine and lance. Norman, 1937. 441 p.

Opler, M. E. The kinship systems of the Southern Athabaskan-speaking tribes.

American Anthropologist, n.s., 38
(1936): 620-633.

Opler, Morris E.   Cultural evolution,
Southern Athapaskans, and chronology in
theory. Southwestern Journal of
Anthropology, 17 (1961): 1-20.

Opler, Morris E.   The death practices and
eschatology of the Kiowa Apache. By
Morris E. Opler and William E. Bittle.
Southwestern Journal of Anthropology, 17
(1961): 383-394.

Opler, Morris E.   Western Apache and Kiowa
Apache materials relating to ceremonial
payment. Ethnology, 8 (1969): 122-124.

Oswald, James M.   History of Fort Elliott.
Panhandle-Plains Historical Review, 32
(1959): 1-59.

Sanford, Margaret Sellers.   Present day
death practices and eschatology of the
Kiowa Apache. Papers in Anthropology,
12, no. 2 (1971): 81-131.

Smith, R. A.   Account of the journey of
Bénard de la Harpe. Southwestern
Historical Quarterly, 62 (1958/1959):
75-86, 246-259, 371-385, 525-541.

Tweedie, M. Jean.   Notes on the history
and adaptation of the Apache tribes.
American Anthropologist, 70 (1968):
1132-1142.

Wedel, W. R.   The Kiowa and Kiowa Apache.
U.S. Bureau of American Ethnology,
Bulletin, 174 (1959): 78-80.

White, Lonnie J.   Indian battles in the
Texas Panhandle, 1874. Journal of the
West, 6 (1967): 278-309.

White, Lonnie J.   Winter campaigning with
Sheridan and Custer: the expedition of
the Nineteenth Kansas Volunteer Cavalry.
Journal of the West, 6 (1967): 68-98.

Whitewolf, Jim.   Jim Whitewolf: the life
of a Kiowa Apache Indian. Edited by
Charles S. Brant.   New York, Dover
Publications, 1969.   11, 144 p.   map.

09-15   Mandan

Anonymous.   South Dakota physical types.
South Dakota, University, William H.
Over Museum, Museum News, 12, no. 5
(1952): 1.

Bass, William M.   The first human skeletal
material from the Huff Site, 32MO11, and
a summary of putative Mandan skeletal
material. By William M. Bass and Walter

H. Birkby. Plains Anthropologist, 7
(1962): 164-177.

Beckwith, M. W.   Mandan and Hidatsa tales.
Folk-Lore Foundation, Publications, 14
(1934): 269-320.

Beckwith, M. W.   Mandan-Hidatsa myths and
ceremonies. American Folk-Lore Society,
Memoirs, 32 (1938): 1-320.

Beckwith, M. W.   Myths and ceremonies of
the Mandan and Hidatsa. Folk-Lore
Foundation, Publications, 12 (1932):
117-267.

Beckwith, M. W.   Myths and hunting stories
of the Mandan and Hidatsa Sioux. Folk-
Lore Foundation, Publications, 10
(1930): 1-116.

Befu, Harumi.   Political complexity and
village community: test of an
hypothesis. Anthropological Quarterly,
39 (1966): 43-52.

Boas, F.   Zur Anthropologie der
nordamerikanischen Indianer. Berliner
Gesellschaft für Anthropologie,
Ethnologie und Urgeschichte,
Verhandlungen (1895): 367-411.

*Bowers, A. W.   Mandan social and
ceremonial organization.   Chicago, 1950.
512 p.

Brower, J. V.   Mandan.   St. Paul, 1904.
158 p.

Brown, C. E.   The Huff Mandan village
site. Wisconsin Archeologist, 9 (1930):
120-122.

Bruner, E. M.   Assimilation among Fort
Berthold Indians. American Indian, 6,
no. 4 (1953): 21-29.

Bruner, E. M.   Cultural transmission and
cultural change. Southwestern Journal of
Anthropology, 12 (1956): 191-199.

Bruner, E. M.   Primary group experience
and the processes of acculturation.
American Anthropologist, 58 (1956): 605-
623.

Bruner, E. M.   Two processes of change in
Mandan-Hidatsa kinship terminology.
American Anthropologist, 57 (1955): 840-
850.

Bruner, Edward M.   Cultural transmission
and cultural change. In Deward E.
Walker, Jr., ed. The Emergent Native
Americans.   Boston, Little, Brown, 1972:
69-75.

Bushnell, D. I.   Burials of the
Algonquian, Siouan and Caddoan tribes.

U.S. Bureau of American Ethnology, Bulletin, 83 (1927): 65-73.

Bushnell, D. I.   Villages of the Algonquian, Siouan and Caddoan tribes. U.S. Bureau of American Ethnology, Bulletin, 77 (1922): 122-140.

Butterfly.   Butterfly's Mandan winter count: 1833-1876. Edited by James H. Howard. Ethnohistory, 7 (1960): 28-43.

Catlin, G.   An account of an annual religious ceremony practised by the Mandan tribe. Miscellanies of the Philobiblon Society, 8, no. 10 (1864): 1-67.

Catlin, G.   Illustrations of the manners, customs and condition of the North American Indians, Vol. 1: 80-184.   New York, 1841.

Catlin, G.   O-Kee-Pa.   Philadelphia, 1867. 52 p.

Catlin, George.   O-kee-pa, a religious ceremony, and other customs of the Mandans. Edited by John C. Ewers.   New Haven, Yale University Press, 1967. 106 p.   illus.

Chardon, Francis A.   Chardon's journal at Fort Clark, 1834-1839.   Freeport, N.Y., Books for Libraries Press, 1970.   46, 458 p.   illus.

Coues, E., ed.   Manuscript journals of Alexander Henry and of David Thompson. New York, 1897.   3 v.

Crawford, K.   A brief sketch of the Mandan Indians. Minnesota Archaeologist, 2, no. 3 (1936): 1-5.

Crawford, L. F.   Flint quarries on Knife River. Minnesota Archaeologist, 2, no. 4 (1936): 1-4.

Culbertson, T. A.   Journal of an expedition to the mauvaises terres and the Upper Missouri in 1850. U.S. Bureau of American Ethnology, Bulletin, 147 (1952): 1-172.

Curtis, E. S.   The North American Indian, Vol. 5: 3-55, 143-148, 169-177. Cambridge, 1909.

*DeLand, C. E.   The aborigines of South Dakota. South Dakota Historical Collections, 3 (1906): 269-586; 4 (1908): 273-730.

Densmore, F.   Mandan and Hidatsa music. U.S. Bureau of American Ethnology, Bulletin, 80 (1923): 1-186.

Densmore, Frances.   Mandan and Hidatsa music.   New York, Da Capo Press, 1972. 20, 192 p.   illus.

Donaldson, T.   The George Catlin Indian Gallery. United States National Museum, Reports (1885): 80-88, 349-383, 398-406.

Dorsey, J. O.   A study of Siouan cults. U.S. Bureau of American Ethnology, Annual Reports, 11 (1890): 501-513.

Dorsey, J. O.   Preface. Contributions to North American Ethnology, 9 (1893): xviii-xxx.

Dorsey, J. O. and C. Thomas.   Mandan. U.S. Bureau of American Ethnology, Bulletin, 30, vol. 1 (1907): 796-799.

Eschambault, A. d'.   La voyage de Vérendrye au pays des Mandannes. Revue d'Histoire de l'Amérique Française, 2 (1948): 424-431.

Ewers, J. C.   Early White influence upon Plains Indian painting. Smithsonian Miscellaneous Collections, 134, no. 7 (1957): 1-11.

Ewers, J. C.   Three ornaments worn by Upper Missouri Indians a century and a quarter ago. New York Historical Society Quarterly, 41 (1957): 24-33.

Ewers, John C.   Mothers of the mixed-bloods. El Palacio, 69 (1962): 20-29.

Fay, George E., ed.   Charters, constitutions and by-laws of the Indian tribes of North America. Part IIa: The Northern Plains.   Greeley, 1967.   6, 141 l.   maps.   (University of Northern Colorado, Museum of Anthropology, Occasional Publications in Anthropology, Ethnology Series, 3)   ERIC ED051923.

Field, Gabriel.   The Camp Missouri-Chariton Road, 1819: the journal of Lt. Gabriel Field. Edited by Roger L. Nichols. Missouri Historical Society, Bulletin, 24 (1967/1968): 139-152.

Frobenius, L.   Geographische Kulturkunde, 581-602.   Leipzig, 1904.

Gaskin, L.   A rare pamphlet on the Mandan religious ceremony. Man, 39 (1939): 141-142.

Gebhard, David.   The shield motif in Plains rock art. American Antiquity, 31 (1965/1966): 721-732.

Gesner, A. T.   Prehistoric Mandan remains in North Dakota. Records of the Past, 4 (1905): 363-367.

Gilmore, M. R. A Mandan monument to a national hero. Indian Notes, 6 (1929): 147-151.

Goplen, A. O. The Mandan Indians. North Dakota History, 13 (1946): 153-175.

Gregg, John B. Ear disease in the Indian skulls at the Museum of the State Historical Society of North Dakota. North Dakota History, 32 (1965): 233-242.

Gregg, John B. Exostoses in the external auditory canals. By John B. Gregg and William M. Bass. Annals of Otology, Rhinology and Laryngology, 79 (1970): 834-839.

Hanson, Charles E., Jr. The Indian garden project. Museum of the Fur Trade Quarterly, 2, no. 3 (1966): 3-6.

Hartle, Donald D. The dance hall of the Santee Bottoms on the Fort Berthold Reservation, Garrison Reservoir, North Dakota. Washington, D.C., Government Printing Office, 1963. 123-132 p. illus. (U.S., Bureau of American Ethnology, River Basin Surveys Papers, 28. U.S., Bureau of American Ethnology, Bulletin, 185)

Hayden, F. V. A sketch of the Mandan Indians. American Journal of Science and Arts, 34 (1862): 57-66.

Hayden, F. V. Contributions to the ethnography and philology of the Indian tribes of the Missouri Valley. American Philosophical Society, Transactions, n.s., 12 (1863): 426-444.

Hiller, W. R. Indian village at Fort Berthold. Minnesota Archaeologist, 17 (1951): 3-9.

Hiller, W. R. The manufacture of bone fish-hooks and stone net sinkers by the Mandans. Minnesota Archaeologist, 6 (1940): 144-148.

Hiller, W. R. X-marked Mandan game pieces. Minnesota Archaeologist, 8 (1942): 126-127.

Hopkins, W. J. The Indian book. Boston, 1911. 239 p.

Howard, James H. A Mandan-Hidatsa headdress and its origin legend. South Dakota, University, Museum, Museum News, 13, no. 2 (1952): 1-5.

Jackson, Donald. A new Lewis and Clark map. Missouri Historical Society, Bulletin, 17 (1960/1961): 117-132.

Jackson, Donald. Journey to the Mandans, 1809; the lost narrative of Dr. Thomas. Missouri Historical Society Bulletin, 20 (1963/1964): 179-192.

Jaques. Notes of a tourist through the Upper Missouri region. Missouri Historical Society, Bulletin, 22 (1965/1966): 393-409.

Jensen, Marguerite. The Mandan tragedy. Indian Historian, 5, no. 3 (1972): 18-22.

Kehoe, Alice B. The function of ceremonial sexual intercourse among the Northern Plains Indians. Plains Anthropologist, 15 (1970): 99-103.

Kennard, E. Mandan grammar. International Journal of American Linguistics, 9, no. 1 (1936): 1-43.

Kessel, Ralph. A structural analysis of a Mandan myth. Plains Anthropologist, 17 (1972): 11-19.

Kipp, J. Mandan. In H. R. Schoolcraft, ed. Information respecting the History, Condition, and Prospects of the Indian Tribes of the United States. Vol. 3. Philadelphia, 1853: 446-459.

Kipp, J. On the accuracy of Catlin's account of the Mandan ceremonies. Smithsonian Institution, Annual Reports of the Board of Regents (1872): 436-438.

Kruse, H. A remarkable aerial photograph of a Mandan Village site. Minnesota Archaeologist, 8 (1942): 80-81.

Lévi-Strauss, Claude. Rapports de symétrie entre rites et mythes de peuples voisins. In Thomas O. Beidelman, ed. The Translation of Culture. London, Tavistock, 1971: 161-178.

Lewis, M. and W. Clark. Travels. London, 1815. 3 v.

Libby, O. G. Typical villages of the Mandans, Arikara, and Hidatsa. North Dakota, State Historical Society, Collections, 2 (1908): 498-508.

Lowie, R. H. Societies of the Hidatsa and Mandan Indians. American Museum of Natural History, Anthropological Papers, 11 (1913): 294-358.

Lowie, R. H. Some problems in the ethnology of the Crow and village Indians. American Anthropologist, n.s., 14 (1912): 60-71.

Lowie, Robert H. Notes on the social organization and customs of the Mandan, Hidatsa, and Crow Indians. New York,

1917. 1-99 p. (American Museum of Natural History, Anthropological Papers, 21, pt. 1)

Matthews, W. The Catlin collection of Indian paintings. United States National Museum, Reports (1890): 593-610.

Matthews, W. Two Mandan chiefs. American Antiquarian and Oriental Journal, 10 (1888): 269-272.

McGee, W J. The Siouan Indians. U.S. Bureau of American Ethnology, Annual Reports, 15 (1894): 157-204.

Metcalf, George. Small sites on and about Fort Berthold Indian Reservation, Garrison Reservoir, North Dakota. Washington, D.C., Government Printing Office, 1963. 1-56 p. illus., map. (U.S., Bureau of American Ethnology, River Basin Surveys Papers, 26. U.S., Bureau of American Ethnology, Bulletin, 185)

Morgan, L. H. Systems of consanguinity and affinity. Smithsonian Contributions to Knowledge, 17 (1871): 291-382.

Morgan, L. H. The Indian journals, 1859-62: p. 169. Ann Arbor, 1959.

Morice, A. G. Disparus et survivants. Société de Géographie (Québec), Bulletin, 21 (1927): 11-49.

Mulloy, W. The Northern Plains. In J. B. Griffin, ed. Archeology of Eastern United States. Chicago, 1952: 124-138.

Nasatir, A. P. Before Lewis and Clark. St. Louis, 1952. 2 v. (882 p.).

Neill, E. D. Life among the Mandans eighty years ago. American Antiquarian and Oriental Journal, 6 (1884): 248-253, 377-384.

Neuman, Robert W. Check-stamped pottery on the northern and central Great Plains. American Antiquity, 29 (1963/1964): 17-26.

Newman, M. T. The blond Mandan. Southwestern Journal of Anthropology, 6 (1950): 255-272.

Nichols, Roger L. Martin Cantonment and American expansion in the Missouri Valley. Missouri Historical Review, 64 (1969/1970): 1-17.

Parker, John. The fur trader and the emerging geography of North America. Museum of the Fur Trade Quarterly, 2, no. 3 (1966): 6-10; 2, no. 4 (1966): 7-11.

Powell, W. Mandan village visited by Verendrye in 1738. Minnesota Archaeologist, 2, no. 10 (1936): 4-6.

Preuss, K. T. Das Frühlingsfest im alten Mexiko und bei den Mandan Indianern. In Donum Natalicium Schrijnen. Nijmegen-Utrecht, 1929: 825-837.

Read, Catherine E. Predicting acculturative behavior of the Mandan, Hidatsa, and Arickara Indians. Anthropology UCLA, 2, no. 2 (1970): 1-5.

Reid, R. The earth lodge. North Dakota Historical Quarterly, 4 (1930): 174-185.

Reid, Russell. Verendrye's journal to North Dakota in 1738. North Dakota History, 32 (1965): 117-129.

Riggs, S. R. Dakota grammar, texts and ethnography. Contributions to North American Ethnology, 9 (1893): xviii-xxix.

Romney, A. K. and D. Metzger. On the processes of change in kinship terminology [with rejoinder by E. M. Bruner]. American Anthropologist, 58 (1956): 551-556.

Simpson, R. de E. A Mandan bull-boat. Masterkey, 23 (1949): 174-175.

Smith, C. S. An analysis of the firearms and related specimens from Like-A-Fishhook village and Fort Berthold I. Plains Anthropologist, 4 (1955): 3-12.

Smith, Marian. Mandan "history" as reflected in Bufferfly's winter count. Ethnohistory, 7 (1960): 199-205.

Soulen, H. A resume of bone materials found in our Mandan site exploratory trip. Minnesota Archaeologist, 6 (1940): 82-87.

Steele, James P., et al. Paleopathology in the Dakotas. South Dakota Journal of Medicine, 18, no. 10 (1965): 17-29.

Steinbreuck, E. R. Indian fireplaces and pots. Archaeological Bulletin, 3 (1912): 22-23.

Stockman, Wallace Henry. Historical perspectives of federal educational promises and performance among the Fort Berthold Indians. Dissertation Abstracts International, 33 (1972/1973): 1475A-1476A. UM 72-25,221.

Strong, W. D. An unusual side-bladed knife from a proto-historic Mandan site. American Antiquity, 11 (1945): 60-61.

Taylor, Colin. Early Plains Indian quill
   techniques in European museum
   collections. Plains Anthropologist, 7
   (1962): 58-69.

Thompson, David. David Thompson's
   narrative 1784-1812. Edited by Richard
   Glover. Toronto, 1962. 102, 410 p.
   map. (Champlain Society, Publications,
   40)

Thompson, Ralph Stanton. The final story
   of the Deapolis Mandan Indian village
   site. North Dakota History, 28 (1961):
   143-153.

Tyrrell, J. B., ed. David Thompson's
   narrative of his explorations in western
   America. Champlain Society,
   Publications, 12 (1916): 225-237.

Vérendrye, P. G. La Verendrye's journal.
   Minnesota Archaeologist, 2, no. 10
   (1936): 7-10.

Wedel, W. R. Observations on some
   nineteenth-century pottery vessels from
   the Upper Missouri. U.S. Bureau of
   American Ethnology, Bulletin, 164
   (1957): 87-114.

Whitehouse, Joseph. The journal of
   Private Joseph Whitehouse, a soldier
   with Lewis and Clark. Edited by Paul
   Russell Cutright. Missouri Historical
   Society, Bulletin, 28 (1971/1972): 143-
   161.

Wied-Neuwied, M. zu. Reise in das innere
   Nordamerika. Coblenz, 1839-1841. 2 v.

Wied-Neuwied, M. zu. Travels in the
   interior of North America. Early Western
   Travels, 22 (1906): 345-351; 23 (1906):
   252-366; 24 (1906): 39-53, 73-75, 234-
   261.

Will, G. F. Archaeology of the Missouri
   Valley. American Museum of Natural
   History, Anthropological Papers, 22
   (1924): 285-344.

Will, G. F. No-Tongue, a Mandan tale.
   Journal of American Folklore, 26 (1913):
   331-337; 29 (1916): 402-406.

Will, G. F. The Bourgeois village site.
   American Anthropologist, 12 (1910): 473-
   476.

Will, G. F. The Mandan lodge at Bismarck.
   North Dakota Historical Quarterly, 5
   (1930): 38-48.

Will, G. F. and G. E. Hyde. Corn among
   the Indians of the Upper Missouri. St.
   Louis, 1917. 317 p.

*Will, G. F. and H. J. Spinden. The
   Mandans. Harvard University, Peabody
   Museum of American Archaeology and
   Ethnology, Papers, 3 (1906): 81-219.

Wood, W. Raymond. A stylistic and
   historical analysis of shoulder patterns
   on Plains Indian pottery. American
   Antiquity, 28 (1962/1963): 25-40.

Wood, W. Raymond. An interpretation of
   Mandan culture history. Washington,
   D.C., Government Printing Office, 1967.
   14, 232 p. illus., maps. (U.S., Bureau
   of American Ethnology, River Basin
   Surveys Papers, 39. U.S., Bureau of
   American Ethnology, Bulletin, 198)

Wood, W. Raymond. An interpretation of
   Mandan culture history. Dissertation
   Abstracts, 22 (1961/1962): 1349-1350.
   UM 61-4521.

Wood, W. Raymond. Mandan culture history.
   Plains Anthropologist, 7 (1962): 93-94.

Woolworth, Alan R. Excavations at Kipp's
   Post. By Alan R. Woolworth and W.
   Raymond Wood. North Dakota History, 29
   (1962): 237-252.

Woolworth, Alan R. The archeology of a
   small trading post (Kipp's Post, 32MN1)
   in the Garrison Reservoir, North Dakota.
   By Alan R. Woolworth and W. Raymond
   Wood. Washington, D.C., Government
   Printing Office, 1960. 239-306 p.
   illus., map. (U.S., Bureau of American
   Ethnology, River Basin Surveys Papers,
   20. U.S., Bureau of American Ethnology,
   Bulletin, 176)

09-16 Missouri

Bannon, John F. Missouri, a borderland.
   Missouri Historical Review, 63
   (1968/1969): 227-240.

Berry, J. B. The Missouri Indians.
   Southwestern Social Science Quarterly,
   17 (1936): 113-124.

Bray, Robert T. The Missouri Indian tribe
   in archaeology and history. Missouri
   Historical Review, 55 (1960/1961): 213-
   225.

Bray, Robert T. University of Missouri
   field school at Van Meter Park. Plains
   Anthropologist, 6 (1961): 64-65.

Briggs, John Ely. Omaha, Oto and
   Missouri. Palimpsest, 50 (1969): 219-
   221.

Bushnell, D. I. Burials of the
   Algonquian, Siouan and Caddoan tribes.

U.S. Bureau of American Ethnology, Bulletin, 33 (1927): 63-65.

Chapman, Berlin B. The Barnes family of Barneston. Nebraska History, 47 (1966): 57-83.

Chapman, Berlin B. The Otoes and Missourias; a study of Indian removal and the legal aftermath. Oklahoma City, Times Journal, 1965. 18, 405 p. illus.

Chapman, C. H. Culture sequence in the Lower Missouri Valley. In J. B. Griffin, ed. Archeology of Eastern United States. Chicago, 1952: 139-151.

Chapman, Carl H. Digging up Missouri's past. Missouri Historical Review, 66 (1966/1967): 348-363.

Chapman, Carl H. Indians and archaeology of Missouri. By Carl H. Chapman and Eleanor F. Chapman. Columbia, University of Missouri Press, 1964. 161 p. illus., maps. (Missouri Handbook, 6)

Chapman, Carl H. The Little Osage and Missouri Indian village sites ca. 1727-1777 A.D. Missouri Archaeologist, 21, no. 1 (1959): 1-67.

Chapman, Carl Haley. The origin of the Osage Indian tribe: an ethnographical, historical and archaeological study. Dissertation Abstracts, 20 (1959/1960): 1525. UM 59-4894.

Dorsey, J. O. and C. Thomas. Missouri. U.S. Bureau of American Ethnology, Bulletin, 30, vol. 1 (1907): 911-912.

Fay, George E., ed. Treaties, and land cessions, between the bands of the Sioux and the United States of America, 1805-1906. Greeley, 1972. 7, 139 l. (University of Northern Colorado, Museum of Anthropology, Occasional Publications in Anthropology, Ethnology Series, 24)

Floyd, Charles. Sergeant Floyd's journal. Edited by William J. Petersen. Palimpsest, 45 (1964): 130-144.

Foreman, G. The last trek of the Indians, 258-262. Chicago, 1946.

Grinnell, George B. Pawnee, Blackfoot, and Cheyenne: history and folklore of the Plains. New York, Scribner, 1961. 301 p.

Holtz, Milton E. Early settlement and public land disposal in the Elkhorn River Valley, Cuming County, Nebraska Territory. Nebraska History, 52 (1971): 113-132.

M. H. W. Chief Moses George Harragarra, last medal chief of the Oto and Missouri tribe. Chronicles of Oklahoma, 45 (1967): 220-222.

McGee, W J. The Siouan Indians. U.S. Bureau of American Ethnology, Annual Reports, 15 (1894): 157-204.

Nasatir, A. P. Before Lewis and Clark. St. Louis, 1952. 2 v. (882 p.).

Petersen, William J. Lewis and Clark expedition. Palimpsest, 45 (1964): 108-129.

Sibley, George C. George C. Sibley's journal of a trip to the Salines in 1811. Edited by George R. Brooks. Missouri Historical Society, Bulletin, 21 (1964/1965): 167-207.

Vincent, John R. Midwest Indians and frontier photography. Annals of Iowa, 38 (1965): 26-35.

Vogel, Virgil J. The origin and meaning of "Missouri". Missouri Historical Society, Bulletin, 16 (1959/1960): 213-222.

Zoltvany, Yves F. New France and the West, 1701-1713. Canadian Historical Review, 46 (1965): 301-322.

09-17   Omaha

Anonymous. Indians are helping themselves. Boletín Indigenista, 19 (1959): 99, 101, 103.

Anonymous. South Dakota physical types. South Dakota, University, William H. Over Museum, Museum News, 12, no. 5 (1952): 1.

Anonymous. The Omaha Tribe proyects [sic!]. Boletín Indigenista, 20 (1960): 31, 33.

Arth, M. J. A functional view of peyotism in Omaha culture. Plains Anthropologist, 7 (1956): 25-29.

Audubon, John James. Barging down from Fort Union. Edited by William J. Petersen. Palimpsest, 52 (1971): 571-583.

Audubon, John James. Birds along the Missouri. Edited by William J. Petersen. Palimpsest, 52 (1971): 550-570.

Becker, David A. Enteric parasites of Indians and Anglo-Americans, chiefly on the Winnebago and Omaha Reservations in Nebraska. Nebraska State Medical

Journal, 53 (1968): 293-296, 347-349,
380-383, 421-423.

Berg, David E. Association between serum
and secretory immunoglobins and chronic
otitis media in Indian children. By
David E. Berg, Arden E. Larsen, and C.
T. Yarington, Jr. Annals of Otology,
Rhinology and Laryngology, 80 (1971):
766-772.

Bibaud, F. M. Biographie des sagamos
illustrés de l'Amérique Septentrionale,
271-274. Montreal, 1848.

Boas, F. Zur Anthropologie der
nordamerikanischen Indianer. Berliner
Gesellschaft für Anthropologie,
Ethnologie und Urgeschichte,
Verhandlungen (1895): 367-411.

Briggs, John Ely. Omaha, Oto and
Missouri. Palimpsest, 50 (1969): 219-
221.

Brown, C. Omaha arrowmakers. Wisconsin
Archeologist, 10 (1911): 123-124.

Bushnell, D. I. Burials of the
Algonquian, Siouan and Caddoan tribes.
U.S. Bureau of American Ethnology,
Bulletin, 83 (1927): 50-52.

Bushnell, D. I. Villages of the
Algonquian, Siouan, and Caddoan tribes.
U.S. Bureau of American Ethnology,
Bulletin, 77 (1922): 77-87.

Conway, William David. A transformational
analysis of the written and oral syntax
of fourth, sixth, and eighth grade Omaha
Indian children. Dissertation Abstracts
International, 32 (1971/1972): 3975A-
3976A. UM 72-3948.

Densmore, F. The survival of Omaha songs.
American Anthropologist, n.s., 46
(1944): 418-420.

Dorsey, J. O. A study of Siouan cults.
U.S. Bureau of American Ethnology,
Annual Reports, 11 (1890): 361-422.

Dorsey, J. O. Abstracts of Omaha and
Ponka myths. Journal of American
Folklore, 1 (1888): 74-78, 204-208.

Dorsey, J. O. How the rabbit caught the
sun in a trap. U.S. Bureau of American
Ethnology, Annual Reports, 1 (1880):
581-583.

Dorsey, J. O. How the rabbit killed the
(male) winter. American Antiquarian and
Oriental Journal, 2 (1879): 128-132.

Dorsey, J. O. Indian personal names.
American Association for the Advancement

of Science, Proceedings, 34 (1886): 393-
399.

Dorsey, J. O. Omaha and Ponca letters.
U.S. Bureau of American Ethnology,
Bulletin, 11 (1891): 1-123.

Dorsey, J. O. Omaha clothing and personal
ornaments. American Anthropologist, 3
(1890): 71-78.

Dorsey, J. O. Omaha dwellings, furniture,
and implements. U.S. Bureau of American
Ethnology, Annual Reports, 13 (1892):
263-288.

Dorsey, J. O. Omaha folk-lore notes.
Journal of American Folklore, 1 (1888):
213-214; 2 (1889): 190.

*Dorsey, J. O. Omaha sociology. U.S.
Bureau of American Ethnology, Annual
Reports, 3 (1882): 205-370.

Dorsey, J. O. Omaha songs. Journal of
American Folklore, 1 (1888): 209-213.

Dorsey, J. O. On the gentile system of
the Omahas. American Antiquarian and
Oriental Journal, 5 (1883): 312-318.

Dorsey, J. O. Ponka and Omaha songs.
Journal of American Folklore, 2 (1889):
271-276.

Dorsey, J. O. Preface. Contributions to
North American Ethnology, 9 (1893):
xviii-xxx.

Dorsey, J. O. Siouan folk-lore and
mythologic notes. American Antiquarian
and Oriental Journal, 6 (1884): 174-176;
7 (1885): 105-108.

Dorsey, J. O. The religion of the Omahas
and Ponkas. American Antiquarian and
Oriental Journal, 5 (1883): 271-275.

Dorsey, J. O. The social organization of
the Siouan tribes. Journal of American
Folklore, 4 (1891): 264-266.

Dorsey, J. O. The young chief and the
thunders. American Antiquarian and
Oriental Journal, 3 (1883): 303-307.

Dorsey, J. O. and C. Thomas. Omaha. U.S.
Bureau of American Ethnology, Bulletin,
30, vol. 2 (1910): 119-121.

*Dorsey, James O. Omaha sociology. New
York, Johnson Reprint, 1970. 205-370,
595-606 p. illus., map.

Dorsey, James Owen. Songs of the Heḍucka
Society. Journal of American Folk-Lore,
1 (1888): 65-68.

Dorsey, James Owen. The Çegiha language. Washington, D.C., Government Printing Office, 1890. 18, 794 p. (Contributions to North American Ethnology, 6)

Dorsey, James Owen. The orphan and the buffalo woman. Anthropological Society of Washington, Transactions, 1 (1879/1882): 69.

Dorsey, James Owen. The young chief and the thunders. Anthropological Society of Washington, Transactions, 1 (1879/1882): 52-55.

Ewers, John C. Bodily proportions as guides to lineal measurements among the Blackfoot Indians. American Anthropologist, 72 (1970): 561-562.

Fay, George E., ed. Treaties, and land cessions, between the bands of the Sioux and the United States of America, 1805-1906. Greeley, 1972. 7, 139 l. (University of Northern Colorado, Museum of Anthropology, Occasional Publications in Anthropology, Ethnology Series, 24)

Fletcher, A. C. A study from the Omaha tribe: the import of the totem. Smithsonian Institution, Annual Reports of the Board of Regents (1897): 577-586.

Fletcher, A. C. A study from the Omaha tribe: the import of the totem. American Association for the Advancement of Science, Proceedings, 46 (1897): 325-334.

Fletcher, A. C. Glimpses of child-life among the Omaha tribe of Indians. Journal of American Folklore, 1 (1888): 115-123.

Fletcher, A. C. Hae-thu-ska society of the Omaha tribe. Journal of American Folklore, 5 (1892): 135-144.

Fletcher, A. C. Häusliches Leben bei den Indianern. Globus, 73 (1898): 252-259.

Fletcher, A. C. Historical sketch of the Omaha tribe. Washington, D.C., 1885. 12 p.

Fletcher, A. C. Home life among the Indians. Century Magazine, 54 (1897): 252-263.

Fletcher, A. C. Indian story and song from North America. Boston, 1900. 126 p.

Fletcher, A. C. Lands in severalty to Indians. American Association for the Advancement of Science, Proceedings, 33 (1884): 654-665.

Fletcher, A. C. Leaves from my Omaha note-book: courtship and marriage. Journal of American Folklore, 2 (1889): 219-226.

Fletcher, A. C. Love songs among the Omaha Indians. International Congress of Anthropology, Memoirs (1893): 153-157.

Fletcher, A. C. Nature and the Indian tribe. Art and Archaeology, 4 (1916): 291-296.

Fletcher, A. C. Observations on the laws and privileges of the gens in Indian society. American Association for the Advancement of Science, Proceedings, 32 (1883): 395-396.

Fletcher, A. C. Observations on the usage, symbolism and influence of the sacred pipes of fellowship among the Omahas. American Association for the Advancement of Science, Proceedings, 33 (1884): 615-617.

Fletcher, A. C. The child and the tribe. National Academy of Sciences, Proceedings, 1 (1915): 569-574.

Fletcher, A. C. The emblematic use of the tree in the Dakotan group. Science, n.s., 4 (1896): 475-487.

Fletcher, A. C. The emblematic use of the tree in the Dakotan group. American Association for the Advancement of Science, Proceedings, 45 (1896): 191-209.

Fletcher, A. C. The Indian and nature. National Academy of Sciences, Proceedings, 1 (1915): 467-473.

Fletcher, A. C. The "lazy man" in Indian lore. Journal of American Folklore, 14 (1901): 100-104.

Fletcher, A. C. The sacred pole of the Omaha tribe. American Antiquarian and Oriental Journal, 17 (1895): 257-268.

Fletcher, A. C. The sacred pole of the Omaha tribe. American Association for the Advancement of Science, Proceedings, 44 (1895): 270-280.

Fletcher, A. C. The significance of the scalp-lock. Royal Anthropological Institute of Great Britain and Ireland, Journal, 27 (1897): 436-450.

Fletcher, A. C. The "wawan," or pipe dance of the Omahas. Harvard University, Peabody Museum of American Archaeology and Ethnology, Reports, 16/17 (1883): 308-333.

Fletcher, A. C.   Tribal life among the Omahas. Century Magazine, 51 (1896): 450-457.

Fletcher, A. C.   Tribal structure. In Putnam Anniversary Volume. New York, 1909: 252-267.

Fletcher, A. C.   Wakondagi. American Anthropologist, n.s., 14 (1912): 106-108.

Fletcher, A. C. and F. La Flesche.   A study of Omaha Indian music. Harvard University, Peabody Museum of American Archaeology and Ethnology, Papers, 1, no. 5 (1893): 1-152.

*Fletcher, A. C. and F. La Flesche.   The Omaha tribe. U.S. Bureau of American Ethnology, Annual Reports, 27 (1906): 17-654.

Fletcher, Alice C.   An Indian boy's initiation into manhood in the Omaha tribe. By Alice C. Fletcher and Francis La Flesche. In Francis Lee Utley, et al., eds. Bear, Man and God. New York, Random House, 1964: 193-196.

*Fletcher, Alice C.   The Omaha tribe. By Alice C. Fletcher and Francis La Flesche. Lincoln, University of Nebraska Press, 1972. 2 v. (660 p.) illus.

*Fletcher, Alice C.   The Omaha tribe. By Alice C. Fletcher and Francis La Flesche. New York, Johnson Reprint, 1970. 17-672 p. illus., maps.

Fontenelle, H.   History of the Omaha Indians. Nebraska State Historical Society, Transactions and Reports, 1 (1885): 76-83.

Fortune, R. F.   Omaha secret societies. Columbia University Contributions to Anthropology, 14 (1932): 1-193.

Fortune, Reo F.   Omaha secret societies. New York, AMS Press, 1969. 6, 193 p. illus.

Giffen, F. R.   Oo-mah-ha Ta-wa-tha (Omaha City). Lincoln, 1898. 94 p.

Gilmore, M. R.   A study in the ethnobotany of the Omaha Indians. Nebraska State Historical Society, Collections, 17 (1913): 314-357.

Gilmore, M. R.   Indian tribal boundary-lines and monuments. Indian Notes, 5 (1928): 59-63.

Gilmore, M. R.   Methods of Indian buffalo hunts. Michigan Academy of Science, Arts and Letters, Papers, 16 (1931): 17-32.

Gilmore, M. R.   Teokanha's sacred bundle. Indian Notes, 1 (1924): 52-62.

Gilmore, M. R.   The Mescal Society among the Omaha Indians. Nebraska State Historical Society, Publications, 19 (1919): 163-167.

Gilmore, M. R.   Uses of plants by the Indians of the Missouri River region. U.S. Bureau of American Ethnology, Annual Reports, 33 (1912): 43-154.

Graebner, Norman A.   Nebraska's Missouri River frontier, 1854-1860. Nebraska History, 42 (1961): 213-235.

Green, Norma Kidd.   Four sisters: daughters of Joseph La Flesche. Nebraska History, 45 (1964): 165-176.

Green, Norma Kidd.   Iron Eye's family: the children of Joseph La Flesche. Lincoln, Johnsen Publishing, 1969. 15, 225 p. illus.

Green, Norma Kidd.   The Presbyterian Mission to the Omaha Indian tribe. Nebraska History, 48 (1967): 267-288.

Gunnerson, Dolores A.   An unusual method of flint chipping. Plains Anthropologist, 14 (1969): 71-72.

Hayden, F. V.   Brief notes on the Pawnee, Winnebago, and Omaha languages. American Philosophical Society, Proceedings, 10 (1868): 406-411.

Hayden, F. V.   Contributions to the ethnography and philology of the Indian tribes of the Missouri Valley. American Philosophical Society, Transactions, n.s., 12 (1863): 444-452.

Holmer, N. M.   Sonant-surds in Ponca-Omaha. International Journal of American Linguistics, 11 (1945): 75-85.

Holtz, Milton E.   Early settlement and public land disposal in the Elkhorn River Valley, Cuming County, Nebraska Territory. Nebraska History, 52 (1971): 113-132.

Howard, J. H.   An Oto-Omaha peyote ritual. Southwestern Journal of Anthropology, 12 (1956): 432-436.

Howard, James H.   An Omaha dancing ornament. South Dakota, University, Museum, Museum News, 12, no. 1 (1950): 1-2.

Howard, James H.   An Omaha medicine packet. Plains Archeological Conference, News Letter, 5, no. 4 (1953): 55-57.

Howard, James H. Notes on the Omaha
Peyote Cult. South Dakota, University,
Museum, Museum News (Apr. 1950): 1-3.

Howard, James H. The Omaha hand game and
gourd dance. Plains Archeological
Conference, News Letter, 3, no. 3
(1950): 3-6.

Jackson, Donald. Journey to the Mandans,
1809; the lost narrative of Dr. Thomas.
Missouri Historical Society Bulletin, 20
(1963/1964): 179-192.

James, E. Account of an expedition from
Pittsburgh to the Rocky Mountains. Early
Western Travels, 14 (1905): 288-321; 15
(1905): 11-130; 17 (1905): 290-298.

James, Edwin. Account of an expedition
from Pittsburgh to the Rocky Mountains.
Ann Arbor, University Microfilms, 1966.
2 v. illus., maps.

Kercheval, G. T. An Otoe and an Omaha
tale. Journal of American Folklore, 6
(1893): 199-204.

Kobelt, W. Das Volk der Omaha. Globus, 1
(1886): 347-351.

Kuttner, Robert E. Alcohol and addiction
in urbanized Sioux Indians. By Robert E.
Kuttner and Albert B. Lorincz. Mental
Hygiene, 51 (1967): 530-542.

Kuttner, Robert E. Promiscuity and
prostitution in urbanized Indian
communities. By Robert E. Kuttner and
Albert B. Lorincz. Mental Hygiene, 54
(1970): 79-91.

La Flesche, F. Death and funeral customs
among the Omahas. Journal of American
Folklore, 2 (1889): 3-11.

La Flesche, F. Omaha and Osage traditions
of separation. International Congress of
Americanists, Proceedings, 19 (1915):
459-462.

La Flesche, F. Omaha bow and arrow
makers. Smithsonian Institution, Annual
Reports of the Board of Regents (1926):
487-494.

La Flesche, F. Omaha bow and arrowmakers. International Congress of
Americanists, Proceedings, 20, vol. 1
(1922): 111-116.

La Flesche, F. The Omaha buffalo
medicine-men. Journal of American
Folklore, 3 (1890): 215-221.

La Flesche, F. The sacred pipes of
friendship. American Association for the
Advancement of Science, Proceedings, 33
(1884): 613-615.

La Flesche, F. Who was the medicine man?
Fairmount Park Art Association, Annual
Report, 32 (1904): 3-13.

La Flesche, Francis. The Middle Five;
Indian schoolboys of the Omaha Tribe.
Madison, University of Wisconsin Press,
1963. 152 p. illus.

Lehmer, Donald J. The Plains bison hunt--
prehistoric and historic. Plains
Anthropologist, 8 (1963): 211-217.

Lowie, R. H. The Omaha and Crow kinship
terminologies. International Congress of
Americanists, Proceedings, 24 (1934):
102-108.

Lurie, Nancy Oestreich. The lady from
Boston and the Omaha Indians. American
West, 3, no. 4 (1966): 31-33, 80-85.

Matson, G. A. Distribution of blood
groups among the Sioux, Omaha, and
Winnebago Indians. American Journal of
Physical Anthropology, 28 (1941): 313-
318.

McGee, W J. The Siouan Indians. U.S.
Bureau of American Ethnology, Annual
Reports, 15 (1894): 157-204.

McGinty, Idie. Omaha Indian child rearing
and culture change. Nebraska Academy of
Science, Proceedings, 80 (1970): 7.

Mead, M. The changing culture of an
Indian tribe. Columbia University
Contributions to Anthropology, 15
(1932): 1-313.

Mead, Margaret. The changing culture of
an Indian tribe. New York, AMS Press,
1969. 14, 313 p.

Mead, Margaret. The changing culture of
an Indian tribe. New York, Capricorn
Books, 1966. 23, 313 p.

Morgan, L. H. Systems of consanguinity
and affinity. Smithsonian Contributions
to Knowledge, 17 (1871): 291-382.

Morgan, L. H. The Indian Journals, 1859-
62, p. 66, 87-92, 138. Ann Arbor, 1959.

Myer, W. E. Archeological field-work in
South Dakota and Missouri. Smithsonian
Miscellaneous Collections, 72, no. 15
(1922): 117-125.

Nasatir, A. P. Before Lewis and Clark.
St. Louis, 1952. 2 v. (882 p.).

Nebraska Writers' Project. Indian place
legends. Nebraska Folklore Pamphlets, 2
(1937): 1-15.

Neuman, Robert W.   Another tipi ring
reference. Plains Anthropologist, 7
(1962): 269-270.

Omaha Tribe of Indians.   Code of laws.
Omaha, 1860.   4 p.

Riggs, S. R. Dakota grammar, texts and
ethnography. Contributions to North
American Ethnology, 9 (1893): xviii-
xxix.

Ross, Donald David.   The Omaha people.
Indian Historian, 3, no. 3 (1970): 19-
22.

Schmidt, W.   Die Omaha und die Ponca. In
his Die Ursprung der Göttesidee. Bd. 2.
Münster i. W., 1929: 657-658.

Swanson, Guy E. Rules of descent: studies
in the sociology of parentage. Ann
Arbor, University of Michigan, 1969.   5,
108 p. (Michigan, University, Museum of
Anthropology, Anthropological Papers,
39)

Vincent, John R.   Midwest Indians and
frontier photography. Annals of Iowa, 38
(1965): 26-35.

Wardle, H. N.   Indian gifts in relation to
primitive law. International Congress of
Americanists, Proceedings, 23 (1928):
463-469.

Will, G. F. and G. E. Hyde.   Corn among
the Indians of the Upper Missouri. St.
Louis, 1917.   317 p.

09-18 Osage

Anonymous. Extracts from the diary of
Major Sibley. Chronicles of Oklahoma, 5
(1927): 196-218.

Anonymous.   Senor Don Manuel Lisa.
Missouri Historical Society, Bulletin,
23 (1966/1967): 52-58.

Anonymous.   The Lord's Prayer in Osage.
American Indian, 3, no. 12 (1929): 4.

Ashcraft, Allan C.   Confederate Indian
Department conditions in August, 1864.
Chronicles of Oklahoma, 41 (1963): 270-
285.

Ashley-Montagu, M. F.   An Indian tradition
relating to the mastodon. American
Anthropologist, 46 (1944): 569-571.

Atherton, Lewis E.   Missouri's society and
economy in 1821. Missouri Historical
Review, 65 (1970/1971): 450-477.

Bailey, Garrick A.   The Osage roll: an
analysis. Indian Historian, 5, no. 1
(1972): 26-29.

Bailey, Garrick Alan.   Changes in Osage
social organization: 1673-1969.
Dissertation Abstracts International, 31
(1970/1971): 3812B.   UM 71-1292.

Baird, Donald.   Some eighteenth century
gun barrels from Osage village sites.
Great Plains Journal, 4 (1964/1965): 49-
62.

Baird, W. David.   Fort Smith and the Red
Man. Arkansas Historical Quarterly, 30
(1971): 337-348.

Barney, R. A.   Laws relating to Osage
Tribe of Indians.   Pawhuska, 1929.
112 p.

Bearss, Edwin C.   In quest of peace on the
Indian border: the establishment of Fort
Smith. Arkansas Historical Quarterly, 23
(1964): 123-153.

Bearss, Edwin C.   The Arkansas whiskey
war: a Fort Smith case study. Journal of
the West, 7 (1968): 143-172.

Berry, B., C. Chapman, and J. Mack.
Archaeological remains of the Osage.
American Antiquity, 10 (1944): 1-12.

Boas, F. Zur Anthropologie der
nordamerikanischen Indianer. Berliner
Gesellschaft für Anthropologie,
Ethnologie und Urgeschichte,
Verhandlungen (1895): 367-411.

Bradbury, J. Travels in the interior of
America. Early Western Travels, 5
(1904): 1-320.

Bradbury, John.   Travels in the interior
of America. Ann Arbor, University
Microfilms, 1966.   12, 364 p.

Burbank, E. A. and E. Royce.   Burbank
among the Indians, 197-200. Caldwell,
1946.

Burchardt, Bill.   Osage oil. Chronicles of
Oklahoma, 41 (1963): 253-269.

Burrill, Robert M.   The establishment of
ranching on the Osage Indian
Reservation. Geographical Review, 62
(1972): 524-543.

Busby, Orel.   Buffalo Valley: an Osage
hunting ground. Chronicles of Oklahoma,
40 (1962): 22-35.

Bushnell, D. I.   Burials of the
Algonquian, Siouan and Caddoan tribes.
U.S. Bureau of American Ethnology,
Bulletin, 83 (1927): 55-60.

Bushnell, D. I. Villages of the Algonquian, Siouan, and Caddoan tribes. U.S. Bureau of American Ethnology, Bulletin, 77 (1922): 98-108.

Chapman, B. B. Dissolution of the Osage Reservation. Chronicles of Oklahoma, 20 (1942): 244-254, 375-386; 21 (1943): 78-87, 171-182.

Chapman, B. B. Removal of the Osages from Kansas. Kansas Historical Quarterly, 7 (1938): 287-305.

Chapman, C. H. Culture sequence in the Lower Missouri Valley. In J. B. Griffin, ed. Archeology of Eastern United States. Chicago, 1952; 139-151.

Chapman, Carl H. Continued excavations on the Little Osage Indian Village Site in the Kaysinger Bluff Reservoir area. Plains Anthropologist, 10 (1965): 51.

Chapman, Carl H. Digging up Missouri's past. Missouri Historical Review, 66 (1966/1967): 348-363.

Chapman, Carl H. Indians and archaeology of Missouri. By Carl H. Chapman and Eleanor F. Chapman. Columbia, University of Missouri Press, 1964. 161 p. illus., maps. (Missouri Handbook, 6)

Chapman, Carl H. Osage prehistory. Plains Anthropologist, 7 (1962): 99-100.

Chapman, Carl H. The Little Osage and Missouri Indian village sites ca. 1727-1777 A.D. Missouri Archaeologist, 21, no. 1 (1959): 1-67.

Chapman, Carl Haley. The origin of the Osage Indian tribe: an ethnographical, historical and archaeological study. Dissertation Abstracts, 20 (1959/1960): 1525. UM 59-4894.

Chase, Charles Monroe. An editor looks at early-day Kansas; the letters of Charles Monroe Chase. Edited by Lela Barnes. Kansas Historical Quarterly, 26 (1960): 118-151.

Christianson, James R. A study of Osage history prior to 1876. Dissertation Abstracts International, 30 (1969/1970): 639A. UM 69-11,202.

Connelley, W. E. Notes on the early Indian occupancy of the Great Plains. Kansas State Historical Society, Collections, 14 (1918): 438-470.

Corbitt, D. C., tr. and ed. Papers from the Spanish archives relating to Tennessee and the Old Southwest. Translated and edited by D. C. Corbitt

and Roberta Corbitt. East Tennessee Historical Society, Publications, 31 (1959): 63-82; 32 (1960): 72-93; 33 (1961): 61-78; 34 (1962): 86-105; 35 (1963): 85-95; 36 (1964): 70-80; 37 (1965): 89-105; 38 (1966): 70-82; 39 (1967): 87-102; 40 (1968): 101-118; 41 (1969): 100-116; 42 (1970): 96-107; 43 (1971): 94-111; 44 (1972): 104-113.

Cutler, J. A topographical description of the State of Ohio, Indiana Territory, and Louisiana, 115-120. Boston, 1812.

DeRosier, Arthur H., Jr. William Dunbar, explorer. Journal of Mississippi History, 25 (1963): 165-185.

Dickerson, P. J. History of the Osage nation. 1906. 144 p.

Dodge, Henry. Journal of Colonel Dodge's expedition from Fort Gibson to the Pawnee Pict village. American State Papers, Military Affairs, 5 (1860): 373-382.

Donaldson, T. The George Catlin Indian Gallery. United States National Museum, Reports (1885): 42-46.

Dorsey, G. A. The Osage mourning-war ceremony. American Anthropologist, n.s., 4 (1902): 404-411.

Dorsey, G. A. Traditions of the Osage. Field Museum, Anthropological Series, 7 (1904): 9-60.

Dorsey, J. O. A study of Siouan cults. U.S. Bureau of American Ethnology, Annual Reports, 11 (1890): 361-422.

Dorsey, J. O. An account of the war customs of the Osages. American Naturalist, 18 (1884): 113-133.

Dorsey, J. O. An Osage secret society. Anthropological Society of Washington, Transactions, 3 (1885): 3-4.

Dorsey, J. O. On the comparative phonology of four Siouan languages. Smithsonian Institution, Annual Reports of the Board of Regents (1883): 919-929.

Dorsey, J. O. Osage traditions. U.S. Bureau of American Ethnology, Annual Reports, 6 (1885): 373-397.

Dorsey, J. O. Preface. Contributions to North American Ethnology, 9 (1893): xviii-xxx.

Dorsey, J. O. Siouan sociology. U.S. Bureau of American Ethnology, Annual Reports, 15 (1894): 233-238.

Dorsey, J. O. The social organization of the Siouan tribes. Journal of American Folklore, 4 (1891): 334-336.

Douglas, F. H. An Osage yarn bag. Denver Art Museum, Material Culture Notes, 7 (1938): 26-30.

Drinnon, Richard. White savage; the case of John Dunn Hunter. New York, Schocken Books, 1972. 19, 282 p. illus.

Fay, George E., ed. Charters, constitutions and by-laws of the Indian tribes of North America. Part V: The Indian tribes of Oklahoma. Greeley, 1968. 14, 104 l. map. (University of Northern Colorado, Museum of Anthropology, Occasional Publications in Anthropology, Ethnology Series, 6) ERIC ED046555.

Finney, F. F. Old Osage customs die with the last Pah-hue-skah. Chronicles of Oklahoma, 36 (1958): 131-136.

Finney, F. F. The Osage Indians and the liquor problem before statehood. Chronicles of Oklahoma, 34 (1956): 456-464.

Finney, Frank F. The Osages and their agency during the term of Isaac T. Gibson, Quaker agent. Chronicles of Oklahoma, 36 (1958/1959): 416-428.

Finney, Frank F., Sr. Marie Tallchief, in history: Oklahoma's own ballerina. Chronicles of Oklahoma, 38 (1960): 8-11.

Finney, Frank F., Sr. Progress in the civilization of the Osage and their government. Chronicles of Oklahoma, 40 (1962): 2-21.

FitzGerald, M. P. Beacon on the Plains. Leavenworth, 1939. 297 p.

Fletcher, A. C. and F. La Flesche. The Omaha tribe. U.S. Bureau of American Ethnology, Annual Reports, 28 (1906): 57-66.

Foreman, G. Indians and pioneers. Rev. ed. Norman, 1936. 285 p.

Foreman, G. The last trek of the Indians, 266-277. Chicago, 1946.

Gabler, Mrs. Ina. Lovely's purchase and Lovely County. Arkansas Historical Quarterly, 19 (1960): 31-39.

Gatschet, A. S. Die Osageindianer. Globus, 83 (1898): 349-355.

Gibson, A. M. An Indian Territory United Nations: the Creek Council of 1845.

Chronicles of Oklahoma, 39 (1961): 398-413.

Goodrich, James W. In the earnest pursuit of wealth: David Waldo in Missouri and the Southwest, 1820-1878. Missouri Historical Review, 66 (1971/1972): 155-184.

Graves, W. W. The First Protestant Osage missions, 1820-1837. Oswego, Kansas, 1949. 272 p.

Gregg, K. L. Westward with dragoons. Fulton, 1937. 97 p.

Hargrett, L. A bibliography of the constitutions and laws of the American Indians, 99-100. Cambridge, 1947.

Harner, J. The village of the Big Osage. Missouri Archaeologist, 5 (1939): 19-20.

Holway, Hope. Union Mission, 1826-1837. Chronicles of Oklahoma, 40 (1962): 355-378.

Howard, James H. Known village sites of the Ponca. Plains Anthropologist, 15 (1970): 109-134.

Howard, James H. The Osage Tribe; divisions and locations, history, and numbers. Kansas City, Mo., 1956. (Kansas City, Museum, Museum Leaflets, 1)

Hunter, J. D. Memoirs of a captivity among the Indians of North America. London, 1823. 447 p.

Irving, Washington. A tour on the prairies. New York, Pantheon Books, 1967. 15, 240 p. illus., map.

Jackson, Donald. A new Lewis and Clark map. Missouri Historical Society, Bulletin, 17 (1960/1961): 117-132.

La Barre, W. A cultist drug addiction in an Indian alcoholic. Menninger Clinic, Bulletin, 5 (1941): 40-46.

La Barre, Weston. The peyote cult. New Haven, Yale University, Department of Anthropology, 1938. 188 p. illus. (Yale University Publications in Anthropology, 19)

La Flesche, F. A dictionary of the Osage language. U.S. Bureau of American Ethnology, Bulletin, 109 (1932): 1-406.

La Flesche, F. Ceremonies and rituals of the Osage. Smithsonian Miscellaneous Collections, 63, no. 8 (1914): 66-69.

La Flesche, F. Ethnology of the Osage Indians. Smithsonian Miscellaneous Collections, 76, no. 10 (1924): 104-107.

La Flesche, F. Omaha and Osage traditions of separation. International Congress of Americanists, Proceedings, 19 (1915): 459-462.

La Flesche, F. Osage marriage customs. American Anthropologist, n.s., 14 (1912): 127-130.

La Flesche, F. Osage songs and rituals. Smithsonian Miscellaneous Collections, 65, no. 6 (1915): 78-81.

La Flesche, F. Osage tribal rites. Smithsonian Miscellaneous Collections, 72, no. 1 (1920): 71-73.

La Flesche, F. Researches among the Osage. Smithsonian Miscellaneous Collections, 70, no. 2 (1919): 110-113.

La Flesche, F. Right and left in Osage ceremonies. In Holmes Anniversary Volume. Washington, D.C., 1916: 278-287.

La Flesche, F. The symbolic man of the Osage tribe. Art and Archaeology, 9 (1920): 68-72.

La Flesche, F. Tribal rites of Osage Indians. Smithsonian Miscellaneous Collections, 68, no. 12 (1918): 84-90.

La Flesche, F. War ceremony and peace ceremony of the Osage Indians. U.S. Bureau of American Ethnology, Bulletin, 101 (1939): 1-280.

La Flesche, F. Work among the Osage Indians. Smithsonian Miscellaneous Collections, 66, no. 17 (1917): 118-121.

La Flesche, Francis. The Osage tribe: rite of the chiefs; sayings of the ancient men. U.S., Bureau of American Ethnology, Annual Report, 35 (1914/1915): 37-604.

La Flesche, Francis. The Osage tribe: rite of the chiefs; sayings of the ancient men. New York, Johnson Reprint, 1970. 604 p. illus.

La Flesche, Francis. The Osage tribe: rite of the Wa-xo'-be. U.S., Bureau of American Ethnology, Annual Report, 45 (1927/1928): 528-833.

La Flesche, Francis. The Osage tribe: the rite of vigil. U.S., Bureau of American Ethnology, Annual Report, 39 (1917/1918): 31-636.

La Flesche, Francis. The Osage tribe: two versions of the child-naming rite. U.S., Bureau of American Ethnology, Annual Report, 43 (1925/1926): 23-164.

Lamb, A. H. The Osage people. Pawhuska, 1930. 31 p.

Lesser, Alexander. Siouan kinship. Dissertation Abstracts, 19 (1958/1959): 208. UM 58-2596.

Littlefield, Daniel F., Jr. The Cherokee Agency Reserve, 1828-1886. By Daniel F. Littlefield, Jr. and Lonnie E. Underhill. Arkansas Historical Review, 31 (1972): 166-180.

MacRitchie, D. A Red Indian coiffure. Man, 17 (1917): 7-9.

Mathews, J. J. Talking to the moon. Chicago, 1945. 243 p.

Mathews, J. J. Wah'kon-tah: the Osage and the White man's road. Norman, 1932. 359 p.

Mathews, John J. The Osages, children of the Middle Waters. Norman, University of Oklahoma Press, 1961. 20, 826 p. illus., maps.

McDermott, J. F., ed. Tixier's travels on the Osage prairies. Norman, 1940. 309 p.

McDermott, John Francis. The Indian as human being. Nebraska History, 52 (1971): 45-49.

McGee, W J. The Siouan Indians. U.S. Bureau of American Ethnology, Annual Reports, 15 (1894): 157-204.

McGimsey, Charles R., III. Indians of Arkansas. Fayetteville, Arkansas Archeological Survey, 1969. 7, 1-47 p. illus., maps. (Arkansas Archeological Survey, Publications on Archeology, Popular Series, 1)

McRill, Leslie A. Ferdinandina: first White settlement in Oklahoma. Chronicles of Oklahoma, 41 (1963): 126-159.

Mead, J. R. The Little Arkansas. Kansas State Historical Society, Transactions, 10 (1908): 7-14.

Miner, Craig. The struggle for an East-West railway into the Indian Territory, 1870-1882. Chronicles of Oklahoma, 47 (1969): 560-581.

Mitchell, Michael Dan. Acculturation problems among the Plains tribes of the government agencies in Western Indian

Territory. Chronicles of Oklahoma, 44
(1966): 281-289.

Montgomery, W. B. Washashe wageressa
pahvgreh tse. Boston, 1834. 126 p.

Morfi, J. A. de. Memorias for the history
of the Province of Texas. Ed. by F. M.
Chabot. San Antonio, 1932. 85 p.

Morgan, L. H. Systems of consanguinity
and affinity. Smithsonian Contributions
to Knowledge, 17 (1871): 291-382.

Morgan, L. H. The Indian journals, 1859-
62: p. 82. Ann Arbor, 1959.

Morris, Wayne. Auguste Pierre Chouteau,
merchant prince at the three forks of
the Arkansas. Chronicles of Oklahoma, 48
(1970): 155-163.

Morris, Wayne. Traders and factories on
the Arkansas frontier, 1805-1822.
Arkansas Historical Quarterly, 28
(1969): 28-48.

Morse, J. A report to the Secretary of
War. New Haven, 1822. 400 p.

Nasatir, A. P. Before Lewis and Clark.
St. Louis, 1952. 2 v. (882 p.).

Nett, B. R. Historical changes in the
Osage kinship system. Southwestern
Journal of Anthropology, 8 (1952): 164-
181.

Nuttall, T. A journal of travels into the
Arkansa Territory. Philadelphia, 1821.
296 p.

Nuttall, Thomas. A journal of travels
into the Arkansa Territory. Ann Arbor,
University Microfilms, 1966. 12,
296 p. illus., map.

Pourtalès, Albert von. On the western
tour with Washington Irving. Norman,
University of Oklahoma Press, 1968. 14,
96 p. illus., map.

Riggs, S. R. Dakota grammar, texts and
ethnography. Contributions to North
American Ethnology, 9 (1893): xviii-
xxix.

Rohrer, J. H. The test intelligence of
Osage Indians. Journal of Social
Psychology, 16 (1942): 99-105.

Roper, James E. Isaac Rawlings, frontier
merchant. Tennessee Historical
Quarterly, 20 (1961): 262-281.

Sebbelov, G. The Osage war dance. Museum
Journal, 2 (1911): 71-74.

Shoemaker, Floyd C. Osceola, land of
Osage River lore. Missouri Historical
Review, 54 (1959/1960): 327-334.

Sibley, George C. George C. Sibley's
journal of a trip to the Salines in
1811. Edited by George R. Brooks.
Missouri Historical Society, Bulletin,
21 (1964/1965): 167-207.

Skinner, A. B. An Osage war party. Public
Museum of the City of Milwaukee,
Yearbook, 2 (1923): 165-169.

Speck, F. G. Notes on the ethnology of
the Osage Indians. Pennsylvania,
University, Free Museum of Science and
Art, Transactions, 2 (1907): 159-171.

Swanton, J. R. Osage. U.S. Bureau of
American Ethnology, Bulletin, 30, vol. 2
(1910): 156-158.

Synder, J. F. Were the Osages mound
builders? Smithsonian Institution,
Annual Reports of the Board of Regents
(1888): 587-596.

Tedlock, Barbara. From Ceremony of
sending: a simultaneity for twenty
choruses. Alcheringa, 1 (1970): 52-56.

Tedlock, Barbara. Planting song.
Alcheringa, 2 (1971): 35.

Tracy, Valerie. The Indian in transition:
the Neosho Agency, 1850-1861. Chronicles
of Oklahoma, 48 (1970): 164-183.

U.S., Bureau of Indian Affairs, Osage
Agency. The Osage people and their
trust property, a field report.
Pawhuska, Okla., 1953. 49, 192 p.
illus.

U.S., Congress, Senate, Committee on
Interior and Insular Affairs,
Subcommittee on Indian Affairs. Osage
Nation of Indians judgment funds.
Hearing, Ninety-second Congress, second
session, on S. 1456 and S. 3234 . . .
March 28, 1972. Washington, D.C.,
Government Printing Office, 1972. 3,
174 p. illus.

Vissier, P. Histoire de la tribu des
Osages. Paris, 1827. 92 p.

Wedel, W. R. The Osage. U.S. Bureau of
American Ethnology, Bulletin, 174
(1959): 54-58.

White Horse Eagle. We Indians. New York,
1931. 255 p.

White, Lonnie J. Arkansas territorial
Indian affairs. Arkansas Historical
Quarterly, 21 (1962): 193-212.

White, Lonnie J. The election of 1827 and the Conway-Crittenden duel. Arkansas Historical Quarterly, 19 (1960): 293-313.

Whitehouse, Joseph. The journal of Private Joseph Whitehouse, a soldier with Lewis and Clark. Edited by Paul Russell Cutright. Missouri Historical Society, Bulletin, 28 (1971/1972): 143-161.

Williams, Alfred M. The giants of the plain. Lippincott's Magazine of Popular Literature and Science, 32 (1883): 362-371.

Wilson, Wesley C. General John B. S. Todd, first delegate, Dakota Territory. North Dakota History, 31 (1964): 189-194.

Wolff, H. An Osage graphemic experiment. International Journal of American Linguistics, 24 (1958): 30-35.

Wolff, H. Osage. International Journal of American Linguistics, 18 (1952): 63-68, 231-237.

Wolff, Hans. An Osage graphemic experiment. International Journal of American Linguistics, 24 (1958): 30-35.

Zoltvany, Yves F. New France and the West, 1701-1713. Canadian Historical Review, 46 (1965): 301-322.

09-19 Oto

Anderson, B. G. Indian sleep man tales. Caldwell, 1940. 145 p.

Anonymous. Extracts from the diary of Rev. Moses Merrill. Nebraska State Historical Society, Transactions and Reports, 4 (1892): 160-191.

Anonymous. Oto. U.S. Bureau of American Ethnology, Bulletin, 30, vol. 2 (1910): 164-166.

Briggs, John Ely. Omaha, Oto and Missouri. Palimpsest, 50 (1969): 219-221.

Bushnell, D. I. Villages of the Algonquian, Siouan and Caddoan tribes. U.S. Bureau of American Ethnology, Bulletin, 77 (1922): 114-121.

Chapman, Berlin B. The Barnes family of Barneston. Nebraska History, 47 (1966): 57-83.

Chapman, Berlin B. The Otoes and Missourias; a study of Indian removal and the legal aftermath. Oklahoma City, Times Journal, 1965. 18, 405 p. illus.

Chapman, Carl Haley. The origin of the Osage Indian tribe: an ethnographical, historical and archaeological study. Dissertation Abstracts, 20 (1959/1960): 1525. UM 59-4894.

Culbertson, T. A. Journal of an expedition to the mauvaises terres and the Upper Missouri in 1850. U.S. Bureau of American Ethnology, Bulletin, 147 (1952): 1-172.

Curtis, E. S. The North American Indian, Vol. 19: 25-26, 151-177, 226-228, 230-238. Norwood, 1930.

Dorsey, J. O. On the comparative phonology of four Siouan languages. Smithsonian Institution, Annual Reports of the Board of Regents (1883): 919-929.

Dorsey, J. O. Preface. Contributions to North American Ethnology, 9 (1893): xviii-xxx.

Dorsey, J. O. The rabbit and the grasshopper. American Antiquarian and Oriental Journal, 3 (1880): 24-27.

Fay, George E., ed. Treaties, and land cessions, between the bands of the Sioux and the United States of America, 1805-1906. Greeley, 1972. 7, 139 l. (University of Northern Colorado, Museum of Anthropology, Occasional Publications in Anthropology, Ethnology Series, 24)

Fletcher, A. C. A birthday wish from Native America. In Holmes Anniversary Volume. Washington, D.C., 1916: 118-122.

Floyd, Charles. Sergeant Floyd's journal. Edited by William J. Petersen. Palimpsest, 45 (1964): 130-144.

Foreman, G. The last trek of the Indians, 258-262. Chicago, 1946.

Graebner, Norman A. Nebraska's Missouri River frontier, 1854-1860. Nebraska History, 42 (1961): 213-235.

Green, Norma Kidd. The Presbyterian Mission to the Omaha Indian tribe. Nebraska History, 48 (1967): 267-288.

Green, T. L., ed. Notes on a buffalo hunt--the diary of Mordecai Bartram. Nebraska History, 35 (1954): 193-222.

Griffin, J. B. The archaeological remains of the Chiwere Sioux. American Antiquity, 2 (1937): 180-181.

Harrington, M. R.   A sacred warclub of the Oto. Indian Notes and Monographs, 10 (1920): 25-27.

Harrington, M. R.   A visit to the Otoe Indians. Museum Journal, 4 (1913): 107-113.

Hayden, F. V.   Brief notes on the present condition of the Otoe Indians. United States Geological and Geographical Survey of the Territories, Annual Reports, 1 (1867): 32-35.

Hayden, F. V.   Contributions to the ethnography and philology of the Indian tribes of the Missouri Valley. American Philosophical Society, Transactions, n.s., 12 (1863): 444-456.

Holtz, Milton E.   Early settlement and public land disposal in the Elkhorn River Valley, Cuming County, Nebraska Territory. Nebraska History, 52 (1971): 113-132.

Howard, J. H.   An Oto-Omaha peyote ritual. Southwestern Journal of Anthropology, 12 (1956): 432-436.

Irving, J. T.   Indian sketches. Philadelphia, 1835. 2 v.

Irving, J. T.   Indian sketches taken during an expedition to the Pawnee Tribes (1833). Norman, 1955. 317 p.

Jackson, Donald.   Journey to the Mandans, 1809; the lost narrative of Dr. Thomas. Missouri Historical Society Bulletin, 20 (1963/1964): 179-192.

Jackson, Donald.   Lewis and Clark among the Oto. Nebraska History, 41 (1960): 237-248.

Kercheval, G. T.   An Otoe and an Omaha tale. Journal of American Folklore, 6 (1893): 199-204.

Lesser, Alexander.   Siouan kinship. Dissertation Abstracts, 19 (1958/1959): 208.   UM 58-2596.

Lieberkühn, S.   The history of our Lord and Saviour Jesus Christ. Tr. into Oto by M. Merrill and L. Dorion. Rochester, 1888. 32 p.

M. H. W.   Chief Moses George Harragarra, last medal chief of the Oto and Missouri tribe. Chronicles of Oklahoma, 45 (1967): 220-222.

McGee, W J.   The Siouan Indians. U.S. Bureau of American Ethnology, Annual Reports, 15 (1894): 157-204.

Merrill, M.   Extracts from the diary of Rev. Moses Merrill. Nebraska State Historical Society, Transactions and Reports, 4 (1892): 160-191.

Möllhausen, B.   Diary of a journey from the Mississippi to the coasts of the Pacific, Vol. 1: 171-181, 198-212, 243-249. London, 1858.

Morgan, L. H.   Systems of consanguinity and affinity. Smithsonian Contributions to Knowledge, 17 (1871): 291-382.

Morgan, L. H.   The Indian journals, 1859-62: p. 67, 99.   Ann Arbor, 1959.

Nasatir, A. P.   Before Lewis and Clark. St. Louis, 1952. 2 v. (882 p.).

Nebraska Writers' Project.   Indian place legends. Nebraska Folklore Pamphlets, 2 (1937): 1-15.

Petersen, William J.   Lewis and Clark expedition. Palimpsest, 45 (1964): 108-129.

Riggs, S. R.   Dakota grammar, texts and ethnography. Contributions to North American Ethnology, 9 (1893): xviii-xxix.

Shunatona, R.   Otoe Indian lore. Nebraska History and Record of Pioneer Days, 5 (1922): 60-64.

Sibley, George C.   George C. Sibley's journal of a trip to the Salines in 1811. Edited by George R. Brooks. Missouri Historical Society, Bulletin, 21 (1964/1965): 167-207.

Skinner, A.   Remarkable Oto necklace. Indian Notes, 2 (1925): 36-38.

Vincent, John R.   Midwest Indians and frontier photography. Annals of Iowa, 38 (1965): 26-35.

Whitehouse, Joseph.   The journal of Private Joseph Whitehouse, a soldier with Lewis and Clark. Edited by Paul Russell Cutright. Missouri Historical Society, Bulletin, 28 (1971/1972): 143-161.

Whitman, W.   Descriptive grammar of Ioway-Oto. International Journal of American Linguistics, 13 (1947): 233-248.

Whitman, W.   Origin legends of the Oto. Journal of American Folklore, 51 (1938): 173-205.

*Whitman, W.   The Oto. Columbia University Contributions to Anthropology, 28 (1937): 1-32.

Wied-Neuwied, M. zu. Reise in das innere
Nordamerika. Coblenz, 1839-1841. 2 v.

Wied-Neuwied, M. zu. Travels in the
interior of North America. Early Western
Travels, 24 (1906): 101-112, 285-293,
313-314.

09-20 Pawnee

Allis, Samuel. Forty years among the
Indians and on the eastern borders of
Nebraska. Nebraska State Historical
Society, Transactions and Reports, 2
(1887): 133-166.

Anonymous. Extracts from the diary of
Major Sibley. Chronicles of Oklahoma, 5,
no. 2 (1927): 196-218.

Bass, William M., III. The variation in
physical types of the prehistoric Plains
Indians. Lincoln, Plains Conference,
1964. 65-145 p. illus. (Plains
Anthropologist, Memoir, 1)

Bass, William Marvin, III. The variation
in physical type of the prehistoric
Plains Indians. Dissertation Abstracts,
22 (1961/1962): 967-968. UM 61-3485.

Befu, Harumi. Political complexity and
village community: test of an
hypothesis. Anthropological Quarterly,
39 (1966): 43-52.

Boas, Franz. Zur Anthropologie der
nordamerikanischen Indianer. Zeitschrift
für Ethnologie, 27 (1895): 366-411.

Bowman, Peter W. Coal-oil Canyon (14LO1),
report on a preliminary investigation.
Hays, Kansas Anthropological
Association, 1960. 2, 79 p. illus.

Bruce, Robert. Pawnee naming ceremonial.
New York, 1933. 36 p.

Bruce, Robert, ed. The fighting Norths
and Pawnee scouts: narratives and
reminiscences of military service on the
old frontier. Lincoln, published with
the cooperation and approval of the
Nebraska State Historical Society, 1932.
72 p. illus.

Brugge, David M. Some Plains Indians in
the church records of New Mexico. Plains
Anthropologist, 10 (1965): 181-189.

Buck, Royal. Red Willow County letters of
Royal Buck, 1872-1873. Edited by Paul D.
Riley. Nebraska History, 47 (1966): 371-
397.

Buckstaff, Ralph N. Stars and
constellations of a Pawnee sky map.

American Anthropologist, n.s., 29
(1927): 279-285.

Burlin, Natalie Curtis. Pawnee Indians.
Acknowledges the assistance of Sakuruta
(Coming Sun, James R. Murie). In Natalie
Curtis. The Indians' Book. New York and
London, Harper and Brothers, 1907: 91-
143.

Burton, O. Pawnee camp ground. Nebraska
History Magazine, 16 (1935): 81.

Bushnell, David I., Jr. Burials of the
Algonquian, Siouan and Caddoan tribes
west of the Mississippi. Washington,
D.C., Government Printing Office, 1927.
10, 103 p. illus. (U.S., Bureau of
American Ethnology, Bulletin, 83)

Cardenal, Ernesto, tr. Poesía de los
indios de Norteamérica. América
Indígena, 21 (1961): 355-362.

Carleton, James Henry. The prairie
logbooks: dragoon campaigns to the
Pawnee villages in 1844, and to the
Rocky Mountains in 1845. Edited with an
introduction by Louis Pelzer. Chicago,
Caxton Club, 1943. 18, 295 p.

Catlin, George. Illustrations of the
manners, customs, and condition of the
North American Indians. Vol. 2. London,
Chatto and Windus, 1876. 8, 266 p.
illus., maps.

Clark, J. S. A Pawnee buffalo-hunt.
Chronicles of Oklahoma, 20, no. 4
(1942): 387-395.

Clayton, Lawrence. William Clayton's
journal. Salt Lake City, Clayton Family
Association, 1921. 10, 376 p.

Connelley, William Elsey. Notes on the
early Indian occupancy of the Great
Plains. Kansas State Historical Society,
Collections, 14 (1915/1918): 438-470.

Culbertson, Thaddeus A. Journal of an
expedition to the Mouvaises Terres and
the Upper Missouri in 1850. Edited by
John Francis McDermott. Washington,
D.C., Government Printing Office, 1952.
8, 164 p. (U.S., Bureau of American
Ethnology, Bulletin, 147)

Cutright, Paul Russell. Lewis and Clark
and Cottonwood. Missouri Historical
Society, Bulletin, 21 (1965/1966): 35-
44.

Dangel, Richard. Tirawa, der höchste Gott
der Pawnee. Archiv für
Religionswissenschaft, 27 (1929): 113-
144.

Danker, Donald F. The North brothers and the Pawnee scouts. Nebraska History, 42 (1961): 161-179.

Densmore, Frances. Communication with the dead as practised by the American Indians. Man, 50 (1950): 40-41.

Densmore, Frances. Pawnee music. Washington, D.C., Government Printing Office, 1929. 18, 129 p. illus. (U.S., Bureau of American Ethnology, Bulletin, 93)

Densmore, Frances. Pawnee music. New York, Da Capo Press, 1972. 18, 129 p. illus.

Dodge, Henry. Colonel Dodge's journal, . . . report of the Secretary of War . . . transmitting a report of the expedition of dragoons, under the command of Colonel Henry Dodge, to the Rocky Mountains during the summer of 1835. Washington, D.C., Blair and Rives, Printers, 1836. 37 p. maps. (U.S., 24th Congress, 1st Session, House, Document, 181)

Dodge, Henry. Report on the expedition of dragoons, under Colonel Henry Dodge, to the Rocky Mountains in 1835. American State Papers, Military Affairs, 6 (1861): 130-146.

Dorsey, George Amos. A Pawnee personal medicine shrine. American Anthropologist, n.s., 7 (1905): 496-498.

Dorsey, George Amos. A Pawnee ritual of instruction. In Berthold Laufer, ed. Boas Anniversary Volume. New York, G. E. Stechert, 1906: 350-353.

Dorsey, George Amos. How the Pawnee captured the Cheyenne medicine arrows. American Anthropologist, n.s., 5 (1903): 644-658.

Dorsey, George Amos. Notes on Skidi Pawnee society. By George A. Dorsey and James R. Murie. Chicago, 1940. 65-119 p. (Field Museum of Natural History, Anthropological Series, 27, no. 2)

Dorsey, George Amos. One of the sacred altars of the Pawnee. In International Congress of Americanists, 13th. 1902, New York. Proceedings. New York, 1902: 67-74.

Dorsey, George Amos. Pawnee war tales. American Anthropologist, n.s., 8 (1906): 337-345.

Dorsey, George Amos. Social organization of the Skidi Pawnee. In International Congress of Americanists, 15th. 1906, Quebec. Proceedings. Quebec, 1906: 71-77.

Dorsey, George Amos. The Pawnee: mythology. Washington, D.C., Carnegie Institution of Washington, 1906. 546 p.

Dorsey, George Amos. The Skidi rite of human sacrifice. In International Congress of Americanists, 15th. 1906, Quebec. Proceedings. Quebec, 1906: 65-70.

Dorsey, George Amos. Traditions of the Skidi Pawnee. Boston and New York, For the American Folk-Lore Society by Houghton, Mifflin, 1904. 26, 366 p. illus. (American Folk-Lore Society, Memoirs, 8)

Dunbar, John B. Lone Chief and Medicine Bull. Magazine of American History, 8, no. 11 (1882): 754-756.

Dunbar, John B. Missionary life among the Pawnee. Nebraska State Historical Society, Proceedings and Collections, 16 (1911): 268-287.

Dunbar, John B. Pitalesharu: chief of the Pawnees. Magazine of American History, 5, no. 5 (1880): 343-345.

Dunbar, John B. The Pawnee Indians. Magazine of American History, 4, no. 4 (1880): 241-281.

Dunbar, John B. The Pawnee Indians: their habits and customs. Magazine of American History, 5, no. 5 (1880): 321-342; 8, no. 11 (1882): 734-754.

Dunbar, John B. The Pawnee language. In George B. Grinnell. Pawnee Hero Stories and Folk-Tales. 2d ed. New York, Charles Scribner's Sons, 1893: 409-437.

Dunbar, John B. The Presbyterian Mission among the Pawnee Indians in Nebraska, 1834 to 1836. Kansas State Historical Society, Collections, 11 (1909/1910): 323-332.

Dunbar, John B., et al. Letters concerning the Presbyterian Mission in the Pawnee country, near Bellevue, Neb., 1831-1849. Kansas State Historical Society, Collections, 14 (1915/1918): 570-784.

Fay, George E., ed. Charters, constitutions and by-laws of the Indian tribes of North America. Part VI: The Indian tribes of Oklahoma (cont'd.). Greeley, 1968. 5, 129 l. map. (University of Northern Colorado, Museum of Anthropology, Occasional Publications in Anthropology, Ethnology Series, 7) ERIC ED046556.

Fletcher, Alice Cunningham. A Pawnee
    ritual used when changing a man's name.
    American Anthropologist, n.s., 1 (1899):
    82-97.

Fletcher, Alice Cunningham. Giving
    thanks: a Pawnee ceremony. Journal of
    American Folk-Lore, 13 (1900): 261-266.

Fletcher, Alice Cunningham. Indian story
    and song from North America. Boston,
    Small, Maynard, 1900. 14, 126 p.

Fletcher, Alice Cunningham. Pawnee. In
    Frederick Webb Hodge, ed. Handbook of
    American Indians North of Mexico. Pt. 2.
    Washington, D.C., Government Printing
    Office, 1910: 213-216. (U.S., Bureau of
    American Ethnology, Bulletin, 30, pt. 2)

Fletcher, Alice Cunningham. Pawnee. In
    James Hastings, ed. Encyclopaedia of
    Religion and Ethics. Vol. 9. New York,
    Charles Scribner's Sons, 1955: 698-700.

Fletcher, Alice Cunningham. Pawnee star
    lore. Journal of American Folk-Lore, 16
    (1903): 10-15.

Fletcher, Alice Cunningham. Skidi. In
    Frederick Webb Hodge, ed. Handbook of
    American Indians North of Mexico. Pt. 2.
    Washington, D.C., Government Printing
    Office, 1910: 589-590. (U.S., Bureau of
    American Ethnology, Bulletin, 30, pt. 2)

Fletcher, Alice Cunningham. Star cult
    among the Pawnee: a preliminary report.
    American Anthropologist, n.s., 4 (1902):
    730-736.

*Fletcher, Alice Cunningham. The Hako: a
    Pawnee ceremony. Washington, D.C.,
    Smithsonian Institution, 1904. 372 p.
    illus. (U.S., Bureau of American
    Ethnology, Annual Report, 22, pt. 2)

Fletcher, Alice Cunningham. The Hako: a
    Pawnee ceremony. In Margaret Mead and
    Ruth L. Bunzel, eds. The Golden Age of
    American Anthropology. New York, George
    Braziller, 1960: 239-245.

Floyd, Charles. Sergeant Floyd's journal.
    Edited by William J. Petersen.
    Palimpsest, 45 (1964): 130-144.

Foreman, Grant. The last trek of the
    Indians. Chicago, University of Chicago
    Press, 1946. 382 p.

Gebhard, David. The shield motif in
    Plains rock art. American Antiquity, 31
    (1965/1966): 721-732.

Gibson, A. M. An Indian Territory United
    Nations: the Creek Council of 1845.
    Chronicles of Oklahoma, 39 (1961): 398-
    413.

Gilmore, Melvin R. Methods of Indian
    buffalo hunts, with the itinerary of the
    last tribal hunt of the Omaha. Michigan
    Academy of Science, Arts and Letters,
    Papers, 16 (1932): 17-32.

Gilmore, Melvin R. Uses of plants by the
    Indians of the Missouri River region.
    U.S., Bureau of American Ethnology,
    Annual Report, 33 (1911/1912): 43-154.

Graebner, Norman A. Nebraska's Missouri
    River frontier, 1854-1860. Nebraska
    History, 42 (1961): 213-235.

Grange, Roger T., Jr. Pawnee and Lower
    Loup pottery. Lincoln, 1968. 13,
    235 p. illus. (Nebraska Historical
    Society, Publications in Anthropology,
    3)

Grange, Roger T., Jr. Pawnee pottery
    sequences: an interpretation. Plains
    Anthropologist, 8 (1963): 126.

Grange, Roger Tibbetts, Jr. Ceramic
    relationships in the Central Plains.
    Dissertation Abstracts, 23 (1962/1963):
    1335-1336. UM 62-4197.

Gray, Margery P. Blood groups of Caddoan
    Indians of Oklahoma. By Margery P. Gray
    and William S. Laughlin. American
    Journal of Human Genetics, 12 (1960):
    86-94.

Gregg, Josiah. Commerce of the prairies.
    Edited by Max L. Moorhead. Norman,
    University of Oklahoma Press, 1954. 38,
    469 p. illus.

Gregg, Josiah. Commerce of the prairies;
    or, the journal of a Santa Fé trader,
    during eight expeditions across the
    great western prairies, and a residence
    of nearly nine years in northern Mexico.
    New York, H. G. Langley, 1844. 2 v.
    illus., maps.

Grinnell, George B. Pawnee, Blackfoot,
    and Cheyenne: history and folklore of
    the Plains. New York, Scribner, 1961.
    301 p.

Grinnell, George B. Pawnee hero stories
    and folk-tales. Lincoln, University of
    Nebraska Press, 1961. 13, 417 p.
    illus. (Bison Book, BB116)

Grinnell, George Bird. A Pawnee star
    myth. Journal of American Folk-Lore, 7
    (1894): 197-200.

Grinnell, George Bird. Development of a
    Pawnee myth. Journal of American Folk-
    Lore, 5 (1892): 127-134.

Grinnell, George Bird.   Marriage among the Pawnees. American Anthropologist, 4 (1891): 275-281.

*Grinnell, George Bird.   Pawnee hero stories and folk-tales. New York, Forest and Stream, 1889. 417 p.

Grinnell, George Bird. Pawnee mythology. Journal of American Folk-Lore, 6 (1893): 113-130.

Grinnell, George Bird. The punishment of the stingy and other Indian stories. New York, London, Harper and Brothers, 1901. 10, 235 p. illus.

Grinnell, George Bird. The Young Dog's dance. Journal of American Folk-Lore, 4 (1891): 307-313.

Grinnell, George Bird. Two great scouts and their Pawnee battalion. Cleveland, Arthur H. Clark, 1928. 5, 15-299 p. map.

Grinnell, George Bird. Two Pawnian tribal names. American Anthropologist, 4 (1891): 197-199.

Hamilton, James Cleland. The Panis: an historical outline of Canadian Indian slavery in the eighteenth century. Canadian Institute, Proceedings, n.s., 1 (1898): 19-27.

Harris, Earl R. Courthouse and Jail Rocks: landmarks on the Oregon Trail. Nebraska History, 43 (1962): 29-51.

Hayden, Ferdinand V. Brief notes on the Pawnee, Winnebago, and Omaha languages. American Philosophical Society, Proceedings, 10 (1868): 389-406.

Hayden, Ferdinand V. Contributions to the ethnography and philology of the Indian tribes of the Missouri Valley. Philadelphia, C. Sherman and Son, 1862. 231-462 p. illus., map.

Hayden, Ferdinand V. Contributions to the ethnography and philology of the Indian tribes of the Missouri Valley. American Philosophical Society, Transactions, n.s., 12 (1863): 231-462.

Hazen, Reuben W. History of the Pawnee Indians. Fremont, Neb., Fremont Tribune, 1893. 80 p. illus.

Hodge, Frederick Webb. Pitalesharu and his medal. Masterkey, 24 (1950): 111-119.

Hoffman, J. J. Molstad Village. Lincoln, Smithsonian Institution, River Basin Surveys, 1967. 6, 123 p. illus., maps. (Smithsonian Institution, River Basin Surveys, Publications in Salvage Archeology, 4)

Hoffmann, Hans. Symbolic logic and the analysis of social organization. Behavioral Science, 4 (1959): 288-298.

Hotz, Gottfried. Indian skin paintings from the American Southwest. Translated by Johannes Malthauer. Norman, University of Oklahoma Press, 1970. 14, 248 p. illus.

Hotz, Gottfried. Indianische Bilderschriftszenen auf einer Wapitihaut. Baessler-Archiv, n.F., 5 (1957): 209-224.

Hotz, Gottfried. Indianische Ledermalereien; Figurenreiche Darstellungen von Grenzkonflikten zwischen Mexiko und dem Missouri um 1720. Berlin, Reimer, 1960. 384 p. illus., maps.

Hudson, Henry James. Henry James Hudson and the Genoa settlement. Edited by Marguerette R. Burke. Nebraska History, 41 (1960): 201-235.

Hughes, Jack Thomas. Prehistory of the Caddoan-speaking tribes. Dissertation Abstracts International, 30 (1969/1970): 950B. UM 69-9198.

Hungate, Mary. Religious beliefs of the Nebraska Indian. Nebraska History Magazine, 19, no. 3 (1938): 207-225.

*Hyde, George E. Pawnee Indians. Denver, University of Denver Press, 1951. 10, 304 p. illus.

Hyde, George E. The Pawnee Indians, part one, 1500-1680. Denver, John Van Male, 1934. 54 p. (The Old West Series, 4)

Hyde, George E. The Pawnee Indians, part two, 1680-1770. Denver, John Van Male, 1934. 50 p. (The Old West Series, 5)

Irving, John Treat, Jr. Indian sketches taken during an expedition to the Pawnee tribes. Norman, University of Oklahoma Press, 1955. 42, 275 p. illus.

Irving, John Treat, Jr. Indian sketches, taken during an expedition to the Pawnee tribes. Philadelphia, Carey, Lea and Blanchard, 1835. 2 v.

Irving, Washington. A tour on the prairies. New York, Pantheon Books, 1967. 15, 240 p. illus., map.

Jackson, Donald. Journey to the Mandans, 1809; the lost narrative of Dr. Thomas. Missouri Historical Society Bulletin, 20 (1963/1964): 179-192.

Jones, Dorothy V. John Dougherty and the Pawnee rite of human sacrifice: April, 1827. Missouri Historical Review, 63 (1968/1969): 293-316.

King, James T. The Republican River Expedition, June-July, 1869. Nebraska History, 41 (1960): 165-199, 281-297.

Läng, H. Die Pawnee: Beiträge zu einer Stammesmonographie. Ethnologische Zeitschrift Zürich, 1 (1972): 243-258.

Lee, John D. Diary of the Mormon Battalion Mission. Edited by Juanita Brooks. New Mexico Historical Review, 42 (1967): 165-209, 281-332.

Lesser, Alexander. Composition of the Caddoan linguistic stock. By Alexander Lesser and Gene Weltfish. Washington, D.C., Smithsonian Institution, 1932. (Smithsonian Miscellaneous Collections, 87, no. 6)

Lesser, Alexander. Cultural significance of the Ghost Dance. American Anthropologist, n.s., 35 (1933): 108-115.

Lesser, Alexander. Levirate and fraternal polyandry among the Pawnees. Man, 30 (1930): 98-101.

*Lesser, Alexander. The Pawnee Ghost Dance hand game. New York, Columbia University Press, 1933. 10, 337 p. (Columbia University Contributions to Anthropology, 16)

*Lesser, Alexander. The Pawnee ghost dance hand game; a study of cultural change. New York, AMS Press, 1969. 10, 337 p. illus.

Lillie, Gordon William. Indian burials. American Antiquarian and Oriental Journal, 8, no. 1 (1886): 28-30.

Lillie, Gordon William. Sacred dances of the Pawnees. American Antiquarian and Oriental Journal, 7, no. 4 (1885): 210-212.

Linton, Ralph. Annual ceremony of the Pawnee medicine men. Field Museum of Natural History, Department of Anthropology, Leaflet, 8 (1923): 1-20.

Linton, Ralph. Purification of the sacred bundles: a ceremony of the Pawnee. Field Museum of Natural History, Department of Anthropology, Leaflet, 7 (1923): 1-11.

Linton, Ralph. The origin of the Skidi Pawnee sacrifice to the morning star. American Anthropologist, n.s., 28 (1926): 457-466.

Linton, Ralph. The sacrifice to the morning star by the Skidi Pawnee. Field Museum of Natural History, Department of Anthropology, Leaflet, 6 (1922): 1-18.

Linton, Ralph. The thunder ceremony of the Pawnee. Field Museum of Natural History, Department of Anthropology, Leaflet, 5 (1922): 3-19.

Lounsbury, Floyd G. A semantic analysis of the Pawnee kinship usage. Language, 32 (1956): 158-194.

McRill, Leslie A. Ferdinandina: first White settlement in Oklahoma. Chronicles of Oklahoma, 41 (1963): 126-159.

Mead, James R. The Pawnees as I knew them. Kansas State Historical Society, Transactions, 10 (1907/1908): 106-111.

Meleen, Elmer E. A report on an investigation of the La Roche Site, Stanley County, South Dakota. Vermillion, S.D., University of South Dakota Museum, 1948. 32 p. illus., plates, table. (South Dakota, University, Archaeological Studies, Circular, 5)

Miller, Alfred Jacob. The West of Alfred Jacob Miller (1837) from the notes and water colors in the Walters Art Gallery. With an account of the artist by Marvin C. Ross. Norman, University of Oklahoma Press, 1951. 28, 200, 33-54 p. illus.

Moore, Guy Rowley. Pawnee traditions and customs. Chronicles of Oklahoma, 17, no. 2 (1939): 151-169.

Morgan, Lewis Henry. Systems of consanguity and affinity of the human family. Washington, D.C., Smithsonian Institution, 1871. 12, 509 p. plates. (Smithsonian Contributions to Knowledge, 17)

Morgan, Lewis Henry. The Indian journals 1859-62. Ann Arbor, University of Michigan Press, 1959. 12, 229 p. illus., maps.

Morse, Jedidiah. A report to the Secretary of War of the United States on Indian affairs, comprising a narrative of a tour performed in the summer of 1820, under a commission from the President of the United States, for the purpose of ascertaining, for the use of the government, the actual state of the Indian tribes in our country. New Haven, Printed by S. Converse, 1822. 400 p. map.

Mullin, Cora Phebe (Smith). Pita-le-Sharu and the Hako. Omaha, Citizen Printing, 1931. 4, 11-72 p. illus.

Munkres, Robert L.   The Plains Indian
    threat on the Oregon Trail before 1860.
    Annals of Wyoming, 40 (1968): 193-221.

Murie, James R.   Pawnee Indian societies.
    New York, 1914.   543-644 p. (American
    Museum of Natural History,
    Anthropological Papers, 11, pt. 7)

Murray, Charles Augustus.   Travels in
    North America, including a summer
    residence with the Pawnee tribe of
    Indians, in the remote prairies of the
    Missouri, and a visit to Cuba and the
    Azore Islands. 3d ed. rev.   London,
    Richard Bentley, 1854.   2 v.

Nasatir, Abraham P.   Before Lewis and
    Clark.   St. Louis, St. Louis Historical
    Documents Foundation, 1952.   2 v. (15,
    853 p.) illus.

Nebraska History Magazine.   The war
    between Nebraska and Kansas, both sides
    of the dispute over the true location of
    the Pike-Pawnee Indian village where the
    Spanish flag came down and the Stars and
    Stripes went up. Nebraska History
    Magazine, 10, no. 3 (1927): 155-261.

Nebraska Writers' Project.   Animal
    legends. Nebraska Folklore Pamphlets, 6
    (1937): 1-11.

Nebraska Writers' Project.   Indian ghost
    legends. Nebraska Folklore Pamphlets, 12
    (1937): 1-11.

Nebraska Writers' Project.   Indian place
    legends. Nebraska Folklore Pamphlets, 2
    (1937): 1-15.

Neuman, Robert W.   Check-stamped pottery
    on the northern and central Great
    Plains. American Antiquity, 29
    (1963/1964): 17-26.

Nichols, Roger L.   Stephen Long and
    scientifific [sic] exploration on the
    Plains. Nebraska History, 52 (1971): 51-
    64.

North, Luther H.   Man of the Plains:
    recollections of Luther North, 1856-
    1882. Edited by Donald F. Danker.
    Lincoln, University of Nebraska Press,
    1961.   20, 350 p.   maps.

Oehler, Gottlieb.   Description of a
    journey and visit to the Pawnee Indians.
    By Gottlieb Oehler and David Z. Smith.
    New York, 1914.   32 p.

Oehler, Gottlieb.   Description of a
    journey to the Pawnee Indians, who live
    on the Platte River, a tributary of the
    Missouri, 70 miles from its mouth. By
    Gottlieb Oehler and David Z. Smith.

Moravian Church Miscellany, 2, no. 8
    (1851): 217-225; 3 (1852): 55-69.

Oswalt, Wendell H.   The Pawnee: horsemen
    and farmers of the western prairies. In
    his This Land Was Theirs.   New York,
    John Wiley and Sons, 1966: 239-289.

Parsons, Elsie Clews.   Ritual parallels in
    Pueblo and Plains cultures, with a
    special reference to the Pawnee.
    American Anthropologist, n.s., 31
    (1929): 642-654.

Pattie, James O.   The personal narrative
    of James O. Pattie. Edited by Timothy
    Flint.   Cincinnati, Printed and
    Published by John H. Wood, 1831.   11,
    13-300 p.   illus.

Pattie, James O.   The personal narrative
    of James O. Pattie. The 1831 edition,
    unabridged. Introduction by William H.
    Goetzmann.   Philadelphia and New York,
    J. B. Lippincott, 1962.   13, 269 p.
    map.   (Keystone Western Americana, KB50)

Pike, Albert.   Albert Pike's journeys in
    the prairie, 1831-1832. Edited by J.
    Evetts Haley. Panhandle-Plains
    Historical Review, 41 (1968): 1-84.

Platt, Elvira Gaston.   Reminiscences of a
    teacher among the Nebraska Indians,
    1843-1885. Nebraska State Historical
    Society, Transactions and Reports, 3
    (1892): 125-143.

Platt, Elvira Gaston.   Some experiences as
    a teacher among the Pawnees. Kansas
    State Historical Society, Collections,
    14 (1915/1918): 784-794.

Pourtalès, Albert von.   On the western
    tour with Washington Irving.   Norman,
    University of Oklahoma Press, 1968.   14,
    96 p.   illus., map.

Prucha, Francis Paul.   Early Indian peace
    medals. Wisconsin Magazine of History,
    45 (1961): 279-289.

Pruitt, O. J.   Some Iowa Indian tales.
    Annals of Iowa, 3d ser., 32 (1953/1955):
    203-216.

Rawlings, Charles.   General Connor's
    Tongue River battle. Annals of Wyoming,
    36 (1964): 73-77.

Riley, Paul D.   Dr. David Franklin Powell
    and Fort McPherson. Nebraska History, 51
    (1970): 153-170.

Roberts, George H.   Ancestry of Latakuts
    Kalahar (Fancy Eagle). Edited by George
    E. Hyde. Nebraska History, 40 (1959):
    67-73.

Robinett, Paul M. The military career of
James Craig. By Paul M. Robinett and
Howard V. Canan. Missouri Historical
Review, 66 (1971/1972): 49-75.

Shirk, Georg H. Peace on the Plains.
Chronicles of Oklahoma, 28, no. 1
(1950): 2-41.

Sibley, George C. George C. Sibley's
journal of a trip to the Salines in
1811. Edited by George R. Brooks.
Missouri Historical Society, Bulletin,
21 (1964/1965): 167-207.

Smith, David Z. Description of the
manners and customs of the Pawnee
Indians. Moravian Church Miscellany, 3
(1852): 86-94.

Strong, William Duncan. An introduction
to Nebraska archeology. Washington,
D.C., 1935. 7, 315 p. illus., plates.
(Smithsonian Miscellaneous Collections,
93, no. 10)

Sunder, John E. British Army officers on
the Santa Fe Trail. Missouri Historical
Society, Bulletin, 23 (1966/1967): 147-
157.

Swanson, Guy E. Rules of descent: studies
in the sociology of parentage. Ann
Arbor, University of Michigan, 1969. 5,
108 p. (Michigan, University, Museum of
Anthropology, Anthropological Papers,
39)

Taylor, Allan R. The classification of
the Caddoan languages. American
Philosophical Society, Proceedings, 107
(1963): 51-59.

Thurman, Melburn D. A case of historical
mythology: the Skidi Pawnee Morning Star
Sacrifice of 1833. Plains
Anthropologist, 15 (1970): 309-311.

Thurman, Melburn D. The Skidi Pawnee
Morning Star Sacrifice of 1827. Nebraska
History, 51 (1970): 269-280.

Troike, Rudolph C. A Pawnee visit to San
Antonio in 1795. Ethnohistory, 11
(1964): 380-393.

Troike, Rudolph C. The Caddo word for
"water". International Journal of
American Linguistics, 30 (1964): 96-98.

Turner, Charles W., ed. Reuben Knox
letters. North Carolina Historical
Review, 37 (1960): 66-93.

United States, Department of the Interior,
Office of Indian Affairs. Constitution
and by-laws of the Pawnee Indians of
Oklahoma. Washington, D.C., Government
Printing Office, 1938. 5 p.

*Wedel, Waldo Rudolph. An introduction to
Pawnee archeology. Washington, D.C.,
Government Printing Office, 1936. 11,
122 p. illus., maps. (U.S., Bureau of
American Ethnology, Bulletin, 112)

Wedel, Waldo Rudolph. Historic Indian
tribes in Kansas. The Pawnee. In Waldo
R. Wedel. An Introduction to Kansas
Archeology. Washington, D.C.,
Government Printing Office, 1959: 58-60.
(U.S., Bureau of American Ethnology,
Bulletin, 174)

Wedel, Waldo Rudolph. Prehistoric man on
the Great Plains. Norman, University of
Oklahoma Press, 1961. 18, 355 p.
illus., plates.

Wedel, Waldo Rudolph. The direct-
historical approach in Pawnee
archeology. Washington, D.C., 1938.
21 p. illus. (Smithsonian
Miscellaneous Collections, 97, no. 7)

Weltfish, Gene. Caddoan texts: Pawnee,
south band dialect. New York, G. E.
Stechert, 1937. 10, 251 p.
(Publications of the American
Ethnological Society, 17)

Weltfish, Gene. Coiled gambling baskets
of the Pawnee and other Plains tribes.
Indian Notes, 7, no. 3 (1930): 277-295.

Weltfish, Gene. The linguistic study of
material culture. International Journal
of American Linguistics, 24 (1958): 301-
311.

*Weltfish, Gene. The lost universe. New
York, Basic Books, 1965. 20, 506 p.
illus., map.

Weltfish, Gene. The question of ethnic
identity, an ethnohistorical approach.
Ethnohistory, 6 (1959): 321-346.

Weltfish, Gene. The vision story of Fox-
Boy, a south band Pawnee text.
International Journal of American
Linguistics, 9 (1936): 44-76.

White, Lonnie J. Disturbances on the
Arkansas-Texas border, 1827-1831.
Arkansas Historical Quarterly, 19
(1960): 95-110.

Will, George Francis. Corn among the
Indians of the Upper Missouri. By George
F. Will and George E. Hyde. St. Louis,
William Harvey Miner, 1917. 323 p.
illus. (Little Histories of North
American Indians, 5)

Wissler, Clark. Comparative study of
Pawnee and Blackfoot rituals. In
International Congress of Americanists,
19th. 1915, Washington, D.C.

Proceedings. Washington, D.C., 1915:
335-339.

Wissler, Clark. The Pawnee human
sacrifice to the morningstar. By Clark
Wissler and Herbert J. Spinden. American
Museum Journal, 16 (1916): 49-55.

Wissler, Clark. The sacred bundles of the
Pawnee. Natural History, 20 (1920): 569-
571.

Wood, W. Raymond. A stylistic and
historical analysis of shoulder patterns
on Plains Indian pottery. American
Antiquity, 28 (1962/1963): 25-40.

Wooster, Charles. The letters of Charles
and Helen Wooster: the problems of
settlement. By Charles and Helen
Wooster. Edited by William F. Schmidt.
Nebraska History, 46 (1965): 121-137.

                    09-21 Ponca

Anonymous. South Dakota physical types.
South Dakota, University, William H.
Cver Museum, Museum News, 12, no. 5
(1952): 1.

Boas, F. Notes on the Ponka grammar.
International Congress of Americanists,
Proceedings, 15, vol. 2 (1906): 317-337.

Boas, F. and J. R. Swanton. Siouan. U.S.
Bureau of American Ethnology, Bulletin,
40, vol. 1 (1911): 875-966.

Clark, J. Stanley. The killing of Big
Snake. Chronicles of Oklahoma, 49
(1971/1972): 302-314.

Dorsey, G. A. The Ponca sun dance. Field
Museum, Anthropological Series, 7
(1905): 67-88.

Dorsey, J. O. A study of Siouan cults.
U.S. Bureau of American Ethnology,
Annual Reports, 11 (1890): 361-422.

Dorsey, J. O. Abstracts of Omaha and
Ponka myths. Journal of American
Folklore, 1 (1888): 74-78, 204-208.

Dorsey, J. O. Omaha and Ponca letters.
U.S. Bureau of American Ethnology,
Bulletin, 11 (1891): 1-123.

Dorsey, J. O. On the comparative
phonology of four Siouan languages.
Smithsonian Institution, Annual Reports
of the Board of Regents (1883): 919-929.

Dorsey, J. O. Ponka and Omaha songs.
Journal of American Folklore, 2 (1889):
271-276.

Dorsey, J. O. Ponka stories. Journal of
American Folklore, 1 (1888): 73.

Dorsey, J. O. Preface. Contributions to
North American Ethnology, 9 (1893):
xviii-xxx.

Dorsey, J. O. The myths of the raccoon
and the crawfish. American Antiquarian
and Oriental Journal, 6 (1884): 237-240.

Dorsey, J. O. The religion of the Omahas
and Ponkas. American Antiquarian and
Oriental Journal, 5 (1883): 271-275.

Dorsey, J. O. The social organization of
the Siouan tribes. Journal of American
Folklore, 4 (1891): 331-332.

Dorsey, J. O. and C. Thomas. Ponca. U.S.
Bureau of American Ethnology, Bulletin,
30, vol. 2 (1910): 278-279.

Dorsey, James Owen. The Ȼegiha language.
Washington, D.C., Government Printing
Office, 1890. 18, 794 p.
(Contributions to North American
Ethnology, 6)

Ellis, Richard N., ed. The Western
American Indian: case studies in tribal
history. Lincoln, University of
Nebraska Press, 1972. 203 p.

Fay, George E., ed. Charters,
constitutions and by-laws of the Indian
tribes of North America. Part VI: The
Indian tribes of Oklahoma (cont'd.).
Greeley, 1968. 5, 129 l. map.
(University of Northern Colorado, Museum
of Anthropology, Occasional Publications
in Anthropology, Ethnology Series, 7)
ERIC ED046556.

Fay, George E., ed. Charters,
constitutions and by-laws of the Indian
tribes of North America. Part XIII:
Midwestern tribes. Greeley, 1972. 3,
101 l. map. (University of Northern
Colorado, Museum of Anthropology,
Occasional Publications in Anthropology,
Ethnology Series, 14)

Fletcher, A. C. Indian story and song
from North America. Boston, 1907.
126 p.

Fletcher, A. C. The emblematic use of the
tree in the Dakotan group. Science,
n.s., 4 (1896): 475-487.

Fletcher, A. C. and F. La Flesche. The
Omaha tribe. U.S. Bureau of American
Ethnology, Annual Reports, 27 (1906):
37-57.

Foreman, G. The last trek of the Indians,
247-258. Chicago, 1946.

Gilmore, M. R. Uses of plants by the Indians of the Missouri River region. U.S. Bureau of American Ethnology, Annual Reports, 33 (1912): 43-154.

Graebner, Norman A. Nebraska's Missouri River frontier, 1854-1860. Nebraska History, 42 (1961): 213-235.

Green, Norma Kidd. Four sisters: daughters of Joseph La Flesche. Nebraska History, 45 (1964): 165-176.

Harkins, Arthur M. Indian Americans in Omaha and Lincoln. By Arthur M. Harkins, Mary L. Zemyan, and Richard G. Woods. Minneapolis, University of Minnesota, Training Center for Community Programs, 1970. 42, 24 p. ERIC ED047860.

Holmer, N. M. Sonant-surds in Ponca-Omaha. International Journal of American Linguistics, 11 (1945): 75-85.

Howard, James H. Peter Le Claire's buffalo headdress. American Indian Tradition, 8, no. 1 (1961): 19-20.

Howard, James H. Ponca dances, ceremonies and music. By James H. Howard and Gertrude P. Kurath. Ethnomusicology, 3 (1959): 1-14.

Howard, James H. The Ponca shinny game. Indian Historian, 4, no. 3 (1971): 10-15.

*Howard, James H., et al. The Ponca tribe. Washington, D.C., Government Printing Office, 1965. 12, 191 p. illus., map. (U.S., Bureau of American Ethnology, Bulletin, 195)

Jackson, Donald. Journey to the Mandans, 1809; the lost narrative of Dr. Thomas. Missouri Historical Society Bulletin, 20 (1963/1964): 179-192.

King, James T. "A better way": General George Crook and the Ponca Indians. In Richard N. Ellis, ed. The Western American Indian. Lincoln, University of Nebraska Press, 1972: 76-87.

King, James T. "A better way": General George Crook and the Ponca Indians. Nebraska History, 50 (1969): 239-256.

Krámský, Jiři. The article and the concept of definiteness in language. The Hague, Mouton, 1972. 212 p. (Janua Linguarum, Series Minor, 125)

Kuttner, Robert E. Alcohol and addiction in urbanized Sioux Indians. By Robert E. Kuttner and Albert B. Lorincz. Mental Hygiene, 51 (1967): 530-542.

Kuttner, Robert E. Promiscuity and prostitution in urbanized Indian communities. By Robert E. Kuttner and Albert B. Lorincz. Mental Hygiene, 54 (1970): 79-91.

Le Claire, Peter. Peter Le Claire--Northern Ponca. An autobiographical sketch. With an introduction and comments by James H. Howard. American Indian Tradition, 8, no. 1 (1961): 17-19.

McGee, W J. Ponka feather symbolism. American Anthropologist, 11 (1898): 156-159.

McGee, W J. The Siouan Indians. U.S. Bureau of American Ethnology, Annual Reports, 15 (1894): 157-204.

Morgan, L. H. Systems of consanguinity and affinity. Smithsonian Contributions to Knowledge, 17 (1871): 291-382.

Morgan, L. H. The Indian journals, 1859-62: p. 147. Ann Arbor, 1959.

Nasatir, A. P. Before Lewis and Clark. St. Louis, 1952. 2 v. (882 p.).

Neuman, Robert W. Check-stamped pottery on the northern and central Great Plains. American Antiquity, 29 (1963/1964): 17-26.

Nieberding, Velma. The Nez Perce in the Quapaw Agency 1878-1879. Chronicles of Oklahoma, 44 (1966): 22-30.

Riggs, S. R. Dakota grammar, texts and ethnography. Contributions to North American Ethnology, 9 (1893): 1-232.

Schmidt, W. Die Omaha und die Ponca. In his Die Ursprung der Göttesidee. Bd. 2. Münster i. W., 1929: 657-658.

Skinner, A. B. Medicine ceremony of the Menomini, Iowa, and Wahpeton Dakota. Indian Notes and Monographs, 4 (1920): 306-308.

Skinner, A. B. Ponca societies and dances. American Museum of Natural History, Anthropological Papers, 11 (1915): 777-801.

Tibbles, Thomas H. The Ponca chiefs; an account of the trial of Standing Bear. Edited by Kay Graber. Lincoln, University of Nebraska Press, 1972. 13, 143 p.

Todd, John B. S. The Harney expedition against the Sioux: the journal of Capt. John B. S. Todd. Edited by Ray H. Mattison. Nebraska History, 43 (1962): 89-130.

Welsh, W. Report of a visit to the Sioux and Ponka Indians of the Missouri River. Philadelphia, 1872. 36 p.

Whitman, W. Xube, a Ponca autobiography. Journal of American Folklore, 52 (1939): 180-193.

Wied-Neuwied, M. zu. Reise in das innere Nordamerika. Coblenz, 1839-1841. 2 v.

Wied-Neuwied, M. zu. Travels in the interior of North America. Early Western Travels, 22 (1906): 283-290.

Will, G. F. and G. E. Hyde. Corn among the Indians of the Upper Missouri. St. Louis, 1917. 317 p.

Wood, W. Raymond. Notes on Ponca ethnohistory, 1785-1804. Ethnohistory, 6 (1959): 1-27.

Wood, W. Raymond. The Redbird Focus and the problem of Ponca prehistory. Lincoln, Plains Conference, 1965. 2, 79-145 p. illus. (Plains Anthropologist, Memoir, 2)

Zimmerman, C. L. White Eagle. Harrisburg, 1941. 273 p.

09-22   Quapaw

Anonymous. The Quapaw pow wow in Ottawa County. Chronicles of Oklahoma, 43 (1965): 208-209.

Baird, W. David. Fort Smith and the Red Man. Arkansas Historical Quarterly, 30 (1971): 337-348.

Baird, W. David. The Quapaw Indians. American Philosophical Society, Yearbook (1972): 416-417.

Banks, Dean. Civil-War refugees from Indian Territory, in the North, 1861-1864. Chronicles of Oklahoma, 41 (1963): 286-298.

Bossu, J. B. Nouveaux voyages aux Indes Occidentales, Vol. 1: 108-124. Paris, 1768.

Bossu, J. B. Travels through that part of North America formerly called Louisiana, Vol. 2: 91-109. London, 1771.

Bushnell, D. I. Villages of the Algonquian, Siouan and Caddoan tribes. U.S. Bureau of American Ethnology, Bulletin, 77 (1922): 108-112.

Chase, Charles Monroe. The letters of Charles Monroe Chase. Kansas Historical Quarterly, 26 (1960): 267-301.

Dorsey, J. O. Kwapa folk-lore. Journal of American Folklore, 8 (1895): 130-131.

Dorsey, J. O. Preface. Contributions to North American Ethnology, 9 (1893): xviii-xxx.

Dorsey, J. O. Siouan sociology. U.S. Bureau of American Ethnology, Annual Reports, 15 (1894): 229-230.

Fletcher, A. C. and F. La Flesche. The Omaha tribe. U.S. Bureau of American Ethnology, Annual Reports, 27 (1906): 67-68.

Ford, James A. Menard Site: the Quapaw village of Osotony on the Arkansas River. New York, 1961. 133-191 p. illus., maps. (American Museum of Natural History, Anthropological Papers, 48, pt. 2)

Foreman, G. The last trek of the Indians, 308-314. Chicago, 1946.

Gibson, A. M. An Indian Territory United Nations: the Creek Council of 1845. Chronicles of Oklahoma, 39 (1961): 398-413.

Harris, Frank H. Neosho Agency 1838-1871. Chronicles of Oklahoma, 43 (1965): 35-57.

Harris, Frank H. Seneca Sub-Agency, 1832-1838. Chronicles of Oklahoma, 42 (1964): 75-93.

Joutel, H. Journal of La Salle's last voyage. New ed. Albany, 1906. 258 p.

Joutel, H. Relation. In P. Margry, ed. Découvertes et Établissements des Français dans l'Ouest et dans le Sud de l'Amérique Septentrionale. Vol. 3. Paris, 1879: 91-534.

La Flesche, F. Omaha and Osage traditions of separation. International Congress of Americanists, Proceedings, 19 (1915): 459-462.

Lane, J. Federal-Quapaw relations, 1800-1833. Arkansas Historical Quarterly, 19 (1960): 61-74.

Lane, Jack. Federal-Quapaw relations, 1800-1833. Arkansas Historical Quarterly, 19 (1960): 61-74.

Laurence, M. A trip to Quapaw in 1903. Chronicles of Oklahoma, 31 (1953): 142-167.

Lesser, Alexander. Siouan kinship. Dissertation Abstracts, 19 (1958/1959): 208. UM 58-2596.

Lyon, O. The trail of the Quapaw. Arkansas Historical Quarterly, 9 (1950): 205-213.

McGee, W J. The Siouan Indians. U.S. Bureau of American Ethnology, Annual Reports, 15 (1894): 157-204.

McGimsey, Charles R., III. Indians of Arkansas. Fayetteville, Arkansas Archeological Survey, 1969. 7, 1-47 p. illus., maps. (Arkansas Archeological Survey, Publications on Archeology, Popular Series, 1)

Mereness, N. D., ed. Travels in the American colonies, 57-58. New York, 1916.

Morris, Wayne. Traders and factories on the Arkansas frontier, 1805-1822. Arkansas Historical Quarterly, 28 (1969): 28-48.

Nasatir, A. P. Before Lewis and Clark. St. Louis, 1952. 2 v. (882 p.).

Nieberding, V. St. Mary's of the Quapaws. Chronicles of Oklahoma, 31 (1953): 2-14.

Nieberding, Velma. The Nez Perce in the Quapaw Agency 1878-1879. Chronicles of Oklahoma, 44 (1966): 22-30.

Nuttall, T. A journal of travels into the Arkansa Territory. Philadelphia, 1821. 296 p.

Nuttall, Thomas. A journal of travels into the Arkansa Territory. Ann Arbor, University Microfilms, 1966. 12, 296 p. illus., map.

Phillips, P., et al. Archaeological survey of the lower Mississippi alluvial valley, 1940-1947. Harvard University, Peabody Museum of American Archaeology and Ethnology, Papers, 25 (1951): 392-421.

Riggs, S. R. Dakota grammar, texts and ethnography. Contributions to North American Ethnology, 9 (1893): xviii-xxix.

Swanton, J. R. Indians of the Southeastern United States. U.S. Bureau of American Ethnology, Bulletin, 137 (1946): 11-832.

Thomas, C. Quapaw. U.S. Bureau of American Ethnology, Bulletin, 30, vol. 2 (1910): 333-336.

Thompson, V. H. A history of the Quapaw. Chronicles of Oklahoma, 33 (1955): 360-383.

Tonti, H. de. An account of Monsieur de la Salle's last expedition. New York Historical Society, Collections, 2 (1814): 217-341.

Tracy, Valerie. The Indian in transition: the Neosho Agency, 1850-1861. Chronicles of Oklahoma, 48 (1970): 164-183.

Weer, P. Passamaquoddy and Quapaw mnemonic records. Indiana Academy of Science, Proceedings, 55 (1946): 29-32.

White, Lonnie J. Arkansas territorial Indian affairs. Arkansas Historical Quarterly, 21 (1962): 193-212.

White, Lonnie J. The election of 1827 and the Conway-Crittenden duel. Arkansas Historical Quarterly, 19 (1960): 293-313.

Wright, M. H. American Indian corn dishes. Chronicles of Oklahoma, 36 (1958): 155-166.

09-23   Santee

DeMallie, Raymond J. Bibliography: the Sioux. Indian Historian, 2, no. 3 (1969): 49-50.

Adams, M. N. The Sioux outbreak in the year 1862. Minnesota Historical Society, Collections, 9 (1901): 431-452.

Allen, Clifford, et al. History of the Flandreau Santee Sioux Tribe. Flandreau, S.D., Flandreau Santee Sioux Tribe, Tribal History Program, 1971. 194 p.

Ames, J. H. The Sioux or Nadouesis. Macalester College Contributions, 1 (1890): 229-240.

Andros, F. The medicine and surgery of the Winnebago and Dakota Indians. American Medical Association, Journal, 1 (1883): 116-118.

Anonymous. Dakota. U.S. Bureau of American Ethnology, Bulletin, 30, vol. 1 (1907): 376-380.

Anonymous. Fur trade in Minnesota--1856. Museum of the Fur Trade Quarterly, 1, no. 1 (1965): 9-10.

Anonymous. Sioux treaty of 1868. Indian Historian, 3, no. 1 (1970): 13-17.

Anonymous. Wahpeton. U.S. Bureau of American Ethnology, Bulletin, 30, vol. 2 (1910): 891-893.

Atwater, C. Remarks made on a tour to Prairie du Chien. Columbus, 1831. 296 p.

Babcock, W. M. Sioux villages in Minnesota prior to 1837. Minnesota Archaeologist, 11 (1945): 126-146.

Babcock, Willoughby M. Minnesota's Indian War. Minnesota History, 38 (1962/1963): 93-98.

Baker, Miriam Hawthorn. Inkpaduta's camp at Smithland. Annals of Iowa, 39 (1967): 81-104.

Beaulieu, David. The formal education of Minnesota Indians; historical perspective until 1934. Minneapolis, University of Minnesota, Training Center for Community Programs, 1971. 38 l. maps. ERIC ED050873.

Beckwith, P. Notes on customs of the Dakotahs. Smithsonian Institution, Annual Reports of the Board of Regents (1886): 245-257.

Beltrami, J. C. A pilgrimage in Europe and America, Vol. 2: 206-300. London, 1828.

Bibaud, F. M. Biographie des sagamos illustrés de l'Amérique Septentrionale, 257-264. Montréal, 1848.

Bishop, Harriet E. Dakota war whoop; Indian massacres and war in Minnesota. Chicago, Lakeside Press, 1965. 34, 395 p. map.

Blackthunder, Elijah, et al. Ehanna Woyakapi (history); Sisseton-Wahpeton Sioux Tribe of the Lake Traverse Reservation, Sisseton, South Dakota. Rev. ed. Sisseton, Sisseton-Wahpeton Sioux Tribe, 1972. 130 l. illus., maps.

Blackwell, R. Quentin. Hemoglobin variant found in Koreans, Chinese, and North American Indians: $a_2\beta^{22Glu>Ala}$. By R. Quentin Blackwell, Ihl-Hyeob Ro, Chen-Sheng Liu, Hung-Ju Yang, Chen-Chang Wang, and Jeanette Tung-Hsiang Huang. American Journal of Physical Anthropology, n.s., 30 (1969): 389-391.

Blackwell, R. Quentin, et al. Hemoglobin variant common to Chinese and North American Indians. Science, 161 (1968): 381-382.

Boas, F. and E. Deloria. Dakota grammar. National Academy of Sciences, Memoirs, 23, no. 2 (1941): 1-183.

Boas, F. and J. R. Swanton. Siouan. U.S. Bureau of American Ethnology, Bulletin, 41, vol. 1 (1911): 875-966.

Bradley, J. H. History of the Sioux. Historical Society of Montana, Contributions, 9 (1923): 29-140.

Brown, Geoge A. The settlement of Cherokee County. Annals of Iowa, 36 (1963): 539-556.

Buechel, Eugene. A dictionary of the Teton Dakota Sioux Language: Lakota-English, English-Lakota, with considerations given to Yankton and Santee. Ed. by Paul Manhart. Pine Ridge, Red Cloud Indian School, Holy Rosary Mission, 1970. 6, 852 p.

Bushnell, D. I. Burials of the Algonquian, Siouan and Caddoan tribes. U.S. Bureau of American Ethnology, Bulletin, 83 (1927): 17-27.

Bushnell, D. I. Villages of the Algonquian, Siouan and Caddoan tribes. U.S. Bureau of American Ethnology, Bulletin, 77 (1922): 44-55.

Carley, Kenneth, ed. As Red Men viewed it; three Indian accounts of the uprising. Minnesota History, 38 (1962/1963): 126-149.

Carver, J. Travels through the interior parts of North America. 2d ed. London, 1779.

Crooker, G. George Crooker's letter to President Abraham Lincoln concerning the Sioux outbreak, October 7, 1862. Minnesota Archaeologist, 19, no. 3 (1954): 3-17.

Culbertson, T. A. Journal of an expedition to the mauvaises terres and the Upper Missouri in 1850. U.S. Bureau of American Ethnology, Bulletin, 147 (1952): 1-172.

Dally, N. Tracks and trails. Walker, 1931. 138 p.

Daniels, A. W. Reminiscences of Little Crow. Minnesota Historical Society, Collections, 12 (1908): 513-530.

Deloria, E. C. Speaking of Indians. New York, 1944. 163 p.

Deloria, Ella C. Some notes on the Santee. South Dakota, University, Museum, Museum News, 28, nos. 5/6 (1967): 1-21.

Deloria, Ella C., tr. "The origin of the courting-flute" a legend in the Santee Dakota dialect. Translated by Ella C.

Deloria and Jay Brandon. South Dakota, State University, W. H. Over Museum, Museum News, 22, no. 6 (1961): 1-7.

Donaldson, T. The George Catlin Indian Gallery. United States National Museum, Reports (1885): 53-63.

Dorsey, J. O. A study of Siouan cults. U.S. Bureau of American Ethnology, Annual Reports, 11 (1890): 351-544.

Dorsey, J. O. Preface. Contributions to North American Ethnology, 9 (1893): xi-xxxii.

Dorsey, J. O. The social organization of the Siouan tribes. Journal of American Folklore, 4 (1891): 257-260.

Dorsey, J. O. and C. Thomas. Mdewakanton. U.S. Bureau of American Ethnology, Bulletin, 30, vol. 1 (1907): 826-828.

Douglas, F. H. The Sioux or Dakota Indians. Denver Art Museum, Indian Leaflet Series, 41 (1932): 1-4.

Duratschek, M. C. Crusading along Sioux trails. St. Meinrad, Indiana, 1947. 334 p.

Eastman, C. A. From the deep woods to civilization. Boston, 1916. 206 p.

Eastman, C. A. Indian boyhood. New York, 1902. 289 p.

Eastman, C. A. Indian child life. Boston, 1913. 162 p.

Eastman, C. A. Indian heroes and great chieftains. Boston, 1918. 241 p.

Eastman, C. A. Old Indian days. New York, 1907. 275 p.

Eastman, C. A. The soul of the Indian. Boston, 1911. 171 p.

Eastman, C. A. and E. G. Eastman. Wigwam evenings. Boston, 1909. 253 p.

Eastman, Charles A. The soul of an Indian. New York, Johnson Reprint, 1971. 13, 170 p.

Eastman, M. Dacotah. New York, 1849. 268 p.

Fay, George E., ed. Charters, constitutions and by-laws of Indian tribes of North America. Part I: The Sioux tribes of South Dakota. Greeley, 1967. 12, 120 l. map. (University of Northern Colorado, Museum of Anthropology, Occasional Publications in Anthropology, Ethnology Series, 1) ERIC ED046551.

Fay, George E., ed. Charters, constitutions and by-laws of the Indian tribes of North America. Part XIV: Great Lakes Agency: Minnesota-Michigan. Greeley, 1972. 4, 84 l. map. (University of Northern Colorado, Museum of Anthropology, Occasional Publications in Anthropology, Ethnology Series, 15)

Fay, George E., ed. Charters, constitutions and by-laws of the Indian tribes of North America. Part XIII: Midwestern tribes. Greeley, 1972. 3, 101 l. map. (University of Northern Colorado, Museum of Anthropology, Occasional Publications in Anthropology, Ethnology Series, 14)

Fay, George E., ed. Charters, constitutions and by-laws of the Indian tribes of North America. Part XIV: Great Lakes Agency: Minnesota-Michigan. Greeley, 1972. 4, 84 l. map. (University of Northern Colorado, Museum of Anthropology, Occasional Publications in Anthropology, Ethnology Series, 15)

Fay, George E., ed. Treaties, and land cessions, between the bands of the Sioux and the United States of America, 1805-1906. Greeley, 1972. 7, 139 l. (University of Northern Colorado, Museum of Anthropology, Occasional Publications in Anthropology, Ethnology Series, 24)

Federal Writers' Projects. Wisconsin Indian place legends, 28-29. Milwaukee, 1936.

Feraca, Stephen E. The identity and demography of the Dakota or Sioux tribe. By Stephen E. Feraca and James H. Howard. Plains Anthropologist, 8 (1963): 80-84.

Fernberger, S. W. and F. G. Speck. Two Sioux shields and their psychological interpretation. Journal of Abnormal and Social Psychology, 33 (1938): 168-178.

Fletcher, A. C. The religious ceremony of the four winds or quarters, as observed by the Santee Sioux. Harvard University, Peabody Museum of American Archaeology and Ethnology, Reports, 16/17 (1883): 289-295.

Forbes, W. H. Traditions of Sioux Indians. Minnesota Historical Society, Collections, 6 (1894): 413-416.

Fugle, Eugene. The Nebraska Santee. By Eugene Fugle and James H. Howard. American Indian Tradition, 8, no. 5 (1962): 215-217.

Furnas, Robert W. The Second Nebraska's campaign against the Sioux. By Robert W. Furnas and Henry W. Pierce. Edited by

Richard D. Rowen. Nebraska History, 44 (1963): 3-53.

Gabetentz, H. G. C. von der. Grammatik der Dakota-Sprache. Leipzig, 1852. 64 p.

Gardner, W. H. Ethnology of the Indians of the valley of the Red River. Smithsonian Institution, Annual Reports of the Board of Regents (1870): 369-373.

Garvie, J. Abraham Lincoln toni Kin. Santee Agency, 1893. 17 p.

Gates, C. M. The Lac qui Parle Indian Mission. Minnesota History, 16 (1935): 133-151.

Gates, C. M., ed. Five fur traders of the Northwest. Minneapolis, 1933. 298 p.

Gatschet, A. S. Adjectives of color in Indian languages. American Naturalist, 13 (1879): 475-485.

Gilman, Rhoda R. Last days of the Upper Mississippi fur trade. Minnesota History, 42 (1970/1971): 123-140.

Gilmore, M. R. Uses of plants by the Indians of the Missouri River region. U.S. Bureau of American Ethnology, Annual Reports, 33 (1912): 43-154.

Goetzinger, William M. Pomme de Terre; a frontier outpost in Grant County. Minnesota History, 38 (1962/1963): 63-71.

Goodrich, A. M. Early Dakota trails and settlements at Centerville, Minn. Minnesota Historical Society, Collections, 15 (1915): 315-322.

Gordon, H. H. Legends of the Northwest. St. Paul, 1881. 143 p.

Guenther, Richard L. The Santee Normal Training School. Nebraska History, 51 (1970): 359-378.

Hans, F. M. The great Sioux nation. Chicago, 1907. 575 p.

Harkins, Arthur M. Indian Americans in Omaha and Lincoln. By Arthur M. Harkins, Mary L. Zemyan, and Richard G. Woods. Minneapolis, University of Minnesota, Training Center for Community Programs, 1970. 42, 24 p. ERIC ED047860.

Harkins, Arthur M. Public education of the Prairie Island Sioux: an interim report. Chicago, University of Chicago, 1969. 91 p. (National Study of American Indian Education, Series I, 10) ERIC ED040797.

Heard, I. V. D. History of the Sioux war and massacres of 1862 and 1863. New York, 1863. 354 p.

Heilbron, B. L. Some Sioux legends in pictures. Minnesota History, 36, no. 1 (1958): 18-23.

Hennepin, L. A new discovery of a vast country in America. Ed. by R. G. Thwaites. Chicago, 1903. 2 v.

Hennepin, L. Nouvelle decouverte d'un tres grand pays situé dans l'Amérique. Utrecht, 1697.

Hickerson, Harold E. The Virginia deer and intertribal buffer zones in the Upper Mississippi Valley. In Anthony Leeds and Andrew P. Vayda, eds. Man, Culture, and Animals. Washington, D.C., 1965: 43-65. (American Association for the Advancement of Science, Publication, 78)

Hofmann, C. American Indian music in Wisconsin. Journal of American Folklore, 60 (1947): 289-293.

Howard, James H. Dakota winter counts as a source of Plains history. Washington, D.C., Government Printing Office, 1960. 335-416 p. illus. (U.S., Bureau of American Ethnology, Anthropological Papers, 61. U.S., Bureau of American Ethnology, Bulletin, 173)

Howard, James H. John F. Lenger: music man among the Santee. Nebraska History, 53 (1972): 194-215.

Howard, James H. The Dakota or Sioux Indians; a study in human ecology. Vermillion, 1966. illus., map. (South Dakota, University, South Dakota Museum, Anthropological Papers, 2)

Howard, James H. The Dakota or Sioux Tribe; a study in human ecology. Part I: The Santee or Eastern Dakota. Powwow Trails, 7, no. 1 (1970): 5-16.

Howard, James H. The Dakota or Sioux tribe. South Dakota, University, Museum, Museum News, 27, nos. 5/6 (1966): 1-10; 27, nos. 7/8 (1966): 1-9; 27, nos. 9/10 (1966): 1-9.

Howard, James H. The Nebraska Santee. By James H. Howard and Eugene Fugle. American Indian Tradition, 8, no. 5 (1962): 215-217.

Huggan, N. The Story of Nancy McClure. Minnesota Historical Society, Collections, 6 (1894): 439-460.

Hurt, W. R. House types of the Santee Indians. South Dakota, University,

Museum, Museum Notes, 14, no. 11 (1953): 1-3.

Hurt, W. R. The urbanization of the Yankton Indians. South Dakota, University, Museum, Museum Notes, 21, no. 3 (1960): 1-6.

Hurt, Wesley R. Factors in the persistence of peyote in the Northern Plains. Plains Anthropologist, 5 (1960): 16-27.

Jenks, A. E. The wild rice gatherers of the Upper Lakes. U.S. Bureau of American Ethnology, Annual Reports, 19, vol. 2 (1898): 1013-1137.

Johnson, Roy P. Fur trader Chaboillez at Pembina. North Dakota History, 32 (1965): 83-99.

Keating, W. H. Narrative of an expedition to the source of St. Peter's River, Vol. 1: 376-439. Philadelphia, 1824.

Krámský, Jiři. The article and the concept of definiteness in language. The Hague, Mouton, 1972. 212 p. (Janua Linguarum, Series Minor, 125)

Landes, R. Dakota warfare. Southwestern Journal of Anthropology, 15 (1959): 43-52.

*Landes, Ruth. The Mystic Lake Sioux; sociology of the Mdewakanton-Santee. Madison, University of Wisconsin Press, 1968. 10, 224 p. map.

Lass, William E. The "Moscow Expedition". Minnesota History, 39 (1964/1965): 227-240.

Lass, William E. The removal from Minnesota of the Sioux and Winnebago Indians. Minnesota History, 38 (1962/1963): 353-364.

League of Women Voters of Minnesota. Indians in Minnesota. 2d ed. St. Paul, 1971. 165 p. illus., maps.

Letterman, Edward J. From whole log to no log. Minneapolis, Dillon Press, 1970. 3, 291 p. illus.

Lockwood, J. H. Early times in Wisconsin. State Historical Society of Wisconsin, Collections, 2 (1855): 178-195.

Long, S. H. Voyage in a six-oared skiff to the Falls of Saint Anthony in 1817. Minnesota Historical Society, Collections, 2, no. 1 (1860): 9-88.

Lowie, R. H. Dance associations of the Eastern Dakota. American Museum of Natural History, Anthropological Papers, 11 (1913): 101-142.

Lynd, J. W. The religion of the Dakotas. Minnesota Historical Society, Collections, 2 (1864): 63-84.

Matson, G. A. Distribution of blood groups among the Sioux, Omaha, and Winnebago Indians. American Journal of Physical Anthropology, 28 (1941): 313-318.

Mayer, Catherine M., et al., comps. Minnesota Indian resources directory. 2d ed. Minneapolis, University of Minnesota, Center for Urban and Regional Affairs, 1970. 173 p. ERIC ED043435.

Mayer, F. B. With pen and pencil on the frontier. Minnesota Historical Society, Narratives and Documents, 1 (1932): 1-214.

McGee, W J. The Siouan Indians. U.S. Bureau of American Ethnology, Annual Reports, 15 (1894): 157-204.

McKern, Waldo C. The Clam River Focus. Milwaukee, 1963. 10, 77 p. (Milwaukee, Public Museum, Publications in Anthropology, 9)

McLaughlin, J. My friend the Indian. Boston, 1910. 417 p.

McLaughlin, M. L. Myths and legends of the Sioux. Bismarck, 1916. 200 p.

Meyer, Roy W. History of the Santee Sioux; United States Indian policy on trial. Lincoln, University of Nebraska Press, 1968. 16, 434 p. illus., maps.

Meyer, Roy W. The establishment of the Santee Reservation, 1866-1869. Nebraska History, 45 (1964): 59-97.

Meyer, Roy W. The Prairie Island community; a remnant of Minnesota Sioux. Minnesota History, 37 (1960/1961): 271-282.

Meyer, Roy W. The Santee Sioux, 1934-1965. In Richard N. Ellis, ed. The Western American Indian. Lincoln, University of Nebraska Press, 1972: 165-172.

Milroy, Thomas W. A physician by the name of Ohiyesa; Charles Alexander Eastman, M.D. Minnesota Medicine, 54 (1971): 569-572.

Minnesota, Governor's Human Rights Commission. Minnesota's Indian citizens, yesterday and today. St. Paul, 1965. 136 p. map.

Minnesota, Governor's Human Rights
    Commission. Race relations in
    Minnesota; reports of the commission.
    St. Paul, 1948. illus., maps.

Minnesota, Governor's Human Rights
    Commission. The Indian in Minnesota; a
    report to Governor Luther W. Youngdahl
    of Minnesota by the Governor's
    Interracial Commission. St. Paul, 1947.
    80 p. map.

Minnesota, Governor's Human Rights
    Commission. The Indian in Minnesota; a
    report to Governor C. Elmer Anderson of
    Minnesota by the Governor's Interracial
    Commission. Rev. St. Paul, 1952. 79 p.

Minnesota, Indian Affairs Commission.
    Report. St. Paul, 1967. 51 p.

Minnesota, Interim Commission on Indian
    Affairs. Report of the Interim
    Commission on Indian Affairs. St. Paul,
    1957. 18 p.

Minnesota, Interim Commission on Indian
    Affairs. Report submitted to the
    Legislature of the State of Minnesota.
    St. Paul, 1961. 27 l.

Morgan, L. H. Systems of consanguinity
    and affinity. Smithsonian Contributions
    to Knowledge, 17 (1871): 291-382.

Morgan, L. H. The Indian journals, 1859-
    62: p. 60-61, 110-111, 151-152, 198.
    Ann Arbor, 1959.

Morton, Thomas F. The Civil War of
    Private Morton. Edited by James T. King.
    North Dakota History, 35 (1868): 9-19.

Nebraska Writers' Project. Santee-Sioux
    Indian legends. Nebraska Folklore
    Pamphlets, 21 (1937): 1-15; 23 (1937):
    1-14.

Neill, E. D. Dakota land and Dakota life.
    Minnesota Historical Society,
    Collections, 1 (1872): 254-294.

Neill, E. D. Memoir of the Sioux.
    Macalester College Contributions, 1
    (1890): 223-240.

Neill, E. D. The history of Minnesota,
    49-98. Philadelphia, 1858.

Neuman, Robert W. Porcupine quill
    flatteners from central United States.
    American Antiquity, 26 (1960/1961): 99-
    102.

Newton, R. The king's highway. Yankton
    Agency, 1879. 427 p.

Oehler, C. M. The great Sioux uprising.
    New York, 1959. 272 p.

Peet, S. D. The Snake Clan among the
    Dakotas. American Antiquarian and
    Oriental Journal, 12 (1890): 237-242.

Petersen, William J. Massacre on the
    Okobojis. Palimpsest, 42 (1961): 445-
    459.

Pfaller, Louis. The forging of an Indian
    agent. North Dakota History, 34 (1967):
    62-76.

Pike, Z. M. Pike's explorations in
    Minnesota, 1825-6. Minnesota Historical
    Society, Collections, 1 (1872): 368-416.

Pond, G. H. Dakota superstitions.
    Minnesota Historical Society,
    Collections, 2 (1867): 32-62.

Pond, G. H. Power and influence of Dakota
    medicine-men. In H. R. Schoolcraft, ed.
    Information respecting the History,
    Condition, and Prospects of the Indian
    Tribes of the United States. Vol. 4.
    Philadelphia, 1854: 641-651.

Pond, S. W. Indian warfare in Minnesota.
    Minnesota Historical Society,
    Collections, 3 (1880): 129-138.

Pond, S. W. The Dakotas or Sioux in
    Minnesota. Minnesota Historical Society,
    Collections, 12 (1908): 319-501.

Prescott, P. Contributions to the
    history, customs and opinions of the
    Dacota tribe. In H. H. Schoolcraft, ed.
    Information respecting the History,
    Condition, and Prospects of the Indian
    Tribes of the United States.
    Philadelphia, 1852, 1853, 1854: (v. 2)
    168-199; (v. 3) 225-246; (v. 4) 59-72.

Ridgley, Mary H. Reminiscences of the
    John Bair family. Michigan History, 47
    (1963): 363-368.

*Riggs, S. R. Dakota grammar, texts and
    ethnography. Contributions to North
    American Ethnology, 9 (1893): 1-232.

Riggs, S. R. Dakota portraits. Minnesota
    History Bulletin, 2 (1918): 481-568.

Riggs, S. R. Mary and I. Chicago, 1880.
    388 p.

Riggs, S. R. Mythology of the Dakotas.
    American Antiquarian and Oriental
    Journal, 5 (1883): 147-149.

Riggs, S. R. Protestant missions in the
    Northwest. Minnesota Historical Society,
    Collections, 6 (1894): 117-188.

Riggs, S. R. Tah-koo Wah-kan. Boston,
    1869. 491 p.

Riggs, S. R. The Dakota language. Minnesota Historical Society, Collections, 1 (1872): 89-107.

Riggs, S. R. The Dakota mission. Minnesota Historical Society, Collections, 3 (1870): 114-128.

Riggs, S. R. The theogony of the Sioux. American Antiquarian and Oriental Journal, 2 (1880): 265-270.

Ritzenthaler, R. E. Evidence of the ancestors of the Chiwere Sioux. Wisconsin Archeologist, n.s., 27 (1946): 89.

Robinson, D. A history of the Dakota or Sioux Indians. South Dakota Historical Collections, 2 (1904): 1-523.

Roddis, L. H. The Indian wars of Minnesota. Cedar Rapids, 1956. 329 p.

Roehrig, F. L. O. On the language of the Dakota or Sioux Indians. Smithsonian Institution, Annual Reports of the Board of Regents (1871): 434-450.

Schmidt, W. Die Wahpeton-Dakota. In Wilhelm Schmidt. Die Ursprung der Göttesidee. Bd. 2. Münster i. W., 1929: 653-657.

Schusky, Ernest L. Mission and government policy in Dakota Indian communities. Practical Anthropology, 10 (1963): 109-114.

Seymour, E. S. Sketches of Minnesota. New York, 1850. 281 p.

Shea, J. G., ed. Early voyages up and down the Mississippi. Albany, 1861. 191 p.

Skinner, A. A sketch of Eastern Dakota ethnology. American Anthropologist, n.s., 21 (1919): 164-174.

Skinner, A. Medicine ceremony of the Menomini, Iowa, and Wahpeton Dakota. Indian Notes and Monographs, 4 (1920): 262-305.

Skinner, A. Notes on the sun dance of the Sisseton Dakota. American Museum of Natural History, Anthropological Papers, 16 (1919): 381-385.

Skinner, A. Tree-dweller bundle of the Wahpeton Dakota. Indian Notes, 2 (1925): 66-73.

Snelling, W. J. Tales of the North-West. Boston, 1830. 288 p.

Stark, Donald S. Boundary markers in Dakota. International Journal of American Linguistics, 28 (1962): 19-35.

Stipe, Claude E. Eastern Dakota clans: the solution of a problem. American Anthropologist, 73 (1971): 1031-1035.

Stipe, Claude Edwin. Eastern Dakota acculturation: the role of agents of culture change. Dissertation Abstracts, 29 (1968/1969): 2720B. UM 69-1537.

Taoyateduta. "Taoyateduta is not a coward". Minnesota History, 38 (1962/1963): 115.

Telford, C. W. Test performance of full and mixed-blood North Dakota Indians. Journal of Comparative Psychology, 14 (1932): 123-145.

Thayer, B. W. A comparison of Dakota and Ojibway steel implements with their prehistoric equivalents. Minnesota Archaeologist, 1, no. 6 (1935): 1-6.

Thomson, William D. History of Fort Pembina: 1870-1895. North Dakota History, 36 (1969): 5-39.

Thwaites, R. G., ed. Radisson and Groseilliers in Wisconsin. State Historical Society of Wisconsin, Collections, 11 (1888): 64-96.

Upham, W. Mounds built by the Sioux in Minnesota. American Antiquarian and Oriental Journal, 27 (1905): 217-223.

U.S., Congress, Senate, Committee on Interior and Insular Affairs, Subcommittee on Indian Affairs. Federal lands in trust for tribes in Minnesota and Wisconsin. Hearing, Ninety-second Congress, first session, on S. 1217 . . . S. 1230 . . . March 26, 1971. Washington, D.C., Government Printing Office, 1971. 3, 72 p.

Vella, F. Hemoglobin G Saskatoon. By F. Vella, W. A. Isaacs, and H. Lehmann. Canadian Journal of Biochemistry, 45 (1967): 351-353.

Vincent, John R. Midwest Indians and frontier photography. Annals of Iowa, 38 (1965): 26-35.

Wallis, R. S. The changed status of twins among the Eastern Dakota. Anthropological Quarterly, 3 (1955): 116-120.

Wallis, R. S. The overt fears of Dakota Indian children. Child Development, 25 (1954): 185-192.

Wallis, R. S. and W. D. Wallis. The sins of the fathers. Southwestern Journal of Anthropology, 9 (1953): 431-436.

Wallis, W. D. Beliefs and tales of the Canadian Dakota. Journal of American Folklore, 36 (1923): 36-101.

*Wallis, W. D. The Canadian Dakota. American Museum of Natural History, Anthropological Papers, 41, no. 1 (1947): 1-225.

Wallis, W. D. The sun dance of the Canadian Dakota. American Museum of Natural History, Anthropological Papers, 16 (1921): 317-380.

Wamditanka, Big Eagle. A Sioux story of the war. Minnesota Historical Society, Collections, 6 (1894): 382-400.

Warren, G. K. Explorations in the Dacota country. Washington, D.C., 1856. 79 p.

Watrall, Charles R. Virginia deer and the buffer zone in the Late Prehistoric-Early Protohistoric periods in Minnesota. Plains Anthropologist, 13 (1968): 81-86.

Wertenberger, Mildred, ed. Fort Totten, Dakota Territory, 1867. North Dakota History, 34 (1967): 125-146.

White, N. D. Captivity among the Sioux. Minnesota Historical Society, Collections, 9 (1901): 396-426.

Williamson, A. W. The Dakotas and their traditions. American Antiquarian and Oriental Journal, 13 (1891): 54-55.

Williamson, J. P. An English-Dakota dictionary. New York, 1902.

Williamson, J. P. The letters of John P. Williamson. Minnesota Archaeologist, 20, no. 1 (1956): 2-21.

Williamson, T. S. Dacotas of the Mississippi. In H. R. Schoolcraft, ed. Information respecting the History, Condition, and Prospects of the Indian Tribes of the United States. Vol. 1. Philadelphia, 1851: 247-256.

Wilson, Peter. The letters of Peter Wilson, first resident agent among the Teton Sioux. Edited by Harry H. Anderson. Nebraska History, 42 (1961): 237-264.

Winchell, N. H. Habitations of the Sioux in Minnesota. Wisconsin Archeologist, 7 (1908): 155-164.

*Winchell, N. H. The aborigines of Minnesota. St. Paul, 1911. 761 p.

Wisconsin, Governor's Commission on Human Rights. Handbook on Wisconsin Indians. Compiled and written by Joyce M. Erdman. Madison, 1966. 103 p. illus., maps. ERIC ED033816.

Wissler, C. Decorative art of the Sioux Indians. American Museum of Natural History, Bulletin, 18 (1904): 231-277.

Woolworth, Nancy L. Captain Edwin V. Sumner's expedition to Devil's Lake in the summer of 1845. North Dakota History, 28 (1961): 79-98.

09-24   Teton

DeMallie, Raymond J. Bibliography: the Sioux. Indian Historian, 2, no. 3 (1969): 49-50.

Abel, A. H., ed. Tabeau's narrative of Loisel's expedition to the Upper Missouri. Norman, 1939. 272 p.

Ablon, Joan. Cultural conflict in American Indians. Mental Hygiene, 55 (1971): 199-205.

Anderson, H. An investigation of the early bands of the Saone group of Teton Sioux. Washington Academy of Sciences, Journal, 46 (1956): 87-94.

Anderson, Harry H. Indian peace-talkers and the conclusion of the Sioux War of 1876. Nebraska History, 44 (1963): 233-254.

Anderson, Harry H. The war club of Sitting Bull, the Oglala. Nebraska History, 42 (1961): 55-61.

Anderson, John A. The Sioux of the Rosebud; a history in pictures. Photographs by John A. Anderson. Text by Henry W. Hamilton and Jean Tyree Hamilton. Norman, University of Oklahoma Press, 1971. 32, 320 p. illus., maps.

Anonymous. An Oglala ghost story. South Dakota, University, William H. Over Museum, Museum News, 18, no. 1/2 (1956): 2.

Anonymous. Brule childrens' games. South Dakota, State University, W. H. Over Museum, Museum News, 20, no. 8 (1959): 1.

Anonymous. Brule death and mourning customs. South Dakota, State University, W. H. Over Museum, Museum News, 20, no. 6 (1959): 1-2.

Anonymous. Dakota. U.S. Bureau of American Ethnology, Bulletin, 30, vol. 1 (1907): 376-380.

Anonymous. Oglala tales. South Dakota, University, William H. Over Museum, Museum News, 18, no. 3/4 (1956): 4-5.

Anonymous. Sioux technology and customs. South Dakota, State University, W. H. Over Museum, Museum News, 21, no. 2 (1960): 1-4.

Anonymous. Sioux treaty of 1868. Indian Historian, 3, no. 1 (1970): 13-17.

Anonymous. The Dakota Indian feast at the Big Bend. South Dakota, University, William H. Over Museum, Museum News, 13, no. 7 (1952): 3.

Anonymous. Two Teton Dakota winter count texts. Edited by James H. Howard. North Dakota History, 27 (1960): 67-79.

Bad Heart Bull, Amos. A pictographic history of the Oglala Sioux. Text by Helen H. Blish. Lincoln, University of Nebraska Press, 1967. 22, 530 p. illus.

Ballas, Donald Joseph. A cultural geography of Todd County, South Dakota, and the Rosebud Sioux Indian Reservation. Dissertation Abstracts International, 31 (1970/1971): 2048B. UM 70-17,698.

Bate, Walter N. Eyewitness reports of the Wagon Box fight. Annals of Wyoming, 41 (1969): 193-202.

Beckwith, M. W. Mythology of the Oglala Dakota. Journal of American Folklore, 43 (1930): 339-442.

Beckwith, P. Notes on customs of the Dakotahs. Smithsonian Institution, Annual Reports of the Board of Regents (1886): 245-257.

Bessaignet, P. Histoires Sioux. Société des Américanistes, Journal, n.s., 44 (1955): 49-54.

Black Elk. Black Elk speaks. As told through John G. Neihardt. Lincoln, University of Nebraska Press, 1961. 280 p. illus. (Bison Book, 119)

Black Elk, Benjamin. Black Elk's notes on Teton Sioux culture. South Dakota, State University, W. H. Over Museum, Museum News, 23, no. 3 (1962): 1-6, 8.

Blakeslee, C. Some observations on the Indians of Crow Creek Reservation, South Dakota. Plains Anthropologist, 5 (1955): 31-35.

Blish, H. H. Ethical conceptions of the Oglala Dakota. Nebraska, University, Studies, 26, nos. 3/4 (1926): 1-47.

Blish, H. H. The ceremony of the sacred bow of the Oglala Dakota. American Anthropologist, n.s., 36 (1934): 180-187.

Boas, F. Some traits of the Dakota language. Language, 13 (1937): 137-141.

Boas, F. Teton Sioux music. Journal of American Folklore, 38 (1925): 319-324.

Boas, F. and E. Deloria. Notes on the Dakota, Teton dialect. International Journal of American Linguistics, 7 (1933): 97-121.

Boas, F. and J. R. Swanton. Siouan. U.S. Bureau of American Ethnology, Bulletin, 40, vol. 1 (1911): 875-966.

Brackett, A. G. The Sioux or Dakota Indians. Smithsonian Institution, Annual Reports of the Board of Regents, 31 (1876): 466-472.

Bradley, J. H. History of the Sioux. Historical Society of Montana, Contributions, 9 (1923): 29-140.

Brady, C. T. Indian fights and fighters. New York, 1904. 423 p.

Brininstool, E. A. Fighting Red Cloud's warriors. Columbus, 1926. 241 p.

Brininstool, E. A., et al. Chief Crazy Horse, his career and death. Nebraska History, 12, no. 1 (1929): 4-78.

Brown, J. E. The sacred pipe. Norman, 1953. 164 p.

Brown, Joseph Epes. The unlikely associates: a study in Oglala Sioux magic and metaphysic. Ethnos, 35 (1970): 5-15.

Bryde, John Francis. The Sioux Indian student: a study of scholastic failure and personality conflict. Dissertation Abstracts, 26 (1965/1966): 4792. UM 66-1594.

Buechel, E. A grammar of Lakota. St. Louis, 1939. 374 p.

Buechel, Eugene. A dictionary of the Teton Dakota Sioux Language: Lakota-English, English-Lakota, with considerations given to Yankton and Santee. Ed. by Paul Manhart. Pine Ridge, Red Cloud Indian School, Holy Rosary Mission, 1970. 6, 852 p.

Burbank, E. A. and E. Royce. Burbank among the Indians, 126-146. Caldwell, 1946.

Burdick, U. L. The last battle of the Sioux nation. Fargo, 1929. 164 p.

Bushnell, D. I. Burials of the Algonquian, Siouan and Caddoan tribes. U.S. Bureau of American Ethnology, Bulletin, 83 (1927): 29-42.

Bushnell, D. I. Villages of the Algonquian, Siouan, and Caddoan tribes. U.S. Bureau of American Ethnology, Bulletin, 77 (1922): 59-71.

Bushotter, G. A Teton Dakota ghost story. Journal of American Folklore, 1 (1888): 68-72.

Bushotter, G. Oath-taking among the Dakota. Indian Notes, 4 (1927): 81-83.

Byrne, P. E. Soldiers of the Plains. New York, 1926. 260 p.

Byron, Elsa Spear. The Fetterman fight. Annals of Wyoming, 36 (1964): 63-66.

Catlin, G. Illustrations of the manners, customs and condition of the North American Indians, Vol. 1: 208-246. New York, 1841.

Chief Eagle, D. Winter count. Colorado Springs, Dentan-Berkeland, 1967. 4, 230 p. illus.

Clark, A. About the Pine Ridge porcupine. Indian Life Readers, Sioux Series, 1 (1941): 1-73.

Clark, A. Brave against the enemy. Indian Life Readers, Sioux Series, 7 (1944): 1-215.

Clark, A. Bringer of the mystery dog. Indian Life Readers, Sioux Series, 6 (1944): 1-84.

Clark, A. Buffalo caller. Evanston, 1942. 36 p.

Clark, A. Singing Sioux cowboy reader. Indian Life Readers, Sioux Series, 9 (1947): 1-114.

Clark, A. The Grass Mountain mouse. Indian Life Readers, Sioux Series, 3 (1943): 1-108.

Clark, A. The hen of Wahpeton. Indian Life Readers, Sioux Series, 4 (1943): 1-97.

Clark, A. The Slim Butte raccoon. Indian Life Readers, Sioux Series, 2 (1942): 1-81.

Clark, A. There still are buffalo. Indian Life Readers, Sioux Series, 5 (1942): 1-86.

Clark, D. W. A note on the function of Christianity among Indians. In O. La Farge, ed. The Changing Indian. Norman, 1942: 163-165.

Clough, Wilson O. Mini-Aku, daughter of Spotted Tail. Annals of Wyoming, 39 (1967): 187-216.

Cohen, L. K. Big Missouri's winter count - a Sioux calendar 1796-1926. Indians at Work, 6, no. 6 (1939): 16-20.

Cohen, L. K. Even in those days pictures were important. Indians at Work, 9, no. 5 (1942): 19-21.

Cohen, L. K. Swift Bear's winter count. Indians at Work, 9, no. 6 (1942): 30-31; 9, no. 7 (1942): 29-30.

Colby, L. W. The ghost songs of the Dakotas. Nebraska State Historical Society, Proceedings and Collections, ser. 2, 1 (1895): 131-150.

Culbertson, T. A. Journal of an expedition to the mauvaises terres and the Upper Missouri in 1850. U.S. Bureau of American Ethnology, Bulletin, 147 (1952): 1-172.

*Curtis, E. S. The North American Indian, Vol. 3: 3-118, 137-190. Cambridge, 1908.

Curtis, N., ed. The Indians' book, 39-90. New York, 1907.

Dangberg, G. M. Letters to Jack Wilson, the Paiute prophet. U.S. Bureau of American Ethnology, Bulletin, 164 (1957): 279-296.

DeLand, C. E. The aborigines of South Dakota. South Dakota Historical Collections, 3 (1904/1906): 269-586.

Deloria, E. Dakota texts. American Ethnological Society, Publications, 14 (1932): 1-279.

Deloria, E. Short Dakota texts including conversation. International Journal of American Linguistics, 20 (1954): 17-22.

Deloria, E. The sun dance of the Oglala Sioux. Journal of American Folklore, 42 (1929): 354-413.

Densmore, F. A collection of specimens from the Teton Sioux. Indian Notes and Monographs, 11 (1948): 163-204.

Densmore, F. Music in its relation to the religious thought of the Teton Sioux. In Holmes Anniversary Volume. Washington, D.C., 1916: 67-79.

Densmore, F. Poems from Sioux and Chippewa songs. Washington, D.C., 1917. 24 p.

Densmore, F. Teton Sioux music. U.S. Bureau of American Ethnology, Bulletin, 61 (1918): 1-533.

Densmore, F. The importance of the mental concept in Indian art. Masterkey, 22 (1948): 96-99.

Densmore, F. The rhythm of Sioux and Chippewa music. Art and Archaeology, 9 (1920): 59-67.

Donaldson, T. The George Catlin Indian Gallery. United States National Museum, Reports (1885): 53-63.

Dorsey, G. A. Legend of the Teton Sioux medicine pipe. Journal of American Folklore, 19 (1906): 326-329.

Dorsey, J. O. A study of Siouan cults. U.S. Bureau of American Ethnology, Annual Reports, 11 (1890): 351-544.

Dorsey, J. O. Games of Teton Dakota children. American Anthropologist, 4 (1891): 329-345.

Dorsey, J. O. Preface. Contributions to North American Ethnology, 9 (1893): xi-xxxii.

Dorsey, J. O. Siouan sociology. U.S. Bureau of American Ethnology, Annual Reports, 15 (1894): 218-222.

Dorsey, J. O. Teton folk-lore. American Anthropologist, 2 (1889): 143-158.

Dorsey, J. O. Teton folk-lore notes. Journal of American Folklore, 2 (1889): 133-139.

Dorsey, J. O. The social organization of the Siouan tribes. Journal of American Folklore, 4 (1891): 260-263.

Dorsey, J. O. and C. Thomas. Brulé. U.S. Bureau of American Ethnology, Bulletin, 30, vol. 1 (1907): 166-167.

Dorsey, J. O. and C. Thomas. Oglala. U.S. Bureau of American Ethnology, Bulletin, 30, vol. 2 (1910): 109-111.

Douglas, F. H. The Sioux or Dakota Indians. Denver Art Museum, Indian Leaflet Series, 41 (1932): 1-4.

Duratschek, M. C. Crusading along Sioux trails. St. Meinrad, Indiana, 1947. 334 p.

Dyck, Paul. Brulé: the Sioux people of the Rosebud. Flagstaff, Northland Press, 1971. 12, 365 p.

Eggleston, Edward. George W. Northrup: the Kit Carson of the Northwest; the-man-that-draws-the-handcart. Edited by Louis Pfaller. North Dakota History, 33 (1966): 4-21.

Ellis, Everett L. To take a scalp. Annals of Wyoming, 31 (1959): 140-143.

Erikson, E. H. Observations on Sioux education. Journal of Psychology, 7 (1939): 101-156.

Ewers, J. C. Edwin T. Denig's "Of the Sioux". Missouri Historical Society, Bulletin, 7 (1951): 185-215.

Ewers, J. C. Teton Dakota ethnology and history. Berkeley, 1938. 108 p.

Farrell, R. C. The burial of Sitting Bull. South Dakota, University, William H. Over Museum, Museum News, 15, no. 1 (1954): 1-2.

Fay, George E., ed. Charters, constitutions and by-laws of Indian tribes of North America. Part I: The Sioux tribes of South Dakota. Greeley, 1967. 12, 120 l. map. (University of Northern Colorado, Museum of Anthropology, Occasional Publications in Anthropology, Ethnology Series, 1) ERIC ED046551.

Fay, George E., ed. Military engagements between United States troops and Plains Indians; documentary inquiry by the U.S. Congress. Part I: 1854-1867. Greeley, 1972. 2 v. (236 l.). (University of Northern Colorado, Museum of Anthropology, Occasional Publications in Anthropology, Ethnology Series, 26)

Fay, George E., ed. Treaties, and land cessions, between the bands of the Sioux and the United States of America, 1805-1906. Greeley, 1972. 7, 139 l. (University of Northern Colorado, Museum of Anthropology, Occasional Publications in Anthropology, Ethnology Series, 24)

Fenenga, F. The interdependence of archaeology and ethnology as illustrated by the ice-glider game of the Northern Plains. Plains Anthropologist, 1 (1954): 31-38.

Feraca, Stephen E. Crucifix and moccasin of Sitting Bull, Hunkpapa Teton chief.

South Dakota, University, Museum, Museum
News, 27, nos. 11/12 (1966): 17-18.

Feraca, Stephen E.   Reply to Hurt's review
of "Wakinyan: contemporary Teton Dakota
religion". American Anthropologist, 67
(1965): 506-507.

Feraca, Stephen E.   The identity and
demography of the Dakota or Sioux tribe.
By Stephen E. Feraca and James H.
Howard. Plains Anthropologist, 8 (1963):
80-84.

Feraca, Stephen E.   The political status
of the early bands and modern
communities of the Oglala Dakota. South
Dakota, University, Museum, Museum News,
27, nos. 1/2 (1966): 1-26.

Feraca, Stephen E.   The Teton Sioux Eagle
Medicine Cult. American Indian
Tradition, 8, no. 5 (1962): 195-196.

Feraca, Stephen E.   The Yuwipi Cult of the
Oglala and Sicangu Teton Sioux. Plains
Anthropologist, 6 (1961): 155-163.

Feraca, Stephen E.   Wakinyan; contemporary
Teton Dakota religion. Browning, Museum
of the Plains Indian, 1963.   72 p.

Finster, David.   The Hardin winter count.
South Dakota, University, Museum, Museum
News, 29, nos. 3/4 (1968): 1-57.

Fire, John.   Lame Deer, seeker of visions.
By John Fire/Lame Deer and Richard
Erdoes.   New York, Simon and Schuster,
1972.   288 p.   illus.

Fletcher, A. C.   Indian story and song
from North America.   Boston, 1907.
126 p.

Fletcher, A. C.   The elk mystery or
festival. Harvard University, Peabody
Museum of American Archaeology and
Ethnology, Reports, 16/17 (1883): 276-
288.

Fletcher, A. C.   The shadow or ghost
lodge. Harvard University, Peabody
Museum of American Archaeology and
Ethnology, Reports, 16/17 (1883): 296-
307.

Fletcher, A. C.   The white buffalo
festival of the Uncpapas. Harvard
University, Peabody Museum of American
Archaeology and Ethnology, Reports,
16/17 (1883): 260-275.

Ford, Virginia.   Cultural criteria and
determinants for acceptance of modern
medical theory and practice among the
Teton Dakota. Dissertation Abstracts, 27
(1966/1967): 4223B.   UM 67-7497.

Fugle, Eugene.   The nature and function of
the Lakota night cults. South Dakota,
University, Museum, Museum News, 27,
nos. 3/4 (1966): 1-38.

Furnas, Robert W.   The Second Nebraska's
campaign against the Sioux. By Robert W.
Furnas and Henry W. Pierce. Edited by
Richard D. Rowen. Nebraska History, 44
(1963): 3-53.

Gaul, G.   Standing Rock Agency. In United
States, Department of the Interior,
Census Office, Eleventh Census, Report
on Indians Taxed and Indians not Taxed.
Washington, D.C., 1890: 519-526.

Gauvreau, E.   Les Dakotas. International
Congress of Americanists, Proceedings,
15, vol. 1 (1907): 311-313.

Gilmore, M. R.   Dakota mourning customs.
Indian Notes, 3 (1926): 295-296.

Gilmore, M. R.   Oath-taking among the
Dakota. Indian Notes, 4 (1927): 81-83.

Gilmore, M. R.   Prairie smoke.   New York,
1929.   208 p.

Gilmore, M. R.   Some native Nebraska
plants with their uses by the Dakota.
Nebraska State Historical Society,
Collections, 17 (1913): 358-370.

Gilmore, M. R.   The Dakota ceremony of
Hunka. Indian Notes, 6 (1929): 75-79.

Gilmore, M. R.   The Dakota ceremony of
presenting a pipe. Michigan Academy of
Science, Arts and Letters, Papers, 18
(1932): 15-21.

Gilmore, M. R.   The old-time method of
rearing a Dakota boy. Indian Notes, 6
(1929): 367-372.

Gilmore, M. R.   The victory dance of the
Dakota Indians. Michigan Academy of
Science, Arts and Letters, Papers, 18
(1932): 23-30.

Gilmore, M. R.   Uses of plants by the
Indians of the Missouri River region.
U.S. Bureau of American Ethnology,
Annual Reports, 33 (1912): 43-154.

Goldfrank, E. S.   Historic change and
social character: a study of the Teton
Dakota. American Anthropologist, n.s.,
45 (1943): 67-83.

Grange, Roger T., Jr.   The Garnier Oglala
winter count. Plains Anthropologist, 8
(1963): 74-79.

Grinnell, Ira H.   The tribal government of
the Oglala Sioux of Pine Ridge, South
Dakota. Vermillion, 1967.   83 l.

illus. (South Dakota, University, Government Research Bureau, Special Project, 22)

Hallam, J. A Sioux vision. In W. W. Beach, ed. Indian Miscellany. Albany, 1877: 127-144.

Hans, F. W. The great Sioux nation. Chicago, 1907. 575 p.

Hanson, Charles E., Jr. The battle of Crow Butte. Museum of the Fur Trade Quarterly, 5, no. 3 (1969): 2-4.

Hanson, James. The Oglala Sioux sun dance. Museum of the Fur Trade Quarterly, 1, no. 3 (1965): 3-5.

Hassrick, R. B. Teton Dakota kinship system. American Anthropologist, n.s., 46 (1944): 338-347.

Hayden, F. V. Contributions to the ethnography and philology of the Indian tribes of the Missouri Valley. American Philosophical Society, Transactions, n.s., 12 (1863): 364-378.

Hebard, G. R. and E. A. Brininstool. The Bozeman Trail. Cleveland, 1922. 2 v.

Heilbron, B. L. Some Sioux legends in pictures. Minnesota History, 36, no. 1 (1958): 18-23.

Hill, Burton S. Bozeman and the Bozeman Trail. Annals of Wyoming, 36 (1964): 204-233.

Howard, J. H. Dakota fishing practices. South Dakota, University, Museum, Museum Notes, 12, no. 5 (1951): 1-4.

Howard, J. H. New notes on the Dakota earth lodge. Plains Archaeological Conference, News Letter, 4, no. 1 (1951): 4-10.

Howard, J. H. Notes on the Dakota grass dance. Southwestern Journal of Anthropology, 7 (1951): 82-85.

Howard, J. H. The Dakota Heyoka cult. Scientific Monthly, 78 (1954): 254-258.

Howard, J. H. The tree dweller cults of the Dakota. Journal of American Folklore, 68 (1955): 462-472.

Howard, J. H. Two Dakota dream headdresses. South Dakota, University, Museum, Museum Notes, 12, no. 4 (1951): 1-4.

Howard, J. H. Two Dakota winter count texts. Plains Anthropologist, 5 (1955): 13-30.

Howard, James H. Dakota winter counts as a source of Plains history. Washington, D.C., Government Printing Office, 1960. 335-416 p. illus. (U.S., Bureau of American Ethnology, Anthropological Papers, 61. U.S., Bureau of American Ethnology, Bulletin, 173)

Howard, James H. Dance at Cheyenne River Agency, South Dakota, 1939. American Indian Crafts and Culture, 6, no. 2 (1972): 10-12.

Howard, James H. Fire Cloud's Omaha or Grass Dance costume. American Indian Crafts and Culture, 6, no. 2 (1972); 6, no. 3 (1972): 2-8.

Howard, James H. Notes on Dakota archery. South Dakota, University, Museum, Museum News, 12, no. 2 (1950): 1-3.

Howard, James H. The Dakota Indian victory dance, World War II. North Dakota History, 18, no. 1 (1951): 31-40.

Howard, James H. The Dakota or Sioux Indians; a study in human ecology. Vermillion, 1966. illus., map. (South Dakota, University, South Dakota Museum, Anthropological Papers, 2)

Howard, James H. The Dakota or Sioux tribe. South Dakota, University, Museum, Museum News, 27, nos. 5/6 (1966): 1-10; 27, nos. 7/8 (1966): 1-9; 27, nos. 9/10 (1966): 1-9.

Howard, James H. The four worst things. Oklahoma Anthropological Society, Newsletter, 18, no. 5 (1970): 14-16.

Howard, James H. The music man among the Santee, or the Bohemian bandmaster's brainstorm. American Indian Crafts and Culture, 6, no. 8 (1972): 6-9, 16-17; 6, no. 9 (1972): 6-9.

Howard, James H. The White Bull manuscript. Linguistic Circle of Manitoba and North Dakota, Proceedings, 3, no. 1 (1961): 7-9.

Howard, James H. The White Bull manuscript. Plains Anthropologist, 6 (1961): 115-116.

Howard, James H. The White Bull manuscript. Plains Anthropologist, 6 (1961): 68.

Hrdlička, A. Anthropology of the Sioux. American Journal of Physical Anthropology, 16 (1931): 123-170.

Hrdlička, A. Ritual ablation of front teeth in Siberia and America. Smithsonian Miscellaneous Collections, 99, no. 3 (1940): 1-32.

Hrdlička, A. Tuberculosis among certain
Indian tribes. U.S. Bureau of American
Ethnology, Bulletin, 42 (1909): 11-14.

Hulsizer, A. Region and culture in the
curriculum of the Navaho and the Dakota.
Federalsburg, 1940. 344 p.

Hultkrantz, Åke. The Indians in
Yellowstone Park. Annals of Wyoming, 29
(1957): 125-149.

Humfreville, J. L. Twenty years among our
savage Indians. Hartford, 1897. 674 p.

Hurt, W. R. Additional notes on Dakota
house types of South Dakota. South
Dakota, University, William H. Over
Museum, Museum News, 15, no. 1 (1954):
3.

Hurt, W. R. and J. H. Howard. A Dakota
conjuring ceremony. Southwestern Journal
of Anthropology, 8 (1952): 286-296.

Hurt, W. R. and J. H. Howard. Two newly-
recorded Dakota house types.
Southwestern Journal of Anthropology, 6
(1950): 423-426.

Hurt, Wesley R. Correction on Yuwipi
color symbolism. Plains Anthropologist,
6 (1961): 43.

Hurt, Wesley R. Factors in the
persistence of peyote in the Northern
Plains. Plains Anthropologist, 5 (1960):
16-27.

Hyde, G. E. A Sioux chronicle. Norman,
1956. 353 p.

Hyde, G. E. Red Cloud's folk: a history
of the Oglala Sioux Indians. Norman,
1937. 331 p.

Hyde, George E. Spotted Tail's folk; a
history of the Brulé Sioux. Norman,
University of Oklahoma Press, 1961. 19,
329 p. illus., maps.

Hyer, J. K. Dictionary of the Sioux
language. New York, 1931. 34 p.

Jackson, Donald. Journey to the Mandans,
1809; the lost narrative of Dr. Thomas.
Missouri Historical Society Bulletin, 20
(1963/1964): 179-192.

Jaques. Notes of a tourist through the
Upper Missouri region. Missouri
Historical Society, Bulletin, 22
(1965/1966): 393-409.

Johnson, W. F. Life of Sitting Bull and
history of the Indian war. Edgewood,
1891. 545 p.

Johnston, M. A. Federal relations with
the great Sioux Indians of South Dakota,
1887-1933. Washington, D.C., 1949.
137 p.

Jones, Robert Huhn. The Northwestern
Frontier and the impact on the Sioux
War, 1862. Mid-America, 41 (1959): 131-
153.

Kane, L. M. The Sioux treaties and the
traders. Minnesota History, 32 (1951):
65-80.

Keegan, J. J. The Indian brain. American
Journal of Physical Anthropology, 3
(1920): 25-62.

Kehoe, Alice B. The Ghost Dance religion
in Saskatchewan, Canada. Plains
Anthropologist, 13 (1968): 296-304.

Kelly, F. Narrative of my captivity among
the Sioux Indians. Toronto, 1872.
304 p.

Kelly, Fanny W. My captivity among the
Sioux Indians. New York, Corinth Books,
1962. 285 p. illus.

Kemnitzer, Luis S. The cultural
provenience of objects used in Yuwipi: a
modern Teton Dakota healing ritual.
Ethnos, 35 (1970): 40-75.

Kemnitzer, Luis S. The structure of
country drinking parties on Pine Ridge
Reservation, South Dakota. Plains
Anthropologist, 17 (1972): 134-142.

Kemnitzer, Luis S. Yuwipi: a modern
Dakota healing ritual. Dissertation
Abstracts, 29 (1968/1969): 3595B. UM
69-5635.

King, James T. General Crook at Camp
Cloud Peak: "I am at a loss what to do".
Journal of the West, 11 (1972): 114-127.

Kirkus, Peggy Dickey. Fort David A.
Russell: a study of its history from
1867 to 1890; with a brief summary of
events from 1890 to the present. Annals
of Wyoming, 41 (1969): 83-111.

Krámský, Jiři. The article and the
concept of definiteness in language.
The Hague, Mouton, 1972. 212 p. (Janua
Linguarum, Series Minor, 125)

Kroeber, A. L. Recent ethnic spreads.
California, University, Publications in
American Archaeology and Ethnology, 47
(1959): 259-281.

Krusche, Rolf. "Custer's massacre".
Leipzig, Museum für Völkerkunde,
Mitteilungen, 35 (1971): 13-20.

Lagasse, Jean H. Community development in Manitoba. Human Organization, 20 (1961/1962): 232-237.

Larson, T. A., ed. Across the Plains in 1864. Annals of Wyoming, 40 (1968): 267-281.

Larson, T. A., ed. Across the Plains in 1864 with George Forman. Annals of Wyoming, 40 (1968): 5-21.

Laymon, O. F. Tribal law for Oglala Sioux. Pierre, 1953.

Lee, D. D. Freedom and culture, 59-69. Englewood Cliffs, 1959.

Leigh, R. W. Dental pathology of Indian tribes. American Journal of Physical Anthropology, 8 (1925): 179-199.

Lesser, A. Some aspects of Siouan kinship. International Congress of Americanists, Proceedings, 23 (1928): 563-571.

Lesser, Alexander. Siouan kinship. Dissertation Abstracts, 19 (1958/1959): 208. UM 58-2596.

Lewis, Thomas H. The Oglala (Teton Dakota) sun dance: vissicitudes [sic] of its structures and functions. Plains Anthropologist, 17 (1972): 44-49.

Lord, M. P. Wowapi wakan kin token eya he, What saith the Scripture. Santee, 1894. 45 p.

Lyford, C. A. Quill and beadwork of the Western Sioux. Indian Handcrafts, 1 (1940): 1-116.

*Macgregor, G. Warriors without weapons. Chicago, 1946. 228 p.

*Malan, V. D. The Dakota Indian family. South Dakota, Agricultural Experiment Station, Bulletin, 470 (1958): 1-71.

Malan, V. D. and C. J. Jesser. The Dakota Indian religion. South Dakota, Agricultural Experiment Station, Bulletin, 473 (1959): 1-64.

Malan, V. D. and M. Kallich. Changing Dakota Indian culture. South Dakota, Agricultural Experiment Station, Farm and Home Research, 8 (1957): 11-15.

Malan, Vernon D. The time concept, perspective, and premise in the socio-cultural order of the Dakota Indians. By Vernon D. Malan and R. Clyde McCone. Plains Anthropologist, 5 (1960): 12-15.

Malan, Vernon D. Theories of culture change relevant to the study of the Dakota Indians. Plains Anthropologist, 6 (1961): 13-20.

Mallery, G. A calendar of the Dakota nation. United States Geological and Geographical Survey of the Territories, Bulletin, 3 (1877): 3-25.

Marion, William. Fort Stambaugh. Annals of Wyoming, 40 (1968): 118-119.

Mathews, G. H. Phonemic analysis of a Dakota dialect. International Journal of American Linguistics, 21 (1955): 56-59.

Matson, G. A. Distribution of blood groups among the Sioux, Omaha, and Winnebago Indians. American Journal of Physical Anthropology, 28 (1941): 313-318.

Mattes, Merrill J. The enigma of Wounded Knee. Plains Anthropologist, 5 (1960): 1-11.

Maynard, Eileen. Hechel lena oyate kin nipi kte. That these people may live; conditions among the Oglala Sioux of the Pine Ridge Reservation, By Eileen Maynard and Gayla Twiss. Pine Ridge, S.D., U.S. Indian Health Service, Community Mental Health Program, 1969. 183 p. illus., maps. ERIC ED035471.

McAllister, Frances Alberta. The Lakota Sioux: their ceremonies and recreations. Dissertation Abstracts, 29 (1968/1969): 1183A. UM 68-14,072.

McBride, Dorothy McFatridge. Hoosier schoolmaster among the Sioux. Montana, the Magazine of Western History, 20, no. 4 (1970): 78-97.

McCone, R. Clyde. Death and the persistence of basic personality structure among the Lakota. Plains Anthropologist, 13 (1968): 305-309.

McGee, W J. The Siouan Indians. U.S. Bureau of American Ethnology, Annual Reports, 15 (1894): 157-204.

McGillycuddy, J. B. McGillycuddy agent. Stanford, 1941. 291 p.

McLaughlin, J. My friend the Indian. Boston, 1910. 417 p.

Meeker, L. L. Oglala games. Pennsylvania, University, Free Museum of Science and Art, Bulletin, 3 (1901): 23-46.

Meeker, L. L. Siouan mythological tales. Journal of American Folklore, 14 (1901): 161-164.

Meeker, L. L.   White man, a Siouan myth. Journal of American Folklore, 15 (1902): 84-87.

Mekeel, H. Scudder.   The economy of a modern Teton Dakota community. New Haven, Human Relations Area Files Press, 1970.   14 p.   map.   (Yale University Publications in Anthropology, 6)

Mekeel, H. Scudder.   The economy of a modern Teton Dakota community. New Haven, 1936.   14 p. map.   (Yale University Publications in Anthropology, 6)

Mekeel, S.   A discussion of culture change as illustrated by material from a Teton-Dakota community. American Anthropologist, n.s., 34 (1932): 274-285.

Mekeel, S.   A short history of the Teton-Dakota. North Dakota Historical Quarterly, 10 (1943): 136-205.

Metcalf, George.   Two relics of the Wounded Knee massacre. Museum of the Fur Trade Quarterly, 2, no. 4 (1966): 1-4.

Meyer, Roy W.   The establishment of the Santee Reservation, 1866-1869. Nebraska History, 45 (1964): 59-97.

Mirsky, J.   The Dakota. In M. Mead, ed. Cooperation and Competition among Primitive Peoples.   New York, 1937: 382-427.

Montgomery, G.   A method of studying the structure of primitive verse applied to the songs of the Teton-Sioux. California, University, Publications in Modern Philology, 11 (1922): 269-283.

Mooney, J.   The ghost-dance religion. U.S. Bureau of American Ethnology, Annual Reports, 14, vol. 2 (1893): 796-927, 1058-1078.

Moorehead, W. K.   Sioux women at home. Illustrated American, 5 (1891): 481-484.

Moorehead, W. K.   The Indian messiah and the ghost dance. American Antiquarian and Oriental Journal, 13 (1891): 161-167.

Moorehead, W. K.   The passing of Red Cloud. Kansas State Historical Society, Transactions, 10 (1908): 295-311.

Moorehead, W. K.   Wanneta, the Sioux. New York, 1890.

Morgan, A.   A description of a Dakotan calendar. Literary and Philosophical Society of Liverpool, Proceedings, 33 (1879): 233-253.

Morgan, L. H.   Systems of consanguinity and affinity. Smithsonian Contributions to Knowledge, 17 (1871): 291-382.

Morgan, L. H.   The Indian journals, 1859-62: p. 60-61, 198.   Ann Arbor, 1959.

Morton, Thomas F.   The Civil War of Private Morton. Edited by James T. King. North Dakota History, 35 (1968): 9-19.

Munkres, Robert L.   The Plains Indian threat on the Oregon Trail before 1860. Annals of Wyoming, 40 (1968): 193-221.

Murphy, James C.   The place of the Northern Arapahoes in the relations between the United States and the Indians of the Plains 1851-1879. Annals of Wyoming, 41 (1969): 33-61, 203-259.

Murray, Robert A.   The Wagon Box fight: a centennial appraisal. Annals of Wyoming, 39 (1967): 104-107.

Nasatir, A. P.   Before Lewis and Clark. St. Louis, 1952.   2 v. (882 p.).

Neihardt, J. G.   When the tree flowered. New York, 1951.

Nevins, A., ed.   Narratives of exploration and adventure by John Charles Frémont. New York, 1956.   542 p.

O'Leary, Mrs. James L.   Henry Chatillon. Missouri Historical Society, Bulletin, 22 (1965/1966): 123-142.

Olson, James C.   Red Cloud and the Sioux problem. Lincoln, University of Nebraska Press, 1965.   13, 375 p. illus., map.

Olson, James C.   Red Cloud vs. McGillycuddy. In Richard N. Ellis, ed. The Western American Indian. Lincoln, University of Nebraska Press, 1972: 97-116.

Orata, Pedro T.   Fundamental education in an Amerindian community.   Lawrence, Kan., U.S. Bureau of Indian Affairs, Haskell Press, 1953.   220 p.   illus.

Curada, Patricia K., ed.   The hat Sitting Bull wears. Told by Andrew Fox. Annals of Wyoming, 41 (1969): 272-274.

Paige, Harry W.   Songs of the Teton Sioux. Los Angeles, Westernlore Press, 1970. 15, 201 p.   illus.   (Great West and Indian Series, 39)

Paige, Harry Worthington.   The songs of the Teton Sioux. Dissertation Abstracts, 28 (1967/1968): 4607A.   UM 68-5272.

Parkman, F. The Oregon Trail. 5th ed.
Boston, 1873. 381 p.

Patrie, Lewis E. A multiphasic screening
project on the Pine Ridge Indian
Reservation. Journal--Lancet, 82 (1962):
511-514.

Pennanen, Gary. Sitting Bull, Indian
without a country. Canadian Historical
Review, 51 (1970): 123-140.

Petersen, Karen Daniels. On Hayden's list
of Cheyenne military societies. American
Anthropologist, 67 (1965): 469-472.

Plant, W. G. A Hebrew-Dakota dictionary.
American Jewish Historical Society,
Proceedings, 42 (1953): 361-370.

Pond, S. W. Two volunteer missionaries
among the Dakotas. Chicago, 1893.
287 p.

Poole, D. C. Among the Sioux of Dakota.
New York, 1881. 235 p.

Powers, William K. Contemporary Oglala
music and dance: Pan-Indianism versus
Pan-Tetonism. Ethnomusicology, 12
(1968): 352-372.

Primbs, C. The sunflower dance of the
Sioux Indians of the Upper Missouri.
Norfolk, 1876. 15 p.

Rabeau, E. S. Health auxilary training,
instructor's guide. Washington, D.C.,
U.S. Public Health Service, Division of
Indian Health, 1966. 261 p. ERIC
ED023827.

Red Horse Owner, Moses. Red Horse Owner's
winter count; the Oglala Sioux, 1786-
1968. Edited by Joseph S. Karol.
Martin, S.D., Booster Publishing, 1969.
68 p.

Reynolds, Sam. A Dakota tipi. North
Dakota History, 40, no. 4 (1973): 20-29.

Riggs, M. A. C. An English and Dakota
vocabulary. New York, 1852. 120 p.

Riggs, S. R. A Dakota-English dictionary.
Contributions to North American
Ethnology, 7 (1890): 1-665.

Riggs, S. R. Dakota grammar, texts and
ethnography. Contributions to North
American Ethnology, 9 (1893): 1-232.

Riggs, S. R. Grammar and dictionary of
the Dakota language. Smithsonian
Contributions to Knowledge, 4 (1852): 1-
338.

Riley, Paul D. Dr. David Franklin Powell
and Fort McPherson. Nebraska History, 51
(1970): 153-170.

Ripich, Carol A. Joseph W. Wham and the
Red Cloud Agency, 1871. Arizona and the
West, 12 (1970): 325-338.

Ritzenthaler, Robert F. Sioux Indian
drawings. Milwaukee, Milwaukee Public
Museum, 1961. 8 p. illus.

Roberts, W. O. Successful agriculture
within the reservation framework. Human
Organization, 2, no. 3 (1943): 37-44.

Robinson, D. A history of the Dakota or
Sioux Indians. South Dakota Historical
Collections, 2 (1904): 1-523.
[Reprinted, 1956.]

Robinson, D. Sioux Indians. Cedar
Rapids, 1908.

Robinson, D. The Sioux of the Dakotas.
Home Geographic Monthly, 2, no. 5
(1932): 7-12.

Rood, David S. Preparing Lakhota teaching
materials; a progress report. By David
S. Rood and Allan R. Taylor. Colorado
Research in Linguistics, 3 (1973): RT1-
RT9.

Ruby, R. H. The Oglala Sioux. New York,
1955. 115 p.

Ruby, Robert H. Yuwipi; ancient rite of
the Sioux. Montana, the Magazine of
Western History, 16, no. 4 (1966): 74-
79.

Saint-Paul, C. Die Dakotahs oder Sioux.
Ausland, 64 (1891): 121-126.

Sanderson, James F. Indian tales of the
Canadian prairies. Alberta Historical
Review, 13, no. 3 (1965): 7-21.

Sandoz, M. Crazy Horse. New York, 1942.
428 p.

Sayre, Robert F. Vision and experience in
Black Elk Speaks. College English, 32
(1970/1971): 509-535.

Schmidt, M. F. and D. Brown. Fighting
Indians of the West, 15-40, 113-228.
New York, 1948.

Schusky, Ernest L. Contemporary migration
and culture change in two Dakota
reservations. Plains Anthropologist, 7
(1962): 178-183.

Schusky, Ernest L. Mission and government
policy in Dakota Indian communities.
Practical Anthropology, 10 (1963): 109-
114.

Schusky, Ernest L. Politics and planning in a Dakota Indian community; a case study of views on termination and plans for rehabilitation on the Lower Brule Reservation in South Dakota. Vermillion, State University of South Dakota, Institute of Indian Studies, 1959. 89 p. illus., map.

Schwarzer, H. Die Heilige Pfeife. Olten, 1956. 234 p.

Schwatka, F. The sun-dance of the Sioux. Century Magazine, 39 (1890): 753-759.

Scudder, Ralph E. Custer country. Portland, Or., Binfords and Mort, 1963. 63 p. illus., maps.

Seagle, William. The murder of Spotted Tail. Indian Historian, 3, no. 4 (1970): 10-22.

Smith, Cornelius C., Jr. Crook and Crazy Horse. Montana, the Magazine of Western History, 16, no. 2 (1966): 14-26.

Smith, DeC. Indian experiences. Caldwell, 1943. 387 p.

Smith, G. Hubert. Big Bend historic sites. Lincoln, Smithsonian Institution, River Basin Surveys, 1968. 4, 111 p. illus., maps. (Smithsonian Institution, River Basin Surveys, Publications in Salvage Archeology, 9)

Smith, J. L. A ceremony for the preparation of the offering cloths for presentation to the Sacred Calf Pipe of the Teton Sioux. Plains Anthropologist, 9 (1964): 190-196.

Smith, J. L. A short history of the Sacred Calf Pipe of the Teton Dakota. South Dakota, University, Museum, Museum News, 28, nos. 7/8 (1967): 1-37.

Smith, J. L. Interview with Robert Holy Dance. South Dakota, University, Museum, Museum News, 26, nos. 9/10 (1965): 5-8.

Smith, J. L. The Sacred Calf Pipe Bundle: it's [sic] effect on the present Teton Dakota. Plains Anthropologist, 15 (1970): 87-93.

Snelling, W. J. Tales of the Northwest. Boston, 1830. 294 p.

South Dakota Writers' Project, Work Projects Administration. Legends of the mighty Sioux. Chicago, 1941. 158 p.

Speck, F. G. Notes on the functional basis of decoration and the feather technique of the Oglala Sioux. Indian Notes, 5 (1928): 1-42.

Speck, F. G. and R. B. Hassrick. A Plains Indian shield and its interpretation. Primitive Man, 21 (1948): 74-79.

Speck, F. G. and S. W. Fernberger. Two Sioux shields and their psychological interpretation. Journal of Abnormal and Social Psychology, 35 (1938): 168-178.

Spindler, W. H. Tragedy strikes at Wounded Knee. Gordon, Nebraska, 1955. 80 p.

Spindler, Will H. Tragedy strikes at Wounded Knee, and other essays on Indian life in South Dakota and Nebraska. Vermillion, University of South Dakota, 1972. 138 p. illus.

Spindler, Will H. Yesterday's trails. Gordon, Neb., Gordon Journal Publishing, 1961. 80 p. illus.

Standing Bear, L. Land of the spotted eagle. Boston, 1933. 259 p.

Standing Bear, L. My people the Sioux. Boston, 1928. 288 p.

Standing Bear, L. Stories of the Sioux. Boston, 1934.

Sullivan, L. R. Anthropometry of the Siouan tribes. American Museum of Natural History, Anthropological Papers, 23 (1920): 81-174.

Thane, James L., Jr. The Montana "Indian War" of 1867. Arizona and the West, 10 (1968): 153-170.

"The Engagees". Stinking Bear's bonnet. Museum of the Fur Trade Quarterly, 5, no. 1 (1969): 21-23.

Thomas, C. Teton. U.S. Bureau of American Ethnology, Bulletin, 30, vol. 2 (1910): 736-737.

Thompson, Edith. The Powder River forts: Connor and Reno. Annals of Wyoming, 36 (1964): 51-53.

Thompson, L. Attitudes and acculturation. American Anthropologist, n.s., 50 (1948): 200-215.

Todd, John B. S. The Harney expedition against the Sioux: the journal of Capt. John B. S. Todd. Edited by Ray H. Mattison. Nebraska History, 43 (1962): 89-130.

Tomkins, W. Universal Indian sign language. San Diego, 1927. 96 p.

Trudeau, J. B. Description of the Upper Missouri. Mississippi Valley Historical Review, 8 (1921): 149-179.

Urvant, Ellen. Native son. Vista volunteer. Washington, D.C., Office of Economic Opportunity, 1969. 31 p. ERIC ED032161.

U.S., Congress, Senate, Committee on Interior and Insular Affairs. Providing for payment for individual Indian and tribal lands of the Lower Brule Sioux Reservation in South Dakota . . . Report to accompany H.R. 5144. Washington, D.C., Government Printing Office, 1962. 35 p. (U.S., Congress, 87th Congress, 2d Session, Senate, Report, 1636)

Useem, J., G. MacGregor, and R. H. Useem. Wartime employment and cultural adjustments of the Rosebud Sioux. Human Organization, 2, no. 2 (1943): 1-9.

Vestal, S. New sources of Indian history. Norman, 1934. 351 p.

Vestal, S. Sitting Bull. 2d ed. Norman, 1957. 376 p.

Vestal, S. Warpath. Boston, 1934. 291 p.

Vogt, K. The Dakota-Sioux. Smoke Signals, 5, no. 2 (1953): 4-7.

Walker, J. D. Tuberculosis among the Oglala Sioux Indians. Southern Workman, 35 (1906): 378-384.

Walker, J. R. Dakota offering sticks. Indian Notes, 3 (1926): 199-200.

Walker, J. R. Oglala kinship terms. American Anthropologist, n.s., 16 (1914): 96-109.

Walker, J. R. Sioux games. Journal of American Folklore, 18 (1905): 277-290; 19 (1906): 29-36.

Walker, J. R. The sun dance and other ceremonies of the Oglala. American Museum of Natural History, Anthropological Papers, 16 (1917): 51-221.

Watson, Elmo Scott. Orlando Scott Goff, pioneer Dakota photographer. North Dakota History, 29 (1962): 211-215.

Wax, Murray L. Cultural deprivation as an educational ideology. By Murray L. Wax and Rosalie H. Wax. In Eleanor B. Leacock, ed. The Culture of Poverty: a Critique. New York, Simon and Schuster, 1971: 127-139.

Wax, Murray L., et al. Formal education in an American Indian community. Atlanta, Emory University, 1964. 10, 126 p. illus. (Society for the Study of Social Problems, Monograph, 1)

Wax, Rosalie H. The warrior dropouts. Trans-Action, 4, no. 6 (1967): 40-46. ERIC ED016529.

Wedel, W. R. and G. B. Griffenhagen. An English balsam among the Dakota aborigines. American Journal of Pharmacy, 126, no. 12 (1954): 409-415.

Welsh, H. Civilization among the Sioux Indians. Philadelphia, 1893. 58 p.

Welsh, H. Four weeks among some of the Sioux tribes of Dakota and Nebraska. Philadelphia, 1882. 31 p.

Welsh, H. Report of a visit to the great Sioux reserve. Philadelphia, 1883. 49 p.

Werden, Patricia Lucille Kilroy. Study of health needs of Oglala Sioux Indian students. Dissertation Abstracts International, 34 (1973/1974): 2104B-2105B. UM 73-26,524.

Weygold, F. Die Hunkazeremonie. Archiv für Anthropologie, 39 (1912): 145-160.

White Bull, Joseph. The warrior who killed Custer; the personal narrative of Chief Joseph White Bull. Translated and edited by James H. Howard. Lincoln, University of Nebraska Press, 1968. 14, 84 p. illus.

Wilson, E. P. The story of Oglala and Brule Sioux in the Pine Ridge country of Northwest Nebraska in the middle seventies. Nebraska History, 22 (1941): 15-33.

Wilson, Peter. The letters of Peter Wilson, first resident agent among the Teton Sioux. Edited by Harry H. Anderson. Nebraska History, 42 (1961): 237-264.

Wilson, Wesley C. Doctor Walter A. Burleigh: Dakota Territorial delegate to 39th and 40th Congress: politician, extraordinary. North Dakota History, 33 (1966): 93-104.

Wissler, C. Decorative art of the Sioux Indians. American Museum of Natural History, Bulletin, 18 (1905): 231-275.

Wissler, C. Distribution of deaths among American Indians. Human Biology, 8 (1936): 223-231.

Wissler, C. Measurements of Dakota Indian children. New York Academy of Sciences, Annals, 20 (1911): 355-364.

Wissler, C. Societies and ceremonial associations in the Oglala division of the Teton Dakota. American Museum of

Natural History, Anthropological Papers,
11 (1912): 1-97.

Wissler, C. Some Dakota myths. Journal of
American Folklore, 20 (1907): 121-131,
195-206.

Wissler, C. Some protective designs of
the Dakota. American Museum of Natural
History, Anthropological Papers, 1
(1907): 21-53.

Wissler, C. Symbolism in the decorative
art of the Sioux. International Congress
of Americanists, Proceedings, 13 (1902):
339-345.

Wissler, C. The whirlwind and the elk in
the mythology of the Dakotas. Journal of
American Folklore, 18 (1905): 257-268.

Yarrow, H. C. Some supersititions of the
live Indians. American Antiquarian and
Oriental Journal, 4 (1882): 136-144.

                09-25 Wichita

Barry, L. With the First U.S. Cavalry in
Indian country, 1859-1861. Kansas
Historical Quarterly, 24 (1958): 257-
284.

Boas, F. Zur Anthropologie der
nordamerikanischen Indianer. Berliner
Gesellschaft für Anthropologie,
Ethnologie und Urgeschichte,
Verhandlungen (1895): 367-411.

Bolton, H. E. Athanase de Mezières and
the Louisiana-Texas frontier.
Cleveland, 1914. 2 v.

Bolton, H. E. Tawakoni. U.S. Bureau of
American Ethnology, Bulletin, 30, vol. 2
(1910): 701-704.

Bolton, H. E. Tawehash. U.S. Bureau of
American Ethnology, Bulletin, 30, vol. 2
(1910): 705-707.

Bolton, H. E. Waco. U.S. Bureau of
American Ethnology, Bulletin, 30, vol. 2
(1910): 887-888.

Bolton, H. E. Yscanis. U.S. Bureau of
American Ethnology, Bulletin, 30, vol. 2
(1910): 1002-1003.

Bucca, Salvador. Kitsai phonology and
morphophonemics. By Salvador Bucca and
Alexander Lesser. International Journal
of American Linguistics, 35 (1969): 7-
19.

Bushnell, D. I. Villages of the
Algonquian, Siouan and Caddoan tribes.

U.S. Bureau of American Ethnology,
Bulletin, 77 (1922): 179-182.

Chapman, B. B. Dissolution of the Wichita
Reservation. Chronicles of Oklahoma, 22
(1944): 192-209, 300-314.

Curtis, E. S. The North American Indian,
Vol. 19: 35-104, 223-224, 230-238.
Norwood, 1930.

Davis, William Robert. The Spanish
borderlands of Texas and Chihuahua.
Texana, 9 (1971): 142-155.

Day, James M. James Kerr: frontier
Texian. Texana, 2 (1964): 24-43.

Derbanne, François Dion Deprez.
Natchitoches and the trail to the Rio
Grande: two early eighteenth-century
accounts by the Sieur Derbanne.
Translated and edited by Katherine
Briggs and Winston De Ville. Louisiana
History, 8 (1967): 239-259.

Dodge, Henry. Journal of Colonel Dodge's
expedition from Fort Gibson to the
Pawnee Pict village. American State
Papers, Military Affairs, 5 (1860): 373-
382.

Dorsey, G. A. Hand or guessing game among
the Wichitas. American Antiquarian and
Oriental Journal, 23 (1901): 363-370.

Dorsey, G. A. The mythology of the
Wichita. Washington, D.C., 1904.
351 p.

Dorsey, G. A. Wichita tales. Journal of
American Folklore, 15 (1902): 215-239;
16 (1903): 160-179; 17 (1904): 153-160.

Douglas, F. H. The grass house of the
Wichita and Caddo. Denver Art Museum,
Indian Leaflet Series, 42 (1932): 1-4.

Douglas, F. H. The Wichita Indians and
allied tribes. Denver Art Museum, Indian
Leaflet Series, 40 (1932): 1-4.

Duffield, Lathel F. The Taovayas village
of 1759: in Texas or Oklahoma? Great
Plains Journal, 4 (1964/1965): 39-48.

Elam, Earl Henry. The history of the
Wichita Indian confederacy to 1868.
Dissertation Abstracts International, 33
(1972/1973): 249A. UM 72-20,295.

Estep, Raymond. Lieutenant William E.
Burnet letters: removal of the Texas
Indians and the founding of Fort Cobb.
Chronicles of Oklahoma, 38 (1960): 369-
396.

Estep, Raymond. Lieutenant Wm. E. Burnet:
notes on removal of Indians from Texas

to Indian Territory. Chronicles of
Oklahoma, 38 (1960): 274-309.

Ethridge, A. N.   Indians of Grant Parish.
Louisiana Historical Quarterly, 23
(1940): 1108-1131.

Fay, George E., ed. Charters,
constitutions and by-laws of the Indian
tribes of North America. Part VI: The
Indian tribes of Oklahoma (cont'd.).
Greeley, 1868. 5, 129 l. map.
(University of Northern Colorado, Museum
of Anthropology, Occasional Publications
in Anthropology, Ethnology Series, 7)
ERIC ED046556.

Fletcher, A. C.   Kichai. U.S. Bureau of
American Ethnology, Bulletin, 30, vol. 1
(1907): 682-683.

Foreman, G.   The last trek of the Indians,
282-286, 290-291, 302-304. Chicago,
1946.

Garvin, P. L. Wichita. International
Journal of American Linguistics, 16
(1950): 179-184.

Gatschet, A. S. Migration of the Wichita
Indians. American Antiquarian and
Oriental Journal, 13 (1891): 249-252.

Gatschet, A. S.   Two Indian Documents.
American Antiquarian and Oriental
Journal, 13 (1891): 249-254.

Gray, Margery P.   Blood groups of Caddoan
Indians of Oklahoma. By Margery P. Gray
and William S. Laughlin. American
Journal of Human Genetics, 12 (1960):
86-94.

Haas, M. R.   Comments on the name
"Wichita". American Anthropologist,
n.s., 44 (1942): 164-165.

Harper, E. A.   The Taovayas Indians in
frontier trade and diplomacy, 1779-1835.
Panhandle-Plains Historical Review, 26
(1953): 41-72.

Harper, E. A.   The Taovayas Indians in
frontier trade and diplomacy, 1769-1779.
Southwestern Historical Quarterly, 57
(1953): 181-201.

Harper, E. A.   The Taovayas Indians in
frontier trade and diplomacy. Chronicles
of Oklahoma, 31 (1953): 268-289.

Havins, T. R.   Noah T. Byars at Torrey's
Trading Post. Texana, 8 (1970): 328-340.

Hughes, Jack Thomas.   Prehistory of the
Caddoan-speaking tribes. Dissertation
Abstracts International, 30 (1969/1970):
950B. UM 69-9198.

Hungate, M.   Religious beliefs of the
Nebraska Indian. Nebraska History, 14,
no. 3 (1938): 207-226.

Jelks, Edward B.   The Norteño Focus: a
historic complex of North Central Texas.
Plains Anthropologist, 7 (1962): 95-96.

Lesser, A.   Levirate and fraternal
polyandry among the Pawnees. Man, 30
(1930): 98-101.

Lesser, A. and G. Weltfish.   Composition
of the Caddoan linguistic stock.
Smithsonian Miscellaneous Collections,
87, no. 6 (1932): 1-15.

McLean, Malcolm D.   Tenoxtitlan, dream
capital of Texas. Southwestern
Historical Quarterly, 70 (1966/1967):
23-43.

Mead, J. R.   The Little Arkansas. Kansas
State Historical Society, Transactions,
10 (1908): 7-14.

Middlebrooks, Audy J.   Holland Coffee of
Red River. By Audy J. and Glenna
Middlebrooks. Southwestern Historical
Quarterly, 69 (1965/1966): 145-162.

Mooney, J.   Wichita. U.S. Bureau of
American Ethnology, Bulletin, 30, vol. 2
(1910): 947-950.

Nasatir, A. P.   Before Lewis and Clark.
St. Louis, 1952. 2 v. (882 p.).

Neighbours, Kenneth F.   Jose Maria:
Anadarko chief. Chronicles of Oklahoma,
44 (1966): 254-274.

Neuman, Robert W.   Check-stamped pottery
on the northern and central Great
Plains. American Antiquity, 29
(1963/1964): 17-26.

Nye, W. S.   Carbine and lance. Norman,
1937. 441 p.

O'Bryant, A.   Differences in Wichita
Indian camp sites as revealed by stone
artifacts. Kansas Historical Quarterly,
15 (1947): 143-150.

Oklahoma, University, Bureau of Business
Research.   The utilization of property
of specified Wichita, Caddo, and
Delaware Indian tribes' land in Caddo
County, Oklahoma. Norman, 1964. 9,
108 p. map.

Rood, David S.   Agent and object in
Wichita. Lingua, 28 (1971): 100-107.

Rood, David Stanley.   Wichita grammar: a
generative semantic sketch. Dissertation
Abstracts International, 31 (1970/1971):
746A. UM 70-13,152.

Sayles, E. B. An archaeological survey of
Texas. Medallion Papers, 17 (1935): 1-
164.

Scarborough, D. Traditions of the Waco
Indians. Texas Folk-Lore Society,
Publications, 1 (1916): 50-54.

Schmitt, K. Wichita death customs.
Chronicles of Oklahoma, 30 (1952): 200-
206.

Schmitt, K. Wichita-Kiowa relations and
the 1874 outbreak. Chronicles of
Oklahoma, 28 (1950): 154-160.

*Schmitt, K. and I. A. Schmitt. Wichita
kinship past and present. Norman, 1952.
82 p.

Smith, R. A. Account of the journey of
Bénard de la Harpe. Southwestern
Historical Quarterly, 62 (1958/1959):
75-86, 246-259, 371-385, 525-541.

Smith, R. A. The Tawehash in French,
Spanish, English, and American imperial
affairs. West Texas Historical
Association Yearbook, 28 (1952): 18-49.

Spier, L. Wichita and Caddo relationship
terms. American Anthropologist, n.s., 26
(1924): 258-263.

Steen, C. R. Two early historic sites on
the Southern Plains. Texas Archeological
and Paleontological Society, Bulletin,
24 (1953): 177-188.

Taylor, Allan R. The classification of
the Caddoan languages. American
Philosophical Society, Proceedings, 107
(1963): 51-59.

Tilghman, Z. A. Origin of the name
Wichita. American Anthropologist, n.s.,
43 (1941): 488-489.

Troike, Rudolph C. The Caddo word for
"water". International Journal of
American Linguistics, 30 (1964): 96-98.

Watt, Frank H. The Waco Indian village
and its peoples. Texana, 6 (1968): 195-
243.

Webb, Murl L. Religious and educational
efforts among Texas Indians in the
1850's. Southwestern Historical
Quarterly, 69 (1965/1966): 22-37.

Wedel, Mildred Mott. J.-B. Bénard, Sieur
de la Harpe: visitor to the Wichitas in
1719. Great Plains Journal, 10
(1970/1971): 37-70.

Wedel, W. R. The Wichita. U.S. Bureau of
American Ethnology, Bulletin, 174
(1959): 60-68.

Wedel, Waldo R. The council circles of
Central Kansas: were they solstice
registers? American Antiquity, 32
(1967): 54-63.

White, Lonnie J. Winter campaigning with
Sheridan and Custer: the expedition of
the Nineteenth Kansas Volunteer Cavalry.
Journal of the West, 6 (1967): 68-98.

Winfrey, Dorman H., ed. The Indian papers
of Texas and the Southwest, 1825-1916.
Edited by Dorman H. Winfrey and James M.
Day. Austin, Pemberton Press, 1966.
412 p.

09-26   Yankton

DeMallie, Raymond J. Bibliography: the
Sioux. Indian Historian, 2, no. 3
(1969): 49-50.

Agogino, George. Oscar Howe Sioux artist.
By George Agogino and Heidi Howe. South
Dakota, State University, W. H. Over
Museum, Museum News, 20, no. 4 (1959):
1-5.

Anonymous. Dakota. U.S. Bureau of
American Ethnology, Bulletin, 30, vol. 1
(1907): 376-380.

Anonymous. Sioux treaty of 1868. Indian
Historian, 3, no. 1 (1970): 13-17.

Belden, G. P. Belden, the White chief.
Cincinnati, 1870. 511 p.

Bigart, Robert James. Indian culture and
industrialization. American
Anthropologist, 74 (1972): 1180-1188.

Bradley, J. H. History of the Sioux.
Historical Society of Montana,
Contributions, 9 (1923): 29-140.

Buechel, Eugene. A dictionary of the
Teton Dakota Sioux Language: Lakota-
English, English-Lakota, with
considerations given to Yankton and
Santee. Ed. by Paul Manhart. Pine
Ridge, Red Cloud Indian School, Holy
Rosary Mission, 1970. 6, 852 p.

Culbertson, T. A. Journal of an
expedition to the mauvaises terres and
the Upper Missouri in 1850. U.S. Bureau
of American Ethnology, Bulletin, 147
(1952): 1-172.

Culin, S. A summer trip among the Western
Indians. Pennsylvania, University, Free
Museum of Science and Art, Bulletin, 3
(1901): 166-172.

Curtis, E. S. The North American Indian,
    Vol. 3: 121-123, 152-159. Cambridge,
    1908.

Dangberg, G. M. Letters to Jack Wilson,
    the Paiute prophet. U.S. Bureau of
    American Ethnology, Bulletin, 174
    (1957): 279-296.

Danziger, Edmund J., Jr. The Crow Creek
    experiment: an aftermath of the Sioux
    War of 1862. North Dakota History, 37
    (1970): 105-123.

Deloria, Ella C. Some notes on the
    Yankton. South Dakota, University,
    Museum, Museum News, 28, nos. 3/4
    (1967): 1-30.

Dorsey, J. O. A study of Siouan cults.
    U.S. Bureau of American Ethnology,
    Annual Reports, 11 (1890): 431-500.

Dorsey, J. O. Preface. Contributions to
    North American Ethnology, 9 (1893): xi-
    xxxii.

Dorsey, J. O. Siouan sociology. U.S.
    Bureau of American Ethnology, Annual
    Reports, 15 (1894): 217-218.

Douglas, F. H. The Sioux or Dakota
    Indians. Denver Art Museum, Indian
    Leaflet Series, 41 (1932): 1-4.

Ducheneaux, F. The Cheyenne River Sioux.
    American Indian, 7, no. 3 (1956): 20-29.

Duratschek, M. C. Crusading along Sioux
    trails. St. Meinrad, Indiana, 1947.
    334 p.

Eggleston, Edward. George W. Northrup:
    the Kit Carson of the Northwest; the-
    man-that-draws-the-handcart. Edited by
    Louis Pfaller. North Dakota History, 33
    (1966): 4-21.

Fay, George E., ed. Charters,
    constitutions and by-laws of Indian
    tribes of North America. Part I: The
    Sioux tribes of South Dakota. Greeley,
    1967. 12, 120 l. map. (University of
    Northern Colorado, Museum of
    Anthropology, Occasional Publications in
    Anthropology, Ethnology Series, 1) ERIC
    ED046551.

Fay, George E., ed. Military engagements
    between United States troops and Plains
    Indians; documentary inquiry by the U.S.
    Congress. Part I: 1854-1867. Greeley,
    1972. 2 v. (236 l.). (University of
    Northern Colorado, Museum of
    Anthropology, Occasional Publications in
    Anthropology, Ethnology Series, 26)

Fay, George E., ed. Treaties, and land
    cessions, between the bands of the Sioux

and the United States of America, 1805-
    1906. Greeley, 1972. 7, 139 l.
    (University of Northern Colorado, Museum
    of Anthropology, Occasional Publications
    in Anthropology, Ethnology Series, 24)

Feraca, Stephen E. The identity and
    demography of the Dakota or Sioux tribe.
    By Stephen E. Feraca and James H.
    Howard. Plains Anthropologist, 8 (1963):
    80-84.

Fleetwood, Mary. Moses K. Armstrong.
    North Dakota History, 28 (1961): 13-22.

Furnas, Robert W. The Second Nebraska's
    campaign against the Sioux. By Robert W.
    Furnas and Henry W. Pierce. Edited by
    Richard D. Rowen. Nebraska History, 44
    (1963): 3-53.

Gaul, G. Standing Rock Agency. In United
    States Department of the Interior,
    Census Office, Eleventh Census, Report
    on Indians Taxed and Indians not Taxed.
    Washington, D.C., 1890: 519-526.

Glatfelter, Noah M. Letters from Dakota
    Territory, 1865. Missouri Historical
    Society, Bulletin, 18 (1961/1962): 104-
    134.

Green, Norma Kidd. Four sisters:
    daughters of Joseph La Flesche. Nebraska
    History, 45 (1964): 165-176.

Hafen, Le Roy R. Etienne Provost,
    mountain man and Utah pioneer. Utah
    Historical Quarterly, 36 (1968): 99-112.

Hayden, F. V. Contributions to the
    ethnography and philology of the Indian
    tribes of the Missouri Valley. American
    Philosophical Society, Transactions,
    n.s., 12 (1863): 364-378.

Hayes, J. Christ Church? Dakota people of
    Yankton. The B.C.U. Digest, 1, no. 3
    (1957): 1-3.

Heilbron, B. L. Some Sioux legends in
    pictures. Minnesota History, 36, no. 1
    (1958): 18-23.

Horsman, Reginald. Wisconsin and the War
    of 1812. Wisconsin Magazine of History,
    46 (1962): 3-15.

Howard, J. H. A Yanktonai Dakota mide
    bundle. North Dakota Historical
    Quarterly, 19, no. 2 (1952): 132-139.

Howard, J. H. Drifting Goose's village.
    South Dakota, University, William H.
    Over Museum, Museum News, 15, no. 1
    (1954): 2.

Howard, J. H. Notes on two Dakota "holy
    dance" medicines and their uses.

American Anthropologist, 55 (1953): 608-609.

Howard, J. H. Yanktonai Dakota eagle trapping. Southwestern Journal of Anthropology, 10 (1954): 69-74.

Howard, James H. A note on the Dakota Water Drinking Society. American Indian Tradition, 7, no. 3 (1961): 96.

Howard, James H. Dakota interpretations of bird calls. South Dakota, University, Museum, Museum News, 27, nos. 11/12 (1966): 19.

Howard, James H. Dakota winter counts as a source of Plains history. Washington, D.C., Government Printing Office, 1960. 335-416 p. illus. (U.S., Bureau of American Ethnology, Anthropological Papers, 61. U.S., Bureau of American Ethnology, Bulletin, 173)

Howard, James H. Grandpa Saul remembers: a Sioux Indian paints his people's past. Oklahoma Anthropological Society, Newsletter, 19, no. 1 (1971): 1-17; 19, no. 2 (1971): 3-6; 19, no. 3 (1971): 23-28; 19, no. 4 (1971): 11-14; 19, no. 5 (1971): 5-10; 19, no. 6 (1971): 5-6.

Howard, James H. Notes on Dakota archery. South Dakota, University, Museum, Museum News, 12, no. 2 (1950): 1-3.

Howard, James H. Notes on the ethnogeography of the Yankton Dakota. Plains Anthropologist, 17 (1972): 281-307.

Howard, James H. The Dakota or Sioux Indians; a study in human ecology. Vermillion, 1966. illus., map. (South Dakota, University, South Dakota Museum, Anthropological Papers, 2)

Howard, James H. The Dakota or Sioux tribe. South Dakota, University, Museum, Museum News, 27, nos. 5/6 (1966): 1-10; 27, nos. 7/8 (1966): 1-9; 27, nos. 9/10 (1966): 1-9.

Howard, James H. Upper Yanktonai Sioux. American Indian Tradition, 7, no. 4 (1961): 138-139.

Hurt, W. R. The urbanization of the Yankton Indians. South Dakota, University, Museum, Museum Notes, 21, no. 3 (1960): 1-6.

Hurt, Wesley R. Factors in the persistence of peyote in the Northern Plains. Plains Anthropologist, 5 (1960): 16-27.

Hurt, Wesley R. Social drinking patterns of the Yankton Sioux. By Wesley R. Hurt and Richard M. Brown. Human Organization, 24 (1965): 222-230.

Hurt, Wesley R. The urbanization of the Yankton Indians. South Dakota, State University, W. H. Over Museum, Museum News, 21, no. 3 (1960): 1-6.

Hurt, Wesley R. The urbanization of the Yankton Indians. In Staten W. Webster, ed. The Disadvantaged Learner. San Francisco, Chandler, 1966: 77-88.

Hurt, Wesley R., Jr. The urbanization of the Yankton Indians. Human Organization, 20 (1961/1962): 226-231.

Jaques. Notes of a tourist through the Upper Missouri region. Missouri Historical Society, Bulletin, 22 (1965/1966): 393-409.

Jones, Robert Huhn. The Northwestern Frontier and the impact on the Sioux War, 1862. Mid-America, 41 (1959): 131-153.

Keating, W. H. Narrative of an expedition to the source of St. Peter's River, Vol. 1: 376-439. Philadelphia, 1824.

Keen, R. Hunter. Dakota patterns of giving. Practical Anthropology, 11 (1964): 273-276.

Lass, William E. The "Moscow Expedition". Minnesota History, 39 (1964/1965): 227-240.

Laviolette, G. The Sioux Indians in Canada. Regina, 1944. 138 p.

Lesser, Alexander. Siouan kinship. Dissertation Abstracts, 19 (1958/1959): 208. UM 58-2596.

Levin, Norman Balfour. Problems in the linguistic description of Nakota. In Congreso Internacional de Americanistas, 36th. 1964, España. Actas y Memorias. Tomo 2. Sevilla, 1966: 213-215.

Lockwood, J. H. Early times and events in Wisconsin. State Historical Society of Wisconsin, Collections, 2 (1855): 98-196.

Malan, Vernon D. The Crow Creek Indian family. By Vernon D. Malan and Joseph F. Powers. Brookings, 1960. 35 p. illus. (South Dakota State College, Agricultural Experiment Station, Bulletin, 487)

McGee, W J. The Siouan Indians. U.S. Bureau of American Ethnology, Annual Reports, 15 (1894): 157-204.

McLaughlin, J. My friend the Indian. Boston, 1910. 417 p.

Meyer, Roy W. The establishment of the Santee Reservation, 1866-1869. Nebraska History, 45 (1964): 59-97.

Morgan, L. H. Systems of consanguinity and affinity. Smithsonian Contributions to Knowledge, 17 (1871): 167-176, 291-382.

Morgan, L. H. The Indian journals, 1859-62: p. 60-61, 110-111, 148-149, 151-152, 195, 198. Ann Arbor, 1959.

Neuman, Robert W. Porcupine quill flatteners from central United States. American Antiquity, 26 (1960/1961): 99-102.

Olden, S. E. The people of Tipi Sapa. Milwaukee, 1918. 158 p.

Petersen, William J. Captives of the Sioux. Palimpsest, 42 (1961): 460-477.

Pfaller, Louis. The Brave Bear murder case. North Dakota History, 36 (1969): 121-139.

Pfaller, Louis. The forging of an Indian agent. North Dakota History, 34 (1967): 62-76.

Pruitt, O. J. Smutty Bear tribe. Annals of Iowa, 3rd ser., 31 (1953): 544-547.

Reynolds, Sam. A Dakota tipi. North Dakota History, 40, no. 4 (1973): 20-29.

Riggs, S. R. A Dakota-English dictionary. Contributions to North American Ethnology, 7 (1890): 1-665.

Riggs, S. R. Dakota grammar, texts and ethnography. Contributions to North American Ethnology, 9 (1893): 1-232.

Riggs, S. R. Grammar and dictionary of the Dakota language. Smithsonian Contributions to Knowledge, 4 (1852): 1-338.

Robinson, D. A history of the Dakota or Sioux Indians. South Dakota Historical Collections, 2 (1904): 1-523.

Roddis, L. H. The Indian wars of Minnesota. Cedar Rapids, 1956. 329 p.

Schusky, Ernest L. Mission and government policy in Dakota Indian communities. Practical Anthropology, 10 (1963): 109-114.

Shields, J. Thrilling adventures among the Sioux and Chippewas. Missouri Historical Society, Bulletin, 13 (1957): 275-282.

Sibley, H. H. Iron Face. Chicago, 1950. 230 p.

Snelling, W. J. Tales of the North-West. Boston, 1830. 288 p.

Sullivan, L. R. Anthropometry of the Siouan tribes. American Museum of Natural History, Anthropological Papers, 23 (1920): 81-174.

Thomas, C. Yankton. U.S. Bureau of American Ethnology, Bulletin, 30, vol. 2 (1910): 988-990.

Thomas, C. Yanktonai. U.S. Bureau of American Ethnology, Bulletin, 30, vol. 2 (1910): 990-991.

Todd, John B. S. The Harney expedition against the Sioux: the journal of Capt. John B. S. Todd. Edited by Ray H. Mattison. Nebraska History, 43 (1962): 89-130.

Umber, Harold. Interdepartmental conflict between Fort Yates and Standing Rock: problems of Indian administration, 1870-1881. North Dakota History, 39, no. 3 (1972): 4-13.

Weston, M. C. and J. W. Cook. Calvary wiwicawangapi kin, qa wokiksuye anpetu kin koya. Madison, South Dakota, 1893. 32 p.

Whitehouse, Joseph. The journal of Private Joseph Whitehouse, a soldier with Lewis and Clark. Edited by Paul Russell Cutright. Missouri Historical Society, Bulletin, 28 (1971/1972): 143-161.

Wied-Neuwied, M. zu. Reise in das innere Nordamerika. Coblenz, 1839-1841. 2 v.

Wied-Neuwied, M. zu. Travels in the interior of North America. Early Western Travels, 22 (1906): 304-311, 341-344; 24 (1906): 223-226.

Williamson, J. P. An English-Dakota dictionary. New York, 1902.

Wilson, Peter. The letters of Peter Wilson, first resident agent among the Teton Sioux. Edited by Harry H. Anderson. Nebraska History, 42 (1961): 237-264.

Wilson, Wesley C. Doctor Walter A. Burleigh: Dakota Territorial delegate to 39th and 40th Congress: politician, extraordinary. North Dakota History, 33 (1966): 93-104.

Wilson, Wesley C. General John B. S.
    Todd, first delegate, Dakota Territory.
    North Dakota History, 31 (1964): 189-
    194.

09-27 Sioux

Minnesota Historical Society. Chippewa
    and Dakota Indians; a subject catalog of
    books, pamphlets, periodical articles,
    and manuscripts in the Minnesota
    Historical Society. St. Paul, 1969.

Anderson, Harry H. A challenge to Brown's
    Sioux Indian wars thesis. Montana, the
    Magazine of Western History, 12, no. 1
    (1962): 40-49.

Anderson, John A. The Sioux of the
    Rosebud; a history in pictures.
    Photographs by John A. Anderson. Text by
    Henry W. Hamilton and Jean Tyree
    Hamilton. Norman, University of
    Oklahoma Press, 1971. 32, 320 p.
    illus., maps.

Anonymous. Naming of Medicine Hat.
    Alberta Historical Review, 9, no. 1
    (1961): 7.

Anonymous. Senor Don Manuel Lisa.
    Missouri Historical Society, Bulletin,
    23 (1966/1967): 52-58.

Anonymous. Standing Rock Sioux Tribe:
    progress in planning. HUD Challenge, 11
    (Oct. 1971): 16-19.

Artichoker, John, Jr. Indians of South
    Dakota. Pierre, South Dakota State
    Department of Public Instruction, 1956.
    101 p. ERIC ED011467.

Artichoker, John, Jr. The Sioux Indian
    goes to college; an analysis of selected
    problems of South Dakota Indian college
    students. By John Artichoker, Jr. and
    Neil M. Palmer. Vermillion, Institute
    of Indian Studies, 1959. 47 p.

Audubon, John James. Barging down from
    Fort Union. Edited by William J.
    Petersen. Palimpsest, 52 (1971): 571-
    583.

Audubon, John James. Birds along the
    Missouri. Edited by William J. Petersen.
    Palimpsest, 52 (1971): 550-570.

Babcock, Willoughby M. With Ramsey to
    Pembina; a treaty-making trip in 1851.
    Minnesota History, 38 (1962/1963): 1-10.

Ballas, Donald Joseph. A cultural
    geography of Todd County, South Dakota,

and the Rosebud Sioux Indian
    Reservation. Dissertation Abstracts
    International, 31 (1970/1971): 2048B.
    UM 70-17,698.

Bass, Mary Anna Owen. Food and nutrient
    intake patterns on the Standing Rock
    Reservation, North and South Dakota.
    Dissertation Abstracts International, 33
    (1972/1973): 2171B. UM 72-28,827.

Bebeau, Donald E. Administration of a
    TOEFL test to Sioux Indian high school
    students. Journal of American Indian
    Education, 9, no. 1 (1969/1970): 7-16.

Becker, David A. Enteric parasites of
    Indians and Anglo-Americans, chiefly on
    the Winnebago and Omaha Reservations in
    Nebraska. Nebraska State Medical
    Journal, 53 (1968): 293-296, 347-349,
    380-383, 421-423.

Benndorf, Helga, ed. Indianer
    Nordamerikas 1760-1860 aus der Sammlung
    Speyer. Edited by Helga Benndorf and
    Arthur Speyer. Offenbach a.M.,
    Deutsches Ledermuseum, Deutsches
    Schuhmuseum, 1968. 141 p. illus.

Berg, David E. Association between serum
    and secretory immunoglobins and chronic
    otitis media in Indian children. By
    David E. Berg, Arden E. Larsen, and C.
    T. Yarington, Jr. Annals of Otology,
    Rhinology and Laryngology, 80 (1971):
    766-772.

Berg, Lillie Clara. Early pioneers and
    Indians of Minnesota and Rice County.
    San Leandro, Calif., 1959. 220 p.
    illus.

Berrien, Joseph Waring. Overland from St.
    Louis to the California gold field in
    1849: the diary of Joseph Waring
    Berrien. Edited by Ted and Caryl
    Hinckley. Indiana Magazine of History,
    56 (1960): 273-351.

Boudens, Robrecht. La mission
    conciliatrice du P. Alexis André auprès
    des Sioux 1863-1865. Études Oblates, 18
    (1959): 404-414.

Bronson, Edgar B. Reminiscences of a
    ranchman. Lincoln, University of
    Nebraska Press, 1962. 369 p. (Bison
    Book, BB127)

Brown, D. Alexander. The Ghost Dance and
    the Battle of Wounded Knee. In Roger L.
    Nichols and George R. Adams, eds. The
    American Indian: Past and Present.
    Waltham, Xerox College Publishing, 1971:
    221-229.

Brown, Mark H.   A new focus on the Sioux War. Montana, the Magazine of Western History, 11, no. 4 (1961): 76-85.

Brown, Richard Ellsworth.   The planning process on the Pine Ridge and Rosebud Indian Reservations: a comparative analysis. Public Affairs (May 15, 1969): 1-8.

Buck, Daniel.   Indian outbreaks. Minneapolis, Ross and Haines, 1965. 284 p.   illus.

Buck, Royal.   Red Willow County letters of Royal Buck, 1872-1873. Edited by Paul D. Riley. Nebraska History, 47 (1966): 371-397.

Burnette, Robert.   The tortured Americans. Englewood Cliffs, Prentice-Hall, 1971. 176, 48 p.   illus.

Cardenal, Ernesto, tr.   Poesía de los indios de Norteamérica. América Indígena, 21 (1961): 355-362.

Carley, Kenneth.   The Sioux uprising of 1862.   St. Paul, Minnesota Historical Society, 1961.   80 p.   illus., maps.

Cash, Joseph H.   The Sioux people (Rosebud).   Phoenix, Indian Tribal Series, 1971.   106 p.

Chaboillez, Charles Jean Baptiste. Journal of Charles Jean Baptiste Chaboillez, 1797-1798. Edited by Harold Hickerson. Ethnohistory, 6 (1959): 265-316, 363-427.

Chafe, Wallace L.   Another look at Siouan and Iroquoian. American Anthropologist, 66 (1964): 852-862.

Chapman, William M.   Remember the wind; a prairie memoir.   Philadelphia, Lippincott, 1965.   239 p.   map.

Corbusier, William T.   Camp Sheridan, Nebraska. Nebraska History, 42 (1961): 29-51.

Danziger, Edmund J., Jr.   The Crow Creek experiment: an aftermath of the Sioux War of 1862. North Dakota History, 37 (1970): 105-123.

Davis, Jane S.   Two Sioux war orders: a mystery unraveled. Minnesota History, 41 (1968/1969): 117-125.

Denig, Edwin T.   Five Indian tribes of the Upper Missouri: Sioux, Arickaras, Assiniboines, Crees, Crows. Edited by John C. Ewers.   Norman, University of Oklahoma Press, 1961.   217 p.   illus.

Dyck, Paul.   Brulé: the Sioux people of the Rosebud.   Flagstaff, Northland Press, 1971.   12, 365 p.

Eastman, Marg H.   Dahcotah: or, Life and legends of the Sioux around Fort Snelling.   Minneapolis, Ross and Haines, 1962.   268 p.   illus.

Eicher, Carl K.   An approach to income improvement on the Rosebud Sioux Indian Reservation. Human Organization, 20 (1961/1962): 191-196.

Ellis, Richard N., ed.   The Western American Indian: case studies in tribal history.   Lincoln, University of Nebraska Press, 1972.   203 p.

Ellis, Richard Nathaniel.   General John Pope and the development of federal Indian policy, 1862-1886. Dissertation Abstracts, 29 (1968/1969): 528A.   UM 68-10,609.

Elmendorf, William W.   Item and set comparison in Yuchi, Siouan, and Yukian. International Journal of American Linguistics, 30 (1964): 328-340.

Elmendorf, William W.   Yukian-Siouan lexical similarities. International Journal of American Linguistics, 29 (1963): 300-309.

Englund, Eric U.   Siouxerna--ett krigarfolk på prärierna.   Stockholm, Natur och Kultur, 1967.   182 p.   illus.

Fay, George E., ed.   Charters, constitutions and by-laws of Indian tribes of North America. Part I: The Sioux tribes of South Dakota.   Greeley, 1967.   12, 120 l.   map.   (University of Northern Colorado, Museum of Anthropology, Occasional Publications in Anthropology, Ethnology Series, 1)   ERIC ED046551.

Fay, George E., ed.   Charters, constitutions and by-laws of the Indian tribes of North America. Part IIa: The Northern Plains.   Greeley, 1967.   6, 141 l.   maps.   (University of Northern Colorado, Museum of Anthropology, Occasional Publications in Anthropology, Ethnology Series, 3)   ERIC ED051923.

Fay, George E., ed.   Treaties, and land cessions, between the bands of the Sioux and the United States of America, 1805-1906.   Greeley, 1972.   7, 139 l. (University of Northern Colorado, Museum of Anthropology, Occasional Publications in Anthropology, Ethnology Series, 24)

Feder, Norman.   Old time Sioux costume. American Indian Hobbyist, 4, nos. 3/4 (1957): 23-31.

Feder, Norman. Sioux kettle dance.
American Indian Hobbyist, 4, nos. 3/4
(1957): 37-38.

Field, Gabriel. The Camp Missouri-
Chariton Road, 1819: the journal of Lt.
Gabriel Field. Edited by Roger L.
Nichols. Missouri Historical Society,
Bulletin, 24 (1967/1968): 139-152.

Finerty, John F. War-path and bivouac.
Norman, University of Oklahoma Press,
1961. 358 p. illus.

Flanagan, Vincent J. Gouverneur Kemble
Warren, explorer of the Nebraska
Territory. Nebraska History, 51 (1970):
171-198.

Flying Hawk. Chief Flying Hawk's tales:
the true story of Custer's last fight.
By Flying Hawk and Milton I. McCreight.
In Thomas Rose, ed. Violence in America.
New York, Random House, 1970: 81-85.

Ford, Virginia. Cultural criteria and
determinants for acceptance of modern
medical theory and practice among the
Teton Dakota. Dissertation Abstracts, 27
(1966/1967): 4223B. UM 67-7497.

Fridley, Russell W., ed. Charles E.
Flandrau and the defense of New Ulm.
Edited by Russell W. Fridley, Leota M.
Kellett, and June D. Holmquist. New
Ulm, Brown County Historical Society,
1962. 62 p. illus., maps.

Gallaher, William H. Up the Missouri in
1865; the journal of William H.
Gallaher. Edited by James E. Moss.
Missouri Historical Review, 57
(1962/1963): 156-183, 261-284.

Georgakas, D. They have not spoken:
American Indians in film. Film
Quarterly, 25, no. 3 (1972): 26-32.

Gerber, Max E. The Custer Expedition of
1874: a new look. North Dakota History,
40, no. 1 (1973): 4-23.

Gerhardt, Alfred C. P., Jr. 1665-1965:
three hundred years of missionary work
among the Sioux Indians. Dunmore, Pa.,
F. Pane Offset Printing, 1969. 7,
103 l.

Gilmore, Melvin R. Prairie smoke. New
York, AMS Press, 1966. 13, 208 p.
illus.

Glazier, Willard. Down the great river.
Edited by William J. Petersen.
Palimpsest, 51 (1970): 355-417.

Goodman, Julia Cody. Julia Cody Goodman's
memoirs of Buffalo Bill. Edited by Don

Russell. Kansas Historical Quarterly, 28
(1962): 442-496.

Goshe, Frederick. Sioux Indian language.
Palo Alto, 1967. 86 p.

Green, Jerome A. The Hayfield Fight; a
reappraisal of a neglected action.
Montana, the Magazine of Western
History, 22, no. 4 (1972): 30-43.

Greene, Jerome A. The Sioux land
commission of 1889: prelude to Wounded
Knee. South Dakota History, 1
(1970/1971): 41-72.

Gregg, John B. Exostoses in the external
auditory canals. By John B. Gregg and
William M. Bass. Annals of Otology,
Rhinology and Laryngology, 79 (1970):
834-839.

Gregg, John B. Roentgenographic
evaluation of temporal bones from South
Dakota Indian burials. By John B. Gregg,
James P. Steele, and Ann Holzhueter.
American Journal of Physical
Anthropology, n.s., 23 (1965): 51-61.

Guenther, Richard L. The Santee Normal
Training School. Nebraska History, 51
(1970): 359-378.

Haas, Mary R. Athapaskan, Tlingit, Yuchi,
and Siouan. In Congreso Internacional de
Americanistas, 35th. 1962, Mexico. Actas
y Memorias. Tomo 2. Mexico, 1964: 495-
500.

Hady, Walter M. Indian migrations in
Manitoba and the West. Historical and
Scientific Society of Manitoba, Papers,
ser. 3, 17 (1960/1961): 24-53.

Hagen, E. E. The Sioux on the
reservations: the American colonial
problem. Preliminary edition. By E. E.
Hagen and Louis C. Shaw. Cambridge,
Massachusetts Institute of Technology,
Center for International Studies, 1960.
ERIC ED024505.

Hans, Frederick M. The great Sioux
Nation; a complete history of Indian
life and warfare in America.
Minneapolis, Ross and Haines, 1964.
586 p. illus.

Harper's Weekly. Outstanding historical
events: the massacre of General Custer
and his men in Montana, June 25, 1876.
Cleveland, Bloch, 1959. illus., map.

Harris, Earl R. Courthouse and Jail
Rocks: landmarks on the Oregon Trail.
Nebraska History, 43 (1962): 29-51.

Hassrick, Royal B. The Sioux; life and
customs of a warrior society. In

collaboration with Dorothy Maxwell and Cile M. Bach. Norman, University of Oklahoma Press, 1964. 20, 337 p. illus., maps.

Henningsen, Charles Frederick. The Custer battle and the critique of an adventurer. Edited by Harold D. Langley. Montana, the Magazine of Western History, 22, no. 2 (1972): 20-33.

Holy Dance, Robert. The seven pipes of the Dakota Sioux. Plains Anthropologist, 15 (1970): 81-82.

Holzhueter, Ann M. A search for stapes footplate fixation in an Indian population, prehistoric and historic. By A. M. Holzhueter, J. B. Gregg, and S. Clifford. American Journal of Physical Anthropology, n.s., 23 (1965): 35-40.

Howard, James H. Archeological investigations at the Spawn Mound, 39LK201, Lake County, South Dakota. Plains Anthropologist, 13 (1968): 132-145.

Howard, James H. The Dakota or Sioux Indians; a study in human ecology. Vermillion, 1966. illus., map. (South Dakota, University, South Dakota Museum, Anthropological Papers, 2)

Hudson, Henry James. Henry James Hudson and the Genoa settlement. Edited by Marguerette R. Burke. Nebraska History, 41 (1960): 201-235.

Hurt, Wesley R. A Yuwipi ceremony at Pine Ridge. Plains Anthropologist, 5 (1960): 48-52.

Hurt, Wesley R. Factors in the persistence of peyote in the Northern Plains. Plains Anthropologist, 5 (1960): 16-27.

Jackson, Donald. A new Lewis and Clark map. Missouri Historical Society, Bulletin, 17 (1960/1961): 117-132.

Jackson, Donald D. Custer's gold; the United States Cavalry expedition of 1874. New Haven, Yale University Press, 1966. 6, 152 p. illus., maps.

Jacobsen, Ethel C. Life in an Indian village. North Dakota History, 26 (1959): 45-92.

Jessett, Frederick E. Sioux farming today. Indian Historian, 3, no. 1 (1970): 34-36.

Johnson, Roy P. Sitting Bull: hero or monster? North Dakota History, 29 (1962): 217-221.

Jones, Robert H. The Civil War in the Northwest: Nebraska, Wisconsin, Iowa, Minnesota, and the Dakotas. Norman, University of Oklahoma Press, 1960. 216 p. illus.

Jones, Robert Huhn. The Northwestern Frontier and the impact on the Sioux War, 1862. Mid-America, 41 (1959): 131-153.

Julien, Henri. Expedition to the North-West. Alberta Historical Review, 9, no. 1 (1961): 8-26.

Keenan, Jerry. The Wagon Box Fight. Journal of the West, 11 (1972): 51-74.

Kelley, William Fitch. Pine Ridge 1890. San Francisco, Pierre Bovis, 1971. 267 p. illus., map.

Kelly, Fanny W. My captivity among the Sioux Indians. New York, Corinth Books, 1962. 285 p. illus.

Kemnitzer, Luis S. The structure of country drinking parties on Pine Ridge Reservation, South Dakota. Plains Anthropologist, 17 (1972): 134-142.

Kent, Calvin A. Indian poverty in South Dakota. By Calvin A. Kent and Jerry W. Johnson. Vermillion, S.D., 1969. 96 p. (South Dakota, University, Vermillion Institute of Indian Studies, Bulletin, 99) ERIC ED042529.

King, James T. The Republican River Expedition, June-July, 1869. Nebraska History, 41 (1960): 165-199, 281-297.

Köbben, André J. F. Prophetic movements as an expression of social protest. International Archives of Ethnography, 49 (1960): 117-164.

Kuske, Irwin I., Jr. Psycholinguistic abilities of Sioux Indian children. Dissertation Abstracts International, 30 (1969/1970): 4280A. UM 70-5304.

Kuttner, Robert E. Alcohol and addiction in urbanized Sioux Indians. By Robert E. Kuttner and Albert B. Lorincz. Mental Hygiene, 51 (1967): 530-542.

Kuttner, Robert E. Promiscuity and prostitution in urbanized Indian communities. By Robert E. Kuttner and Albert B. Lorincz. Mental Hygiene, 54 (1970): 79-91.

Kutzleb, Charles R. Educating the Dakota Sioux, 1876-1890. North Dakota History, 32 (1965): 197-215.

Lanegraff, T. G.   Pioneering among the
Indians.   Utica, N.Y., N. T. Lewis,
1961.   20 p.   illus.

Larned, William L.   The Fisk Expedition of
1864: the diary of William L. Larned.
Edited by Ray H. Mattison. North Dakota
History, 36 (1969): 209-274.

Lee, Dorothy D.   Education and cultural
values. National Elementary Principal,
42, no. 2 (1962/1963): 13-17.

Lesser, Alexander.   Siouan kinship.
Dissertation Abstracts, 19 (1958/1959):
208.   UM 58-2596.

Lind, Robert William.   Familistic
attitudes and marriage role expectations
of American Indian and White
adolescents. Dissertation Abstracts
International, 32 (1971/1972): 5288B.
UM 72-10,035.

Mahan, Bruce E.   Fort Shelby and Fort
McKay. Palimpsest, 42 (1961): 454-461.

Malan, Vernon D.   The Dakota Indian
community. By Vernon D. Malan and Ernest
L. Schusky.   Brookings, 1962.   48 p.
illus., map.   (South Dakota,
Agricultural Experiment Station,
Bulletin, 505)

Malan, Vernon D.   The Dakota Indian
economy. Brookings, 1963.   56 p.
illus. (South Dakota, Agricultural
Experiment Station, Bulletin, 509)

Malan, Vernon D.   The value system of the
Dakota Indians; harmony with nature,
kinship, and animism. Journal of
American Indian Education, 3, no. 1
(1963/1964): 21-25.

Malm, Einar.   De kämpade förgäves.
Stockholm, Rabén and Sjögren, 1967.
213 p.   illus.

Mardock, Robert W.   The Plains frontier
and the Indian peace policy, 1865-1880.
Nebraska History, 49 (1968): 187-201.

Martin, Harry W.   Correlates of adjustment
among American Indians in an urban
environment. Human Organization, 23
(1964): 290-295.

Matthew, William Diller.   The letters of
William Diller Matthew. Edited by
Charles L. Camp. Journal of the West, 8
(1969): 263-290, 454-476.

Matthews, G. H.   Some notes on the Proto-
Siouan continuants. International
Journal of American Linguistics, 36
(1970): 98-109.

Maynard, Eileen.   Hechel lena oyate kin
nipi kte. That these people may live;
conditions among the Oglala Sioux of the
Pine Ridge Reservation. By Eileen
Maynard and Gayla Twiss.   Pine Ridge,
S.D., U.S. Indian Health Service,
Community Mental Health Program, 1969.
183 p.   illus., maps.   ERIC ED035471.

McBride, Dorothy McFatridge.   Hoosier
schoolmaster among the Sioux. Montana,
the Magazine of Western History, 20,
no. 4 (1970): 78-97.

McGrew, Robert N.   Anomalous fusion of the
malleus to the tympanic ring. By Robert
N. McGrew and John B. Gregg. Annals of
Otology, Rhinology and Laryngology, 80
(1971): 138-140.

McKelvie, Martha G.   The hills of
yesterday.   Philadelphia, Dorrance,
1960.   117 p.   illus.

McNeilly, Marie M.   The wonderful years;
experiences of a nurse among the
Indians.   New York, Exposition Press,
1961.   114 p.   illus.

Meyer, Roy W.   The Canadian Sioux;
refugees from Minnesota. Minnesota
History, 41 (1968/1969): 13-28.

Meyer, Roy W.   The Canadian Sioux,
refugees from Minnesota. In Roger L.
Nichols and George R. Adams, eds. The
American Indian: Past and Present.
Waltham, Xerox College Publishing, 1971:
168-182.

Miller, David Humphreys.   Sitting Bull's
white squaw. Montana, the Magazine of
Western History, 14, no. 2 (1964): 54-
71.

Miller, Wick R.   A lexicostatistic study
of Shoshoni dialects. By Wick R. Miller,
James L. Tanner, and Lawrence P. Foley.
Anthropological Linguistics, 13 (1971):
142-164.

Misch, Jürgen.   Der letzte Kriegspfad; der
Schicksalskampf der Sioux und Apachen.
Stuttgart, Union, 1970.   223 p.   illus.,
maps.

Mooney, James.   The ghost-dance religion
and the Sioux outbreak of 1890. Edited
and abridged with an introduction by
Anthony F. C. Wallace.   Chicago,
University of Chicago Press, 1965.   23,
359 p.   illus.

Morton, Desmond, ed.   Telegrams of the
North-West Campaign 1885. Edited by
Desmond Morton and Reginald H. Roy.
Toronto, 1972.   103, 431 p.   illus.,
maps.   (Champlain Society, Publications,
47)

Morton, William. The battle at the Grand Coteau, July 13 and 14, 1851. Historical and Scientific Society of Manitoba, Papers, ser. 3, 16 (1961): 37-49.

Mueller, Richard E. Jefferson Barracks: the early years. Missouri Historical Review, 67 (1972/1973): 7-30.

Müller, Werner. Glauben und Denken der Sioux. Berlin, Reimer, 1970. 12, 419 p. illus., maps.

Müller, Werner. The "passivity" of language and the experience of nature: a study in the structure of the primitive mind. In Joseph M. Kitagawa, et al., eds. Myths and Symbols. Chicago, University of Chicago Press, 1969: 227-239.

Munn, Fred M. Fred Munn, veteran of frontier experiences, remembered the days he rode with Miles, Howard and Terry. As told to Robert A. Griffen. Montana, the Magazine of Western History, 16, no. 2 (1966): 50-64.

Nadeau, Remi A. Fort Laramie and the Sioux Indians. Englewood Cliffs, Prentice-Hall, 1967. 12, 335 p. illus., maps.

Nelson, John Young. Fifty years on the trail; a true story of western life. New ed. Norman, University of Oklahoma Press, 1963. 291 p.

Neuman, Robert W. The brother-of-all document. Plains Anthropologist, 6 (1961): 68-69.

Nichols, Roger L., ed. The Black Hawk War; another view. Annals of Iowa, 36 (1963): 525-533.

Nicolay, John G. Lincoln's secretary goes West. La Crosse, Wis., Sumac Press, 1965. 69 p. map.

Nurge, Ethel. The Sioux Sun Dance in 1962. In Congreso Internacional de Americanistas, 36th. 1964, España. Actas y Memorias. Tomo 3. Sevilla, 1966: 105-114.

Oehler, Chester M. The great Sioux uprising. New York, Oxford University Press, 1959. 272 p. illus.

Ohannessian, Sirarpi. The study of the problems of teaching English to American Indians, report and recommendations. Washington, D.C., Center for Applied Linguistics, 1967. 46 p. ERIC ED014727.

Olson, James C. "A lasting peace"--Fort Laramie, 1866. In Richard N. Ellis, ed.

The Western American Indian. Lincoln, University of Nebraska Press, 1972: 23-35.

O'Neil, Floyd A. An anguished odyssey: the flight of the Utes, 1906-1908. Utah Historical Quarterly, 36 (1968): 315-327.

Parker, Watson. The Black Hills gold rush, 1874-1879. Dissertation Abstracts, 26 (1965/1966): 1617. UM 65-9756.

Partridge, William L. An analysis of Crow enculturation (as compared to Sioux enculturation) 1868 to 1880. Florida Anthropologist, 18 (1965): 225-234.

Patrie, Lewis E. A multiphasic screening project on the Pine Ridge Indian Reservation. Journal--Lancet, 82 (1962): 511-514.

Paulson, Howard W. The allotment of land in severalty to the Dakota Indians before the Dawes Act. South Dakota History, 1 (1970/1971): 132-153.

Peirce, Parker I. Antelope Bill. Minneapolis, Ross and Haines, 1962. 196 p. illus.

Petersen, William J. Buffalo hunting with Keokuk. Palimpsest, 46 (1965): 257-272.

Petersen, William J. The Winnebago leave Iowa. Palimpsest, 41 (1960): 351-356.

Petrakis, Nicholas L. Cerumen in American Indians: genetic implications of sticky and dry types. By Nicholas L. Petrakis, Kathryn T. Molohon, and David J. Tepper. Science, 158 (1967): 1192-1193.

Pfaller, Louis. Father De Smet in Dakota. Richardton, N.D., Assumption Abbey, 1962. 79 p. illus.

Pfaller, Louis. The Brave Bear murder case. North Dakota History, 36 (1969): 121-139.

Pfaller, Louis. The peace mission of 1863-1864. North Dakota History, 37 (1970): 293-313.

Praus, Alexis A. The Sioux, 1798-1922, a Dakota winter count. Bloomfield Hills, 1962. 4, 31 p. illus. (Cranbrook Institute of Science, Bulletin, 44)

Pruitt, O. J. John Y. Nelson: plainsman. Annals of Iowa, 35 (1960): 294-303.

Query, William T. Aggressive responses to the Holtzman Inkblot technique by Indian and White alcoholics. By William T. Query and Joy M. Query. Journal of

Cross-Cultural Psychology, 3 (1972): 413-416.

Rabeau, E. S.   Health auxilary training, instructor's guide.   Washington, D.C., U.S. Public Health Service, Division of Indian Health, 1966.   261 p.   ERIC ED023827.

Rahill, Peter J.   The Catholic Indian missions and Grant's peace policy 1870-1884.   Washington, D.C., Catholic University of America Press, 1953.   20, 396 p.   (Catholic University of America, Studies in American Church History, 41)

Rickey, Don, Jr.   The British-Indian attack on St. Louis, May 26, 1780.   Missouri Historical Review, 55 (1960/1961): 35-45.

Riegert, Wilbur A.   I am a Sioux Indian.   Rapid City, S.D., Fenwyn Press, 1967.   24 p.   illus.

Riggs, Theodore F.   A log house was home.   New York, Exposition Press, 1961.   208 p.   illus.

Robinett, Paul M.   The military career of James Craig. By Paul M. Robinett and Howard V. Canan. Missouri Historical Review, 66 (1971/1972): 49-75.

Rolston, Alan.   The Yellowstone Expedition of 1873. Montana, the Magazine of Western History, 20, no. 2 (1970): 20-29.

Ruby, Robert H.   Yuwipi; ancient rite of the Sioux. Montana, the Magazine of Western History, 16, no. 4 (1966): 74-79.

Russell, Don.   Custer's last or, The battle of the Little Big Horn.   Fort Worth, Amon Carter Museum of Western Art, 1968.   5, 67 p.   illus.

Russell, Don.   Custer's list: a checklist of pictures relating to the battle of the Little Big Horn. Fort Worth, Amon Carter Museum of Western Art, 1969.   10, 88 p.

Sandoz, Mari.   These were the Sioux.   New York, Hastings House, 1961.   118 p.   illus.

Schuck, Cecilia.   Nutritive value of the boarding school diets of Sioux Indian children. By Cecilia Schuck, Burness Wenberg, and Margaret Talcott. Federation Proceedings, 21, no. 2 (1962): 387.

Schusky, Ernest L.   Contemporary migration and culture change in two Dakota

reservations. Plains Anthropologist, 7 (1962): 178-183.

Sheehan, John F.   Carcinoma of the cervix in Indian women. By John F. Sheehan, George J. Basque, and Harle V. Barrett. Nebraska State Medical Journal, 50 (1965): 553-558.

Ship, Irwin I.   Dental caries incidence in North and South Dakota Indian school children during 30 years. Journal of Dental Research, 45 (1966): 359-363.

Sibley, Henry Hastings.   The Sioux Campaign of 1862; Sibley's letters to his wife. Edited by Kenneth Carley. Minnesota History, 38 (1962/1963): 99-114.

Sievers, Michael A.   The administration of Indian affairs on the Upper Missouri, 1858-1865. North Dakota History, 38 (1971): 366-394.

Silverman, Jane.   Sioux Indians of Standing Rock in North and South Dakota pioneer HUD's new "rural development strategy". Journal of Housing, 29 (1972): 18-22.

Singh, Devendra.   Preference for work over "freeloading" in children. By Devendra Singh and William T. Query. Psychonomic Science, 24 (1971): 77-79.

Smith, Duane A.   Gold, silver, and the Red Man. Journal of the West, 5 (1966): 114-121.

Snow, Fred S.   Fred Snow's account of the Custer Expedition of 1874. Edited by Ernest J. Moyne. North Dakota History, 27 (1960): 143-151.

Spencer, Milton.   The letters of Private Milton Spencer, 1862-1865: a soldier's view of military life on the Northern Plains. Edited by Carol G. Goodwin. North Dakota History, 37 (1970): 233-269.

Spindler, Will H.   Tragedy strikes at Wounded Knee, and other essays on Indian life in South Dakota and Nebraska. Vermillion, University of South Dakota, 1972.   138 p.   illus.

Springer, Charles H.   Soldiering in Sioux country: 1865. Edited by Benjamin Franklin Cooling, III.   San Diego, Frontier Heritage Press, 1971.   82 p.   illus., maps.

Spry, Irene M., ed.   The papers of the Palliser Expedition 1857-1860.   Toronto, 1968.   138, 694 p.   illus., map. (Champlain Society, Publications, 44)

Steele, James P., et al. Paleopathology in the Dakotas. South Dakota Journal of Medicine, 18, no. 10 (1965): 17-29.

Sterling, Everett W. The Indian reservation system on the North Central Plains. Montana, the Magazine of Western History, 14, no. 2 (1964): 92-100.

Stewart, William J. Settler, politician, and speculator in the sale of the Sioux Reserve. Minnesota History, 39 (1964/1965): 85-92.

Swisher, J. A. The Sioux. Palimpsest, 50 (1969): 227-230.

Talcott, Margaret I. Diets and nutritional status of adolescent Indian girls in boarding schools of the Dakotas. By Margaret I. Talcott and Cecilia Schuck. South Dakota Academy of Sciences, Proceedings, 40 (1961): 245-246.

Taunton, Francis B., ed. Sidelights of the Sioux wars. London, 1967. 78 p. illus., map. (English Westerners' Special Publication, 2)

Taylor, Calvin. Overland to the gold fields of California in 1850: the journal of Calvin Taylor. Edited by Burton J. Williams. Nebraska History, 50 (1969): 125-149.

Thompson, Ralph Stanton. The final story of the Deapolis Mandan Indian village site. North Dakota History, 28 (1961): 143-153.

Thomson, William D. History of Fort Pembina: 1870-1895. North Dakota History, 36 (1969): 5-39.

Throne, Mildred, ed. Iowa troops in Dakota territory, 1861-1864. Based on the diaries and letters of Henry J. Wieneke. Iowa Journal of History, 57 (1959): 97-190.

Thwaites, Reuben G., ed. The French regime in Wisconsin [1634-1748]. Madison, 1902, 1906. 2 v. illus. (Wisconsin, State Historical Society, Collections, 16-17)

Thwaites, Reuben G., ed. The French regime in Wisconsin [1743-1760]. Madison, 1908. 25, 1-222 p. (Wisconsin, State Historical Society, Collections, 18)

Todd, John B. S. The Harney expedition against the Sioux: the journal of Capt. John B. S. Todd. Edited by Ray H. Mattison. Nebraska History, 43 (1962): 89-130.

Umber, Harold. Interdepartmental conflict between Fort Yates and Standing Rock: problems of Indian administration, 1870-1881. North Dakota History, 39, no. 3 (1972): 4-13.

Utley, Robert M. The last days of the Sioux Nation. New Haven, Yale University Press, 1963. 314 p. illus. (Yale Western Americana Series, 3)

Vaughn, J. W. Sergeant Custard's wagon train fight. Annals of Wyoming, 32 (1960): 227-234.

Vogdes, Ada A. The journal of Ada A. Vogdes, 1868-71. Edited by Donald K. Adams. Montana, the Magazine of Western History, 13, no. 3 (1963): 2-18.

Wax, Murray L. Cultural deprivation as an educational ideology. By Murray and Rosalie Wax. Journal of American Indian Education, 3, no. 2 (1963/1964): 15-18.

Wax, Murray L. Formal education in an American Indian community. By Murray L. Wax, Rosalie H. Wax, and Robert V. Dumont. In Deward E. Walker, Jr., ed. The Emergent Native Americans. Boston, Little, Brown, 1972: 627-642.

Wax, Murray L., et al. Indian communities and Project Head Start. Summary and observations in the Dakotas and Minnesota, together with an appraisal of possibilities for a Head Start program among the Potawatomi Indians of Kansas. Washington, D.C., 1967. 65 p. (U.S., Office of Economic Opportunity, Report, 520) ERIC ED016510.

Wax, Rosalie H. Doing fieldwork; warnings and advice. Chicago, University of Chicago Press, 1971. 10, 395 p.

Wax, Rosalie H. Indian education for what? By Rosalie and Murray Wax. Midcontinent American Studies Journal, 6 (1965): 164-170.

Webb, Frances Seely. The Indian version of the Platte Bridge fight. Annals of Wyoming, 32 (1960): 234-236.

Webb, Wayne E. Uprising; a newspaper story of the Sioux uprising of 1862. Redwood Falls, Minn., 1962. 27 p. illus.

Wertenberger, Mildred, ed. Fort Totten, Dakota Territory, 1867. North Dakota History, 34 (1967): 125-146.

Wetmore, Alphonso, ed. Biographical notice of Genl. William H. Ashley. Edited by Alphonso Wetmore and Charles Keemle. Missouri Historical Society, Bulletin, 24 (1967/1968): 348-354.

Whittaker, James O. Alcohol and the
Standing Rock Sioux tribe. Quarterly
Journal of Studies on Alcohol, 23
(1962): 468-479; 24 (1963): 80-90.

Willand, Jon. Lac qui Parle and the
Dakota Mission. Madison, Minn., Lac qui
Parle County Historical Society, 1964.
10, 306 p. illus., map.

Woodward, George A. The Northern Cheyenne
at Fort Fetterman; Colonel Woodward
describes some experiences of 1871.
Edited by John E. Parsons. Montana, the
Magazine of Western History, 9, no. 2
(1959): 16-27.

Woodyard, Darrel. Dakota Indian lore.
San Antonio, Naylor, 1968. 16, 164 p.
illus.

Woolworth, Nancy L. The Grand Portage
Mission: 1731-1965. Minnesota History,
39 (1964/1965): 301-310.

Wright, Dana. The Sibley trail of 1863.
North Dakota History, 29 (1962): 283-
296.

Wright, Peter M. The pursuit of Dull
Knife from Fort Reno in 1878-1879.
Chronicles of Oklahoma, 46 (1968): 141-
154.

Writers' Program, South Dakota. Legends
of the mighty Sioux. Sioux Falls,
Fantah, 1960. 158 p.

09-28   Oklahoma Indians

Andrews, Thomas F. Freedmen in Indian
Territory: a post-Civil War dilemma.
Journal of the West, 4 (1965): 367-376.

Ashcraft, Allan C. Confederate Indian
Department conditions in August, 1864.
Chronicles of Oklahoma, 41 (1963): 270-
285.

Avera, William Franklin. Extracts from
the memoirs of William Franklin Avera.
Edited by Henry Cathey. Arkansas
Historical Quarterly, 22 (1963): 99-116.

Bailey, Minnie Elizabeth Thomas.
Reconstruction in Indian Territory; a
story of avarice, discrimination, and
opportunism. Port Washington, Kennikat
Press, 1972. 225 p. illus.

Baird, W. David. Fort Smith and the Red
Man. Arkansas Historical Quarterly, 30
(1971): 337-348.

Bearss, Edwin C. Confederate action
against Fort Smith Post: early 1864.

Arkansas Historical Quarterly, 29
(1970): 226-251.

Bearss, Edwin C. The Civil War comes to
Indian Territory, 1861: the flight of
Opothleyoholo. Journal of the West, 11
(1972): 9-42.

Bearss, Edwin C. The Confederate attempt
to regain Fort Smith, 1863. Arkansas
Historical Quarterly, 28 (1969): 342-
380.

Bearss, Edwin C. The Federals capture
Fort Smith, 1863. Arkansas Historical
Quarterly, 28 (1969): 156-190.

Burrill, Robert Meredith. Grassland
empires: the geography of ranching in
Osage County, Oklahoma, 1872-1965.
Dissertation Abstracts International, 31
(1970/1971): 3471B-3472B. UM 70-25,309.

Butcher, Thomas. Touring the Southeast
Kansas area in 1896: from the diary of
Thomas Butcher. Edited by Betty
Littleton. Kansas Historical Quarterly,
35 (1969): 143-154.

Carriker, Robert Charles. Fort Supply,
Indian Territory: frontier outpost on
the Southern Plains, 1868-1894.
Dissertation Abstracts, 28 (1967/1968):
2158A. UM 67-15,910.

Cole, Helen Joyce. A comparison of
associative learning rates of Indian and
White adolescents. Dissertation
Abstracts International, 32 (1971/1972):
3779A-3780A. UM 72-3382.

Cuyler, Telamon. Telamon Cuyler's diary:
to Texas in 1888. Edited by John Hammond
Moore. Southwestern Historical
Quarterly, 70 (1966/1967): 474-488.

Danziger, Edmund J., Jr. The Office of
Indian Affairs and the problem of Civil
War Indian refugees in Kansas. Kansas
Historical Quarterly, 35 (1969): 257-
275.

Davis, Carl L. Dragoon life in Indian
Territory, 1833-1846. By Carl L. Davis
and LeRoy H. Fischer. Chronicles of
Oklahoma, 48 (1970/1971): 2-24.

DeMorse, Charles. Indians for the
Confederacy. Chronicles of Oklahoma, 50
(1972): 474-478.

Fay, George E., ed. Charters,
constitutions and by-laws of the Indian
tribes of North America. Part V: The
Indian tribes of Oklahoma. Greeley,
1968. 14, 104 l. map. (University of
Northern Colorado, Museum of
Anthropology, Occasional Publications in

Anthropology, Ethnology Series, 6) ERIC ED046555.

Fischer, LeRoy H. Confederate victory at Chusto-Talasah. By LeRoy H. Fischer and Kenny A. Franks. Chronicles of Oklahoma, 49 (1971/1972): 452-476.

Fischer, LeRoy H. United States Indian agents to the Five Civilized Tribes. Chronicles of Oklahoma, 50 (1972): 410-414.

Gage, Duane. Oklahoma: a resettlement area for Indians. Chronicles of Oklahoma, 47 (1969): 282-287.

Gibson, A. M. Confederates on the Plains: the Pike mission to Wichita Agency. Great Plains Journal, 4 (1964/1965): 7-16.

Goode, William H. Outposts of Zion, with limnings of mission life. Cincinnati, Poe and Hitchcock, 1863. 464 p.

Gordon, Ralph C. Natal teeth in American Indian children. By Ralph C. Gordon and Rex N. Langley. Journal of Pediatrics, 76 (1970): 613-614.

Harlow, Victor E. Oklahoma history. Oklahoma City, Harlow, 1961. 596 p. illus.

Horton, L. W. General Sam Bell Maxey: his defense of North Texas and the Indian Territory. Southwestern Historical Quarterly, 74 (1970/1971): 507-524.

Howard, James H. The compleat stomp dancer. South Dakota, University, Museum, Museum News, 26, nos. 5/6 (1965): 1-23.

Hubbard, Mary. A letter from Wyandotte Mission, postmarked Grand River, Indian Territory, 1888. Chronicles of Oklahoma, 48 (1970/1971): 353-355.

Jordan, Julia A. Oklahoma's oral history collection: new source for Indian history. Chronicles of Oklahoma, 49 (1971/1972): 150-172.

Kansas City Star. Report on the Five Civilized Tribes 1897. Chronicles of Oklahoma, 48 (1970/1971): 416-430.

Littlefield, Daniel F., Jr. Utopian dreams of the Cherokee fullbloods: 1890-1934. Journal of the West, 10 (1971): 404-427.

Lough, Jean C. Gateways to the promised land; the role played by the southern Kansas towns in the opening of the Cherokee Strip to settlement. Kansas Historical Quarterly, 25 (1959): 17-31.

Martin, Harry W. Mental health of Eastern Oklahoma Indians: an exploration. By Harry W. Martin, Sara Smith Sutker, Robert L. Leon, and William M. Hales. Human Organization, 27 (1968): 308-315.

McCoy, Isaac. History of Baptist Indian missions. Washington, D.C., W. M. Morrison; New York, H. and S. Raynor, 1840. 5, 611 p.

Michalicka, John. First Catholic church in Indian Territory--1872; St. Patrick's Church at Atoka. Chronicles of Oklahoma, 50 (1972): 479-485.

Nolan, Charles E. Recollections of Tulsa, Indian Territory, from Sister Mary Agnes Newchurch, O. Carm. Chronicles of Oklahoma, 49 (1971/1972): 92-99.

Oklahoma, Employment Security Commission, Research and Planning Division. Indians in Oklahoma: social and economic statistical data. By Bill Hunter and Tim Tucker. Oklahoma City, 1966. 5, 37 p. illus., maps. ERIC ED020052.

Owens, Charles S. The American Indian high school dropout in the Southwest. By Charles S. Owens and Willard P. Bass. Albuquerque, Southwestern Cooperative Educational Laboratory, 1969. 43 p. ERIC ED026195.

Perkins, Larry M. Ponca City and White Eagle, Oklahoma. Chicago, University of Chicago, 1970. 14 p. (National Study of American Indian Education, Series I, 4, Final Report) ERIC ED039975.

Quinten, B. T. Oklahoma tribes, the great depression and the Indian Bureau. In Roger L. Nichols and George R. Adams, eds. The American Indian: Past and Present. Waltham, Xerox College Publishing, 1971: 243-254.

Quinten, B. T. Oklahoma tribes, the Great Depression and the Indian Bureau. Mid-America, 49 (1967): 29-43.

Rachlin, Carol K. The Native American Church in Oklahoma. Chronicles of Oklahoma, 42 (1964): 262-272.

Rachlin, Carol K. Tight shoe night. Midcontinent American Studies Journal, 6 (1965): 84-100.

Ramp, Lary C. Civil War battle of Barren Creek, Indian Territory, 1863. Chronicles of Oklahoma, 48 (1970/1971): 74-82.

Simms, Ruthanna M. As long as the sun gives light. Richmond, Ind., Associated Executive Committee of Friends on Indian Affairs, 1970. 146 p. illus., map.

Taylor, Floyd L. An investigation of environmental conditions which characterize Indians in the Oklahoma City School District and a background for understanding contemporary Indian attitudes and behaviors. Dissertation Abstracts, 29 (1968/1969): 2501A. UM 69-1995.

Tracy, Valerie. The Indian in transition: the Neosho Agency 1850-1861. Chronicles of Oklahoma, 48 (1970/1971): 164-183.

Trimble, Joseph E. An index of the social indicators of the American Indian in Oklahoma. Oklahoma City, State Office of Community Affairs and Planning, 1972. 13, 564 p.

Tyler, Carl W., Jr. Maternal health and socioeconomic status of nonreservation Indians. By Carl W. Tyler, Jr. and Armin L. Saeger, Jr. U.S., Public Health Service, Public Health Reports, 83 (1968): 465-473.

Underhill, Lonnie E. Classification of Oklahoma Indian tribes: language stocks, population, and locations. By Lonnie E. Underhill and John H. Battle. Chronicles of Oklahoma, 48 (1970): 197-208.

Underhill, Lonnie E. Wild turkeys in Oklahoma. By Lonnie E. Underhill and Daniel F. Littlefield, Jr. Chronicles of Oklahoma, ·48 (1970/1971): 376-388.

U.S., Bureau of Indian Affairs. Indians of Oklahoma. Washington, D.C., Government Printing Office, 1968. 19 p. ERIC ED028864.

Ward, Allen T. Letters of Allen T. Ward, 1842-1851, from the Shawnee and Kaw (Methodist) Missions. Edited by Lela Barnes. Kansas Historical Quarterly, 33 (1967): 321-376.

Watt, Frank H. The Waco Indian village and its peoples. Texana, 6 (1968): 195-243.

Wax, Rosalie H. Doing fieldwork; warnings and advice. Chicago, University of Chicago Press, 1971. 10, 395 p.

Willson, Walt. Freedmen in Indian Territory during Reconstruction. Chronicles of Oklahoma, 49 (1971/1972): 230-244.

Wilson, Charles B., ed. Indians of eastern Oklahoma. Afton, Okla., Buffalo Publishing, 1964. 43 p. illus.

Wright, Muriel H. The Indian International Fair at Muskogee. Chronicles of Oklahoma, 49 (1971/1972): 14-50.

Wright, Peter M. John Collier and the Oklahoma Indian Welfare Act of 1936. Chronicles of Oklahoma, 50 (1972): 347-371.

Zolotarevskaia, I. A. Nekotorye materialy ob assimiliatsii indeĭtsev oklakhomy. Akademiia Nauk SSSR, Institut Etnografii imeni N.N. Miklukho-Maklaia, Kratkie Soobshcheniia, 33 (1960): 84-89.

Zolotarevskaia, I. A. Poezdka k indeĭtsev SSHA. Sovetskaia Etnografiia, no. 6 (1959): 162-172.

Zolotarevskaia, I. A. Some materials on the assimilation of Oklahoma Indians. Translated by William Andrews. Edited by William E. Bittle. By I. A. Zolotarevskaja. Plains Anthropologist, 6 (1961): 1-6.

09-30   Red River Métis

Anderson, Frank W. Gabriel Dumont. Alberta Historical Review, 7, no. 3 (1959): 1-6.

Belcourt, George Antoine. Hunting buffalo on the northern Plains: a letter from Father Belcourt. North Dakota History, 38 (1971): 332-348.

Berry, J. P. Canada's debt to the fur traders. Alberta Historical Review, 7, no. 3 (1959): 11-20.

Bowsfield, Hartwell. Louis Riel, the rebel and the heros. Toronto, Oxford University Press, 1971. 160 p. illus., maps.

Breen, David H. "Timber Tom" and the North-West rebellion. Alberta Historical Review, 19, no. 3 (1971): 1-7.

Buckley, Helen. The Indians and Metis of Northern Saskatchewan. A report on economic and social development. Saskatoon, Canadian Centre for Community Studies, 1963. 114 p. ERIC ED026197.

Canadian Corrections Association. Indians and the law. Journal of Canadian Studies, 3, no. 2 (1968): 31-55.

Cass-Beggs, Barbara, comp. Seven Métis songs of Saskatchewan. Don Mills, Ont., BMI Canada, 1967. 31 p. illus.

Cerbelaud Salagnac, Georges. La révolte des métis; Louis Riel, héros ou rebelle? Montréal, HMH, 1971. 205 p. illus.

Cerbelaud Salagnac, Georges. La révolte des métis: Louis Riel, héros ou rebelle? Tours, Mame, 1971. 205 p. illus., map.

De Tremaudan, Auguste-Henri. Histoire de la nation métisse dans l'ouest canadien. Montréal, A. Levesque, 1935. 450 p.

Drouin, Emeric O. St. Paul des Metis. Alberta Historical Review, 11, no. 4 (1963): 12-14.

Elliott, Jack. Tobacco pipes among the Hivernant hide hunters: A.D. 1860-1882. Western Canadian Journal of Anthropology, 3, no. 1 (1972): 146-157.

Foster, John E. Missionaries, mixed-bloods and the fur trade: four letters of the Rev. William Cockran, Red River Settlement, 1830-1833. Western Canadian Journal of Anthropology, 3, no. 1 (1972): 94-125.

Foster, John E. Program for the Red River Mission: the Anglican clergy 1820-1826. Histoire Sociale, 4 (1969): 49-75.

*Giraud, Marcel. Le Métis Canadien: son rôle dans l'histoire des Provinces de l'Ouest. Paris, 1945. 56, 1,296 p. illus., maps. (Paris, Université, Institut d'Ethnologie, Travaux et Mémoires, 44)

Gray, John S. The Northern Overland pony express. Montana, the Magazine of Western History, 16, no. 4 (1966): 58-73.

Hatt, F. K. The Canadian Métis: recent interpretations. Canadian Ethnic Studies, 3 (1971): 1-16.

Heilbron, Bertha L. Artist as buffalo hunter; Paul Kane and the Red River half-breeds. Minnesota History, 36 (1958/1959): 300-314.

Hendrie, Hugh C. A comparative study of the psychiatric care of Indian and Metis. By Hugh C. Hendrie and Diane Hanson. American Journal of Orthopsychiatry, 42 (1972): 480-489.

Howard, James H. The identity and demography of the Plains-Ojibwa. Plains Anthropologist, 6 (1961): 171-178.

Hurt, Wesley R. Factors in the persistence of peyote in the Northern Plains. Plains Anthropologist, 5 (1960): 16-27.

Ironside, R. G. Development of Victoria settlement. By R. G. Ironside and E. Tomasky. Alberta Historical Review, 19, no. 2 (1971): 20-29.

Jamieson, Frederick. The Edmonton Hunt. Pioneer West, 1 (1969): 10-18.

Kreutzweiser, Erwin E. The Red River insurrection; its causes and events. Gardenvale, Que., Garden City Press, 1936. 9, 166 p.

Lagasse, Jean H. Community development in Manitoba. Human Organization, 20 (1961/1962): 232-237.

Legasse, Jean. The Métis in Manitoba. Historical and Scientific Society of Manitoba, Papers, ser. 3, 15 (1960): 39-57.

Manitoba, Indian and Métis Conference Committee, Health and Welfare Subcommittee. A survey of welfare services for Indian and Métis people in Manitoba. Winnipeg, 1967. 3, 22, 12 p.

Morton, Thomas F. The Civil War of Private Morton. Edited by James T. King. North Dakota History, 35 (1968): 9-19.

Morton, W. L. A century of plain and parkland. Alberta Historical Review, 17, no. 2 (1969): 1-10.

Morton, William. The battle at the Grand Coteau, July 13 and 14, 1851. Historical and Scientific Society of Manitoba, Papers, ser. 3, 16 (1961): 37-49.

Normandeau, Louis. 65th Mount Royal Regiment and the Riel rebellion. Alberta Historical Review, 9, no. 4 (1961): 22-26.

Pfaller, Louis. The peace mission of 1863-1864. North Dakota History, 37 (1970): 293-313.

Ross, Alexander. The Red River settlement: its rise, progress, and present state. Burlington, Vt., C. E. Tuttle, 1972. 28, 416 p.

Shera, John W. Poundmaker's capture of a wagon train. Pioneer West, 1 (1969): 7-9.

Shrive, F. N. Charles Mair: a document on the Red River rebellion. Canadian Historical Review, 40 (1959): 218-226.

Silver, A. I. French Canada and the prairie frontier, 1870-1890. Canadian Historical Review, 50 (1969): 11-36.

Spaulding, Philip Taft. The Metis of Ile-a-la-Crosse. Dissertation Abstracts International, 31 (1970/1971): 2434B-2435B. UM 70-19,659.

Sprenger, G. Herman. The Metis Nation: buffalo hunting vs. agriculture in the Red River Settlement (circa 1810-1870). Western Canadian Journal of Anthropology, 3, no. 1 (1972): 158-178.

Sydiaha, D. Motivational and attitudinal
  characteristics of Indian school
  children as measured by the Thematic
  Apperception Test. By D. Sydiaha and J.
  Rempel. Canadian Psychologist, 5a, no. 3
  (1964): 139-148.

Thomson, William D. History of Fort
  Pembina: 1870-1895. North Dakota
  History, 36 (1969): 5-39.

Woolworth, Nancy L. Captain Edwin V.
  Sumner's expedition to Devil's Lake in
  the summer of 1845. North Dakota
  History, 28 (1961): 79-98.

14 Gulf

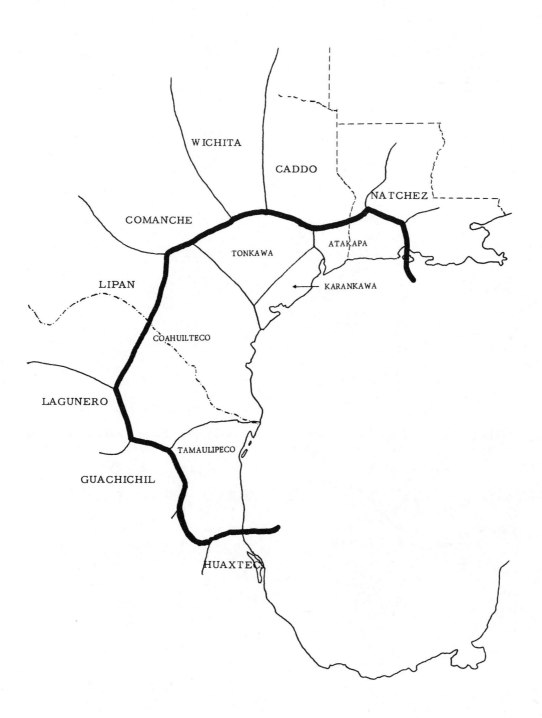

WICHITA

CADDO

COMANCHE

NATCHEZ

TONKAWA

ATAKAPA

LIPAN

KARANKAWA

COAHUILTECO

LAGUNERO

TAMAULIPECO

GUACHICHIL

HUAXTEC

14 Gulf

This area includes the territory between approximately the Río Pánuco in northeastern Mexico and the Vermilion River in southern Louisiana, including part of southwestern Louisiana, southeastern Texas as far west as the Edwards Plateau, northeastern Coahuila, northern Nuevo León, and most of Tamaulipas. The groups inhabiting this large area were mostly hunters and gatherers who utilized a very limiting, semiarid environment. Small bands united by kinship bonds were the basic social units, with little social differentiation by status or rank. Groups so characterized inhabited what has been termed the Western Gulf Area, which is generally the region from the Trinity River in northeast Texas southward to the Río Pánuco. The Tonkawa and Atakapa, whose territorials lie outside this region, are culturally peripheral to the Plains and the Southeast respectively. Tonkawa culture developed toward the typical bison-hunting, horse-nomad Plains type, but they were hindered by the relative lack of bison and the appearance of the hostile Comanche and Kiowa on the edge of their territory. The Atakapa were basically horticulturalists with a social organization reflecting the nearby climax area of the Southeast. As a whole, these groups are very poorly known, most having become extinct as functioning cultures by the nineteenth century. A few Tonkawa are still living in a Federal trust area in northern Oklahoma.

14-01. Atakapa. The Atakapa, plus the Akokisa (Arkokisa), the Bidai, the Opelousa, and the Deadose, lived along the Gulf coast in southwestern Louisiana and northeastern Texas between Vermilion Bay and Trinity Bay, near Baytown, Texas. They spoke a language isolate in the Macro-Algonquian phylum and became extinct as a group in the nineteenth century.

Sjöberg, Andrée F. The Bidai Indians of southeastern Texas. Southwestern Journal of Anthropology, 7 (1951): 391-400.

14-02. Coahuilteco. The Coahuilteco (Coahuiltec, Tejanos), including a large number of autonomous bands, such as the Alasapa (Alazapa), Borrado (Quinigua, Quinicuano, Guinigua), Comecrudo, Mescal, Orejon, Pakawa, Pampopa, Pausane, Pihuique, Sanipao, Tecame (Tacame), Tilijayo, (Tilijaes), and Venado, ranged over a large area of the interior of northeastern Mexico and along the coast of southern Texas to Aransas Bay. They spoke a language isolate in the Hokan phylum and are extinct as groups.

14-03. Karankawa. The Karankawa, including the Coapite, Coaque (Coco), Kohani, Pataquilla, Quilotes, Tiopane, and Tups, lived on the Gulf Coast of Texas between Trinity Bay and Aransas Bay. They spoke a language isolate perhaps related to Coahuiltecan and are extinct.

14-04. Tamaulipeco. The Tamaulipeco (Tamaulipec), plus the Janambre and Pisone, and a number of other small groups, lived along the coast and in part of the interior of the Mexican state of Tamaulipas from the Texas border to the Río Pánuco. They probably spoke languages related to Coahuiltecan and are extinct.

14-05. Tonkawa. The Tonkawa (Konkone), including the Cava, Emet, Ervipiame, Mayeye, Sana, Tohaha, Toho, Tonkawa, Tusolivi, Ujuiap, and Yojuane, lived in central Texas from Cibolo Creek on the southwest to near the Trinity River in the northeast. Their descendants now live in a Federal trust area in north-central Oklahoma. They spoke a language isolate in the Macro-Algonquian phylum and numbered 40 in 1972.

14-00   Gulf Area Bibliography

Bancroft, H. H.   The native races of the
Pacific States, Vol. 1: 615-644.   New
York, 1875.

Bandelier, A. F., ed.   The journey of
Alvar Nuñez Cabeza de Vaca.   New York,
1922.   230 p.

Beals, R. L.   The comparative ethnology of
northern Mexico.   Ibero-Americana, 2
(1932): 93-225.

Berlandier, Luis.   The Indians of Texas in
1830.   By Jean Louis Berlandier.
Translated by Patricia Reading Leclercq.
Edited by John C. Ewers.   Washington,
D.C., Smithsonian Institution Press,
1969.   11, 209 p.   illus., maps.

Bollaert, W.   Observations on the Indian
tribes in Texas.   Ethnological Society
(London), Journal, 2 (1850): 262-283.

Bolton, H. E.   Texas in the middle
eighteenth century.   California,
University, Publications in History, 3
(1915): 1-501.

Bonnell, George W.   Topographical
description of Texas.   To which is added
an account of the Indian tribes.   Waco,
Texian Press, 1964.   150 p.

Cortes Alonso, V.   Noticias sobre las
tribus de las costas de Tejas durante el
siglo XVIII.   Seminario de Estudios
Americanistas, Trabajos y Conferencias,
4 (1954): 133-140.

Eckhart, George B.   Spanish missions of
Texas, 1680-1800.   Kiva, 32, no. 3
(1966/1967): 73-95.

Galaviz de Capdevielle, María Elena.
Rebeliones indígenas en el norte del
reino de la Nueva España; siglos xvi y
xvii.   México, Editorial Campesina,
1967.   219 p.   maps.

Gursky, Karl-Heinz.   Ein Vergleich der
grammatikalischen Morpheme der Golf-
Sprachen und der Hoka-Subtiaba-Sprachen.
Orbis, 15 (1966): 511-537.

Gursky, Karl-Heinz.   Gulf and Hokan-
Subtiaban: new lexical parallels.
International Journal of American
Linguistics, 34 (1968): 21-41.

Haas, M. R.   A new linguistic relationship
in North America.   Southwestern Journal
of Anthropology, 14 (1958): 231-264.

Haas, M. R.   The proto-Gulf word for land.
International Journal of American
Linguistics, 18 (1952): 238-240.

Haas, M. R.   The proto-Gulf word for
water.   International Journal of American
Linguistics, 17 (1951): 71-79.

Hrdlička, A.   Catalogue of human crania in
the United States National Museum
collections.   United States National
Museum, Proceedings, 87 (1940): 315-464.

Huerta Preciado, María Teresa.   Rebeliones
indígenas en el Noreste de México en la
época colonial.   México, 1966.   108 p.
(Instituto Nacional de Antropología e
Historia, Publicaciones, Serie Historia,
15)

Jackson, A. T.   Ornaments of East Texas
Indians.   Texas Archeological and
Paleontological Society, Bulletin, 7
(1935): 11-28.

Jackson, A. T.   Picture-writing of Texas
Indians.   Texas, University,
Publications, Anthropological Papers, 2
(1938): 1-490.

Jimenez Moreno, W.   Tribus e idiomas del
norte de Mexico.   In El Norte de México y
el Sur de Estados Unidos.   México, 1943:
121-133.

Kirchhoff, P.   Los recolectores-cazadores
del norte de Mexico.   In El Norte de
México y el Sur de Estados Unidos.
México, 1943: 133-144.

Krieger, A. D.   Food habits of Texas
coastal Indians in the early sixteenth
century.   Texas Archeological and
Paleontological Society, Bulletin, 27
(1956): 47-58.

Kunkel, P. A.   The Indians of Louisiana
about 1700.   Louisiana Historical
Quarterly, 34 (1951): 175-204.

Mason, J. A.   The place of Texas in pre-
Columbian relationships between the
United States and Mexico.   Texas
Archeological and Paleontological
Society, Bulletin, 7 (1935): 29-46.

Morfi, J. A. de.   Memorias for the history
of the Province of Texas.   Ed. by F. M.
Chabot.   San Antonio, 1932.   85 p.

Newcomb, William W., Jr.   The Indians of
Texas, from prehistoric to modern times.
Austin, University of Texas Press, 1961.
404 p.   illus.

O'Rourke, T. P.   The Franciscan missions
in Texas (1690-1793).   Catholic
University of America, Studies in
American Church History, 5 (1927): 1-
107.

Ortiz, Francisco Xavier.   Razón de la
visita a las misiones de la Provincia de

Texas: 2. México, Vargas Rea, 1955.
38 p.

Powell, Philip W., comp. War and peace on
the North Mexican frontier: a
documentary record. Vol. 1. Madrid,
Ediciones Jose Porrua Turanzas, 1971.
27, 276 p. illus. (Colección
Chimalistac de Libros y Documentos
acerca de la Nueva España, 32)

Rea, Robert R. Redcoats and Redskins on
the lower Mississippi, 1763-1776: the
career of Lt. John Thomas. Louisiana
History, 11 (1970): 5-35.

Sapir, E. The Hokan and Coahuiltecan
languages. International Journal of
American Linguistics, 1 (1920): 280-290.

Sibley, J. A report from Natchitoches in
1807. Indian Notes and Monographs, n.s.,
25 (1922): 5-102.

Smith, R. A. Account of the journey of
Bénard de la Harpe. Southwestern
Historical Quarterly, 62 (1958/1959):
75-86, 246-259, 371-385, 525-541.

Swanton, J. R. Linguistic position of the
tribes of southern Texas and
northeastern Mexico. American
Anthropologist, n.s., 17 (1915): 17-40.

Swanton, J. R. Relations between northern
Mexico and the southeast of the United
States from the point of view of
ethnology and history. In El Norte de
México y el Sur de Estados Unidos.
México, 1943: 259-276.

Taylor, V. H. and J. Hammons. The letters
of Antonio Martinez. Austin, 1957.
374 p.

Texas, State Library, Austin, Archives
Division. Texas Indian papers. Edited
by Dorman H. Winfrey, et al. Austin,
1959-1966. 5 v. illus., maps.

Weddle, Robert S. La Salle's survivors.
Southwestern Historical Quarterly, 75
(1971/1972): 413-433.

Weitlaner, R. J. Las lenguas del sur de
Estados Unidos y el norte de México. In
El Norte de México y el Sur de Estados
Unidos. México, 1943: 181-185.

Weitlaner, Roberto J. Lenguas del sur de
Estados Unidos y el norte de México. Un
suplemento. México, Instituto Nacional
de Antropología e Historia, Anales, 16
(1963): 193-195.

14-01 Atakapa

Bolton, H. E. Athanase de Mézières and
the Louisiana-Texas frontier.
Cleveland, 1914. 2 v.

Bossu, Jean B. Travels in the interior of
North America, 1751-1762. Translated and
edited by Seymour Feiler. Norman,
University of Oklahoma Press, 1962. 17,
243 p. illus., maps.

Bossu, M. Travels through that part of
North America formerly called Louisiana,
Vol. 1: 337-345. London, 1771.

Burch, M. C. The indigenous Indians of
the lower Trinity area of Texas.
Southwestern Historical Quarterly, 60
(1956): 36-52.

Bushnell, D. I. Drawings by A. DeBatz in
Louisiana. Smithsonian Miscellaneous
Collections, 80, no. 5 (1927): 1-14.

Butler, Joseph T., Jr. The Atakapa
Indians: cannibals of Louisiana.
Louisiana History, 11 (1970): 167-176.

Campbell, T. N. Archeological
investigations at the Caplen Site,
Galveston County, Texas. Texas Journal
of Science, 9 (1957): 448-471.

Dyer, J. O. The Lake Charles Atakapas.
Galveston, 1917.

Gatschet, A. S. and J. R. Swanton. A
dictionary of the Atakapa language. U.S.
Bureau of American Ethnology, Bulletin,
108 (1932): 1-181.

Gilmore, Kathleen K. The San Xavier
Missions: a study in historical site
identification. Austin, Tex., State
Building Commission, 1969. 6, 151 p.
illus. (Texas, State Building
Commission Archeological Program, 16)

Gursky, Karl-Heinz. A lexical comparison
of Atakapa, Chitimacha, and Tunica
languages. International Journal of
American Linguistics, 35 (1969): 83-107.

Haas, Mary R. Historical linguistics and
the genetic relationship of languages.
In Theoretical Foundations. The Hague,
Mouton, 1966: 113-153. (Current Trends
in Linguistics, 3)

Hewitt, J. N. B. Attacapa. U.S. Bureau of
American Ethnology, Bulletin, 30, vol. 1
(1907): 114-115.

Holmes, Jack D. L. Three early Memphis
commandants: Beauregard, Deville
Degoutin, and Folch. West Tennessee

Historical Society, Papers, 18 (1964):
5-38.

Jelks, Edward B.   The archeology of McGee
Bend Reservoir, Texas. Dissertation
Abstracts, 26 (1965/1966): 1861.   UM 65-
8055.

Newcomb, W. W.   A reappraisal of the
"Cultural Sink" of Texas. Southwestern
Journal of Anthropology, 12 (1956): 145-
153.

Post, Lauren C.   Some notes on the
Attakapas Indians of Southwest
Louisiana. Louisiana History, 3 (1962):
221-242.

Sayles, E. B.   An archaeological survey of
Texas. Medallion Papers, 17 (1935): 1-
164.

*Sjöberg, Andrée F.   The Bidai Indians of
southeastern Texas. Southwestern Journal
of Anthropology, 7 (1951): 391-400.

Swadesh, M.   Atakapa-Chitimacha *kw.
International Journal of American
Linguistics, 13 (1947): 120-121.

Swadesh, M.   Phonologic formulas for
Atakapa-Chitimacha. International
Journal of American Linguistics, 12
(1946): 113-132.

Swanton, J. R.   A sketch of the Atakapa
Language. International Journal of
American Linguistics, 5 (1929): 121-149.

Swanton, J. R.   A structural and lexical
comparison of the Tunica, Chitimacha,
and Atakapa Languages. U.S. Bureau of
American Ethnology, Bulletin, 68 (1919):
1-56.

Swanton, J. R.   Indian language studies in
Louisiana. Smithsonian Institution,
Explorations and Field-Work (1930): 195-
200.

Swanton, J. R.   Indian tribes of the lower
Mississippi valley and adjacent coast of
the Gulf of Mexico. U.S. Bureau of
American Ethnology, Bulletin, 43 (1911):
360-364.

Swanton, J. R.   Indians of the
Southeastern United States. U.S. Bureau
of American Ethnology, Bulletin, 137
(1946): 11-830.

Swanton, J. R.   Mythology of the Indians
of Louisiana and the Texas coast.
Journal of American Folklore, 20 (1907):
285-289.

Vila Vilar, Luisa.   Aculturacion de los
grupos indigenas de Texas segun la
documentacion española del siglo XVIII.

In Congreso Internacional de
Americanistas, 36th. 1964, España. Actas
y Memorias. Tomo 2.   Sevilla, 1966: 161-
165.

Villiers du Terrage, M. de and P. Rivet.
Les Indiens du Texas. Société des
Américanistes, Journal, n.s., 11 (1919):
403-442.

Wheat, J. B.   The Addicks Dam Site. U.S.
Bureau of American Ethnology, Bulletin,
154 (1953): 143-252.

14-02   Coahuilteco

Anderson, A. E.   Artifacts of the Rio
Grande Delta region. Texas Archeological
and Paleontological Society, Bulletin, 4
(1932): 29-31.

Ayala-Vallejo, Reynaldo.   An historical
geography of Parras de la Fuente,
Coahuila-Mexico, or the changing man-
land relationship in Parras de la
Fuente, Coahuila-Mexico. Dissertation
Abstracts International, 32 (1971/1972):
4660B.   UM 72-5357.

Beals, Ralph L.   The comparative ethnology
of northern Mexico before 1750.
Berkeley, University of California
Press, 1932.   6, 93-225 p.   maps.
(Ibero-Americana, 2)

Bishop, M.   The odyssey of Cabeza de Vaca.
New York, 1933.   306 p.

Daniel, James M.   The Spanish frontier in
West Texas and northern Mexico.
Southwestern Historical Quarterly, 71
(1967/1968): 481-495.

Dávila Aguirre, J. de Jesús.
Chichimécatl; origen, cultura, lucha y
extinción de los gallardos, bárbaros del
Norte.   Saltillo, Universidad de
Coahuila y el Ateneo Guente, 1967.
127 p.   illus., maps.

Del Hoyo, Eugenio, ed.   El Cuadernillo de
la lengua de los Indios Pajalates (1732)
por Gabriel de Vergara, y El
Confesonario de Indios en lengua
coahuilteca.   Monterey, Instituto
Tecnológico y de Estudios Superiores de
Monterey, 1965.   5, 86 p.   (Materiales
para la Etnohistoria del Noreste de
Mexico, 1)

Duaine, Carl L., comp.   Caverns of
oblivion.   Corpus Christi, 1971.   17,
245 p.   illus.

Eguilaz de Prado, Isabel.   Los indios del
nordeste de Méjico en el siglo XVIII.
Sevilla, 1965.   128 p.   (Sevilla,

Universidad, Seminario de Antropología Americana, Publicaciones, 7)

Eguilaz de Prado, Isabel. Los indios del nordeste de Mexico en el siglo XVIII: areas de poblacion y areas culturales. In Congreso Internacional de Americanistas, 36th. 1964, España. Actas y Memorias. Tomo 2. Sevilla, 1966: 177-194.

Gatschet, A. S. and C. Thomas. Coahuiltecan. U.S. Bureau of American Ethnology, Bulletin, 30, vol. 1 (1907): 314-315.

Griffen, William B. Culture change and shifting populations in central northern Mexico. Tucson, 1969. 12, 196 p. maps. (Arizona, University, Anthropological Papers, 13)

Griffen, William B. Procesos de extinción y continuidad social y cultural en el norte de México durante la Colonia. América Indígena, 30 (1970): 689-724.

Gursky, Karl-Heinz. Algonkian and the languages of southern Texas. Anthropological Linguistics, 5, no. 9 (1963): 17-21.

Gursky, Karl-Heinz. The linguistic position of the Quinigua Indians. International Journal of American Linguistics, 30 (1964): 325-327.

Haas, M. R. The proto-Hokan-Coahuiltecan word for "Water". California, University, Publications in Linguistics, 10 (1954): 57-62.

Haas, Mary R. Tonkawa and Algonkian. Anthropological Linguistics, 1, no. 2 (1959): 1-6.

Hester, Thomas Roy. Aboriginal watercraft on the lower Rio Grande of Texas. Masterkey, 46 (1972): 108-111.

Hester, Thomas Roy. Archeological materials from the Oulline Site (41LS3) and other sites in La Salle County, Southwest Texas. By Thomas Roy Hester, L. D. White, and Joy White. Texas Journal of Science, 21 (1969/1970): 131-166.

Hoyo, Eugenio del. Vocablos de la lengua quinigua de los indios borrados del noreste de México. Humanitas (Monterrey), 1 (1960): 489-515.

Jacobsen, William H., Jr. Switch-reference in Hokan-Coahuiltecan. In Dell H. Hymes and William E. Bittle, eds. Studies in Southwestern Ethnolinguistics. The Hague, Mouton,

1967: 238-263. (Studies in General Anthropology, 3)

Landar, Herbert J. The Karankawa invasion of Texas. International Journal of American Linguistics, 34 (1968): 242-258.

Martin, G. C. The Indian tribes of the Mission Nuestra Senora del Refugio. San Antonio, 1936. 82 p.

Newcomb, W. W. A reappraisal of the "Cultural Sink" of Texas. Southwestern Journal of Anthropology, 12 (1956): 145-153.

Opler, M. E. The use of peyote by the Carrizo and Lipan Apache tribes. American Anthropologist, n.s., 40 (1938): 271-285.

Portillo, Esteban L. Apuntes para la historia antigua de Coahuila y Texas. Saltillo, Tip. "El Golfo de México" de S. Fernandez, 1886. 482 p.

Ruecking, F. Bands and band-clusters of the Coahuiltecan Indians. Student Papers in Anthropology, 1, no. 2 (1954): 1-24.

Ruecking, F. The economic system of the Coahuiltecan Indians of southern Texas. Texas Journal of Science, 5 (1953): 480-497.

Ruecking, F. The social organization of the Coahuiltecan Indians of southern Texas. Texas Journal of Science, 7 (1955): 357-388.

Ruecking, Frederick, Jr. Ceremonies of the Coahuiltecan Indians of southern Texas and northeastern Mexico. Texas Journal of Science, 6 (1954): 330-339.

Sapir, E. The Hokan and Coahuiltecan languages. International Journal of American Linguistics, 1 (1920): 280-290.

Sayles, E. B. An archaeological survey of Texas. Medallion Papers, 17 (1935): 1-164.

Schuetz, Mardith K. Historic background of the Mission San Antonio de Valero. Austin, Tex., State Building Commission, 1966. 46 p. illus., maps. (Texas, State Building Commission Archeological Program, 1)

Schuetz, Mardith K. The history and archeology of Mission San Juan Capistrano, San Antonio, Texas. Vol. 1. Historical documentation and description of the structures. Austin, Tex., State building Commission, 1968. 2, 263 p. illus., maps. (Texas, State Building Commission Archeological Program, 10)

Schuetz, Mardith K. The history and archeology of Mission San Juan Capistrano, San Antonio, Texas. Vol. 2. Description of the artifacts and ethnohistory of the Coahuiltecan Indians. Austin, Tex., State Building Commission, 1969. 2, 133 p. illus. (Texas, State Building Commission Archeological Program, 11)

Swadesh, Mauricio. Las lenguas indígenas del noreste de México. Anales de Antropología, 5 (1968): 75-86.

Swanton, J. R. Linguistic material from the tribes of southern Texas and northeastern Mexico. U.S. Bureau of American Ethnology, Bulletin, 127 (1940): 1-145.

Thomas, Cyrus. Indian languages of Mexico and Central America and their geographical distribution. By Cyrus Thomas assisted by John R. Swanton. Washington, D.C., Government Printing Office, 1911. 7, 108 p. map. (U.S., Bureau of American Ethnology, Bulletin, 44)

Troike, Rudolph C. A structural comparison of Tonkawa and Coahuilteco. In Dell H. Hymes and William E. Bittle, eds. Studies in Southwestern Ethnolinguistics. The Hague, Mouton, 1967: 321-332. (Studies in General Anthropology, 3)

Troike, Rudolph C. Notes on Coahuiltecan ethnography. Texas Archeological Society, Bulletin, 32 (1961): 57-63.

Troike, Rudolph Charles, Jr. A descriptive phonology and morphology of Coahuilteco. Dissertation Abstracts, 20 (1959/1960): 2793. UM 59-6728.

Vergara, Gabriel de. El cuadernillo de la lengua de los indios pajalates (1732), y Confesionario de indios en lengua coahuilteco. Edited by Eugenio del Hoyo. Monterrey, N.L., 1965. 86 p. (Monterrey, Instituto Technologico y de Estudios Superiores de Monterrey, Publicaciones, Serie: Historia, 3)

Vila Vilar, Luisa. Aculturacion de los grupos indigenas de Texas segun la documentacion española del siglo XVIII. In Congreso Internacional de Americanistas, 36th. 1964, España. Actas y Memorias. Tomo 2. Sevilla, 1966: 161-165.

Villiers du Terrage, M. de and P. Rivet. Les Indiens du Texas. Société des Américanistes, Journal, n.s., 11 (1919): 403-442.

Weddle, Robert S. San Juan Bautista: mother of Texas missions. Southwestern Historical Quarterly, 71 (1967/1968): 542-563.

14-03 Karankawa

Atkinson, M. J. The Texas Indians, 193-207. San Antonio, 1935.

Bedichek, R. Karankaway County. Southwest Review, 35 (1950): 259-264.

Bishop, M. The odyssey of Cabeza de Vaca. New York, 1933. 306 p.

Bolton, H. E. Athanase de Mézières and the Louisiana-Texas frontier. Cleveland, 1914. 2 v.

Burch, M. C. The indigenous Indians of the lower Trinity area of Texas. Southwestern Historical Quarterly, 60 (1956): 36-52.

Cabeza de Vaca, Alvar Núñez. Adventures in the unknown interior of America. New York, Collier, 1961. 152 p. (Collier Books, AS117)

Carter, James D. Background of Anglo-American colonization of Texas. Texana, 4 (1966): 75-92.

Cavazos Garza, Israel. Las incursiones de los bárbaros en el noreste de México, durante el siglo XIX. Humanitas (Monterrey), 5 (1964): 343-356.

Clauser, C. E. The relationship between a Coastal Algonkin and a Karankawa cranial series. Indiana Academy of Science, Proceedings, 57 (1948): 18-23.

Day, James M. James Kerr: frontier Texian. Texana, 2 (1964): 24-43.

Faulk, Odie B. Spanish-Comanche relations and the Treaty of 1785. Texana, 2 (1964): 44-53.

Faulk, Odie B., tr. and ed. A description of Texas in 1803. Southwestern Historical Quarterly, 66 (1962/1963): 513-515.

Fletcher, A. C. Coaque. U.S. Bureau of American Ethnology, Bulletin, 30, vol. 1 (1907): 315-316.

Fletcher, A. C. and J. R. Swanton. Karankawa. U.S. Bureau of American Ethnology, Bulletin, 30, vol. 1 (1907): 657-658.

Gatschet, A. S. Die Karankawa-Indianer. Globus, 49 (1886): 123-125.

Gatschet, A. S. The Karankawa Indians. Harvard University, Peabody Museum of American Archaeology and Ethnology, Papers, 1, no. 2 (1891): 5-103.

Gilmore, Kathleen K. The San Xavier Missions: a study in historical site identification. Austin, Tex., State Building Commission, 1969. 6, 151 p. illus. (Texas, State Building Commission Archeological Program, 16)

Gursky, Karl-Heinz. Algonkian and the languages of southern Texas. Anthropological Linguistics, 5, no. 9 (1963): 17-21.

Gursky, Karl-Heinz. The linguistic position of the Quinigua Indians. International Journal of American Linguistics, 30 (1964): 325-327.

Hasdorff, James Curtis. Four Indian tribes of Texas 1758-1858: a reevaluation of historical sources. Dissertation Abstracts International, 32 (1971/1972): 4512A. UM 72-4805.

Landar, Herbert J. The Karankawa invasion of Texas. International Journal of American Linguistics, 34 (1968): 242-258.

Leutenegger, Benedict, tr. and ed. New documents on Father José Mariano Reyes. Southwestern Historical Quarterly, 71 (1967/1968): 583-602.

Martin, G. C. Notes on some Texas coast campsites and other remains. Texas Archeological and Paleontological Society, Bulletin, 1 (1929): 50-57.

Martin, G. C. Texas coast pottery. Texas Archeological and Paleontological Society, Bulletin, 3 (1931): 53-56.

Martin, G. C. The Indian tribes of the Mission Nuestra Señora del Refugio. San Antonio, 1936. 82 p.

Newcomb, W. W. A reappraisal of the "Cultural Sink" of Texas. Southwestern Journal of Anthropology, 12 (1956): 145-153.

Potter, W. H. Ornamentation on the pottery of the Texas coastal tribes. Texas Archeological and Paleontological Society, Bulletin, 2 (1930): 41-44.

Roessler, A. R. Antiquities and aborigines of Texas. Smithsonian Institution, Annual Report of the Board of Regents (1881): 613-616.

Sayles, E. B. An archaeological survey of Texas. Medallion Papers, 17 (1935): 1-164.

Schaedel, R. P. The Karankawa of the Texas Gulf Coast. Southwestern Journal of Anthropology, 5 (1949): 117-137.

Straley, W. The Karankawas. National Archaeological News, 1, no. 8 (1937): 5-11.

Swanton, J. R. Linguistic material from the tribes of southern Texas and northeastern Mexico. U.S. Bureau of American Ethnology, Bulletin, 127 (1940): 124-133.

Vila Vilar, Luisa. Aculturacion de los grupos indigenas de Texas segun la documentacion española del siglo XVIII. In Congreso Internacional de Americanistas, 36th. 1964, España. Actas y Memorias. Tomo 2. Sevilla, 1966: 161-165.

Villiers du Terrage, M. de and P. Rivet. Les Indiens du Texas. Société des Américanistes, Journal, n.s., 11 (1919): 403-442.

Vizcaya Canales, Isidro. La invasión de los indios bárbaros al noreste de México, en los años de 1840 y 1841. Monterrey, N.L., 1968. 296 p. (Monterrey, Instituto Tecnologico y de Estudios Superiores de Monterrey, Publicaciones, Serie: Historia, 7)

Wolff, Thomas. The Karankawa Indians: their conflict with the White Man in Texas. Ethnohistory, 16 (1969): 1-32.

14-04 Tamaulipeco

Beals, R. L. The comparative ethnology of northern Mexico. Ibero-Americana, 2 (1932): 93-225.

Calleja, Félix. Nuevo Santander in 1795: a provincial inspection by Félix Calleja. Translated and edited by David M. Vigness. Southwestern Historical Quarterly, 75 (1971/1972): 461-506.

Duaine, Carl L., comp. Caverns of oblivion. Corpus Christi, 1971. 17, 245 p. illus.

Eguilaz de Prado, Isabel. Los indios del nordeste de Méjico en el siglo XVIII. Sevilla, 1965. 128 p. (Sevilla, Universidad, Seminario de Antropología Americana, Publicaciones, 7)

Eguilaz de Prado, Isabel. Los indios del nordeste de Mexico en el siglo XVIII: areas de poblacion y areas culturales. In Congreso Internacional de Americanistas, 36th. 1964, España. Actas y Memorias. Tomo 2. Sevilla, 1966: 177-194.

Lopez Prieto, A. Historia y estadística del estado de Tamaulipas. México, 1873.

MacNeish, R. S. Preliminary archaeological investigations in the Sierra de Tamaulipas. American Philosophical Society, Transactions, n.s., 44, no. 6 (1958): 1-210.

Martin, G. C. The Indian tribes of the Mission Nuestra Señora del Refugio. San Antonio, 1936. 82 p.

Prieto, Alejandro. Historia, geografía y estadística del estado de Tamaulipas. México, Tip. Escalerillas, 1873. 4, 361 p. map.

Saldivar, G. Historia compendiada de Tamaulipas. Mexico, 1945. 358 p.

Saldivar, G. Los Indios de Tamaulipas. In El Norte de México y el Sur de Estados Unidos. México, 1943: 49-52.

Saldivar, G. Los Indios de Tamaulipas. Instituto Panamericano de Geografía e Historia, Publicación, 70 (1943): 1-36.

Swadesh, Mauricio. Las lenguas indígenas del noreste de México. Anales de Antropología, 5 (1968): 75-86.

Swadesh, Morris. El Tamaulipeco. Revista Mexicana de Estudios Antropológicos, 19 (1963): 93-103.

Thomas, Cyrus. Indian languages of Mexico and Central America and their geographical distribution. By Cyrus Thomas assisted by John R. Swanton. Washington, D.C., Government Printing Office, 1911. 7, 108 p. map. (U.S., Bureau of American Ethnology, Bulletin, 44)

14-05 Tonkawa

Atkinson, M. J. The Texas Indians, 211-224. San Antonio, 1935.

Bishop, M. The odyssey of Cabeza de Vaca. New York, 1933. 306 p.

Bolton, H. E. Athanase de Mézières and the Louisiana-Texas frontier. Cleveland, 1914. 2 v.

Bolton, H. E. Sana. U.S. Bureau of American Ethnology, Bulletin, 30, vol. 2 (1910): 422-423.

Bolton, H. E. Tonkawa. U.S. Bureau of American Ethnology, Bulletin, 30, vol. 2 (1910): 778-783.

Bolton, H. E. Yojuane. U.S. Bureau of American Ethnology, Bulletin, 30, vol. 2 (1910): 998-999.

Borgström, C. H. Tonkawa and Indo-European vowel gradation. Norsk Tidsskrift for Sprogvidenskap, 17 (1954): 119-128.

Cabeza de Vaca, Alvar Núnez. Adventures in the unknown interior of America. New York, Collier, 1961. 152 p. (Collier Books, AS117)

Day, James M. James Kerr: frontier Texian. Texana, 2 (1964): 24-43.

Dixon, Ford. Cayton Erhard's reminiscences of the Texan Santa Fe expedition, 1841. Southwestern Historical Quarterly, 66 (1962/1963): 424-456.

Estep, Raymond. Lieutenant William E. Burnet letters: removal of the Texas Indians and the founding of Fort Cobb. Chronicles of Oklahoma, 38 (1960): 369-396.

Estep, Raymond. Lieutenant Wm. E. Burnet: notes on removal of Indians from Texas to Indian Territory. Chronicles of Oklahoma, 38 (1960): 274-309.

Faulk, Odie B., tr. and ed. A description of Texas in 1803. Southwestern Historical Quarterly, 66 (1962/1963): 513-515.

Fay, George E., ed. Charters, constitutions and by-laws of the Indian tribes of North America. Part VI: The Indian tribes of Oklahoma (cont'd.). Greeley, 1968. 5, 129 l. map. (University of Northern Colorado, Museum of Anthropology, Occasional Publications in Anthropology, Ethnology Series, 7) ERIC ED046556.

Fleming, Elvis Eugene. Captain Nicholas Nolan; lost on the Staked Plains. Texana, 4 (1966): 1-13.

Fletcher, A. C. Yguases. U.S. Bureau of American Ethnology, Bulletin, 30, vol. 2 (1910): 997.

Foreman, G. The last trek of the Indians, 286-290. Chicago, 1946.

Gatschet, A. S. Die Sprache der Tonkawas. Zeitschrift für Ethnologie, 9 (1877): 64-73.

Gatschet, A. S. Remarks upon the Tónkawa language. American Philosophical Society, Proceedings, 16 (1876): 318-327.

Gatschet, A. S. Zwölf Sprachen aus dem Südwesten Nordamerikas. Weimar, 1876. 150 p.

Gilmore, Kathleen K. A documentary and archeological investigation of Presidio San Luis de las Amarillas and Mission Santa Cruz de San Sabá. Austin, Tex., State Building Commission, 1967. 1, 72 p. illus., map. (Texas, State Building Commission Archeological Program, 9)

Gilmore, Kathleen K. The San Xavier Missions: a study in historical site identification. Austin, Tex., State Building Commission, 1969. 6, 151 p. illus. (Texas, State Building Commission Archeological Program, 16)

Gursky, Karl-Heinz. The linguistic position of the Quinigua Indians. International Journal of American Linguistics, 30 (1964): 325-327.

Haas, Mary R. On the relations of Tonkawa. In Dell H. Hymes and William E. Bittle, eds. Studies in Southwestern Ethnolinguistics. The Hague, Mouton, 1967: 310-320. (Studies in General Anthropology, 3)

Haas, Mary R. Tonkawa and Algonkian. Anthropological Linguistics, 1, no. 2 (1959): 1-6.

Hasdorff, James Curtis. Four Indian tribes of Texas 1758-1858: a reevaluation of historical sources. Dissertation Abstracts International, 32 (1971/1972): 4512A. UM 72-4805.

Hasskarl, Robert A., Jr. The culture and history of the Tonkawa Indians. Plains Anthropologist, 7 (1962): 217-231.

Hoijer, H. Analytical dictionary of the Tonkawa language. California, University, Publications in Linguistics, 5 (1949): 1-74.

Hoijer, H. Tonkawa. In F. Boas, ed. Handbook of American Indian Languages. Vol. 3. Washington, D.C., 1931: 1-148.

Hoijer, H. Tonkawa syntactic suffixes and anaphoric particles. Southwestern Journal of Anthropology, 5 (1949): 37-55.

Hoijer, H. Tonkawa. Viking Fund Publications in Anthropology, 6 (1946): 239-311.

Howard, J. H. A Tonkawa peyote legend. South Dakota, University, Museum, Museum Notes, 12, no. 4 (1951): 1-4.

Hymes, Dell H. Interpretation of a Tonkawa paradigm. In Dell H. Hymes and William E. Bittle, eds. Studies in Southwestern Ethnolinguistics. The Hague, Mouton, 1967: 264-278. (Studies in General Anthropology, 3)

Jacobsen, William H., Jr. Switch-reference in Hokan-Coahuiltecan. In Dell H. Hymes and William E. Bittle, eds. Studies in Southwestern Ethnolinguistics. The Hague, Mouton, 1967: 238-263. (Studies in General Anthropology, 3)

Jones, William K. Notes on the history and material culture of the Tonkawa Indians. Washington, D.C., Smithsonian Press, 1969. 5, 65-81 p. illus., maps. (Smithsonian Contributions to Anthropology, 2, no. 5)

Kissenberth, Charles W. Vowel elision in Tonkawa and derivational constraints. In Jerrold M. Sadock and Anthony L. Vanek, eds. Studies Presented to Robert B. Lees by His Students. Edmonton, Linguistic Research, 1970: 109-137.

Landar, Herbert J. The Karankawa invasion of Texas. International Journal of American Linguistics, 34 (1968): 242-258.

McLane, William. William McLane's narrative of the Magee-Gutierrez expedition, 1812-1813. Edited by Henry P. Walker. Southwestern Historical Quarterly, 66 (1962/1963): 457-479, 569-588.

Mooney, J. Die Tonkawas. Globus, 82 (1902): 76-79.

Nance, B. H. D. A. Nance and the Tonkawa Indians. West Texas Historical Association Yearbook, 28 (1952): 87-95.

Newcomb, W. W. A reappraisal of the "Cultural Sink" of Texas. Southwestern Journal of Anthropology, 12 (1956): 145-153.

Opler, M. E. A description of a Tonkawa peyote meeting. American Anthropologist, n.s., 41 (1939): 433-439.

Roessler, A. R. Antiquities and aborigines of Texas. Smithsonian Institution, Annual Report of the Board of Regents (1881): 613-616.

Sayles, E. B. An archaeological survey of Texas. Medallion Papers, 17 (1935): 1-164.

Schuetz, Mardith K.   Historic background
of the Mission San Antonio de Valero.
Austin, Tex., State Building Commission,
1966. 46 p. illus., maps. (Texas,
State Building Commission Archeological
Program, 1)

Schuetz, Mardith K. The history and
archeology of Mission San Juan
Capistrano, San Antonio, Texas. Vol. 1.
Historical documentation and description
of the structures. Austin, Tex., State
building Commission, 1968. 2, 263 p.
illus., maps. (Texas, State Building
Commission Archeological Program, 10)

Sjoberg, A. F. The culture of the
Tonkawa. Texas Journal of Science, 5
(1953): 280-304.

Troike, Rudolph C. A structural
comparison of Tonkawa and Coahuilteco.
In Dell H. Hymes and William E. Bittle,
eds. Studies in Southwestern
Ethnolinguistics. The Hague, Mouton,
1967: 321-332. (Studies in General
Anthropology, 3)

Vila Vilar, Luisa. Aculturacion de los
grupos indigenas de Texas segun la
documentacion española del siglo XVIII.
In Congreso Internacional de
Americanistas, 36th. 1964, España. Actas
y Memorias. Tomo 2. Sevilla, 1966: 161-
165.

Villiers du Terrage, M. de and P. Rivet.
Les Indiens du Texas. Société des
Américanistes, Journal, n.s., 11 (1919):
403-442.

Winfrey, Dorman H., ed. The Indian papers
of Texas and the Southwest, 1825-1916.
Edited by Dorman H. Winfrey and James M.
Day. Austin, Pemberton Press, 1966.
412 p.

15 Southwest

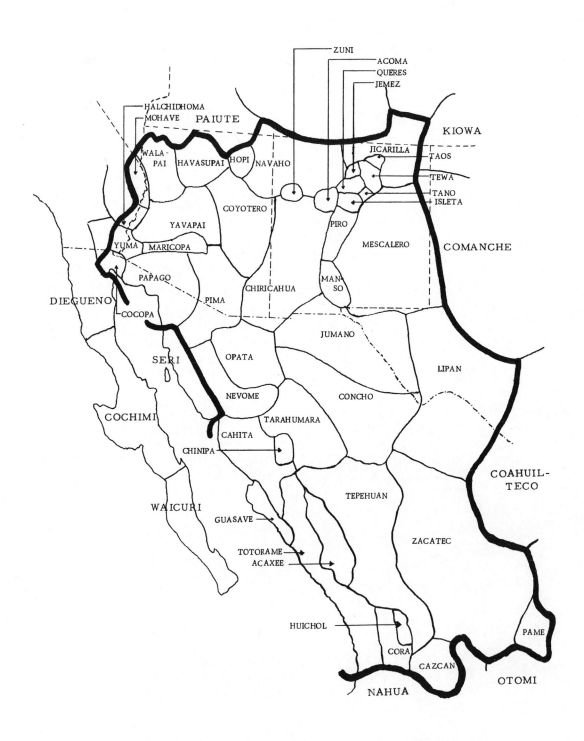

15 Southwest

This area includes most of Arizona and New Mexico, parts of Texas, Colorado, Utah, and California, all of the Mexican 'states of Sinaloa, Chihuahua, Durango, Nayarit, Zacatecas, and San Luís Potosí, and parts of Sonora, Coahuila, Nuevo León, Guanajuato, Querétaro, Hidalgo, and Jalisco. Most of the area is desert or mountainous and is generally semiarid to arid in climate. Settlements tend to cluster close to water supply as a result. Most of the Indians were farmers, although there were hunters and collectors in the eastern parts as well. Maize agriculture was the basis of subsistence throughout most of the area, with reliance on maize being greatest among the Puebloan peoples of Arizona and New Mexico, and among Mexican groups in the southwestern part of the area. Squashes, beans, and sunflower seeds also characterized the diet. Meat was not plentiful in most of the area, but fish was a regular part of the diet on the West Mexican coast. In the arid areas, plant collecting formed a large part of the subsistence base.

There was a wide range of sociopolitical organization, from a weak band organization among the Desert Yumans and the Athabascans (Apache and Navajo), through the village and town organizations of the Puebloan and Mexican peoples, to the true tribes of the River Yumans. Raiding and warfare were endemic until the Spanish government managed to put an end to most of these activities. Some of the Mexican groups kept armies.

In the U.S. part of the area, dislocation and reduction of the population has not been as great as in other parts of the country. The Navajo, for instance, are now the largest Indian population group in the United States, and most of the other groups have a relatively stable population. On the other hand, in Mexico many aboriginal groups have become extinct as a result of warfare with the Spanish and Mexican governments and disease. However, a strong element in the disappearance of these groups has been their assimilation into the general Mexican population. The Mayo and the Tarahumara still have quite large populations, but other groups are approaching cultural extinction.

Swadesh, Frances L. 20,000 years of history; a New Mexico bibliography. Santa Fe, Sunstone Press, 1973. 128 p.

15-01. Acoma. The pueblos of Acoma (Kawaiko, Sitsime), including Acomita, Heashhowa, and Pueblito, and Laguna are in west-central New Mexico, about 40 miles west of Albuquerque. The inhabitants speak Western Keresan languages and numbered 4,408 in 1970 (1,944 in Acoma and 2,464 in Laguna).

15-02. Cahita. The Cahita group, which includes the Baciroa, Conicari, Macoyahui, Mayo, Tepahue, Yaqui, Tehueco, Sinaloa (Cinaloa), Nio, Zoque, and Zuaque, live in southwestern Sonora and northwestern Sinaloa, from the Gulf of California to the Sierra Madre. A number of Yaqui also live in barrios in the Arizona cities of Tucson and Phoenix. Many of the groups named are extinct. The remainder speak languages of the Yaqui-Mayo group of Uto-Aztecan and probably number around 50,000.

15-03. Chinipa. The Chinipa, with the Huite and the Tubar (Tubare), lived in southwestern Chihuahua on the upper Río Fuerte and Río Otero. They spoke Uto-Aztecan languages and are extinct.

15-04. Chiricahua. The Chiricahua Apache (Aiaha), with the Gila (Xila, Gileño), Mimbreño (Coppermine Apache), Mogollon Apache, and Warm Spring Apache, lived in southeastern Arizona and southwestern New Mexico. Most of them now live on the Mescalero Indian Reservation in southern New Mexico and on the Fort Apache Indian Reservation in Arizona, but a few live in the Fort Sill area of southwestern Oklahoma. They speak an Athabascan language and probably number around ·900, with 60 in Oklahoma in 1972.

15-05. Cocopa. The Cocopa (Hagiopas), with the Kohuana (Cajuenche, Coana, Cutganes, Quokim), lived around the mouth of the Colorado River in southwestern Arizona and northwestern Sonora. They now live on the Cocopah Indian Reservation in Arizona. They speak a Yuman language and numbered 441 on the reservation in 1972.

15-06. Concho. The Concho, with the Chinarra and Chizo, lived in northern Chihuahua between Casas Grandes to the west and the Big Bend of the Rio Grande to the east. They spoke Uto-Aztecan languages and are extinct.

15-07. Coyotero. The Coyotero (Western Apache), including the San Carlos Apache, Apache Peaks Apache, Arivaipa, Pinaleño (Pinal), White Mountain Apache (Sierra Blanca Apache), Cibecue Apache, Canyon Creek Apache, Carrizo Apache, Tonto Apache, Mazatzal, Bald Mountain Apache, Fossil Creek Apache, Mormon Lake Apache, and Oak Creek Apache, lived in east-central Arizona. They now live on two contiguous reservations in the same area, the San Carlos Indian Reservation and the

Fort Apache Indian Reservation. They speak Athabascan languages and probably number around 7,500.

15-08. Guasave. The Guasave (Guazave), with the Achire, Ahome, Comopori, and Vacoregue, lived on the Pacific coast of Sinaloa from Approximately the Sonora-Sinaloa border south to the Rio San Lorenzo. They spoke Uto-Aztecan languages and are extinct as groups.

15-09. Halchidhoma. The Halchidhoma lived along the Colorado River in Arizona near the mouth of the Gila River. They spoke a Yuman language and now live with the Maricopa in Arizona on the Gila River Indian Reservation.

15-10. Havasupai. The Havasupai (Coconino, Kanina, Kokonino, Supai, Nation of the Willows) live in Cataract Canyon, formed by Havasu Creek near its confluence with the Colorado River in northwestern Arizona. They are now on the Havasupai Indian Reservation in the same place. They speak a Yuman language and numbered 370 in 1972.

15-11. Hopi. The Hopi (Moki, Moqui, Tusayan), including the pueblos of Homolobi, Hotevila, Mishongnovi, Oraibi (Old Oraibi), New Oraibi, Shipaulovi, Shongopovi, Sichomovi, and Walpi, and the towns of Bacavi and Moenkopi (Moenkapi), live on the Hopi Indian Reservation in northeastern Arizona. They speak a Shoshonean language and numbered 7,236 in 1970, with 6,423 living on the reservation in 1972.

15-12. Isleta. The Isleta division of the bibliography includes citations on the southern Tiwa (Tigua, Tiguex) pueblos of Isleta, Isleta del Sur (Ysleta del Sur), Sandia, and Senecu del Sur. These pueblos are in central New Mexico on the Sandia Indian Reservation and the Isleta Indian Reservation and in the vicinity of El Paso, Texas, where the inhabitants now live in the Ysleta Tigua community. They speak a Tanoan language and numbered about 2,300 in 1970.

Steiner, Stanley. The Tiguas; the lost tribe of city Indians. New York, Crowell-Collier, 1972. 90 p.

15-13. Jemez. The pueblo of Jemez is in central New Mexico about 20 miles northwest of Bernalillo. This bibliographic division also includes citations on the abandoned pueblo of Pecos, which is on the upper Pecos River southeast of Albuquerque. The inhabitants of Pecos Pueblo joined those of Jemez Pueblo in 1838. They speak a Tanoan language and numbered 1,448 in 1970.

15-14. Jicarilla. The Jicarilla Apache (Tinde) lived in southeastern Colorado and northeastern New Mexico but ranged into Texas, Oklahoma, and Kansas. They now live on the Jicarilla Indian Reservation in northwestern New Mexico. They speak an Athabascan language and numbered 1,928 in 1972.

Gunnerson, Dolores A. The Jicarilla Apache; a study in survival. DeKalb, Ill., Northern Illinois University Press, 1974. 326 p. illus., map.

15-15. Jumano. The Jumano (Chouman, Humano, Shuman), with the Suma, lived in southwestern Texas and northeastern Chihuahua in the Rio Grande Valley area, to the north of the Concho. They probably spoke a Uto-Aztecan language and are now extinct.

15-16. Lipan. The Lipan Apache (Ipan'de, Naizhan, Yabupai Lipan) lived in southeastern New Mexico, southwestern Texas, and adjacent Mexico, ranging as far as the Gulf of Mexico at times. Their descendants now live on the Mescalero Indian Reservation in New Mexico and with the Tonkawa and Kiowa Apache in Oklahoma. They spoke an Athabascan language and probably number less than 50.

15-17. Manso. The Manso (Gorretas, Lanos) lived in the Mesilla Valley in southern New Mexico near Las Cruces. Their descendants now live in the vicinity of El Paso with the Piro and Tiwa. They may have spoken an Athabascan or a Tanoan language and are now extinct as a group.

15-18. Maricopa. The Maricopa (Cocomaricopa, Papatsje), with the Kaveltcadom, lived on the lower Gila River in Arizona near its confluence with the Colorado River. They now live on the Salt River Indian Reservation and on the Gila River Indian Reservation in Arizona. They speak a Yuman language and probably number around 200.

15-19. Mescalero. The Mescalero Apache, with the Faraon Apache (Pharaoh), Janos, Jocomes, and Toboso, lived in southeastern New Mexico east of the Rio Grande River, and into northern Mexico. They now live on the Mescalero Indian Reservation in New Mexico. They speak an Athabascan language and probably number around 700.

15-20. Mohave. The Mohave (Amojave, Jamajabs, Soyopas, Mojave) lived on both sides of the Colorado River in northwestern Arizona and in southeastern California in the vicinity of Needles. They now live on the Fort Mojave Indian Reservation in the same area, and on the Colorado River Indian Reservation at Parker, Arizona. They speak a Yuman language and probably number about 1,000.

15-21. Navajo. The Navajo (Navaho, Apaches de Nabaju, Dine, Yabipais Nabajay) live in a large area in northern New Mexico, northern Arizona, southeastern Utah, and southwestern Colorado. They live principally on the main Navajo Indian Reservation, but also on the Canoncito Navajo Indian Reservation and the Alamo Navajo Indian Reservation in New Mexico, with substantial populations in Albuquerque and Denver. They speak an Athabascan language and numbered about 135,000 in 1972.

> Correll, J. Lee, et al. Navajo bibliography with subject index. Rev. ed. Window Rock, Ariz., Navajo Tribe, 1969, 1973. 2 v. (Navajo Parks and Recreation, Research Section, Research Report, 2)

15-22. Nevome. The Nevome (Lower Pima, Pima Bajo), including the Yecora and Ure, live in the upper Río Yaqui region in Sonora, extending eastward into Chihuahua. They speak a Uto-Aztecan language and probably number about 1,500.

15-23. Opata. The Opata (Baviapes, Cipias, Hipotlapiguas, Ypotlapiguas), with the Heve (Eudeve) and Jova (Joba), lived in northeastern Sonora to the east of the Pima and to the east and north of the Nevome, north from the upper Río Yaqui to the international border. They spoke a Uto-Aztecan language and number about 4,000.

15-24. Papago. The Papago (Tonooohtam), including the Soba (Piato), Pinacate, and Sand Papago (Areñenos), live in southern Arizona and northwestern Sonora. They now live on the Papago Indian Reservation, the Gila Bend Indian Reservation, the San Xavier Papago Indian Reservation, the Ak Chin Indian Reservation, and the Maricopa Indian Reservation in Arizona, and in various other localities in Arizona and Sonora. They speak a Uto-Aztecan language and probably number about 10,000.

15-25. Pima. The Pima (Aa'tam), including the Pima Alto (Upper Pima, Himeri, Hymeris, Himides), Quahatika (Kohatk, Qahatika), and the Sobaipuri, lived to the east and south of the Papago in the valleys of the Gila and the Salt Rivers in southern Arizona, and in northern Sonora. They now live on the Salt River Indian Reservation and the Gila River Indian Reservation in Arizona and in other scattered locations in Arizona and Sonora. They speak a Uto-Aztecan language and probably number around 7,000.

> Bahr, Donald M., et al. Piman shamanism and staying sickness (Ká:cim Múmkidag). Tucson, University of Arizona Press, 1974. 11, 332 p.

15-26. Piro. The Piro lived in the Rio Grande valley in New Mexico south of Albuquerque but eventually moved to the pueblos of Senecu del Sur and Socorro del Sur south of El Paso. They spoke a Tanoan language and are probably extinct as a group.

15-27. Queres. This bibliographical division includes the Eastern Keresan (K'eres, Queres, Cherechos) pueblos of Cochiti, San Felipe, Santa Ana, Santo Domingo, and Sia (Zia). The towns are located along the Rio Grande in north-central New Mexico between the Río de los Frijoles and the Río Jemez, and on the Río Jemez from Bernalillo upstream to Sia Pueblo. Each of these pueblos is on a separate reservation. They speak a language isolate in the Hokan-Siouan phylum and numbered 4,469 in 1970.

15-28. Tano. The Tano (Southern Tewa) lived in the region to the south of Santa Fe, New Mexico, and occupied a number of pueblos. They spoke a Tanoan language and became extinct as a group in the nineteenth century, although a few descendants are still living in some of the Rio Grande pueblos, especially Santo Domingo.

15-29. Taos. This bibliographical division includes the Northern Tiwa pueblos of Taos and Picuris; the latter being on the Rio Grande about 40 miles north of Santa Fe, while Taos Pueblo is about 20 miles northeast of Picuris on the Taos River. Each is the focus of a separate Indian reservation. They speak Tanoan languages and numbered 1,683 in 1972.

15-30. Tarahumara. The Tarahumara (Tarahumare, Raramuri, Ralamuri), with the Pachero and the Varohio (Warohio, Warihio, Guarijio), live in the Sierra Madre Mountains in southeastern Sonora and southwestern Chihuahua. They speak a Uto-Aztecan language and number about 50,000.

15-31. Tewa. The Tewa (i.e. Northern Tewa), including the pueblos of Nambe, Pojoaque (Pojuaque), San Ildefonso, San Juan, Santa Clara, Tesuque, and Hano, live in the Rio Grande valley of New Mexico north of Santa Fe, except for the pueblo of Hano which is on First Mesa in the Hopi Indian Reservation in Arizona. They speak Tanoan languages and numbered 4,778 in 1972.

15-32. Walapai. The Walapai (E-pa, Gualiba, Hawalapai, Hualapai) live in the middle valley of the Colorado River in northwestern Arizona, principally on the Hualapai Indian Reservation. They speak a Yuman language and number about 1,000, with 969 on the reservation in 1972.

15-33. Yavapai. The Yavapai (Apaches-Mohaves, Mohave-Apache, Yampaos, Cruzados, Enyaevapai), with the Tolkepaya (Tulkepaia, Western Yavapai, Apache-Yuma), lived in a large area of west-central

Arizona to the north and west of Phoenix. They now live on the Yavapai Indian Reservation near Prescott and on the Camp Verde Indian Reservation. They speak a Yuman language and number about 1,000.

15-34. Yuma. The Yuma (Cetguanes, Chirumas, Cuchan, Quechan, Kwitcyana) lived on both sides of the lower Colorado River at and below its junction with the Gila River in southwestern Arizona and southeastern California. They now live on the Fort Yuma Indian Reservation in southeastern California. They speak a Yuman language and numbered 1,290 in 1972.

15-35. Zuni. The Zuni (Ashiwi, Cibola, Juñi), including the towns of Nutria, Pescado, and Ojo Caliente, and the former pueblos of Hawikuh, Halona, Kwakina, and Matsaki, live in northwestern New Mexico on the Zuni Indian Reservation. They speak a language isolate within the Penutian phylum and numbered 5,155 in 1972.

15-36. Acaxee. The Acaxee, including the Papudo Sobaibo (Sabaibo), Tebaca, and Tecaya, with the Xixime, including the Aibine and Hume, lived on the headwaters of the Culiacan, San Lorenzo, Piaxtla, Presidio, and Baluarte Rivers in the Mexican states of Durango and Sinaloa. They spoke Uto-Aztecan languages and are extinct.

15-37. Cazcan. The Cazcan, including the Coca and Tecuexe (Tehuexe), lived in the southern part of the Mexican state of Zacatecas, and in northern Jalisco, extending south to Lake Chapala. They spoke a Nahuatl language and are extinct.

15-38. Tepehuan. The Tepehuan (Tepehua, Tepehuane), with the Tepecano, live on the eastern slopes of the Sierra Madre mainly in the Mexican state of Durango, but also extending into Chihuahua, Zacatecas, and northern Jalisco. They speak Piman languages and number about 7,000.

15-39. Totorame. The Totorame, with the Mocorito and the Tahue, lived on the coast of the West Mexican state of Sinaloa from the Sinaloa-Nayarit border northward to the Río San Lorenzo and then inland and north to the vicinity of the town of Mocorito. They spoke Uto-Aztecan languages and are extinct.

15-40. Zacatec. The Zacatec (Zacateco), with the Guachichil (Guachichile) and Lagunero, lived in a large area of northern Mexico in the states of Zacatecas, Durango, Guanajuato, Querétaro, San Luís Potosí, and southern Coahuila. They spoke Uto-Aztecan languages and are nearly extinct.

15-41. Chichimec. The Chichimec, with the Guamares and the Jonaz, lived in small groups through much of northeastern Mexico and therefore have not been indicated on the maps. The term "Chichimec" has meant various things through the historical period. It probably refers to peoples speaking a number of different languages and probably includes some of the other groups listed in this bibliography. Therefore, this bibliographical division is primarily a residual category for citations on the Chichimec which cannot easily be referred to a specific group. The Jonaz live in San Luís de la Paz in Guanajuato. There were about 800 Jonaz speaking an Otomian language in 1956.

15-42. Pame. The Pame lived in the southeastern part of the Mexican state of San luis Potosí and adjoining areas of Tamaulipas, Querétaro, and Hidalgo. They speak an Otomian language and number about 2,800.

15-43. Cora. The Cora (Nayarit, Nayariti), includin the Coano, Huaynamota, Zayahueco, and Tecual (Tecualm), live in the northeastern part of Nayarit in the Sierra Madre Occidentale. They speak a Shoshonean language and numbered about 8,600 in 1960.

15-44. Huichol. The Huichol (Guichol, Guisar, Usilique) live in the mountains of eastern Nayarit and western Jalisco states in Mexico. They speak a Shoshonean language and number about 7,000.

Myerhoff, Barbara G. Peyote hunt; the sacred journey of the Huichol Indians. Ithaca, Cornell University Press, 1974. 285 p. illus.

15-00 Southwest Area Bibliography

Ayala Echávarri, Rafael. Bibliografía histórica y geográfica de Querétaro. México, Secretaría de Relaciones Exteriores, Departamento de Información para el Extranjero, 1949. 13, 387 p. (Monografías, Bibliográficas Mexicanas, Seg. Serie, 2)

Bernal, Ignacio. Bibliografía de arqueología y etnografía: Mesoamérica y Norte de México, 1514-1960. México, 1962. 16, 634 p. map. (México, Instituto Nacional de Antropología e Historia, Memorias, 7)

Carlson, Alvar W. A bibliography of the geographers' contributions to understanding the American Southwest (Arizona and New Mexico), 1920-1971. Arizona Quarterly, 28 (1972): 101-141.

Dobyns, Henry F. Sonoran missionaries in 1790. By Henry F. Dobyns and Paul H. Ezell. New Mexico Historical Review, 34 (1959): 52-54.

Evans, G. Edward. A guide to pre-1750 manuscripts in the United States relating to Mexico and the Southwestern United States, with emphasis on their value to anthropologists. Ethnohistory, 17 (1970): 63-90.

Fraser, James H. Indian mission printing in Arizona: an historical sketch and bibliography. Journal of Arizona History, 10 (1969): 67-102.

Hopkins, Jean. Southwestern Indian art, summary charts and bibliography. [n.p.] 1962. 19 l.

Lopez, E. Y. Bibliografía de Sonora. Hermosillo, Ediciones Fátima, 1960. 200 p.

Pilling, J. C. Bibliography of the Athapascan languages. U.S. Bureau of American Ethnology, Bulletin, 14 (1892): 1-125.

Pinnow, Heinz-Jürgen. Einige Züge indianischen Denkens dargelegt an den Sprachen der Athapasken. Anthropos, 61 (1966): 9-32.

Powell, Donald M. Materials relating to New Mexico and Arizona in the Serial Set 1846-1861. New Mexico Historical Review, 44 (1969): 315-342; 45 (1970): 47-77.

Rittenhouse, Jack D. The Santa Fe Trail; a historical bibliography. Albuquerque, University of New Mexico Press, 1971. 271 p. illus., map.

Saunders, L. A guide to materials bearing on cultural relations in New Mexico. Albuquerque, 1944. 528 p.

Villaseñor y Villaseñor, Ramiro. Bibliografía general de Jalisco. Tomo 1. Guadalajara, 1958.

Whiting, Alfred F. The present status of ethnobotany in the Southwest. Economic Botany, 20 (1966): 316-325.

Abel, A. H., ed. Indian affairs in New Mexico under the administration of William Carr Lane. New Mexico Historical Review, 16 (1941): 206-232, 328-358.

Aberle, S. D. The Pueblo Indians of New Mexico. American Anthropological Association, Memoirs, 70 (1948): 1-93.

Adair, J. Navaho and Pueblo silversmiths. Norman, 1944. 220 p.

Adair, J. The Navajo and Pueblo veteran. American Indian, 4, no. 1 (1947): 5-11.

Adair, John. The changing economy of Southwest Indian arts and crafts. New Mexico Quarterly, 29 (1959): 97-103.

Adams, David Bergen. The Tlaxcalan colonies of Spanish Coahuila and Nuevo León: an aspect of the settlement of northern Mexico. Dissertation Abstracts International, 32 (1971/1972): 5698A. UM 72-11,293.

Adams, E. B. Bishop Tamaron's visitation of New Mexico, 1760. New Mexico Historical Review, 28 (1953): 81-114, 192-221, 291-315; 29 (1954): 41-47.

Adams, Eleanor B. Fray Silvestre and the obstinate Hopi. New Mexico Historical Review, 38 (1963): 97-138.

Aguirre Beltran, Gonzalo. Medicina y magia. México, Instituto Nacional Indigenista, 1963.

Alcina Franch, José. Etnohistoria del Norte de Méjico: un proyecto en marcha. Runa, 10, no. 1/2 (1960/1965): 98-122.

Alexander, H. B. Pueblo Indian painting. Nice, 1932.

Alexander, H. B. The ritual dances of the Pueblo Indians. Denver, 1927.

Allen, F. W. and H. D. Larsen. Heredity of agglutinogens M and N among Pueblo and Blackfeet Indians. Journal of Immunology, 32 (1937): 301-305.

Allen, F. W. and W. Schaeffer. The distribution of the human blood groups among the Navajo and Pueblo Indians. New Mexico, University, Bulletin, Biological Series, 4, no. 2 (1935): 3-29.

Almstedt, Ruth F. Diegueño tree: an ecological approach to a linguistic problem. International Journal of American Linguistics, 34 (1968): 9-15.

Amsden, C. A. Arts and crafts of the Southwestern Indians. Masterkey, 15 (1941): 74-80.

Amsden, C. A. Prehistoric Southwesterners from Basketmaker to Pueblo. Los Angeles, 1949. 163 p.

Anderson, F. G. Intertribal relations in the Pueblo kachina cult. International Congress of the Anthropological and Ethnological Sciences, Acts, 5 (1960): 377-383.

Anderson, F. G. The Pueblo kachina cult. Southwestern Journal of Anthropology, 11 (1955): 404-419.

Andrews, E. Military surgery among the Apache Indians. Chicago Medical Examiner, 10 (1869): 599-601.

Angle, Jerry. Federal, State and tribal jurisdiction on Indian reservations in Arizona. Tucson, 1959. 7, 46 p. (Arizona, University, Bureau of Ethnic Research, American Indian Series, 2)

Anonymous. Higher education of Southwestern Indians with reference to success and failure. Journal of American Indian Education, 4, no. 2 (1964/1965): 5-13.

Anonymous. The All-Indian Pow Wow at Flagstaff. Arizona Highways, 48, no. 6 (1972): 44-45.

Anza, Juan Bautista de. Anza damns the missions: a Spanish soldier's criticism of Indian policy, 1772. Edited by John L. Kessell. Journal of Arizona History, 13 (1972): 53-63.

Anza, Juan Bautista de. Anza, Indian fighter; the spring campaign of 1766. Edited by John L. Kessell. Journal of Arizona History, 9 (1968): 155-163.

Applegate, F. G. Native tales of New Mexico. Philadelphia, 1932. 263 p.

Ariss, R. Distribution of smoking pipes in the Pueblo area. New Mexico Anthropologist, 3 (1939): 53-57.

Arizona, Commission of Indian Affairs. Survey of the Camp Verde Reservation. Phoenix [1968?].

Arizona, Commission of Indian Affairs. Tribal directory. Phoenix, 1971. 72 p. tables. ERIC ED051945.

Arizona Highways. Arizona Highways presents a treasury of Arizona's colorful Indians. Phoenix, 1967. illus.

Arizona, Library Extension Service. Final report to the Four Corners Regional Commission. Phoenix, 1971. 22, 7 l. illus.

Arizona, State University, Tempe, Indian Education Center. Indian education workshops. Edited by Robert A. Roessel, Jr., and Nicholas Lee. Tempe, 1962-1964. 2 v. illus., maps.

Armstrong, S. C. Indian reservations of the Southwest. Philadelphia, 1884. 28 p.

Arny, William F. M. Indian agent in New Mexico; the journal of special agent W. F. M. Arny, 1870. Introduction and notes by Lawrence R. Murphy. Santa Fe, Stagecoach Press, 1967. 62 p. (Southwestern Series, 5)

Arriquibar, Pedro Antonio de. Fray Pedro de Arriquibar's census of Tucson, 1820. Edited by Karen Sikes Collins. Journal of Arizona History, 11 (1970): 14-22.

Atkinson, Mary J. Indians of the Southwest. 4th ed. San Antonio, Naylor, 1963. 20, 343 p. illus., map.

Ayer, Mrs. E. E., ed. The memorial of Fray Alonso de Benavides. Land of Sunshine, 13 (1900): 277-290, 337-340, 345-358, 419-420, 435-444; 14 (1901): 39-52, 137-148, 227-232.

Ayer, Mrs. E. E., ed. The memorial of Fray Alonso de Benavides. Chicago, 1916. 309 p.

Bahti, Tom. An introduction to Southwestern Indian arts and crafts. Flagstaff, KC Publications, 1964. 32 p. illus.

Bahti, Tom. Southwestern Indian tribes. Flagstaff, KC Publications, 1968. 72 p. illus., maps.

Bailey, Lynn R. Indian slave trade in the Southwest. Los Angeles, Westernlore Press, 1966. 16, 236 p. illus., map.

Bailey, Lynn R. Thomas Varker Keam:
Tusayan trader. Arizoniana, 2, no. 4
(1961): 15-19.

Bailey, Paul D. The Navajo wars.
Arizoniana, 2, no. 2 (1961): 3-12.

Bain, James G. Rock art. El Palacio, 77,
no. 1 (1970): 1-13.

Baldwin, P. M. Fray Marcos de Niza and
his discovery of the seven cities of
Cibola. New Mexico Historical Review, 1
(1926): 193-223.

Ballinger, Thomas O. Some notes on
directional movements in the drawings
and paintings of Pueblo and Navajo
children. American Anthropologist, 66
(1964): 880-883.

Bancroft, H. H. The native races of the
Pacific States, Vol. 1: 471-614. New
York, 1875.

Bandelier, A. F. Contributions to the
history of the southwestern portion of
the United States. Archaeological
Institute of America, Papers, American
Series, 5 (1890): 1-206.

Bandelier, A. F. Documentary history of
the Rio Grande Pueblos. New Mexico
Historical Review, 4 (1929): 303-334; 5
(1930): 38-66, 154-185, 240-262, 333-
385.

Bandelier, A. F. Documentary history of
the Rio Grande Pueblos. Archaeological
Institute of America, School of American
Archaeology, Santa Fe, Papers, 13
(1910): 1-27.

Bandelier, A. F. Final report of
investigations among the Indians of the
Southwestern United States.
Archaeological Institute of America,
Papers, American Series, 3 (1890): 1-
323; 4 (1892): 1-591.

Bandelier, A. F. Historical introduction
to studies among the sedentary Indians
of New Mexico. Archaeological Institute
of America, Papers, American Series, 1
(1881): 1-33.

Bandelier, A. F. Kin and clan. New Mexico
Historical Review, 8 (1933): 165-175.

Bandelier, A. F. The gilded man. New
York, 1893. 302 p.

Bandelier, A. F. The "Montezuma" of the
Pueblo Indians. American Anthropologist,
5 (1892): 319-326.

Bandelier, A. F. and E. L. Hewitt.
Indians of the Rio Grande Valley.
Albuquerque, 1937. 274 p.

Bandelier, A. F. and F. R. Bandelier.
Historical documents relating to New
Mexico, Nueva Viscaya, and approaches
thereto. Ed. by C. W. Hackett.
Washington, D.C., 1923-1937. 3 v.

Bandelier, Adolph F. A. A history of the
Southwest. Edited by Ernest J. Burrus.
Città del Vaticano, Biblioteca
Apostolica Vaticana, 1969. 2 v.

Bandelier, Adolph F. A. A scientist on
the trail; travel letters of A. F.
Bandelier, 1880-1881. Berkeley, Calif.,
1949. 11, 142 p. (Quivira Society,
Publications, 10)

Bandelier, Adolph F. A. Correspondencia
de Adolfo F. Bandelier. México, 1960.
322 p. (México, Instituto Nacional de
Antropología e Historia, Serie Historia,
4)

Bandelier, Adolph F. A. The Southwestern
journals of Adolph F. Bandelier. Edited
by Charles H. Lange and Carroll L.
Riley. Albuquerque, University of New
Mexico Press, 1966.

Barbastro, Francisco A. Sonora hacia
fines del siglo XVIII. Estudio
preliminar . . . por Lino Gómez Canedo.
Guadalajara, Librería Font, 1971.
133 p. map. (Documentación Histórica
Mexicana, 3)

Barber, B. A socio-cultural
interpretation of the peyote cult.
American Anthropologist, n.s., 43
(1941): 673-675.

Barber, E. A. On the ancient and modern
Pueblo tribes. American Naturalist, 11
(1877): 591-599.

Barber, E. A. Pueblo pottery. American
Naturalist, 15 (1881): 453-462.

Barker, G. C. Some functions of Catholic
processions in Pueblo and Yaqui culture
change. American Anthropologist, 60
(1958): 449-455.

Bartlett, K. The distribution of the
Indians of Arizona in 1848. Plateau, 17
(1945): 41-45.

Bartlett, K. The Indians of northern
Arizona. Flagstaff, Ariz., Museum of
Northern Arizona, Museum Notes, 5
(1933): 65-71.

Bass, Willard P. The American Indian high
school graduate in the Southwest.
Albuquerque, Southwestern Cooperative
Education Laboratory, 1969. 106 p.
ERIC ED031362.

Basso, Keith H., ed. Apachean culture history and ethnology. Edited by Keith H. Basso and Morris E. Opler. Tucson, University of Arizona Press, 1971. 8, 168 p. illus. (Arizona, University, Anthropological Papers, 21)

Baumann, G. Frijoles Canyon pictographs. Santa Fe, 1939. 43 p.

Beals, R. L. An ecological interpretation of the Southwestern culture area. In Estudios Antropológicas Publicados en Homenaje al Doctor Manual Gamio. México, 1956: 255-260.

Beals, R. L. Northern Mexico and the Southwest. In El Norte de México y el Sur de Estados Unidos. México, 1943: 191-199.

Beals, R. L. Preliminary report on the ethnography of the Southwest. Berkeley, 1935. 120 p.

Beals, R. L. Relations between Meso America and the Southwest. In El Norte de México y el Sur de Estados Unidos. México, 1943: 245-252.

Beals, R. L. The comparative ethnology of northern Mexico. Ibero-Americana, 2 (1932): 93-225.

Beals, Ralph L. Anthropological research problems with reference to the contemporary peoples of Mexico and Guatemala. By Ralph L. Beals, Robert Redfield, and Sol Tax. American Anthropologist, n.s., 45 (1943): 1-22.

Bean, Lowell John, ed. Diaries and accounts of the Romero expeditions in Arizona and California, 1823-1826. Edited by Lowell John Bean and William Marvin Mason. Los Angeles, Published for the Palm Springs Desert Museum by the W. Ritchie Press, 1962. 17, 117 p. illus., map.

Beidleman, R. C. Ethno-zoology of the Pueblo Indians in historic times. Southwestern Lore, 22 (1956): 5-13, 17-28.

Bell, C. C., Jr., et al. Relationship of bile acid pool size to the formation of lithogenous bile in male Indians of the Southwest. Surgery, Gynecology and Obstetrics, 134 (1972): 473-478.

Bell, Sandra. The legend of Quivira. Western Folklore, 22 (1963): 113-116.

Bell, W. A. New tracks in North America. London, 1869. 2 v.

Bell, W. A. On the native races of New Mexico. Ethnological Society (London), Journal, n.s., 1 (1869): 222-274.

Bell, W. H. and E. F. Castetter. The utilization of mesquite and screwbean by the aborigines in the American Southwest. New Mexico, University, Bulletin, Biological Series, 5, no. 2 (1937): 3-55.

Bell, W. H. and E. F. Castetter. The utilization of yucca, sotol, and beargrass by the aborigines in the American Southwest. New Mexico, University, Bulletin, Biological Series, 5, no. 5 (1941): 1-74.

Bell, William A. New tracks in North America. Albuquerque, Horn and Wallace, 1965. 69, 564 p. illus., maps.

Benavides, Alonso de. Fray Alonso de Benavides' revised memorial of 1634, with numerous supplementary documents, elaborately annotated. Edited by Frederick Webb Hodge, George P. Hammond, and Agapito Rey. Albuquerque, University of New Mexico Press, 1945. 16, 368 p.

Benavides, Alonso de. The memorial of Fray Alonso de Benavides, 1630. Translated by Mrs. Edward E. Ayer. Albuquerque, Horn and Wallace, 1965. 13, 309 p. illus., map.

Benedict, R. Psychological types in the cultures of the Southwest. International Congress of Americanists, Proceedings, 23 (1928): 572-581.

Benes, Ronald J. Anza and Concha in New Mexico, 1787-1793: a study in new colonial techniques. Journal of the West, 4 (1965): 63-76.

Bennett, J. W. The interpretation of Pueblo culture. Southwestern Journal of Anthropology, 2 (1946): 361-374.

Bennett, Wendell C. The Tarahumara; an Indian tribe of northern Mexico. By Wendell C. Bennett and Robert M. Zingg. Chicago, University of Chicago Press, 1935. 19, 412 p. illus.

Berge, Dale LeRoy. Historical archaeology in the American Southwest. Dissertation Abstracts, 29 (1968/1969): 1243B. UM 68-14,507.

Berlandier, Luis. The Indians of Texas in 1830. By Jean Louis Berlandier. Translated by Patricia Reading Leclercq. Edited by John C. Ewers. Washington, D.C., Smithsonian Institution Press, 1969. 11, 209 p. illus., maps.

Berlin, Brent. Categories of eating in Tzeltal and Navaho. International Journal of American Linguistics, 33 (1967): 1-6.

Berman, Mark L. Some considerations in the education of indigenous groups in the Southwest. Santa Monica, Calif., System Development, 1965. 16 p. (System Development Corporation, Report, SP-2148) ERIC ED016387.

Bettman, Jerome W., et al. Inclusion conjunctivitis in American Indians of the Southwest. American Journal of Ophthalmology, 70 (1970): 363-366.

Bewley, M. A résumé of the pre-Civil War Indian situation in New Mexico. University of New Mexico, Research, 3, no. 1 (1939): 33-41.

Biasutti, R. Le razzi e i popoli della terra, 2d ed., Vol. 4: 445-453. Torino, 1957.

Biggs, B. Testing intelligibility among Yuman languages. International Journal of American Linguistics, 23 (1957): 57-62.

Birket-Smith, K. An early American skin garment in the Danish National Museum. In Miscellanea Paul Rivet Octogenario Dicata. Vol. 1. México, 1958: 219-226.

Biswell, Roderick. Keratoplasty and trachoma in the Southwestern American Indian. Archives of Ophthalmology, 81 (1969): 791-796.

Bivens, Melvin D., et al. Carcinoma of the cervix in the Indians of the Southwest. A preliminary report. American Journal of Obstetrics and Gynecology, 83 (1962): 1203-1207.

Blackwood, B. A study of mental testing in relation to anthropology. Mental Measurement Monographs, 4 (1927): 1-120.

Bleeker, S. The Pueblo Indians. New York, 1955.

Bloom, L. B. Bourke on the Southwest. New Mexico Historical Review, 8 (1933): 1-30; 9 (1934): 33-77, 159-183, 273-289, 375-435; 10 (1935): 1-35, 271-322; 11 (1936): 77-122, 188-207, 217-282; 12 (1937): 41-77, 337-379; 13 (1938): 192-238.

Bloom, L. B. Early bridges in New Mexico. El Palacio, 18 (1925): 163-175.

Bloom, L. B. Early weaving in New Mexico. New Mexico Historical Review, 2 (1927): 228-238.

Bolton, H. E. Pageant in the wilderness. Utah Historical Quarterly, 18 (1950): 1-283.

Bolton, H. E. Rim of Christendom, a biography of Eusebio Francisco Kino. New York, 1936. 627 p.

Bolton, H. E. Spanish exploration in the Southwest, 1542-1706. New York, 1916.

Bonnell, George W. Topographical description of Texas. To which is added an account of the Indian tribes. Waco, Texian Press, 1964. 150 p.

Bouman, William. Xg blood groups of American Indians. By William Bouman, J. D. Mann, and William J. Dewey. Nature, 209 (1966): 411.

Bourke, J. G. The snake ceremonials at Walpi. American Anthropologist, 8 (1895): 192-196.

Bowen, Thomas. Material and functional aspects of Seri instrumental music. By Thomas Bowen and Edward Moser. Kiva, 35, no. 4 (1969/1970): 178-200.

Bowman, J. N. Anza and the northwest frontier of New Spain. By J. N. Bowman and Robert F. Heizer. Los Angeles, 1967. 19, 182 p. illus., maps. (Southwest Museum, Papers, 20)

Boyd, E. Rio Grande blankets containing hand spun cotton yarns. El Palacio, 71, no. 4 (1964): 22-28.

Bradley, C. E. Yerba de la fleche. Economic Botany, 10 (1956): 362-366.

Brayer, H. O. Pueblo Indian land grants of the "Rio Abajo". New Mexico, University, Bulletin, Historical Series, 1, no. 1 (1938): 1-135.

Brennan, Jose Lewis. Jose Lewis Brennan's account of Papago "customs and other references". Edited by Bernard L. Fontana. Ethnohistory, 6 (1959): 226-237.

Brewer, I. W. Tuberculosis among the Indians of Arizona and New Mexico. New York Medical Journal, 84 (1906): 981-983.

Briggs, Jerome Robert. A steppe-oasis association in native North America. Dissertation Abstracts, 29 (1968/1969): 1911B-1912B. UM 68-16,898.

Bright, W. L. A note on Southwestern words for cat. International Journal of American Linguistics, 26 (1960): 167-168.

Bright, William.   A note on the
Southwestern words for cat.
International Journal of American
Linguistics, 26 (1960): 167-168.

Brinckerhoff, Sidney B.   "Steadfast" Gregg
in Arizona. Arizoniana, 5, no. 2 (1964):
31-37.

Brown, Christine.   Pima Central School and
Blackwater School, Sacaton, Arizona. By
Christine Brown and Robert J.
Havighurst.   Chicago, University of
Chicago, 1970.   6 p.   (National Study of
American Indian Education, Series I, 22,
Final Report)   ERIC ED044211.

Brugge, David M.   Linguistic distributions
in northwestern Mexico, 1761 to 1763.
Katunob, 2, no. 1 (1961): 65-67.

Brugge, David M.   Navajos in the Catholic
Church records of New Mexico, 1694-1785.
Window Rock, Navajo Tribe, 1968.   16,
160 p.   (Research Reports, 1)

Brugge, David M.   Notes on the Apaches in
the late 18th century. Katunob, 2, no. 1
(1961): 59-63.

Brugge, David M.   Pueblo factionalism and
external relations. Ethnohistory, 16
(1969): 191-200.

Bryan, K.   Pre-Columbian agriculture in
the Southwest as conditioned by periods
of alluviation. American Scientific
Congress, 8th, Proceedings, 2 (1942):
57-74.

Bunker, R.   Other men's skies.
Bloomington, 1956.   256 p.

Burbank, E. A. and E. Royce.   Burbank
among the Indians, 57-87.   Caldwell,
1946.

Burger, Henry G., ed.   Ethnics on
education: report on a conference of
Spanish-speaking, Amerindian, and Negro
Cultural leaders on Southwestern
teaching and learning.   Albuquerque,
Southwestern Cooperative Educational
Laboratory, 1969.   42 p.   (U.S., Office
of Education, Bureau of Research, Bureau
BR-6-2827)   ERIC ED032440.

Burrus, Ernest J.   An introduction to
bibliographical tools in Spanish
archives and manuscript collections
relating to Hispanic America. Hispanic
American Historical Review, 35 (1955):
443-483.

Burrus, Ernest J.   Kino and Manje:
explorers of Sonora and Arizona.   Rome,
Jesuit Historical Institute, 1971.
793 p.

Buschmann, J. C. E.   Die Verwandtschafts-
Verhältnisse der athapaskischen
Sprachen. Berlin, Königliche Akademie
der Wissenschaften, Abhandlungen, no. 2
(1862): 195-252.

Buschmann, J. C. E.   Die Völker und
Sprachen Neu-Mexico's und der Westseite
des britischen Nordamerika. Berlin,
Königliche Akademie der Wissenschaften,
Abhandlungen (1857): 209-404.

Bushnell, G. H. S. and A. Digby.   Ancient
American pottery.   London, 1955.   64 p.

Butcher, Russell D.   Winged messengers. El
Palacio, 75, no. 1 (1968): 39-43.

Byrne, E.   The Pueblo Indians of New
Mexico. America, 82 (1950): 717-719.

Campa, A. L.   Piñon as an economic and
social factor. New Mexico Business
Review, 1 (1932): 144-147.

Cardenal, Ernesto, tr.   Poesía de los
indios de Norteamérica. América
Indígena, 21 (1961): 355-362.

Carleton, James Henry.   Diary of an
excursion to the ruins of Abó, Quarra,
and Gran Quivira in New Mexico in 1853.
Santa Fe, Stagecoach Press, 1965.
61 p.   map.

Carlson, Alvar Ward.   New Mexico's sheep
industry, 1850-1900: its role in the
history of the Territory. New Mexico
Historical Review, 44 (1969): 25-49.

Carlson, Roy L.   Eighteenth century Navajo
fortresses of the Gobernador District.
Boulder, University of Colorado Press,
1965.   2, 116 p.   (Colorado, University,
Studies, Series in Anthropology, 10)

Carranco, Lynwood.   Anza's bones in
Arizpe. Journal of the West, 8 (1969):
416-428.

Carroll, H. B.   The Texan Santa Fe Trail.
Panhandle-Plains Historical Review, 24
(1954): 1-201.

Carroll, Terry Lee.   Gallup and her
ceremonials. Dissertation Abstracts
International, 33 (1972/1973): 3527A.
UM 73-1548.

Carter, G. F.   Plant geography and culture
history in the American Southwest.
Viking Fund Publications in
Anthropology, 5 (1945): 1-140.

Carter, G. F. and E. Anderson.   A
preliminary survey of maize in the
South-Western United States. Missouri
Botanical Garden, Annals, 32 (1945):
297-322.

Caso, Alfonso. Densidad de la población de habla indígena en la República Mexicana. By Alfonso Caso and Manuel German Parra. México, 1950. 76 p. maps. (México, Instituto Nacional Indigenista, Memoria, 1, no. 1)

Cassidy, I. S. Some Pueblo ideas. Western Folklore, 10 (1951): 78.

Castaño de Sosa, Gaspar. A colony on the move; Gaspar Castaño de Sosa's journal, 1590-1591. Translated by Dan S. Matson. Edited by Albert H. Schroeder. Santa Fe, School of American Research, 1965. 11, 196 p. illus., maps.

Castelló Yturbide, Teresa. El traje indígena de México. México, Instituto Nacional de Antropología e Historia, 1965-1966. 3 v. illus.

Castetter, E. F. Early tobacco utilization and cultivation in the American Southwest. American Anthropologist, n.s., 45 (1943): 320-325.

Castetter, E. F. Uncultivated native plants used as sources of food. New Mexico, University, Bulletin, Biological Series, 4, no. 1 (1935): 3-62.

Castetter, E. F. and W. H. Bell. The aboriginal utilization of the tall cacti in the American Southwest. New Mexico, University, Bulletin, Biological Series, 5, no. 1 (1937): 1-48.

Castetter, E. F., W. H. Bell, and A. R. Grove. The early utilization and distribution of agave in the American Southwest. New Mexico, University, Bulletin, Biological Series, 5, no. 4 (1938): 1-92.

Cavazos Garza, Israel. La obra franciscana en Nuevo León. Humanitas (Monterrey), 2 (1961): 437-452.

Cazeneuve, J. Indiens du Nouveau-Mexique. Connaissance du Monde, 12, no. 6 (1957): 19-30.

Cazeneuve, J. Noël chez les Pueblos du Rio Grande. Ethnographie, 50 (1955): 163-168.

Chapin, F. H. The land of cliff dwellers. Boston, 1892. 188 p.

Chapman, K. M. Decorative art of the Indians of the Southwest. Santa Fe, Laboratory of Anthropology, Bulletin, General Series, 1 (1934): 1-11.

Chapman, K. M. Life forms in Pueblo pottery decoration. Art and Archaeology, 13 (1922): 120-122.

Chapman, K. M. Pueblo Indian pottery. Nice, 1933. 2 v.

Chapman, K. M. Pueblo Indian pottery of the post-Spanish period. Santa Fe, Laboratory of Anthropology, Bulletin, General Series, 4 (1938): 1-14.

Chapman, K. M. and B. T. Ellis. The line-break. El Palacio, 58 (1951): 251-289.

Chaput, Donald. Babes in arms. Journal of Arizona History, 13 (1972): 197-204.

Chavez, Angelico. Pohé-Yemo's representative and the Pueblo Revolt of 1680. New Mexico Historical Review, 42 (1967): 85-126.

Chavez, Tibo J. Early witchcraft in New Mexico. El Palacio, 76, no. 3 (1969): 7-9.

Chesky, J. Indian music of the Southwest. Kiva, 7 (1941): 9-12.

Christiansen, Paige W. The myth of Robledo. El Palacio, 71, no. 3 (1964): 30-34.

Christinger, R. Mythes et légendes des Pueblos du Nouveau Mexique et de l'Arizona. Société Suisse des Américanistes, Bulletin, 1 (1950): 11-14.

Clark, Geoffrey A. A preliminary analysis of burial clusters at the Grasshopper site, East Central Arizona. Kiva, 35, no. 2 (1969/1970): 86.

Cobb, John C. Trachoma among Southwestern Indians. By John C. Cobb and Chandler R. Dawson. American Medical Association, Journal, 175 (1961): 405-406.

Cohen, Burton M. Diabetes mellitus among Indians of the American Southwest: its prevalence and clinical characteristics in a hospitalized population. Annals of Internal Medicine, 40 (1954): 588-599.

Colee, Philip S. Rio Abajo population movements: 1670-1750. Ethnohistory, 18 (1971): 353-360.

Collier, John. American Indian ceremonial dances: Navajo, Pueblo, Apache, Zuni. New York, Bounty Books, 1972. 192 p. illus.

Collier, John. On the gleaming way. Denver, Sage Books, 1962. 163 p. illus.

Collins, G. N. Pueblo Indian maize breeding. Journal of Heredity, 5 (1914): 255-268.

Colton, H. S. Prehistoric trade in the Southwest. Scientific Monthly, 52 (1941): 308-319.

Colton, H. S. and L. L. Hargrave. Handbook of northern Arizona pottery wares. Flagstaff, Ariz., Museum of Northern Arizona, Bulletin, 11 (1937): 1-267.

Colton, Harold S. Check list of Southwestern pottery types. Flagstaff, Northern Arizona Society of Science and Art, 1965. 4, 55 p. map.

Concha, Fernando de la. Colonel Don Fernando de la Concha diary, 1788. Edited by Adlai Feather. New Mexico Historical Review, 34 (1959): 285-304.

Confederation of Colorado River Tribes. Blueprint for action by the Confederation of Colorado River Tribes. Long Beach, 1972. 80 p. illus., maps.

Cook de Leonard, Carmen. Distribución de los pueblos sonorenses en el siglo XVIII según Pfefferkorn. Tlatoani, 1, no. 1/2 (1952): 19-20.

Coolidge, M. R. The rain-makers. Boston, 1929. 313 p.

Corbella de la Immaculada, Carmelo. Quipata; libro histórico misional de Indios. Lérida, Artis Estudios Gráficos, 1970. 283 p. illus.

Corbusier, William T. Verde to San Carlos: recollections of a famous Army surgeon and his observant family on the western frontier, 1869-1886. Tucson, Dale Stuart King, 1969. 310 p.

Cordry, Donald B. Mexican Indian costumes. By Donald and Dorothy Cordry. Austin, University of Texas Press, 1968. 20, 373 p. illus., maps.

Coues, E., ed. On the trail of a Spanish pioneer. New York, 1900. 2 v.

Covington, James W., ed. Correspondence between Mexican officials at Santa Fe and officials in Missouri: 1823-1825. Missouri Historical Society, Bulletin, 16 (1959/1960): 20-32.

Coze, P. Southwestern Indian hair-dos. Arizona Highways, 26, no. 7 (1950): 26-35.

Cozzens, Samuel W. The marvelous country; or, Three years in Arizona and New Mexico, the Apache's home. Minneapolis, Ross and Haines, 1967. 540 p. illus.

Crampton, C. Gregory. Indian country. Utah Historical Quarterly, 39 (1971): 90-94.

Crampton, C. Gregory. Military reconnaissance in southern Utah, 1866. Utah Historical Quarterly, 32 (1964): 145-161.

Crane, L. Desert drums. Boston, 1928. 393 p.

Crane, Leo. Desert drums; the Pueblo Indians of New Mexico, 1540-1928. Glorieta, N.M., Rio Grande Press, 1972. 10, 402 p. illus.

Cremony, John C. Life among the Apaches. Glorieta, N.M., Rio Grande Press, 1969. 327 p. illus., map.

Crimmins, M. L. The Aztec influence on the primitive culture of the Southwest. Texas Archeological and Paleontological Society, Bulletin, 4 (1932): 32-39.

Crocchiola, Stanley F. L. The Apaches of New Mexico, 1540-1940. By F. Stanley. Pampa, Tex., Pampa Print Shop, 1962. 449 p.

Crook, George. Crook's resumé of operations against Apache Indians, 1882 to 1886. London, Johnson-Taunton Military Press, 1971. 28 p.

Crowley, Cornelius Crowley. Some remarks on the etymology of the Southwestern words for cat. International Journal of American Linguistics, 28 (1962): 149-151.

Cruz, Raúl de la. Ritos y costumbres de nuestros pueblos primitivos. México, 1964. 143 p. illus.

Cundick, Bert P. Measures of intelligence on Southwest Indian students. Journal of Social Psychology, 81 (1970): 151-156.

Current, William. Pueblo architecture of the Southwest; a photographic essay. Text by Vincent Scully. Austin, University of Texas Press, 1971. 97 p. illus.

Curtin, L. S. M. Healing herbs of the Upper Rio Grande. Santa Fe, 1948. 381 p.

Curtis, W. E. Education and morals among the Navajos and Pueblos. American Antiquarian and Oriental Journal, 27 (1905): 259-264.

Dale, E. E. The Indians of the Southwest. Norman, 1949. 283 p.

Daniel, James M. The Spanish frontier in West Texas and northern Mexico. Southwestern Historical Quarterly, 71 (1967/1968): 481-495.

Daniels, David. Photography's wet-plate interlude in Arizona Territory: 1864-1880. Journal of Arizona History, 9 (1968): 171-194.

Danziger, Edmund J., Jr. The Steck-Carleton controversy in Civil War New Mexico. Southwestern Historical Quarterly, 74 (1970/1971): 189-203.

Davidson, William. A preliminary analysis of active verbs in Dogrib. In Harry Hoijer, et al., eds. Studies in the Athapaskan Languages. Berkeley, Los Angeles, University of California Press, 1963: 48-55. (California, University, Publications in Linguistics, 29)

Dávila Garibi, José Ignacio Paulino. Los idiomas nativos de Jalisco y el problema de filiación de los ya desaparecidos. México, 1945. 9-104 p.

Davis, W. W. H. The Pueblo Indians of New Mexico. El Palacio, 26 (1929): 259-286.

Davis, William Robert. The Spanish borderlands of Texas and Chihuahua. Texana, 9 (1971): 142-155.

Davis, William W. H. El Gringo; or, New Mexico and her people. Chicago, Rio Grande Press, 1962. 332 p. illus.

Dawson, Chandler R. Controlled treatment trials of trachoma in American Indian children. By Chandler R. Dawson, Lavelle Hanna, and Ernest Jawetz. Lancet, 2 (1967): 961-964.

Decorme, Gerard. La obra de los jesuítas mexicanas durante la época colonial, 1572-1767. México, Antigua Librería Robredo de J. Porrúa e Hijos, 1941. 2 v.

DeHuff, J. The intelligence quotient of the Pueblo Indian. El Palacio, 22 (1927): 422-432.

Delaney, Robert W. The Southern Utes a century ago. Utah Historical Quarterly, 39 (1971): 114-128.

Demeke, Howard J., comp. In-service education series and consultant services. Final report. Tempe, Arizona State University, College of Education, Bureau of Educational Research and Services, 1967. 47 p. ERIC ED046591.

Dennis, W. and M. G. Dennis. Cradles and cradling practices of the Pueblo Indians. American Anthropologist, n.s., 42 (1940): 107-115.

Densmore, F. A resemblance between Yuman and Pueblo songs. American Anthropologist, n.s., 34 (1932): 694-700.

DiPeso, C. C. A Guaraheo potter. Kiva, 16, no. 3 (1950): 1-5.

Ditzler, Robert E. The Indian people of Arizona. New York, Vantage Press, 1967. 177 p.

Dobie, James Frank, ed. Southwestern lore. Hatboro, Pa., Folklore Associates, 1965. 5, 198 p. (Texas Folklore Society, Publications, Reprint Edition, 9)

Dobyns, Henry F. The Apache people. Phoenix, Indian Tribal Series, 1971. 5, 106 p. illus.

Dobyns, Henry F. The 1797 population of the Presidio of Tucson. Journal of Arizona History, 13 (1972): 205-209.

Dobyns, Henry F. What were Nixoras? By Henry F. Dobyns, Paul H. Ezell, Alden W. Jones, and Greta S. Ezell. Southwestern Journal of Anthropology, 16 (1960): 230-258.

Dockstader, F. J. The kachina and the White Man. Cranbrook Institute of Science, Bulletin, 35 (1954): 1-202.

Dodge, N. N. and H. S. Zim. The American Southwest. New York, 1955. 160 p.

Doerner, Rita. Sinew Riley, Apache scout. Journal of Arizona History, 14 (1973): 271-280.

Dolch, E. W. and M. P. Dolch. Pueblo stories, in basic vocabulary. Champaign, 1956. 160 p.

Dominguez, F. A. The missions of New Mexico, 1776. Albuquerque, 1956. 408 p.

Donohue, John A. After Kino: Jesuit missions in northwestern New Spain, 1711-1767. Rome, Jesuit Historical Institute; St. Louis, St. Louis University, 1969. 4, 183 p. map.

Dorsey, G. A. Indians of the Southwest. 1903. 223 p.

Douglas, F. H. Indian sand-painting. Denver Art Museum, Indian Leaflet Series, 43/44 (1932): 1-8.

Douglas, F. H.   Kachinas and kachina
dolls. Denver Art Museum, Indian Leaflet
Series, 111 (1951): 1-3.

Douglas, F. H.   Modern Pueblo Indian
villages. Denver Art Museum, Indian
Leaflet Series, 45/46 (1932): 1-8.

Douglas, F. H.   Modern Pueblo pottery
types. Denver Art Museum, Indian Leaflet
Series, 53/54 (1935): 10-16.

Douglas, F. H.   Notes on distinguishing
similar objects. Denver Art Museum,
Indian Leaflet Series, 86 (1939): 141-
144.

Douglas, F. H.   Periods of Pueblo culture
and history. Denver Art Museum, Indian
Leaflet Series, 11 (1930): 1-4.

Douglas, F. H.   Pottery of the
Southwestern tribes. Denver Art Museum,
Indian Leaflet Series, 69/70 (1935): 74-
80.

Douglas, F. H.   Pueblo Indian clothing.
Denver Art Museum, Indian Leaflet
Series, 4 (1930): 1-4.

Douglas, F. H.   Pueblo Indian foods.
Denver Art Museum, Indian Leaflet
Series, 8 (1930): 1-4.

Douglas, F. H.   Pueblo Indian pottery
making. Denver Art Museum, Indian
Leaflet Series, 6 (1930): 1-4.

Douglas, F. H.   Southwestern Indian
dwellings. Denver Art Museum, Indian
Leaflet Series, 9 (1930): 1-4.

Douglas, F. H.   Southwestern twined,
wicker, and plaited basketry. Denver Art
Museum, Indian Leaflet Series, 99/100
(1940): 194-199.

Douglas, F. H.   Tribes of the Southwest.
Denver Art Museum, Indian Leaflet
Series, 55 (1933): 1-4.

Douglas, F. H.   Types of Southwestern
coiled basketry. Denver Art Museum,
Indian Leaflet Series, 88 (1939): 150-
152.

Douglas, F. H. and A. Marriott.   Metal
jewelry of the peyote cult. Denver Art
Museum, Material Culture Notes, 17
(1942): 17-82.

Douglass, A. E.   Dating Pueblo Bonito and
other ruins of the Southwest. National
Geographic Society, Contributed
Technical Papers, Pueblo Bonito Series,
1 (1935): 1-74.

Douglass, A. E.   The secret of the
Southwest solved by talkative tree

rings. National Geographic Magazine, 65
(1929): 737-770.

Douglass, A. E.   Tree rings and
chronology. Arizona, University,
Bulletin, 8, no. 4 (1937): 1-36.

Downing, George L.   Native pottery of the
Southwest. Natural History, 78, no. 6
(1969): 34-39.

Dozier, E. P.   Ethnological clues for the
sources of Rio Grande population. [With
comment by L. A. White]. Arizona,
University, Social Science Bulletin, 27
(1958): 21-32.

Dozier, E. P.   Spanish-Catholic influences
on Rio Grande pueblo religion. American
Anthropologist, 60 (1958): 441-448.

Dozier, Edward P.   Linguistic
acculturation in the Southwestern United
States. In Congreso Internacional de
Americanistas, 36th. 1964, España. Actas
y Memorias. Tomo 2.   Sevilla, 1966: 253-
259.

Dozier, Edward P.   Linguistic
acculturation studies in the Southwest.
In Dell H. Hymes and William E. Bittle,
eds. Studies in Southwestern
Ethnolinguistics.   The Hague, Mouton,
1967: 389-402.   (Studies in General
Anthropology, 3)

Dozier, Edward P.   Los indios pueblo de
Arizona y Nuevo México. Anuario
Indigenista, 28 (1968): 191-197.

Dozier, Edward P.   Pueblo Indian response
to culture contact. In M. Estellie
Smith, ed. Studies in Linguistics in
Honor of George L. Trager.   The Hague,
Mouton, 1972: 457-467.   (Janua
Linguarum, Series Maior, 52)

Dozier, Edward P.   Southwestern social
units and archaeology. American
Antiquity, 31 (1965/1966): 38-47.

Dozier, Edward P.   The American Southwest.
In Eleanor Burke Leacock and Nancy
Oestreich Lurie, eds. North American
Indians in Historical Perspective.   New
York, Random House, 1971: 228-256.

Dozier, Edward P.   The Pueblo Indians of
North America.   New York, Holt, Rinehart
and Winston, 1970.   15, 224 p.   illus.,
maps.

Dozier, Edward P.   The Pueblo Indians of
the Southwest. Current Anthropology, 5
(1964): 79-97.

Driver, H. E.   Girls' puberty rites in
western North America. Anthropological
Records, 6 (1941): 21-90.

Driver, Harold E. Reply to Opler on Apachean subsistence, residence, and girls' puberty rites. American Anthropologist, 74 (1972): 1147-1151.

Duffen, William A., ed. Overland via "jackass mail" in 1858; the diary of Phocion R. Way. Part two. Arizona and the West, 2 (1960): 147-164.

Dumbier, Roger. The Sonoran desert; its geography, economy and people. Tucson, University of Arizona Press, 1968. 13, 426 p. illus., maps.

Dunn, D. The development of modern American painting in the Southwest and Plains areas. El Palacio, 58 (1951): 331-353.

Dunn, D. The studio of painting: Santa Fe Indian School. El Palacio, 67 (1960): 16-27.

Dunn, Dorothy. A documented chronology of modern American Indian paintings of the Southwest. Plateau, 44 (1970): 150-162.

Dunn, Dorothy. American Indian painting of the Southwest and Plains areas. Santa Fe, University of New Mexico Press, 1968. 27, 429 p. illus.

Dunn, Dorothy. The Studio of Painting, Santa Fe Indian School. El Palacio, 67 (1960): 16-27.

Dutton, B. P. New Mexico Indians and their Arizona neighbors. Santa Fe, 1955.

Dutton, Bertha P. Indian artistry in wood and other media. El Palacio, 64 (1957): 3-28.

Dutton, Bertha P. Indian villages, past and present. Santa Fe, Museum of New Mexico Press, 1962. illus.

Dutton, Bertha P. Indians of the Southwest; pocket handbook. Santa Fe, Southwestern Association on Indian Affairs, 1963. 160 p. illus., map.

Dutton, Bertha P. Let's explore Indian villages, past and present; tour guide for Santa Fe area. Rev. ed. Santa Fe, Museum of New Mexico Press, 1970. 65 p. illus., maps.

Dutton, Bertha P. Sun father's way: the kiva murals of Kuaua. Albuquerque, University of New Mexico Press, 1963. 8, 237 p. illus.

Dutton, Bertha P. The New Year of the Pueblo Indians of New Mexico. El Palacio, 78, no. 1 (1972): 3-13.

Duty, Tony E. The Coronado Expedition (1540-1542). Texana, 8 (1970): 121-139.

Dyreson, Delmar A. Settlement pattern changes and self-organizing systems in the central Rio Grande watershed of New Mexico, A.D. 1350-1968. Dissertation Abstracts International, 32 (1971/1972): 4001B. UM 72-3050.

Eckhart, George B. Some little-known missions in Texas. Masterkey, 36 (1962): 127-136; 37 (1963): 9-14.

Eckhart, George B. Spanish missions of Texas, 1680-1800. Kiva, 32, no. 3 (1966/1967): 73-95.

Eddy, Frank W. Excavations at Los Pinos Phase sites in the Navajo Reservoir district. By Frank W. Eddy with a section by Beth L. Dickey. Santa Fe, 1961. 107 p. illus., maps. (Museum of New Mexico, Papers in Anthropology, 4)

Eddy, Frank W. Prehistory in the Navajo Reservoir district: northwestern New Mexico. Santa Fe, 1966. 631 p. illus. (Museum of New Mexico, Papers in Anthropology, 15)

Eddy, Frank Warren. Culture ecology and the prehistory of the Navajo Reservoir District. Dissertation Abstracts, 29 (1968/1969): 1245B. UM 68-14,377.

Eggan, F. Social organization of the Western Pueblos. Chicago, 1951. 401 p.

Eguilaz de Prado, Isabel. Los indios del nordeste de Méjico en el siglo XVIII. Sevilla, 1965. 128 p. (Sevilla, Universidad, Seminario de Antropología Americana, Publicaciones, 7)

Eickemeyer, C. and L. W. Eickemeyer. Among the Pueblo Indians. New York, 1895. 195 p.

Eickhoff, H. Die Kultur der Pueblos in Arizona und New Mexico. Studien und Forschungen zur Menschen- und Völkerkunde, 4 (1908): 1-78.

Elias, E. El terrible veneno. Tactica guerrera de los Indios Apaches. Sociedad Chihuahuense de Estudios Históricos, Boletín, 7 (1950): 392-393.

Ellis, F. H. Patterns of aggression and the war cult in Southwestern Pueblos. Southwestern Journal of Anthropology, 7 (1951): 177-201.

Ellis, F. H. Pueblo social organization and Southwestern archaeology. American Antiquity, 17 (1951): 148-151.

Ellis, Florence Hawley. Differential Pueblo specialization in fetishes and shrines. México, Instituto Nacional de Antropología e Historia, Anales, Época 7, 1 (1967/1968): 159-179.

Ellis, Florence Hawley. On distinguishing Laguna from Acoma polychrome. El Palacio, 73, no. 3 (1966): 37-39.

Ellis, Florence Hawley. Use and significance of the Tcamahia. El Palacio, 74, no. 1 (1967): 35-43.

Ellis, Florence Hawley. Where did the Pueblo people come from? El Palacio, 74, no. 3 (1967): 35-43.

Ellis, Richard N. Copper-skinned soldiers: the Apache scouts. Great Plains Journal, 5 (1965/1966): 51-67.

Ellis, Richard N., ed. New Mexico past and present: a historical reader. Albuquerque, University of New Mexico Press, 1971. 5, 250 p.

Ellis, Richard N., ed. The Western American Indian: case studies in tribal history. Lincoln, University of Nebraska Press, 1972. 203 p.

Ellis, Richard Nathaniel. General John Pope and the development of federal Indian policy, 1862-1886. Dissertation Abstracts, 29 (1968/1969): 528A. UM 68-10,609.

Elmore, F. H. Ethnobiology and climate in the Southwest. El Palacio, 59 (1952): 315-319.

Erasmus, Charles J. Man takes control; cultural development and American aid. Minneapolis, University of Minnesota Press, 1961. 365 p. illus.

Erskine, M. H. A cattle drive from Texas to California: the diary of M. H. Erskine, 1854. Edited by Walter S. Sanderlin. Southwestern Historical Quarterly, 67 (1963/1964): 397-412.

Espinosa, A. M. Pueblo Indian folk tales. Journal of American Folklore, 49 (1936): 69-133.

Espinosa, A. M. Spanish tradition among the Pueblo Indians. In Estudios Hispánicos, Homenaje a Archer M. Huntington. Wellesley, 1952: 131-141.

Espinosa, J. M., ed. First expedition of Vargas into New Mexico. Albuquerque, 1940. 319 p.

Estabrook, Emma F. Ancient lovers of peace. Boston, 1959. 22, 90 p. illus.

Euler, R. C. and V. H. Jones. Hermetic sealing as a technique of food preservation among the Indians of the American Southwest. American Philosophical Society, Proceedings, 100 (1956): 87-89.

Evans, B. and M. G. Evans. American Indian dance steps. New York, 1931. 122 p.

Ewton, Ralph W., Jr., ed. Studies in language and linguistics, 1969-1970. Edited by Ralph W. Ewton, Jr. and Jacob Ornstein. El Paso, University of Texas at El Paso, Texas Western Press, 1970. 232 p. ERIC ED038653.

Ezell, Paul H. Indians under the law; Mexico, 1821-1847. América Indígena, 15 (1955): 199-214.

Fages, P. Diary. Academy of Pacific Coast History, Publications, 3 (1913): 133-233.

Fages, P. Voyage en Californie. Nouvelles Annales des Voyages, 101 (1844): 145-182, 311-347.

Farmer, M. M. A suggested typology for defensive systems of the Southwest. Southwestern Journal of Anthropology, 13 (1957): 249-266.

Faulk, Odie B. Spanish-Comanche relations and the Treaty of 1785. Texana, 2 (1964): 44-53.

Faulk, Odie B. The Presidio: fortress or farce? Journal of the West, 8 (1969): 22-28.

Fay, G. E. A calendar of Indian ceremonies. El Palacio, 57 (1950): 166-172.

Fay, George E., ed. Charters, constitutions and by-laws of the Indian tribes of North America. Part IV: The Southwest (Navajo-Zuni). Greeley, 1967. 5, 120 l. maps. (University of Northern Colorado, Museum of Anthropology, Occasional Publications in Anthropology, Ethnology Series, 5) ERIC ED046554.

Feather, Adlai. Origin of the name Arizona. New Mexico Historical Review, 39 (1964): 89-100.

Feder, Norman. North American Indian painting. New York, Museum of Primitive Art, 1967. illus.

Ferdon, Edwin N., Jr. The Hohokam "ball court"; an alternative view of its function. Kiva, 33, no. 1 (1967/1968): 1-14.

Fergusson, Erna. New Mexico, a pageant of three peoples. 2d ed. New York, Knopf, 1964. 12, 408 p. illus., maps.

Ferris, Robert G., ed. The Indians of New Mexico: Apache, Navaho, Pueblo, Ute. Santa Fe, Museum of New Mexico Press, 1963. 34 p. ERIC ED024518.

Fewkes, J. W. Ancient Pueblo and Mexican water symbol. American Anthropologist, n.s., 6 (1904): 535-538.

Fierman, Floyd S. Nathan Bibo's reminiscences of early New Mexico. El Palacio, 68 (1961): 231-257; 69 (1962): 40-60.

Finch, Boyd. Sherod Hunter and the Confederates in Arizona. Journal of Arizona History, 10 (1969): 137-206.

Fisher, R. G. An outline of Pueblo government. In D. D. Brand and F. E. Harvey, eds. So Live the Works of Men. Albuquerque, 1939: 147-157.

Fleming, Elvis Eugene. Captain Nicholas Nolan; lost on the Staked Plains. Texana, 4 (1966): 1-13.

Fontana, Bernard L. Johnny Ward's ranch: a study in historic archaeology. By Bernard L. Fontana and J. Cameron Greenleaf. Kiva, 28, nos. 1/2 (1962/1963): 1-115.

Forbes, A. A survey of current Pueblo Indian painting. El Palacio, 57 (1950): 235-252.

Forbes, J. D. The appearance of the mounted Indian in northern Mexico and the Southwest, to 1680. Southwestern Journal of Anthropology, 15 (1959): 189-212.

Forbes, Jack D. Apache, Navaho, and Spaniard. Norman, University of Oklahoma Press, 1960. 304 p. illus.

Forbes, Jack D. Indian horticulture west and northwest of the Colorado River. Journal of the West, 2 (1963): 1-14.

Forbes, Jack D. The early Western Apache, 1300-1700. Journal of the West, 5 (1966): 336-354.

Forbes, Jack D. The ethnohistorian in the Southwest. Journal of the West, 3 (1964): 430-439.

Forbes, Jack Douglas. Apache, Navaho, and Spaniard: a history of the Southern Athapaskans and their relations with the Spanish Empire, 1540-1698. Dissertation Abstracts, 22 (1961/1962): 3173-3174. UM 61-6283.

Ford, Richard I. Barter, gift, or violence: an analysis of Tewa intertribal exchange. In Edwin N. Wilmsen, ed. Social Exchange and Interaction. Ann Arbor, University of Michigan, 1972: 24-45. (Michigan, University, Musuem of Anthropology, Anthropological Papers, 46)

Forrest, E. R. Missions and Pueblos of the old Southwest. Cleveland, 1929.

Forrest, Earle Robert. Missions and pueblos of the old Southwest. Chicago, Rio Grande Press, 1962. 386 p. illus.

Foster, James Monroe, Jr. Fort Bascom, New Mexico. New Mexico Historical Review, 35 (1960): 30-62.

Fowler, Don D., ed. "Photographed all the best scenery": Jack Hillers's diary of the Powell expeditions, 1871-1875. Salt Lake City, University of Utah, 1972. 225 p. illus., maps.

Fox, J. Robin. Multilingualism in two communities. By Robin Fox. Man, n.s., 3 (1968): 457-464.

Francis, E. K. Multiple intergroup relations in the Upper Rio Grande region. American Sociological Review, 21 (1956): 84-87.

Frank, M. L. and C. A. Elkin. Scarlet fever among Pueblo Indians. American Journal of Diseases of Children, 71 (1946): 477-481.

Frazer, Robert W. Fort Butler: the fort that almost was. New Mexico Historical Review, 43 (1968): 253-270.

Freeman, G. F. Southwestern beans and teparies. Arizona, State Agricultural Experiment Station, Bulletin, 68 (1912): 573-619.

Freise, Reinhilde. Studie zum Feuer in Vorstellungswelt und Praktiken der Indianer des südwestlichen Nordamerika. Tübingen, 1969. 335 p.

Fynn, A. J. The Pueblo Indian as a product of environment. New York, 1907. 275 p.

Galaviz de Capdevielle, María Elena. Rebeliones indígenas en el norte del reino de la Nueva España; siglos xvi y xvii. México, Editorial Campesina, 1967. 219 p. maps.

Gallenkamp, C. The Pueblo Indians of New Mexico. Canadian Geographical Journal, 50 (1955): 206-215.

Galvez, B. de.   Instructions for governing the interior provinces of New Spain, 1786. Quivira Society, Publications, 12 (1951): 1-164.

Garland, Hamlin.   Hamlin Garland and the Navajos. By Lonnie E. Underhill and Daniel F. Littlefield, Jr. Journal of Arizona History, 13 (1972): 275-285.

Garth, T. R.   A comparison of the intelligence of Mexican and mixed and full blood Indian children. Psychological Review, 30 (1923): 388-401.

Garth, T. R.   The intelligence of full blood Indians. Journal of Applied Psychology, 9 (1925): 382-389.

Garth, T. R. and M. A. Barnard.   The will-temperament of Indians. Journal of Applied Psychology, 11 (1927): 512-518.

Garth, Thomas R.   The Plateau whipping complex and its relationship to Plateau-Southwest contacts. Ethnohistory, 12 (1965): 141-170.

Gates, John Morgan.   General George Crook's first Apache campaign; (the use of mobile, self-contained units against the Apache in the Military Department of Arizona, 1871-1873). Journal of the West, 6 (1967): 310-320.

Gatschet, A. S.   Der Yuma-Sprachstamm. Zeitschrift für Ethnologie, 24 (1892): 1-18.

Gerheim, E. B.   Incidence of Rh factor among the Indians of the Southwest. Society for Experimental Biology and Medicine, Proceedings, 66 (1947): 419-420.

Germann, F. E. E.   Ceramic pigments of the Indians of the Southwest. El Palacio, 20 (1926): 222-226.

Gershowitz, H.   The Diego factor among Asiatic Indians, Apaches and West African Negroes. American Journal of Physical Anthropology, n.s., 17 (1959): 195-200.

Getty, H. T.   Some characteristics of the folklore of the Indians of Arizona. Arizona, University, Bulletin, 16, no. 1 (1945): 29-32.

Gifford, E. W.   Cultural relations of the Gila River and Lower Colorado tribes. American Anthropologist, n.s., 38 (1936): 679-682.

Gifford, E. W.   Pottery-making in the Southwest. California, University,

Publications in American Archaeology and Ethnology, 23 (1928): 253-273.

Gila River Indian Community.   Constitution and bylaws. Approved March 17, 1960. Washington, D.C., Government Printing Office, 1960.   15 p.

Gill, George A.   The changing Indians of the Southwest. Journal of American Indian Education, 6, no. 2 (1966/1967): 20-25.

Gilmore, Kathleen K.   A documentary and archeological investigation of Presidio San Luis de las Amarillas and Mission Santa Cruz de San Sabá.   Austin, Tex., State Building Commission, 1967.   1, 72 p.   illus., map. (Texas, State Building Commission Archeological Program, 9)

Gilpin, L.   The Pueblos, a camera chronicle.   New York, 1941.   124 p.

Gladwin, H. S.   A history of the ancient Southwest.   Portland, Maine, 1957. 403 p.

Goddard, P. E.   Assimilation to environment as illustrated by Athapascan peoples. International Congress of Americanists, Proceedings, 15, vol. 1 (1906): 337-359.

Goddard, P. E.   Indians of the Southwest. New York, 1931.   188 p.

Goddard, P. E.   Pottery of the Southwestern Indians. American Museum of Natural History, Guide Leaflet Series, 73 (1928): 1-30.

Goddard, P. E.   Similarities and diversities within Athapascan linguistic stocks. International Congress of Americanists, Proceedings, 22, vol. 2 (1926): 489-494.

Goddard, P. E.   The cultural and somatic correlations of Uto-Aztecan. American Anthropologist, n.s., 22 (1920): 244-247.

Goggin, J. M.   Additional Pueblo ceremonies. New Mexico Anthropologist, 3 (1939): 62-63.

Goggin, John M.   Spanish majolica in the New World; types of the sixteenth to eighteenth centuries.   New Haven, Yale University, Department of Anthropology, 1968.   240 p.   illus. (Yale University Publications in Anthropology, 72)

Goldfrank, E. S.   The different patterns of Blackfoot and Pueblo adaptation to White authority. International Congress of Americanists, Proceedings, 29, vol. 2 (1952): 74-79.

Goldman, Henry H. General James H. Carleton and the New Mexico Indian campaigns, 1862-1866. Journal of the West, 2 (1963): 156-165.

Goldman, Stanford M., et al. Roentgen manifestations of diseases in Southwestern Indians. Radiology, 103 (1972): 303-306.

Gómez Canedo, Lino. De México a la Alta California: una gran epopeya misional. México, Editorial Jus., 1969. 37, 240 p. (México Heróico, 103)

González Dávila, Amado. Dicionario geográfico, histórico, biográfico y estadístico del estado de Sinaloa. Culiacán, 1959.

Gonzalez de Cossio, F., ed. Estado y descripción de la provincia de Sonora 1730. México, Archivo General de la Nación, Boletín, 16 (1945): 587-636.

Goodrich, James W. In the earnest pursuit of wealth: David Waldo in Missouri and the Southwest, 1820-1878. Missouri Historical Review, 66 (1971/1972): 155-184.

Goodwin, G. The Southern Athapaskans. Kiva, 4, no. 2 (1938): 5-10.

Goss, James A. Ute linguistics and Anasazi abandonment of the Four Corners area. In Douglas Osborne, assembler. Contributions of the Wetherill Mesa Archeological Project. Salt Lake City, 1965: 73-81. (Society for American Archaeology, Memoir, 19)

Graham, Patrick E. Reservations and tribal customs, history and language. By Patrick E. Graham and Judson H. Taylor. Journal of American Indian Education, 8, no. 3 (1968/1969): 19-26.

Graves, Theodore D. Psychological acculturation in a tri-ethnic community. Southwestern Journal of Anthropology, 23 (1967): 337-350.

Gray, J. R. Appraisal of Bureau of Indian Affairs credit program, Gallup area, New Mexico, 1958. Albuquerque, 1959. 46 p. (New Mexico, Agricultural Experiment Station, Research Report, 26)

Greene, A. C. The last captive. Austin, Encino Press, 1972. 21, 161 p. illus.

Greenleaf, Richard E. Land and water in Mexico and New Mexico 1700-1821. New Mexico Historical Review, 47 (1972): 85-112.

Greenleaf, Richard E. The Nueva Vizcaya frontier, 1787-1789. Journal of the West, 8 (1969): 56-66.

Greenwood, N. H. Sol Barth: a Jewish settler on the Arizona frontier. Journal of Arizona History, 14 (1973): 363-378.

Griffen, William B. A North American nativistic movement, 1684. Ethnohistory, 17 (1970): 95-116.

Griffith, James S. Legacy of conquest; the arts of Northwest Mexico. Colorado Springs, Taylor Museum of the Colorado Springs Fine Arts Center, 1967. 32 p. illus.

Gunnerson, D. A. The Southern Athabascans. El Palacio, 63 (1956): 346-365.

Gunnerson, Dolores A. Man and bison on the Plains in the protohistoric period. Plains Anthropologist, 17 (1972): 1-10.

Gursky, Karl-Heinz. Gulf and Hokan-Subtiaban: new lexical parallels. International Journal of American Linguistics, 34 (1968): 21-41.

Gursky, Karl-Heinz. The linguistic position of the Quinigua Indians. International Journal of American Linguistics, 30 (1964): 325-327.

Haas, Mary R. Notes on a Chipewyan dialect. International Journal of American Linguistics, 34 (1968): 165-175.

Habig, Marion A. Mission San José y San Miguel de Aguayo, 1720-1824. Southwestern Historical Quarterly, 71 (1967/1968): 496-516.

Hackett, C. W. The revolt of the Pueblo Indians of New Mexico in 1680. Texas State Historical Association Quarterly, 15 (1911): 93-147.

Hackett, C. W. and G. P. Hammond, et al, eds. New Spain and the Anglo-American West. Los Angeles, 1932. 2 v.

Hackett, C. W., ed. Revolt of the Pueblo Indians of New Mexico and Otermin's attempted reconquest, 1680-1682. Albuquerque, 1942. 2 v.

Haeberlin, H. K. Das Flachenornament in der Keramik der alten Pueblo-Kultur. Baessler-Archiv, 6 (1922): 1-35.

Haeberlin, H. K. The idea of fertilization in the culture of the Pueblo Indians. American Anthropological Association, Memoirs, 3 (1916): 1-55.

Haekel, J. Das Mutterrecht bei den
Indianerstämmen im südwestlichen
Nordamerika. Zeitschrift für Ethnologie,
68 (1936): 227-249.

Hafen, L. R. and A. W. Hafen, eds. Rufus
B. Sage, his letters and papers, 1836-
1847. The Far West and the Rockies
Historical Series 1820-1875, 4 (1956):
1-354; 5 (1956): 1-360.

Hafner, Gertrude. Das Calumet und seine
Beziehungen zum nordamerikanischen
Südwesten. In Internationale
Amerikanistenkongress, 34th. 1960, Wien.
Akten. Horn-Wien, Berger, 1962: 564-
568.

Hagemann, E. R. Scout out from Camp
McDowell. Arizoniana, 5, no. 3 (1964):
29-47.

Hale, Kenneth. The sub-grouping of Uto-
Aztecan languages: lexical evidence for
Sonoran. In Congreso Internacional de
Americanistas, 35th. 1962, Mexico. Actas
y Memorias. Tomo 2. Mexico, 1964: 511-
518.

Hall, E. T. Recent clues to Athapascan
prehistory in the Southwest. American
Anthropologist, n.s., 46 (1944): 98-105.

Hall, H. U. Some shields of the Plains
and Southwest. Museum Journal, 17
(1926): 37-61.

Halseth, O. S. Revival of Pueblo pottery-
making. El Palacio, 21 (1926): 135-154.

Halseth, O. S. The acculturation of the
Pueblo Indians. El Palacio, 18 (1925):
254-268.

Halseth, O. S. The Pueblo Indians. El
Palacio, 22 (1927): 238-251.

Hammack, Laurens C. Archaeology of the
Ute dam and reservoir. Santa Fe, 1965.
69 p. illus., maps. (Museum of New
Mexico, Papers in Anthropology, 14)

Hammond, D. Corydon. Cross-cultural
rehabilitation. Journal of
Rehabilitation, 37, no. 5 (1971): 34-36,
44.

Hammond, G. P. Don Juan de Onate and the
founding of New Mexico. New Mexico
Historical Review, 1 (1926): 42-77, 156-
192, 292-323, 445-477; 2 (1927): 37-66,
134-174.

Hammond, G. P. and A. Rey, eds.
Expedition into New Mexico by Antonio de
Espejo. Quivira Society, Publications, 1
(1929): 1-143.

Hammond, G. P. and A. Rey, eds. The
Gallegos relation of the Rodriquez
expedition. New Mexico Historical
Review, 2 (1927): 239-268, 334-362.

Hanna, Lavelle. Immunofluorescence in
chronic TRIC infections of American
Indians and Tunisians: influence of
trauma on results of tests. Society for
Experimental Biology and Medicine,
Proceedings, 136 (1971): 655-659.

Harcourt, R. d'. Arts de l'Amérique, 43-
48. Paris, 1948.

Hardy, B. Carmon. The trek south: how the
Mormons went to Mexico. Southwestern
Historical Quarterly, 73 (1969/1970): 1-
16.

Harlow, Francis H. Contemporary Pueblo
Indian pottery. By Frances H. Harlow and
John V. Young. Santa Fe, Museum of New
Mexico Press, 1965. 24 p. illus.

Harlow, Francis H. Historic Pueblo Indian
pottery; painted jars and bowls of the
period 1600-1900. Los Alamos, N.M.,
Monitor Press, 1967. 49 p. illus.

Harrington, J. P. Southern peripheral
Athapaskawan origins, divisions and
migrations. Smithsonian Miscellaneous
Collections, 100 (1940): 503-532.

Harris, W. R. The Catholic Church in
Utah. Salt Lake City, 1909. 350 p.

Harvey, Byron, III. New Mexico kachina
dolls. Masterkey, 37 (1963): 4-8.

Haskell, M. L. Rubi's inspection of the
frontier presidios of New Spain, 1766-
1768. Southern California Historical
Society, Publications, 5 (1917): 33-43.

Hastings, James Rodney. People of reason
and others: the colonization of Sonora
to 1767. Arizona and the West, 3 (1961):
321-340.

Haught, B. F. Mental growth of the
Southwestern Indian. Journal of Applied
Psychology, 18 (1934): 137-142.

Hawley, F. M. Big kivas, little kivas,
and moiety houses in historical
reconstruction. Southwestern Journal of
Anthropology, 6 (1950): 286-302.

Hawley, F. M. Mechanics of perpetuation
of Pueblo witchcraft. In For the Dean.
Essays in Anthropology in Honor of Byron
Cummings. Tucson, 1950: 143-158.

Hawley, F. M. Pueblo social organization
as a lead to Pueblo history. American
Anthropologist, n.s., 39 (1937): 504-
522.

Hawley, F. M. Some factors in the Indian problem in New Mexico. New Mexico, University, Department of Government, Publications, 15 (1948): 1-48.

Hawley, F. M. The role of Pueblo social organization in the dissemination of Catholicism. American Anthropologist, n.s., 48 (1946): 407-415.

Hayes, William D. Indian tales of the desert people. New York, D. McKay, 1957. 110 p. illus.

Heaston, Michael D. The governor and the Indian agent: 1855-1857. New Mexico Historical Review, 45 (1970): 137-146.

Heaston, Michael D. Whiskey regulations and Indian land titles in New Mexico Territory, 1851-1861. Journal of the West, 10 (1971): 474-483.

Hedrick, Basil C., ed. The North Mexican frontier; readings in archaeology, ethnohistory, and ethnography. Edited by Basil C. Hedrick, J. Charles Kelley, and Carroll L. Riley. Carbondale, Southern Illinois University Press, 1971. 16, 255 p.

Heizer, R. F. Ancient grooved clubs and modern rabbit sticks. American Antiquity, 8 (1942): 41-56.

Hemmings, E. Thomas. Cruciform and related artifacts of Mexico and the Southwestern United States. Kiva, 32, no. 4 (1966/1967): 150-169.

Henderson, A. C. Indian artists of the Southwest. American Indian, 2, no. 3 (1945): 21-27.

Henderson, A. C. Why Pueblo culture is dying. American Indian, 5 (1949): 13-16.

Henderson, Patrick C. The public domain in Arizona: 1863-1891. Dissertation Abstracts, 27 (1966/1967): 1007A. UM 66-8507.

Herzog, G. A comparison of Pueblo and Pima musical styles. Journal of American Folklore, 49 (1936): 283-417.

Hester, James J. Early Navajo migrations and acculturation in the Southwest. Santa Fe, 1962. 10, 138 p. illus., maps. (Museum of New Mexico, Papers in Anthropology, 6)

Hester, James Jean. Early Navajo migrations and acculturation in the Southwest. Dissertation Abstracts, 22 (1961/1962): 1348. UM 61-3846.

Hewett, E. L. Ancient life in the American Southwest. Indianapolis, 1930. 392 p.

Hewett, E. L. My neighbors, the Pueblo Indians. Art and Archaeology, 16 (1924): 3-25.

Hewett, E. L. Native American artists. Art and Archaeology, 13 (1922): 103-113.

Hewett, E. L. Pueblo water color painting. Art and Archaeology, 13 (1922): 103-111.

Hewett, E. L. and B. P. Dutton. The Pueblo Indian world. Albuquerque, 1945. 176 p.

Hewett, E. L., J. Henderson, and W. W. Robbins. The physiography of the Rio Grande Valley, New Mexico, in relation to Pueblo culture. U.S. Bureau of American Ethnology, Bulletin, 54 (1913): 1-76.

Hewett, Edgar Lee. Ancient life in the American Southwest. New York, Biblo and Tannen, 1968. 392 p. illus., map.

Hewitt, Harry Paxton. The historical development of Nueva Vizcaya's defenses to 1646. Dissertation Abstracts International, 32 (1971/1972): 2013A. UM 71-25,011.

Higgins, James M. The Southwestern Indian in fact and fiction: an ethnohistorical study of the novels of Frank Waters and Oliver LaFarge. Masters Abstracts, 10 (1972): 56. UM M-3072.

Hill, Jane A. A note on Uto-Aztecan color terminologies. By Jane A. Hill and Kenneth C. Hill. Anthropological Linguistics, 12 (1970): 231-237.

Hillary, Frank M. Cajeme, and the Mexico of his time. Journal of Arizona History, 8 (1967): 120-136.

Hodge, F. W. How old is Southwestern Indian silverwork? El Palacio, 25 (1928): 224-232.

Hodge, F. W. Masked kachinas in Spanish times. Masterkey, 26 (1952): 17-20.

Hodge, F. W. Pueblo Indian clans. American Anthropologist, 9 (1896): 345-352.

Hodge, F. W. Pueblo Indian government. Masterkey, 7 (1933): 124-126.

Hodge, F. W. Pueblo names in the Onate documents. New Mexico Historical Review, 10 (1935): 36-47.

Hodge, F. W. Pueblo snake ceremonials.
American Anthropologist, 9 (1896): 133-
136.

Hodge, F. W. Pueblos. U.S. Bureau of
American Ethnology, Bulletin, 30, vol. 2
(1910): 318-324.

Hodge, G. M. The kachinas are coming.
Los Angeles, 1937. 129 p.

Hoebel, E. Adamson. The authority systems
of the Pueblos of the Southwestern
United States. In Internationale
Amerikanistenkongress, 34th. 1960, Wien.
Akten. Horn-Wien, Berger, 1962: 555-
563.

Hoffman, W. J. The practice of medicine
and surgery by the aboriginal races of
the Southwest. Medical and Surgical
Reporter, 40 (1879): 157-160.

Hoijer, H. The Southern Athapaskan
languages. American Anthropologist,
n.s., 40 (1938); 75-87.

Hoijer, H. The structure of the noun in
Apachean languages. International
Congress of Americanists, Proceedings,
28 (1948): 173-184.

Hoijer, Harry. Athapaskan morphology. In
Jesse Sawyer, ed. Studies in American
Indian Languages. Berkeley and Los
Angeles, University of California Press,
1971: 113-147. (California, University,
Publications in Linguistics, 65)

Hoijer, Harry. Internal reconstruction in
Navaho. Word, 25 (1969): 155-159.

Hoijer, Harry. Linguistic sub-groupings
by glottochronology and by the
comparative method: the Athapaskan
languages. Lingua, 11 (1962): 192-198.

Hoijer, Harry. Studies in the Athapaskan
languages. By Harry Hoijer, et al.
Berkeley and Los Angeles, University of
California Press, 1963. 6, 154 p.
(California, University, Publications in
Linguistics, 29)

Hoijer, Harry. The Athapaskan languages.
In Harry Hoijer, et al., eds. Studies in
the Athapaskan Languages. Berkeley and
Los Angeles, University of California
Press, 1963: 1-29. (California,
University, Publications in Linguistics,
29)

Holien, Elaine Baran. Kachinas. El
Palacio, 76, no. 4 (1970): 1-15.

Holling, H. C. The book of Indians, 73-
96. New York, 1935.

Hopkins, Richard C. Kit Carson and the
Navajo Expedition. Montana, the Magazine
of Western History, 18, no. 2 (1968):
52-61.

Horn, Tom. Life of Tom Horn, Government
scout and interpreter, written by
himself. New ed. Norman, University of
Oklahoma Press, 1964. 18, 277 p.

Hotz, Gottfried. Indian skin paintings
from the American Southwest. Translated
by Johannes Malthauer. Norman,
University of Oklahoma Press, 1970. 14,
248 p. illus.

Hotz, Gottfried. Indianische
Ledermalereien; Figurenreiche
Darstellungen von Grenzkonflikten
zwischen Mexiko und dem Missouri um
1720. Berlin, Reimer, 1960. 384 p.
illus., maps.

Hough, W. Pueblo environment. American
Association for the Advancement of
Science, Proceedings, 55 (1906): 447-
454.

Houghton, N. D. "Wards of the United
States"--Arizona applications. Arizona,
University, Social Science Bulletin, 14
(1945): 5-19.

Houser, Nicholas P. The Tigua settlement
of Ysleta del Sur. Kiva, 36, no. 1
(1970/1971): 23-39.

Howells, W. W. and H. Hotelling.
Measurements and correlations on pelves
of Indians of the Southwest. American
Journal of Physical Anthropology, 21
(1936): 91-106.

Hoyt, Elizabeth E. Young Indians: some
problems and issues of mental hygiene.
Mental Hygiene, 46 (1962): 41-47.

Hrdlička, A. Catalogue of human crania in
the United States National Museum
collections. United States National
Museum, Proceedings, 78, no. 2 (1931):
1-95.

Hrdlička, A. Diseases of the Indians.
Washington Medical Annals, 4
(1905/1906): 372-382.

Hrdlička, A. On the stature of the
Indians of the Southwest and of Northern
Mexico. In Putnam Anniversary Volume.
New York, 1909: 405-426.

Hrdlička, A. Physiological and medical
observations among the Indians of
Southwestern United States and Northern
Mexico. U.S. Bureau of American
Ethnology, Bulletin, 24 (1908): 1-425.

Hrdlička, A. Ritual ablation of front teeth in Siberia and America. Smithsonian Miscellaneous Collections, 99, no. 3 (1940): 1-32.

Hrdlička, A. The Pueblos. American Journal of Physical Anthropology, 20 (1935): 235-460.

Huerta Preciado, María Teresa. Rebeliones indígenas en el Noreste de México en la época colonial. México, 1966. 108 p. (Instituto Nacional de Antropología e Historia, Publicaciones, Serie Historia, 15)

Hughes, John T. Doniphan's Expedition; an account of the U.S. Army operations in the great American Southwest. Chicago, Rio Grande Press, 1962. 407 p. illus., map.

Hunt, W. B. Kachina dolls. Public Museum of the City of Milwaukee, Popular Science Handbook, 7 (1957): 1-36.

Hurt, W. R. Christmas Eve ceremonies of the Pueblo Indians of New Mexico. South Dakota, University, Museum, Museum Notes, 12, no. 4 (1951): 4-7.

Huscher, B. H. and H. A. Huscher. Athapaskan migration via the intermontane region. American Antiquity, 8 (1942): 80-88.

Huscher, Harold A. Deer Raiser and Corn Mother: the corn origin myth of the Upper Missouri and the Athapaskan Southwest. Plains Anthropologist, 10 (1965): 56.

Huscher, Harold A. Salt traders of Cibola. Great Plains Journal, 5 (1965/1966): 73-83.

Huscher, Harold A. Southern Athapaskan names in early Spanish records. Plains Anthropologist, 8 (1963): 128.

Hutchins, James S. "Bald Head" Ewell, frontier dragoon. Arizoniana, 3, no. 1 (1962): 18-23.

Indian Arts and Crafts Board. Pottery of the Pueblo Indian. Washington, D.C., 1956. 7 p.

Indian Arts and Crafts Board. Silver jewelry of the Navajo and Pueblo Indians. Washington, D.C., 1956. 7 p.

Ingstad, H. Apache-Indianerne. Oslo, 1939. 329 p.

Ingstad, Helge M. Apache-indianerne. Oslo, Gyldendal, 1972. 228 p. illus., maps.

Institute of Texan Cultures. The Indian Texans. San Antonio, 1970.

Ivancovich, Byron. Juan Bautista de Anza: pioneer of Arizona. Arizoniana, 1, no. 4 (1960): 21-24.

Ives, R. L. Sonoran mission languages in 1730. Masterkey, 22 (1948): 93-95.

Ives, Ronald L. Manje's mercury mines. Journal of Arizona History, 6 (1965): 165-176.

James, H. L. Ácoma: the people of the white rock. Glorieta, Rio Grande Press, 1970. 96 p. illus., map.

Jaquith, James R. The present status of the Uto-Aztekan language of Mexico. Greeley, 1970. 80 l. (University of Northern Colorado, Museum of Anthropology, Occasional Publications in Anthropology, Linguistics Series, 1)

Jeancon, J. A. Indian music of the Southwest. El Palacio, 23 (1927): 438-447.

Jeancon, J. A. Pueblo beads and inlay. Denver Art Museum, Indian Leaflet Series, 30 (1931): 1-4.

Jenkins, Myra Ellen. Taos Pueblo and its neighbors; 1540-1847. New Mexico Historical Review, 41 (1966): 85-114.

Jenkins, Myra Ellen. The Baltasar Baca "Grant": history of an encroachment. El Palacio, 68 (1961): 47-64, 87-105.

Jennings, Jesse D. The Glen Canyon: a multi-discipline project. By Jesse D. Jennings and Floyd W. Sharrock. Utah Historical Quarterly, 33 (1965): 34-50.

Jett, Stephen C. Comment on Davis' hypothesis of Pueblo Indian migrations. American Antiquity, 31 (1965/1966): 276-277.

Jett, Stephen C. Pueblo Indian migrations: an evaluation of the possible physical and cultural determinants. American Antiquity, 29 (1963/1964): 281-300.

Jimenez Moreno, W. Tribus e idiomas del norte de México. In El Norte de México y el Sur de Estados Unidos. México, 1943: 121-133.

Johnson, Charles Clark. A study of modern Southwestern Indian leadership. Dissertation Abstracts, 25 (1964/1965): 751. UM 64-4359.

Johnson, Fred. The linguistic map of Mexico and Central America. In Clarence

L. Hay, et al., eds. The Maya and Their Neighbors. New York, 1940: 88-114.

Johnson, J. B. Sonora dance regalia. El México Antiguo, 1/2 (1940): 54-56.

Johnson, J. R. Colonel John Miller Stotsenburg: a man of valor. Nebraska History, 50 (1969): 339-357.

Johnston, Bernice E. Speaking of Indians, with an accent on the Southwest. Tucson, University of Arizona Press, 1970. 112 p. illus., map.

Johnston, Francis E., et al. Alloalbuminemia in Southwestern U.S. Indians: polymorphism of albumen Naskapi and albumin Mexico. Human Biology, 41 (1969): 263-270.

Johnston, Francis J. Stagecoach travel through San Gorgonio Pass. Journal of the West, 11 (1972): 616-635.

Jones, J. A. Rio Grande Pueblo albinism. American Journal of Physical Anthropology, n.s., 22 (1964): 265-270.

Jones, J. A. Variables influencing behavior in indigenous non-Western cultures. Final progress report. Tempe, Arizona State University, Department of Anthropology, 1968. 219 p. ERIC ED035477.

Jones, Oakah L., Jr. Pueblo Indian auxiliaries and the reconquest of New Mexico, 1692-1704. Journal of the West, 2 (1963): 257-280.

Jones, Oakah L., Jr. Pueblo Indian auxiliaries and the Spanish defense of New Mexico, 1692-1794. Dissertation Abstracts, 26 (1965/1966): 6675. UM 66-5980.

Jones, Oakah L., Jr. Pueblo Indian auxiliaries in New Mexico, 1763-1821. New Mexico Historical Review, 37 (1962): 81-109.

Jones, Oakah L., Jr. Pueblo warriors and Spanish conquest. Norman, University of Oklahoma Press, 1966. 21, 225 p. illus., maps.

Jones, Paul. Reclamation and the Indian. Utah Historical Quarterly, 27 (1959): 50-56.

Jordan, Scott W. Carcinoma of the cervix in American Indian women. By Scott W. Jordan, Robert A. Munsick, and Robert S. Stone. Cancer, 23 (1969): 1227-1232.

Jordan, Scott W., et al. Carcinoma of the cervix in Southwestern American Indian women. Cancer, 29 (1972): 1235-1241.

Kaemlein, Wilma R. An inventory of Southwestern American Indian specimens in European museums. Tucson, Arizona State Museum, 1967. 11, 229 p.

Kaplan, L. The cultivated beans of the prehistoric Southwest. Missouri Botanical Garden, Annals, 43 (1956): 189-251.

Kate, H. F. C. ten. Notes on the hands and feet of American natives. American Anthropologist, n.s., 20 (1918): 187-202.

Kate, H. F. C. ten. Sur la synonymie ethnique et la toponymie chez les Indiens de l'Amérique du Nord. Amsterdam, Koninklijke Akademie van Wetenschappen, Afdeeling Letterkunde, Verslagen en Mededeelingen, ser. 3, 1 (1884): 353-363.

Kayser, Joan. Phantoms in the pinyon: an investigation of Ute-Pueblo contacts. In Douglas Osborne, assembler. Contributions of the Wetherill Mesa Archeological Project. Salt Lake City, 1965: 82-91. (Society for American Archaeology, Memoir, 19)

Keech, R. A. Christianity and the Pueblo Indians. El Palacio, 34 (1933): 143-146.

Keech, R. A. Pueblo dwelling architecture. El Palacio, 36 (1934): 49-53.

Kelly, Roger E. American Indians in small cities: a survey of urban acculturation in two northern Arizona communities. By Roger E. Kelly and John O. Cramer. Flagstaff, Northern Arizona University, Department of Rehabilitation, 1966. 90 p. illus.

Kelly, W. H. Applied anthropology in the Southwest. American Anthropologist, 56 (1954): 709-714.

Kelly, W. H. Indians of the Southwest. Arizona, University, Bureau of Ethnic Research, Reports, 1 (1953): 1-129.

Kendrick, Edith Johnston. Regional dances of Mexico. By Edith Johnston. Lincolnwood, Ill., B. Upshaw, 1966. 58 p. illus.

Kennard, Edward A. Metaphor and magic: key concepts in Hopi culture and their linguistic forms. In M. Estellie Smith, ed. Studies in Linguistics in Honor of George L. Trager. The Hague, Mouton, 1972: 468-473. (Janua Linguarum, Series Maior, 52)

Kenner, Charles L. A history of New Mexican-Plains Indian relations.

Norman, University of Oklahoma Press, 1969. 9, 250 p. illus., maps.

Kent, K. P. A comparison of prehistoric and modern Pueblo weaving. Kiva, 10 (1945): 14-20.

Kent, K. P. Notes on the weaving of prehistoric Pueblo textiles. Plateau, 14 (1941): 1-11.

Kent, K. P. The cultivation and weaving of cotton in the prehistoric Southwestern United States. American Philosophical Society, Transactions, 47 (1957): 457-732.

Kent, Kate Peck. Archaeological clues to early historic Navajo and Pueblo weaving. Plateau, 39 (1966): 46-70.

Kessell, John L. Campaigning on the Upper Gila, 1756. New Mexico Historical Review, 46 (1971): 133-160.

Kessell, John L. Father Ramón and the big debt, Tumacácori, 1821-1823. New Mexico Historical Review, 44 (1969): 53-72.

Kessell, John L. The puzzling Presidio; San Phelipe de Guevava, alias Terrenate. New Mexico Historical Review, 41 (1966): 21-46.

Khoroshaeva, I. F. Sovremennoe indeĭskoe naselenie Meksiki. Akademiĭa Nauk SSSR, Institut Etnografii imeni N.N. Miklukho-Maklaĭa, Trudy, novaĭa seriĭa, 58 (1960): 156-202.

Kidder, A. V. An introduction to the study of Southwestern archaeology. New Haven, 1924. 151 p.

Kidder, A. V. and S. J. Guernsey. Archaeological explorations in northeastern Arizona. U.S. Bureau of American Ethnology, Bulletin, 65 (1919): 1-228.

Kiddle, Lawrence B. American Indian reflexes of two Spanish words for cat. International Journal of American Linguistics, 30 (1964): 299-305.

King, Charles. Campaigning with Crook, and stories of army life. Ann Arbor, University Microfilms, 1966. 5, 295 p. illus.

King, Charles. Campaigning with Crook. New ed. Norman, University of Oklahoma Press, 1964. 25, 166 p. illus., map.

King, Patrick. Pueblo Indian religious architecture; a photographic study. Salt Lake City, Printed by Planning and Research Associates, 1971. 108 p. illus., map.

Kino, Eusebio Francisco. Correspondencia del P. Kino con los generales de la Compañía de Jesús 1682-1707. Prólogo y notas de Ernest J. Burrus, S.J. México, Editorial Jus, 1961. 95 p. illus., maps. (Testimonio Historica, 5)

Kino, Eusebio Francisco. Kino reports to headquarters; correspondence . . . from New Spain with Rome. Original Spanish text of fourteen unpublished letters and reports. With English translation and notes by Ernest J. Burrus, S.J. Rome, Institutum Historicum Societatis Jesu, 1954. 135 p.

Kirchhoff, P. Gatherers and farmers in the greater Southwest. American Anthropologist, 56 (1954): 529-550.

Kirchhoff, P. Los recolectores-cazadores del Norte de México. In El Norte de México y el Sur de Estados Unidos. México, 1943: 133-144.

Kirchhoff, P. Versuch einer Gliederung der Südgruppe des Athapaskischen. International Congress of Americanists, Proceedings, 24 (1930): 258-263.

Kirkland, F. A study of Indian pictures in Texas. Texas Archeological and Paleontological Society, Bulletin, 9 (1937): 89-119.

Kluckhohn, C. Southwestern studies of culture and personality. American Anthropologist, 56 (1954): 685-697.

Kluckhohn, Clyde. Conceptions of death among the Southwestern Indians. In Richard Kluckhohn, ed. Culture and Behavior. New York, Free Press, 1962: 134-149.

Kluckhohn, Clyde. Conceptions of death among the Southwestern Indians. Harvard University, Divinity School, Bulletin, 66 (1948): 5-19.

Kluckhohn, Clyde. To the foot of the rainbow; a tale of twenty-five hundred miles of wandering on horseback through the Southwest enchanted land. Glorieta, Rio Grande Press, 1967. 10, 276 p. map.

Knight, Margaret E. The nature of teacher-community contact in schools serving Southwest Indian children. Tuscon, University of Arizona, Department of Anthropology, 1970. 8 p. (American Indian Education Papers, 2) ERIC ED052880.

Knowlton, Clark S., ed. Indian and Spanish American adjustments to arid and semiarid environments. Lubbock, Texas

Technological College, 1964. 97 p.
ERIC ED024478.

Koenig, Seymour H. Sky, sand, and
spirits; Navaho and Pueblo Indian art
and culture. Yonkers, N.Y., Hudson
River Museum, 1972. 90 p. illus.

Krámský, Jiři. The article and the
concept of definiteness in language.
The Hague, Mouton, 1972. 212 p. (Janua
Linguarum, Series Minor, 125)

Kraus, B. S. and B. M. Jones. Indian
health in Arizona. Arizona, University,
Bureau of Ethnic Research, Reports, 2
(1954): 1-164.

Krause, F. Die Pueblo-Indianer. Halle,
1907. 98 p.

Kravagna, Paul Warren. An ethnological
approach to art education programming
for Navajo and Pueblo students.
Dissertation Abstracts International, 32
(1971/1972): 5107A-5108A. UM 72-8369.

Kravetz, Robert E. Etiology of biliary
tract disease in Southwestern American
Indians: analysis of 105 consecutive
cholecystectomies. Gastroenterology, 46
(1964): 392-398.

Krickeberg, W. Blood-letting and bloody
castigation among the American Indians.
Ciba Symposia, 1 (1939): 26-34.

Krickeberg, W. The Indian sweat bath.
Ciba Symposia, 1 (1939): 19-25.

Kroeber, A. L. Athabascan kin term
systems. American Anthropologist, n.s.,
39 (1937): 602-608.

Kroeber, A. L. Native culture of the
Southwest. California, University,
Publications in American Archaeology and
Ethnology, 23 (1928): 375-398.

Kroeber, A. L. Salt, dogs, tobacco.
Anthropological Records, 6 (1941): 1-20.

Kroeber, A. L. Stepdaughter marriage.
American Anthropologist, n.s., 42
(1940): 562-570.

Kroeber, A. L. The classification of the
Yuman languages. California, University,
Publications in Linguistics, 1 (1943):
21-40.

Kroeber, A. L. Uto-Aztecan languages of
Mexico. Ibero-Americana, 8 (1934): 1-27.

Kroeber, Alfred L. Semantic contributions
of lexicostatistics. International
Journal of American Linguistics, 27
(1961): 1-8.

Kroeber, Clifton B. The Mohave as
nationalist, 1859-1874. American
Philosophical Society, Proceedings, 109
(1965): 173-180.

Kurath, G. P. Game animal dances of the
Rio Grande Pueblos. Southwestern Journal
of Anthropology, 14 (1958): 438-448.

Kurath, G. P. Notation of a Pueblo Indian
corn dance. Dance Notation Record, 8,
no. 4 (1957): 9-11.

Kurath, G. P. The origin of the Pueblo
Indian Matachines. El Palacio, 64
(1957): 259-264.

Kurath, Gertrude P. A comparison of
Plains and Pueblo songs.
Ethnomusicology, 13 (1969): 512-517.

LaFarge, Oliver. Chronic peculiarity. In
Harold Peter Simonson, ed. Cross
Currents. New York, Harper, 1959: 83-
91.

Lamb, Sydney M. The classification of the
Uto-Aztecan languages: an historical
survey. In William Bright, ed. Studies
in Californian Linguistics. Berkeley
and Los Angeles, University of
California Press, 1964: 106-125.
(California, University, Publications in
Linguistcs, 34)

Lambert, Marjorie F. Southwestern Indians
today; a gallery guide. Santa Fe,
Museum of New Mexico Press, 1965.
23 p. illus.

Landar, Herbert J. The diffusion of some
Southwestern words for cat.
International Journal of American
Linguistics, 25 (1959): 273-274.

Landar, Herbert J. The loss of Athapaskan
words for fish in the Southwest.
International Journal of American
Linguistics, 26 (1960): 75-77.

Landar, Herbert J. The Southwestern words
for cat. International Journal of
American Linguistics, 27 (1961): 370-
371.

Lange, C. H. A reappraisal of evidence of
Plains influences among the Rio Grande
Pueblos. Southwestern Journal of
Anthropology, 9 (1953): 212-230.

Lange, C. H. Comparative notes on
Southwestern medical practices. Texas
Journal of Science, 6 (1954): 62-71.

Lange, C. H. Notes on the use of turkeys
by Pueblo Indians. El Palacio, 57
(1950): 204-209.

Lange, C. H. Plains-Southwestern intercultural relations during the historic
period. Ethnohistory, 4 (1957): 150-173.

Lange, C. H. Tablita, or corn, dances of
the Rio Grande Pueblo Indians. Texas
Journal of Science, 9 (1957): 59-74.

Lange, C. H. The Keresan component of
Southwestern Pueblo culture.
Southwestern Journal of Anthropology, 14
(1958): 34-50.

Lange, Charles H. Adolph F. Bandelier as
a Pueblo ethnologist. Kiva, 29, no. 1
(1963/1964): 28-34.

Leap, William L. Who were the Piro?
Anthropological Linguistics, 13 (1971):
321-330.

Lebrija Celay, Antonio. Misiones y
misioneros en Nueva España. México,
Instituto Nacional de Antropología e
Historia, Anales, 5 (1951): 89-110.

Lecompte, Janet. The Manco Burro Pass
Massacre. New Mexico Historical Review,
41 (1966): 305-318.

Lee, B. J. Cancer among the Indians of
the Southwest. Liga Contra el Cancer,
Boletín, Edición Social, 1 (1930): 234-
241.

Lee, B. J. The incidence of cancer among
the Indians of the Southwest. Surgery,
Gynecology, and Obstetrics, 50 (1930):
196-199.

Leonard, I. A., ed. The Mercurio Volante
of Don Carlos de Sigüenza y Góngora.
Los Angeles, 1932. 136 p.

Leupp, F. E. Notes of a summer tour among
the Indians of the Southwest.
Philadelphia, 1897.

Levy, Walter J. A study of the refractive
state of a group of American Pueblo
Indians. By Walter J. Levy and Francis
J. Wall. Rocky Mountain Medical Journal,
66, no. 9 (1969): 40-42.

Lindig, Wolfgang H. Die "zweite Ernte"
bei den Wildbeutern Nordwest-Mexikos.
Anthropologische Gesellschaft in Wien,
Mitteilungen, 90 (1960): 98-104.

Lindig, Wolfgang H. Recht und Sitte,
einige Bemerkungen zu einem rechts
ethnologischen Problem. Baessler-Archiv,
n.F., 7 (1959): 247-255.

Linton, R. Nomad raids and fortified
pueblos. American Antiquity, 10 (1944):
28-32.

Lister, Florence C. Chihuahua; storehouse
of storms. By Florence C. Lister and
Robert H. Lister. Albuquerque,
University of New Mexico Press, 1966.
8, 360 p. illus., maps.

Longacre, Robert E. Grammar discovery
procedures; a field manual. The Hague,
Mouton, 1964. 162 p. (Janua Linguarum,
Series Minor, 33)

Longman, Doris P. Working with Pueblo
Indians in New Mexico. American Dietetic
Association, Journal, 47 (1965): 470-
473.

Loomis, Noel M. Early cattle trails in
southern Arizona. Arizoniana, 3, no. 4
(1962): 18-24.

Lummis, C. F. Land of poco tiempo. New
York, 1893. 310 p.

Lummis, Charles F. General Crook and the
Apache wars. Edited by Turbesé Lummis
Fiske. Flagstaff, Northland Press,
1966. 19, 148 p. illus.

Lummis, Charles F. The land of poco
tiempo. Illus. facsimile ed.
Albuquerque, University of New Mexico
Press, 1966. 9, 310 p. illus.

Lyman, T. S. and T. H. Darrel. Report of
Fray Alonso de Posada. New Mexico
Historical Review, 33 (1958): 285-314.

MacGregor, J. C. Southwestern
archaeology. New York, 1941. 403 p.

Marcson, S. Some methodological
consequences of correlational analysis
in anthropology. American
Anthropologist, n.s., 45 (1943): 588-
601.

Marino Flores, Anselmo. Distribución
municipal de los hablantes de lenguas
indígenas en la República Mexicana.
México, 1963. 70 p. maps. (México,
Instituto Nacional de Antropología e
Historia, Departamento de
Investigaciones Antropologicas,
Publicaciones, 12)

Marinsek, Edward A., et al. The effect of
cultural differences in the education of
Pueblo, [Apache, and Navajo] Indians
[and Spanish Americans]. Albuquerque,
University of New Mexico, College of
Education, 1958-1960. 4 v.

Marriott, A. L. Indians of the Four
Corners. New York, 1952. 229 p.

Marsh, Dick E. Two contemporary Papago
recipes of indigenous plants and the
American Southwest botanical

implication. Kiva, 34, no. 4
(1968/1969): 242-245.

Marti, S. Musica primitiva en Sonora.
YAN, 1 (1953): 10-17.

Martin, D. D. H. Lawrence and Pueblo
religion. Arizona Quarterly, 9 (1953):
219-234.

Mason, J. A. Turquoise mosaics from
northern Mexico. Museum Journal, 20
(1929): 157-175.

Mason, J. Alden. The classification of
the Sonoran languages. In Robert H.
Lowie, ed. Essays in Anthropology
Presented to A. L. Kroeber. Berkeley,
1936: 183-198.

Mason, J. Alden. The native languages of
Middle America. In Clarence L. Hay, et
al., eds. The Maya and Their Neighbors.
New York, 1940: 52-87.

Mason, Joyce Evelyn. The use of Indian
scouts in the Apache wars, 1870-1886.
Dissertation Abstracts International, 31
(1970/1971): 2286A. UM 70-22,837.

Matis, John A. Odontognathic
discrimination of United States Indian
and Eskimo groups. By John A. Matis and
Thomas J. Zwemer. Journal of Dental
Research, 50 (1971): 1245-1248.

Maughan, Scott Jarvis. Francisco Garcés
and New Spain's northwestern frontier,
1768-1781. Dissertation Abstracts, 29
(1968/1969): 2647A-2648A. UM 69-3508.

Mauzy, Wayne L. The Old Palace and the
Pueblo revolt of 1680. El Palacio, 68
(1961): 201-214.

Maxon, James C. Indians of the Lake Mead
Country. Globe, Ariz., Southwest Parks
and Monuments Association, 1971. 64 p.
illus.

Maxon, Mason M. Maxon, scout. Compiled by
James C. Cage. San Antonio, Naylor,
1968. 25 p. map.

McCleneghan, Thomas J. Vh-thaw-hup-ea-ju
(it must happen) promises Gila River
Indians new prosperity. By Thomas J.
McCleneghan and Nancy Gale. Arizona
Review, 17, no. 4 (1968): 1-9.

McGaw, William C. Savage scene; the life
and times of James Kirker, frontier
king. New York, Hastings House, 1972.
11, 242 p. illus.

McGee, W J. The beginning of zooculture.
American Anthropologist, 10 (1897): 215-
230.

McGiboney, J. R. Trachoma among Indians
of the United States of America. América
Indígena, 2, no. 3 (1942): 20-23.

McGrath, G. D., et al. Higher education
of Southwestern Indians with reference
to success and failure. Tempe, 1962-
1963. 2 v. [275 p.]. (Arizona State
University, Indian Education Center,
Cooperative Research Project, 938)

McKelvie, Martha G. Quien sabe? (Who
knows?). Philadelphia, Franklin, 1965.
13, 160 p. illus.

McNitt, Frank. Fort Sumner: a study in
origins. New Mexico Historical Review,
45 (1970): 101-117.

Meaders, Margaret. Some aspects of Indian
affairs in New Mexico. New Mexico
Business, 16, no. 1 (1962): 3-19; 16,
no. 3 (1962): 3-15; 16, no. 7 (1962): 2-
17; 16, no. 8 (1962): 3-23.

Meaders, Margaret. The Indian situation
in New Mexico. Albuquerque, University
of New Mexico, Bureau of Business
Research, 1963. 5, 66 p. illus., map.

Mecham, J. L. The second Spanish
expedition in New Mexico. New Mexico
Historical Review, 1 (1926): 265-291.

Meggers, Betty J. Field testing of
cultural law: a reply to Morris Opler.
Southwestern Journal of Anthropology, 17
(1961): 352-354.

Meinig, D. W. Southwest: three peoples in
geographical change, 1600-1970. New
York, Oxford University Press, 1971.
12, 151 p. illus., maps.

Meline, James F. Two thousand miles on
horseback, Santa Fé and back.
Albuquerque, Horn and Wallace, 1966.
10, 317 p. map.

Melvin, Dorothy M. Parasitologic surveys
on Indian reservations in Montana, South
Dakota, New Mexico, Arizona, and
Wisconsin. By Dorothy M. Melvin and M.
M. Brooke. American Journal of Tropical
Medicine and Hygiene, 11 (1962): 765-
772.

Mendinueta, Pedro Fermín de. Indian and
mission affairs in New Mexico, 1773.
Edited and translated by Marc Simmons.
Santa Fe, Stagecoach Press, 1965.
23 p. map.

Mendizábal, Miguel Othón de. La evolución
del noroeste de México. In his Obras
Completas. Tomo 3. México, 1946: 7-86.

Mera, H. P. Indian silverwork of the
Southwest. Globe, 1959. 128 p.

Mera, H. P. Indian silverwork of the Southwest. Santa Fe, Laboratory of Anthropology, Bulletin, General Series, 17/19 (1944/1945): 1-59.

Mera, H. P. Pueblo Indian embroidery. Santa Fe, Laboratory of Anthropology, Memoirs, 4 (1943): 1-73.

Mera, H. P. Style trends of Pueblo pottery. Santa Fe, Laboratory of Anthropology, Memoirs, 3 (1939): 1-165.

Mera, H. P. The "rain bird": a study in Pueblo design. Santa Fe, Laboratory of Anthropology, Memoirs, 2 (1937): 1-113.

Mera, Harry P. Indian silverwork of the Southwest, illustrated. 2d ed. Globe, Ariz., D. S. King, 1960. 122 p. illus.

Mera, Harry P. Pueblo designs. New York, Dover Publications, 1970. 113 p. illus.

Merbs, Charles F. Anterior tooth loss in Arctic populations. Southwestern Journal of Anthropology, 24 (1968): 20-32.

Mertins, Marshall Louis. The blue god; an epic of Mesa Verde. By Louis Mertins. Los Angeles, W. Ritchie Press, 1968. 256 p.

Mesa Verde Museum. The Mesa Verde Museum. By Richard M. Howard. Mesa Verde National Park, Mesa Verde Museum Association, 1968. 40 p. illus.

Milford, S. J. The twin war god myth cycle. El Palacio, 43 (1937): 1-12, 19-28.

Milke, Wilhelm. Athapaskische chronologie: versuch einer revision. International Journal of American Linguistics, 25 (1959): 182-188.

Miller, David H. The Ives Expedition revisited; a Prussian's impressions. Journal of Arizona History, 13 (1972): 1-25.

Miller, Julius J. The anthropology of Keres identity. Dissertation Abstracts International, 33 (1972/1973): 1361B. UM 72-27,578.

Miller, M. R. T. Pueblo Indian culture as seen by the early Spanish explorers. Los Angeles, 1941. 30 p.

Miller, Marjorie A. Indian arts and crafts. Los Angeles, Nash, 1972. 118 p. illus.

Miller, Wick R. Spanish loanwords in Acoma. International Journal of American Linguistics, 25 (1959): 147-153; 26 (1960): 41-49.

Miller, Wick R. The Shoshonean languages of Uto-Aztecan. In William Bright, ed. Studies in Californian Linguistics. Berkeley and Los Angeles, University of California Press, 1964: 145-148. (California, University, Publications in Linguistics, 34)

Miller, Wick R. Uto-Aztecan cognate sets. Berkeley and Los Angeles, University of California Press, 1967. 5, 83 p. map. (California, University, Publications in Linguistics, 48)

Mindeleff, C. Aboriginal architecture in the United States. American Geographical Society, Bulletin, 30 (1898): 414-427.

Misch, Jürgen. Der letzte Kriegspfad; der Schicksalskampf der Sioux und Apachen. Stuttgart, Union, 1970. 223 p. illus., maps.

Mohr, A. The hunting crook. Masterkey, 25 (1951): 145-154.

Möllhausen, B. Diary of a journey from the Mississippi to the coasts of the Pacific. London, 1858. 2 v.

Monahan, Forrest D., Jr. The Kiowas and New Mexico, 1800-1845. Journal of the West, 8 (1969): 67-75.

Moncus, Herman H. Prairie schooner pirates. New York, Carlton Press, 1963. 191 p. illus.

Monongye, Preston. The new Indian jewelry art of the Southwest. Arizona Highways, 48, no. 6 (1972): 6-11, 46-47.

Moorhead, Max L. The Apache frontier; Jacobo Ugarte and Spanish-Indian relations in northern New Spain, 1769-1791. Norman, University of Oklahoma Press, 1968. 13, 309 p. illus.

Morgan, L. H. Houses and house-life of the American aborigines. Contributions to North American Ethnology, 4 (1881): 1-281.

Morice, A. G. The great Déné race. Anthropos, 1 (1906): 229-277, 483-508, 695-730; 2 (1907): 1-34, 181-196; 4 (1909): 582-606; 5 (1910): 113-142, 419-443, 643-653, 969-990.

Morris, Joyce. An investigation into language-concept development of primary school Pueblo Indian children. Dissertation Abstracts, 27 (1966/1967): 1716A. UM 66-11,723.

Munsell, Marvin Robert. Land and labor at Salt River: household organization in a changing economy. Dissertation Abstracts, 28 (1967/1968): 2243B. UM 67-16,171.

Murphy, Lawrence R. Rayado: pioneer settlement in northeastern New Mexico, 1848-1857. New Mexico Historical Review, 46 (1971): 37-56.

Murphy, Lawrence R. The Beaubien and Miranda land grant; 1841-1846. New Mexico Historical Review, 42 (1967): 27-47.

Neighbours, Kenneth F. The German-Comanche Treaty. Texana, 2 (1964): 311-322.

Nelson, N. C. The Southwest problem. El Palacio, 6 (1919): 132-135.

Neumann, D. L. Southwestern Indians enter modern money economy. El Palacio, 63 (1956): 233-235.

New Mexico Association on Indian Affairs. New Mexico Indians. Santa Fe, 1941. 36 p.

New Mexico, Commission on Alcoholism. BX project: proposed Indian program to combat alcoholism in New Mexico. By Robert Boissiere. Santa Fe, 1960. 39 l.

New Mexico, State Planning Board. Indian lands in New Mexico. Santa Fe, 1936. 176 p.

New Mexico, University, College of Education. The Indian research study: the adjustment of Indian and non-Indian children in the public schools of New Mexico, final report. Albuquerque, 1961. 2 v. (16, 279 l.) illus.

Newcomb, William W., Jr. The Indians of Texas, from prehistoric to modern times. Austin, University of Texas Press, 1961. 404 p. illus.

Newcomb, William W., Jr. The rock art of Texas Indians. Paintings by Forrest Kirkland. Austin, University of Texas Press, 1967. 14, 239 p. illus., maps.

Newman, S. American Indian linguistics in the Southwest. American Anthropologist, 56 (1954): 626-634.

Niswander, Jerry D., et al. Population studies on Southwestern Indian trbies: I. History, culture and genetics of the Papago. American Journal of Human Genetics, 22 (1970): 7-23.

Nitz, H. C. Trophies of grace; echoes from Apacheland. Milwaukee, Northwestern Publishing House, 1962. 65 p.

Nolasco Armas, Margarita. Continuidad y cambio sociocultural en el norte de México. América Indígena, 31 (1971): 323-333.

Nolasco Armas, Margarita. Problemas indígenas en los zonas áridas de México. By Margarita Nolasco, Cecilia Ramírez Cardoso, and Sergio Vivanco. Anuario Indigenista, 28 (1968): 202-213.

Norris, Robert. The effects of selected cultural variables influencing the college performances of Native American Indians. Dissertation Abstracts International, 32 (1971/1972): 6783A. UM 72-13,775.

Nuttall, Donald Andrew. Pedro Fages and the advance of the northern frontier of New Spain, 1767-1782. Dissertation Abstracts, 25 (1964/1965): 3542. UM 64-13,532.

Obregón, B. de. History of 16th century explorations in western America. Ed. by G. P. Hammond and A. Ray. Los Angeles, 1928. 351 p.

Ocaranza, F. Parva crónica de la Sierra Madre y les Pimerias. Instituto Panamericano de Geografía e Historia, Publicación, 64 (1942): 1-156.

Ocaranza, Fernando. Las misiones de Sonora en el año de 1658. Academia Mexicana de la Historia, Memorias, 14 (1955): 119-129.

Och, Joseph. Missionary in Sonora; the travel reports of Joseph Och, S.J., 1755-1767. Translated by Theodore E. Treutlein. San Francisco, 1965. 18, 196 p. maps. (California Historical Society, Special Publication, 40)

O'Conor, Hugo. The interior provinces of New Spain; the report of Hugo O'Conor, January 30, 1776. Translated and edited by Mary Lu Moore and Delmar L. Beene. Arizona and the West, 13 (1971): 265-282.

Officer, J. E. Indians in school. Arizona, University, Bureau of Ethnic Research, American Indian Series, 1 (1956): 1-148.

Ogle, Ralph H. The end of Apache resistance. In Richard N. Ellis, ed. The Western American Indian. Lincoln, University of Nebraska Press, 1972: 90-95.

Oglesby, C. Modern primitive arts, 21-95. New York, 1939.

Oglesby, Catharine. Modern primitive arts of Mexico, Guatemala, and the Southwest. Freeport, N.Y., Books for Libraries Press, 1969. 226 p. illus.

Olsen, Robert W., Jr. Pipe Spring, Arizona, and thereabouts. Journal of Arizona History, 6 (1965): 11-20.

Opler, Morris E. Cultural evolution, Southern Athapaskans, and chronology in theory. Southwestern Journal of Anthropology, 17 (1961): 1-20.

Orozco y Berra, Manuel. Geografía de las lenguas y carta etnográfica de México. México, Impr. de J. M. Andrade y F. Escalante, 1864. 14, 392 p. map.

Ortega, José de. Apostolicos afanes de la Compañía de Jesús. By José de Ortega and Juan Antonio Baltasar. México, Editorial Lagac, 1944. 24, 445 p.

Ortega, José de. Historia del Nayarit, Sonora, Sinaloa y ambas Californias. México, Tipografía de E. Abadiano, 1887. 9, 564 p.

Ortiz, Alfonso. Anecdotes from the Southwest. Anthropology Tomorrow, 9, no. 2 (1963): 44-49.

Ortiz, Alfonso. Dual organization as an operational concept in the Pueblo Southwest. Ethnology, 4 (1965): 389-396.

Ortiz, Alfonso, ed. New perspectives on the Pueblos. Albuquerque, University of New Mexico Press, 1972. 20, 340 p. maps.

Ortiz, Francisco Xavier. Razón de la visita a las misiones de la Provincia de Texas: 2. México, Vargas Rea, 1955. 38 p.

Otermín, Antonio de. Documentos que sobre el levantamiento de los indios del año de 1680. México, Vargas Rea, 1947. 47 p.

Otis, R. Indian art of the Southwest. Santa Fe, 1931.

Owen, Roger C. Notes on remaining indigenous languages in northern Sonora and Baja California Norte, Mexico. Katunob, 1, no. 4 (1960): 14-15.

Owens, Charles S. The American Indian high school dropout in the Southwest. By Charles S. Owens and Willard P. Bass. Altuquerque, Southwestern Cooperative Educational Laboratory, 1969. 43 p. ERIC ED026195.

Packard, Gar. Southwest 1880 with Ben Wittick, pioneer photographer of Indian and frontier life. By Gar and Maggy Packard. Santa Fe, Packard Publications, 1970. 47 p.

Packard, Robert C. Demographic discrimination of American Indian and Alaskan Eskimo groups by means of Bjork analysis. By Robert C. Packard and Thomas J. Zwemer. Journal of Dental Research, 50 (1971): 364-370.

Padfield, Harland Irvine. Technological and social change in farm industries of Arizona. Dissertation Abstracts, 26 (1965/1966): 1861. UM 65-5391.

Paloheimo, L. C. The antelope are fat in summer. Masterkey, 24 (1950): 73-78.

Parman, Donald Lee. The Indian Civilian Conservation Corps. Dissertation Abstracts, 27 (1966/1967): 3819A-3820A. UM 67-3978.

Parsons, E. C. Der spanische Einfluss auf die Märchen der Pueblo-Indianer. Zeitschrift für Ethnologie, 58 (1926): 16-28.

Parsons, E. C. Pueblo Indian religion. Chicago, 1939. 2 v.

Parsons, E. C. Ritual parallels in Pueblo and Plains cultures. American Anthropologist, n.s., 31 (1929): 642-654.

Parsons, E. C. Some Aztec and Pueblo parallels. American Anthropologist, n.s., 35 (1933): 611-631.

Parsons, E. C. Spanish elements in the kachina cult of the Pueblos. International Congress of Americanists, Proceedings, 23 (1928): 582-603.

Parsons, E. C. The house-clan complex of the Pueblos. In Essays in Anthropology Presented to A. L. Kroeber. Berkeley, 1936: 229-231.

Parsons, E. C. The Pueblo Indian clan in folk-lore. Journal of American Folklore, 34 (1921): 209-216.

Parsons, E. C. The religion of the Pueblo Indians. International Congress of Americanists, Proceedings, 21, vol. 1 (1924): 140-161.

Parsons, E. C. Witchcraft among the Pueblos: Indian or Spanish. Man, 27 (1927): 106-112, 125-128.

Parsons, E. C. and R. L. Beals. The sacred clowns of the Pueblo and Mayo-

Yaqui Indians. American Anthropologist, n.s., 36 (1934): 491-514.

Parsons, Mark L. Archeological investigations in Crosby and Dickens counties, Texas during the winter, 1966-1967. Austin, Texas State Building Commission, 1967. 108 p. illus., maps. (Texas, State Building Commission, Archeological Program, 7)

Paxton, S. Gabe, Jr. A study of the composite self-concept of the Southwestern Indian adolescent; an inservice action research project of Sherman Institute. Washington, D.C., Bureau of Indian Affairs, 1966. 32 p. ERIC ED052878.

Pearson, Keith L. "Watch out, you might assimilate". Natural History, 80, no. 6 (1971): 24-33.

Pedersen, Gilbert J. "The townsite is now secure": Tucson incorporates, 1871. Journal of Arizona History, 11 (1970): 151-174.

Peet, S. D. The cliff dwellers and Pueblos. Chicago, 1899.

Pérez de Ribas, Andrés. Historia de los triunfos de nuestra santa fe entre gentes las más bárbaras y fieras del nuevo orbe. Madrid, A. de Paredes, 1645. 20, 763 p.

Pérez de Ribas, Andrés. My life among the savage nations of New Spain. Translated by Tomás Antonio Robertson. Los Angeles, Ward Ritchie Press, 1968. 16, 256 p. illus., maps.

Perrigo, Lynn I. The American Southwest: its people and cultures. New York, Holt, Rinehart and Winston, 1971. 469 p.

Petersen, Karen Daniels. Plains Indian art from Fort Marion. Norman, University of Oklahoma Press, 1971. 20, 340 p. illus.

Peterson, Charles S. The Hopi and the Mormons; 1858-1873. Utah Historical Quarterly, 39 (1971): 179-194.

Peterson, Charles Sharon. Settlement on the Little Colorado 1873-1900: a study of the processes and institutions of Mormon expansion. Dissertation Abstracts, 28 (1967/1968): 2629A-2630A. UM 67-17,089.

Petrakis, Nicholas L. Cerumen in American Indians: genetic implications of sticky and dry types. By Nicholas L. Petrakis, Kathryn T. Molohon, and David J. Tepper. Science, 158 (1967): 1192-1193.

Philp, Kenneth. Albert B. Fall and the protest from the Pueblos, 1921-23. Arizona and the West, 12 (1970): 237-254.

Pinnow, Heinz-Jürgen. Genetic relationship vs. borrowing in Na-dene. International Journal of American Linguistics, 34 (1968): 204-211.

Pinnow, Heinz-Jürgen. Grundzüge einer historischen Lautlehre des Tlingit. Ein Versuch. Wiesbaden, Otto Harrassowitz, 1966. 166 p.

Pinnow, Heinz-Jürgen. On the historical position of Tlingit. International Journal of American Linguistics, 30 (1964): 155-164.

Pi-Sunyer, Oriol. Religion and witchcraft: Spanish attitudes and Pueblo reactions. Anthropologica, n.s., 2 (1960): 66-75.

Poehlman, Charles H., et al. Know your Nevada Indians. Carson City, Nevada State Department of Education, 1967. 87 l. illus., maps. ERIC ED011219.

Pogue, J. E. The aboriginal use of turquoise in North America. American Anthropologist, n.s., 14 (1912): 437-466.

Polzer, Charles William. The evolution of the Jesuit mission system in northwestern New Spain, 1600-1767. Dissertation Abstracts International, 33 (1972/1973): 5102A. UM 73-6731.

Posey, W. C. Trachoma among the Indians of the Southwest. American Medical Association, Journal, 88 (1927): 1618-1619.

Pospisil, F. Etnologické materiálie z jihozápadu U.S.A. Brno, 1932. 256 p.

Poston, William K., Jr., ed. Teaching Indian pupils in public schools. (Proceedings of a seminar, April 27-May 2, 1967). Mesa, Ariz., Mesa Public Schools, 1967. 69 p. (U.S., Office of Education, Division of Plans and Supplementary Centers, Report, DPSC-66-1284) ERIC ED021664.

Potts, Alfred M., 2d. Developing curriculum for Indian children. By Alfred M. Potts, 2d. and Mamie Sizemore. Alamosa, Colo., Adams State College, Center for Cultural Studies, 1964. 106 l. ERIC ED012188.

Pourade, Richard F. Anza conquers the desert: the Anza expeditions from Mexico to California and the founding of San Francisco: 1774 to 1776. San Diego,

Copley Press, 1971. 224 p. illus., maps.

Powell, J. W. Canyons of the Colorado. Meadville, 1895. 400 p.

Powell, Philip W., comp. War and peace on the North Mexican frontier: a documentary record. Vol. 1. Madrid, Ediciones Jose Porrua Turanzas, 1971. 27, 276 p. illus. (Colección Chimalistac de Libros y Documentos acerca de la Nueva España, 32)

Pradeau, Alberto Francisco. Descripción de Sonora del Padre Nentuig. México, Archivo General de la Nación, Boletín, 26 (1955): 237-257.

Pradeau, Alberto Francisco. Nentuig's "Description of Sonora". Mid-America, 35 (1953): 81-90.

Prestwich, Sheldon. The influence of two counseling methods on the physical and verbal aggression of preschool Indian children. Part of the final report on Head Start evaluation and research: 1968-1969 to the Office of Economic Opportunity. Austin, University of Texas, Child Development Evaluation and Research Center, 1969. 93 p. (U.S., Office of Economic Opportunity, Report, OEO-4115) ERIC ED037243.

Prosnitz, Leonard R. Unusual features of postpartum hypopituitarism among American Indians of the Southwest. By Leonard R. Prosnitz and Edward E. Wallach. Obstetrics and Gynecology, 29 (1967): 351-357.

Putnam, F. W. Archaeological and ethnological collections. In Report upon United States Geographical Surveys West of the One Hundredth Meridian. Vol. 7. Washington, D.C., 1879: 1-497.

Quinn, Charles R., ed. Edward H. Davis and the Indians of the Southwest United States and Northwest Mexico. Edited by Charles R. Quinn and Elena Quinn. Downey, Calif., E. Quinn, 1965. 224 p. illus.

Ramos, Antonio. Mission San Jose de Tumacacori and San Xavier del Bac in 1774. Edited by Louis Baldonado. Kiva, 24, no. 4 (1958/1959): 21-24.

Rasch, Philip J. Alias "Whiskey Jim". Panhandle-Plains Historical Review, 36 (1963): 103-114.

Reagan, A. B. Don Diego. New York, 1914. 352 p.

Reed, E. K. Aspects of acculturation in the Southwest. Acta Americana, 2 (1944): 62-69.

Reed, E. K. Transition to history in the Pueblo Southwest. American Anthropologist, 56 (1954): 592-603.

Reed, E. K. Turkeys in Southwestern archaeology. El Palacio, 58 (1951): 195-205.

Reed, Erik K. Cultural continuity from pre-Spanish archeological groups to modern Indian tribes in the Southwestern United States. In Internationale Amerikanistenkongress, 34th. 1960, Wien. Akten. Horn-Wien, Berger, 1962: 298-300.

Reeve, F. D. Federal Indian policy in New Mexico, 1858-80. New Mexico Historical Review, 12 (1937): 218-269; 13 (1938): 14-62, 146-191, 261-313.

Reeve, Frank D. Navaho foreign affairs, 1795-1846. Edited by Eleanor B. Adams and John L. Kessell. New Mexico Historical Review, 46 (1971): 101-132, 223-251.

Reeve, Frank D. Navaho-Spanish diplomacy, 1770-1790. New Mexico Historical Review, 35 (1960): 200-235.

Reeve, Frank D. The Navaho-Spanish peace: 1720's-1770's. New Mexico Historical Review, 34 (1959): 9-40.

Reichard, G. A. A few instances of cultural resistance in Southwest North America. International Congress of Americanists, Proceedings, 22, vol. 2 (1926): 289-297.

Reichenbach, Dennis D. Autopsy incidence of diseases among Southwestern American Indians. Archives of Pathology, 84 (1967): 81-86.

Renaud, E. B. Evolution of population and dwelling in the Indian Southwest. Social Forces, 7 (1928): 263-270.

Renaud, E. B. Fabrication de la céramique indienne du sud-ouest des États-Unis. Société des Américanistes, Journal, n.s., 17 (1925): 101-117.

Renaud, E. B. Notes sur le céramique indienne du sud-ouest des États-Unis. Société des Américanistes, Journal, n.s., 17 (1925): 85-100.

Reno, Philip. Rebellion in New Mexico--1837. New Mexico Historical Review, 40 (1965): 197-213.

Ricard, Robert. The spiritual conquest of Mexico. Translated by Lesley Byrd Simpson. Berkeley, University of California Press, 1966. 12, 423 p.

Rice, Josiah M. A cannoneer in Navajo country; journal of Private Josiah M. Rice, 1851. Edited by Richard H. Dillon. Denver, Published for the Denver Public Library by the Old West Publishing, 1970. 123 p. illus., map.

Riley, Carroll L. Color-direction symbolism. An example of Mexican-Southwestern contacts. América Indígena, 23 (1963): 49-60.

Riley, Carroll L. Early Spanish-Indian communication in the greater Southwest. New Mexico Historical Review, 46 (1971): 285-314.

Rister, Carl C. The Southwestern frontier, 1865-1881. New York, Russell and Russell, 1969. 336 p. illus., maps.

Robbins, W. J. Some aspects of Pueblo Indian religion. Harvard Theological Review, 34 (1941): 25-49.

Roberts, Alan H. Cross-cultural study of relationships among four dimensions of time perspective. By Alan H. Roberts and Joel E. Greene. Perceptual and Motor Skills, 33 (1971): 163-173.

Roberts, Don L. A brief guide to Rio Grande Pueblo dances. Southwestern Association on Indian Affairs, Quarterly, 1, no. 2 (1964): 12-15.

Roberts, F. H. H. A survey of Southwestern archaeology. American Anthropologist, n.s., 37 (1935): 1-35.

Roberts, F. H. H. Archaeology in the Southwest. American Antiquity, 3 (1937): 3-33.

Roberts, F. H. H. The ruins at Kiatuthlanna. U.S. Bureau of American Ethnology, Bulletin, 100 (1931): 1-195.

Roberts, H. H. Indian music from the Southwest. Natural History, 27 (1927): 257-265.

Robinson, B. Basketmakers of Arizona. Arizona Highways, 27, no. 8 (1951): 30-39.

Robinson, B. The basket weavers of Arizona. Albuquerque, 1955. 176 p.

Roediger, V. M. Ceremonial costumes of the Pueblo Indians. New York, 1938. 136 p.

Roediger, V. M. Ceremonial costumes of the Pueblo Indians. Berkeley, 1941. 234 p.

Roessel, Robert A., Jr. Indian education in Arizona. Journal of American Indian Education, 1, no. 1 (1961/1962): 33-38.

Roessel, Robert L. Education for the adult Indian community. Tempe, Arizona State University, College of Education, 1964. 338 p. ERIC ED017350.

Romer, Margaret. General Howard made Apache peace in pow-wow. Journal of the West, 1 (1962): 98-102.

Rosenbaum, Louis J. Dexamethasone testing in Southwestern Indians. By Louis J. Rosenbaum, Ellen Alton, and Bernard Becker. Investigative Ophthalmology, 9 (1970): 325-330.

Rubín de la Borbolla, D. F. La antropología física y el norte de México. In El Norte de México y el Sur de Estados Unidos. México, 1943: 166-171.

Ruby, Jay William. Culture contact between aboriginal Southern California and the Southwest. Dissertation Abstracts International, 31 (1970/1971): 1673B. UM 70-19,890.

Rudolph, Ross. Biliary cancer among Southwestern American Indians. By Ross Rudolph, J. J. Cohen, and R. H. Gascoigne. Arizona Medicine, 27, no. 10 (1970): 1-4.

Rue, Norman L. Pesh-Bi-Yalti speaks White Man's talking wire in Arizona. Journal of Arizona History, 12 (1971): 229-262.

Ruiz, José Francisco. Report on the Indian tribes of Texas in 1828. Translated by Georgette Dorn. Edited by John C. Ewers. New Haven, Yale University Library, 1972. 18 p.

Rund, Nadine H. Demographic and socio-cultural characteristics. By Nadine H. Rund, Ella G. Rumley, and Herman Siegel. Tucson, Arizona Division of Indian Health, Health Program Systems Center, 1968. 2 v.

Russell, Traylor. Kendall Lewis. Texana, 9 (1971): 17-32.

Ryan, Pat M. John P. Clum: "boss-with-the-white-forehead". Arizoniana, 5, no. 3 (1964): 48-60.

Saldaña, Nancy H. La Malinche: her representation in dances of Mexico and the United States. Ethnomusicology, 10 (1966): 298-309.

Salpointe, Jean Baptiste. Soldiers of the cross; notes on the ecclesiastical history of New Mexico, Arizona, and Colorado. Albuquerque, C. Horn, 1967. 14, 299 p. illus.

Salpointe, John Baptiste. Arizona Catholicism in 1878: a report by John Baptiste Salpointe. Edited by Francis J. Weber. Journal of Arizona History, 9 (1968): 119-139.

Salwen, Bert. The introduction of leather footgear in the Pueblo area. Ethnohistory, 7 (1960): 206-238.

Sando, Joe S. The Pueblo pueblo . . . leadership and government. Indian Historian, 2, no. 3 (1969): 19-21.

Sando, Joseph. Joseph Naranjo, Capitan-Mayor de la Guerra. Indian Historian, 3, no. 3 (1970): 46-48.

Sauer, C. O. Aboriginal population of northwestern Mexico. Ibero-Americana, 10 (1935): 1-33.

Sauer, C. O. The distribution of aboriginal tribes and languages in northwestern Mexico. Ibero-Americana, 5 (1934): 1-90.

Sauer, C. O. The road to Cibola. Ibero-Americana, 3 (1932): 1-58.

Sauer, J. Amaranths as dye plants among the Pueblo peoples. Southwestern Journal of Anthropology, 6 (1950): 412-415.

Schaafsma, Polly. Rock art in the Navajo reservoir district. Santa Fe, Museum of New Mexico Press, 1963. 74 p. illus., maps. (Museum of New Mexico, Papers in Anthropology, 7)

Schäfer, Georg. Im Reiche des Mescál; eine indianische Legende. Eremen, Schünemann, 1968. 36 p. illus.

Schellie, Don. Vast domain of blood; the story of the Camp Grant massacre. Los Angeles, Westernlore Press, 1968. 17, 268 p. map. (Great West and Indian Series, 37)

Schilling, Frank A. Military posts of the old frontier: Arizona-New Mexico. Southern California Quarterly, 42 (1960): 133-149.

Schmutz, Richard. Jesuit missionary methods in northwestern Mexico. Journal of the West, 8 (1969): 76-89.

Scholes, F. V. Civil government and society in New Mexico in the seventeenth century. New Mexico Historical Review, 10 (1935): 71-111.

Schroeder, Albert H. Navajo and Apache relationships west of the Rio Grande. El Palacio, 70, no. 3 (1963): 5-23.

Schroeder, Albert H. Shifting for survival in the Spanish Southwest. New Mexico Historical Review, 43 (1968): 291-310.

Schroeder, Albert H. Spanish entradas, the big houses, and the Indian groups of northern Mexico. Artifact, 7, no. 4 (1969): 15-22.

Schroeder, Albert H. The language of the Saline Pueblos; Piro or Tiwa? New Mexico Historical Review, 39 (1964): 235-249.

Schroeder, Gail D. San Juan pottery: methods and incentives. El Palacio, 71, no. 1 (1964): 45-51.

Schuetz, Mardith K. Historic background of the Mission San Antonio de Valero. Austin, Tex., State Building Commission, 1966. 46 p. illus., maps. (Texas, State Building Commission Archeological Program, 1)

Schuetz, Mardith K. The history and archeology of Mission San Juan Capistrano, San Antonio, Texas. Vol. 1. Historical documentation and description of the structures. Austin, Tex., State building Commission, 1968. 2, 263 p. illus., maps. (Texas, State Building Commission Archeological Program, 10)

Scott, George Richard. Dental morphology: a genetic study of American White families and variation in living Southwest Indians. Dissertation Abstracts International, 34 (1973/1974): 2436B. UM 73-28,655.

Sebag, Lucien. L'invention du monde chez les Indiens Pueblos. Paris, F. Maspero, 1971. 506 p. illus.

Secoy, F. R. The identity of the "Paduca". American Anthropologist, 53 (1951): 525-542.

Seltzer, C. C. Racial prehistory in the Southwest and the Hawikuh Zunis. Harvard University, Peabody Museum of American Archaeology and Ethnology, Papers, 23 (1944): 1-37.

Serven, James E. The gun: an instrument of destiny in Arizona. Arizoniana, 5, no. 3 (1964): 14-28.

Shimkin, D. B. The Uto-Aztecan system of kinship terminology. American Anthropologist, n.s., 43 (1941): 223-245.

Sides, D. S. Decorative art of the Southwestern Indians. Santa Ana, 1936.

Sides, Dorothy S. Decorative art of the Southwestern Indians. New York, Dover, 1961. 18, 50 p. illus.

Sievers, Maurice L. A study of achlorhydria among Southwestern American Indians. American Journal of Gastroenterology, 45 (1966): 99-108.

Sievers, Maurice L. Cigarette and alcohol usage by Southwestern American Indians. American Journal of Public Health, 58 (1968): 71-82.

Sievers, Maurice L. Coccidioidomycosis among Southwestern American Indians. American Review of Respiratory Diseases, 90 (1964): 920-926.

Sievers, Maurice L. Disease patterns among Southwestern Indians. U.S., Public Health Service, Public Health Reports, 81 (1966): 1075-1083.

Sievers, Maurice L. Duodenal ulcer among Southwestern American Indians. By Maurice L. Sievers and James R. Marquis. Gastroenterology, 42 (1962): 566-569.

Sievers, Maurice L. Lung cancer among Indians of the Southwestern United States. By Maurice L. Sievers and Samuel L. Cohen. Annals of Internal Medicine, 54 (1961): 912-915.

Sievers, Maurice L. Myocardial infarction among Southwestern American Indians. Annals of Internal Medicine, 67 (1967): 800-807.

Sievers, Maurice L. Serum cholesterol levels in Southwestern American Indians. Journal of Chronic Diseases, 21 (1968): 107-115.

Sievers, Maurice L. The new Phoenix Indian Medical Center: a history of its predecessors. Arizona Medicine, 28 (1971): 435-438.

Sievers, Maurice L. The Southwestern American Indian's burden: biliary disease. By Maurice L. Sievers and James R. Marquis. American Medical Association, Journal, 182 (1962): 570-572.

Silverberg, Robert. The old ones: Indians of the American Southwest. Greenwich, Conn., New York Graphic Society, 1965. 269 p. illus., map.

Silverberg, Robert. The Pueblo Revolt. New York, Weybright and Talley, 1970. 216 p. map.

Simmons, Marc. Settlement patterns and village plans in colonial New Mexico. Journal of the West, 8 (1969): 7-21.

Simmons, Marc. Tlascalans in the Spanish borderlands. New Mexico Historical Review, 39 (1964): 101-110.

Simpson, J. H. Journal of a military reconnaissance from Santa Fe, New Mexico, to the Navajo country. Philadelphia, 1852.

Simpson, James Hervey. Navaho expedition; journal of a military reconnaissance from Santa Fe, New Mexico, to the Navaho country made in 1849. Edited by Frank McNitt. Norman, University of Oklahoma Press, 1964. 79, 296 p. illus.

Simpson, R. D. The coyote in Southwestern Indian tradition. Masterkey, 32 (1958): 43-54.

Sizemore, Mamie. Closing the gap in Indian education. Phoenix, Arizona State Department of Education, 1967. 16 p. ERIC ED011475.

Smiley, Winn Whiting. Ammon M. Tenney, Mormon missionary to the Indians. Journal of Arizona History, 13 (1972): 82-108.

Smith, Anne M. Indian Head Start. El Palacio, 75, no. 4 (1968): 12-28.

Smith, Anne Marie. Indian education in New Mexico. Albuquerque, 1968. 8, 52 p. map. (New Mexico, University, Division of Government Research, Publications, 77) ERIC ED025345.

Smith, Anne Marie. New Mexico Indians; economic, educational, and social problems. Santa Fe, Museum of New Mexico, 1966. 165 p. (Museum of New Mexico, Research Records, RR-1) ERIC ED019172.

Smith, M. Estellie. Notes on an ethnolinguistic study of governing. In M. Estellie Smith, ed. Studies in Linguistics in Honor of George L. Trager. The Hague, Mouton, 1972: 487-501. (Janua Linguarum, Series Maior, 52)

Smith, M. Estellie. Southwestern studies: a view to the future. Human Organization, 30 (1971): 427-436.

Smith, Ralph A. Apache plunder trails southward, 1831-1840. New Mexico Historical Review, 37 (1962): 20-42.

Smith, Ralph A. Apache "ranching" below the Gila, 1841-1845. Arizoniana, 3, no. 4 (1962): 1-17.

Smith, Ralph A. The "King of New Mexico" and the Doniphan Expedition. New Mexico Historical Review, 38 (1963): 29-55.

Smith, Ralph A. The scalp hunt in Chihuahua--1849. New Mexico Historical Review, 40 (1965): 116-140.

Smith, Ralph A. The scalp hunter in the borderlands 1835-1850. In Roger L. Nichols and George R. Adams, eds. The American Indian: Past and Present. Waltham, Xerox College Publishing, 1971: 156-167.

Snyder, Richard G. Hyperodontia in prehistoric Southwest Indians. Southwestern Journal of Anthropology, 16 (1960): 492-502.

Sowell, Andrew J. Early settlers and Indian fighters of Southwest Texas. New York, Argosy-Antiquarian, 1964. 2 v. (8, 844 p.) illus.

Spencer, F. C. Education of the Pueblo child. New York, 1899. 93 p.

Spicer, E. H. Spanish-Indian acculturation in the Southwest. American Anthropologist, 56 (1954): 663-678.

Spicer, E. H. Worlds apart--cultural differences in the modern Southwest. Arizona Quarterly, 13 (1957): 197-229.

Spicer, Edward H. Cycles of conquest. Tucson, University of Arizona Press, 1962. 12, 609 p. illus., maps.

Spicer, Edward H. European expansion and the enclavement of Southwestern Indians. In Roger L. Nichols and George R. Adams, eds. The American Indian: Past and Present. Waltham, Xerox College Publishing, 1971: 86-95.

Spicer, Edward H. Northwest Mexico: introduction. In Evon Z. Vogt, volume editor. Handbook of Middle American Indians. Vol. 8. Austin, University of Texas Press, 1969: 777-791.

Spicer, Edward H. Paths to civilization. In Deward E. Walker, Jr., ed. The Emergent Native Americans. Boston, Little, Brown, 1972: 97-115.

Spicer, Edward H., ed. Plural society in the Southwest. Edited by Edward H. Spicer and Raymond H. Thompson. New York, Interbook, 1972. 8, 367 p. illus., maps.

Spier, L. Havasupai ethnography. American Museum of Natural History, Anthropological Papers, 29 (1928): 81-392.

Spier, L. Problems arising from the cultural position of the Havasupai. American Anthropologist, n.s., 31 (1929): 213-222.

Spinden, H. J. Indian dances of the Southwest. American Museum Journal, 15 (1915): 103-115.

Spring, John A. John Spring's Arizona. Edited by A. M. Gustafson. Tucson, University of Arizona Press, 1966. 326 p. illus.

Spuhler, J. N. Some problems in the physical anthropology of the American Southwest. American Anthropologist, 56 (1954): 604-619.

Standley, P. C. Some useful native plants of New Mexico. Smithsonian Institution, Annual Report of the Board of Regents (1911): 447-463.

Starnes, Gary Bertram. Juan de Ugalde (1729-1816) and the Provincias Internas of Coahuila and Texas. Dissertation Abstracts International, 32 (1971/1972): 5722A. UM 72-12,491.

Steece, H. M. Corn culture among the Indians of the Southwest. Natural History, 21 (1921): 414-424.

Steen, Charlie R. Tumacacori interior decorations. By Charlie R. Steen and Rutherford J. Gettens. Arizoniana, 3, no. 3 (1962): 7-33.

Steward, J. H. Ecological aspects of Southwestern society. Anthropos, 32 (1937): 87-104.

Steward, J. H. Lineage to clan. In his Theory of Culture Change. Urbana, 1955: 151-172.

Stewart, G. R. Conservation in Pueblo culture. Scientific Monthly, 51 (1940): 201-220, 329-340.

Stewart, G. R. and M. Donnelly. Soil and water economy in the Pueblo Southwest. Scientific Monthly, 56 (1943): 31-44, 134-144.

Stewart, Kenneth M. A brief history of the Chemehuevi Indians. Kiva, 34, no. 1 (1968/1969): 9-27.

Stewart, Kenneth M. A brief history of the Mohave Indians since 1850. Kiva, 34, no. 4 (1968/1969): 219-236.

Stewart, Kenneth M. Scalps and scalpers in Mohave Indian culture. El Palacio, 76, no. 2 (1969): 26-30.

Stewart, Omer C. Ute Indians: before and after White contact. Utah Historical Quarterly, 34 (1966): 40-61.

Strong, W. D. An analysis of Southwestern society. American Anthropologist, n.s., 29 (1927): 1-61.

Stucki, Larry Roland. The entropy theory of human behavior: Indian miners in search of the ultrastable state during a prolonged copper strike. Dissertation Abstracts International, 32 (1971/1972): 685B-686B. UM 71-21,627.

Summerhayes, Martha. Vanished Arizona: recollections of the Army life of a New England woman. Glorieta, N.M., Rio Grande Press, 1970. 319 p.

Swadesh, Morris. Linguistic classification in the Southwest. In Dell H. Hymes and William E. Bittle, eds. Studies in Southwestern Ethnolinguistics. The Hague, Mouton, 1967: 281-309. (Studies in General Anthropology, 3)

Swadesh, Morris. Mapas de clasificación lingüística de México y las Américas. México, 1959. 36 p. illus., maps. (México, Universidad Nacional Autónoma de México, Instituto de Historia, Publicaciones, 51)

Switzer, Ronald R. The origin and significance of snake-lightning cults in the Pueblo Southwest. El Paso, 1972. 3, 48 p. illus. (El Paso Archaeological Society, Special Report, 11)

Szasz, Margaret Garretson. Indian reform in a decade of prosperity. Montana, the Magazine of Western History, 20, no. 1 (1970): 16-27.

Tanner, C. L. Basketry of the modern Southwest Indians. Kiva, 9 (1944): 18-26.

Tanner, C. L. Contemporary Southwest Indian silver. Kiva, 25, no. 3 (1960): 1-22.

Tanner, C. L. Coral among Southwestern Indians. In For the Dean. Essays in Anthropology in Honor of Byron Cummings. Tucson, 1950: 117-132.

Tanner, C. L. Life forms in prehistoric pottery of the Southwest. Kiva, 8 (1943): 26-32.

Tanner, C. L. Pottery of the modern Southwestern Indians. Kiva, 10 (1944): 3-12.

Tanner, C. L. Southwest Indian painting. Tucson, 1957. 175 p.

Tanner, C. L. and F. Connolly. Petroglyphs in the Southwest. Kiva, 3 (1938): 13-16.

Tanner, Clara Lee. Southwest Indian craft arts. Tucson, University of Arizona Press, 1968. 206 p. illus., map.

Tanner, Clara Lee. The influence of the White Man on Southwest Indian art. Ethnohistory, 7 (1960): 137-150.

Taub, A. Southwestern Indian poetry. Arizona Quarterly, 6 (1950): 236-243.

Taylor, Benjamin J. Arizona Indian demographic data: needs and recommendations. By Benjamin J. Taylor and John Helmkamp. Phoenix, Arizona Department of Economic Planning and Development [n.d.]. 4, 105 p.

Taylor, Benjamin J. Indian manpower resources in the Southwest: a pilot study. By Benjamin J. Taylor and Dennis J. O'Connor. Tempe, Arizona State University, 1969. 26, 374 p.

Taylor, Benjamin J. The reservation Indian and mainstream economic life. Arizona Business Bulletin, 17 (Dec. 1970): 12-22.

Taylor, Joe F., ed. The Indian campaign on the Staked Plains, 1874-1875. Panhandle-Plains Historical Review, 34 (1961): 1-216; 35 (1962): 215-368.

Taylor, Morris F. Campaigns against the Jicarilla Apache, 1854. New Mexico Historical Review, 44 (1969): 269-291.

Taylor, Morris F. Campaigns against the Jicarilla Apache, 1855. New Mexico Historical Review, 45 (1970): 119-136.

Taylor, Morris F. Fort Massachusetts. Colorado Magazine, 45 (1968): 120-142.

Taylor, Morris F. Plains Indians on the New Mexico-Colorado border: the last phase, 1870-1876. New Mexico Historical Review, 46 (1971): 315-336.

Taylor, V. H. and J. Hammons. The letters of Antonio Martinez. Austin, 1957. 374 p.

Taylor, Walter W. Archaeology and language in western North America. American Antiquity, 27 (1961/1962): 71-81.

Terrell, John U. Apache chronicle. New York, World, 1972. 15, 411 p. illus.

Texas, State Library, Austin, Archives Division. Texas Indian papers. Edited by Dorman H. Winfrey, et al. Austin, 1959-1966. 5 v. illus., maps.

Thiel, Richard Henry. An analysis of social-cultural factors and performance of primary grade children. Dissertation Abstracts, 29 (1968/1969): 4394A. UM 69-9043.

Thomas, A. B. After Coronado. Norman, 1935. 307 p.

Thomas, A. B. The Plains Indians and New Mexico, 1751-1778. Albuquerque, 1940. 232 p.

Thomas, C. and J. R. Swanton. Indian languages of Mexico and Central America. U.S. Bureau of American Ethnology, Bulletin, 44 (1911): 1-108.

Thompson, H. Atoms and the morning star. Land, 9 (1950): 41-45.

Thrapp, Dan L. General Crook and the Sierra Madre adventure. Norman, University of Oklahoma Press, 1971. 25, 196 p.

Thrapp, Dan L. The conquest of Apacheria. Norman, University of Oklahoma Press, 1967. 16, 405 p. illus., maps.

Toulouse, J. H., Jr. Cremation among the Indians of New Mexico. American Antiquity, 10 (1944): 65-74.

Townsend, Irving D. Reading achievement of eleventh and twelfth grade Indian students. Journal of American Indian Education, 3, no. 1 (1963/1964): 9-10.

Trager, G. L. Linguistic history and ethnologic history in the Southwest. Washington Academy of Sciences, Journal, 41 (1951): 341-343.

Trager, George L. The Tanoan settlement of the Rio Grande area: a possible chronology. In Dell H. Hymes and William E. Bittle, eds. Studies in Southwestern Ethnolinguistics. The Hague, Mouton, 1967: 335-350. (Studies in General Anthropology, 3)

Turner, Christy G., II. Household size of prehistoric Western Pueblo Indians. By Christy G. Turner, II and Laurel Lofgren. Southwestern Journal of Anthropology, 22 (1966): 117-132.

Tweedie, M. Jean. Notes on the history and adaptation of the Apache tribes. American Anthropologist, 70 (1968): 1132-1142.

Twitchell, R. E. Pueblo Indian land tenures in New Mexico and Arizona. El Palacio, 12 (1922): 31-33, 38-61.

Tyler, Barbara Ann. Cochise: Apache war leader, 1858-1861. Journal of Arizona History, 6 (1965): 1-10.

Tyler, Hamilton A. Pueblo gods and myths. Norman, University of Oklahoma Press, 1964. 22, 313 p. illus., map.

Tyler, S. Lyman. The report of Fray Alonso de Posada in relation to Quivira and Teguayo. By S. Lyman Tyler and H. Darrel Taylor. New Mexico Historical Review, 33 (1958): 285-314.

Underhill, R. M. Ceremonial patterns in the greater Southwest. American Ethnological Society, Monographs, 13 (1948): 1-62.

Underhill, R. M. First penthouse dwellers of America. Rev. ed. Santa Fe, 1946. 161 p.

Underhill, R. M. Intercultural relations in the greater Southwest. American Anthropologist, 56 (1954): 645-656.

Underhill, R. M. Pueblo crafts. Indian Handcrafts, 7 (1944): 1-147.

Underhill, R. M. Workaday life of the Pueblos. Indian Life and Customs Pamphlets, 4 (n.d.): 1-174.

Underhill, Ruth M. Indians of the Southwest. Garden City, N. Doubleday, 1966. 64 p. illus., maps.

U.S., Army, Corps of Topographical Engineers. Abert's New Mexico report, 1846-'47. Albuquerque, Horn and Wallace, 1962. 7, 182 p. illus., map.

U.S., Board of Indian Commissioners. Peace with the Apaches of New Mexico and Arizona. Report of Vincent Colyer. Freeport, N.Y., Books for Libraries Press, 1971. 58 p.

U.S., Bureau of Indian Affairs. Indians of Arizona. Washington, D.C., Government Printing Office, 1968. 28 p. ERIC ED028872.

Utley, Robert M. Fort Davis National Historic Site, Texas. Washington, D.C., 1965. 62 p. illus., maps. (National Park Service Historical Handbook Series, 38)

Utley, Robert M. The range cattle industry in the Big Bend of Texas. Southwestern Historical Quarterly, 69 (1965/1966): 419-441.

Utley, Robert M. The reservation trader in Navajo history. El Palacio, 68 (1961): 5-27.

Villaseñor, David V. Tapestries in sand; the spirit of Indian sandpainting. Rev. ed. Healdsburg, Calif., Naturegraph, 1966. 112 p. illus.

Vivo Escoto, Jorge A. Caracteres de las culturas del norte de México. In Jorge A. Vivó, ed. México Prehispánico. México, 1946: 323-330.

Vlahcevic, Z. R., et al. Relation of bile acid pool size to the formation of lithogenic bile in female Indians of the Southwest. Gastroenterology, 62 (1972): 73-83.

Voegelin, Carl F. Languages of the world: Ibero-Caucasian and Pidgin-Creole. Fascicle one. By C. F. Voegelin and F. M. Voegelin. Anthropological Linguistics, 6, no. 8 (1964): 1-71.

Voegelin, Carl F. The language situation in Arizona as part of the Southwest culture area. By C. F. Voegelin, F. M. Voegelin, and Noel W. Schutz, Jr. In Dell H. Hymes and William E. Bittle, eds. Studies in Southwestern Ethnolinguistics. The Hague, Mouton, 1967: 403-454. (Studies in General Anthropology, 3)

Wadsworth, B. Design motifs of the Pueblo Indians. San Antonio, 1957. 96 p.

Wagner, G. Entwicklung und Verbreitung des Peyote-Kultes. Baessler-Archiv, 15 (1932): 59-144.

Walker, Henry P. George Crook--"the Gray Fox"; prudent, compassionate Indian fighter. Montana, the Magazine of Western History, 17, no. 2 (1967): 2-13.

Wallace, Andrew. General August V. Kautz in Arizona, 1874-1878. Arizoniana, 4, no. 4 (1963): 54-65.

Wallace, Andrew. The image of Arizona; pictures from the past. Albuquerque, University of New Mexico Press, 1971. 224 p.

Wallach, Edward E. Patient acceptance of oral contraceptives. I. The American Indian. By Edward E. Wallach, Alan E. Beer, and Celso-Ramon Garcia. American Journal of Obstetrics and Gynecology, 97 (1967): 984-991.

Wallen, Henry Davies. Prisoners without walls; Fort Sumner in 1864. Edited by John Wilson. El Palacio, 74, no. 1 (1967): 10-28.

Ward, J. Report. U.S. Commissioner of Indian Affairs, Annual Reports (1864): 187-195.

Warner, H. J. Notes on the results of trachoma work by the Indian Service in Arizona and New Mexico. United States Public Health Service, Public Health Reports, 44 (1929): 2913-2920.

Warner, Michael J. Protestant missionary activity among the Navajo, 1890-1912. New Mexico Historical Review, 45 (1970): 209-232.

Warner, Ted J. Don Félix Martínez and the Santa Fe Presidio, 1693-1730. New Mexico Historical Review, 45 (1970): 269-310.

Warner, Ted J. Frontier defense. New Mexico Historical Review, 41 (1966): 5-19.

Warren, Helene. Tonque: one pueblo's glaze pottery industry dominated Middle Rio Grande commerce. El Palacio, 76, no. 2 (1969): 36-42.

Waterman, T. T. Ornamental designs in Southwestern pottery. Indian Notes, 7 (1930): 497-522.

Waters, F. Masked gods. Albuquerque, 1950. 438 p.

Watkins, F. E. Southwestern Athapascan women. Southwestern Lore, 10 (1944): 32-35.

Watson, E. L. The cult of the mountain lion. El Palacio, 34 (1933): 95-109.

Wayland, Virginia. Apache playingcards. Masterkey, 35 (1961): 84-98.

Weber, David Joseph. The Taos trappers: the fur trade from New Mexico, 1540-1846. Dissertation Abstracts, 28 (1967/1968): 3622A. UM 68-3488.

Weddle, Robert S. San Juan Bautista; gateway to Spanish Texas. Austin, University of Texas Press, 1968. 14, 469 p. illus., maps.

Wedel, Waldo R. Coronado's route to Quivira 1541. Plains Anthropologist, 15 (1970): 161-168.

Wellman, Klaus F. Kokopelli of Indian paleology. Hunchbacked rain priest, hunting magician, and Don Juan of the old Southwest. American Medical Association, Journal, 212 (1970): 1678-1682.

Welsh, Dean C. Colorado River Tribes public library first in the nation.

Indian Historian, 2, no. 1 (1969): 8, 38.

Wendorf, Fred. The archaeology of northeastern New Mexico. El Palacio, 67 (1960): 55-65.

Werner, David. Healing in the Sierra Madre. Natural History, 79, no. 9 (1970): 60-67.

Werner, Oswald. Semantics of Navaho medical terms: I. International Journal of American Linguistics, 31 (1965): 1-17.

Westley, C. R. Familial nephritis and associated deafness in a Southwestern Apache Indian family. Southern Medical Journal, 63 (1970): 1415-1419.

Wharfield, H. B. Apache Indian scouts. El Cajon, Calif., 1964. 5, 113 p. illus.

Wharfield, H. B. With scouts and cavalry at Fort Apache. Edited by John A. Carroll. Tucson, Arizona Pioneers' Historical Society, 1965. 12, 124 p. illus., map.

Wheat, J. B. Kroeber's formulation of the Southwestern culture area. Colorado, University, Studies, Series in Anthropology, 4 (1954): 23-44.

Wheeler, R. P. Danton, Leslie and Cynoamp English merchants. International Congress of Americanists, Proceedings, 26, vol. 2 (1948): 369-372.

Whipple, A. W., T. Ewbank, and W. M. Turner. Report upon the Indian tribes. In Reports of Explorations and Surveys to Ascertain the Most Practicable and Economical Route for a Railroad from the Mississippi River to the Pacific Ocean (33d Congress, 2d Session, H.R. Ex. Doc. 91). Vol. 3. Washington, D.C., 1855: 7-127.

Whipple, Amiel W. The Whipple report. Edited by E. I. Edwards. Los Angeles, Westernlore Press, 1961. 100 p. illus.

White, C. B. A comparison of theories on Southern Athapaskan kinship systems. American Anthropologist, 59 (1957): 434-448.

White, L. A. A ceremonial vocabulary among the Pueblos. International Journal of American Linguistics, 10 (1944): 161-167.

White, L. A. The impersonation of saints among the Pueblos. Michigan Academy of Science, Arts and Letters, Papers, 27 (1941): 559-564.

Whorf, B. L. The comparative linguistics of Uto-Aztecan. American Anthropologist, n.s., 37 (1935): 600-608.

Williams, Lillie Evaline. The relationships between dogmatism, academic adjustment, and grade point averages for American Indian college students. Dissertation Abstracts International, 31 (1970/1971): 2028A. UM 70-21,965.

Williams, Lyle Wayne. Struggle for survival: the hostile frontier of New Spain, 1750-1800. Dissertation Abstracts International, 31 (1970/1971): 2820A. UM 70-25,179.

Wilson, C. R. Navajos, Apaches and western Canada? An introduction. Western Canadian Journal of Anthropology, 2, no. 1 (1970): 176-179.

Wilson, Edward. An unwritten history; a record from the exciting days of early Arizona. Santa Fe, Stagecoach Press, 1966. 62 p.

Winfrey, Dorman H., et al. Indian tribes of Texas. Waco, Texian Press, 1971. 7, 178 p. illus.

Winship, G. P. The Coronado expedition. U.S. Bureau of American Ethnology, Annual Reports, 14, vol. 1 (1893): 339-613.

Winter, W. Yuman languages. International Journal of American Linguistics, 23 (1957): 18-24.

Witt, Shirley Hill. Migration into San Juan Indian Pueblo, 1726-1968. Dissertation Abstracts International, 31 (1970/1971): 1034B-1035B. UM 70-17,249.

Wittfogel, K. A. and E. S. Goldfrank. Some aspects of Pueblo mythology and society. Journal of American Folklore, 56 (1943): 17-30.

Wolman, Carol S. The cradleboard of the Western Indians. A baby-tending device of cultural importance. Clinical Pediatrics, 9 (1970): 306-308.

Wood, Raymund F. Francisco Garcés, explorer of Southern California. Southern California Quarterly, 51 (1969): 185-209.

Woodbury, Richard B. A reconsideration of Pueblo warfare in the Southwestern United States. In Congreso Internacional de Americanistas, 33d. 1958, San José. Actas. Tomo 2. San José, Lehmann, 1959: 124-133.

Woodward, Arthur.   Side lights on fifty
    years of Apache warfare, 1836-1886.
    Arizoniana, 2, no. 3 (1961): 3-14.

Woody, Clara T., ed.   The Woolsey
    expeditions of 1864. Arizona and the
    West, 4 (1962): 157-176.

Worcester, D. C.   Early Spanish accounts
    of the Apache Indians. American
    Anthropologist, n.s., 43 (1941): 308-
    312.

Worcester, D. E.   The spread of Spanish
    horses in the Southwest. New Mexico
    Historical Review, 19 (1944): 225-232;
    20 (1945): 1-13.

Wormington, H. M.   The story of Pueblo
    pottery. Denver Museum of Natural
    History, Museum Pictorial, 2 (1951): 1-
    61.

Wright, Bessie L., ed.   Diary of a member
    of the first mule pack train to leave
    Fort Smith for California in 1849.
    Panhandle-Plains Historical Review, 42
    (1969): 61-119.

Wyman, Leland C.   Snakeskins and hoops.
    Plateau, 39 (1966): 4-25.

Yarnell, R. A.   Prehistoric Pueblo use of
    datura. El Palacio, 66 (1959): 176-178.

Yurchenko, Henrietta.   La recopilación de
    música indígena. América Indígena, 6
    (1946): 320-331.

Zárate-Salmerón, G. de.   Relating all the
    things that have been seen and known in
    New Mexico. Land of Sunshine, 11 (1899):
    337-356; 12 (1900): 39-48, 104-113, 180-
    187.

Zbinden, Ernst A.   Nördliche und südliche
    Elemente im Kulturheroenmythus der
    Südathapasken. Anthropos, 55 (1960):
    689-733.

Zerwekh, Edward Mary.   John Baptist
    Salpointe, 1825-1894. New Mexico
    Historical Review, 37 (1962): 1-19, 132-
    154, 214-229.

Zingg, R. M.   A reconstruction of Uto-
    Aztekan history. Denver, University,
    Contributions to Ethnography, 2 (1939):
    1-274.

Zintz, Miles V.   Problems of classroom
    adjustment of Indian children in public
    elementary schools in the Southwest.
    Science Education, 46 (1962): 261-269.

Zintz, Miles V.   The Indian Research
    Study; the adjustment of Indian and non-
    Indian children in the public schools of
    New Mexico. Albuquerque, University of

New Mexico, College of Education, 1957-
    1960. 2 v. (17, 279 p.).

Zolotarevskaïa, I. A.   Indeïtsy ïugo-
    zapada. By I. A. Zolotarevskaïa and M.
    V. Stepanova. In A. V. Efimov and S. A.
    Tokarev, eds. Narody Ameriki. Vol. 1.
    Moskva, Izdatel'stvo Akademiïa Nauk
    SSSR, 1959: 284-305.

Zolotarevskaïa, I. A.   Indeïtsy Pueblo.
    Akademiïa Nauk SSSR, Institut Etnografiï
    Imeni N. N. Miklukho-Maklaïa, Trudy, 25
    (1955): 119-134.

Zonis, Richard D.   Chronic otitis media in
    the Arizona Indian. Arizona Medicine,
    27, no. 6 (1970): 1-6.

Zonis, Richard D.   Chronic otitis media in
    the Southwestern American Indian.
    Archives of Otolaryngology, 88 (1968):
    360-369.

15-01   Acoma

Fraser, James H.   Indian mission printing
    in New Mexico: a bibliography. New
    Mexico Historical Review, 43 (1968):
    311-318.

Anonymous.   Acoma the sky pueblo. El
    Palacio, 47 (1940): 160-161.

Bandelier, A. F.   Ein Brief über Akoma.
    Ausland, 57 (1884): 241-243.

Beckwith, F.   A day in Acoma. El Palacio,
    35 (1933): 201-210.

Benedict, R.   Eight stories from Acoma.
    Journal of American Folklore, 43 (1930):
    59-87.

Bercovitz, M.   Laguna Indian translations.
    Laguna [c. 1880].   27 p.

Bloom, L. B., ed.   Bourke on the
    Southwest. New Mexico Historical Review,
    12 (1937): 337-379.

Boas, F.   A Keresan text. International
    Journal of American Linguistics, 2
    (1923): 171-180.

Boas, F.   Abstract characteristics of
    Keresan folktales. International
    Congress of Americanists, Proceedings,
    20, vol. 1 (1922): 223-224.

Boas, F.   Keresan texts. American
    Ethnological Society, Publications, 8,
    no. 1 (1928): 1-300.

Boke, R. L. Laguna Indians pin their hopes on better land use. Soil Conservation, 2 (1937): 199-200.

Brandfonbrener, Martin. Cardiomyopathy in the Southwest American Indian. By M. Brandfonbrener, W. S. Lovekin, and J. K. Leach. British Heart Journal, 32 (1970): 491-496.

Brayer, H. O. The land grants of Laguna. Research, 1 (1936): 5-22.

Bunzel, R. L. The Pueblo potter. Columbia University Contributions to Anthropology, 8 (1929): 1-134.

Bunzel, Ruth L. The Pueblo potter. New York, AMS Press, 1969. 134 p. illus.

Chilcott, John H. Laguna Indian Reservation and Acoma Indian Reservation, Laguna-Acoma Junior and Senior High School: community background reports. By John H. Chilcott and Jerry P. Garcia. Chicago, University of Chicago, 1970. 11 p. maps. (National Study of American Indian Education, Series 1, 16) ERIC ED047874.

Christinger, Raymond. Acoma, mythe d'origine. Société Suisse des Américanistes, Bulletin, 23 (1962): 2-12.

Christinger, Raymond. L'origine des katchinas. Société Suisse des Américanistes, Bulletin, 26 (1963): 10-18.

Cobb, John C. Trachoma among Southwestern Indians. By John C. Cobb and Chandler R. Dawson. American Medical Association, Journal, 175 (1961): 405-406.

Concha, Fernando de la. Colonel Don Fernando de la Concha diary, 1788. Edited by Adlai Feather. New Mexico Historical Review, 34 (1959): 285-304.

Corbett, Thomas H. Iron deficiency anemia in a Pueblo Indian village. American Medical Association, Journal, 205 (1968): 186.

*Curtis, E. S. The North American Indian, Vol. 16: 65-248. Norwood, 1926.

Curtis, N., ed. The Indians' book, 447-470. New York, 1907.

Curtis, N., ed. Two Pueblo Indian grinding songs. Craftsman, 7 (1904): 35-41.

DeHuff, E. W. More Pueblo tales. El Palacio, 11 (1921): 140-144.

DeHuff, E. W. Myths told by the Pueblos. El Palacio, 11 (1921): 86-92.

DeHuff, E. W. Taytay's memories, 25-40, 55-82, 158-160, 187-197, 229-247. New York, 1924.

DeHuff, E. W. Taytay's tales, 40-50, 88-91, 95-111, 132-140, 165-167, 172-182, 191-197. New York, 1922.

Densmore, F. Music of Acoma, Isleta, Cochiti and Zuñi Pueblos. U.S. Bureau of American Ethnology, Bulletin, 165 (1957): 1-129.

Densmore, Frances. Music of Acoma, Isleta, Cochiti, and Zuñi Pueblos. New York, Da Capo Press, 1972. 12, 117 p. illus.

Dismuke, D. Acoma and Laguna Indians adjust their livestock to their range. Soil Conservation, 6 (1940): 130-132.

Dittert, Alfred Edward, Jr. Culture change in the Cebolleta Mesa region, central western New Mexico. Dissertation Abstracts, 20 (1959/1960): 645-646. UM 59-2682.

Donaldson, T. Moqui Indians of Arizona and Pueblo Indians of New Mexico. U.S. Census Office, Eleventh Census, Extra Bulletin (1893): 1-136.

Douglas, F. H. Acoma Pueblo weaving and embroidery. Denver Art Museum, Indian Leaflet Series, 89 (1939): 154-156.

Douglas, F. H. An embroidered cotton garment from Acoma. Denver Art Museum, Material Culture Notes, 1 (1937): 1-4.

Downing, George L. Native pottery of the Southwest. Natural History, 78, no. 6 (1969): 34-39.

Dozier, Edward P. Autogobierno y los pueblo del suroeste de los Estados Unidos. Anuario Indigenista, 29 (1969): 65-72.

Dozier, Edward P. Pueblo Indian response to culture contact. In M. Estellie Smith, ed. Studies in Linguistics in Honor of George L. Trager. The Hague, Mouton, 1972: 457-467. (Janua Linguarum, Series Maior, 52)

Dutton, B. P. and M. A. Marmon. The Laguna calendar. New Mexico, University, Bulletin, Anthropological Series, 1, no. 2 (1936): 1-21.

*Eggan, F. Social organization of the Western Pueblos, 223-290. Chicago, 1950.

Ellis, F. H. An outline of Laguna Pueblo history and social organization. Southwestern Journal of Anthropology, 15 (1959): 325-347.

Ellis, F. H. Laguna bows and arrows. El Palacio, 66 (1959): 91.

Ellis, Florence Hawley. On distinguishing Laguna from Acoma polychrome. El Palacio, 73, no. 3 (1966): 37-39.

Espinosa, A. M. All-Souls' Day at Zuni, Acoma, and Laguna. Journal of American Folklore, 31 (1918): 550-552.

Espinosa, A. M. El desarrollo de la palabra castilla en la lengua de los Indios Queres de Nuevo Méjico. Revista de Filología Española, 19 (1932): 261-277.

Fay, George E., ed. Charters, constitutions and by-laws of the Indian tribes of North America. Part IV: The Southwest (Navajo-Zuni). Greeley, 1967. 5, 120 l. maps. (University of Northern Colorado, Museum of Anthropology, Occasional Publications in Anthropology, Ethnology Series, 5) ERIC ED046554.

Forde, C. D. A creation myth from Acoma. Folk-Lore, 41 (1930): 370-387.

Gatschet, A. S. Classification into seven linguistic stocks of Western Indian dialects. In Report upon United States Geographical Surveys West of the One Hundredth Meridian. Vol. 7. Washington, D.C., 1879: 403-485.

Goldfrank, E. S. Notes on deer-hunting practices at Laguna Pueblo. Texas Journal of Science, 6 (1954): 407-421.

Goldfrank, E. S. Notes on two Pueblo feasts. American Anthropologist, n.s., 25 (1923): 188-196.

Gordon, Dudley. An early fiesta at Laguna. Masterkey, 46 (1972): 34-37.

Gunn, J. M. History, traditions, and narratives of the Queres Pueblos of Laguna and Acoma. Records of the Past, 3 (1904): 291-310, 323-344.

Gunn, J. M. Schat-chen. Albuquerque, 1917. 222 p.

Halseth, Odd S., et al. The Laguna santero. El Palacio, 77, no. 3 (1971): 19-22.

Harrington, J. P. Haáko, original form of the Keresan name of Acoma. El Palacio, 56 (1949): 141-144.

Harvey, Byron, III. Masks at a maskless pueblo: the Laguna colony Kachina organization at Isleta. Ethnology, 2 (1963): 478-489.

Hawley, F. Keresan patterns of kinship and social organization. American Anthropologist, n.s., 52 (1950): 499-512.

Hodge, F. W. Acoma. U.S. Bureau of American Ethnology, Bulletin, 30, vol. 1 (1907): 10-11.

Hodge, F. W. Laguna. U.S. Bureau of American Ethnology, Bulletin, 30, vol. 1 (1907): 752-753.

Hodge, F. W. Pueblo snake ceremonials. American Anthropologist, 9 (1896): 133-136.

Hodge, F. W. The verification of a tradition. American Anthropologist, 10 (1897): 299-302.

Hrdlička, A. A Laguna ceremonial language. American Anthropologist, n.s., 5 (1903): 730-732.

Hunt, Irvin. Christmas among the Pueblos. Indian Historian, 1, no. 1 (1967/1968): 7-8.

James, H. L. Ácoma: the people of the white rock. Glorieta, Rio Grande Press, 1970. 96 p. illus., map.

Jenkins, Myra Ellen. The Baltasar Baca "Grant": history of an encroachment. El Palacio, 68 (1961): 47-64, 87-105.

Kroeber, A. L. Zuni kin and clan. American Museum of Natural History, Anthropological Papers, 18 (1917): 83-88.

Lemos, P. J. Marvelous Acoma and its craftsmen. El Palacio, 24 (1928): 234-244.

Lomax, Alan. Special features of the sung communication. In June Helm, ed. Essays on the Verbal and Visual Arts. Seattle, University of Washington Press, 1967: 109-127. (American Ethnological Society, Proceedings of the Annual Spring Meeting, 1966)

Lummis, C. F. A week of wonders. Land of Sunshine, 15 (1901): 315-332, 425-437.

Maring, Ester Gayo. The religio-political organization, customary law and values of the Acoma (Keresan) Pueblo Indians: a study in acculturation and social control. Dissertation Abstracts International, 30 (1969/1970): 4888B-4889B. UM 70-7479.

Maring, Joel Marvyl. Grammar of Acoma Keresan. Dissertation Abstracts, 28 (1967/1968): 2242B-2243B. UM 67-15,135.

Mickey, B. H. Acoma kinship terms. Southwestern Journal of Anthropology, 12 (1956): 249-256.

Miller, W. R. Some notes on Acoma kinship terminology. Southwestern Journal of Anthropology, 15 (1959): 179-184.

Miller, Wick R. Acoma grammar and texts. Berkeley and Los Angeles, University of California Press, 1965. 8, 259 p. (California, University, Publications in Linguistics, 40)

Miller, Wick R. Spanish loanwords in Acoma. International Journal of American Linguistics, 25 (1959): 147-153; 26 (1960): 41-49.

Morgan, L. H. Systems of consanguinity and affinity. Smithsonian Contributions to Knowledge, 17 (1871): 291-382.

Ortiz, Simon. Out of the canyon near Two Turkey ruin. Alcheringa, 2 (1971): 18.

Parsons, E. C. All-Souls' Day at Zuni, Acoma, and Laguna. Journal of American Folklore, 30 (1917): 495-496.

Parsons, E. C. Early relations between Hopi and Keres. American Anthropologist, n.s., 38 (1936): 554-560.

Parsons, E. C. Laguna genealogies. American Museum of Natural History, Anthropological Papers, 19 (1923): 133-292.

Parsons, E. C. Laguna tales. Journal of American Folklore, 44 (1931): 137-142.

Parsons, E. C. Mothers and children at Laguna. Man, 19 (1919): 34-38.

Parsons, E. C. Nativity myth at Laguna and Zuni. Journal of American Folklore, 31 (1918): 256-263.

Parsons, E. C. Notes on Acoma and Laguna. American Anthropologist, n.s., 20 (1918): 162-186.

Parsons, E. C. Notes on ceremonialism at Laguna. American Museum of Natural History, Anthropological Papers, 19 (1920): 85-131.

Parsons, E. C. Notes on Isleta, Santa Ana, and Acoma. American Anthropologist, n.s., 22 (1920): 56-69.

Parsons, E. C. Pueblo Indian religion. Chicago, 1939. 2 v.

Parsons, E. C. Pueblo-Indian folk-tales, probably of Spanish provenience. Journal of American Folklore, 31 (1918): 216-255.

Parsons, E. C. The antelope clan in Keresan custom and myth. Man, 17 (1917): 190-193.

Parsons, E. C. The kinship nomenclature of the Pueblo Indians. American Anthropologist, n.s., 34 (1932): 377-389.

Parsons, E. C. The Laguna migration to Isleta. American Anthropologist, n.s., 30 (1928): 602-613.

Parsons, E. C. War god shrines of Laguna and Zuni. American Anthropologist, n.s., 20 (1918): 381-405.

Parsons, E. C. and F. Boas. Spanish tales from Laguna and Zuni. Journal of American Folklore, 33 (1920): 47-72.

Paytiamo, J. Flaming Arrow's people. New York, 1932. 157 p.

Pradt, G. H. Shakok and Miochin: origin of summer and winter. Journal of American Folklore, 15 (1902): 88.

Reuter, B. A. Restoration of Acoma mission. El Palacio, 22 (1927): 79-87.

Roberts, H. H. Chakwena songs of Zuni and Laguna. Journal of American Folklore, 36 (1923): 177-184.

Ruppe, R. J. and A. E. Dittert. Acoma archaeology. El Palacio, 60 (1953): 259-274.

Ruppe, R. J. and A. E. Dittert. The archaeology of Cebolleta Mesa and Acoma Pueblo. El Palacio, 59 (1952): 191-219.

Ruppé, Reynold J. The archaeological survey: a defense. American Antiquity, 31 (1965/1966): 313-333.

Sampliner, James E. Biliary surgery in the Southwestern American Indian. By James E. Sampliner and Daniel J. O'Connell. Archives of Surgery, 96 (1968): 1-3.

Schiff, E. A note on twins. American Anthropologist, n.s., 23 (1921): 387-388.

Sedgwick, Mrs. W. T. Acoma, the sky city. Cambridge, 1926. 295 p.

Smith, D. M. Indian tribes of the Southwest, 1-15. Stanford, 1933.

Spencer, R. F.   A sketch of Laguna land ways. El Palacio, 47 (1940): 214-227.

Spencer, R. F.   The phonemes of Keresan. International Journal of American Linguistics, 12 (1946): 229-236.

Stevenson, J.   Illustrated catalogue of the collections obtained from the Indians of New Mexico and Arizona. U.S. Bureau of American Ethnology, Annual Reports, 2 (1883): 399-405.

*Stirling, M. W.   Origin myth of Acoma. U.S. Bureau of American Ethnology, Bulletin, 135 (1942): 1-123.

Taylor, Benjamin J.   Indian manpower resources in the Southwest: a pilot study. By Benjamin J. Taylor and Dennis J. O'Connor.   Tempe, Arizona State University, 1969.   26, 374 p.

Toomey, T. N.   Grammatical and lexical notes on the Keres language. Hervas Laboratories of American Linguistics, Bulletin, 5 (1914): 1-11.

U.S., General Accounting Office. Deficient financial analysis which resulted in approval of unneeded grant, Area Redevelopment Administration, Department of Commerce.   Washington, D.C., 1965.   2, 13 l.

Warner, Michael J.   Protestant missionary activity among the Navajo, 1890-1912. New Mexico Historical Review, 45 (1970): 209-232.

White, L. A.   A comparative study of Keresan medicine societies. International Congress of Americanists, Proceedings, 23 (1928): 604-619.

White, L. A.   Miscellaneous notes on the Keresan Pueblos. Michigan Academy of Science, Arts and Letters, Papers, 32 (1946): 365-376.

*White, L. A.   New material from Acoma. U.S. Bureau of American Ethnology, Bulletin, 136 (1943): 301-359.

White, L. A.   Notes on the ethnobotany of the Keres. Michigan Academy of Science, Arts and Letters, Papers, 30 (1944): 557-570.

White, L. A.   Notes on the ethnozoology of the Keresan Pueblo Indians. Michigan Academy of Science, Arts and Letters, Papers, 31 (1945): 223-246.

White, L. A.   "Rohona" in Pueblo culture. Michigan Academy of Science, Arts and Letters, Papers, 29 (1943): 439-443.

White, L. A.   Summary report of field work at Acoma. American Anthropologist, n.s., 30 (1928): 559-568.

*White, L. A.   The Acoma Indians. U.S. Bureau of American Ethnology, Annual Reports, 47 (1930): 17-192.

Whitener, H. C., tr.   Jesus Christo niya tawa-mani.   Albuquerque, 1935.   72 p.

Wittick, Ben.   Ben Wittick views the Pueblos. Edited by Carol Scott Alley. El Palacio, 73, no. 2 (1966): 4-9.

Woolf, Charles M.   Albinism among Indians in Arizona and New Mexico. American Journal of Human Genetics, 17 (1965): 23-35.

Zbinden, Ernst A.   Nördliche und südliche Elemente im Kulturheroenmythus der Südathapasken. Anthropos, 55 (1960): 689-733.

15-02   Cahita

Acosta, Roberto.   Apuntes históricos Sonorenses. La conquista temporal y espiritual del Yaqui y del Mayo. México, Imprenta Aldina-Rosell y Sordo Noviega, 1949.   140 p.

Acosta, Roberto.   Apuntes históricos Sonorenses. La conquista temporal y espiritual del Yaqui y del Mayo. Academia Mexicana de la Historia, Memorias, 6 (1947): 112-125, 269-300; 7 (1948): 72-96, 100-108, 229-263.

Altman, G. J.   The Yaqui Easter play of Guadalupe, Arizona. Masterkey, 20 (1946): 181-189; 21 (1947): 19-23, 67-72.

Alvar Loría, Q. B. P.   Estudios sobre algunas caracteristicas hematologicas hereditarias en la población mexicana. III. Deficiencia en la glucosa 6-fosfato deshidrogenasa eritrocítica en 7 grupos indígenas y algunos mestizos. Gaceta Médica de México, 93 (1963): 299-303.

Anonymous.   The President of the Republic visits the Yaqui tribes. Boletín Indigenista, 20 (1960): 221, 223.

Bannon, John Francis.   The mission frontier in Sonora, 1620-1687. Edited by James A. Reynolds.   New York, United States Catholic Historical Society, 1955.   4, 160 p.   (United States Catholic Historical Society, Monograph Series, 26)

Barker, G. C.   Some aspects of penitential processions in Spain and the American

Southwest. Journal of American Folklore, 70 (1957): 137-142.

Barker, G. C. Some functions of Catholic processions in Pueblo and Yaqui culture change. American Anthropologist, 60 (1958): 449-455.

Barker, G. C. The Yaqui Easter Ceremony at Hermosillo. Western Folklore, 16 (1957): 256-262.

Bartell, Gilbert Duke. Directed culture change among the Sonoran Yaquis. Dissertation Abstracts, 26 (1965/1966): 1860. UM 65-5392.

Bartell, Gilberto D. The consequences of differing perceived reality: a case study of a directed change program in Sonora, Mexico. America Latina, 9, no. 2 (1966): 67-76.

Basauri, Carlos. Familia "Pimana": Mayos. In his La Poblacion Indigena de Mexico. Tomo I. Mexico, Secretaria de Educacion Publica, 1940: 285-298.

Basauri, Carlos. Familia "Pimana": Yaquis. In his La Poblacion Indigena de Mexico. Tomo 1. Mexico, Secretaria de Educacion Publica, 1940: 243-284.

Basilio, Tommaso. Arte de la lengua cáhita, por un padre de la Compañia de Jesús. Edited by Eustaquio Euelna. México, Impr. del Gobierno Federal, 1890. 63, 264 p.

Beals, R. L. Aboriginal survivals in Mayo culture. American Anthropologist, n.s., 34 (1932): 28-39.

*Beals, R. L. The aboriginal culture of the Cahita Indians. Ibero-Americana, 19 (1943): 1-86.

*Beals, R. L. The contemporary culture of the Cahita Indians. U.S. Bureau of American Ethnology, Bulletin, 142 (1945): 1-244.

Beals, Ralph L. Kinship terminology and social structure. Kroeber Anthropological Society Papers, 25 (1961): 129-148.

Beals, Ralph L. The comparative ethnology of northern Mexico before 1750. Berkeley, University of California Press, 1932. 6, 93-225 p. maps. (Ibero-Americana, 2)

Bogan, P. M. Yaqui Indian dances. Tucson, 1925. 69 p.

Bowen, Thomas. Seri headpieces and hats. By Thomas Bowen and Edward Moser. Kiva, 35, no. 4 (1969/1970): 168-177.

Brown, E. The passion at Pascua. Tucson, 1941. 28 p.

Buschmann, J. C. Grammatik der Sonorischen Sprache. Berlin, Königliche Akademie der Wissenschaften, Abhandlungen, 47 (1863): 369-454; 51 (1867): 23-216; 53, no. 1 (1869): 67-266.

Cámara Barbachano, Fernando. El papel de la religión en la integración y desintegración de la sociedad y cultura yaqui. In Congreso Internacional de Americanistas, 35th. 1962, Mexico. Actas y Memorias. Tomo 2. Mexico, 1964: 575-593.

Cardenal, Ernesto, tr. Poesía de los indios de Norteamérica. América Indígena, 21 (1961): 355-362.

Castaneda, Carlos. A separate reality; further conversations with Don Juan. New York, Simon and Schuster, 1971. 317 p.

Castaneda, Carlos. Sorcery: a description of the world. Dissertation Abstracts International, 33 (1972/1973): 5625B.

Castaneda, Carlos. The teachings of Don Juan; a Yaqui way of knowledge. Berkeley, University of California Press, 1968. 8, 196 p.

Cazeneuve, L. Les Indiens de la région de Tucson. Ethnographie, 51 (1956): 37-45.

Chavez, A. The Penitentes of New Mexico. New Mexico Historical Review, 29 (1954): 97-123.

Clark, C. U. Excerpts from the journals of Prince Paul of Wurtemberg, Year 1850. Southwestern Journal of Anthropology, 15 (1959): 291-299.

Collard, H. and B. Collard. Folleto sobre el Paludismo. México, 1956.

Corbella de la Immaculada, Carmelo. Quipata; libro histórico misional de Indios. Lérida, Artis Estudios Gráficos, 1970. 283 p. illus.

Corey, Herbert. Adventuring down the West Coast of Mexico. National Geographic Magazine, 42 (1922): 449-503.

Crumrine, Lynne S. Ceremonial exchange as a mechanism in tribal integration among the Mayos of Northwest Mexico. Tucson, University of Arizona Press, 1967. 12, 52 p. illus., maps. (Arizona, University, Anthropological Papers, 14)

Crumrine, Lynne S. Mundo de la selva vs. tractor: sistema económico moderno de los indios mayo, en el noroeste de México. By Lynne S. Crumrine and N. Ross Crumrine. América Indígena, 27 (1967): 715-733.

Crumrine, Lynne S. The phonology of Arizona Yaqui: with texts. Tucson, University of Arizona Press, 1961. 1, 43 p. (Arizona, University, Anthropological Papers, 5)

Crumrine, Lynne Scoggins. Ceremonial exchange as a mechanism in tribal integration among the Mayos of Northwest Mexico. Dissertation Abstracts, 26 (1965/1966): 6297-6298. UM 66-5138.

Crumrine, N. Ross. Ancient and modern Mayo fishing practices. By N. Ross Crumrine and Lynne S. Crumrine. Kiva, 33, no. 1 (1967/19..): 25-33.

Crumrine, N. Ross. Anthropological antinomy: the importance of an empirical basis for a concept of anthropological fact. Anthropological Quarterly, 41 (1968): 34-46.

Crumrine, N. Ross. Capakoba, the Mayo Easter ceremonial impersonator: explanations of ritual clowning. Journal for the Scientific Study of Religion, 8 (1969): 1-22.

Crumrine, N. Ross. Función del ritual y del simbolismo sagrado en la aculturación y el pluralismo. Con especial referencia al ceremonial Mayo. Anuario Indigenista, 29 (1969): 331-346.

Crumrine, N. Ross. Mayo ritual impersonation: the mask, arousal, and enculturation. Anthropos, 63/64 (1968/1969): 976-977.

Crumrine, N. Ross. The Easter ceremonial in the socio-cultural identity of Mayos, Sonora, Mexico. Dissertation Abstracts, 29 (1968/1969): 1244B. UM 68-13,680.

Crumrine, N. Ross. The house cross of the Mayo Indians of Sonora, Mexico; a symbol in ethnic identity. Tucson, 1964. 57 p. illus., maps. (Arizona, University, Anthropological Papers, 8)

Davila Garibi, J. I. Es el Coca un idioma taracahita. In Homenaje al Doctor Alfonso Caso. México, 1951: 143-152.

Dávila Garibi, José Ignacio. Algunas afinidades entre las lenguas coca y cahita. El México Antiguo, 6 (1942): 47-60.

Dedrick, J. M. How Jobe'eso Ro'i got his name. Tlalocan, 2 (1946): 163-166.

DeGrazia, Ted E. De Grazia paints the Yaqui Easter; forty days of Lent in forty paintings, with a personal commentary. Tucson, University of Arizona Press, 1968. 92 p. illus.

Delgado Hernandez, Felipe. Estudio sobre la rehabilitación económico-agrícola de la zona correspondiente a las tribus yaquis. Sociedad Mexicana de Geografía y Estadística, Boletín, 72 (1951): 115-144.

Densmore, F. Native songs of two hybrid ceremonies. American Anthropologist, n.s., 43 (1941): 77-82.

Densmore, F. Yuman and Yaqui music. U.S. Bureau of American Ethnology, Bulletin, 110 (1932): 1-216.

Densmore, Frances. Yuman and Yaqui music. New York, Da Capo Press, 1972. 18, 216 p. illus.

Dobyns, Henry F. Indian extinction in the middle Santa Cruz River Valley, Arizona. New Mexico Historical Review, 38 (1963): 163-181.

Dominguez, F. Costumbres Yaquis. Mexican Folkways, Special Yaqui Number (1937): 6-25.

Dominguez, F. Musica Yaqui. Mexican Folkways, Special Yaqui Number (1937): 32-44.

Dozier, E. P. Two examples of linguistic acculturation. Language, 32 (1956): 146-157.

Dozier, Edward P. Pueblo Indian response to culture contact. In M. Estellie Smith, ed. Studies in Linguistics in Honor of George L. Trager. The Hague, Mouton, 1972: 457-467. (Janua Linguarum, Series Maior, 52)

Drucker, Philip. Culture element distributions: XVII Yuman-Piman. Berkeley, 1941. 91-230 p. illus., map. (California, University, Publications, Anthropological Records, 6, no. 3)

Erasmus, Charles J. Man takes control; cultural development and American aid. Minneapolis, University of Minnesota Press, 1961. 365 p. illus.

Escudero, J. A. de. Noticias estadísticas de Sonora y Sinaloa. México, 1849.

Fabila, A. Las tribus yaquis de Sonora. México, 1940. 313 p.

Fabila, A. Los Indios Yaquis de Sonora. México, 1945. 87 p.

Fabila, A. Los Indios Yaquis del Estado
Sonora. Sociologia en Mexico, 1, no. 4
(1951): 1-27.

Fay, G. E. Indian house types of Sonora,
I: Yaqui. Masterkey, 29 (1955): 196-199.

Fay, G. E. Indian house types of Sonora,
II: Mayo. Masterkey, 30 (1956): 25-28.

Fay, G. E. Uses of the tamarindo fruit.
El Palacio, 63 (1956): 58.

Fay, George E. An Indian-Mexican house
type in Sonora, Mexico. Greeley, 1969.
9 l. illus. (Colorado State College,
Museum of Anthropology, Miscellaneous
Series, 5)

Feather, Adlai. Origin of the name
Arizona. New Mexico Historical Review,
39 (1964): 89-100.

Forbes, J. D. Historical survey of the
Indians of Sonora, 1821-1910.
Ethnohistory, 4 (1957): 335-368.

Fraenkel, Gerd. Yaqui phonemics.
Anthropological Linguistics, 1, no. 5
(1959): 7-18.

Gámez, Ernesto. El valle del Fuerte.
Mochis, 1955. 128 p. illus.

Getty, H. T. Some characteristics of the
folklore of the Indians of Arizona.
Arizona, University, Bulletin, 16, no. 1
(1945): 29-42.

Giddings, Ruth W. Yaqui myths and
legends. Tucson, 1959. 73 p.
(Arizona, University, Anthropological
Papers, 2)

Giddings, Ruth W. Yaqui myths and
legends. Tucson, University of Arizona
Press, 196-. 180 p. illus.

González Bonilla, L. A. Los Yaquis.
Revista Mexicana de Sociología, 2, no. 1
(1940): 57-88.

Griffin, William B. Seventeenth century
Seri. Kiva, 27, no. 2 (1961/1962): 12-
21.

Griffith, James. Cahitan Pascola masks.
Kiva, 37 (1972): 185-198.

Griffith, James A. Mochicahui Judio
masks: a type of Mayo Fariseo mask from
northern Sinaloa, Mexico. Kiva, 32,
no. 4 (1966/1967): 143-149.

Griffith, James S. Magdalena revisited:
the growth of a fiesta. Kiva, 33, no. 2
(1967/1968): 82-86.

Hamy, E. T. Algunas observaciones sobre
la distribución geográfica de los
Ópatas, de los Tarahumares y de los
Pimas. Museo de Arqueología, Historia y
Etnografía, Anales, época 4a, 5 (1922):
93-98.

Hanna, Bertram L. The biological
relationships among Indian groups of the
Southwest: analysis of morphological
traits. American Journal of Physical
Anthropology, n.s., 20 (1962): 499-508.

Hanna, Joel M. Responses of native and
migrant desert residents to arid heat.
American Journal of Physical
Anthropology, n.s., 32 (1970): 187-195.

Hardy, B. Carmon. Cultural "encystment"
as a cause of the Mormon exodus from
Mexico in 1912. Pacific Historical
Review, 34 (1965): 439-454.

Hastings, James Rodney. People of reason
and others: the colonization of Sonora
to 1767. Arizona and the West, 3 (1961):
321-340.

Hernandez, F. Las razas indígenas de
Sonora y la guerra del Yaqui, 77-233.
México, 1902.

Hodge, F. W. Cahita. U.S. Bureau of
American Ethnology, Bulletin, 30, vol. 1
(1907): 184-185.

Hodge, F. W. Yaqui. U.S. Bureau of
American Ethnology, Bulletin, 30, vol. 2
(1910): 991-992.

*Holden, W. C., C. C. Seltzer, R. A.
Studhalter, C. J. Wagner, and W. G.
McMillan. Studies of the Yaqui Indians
of Sonora. Texas Technological College,
Bulletin, 12, no. 1 (1936): 1-142.

Honigmann, J. J. An interpretation of the
social-psychological functions of the
ritual clown. Character and Personality,
10 (1942): 220-226.

Hrdlička, A. Notes on the Indians of
Sonora. American Anthropologist, n.s., 6
(1904): 59-71.

Jensen, Marguerite. The Yaqui. Indian
Historian, 4, no. 3 (1971): 41-43.

Johnson, Barbara. Holy Saturday: a Yaqui
ceremony in Pascua Village. El Palacio,
67 (1960): 102-104.

Johnson, J. B. A clear case of linguistic
acculturation. American Anthropologist,
n.s., 45 (1943): 427-434.

Johnson, Jean B. El idioma yaqui.
México, 1962. 303 p. (México,
Instituto Nacional de Antropología e

Historia, Departamento de
Investigaciones Antropológicas,
Publicaciones, 10)

Jones, J. A. Variables influencing
behavior in indigenous non-Western
cultures. Final progress report. Tempe,
Arizona State University, Department of
Anthropology, 1968. 219 p. ERIC
ED035477.

Kelly, Marsha C. Las fiestas como reflejo
del orden social: el caso de San Xavier
del Bac. América Indígena, 31 (1971):
141-161.

Kraus, B. S. Occurrence of the Carabelli
trait in Southwest ethnic groups.
American Journal of Physical
Anthropology, n.s., 17 (1959): 117-123.

Kroeber, A. L. Uto-Aztecan languages of
Mexico. Ibero-Americana, 8 (1934): 1-27.

Kurath, Gertrude P. The sena'asom rattle
of the Yaqui Indian Pascolas.
Ethnomusicology, 4 (1960): 60-63.

Kurath, W. and E. H. Spicer. A brief
introduction to Yaqui. Arizona,
University, Social Science Bulletin, 15
(1947): 1-46.

León-Portilla, Miguel. Panorama de la
población indígena de México. América
Indígena, 19 (1959): 43-73.

Lindenfeld, Jacqueline. Semantic
categorization as a deterrent to
grammatical borrowing: a Yaqui example.
International Journal of American
Linguistics, 37 (1971): 6-14.

Lindenfeld, Jacqueline Marie. A
transformational grammar of Yaqui.
Dissertation Abstracts International, 30
(1969/1970): 4966A-4967A. UM 70-8172.

Lisker, Rubén. Estudios sobre algunas
caracteristicas hematologicas
hereditarias en la población mexicana.
II. Hemoglobinas anormales en 7 grupos
indígenas y algunos mestizos. Gaceta
Médica de México, 93 (1963): 289-297.

Lisker, Rubén. Frecuencia de algunas
características hereditarias en la
población indígena de México. By Rubén
Lisker, Alvar Loría and Héctor
Rodríguez. In Congreso Internacional de
Americanistas, 35th. 1962, Mexico. Actas
y Memorias. Tomo 3. Mexico, 1964: 109-
113.

MacKenzie, A. S. Yaqui of Mexico.
American Anthropologist, 2 (1889): 299-
300.

Makarius, Laura. The Capakobam of Sonora,
Mexico. Anthropos, 67 (1972): 595-596.

Mason, J. A. A preliminary sketch of the
Yaqui language. California, University,
Publications in American Archaeology and
Ethnology, 20 (1923): 195-212.

Miller, Wick R. Uto-Aztecan cognate sets.
Berkeley and Los Angeles, University of
California Press, 1967. 5, 83 p. map.
(California, University, Publications in
Linguistics, 48)

Moisés, Rosalio. The tall candle; the
personal chronicle of a Yaqui Indian. By
Rosalio Moisés, Jane Holden Kelley, and
William Curry Holden. Lincoln,
University of Nebraska Press, 1971. 58,
251 p. illus., map.

Montell, G. Yaqui dances. Ethnos, 3,
no. 6 (1938): 145-166.

Nalven, Joseph G. What is Yaqui in A
Yaqui Way of Knowledge? New Scholar, 3,
no. 1 (1972): 6-33.

Nolasco Armas, Margarita. Seris, yaquis y
tarahumaras. México, 1968. 30 p.
illus. (México, Museo Nacional de
Antropología, Servicios Educativos,
Colección Breve, 6)

Packard, Robert C. Demographic
discrimination of American Indian and
Alaskan Eskimo groups by means of Bjork
analysis. By Robert C. Packard and
Thomas J. Zwemer. Journal of Dental
Research, 50 (1971): 364-370.

Painter, M. T. The Yaqui Easter ceremony
at Pascua. Tucson, 1950.

Painter, M. T., et al. A Yaqui Easter
sermon. Arizona, University, Social
Science Bulletin, 26 (1955): 1-89.

Painter, Muriel T. Easter at Pascua
Village. 2d ed. Tucson, University of
Arizona Press, 1960. 35 p. illus.

Painter, Muriel Thayer. A Yaqui Easter.
Tucson, University of Arizona Press,
1971. 40 p. illus.

Parsons, E. C. and R. L. Beals. The
sacred clowns of the Pueblo and Mayo-
Yaqui Indians. American Anthropologist,
n.s., 36 (1934): 491-514.

Parsons, Elsie Clews. Pueblo Indian
religion. Vol. 2. Chicago, University
of Chicago Press, 1939. 551-1275 p.

Passin, Herbert. Some relationships in
Northwest Mexican kinship systems. El
México Antiguo, 6, no. 7/8 (July 1944):
205-218.

Pemex Travel Club. Mexico's music: its past and present. Katunob, 4, no. 4 (1963): 30-52.

Perez de Ribas, A. Historia de los triumphos de novestra santa fee en los missiones de la provincia de Nueva Espana. Madrid, 1645.

Pérez de Ribas, Andrés. My life among the savage nations of New Spain. Translated by Tomás Antonio Robertson. Los Angeles, Ward Ritchie Press, 1968. 16, 256 p. illus., maps.

Putnam, Frank Bishop. Teresa Urrea, "the Saint of Cabora". Southern California Quarterly, 45 (1963): 245-264.

Rehm, Pierre. Anomalie encephalique chez un indien yaqui. Société d'Anthropologie de Paris, Bulletins et Mémoires, 6 série, 5 (1914): 277-281.

Sauer, C. The distribution of aboriginal tribes and languages in northwestern Mexico. Ibero-Americana, 5 (1934): 23-26, 31-32.

Schmutz, Richard. Jesuit missionary methods in northwestern Mexico. Journal of the West, 8 (1969): 76-89.

Seiler, Hansjakob. Accent and morphophonemics in Cahuilla and in Uto-Aztecan. International Journal of American Linguistics, 31 (1965): 50-59.

Shutler, Mary Elizabeth. Persistence and change in the health beliefs and practices of an Arizona Yaqui community. Dissertation Abstracts, 28 (1967/1968): 34B. UM 67-8811.

Skaggs, Jimmy M., ed. Chronicles of the Yaqui Expedition. Edited by Jimmy M. Skaggs, Fane Downs, and Winifred Vigness. Lubbock, West Texas Museum Association, 1972. 230 p. illus. (West Texas Museum Association, Museum Journal, 13)

Spicer, E. H. El problema yaqui. América Indígena, 5 (1945): 273-286.

Spicer, E. H. Linguistic aspects of Yaqui acculturation. American Anthropologist, n.s., 45 (1943): 410-426.

*Spicer, E. H. Pascua: a Yaqui village in Arizona. Chicago, 1940. 319 p.

*Spicer, E. H. Potam. American Anthropological Association, Memoirs, 77 (1954): 1-226.

Spicer, E. H. Social organization and disorganization in an Arizona Yaqui village. Chicago, 1946.

Spicer, E. H. Social structure and cultural process in Yaqui religious acculturation. American Anthropologist, 60 (1958): 433-441.

Spicer, E. H. The military orientation in Yaqui culture. In For the Dean. Essays in Anthropology in Honor of Byron Cummings. Tucson, 1950: 171-188.

Spicer, E. H. Yaqui militarism. Arizona Quarterly, 3 (1947): 40-48.

Spicer, E. H. Yaqui villages past and present. Kiva, 13 (1947): 2-12.

Spicer, Edward H. Apuntes sobre el tipo de religión de los Yuto-Aztecas Centrales. In Congreso Internacional de Americanistas, 35th. 1962, Mexico. Actas y Memorias. Tomo 2. Mexico, 1964: 27-38.

Spicer, Edward H. European expansion and the enclavement of Southwestern Indians. Arizona and the West, 1 (1959): 132-145.

Spicer, Edward H. La danza yaqui del venado en la cultura mexicana. América Indígena, 25 (1965): 117-139.

Spicer, Edward H. Social structure and the acculturation process. In Deward E. Walker, Jr., ed. The Emergent Native Americans. Boston, Little, Brown, 1972: 362-369.

Spicer, Edward H. The Yaqui and Mayo. In Evon Z. Vogt, volume editor. Handbook of Middle American Indians. Vol. 8. Austin, University of Texas Press, 1969: 830-845.

Stevens, Robert Conway. Mexico's forgotten frontier: a history of Sonora, 1821-1846. Dissertation Abstracts, 24 (1963/1964): 3719-3720. UM 64-2142.

Stout, Joe A., Jr. Joseph C. Morehead and manifest destiny: a filibuster in Sonora, 1851. Pacific Historian, 15, no. 1 (1971): 62-71.

Thomas, Cyrus. Indian languages of Mexico and Central America and their geographical distribution. By Cyrus Thomas assisted by John R. Swanton. Washington, D.C., Government Printing Office, 1911. 7, 108 p. map. (U.S., Bureau of American Ethnology, Bulletin, 44)

Toor, F. Apuntes sobre costumbres yaquis. Mexican Folkways, Special Yaqui Number (1937): 52-63.

Toor, Frances. A treasury of Mexican folkways. New York, Crown, 1947. 32, 566 p. illus.

Velasco, J. B. de. Arte de la lengua
    cahita. México, 1890.

Warner, R. E. Yaquis of Mexico and their
    folk literature. Kiva, 8 (1943): 18-22.

Wharfield, H. B. A fight with the Yaquis
    at Bear Valley, 1918. Arizoniana, 4,
    no. 3 (1963): 1-8.

Whiting, A. F. The Tumacacori census of
    1796. Kiva, 29, no. 1 (1953): 1-12.

Wilder, Carleton Stafford. The Yaqui Deer
    Dance: a study in cultural change.
    Washington, D.C., Government Printing
    Office, 1963. 145-210 p. illus.
    (U.S., Bureau of American Ethnology,
    Anthropological Papers, 66. U.S., Bureau
    of American Ethnology, Bulletin, 186)

Willard, William. The community
    development worker in an Arizona Yaqui
    project. Dissertation Abstracts
    International, 31 (1970/1971): 2436B-
    2437B. UM 70-22,318.

Zingg, Robert M. A reconstruction of Uto-
    Aztekan history. New York, G. E.
    Stechert, 1939. 4, 274 p. (Denver,
    University, Contributions to
    Ethnography, 2)

                    15-03   Chinipa

Anonymous. Tubare. U.S. Bureau of
    American Ethnology, Bulletin, 30, vol. 2
    (1910): 830.

Lumholtz, Carl. Unknown Mexico. New
    York, Charles Scribner's Sons, 1902.
    2 v.

Pérez de Ribas, Andrés. Historia de los
    triunfos de nuestra santa fe entre
    gentes las más bárbaras y fieras del
    nuevo orbe. Madrid, A. de Paredes,
    1645. 20, 763 p.

Pérez de Ribas, Andrés. My life among the
    savage nations of New Spain. Translated
    by Tomás Antonio Robertson. Los
    Angeles, Ward Ritchie Press, 1968. 16,
    256 p. illus., maps.

Sauer, C. The distribution of aboriginal
    tribes and languages in northwestern
    Mexico. Ibero-Americana, 5 (1934): 32-
    36.

Thomas, Cyrus. Indian languages of Mexico
    and Central America and their
    geographical distribution. By Cyrus
    Thomas assisted by John R. Swanton.
    Washington, D.C., Government Printing
    Office, 1911. 7, 108 p. map. (U.S.,

Bureau of American Ethnology, Bulletin,
    44)

                    15-04   Chiricahua

Adams, Alexander B. Geronimo, a
    biography. New York, Putnam, 1971.
    381 p. illus.

Anonymous. Apache. U.S. Bureau of
    American Ethnology, Bulletin, 30, vol. 1
    (1907): 63-67.

Anonymous. Chiricahua. U.S. Bureau of
    American Ethnology, Bulletin, 30, vol. 1
    (1907): 282-285.

Arnold, E. Blood brother. New York,
    1947. 558 p.

Arriquibar, Pedro Antonio de. Fray Pedro
    de Arriquibar's census of Tucson, 1820.
    Edited by Karen Sikes Collins. Journal
    of Arizona History, 11 (1970): 14-22.

Baldwin, Gordon C. The warrior Apaches; a
    story of the Chiricahua and Western
    Apache. Tucson, D. S. King, 1965.
    144 p. illus., map.

Ball, E. Chiricahua legends. Western
    Folklore, 15 (1956): 110-112.

Ball, Eve. In the days of Victorio;
    recollections of a Warm Springs Apache.
    Tucson, University of Arizona Press,
    1970. 222 p.

Ball, Eve. The Apache Scouts; a
    Chiricahua appraisal. Arizona and the
    West, 7 (1965): 315-328.

Barrett, S. M., ed. Geronimo's story of
    his life. New York, 1906. 216 p.

Bartoli, J. F. The Apache "devil dance".
    Musical Courier, 152, no. 8 (1955): 8-
    10.

Baur, John E. The Senator's happy
    thought. American West, 10, no. 1
    (1973): 34-39, 62-63.

Bellah, R. N. Apache kinship systems.
    Cambridge, 1952. 151 p.

Betzinez, J. and W. S. Nye. I fought with
    Geronimo. Harrisburg, Pennsylvania,
    1959. 214 p.

Bigelow, J. On the bloody trail of
    Geronimo. Los Angeles, 1958. 237 p.

Bigelow, John. On the bloody trail of
    Geronimo. Los Angeles, Westernlore
    Press, 1968. 25, 237 p. illus., map.

Bourke, J. G. An Apache campaign in the Sierra Madre. New York, 1886. 112 p.

Bourke, J. G. Notes on Apache mythology. Journal of American Folklore, 3 (1890): 209-212.

Bourke, J. G. Notes upon the gentile organization of the Apaches of Arizona. Journal of American Folklore, 3 (1890): 111-126.

Bourke, J. G. Notes upon the religion of the Apache Indians. Folk-Lore, 2 (1891): 419-454.

Bourke, J. G. On the border with Crook. New York, 1892. 491 p.

Bourke, J. G. The medicine men of the Apache. U.S. Bureau of American Ethnology, Annual Reports, 9 (1892): 451-595.

Bourke, J. G. Vesper hours of the stone age. American Anthropologist, 3 (1890): 55-63.

Bourke, John G. On the border with Crook. Lincoln, University of Nebraska Press, 1971. 6, 491 p.

Bourke, John G. On the border with Crook. Chicago, Rio Grande Press, 1962. 491 p. illus.

Bourke, John G. The medicine men of the Apache. Glorieta, N.M., Rio Grande Press, 1970. 443-617 p. illus.

Boyer, L. Bryce. Effects of acculturation on the vicissitudes of the aggressive drive among the Apaches of the Mescalero Indian Reservation. By L. Bryce Boyer and Ruth M. Boyer. In Warner Muensterberger and Aaron Esman, eds. The Psychoanalytic Study of Society. Vol. 5. New York, International Universities Press, 1972: 40-82.

Boyer, L. Bryce. Folk psychiatry of the Apaches of the Mescalero Indian Reservation. In Ari Kiev, ed. Magic, Faith, and Healing. New York, Free Press, 1964: 384-419.

Boyer, L. Bryce. Further remarks concerning shamans and shamanism. Israel Annals of Psychiatry and Related Disciplines, 2 (1964): 235-257.

Boyer, L. Bryce. Remarks on the personality of shamans with special reference to the Apache of the Mescalero Indian Reservation. In Warner Muensterberger and Sidney Axelrad, eds. The Psychoanalytic Study of Society. Vol. 2. New York, International Universities Press, 1962: 233-254.

Boyer, L. Bryce. Stone as a symbol in Apache mythology. American Imago, 22 (1965): 14-39.

Boyer, L. Bryce, et al. Apache age groups. Journal of Projective Techniques and Personality Assessment, 28 (1964): 397-402.

Boyer, L. Bryce, et al. Apache "learners" and "nonlearners". II. Quantitative Rorschach signs of influential adults. Journal of Projective Techniques and Personality Assessment, 32 (1968): 146-159.

Boyer, L. Bryce, et al. Apache "learners" and "nonlearners". Journal of Projective Techniques and Personality Assessment, 31, no. 6 (1967): 22-29.

Boyer, L. Bryce, et al. Comparisons of the shamans and pseudoshamans of the Apaches of the Mescalero Indian Reservation: a Rorschach study. Journal of Projective Techniques and Personality Assessment, 28 (1964): 173-180.

Boyer, L. Bryce, et al. Effects of acculturation on the personality traits of the old people of the Mescalero and Chiricahua Apaches. International Journal of Social Psychiatry, 11 (1965): 264-271.

Brinckerhoff, Sidney B. The last years of Spanish Arizona 1786-1821. Arizona and the West, 9 (1966): 5-20.

Brugge, David M. History, huki, and warfare--some random data on the Lower Pima. Kiva, 26, no. 4 (1960/1961): 6-16.

Castetter, E. F. and M. E. Opler. The ethnobiology of the Chiricahua and Mescalero Apache. New Mexico, University, Bulletin, Biological Series, 4, no. 5 (1936): 3-63.

Cavazos Garza, Israel. Las incursiones de los bárbaros en el noreste de México, durante el siglo XIX. Humanitas (Monterrey), 5 (1964): 343-356.

Chapel, William L. Camp Rucker: outpost in Apachería. Journal of Arizona History, 14 (1973): 95-112.

Clark, LaVerne Harrell. Early horse trappings of the Navajo and Apache Indians. Arizona and the West, 5 (1963): 233-248.

Clark, LaVerne Harrell. They sang for horses; the impact of the horse on Navajo and Apache folklore. Tucson, University of Arizona Press, 1966. 20, 225 p. illus., maps.

Clum, John P. "All about courtesy"; in a verbal war, John P. Clum has a parting shot. Arizoniana, 4, no. 2 (1963): 11-18.

Cochise, Ciyé. The first hundred years of Niño Cochise. New York, Abelard-Schuman, 1971. 346 p. illus.

Concha, Fernando de la. Colonel Don Fernando de la Concha diary, 1788. Edited by Adlai Feather. New Mexico Historical Review, 34 (1959): 285-304.

Cremony, J. C. Life among the Apaches. San Francisco, 1868. 322 p.

Curtis, E. S. The North American Indian, Vol. 1: 3-51. Cambridge, 1907.

Curtis, N., ed. The Indians' book, 323-328. New York, 1907.

Dana, R. W. An echo of Apache days. Indian Notes, 6 (1929): 250-254.

Davisson, Lori. The Apaches at home; a photographic essay. Journal of Arizona History, 14 (1973): 113-132.

Devereux, G. and E. M. Loeb. Some notes on Apache criminality. Journal of Criminal Psychopathology, 4 (1943): 424-430.

Dorr, L. L. The fight at Chiricahua Pass in 1869 as described by L. L. Dorr, M.D. Edited by Marion E. Valputic and Harold H. Longfellow. Arizona and the West, 13 (1971): 369-378.

East, O. G. and A. C. Manucy. Arizona Apaches as "guests" in Florida. Florida Historical Quarterly, 30 (1952): 294-300.

Edgerton, Faye E. The tagmemic analysis of sentence structure in Western Apache. In Harry Hoijer, et al., eds. Studies in the Athapaskan Languages. Berkeley and Los Angeles, University of California Press, 1963: 102-148. (California, University, Publications in Linguistics, 29)

Ellis, Richard N., ed. "The Apache Chronicle". New Mexico Historical Review, 47 (1972): 275-282.

Feather, Adlai. The territories of Arizona. New Mexico Historical Review, 39 (1964): 16-31.

Forrest, Earle R. The fabulous Sierra Bonita. Journal of Arizona History, 6 (1965): 132-146.

Gardner, H. Philip St. George Cooke and the Apache, 1854. New Mexico Historical Review, 28 (1953): 115-132.

Gatewood, Charles B. Gatewood reports to his wife from Geronimo's camp. Edited by Charles Byars. Journal of Arizona History, 7 (1966): 76-81.

Gatschet, A. S. The Chiricahua Apache "sun circle". Smithsonian Miscellaneous Collections, 34, no. 2 (1885): 144-147.

Geronimo. Geronimo: his own story. Newly edited with an introduction and notes by Frederik W. Turner III. New York, Dutton, 1970. 190 p. illus., map.

Gershowitz, H. The Diego factor among Asiatic Indians, Apaches and West African Negroes. American Journal of Physical Anthropology, n.s., 17 (1959): 195-200.

Gifford, E. W. Apache-Pueblo. Anthropological Records, 4 (1940): 1-207.

Goodman, David Michael. Apaches as prisoners of war, 1886-1894. Dissertation Abstracts International, 30 (1969/1970): 655A. UM 69-13,248.

Greenberg, Joseph H. Language universals. In Theoretical Foundations. The Hague, Mouton, 1966: 61-112. (Current Trends in Linguistics, 3)

Greenberg, Joseph H. Language universals; with special reference to feature hierarchies. The Hague, Mouton, 1966. 89 p. (Janua Linguarum, Series Minor, 59)

Greene, Jerome A. The Crawford Affair: international implications of the Geronimo Campaign. Journal of the West, 11 (1972): 143-153.

Greenfeld, Philip J. Playing card names in Western Apache. International Journal of American Linguistics, 37 (1971): 195-196.

Greenleaf, Richard E. The Nueva Vizcaya frontier, 1787-1789. Journal of the West, 8 (1969): 56-66.

Griswold, Gillett. Application of ethnographic data in identification of historic graves. Plains Anthropologist, 7 (1962): 96-97.

Harrington, J. P. Southern peripheral Athapaskawan origins, divisions, and migrations. Smithsonian Miscellaneous Collections, 100 (1940): 503-532.

Harrington, M. R. The devil dance of the Apaches. Museum Journal, 3 (1912): 6-10.

Hayes, J. G. Apache vengeance. Albuquerque, 1954. 185 p.

Heald, Weldon F. The great Cochise. Pacific Discovery, 17, no. 5 (1964): 27-31.

Helms, Mary W. Matrilocality, social solidarity, and culture contact: three case histories. Southwestern Journal of Anthropology, 26 (1970): 197-212.

Hoijer, H. Chiricahua and Mescalero Apache texts. Chicago, 1938. 219 p.

Hoijer, H. Chiricahua Apache. Viking Fund Publications in Anthropology, 6 (1946): 9-29.

Hoijer, H. Chiricahua loan-words from Spanish. Language, 15 (1939): 100-115.

Hoijer, H. Classificatory verb stems in the Apachean languages. International Journal of American Linguistics, 11 (1945): 13-23.

Hoijer, H. Phonetic and phonemic change in the Athapaskan languages. Language, 18 (1942): 218-220.

Hoijer, H. Pitch accent in the Apachean languages. Language, 19 (1943): 38-41.

Hoijer, H. The Apachean verb. International Journal of American Linguistics, 11 (1945): 193-203; 12 (1946): 1-13, 51-59; 14 (1948): 247-259; 15 (1949): 12-22.

Jerome, Lawrence R. Soldiering and suffering in the Geronimo Campaign: reminiscences of Lawrence R. Jerome. Edited by Joe A. Stout, Jr. Journal of the West, 11 (1972): 154-169.

Jozhe, Benedict. A brief history of the Fort Sill Apache tribe. Chronicles of Oklahoma, 39 (1961): 427-432.

Kate, H. F. C. ten. Reizen en onderzoekingen in Noord-Amerika, 165-208. Leiden, 1885.

Kraus, B. S. Indian health in Arizona. Arizona, University, Bureau of Ethnic Research, Reports, 2 (1954): 1-164.

Landar, Herbert J. Theme of incest in Navaho folklore. In Samir K. Ghosh, ed. Man, Language and Society; Contributions to the Sociology of Language. The Hague, Mouton, 1972: 118-133. (Janua Linguarum, Series Minor, 109)

Lane, William Carr. William Carr Lane, diary. Edited by Wm. G. B. Carson. New Mexico Historical Review, 39 (1964): 181-234, 274-332.

Leftwich, Regal H. Chiricahua anniversary. Alamagordo, 1963. 51 p. illus.

Lehmann, H. Nine years among the Indians. Austin, 1927. 235 p.

Lockwood, F. C. The Apache Indians. New York, 1938. 348 p.

Loeb, E. M. A note on two far-travelled kachinas. Journal of American Folklore, 56 (1943): 192-199.

Lummis, Charles F. Chiricahua Apache costume in the 1880's. Masterkey, 36 (1962): 33-34.

MacLachlan, Bruce B. The Mescalero Apache quest for law and order. Journal of the West, 3 (1964): 441-458.

Matson, D. S. and A. H. Schroeder. Cordero's description of the Apache-1796. New Mexico Historical Review, 32 (1957): 335-356.

Mattison, Ray H. The tangled web: the controversy over the Tumacácori and Baca land grants. Journal of Arizona History, 8 (1967): 71-90.

Meyers, Lee. Military establishments in southwestern New Mexico: stepping stones to settlement. New Mexico Historical Review, 43 (1968): 5-48.

Mierau, Eric. Concerning Yavapai-Apache bilingualism. International Journal of American Linguistics, 29 (1963): 1-3.

Mozer, Corinne C. A brief history of Fort Fillmore 1851-1862. El Palacio, 74, no. 2 (1967): 5-18.

Myers, Lee. Fort Webster on the Mimbres River. New Mexico Historical Review, 41 (1966): 47-57.

Myers, Lee. The enigma of Mangas Coloradas' death. New Mexico Historical Review, 41 (1966): 287-304.

Ogle, R. H. The Apache and the government-1870's. New Mexico Historical Review, 34 (1959): 81-102.

Opler, M. E. A note on the cultural affiliations of northern Mexican nomads. American Anthropologist, n.s., 37 (1935): 702-706.

Opler, M. E. An analysis of Mescalero and Chiricahua Apache social organization in the light of their systems of relationship. Chicago, 1936. 19 p.

*Opler, M. E. An Apache life-way. Chicago, 1941. 500 p.

Opler, M. E. An interpretation of ambivalence of two American Indian tribes. Journal of Social Psychology, 7 (1936): 82-116.

Opler, M. E. An outline of Chiricahua Apache social organization. In F. Eggan, ed. Social Anthropology of North American Tribes. 2d ed. Chicago, 1955: 173-242.

Opler, M. E. Apache data concerning the relation of kinship terminology to social classification. American Anthropologist, n.s., 39 (1937): 201-212.

Opler, M. E. Chiricahua Apache material relating to sorcery. Primitive Man, 19 (1946): 81-92.

Opler, M. E. Examples of ceremonial interchanges among Southwestern tribes. Masterkey, 16 (1942): 77-80.

Opler, M. E. Further comparative anthropological data bearing on the solution of a psychological problem. Journal of Social Psychology, 9 (1938): 477-483.

Opler, M. E. Mountain spirits of the Chiricahua Apache. Masterkey, 20 (1946): 125-131.

*Opler, M. E. Myths and tales of the Chiricahua Apache Indians. American Folk-Lore Society, Memoirs, 37 (1942): 1-114.

Opler, M. E. Notes on Chiricahua Apache culture. Primitive Man, 20 (1947): 1-14.

Opler, M. E. Some points of comparison and contrast between the treatment of functional disorders by Apache shamans and modern psychiatric practice. American Journal of Psychiatry, 92 (1936): 1371-1387.

Opler, M. E. The concept of supernatural power among the Chiricahua and Mescalero Apache. American Anthropologist, n.s., 37 (1935): 65-70.

Opler, M. E. The identity of the Apache Mansos. American Anthropologist, n.s., 44 (1942): 725.

Opler, M. E. The kinship systems of Southern Athabaskan-speaking tribes. American Anthropologist, n.s., 38 (1936): 620-633.

Opler, M. E. The sacred clowns of the Chiricahua and Mescalero Indians. El Palacio, 44 (1938): 75-79.

Opler, M. E. and H. Hoijer. The raid and warpath language of the Chiricahua Apache. American Anthropologist, n.s., 42 (1940): 617-634.

*Opler, Morris E. An Apache life-way; the economic, social, and religious institutions of the Chiricahua Indians. New York, Cooper Square Publishers, 1965. 17, 500 p. illus., map.

Opler, Morris E. Cause and effect in Apachean agriculture, division of labor, residence patterns, and girls' puberty rites. American Anthropologist, 74 (1972): 1133-1146.

Opler, Morris E. Cultural evolution, Southern Athapaskans, and chronology in theory. Southwestern Journal of Anthropology, 17 (1961): 1-20.

Opler, Morris E. Remuneration to supernaturals and man in Apachean ceremonialism. Ethnology, 7 (1968): 356-393.

Park, Joseph F. Spanish Indian policy in northern Mexico, 1765-1810. Arizona and the West, 4 (1962): 325-344.

Park, Joseph F. The Apaches in Mexican-American relations, 1848-1861: a footnote to the Gadsden Treaty. Arizona and the West, 3 (1961): 129-146.

Pennington, William David. Government policy and farming on the Kiowa Reservation: 1869-1901. Dissertation Abstracts International, 33 (1972/1973): 1123A. UM 72-23,107.

Pinnow, Heinz-Jürgen. Zu den Eigennamen der Apachen-Häuptlinge. Anthropos, 63/64 (1968/1969): 441-456.

Powers, Nellie Brown. A ride from Geronimo, the Apache. New Mexico Historical Review, 36 (1961): 89-96.

Ross, William T. Some guidance problems among the Mescalero Apache Indians. In Internationale Amerikanistenkongress, 34th. 1960, Wien. Akten. Horn-Wien, Berger, 1962: 569-577.

Sacks, Benjamin H., ed. New evidence on the Bascom affair. Arizona and the West, 4 (1962): 261-278.

Salzman, M., Jr. Geronimo, the Napoleon of Indians. Journal of Arizona History, 8 (1967): 215-247.

Santee, R. Apache land. New York, 1947. 216 p.

Sauer, C. The distribution of aboriginal tribes and languages in northwestern Mexico. Ibero-Americana, 5 (1934): 75-76.

Schmidt, M. F. and D. Brown. Fighting Indians of the West, 301-330. New York, 1948.

Schmitz, O. Die Apachen. Ausland, 44 (1871): 347-351.

Schroeder, Albert H. Navajo and Apache relationships west of the Rio Grande. El Palacio, 70, no. 3 (1963): 5-23.

Smith, Ralph A. The scalp hunter in the borderlands 1835-1850. In Roger L. Nichols and George R. Adams, eds. The American Indian: Past and Present. Waltham, Xerox College Publishing, 1971: 156-167.

Smith, Ralph A. The scalp hunter in the borderlands 1835-1850. Arizona and the West, 6 (1964): 5-22.

Spicer, Edward H. European expansion and the enclavement of Southwestern Indians. Arizona and the West, 1 (1959): 132-145.

Stevens, Robert C. The Apache menace in Sonora 1831-1849. Arizona and the West, 6 (1964): 211-222.

Tatje, Terrence. Variations in ancestor worship beliefs and their relation to kinship. By Terrence Tatje and Francis L. K. Hsu. Southwestern Journal of Anthropology, 25 (1969): 153-172.

Thompson, Erwin N. The Negro soldier on the frontier: a Fort Davis case study. Journal of the West, 7 (1968): 217-235.

Turcheneske, John A., Jr. The Arizona press and Geronimo's surrender. Journal of Arizona History, 14 (1973): 133-148.

Tweedie, M. Jean. Notes on the history and adaptation of the Apache tribes. American Anthropologist, 70 (1968): 1132-1142.

Tyler, Barbara Ann. Cochise: Apache war leader, 1858-1861. Journal of Arizona History, 6 (1965): 1-10.

Utley, Robert M. The Bascom affair: a reconstruction. Arizona and the West, 3 (1961): 59-68.

Utley, Robert M. The surrender of Geronimo. Arizoniana, 4, no. 1 (1963): 1-9.

Utley, Robert M., ed. Captain John Pope's plan of 1853 for the frontier defense of New Mexico. Arizona and the West, 5 (1963): 149-163.

Verdín, Trini. Trini Verdín and the "truth" of history. Edited and translated by Kieran McCarty. Journal of Arizona History, 14 (1973): 149-164.

Vizcaya Canales, Isidro. La invasión de los indios bárbaros al noreste de México, en los años de 1840 y 1841. Monterrey, N.L., 1968. 296 p. (Monterrey, Instituto Tecnologico y de Estudios Superiores de Monterrey, Publicaciones, Serie: Historia, 7)

Wayland, Virginia. Apache playing cards. Expedition, 4, no. 3 (1962): 34-39.

Wharfield, H. B. Footnotes to history: Apache Kid and the record. Journal of Arizona History, 6 (1965): 37-46.

Wood, Leonard. Chasing Geronimo; the journal of Leonard Wood, May-September, 1886. Edited by Jack C. Lane. Albuquerque, University of New Mexico Press, 1970. 8, 152 p. illus., map.

Woodward, A. John G. Bourke on the Arizona Apache, 1874. Plateau, 16 (1943): 33-44.

15-05   Cocopa

Chittenden, N. H. Among the Cocopahs. Land of Sunshine, 14 (1901): 196-204.

Crawford, James M. Cocopa baby talk. International Journal of American Linguistics, 36 (1970): 9-13.

Crawford, James Mack, Jr. The Cocopa language. Dissertation Abstracts, 27 (1966/1967): 3440A. UM 67-5037.

Densmore, F. Field work among the Yuma, Cocopa, and Yaqui Indians. Smithsonian Miscellaneous Collections, 74, no. 5 (1925): 147-154.

Densmore, F. Yuman and Yaqui music. U.S. Bureau of American Ethnology, Bulletin, 110 (1932): 1-216.

Dobyns, H. F., et al. Thematic changes in Yuman warfare. In V. F. Ray, ed. Cultural Stability and Cultural Change. Seattle, 1957: 46-71.

Drucker, Philip. Culture element distributions: XVII Yuman-Piman. Berkeley, 1941. 91-230 p. illus., map. (California, University, Publications, Anthropological Records, 6, no. 3)

Fay, George E., ed. Charters, constitutions and by-laws of the Indian tribes of North America. Part III: The Southwest (Apache-Mohave). Greeley, 1967. 6, 118 l. maps. (University of Northern Colorado, Museum of Anthropology, Occasional Publications in Anthropology, Ethnology Series, 4) ERIC ED046553.

Gatschet, A. S. Der Yuma-Sprachstamm. Zeitschrift für Ethnologie, 9 (1887): 382-383, 392-406.

Gifford, E. W. Californian kinship terminologies. California, University, Publications in American Archaeology and Ethnology, 18 (1922): 67-68.

Gifford, E. W. Clans and moieties in southern California. California, University, Publications in American Archaeology and Ethnology, 14 (1918): 156-167.

*Gifford, E. W. The Cocopa. California, University, Publications in American Archaeology and Ethnology, 31 (1933): 257-334.

Henry, R. E., et al. Diabetes in the Cocopah Indians. Diabetes, 18 (1969): 33-37.

Henshaw, H. W. Cajuenche. U.S. Bureau of American Ethnology, Bulletin, 30, vol. 1 (1907): 187.

Hicks, Frederic Noble. Ecological aspects of aboriginal culture in the western Yuman area. Dissertation Abstracts, 24 (1963/1964): 1333-1334. UM 63-6591.

Hodge, F. W. Cocopa. U.S. Bureau of American Ethnology, Bulletin, 30, vol. 1 (1907): 319-320.

Ives, J. C. Report upon the Colorado River of the West. Washington, D.C., 1861. 131 p.

Joel, Judith. Classification of the Yuman languages. In William Bright, ed. Studies in Californian Linguistics. Berkeley and Los Angeles, University of California Press, 1964: 99-105. (California, University, Publications in Linguistics, 34)

Kelly, D. S. A brief history of the Cocopa Indians. In For the Dean. Essays in Anthropology in Honor of Byron Cummings. Tucson, 1950: 159-170.

Kelly, W. H. Cocopa gentes. American Anthropologist, n.s., 44 (1942): 675-691.

Kelly, W. H. The place of scalps in Cocopa warfare. El Palacio, 56 (1949): 85-91.

Kino, Eusebio Francisco. Correspondencia del P. Kino con los generales de la Compañía de Jesús 1682-1707. Prólogo y notas de Ernest J. Burrus, S.J. México, Editorial Jus, 1961. 95 p. illus., maps. (Testimonio Historica, 5)

Kino, Eusebio Francisco. Kino reports to headquarters; correspondence . . . from New Spain with Rome. Original Spanish text of fourteen unpublished letters and reports. With English translation and notes by Ernest J. Burrus, S.J. Rome, Institutum Historicum Societatis Jesu, 1954. 135 p.

Kino, Eusebio Francisco. Salida para los Quiquimas de la California. México, Vargas Rea, 1954. 52 p.

Kniffen, F. B. The primitive cultural landscape of the Colorado delta. California, University, Publications in Geography, 5 (1931): 43-66.

Kroeber, A. L. Yuman tribes of the Lower Colorado. California, University, Publications in American Archaeology and Ethnology, 16 (1920): 475-482.

Langdon, Margaret. Sound symbolism in Yuman languages. In Jesse Sawyer, ed. Studies in American Indian Languages. Berkeley and Los Angeles, University of California Press, 1971: 149-173. (California, University, Publications in Linguistics, 65)

Law, Howard W. A reconstructed proto-culture derived from some Yuman vocabularies. Anthropological Linguistics, 3, no. 4 (1961): 45-57.

Moriarty, James Robert, III. The environmental variations of the Yuman culture area of Southern California. Anthropological Journal of Canada, 6, no. 2 (1968): 2-20; 6, no. 3 (1968): 9-23.

Nichols, Johanna. Diminutive consonant symbolism in western North America. Language, 47 (1971): 826-848.

North, A. W. The native tribes of Lower California. American Anthropologist, n.s., 10 (1908): 236-250.

Polesky, Herbert F. Serum albumin polymorphism in Indians of the South-western United States. By Herbert F. Polesky, Dwight A. Rokala, and Thomas A. Burch. Nature, 220 (1968): 175-176.

Romer, Margaret. Aboard ship on dry land. Journal of the West, 8 (1969): 606-612.

Romney, A. Kimball. Internal reconstruction of Yuman kinship terminology. In Dell H. Hymes and William E. Bittle, eds. Studies in Southwestern Ethnolinguistics. The Hague, Mouton, 1967: 379-386. (Studies in General Anthropology, 3)

Sedelmayr, Jacobo. Jacobo Sedelmayr missionary frontiersman explorer in Arizona and Sonora. Four original manuscript narratives 1744-1751. Translated and annotated by Peter Masten Dunne. [n.p.] Arizona Pioneers' Historical Society, 1955. 4, 82, 7 p. map.

Spier, Leslie. Cultural relations of the Gila River and Lower Colorado tribes. New Haven, Human Relations Area Files Press, 1970. 22 p. (Yale University Publications in Anthropology, 3)

Thomas, Cyrus. Indian languages of Mexico and Central America and their geographical distribution. By Cyrus Thomas assisted by John R. Swanton. Washington, D.C., Government Printing Office, 1911. 7, 108 p. map. (U.S., Bureau of American Ethnology, Bulletin, 44)

Wares, Alan Campbell. A comparative study of Yuman consonantism. The Hague, Mouton, 1968. 100 p. map. (Janua Linguarum, Series Practica, 57)

Wares, Alan Campbell. A comparative study of Yuman consonantism. Dissertation Abstracts, 26 (1964/1965): 2200. UM 65-10,774.

15-06   Concho

Beals, R. L. The comparative ethnology of northern Mexico. Ibero-Americana, 2 (1932): 93-225.

Davis, William Robert. The Spanish borderlands of Texas and Chihuahua. Texana, 9 (1971): 142-155.

Griffen, William B. Culture change and shifting populations in central northern Mexico. Tucson, 1969. 12, 196 p. maps. (Arizona, University, Anthropological Papers, 13)

Griffen, William B. Procesos de extinción y continuidad social y cultural en el norte de México durante la Colonia. América Indígena, 30 (1970): 689-724.

Hammond, G. P. and A. Rey, eds. Expedition into New Mexico made by Antonio de Espejo, 49-54. Los Angeles, 1929.

Hammond, G. P. and A. Rey, eds. The Gallegos relation of the Rodriguez expedition. New Mexico Historical Review, 2 (1927): 251-252.

Kelley, J. C. The historic Indian pueblos of La Junta de los Rios. New Mexico Historical Review, 27 (1952): 257-295; 28 (1953): 21-51.

Sauer, C. The distribution of aboriginal tribes and languages in northwestern Mexico. Ibero-Americana, 5 (1934): 59-64.

Spicer, Edward H. European expansion and the enclavement of Southwestern Indians. Arizona and the West, 1 (1959): 132-145.

Thomas, Cyrus. Indian languages of Mexico and Central America and their geographical distribution. By Cyrus Thomas assisted by John R. Swanton. Washington, D.C., Government Printing Office, 1911. 7, 108 p. map. (U.S., Bureau of American Ethnology, Bulletin, 44)

15-07   Coyotero

Allen, Robert J. The story of Superstition Mountain and the Lost Dutchman Gold Mine. New York, Pocket Books, 1971. 212 p.

Anderson, Ned. Formal education on the White Mountain Apache Reservation; report of a self-study conference. By Ned Anderson and John H. Chillcott. Chicago, University of Chicago, 1970. 48 p. (National Study of American Indian Education, Series I, 25, Final Report) ERIC ED046603.

Anonymous. Apache. U.S. Bureau of American Ethnology, Bulletin, 30, vol. 1 (1907): 63-67.

Arnold, E. The ceremony of the big wickiup. Arizona Highways, 27, no. 8 (1951): 8-15.

Baldwin, Gordon C. The warrior Apaches; a story of the Chiricahua and Western Apache. Tucson, D. S. King, 1965. 144 p. illus., map.

Bartell, Gilbert D. Apache suicide patterns: affective magical acts. In Congreso Internacional de Americanistas, 36th. 1964, España. Actas y Memorias. Tomo 3. Sevilla, 1966: 471-477.

Bartoli, J. F.   The Apache "devil dance".
Musical Courier, 152, no. 8 (1955): 8-
10.

Basso, Keith H.   Semantic aspects of
linguistic acculturation. American
Anthropologist, 69 (1967): 471-477.

*Basso, Keith H.   The Cibecue Apache.   New
York, Holt, Rinehart and Winston, 1970.
16, 106 p.   illus., maps.

Basso, Keith H.   The gift of Changing
Woman.   Washington, D.C., Government
Printing Office, 1966.   113-173 p.
illus., map.   (U.S., Bureau of American
Ethnology, Anthropological Papers, 76.
U.S., Bureau of American Ethnology,
Bulletin, 196)

Basso, Keith H.   The Western Apache
classificatory verb system: a formal
analysis. Southwestern Journal of
Anthropology, 24 (1968): 252-266.

Basso, Keith H.   "To give up on words":
silence in Western Apache culture.
Southwestern Journal of Anthropology, 26
(1970): 213-230.

Basso, Keith H.   'To give up on words':
silence in Western Apache culture. In
Pier Paolo Giglioli, ed. Language and
Social Context: Selected Readings.
Baltimore, Penguin Books, 1972: 67-86.

Basso, Keith H.   Western Apache
witchcraft.   Tucson, 1969.   75 p.   maps.
(Arizona, University, Anthropological
Papers, 15)

Basso, Keith Hamilton.   Heavy with hatred:
an ethnographic study of Western Apache
witchcraft. Dissertation Abstracts, 28
(1967/1968): 2699B.   UM 67-17,394.

Beals, R. L.   Material culture of the
Pima, Papago, and Western Apache.
Berkeley, 1934.   44 p.

Bellah, R. N.   Apache kinship systems.
Cambridge, 1952.   151 p.

Bernardoni, Louis C.   Apache parents and
vocational choice. Journal of American
Indian Education, 2, no. 2 (1962/1963):
1-8.

Bloom, L. B., ed.   Bourke on the
Southwest. New Mexico Historical Review,
9 (1934): 159-183, 375-435; 10 (1935):
1-35.

Bourke, J. G.   Notes upon the gentile
organization of the Apaches of Arizona.
Journal of American Folklore, 3 (1890):
111-126.

Bourke, J. G.   Notes upon the religion of
the Apache Indians. Folk-Lore, 2 (1891):
419-454.

Bourke, J. G.   The medicine men of the
Apache. U.S. Bureau of American
Ethnology, Annual Reports, 9 (1892):
451-595.

Bourke, J. G.   Vesper hours of the stone
age. American Anthropologist, 3 (1890):
55-63.

Bret Harte, John.   The San Carlos Indian
Reservation, 1872-1886: an
administrative history. Dissertation
Abstracts International, 33 (1972/1973):
5080A.   UM 73-7802.

Brinckerhoff, Sidney B.   The last years of
Spanish Arizona 1786-1821. Arizona and
the West, 9 (1966): 5-20.

Brodhead, Michael J.   Elliot Coues and the
Apaches. Journal of Arizona History, 14
(1973): 87-94.

Brugge, David M.   A linguistic approach to
demographic problems: the Tonto-Yavapai
boundary. Ethnohistory, 12 (1965): 355-
372.

Burbank, E. A. and E. Royce.   Burbank
among the Indians, 17-39.   Caldwell,
1946.

Buschmann, J. C. E.   Die Spuren der
aztekischen Sprache im nördlichen Mexico
und höheren amerikanischen Norden.
Berlin, Königliche Akademie der
Wissenschaften, Abhandlungen,
Supplement-Band, 2 (1854): 298-322.

Cassel, Russell N.   A comparative analysis
of scores from two leadership tests for
Apache Indian and Anglo American youth.
By Russell N. Cassel and Richard A.
Sanders. Journal of Educational
Research, 55 (1961/1962): 19-23.

Cavazos Garza, Israel.   Las incursiones de
los bárbaros en el noreste de México,
durante el siglo XIX. Humanitas
(Monterrey), 5 (1964): 343-356.

Chaput, Donald.   Babes in arms. Journal of
Arizona History, 13 (1972): 197-204.

Clark, LaVerne Harrell.   They sang for
horses; the impact of the horse on
Navajo and Apache folklore.   Tucson,
University of Arizona Press, 1966.   20,
225 p.   illus., maps.

Clifford, Nathan J., et al.   Coronary
heart disease and hypertension in the
White Mountain Apache tribe.
Circulation, 28 (1963): 926-931.

Clum, J. P. Es-kim-in-zin. New Mexico Historical Review, 3 (1928): 399-420; 4 (1929): 1-28.

Clum, J. P. The San Carlos Apache police. New Mexico Historical Review, 4 (1929): 203-220; 5 (1930): 67-93.

Clum, John P. "All about courtesy"; in a verbal war, John P. Clum has a parting shot. Arizoniana, 4, no. 2 (1963): 11-18.

Clum, W. Apache agent. Boston, 1936. 297 p.

Colton, Harold S. Principal Hopi trails. Plateau, 36 (1964): 91-94.

Corrigan, Francis Vincent. A comparison of self-concepts of American-Indian students from public or federal school backgrounds. Dissertation Abstracts International, 31 (1970/1971): 2679A-2680A. UM 70-24,959.

Curtis, E. S. The North American Indian, Vol. 1: 3-51. Cambridge, 1907.

Davisson, Lori. The Apaches at home; a photographic essay. Journal of Arizona History, 14 (1973): 113-132.

Dodge, K. T. White Mountain Apache baskets. American Anthropologist, n.s., 2 (1900): 193-194.

Douglas, F. H. Apache Indian coiled basketry. Denver Art Museum, Indian Leaflet Series, 64 (1934): 54-56.

Douglas, F. H. The Apache Indians. Denver Art Museum, Indian Leaflet Series, 16 (1930): 1-4.

Durbin, Marshall Elza. A componontial analysis of the San Carlos dialect of Western Apache: a study based on the analysis of the phonology, morphophonics, and morphemics. Dissertation Abstracts, 27 (1966/1967): 1357B-1358B. UM 65-3743.

East, O. G. and A. C. Manucy. Arizona Apaches as "guests" in Florida. Florida Historical Quarterly, 30 (1952): 294-300.

Edgerton, F. and F. Hill. Primers I, II. Glendale, 1958.

Edgerton, Faye E. The tagmemic analysis of sentence structure in Western Apache. In Harry Hoijer, et al., eds. Studies in the Athapaskan Languages. Berkeley and Los Angeles, University of California Press, 1963: 102-148. (California, University, Publications in Linguistics, 29)

Edwards, Newton. Economic development of Indian reserves. Human Organization, 20 (1961/1962): 197-202.

Ellinwood, Sybil. Calabasas. Arizoniana, 5, no. 4 (1964): 27-41.

Everett, M. W. Pathology in the White Mountain Apache culture: a preliminary analysis. Western Canadian Journal of Anthropology, 2, no. 1 (1970): 180-203.

Everett, Michael W. Cooperación en el cambio? El caso de los apaches occidentales. Anuario Indigenista, 29 (1969): 97-107.

Everett, Michael Wayne. White Mountain Apache health and illness: an ethnographic study of medical decision-making. Dissertation Abstracts International, 31 (1970/1971): 7056B-7057B. UM 71-14,512.

Fay, George E., ed. Charters, constitutions and by-laws of the Indian tribes of North America. Part III: The Southwest (Apache-Mohave). Greeley, 1967. 6, 118 l. maps. (University of Northern Colorado, Museum of Anthropology, Occasional Publications in Anthropology, Ethnology Series, 4) ERIC ED046553.

Federal Writers' Project. The Apache. Arizona State Teachers College, Bulletin, 20, no. 1 (1939): 1-16.

Forbes, J. D. Historical survey of the Indians of Sonora, 1821-1910. Ethnohistory, 4 (1957): 355-368.

Forbes, Jack D. The early Western Apache, 1300-1700. Journal of the West, 5 (1966): 336-354.

Frazer, R. The Apaches of the White Mountain Reservation. Philadelphia, 1885. 22 p.

Gatewood, Charles B. Gatewood reports to his wife from Geronimo's camp. Edited by Charles Byars. Journal of Arizona History, 7 (1966): 76-81.

Gatschet, A. S. Classification into seven linguistic stocks of Western Indian dialects. In Report upon United States Geographical Surveys West of the One Hundredth Meridian. Vol. 7. Washington, D.C., 1879: 403-485.

Gatschet, A. S. Zwölf Sprachen aus dem Südwesten Nord-amerikas. Weimar, 1876. 150 p.

Gerald, R. E. Two wickiups on the San Carlos Indian Reservation. Kiva, 23, no. 3 (1958): 5-11.

Gershowitz, H. The Diego factor among Asiatic Indians, Apaches and West African Negroes. American Journal of Physical Anthropology, n.s., 17 (1959): 195-200.

Getty, Harry T. San Carlos Apache cattle industry. Human Organization, 20 (1961/1962): 181-186.

Getty, Harry T. The San Carlos Indian cattle industry. Tucson, University of Arizona Press, 1963. 87 p. illus., maps. (Arizona, University, Anthropological Papers, 7)

Gifford, E. W. Apache-Pueblo. Anthropological Records, 4 (1940): 1-207.

Goddard, P. E. Myths and tales from the San Carlos Apache. American Museum of Natural History, Anthropological Papers, 24 (1918): 1-86.

Goddard, P. E. Myths and tales from the White Mountain Apache. American Museum of Natural History, Anthropological Papers, 24 (1919): 87-139.

Goddard, P. E. San Carlos Apache texts. American Museum of Natural History, Anthropological Papers, 24 (1919): 141-367.

Goddard, P. E. Slender-maiden of the Apache. In E. C. Parsons, ed. American Indian Life. New York, 1925: 147-151.

Goddard, P. E. White Mountain Apache texts. American Museum of Natural History, Anthropological Papers, 24 (1920): 369-527.

Goldman, Stanford M., et al. Roentgen manifestations of diseases in Southwestern Indians. Radiology, 103 (1972): 303-306.

Goodwin, G. A comparison of Navaho and White Mountain ceremonial forms and categories. Southwestern Journal of Anthropology, 1 (1945): 498-506.

Goodwin, G. Clans of the Western Apache. New Mexico Historical Review, 8 (1933): 176-182.

Goodwin, G. Myths and tales of the White Mountain Apache. American Folk-Lore Society, Memoirs, 33 (1939): 1-223.

Goodwin, G. The characteristics and function of clan in a Southern Athapascan culture. American Anthropologist, n.s., 39 (1937): 394-407.

Goodwin, G. The social divisions and economic life of the Western Apache. American Anthropologist, n.s., 37 (1935): 55-64.

*Goodwin, G. The social organization of the Western Apache. Chicago, 1942. 791 p.

Goodwin, G. White Mountain Apache religion. American Anthropologist, n.s., 40 (1938): 24-37.

Goodwin, G. and C. Kaut. A native religious movement among the White Mountain and Cibecue Apache. Southwestern Journal of Anthropology, 10 (1954): 385-404.

*Goodwin, Grenville. The social organization of the Western Apache. With a preface by Keith H. Basso. Tucson, University of Arizona Press, 1969. 22, 701 p. illus., maps.

*Goodwin, Grenville. Western Apache raiding and warfare. Edited by Keith H. Basso. Tucson, University of Arizona Press, 1971. 12, 330 p. illus.

Greene, Jerome A. The Crawford Affair: international implications of the Geronimo Campaign. Journal of the West, 11 (1972): 143-153.

Greenfeld, Philip J. Playing card names in Western Apache. International Journal of American Linguistics, 37 (1971): 195-196.

Greenfeld, Philip John. The phonological hierarchy of the White Mountain dialect of Western Apache. Dissertation Abstracts International, 33 (1972/1973): 2450B. UM 72-31,852.

Hanna, Bertram L. The biological relationships among Indian groups of the Southwest: analysis of morphological traits. American Journal of Physical Anthropology, n.s., 20 (1962): 499-508.

Harrington, J. P. Southern peripheral Athapaskawan origins, divisions, and migrations. Smithsonian Miscellaneous Collections, 100 (1940): 503-532.

Hastings, James R. The tragedy at Camp Grant in 1871. Arizona and the West, 1 (1959): 146-160.

Hildburgh, W. L. On the flint implements attached to some Apache "medicine cords". Man, 19 (1919): 81-87.

Hill, Faith. Some comparisons between the San Carlos and White Mountain dialects of Western Apache. In Harry Hoijer, et al., eds. Studies in the Athapaskan

Languages. Berkeley and Los Angeles, University of California Press, 1963: 149-154. (California, University, Publications in Linguistics, 29)

Hoffman, W. J. Miscellaneous ethnographic observations. United States Geological and Geographical Survey of the Territories, Annual Reports, 10 (1876): 461-478.

Hoijer, H. Phonetic and phonemic change in the Athapaskan languages. Language, 18 (1942): 218-220.

Hoijer, H. Pitch accent in the Apachean languages. Language, 19 (1943): 38-41.

Hoijer, H. The Apachean verb. International Journal of American Linguistics, 11 (1945): 193-203; 12 (1946): 1-13, 51-59.

Houser, Nicholas P. 'The camp': an Apache community of Payson, Arizona. Kiva, 37 (1971/1972): 65-73.

Hrdlička, A. Notes on the San Carlos Apache. American Anthropologist, n.s., 7 (1905): 480-495.

James, G. W. Basket makers of the Palomas Apaches. Sunset Magazine, 11 (1903): 146-153.

Jerome, Lawrence R. Soldiering and suffering in the Geronimo Campaign: reminiscences of Lawrence R. Jerome. Edited by Joe A. Stout, Jr. Journal of the West, 11 (1972): 154-169.

Kate, H. F. C. ten. Reizen en onderzoekingen in Noord-Amerika, 165-208. Leiden, 1885.

Kaut, C. R. Notes on Western Apache religious and social organization. American Anthropologist, 61 (1959): 99-102.

*Kaut, C. R. The Western Apache clan system. New Mexico, University, Publications in Anthropology, 9 (1957): 1-99.

Kaut, C. R. Western Apache clan and phratry organization. American Anthropologist, 58 (1956): 140-146.

Keegan, J. J. The Indian brain. American Journal of Physical Anthropology, 3 (1920): 25-62.

Kelly, Roger E. Flagstaff's frontier fort: 1881-1920. Plateau, 36 (1964): 101-106.

Kraus, B. S. Occurrence of the Carabelli trait in Southwest ethnic groups.

American Journal of Physical Anthropology, n.s., 17 (1959): 117-123.

Kraus, B. S. and B. M. Jones. Indian health in Arizona. Arizona, University, Bureau of Ethnic Research, Reports, 2 (1954): 1-164.

Kraus, B. S. and C. B. White. Micro-evolution in a human population. American Anthropologist, 58 (1956): 1017-1043.

Kraus, Bertram S. The Western Apache: some anthropometric observations. American Journal of Physical Anthropology, n.s., 19 (1961): 227-236.

Kunitz, S. J., et al. The epidemiology of alcoholic cirrhosis in two Southwestern Indian tribes. Quarterly Journal of Studies on Alcohol, 32 (1971): 706-720, 865.

Kunitz, Stephen Joshua. Navajo drinking patterns. Dissertation Abstracts International, 31 (1970/1971): 3666A. UM 70-26,174.

LaFarge, O. Apache chief--1949 model. American Indian, 5, no. 3 (1950): 3-16.

Lane, William Carr. William Carr Lane, diary. Edited by Wm. G. B. Carson. New Mexico Historical Review, 39 (1964): 181-234, 274-332.

Leo, Thomas F. Cardiovascular survey in a population of Arizona Indians. By Thomas F. Leo, John J. Kelly, Jr., and Howard A. Eder. Circulation, 18 (1958): 748.

Levy, Jerrold E. Notes on some White Mountain Apache social pathologies. By Jerrold E. Levy and Stephen J. Kunitz. Plateau, 42 (1969): 11-19.

Lockwood, F. C. The Apache Indians. New York, 1938. 348 p.

Loew, O. Vocabulary of the Apache and of the Navajo. In Report upon United States Geographical Surveys West of the One Hundredth Meridian. Vol. 7. Washington, D.C., 1879: 424-465, 469.

Longacre, William A. Archeological lessons from an Apache wickiup. By William A. Lonacre and James E. Ayres. In Sally R. Binford and Lewis R. Binford, eds. New Perspectives in Archeology. Chicago, Aldine, 1968: 151-159.

Lyon, Juana Fraser. Archie McIntosh, the Scottish Indian scout. Journal of Arizona History, 7 (1966): 103-122.

MacLachlan, Bruce B. The Mescalero Apache quest for law and order. Journal of the West, 3 (1964): 441-458.

Martin, Douglas D., ed. An Apache's epitaph; the last legal hanging in Arizona--1936. Arizona and the West, 5 (1963): 352-360.

Matson, D. S. and A. H. Schroeder. Cordero's description of the Apache-- 1796. New Mexico Historical Review, 32 (1957): 335-356.

McAllester, D. P. The role of music in Western Apache culture. International Congress of the Anthropological and Ethnological Sciences, Acts, 5 (1960): 468-472.

McNevins, Margaret. A good preschool program. Whiteriver, Ariz., Whiteriver Public Schools, 1965. 57 p. ERIC ED011468.

Meader, Forrest W., Jr. Na'ilde': the ghost dance of the White Mountain Apache. Kiva, 33, no. 1 (1967/1968): 15-24.

Meyers, Lee. Military establishments in southwestern New Mexico: stepping stones to settlement. New Mexico Historical Review, 43 (1968): 5-48.

Miller, Peter S. Secular changes among the Western Apache. American Journal of Physical Anthropology, n.s., 33 (1970): 197-206.

Miller, Peter Springer. Secular change among the Western Apache, 1940 to 1967. Dissertation Abstracts International, 30 (1969/1970): 1997B-1998B. UM 69-19,258.

Moore, Richard T. Mineral deposits of the Fort Apache Indian Reservation, Arizona. Tucson, 1968. 6, 84 p. maps. (Arizona, Bureau of Mines, Bulletin, 177)

Morris, Clyde P. A brief economic history of the Camp and Middle Verde reservations. Plateau, 44 (1971): 43-51.

Morris, Clyde P. Yavapai-Apache family organization in a reservation context. Plateau, 44 (1972): 105-110.

Murphy, Ralph. I was there when the old fort was built. By Ralph Murphy and annotated by Roger E. Kelly. Plateau, 36 (1964): 107-109.

Ogle, R. H. Federal control of the Western Apaches, 1848-1886. Historical Society of New Mexico, Publications in History, 9 (1940): 1-268.

Ogle, R. H. The Apache and the government--1870's. New Mexico Historical Review, 34 (1959): 81-102.

Ogle, Ralph H. Federal control of the Western Apaches, 1848-1886. Albuquerque, University of New Mexico Press, 1970. 30, 259 p.

Opler, M. E. The kinship systems of the Southern Athabaskan-speaking tribes. American Anthropologist, n.s., 38 (1936): 620-633.

Opler, Morris E. Cause and effect in Apachean agriculture, division of labor, residence patterns, and girls' puberty rites. American Anthropologist, 74 (1972): 1133-1146.

Opler, Morris E. Remuneration to supernaturals and man in Apachean ceremonialism. Ethnology, 7 (1968): 356-393.

Opler, Morris E. Western Apache and Kiowa Apache materials relating to ceremonial payment. Ethnology, 8 (1969): 122-124.

Owen, George M., et al. Nutritional survey of White Mountain Apache preschool children. Columbus, Ohio, Childrens Hospital Research Foundation and Ohio State University, 1970. 22 p. ERIC ED046508.

Palmer, E. Customs of the Coyotero Apaches. Zoe, 1 (1890): 161-172.

Palmer, E. Notes on Indian manners and customs. American Naturalist, 12 (1878): 308-313.

Parmee, Edward A. Formal education and culture change; a modern Apache Indian community and government education programs. Tuscon, University of Arizona Press, 1968. 10, 132 p. ERIC ED024510.

Perry, Richard. Structural resiliency and the danger of the dead: the Western Apache. Ethnology, 11 (1972): 380-385.

Perry, Richard John. The Apache continuum: an analysis of continuity through change in San Carlos Apache culture and society. Dissertation Abstracts International, 32 (1971/1972): 5589B. UM 72-11,857.

Pinnow, Heinz-Jürgen. Zu den Eigennamen der Apachen-Häuptlinge. Anthropos, 63/64 (1968/1969): 441-456.

Reagan, A. B. Apache medicine ceremonies. Indiana Academy of Science, Proceedings, 14 (1904): 275-283.

Reagan, A. B. Archaeological notes on the Fort Apache region. Indiana Academy of Science, Proceedings, 33 (1930): 111-131.

Reagan, A. B. Naezhosh, or the Apache pole game. Indiana Academy of Science, Proceedings, 12 (1902): 68-71.

Reagan, A. B. Notes on the Indians of the Fort Apache region. American Museum of Natural History, Anthropological Papers, 31 (1930): 281-345.

Reagan, A. B. Plants used by the White Mountain Apache Indians. Wisconsin Archeologist, n.s., 8 (1929): 143-161.

Reagan, A. B. Sketches of Indian life and character. Kansas Academy of Science, Transactions, 21 (1908): 207-215.

Reagan, A. B. Some notes on the occult and hypnotic ceremonies of Indians. Utah Academy of Sciences, Arts, and Letters, Proceedings, 11 (1934): 65-71.

Reagan, A. B. The Apache stick game. Indiana Academy of Science, Proceedings, 13 (1903): 197-199.

Reed, A. C. Apache cattle, horses and men. Arizona Highways, 30, no. 7 (1954): 16-25.

Roberts, H. H. Basketry of the San Carlos Apache. American Museum of Natural History, Anthropological Papers, 31 (1929): 121-218.

Roberts, H. H. San Carlos Apache double coiled basket. American Anthropologist, n.s., 18 (1916): 601-602.

Roberts, Helen H. Basketry of the San Carlos Apache Indians. Glorieta, N.M., Rio Grande Press, 1972. 121-218 p. illus.

Roessel, Robert A., Jr., ed. San Carlos Apache Indian education. Tempe, Arizona State University, Indian Education Center, 1963. 186 l. ERIC ED015810.

Roessel, Robert A., Jr., et al. Indian communities in action. Tempe, Arizona State University, Bureau of Publications, 1967. 223 p. illus.

Roessel, Ruth, comp. Papers on Navajo culture and life. Many Farms, Ariz., Navajo Community College Press, 1970. 2, 193 p. illus., map.

Romero, M. Correrias de los Apaches "Los Amarillos". Sociedad Chihuahuense de Estudios Históricos, Boletín, 7, no. 11 (1952): 567-570.

Ryan, Pat M. Trail-blazer of civilization: John P. Clum's Tucson and Tombstone years. Journal of Arizona History, 6 (1965): 53-70.

Sabre. Tour in Arizona: footprints of an Army officer. Edited by Henry Winfred Splitter. Journal of the West, 1 (1962): 74-97.

Sampliner, James E. Biliary surgery in the Southwestern American Indian. By James E. Sampliner and Daniel J. O'Connell. Archives of Surgery, 96 (1968): 1-3.

Santee, R. Apache land. New York, 1947. 216 p.

Sapir, E. An Apache basket jar. Museum Journal, 1 (1910): 13-15.

Schaeffer, M. W. M. The construction of a wickiup on the Fort Apache Indian Reservation. Kiva, 24, no. 2 (1958): 14-20.

Schmidt, M. F. and D. Brown. Fighting Indians of the West, 89-112. New York, 1948.

Schoolcraft, H. R. Apaches. In his Information respecting the History, Condition, and Prospects of the Indian Tribes of the United States. Vol. 5. Philadelphia, 1855: 202-214.

Schroeder, Albert H. The language of the Saline Pueblos; Piro or Tiwa? New Mexico Historical Review, 39 (1964): 235-249.

Sievers, Maurice L. Coccidioidomycosis among Southwestern American Indians. American Review of Respiratory Diseases, 90 (1964): 920-926.

Sievers, Maurice L. Serum cholesterol levels in Southwestern American Indians. Journal of Chronic Diseases, 21 (1968): 107-115.

Silvaroli, Nicholas. Educating Apache Indian children in a public school system. Final report of the Fort Thomas Diverse Capacity Project. By Nicholas Silvaroli and John M. Zuchowski. Phoenix, Western States Small Schools Project, 1968. 21 p. ERIC ED026182.

Smart, C. Notes on the "Tonto" Apaches. Smithsonian Institution, Annual Report of the Board of Regents, 22 (1867): 417-419.

Smart, Charles. Surgeon Smart and the Indians; an 1866 Apache word-list. Journal of Arizona History, 11 (1970): 126-140.

Smith, D. M.   Indian tribes of the
Southwest, 16-33.   Stanford, 1933.

Smith, Ralph A.   Apache plunder trails
southward, 1831-1840. New Mexico
Historical Review, 37 (1962): 20-42.

Smith, Ralph A.   The scalp hunter in the
borderlands 1835-1850. Arizona and the
West, 6 (1964): 5-22.

Stevens, Robert C.   The Apache menace in
Sonora 1831-1849. Arizona and the West,
6 (1964): 211-222.

Stratton, R. B.   Captivity of the Oatman
girls.   New York, 1857.   288 p.

Talbot, Steve.   Community development in
Bylas. By Steve and Helen Talbot.
Journal of American Indian Education, 2,
no. 2 (1962/1963): 9-15.

Taylor, Benjamin J.   Fort Apache
Reservation manpower resources; Indian
manpower resources in the Southwest. A
pilot study. By Benjamin J. Taylor and
Dennis J. O'Connor.   Tempe, Arizona
State University, College of Business
Administration, 1969.   43 p.   ERIC
ED043444.

Taylor, Benjamin J.   Fort Apache
Reservation manpower resources. By
Benjamin J. Taylor and Dennis J.
O'Connor.   Tempe, 1969.   11, 73 p.
(Arizona State University, Bureau of
Business and Economic Research,
Occasional Paper, 3)

Taylor, Benjamin J.   Indian manpower
resources in the Southwest: a pilot
study. By Benjamin J. Taylor and Dennis
J. O'Connor.   Tempe, Arizona State
University, 1969.   26, 374 p.

Taylor, Benjamin J.   San Carlos
Reservation resources. Indian manpower
resources in the Southwest. A pilot
study. By Benjamin J. Taylor and Dennis
J. O'Connor.   Tempe, Arizona State
University, College of Business
Administration, 1969.   77 p.   ERIC
ED044198.

Thompson, Erwin N.   The Negro soldier on
the frontier: a Fort Davis case study.
Journal of the West, 7 (1968): 217-235.

Tuohy, Donald R.   Two more wickiups on the
San Carlos Indian Reservation, Arizona.
Kiva, 26, no. 2 (1960/1961): 27-30.

Turcheneske, John A., Jr.   The Arizona
press and Geronimo's surrender. Journal
of Arizona History, 14 (1973): 133-148.

Tweedie, M. Jean.   Notes on the history
and adaptation of the Apache tribes.

American Anthropologist, 70 (1968):
1132-1142.

Utley, Robert M.   The surrender of
Geronimo. Arizoniana, 4, no. 1 (1963):
1-9.

Variakojis, Danguole Jurate.   Concepts of
secular and sacred among the White
Mountain Apache as illustrated by
musical practice. Dissertation Abstracts
International, 30 (1969/1970): 1474B.
UM 69-12,853.

Vivian, R. Gwinn.   An Apache site on Ranch
Creek, Southeast Arizona. Kiva, 35,
no. 3 (1969/1970): 125-130.

Vizcaya Canales, Isidro.   La invasión de
los indios bárbaros al noreste de
México, en los años de 1840 y 1841.
Monterrey, N.L., 1968.   296 p.
(Monterrey, Instituto Tecnologico y de
Estudios Superiores de Monterrey,
Publicaciones, Serie: Historia, 7)

Wesley, C.   From the Apache Indians of San
Carlos. Boletín Indigenista, 14 (March
1954): 31-36.

Wesley, Clarence.   Indian education.
Journal of American Indian Education, 1,
no. 1 (1961/1962): 4-7.

Wesley, Clarence.   Integración social de
los Apaches de San Carlos. América
Indígena, 19 (1959): 305-309.

Wharfield, H. B.   Footnotes to history:
Apache Kid and the record. Journal of
Arizona History, 6 (1965): 37-46.

Whitaker, Kathleen.   Na ih es: an Apache
puberty ceremony. Masterkey, 45 (1971):
4-12.

Whitaker, Kathleen.   Na Ih Es at San
Carlos. Masterkey, 43 (1969): 151.

White, C. B.   The Western Apache and
cross-cousin marriage. American
Anthropologist, 59 (1957): 131-133.

Whiting, A. F.   The Tumacacori census of
1796. Kiva, 29, no. 1 (1953): 1-12.

Woodward, A.   John G. Bourke on the
Arizona Apache, 1874. Plateau, 16
(1943): 33-44.

Woody, Clara T., ed.   The Woolsey
expeditions of 1864. Arizona and the
West, 4 (1962): 157-176.

Zonis, Richard D.   Chronic otitis media in
the Arizona Indian. Arizona Medicine,
27, no. 6 (1970): 1-6.

15-08 Guasave

Beals, Ralph L. The comparative ethnology
of northern Mexico before 1750.
Berkeley, University of California
Press, 1932. 6, 93-225 p. maps.
(Ibero-Americana, 2)

Ekholm, G. F. Excavations at Guasave,
Sinaloa, Mexico. American Museum of
Natural History, Anthropological Papers,
38, no. 2 (1942): 23-139.

Pérez de Ribas, Andrés. Historia de los
triunfos de nuestra santa fe entre
gentes las más bárbaras y fieras del
nuevo orbe. Madrid, A. de Paredes,
1645. 20, 763 p.

Pérez de Ribas, Andrés. My life among the
savage nations of New Spain. Translated
by Tomás Antonio Robertson. Los
Angeles, Ward Ritchie Press, 1968. 16,
256 p. illus., maps.

Sauer, C. The distribution of aboriginal
tribes and languages in northwestern
Mexico. Ibero-Americana, 5 (1934): 28-
30.

Thomas, Cyrus. Indian languages of Mexico
and Central America and their
geographical distribution. By Cyrus
Thomas assisted by John R. Swanton.
Washington, D.C., Government Printing
Office, 1911. 7, 108 p. map. (U.S.,
Bureau of American Ethnology, Bulletin,
44)

15-09 Halchidhoma

Dobyns, Henry F. Death of a society. By
Henry F. Dobyns, Paul H. Ezell, and
Greta S. Ezell. In Deward E. Walker,
Jr., ed. The Emergent Native Americans.
Boston, Little, Brown, 1972: 192-217.

Dobyns, Henry F. Death of a society. By
Henry F. Dobyns, Paul H. Ezell, and
Greta S. Ezell. Ethnohistory, 10 (1963):
105-161.

Hicks, Frederic Noble. Ecological aspects
of aboriginal culture in the western
Yuman area. Dissertation Abstracts, 24
(1963/1964): 1333-1334. UM 63-6591.

Johnston, Francis J. San Gorgonio Pass:
forgotten route of the Californios?
Journal of the West, 8 (1969): 125-136.

Kelly, M. C. The society that did not
die. Ethnohistory, 19 (1972): 261-265.

Kroeber, A. L. Handbook of the Indians of
California. U.S. Bureau of American
Ethnology, Bulletin, 78 (1925): 799-802.

Kroeber, A. L. Yuman tribes of the Lower
Colorado. California, University,
Publications in American Archaeology and
Ethnology, 16 (1920): 478-482.

Kroeber, Clifton B., ed. The route of
James O. Pattie on the Colorado in 1826.
A reappraisal by A. L. Kroeber. [With
comments by R. C. Euler and A. H.
Schroeder]. Arizona and the West, 6
(1964): 119-136.

Moriarty, James Robert, III. The
environmental variations of the Yuman
culture area of Southern California.
Anthropological Journal of Canada, 6,
no. 2 (1968): 2-20; 6, no. 3 (1968): 9-
23.

Romney, A. Kimball. Internal
reconstruction of Yuman kinship
terminology. In Dell H. Hymes and
William E. Bittle, eds. Studies in
Southwestern Ethnolinguistics. The
Hague, Mouton, 1967: 379-386. (Studies
in General Anthropology, 3)

Spier, L. Yuman tribes of the Gila River.
Chicago, 1933. 433 p.

Spier, Leslie. Cultural relations of the
Gila River and Lower Colorado tribes.
New Haven, Human Relations Area Files
Press, 1970. 22 p. (Yale University
Publications in Anthropology, 3)

Spier, Leslie. Yuman tribes of the Gila
River. New York, Cooper Square
Publishers, 1970. 18, 433 p. illus.,
maps.

15-10 Havasupai

Alvarado, Anita L. Cultural determinants
of population stability in the Havasupai
Indians. American Journal of Physical
Anthropology, n.s., 33 (1970): 9-14.

Anonymous. Indian village in the Grand
Canyon. Nursing Outlook, 14, no. 3
(1966): 46-47.

Berry, S. S. A shell necklace from the
Havasupai Indians. Plateau, 19 (1946):
29-34.

Casanova, Frank E. Trails to Supai in
Cataract Canyon. Plateau, 39 (1967):
124-130.

Casanova, Frank E., ed. General Crook
visits the Supais. As reported by John

G. Bourke. Arizona and the West, 10 (1968): 253-276.

Colton, Harold S. Principal Hopi trails. Plateau, 36 (1964): 91-94.

Curtis, E. S. The North American Indian, Vol. 2: 97-102. Cambridge, 1908.

Cushing, F. H. The Nation of the Willows. Atlantic Monthly, 50 (1882): 362-374, 541-559.

Cushing, Frank H. The Nation of the Willows. Flagstaff, Northland Press, 1965. 75 p.

Dobyns, Henry F. A brief history of the Northeastern Pai. By Henry F. Dobyns and Robert C. Euler. Plateau, 32 (1960): 49-57.

Dobyns, Henry F. The ghost dance of 1889 among the Pai Indians of northwestern Arizona. By Henry F. Dobyns and Robert C. Euler. Prescott, Prescott College Press, 1967. 12, 67 p. illus., map.

Dobyns, Henry F. The Havasupai people. By Henry F. Dobyns and Robert C. Euler. Phoenix, Indian Tribal Series, 1971. 6, 71 p. illus., maps.

Dobyns, Henry F. Wauba Yuma's people; the comparative socio-political structure of the Pai Indians of Arizona. By Henry F. Dobyns and Robert C. Euler. Prescott, Prescott College Press, 1970. 98 p.

Douglas, F. H. The Havasupai Indians. Denver Art Museum, Indian Leaflet Series, 33 (1931): 1-4.

Emerick, Richard. The Havasupais, people of Cataract Canyon. Pennsylvania, University, University Museum, Bulletin, 18, no. 3 (1954): 32-47.

Ewing, Henry P. The origin of the Pai tribes. Edited by Henry F. Dobyns and Robert C. Euler. Kiva, 26, no. 3 (1961): 8-23.

Ewing, Henry P. The Pai tribes. Edited by Robert C. Euler and Henry F. Dobyns. Ethnohistory, 7 (1960): 61-80.

Fay, George E., ed. Charters, constitutions and by-laws of the Indian tribes of North America. Part III: The Southwest (Apache-Mohave). Greeley, 1967. 6, 118 l. maps. (University of Northern Colorado, Museum of Anthropology, Occasional Publications in Anthropology, Ethnology Series, 4) ERIC ED046553.

Griffin, John I. Today with the Havasupai Indians. Phoenix, Indian Tribal Series, 1972. illus., map.

Hanna, Dan. Havasupai medicine song. By Dan Hanna and Leanne Hinton. Alcheringa, 3 (1971): 68-75.

Henshaw, H. W. Havasupai. U.S. Bureau of American Ethnology, Bulletin, 30, vol. 1 (1907): 537-539.

Iliff, F. G. People of the blue water. New York, 1954. 271 p.

James, G. W. The Indians of the Painted Desert region. Boston, 1903. 268 p.

Janson, Donald. People of the blue-green waters. Audubon Magazine, 68 (1966): 464-469.

Joel, Judith. Classification of the Yuman languages. In William Bright, ed. Studies in Californian Linguistics. Berkeley and Los Angeles, University of California Press, 1964: 99-105. (California, University, Publications in Linguistics, 34)

Kozlowski, Edwin Louis. Havasupai simple sentences. Dissertation Abstracts International, 33 (1972/1973): 741A-742A. UM 72-21,393.

Kroeber, Clifton B., ed. The route of James O. Pattie on the Colorado in 1826. A reappraisal by A. L. Kroeber. [With comments by R. C. Euler and A. H. Schroeder]. Arizona and the West, 6 (1964): 119-136.

Law, Howard W. A reconstructed proto-culture derived from some Yuman vocabularies. Anthropological Linguistics, 3, no. 4 (1961): 45-57.

Martin, John F. A reconsideration of Havasupai land tenure. Ethnology, 7 (1968): 450-460.

Montandon, G. Gravures et peintures rupestres des Indiens du Cataract Canyon. Anthropologie (Paris), 33 (1923): 347-355.

Montandon, G. Une descente chez les Havazoupai. Société des Américanistes, Journal, n.s., 19 (1927): 145-154.

Nag, Moni. Factors affecting human fertility in nonindustrial societies: a cross-cultural study. New Haven, Human Relations Area Files Press, 1968. 227 p. (Yale University Publications in Anthropology, 66)

Nag, Moni. Factors affecting human fertility in nonindustrial societies: a cross-cultural study. New Haven, Yale University, Department of Anthropology, 1962. 227 p. (Yale University Publications in Anthropology, 66)

Reilly, P. T. The disappearing Havasupai corn-planting ceremony. Masterkey, 44 (1970): 30-34.

Romney, A. Kimball. Internal reconstruction of Yuman kinship terminology. In Dell H. Hymes and William E. Bittle, eds. Studies in Southwestern Ethnolinguistics. The Hague, Mouton, 1967: 379-386. (Studies in General Anthropology, 3)

Schroeder, A. H. A brief history of the Havasupai. Plateau, 25 (1953): 45-52.

Schwartz, D. W. Culture area and time depth. American Anthropologist, 61 (1959): 1060-1070.

Schwartz, D. W. The Havasupai 600 A.D.-1955 A.D. Plateau, 28 (1956): 77-85.

Schwartz, Douglas W. A historical analysis and synthesis of Grand Canyon archaeology. American Antiquity, 31 (1965/1966): 469-484.

Schwartz, Douglas W. Prehistoric man in the Grand Canyon. Scientific American, 198, no. 2 (1958): 97-100, 102.

Schwartz, Douglas Wright. Havasupai prehistory: thirteen centuries of cultural development. Dissertation Abstracts, 28 (1967/1968): 776B. UM 67-11,540.

Seiden, William. Havasupai phonology and morphology. Dissertation Abstracts, 24 (1963/1964): 3742-3743. UM 64-514.

Service, Elman. Recent observations on Havasupai land tenure. Southwestern Journal of Anthropology, 3 (1947): 360-366.

Shufeldt, R. W. Some observations on the Havesu-pai Indians. United States National Museum, Proceedings, 14 (1891): 387-390.

Smith, Charline Galloway. Culture and diabetes among the Upland Yuman Indians. Dissertation Abstracts International, 31 (1970/1971): 3821B. UM 71-1045.

*Smithson, Carma Lee. Havasupai religion and mythology. By Carma Lee Smithson and Robert C. Euler. Salt Lake City, University of Utah Press, 1964. 8, 112 p. (Utah, University, Department of Anthropology, Anthropological Papers, 68)

Spier, L. Comparative vocabularies and parallel texts in two Yuman languages of Arizona. New Mexico, University, Publications in Anthropology, 2 (1940): 1-150.

Spier, L. Havasupai days. In E. C. Parsons, ed. American Indian Life. New York, 1925: 179-187.

*Spier, L. Havasupai ethnography. American Museum of Natural History, Anthropological Papers, 29 (1928): 83-392.

Spier, L. Havasupai (Yuman) texts. International Journal of American Linguistics, 3 (1924): 109-116.

Spier, L. Problems arising from the cultural position of the Havasupai. American Anthropologist, n.s., 31 (1929): 213-222.

Spier, L. The Havasupai of Cataract Canyon. American Museum Journal, 18 (1918): 637-645.

Stegner, Wallace E. Packhorse paradise. In his The Sound of Mountain Water. Garden City, Doubleday, 1969: 77-93.

Wampler, Joseph. Whence the Havasupai? Pacific Discovery, 12, no. 4 (1959): 24-27, 31.

Wares, Alan Campbell. A comparative study of Yuman consonantism. Dissertation Abstracts, 26 (1964/1965): 2200. UM 65-10,774.

Wares, Alan Campbell. A comparative study of Yuman consonantism. The Hague, Mouton, 1968. 100 p. map. (Janua Linguarum, Series Practica, 57)

Whiting, A. F. Havasupai characteristics in the Cohonina. Plateau, 30 (1958): 55-60.

Writers' Program of Work Projects Administration. The Havasupai and the Hualapai. Arizona State Teachers College, Bulletin, 21, no. 5 (1940): 1-36.

15-11 Hopi

*Aberle, D. F. The psychosocial analysis of a Hopi life history. Comparative Psychology Monographs, 21, no. 1 (1951): 1-133.

Aberle, David F. The psychosocial analysis of a Hopi life-history. In Robert Hunt, ed. Personalities and

Cultures.   Garden City, Natural History
Press, 1967: 79-138.

Adams, Eleanor B.   Fray Silvestre and the
obstinate Hopi. New Mexico Historical
Review, 38 (1963): 97-138.

Akin, L.   American artist. American Museum
Journal, 13 (1913): 113-118.

Albrecht, Dorothy E.   John Lorenzo
Hubbell, Navajo Indian trader.
Arizoniana, 4, no. 3 (1963): 33-40.

Allen, Terry, ed.   The whispering wind;
poetry by young American Indians.
Garden City, Doubleday, 1972.   16,
128 p.

American Bible Society.   Imuy Matthewt,
Markt, Luket, pu Johnt pumuy
lomatuawiamu.   New York, 1929.   270 p.

American Institutes for Research.
Behavior analysis model of a follow
through program, Oraibi, Arizona;
childhood education.   Palo Alto, Calif.,
American Institutes for Research, 1970.
24 p.   ERIC ED045251.

Anderson, E., et al.   Observations on
three varieties of Hopi maize. American
Journal of Botany, 39 (1952): 597-609.

Anonymous.   Found on Navajo Mountain.
Pacific Discovery, 6 (Sept./Oct. 1953):
12-13, 32.

Anonymous.   Hopi snake dance. Arizona
Highways, 21, no. 7 (1950): 4-7.

Anonymous.   Moqui Pueblos of Arizona. In
United States, Department of the
Interior, Census Office, Eleventh
Census, Report on Indians Taxed and
Indians not Taxed.   Washington, D.C.,
1890: 160-198.

Applegate, Frank G.   Indian stories from
the Pueblos.   Glorieta, N.M., Rio Grande
Press, 1971.   178 p.   illus.

Armer, Laura A.   In Navajo land.   New
York, D. McKay, 1962.   107 p.   illus.

Bahnimptewa, Cliff.   Dancing kachinas; a
Hopi artist's documentary. Original
paintings by Cliff Bahnimptewa.
Phoenix, Heard Museum of Anthropology
and Primitive Art, 1971.   36 p.   illus.

Bailey, Lynn R.   Thomas Varker Keam:
Tusayan trader. Arizoniana, 2, no. 4
(1961): 15-19.

Barber, E. A.   Habits of the Moqui tribe.
American Association for the Advancement
of Science, Proceedings, 26 (1877): 340.

Barber, E. A.   Moqui food preparations.
American Naturalist, 12 (1878): 456-458.

Barber, E. A.   The seven towns of Moqui.
American Naturalist, 11 (1877): 728-731.

Barrett, S. A.   An observation on Hopi
child burial. American Anthropologist,
n.s., 39 (1937): 562-564.

Bartlett, K.   Hopi history, II: the Navajo
wars. Flagstaff, Ariz., Museum of
Northern Arizona, Museum Notes, 8
(1937): 33-37.

Bartlett, K.   Hopi Indian costume.
Plateau, 22 (1949): 1-10.

Bartlett, K.   Spanish contacts with the
Hopi. Flagstaff, Ariz., Museum of
Northern Arizona, Museum Notes, 6
(1934): 55-59.

Baxter, R. H.   The Moqui snake dance.
American Antiquarian and Oriental
Journal, 17 (1895): 205-207.

Beaglehole, E.   Hopi hunting and hunting
ritual. Yale University Publications in
Anthropology, 4 (1936): 1-26.

Beaglehole, E.   Notes on Hopi economic
life. Yale University Publications in
Anthropology, 15 (1937): 1-88.

Beaglehole, E. and P. Beaglehole.   Hopi of
the Second Mesa. American
Anthropological Association, Memoirs, 44
(1935): 1-65.

Beaglehole, Ernest.   Hopi hunting and
hunting ritual.   New Haven, Human
Relations Area Files Press, 1970.   26 p.
(Yale University Publications in
Anthropology, 4)

Beaglehole, P.   Census data from two Hopi
villages. American Anthropologist, n.s.,
37 (1935): 41-54.

Beaver, W. T.   Peyote and the Hopi.
American Anthropologist, 54 (1952): 120.

Beckwith, M. W.   Dance forms of the Moqui
and Kwakiutl Indians. International
Congress of Americanists, Proceedings,
15, vol. 2 (1906): 79-114.

Bell, C. C., Jr., et al.   Relationship of
bile acid pool size to the formation of
lithogenous bile in male Indians of the
Southwest. Surgery, Gynecology and
Obstetrics, 134 (1972): 473-478.

Bennett, C. N.   The elder brother of the
Hopi Indians. Smoke Signals, 4, no. 5
(1952): 4-5.

Biglin, James E. Parental attitudes towards Indian education. By James E. Biglin and Jack Wilson. Journal of American Indian Education, 11, no. 3 (1971/1972): 1-6.

Billingsley, M. W. Behind the scenes in Hopi land. [n.p.] 1971. 10, 134 p. illus.

Black, Robert A. Hopi grievance chants: a mechanism of social control. In Dell H. Hymes and William E. Bittle, eds. Studies in Sothwestern Ethnolinguistics. The Hague, Mouton, 1967: 54-67. (Studies in General Anthropology, 3)

Black, Robert A. Hopi rabbit-hunt chants: a ritualized language. In June Helm, ed. Essays on the Verbal and Visual Arts. Seattle, University of Washington Press, 1967: 7-11. (American Ethnological Society, Proceedings of the Annual Spring Meeting, 1966)

Black, Robert Abner. A content analysis of 81 Hopi Indian chants. Dissertation Abstracts, 26 (1965/1966): 2411. UM 65-10,805.

Bloom, L. B. A campaign against the Moqui pueblos. New Mexico Historical Review, 6 (1931): 158-226.

Bloom, L. B. Bourke on the Southwest. New Mexico Historical Review, 10 (1935): 1-35.

Boas, F. Zur Anthropologie der nordamerikanischen Indianer. Berliner Gesellschaft für Anthropologie, Ethnologie und Urgeschichte, Verhandlungen (1895): 367-411.

Boelter, Homer H. Portfolio of Hopi kachinas. Hollywood, Calif., H. H. Boelter Lithography, 1969. 61 p. illus.

Bogert, C. M. The Hopi snake dance. Natural History, 47 (1941): 276-283.

Bourke, J. G. The snake ceremonials at Walpi. American Anthropologist, 8 (1895): 192-196.

Bourke, J. G. The snake-dance of the Moquis of Arizona. London, 1884. 371 p.

Bourke, John G. The snake dance of the Moquis of Arizona. Chicago, Rio Grande Press, 1962. 16, 371 p. illus.

Bradfield, Maitland. Hopi names for certain common shrubs and their ecology. Plateau, 41 (1968): 61-71.

Bradfield, Maitland. Rodents of the Hopi region, in relation to Hopi farming. Plateau, 44 (1971): 75-77.

Bradfield, Maitland. The changing pattern of Hopi agriculture. London, 1971. 6, 66 p. illus., map. (Royal Anthropological Institute of Great Britain and Ireland, Occasional Paper, 30)

Brainerd, M. The Hopi Indian family. Chicago, 1939. 62 p.

*Brandt, R. B. Hopi ethics. Chicago, 1954. 408 p.

Brandt, Richard Booker. Hopi ethics. In Walter R. Goldschmidt, ed. Exploring the Ways of Mankind. New York, Holt, 1960: 554-556.

Breed, William J. Hopi bowls collected by John Wesley Powell. Plateau, 45 (1972/1973): 44-46.

Breed, William J. Hopi pahos at the South Pole. Plateau, 42 (1970): 125.

Brew, J. O. The first two seasons at Awatovi. American Antiquity, 3 (1937): 122-137.

Brew, J. O. and J. T. Hack. Prehistoric use of coal by Indians of northern Arizona. Plateau, 12 (1939): 8-14.

Brito, Sylvester J. The Hopi in the twentieth century. Keystone Folklore Quarterly, 17, no. 3 (1972): 83-89.

Brugge, David M. Navajos in the Catholic Church records of New Mexico, 1694-1785. Window Rock, Navajo Tribe, 1968. 16, 160 p. (Research Reports, 1)

Bunzel, R. L. The Pueblo potter. Columbia University Contributions to Anthropology, 8 (1929): 1-134.

Bunzel, Ruth L. The Pueblo potter. New York, AMS Press, 1969. 134 p. illus.

Burbank, E. A. and E. Royce. Burbank among the Indians, 88-107. Caldwell, 1946.

Burgh, Robert F. Ceramic profiles in the western mound at Awatavi, northeastern Arizona. American Antiquity, 25 (1959/1960): 184-202.

Buschmann, J. C. E. Die Spuren der aztekischen Sprache im nördlichen Mexico and höheren amerikanischen Norden. Berlin, Königliche Akademie der Wissenschaften, Abhandlungen, Supplement-Band, 2 (1854): 281-293.

Callahan, J. T. The occurrence of ground water in diatremes of the Hopi Buttes area, Arizona. By J. T. Callahan, William Kam, and J. P. Akers. Plateau, 32 (1959): 1-12.

Chapman, K. M. A feather symbol of the ancient Pueblos. El Palacio, 23 (1927): 526-536.

Chavez, Tibo J. Early witchcraft in New Mexico. El Palacio, 76, no. 3 (1969): 7-9.

Christinger, Raymond. La Home Dance des Hopis. Société Suisse des Américanistes, Bulletin, 35 (1971): 19-20.

Clemmer, Richard O. Resistance and the revitalization of anthropologists: a new perspective on cultural change and resistance. In Dell Hymes, ed. Reinventing Anthropology. New York, Panthem Books, 1973: 213-247.

Clemmer, Richard Ora. Directed resistance to acculturation: a comparative study of the effects of non-Indian jurisdiction on Hopi and Western Shoshone communities. Dissertation Abstracts International, 34 (1973/1974): 500B. UM 73-17,158.

Collier, John. On the gleaming way. Denver, Sage Books, 1962. 163 p. illus.

Collins, G. N. A drought-resisting adaptation in seedlings of Hopi maize. Journal of Agricultural Research, 1 (1914): 293-302.

Collins, G. N. Pueblo Indian maize breeding. Journal of Heredity, 5 (1914): 255-268.

Colton, H. S. A brief survey of Hopi common law. Flagstaff, Ariz., Museum of Northern Arizona, Museum Notes, 7 (1934): 21-24.

Colton, H. S. "Fools names like fools faces". Plateau, 19 (1946): 1-8.

Colton, H. S. Hopi deities. Plateau, 20 (1947): 10-16.

Colton, H. S. Hopi kachina dolls. Albuquerque, 1959. 144 p.

Colton, H. S. Hopi number systems. Plateau, 14 (1941): 33-36.

Colton, H. S. Hopi pottery firing temperatures. Plateau, 24 (1951): 73-76.

Colton, H. S. Kachina dolls. Arizona Highways, 21, no. 7 (1950): 8-13.

Colton, H. S. Primitive pottery making. Faenza, 37, no. 6 (1952): 135-139.

Colton, H. S. Troy town on the Hopi mesas. Scientific Monthly, 58 (1944): 129-134.

Colton, H. S. What is a kachina? Plateau, 19 (1947): 40-47.

Colton, H. S. and E. Nequatewa. The ladder dance. Flagstaff, Ariz., Museum of Northern Arizona, Museum Notes, 5 (1932): 4-12.

Colton, H. S., M. R. F. Colton, and E. Nequatewa. Hopi legends of the Sunset Crater region. Flagstaff, Ariz., Museum of Northern Arizona, Museum Notes, 5 (1932): 17-23.

Colton, Harold S. Principal Hopi trails. Plateau, 36 (1964): 91-94.

Colton, M. R. F. Hopi silversmithing. Plateau, 12 (1939): 1-8.

Colton, M. R. F. Technique of the major Hopi crafts. Flagstaff, Ariz., Museum of Northern Arizona, Museum Notes, 3, no. 12 (1931): 1-7.

Colton, M. R. F. The arts and crafts of the Hopi Indians. Flagstaff, Ariz., Museum of Northern Arizona, Museum Notes, 11 (1938): 1-24.

Colton, M. R. F. and E. Nequatewa. Hopi courtship and marriage. Flagstaff, Ariz., Museum of Northern Arizona, Museum Notes, 5, no. 9 (1933): 41-56.

Colton, Mary R. F. Hopi dyes. Flagstaff, 1965. 10, 87 p. illus. (Museum of Northern Arizona, Bulletin, 41)

Coolidge, M. R. The rain-makers. Boston, 1929. 313 p.

Corrigan, Francis Vincent. A comparison of self-concepts of American-Indian students from public or federal school backgrounds. Dissertation Abstracts International, 31 (1970/1971): 2679A-2680A. UM 70-24,959.

Costo, Rupert. Indian water rights: a survival issue. Indian Historian, 5, no. 3 (1972): 4-6.

Courlander, Harold, comp. People of the short blue corn; tales and legends of the Hopi Indians. New York, Harcourt, Brace, Jovanovich, 1970. 189 p. illus.

Courlander, Harold, comp. The fourth world of the Hopis. New York, Crown, 1971. 239 p. illus.

Cox, Bruce A. Hopi trouble cases: cultivation rights and homesteads. Plateau, 39 (1967): 145-156.

Cox, Bruce A. What is Hopi gossip about? Information management and Hopi factions. Man, n.s., 5 (1970): 89-98.

Cox, Bruce Alden. Law and conflict management among the Hopi. Dissertation Abstracts International, 30 (1969/1970): 949B. UM 69-14,865.

Coze, Paul. Hopi glossary. Social Education, 36 (1972): 486.

Crampton, C. Gregory. Historical sites in Glen Canyon, mouth of San Juan River to Lee's Ferry. Salt Lake City, University of Utah Press, 1960. 16, 130 p. illus., maps. (Utah, University, Anthropological Papers, 46)

Crane, L. Indians of the enchanted desert. Boston, 1925. 364 p.

Crane, Leo. Indians of the enchanted desert. Glorieta, N.M., Rio Grande Press, 1972. 10, 368 p. illus.

Crimmins, M. L. The rattlesnake in the art and life of the American Indian. Texas Archeological and Paleontological Society, Bulletin, 17 (1946): 28-41.

Cummings, B. The bride of the sun. Kiva, 1, no. 5 (1936): 1-4.

Curtin, L. S. M. Reminiscences in Southwest archaeology: 3. Kiva, 26, no. 2 (1960/1961): 1-10.

Curtin, L. S. M. Spanish and Indian witchcraft in New Mexico. Masterkey, 45 (1971): 89-101.

*Curtis, E. S. The North American Indian, Vol. 12: 1-291. Norwood, 1922.

Curtis, N., ed. The Indians' book, 473-532. New York, 1907.

Cushing, F. H. Origin myth from Oraibi. Journal of American Folklore, 36 (1923): 163-170.

Cushing, F. H., J. W. Fewkes, and E. C. Parsons. Contributions to Hopi history. American Anthropologist, n.s., 24 (1922): 253-298.

DeHuff, E. W. Taytay's memories, 83-90. New York, 1924.

DeHuff, E. W. Taytay's tales, 18-21, 25-39, 116-121, 125-131, 141-148, 172-182. New York, 1922.

DeHuff, E. W. The witch. El Palacio, 31 (1931): 37-39.

DeHuff, E. W. Two little Hopi. New York, 1936. 224 p.

Dellenbaugh, F. S. The Somaikoli dance at Sichumovi. American Museum Journal, 15 (1915): 256-258.

Denman, Leslie V. N. Sh'a a-la-k'o Mana; ritual of creation (Hopi). San Francisco, printed at the Grabhorn Press for W. and L. Denman, 1957. 48 p. illus.

Dennis, W. Animism and related tendencies in Hopi children. Société des Américanistes, Journal, 38 (1943): 21-36.

Dennis, W. Does culture appreciably affect patterns of infant behavior? Journal of Social Psychology, 12 (1940): 305-317.

Dennis, W. The Hopi child. New York, 1945. 204 p.

Dennis, W. and M. G. Dennis. The effect of cradling practices upon the onset of walking in Hopi children. Journal of Genetic Psychology, 56 (1940): 77-86.

Dennis, Wayne. The Hopi child. New York, Arno Press, 1972. 11, 200 p. illus.

Devereux, Don. The re-location of a Pueblo Emergence Shrine. El Palacio, 73, no. 4 (1966): 21-26.

Devereux, G. La chasse collective au lapin. Société des Américanistes, Journal, n.s., 33 (1941): 63-90.

Dienes, A. de. Costumes of the Southwest Indians. Natural History, 56 (1947): 360-367.

Dockstader, F. J. Christmas--Hopi style. Smoke Signals, 3, no. 6 (1951): 2-5.

Dockstader, F. J. Spanish loanwords in Hopi. International Journal of American Linguistics, 21 (1955): 151-159.

Dockstader, F. J. The Hopi kachina cult. Tomorrow, 4, no. 3 (1956): 57-63.

Donaldson, T. Moqui Indians of Arizona and Pueblo Indians of New Mexico. U.S. Census Office, Eleventh Census, Extra Census Bulletin (1893): 1-136.

Dorsey, G. A. Indians of the Southwest. 1903. 223 p.

Dorsey, G. A. The Hopi Indians of Arizona. Popular Science Monthly, 55 (1899): 732-750.

Dorsey, G. A. and H. R. Voth. The Mishongnovi ceremonies of the Snake and Antelope Fraternities. Field Museum, Anthropological Series, 3 (1902): 165-261.

Dorsey, G. A. and H. R. Voth. The Oraibi soyal ceremony. Field Museum, Anthropological Series, 3 (1901): 5-59.

Douglas, F. H. Hopi Indian basketry. Denver Art Museum, Indian Leaflet Series, 17 (1931): 1-4.

Douglas, F. H. Hopi Indian pottery. Denver Art Museum, Indian Leaflet Series, 47 (1932): 1-4.

Douglas, F. H. Hopi Indian weaving. Denver Art Museum, Indian Leaflet Series, 18 (1931): 1-4.

Douglas, F. H. Hopi pottery. Pasadena, 1933. 15 p.

Douglas, F. H. Main types of Pueblo cotton textiles. Denver Art Museum, Indian Leaflet Series, 92/93 (1940): 166-172.

Douglas, F. H. Main types of Pueblo woolen textiles. Denver Art Museum, Indian Leaflet Series, 94/95 (1940): 174-180.

Douglas, F. H. Notes on Hopi brocading. Flagstaff, Ariz., Museum of Northern Arizona, Museum Notes, 11 (1938): 35-38.

Douglas, F. H. The Hopi Indians. Denver Art Museum, Indian Leaflet Series, 13 (1930): 1-4.

Dozier, E. P. Kinship and linguistic change among the Arizona Tewa. International Journal of American Linguistics, 21 (1955): 242-251.

Dozier, E. P. Resistance to acculturation and assimilation in an Indian pueblo. American Anthropologist, n.s., 53 (1951): 56-66.

Dozier, Edward P. Pueblo Indian response to culture contact. In M. Estellie Smith, ed. Studies in Linguistics in Honor of George L. Trager. The Hague, Mouton, 1972: 457-467. (Janua Linguarum, Series Maior, 52)

Dozier, Edward P. The Hopi and the Tewa. Scientific American, 196, no. 6 (1957): 126-130, 132, 134, 136.

Dozier, Edward P. The Pueblo Indians of the Southwest. Current Anthropology, 5 (1964): 79-97.

Drucker, P. Yuman-Piman. Anthropological Records, 6 (1941): 91-230.

Dutton, Bertha P. Indian artistry in wood and other media. El Palacio, 64 (1957): 3-28.

Earle, E. and E. A. Kennard. Hopi kachinas. New York, 1938. 40 p.

Eggan, D. Hopi marriage and family traditions. Marriage and Family Living, 6 (1944): 1-2.

Eggan, D. Instruction and affect in Hopi cultural continuity. Southwestern Journal of Anthropology, 12 (1956): 347-370.

Eggan, D. The general problem of Hopi adjustment. American Anthropologist, n.s., 45 (1943): 357-373.

Eggan, D. The general problem of Hopi adjustment. In C. Kluckhohn and H. Murray, eds. Personality in Nature, Society and Culture. 2d ed. New York, 1953: 276-291.

Eggan, D. The manifest content of dreams. American Anthropologist, 54 (1952): 469-485.

Eggan, D. The significance of dreams for anthropological research. American Anthropologist, n.s., 51 (1949): 177-198.

Eggan, Dorothy. Hopi dreams in cultural perspective. In Gustav E. von Grunebaum and Roger Caillois, eds. The Dream and Human Societies. Berkeley, University of California Press, 1966: 237-265.

Eggan, Dorothy. Instruction and affect in Hopi cultural continuity. In John Middleton, ed. From Child to Adult. Garden City, Natural History Press, 1970: 109-133.

*Eggan, F. Social organization of the Western Pueblos, 17-138. Chicago, 1950.

Eggan, F. The kinship system of the Hopi Indians. Chicago, 1936. 56 p.

Eggan, Fred. From history to myth: a Hopi example. In Dell H. Hymes and William E. Bittle, eds. Studies in Southwestern Ethnolinguistics. The Hague, Mouton, 1967: 33-53. (Studies in General Anthropology, 3)

Ehrenreich, W. Ein Ausflug nach Tusayan. Globus, 76 (1899): 53-54, 74-78, 91-95, 138-142, 154-155.

Eiseman, Fred B., Jr. Notes on the Hopi ceremonial cycles. Plateau, 34 (1961): 18-22.

Eiseman, Fred B., Jr. The Hopi salt trail. Plateau, 32 (1959): 25-32.

Ellis, Florence Hawley. A reconstruction of basic Jemez pattern of social organization, with comparisons to other Tanoan social structures. Albuquerque, University of New Mexico Press, 1964. 69 p. (New Mexico, University, Publications in Anthropology, 11)

*Emmons, G. L. Hopi hearings. Washington, D.C., 1955. 412 p.

Euler, Robert C. The Hopi people. By Robert C. Euler and Henry F. Dobyns. Phoenix, Indian Tribal Series, 1971. 106 p. illus., maps.

Farmer, M. F. Awatovi bows. Plateau, 28 (1955): 8-10.

Farmer, M. F. Awatovi mural decorations. Plateau, 27, no. 2 (1954): 21-24.

Fay, George E., ed. Charters, constitutions and by-laws of the Indian tribes of North America. Part III: The Southwest (Apache-Mohave). Greeley, 1967. 6, 118 l. maps. (University of Northern Colorado, Museum of Anthropology, Occasional Publications in Anthropology, Ethnology Series, 4) ERIC ED046553.

Federal Writers' Project. The Hopi. Arizona State Teachers College, Bulletin, 18, no. 2 (1937): 1-26.

Fergusson, E. Dancing gods, 115-178. New York, 1931.

Fewkes, J. W. A Central American ceremony which suggests the snake dance of the Tusayan villagers. American Anthropologist, 6 (1893): 285-306.

Fewkes, J. W. A comparison of Sia and Tusayan snake ceremonials. American Anthropologist, 8 (1895): 118-141.

Fewkes, J. W. A contribution to ethno-botany. American Anthropologist, 9 (1896): 14-21.

Fewkes, J. W. A few summer ceremonials at the Tusayan pueblos. Journal of American Ethnology and Archaeology, 2 (1892): 1-160.

Fewkes, J. W. A few Tusayan pictographs. American Anthropologist, 5 (1892): 9-26.

Fewkes, J. W. A study of summer ceremonials at Zuni and Moqui pueblos. Essex Institute (Salem), Bulletin, 22 (1890): 89-113.

Fewkes, J. W. A suggestion as to the meaning of the Moki Snake dance. Journal of American Folklore, 4 (1891): 129-138.

Fewkes, J. W. A theatrical performance at Walpi. Washington Academy of Science, Proceedings, 2 (1900): 605-629.

Fewkes, J. W. An interpretation of katcina worship. Journal of American Folklore, 14 (1901): 81-94.

Fewkes, J. W. Ancestor worship of the Hopi Indians. Smithsonian Institution, Annual Report of the Board of Regents (1921): 485-506.

Fewkes, J. W. Designs on prehistoric Hopi pottery. U.S. Bureau of American Ethnology, Annual Reports, 33 (1919): 207-284.

Fewkes, J. W. Dolls of the Tusayan Indians. Internationales Archiv für Ethnographie, 7 (1894): 45-74.

Fewkes, J. W. Fire worship of the Hopi Indians. Smithsonian Institution, Annual Report of the Board of Regents (1920): 589-610.

Fewkes, J. W. Hopi basket dances. Journal of American Folklore, 12 (1899): 81-96.

Fewkes, J. W. Hopi ceremonial frames. American Anthropologist, n.s., 8 (1906): 664-670.

Fewkes, J. W. Hopi katcinas drawn by native artists. U.S. Bureau of American Ethnology, Annual Reports, 21 (1900): 3-126.

Fewkes, J. W. Hopi katcinas. U.S. Bureau of American Ethnology, Annual Reports, 21 (1903): 3-126.

Fewkes, J. W. Hopi shrines near the East Mesa. American Anthropologist, n.s., 8 (1906): 346-375.

Fewkes, J. W. Hopi snake-washing. American Anthropologist, 11 (1898): 313-318.

Fewkes, J. W. Hopi. U.S. Bureau of American Ethnology, Bulletin, 30, vol. 1 (1907): 560-568.

Fewkes, J. W. Minor Hopi festivals. American Anthropologist, n.s., 4 (1902): 482-511.

Fewkes, J. W. Morphology of Tusayan altars. American Anthropologist, 10 (1897): 129-145.

Fewkes, J. W. On certain personages who appear in a Tusayan ceremony. American Anthropologist, 7 (1894): 32-52.

Fewkes, J. W. Pacific Coast shells from prehistoric Tusayan pueblos. American Anthropologist, 9 (1896): 359-367.

Fewkes, J. W. Prehistoric culture of Tusayan. American Anthropologist, 9 (1896): 151-173.

Fewkes, J. W. Preliminary account of an expedition to the cliff villages of the Red Rock country and the Tusayan ruins of Sikyatki and Awatobi. Smithsonian Institution, Annual Report of the Board of Regents (1895): 557-588.

Fewkes, J. W. Property-right in eagles among the Hopi. American Anthropologist, n.s., 2 (1900): 690-707.

Fewkes, J. W. Provisional list of annual ceremonies at Walpi. Internationales Archiv für Ethnographie, 8 (1895): 215-238.

Fewkes, J. W. Sky-god impersonations in Hopi worship. Journal of American Folklore, 15 (1902): 14-32.

Fewkes, J. W. Snake ceremonials at Walpi. Journal of American Ethnology and Archaeology, 4 (1894): 1-126.

Fewkes, J. W. Southern extension of prehistoric Tusayan. American Anthropologist, 9 (1896): 253.

Fewkes, J. W. Studies in Tusayan archaeology. Internationales Archiv für Ethnographie, 9 (1896): 204-205.

Fewkes, J. W. Sun worship of the Hopi Indians. Smithsonian Institution, Annual Report of the Board of Regents (1918): 493-526.

Fewkes, J. W. The Alósaka Cult of the Hopi Indians. American Anthropologist, n.s., 1 (1899): 522-544.

Fewkes, J. W. The A-wa'-to-bi. American Anthropologist, 6 (1893): 363-376.

Fewkes, J. W. The butterfly in Hopi myth and ritual. American Anthropologist, n.s., 12 (1910): 575-594.

Fewkes, J. W. The ceremonial circuit among the village Indians of north east Arizona. Journal of American Folklore, 5 (1892): 33-42.

Fewkes, J. W. The destruction of the Tusayan monsters. Journal of American Folklore, 8 (1895): 132-137.

Fewkes, J. W. The feather symbol in ancient Hopi designs. American Anthropologist, 11 (1898): 1-14.

Fewkes, J. W. The growth of the Hopi ritual. Journal of American Folklore, 11 (1898): 173-194.

Fewkes, J. W. The katcina altars in Hopi worship. Smithsonian Institution, Annual Report of the Board of Regents (1926): 469-486.

Fewkes, J. W. The kinship of the Tusayan villagers. American Anthropologist, 7 (1894): 394-417.

Fewkes, J. W. The lesser new-fire ceremony at Walpi. American Anthropologist, n.s., 3 (1901): 438-453.

Fewkes, J. W. The Mam-zrau'ti: a Tusayan ceremony. American Anthropologist, 5 (1892): 217-245.

Fewkes, J. W. The Mishongnovi flute altars. Journal of American Folklore, 9 (1896): 241-255.

Fewkes, J. W. The new-fire ceremony at Walpi. American Anthropologist, n.s., 2 (1900): 80-138.

Fewkes, J. W. The Oraibi flute altar. Journal of American Folklore, 8 (1895): 265-282.

Fewkes, J. W. The Owakülti altar at Sichomovi pueblo. American Anthropologist, n.s., 3 (1901): 211-226.

Fewkes, J. W. The Pa-lü-lü-kon-ti. Journal of American Folklore, 6 (1893): 269-282.

Fewkes, J. W. The sacrificial element in Hopi worship. Journal of American Folklore, 10 (1897): 187-201.

Fewkes, J. W. The sun's influence on the form of Hopi pueblos. American Anthropologist, n.s., 8 (1906): 88-100.

Fewkes, J. W. The Tusayan ritual. Smithsonian Institution, Annual Report of the Board of Regents, 1 (1895): 683-700.

Fewkes, J. W. The use of idols in Hopi worship. Smithsonian Institution, Annual

Report of the Board of Regents, 1 (1922): 377-397.

Fewkes, J. W. The Walpi flute observance. Journal of American Folklore, 7 (1894): 265-287.

Fewkes, J. W. The Wa-wac-ka-tci-na, a Tusayan foot race. Essex Institute (Salem), Bulletin, 24 (1892): 113-133.

Fewkes, J. W. The winter solstice ceremony at Walpi. American Anthropologist, 11 (1898): 65-87, 101-115.

Fewkes, J. W. Tusayan flute and snake ceremonies. U.S. Bureau of American Ethnology, Annual Reports, 19, vol. 2 (1900): 957-1011.

Fewkes, J. W. Tusayan katcinas. U.S. Bureau of American Ethnology, Annual Reports, 15 (1897): 245-313.

Fewkes, J. W. Tusayan migration traditions. U.S. Bureau of American Ethnology, Annual Reports, 19, vol. 2 (1900): 573-633.

Fewkes, J. W. Tusayan snake ceremonies. U.S. Bureau of American Ethnology, Annual Reports, 16 (1897): 267-312.

Fewkes, J. W. Tusayan totemic signatures. American Anthropologist, 10 (1897): 1-11.

Fewkes, J. W. Walpi. U.S. Bureau of American Ethnology, Bulletin, 30, vol. 2 (1910): 901-902.

Fewkes, J. W., A. M. Stephen, and J. G. Owens. The snake ceremonials at Walpi. Journal of American Ethnology and Archaeology, 4 (1894): 1-126.

Fewkes, J. W. and J. G. Owens. The Lá-la-kon-ta: a Tusayan dance. American Anthropologist, 5 (1892): 105-129.

Fewkes, Jesse W. Archeological expeditions to Arizona in 1895. Glorieta, N.M., Rio Grande Press, 1971. 15, 521-752 p. illus.

Fewkes, Jesse W. Hopi katcinas, drawn by native artists. Chicago, Rio Grande Press, 1962. 190 p. illus.

Fisher, A. K. A partial list of Moki animal names. American Anthropologist, 9 (1896): 174.

Fontana, Bernard L. The Hopi-Navajo colony on the lower Colorado River: a problem in ethnohistorical interpretation. Ethnohistory, 10 (1963): 162-182.

Forde, C. D. Habitat, economy, and society, 220-259. London, 1934.

Forde, C. D. Hopi agriculture and land ownership. Royal Anthropological Institute of Great Britain and and Ireland, Journal, 61 (1931): 357-405.

Forrest, Earle R. The snake dance of the Hopi Indians. Los Angeles, Westernlore Press, 1961. 172 p. illus. (Great West and Indian Series, 21)

Fraser, Douglas. Village planning in the primitive world. New York, George Braziller, 1968. 128 p. illus.

Frigout, Arlette. L'espace cérémoniel des Indiens Hopi (Arizona--Etats Unis). In Congreso Internacional de Americanistas, 36th. 1964, España. Actas y Memorias. Tomo 3. Sevilla, 1966: 465-470.

Frigout, Arlette. Mission chez les Indiens Hopi d'Arizona. Homme, 5, no. 1 (1965): 113-118.

Gatschet, A. S. Classification into seven linguistic stocks of Western Indian dialects. In Report upon United States Geographical Surveys West of the One Hundredth Meridian. Vol. 7. Washington, D.C., 1879: 403-485.

Gatschet, A. S. Zwolf Sprachen aus dem Sudwesten Nordamerikas. Wiemar, 1876. 150 p.

Gianini, C. A. The Hopi snake dance. El Palacio, 25 (1928): 439-449.

Gifford, E. W. Apache-Pueblo. Anthropological Records, 4 (1940): 1-207.

Gilman, B. I. Hopi songs. Journal of American Ethnology and Archaeology, 5 (1908): 1-226.

Gipper, Helmut. Gibt es ein sprachliche Relativitätsprinzip? Unter-suchungen zur Sapir-Whorf Hypothese. Frankfurt/Main, Fischer, 1971. 20, 349 p.

Goldfrank, E. S. Socialization, personality, and the structure of Pueblo society. American Anthropologist, n.s., 47 (1945): 516-539.

Goldfrank, E. S. The impact of situation and personality on four Hopi emergence myths. Southwestern Journal of Anthropology, 4 (1948): 241-262.

Granzberg, Gary. Hopi initiation rites--a case study of the validity of the Freudian theory of culture. Journal of Social Psychology, 87 (1972): 189-195.

Gray, L. H. Hopi. In J. Hastings, ed.
Encyclopaedia of Religion and Ethics.
Vol. 6. New York, 1914: 782-789.

*Hack, J. T. The changing physical
environment of the Hopi Indians. Harvard
University, Peabody Museum of American
Archaeology and Ethnology, Papers, 35,
no. 1 (1942): 1-85.

Hamer, J. H. An analysis of aggression in
two societies. Anthropology Tomorrow, 5
(1956): 87-94.

Hammond, G. P. and A. Rey, eds.
Expedition into New Mexico made by
Antonio de Espejo, 95-104. Los Angeles,
1929.

Hargrave, L. L. First Mesa. Flagstaff,
Ariz., Museum of Northern Arizona,
Museum Notes, 3, no. 8 (1931): 1-4.

Hargrave, L. L. Oraibi. Flagstaff, Ariz.,
Museum of Northern Arizona, Museum
Notes, 4, no. 7 (1932): 1-8.

Hargrave, L. L. Shungopovi. Flagstaff,
Ariz., Museum of Northern Arizona,
Museum Notes, 2, no. 10 (1931): 1-4.

Hargrave, L. L. The Jeddito Valley and
the first Pueblo towns in Arizona to be
visited by Europeans. Flagstaff, Ariz.,
Museum of Northern Arizona, Museum
Notes, 8 (1935): 17-32.

Harrington, I. L. "The good-bringing," a
tale from the Hopi pueblo of Oraibi. New
Mexico Historical Review, 6 (1931): 227-
230.

Harrington, J. P. Note on the names Moqui
and Hopi. American Anthropologist, n.s.,
47 (1945): 177-178.

Harrington, M. R. Ancient Nevada pueblo
cotton. Masterkey, 11 (1937): 5-7.

Harrison, Michael. First mention in print
of the Hopi Snake Dance. Masterkey, 38
(1964): 150-155.

Harvey, Byron, III. Ritual in Pueblo art;
Hopi life in Hopi painting. New York,
1970. 7, 81 p. illus. (Museum of the
American Indian, Heye Foundation,
Contributions, 24)

Harvey, Byron, III. Song of the Dog
Kachina. Masterkey, 40 (1966): 106-108.

Haury, E. W. and C. M. Conrad. The
comparison of fiber properties of
Arizona cliff-dweller and Hopi cotton.
American Antiquity, 3 (1938): 224-227.

Hayley, Audrey. Symbolic equations: the
ox and the cucumber. Man, n.s., 3
(1968): 262-271.

Heard Museum of Anthropology and Primitive
Art, Phoenix. The Goldwater Kachina
Doll Collection. Tempe, Published for
the Museum by the Arizona Historical
Foundation, 1969. 27 p. illus.

Heizer, R. F. The Hopi snake dance. Ciba
Symposia, 5 (1944): 1681-1684.

Henry, W. E. The thematic apperception
technique in the study of culture-
personality relations. Genetic
Psychology Monographs, 35 (1947): 1-135.

Hieb, Louis Albert. The Hopi ritual
clown: life as it should not be.
Dissertation Abstracts International, 33
(1972/1973): 990B-991B. UM 72-24,681.

Hodge, F. W. Hopi pottery fired with
coal. American Anthropologist, n.s., 6
(1904): 581-582.

Hodge, G. M. The kachinas are coming.
Los Angeles, 1937. 129 p.

Hodge, Gene Meany. The kachinas are
coming; Pueblo Indian kachina dolls,
with related folktales. Flagstaff,
Northland Press, 1967. 27, 129 p.
illus.

Holterman, J. Mission San Bartolome de
Xongopavi. Plateau, 28 (1955): 29-36.

Holterman, Jack. The mission of San
Miguel de Oraibi. Plateau, 32 (1959):
39-48.

Honigmann, John J. Understanding culture.
New York, Harper and Row, 1963. 8,
468 p. illus., maps.

Hoover, J. W. Tusayan: the Hopi Indian
country of Arizona. Geographical Review,
20 (1930): 425-444.

Hough, W. A collection of Hopi ceremonial
pigments. United States National Museum,
Reports (1900): 463-471.

Hough, W. Environmental interrelations in
Arizona. American Anthropologist, 11
(1898): 133-155.

Hough, W. Field work among the Hopi
Indians. Smithsonian Miscellaneous
Collections, 72, no. 6 (1922): 94-96.

Hough, W. Music of the Hopi flute
ceremony. American Anthropologist, 10
(1897): 162-163.

Hough, W. Sacred springs in the Southwest. Records of the Past, 5 (1906): 163-170.

Hough, W. The Hopi in relation to their plant environment. American Anthropologist, 10 (1897): 33-44.

Hough, W. The Hopi Indian collection in the United States National Museum. United States National Museum, Proceedings, 54 (1919): 235-296.

*Hough, W. The Hopi Indians. Cedar Rapids, 1915. 265 p.

Hough, W. The Moki snake dance. Chicago, 1899. 58 p.

Hough, W. The Sio Shalako at the First Mesa. American Anthropologist, n.s., 19 (1917): 410-415.

Hough, Walter. A revival of the ancient Hopi pottery art. In Frederica de Laguna, ed. Selected Papers from the American Anthropologist 1888-1920. Evanston, Row, Peterson, 1960: 246-247.

Houston, Susan H. A survey of psycholinguistics. The Hague, Mouton, 1972. 299 p. illus. (Janua Linguarum, Series Minor, 98)

Hubert, V. An introduction to Hopi pottery design. Flagstaff, Ariz., Museum of Northern Arizona, Museum Notes, 10 (1937): 1-4.

Ives, J. C. Report upon the Colorado River of the West. Washington, D.C., 1861. 131 p.

James, G. W. The Indians of the Painted Desert region. Boston, 1903. 268 p.

James, H. C. Haliksai. El Centro, 1940. 28 p.

James, H. C. The Hopi Indians. Caldwell, 1956. 236 p.

Johnson, J. R. Colonel John Miller Stotsenburg: a man of valor. Nebraska History, 50 (1969): 339-357.

Johnston, Francis E., et al. Alloalbuminemia in Southwestern U.S. Indians: polymorphism of albumin Naskapi and albumin Mexico. Human Biology, 41 (1969): 263-270.

Jones, H. Niman katcina dance at Walpi. El Palacio, 33 (1932): 68-71.

Jones, Paul. Reclamation and the Indian. Utah Historical Quarterly, 27 (1959): 50-56.

Jones, V. H. The establishment of the Hopi Reservation. Plateau, 23 (1950): 17-25.

Judd, B. Ira. Tuba City, Mormon settlement. Journal of Arizona History, 10 (1969): 37-42.

Judd, N. M. Nampeyo, an additional note. Plateau, 24 (1951): 92-96.

Kabotie, F. Designs from the ancient Mimbreños. San Francisco, 1949. 83 p.

Kate, H. F. C. ten. Reizen en onderzoekingen in Noord-Amerika, 245-267. Leiden, 1885.

Kealiinohomoku, Joann. Hopi and Polynesian dance; a study in cross-cultural comparisons. Ethnomusicology, 11 (1967): 343-358.

Kelly, Roger E. An old Hopi "tihu". Plateau, 40 (1967): 62-67.

Kelly, Roger E. Lessons from the Zeyouma Trading Post near Flagstaff, Arizona. By Roger E. Kelly and Albert E. Ward. Historical Archaeology, 6 (1972): 65-76.

Kennard, E. A. Hopi kachinas. New York, 1938. 40 p.

Kennard, E. A. Hopi reactions to death. American Anthropologist, n.s., 39 (1937): 491-496.

Kennard, E. A. Little Hopi Hopihoya. Indian Life Readers, Pueblo Series, 2 (1948): 1-201.

Kennard, Edward A. Hopi kachinas. 2d ed. New York, Museum of the American Indian, Heye Foundation, 1971. 15, 50 p. illus.

Kennard, Edward A. Linguistic acculturation in Hopi. International Journal of American Linguistics, 29 (1963): 36-41.

Kennard, Edward A. Metaphor and magic: key concepts in Hopi culture and their linguistic forms. In M. Estellie Smith, ed. Studies in Linguistics in Honor of George L. Trager. The Hague, Mouton, 1972: 468-473. (Janua Linguarum, Series Maior, 52)

Kennard, Edward A. Post-war economic changes among the Hopi. In June Helm, et al., eds. Essays in Economic Anthropology. Seattle, University of Washington Press, 1965: 25-32. (American Ethnological Society, Proceedings of the Annual Spring Meeting, 1965)

Kent, K. P. The braiding of a Hopi wedding sash. Plateau, 12 (1940): 46-52.

Kewanwytewa, J. A true story. Plateau, 29 (1957): 87-88.

Kewanwytewa, J. and K. Bartlett. Hopi moccasin making. Plateau, 19 (1946): 21-28.

Klauber, L. M. A herpetological review of the Hopi snake dance. Zoological Society of San Diego, Bulletin, 6 (1930): 1-58.

Klauber, L. M. How the Hopi handle rattlesnakes. Plateau, 19 (1947): 37-39.

Kluckhohn, C. Hopi and Navajo. New Mexico Quarterly, 3 (1933): 56-64.

Kluckhohn, C. and K. MacLeish. Moencopi variations from Whorf's Second Mesa Hopi. International Journal of American Linguistics, 21 (1955): 150-156.

Kravagna, Paul Warren. An ethnological approach to art education programming for Navajo and Pueblo students. Dissertation Abstracts International, 32 (1971/1972): 5107A-5108A. UM 72-8369.

Kunitz, S. J., et al. The epidemiology of alcoholic cirrhosis in two Southwestern Indian tribes. Quarterly Journal of Studies on Alcohol, 32 (1971): 706-720, 865.

Kunitz, Stephen Joshua. Navajo drinking patterns. Dissertation Abstracts International, 31 (1970/1971): 3666A. UM 70-26,174.

Kupferer, Harriet J. Couvade: ritual or real illness. American Anthropologist, 67 (1965): 99-102.

Landar, Herbert J. The loss of Athapaskan words for fish in the Southwest. International Journal of American Linguistics, 26 (1960): 75-77.

Lawrence, B. Mammals found at the Awatovi Site. Harvard University, Peabody Museum of American Archaeology and Ethnology, Papers, 35, no. 3 (1951): 1-44.

Lee, D. D. Freedom and culture. Englewood Cliffs, 1959. 187 p.

Levy, Jerrold E. Indian reservations, anomie, and social pathologies. By Jerrold E. Levy and Stephen J. Kunitz. Southwestern Journal of Anthropology, 27 (1971): 97-128.

Lewton, F. L. The cotton of the Hopi Indians. Smithsonian Miscellaneous Collections, 60, no. 6 (1913): 1-15.

Linné, S. Prehistoric and modern Hopi pottery. Ethnos, 11 (1946): 89-98.

List, George. Songs in Hopi culture, past and present. International Folk Music Council, Journal, 14 (1962): 30-35.

List, George. The Hopi and the White Man's music. Sing Out, 14, no. 2 (1964): 47-49.

List, George. The Hopi as composer and poet. In Peter Crossley-Holland, ed. Centennial Workshop in Ethnomusicology. June 19-23, 1967, University of British Columbia, Vancouver. Proceedings. Victoria, Government of the Province of British Columbia, 1968: 43-53.

Lockett, H. G. The unwritten literature of the Hopi. Arizona, University, Social Science Bulletin, 2 (1933): 1-101.

Loeb, S. M. A note on two far-travelled kachinas. Journal of American Folklore, 56 (1943): 192-199.

Lowie, R. H. A woman's ceremony among the Hopi. Natural History, 25 (1925): 178-184.

Lowie, R. H. Hopi kinship. American Museum of Natural History, Anthropological Papers, 30 (1929): 361-388.

Lowie, R. H. Noted in Hopiland. American Museum Journal, 17 (1917): 569-574.

Lowie, R. H. Notes on Hopi clans. American Museum of Natural History, Anthropological Papers, 30 (1929): 303-360.

Lummis, Charles F. Bullying the Moqui. Prescott, Prescott College Press, 1968. 11, 132 p. illus.

Lundahl, W. D. About Hopi kachinas. Masterkey, 32 (1958): 122-126.

MacGregor, J. C. Burial of an early American magician. American Philosophical Society, Proceedings, 86 (1943): 270-292.

MacGregor, J. C. Zwei gegensätzliche Indianer-Stämme in Arizona. Natur und Volk, 68 (1938): 535-544.

MacLeish, K. A few Hopi songs from Moenkopi. Masterkey, 15 (1941): 178-184.

MacLeish, K. Notes on folk medicine in the Hopi village of Moenkopi. Journal of American Folklore, 56 (1943): 62-68.

MacLeish, K. Notes on Hopi belt-weaving
of Moenkopi. American Anthropologist,
n.s., 42 (1940): 291-310.

Marcy, R. B. Thirty years of army life on
the border, 104-111. New York, 1866.

Martin, P. S. and E. S. Willis. Anasazi
painted pottery. Field Museum of Natural
History, Anthropology Memoirs, 5 (1940):
1-284.

Matchett, William F. Repeated
hallucinatory experiences as a part of
the mourning process among Hopi Indian
women. Psychiatry, 35 (1972): 185-194.

McCormick, H. The artist's Southwest.
American Museum Journal, 13 (1913): 119-
125.

McGibbeny, J. H. Hopi jewelry. Arizona
Highways, 21, no. 7 (1950): 18-25.

McIntire, Elliot G. Ten Kate's account of
the Walpi Snake Dance: 1883. By Elliot
G. McIntire and Sandra R. Gordon.
Plateau, 41 (1968): 27-33.

McIntire, Elliot Gregor. The impact of
cultural change on the land use patterns
of the Hopi Indians. Dissertation
Abstracts International, 30 (1969/1970):
475B. UM 69-12,628.

McPhee, J. C. Indians in non-Indian
communities. Window Rock, 1953. 68 p.

Means, Florence C. Sunlight on the Hopi
mesas; the story of Abigail E. Johnson.
Philadelphia, Judson Press, 1960.
171 p. illus.

Mearns, E. A. Ornithological vocabulary
of the Moki Indians. American
Anthropologist, 9 (1896): 391-403.

Milford, S. J. Why the coyote has a black
spot on his tail. El Palacio, 48 (1941):
83-84.

Miller, Mary R. The language and language
beliefs of Indian children.
Anthropological Linguistics, 12 (1970):
51-61.

Miller, Wick R. Uto-Aztecan cognate sets.
Berkeley and Los Angeles, University of
California Press, 1967. 5, 83 p. map.
(California, University, Publications in
Linguistics, 48)

Mindeleff, C. An Indian dance. Science, 7
(1886): 507-514.

Mindeleff, C. Localization of Tusayan
clans. U.S. Bureau of American
Ethnology, Annual Reports, 19, vol. 2
(1900): 635-653.

Mindeleff, V. A study of Pueblo
architecture, Tusayan and Cibola. U.S.
Bureau of American Ethnology, Annual
Reports, 8 (1887): 13-234.

Monongye, Preston. The new Indian jewelry
art of the Southwest. Arizona Highways,
48, no. 6 (1972): 6-11, 46-47.

*Montgomery, R. G., W. Smith, and J. O.
Brew. Franciscan Awatowi. Harvard
University, Peabody Museum of American
Archaeology and Ethnology, Papers, 36
(1949): 1-361.

Mori, Jocelyn Irene. Changes in Hopi
material culture. Dissertation Abstracts
International, 34 (1973/1974): 967B. UM
73-21,464.

Mori, John. Hopi silversmithing. By John
and Joyce Mori. Los Angeles, 1971.
20 p. illus. (Southwest Museum,
Leaflets, 35)

Mori, John. Hopi silversmithing. By John
Mori and Joyce Mori. Masterkey, 44
(1970): 124-142.

Mori, Joyce. Modern Hopi coiled basketry.
By Joyce Mori and John Mori. Masterkey,
46 (1972): 4-17.

Munk, J. A. Arizona sketches, 181-211.
New York, 1905.

Murdock, G. P. Our primitive
contemporaries, 324-358. New York,
1934.

Murphy, M. M. The snake dance people and
their country. Oakland, 1928. 14 p.

*Nagata, Shuichi. Modern transformations
of Moenkopi Pueblo. Urbana, University
of Illinois Press, 1970. 17, 336 p.
illus., maps. (Illinois, University,
Studies in Anthropology, 6)

Nagata, Shuichi. Modern transformations
of Moenkopi Pueblo. Dissertation
Abstracts, 28 (1967/1968): 1324B-1325B.
UM 67-11,892.

Nagata, Shuichi. The reservation
community and the urban community: Hopi
Indians of Moenkopi. In Jack O. Waddell
and O. Michael Watson, eds. The American
Indian in Urban Society. Boston,
Little, Brown, 1971: 114-159.

Nelson, J. L. Rhythm for rain. Boston,
1937. 272 p.

Nequatewa, E. A flute ceremony at
Hotevilla. Plateau, 19 (1946): 35-36.

Nequatewa, E. A Mexican raid on the Hopi pueblo of Oraibi. Plateau, 16 (1944): 45-52.

Nequatewa, E. Chaveyo, the first kachina. Plateau, 20 (1948): 60-62.

Nequatewa, E. Hopi Hopiwime: the Hopi ceremonial calendar. Flagstaff, Ariz., Museum of Northern Arizona, Museum Notes, 3, no. 9 (1931): 1-4.

Nequatewa, E. How the Hopi respect the game animals. Plateau, 18 (1946): 61-62.

Nequatewa, E. Miniature pottery. Plateau, 12 (1939): 18.

Nequatewa, E. Some Hopi recipes for the preparation of wild plant foods. Plateau, 16 (1943): 18-20.

Nequatewa, E. The destruction of Elden Pueblo. Plateau, 28, no. 2 (1955): 37-44.

Nequatewa, E. The morning-echo days. Plateau, 13 (1940): 15-16.

Nequatewa, E. The place of corn and feathers in Hopi ceremonies. Plateau, 19 (1946): 15-16.

Nequatewa, E. Truth of a Hopi and other clan stories of Shungopovi. Flagstaff, Ariz., Museum of Northern Arizona, Bulletin, 8 (1936): 1-113.

Nequatewa, E. and M. R. F. Colton. Hopi courtship and marriage. Flagstaff, Ariz., Museum of Northern Arizona, Museum Notes, 5 (1933): 41-54.

Nusbaum, M. A. Another tower of Babel, a Hopi tale. El Palacio, 18 (1925): 9-12.

Oakden, E. C. and M. Sturt. The snake dance of the Hopi Indians. Scottish Geographical Magazine, 43 (1927): 41-44.

O'Kane, W. C. Sun in the sky. Norman, 1950. 261 p.

O'Kane, W. C. The Hopi. Norman, 1953. 279 p.

Oliver, M. L. The snake dance. National Geographic Magazine, 22 (1911): 107-137.

Olsen, Robert W., Jr. Winsor Castle: Mormon frontier fort at Pipe Spring. Utah Historical Quarterly, 34 (1966): 218-226.

Owens, J. C. Natal ceremonies of the Hopi Indians. Journal of American Ethnology and Archaeology, 2 (1892): 163-175.

Page, G. B. Hopi land patterns. Plateau, 13 (1940): 29-36.

Painter, S. L. Hemophilia (AHG deficiency) and factor VII (stable factor) deficiency in the American Indian. Report of four cases. By S. L. Painter and Rosamond Ellett. Rocky Mountain Medical Journal, 57, no. 1 (1960): 65-68.

Parry, C. C. On a form of the boomerang in use among the Moqui-Pueblo Indians. American Association for the Advancement of Science, Proceedings, 20 (1871): 397-400.

Parsons, E. C. A Pueblo Indian journal. American Anthropological Association, Memoirs, 32 (1925): 1-123.

Parsons, E. C. Early relations between Hopi and Keres. American Anthropologist, n.s., 38 (1936): 554-560.

Parsons, E. C. Getting married on First Mesa. Scientific Monthly, 13 (1921): 259-265.

Parsons, E. C. Hidden ball on First Mesa. Man, 22 (1922): 89-91.

Parsons, E. C. Hopi and Zuni ceremonialism. American Anthropological Association, Memoirs, 39 (1933): 1-108.

Parsons, E. C. Hopi mothers and children. Man, 21 (1921): 98-104.

Parsons, E. C. Naming practices in Arizona. American Anthropologist, n.s., 39 (1937): 561-562.

Parsons, E. C. Pueblo Indian religion. Chicago, 1939. 2 v.

Parsons, E. C. The Hopi buffalo dance. Man, 23 (1923): 21-27.

Parsons, E. C. The Hopi Wowochim ceremony in 1920. American Anthropologist, n.s., 25 (1923): 156-187.

Parsons, E. C. The humpbacked flute player of the Southwest. American Anthropologist, n.s., 40 (1938): 337-338.

Parsons, E. C. The kinship nomenclature of the Pueblo Indians. American Anthropologist, n.s., 34 (1932): 377-389.

Paxton, S. Gabe, Jr. A study of the composite self-concept of the Southwestern Indian adolescent; an inservice action research project of Sherman Institute. Washington, D.C.,

Bureau of Indian Affairs, 1966. 32 p. ERIC ED052878.

Peet, S. D. The worship of the rain-god. American Antiquarian and Oriental Journal, 16 (1894): 341-356.

Peters, Herbert D. Performance of Hopi children on four intelligence tests. Journal of American Indian Education, 2, no. 2 (1962/1963): 27-31.

Peterson, Charles S. The Hopi and the Mormons; 1858-1873. Utah Historical Quarterly, 39 (1971): 179-194.

Phoenix Indian School. The new trail: a book of creative writing by Indian students. Phoenix, 1941. 158 p.

Porvaznik, John. Surgical problems of the Navajo and Hopi Indians. American Journal of Surgery, 123 (1972): 545-548.

Postal, Susan Koessler. Body-image and identity: a comparison of Kwakiutl and Hopi. American Anthropologist, 67 (1965): 455-462.

Prosnitz, Leonard R. Diabetes mellitus among Navajo and Hopi Indians: the lack of vascular complications. By Leonard R. Prosnitz and Gerald L. Mandell. American Journal of the Medical Sciences, 253 (1967): 700-705.

Qoyawayma, Polingaysi. No turning back. By Polingyasi Qoyawayma (Elizabeth Q. White). Albuquerque, University of New Mexico Press, 1964. 180 p. illus.

Reid, F. A. Hopi snake poison. Masterkey, 22 (1948): 10-11.

Renaud, E. B. Kokopelli. Southwestern Lore, 14 (1948): 25-40.

Ressler, John Quenton. Moenkopi: sequent occupance, landscape change, and the view of the environment in an oasis on the western Navajo Reservation, Arizona. Dissertation Abstracts International, 31 (1970/1971): 6059B-6060B. UM 71-10,777.

Rhodes, Willard. North American Indian music in transition. International Folk Music Council, Journal, 15 (1963): 9-14.

Rinaldo, John B. Notes on the origins of historic Zuni culture. Kiva, 29, no. 4 (1963/1964): 86-98.

Roessel, Ruth, comp. Papers on Navajo culture and life. Many Farms, Ariz., Navajo Community College Press, 1970. 2, 193 p. illus., map.

Rubenstein, A., et al. Effect of improved sanitary facilities on infant diarrhea

in a Hopi village. U.S., Public Health Service, Public Health Reports, 84 (1969): 1093-1097.

Rust, H. N. The Moqui snake dance. Land of Sunshine, 4 (1896): 70-76.

Sampliner, James E. Biliary surgery in the Southwestern American Indian. By James E. Sampliner and Daniel J. O'Connell. Archives of Surgery, 96 (1968): 1-3.

Schwartz, Douglas W. A historical analysis and synthesis of Grand Canyon archaeology. American Antiquity, 31 (1965/1966): 469-484.

Sedelmayr, Jacobo. Jacobo Sedelmayr missionary frontiersman explorer in Arizona and Sonora. Four original manuscript narratives 1744-1751. Translated and annotated by Peter Masten Dunne. [n.p.] Arizona Pioneers' Historical Society, 1955. 4, 82, 7 p. map.

Seiler, Hansjakob. Accent and morphophonemics in Cahuilla and in Uto-Aztecan. International Journal of American Linguistics, 31 (1965): 50-59.

Se-kyal-ets-tewa. Indian love letters. Tucson, Omen Press, 1972. 122 p. illus.

Senior, Willoughby F. Smoke upon the winds; adventures in peace. Denver, Sage Books, 1961. 144 p. illus.

Senter, D. and F. Hawley. Hopi and Navajo child burials. American Anthropologist, n.s., 39 (1937): 131-134.

Shepardson, Mary. The traditional authority system of the Navajos. In Ronald Cohen and John Middleton, eds. Comparative Political Systems. Garden City, Natural History Press, 1967: 143-154.

Shufeldt, R. W. A maid of Wolpai. United States National Museum, Proceedings, 15 (1892): 29-33.

Sievers, Maurice L. A study of achlorhydria among Southwestern American Indians. American Journal of Gastroenterology, 45 (1966): 99-108.

Sikorski, Kathryn A. Modern Hopi pottery. Logan, Utah State University Press, 1968. 92 p. illus. (Utah State University, Monograph Series, 15, no. 2)

*Simmons, L. W. Sun Chief. New Haven, 1942. 460 p.

Simmons, Marc. New Mexico's smallpox epidemic of 1780-1781. New Mexico Historical Review, 41 (1966): 319-326.

Simpson, R. D. The Hopi Indians. Southwest Museum Leaflets, 25 (1953): 1-91.

Singer, O. E. Abbot Sakiestewa--Hopi doll maker. Arizona Highways, 31, no. 8 (1955): 8-15.

Smith, D. M. Indian tribes of the Southwest, 39-55. Stanford, 1933.

Smith, W. Kiva mural decorations at Awatovi and Kawaika-a. Harvard University, Peabody Museum of American Archaeology and Ethnology, Papers, 37 (1952): 1-348.

Solberg, O. Gebräuche der Mittelmesa-Hopi (Moqui) bei Namengebung, Heirat und Tod. Zeitschrift für Ethnologie, 37 (1905): 626-636.

Solberg, O. Uber die Báhos der Hopi. Archiv für Anthropologie, 22 (1906): 48-74.

Stanislawski, Michael B. The ethno-archaeology of Hopi pottery making. Plateau, 42 (1969): 27-33.

Stanislawski, Michael B. The ethno-archaeology of Hopi pottery-making. In Jesse D. Jennings and E. Adamson Hoebel, eds. Readings in Anthropology. 3d ed. New York, McGraw-Hill, 1972: 80-84.

Stanislawski, Michael Barr. Wupatki Pueblo: a study in cultural fusion and change in Sinagua and Hopi prehistory. Dissertation Abstracts, 25 (1964/1965): 24-25. UM 64-4280.

Stephen, A. M. Hopi Indians of Arizona. Masterkey, 13 (1939): 197-204; 14 (1940): 20-27, 102-109, 143-149, 170-179, 207-215.

Stephen, A. M. Hopi tales. Journal of American Folklore, 42 (1929): 2-72.

Stephen, A. M. Legend of the Snake Order of the Moquis. Journal of American Folklore, 1 (1888): 109-114.

Stephen, A. M. The Po-boc-tu among the Hopi. American Antiquarian and Oriental Journal, 16 (1894): 212-215.

*Stephen, Alexander M. Hopi journal of Alexander M. Stephen. Edited by Elsie Clews Parsons. New York, AMS Press, 1969. 2 v. (52, 1417 p.) illus., maps.

Stevenson, J. Illustrated catalogue of the collections obtained from the Pueblos of Zuni, New Mexico, and Wolpi, Arizona. U.S. Bureau of American Ethnology, Annual Reports, 3 (1884): 587-594.

Stevenson, J. Illustrated catalogue of the collections obtained from the Indians of New Mexico and Arizona. U.S. Bureau of American Ethnology, Annual Reports, 2 (1883): 375-399.

Stevenson, M. C. Tusayan legends of the snake and flute people. American Association for the Advancement of Science, Proceedings, 41 (1892): 258-271.

Steward, J. H. Notes on Hopi ceremonies in their initiatory form. American Anthropologist, n.s., 33 (1931): 56-79.

Stirling, M. W. Snake bites and the Hopi snake dance. Smithsonian Institution, Annual Report of the Board of Regents (1941): 551-555.

Stocker, J. Indian country. Arizona Highways, 31, no. 7 (1955): 18-29.

Suci, George J. A comparison of semantic structures in American Southwest culture groups. Journal of Abnormal and Social Psychology, 61 (1960): 25-30.

Talayesva, Don C. Twins twisted into one. In Alan Dundes, ed. Every Man His Way. Englewood Cliffs, Prentice-Hall, 1968: 440-448.

Thompson, L. Attitudes and acculturation. American Anthropologist, n.s., 50 (1948): 200-215.

*Thompson, L. Culture in crisis. New York, 1950. 221 p.

Thompson, L. Logico-aesthetic integration in Hopi culture. American Anthropologist, n.s., 47 (1945): 540-553.

Thompson, L. and A. Joseph. The Hopi way. Chicago, 1945. 151 p.

Thompson, Laura. Education of the Hopi child. By Laura Thompson and Alice Joseph. In Walter R. Goldschmidt, ed. Exploring the Ways of Mankind. New York, Holt, 1960: 187-194.

Thompson, Laura. The Hopi way. By Laura Thompson and Alice Joseph. New York, Russell and Russell, 1965. 151 p. illus., maps.

Titiev, M. A Hopi salt expedition. American Anthropologist, n.s., 39 (1937): 244-258.

Titiev, M. A Hopi visit to the afterworld. Michigan Academy of Science, Arts and Letters, Papers, 26 (1940): 495-504.

Titiev, M. Dates of planting at the Hopi Indian pueblo of Oraibi. Flagstaff, Ariz., Museum of Northern Arizona, Museum Notes, 11 (1938): 39-42.

Titiev, M. Hopi racing customs at Oraibi. Michigan Academy of Science, Arts and Letters, Papers, 24, no. 4 (1938): 33-42.

Titiev, M. Hopi snake handling. Scientific Monthly, 57 (1943): 44-51.

Titiev, M. Notes on Hopi witchcraft. Michigan Academy of Science, Arts and Letters, Papers, 28 (1943): 549-557.

*Titiev, M. Old Oraibi. Harvard University, Peabody Museum of American Archaeology and Ethnology, Papers, 22, no. 1 (1944): 1-277.

Titiev, M. Shamans, witches and chiefs among the Hopi. Tomorrow, 4, no. 3 (1956): 51-56.

Titiev, M. Suggestions for the further study of Hopi. International Journal of American Linguistics, 12 (1946): 89-91.

Titiev, M. The Hopi method of baking sweet corn. Michigan Academy of Science, Arts and Letters, Papers, 23 (1937): 87-94.

Titiev, M. The problem of cross-cousin marriage among the Hopi. American Anthropologist, n.s., 40 (1938): 105-111.

Titiev, M. The story of Kokopele. American Anthropologist, n.s., 41 (1939): 91-98.

Titiev, M. The use of kinship terms in Hopi ritual. Flagstaff, Ariz., Museum of Northern Arizona, Museum Notes, 10 (1937): 9-11.

Titiev, M. Two Hopi myths and rites. Journal of American Folklore, 61 (1948): 31-43.

Titiev, M. Two Hopi tales from Oraibi. Michigan Academy of Science, Arts and Letters, Papers, 29 (1943): 425-438.

Titiev, Mischa. Some aspects of clowning among the Hopi Indians. In Mario D. Zamora, et al., eds. Themes in Culture. Quezon City, Kayumanggi, 1971: 326-336.

*Titiev, Mischa. The Hopi Indians of Old Oraibi: change and continuity. Ann Arbor, University of Michigan Press, 1972. 12, 379 p. illus.

Titiev, Mischa. The Hopi use of kinship terms for expressing sociocultural values. Anthropological Linguistics, 9, no. 5 (1967): 44-49.

Turner, Christy G., II. A massacre at Hopi. By Christy G. Turner, II and Nancy T. Morris. American Antiquity, 35 (1970): 320-331.

Turner, Christy G., II. Microevolutionary interpretations from the dentition. American Journal of Physical Anthropology, n.s., 30 (1969): 421-426.

Underhill, R. M. First penthouse dwellers of America, 25-55. New York, 1938.

U.S., Congress, House, Committee on Interior and Insular Affairs, Subcommittee on Indian Affairs. Partition of Navajo and Hopi 1882 reservation. Hearings, Ninety-second Congress, second session, on H.R. 1128, H.R. 4753, and H.R. 4754 . . . April 17 and 18, 1972. Washington, D.C., Government Printing Office, 1972. 6, 284 p. illus.

U.S., Congress, Senate, Committee on Interior and Insular Affairs, Subcommittee on Indian Affairs. Authorize partition of surface rights of Navaho-Hopi Indian land. Hearings . . . on H.R. 11128 . . . September 14 and 15, 1972. Washington, D.C., Government Printing Office, 1972. 6, 266 p. illus.

U.S., General Accounting Office. Assessment of the Teacher Corps program at Northern Arizona University and participating schools on the Navajo and Hopi Indian Reservations. Washington, D.C., 1971. 4, 38 p. illus., map.

Van Duzen, Jean L. Medical practice on the Navajo Reservation. American Medical Women's Association, Journal, 19 (1964): 558-560.

Vestal, P. A. Notes on a collection of plants from the Hopi Indian region. Harvard University, Botanical Museum, Leaflets, 8 (1940): 153-168.

Vlahcevic, Z. R., et al. Relation of bile acid pool size to the formation of lithogenic bile in female Indians of the Southwest. Gastroenterology, 62 (1972): 73-83.

Voegelin, C. F. Phonemicizing for dialect study with reference to Hopi. Language, 32 (1956): 116-135.

Voegelin, C. F. Pregnancy couvade attested by term and text in Hopi. American Anthropologist, 62 (1960): 491-494.

Voegelin, C. F. and F. M. Voegelin. Selection in Hopi ethics, linguistics, and translation. Anthropological Linguistics, 2, no. 2 (1960): 48-78.

Voegelin, C. F. and R. C. Euler. Introduction to Hopi chants. Journal of American Folklore, 70 (1957): 115-136.

Voegelin, Carl F. An expanding language, Hopi. Plateau, 32 (1959): 33-39.

Voegelin, Carl F. Hopi /ʼas/. By C. F. Voegelin and F. M. Voegelin. International Journal of American Linguistics, 35 (1969): 192-202.

Voegelin, Carl F. Hopi names and no names (with reference to households in social organization). By C. F. and F. M. Voegelin. In Earl H. Swanson, Jr., ed. Languages and Cultures of Western North America. Pocatello, Idaho State University Press, 1970: 47-53.

Voegelin, Carl F. Methods for typologizing directly and by distinctive features (in reference to Uto-Aztecan and Kiowa-Tanoan vowel systems). Lingua, 11 (1962): 469-487.

Voegelin, Carl F. Our knowledge of semantics and how it is obtained (with reference to Hopi /ʼas/ and Papago /čim/). By C. F. Voegelin and F. M. Voegelin. International Journal of American Linguistics, 36 (1970): 241-246.

Voegelin, Carl F. Passive transformations from non-transitive bases in Hopi. By C. F. Voegelin and F. M. Voegelin. International Journal of American Linguistics, 33 (1967): 276-281.

Voegelin, Carl F. Pregnancy couvade attested by term and text in Hopi. American Anthropologist, 62 (1960): 491-494.

Voegelin, Carl F. Selection in Hopi ethics, linguistics, and translation. By C. F. Voegelin and F. M. Voegelin. Anthropological Linguistics, 2, no. 2 (1960): 48-78.

Voegelin, Carl F. Sign language analysis on one level or two? International Journal of American Linguistics, 24 (1958): 71-77.

Voegelin, Carl F. The autonomy of linguistics and the dependence of cognitive culture. By C. F. and F. M.

Voegelin. In Jesse Sawyer, ed. Studies in American Indian Languages. Berkeley and Los Angeles, University of California Press, 1971: 303-317. (California, University, Publications in Linguistics, 65)

Voegelin, Carl F. Typology of density ranges, I: introduction. By C. F. Voegelin, A. K. Ramanujan, and F. M. Voegelin. International Journal of American Linguistics, 26 (1960): 198-205.

Voth, H. R. Four Hopi tales. Field Museum, Anthropological Series, 11 (1912): 139-143.

Voth, H. R. Hopi marriage rites on the wedding morning. Field Museum, Anthropological Series, 11 (1912): 145-149.

Voth, H. R. Hopi proper names. Field Museum, Anthropological Series, 6 (1905): 63-113.

Voth, H. R. Notes on modern burial customs of the Hopi. Field Museum, Anthropological Series, 11 (1912): 99-103.

Voth, H. R. Notes on the eagle cult among the Hopi Indians. Field Museum, Anthropological Series, 11 (1912): 105-109.

Voth, H. R. Oraibi marriage customs. American Anthropologist, n.s., 2 (1900): 238-246.

Voth, H. R. Oraibi natal customs and ceremonies. Field Museum, Anthropological Series, 6 (1905): 47-61.

Voth, H. R. Tawa Baholawu of the Oraibi flute ceremony. Field Museum, Anthropological Series, 11 (1912): 121-136.

Voth, H. R. The Oraibi Marau ceremony. Field Museum, Anthropological Series, 11 (1912): 1-88.

Voth, H. R. The Oraibi new year ceremony. Field Museum, Anthropological Series, 11 (1912): 111-119.

Voth, H. R. The Oráibi Oáqöl ceremony. Field Museum, Anthropological Series, 6 (1903): 1-46.

Voth, H. R. The Oraibi Powamu ceremony. Field Museum, Anthropological Series, 3 (1901): 67-158.

Voth, H. R. The Oraibi summer snake ceremony. Field Museum, Anthropological Series, 3 (1903): 267-358.

Voth, H. R. The traditions of the Hopi. Field Museum, Anthropological Series, 8 (1905): 1-319.

Wallace, William Swilling. Lieutenants Pershing and Stotsenberg visit the Grand Canyon: 1887. Arizona and the West, 3 (1961): 265-284.

Wallis, W. D. Folk tales from Shumopovi. Journal of American Folklore, 49 (1936): 1-68.

Wallis, W. D. and M. Titiev. Hopi notes from Chimopovy. Michigan Academy of Science, Arts and Letters, Papers, 30 (1944): 523-556.

Walton, E. L. and T. T. Waterman. American Indian poetry. American Anthropologist, n.s., 27 (1925): 25-52.

Waters, Frank. Book of the Hopi. New York, Viking Press, 1963. 17, 347 p. illus.

Waters, Frank. Pumpkin Seed Point. Chicago, Sage Books, Swallow Press, 1969. 175 p.

Watkins, F. E. Indians at play. Masterkey, 18 (1944): 139-141; 19 (1945): 20-22, 113-115, 162-164; 20 (1946): 81-87.

Watson, J. B. How the Hopi classify their food. Plateau, 15 (1943): 49-52.

Wencker, A. Easy Hopi sentence folder. Glendale, 1959.

Wencker, A. Primer I-II. Glendale, 1959.

Werner, Emmy E. Infants around the world: cross-cultural studies of psychomotor development from birth to two years. Journal of Cross-Cultural Psychology, 3 (1972): 111-134.

White, L. A. "Rohona" in Pueblo culture. Michigan Academy of Science, Arts and Letters, Papers, 29 (1943): 439-443.

Whiting, A. F. Ethnobotany of the Hopi. Flagstaff, Ariz., Museum of Northern Arizona, Bulletin, 15 (1939): 1-120.

Whiting, A. F. Hopi Indian agriculture. Flagstaff, Ariz., Museum of Northern Arizona, Museum Notes, 8, no. 10 (1936): 51-53; 10, no. 5 (1937): 13-16.

Whiting, Alfred F. Ethnobotany of the Hopi. Flagstaff, Museum of Northern Arizona, 1966. 8, 120 p.

Whiting, Alfred F. Father Porras at Awatovi and the flying nun. Plateau, 44 (1971): 60-66.

Whiting, Alfred F. Hopi kachinas. Plateau, 37 (1964): 1-7.

Whiting, Alfred F. Hopi nocturne. Plateau, 37 (1964/1965): 99-105.

Whiting, Alfred F. Leaves from a Hopi doctor's casebook. New York Academy of Medicine, Bulletin, 47 (1971): 125-146.

Whiting, Alfred F. The bride wore white. Plateau, 37 (1965): 128-140.

Whitney, R. Idols of rain. Masterkey, 1 (1927): 14-22.

Whitsell, W. J. New water source for Hopi Indian Reservation. American Water Works Association, Journal, 60 (1968): 816-818.

Whorf, B. L. An American Indian model of the universe. International Journal of American Linguistics, 16 (1950): 67-72.

Whorf, B. L. Linguistic factors in the terminology of Hopi architecture. International Journal of American Linguistics, 19 (1953): 141-145.

Whorf, B. L. Some verbal categories of Hopi. Language, 14 (1938): 275-286.

Whorf, B. L. The Hopi language, Toreva dialect. Viking Fund Publications in Anthropology, 6 (1946): 150-183.

Whorf, B. L. The punctual and segmentative aspects of verbs in Hopi. Language, 12 (1936): 127-131.

Whorf, B. L. The relation of habitual thought and behavior to language. In Essays in Memory of Edward Sapir. Menasha, 1941: 75-93.

Wilson, John P. Awatovi--more light on a legend. Plateau, 44 (1972): 125-130.

Woodbury, R. B. Prehistoric stone implements of northeastern Arizona. Harvard University, Peabody Museum of American Archaeology and Ethnology, Papers, 34 (1954): 1-240.

Woolf, Charles M. Albinism among Indians in Arizona and New Mexico. American Journal of Human Genetics, 17 (1965): 23-35.

Woolf, Charles M. Albinism among the Hopi Indians in Arizona. By Charles M. Woolf and Robert B. Grant. American Journal of Human Genetics, 14 (1962): 391-400.

Wright, Barton. This is a Hopi Kachina. By Barton Wright and Evelyn Roat. Flagstaff, Northern Arizona Society of Science and Art, 1962. 28 p. illus.

Yamada, G., ed. The great resistance.
Mexico, 1957. 79 p.

Yamada, George. The great resistance.
Boletín Indigenista, 12 (1952): 143-151.

Yount, G. C. A sketch of the Hopi in
1828. Masterkey, 16 (1942): 193-199.

Zbinden, Ernst A. Nördliche und südliche
Elemente im Kulturheroenmythus der
Südathapasken. Anthropos, 55 (1960):
689-733.

Zom, E. Die Hopi-Pueblos in Arizona and
ihre Bevölkerung. Erdball, 1 (1927):
108-115.

15-12   Isleta

Bartholomew (Harland) and Associates. A
general development plan for the future
use of the lands of Isleta Pueblo, New
Mexico. St. Louis, 1962. illus., maps.

Bloom, L. B., ed. Bourke on the
Southwest. New Mexico Historical Review,
13 (1938): 192-238.

Brandfonbrener, Martin. Cardiomyopathy in
the Southwest American Indian. By M.
Brandfonbrener, W. S. Lovekin, and J. K.
Leach. British Heart Journal, 32 (1970):
491-496.

Brandt, Elizabeth. On the origins of
linguistic stratification: the Sandia
case. Anthropological Linguistics, 12
(1970): 46-50.

Brandt, Elizabeth Anne. Sandia Pueblo,
New Mexico: a linguistic and
ethnolinguistic investigation.
Dissertation Abstracts International, 31
(1970/1971): 5768B. UM 71-8755.

Chavez, Tibo J. Early witchcraft in New
Mexico. El Palacio, 76, no. 3 (1969): 7-
9.

Curtin, L. S. M. Preparation of sacred
corn meal in the Rio Grande pueblos.
Masterkey, 41 (1967): 124-130; 42
(1968): 10-16.

Curtin, L. S. M. Spanish and Indian
witchcraft in New Mexico. Masterkey, 45
(1971): 89-101.

Curtis, E. S. The North American Indian,
Vol. 16: 3-27. Norwood, 1926.

Densmore, F. Music of Acoma, Isleta,
Cochiti and Zuñi Pueblos. U.S. Bureau of
American Ethnology, Bulletin, 165
(1957): 1-129.

Densmore, Frances. Music of Acoma,
Isleta, Cochiti, and Zuñi Pueblos. New
York, Da Capo Press, 1972. 12, 117 p.
illus.

Dismuke, D. Range management brings
success to Isleta Indians. Soil
Conservation, 5 (1939): 34-35.

Dixon, W. H. Isleta--why the church has a
wooden floor. Scribner's Magazine, 70
(1921): 193-199.

Downing, George L. Native pottery of the
Southwest. Natural History, 78, no. 6
(1969): 34-39.

Dozier, Edward P. Pueblo Indian response
to culture contact. In M. Estellie
Smith, ed. Studies in Linguistics in
Honor of George L. Trager. The Hague,
Mouton, 1972: 457-467. (Janua
Linguarum, Series Maior, 52)

Euler, R. C. Notes on land tenure at
Isleta Pueblo. El Palacio, 61 (1954):
368-373.

Fay, George E., ed. Charters,
constitutions and by-laws of the Indian
tribes of North America. Part IV: The
Southwest (Navajo-Zuni). Greeley, 1967.
5, 120 l. maps. (University of
Northern Colorado, Museum of
Anthropology, Occasional Publications in
Anthropology, Ethnology Series, 5) ERIC
ED046554.

Fergusson, E. Dancing gods, 49-53. New
York, 1931.

Fewkes, J. W. The pueblo settlements near
El Paso. American Anthropologist, n.s.,
4 (1902): 57-72.

French, D. H. Factionalism in Isleta
Pueblo. American Ethnological Society,
Monographs, 14 (1948): 1-48.

Gatschet, A. S. A mythic tale of the
Isleta Indians. American Philosophical
Society, Proceedings, 29 (1891): 207-
217.

Gatschet, A. S. Classification into seven
linguistic stocks of Western Indian
dialects. In Report upon United States
Geographical Surveys West of the One
Hundredth Meridian. Vol. 7. Washington,
D.C., 1879: 403-485.

Gatschet, A. S. The sun worship of Isleta
Pueblo. American Philosophical Society,
Proceedings, 29 (1891): 217-219.

Gatschet, A. S. Zwölf Sprachen aus dem
Südwesten Nordamerikas. Weimar, 1876.
150 p.

Goldfrank, E. S. Isleta variants: a study in flexibility. Journal of American Folklore, 39 (1926): 70-78.

Goldfrank, Esther S. The artist of "Isleta paintings" in Pueblo society. Washington, D.C., Smithsonian Press, 1967. 6, 227 p. illus. (Smithsonian Contributions to Anthropology, 5)

*Goldfrank, Esther S., ed. Isleta paintings. Introduction by Elsie Clews Parsons. Washington, D.C., Government Printing Office, 1962. 16, 299 p. illus. (U.S., Bureau of American Ethnology, Bulletin, 181)

Gordon, Dudley. An example of Indian oratory. Masterkey, 39 (1965): 154-156.

Hale, Kenneth. Toward a reconstruction of Kiowa-Tanoan phonology. International Journal of American Linguistics, 33 (1967): 112-120.

Hammond, G. P. and A. Rey, eds. Expedition into New Mexico made by Antonio de Espejo, 79-82. Los Angeles, 1929.

Harvey, Byron, III. Is pottery making a dying art. Masterkey, 38 (1964): 55-65.

Harvey, Byron, III. Masks at a maskless pueblo: the Laguna colony Kachina organization at Isleta. Ethnology, 2 (1963): 478-489.

Hodge, F. W. Isleta. U.S. Bureau of American Ethnology, Bulletin, 30, vol. 1 (1907): 622-624.

Hodge, F. W. Tigua. U.S. Bureau of American Ethnology, Bulletin, 30, vol. 2 (1910): 747-749.

Houser, Nicholas P. The Tigua settlement of Ysleta del Sur. Kiva, 36, no. 1 (1970/1971): 23-39.

Hurt, W. R. Tortugas. El Palacio, 59 (1952): 104-122.

Lane, William Carr. William Carr Lane, diary. Edited by Wm. G. B. Carson. New Mexico Historical Review, 39 (1964): 181-234, 274-332.

Lange, C. H. Notes on a winter ceremony at Isleta Pueblo, January 7, 1940. El Palacio, 60 (1953): 116-123.

Leap, William L. Tiwa noun class semology: a historical view. Anthropological Linguistics, 12 (1970): 38-45.

Leap, William L. Who were the Piro? Anthropological Linguistics, 13 (1971): 321-330.

Leap, William Lester. The language of Isleta, New Mexico. Dissertation Abstracts International, 31 (1970/1971): 5772B-5773B. UM 71-8763.

Lummis, C. F. Pueblo Indian folk-stories. New York, 1910. 257 p.

Lummis, C. F. The man who married the moon. New York, 1894. 239 p.

Parsons, E. C. Further notes on Isleta. American Anthropologist, n.s., 23 (1921): 149-169.

*Parsons, E. C. Isleta. U.S. Bureau of American Ethnology, Annual Reports, 47 (1930): 193-466.

Parsons, E. C. Notes on Isleta, Santa Ana, and Acoma. American Anthropologist, n.s., 22 (1920): 56-69.

Parsons, E. C. Pueblo Indian religion. Chicago, 1939. 2 v.

Parsons, E. C. The kinship nomenclature of the Pueblo Indians. American Anthropologist, n.s., 34 (1932): 377-389.

Parsons, E. C. The Laguna migration to Isleta. American Anthropologist, n.s., 30 (1928): 602-613.

Schroeder, Albert H. The language of the Saline Pueblos; Piro or Tiwa? New Mexico Historical Review, 39 (1964): 235-249.

Simons, Suzanne Lee. Sandia Pueblo: persistence and change in a New Mexican Indian community. Dissertation Abstracts International, 31 (1970/1971): 35B-36B. UM 70-12,903.

Smith, M. Estellie. Notes on an ethnolinguistic study of governing. In M. Estellie Smith, ed. Studies in Linguistics in Honor of George L. Trager. The Hague, Mouton, 1972: 487-501. (Janua Linguarum, Series Maior, 52)

Stephens, E. L. Steve. West of the Pecos. New Mexico Historical Review, 35 (1960): 81-108, 236-256, 309-326; 36 (1961): 159-174.

Trager, G. L. The kinship and status terms of the Tiwa languages. American Anthropologist, n.s., 45 (1943): 557-571.

Trager, George L. The cardinal directions ~+ Taos and Picuris. By George L. Trager

and Felicia Harben Trager.
Anthropological Linguistics, 12 (1970):
31-37.

White, L. A. Ethnographic notes on Sandia
Pueblo. Michigan Academy of Science,
Arts and Letters, Papers, 31 (1945):
215-222.

Wittick, Ben. Ben Wittick views the
Pueblos. Edited by Carol Scott Alley. El
Palacio, 73, no. 2 (1966): 4-9.

15-13 Jemez

Alexander, H. B. Field notes at Jemez. El
Palacio, 27 (1929): 95-106.

Anza, Juan Bautista de. Governor Anza,
the Lipan Apaches and Pecos Pueblo.
Translated and edited by Marc Simmons.
El Palacio, 77, no. 1 (1970): 35-40.

Bailit, Howard L. Tooth size reduction: a
hominid trend. By Howard L. Bailit and
Jonathan S. Friedlaender. American
Anthropologist, 68 (1966): 665-672.

Bandelier, A. F. A visit to the
aboriginal ruins in the valley of the
Rio Pecos. Archaeological Institute of
America, Papers, American Series, 1
(1883): 37-133.

Bloom, L. B. Bourke on the Southwest. New
Mexico Historical Review, 13 (1938):
192-238.

Bloom, L. B. The West Jemez culture area.
El Palacio, 12 (1922): 19-25.

Bloom, L. B. The West Jemez culture area.
New Mexico Historical Review, 21 (1946):
120-126.

Cobb, John C. Trachoma among Southwestern
Indians. By John C. Cobb and Chandler R.
Dawson. American Medical Association,
Journal, 175 (1961): 405-406.

Concha, Fernando de la. Colonel Don
Fernando de la Concha diary, 1788.
Edited by Adlai Feather. New Mexico
Historical Review, 34 (1959): 285-304.

Cook, Sherburne F. Can pottery residues
be used as an index to population? In
Miscellaneous Papers on Archaeology.
Berkeley, University of California,
1972: 17-39. (California, University,
Archaeological Research Facility,
Contributions, 14)

Curtin, L. S. M. Preparation of sacred
corn meal in the Rio Grande pueblos.
Masterkey, 41 (1967): 124-130; 42
(1968): 10-16.

DeHuff, E. W. Taytay's tales, 162-164,
170-171. New York, 1922.

Douglas, F. H. Weaving of the Tiwa
pueblos and Jemez. Denver Art Museum,
Indian Leaflet Series, 91 (1939): 162-
164.

Dutton, B. P. Hopi dance of the Jemez
Indians. Research, 1 (1936): 70-84.

Ellis, F. H. Authoritative control and
the society system in Jemez Pueblo.
Southwestern Journal of Anthropology, 9
(1953): 385-394.

Ellis, F. H. Jemez kiva magic and its
relation to features of prehistoric
kivas. Southwestern Journal of
Anthropology, 8 (1952): 147-163.

Ellis, Florence Hawley. A reconstruction
of basic Jemez pattern of social
organization, with comparisons to other
Tanoan social structures. Albuquerque,
University of New Mexico Press, 1964.
69 p. (New Mexico, University,
Publications in Anthropology, 11)

Ellis, Florence Hawley. Pueblo boundaries
and their markers. Plateau, 38 (1966):
97-106.

Fergusson, E. Dancing gods, 61-65. New
York, 1931.

Gatschet, A. S. Classification into seven
linguistic stocks of Western Indian
dialects. In Report upon United States
Geographical Surveys West of the One
Hundredth Meridian. Vol. 7. Washington,
D.C., 1879: 403-485.

Gatschet, A. S. Zwölf Sprachen aus dem
Südwesten Nordamerikas. Weimar, 1876.
150 p.

Gunnerson, James H. Evidence of Apaches
at Pecos. By James H. Gunnerson and
Dolores A. Gunnerson. El Palacio, 76,
no. 3 (1969): 1-6.

Hale, Kenneth. Jemez and Kiowa
correspondences in reference to Kiowa-
Tanoan. International Journal of
American Linguistics, 28 (1962): 1-5.

Hewett, E. L. Studies on the extinct
pueblo of Pecos. American
Anthropologist, n.s., 6 (1904): 426-439.

Hodge, F. W. Jemez. U.S. Bureau of
American Ethnology, Bulletin, 30, vol. 1
(1907): 629-631.

Holmes, W. H. Notes on the antiquities of
Jemez Valley. American Anthropologist,
n.s., 7 (1905): 198-212.

Hooton, E. A. The Indians of Pecos Pueblo. New Haven, 1930. 391 p.

Hunt, Edward E., Jr. Cranial deformation in Pecos Pueblo, New Mexico: a comment on "Infant stimulation and adult stature of human males" by Landauer and Whiting. American Anthropologist, 67 (1965): 997-999.

Jones, J. A. Rio Grande Pueblo albinism. American Journal of Physical Anthropology, n.s., 22 (1964): 265-270.

Jones, J. R. A Jemez corn grinding. El Palacio, 54 (1947): 43-44.

Judd, N. M. When the Jemez medicine men came to Zuni. Journal of American Folklore, 40 (1947): 182-184.

Keech, R. A. The Pecos ceremony at Jemez. El Palacio, 36 (1934): 129-134.

Keech, R. A. Two days and nights in a pueblo. El Palacio, 35 (1933): 185-195.

Kenner, Charles Leroy. A history of New Mexican-Plains Indian relations. Dissertation Abstracts, 28 (1967/1968): 595A. UM 66-12,762.

Kidder, A. V. Pecos, New Mexico: archaeological notes. Robert S. Peabody Foundation for Archaeology, Papers, 5 (1958): 1-380.

Kidder, A. V. Pecos Pueblo. El Palacio, 58 (1951): 83-89.

Kidder, A. V. The artifacts of Pecos. New Haven, 1932. 314 p.

Kidder, A. V. and A. Shepard. The pottery of Pecos. New Haven, 1936. 2 v.

Kidder, M. A. and A. V. Kidder. Notes on the pottery of Pecos. American Anthropologist, n.s., 19 (1917): 325-360.

Lambert, M. F. A rare stone humpbacked figurine from Pecos Pueblo. El Palacio, 64 (1957): 93-108.

Lane, William Carr. William Carr Lane, diary. Edited by Wm. G. B. Carson. New Mexico Historical Review, 39 (1964): 181-234, 274-332.

Loew, O. Lieutenant G. M. Wheeler's zweite Expedition nach Neu-Mexiko und Colorado. Petermanns Mitteilungen, 22 (1876): 209-211.

Morris, Donald Harvey. The anthropological utility of dental morphology. Dissertation Abstracts, 26 (1965/1966): 4169. UM 65-13,866.

Nelson, C. T. The teeth of the Indians of Pecos Pueblo. American Journal of Physical Anthropology, 23 (1938): 261-294.

Parsons, E. C. Pueblo Indian religon. Chicago, 1939. 2 v.

Parsons, E. C. The kinship nomenclature of the Pueblo Indians. American Anthropologist, n.s., 34 (1932): 377-389.

*Parsons, E. C. The Pueblo of Jemez. New Haven, 1925. 141 p.

Reagan, A. B. Dances of the Jemez Pueblo Indians. Kansas Academy of Science, Transactions, 23 (1906): 241-272.

Reagan, A. B. Notes on Jemez ethnography. American Anthropologist, n.s., 29 (1927): 719-728.

Reagan, A. B. Sketches of Indian life and character. Kansas Academy of Science, Transactions, 21 (1908): 207-215.

Reagan, A. B. Some paintings from one of the estufas in the Indian village of Jemez. Indiana Academy of Science, Proceedings, 13 (1903): 201-204.

Reagan, A. B. The corn dance at Jemez. Southern Workman, 44 (1915): 481-484.

Reagan, A. B. The Jemez Indians. Annual Archaeological Report, being Part of Appendix to the Report of the Minister of Education, Ontario (1923): 103-108.

Reagan, A. B. The masked dance of the Jemez Indians. Southern Workman, 44 (1915): 423-427.

Reiter, P. The Jemez Pueblo of Unshagi. Archaeological Institute of America, School of American Research, Santa Fe, Monographs, 5 (1938): 1-92; 6 (1938): 97-211.

Reiter, P. The Jemez Pueblo of Unshagi. New Mexico, University, Bulletin, Monograph Series, 1, no. 4/5 (1938): 1-211.

Rihan, H. Y. Dental and orthodontic observations on 289 adult and 53 immature skulls from Pecos. International Journal of Orthodontia and Oral Surgery and Radiography, 18 (1932): 708-713.

Simmons, Marc. Governor Anza, the Lipan Apaches and Pecos Pueblo. El Palacio, 77, no. 1 (1970): 35-40.

Simmons, Marc. New Mexico's smallpox epidemic of 1780-1781. New Mexico Historical Review, 41 (1966): 319-326.

Stubbs, S. A., et al. "Lost" Pecos church. El Palacio, 64 (1957): 67-92.

Thompson, G. An Indian dance at Jemez. American Anthropologist, 2 (1889): 351-355.

Twitchell, R. E. The ancient pueblo of Pecos. Santa Fe Magazine, 4 (1910): 27-32.

Walter, P. Notes on a trip to Jemez. El Palacio, 29 (1930): 206-213.

Weinman, Janice. The influence of Pueblo worldview on the construction of its vocal music. Ethnomusicology, 14 (1970): 313-315.

Williamson, T. B. The Jemez yucca ring basket. El Palacio, 42 (1937): vii-ix.

Wittick, Ben. Ben Wittick views the Pueblos. Edited by Carol Scott Alley. El Palacio, 73, no. 2 (1966): 4-9.

Woolf, Charles M. Albinism among Indians in Arizona and New Mexico. American Journal of Human Genetics, 17 (1965): 23-35.

15-14   Jicarilla

Bartoli, J. F. The Apache "devil dance". Musical Courier, 152, no. 8 (1955): 8-10.

Basehart, Harry W. Changing political organization in the Jicarilla Apache Reservation community. By Harry W. Basehart and Tom T. Sasaki. Human Organization, 23 (1964): 283-289.

Bellah, R. N. Apache kinship systems. Cambridge, 1952. 151 p.

Clark, LaVerne Harrell. They sang for horses; the impact of the horse on Navajo and Apache folklore. Tucson, University of Arizona Press, 1966. 20, 225 p. illus., maps.

Concha, Fernando de la. Colonel Don Fernando de la Concha diary, 1788. Edited by Adlai Feather. New Mexico Historical Review, 34 (1959): 285-304.

Crocchiola, Stanley F. L. The Jicarilla Apaches of New Mexico, 1540-1967. By F. Stanley. Pampa, Tex., Pampa Print Shop, 1967. 5, 376 p.

Curtis, E. S. The North American Indian, Vol. 1: 53-72. Cambridge, 1907.

Daklugie, A. and E. Ball. Coyote and the flies. New Mexico Folklore Record, 10 (1955/1956): 12-13.

Dolan, T. A. Report of council proceedings with the Jicarilla Apache Indians. New Mexico Historical Review, 4 (1929): 59-72.

Douglas, F. H. A Jicarilla Apache beaded cape. Denver Art Museum, Material Culture Notes, 4 (1939): 34-37.

Douglas, F. H. Apache Indian coiled basketry. Denver Art Museum, Indian Leaflet Series, 64 (1934): 54-56.

Douglas, F. H. The Apache Indians. Denver Art Museum, Indian Leaflet Series, 16 (1930): 1-4.

Douglas, F. H., et al. A Jicarilla Apache man's skin leggings. Denver Art Museum, Material Culture Notes, 22 (1953): 1-12.

Douglas, F. H., et al. A Jicarilla Apache man's skin shirt. Denver Art Museum, Material Culture Notes, 21 (1953): 1-10.

Douglas, F. H., et al. A Jicarilla Apache woman's skin dress. Denver Art Museum, Material Culture Notes, 20 (1953): 1-10.

Dunn, D. Nehakije: Apache artist. El Palacio, 59 (1952): 71-76.

Fay, George E., ed. Charters, constitutions and by-laws of the Indian tribes of North America. Part III: The Southwest (Apache-Mohave). Greeley, 1967. 6, 118 l. maps. (University of Northern Colorado, Museum of Anthropology, Occasional Publications in Anthropology, Ethnology Series, 4) ERIC ED046553.

Fergusson, E. Dancing Gods, 269-276. New York, 1931.

Fergusson, E. Modern Apaches of New Mexico. American Indian, 6, no. 1 (1951): 3-13.

Ford, Richard I. Barter, gift, or violence: an analysis of Tewa intertribal exchange. In Edwin N. Wilmsen, ed. Social Exchange and Interaction. Ann Arbor, University of Michigan, 1972: 24-45. (Michigan, University, Musuem of Anthropology, Anthropological Papers, 46)

Gatschet, A. S. Classification into seven linguistic stocks of Western Indian dialects. In Report upon United States Geographical Surveys West of the One

Hundredth Meridian. Vol. 7. Washington, D.C., 1879: 403-485.

Goddard, P. E. Jicarilla Apache texts. American Museum of Natural History, Anthropological Papers, 8 (1911): 1-276.

Gordon, B. L. Heroes and ethos of the Jicarilla Apache. Masterkey, 44 (1970): 54-62.

Greenleaf, Richard E. The Nueva Vizcaya frontier, 1787-1789. Journal of the West, 8 (1969): 56-66.

Grinnell, G. B. Who were the Padouca? American Anthropologist, n.s., 22 (1920): 248-260.

Gunnerson, Dolores Alice. The Jicarilla Apaches: a study in survival. Dissertation Abstracts International, 32 (1971/1972): 3125B. UM 72-1122.

Gunnerson, James H. A human skeleton from an Apache baking pit. Plains Anthropologist, 14 (1969): 46-56.

Gunnerson, James H. An introduction to Plains Apache archeology--the Dismal River Aspect. Washington, D.C., Government Printing Office, 1960. 131-260 p. illus., map. (U.S., Bureau of American Ethnology, Anthropological Papers, 58. U.S., Bureau of American Ethnology, Bulletin, 173)

Gunnerson, James H. Apache archaeology in northeastern New Mexico. American Antiquity, 34 (1969): 23-39.

Gunnerson, James H. Evidence of Apaches at Pecos. By James H. Gunnerson and Dolores A. Gunnerson. El Palacio, 76, no. 3 (1969): 1-6.

Gunnerson, James H. Plains Apache archaeology: a review. Plains Anthropologist, 13 (1968): 167-189.

Harrington, J. P. Southern peripheral Athapaskawan origins, divisions, and migrations. Smithsonian Miscellaneous Collections, 100 (1940): 503-532.

Hodge, F. W. Jicarilla. U.S. Bureau of American Ethnology, Bulletin, 30, vol. 1 (1907): 631-632.

Hoijer, H. Phonetic and phonemic change in the Athapaskan languages. Language, 18 (1942): 218-220.

Hoijer, H. Pitch accent in the Apachean languages. Language, 19 (1943): 38-51.

Hoijer, H. The Apachean verb. International Journal of American Linguistics, 11 (1945): 193-203; 12 (1946): 1-13, 51-59; 14 (1948): 247-259; 15 (1949): 12-22.

Jelinek, Arthur J. Environment and aboriginal population seen through the historical record. In A Prehistoric Sequence in the Middle Pecos Valley, New Mexico. Ann Arbor, University of Michigan, 1967: 18-40. (Michigan, University, Museum of Anthropology, Anthropological Papers, 31)

Jones, G. A Jicarilla Apache family. American Indian, 6, no. 2 (1951): 32-37.

Lane, William Carr. William Carr Lane, diary. Edited by Wm. G. B. Carson. New Mexico Historical Review, 39 (1964): 181-234, 274-332.

Lecompte, Janet. The Manco Burro Pass Massacre. New Mexico Historical Review, 41 (1966): 305-318.

Lockwood, F. C. The Apache Indians. New York, 1938. 348 p.

MacLachlan, Bruce B. The Mescalero Apache quest for law and order. Journal of the West, 3 (1964): 441-458.

Matson, D. S. and A. H. Schroeder. Cordero's description of the Apache-1796. New Mexico Historical Review, 32 (1957): 335-356.

Meston, G. D. Jicarilla Apache Reservation. In United States, Department of the Interior, Census Office, Eleventh Census, Report on Indians Taxed and Indians not Taxed. Washington, D.C., 1890: 404-407.

Mooney, J. The Jicarilla genesis. American Anthropologist, 11 (1898): 197-209.

Mozer, Corinne C. A brief history of Fort Fillmore 1851-1862. El Palacio, 74, no. 2 (1967): 5-18.

Ogle, R. H. The Apache and the government-1870's. New Mexico Historical Review, 34 (1959): 81-102.

Opler, M. E. A Jicarilla Apache expedition and scalp dance. Journal of American Folklore, 54 (1941): 10-23.

*Opler, M. E. A summary of Jicarilla Apache culture. American Anthropologist, n.s., 38 (1936): 202-223.

Opler, M. E. Adolescence rite of the Jicarilla. El Palacio, 49 (1942): 25-38.

Opler, M. E. Apache data concerning the relation of kinship terminology to social classification. American

Anthropologist, n.s., 39 (1937): 201-212.

Opler, M. E. Childhood and youth in Jicarilla Apache society. Frederick Webb Hodge Anniversary Publication Fund, Southwest Museum, Publications, 5 (1946): 1-170.

Opler, M. E. Dirty Boy: a Jicarilla tale of raid and war. American Anthropological Association, Memoirs, 52 (1938): 1-80.

Opler, M. E. Further comparative anthropological data bearing on the solution of a psychological problem. Journal of Social Psychology, 9 (1938): 477-483.

Opler, M. E. Jicarilla Apache fertility aids and practices for preventing conception. American Anthropologist, n.s., 50 (1948): 359-361.

Opler, M. E. Mythology and folk belief in the maintenance of Jicarilla Apache tribal endogamy. Journal of American Folklore, 60 (1947): 126-129.

Opler, M. E. Myths and tales of the Jicarilla Apache Indians. American Folk-Lore Society, Memoirs, 31 (1938): 1-406.

Opler, M. E. Navaho shamanistic practice among the Jicarilla Apache. New Mexico Anthropologist, 6/7 (1943): 13-18.

Opler, M. E. Rule and practice in the behavior between Jicarilla Apache affinal relatives. American Anthropologist, n.s., 49 (1947): 453-462.

*Opler, M. E. The character and derivation of Jicarilla holiness rites. New Mexico, University, Bulletin, Anthropological Series, 4, no. 3 (1943): 1-98.

Opler, M. E. The Jicarilla Apache ceremonial relay race. American Anthropologist, n.s., 46 (1944): 75-97.

Opler, M. E. The kinship systems of the southern Athabaskan-speaking tribes. American Anthropologist, n.s., 38 (1936): 620-633.

Opler, Morris E. Cause and effect in Apachean agriculture, division of labor, residence patterns, and girls' puberty rites. American Anthropologist, 74 (1972): 1133-1146.

Opler, Morris E. Cultural evolution, Southern Athapaskans, and chronology in theory. Southwestern Journal of Anthropology, 17 (1961): 1-20.

Opler, Morris E. Jicarilla Apache territory, economy, and society in 1850. Southwestern Journal of Anthropology, 27 (1971): 309-329.

Opler, Morris E. Remuneration to supernaturals and man in Apachean ceremonialism. Ethnology, 7 (1968): 356-393.

Pinnow, Heinz-Jürgen. Zu den Eigennamen der Apachen-Häuptlinge. Anthropos, 63/64 (1968/1969): 441-456.

Potts, Alfred M., 2d. Developing curriculum for Indian children. By Alfred M. Potts, 2d. and Mamie Sizemore. Alamosa, Colo., Adams State College, Center for Cultural Studies, 1964. 106 l. ERIC ED012188.

Russell, F. An Apache medicine dance. American Anthropologist, 11 (1898): 367-372.

Russell, F. Myths of the Jicarilla Apaches. Journal of American Folklore, 40 (1898): 253-271.

Santee, R. Apache land. New York, 1947. 216 p.

Sasaki, Tom T. Sources of income among Many Farms--Rough Rock Navajo and Jicarilla Apache: some comparisons and comments. By Tom T. Sasaki and Harry W. Basehart. Human Organization, 20 (1961/1962): 187-190.

Schlesier, Karl H. Rethinking the Dismal River Aspect and the Plains Athapaskans, A.D. 1692-1768. Plains Anthropologist, 17 (1972): 101-133.

Schoolcraft, H. R. Apaches. In his Information respecting the History, Condition, and Prospects of the Indian Tribes of the United States. Vol. 5. Philadelphia, 1855: 202-214.

Schroeder, Albert H. Navajo and Apache relationships west of the Rio Grande. El Palacio, 70, no. 3 (1963): 5-23.

Sharp, A. W. The annual Jicarilla Apache encampment, 1951. El Palacio, 59 (1952): 95-96.

Skinner, S. Alan. Two historic period sites in the El Rito Valley, New Mexico. Plains Anthropologist, 13 (1968): 63-70.

Smith, Anne Marie. New Mexico Indians; economic, educational, and social problems. Santa Fe, Museum of New Mexico, 1966. 165 p. (Museum of New Mexico, Research Records, RR-1) ERIC ED019172.

Smith, Ralph A. The scalp hunter in the borderlands 1835-1850. In Roger L. Nichols and George R. Adams, eds. The American Indian: Past and Present. Waltham, Xerox College Publishing, 1971: 156-167.

Stephens, E. L. Steve. West of the Pecos. New Mexico Historical Review, 35 (1960): 81-108, 236-256, 309-326; 36 (1961): 159-174.

Taylor, Morris F. Action at Fort Massachusetts: the Indian campaign of 1855. Colorado Magazine, 42 (1965): 292-310.

Taylor, Morris F. Campaigns against the Jicarilla Apache, 1854. New Mexico Historical Review, 44 (1969): 269-291.

Taylor, Morris F. Campaigns against the Jicarilla Apache, 1855. New Mexico Historical Review, 45 (1970): 119-136.

Taylor, Morris F. Some aspects of historical Indian occupation of southeastern Colorado. Great Plains Journal, 4 (1964/1965): 17-28.

Thomas, A. B. After Coronado. Norman, 1935. 307 p.

Tweedie, M. Jean. Notes on the history and adaptation of the Apache tribes. American Anthropologist, 70 (1968): 1132-1142.

Van Roekel, Gertrude B. Jicarilla Apaches. San Antonio, Naylor, 1971. 17, 86 p. illus.

Wedel, W. R. The Plains Apache. U.S. Bureau of American Ethnology, Bulletin, 174 (1959): 69-75.

Wilson, H. Clyde. Jicarilla Apache political and economic structures. Berkeley, 1964. 5, 297-359 p. maps. (California, University, Publications in American Archaeology and Ethnology, 48, no. 4)

Woodward, A. John G. Bourke on the Arizona Apache, 1874. Plateau, 16 (1943): 33-44.

15-15 Jumano

Bannon, John Francis. The mission frontier in Sonora, 1620-1687. Edited by James A. Reynolds. New York, United States Catholic Historical Society, 1955. 4, 160 p. (United States Catholic Historical Society, Monograph Series, 26)

Bolton, H. E. The Jumano Indians in Texas. Texas State Historical Association Quarterly, 15 (1911): 66-84.

Brugge, David M. Some Plains Indians in the church records of New Mexico. Plains Anthropologist, 10 (1965): 181-189.

Cabeza de Vaca, Alvar Núñez. Adventures in the unknown interior of America. New York, Collier, 1961. 152 p. (Collier Books, AS117)

Chiodo, Beverly Ann. Real County. Southwestern Historical Quarterly, 65 (1961/1962): 348-365.

Clark, LaVerne Harrell. They sang for horses; the impact of the horse on Navajo and Apache folklore. Tucson, University of Arizona Press, 1966. 20, 225 p. illus., maps.

Davis, William Robert. The Spanish borderlands of Texas and Chihuahua. Texana, 9 (1971): 142-155.

Eckhart, George B. Spanish missions of Texas, 1680-1800. Kiva, 32, no. 3 (1966/1967): 73-95.

Forbes, J. D. The Janos, Jocomes, Mansos and Sumas Indians. New Mexico Historical Review, 32 (1957): 319-334.

Forbes, Jack D. Unknown Athapaskans: the identification of the Jano, Jocome, Jumano, Manso, Suma, and other Indian tribes of the Southwest. Ethnohistory, 6 (1959): 97-159.

Griffen, William B. Culture change and shifting populations in central northern Mexico. Tucson, 1969. 12, 196 p. maps. (Arizona, University, Anthropological Papers, 13)

Griffen, William B. Procesos de extinción y continuidad social y cultural en el norte de México durante la Colonia. América Indígena, 30 (1970): 689-724.

Hammond, G. P. and A. Rey. Expedition into New Mexico made by Antonio de Espejo, 54-69. Los Angeles, 1929.

Hammond, G. P. and A. Rey. The Gallegos relation of the Rodriguez expedition. New Mexico Historical Review, 2 (1927): 239-268, 334-362.

Hays, Alden. The missing Convento of San Isidro. El Palacio, 75, no. 4 (1968): 35-40.

Henshaw, F. W. Suma. U.S. Bureau of American Ethnology, Bulletin, 30, vol. 2 (1910): 649.

Hodge, F. W. Jumano. U.S. Bureau of
American Ethnology, Bulletin, 30, vol. 1
(1907): 636.

Hodge, F. W. The Jumano Indians. American
Antiquarian Society, Proceedings, n.s.,
10 (1910): 249-268.

Kelley, J. C. Juan Sabeata and diffusion
in aboriginal Texas. American
Anthropologist, 57 (1955): 981-995.

Kubler, G. Gran Quivira-Humanas. New
Mexico Historical Review, 14 (1939):
418-421.

Naylor, Thomas H. The extinct Suma of
northern Chihuahua: their origin,
cultural identity, and disappearance.
Artifact, 7, no. 4 (1969): 1-14.

Sauer, C. The distribution of aboriginal
tribes and languages in northwestern
Mexico. Ibero-Americana, 5 (1934): 65-
74.

Scholes, F. V. and H. P. Mera. Some
aspects of the Jumano problem. Carnegie
Institution, Contributions to American
Anthropology and History, 6 (1940): 265-
299.

Schroeder, Albert H. A re-analysis of the
routes of Coronado and Oñate into the
Plains in 1541 and 1601. Plains
Anthropologist, 7 (1962): 2-23.

Sedelmayr, Jacobo. Jacobo Sedelmayr
missionary frontiersman explorer in
Arizona and Sonora. Four original
manuscript narratives 1744-1751.
Translated and annotated by Peter Masten
Dunne. [n.p.] Arizona Pioneers'
Historical Society, 1955. 4, 82, 7 p.
map.

15-16 Lipan

Anza, Juan Bautista de. Governor Anza,
the Lipan Apaches and Pecos Pueblo.
Translated and edited by Marc Simmons.
El Palacio, 77, no. 1 (1970): 35-40.

Bartlett, J. R. Personal narrative of
explorations and incidents in Texas, New
Mexico, California, Sonora, and
Chihuahua, Vol. 1: 323-329. New York,
1854.

Beals, R. L. The comparative ethnology of
northern Mexico. Ibero-Americana, 2
(1932): 93-225.

Bellah, R. N. Apache kinship systems.
Cambridge, 1952. 151 p.

Bollaert, W. Observations on the Indian
tribes in Texas. Ethnological Society
(London), Journal, 2 (1850): 262-283.

Bolton, H. E. Athanase de Mézières and
the Louisiana-Texas Frontier.
Cleveland, 1914. 2 v.

Bolton, H. E. Texas in the middle
eighteenth century. California,
University, Publications in History, 3
(1915): 1-501.

Boyer, L. Bryce. Folk psychiatry of the
Apaches of the Mescalero Indian
Reservation. In Ari Kiev, ed. Magic,
Faith, and Healing. New York, Free
Press, 1964: 384-419.

Buckelew, F. M. Life of an Indian
captive. By Lillie M. Ross.
Philadelphia, Dorrance, 1965. 94 p.

Calleja, Félix. Nuevo Santander in 1795:
a provincial inspection by Félix
Calleja. Translated and edited by David
M. Vigness. Southwestern Historical
Quarterly, 75 (1971/1972): 461-506.

Canedo, Lino de. Sangre misionera en
Tejas: II centenario. La breve y tragica
historia de la Misión de los Apaches.
España Misionera, 15 (1958): 127-143.

Carter, James D. Background of Anglo-
American colonization of Texas. Texana,
4 (1966): 75-92.

Cavazos Garza, Israel. Las incursiones de
los bárbaros en el noreste de México,
durante el siglo XIX. Humanitas
(Monterrey), 5 (1964): 343-356.

Chavez, J. C. Los Apaches de Chihuahua.
Sociedad Chihuahuense de Estudios
Históricos, Boletín, 9, no. 2 (1955):
815-820.

Chiodo, Beverly Ann. Real County.
Southwestern Historical Quarterly, 65
(1961/1962): 348-365.

Clark, LaVerne Harrell. They sang for
horses; the impact of the horse on
Navajo and Apache folklore. Tucson,
University of Arizona Press, 1966. 20,
225 p. illus., maps.

Conroy, William. The Llano Estacado in
1541: Spanish perception of a
distinctive physical setting. Journal of
the West, 11 (1972): 573-581.

Daniel, James M. The Spanish frontier in
West Texas and northern Mexico.
Southwestern Historical Quarterly, 71
(1967/1968): 481-495.

Dixon, Ford. Cayton Erhard's reminiscences of the Texan Santa Fe expedition, 1841. Southwestern Historical Quarterly, 66 (1962/1963): 424-456.

Dunn, W. E. Apache relations in Texas. Texas State Historical Association Quarterly, 14 (1910): 198-274.

Edgerton, Faye E. The tagmemic analysis of sentence structure in Western Apache. In Harry Hoijer, et al., eds. Studies in the Athapaskan Languages. Berkeley and Los Angeles, University of California Press, 1963: 102-148. (California, University, Publications in Linguistics, 29)

Gifford, E. W. Apache-Pueblo. Anthropological Records, 4 (1940): 1-207.

Gunnerson, J. H. An introduction to Plains Apache archeology. U.S. Bureau of American Ethnology, Bulletin, 173 (1960): 131-260.

Harrington, J. P. Southern peripheral Athapaskawan origins, divisions, and migrations. Smithsonian Miscellaneous Collections, 100 (1940): 503-532.

Hasdorff, James Curtis. Four Indian tribes of Texas 1758-1858: a reevaluation of historical sources. Dissertation Abstracts International, 32 (1971/1972): 4512A. UM 72-4805.

Hester, Thomas Roy. Aboriginal watercraft on the lower Rio Grande of Texas. Masterkey, 46 (1972): 108-111.

Hodge, F. W. Lipan. U.S. Bureau of American Ethnology, Bulletin, 30, vol. 1 (1907): 768-769.

Hoijer, H. Phonetic and phonemic change in the Athapaskan languages. Language, 18 (1942): 218-220.

Hoijer, H. Pitch accent in the Apachean languages. Language, 19 (1943): 38-41.

Hoijer, H. The Apachean verb. International Journal of American Linguistics, 11 (1945): 193-203; 12 (1946): 1-13, 51-59; 14 (1948): 247-259; 15 (1949): 12-22.

Leutenegger, Benedict, tr. and ed. New documents on Father José Mariano Reyes. Southwestern Historical Quarterly, 71 (1967/1968): 583-602.

Matson, D. S. and A. H. Schroeder. Cordero's description of the Apache-- 1796. New Mexico Historical Review, 32 (1957): 335-356.

McLane, William. William McLane's narrative of the Magee-Gutierrez expedition, 1812-1813. Edited by Henry P. Walker. Southwestern Historical Quarterly, 66 (1962/1963): 457-479, 569-588.

Morfi, J. A. de. Memorias for the history of the Province of Texas. Ed. by F. M. Chabot. San Antonio, 1932. 85 p.

Ogle, R. H. The Apache and the government--1870's. New Mexico Historical Review, 34 (1959): 81-102.

Opler, M. E. An application of the theory of themes in culture. Washington Academy of Sciences, Journal, 36 (1946): 137-166.

Opler, M. E. Apache data concerning the relation of kinship terminology to social classification. American Anthropologist, n.s., 39 (1937): 201-212.

Opler, M. E. Further comparative anthropological data bearing on the solution of a psychological problem. Journal of Social Psychology, 9 (1938): 477-483.

Opler, M. E. Myths and legends of the Lipan Apache Indians. American Folk-Lore Society, Memoirs, 36 (1940): 1-296.

Opler, M. E. The kinship systems of the southern Athabaskan-speaking tribes. American Anthropologist, n.s., 38 (1936): 620-633.

Opler, M. E. The Lipan Apache death complex and its extensions. Southwestern Journal of Anthropology, 1 (1945): 122-141.

Opler, M. E. The use of peyote by the Carrizo and Lipan Apache tribes. American Anthropologist, n.s., 40 (1938): 271-285.

Opler, M. E. Themes as dynamic forces in culture. American Journal of Sociology, 51 (1945): 198-206.

Opler, Morris E. Cause and effect in Apachean agriculture, division of labor, residence patterns, and girls' puberty rites. American Anthropologist, 74 (1972): 1133-1146.

Opler, Morris E. Cultural evolution, Southern Athapaskans, and chronology in theory. Southwestern Journal of Anthropology, 17 (1961): 1-20.

Opler, Morris E. Remuneration to supernaturals and man in Apachean ceremonialism. Ethnology, 7 (1968): 356-393.

Park, Joseph F. Spanish Indian policy in northern Mexico, 1765-1810. Arizona and the West, 4 (1962): 325-344.

Patten, Roderick B., tr. and ed. Miranda's inspection of Los Almagres: his journal, report, and petition. Southwestern Historical Quarterly, 74 (1970/1971): 223-254.

Pinnow, Heinz-Jürgen. Zu den Eigennamen der Apachen-Häuptlinge. Anthropos, 63/64 (1968/1969): 441-456.

Sayles, E. B. An archaeological survey of Texas. Medallion Papers, 17 (1935): 1-164.

Schroeder, Albert H. A re-analysis of the routes of Coronado and Oñate into the Plains in 1541 and 1601. Plains Anthropologist, 7 (1962): 2-23.

Simmons, Marc. Governor Anza, the Lipan Apaches and Pecos Pueblo. El Palacio, 77, no. 1 (1970): 35-40.

Sjoberg, A. F. Lipan Apache culture in historical perspective. Southwestern Journal of Anthropology, 9 (1953): 76-98.

Smith, Ralph A. The scalp hunter in the borderlands 1835-1850. In Roger L. Nichols and George R. Adams, eds. The American Indian: Past and Present. Waltham, Xerox College Publishing, 1971: 156-167.

Thomas, Cyrus. Indian languages of Mexico and Central America and their geographical distribution. By Cyrus Thomas assisted by John R. Swanton. Washington, D.C., Government Printing Office, 1911. 7, 108 p. map. (U.S., Bureau of American Ethnology, Bulletin, 44)

Tunnell, Curtis D. A Lipan Apache mission: San Lorenzo de la Santa Cruz, 1762-1771. By Curtis D. Tunnell and W. W. Newcomb, Jr. Austin, 1969. 191 p. illus. (Texas Memorial Museum, Bulletin, 14)

Tweedie, M. Jean. Notes on the history and adaptation of the Apache tribes. American Anthropologist, 70 (1968): 1132-1142.

Vigness, D. M. Indian raids on the lower Rio Grande, 1836-1837. Southwestern Historical Quarterly, 59 (1955): 14-23.

Vizcaya Canales, Isidro. La invasión de los indios bárbaros al noreste de México, en los años de 1840 y 1841. Monterrey, N.L., 1968. 296 p. (Monterrey, Instituto Tecnologico y de Estudios Superiores de Monterrey, Publicaciones, Serie: Historia, 7)

Wallace, Ernest. R. S. Mackenzie and the Kickapoos; the raid into Mexico in 1873. By Ernest Wallace and Adrian S. Anderson. Arizona and the West, 7 (1965): 105-126.

Weddle, Robert S. San Juan Bautista; gateway to Spanish Texas. Austin, University of Texas Press, 1968. 14, 469 p. illus., maps.

Weddle, Robert S. San Juan Bautista: mother of Texas missions. Southwestern Historical Quarterly, 71 (1967/1968): 542-563.

Weddle, Robert S. The San Sabá Mission: approach to the Great Plains. Great Plains Journal, 4 (1964/1965): 29-38.

Weddle, Robert S. The San Sabá Mission, Spanish pivot in Texas. Austin, University of Texas Press, 1964. 13, 238 p. illus., maps.

Winfrey, Dorman H., ed. The Indian papers of Texas and the Southwest, 1825-1916. Edited by Dorman H. Winfrey and James M. Day. Austin, Pemberton Press, 1966. 412 p.

15-17 Manso

Anonymous. Manso. U.S. Bureau of American Ethnology, Bulletin, 30, vol. 1 (1907): 801-802.

Bandelier, A. F. Final report of investigations among the Indians of the Southwestern United States. Archaeological Institute of America, Papers, American Series, 3 (1890): 1-323; 4 (1892): 1-591.

Davis, William Robert. The Spanish borderlands of Texas and Chihuahua. Texana, 9 (1971): 142-155.

Dobyns, Henry F. Indian extinction in the middle Santa Cruz River Valley, Arizona. New Mexico Historical Review, 38 (1963): 163-181.

Forbes, J. D. The Janos, Jocomes, Mansos and Sumas Indians. New Mexico Historical Review, 32 (1957): 319-334.

Forbes, Jack D. Unknown Athapaskans: the identification of the Jano, Jocome, Jumano, Manso, Suma, and other Indian tribes of the Southwest. Ethnohistory, 6 (1959): 97-159.

Opler, M. E. The identity of the Apache Mansos. American Anthropologist, n.s., 44 (1942): 725.

15-18 Maricopa

Bartlett, J. R. Personal narrative of explorations and incidents in Texas, New Mexico, California, Sonora, and Chihuahua, Vol. 2: 221-238. New York, 1854.

Brown, H. A Pima-Maricopa ceremony. American Anthropologist, n.s., 8 (1906): 688-690.

Buschmann, J. C. E. Die Spuren der aztekischen Sprache im nördlichen Mexico and höheren amerikanischen Norden. Berlin, Königliche Akademie der Wissenschaften, Abhandlungen, Supplement-Band, 2 (1854): 264-267.

Chilcott, John H., comp. Handbook for Pima and Maricopa Indian teacher aides. Tuscon, Ariz., University of Arizona, Bureau of Educational Research and Service, 1970. 20 p. ERIC ED044221.

Curtis, E. S. The North American Indian, Vol. 2: 81-87. Cambridge, 1908.

Demeke, Howard J., comp. In-service education series and consultant services. Final report. Tempe, Arizona State University, College of Education, Bureau of Educational Research and Services, 1967. 47 p. ERIC ED046591.

Dobyns, H. F., et al. Thematic changes in Yuman warfare. In V. F. Ray, ed. Cultural Stability and Cultural Change. Seattle, 1957: 46-71.

Drucker, Philip. Culture element distributions: XVII Yuman-Piman. Berkeley, 1941. 91-230 p. illus., map. (California, University, Publications, Anthropological Records, 6, no. 3)

Ezell, Paul H. The Hispanic acculturation of the Gila River Pimas. Menasha, American Anthropological Association, 1961. 5, 171 p. illus., maps. (American Anthropological Association, Memoir, 90)

Ezell, Paul H. The Maricopas: an identification from documentary sources. Tucson, University of Arizona Press, 1963. 29 p. (Arizona, University, Anthropological Papers, 6)

Fay, George E., ed. Charters, constitutions and by-laws of the Indian tribes of North America. Part IV: The Southwest (Navajo-Zuni). Greeley, 1967. 5, 120 l. maps. (University of Northern Colorado, Museum of Anthropology, Occasional Publications in Anthropology, Ethnology Series, 5) ERIC ED046554.

Frisch, Jack A. Componential analysis and semantic reconstruction: the Proto Central Yuman kinship system. By Jack A. Frisch and Noel W. Schutz, Jr. Ethnology, 6 (1967): 272-293.

Frisch, Jack A. Maricopa foods: a native taxonomic system. International Journal of American Linguistics, 34 (1968): 16-20.

Gatschet, A. S. Der Yuma-Sprachstamm. Zeitschrift für Ethnologie, 9 (1887): 375-377, 390-406.

Gifford, E. W. Clans and moieties in southern California. California, University, Publications in American Archaeology and Ethnology, 14 (1918): 155-219.

Hanna, Bertram L. The biological relationships among Indian groups of the Southwest: analysis of morphological traits. American Journal of Physical Anthropology, n.s., 20 (1962): 499-508.

Harvey, Byron, III. Is pottery making a dying art. Masterkey, 38 (1964): 55-65.

Hodge, F. W. Maricopa. U.S. Bureau of American Ethnology, Bulletin, 30, vol. 1 (1907): 805-807.

Hrdlička, A. Maricopa weaving. American Anthropologist, n.s., 7 (1905): 361.

Ives, Ronald L. Kino's exploration of the Pinacate region. Journal of Arizona History, 7 (1966): 59-75.

Joel, Judith. Classification of the Yuman languages. In William Bright, ed. Studies in Californian Linguistics. Berkeley and Los Angeles, University of California Press, 1964: 99-105. (California, University, Publications in Linguistics, 34)

Johnston, Francis E., et al. Alloalbuminemia in Southwestern U.S. Indians: polymorphism of albumin Naskapi and albumin Mexico. Human Biology, 41 (1969): 263-270.

Johnston, Francis J. San Gorgonio Pass: forgotten route of the Californios? Journal of the West, 8 (1969): 125-136.

Kate, H. F. C. ten. Indiens d'Amérique du Nord. Anthropologie (Paris), 28 (1917): 369-401.

Kate, H. F. C. ten. Somatological observations on Indians of the Southwest. Journal of American Ethnology and Archaeology, 3 (1892): 117-144.

Kayser, David W. Take a smooth pebble, add hard work: that's Maricopa pottery. El Palacio, 77, no. 1 (1970): 25-32.

Kelly, William H. A study of southern Arizona school-age Indian children, 1966-1967. Tucson, University of Arizona, Bureau of Ethnic Research, 1967. 3, 38 p. ERIC ED024485.

Kino, Eusebio Francisco. Correspondencia del P. Kino con los generales de la Compañia de Jesús 1682-1707. Prólogo y notas de Ernest J. Burrus, S.J. México, Editorial Jus, 1961. 95 p. illus., maps. (Testimonio Historica, 5)

Kino, Eusebio Francisco. Kino reports to headquarters; correspondence . . . from New Spain with Rome. Original Spanish text of fourteen unpublished letters and reports. With English translation and notes by Ernest J. Burrus, S.J. Rome, Institutum Historicum Societatis Jesu, 1954. 135 p.

Law, Howard W. A reconstructed proto-culture derived from some Yuman vocabularies. Anthropological Linguistics, 3, no. 4 (1961): 45-57.

Matson, G. Albin. Distribution of hereditary factors in the blood of Indians of the Gila River, Arizona. By G. Albin Matson, Thomas A. Burch, Herbert F. Polesky, Jane Swanson, H. Eldon Sutton, and Abner Robinson. American Journal of Physical Anthropology, n.s., 29 (1968): 311-337.

Miller, Mary R. The language and language beliefs of Indian children. Anthropological Linguistics, 12 (1970): 51-61.

Phoenix Indian School. The new trail; a book of creative writing by Indian students. Phoenix, 1941. 158 p.

Polesky, Herbert F. Serum albumin polymorphism in Indians of the Southwestern United States. By Herbert F. Polesky, Dwight A. Rokala, and Thomas A. Burch. Nature, 220 (1968): 175-176.

Roberts, Shirley J. Minority-group poverty in Phoenix; a socio-economic survey. Journal of Arizona History, 14 (1973): 347-362.

Romney, A. Kimball. Internal reconstruction of Yuman kinship terminology. In Dell H. Hymes and William E. Bittle, eds. Studies in Southwestern Ethnolinguistics. The Hague, Mouton, 1967: 379-386. (Studies in General Anthropology, 3)

Sabre. Tour in Arizona: footprints of an Army officer. Edited by Henry Winfred Splitter. Journal of the West, 1 (1962): 74-97.

Sanford, George Bliss. "Thou art the man"; an address on the Indian question in 1892 by Colonel George Bliss Sanford. Edited by E. R. Hagemann. Journal of Arizona History, 9 (1968): 30-38.

Schroeder, Albert H. An archaeological survey of the Painted Rocks Resevoir, Western Arizona. Kiva, 27, no. 1 (1961/1962): 1-28.

Sedelmayr, Jacobo. Jacobo Sedelmayr missionary frontiersman explorer in Arizona and Sonora. Four original manuscript narratives 1744-1751. Translated and annotated by Peter Masten Dunne. [n.p.] Arizona Pioneers' Historical Society, 1955. 4, 82, 7 p. map.

Spier, L. Comparative vocabularies and parallel texts in two Yuman languages. New Mexico, University, Publications in Anthropology, 2 (1946): 1-150.

Spier, L. Cultural relations of the Gila River and Lower Colorado tribes. Yale University Publications in Anthropology, 3 (1936): 1-22.

*Spier, L. Yuman tribes of the Gila River. Chicago, 1933. 433 p.

Spier, Leslie. Cultural relations of the Gila River and Lower Colorado tribes. New Haven, Human Relations Area Files Press, 1970. 22 p. (Yale University Publications in Anthropology, 3)

*Spier, Leslie. Yuman tribes of the Gila River. New York, Cooper Square Publishers, 1970. 18, 433 p. illus., maps.

Wares, Alan Campbell. A comparative study of Yuman consonantism. The Hague, Mouton, 1968. 100 p. map. (Janua Linguarum, Series Practica, 57)

Wares, Alan Campbell. A comparative study of Yuman consonantism. Dissertation Abstracts, 26 (1964/1965): 2200. UM 65-10,774.

Whited, S. Pima Agency. In United States, Department of the Interior, Census

Office, Eleventh Census, Report on Indians Taxed and Indians not Taxed. Washington, D.C., 1890: 137-146.

Woody, Clara T., ed. The Woolsey expeditions of 1864. Arizona and the West, 4 (1962): 157-176.

                    15-19 Mescalero

Bartoli, J. F. The Apache "devil dance". Musical Courier, 152, no. 8 (1955): 8-10.

*Basehart, Harry W. Mescalero Apache band organization and leadership. Southwestern Journal of Anthropology, 26 (1970): 87-106.

Basehart, Harry W. The resource holding corporation among the Mescalero Apache. Southwestern Journal of Anthropology, 23 (1967): 277-291.

Bellah, Robert N. Apache kinship systems. Cambridge, 1952. 151 p.

Boyer, L. Bryce. Aportes psicoanalíticos y antropológicos a la tarea con minorías étnicas. By L. Bryce Boyer and Ruth M. Boyer. Acta Psiquiátrica y Psicológica de América Latina, 15 (1969): 25-33.

Boyer, L. Bryce. Effects of acculturation on the vicissitudes of the aggressive drive among the Apaches of the Mescalero Indian Reservation. By L. Bryce Boyer and Ruth M. Boyer. In Warner Muensterberger and Aaron Esman, eds. The Psychoanalytic Study of Society. Vol. 5. New York, International Universities Press, 1972: 40-82.

Boyer, L. Bryce. Folk psychiatry of the Apaches of the Mescalero Indian Reservation. In Ari Kiev, ed. Magic, Faith, and Healing. New York, Free Press, 1964: 384-419.

Boyer, L. Bryce. Further remarks concerning shamans and shamanism. Israel Annals of Psychiatry and Related Disciplines, 2 (1964): 235-257.

Boyer, L. Bryce. Remarks on the personality of shamans with special reference to the Apache of the Mescalero Indian Reservation. In Warner Muensterberger and Sidney Axelrad, eds. The Psychoanalytic Study of Society. Vol. 2. New York, International Universities Press, 1962: 233-254.

Boyer, L. Bryce. Shamans: to set the record straight. American Anthropologist, 71 (1969): 307-309.

Boyer, L. Bryce. Stone as a symbol in Apache mythology. American Imago, 22 (1965): 14-39.

Boyer, L. Bryce, et al. Apache age groups. Journal of Projective Techniques and Personality Assessment, 28 (1964): 397-402.

Boyer, L. Bryce, et al. Apache "learners" and "nonlearners". II. Quantitative Rorschach signs of influential adults. Journal of Projective Techniques and Personality Assessment, 32 (1968): 146-159.

Boyer, L. Bryce, et al. Apache "learners" and "nonlearners". Journal of Projective Techniques and Personality Assessment, 31, no. 6 (1967): 22-29.

Boyer, L. Bryce, et al. Comparisons of the shamans and pseudoshamans of the Apaches of the Mescalero Indian Reservation: a Rorschach study. Journal of Projective Techniques and Personality Assessment, 28 (1964): 173-180.

Boyer, L. Bryce, et al. Effects of acculturation on the personality traits of the old people of the Mescalero and Chiricahua Apaches. International Journal of Social Psychiatry, 11 (1965): 264-271.

Boyer, Ruth M. A Mescalero Apache tale: the bat and the flood. Western Folklore, 31 (1972): 189-197.

Boyer, Ruth M. The matrifocal family among the Mescalero: additional data. American Anthropologist, 66 (1964): 593-602.

Calleja, Félix. Nuevo Santander in 1795: a provincial inspection by Félix Calleja. Translated and edited by David M. Vigness. Southwestern Historical Quarterly, 75 (1971/1972): 461-506.

Castetter, E. F. and M. E. Opler. The ethnobiology of the Chiricahua and Mescalero Apache. New Mexico, University, Bulletin, Biological Series, 4, no. 5 (1936): 3-63.

Cavazos Garza, Israel. Las incursiones de los bárbaros en el noreste de México, durante el siglo XIX. Humanitas (Monterrey), 5 (1964): 343-356.

Chris. Apache odyssey; a journey between two worlds. By Morris E. Opler. New York, Holt, Rinehart and Winston, 1969. 16, 301 p. illus., maps.

Clark, LaVerne Harrell. Early horse trappings of the Navajo and Apache

Indians. Arizona and the West, 5 (1963): 233-248.

Clark, LaVerne Harrell.   They sang for horses; the impact of the horse on Navajo and Apache folklore. Tucson, University of Arizona Press, 1966. 20, 225 p. illus., maps.

Conroy, William.   The Llano Estacado in 1541: Spanish perception of a distinctive physical setting. Journal of the West, 11 (1972): 573-581.

Curley, Richard T.   Drinking patterns of the Mescalero Apache. Quarterly Journal of Studies on Alcohol, 27 (1966): 336-337; 28 (1967): 116-131.

Curtis, E. S.   The North American Indian, Vol. 1: 3-51. Cambridge, 1907.

Daniel, James M.   The Spanish frontier in West Texas and northern Mexico. Southwestern Historical Quarterly, 71 (1967/1968): 481-495.

Davisson, Lori.   The Apaches at home; a photographic essay. Journal of Arizona History, 14 (1973): 113-132.

Devereux, G. and E. M. Loeb.   Some notes on Apache criminality. Journal of Criminal Psychopathology, 4 (1943): 424-430.

Dory, W.   The Mescalero Apaches' present condition. Southern Workman, 51 (1922): 413-419, 422.

Douglas, F. H.   Apache Indian coiled basketry. Denver Art Museum, Indian Leaflet Series, 64 (1934): 54-56.

Douglas, F. H.   The Apache Indians. Denver Art Museum, Indian Leaflet Series, 16 (1930): 1-4.

Dunn, W. E.   Apache relations in Texas. Texas State Historical Association Quarterly, 14 (1910): 198-274.

Edgerton, Faye E.   The tagmemic analysis of sentence structure in Western Apache. In Harry Hoijer, et al., eds. Studies in the Athapaskan Languages. Berkeley and Los Angeles, University of California Press, 1963: 102-148. (California, University, Publications in Linguistics, 29)

Fay, George E., ed.   Charters, constitutions and by-laws of the Indian tribes of North America. Part III: The Southwest (Apache-Mohave). Greeley, 1967. 6, 118 l. maps. (University of Northern Colorado, Museum of Anthropology, Occasional Publications in

Anthropology, Ethnology Series, 4)   ERIC ED046553.

Fergusson, E.   Dancing gods, 249-269.   New York, 1931.

Fergusson, E.   Modern Apaches of New Mexico. American Indian, 6, no. 1 (1951): 3-14.

Flannery, R.   The position of woman among the Mescalero Apache. Primitive Man, 5 (1932): 26-33.

Forbes, Jack D.   Unknown Athapaskans: the identification of the Jano, Jocome, Jumano, Manso, Suma, and other Indian tribes of the Southwest. Ethnohistory, 6 (1959): 97-159.

Gardner, H.   Philip St. George Cooke and the Apache, 1854. New Mexico Historical Review, 28 (1953): 115-132.

Gifford, E. W.   Apache-Pueblo. Anthropological Records, 4 (1940): 1-207.

Goddard, P. E.   Gotal--a Mescalero Apache ceremony. In Putnam Anniversary Volume. New York, 1909: 385-394.

Goddard, P. E.   The masked dancers of the Apache. In Holmes Anniversary Volume. Washington, D.C., 1916: 132-136.

Greenleaf, Richard E.   The Nueva Vizcaya frontier, 1787-1789. Journal of the West, 8 (1969): 56-66.

Griffen, William B.   Culture change and shifting populations in central northern Mexico. Tucson, 1969. 12, 196 p. maps. (Arizona, University, Anthropological Papers, 13)

Griffen, William B.   Procesos de extinción y continuidad social y cultural en el norte de México durante la Colonia. América Indígena, 30 (1970): 689-724.

Gunnerson, James H.   Evidence of Apaches at Pecos. By James H. Gunnerson and Dolores A. Gunnerson. El Palacio, 76, no. 3 (1969): 1-6.

Harrington, J. P.   Southern peripheral Athpaskawan origins, divisions, and migrations. Smithsonian Miscellaneous Collections, 100 (1940): 503-532.

Helms, Mary W.   Matrilocality, social solidarity, and culture contact: three case histories. Southwestern Journal of Anthropology, 26 (1970): 197-212.

Hodge, F. W.   Mescaleros. U.S. Bureau of American Ethnology, Bulletin, 30, vol. 1 (1907): 846.

Hoijer, H. Chiricahua and Mescalero
Apache texts. Chicago, 1938. 219 p.

Hoijer, H. Phonetic and phonemic change
in the Athapaskan languages. Language,
18 (1942): 218-220.

Hoijer, H. Pitch accent in the Apachean
languages. Language, 19 (1943): 38-41.

Hoijer, H. The Apachean verb.
International Journal of American
Linguistics, 11 (1945): 193-203; 12
(1946): 1-13, 51-59; 14 (1948): 247-259;
15 (1949): 12-22.

Jelinek, Arthur J. Environment and
aboriginal population seen through the
historical record. In A Prehistoric
Sequence in the Middle Pecos Valley, New
Mexico. Ann Arbor, University of
Michigan, 1967: 18-40. (Michigan,
University, Museum of Anthropology,
Anthropological Papers, 31)

Klopfer, Bruno. Notes on the personality
structure of a North American Indian
shaman: Rorschach interpretation. By
Bruno Klopfer and L. Bryce Boyer.
Journal of Projective Techniques and
Personality Assessment, 25 (1961): 170-
178.

Kunstadter, Peter. A survey of the
consanguine or matrifocal family.
American Anthropologist, 65 (1963): 56-
66.

Kunstadter, Peter. Culture change, social
structure, and health behavior: a
quantitative study of clinic use among
the Apaches of the Mescalero
Reservation. Dissertation Abstracts, 22
(1961/1962): 392. UM 61-2766.

Kunstadter, Peter. Southern Athabaskan
herding patterns and contrasting social
institutions. In Anthony Leeds and
Andrew P. Vayda, eds. Man, Culture, and
Animals. Washington, D.C., 1965: 67-86.
(American Association for the
Advancement of Science, Publication, 78)

La Barre, Weston. The peyote cult. New
Haven, Yale University, Department of
Anthropology, 1938. 188 p. illus.
(Yale University Publications in
Anthropology, 19)

Landar, Herbert J. Theme of incest in
Navaho folklore. In Samir K. Ghosh, ed.
Man, Language and Society; Contributions
to the Sociology of Language. The
Hague, Mouton, 1972: 118-133. (Janua
Linguarum, Series Minor, 109)

Lane, William Carr. William Carr Lane,
diary. Edited by Wm. G. B. Carson. New

Mexico Historical Review, 39 (1964):
181-234, 274-332.

Lockwood, F. C. The Apache Indians. New
York, 1938. 348 p.

MacLachlan, Bruce B. On "Indian Justice".
Plains Anthropologist, 8 (1963): 257-
261.

MacLachlan, Bruce B. The Mescalero Apache
quest for law and order. Journal of the
West, 3 (1964): 441-458.

Matson, D. S. and A. H. Schroeder.
Cordero's description of the Apache--
1796. New Mexico Historical Review, 32
(1957): 335-356.

Mechem, G. B. Mescalero Agency. In United
States, Department of the Interior,
Census Office, Eleventh Census, Report
on Indians Taxed and Indians not Taxed.
Washington, D.C., 1890: 398-404.

Mehren, Lawrence L., ed. Scouting for
Mescaleros; the Price campaign of 1873.
Arizona and the West, 10 (1968): 171-
190.

Mozer, Corinne C. A brief history of Fort
Fillmore 1851-1862. El Palacio, 74,
no. 2 (1967): 5-18.

Nicholas, D. Mescalero Apache girls'
puberty ceremony. El Palacio, 46 (1939):
193-204.

Ogle, R. H. The Apache and the
government--1870's. New Mexico
Historical Review, 34 (1959): 81-102.

Opler, M. E. A Mescalero Apache account
of the origin of the peyote ceremony. El
Palacio, 52 (1945): 210-212.

Opler, M. E. A note on the cultural
affiliations of northern Mexican nomads.
American Anthropologist, n.s., 37
(1935): 702-706.

Opler, M. E. An analysis of Mescalero and
Chiricahua Apache social organization in
the light of their systems of
relationship. Chicago, 1936. 19 p.

Opler, M. E. An interpretation of
ambivalence of two American Indian
tribes. Journal of Social Psychology, 7
(1936): 82-118.

Opler, M. E. Apache data concerning the
relation of kinship terminology to
social classification. American
Anthropologist, n.s., 39 (1937): 201-
212.

Opler, M. E. Further comparative
anthropological data bearing on the

solution of a psychological problem. Journal of Social Psychology, 9 (1938): 477-483.

Opler, M. E. Kinship systems of the southern Athabaskan-speaking tribes. American Anthropologist, n.s., 38 (1936): 620-633.

Opler, M. E. Reaction to death among the Mescalero Apache. Southwestern Journal of Anthropology, 2 (1946): 455-467.

Opler, M. E. Some points of comparison and contrast between the treatment of functional disorders by Apache shamans and modern psychiatric practice. American Journal of Psychiatry, 92 (1936): 1371-1387.

Opler, M. E. The concept of supernatural power among the Chiricahua and Mescalero Apaches. American Anthropologist, n.s., 37 (1935): 65-70.

Opler, M. E. The creative role of shamanism in Mescalero Apache mythology. Journal of American Folklore, 59 (1946): 268-281.

Opler, M. E. The influence of aboriginal pattern and White contact on a recently introduced ceremony, the Mescalero peyote rite. Journal of American Folklore, 49 (1936): 143-166.

Opler, M. E. The sacred clowns of the Chiricahua and Mescalero Indians. El Palacio, 44 (1938): 75-79.

Opler, M. E. The slaying of the monsters. El Palacio, 53 (1946): 215-225, 242-258.

Opler, M. E. and C. H. Opler. Mescalero Apache history in the Southwest. New Mexico Historical Review, 25 (1950): 1-36.

Opler, Marvin K. Plains and Pueblo influences in Mescalero Apache culture. In Mario D. Zamora, et al., eds. Themes in Culture. Quezon City, Kayumanggi, 1971: 73-112.

Opler, Morris E. Cause and effect in Apachean agriculture, division of labor, residence patterns, and girls' puberty rites. American Anthropologist, 74 (1972): 1133-1146.

Opler, Morris E. Cultural evolution, Southern Athapaskans, and chronology in theory. Southwestern Journal of Anthropology, 17 (1961): 1-20.

Opler, Morris E. Remuneration to supernaturals and man in Apachean ceremonialism. Ethnology, 7 (1968): 356-393.

Opler, Morris E. The schooling of an Apache. In Walter R. Goldschmidt, ed. Exploring the Ways of Mankind. 2d ed. New York, Holt, Rinehart and Winston, 1971: 155-161.

Oren, Joseph, et al. Aseptic meningitis on an Indian reservation. An epidemic associated with ECHO 9 virus. American Journal of Diseases of Children, 102 (1961): 843-852.

Park, Joseph F. Spanish Indian policy in northern Mexico, 1765-1810. Arizona and the West, 4 (1962): 325-344.

Pinnow, Heinz-Jürgen. Zu den Eigennamen der Apachen-Häuptlinge. Anthropos, 63/64 (1968/1969): 441-456.

Pokorn, Alfred. Apachen-Indianer; Geschichte, Ansiedlung, Sprache, Sitte und Verwaltung der Mescaleros. München, Oldenbourg, 1960. 72 p. illus. (Orion-Bücher, 136)

Rives, James A. A comparative study of traditional and programmed methods for developing music listening skills in the fifth grade. Journal of Research in Music Education, 18, no. 2 (1970): 126-133.

Ross, William T. Backgrounds of vocational choice: an Apache study. By William T. Ross and Golda V. B. Ross. Personnel and Guidance Journal (1957): 270-275.

Ross, William T. Some guidance problems among the Mescalero Apache Indians. In Internationale Amerikanistenkongress, 34th. 1960, Wien. Akten. Horn-Wien, Berger, 1962: 569-577.

Santee, R. Apache land. New York, 1947. 216 p.

Sauer, Carl O. The distribution of aboriginal tribes and languages in northwestern Mexico. Berkeley, University of California Press, 1934. 6, 94 p. map. (Ibero-Americana, 5)

Schoolcraft, H. R. Apaches. In his Information respecting the History, Condition, and Prospects of the Indian Tribes of the United States. Vol. 5. Philadelphia, 1855: 202-214.

Schroeder, Albert H. The language of the Saline Pueblos; Piro or Tiwa? New Mexico Historical Review, 39 (1964): 235-249.

Scott, Richard B. English language skills of the Mescalero Apache Indians. América Indígena, 20 (1960): 173-181.

Scully, Vincent. In praise of women: the
Mescalero puberty. Art in America, 60,
no. 4 (1972): 70-77.

Smart, Charles. Surgeon Smart and the
Indians; an 1866 Apache word-list.
Journal of Arizona History, 11 (1970):
126-140.

Smith, Anne Marie. New Mexico Indians;
economic, educational, and social
problems. Santa Fe, Museum of New
Mexico, 1966. 165 p. (Museum of New
Mexico, Research Records, RR-1) ERIC
ED019172.

*Sonnichsen, C. L. The Mescalero Apaches.
Norman, 1958. 315 p.

Spicer, Edward H. European expansion and
the enclavement of Southwestern Indians.
Arizona and the West, 1 (1959): 132-145.

Starnes, Gary Bertram. Juan de Ugalde
(1729-1816) and the Provincias Internas
of Coahuila and Texas. Dissertation
Abstracts International, 32 (1971/1972):
5722A. UM 72-12,491.

Tatje, Terrence. Variations in ancestor
worship beliefs and their relation to
kinship. By Terrence Tatje and Francis
L. K. Hsu. Southwestern Journal of
Anthropology, 25 (1969): 153-172.

Thomas, A. B. After Coronado. Norman,
1935. 307 p.

Thompson, Erwin N. The Negro soldier on
the frontier: a Fort Davis case study.
Journal of the West, 7 (1968): 217-235.

Tweedie, M. Jean. Notes on the history
and adaptation of the Apache tribes.
American Anthropologist, 70 (1968):
1132-1142.

Utley, Robert M. The range cattle
industry in the Big Bend of Texas.
Southwestern Historical Quarterly, 69
(1965/1966): 419-441.

Vigness, D. M. Indian raids on the lower
Rio Grande, 1836-1837. Southwestern
Historical Quarterly, 59 (1955): 14-23.

Vigness, David M. Don Hugo Oconor and New
Spain's northeastern frontier, 1764-
1776. Journal of the West, 6 (1967): 27-
40.

Vizcaya Canales, Isidro. La invasión de
los indios bárbaros al noreste de
México, en los años de 1840 y 1841.
Monterrey, N.L., 1968. 296 p.
(Monterrey, Instituto Tecnologico y de
Estudios Superiores de Monterrey,
Publicaciones, Serie: Historia, 7)

Wallace, Ernest. R. S. Mackenzie and the
Kickapoos; the raid into Mexico in 1873.
By Ernest Wallace and Adrian S.
Anderson. Arizona and the West, 7
(1965): 105-126.

Wilson, John P. Lt. H. B. Cushing: Indian
fighter extraordinary. El Palacio, 76,
no. 1 (1969): 40-46.

Woodward, A. John G. Bourke on the
Arizona Apache, 1874. Plateau, 16
(1943): 33-44.

15-20   Mohave

Allen, G. A. Manners and customs of the
Mohaves. Smithsonian Institution, Annual
Report of the Board of Regents (1890):
615-616.

Anonymous. Indians mortgage land for
return of arts. Indian Historian, 3,
no. 2 (1970): 18.

Aschmann, Homer. Historical sources for a
contact ethnography of Baja California.
California Historical Society Quarterly,
44 (1965): 99-121.

Atherton, Warren H. Stockton: supply
bull's-eye for the Mother Lode. Pacific
Historian, 9 (1965): 178-183.

Avillo, Philip J., Jr. Fort Mojave:
outpost on the Upper Colorado. Journal
of Arizona History, 11 (1970): 77-100.

Bean, Lowell John. Cahuilla
ethnobotanical notes: the aboriginal
uses of the mesquite and screwbean. By
Lowell John Bean and Katherine Siva
Saubel. California, University,
University at Los Angeles,
Archaeological Survey, Annual Report
(1962/1963): 51-75.

Boas, F. Zur Anthropologie der
nordamerikanischen Indianer. Berliner
Gesellschaft für Anthropologie,
Ethnologie und Urgeschichte,
Verhandlungen (1895): 367-411.

Bourke, J. G. Notes on the cosmogony and
theogony of the Mojave Indians. Journal
of American Folklore, 2 (1889): 169-189.

Burbank, E. A. and E. Royce. Burbank
among the Indians: 114-117. Caldwell,
1946.

Burch, Thomas A. Epidemiological studies
on rheumatic diseases. Military
Medicine, 131 (1966): 507-511.

Campion, J. S. On the frontier. 2d ed.
London, 1878. 372 p.

Conrad, David E. The Whipple expedition in Arizona 1853-1854. Arizona and the West, 11 (1969): 147-178.

Crawford, James M. Cocopa baby talk. International Journal of American Linguistics, 36 (1970): 9-13.

Curtis, E. S. The North American Indian, Vol. 2: 47-61. Cambridge, 1908.

Davis, Emma Lou. Notes on two sites in eastern California: unusual finds. By Emma Lou Davis, Delbert True, and Gene Sterud. California, University, University at Los Angeles, Archaeological Survey, Annual Report, 7 (1965): 323-331.

Densmore, F. Yuman and Yaqui music. U.S. Bureau of American Ethnology, Bulletin, 110 (1932): 1-216.

Devereux, G. Amusements and sports of Mohave children. Masterkey, 24 (1950): 143-152.

Devereux, G. Atypical and deviant Mohave marriages. Samiksa, Journal of the Indian Psycho-Analytic Society, 4 (1951): 200-215.

Devereux, G. Cultural and characterological traits of the Mohave. Psychoanalytic Quarterly, 20 (1951): 398-422.

Devereux, G. Der Begriff der Vaterschaft bei den Mohave-Indianer. Zeitschrift für Ethnologie, 69 (1937): 72-78.

Devereux, G. Dream learning and individual ritual differences in Mohave shamanism. American Anthropologist, 59 (1957): 1036-1045.

Devereux, G. Education and discipline in Mohave society. Primitive Man, 23 (1950): 85-102.

Devereux, G. Heterosexual behavior of the Mohave Indians. Psychoanalysis and the Social Sciences, 2 (1950): 85-128.

Devereux, G. Institutionalized homosexuality of the Mohave Indians. Human Biology, 9 (1937): 498-527.

Devereux, G. L'envoutement chez les Indiens Mohave. Société des Américanistes, Journal, n.s., 29 (1937): 405-412.

Devereux, G. Magic substances and narcotics of the Mohave Indians. British Journal of Medical Psychology, 22 (1949): 110-116.

Devereux, G. Mohave beliefs concerning twins. American Anthropologist, n.s., 43 (1941): 573-592.

Devereux, G. Mohave chieftainship in action. Plateau, 23 (1951): 33-43.

Devereux, G. Mohave coyote tales. Journal of American Folklore, 61 (1948): 233-255.

Devereux, G. Mohave culture and personality. Character and Personality, 8 (1939): 91-109.

Devereux, G. Mohave dreams of omen and power. Tomorrow, 4, no. 3 (1956): 17-24.

Devereux, G. Mohave etiquette. Masterkey, 22 (1948): 119-127.

Devereux, G. Mohave Indian autoerotic behavior. Psychoanalytic Review, 37 (1950): 201-220.

Devereux, G. Mohave Indian infanticide. Psychoanalytic Review, 35 (1948): 126-139.

Devereux, G. Mohave Indian kamaloty. Journal of Clinical Psychopathology, 9 (1948): 433-457.

Devereux, G. Mohave Indian obstetrics. América Indígena, 5 (1948): 95-139.

Devereux, G. Mohave Indian verbal and motor profanity. Psychoanalysis and the Social Sciences, 3 (1951): 99-127.

Devereux, G. Mohave orality. Psychoanalytic Quarterly, 16 (1947): 519-546.

Devereux, G. Mohave paternity. Samiksa, Journal of the Indian Psycho-Analytic Society, 3 (1949): 162-194.

Devereux, G. Mohave pregnancy. Acta Americana, 6 (1948): 89-116.

Devereux, G. Mohave soul concepts. American Anthropologist, n.s., 39 (1937): 417-422.

Devereux, G. Mohave voice and speech mannerisms. Word, 5 (1949): 268-272.

Devereux, G. Mohave zoophilia. Samiksa, Journal of the Indian Psycho-Analytic Society, 2 (1948): 227-245.

Devereux, G. Notes on the developmental pattern and organic needs of Mohave Indian children. Kansas Academy of Science, Transactions, 53 (1950): 178-185.

Devereux, G. Post-partum parental observances of the Mohave Indians. Kansas Academy of Science, Transactions, 52 (1949): 458-465.

Devereux, G. Primitive psychiatry. Bulletin of the History of Medicine, 8 (1940): 1194-1213; 11 (1942): 522-542.

Devereux, G. Psychodynamics of Mohave gambling. América Indígena, 7 (1950): 55-65.

Devereux, G. Some Mohave gestures. American Anthropologist, n.s., 51 (1949): 325-326.

Devereux, G. Status, socialization and interpersonal relations of Mohave children. Psychiatry, 13 (1950): 489-502.

Devereux, G. The function of alcohol in Mohave society. Quarterly Journal of Studies on Alcohol, 9 (1948): 207-251.

Devereux, G. The Mohave male puberty rite. Samiksa, Journal of the Indian Psycho-Analytic Society, 3 (1949): 11-25.

Devereux, G. The Mohave neonate and its cradle. Primitive Man, 21 (1948): 1-18.

Devereux, G. The primal scene and juvenile heterosexuality in Mohave society. In G. B. Wilbur and W. Muensterberger, eds. Psychoanalysis and Culture. New York, 1951: 90-107.

Devereux, G. The psychology of feminine genital bleeding. International Journal of Psycho-Analysis, 31 (1950): 237-252.

Devereux, G. The social and cultural implications of incest among the Mohave Indians. Psychoanalytic Quarterly, 8 (1939): 510-533.

Devereux, G. and E. M. Loeb. Antagonistic acculturation. American Sociological Review, 8 (1943): 133-147.

Devereux, George. Mohave ethnopsychiatry and suicide: the psychiatric knowledge and the psychic disturbances of an Indian tribe. Washington, D.C., 1961. 6, 586 p. illus. (U.S., Bureau of American Ethnology, Bulletin, 175)

*Devereux, George. Mohave ethnopsychiatry: the psychic disturbances of an Indian tribe. Washington, D.C., Smithsonian Institution Press, 1969. 16, 597 p. illus.

Devereux, George. Pathogenic dreams in non-Western societies. In Gustav E. von Grunebaum and Roger Caillois, eds. The Dream and Human Societies. Berkeley, University of California Press, 1966: 213-228.

Devereux, George. Primitive psychiatric diagnosis; a general theory of the diagnostic process. In Iago Galdston, ed. Man's Image in Medicine and Anthropology. New York, International Universities Press, 1963: 337-373.

Devereux, George. Re Mojave shamans. Masterkey, 44 (1970): 155-156.

Dobyns, H. F. A Mohave potter's experiment. Kiva, 24, no. 3 (1959): 16-17.

Dobyns, H. F., et al. Thematic changes in Yuman warfare. In V. F. Ray, ed. Cultural Stability and Cultural Change. Seattle, 1957: 46-71.

Dobyns, Henry F. A Mohave potter's experiment. Kiva, 24, no. 3 (1958/1959): 16-17.

Downing, George L. Native pottery of the Southwest. Natural History, 78, no. 6 (1969): 34-39.

Drucker, Philip. Culture element distributions: XVII Yuman-Piman. Berkeley, 1941. 91-230 p. illus., map. (California, University, Publications, Anthropological Records, 6, no. 3)

DuBois, C. G. Diegueno myths and their connections with the Mohave. International Congress of Americanists, Proceedings, 15, vol. 2 (1906): 129-133.

Essig, E. O. The value of insects to the California Indians. Scientific Monthly, 38 (1934): 181-186.

Fathauer, G. H. Religion in Mohave social structure. Ohio Journal of Science, 51 (1951): 273-276.

Fathauer, G. H. The structure and causation of Mohave warfare. Southwestern Journal of Anthropology, 10 (1954): 97-118.

Fay, George E., ed. Charters, constitutions and by-laws of the Indian tribes of North America. Part III: The Southwest (Apache-Mohave). Greeley, 1967. 6, 118 l. maps. (University of Northern Colorado, Museum of Anthropology, Occasional Publications in Anthropology, Ethnology Series, 4) ERIC ED046553.

Freed, Stanley A. A comparison of the reactions of Washo and Mohave respondents to an objective technique (role profile test) for measuring role behavior. New York Academy of Sciences, Transactions, ser. 2, 27 (1964/1965): 959-969.

Freed, Stanley A. A technique for studying role behavior. By Stanley A. Freed and Ruth S. Freed. Ethnology, 10 (1971): 107-121.

Freed, Stanley A. Mohave and Washo role behavior. By Stanley A. Freed and Ruth S. Freed. New York, American Museum of Natural History, 1968. 49 p. (American Museum Novitates, 2330)

Freed, Stanley A. Studying role behavior cross-culturally: comparison of a matrilineal and a bilateral society. By Stanley A. Freed and Ruth S. Freed. New York, American Museum of Natural History, 1970. 63 p. (American Museum Novitates, 2437)

Frisch, Jack A. Componential analysis and semantic reconstruction: the Proto Central Yuman kinship system. By Jack A. Frisch and Noel W. Schutz, Jr. Ethnology, 6 (1967): 272-293.

Gatschet, A. S. Classification into seven linguistic stocks of Western Indian dialects. In Report upon United States Geographical Surveys West of the One Hundredth Meridian. Vol. 7. Washington, D.C., 1879: 403-485.

Gatschet, A. S. Der Yuma-Sprachstamm. Zeitschrift für Ethnologie, 9 (1887): 378-380, 391-407, 412-418.

Gifford, E. W. Clans and moieties in southern California. California, University, Publications in American Archaeology and Ethnology, 14 (1918): 156-167.

Grey, Herman. Tales from the Mohaves. Norman, University of Oklahoma Press, 1970. 15, 96 p. map.

Hafen, L. R. and A. W. Hafen. Old Spanish trail. The Far West and the Rockies Historical Series 1820-1875, 1 (1954): 1-377.

Hall, S. M. The burning of a Mojave chief. Out West, 18 (1903): 60-65.

Hanna, Bertram L. The biological relationships among Indian groups of the Southwest: analysis of morphological traits. American Journal of Physical Anthropology, n.s., 20 (1962): 499-508.

Harrington, J. P. The Mohave. El Palacio, 27 (1929): 16-19.

Henshaw, H. W. and F. W. Hodge. Mohave. U.S. Bureau of American Ethnology, Bulletin, 30, vol. 1 (1907): 919-921.

Herzog, G. The Yuman musical style. Journal of American Folklore, 41 (1928): 183-231.

Hicks, Frederic Noble. Ecological aspects of aboriginal culture in the western Yuman area. Dissertation Abstracts, 24 (1963/1964): 1333-1334. UM 63-6591.

Hoffman, W. J. Miscellaneous ethnographic observations. United States Geological and Geographical Survey of the Territories, Annual Reports, 10 (1876): 461-477.

Hrdlička, A. Tuberculosis among certain Indian tribes. U.S. Bureau of American Ethnology, Bulletin, 42 (1909): 17-19.

Ives, J. C. Report upon the Colorado River of the West. Washington, D.C., 1861. 131 p.

Joel, Judith. Classification of the Yuman languages. In William Bright, ed. Studies in Californian Linguistics. Berkeley and Los Angeles, University of California Press, 1964: 99-105. (California, University, Publications in Linguistics, 34)

Johnston, Francis E., et al. Alloalbuminemia in Southwestern U.S. Indians: polymorphism of albumin Naskapi and albumin Mexico. Human Biology, 41 (1969): 263-270.

Kate, H. F. C. ten. Reizen en onderzoekingen in Noord-Amerika, 123-137. Leiden, 1885.

King, Chester. Chumash inter-village economic exchange. Indian Historian, 4, no. 1 (1971): 30-43.

Kroeber, A. L. A Mohave historical epic. Anthropological Records, 11 (1951): 71-176.

Kroeber, A. L. Ad hoc reassurance dreams. California, University, Publications in American Archaeology and Ethnology, 47 (1957): 205-208.

Kroeber, A. L. California kinship systems. California, University, Publications in American Archaeology and Ethnology, 12 (1917): 340-348.

Kroeber, A. L. Desert Mohave: fact or fancy. California, University, Publications in American Archaeology and Ethnology, 47 (1959): 294-307.

Kroeber, A. L. Earth-Tongue, a Mohave. In E. C. Parsons, ed. American Indian Life. New York, 1925: 189-202.

*Kroeber, A. L. Handbook of the Indians of California. U.S. Bureau of American Ethnology, Bulletin, 78 (1925): 726-780.

Kroeber, A. L. Mohave clairvoyance. California, University, Publications in American Archaeology and Ethnology, 47 (1957): 226-233.

Kroeber, A. L. Clive Oatman's return. Kroeber Anthropological Society, Publications, 4 (1951): 1-18.

Kroeber, A. L. Phonetic elements of the Mohave language. California, University, Publications in American Archaeology and Ethnology, 10 (1911): 45-96.

Kroeber, A. L. Preliminary sketch of the Mohave Indians. American Anthropologist, n.s., 4 (1902): 276-285.

Kroeber, A. L. Seven Mohave myths. Anthropological Records, 11 (1948): 1-70.

Kroeber, A. L. Two myths of the Mission Indians. Journal of American Folklore, 19 (1906): 309-321.

Kroeber, A. L. and M. J. Harner. Mohave pottery. Anthropological Records, 16 (1955): 1-35.

Kroeber, Alfred L. More Mohave myths. Berkeley, 1972. 12, 160 p. illus., map. (California, University, Publications, Anthropological Records, 27)

Kroeber, Alfred L. Clive Oatman's first account of her captivity among the Mohave. By A. L. Kroeber and Clifton B. Kroeber. California Historical Society Quarterly, 41 (1962): 309-317.

Kroeber, Alfred L. Preliminary sketch of the Mohave Indians. In Frederica de Laguna, ed. Selected Papers from the American Anthropologist 1888-1920. Evanston, Row, Peterson, 1960: 506-521.

Kroeber, Clifton B. The Mohave as nationalist, 1859-1874. American Philosophical Society, Proceedings, 109 (1965): 173-180.

Kroeber, Clifton B., ed. The route of James O. Pattie on the Colorado in 1826. A reappraisal by A. L. Kroeber. [With comments by R. C. Euler and A. H. Schroeder]. Arizona and the West, 6 (1964): 119-136.

Langdon, Margaret. Sound symbolism in Yuman languages. In Jesse Sawyer, ed. Studies in American Indian Languages. Berkeley and Los Angeles, University of California Press, 1971: 149-173. (California, University, Publications in Linguistics, 65)

Law, Howard W. A reconstructed proto-culture derived from some Yuman vocabularies. Anthropological Linguistics, 3, no. 4 (1961): 45-57.

Lincoln, J. S. The dream in primitive cultures. London, 1935. 359 p.

Loew, O. Notes upon ethnology of southern California and adjacent regions. U.S. Chief of Engineers, Annual Reports, 3 (1876): 541-547.

McNichols, C. L. Crazy weather. New York, 1944. 195 p.

Möllhausen, B. Diary of a journey from the Mississippi to the coasts of the Pacific, Vol. 2: 249-271. London, 1858.

Moriarty, James Robert, III. The environmental variations of the Yuman culture area of Southern California. Anthropological Journal of Canada, 6, no. 2 (1968): 2-20; 6, no. 3 (1968): 9-23.

Pages of History. The Mohave of the Colorado. Sausalito, Calif., 1960. 23 p. illus.

Palmer, E. Fish hooks of the Mohave Indians. American Naturalist, 12 (1878): 403.

Pickerell, A. R. Death of Orawthoma. Masterkey, 31 (1957): 166-169.

Romney, A. Kimball. Internal reconstruction of Yuman kinship terminology. In Dell H. Hymes and William E. Bittle, eds. Studies in Southwestern Ethnolinguistics. The Hague, Mouton, 1967: 379-386. (Studies in General Anthropology, 3)

Sherer, Lorraine M. Great chieftains of the Mojave Indians. Southern California Quarterly, 48 (1966): 1-35.

Sherer, Lorraine M. The clan system of the Fort Mojave Indians: a contemporary survey. Southern California Quarterly, 47 (1965): 1-72.

Sherer, Lorraine M. The clan system of the Fort Mojave Indians. Los Angeles, Historical Society of Southern California, 1965. 8, 85 p. illus., map.

Sherer, Lorraine M. The name Mojave, Mohave: a history of its origin and meaning. Southern California Quarterly, 49 (1967): 1-36.

Sherer, Lorraine M. The name Mojave, Mohave: an addendum. Southern California Quarterly, 49 (1967): 455-458.

Smith, Melvin T. Colorado River exploration and the Mormon War. Utah Historical Quarterly, 38 (1970): 207-223.

Spier, L. Cultural relations of the Gila River and Lower Colorado tribes. Yale University Publications in Anthropology, 3 (1936): 1-22.

Spier, L. Mohave culture items. Flagstaff, 1955. 35 p.

Spier, L. Some observations on Mohave clans. Southwestern Journal of Anthropology, 9 (1953): 324-342.

Stewart, K. M. An account of the Mohave mourning ceremony. American Anthropologist, n.s., 49 (1947): 146-148.

Stewart, K. M. Mohave fishing. Masterkey, 31 (1957): 198-203.

Stewart, K. M. Mohave hunting. Masterkey, 21 (1947): 80-84.

Stewart, K. M. Mohave warfare. Southwestern Journal of Anthropology, 3 (1947): 257-278.

Stewart, Kenneth M. A brief history of the Mohave Indians since 1850. Kiva, 34, no. 4 (1968/1969): 219-236.

Stewart, Kenneth M. Chemehuevi culture changes. Plateau, 40 (1967): 14-21.

Stewart, Kenneth M. Culinary practices of the Mohave Indians. El Palacio, 75, no. 1 (1968): 26-37.

Stewart, Kenneth M. Mohave Indian gathering of wild plants. Kiva, 31, no. 1 (1965/1966): 46-53.

Stewart, Kenneth M. Mojave Indian agriculture. Masterkey, 40 (1966): 4-15.

Stewart, Kenneth M. Mojave Indian shamanism. Masterkey, 44 (1970): 15-24.

Stewart, Kenneth M. Scalps and scalpers in Mohave Indian culture. El Palacio, 76, no. 2 (1969): 26-30.

Stewart, Kenneth M. The aboriginal territory of the Mohave Indians. Ethnohistory, 16 (1969): 257-276.

Stewart, Kenneth M. The Mohave Indians and the fur trappers. Plateau, 39 (1966): 73-79.

Stewart, Kenneth M. The Mohave Indians in Hispanic times. Kiva, 32, no. 1 (1966/1967): 25-38.

Stratton, R. B. Captivity of the Oatman girls. New York, 1857. 288 p.

Stuart, B. R. Paiute surprise the Mohave. Masterkey, 17 (1943): 217-219.

Taylor, E. S. and W. J. Wallace. Mohave tattooing and face-painting. Masterkey, 21 (1947): 183-195.

Walker, Henry Pickering, ed. Teacher to the Mojaves; the experiences of George W. Nock 1887-1889. Arizona and the West, 9 (1967): 143-166, 259-280.

Wallace, W. J. Infancy and childhood among the Mohave Indians. Primitive Man, 21 (1948): 19-37.

Wallace, W. J. Mohave fishing equipment and methods. Anthropological Quarterly, 3 (1955): 87-94.

Wallace, W. J. The dream in Mohave life. Journal of American Folklore, 60 (1947): 252-258.

Wallace, W. J. The girl's puberty rite of the Mohave. Indiana Academy of Science, Proceedings, 57 (1948): 37-40.

Wallace, W. J. Tobacco and its use among the Mohave Indians. Masterkey, 27 (1953): 193-202.

Wallace, William J. Indian use of California's rocks and minerals. Journal of the West, 10 (1971): 35-52.

Wares, Alan Campbell. A comparative study of Yuman consonantism. Dissertation Abstracts, 26 (1964/1965): 2200. UM 65-10,774.

Wares, Alan Campbell. A comparative study of Yuman consonantism. The Hague, Mouton, 1968. 100 p. map. (Janua Linguarum, Series Practica, 57)

Waterman, T. T. Analysis of the Mission Indian creation story. American Anthropologist, n.s., 11 (1909): 41-55.

Woodward, A. Irataba--"Chief of the Mohave". Plateau, 25 (1953): 53-68.

15-21   Navajo

Beidleman, R. G. A partial, annotated bibliography of Colorado ethnology. Colorado College Studies, 2 (1958): 1-55.

Kluckhohn, C. and K. Spencer. A bibliography of the Navaho Indians. New York, 1940. 93 p.

Martin, F. Ellen. The Navajo Indians; bibliography. Tempe, 1968. 40 l.

Powell, Donald M. A preliminary bibliography of the published writings of Berard Haile, O.F.M. Kiva, 26, no. 4 (1960/1961): 44-47.

Abel, T. M. Free designs of limited scope as a personality index. Character and Personality, 7 (1938): 50-63.

Aberle, D. F. Mythology of the Navaho game stick-dice. Journal of American Folklore, 55 (1942): 144-154.

Aberle, D. F. and O. C. Stewart. Navaho and Ute peyotism. Colorado, University, Studies, Series in Anthropology, 6 (1957): 1-138.

Aberle, David F. Some sources of flexibility in Navaho social organization. Southwestern Journal of Anthropology, 19 (1963): 1-8.

Aberle, David F. The Navaho singer's "fee": payment or prestation? In Dell H. Hymes and William E. Bittle, eds. Studies in Southwestern Ethnolinguistics. The Hague, Mouton, 1967: 15-32. (Studies in General Anthropology, 3)

*Aberle, David F. The peyote religion among the Navaho. Chicago, Aldine, 1966. 26, 454 p. illus., maps. (Viking Fund Publications in Anthropology, 42)

Adair, J. Navaho and Pueblo silversmiths. Norman, 1944. 220 p.

Adair, J. The Navajo and Pueblo veteran. American Indian, 4, no. 1 (1947): 5-11.

Adair, J. and E. Vogt. Navaho and Zuni veterans: a study of contrasting modes of culture change. American Anthropologist, n.s., 51 (1949): 547-561.

Adair, J. and K. Deuschle. Some problems of the physicians on the Navajo Reservation. Human Organization, 17, no. 4 (1958): 19-23.

Adair, J., et al. Patterns of health and disease among the Navahos. American Academy of Political and Social Science, Annals, 311 (1957): 80-94.

Adair, John. Physicians, medicine men and their Navaho patients. In Iago Galdston, ed. Man's Image in Medicine and Anthropology. New York, International Universities Press, 1963: 237-257.

Adair, John. The Indian health worker in the Cornell-Navaho project. Human Organization, 19 (1960/1961): 59-63.

Adair, John. The Navajo as filmmaker: a brief report of research in the cross-cultural aspects of film communications. By John Adair and Sol Worth. American Anthropologist, 69 (1967): 76-78.

Adair, John. The People's health; medicine and anthropology in a Navajo community. By John Adair and Kurt W. Deuschle. New York, Appleton-Century-Crofts, 1970. 16, 188 p. illus., maps.

Adair, John J. A rejoinder to Adair: in reply to Downs. American Anthropologist, 69 (1967): 368.

Adams, W. Y. New data on Navajo social organization. Plateau, 30 (1958): 64-70.

Adams, William Y. Navaho automotive terminology. American Anthropologist, 70 (1968): 1181.

Adams, William Y. Navajo and Anglo reconstruction of prehistoric sites in southeastern Utah. American Antiquity, 25 (1959/1960): 269-272.

Adams, William Y. Navajo social organization. American Anthropologist, 73 (1971): 273.

*Adams, William Y. Shonto; a study of the role of the trader in a modern Navaho community. Washington, D.C., Government Printing Office, 1963. 11, 329 p. illus., maps. (U.S., Bureau of American Ethnology, Bulletin, 188)

Adams, William Yewdale. Shonto: a study of the role of the trader in a modern Navajo community. Dissertation Abstracts, 19 (1958/1959): 207. UM 58-2783.

Agogino, George. One Navajo's view of Navajo tribal government. By George Agogino and June Martinez. Masterkey, 44 (1970): 25-29.

Akmajian, Adrian.   On the use of fourth person in Navajo, or Navajo made harder. By Adrian Akmajian and Stephen Anderson. International Journal of American Linguistics, 36 (1970): 1-8.

Albert, E. M.   The classification of values. American Anthropologist, 58 (1956): 221-248.

Albrecht, Dorothy E.   John Lorenzo Hubbell, Navajo Indian trader. Arizoniana, 4, no. 3 (1963): 33-40.

Alexander, Charles Ivan.   An introduction to Navaho sandpaintings.   Santa Fe, Museum of Navaho Ceremonial Art, 1967. 24 p. illus., maps.

Alfred, Braxton Marcellus.   Acculturative stress among Navaho migrants to Denver, Colorado. Dissertation Abstracts, 26 (1965/1966): 6296-6297.   UM 66-2758.

Allen, T. D.   Navahos have five fingers. Norman, University of Oklahoma Press, 1963. 14, 249 p. illus.

Alley, R. D. and M. Pijoan.   Salmonella javiana food infection. Yale Journal of Biology and Medicine, 15 (1942): 229-239.

Altman, G. J.   A Navaho wedding. Masterkey, 20 (1946): 159-164.

American Bible Society, ed.   Mozes bi naltsos alsedihigi Godesziz holyehigi inda yistainilli ba Hani Mark naltsos ye yiki-iscinigi. New York, 1912. 46 p.

Ammons, Madeline, et al., comps.   A Navaho teacher teacher-aide guide. Yuma, Arizona Western College, 1969. 28 p. ERIC ED040965.

Amsden, C. A.   Navaho origins. New Mexico Historical Review, 7 (1932): 193-209.

Amsden, C. A.   Navaho weaving.   Santa Ana, 1934. 261 p.

*Amsden, C. A.   Navaho weaving. Albuquerque, 1949. 263 p.

Amsden, C. A.   Reviving the Navaho blanket. Masterkey, 6 (1932): 137-149.

Amsden, C. A.   When Navaho rugs were blankets. School Arts Magazine, 34 (1935): 387-396.

Amsden, Charles Avery.   Navaho weaving, its techic and history.   Chicago, Rio Grande Press, 1964. 18, 261 p. illus., maps.

Anderson, H. A.   Tribesmen of Tuzigoot. Desert, 13 (June 1950): 16-19.

Anonymous.   Los Indios Navajos. Boletín Indigenista, 17 (1957): 224-231.

Anonymous.   Native America today. Indian Historian, 4, no. 1 (1971): 55-56, 66.

Anonymous.   Navaho baby-carrier. Masterkey, 22 (1948): 99.

Anonymous.   Navaho pottery and basketry. Masterkey, 26 (1952): 109.

Anonymous.   Navahos seem immune to cancer. Hygeia, 9 (1931): 684.

Anonymous.   The Diné, Apache de Navajo; their centennial year. Indian Historian, 1, no. 2 (1967/1968): 4-6.

Arewa, E. Ojo.   Values relevant to family and social relationships among the Navahos, with a special reference to marriage. Kroeber Anthropological Society Papers, 31 (1964): 117-127.

Armer, L. A.   Sand-paintings of the Navaho Indians. Leaflets of the Exposition of Indian Tribal Arts, 5 (1931): 1-9.

Armer, L. A.   The Crawler, Navaho healer. Masterkey, 27 (1953): 5-10.

Armer, L. A.   Two Navaho sand-paintings. Masterkey, 24 (1950): 79-83.

Armer, L. A.   Waterless mountain.   New York, 1931. 212 p.

Armer, Laura A.   In Navajo land.   New York, D. McKay, 1962. 107 p. illus.

Arneklev, Bruce Leon.   The use of defensiveness as a covariate of self-report in the assessment of self-concept among Navajo adolescents. Dissertation Abstracts International, 32 (1971/1972): 3772A-3773A.   UM 72-4752.

Ashe, Robert W.   Survey report--Navajo Community College.   Tempe, Arizona State University, College of Education, 1966. 174 p.   ERIC ED017229.

Astrov, M.   The concept of motion as the psychological leitmotif of Navaho life and literature. Journal of American Folklore, 63 (1950): 45-56.

Babington, S. H.   Navajos, gods and tom-toms.   New York, 1950. 256 p.

Backus, E.   An account of the Navajoes. In H. R. Schoolcraft, ed. Information respecting the History, Condition, and Prospects of the Indian Tribes of the United States. Vol. 4. Philadelphia, 1854: 209-215.

Bailey, F. L. Navaho foods and cooking
methods. American Anthropologist, n.s.,
42 (1940): 270-290.

Bailey, F. L. Navaho motor habits.
American Anthropologist, n.s., 44
(1942): 210-234.

Bailey, F. L. Navaho women and the
sudatory. American Anthropologist, n.s.,
43 (1941): 484-485.

Bailey, F. L. Some sex beliefs and
practices in a Navaho community. Harvard
University, Peabody Museum of American
Archaeology and Ethnology, Papers, 40,
no. 2 (1950): 1-108.

Bailey, F. L. Suggested techniques for
inducing Navaho women to accept
hospitalization during childbirth.
American Journal of Public Health, 38
(1948): 1418-1423.

Bailey, Lynn R. The long walk; a history
of the Navajo wars, 1846-68. Los
Angeles, Westernlore Press, 1964. 13,
252 p. illus., maps.

Bailey, Paul D. The Navajo wars.
Arizoniana, 2, no. 2 (1961): 3-12.

Ballinger, Thomas O. Some notes on
directional movements in the drawings
and paintings of Pueblo and Navajo
children. American Anthropologist, 66
(1964): 880-883.

Barber, B. Acculturation and messianic
movements. American Sociological Review,
4 (1941): 663-669.

Bartlett, K. Hopi history, II: the Navajo
wars. Flagstaff, Ariz., Museum of
Northern Arizona, Museum Notes, 8
(1937): 33-37.

Bartlett, K. Hopi yucca baskets. Plateau,
21 (1949): 33-41.

Bartlett, K. Present trends in weaving on
the western Navajo Reservation. Plateau,
23 (1950): 1-5.

Bartlett, K. Why the Navajos came to
Arizona. Flagstaff, Ariz., Museum of
Northern Arizona, Museum Notes, 5
(1932): 29-32.

Beadle, J. H. The undeveloped West.
Philadelphia, 1873.

Beatty, Willard W. History of Navajo
education. América Indígena, 21 (1961):
7-31.

Bedinger, M. Navajo Indian silver-work.
Old West Series, 8 (1936): 1-43.

Begay, Blanche Bizahaloni. Does your
child have a future? Flagstaff,
Northern Arizona University, 1967.
22 p. ERIC ED035495.

Begaye, John Y. Navajo evaluators look at
Rough Rock Demonstration School.
Chinle, Ariz., Rough Rock Demonstration
School, 1969. 48 p. ERIC ED034612.

Bell, C. C., Jr., et al. Relationship of
bile acid pool size to the formation of
lithogenous bile in male Indians of the
Southwest. Surgery, Gynecology and
Obstetrics, 134 (1972): 473-478.

Bellah, Robert N. Religious sytems. In
Evon Z. Vogt and Ethel M. Albert, eds.
The People of Rimrock. Cambridge,
Harvard University Press, 1966: 227-264.

Bender, Marvin L. Chance CVC
correspondences in unrelated languages.
Language, 45 (1969): 519-531.

Bennett, Benjamin, Jr. Seventh grade
Navaho answer "why education?" Journal
of American Indian Education, 4, no. 1
(1964/1965): 17-19.

Bennett, Kay. Kaibah; recollections of a
Navajo girlhood. Los Angeles,
Westernlore Press, 1964. 253 p. illus.

Bennett, Noël. Working with wool; how to
weave a Navajo rug. By Noël Bennett and
Tiana Bighorse. Flagstaff, Northland
Press, 1971. 13, 105 p.

Bergmann, Robert L. Navajo peyote use:
its apparent safety. American Journal of
Psychiatry, 128 (1971): 695-699.

Berlant, Anthony. The Navajo blanket. By
Anthony Berlant and Mary Kahlenberg. Art
in America, 60, no. 4 (1972): 78-82.

Berlin, Brent. Categories of eating in
Tzeltal and Navaho. International
Journal of American Linguistics, 33
(1967): 1-6.

Berry, R. V. S. The Navajo shaman and his
sacred sand-paintings. Art and
Archaeology, 27 (1929): 3-17.

Biglin, James E. Parental attitudes
towards Indian education. By James E.
Biglin and Jack Wilson. Journal of
American Indian Education, 11, no. 3
(1971/1972): 1-6.

Bivens, Melvin D. A 10-year survey of
cervical carcinoma in Indians of the
Southwest. By Melvin D. Bivens and
Howard O. Fleetwood. Obstetrics and
Gynecology, 32 (1968): 11-16.

Bivens, Melvin D., et al. Carcinoma of the cervix in the Indians of the Southwest. A preliminary report. American Journal of Obstetrics and Gynecology, 83 (1962): 1203-1207.

Blackwood, B. An anthropologist among the Navaho. Natural History, 27 (1927): 223-228.

Blanchard, Kendall Allan. Religious change and economic behavior among the Ramah Navajo. Dissertation Abstracts International, 32 (1971/1972): 6175B-6176B. UM 72-6350.

Bloom, L. B., ed. Bourke on the Southwest. New Mexico Historical Review, 11 (1936): 77-122, 217-282.

Blount, T., et al. Primers I-III. Phoenix, 1947.

Blount, T., et al. Primers I-III, new series. Phoenix, 1957.

Blunn, C. T. Improvement of the Navajo sheep. Journal of Heredity, 31 (1940): 99-112.

Boas, F. Northern elements in the mythology of the Navaho. American Anthropologist, 10 (1897): 371-376.

Boas, F. Zur Anthropologie der nordamerikanischen Indianer. Berliner Gesellschaft für Anthropologie, Ethnologie und Urgeschichte, Verhandlungen (1895): 367-411.

Bohrer, Vorsila L. A Navajo sweathouse. Plateau, 36 (1964): 95-99.

Bollinger, Charles C. Intrauterine contraception in Indians of the American Southwest. By Charles C. Bollinger, Thomas C. Carrier, and William J. Ledger. American Journal of Obstetrics and Gynecology, 106 (1970): 669-675.

Bosch, James Wiley. Measurement of acculturation level with the Guttman scale. Dissertation Abstracts, 27 (1966/1967): 25B. UM 66-6323.

Bouman, William. Xg blood groups of American Indians. By William Bouman, J. D. Mann, and William J. Dewey. Nature, 209 (1966): 411.

Bourke, J. G. The early Navajo and Apache. American Anthropologist, 8 (1895): 287-294.

Boyce, G. A. A primer of Navajo economic problems. Window Rock, 1942. 128 p.

Boyd, W. C. and L. G. Boyd. The blood groups and types of the Ramah Navaho.

American Journal of Physical Anthropology, n.s., 7 (1949): 569-574.

Bradley, Zorro A. The Whitmore-McIntyre dugout, Pipe Spring National Monument. Part I: history. Plateau, 33 (1960): 40-45.

Brandfonbrener, Martin. Cardiomyopathy in the Southwest American Indian. By M. Brandfonbrener, W. S. Lovekin, and J. K. Leach. British Heart Journal, 32 (1970): 491-496.

Brewer, J. Notes on how to build a hogan. Southwestern Monuments Monthly Reports, Supplement (1936): 485-488.

Brewer, S. P. Notes on Navaho astronomy. In For the Dean. Essays in Anthropology in Honor of Byron Cummings. Tucson, 1950: 133-136.

Brodhead, Michael J. Elliot Coues and the Apaches. Journal of Arizona History, 14 (1973): 87-94.

Brown, R. Chris, et al. The epidemiology of accidents among the Navajo Indians. U.S., Public Health Service, Public Health Reports, 85 (1970): 881-888.

Brugge, D. M. Navaho sweat houses. El Palacio, 63 (1956): 101-106.

Brugge, David M. A Sonoran grooved-stone tool. Katunob, 4, no. 1 (1963): 11.

Brugge, David M. Imitation Navajo rugs. Washington Archaeologist, 16, no. 1 (1972): 1-3.

Brugge, David M. Navajo use of agave. Kiva, 31, no. 2 (1965/1966): 88-98.

Brugge, David M. Navajos in the Catholic Church records of New Mexico, 1694-1785. Window Rock, Navajo Tribe, 1968. 16, 160 p. (Research Reports, 1)

Brugge, David M. Revised dates for Navajo hogans near Canyon de Chelly. American Antiquity, 32 (1967): 396-398.

Brugge, David M. Vizcarra's Navajo campaign of 1823. Arizona and the West, 6 (1964): 223-244.

Bryan, N. G. and S. Young. Navaho native dyes. Indian Handcrafts, 2 (1940): 1-75.

Buckland, A. W. Points of contact between Old World myths and customs and the Navajo myth entitled "The Mountain Chant". Royal Anthropological Institute of Great Britain and Ireland, Journal, 22 (1892): 346-355.

Bunker, R. Other men's skies. Bloomington, 1956. 256 p.

Bunker, R. The hunger of the Navajos. New Mexico Quarterly Review, 26 (1956): 133-146.

Burger, Henry G. "Ethno-Janus": utilizing cultural heritage to plan for future employment. Practical Anthropology, 17 (1970): 241-252.

Buschmann, J. C. E. Die Spuren der aztekischen Sprache im nördlichen Mexico and höheren amerikanischen Norden. Berlin, Königliche Akademie der Wissenschaften, Abhandlungen, Supplement-Band, 2 (1854): 293-298.

Buxton, L. H. D. Some Navajo folktales and customs. Folk-Lore, 34 (1923): 293-313.

California, University, School of Public Health. Orientation to health on the Navajo Indian Reservation; a guide for hospital and public health workers. Washington, D.C., U.S. Public Health Service, 1960. 29 p. illus.

Callahan, J. T. The occurrence of ground water in diatremes of the Hopi Buttes area, Arizona. By J. T. Callahan, William Kam, and J. P. Akers. Plateau, 32 (1959): 1-12.

Callaway, Sydney M. Grandfather stories of the Navahos. Chinle, Ariz., Rough Rock Demonstration School, 1968. 42 p.

Callaway, Sydney M., et al. Grandfather stories of the Navahos. Rough Rock, Ariz., Rough Rock Demonstration School, 1968. 77 p. illus.

Campbell, I. Navajo sandpaintings. Southwest Review, 25 (1940): 143-150.

Campbell, Ian Alexander Naysmith. The Shonto Plateau, Arizona: an analysis and comparison of some aspects of the physical geography. Dissertation Abstracts, 29 (1968/1969): 1399B. UM 68-14,235.

Cardenal, Ernesto, tr. Poesía de los indios de Norteamérica. América Indígena, 21 (1961): 355-362.

Carlson, Alvar Ward. New Mexico's sheep industry, 1850-1900: its role in the history of the Territory. New Mexico Historical Review, 44 (1969): 25-49.

Carlson, Roy L. Eighteenth century Navajo fortresses of the Gobernador District. Boulder, University of Colorado Press, 1965. 2, 116 p. (Colorado, University, Studies, Series in Anthropology, 10)

Carpenter, T. M. and M. Steggerda. The food of the present-day Navajo Indians. Journal of Nutrition, 18 (1939): 297-306.

Carr, M., K. Spencer, and D. Woolley. Navaho clans and marriage at Pueblo Alto. American Anthropologist, n.s., 41 (1939): 245-257.

Casagrande, J. B. The Southwest Project in Comparative Psycholinguistics. International Congress of the Anthropological and Ethnological Sciences, Acts, 5 (1960): 777-782.

Casagrande, Joseph B. On "round objects", a Navaho covert category. In International Congress of Anthropological and Ethnological Sciences, 6th. 1960, Paris. Tome II, v. 2. Paris, Musée de l'Homme, 1964: 49-54.

Case, Charles C. Blessing Way, the core ritual of Navajo ceremony. Plateau, 41 (1968): 35-42.

Cata, Juanita. The Navajo Social Studies Project. Albuquerque, University of New Mexico, College of Education, 1968. 61 p. ERIC ED025346.

Chapin, G. A Navajo myth. New Mexico Anthropologist, 4 (1940): 63-67.

Chelf, C. R. Good luck for Gray Head. Masterkey, 32 (1958): 21-28.

Chien, Chiao. The continuation of tradition: Navaho and Chinese models. Dissertation Abstracts International, 30 (1969/1970): 2999B. UM 69-20,970.

Chilcott, John H. The Navajo Bordertown Dormitory in Flagstaff, Arizona. Tuscon, University of Arizona, Department of Anthropology; Flagstaff, Museum of Northern Arizona, 1970. 141 p. ERIC ED051958.

Chilcott, John H. Tuba City, Arizona. By John H. Chilcott and Marjorie Thomas. Chicago, University of Chicago, 1970. 17 p. (National Study of American Indian Education, Series 1, 20) ERIC ED045272.

Christian, Jane MacNab. The Navajo, a people in transition. El Paso, Texas Western College Press, 1964-1965. 2 v. illus., maps. (Southwestern Studies, 2, nos. 3, 4)

Clark, LaVerne Harrell. Early horse trappings of the Navajo and Apache Indians. Arizona and the West, 5 (1963): 233-248.

Clark, LaVerne Harrell. They sang for horses; the impact of the horse on Navajo and Apache folklore. Tucson, University of Arizona Press, 1966. 20, 225 p. illus., maps.

Clute, W. N. Notes on the Navajo region. American Botanist, 26 (1920): 39-47.

Cobb, John C. Trachoma among Southwestern Indians. By John C. Cobb and Chandler R. Dawson. American Medical Association, Journal, 175 (1961): 405-406.

Colby, Benjamin N. A study of thematic apperception tests with the General Inquirer system. El Palacio, 71, no. 4 (1964): 29-36.

Colby, Benjamin N. The analysis of culture content and the patterning of narrative concern in texts. American Anthropologist, 68 (1966): 374-388.

Cole, E. P. Navajo weaving with two- or four-harness looms. Weaver, 2, no. 4 (1937): 11-13.

Collier, J. Navajos. Survey, 2 (1924): 332-339, 363-365.

Collier, John. American Indian ceremonial dances: Navajo, Pueblo, Apache, Zuni. New York, Bounty Books, 1972. 192 p. illus.

Collier, John. On the gleaming way. Denver, Sage Books, 1962. 163 p. illus.

Collier, John. The Navajos. In Samuel B. Rapport and Helen Wright, eds. Anthropology. New York, New York University Press, 1967: 297-318.

Collier, M. C. Leadership at Navajo Mountain and Klagetoh. American Anthropologist, n.s., 48 (1946): 137-138.

Collins, G. N. Pueblo Indian maize breeding. Journal of Heredity, 5 (1914): 255-268.

Colorado Springs, Fine Arts Center, Taylor Museum. Navajo sandpainting; the Huckel collection. Colorado Springs, 1960. 88 p. illus.

Colton, H. S. Troy Town on the Hopi mesas. Scientific Monthly, 58 (1944): 129-134.

Colton, Harold S. Principal Hopi trails. Plateau, 36 (1964): 91-94.

Concha, Fernando de la. Colonel Don Fernando de la Concha diary, 1788.

Edited by Adlai Feather. New Mexico Historical Review, 34 (1959): 285-304.

Conn, Stephen. The bicultural legal education project at Ramah, New Mexico. Indian Historian, 5, no. 3 (1972): 36-39, 50.

Conrad, David E. The Whipple expedition in Arizona 1853-1854. Arizona and the West, 11 (1969): 147-178.

Coolidge, D. and M. R. Coolidge. The Navajo Indians. Boston, 1930. 309 p.

Coolidge, M. R. The rain-makers, 245-290. Boston, 1929.

Corbett, J. M. Navajo house types. El Palacio, 47 (1940): 97-108.

Corcoran, Patricia A. Blood groups of 237 Navajo school children at Pinon Boarding School, Pinon, Arizona (1961). By Patricia A. Corcoran, David L. Rabin, and Fred H. Allen, Jr. American Journal of Physical Anthropology, n.s., 20 (1962): 389-390.

Corle, E. People on the earth. New York, 1937. 401 p.

Cornell, R. D. Four-horned rams. Natural History, 64 (1955): 258-259.

Correll, J. Lee. Navajo frontiers in Utah and troublous times in Monument Valley. Utah Historical Quarterly, 39 (1971): 145-161.

Corrigan, Francis Vincent. A comparison of self-concepts of American-Indian students from public or federal school backgrounds. Dissertation Abstracts International, 31 (1970/1971): 2679A-2680A. UM 70-24,959.

Cowan, J. L. Bedouins of the Southwest. Out West, 35 (1912): 107-116.

Cozzens, S. W. The marvellous country. London, 1874.

Crampton, C. Gregory. Historical sites in Glen Canyon, mouth of San Juan River to Lee's Ferry. Salt Lake City, University of Utah Press, 1960. 16, 130 p. illus., maps. (Utah, University, Anthropological Papers, 46)

Crampton, C. Gregory, ed. Journal of two campaigns by the Utah Territorial Militia against the Navajo Indians, 1869. Edited by C. Gregory Crampton and David E. Miller. Utah Historical Quarterly, 29 (1961): 148-176.

Crane, Leo. Indians of the enchanted desert. Glorieta, N.M., Rio Grande Press, 1972. 10, 368 p. illus.

Crapanzano, Vincent. The fifth world of Enoch Maloney; portrait of a Navaho. New York, Random House, 1970. 242 p.

Crapanzano, Vincent. The fifth world of Forster Bennett; portrait of a Navaho. New York, Viking Press, 1972. 7, 245 p.

Cummings, B. Indians I have known. Tucson, 1952. 75 p.

Cummings, B. Navajo sand paintings. Kiva, 1, no. 7 (1936): 1-2.

Cummins, H. Dermatoglyphics in North American Indians and Spanish-Americans. Human Biology, 13 (1941): 177-188.

Curtin, L. S. M. Reminiscences in Southwest archaeology: 3. Kiva, 26, no. 2 (1960/1961): 1-10.

Curtis, E. S. The North American Indian, Vol. 1: 73-129, 136-144. Cambridge, 1907.

Curtis, E. S. Vanishing Indian types. Scribner's Magazine, 39 (1906): 513-529.

Curtis, N., ed. The Indians' book, 347-421. New York, 1907.

*Darby, W. J., et al. Study of the dietary background and nutrition of the Navajo Indian. Journal of Nutrition, 60, suppl. 2 (1956): 1-85.

Davidson, William. Athapaskan classificatory verbs. By William Davidson, L. W. Elford, and Harry Hoijer. In Harry Hoijer, et al., eds. Studies in the Athapaskan Languages. Berkeley and Los Angeles, University of California Press, 1963: 30-41. (California, University, Publications in Linguistics, 29)

Davis, W. H. El Gringo, 389-432. New York, 1857.

Davis, William W. H. El Gringo; or, New Mexico and her people. Chicago, Rio Grande Press, 1962. 332 p. illus.

DeHuff, E. W. Taytay's memories, 131-134, 175-186, 224-228, 248-255. New York, 1924.

Dellenbaugh, Frederick Samuel. F. S. Dellenbaugh of the Colorado: some letters pertaining to the Powell voyages and the history of the Colorado River. Edited by C. Gregory Crampton. Utah Historical Quarterly, 37 (1969): 214-243.

Denman, L. V. N. Dance with fire. San Francisco, 1952. 8 p.

Dennis, W. Does culture appreciably affect patterns of infant behavior? Journal of Social Psychology, 12 (1940): 305-317.

Deumann, David L. Navajo silversmithing. El Palacio, 77, no. 2 (1971): 13-32.

Deuschle, Kurt. An interdisciplinary approach to public health on the Navajo Indian Reservation: medical and anthropological aspects. By Kurt Deuschle and John Adair. New York Academy of Sciences, Annals, 84 (1960): 887-905.

Deuschle, Kurt. Tuberculosis among the Navajo Indians. Pennsylvania Medical Journal, 63 (1960): 304-305.

Devereux, G. The psychological 'date' of dreams. Psychiatric Quarterly Supplement, 23 (1949): 127-130.

Dietrich, M. S. The Navajo in no-man's land. New Mexico Quarterly Review, 20 (1950): 439-450.

Dietrich, M. S. Urgent Navajo problems. Santa Fe, 1940. 42 p.

Dittmann, A. T. and H. C. Moore. Disturbance in dreams as related to peyotism among the Navaho. American Anthropologist, 59 (1957): 642-649.

Dobyns, Henry F. The Navajo people. By Henry F. Dobyns and Robert C. Euler. Phoenix, Indian Tribal Series, 1972. 106 p. illus.

Dodd, A. Patterns of a culture--The Navaho. Masterkey, 28 (1954): 52-62.

Donald, Leland. Leadership in a Navajo community. Anthropos, 65 (1970): 867-880.

Dory, W. Navajo land. Natural History, 23 (1923): 487-505.

Douglas, F. H. Navaho silversmithing. Denver Art Museum, Indian Leaflet Series, 15 (1930): 1-4.

Douglas, F. H. Seven Navajo pots. Denver Art Museum, Material Culture Notes, 3 (1937): 9-14.

Downs, James F. A rejoinder to Adair. American Anthropologist, 69 (1967): 367-368.

Downs, James F. Animal husbandry in Navajo society and culture. Berkeley, 1964. 104 p. illus., map.

(California, University, Publications in Anthropology, 1)

Downs, James F. The Navajo. New York, Holt, Rinehart and Winston, 1972. 6, 136 p. illus.

Downs, James F. The social consequences of a dry well. American Anthropologist, 67 (1965): 1387-1416.

Dozier, Edward P. Pueblo Indian response to culture contact. In M. Estellie Smith, ed. Studies in Linguistics in Honor of George L. Trager. The Hague, Mouton, 1972: 457-467. (Janua Linguarum, Series Maior, 52)

Dubin, Fraida. Language and attitudes among Navajo adolescents. Dissertation Abstracts International, 32 (1971/1972): 4590A. UM 72-5828.

Durfey, Calvin R. An evaluation of bilingual education with a cross cultural emphasis designed for Navajo and non-Navajo students in San Juan County, Utah, 1969-1971. Dissertation Abstracts International, 32 (1971/1972): 3662A. UM 72-1745.

Dutton, B. P. The Navaho Wind Way ceremonial. El Palacio, 48 (1941): 73-82.

Dutton, Bertha P. Cultural arts of the Navaho Indians. In International Congress of Anthropological and Ethnological Sciences, 8th. 1968, Tokyo and Kyoto. Proceedings. Vol. 2. Tokyo, Science Council of Japan, 1969: 327-329.

Dutton, Bertha P. Navajo weaving today. Santa Fe, Museum of New Mexico Press, 1961. 43 p. illus.

*Dyk, W. A Navaho autobiography. Viking Fund Publications in Anthropology, 8 (1947): 1-218.

Dyk, W. Notes and illustrations of Navaho sex behavior. In G. B. Wilbur and W. Muensterberger, eds. Psychoanalysis and Culture. New York, 1951: 108-119.

Dyk, W. Son of Old Man Hat. New York, 1938. 378 p.

Eaton, J. H. Vocabulary of the language of the Navajo. In H. R. Schoolcraft, ed. Information respecting the History, Condition, and Prospects of the Indian Tribes of the United States. Vol. 4. Philadelphia, 1854: 416-431.

Eddy, Frank W. Excavations at Los Pinos Phase sites in the Navajo Reservoir district. By Frank W. Eddy with a section by Beth L. Dickey. Santa Fe,

1961. 107 p. illus., maps. (Museum of New Mexico, Papers in Anthropology, 4)

Eddy, Frank W. Prehistory in the Navajo Reservoir district: northwestern New Mexico. Santa Fe, 1966. 631 p. illus. (Museum of New Mexico, Papers in Anthropology, 15)

Eddy, Frank Warren. Culture ecology and the prehistory of the Navajo Reservoir District. Dissertation Abstracts, 29 (1968/1969): 1245B. UM 68-14,377.

Edgerton, Faye E. The tagmemic analysis of sentence structure in Western Apache. In Harry Hoijer, et al., eds. Studies in the Athapaskan Languages. Berkeley and Los Angeles, University of California Press, 1963: 102-148. (California, University, Publications in Linguistics, 29)

Edgerton, Robert B. Pokot intersexuality: an East African example of the resolution of sexual incongruity. American Anthropologist, 66 (1964): 1288-1299.

Edmonson, Munro S. A measurement of relative racial difference. Current Anthropology, 6 (1965): 167-198. [With comments].

Edmonson, Munro S. Kinship systems. In Evon Z. Vogt and Ethel M. Albert, eds. The People of Rimrock. Cambridge, Harvard University Press, 1966: 126-159.

Ehrenreich, W. Ein Ausflug nach Tusayan. Globus, 76 (1899): 172-174.

Eickemeyer, C. Over the great Navajo trail. New York, 1900. 270 p.

Eisenman, Russell. Scapegoating the deviant in two cultures. International Journal of Psychology, 2 (1967): 133-138.

Elgin, Patricia Anne Suzette. Some topics in Navajo syntax. Dissertation Abstracts International, 34 (1973/1974): 3370A-3371A. UM 73-24,508.

Ellis, Florence Hawley. A reconstruction of basic Jemez pattern of social organization, with comparisons to other Tanoan social structures. Albuquerque, University of New Mexico Press, 1964. 69 p. (New Mexico, University, Publications in Anthropology, 11)

*Elmore, F. H. Ethnobotany of the Navajo. Archaeological Institute of America, School of American Research, Santa Fe, Monographs, 8 (1944): 1-136.

Elmore, F. H. Food animals of the Navajo.
El Palacio, 44 (1938): 149-154.

Elmore, F. H. The deer, and his
importance to the Navaho. El Palacio, 60
(1953): 371-384.

Emrich, Robert Louis. Style of thinking;
a cross-cultural study of cognition.
Dissertation Abstracts, 23 (1962/1963):
1487-1488. UM 62-4947.

English, Lydia E. By wagon from Kansas to
Arizona in 1875--the travel diary of
Lydia E. English. Edited by Joseph W.
Snell. Kansas Historical Quarterly, 36
(1970): 369-389.

Enochs, J. B. Little Man's family.
Phoenix, 1940. 78 p.

Ervin, Susan M. Navaho word-associations.
By Susan M. Ervin and Herbert Landar.
American Journal of Psychology, 76
(1963): 49-57.

Ervin, Susan M. Semantic shift in
bilingualism. American Journal of
Psychology, 74 (1961): 233-241.

Ervin-Tripp, Susan. Navaho connotative
judgments: the metaphor of person
description. In Dell H. Hymes and
William E. Bittle, eds. Studies in
Southwestern Ethnolinguistics. The
Hague, Mouton, 1967: 91-116. (Studies
in General Anthropology, 3)

Eubank, L. Legends of three Navaho games.
El Palacio, 52 (1945): 138-140.

Euler, R. C. Anthropology, economics, and
the Navaho. Plateau, 23 (1951): 58-60.

Euler, Robert C. Aspects of political
organization among the Puertocito
Navajo. El Palacio, 68 (1961): 118-120.

Euler, Robert C. Ethnic group land rights
in the modern state: three case studies.
By Robert C. Euler and Henry F. Dobyns.
Human Organization, 20 (1961/1962): 203-
207.

Evans, T. Hosteen Bear loses the second
fall. Southwestern Lore, 14 (1948): 3-4.

Evans, T. Navajo folk lore. Southwestern
Lore, 1 (1935): 10-16.

Evans, W. How jackrabbit got his long
ears. Southwestern Lore, 13 (1947): 41-
42.

Evans, W. Navaho folk lore. Southwestern
Lore, 14 (1948): 45-68.

Evans, W. The origins of Navajo
sandpainting. New Mexico Folklore
Record, 9 (1954/1955): 4-7.

Evans, W. The White-haired One wrestles
with Hosteen Bear. Southwestern Lore, 13
(1948): 53-54.

Falls, A. E. The culinary art of the
Navajos. Practical Home Economics, 20
(1942): 349-350.

Farmer, M. F. Navaho archaeology of Upper
Blanco and Largo Canyons. American
Antiquity, 8 (1942): 65-79.

Fasano, R. J. Incidence of dental disease
among the Navajo Indians of Monument
Valley, Utah. By R. J. Fasano and T. J.
Zwemer. Journal of Dental Research, 48
(1969): 328.

Faulkner, H. Wade. Pseudo-exfoliation of
the lens among the Navajo Indians.
American Journal of Ophthalmology, 72
(1971): 206-207.

Fay, George E., ed. Charters,
constitutions and by-laws of the Indian
tribes of North America. Part IV: The
Southwest (Navajo-Zuni). Greeley, 1967.
5, 120 l. maps. (University of
Northern Colorado, Museum of
Anthropology, Occasional Publications in
Anthropology, Ethnology Series, 5) ERIC
ED046554.

Federal Writers' Project. The Navaho.
Arizona State Teachers College,
Bulletin, 18, no. 4 (1937): 1-29.

Ferguson, Frances N. A treatment program
for Navaho alcoholics: results after
four years. Quarterly Journal of Studies
on Alcohol, 31 (1970): 898-919, 1025.

Ferguson, Frances Northend. A stake in
society: its relevance to response by
Navajo alcoholics in a treatment
program. Dissertation Abstracts
International, 34 (1973/1974): 34B. UM
73-16,471.

Ferguson, Frances Northend. Navaho
drinking: some tenative hypotheses.
Human Organization, 27 (1968): 159-167.

Fergusson, E. Dancing gods, 179-247. New
York, 1931.

Ferris, Robert G., ed. The Indians of New
Mexico: Apache, Navaho, Pueblo, Ute.
Santa Fe, Museum of New Mexico Press,
1963. 34 p. ERIC ED024518.

Fewkes, J. W. Clay figurines made by
Navaho children. American
Anthropologist, n.s., 25 (1923): 559-
563.

Fierman, Floyd S. Nathan Bibo's
reminiscences of early New Mexico. El
Palacio, 68 (1961): 231-257; 69 (1962):
40-60.

Filmore, J. C. Songs of the Navajos. Land
of Sunshine, 5 (1896): 238-241.

Findley, David. Some health problems of
the Navajo Indians. Nebraska State
Medical Journal, 49 (1964): 326-332.

Fintzelberg, Nicholas M. Peyote
paraphernalia. San Diego, 1969. 9 l.
illus. (San Diego Museum of Man, Ethnic
Technology Notes, 4)

Firestone, Melvin. Notes on the
derivation of the naja. By Melvin
Firestone and Antonio Rodriguez.
Plateau, 42 (1970): 139-145.

Fisher, Kathy. The forgotten Dodge.
Annals of Iowa, 40 (1970): 296-305.

Fishler, S. A. A Navaho version of the
"bear's son" folktale. Journal of
American Folklore, 66 (1953): 70-74.

Fishler, S. A. In the beginning. Utah,
University, Anthropological Papers, 13
(1953): 1-132.

Fishler, S. A. Navaho buffalo hunting. El
Palacio, 62 (1955): 43-57.

Fishler, S. A. Symbolism of a Navaho
"wedding" basket. Masterkey, 28 (1954):
205-215.

Fonaroff, L. Schuyler. Navajo attitudes
and the Indian Reorganization Act: a new
document. Plateau, 34 (1962): 97-100.

Fontana, Bernard L. The Hopi-Navajo
colony on the lower Colorado River: a
problem in ethnohistorical
interpretation. Ethnohistory, 10 (1963):
162-182.

Forbes, Jack D. Apache, Navaho, and
Spaniard. Norman, University of
Oklahoma Press, 1960. 304 p. illus.

Forbes, Jack Douglas. Apache, Navaho, and
Spaniard: a history of the Southern
Athapaskans and their relations with the
Spanish Empire, 1540-1698. Dissertation
Abstracts, 22 (1961/1962): 3173-3174.
UM 61-6283.

Ford, Richard I. Barter, gift, or
violence: an analysis of Tewa
intertribal exchange. In Edwin N.
Wilmsen, ed. Social Exchange and
Interaction. Ann Arbor, University of
Michigan, 1972: 24-45. (Michigan,
University, Musuem of Anthropology,
Anthropological Papers, 46)

Forrest, Earle R. With a camera in old
Navaholand. Norman, University of
Oklahoma Press, 1970. 17, 274 p.
illus.

Franciscan Fathers. A vocabulary of the
Navaho language. St. Michaels, 1912.
2 v.

*Franciscan Fathers. An ethnologic
dictionary of the Navaho language. St.
Michaels, 1910. 536 p.

Freed, Stanley A. A note on regional
variation in Navajo kinship terminology.
By Stanley A. Freed and Ruth S. Freed.
American Anthropologist, 72 (1970):
1439-1444.

Freed, Stanley A. A technique for
studying role behavior. By Stanley A.
Freed and Ruth S. Freed. Ethnology, 10
(1971): 107-121.

Freed, Stanley A. Studying role behavior
cross-culturally: comparison of a
matrilineal and a bilateral society. By
Stanley A. Freed and Ruth S. Freed. New
York, American Museum of Natural
History, 1970. 63 p. (American Museum
Novitates, 2437)

Frink, Maurice. Fort Defiance and the
Navajos. Boulder, Pruett Press, 1968.
9, 124 p. illus., map.

Frisbie, Charlotte Johnson. Kinaaldá; a
study of the Navajo girl's puberty
ceremony. Middletown, Conn., Wesleyan
University Press, 1967. 13, 437 p.
illus., map.

Frisbie, Charlotte Johnson. The Navajo
House Blessing Ceremonial: a study of
cultural change. Dissertation Abstracts
International, 31 (1970/1971): 5770B-
5771B. UM 71-9274.

Fryer, E. R. Navajo social organization
and land use adjustment. Scientific
Monthly, 55 (1942): 408-422.

Fulmer, Hugh S. Coronary heart disease
among the Navajo Indians. By Hugh S.
Fulmer and Richard W. Roberts. Annals of
Internal Medicine, 59 (1963): 740-764.

Garland, Hamlin. Hamlin Garland and the
Navajos. By Lonnie E. Underhill and
Daniel F. Littlefield, Jr. Journal of
Arizona History, 13 (1972): 275-285.

Gatschet, A. S. Classification into seven
linguistic stocks of Western Indian
dialects. In Report upon United States
Geographical Surveys West of the One
Hundredth Meridian. Vol. 7. Washington,
D.C., 1879: 403-485.

Gatschet, A. S. Zwölf Sprachen aus dem Südwesten Nordamerikas. Weimar, 1876. 150 p.

Gerken, E. A. Development of a health education program: experiences with Navajo Indians. American Journal of Public Health, 30 (1940): 915-920.

Gerken, E. A. How the Navajos improve their health. Childhood Education, 18 (1942): 315-318.

Gifford, E. W. Apache-Pueblo. Anthropological Records, 4 (1940): 1-207.

Gilbert, Jarvey. Absence of coronary thrombosis in Navajo Indians. California Medicine, 82 (1955): 114-115.

Gilbreath, Kent. Business development on the Navajo Reservation. New Mexico Business, 25, no. 3 (1972): 3-10.

Gillmore, F. and L. W. Wetherill. Traders to the Navajos. Boston, 1934. 265 p.

Gilman, M. F. Birds of the Navajo Reservation. Condor, 10 (1908): 146-152.

Gilpin, Laura. The enduring Navaho. Austin, University of Texas Press, 1968. 13, 263 p. illus., map.

Gluckman, Max. Psychological, sociological and anthropological explanations of witchcraft and gossip: a clarification. Man, n.s., 3 (1968): 20-34.

Goddard, P. E. Assimilation to environment as illustrated by Athapascan peoples. International Congress of Americanists, Proceedings, 15 vol. 1 (1906): 337-359.

Goddard, P. E. Navaho blankets. American Museum Journal, 10 (1910): 201-211.

Goddard, P. E. Navajo. In J. Hastings, ed. Encyclopaedia of Religion and Ethics. Vol. 9. New York, 1917: 254-256.

Goddard, P. E. Navajo texts. American Museum of Natural History, Anthropological Papers, 34 (1933): 1-179.

Golden, Archie S. The other poor and their children. Clinical Pediatrics, 10 (1971): 66-68.

Goldfrank, E. S. Irrigation agriculture and Navaho community leadership. American Anthropologist, n.s., 47 (1945): 262-277.

Goldfrank, E. S. More on irrigation agriculture and Navaho community leadership. American Anthropologist, n.s., 48 (1946): 473-476.

Goldstine, Thea. A TAT study of Navajo aging. By Thea Goldstine and David Gutmann. Psychiatry, 35 (1972): 373-384.

Golla, Victor K. An etymological study of Hupa noun stems. International Journal of American Linguistics, 30 (1964): 108-117.

Goodwin, G. A comparison of Navaho and White Mountain Apache ceremonial forms and categories. Southwestern Journal of Anthropology, 1 (1945): 498-506.

Goossen, Irvy W. Navajo made easier; a course in conversational Navajo. Flagstaff, Northland Press, 1967. 15, 271 p.

Grandstaff, J. O. Wool characteristics in relation to Navajo weaving. U.S., Department of Agriculture, Technical Bulletin, 790 (1942): 1-36.

Graves, Theodore D. Acculturation, access, and alcohol in a tri-ethnic community. American Anthropologist, 69 (1967): 306-321.

Graves, Theodore D. Determinants of urban migrant Indian wages. By Theodore D. Graves and Charles A. Lave. Human Organization, 31 (1972): 47-61.

Graves, Theodore D. Drinking and drunkenness among urban Indians. In Jack O. Waddell and O. Michael Watson, eds. The American Indian in Urban Society. Boston, Little, Brown, 1971: 274-311.

Graves, Theodore D. Psychological acculturation in a tri-ethnic community. Southwestern Journal of Anthropology, 23 (1967): 337-350.

Graves, Theodore D. The personal adjustment of Navajo Indian migrants to Denver, Colorado. American Anthropologist, 72 (1970): 35-54.

Graves, Theodore D. The personal adjustment of Navajo Indian migrants to Denver, Colorado. In International Congress of Anthropological and Ethnological Sciences, 8th. 1968, Tokyo and Kyoto. Proceedings. Vol. 2. Tokyo, Science Council of Japan, 1969: 376-377.

Graves, Theodore Dumaine. Time perspective and the deferred gratification pattern in a tri-ethnic community. Dissertation Abstracts, 23 (1962/1963): 1161. UM 62-4294.

Green, E. C. Navajo rugs. Southwestern Lore, 24, no. 2 (1958): 17-24.

Greenfeld, Philip J. Playing card names in Western Apache. International Journal of American Linguistics, 37 (1971): 195-196.

Gregory, H. E. Geology of the Navajo country. U.S., Department of the Interior, Professional Papers, 93 (1917): 1-161.

Gregory, H. E. The Navajo country. American Geographical Society, Bulletin, 47 (1915): 561-577, 652-672.

Gregory, H. E. The Navajo country. U.S., Department of the Interior, Water Supply Papers, 280 (1916): 1-219.

Guernsey, S. J. Notes on a Navajo war dance. American Anthropologist, n.s., 22 (1920): 304-307.

Haile, B. A manual of Navaho grammar. St. Michaels, 1926. 324 p.

Haile, B. A stem vocabulary of the Navaho language. St. Michaels, 1950-1951. 2 v. (727 p.).

Haile, B. Aspects of Navaho life. The Americas, 7 (July 1950): 63-72.

Haile, B. Emergence myth according to the Hanelthmaye or Upward Reaching Rite. Navajo Religion Series, 3 (1949): 1-186.

Haile, B. Head and face masks in Navaho ceremonialism. St. Michaels, 1947. 122 p.

Haile, B. Learning Navaho. St. Michael's, 1941-1948. 4 v.

Haile, B. Legend of the Ghostway ritual. St. Michaels, 1950. 372 p.

Haile, B. Navaho chantways and ceremonials. American Anthropologist, n.s., 40 (1938): 639-652.

Haile, B. Navaho country. Franciscan Missions of the Southwest, 10 (1922): 28-38.

Haile, B. Navaho games of chance and taboo. Primitive Man, 6 (1933): 35-40.

Haile, B. Navaho sacrificial figurines. Chicago, 1947. 100 p.

Haile, B. Navaho upward-reaching way and emergence place. American Anthropologist, n.s., 44 (1942): 407-420.

Haile, B. Origin legend of the Navaho Enemy Way. Yale University Publications in Anthropology, 17 (1938): 1-320.

Haile, B. Origin legend of the Navaho Flintway. Chicago, 1943. 319 p.

Haile, B. Prayer stick cutting in a five night Navaho ceremonial of the male branch of Shootingway. Chicago, 1947. 229 p.

Haile, B. Property concepts of the Navaho Indians. Catholic University of America, Anthropological Series, 17 (1954): 1-64.

Haile, B. Reichard's Chant of Waning Endurance. American Anthropologist, n.s., 45 (1943): 307-311.

Haile, B. Religious concepts of the Navajo Indians. Catholic Philosophical Association, Proceedings, 10 (1935): 84-98.

Haile, B. Some cultural aspects of the Navajo hogan. Fort Wingate, 1937. 9 p.

Haile, B. Some mortuary customs of the Navajo. Franciscan Missions of the Southwest, 5 (1917): 29-33.

Haile, B. Starlore among the Navaho. Santa Fe, 1947. 44 p.

Haile, B. The holy gospels for Sunday and holy days. St. Michaels, 1938. 254 p.

Haile, B. The Navaho fire dance or corral dance. St. Michael's, 1946. 57 p.

Haile, B. The Navaho land question. Franciscan Missions of the Southwest, 10 (1922): 8-16.

Haile, B. The Navaho war dance. St. Michael's, 1946. 50 p.

Haile, B. Why the Navaho hogan? Primitive Man, 15 (1942): 39-56.

Hamamsy, L. S. The role of women in a changing Navaho society. American Anthropologist, 59 (1957): 101-111.

Hamer, J. H. An analysis of aggression in two societies. Anthropology Tomorrow, 5 (1956): 87-94.

Hammond, Blodwen. The "born-between" phenomenon among the Navajo. By Blodwen Hammond and Mary Shepardson. American Anthropologist, 67 (1965): 1516-1517.

Hancock, J. C. Diseases among the Indians. Southwestern Medicine, 17 (1933): 126.

Hannum, A. Paint the wind. New York, 1958. 206 p.

Hannum, A. Spin a silver dollar. 193 p.

Hanson, Charles E., Jr. The deadly arrow. Museum of the Fur Trade Quarterly, 3, no. 4 (1967): 2-5.

Harkins, Arthur M., ed. Problem of cross-cultural educational research and evaluation: the Rough Rock Demonstration School. Edited by Arthur Harkins and Richard Woods. Minneapolis, University of Minnesota, Training Center for Community Programs, 1969. 26 p. ERIC ED040231.

Harman, Robert. Change in a Navajo ceremonial. El Palacio, 71, no. 1 (1964): 20-26.

Harrington, J. P. A field comparison of Northwestern with Southwestern Indians. Smithsonian Institution, Explorations and Field-Work (1940): 91-94.

Harrington, J. P. A key to the Navaho orthography employed by the Franciscan Fathers. American Anthropologist, n.s., 13 (1911): 164-166.

Harrington, J. P. Six common Navaho nouns accounted for. Washington Academy of Sciences, Journal, 35 (1945): 373.

Harrington, J. P. Southern peripheral Athapaskawan origins, divisions, and migrations. Smithsonian Miscellaneous Collections, 100 (1940): 503-532.

Harrington, J. P. The Apache and Navaho. El Palacio, 27 (1929): 37-39.

Harrington, M. R. Swedged Navaho bracelets. Masterkey, 8 (1934): 183-184.

Harris, Z. S. Navaho phonology and Hoijer's analysis. International Journal of American Linguistics, 11 (1945): 239-246.

Harrold, L. L. Floods in the Navajo country. Soil Conservation, 7 (1942): 172-173.

Hartman, L. D. The life and customs of the Navajo women. Wisconsin Archeologist, n.s., 18 (1938): 100-107.

Hassett, Irene D. Popovich. The effects of type of reinforcer on several lower-class cultural groups. Dissertation Abstracts International, 31 (1970/1971): 5200A. UM 71-9276.

Hatcher, Evelyn Payne. Navaho art: a methodological study in visual communication. Dissertation Abstracts, 28 (1967/1968): 4854B. UM 68-7432.

Hatcher, Evelyn Payne. Navaho art; a methodological study in visual communication. Minneapolis, Intermittent Press, 1967. 7, 368 l. illus.

Hayes, F. Chee and his pony. Boston, 1950. 262 p.

Hayes, F. Hosh-ki the Navaho. New York, 1943. 250 p.

Heath, Dwight B. Prohibition and post-repeal drinking patterns among the Navaho. Quarterly Journal of Studies on Alcohol, 25 (1964): 119-135.

Heffernan, W. J. E. M. Kern, the travels of an artist-explorer. Bakersfield, 1953. 120 p.

Hegemann, Elizabeth C. Navaho silver. Los Angeles, 1962. 32 p. illus. (Southwest Museum, Leaflet, 29)

Hegemann, Elizabeth C. Navaho silver. Masterkey, 36 (1962): 45-59, 102-113.

Hegemann, Elizabeth C. Navaho trading days. Albuquerque, University of New Mexico Press, 1963. 388 p. illus.

Heinecke, R. Der Kampf der Navajos. Hannover, 1955. 94 p.

Henderson, Norman B. Cross-cultural action research: some limitations, advantages, and problems. Journal of Social Psychology, 73 (1967): 61-70.

Henderson, Norman B., et al. Cooperative program for rehabilitation of the disabled Indian. Navajo rehabilitation project. Final report. Flagstaff, Northern Arizona University, 1967. 135 p. (Navajo Rehabilitation Project, Report, TR-1) ERIC ED012930.

Henderson, Norman B., et al. Sex of person drawn by Japanese, Navajo, American White, and Negro seven-year-olds. Journal of Personality Assessment, 35 (1971): 261-264.

Henderson, R. Healing ceremonies in Monument Valley. Desert, 13 (March 1950): 24-25.

Henrikson, Craig Ernest. Acculturation, value change, and mental health among the Navajo. Dissertation Abstracts International, 32 (1971/1972): 4992B. UM 72-10,731.

Henry, W. E. Thematic apperception technique in the study of culture-

personality relations. Genetic
Psychology Monographs, 35 (1947): 1-135.

Hester, James J. An ethnohistoric
reconstruction of Navajo culture, 1582-
1824. El Palacio, 69 (1962): 130-138.

Hester, James J. Early Navajo migrations
and acculturation in the Southwest.
Santa Fe, 1962. 10, 138 p. illus.,
maps. (Museum of New Mexico, Papers in
Anthropology, 6)

Hester, James J. Studies at Navajo period
sites in the Navajo Reservoir District.
By James J. Hester and Joel L. Shiner.
Santa Fe, 1963. 77 p. illus., maps.
(Museum of New Mexico, Papers in
Anthropology, 9)

Hester, James Jean. Early Navajo
migrations and acculturation in the
Southwest. Dissertation Abstracts, 22
(1961/1962): 1348. UM 61-3846.

Hill, G. The art of the Navajo
silversmith. Kiva, 2, no. 5 (1937): 17-
21.

Hill, G. The use of turquoise among the
Navajo. Kiva, 4 (1938): 11-14.

Hill, Robert Fred. Intercultural
understanding and planned change: an
analysis of the processes of interaction
and communication between the Navaho and
the Bureau of Indian Affairs during the
stock reduction program of the 1930's.
Masters Abstracts, 6 (1968): 115. UM M-
1500.

Hill, W. W. Navaho humor. General Series
in Anthropology, 9 (1943): 1-28.

Hill, W. W. Navaho rites for dispelling
insanity and delirium. El Palacio, 41
(1936): 71-74.

Hill, W. W. Navaho trading and trading
ritual. Southwestern Journal of
Anthropology, 4 (1948): 371-396.

Hill, W. W. Navaho warfare. Yale
University Publications in Anthropology,
5 (1936): 1-19.

Hill, W. W. Navajo pottery manufacture.
New Mexico, University, Bulletin,
Anthropological Series, 2, no. 3 (1937):
5-23.

Hill, W. W. Navajo salt gathering. New
Mexico, University, Bulletin,
Anthropological Series, 3, no. 4 (1940):
1-25.

Hill, W. W. Navajo use of jimson weed.
New Mexico Anthropologist, 3 (1939): 19-
21.

Hill, W. W. Some aspects of Navajo
political structure. Plateau, 13 (1940):
23-28.

Hill, W. W. Some Navaho culture changes
during two centuries. Smithsonian
Miscellaneous Collections, 100 (1940):
395-415.

Hill, W. W. Stability in culture and
pattern. American Anthropologist, n.s.,
41 (1939): 258-260.

Hill, W. W. The agricultural and hunting
methods of the Navaho Indians. Yale
University Publications in Anthropology,
18 (1938): 1-194.

Hill, W. W. The hand trembling ceremony
of the Navaho. El Palacio, 38 (1935):
65-68.

Hill, W. W. The Navaho Indians and the
ghost dance of 1890. American
Anthropologist, n.s., 46 (1944): 523-
527.

Hill, W. W. The status of the
hermaphrodite and transvestite in Navaho
culture. American Anthropologist, n.s.,
37 (1935): 273-279.

Hill, W. W. and D. W. Hill. Navaho coyote
tales and their position in the Southern
Athabaskan group. Journal of American
Folklore, 58 (1945): 317-343.

Hill, W. W. and D. W. Hill. The legend of
the Navajo Eagle-catching Way. New
Mexico Anthropologist, 6/7 (1943): 31-
36.

Hill, W. W. and D. W. Hill. Two Navajo
myths. New Mexico Anthropologist, 6/7
(1943): 111-115.

Hill, Willard W. Navaho warfare. New
Haven, Human Relations Area Files Press,
1970. 19 p. illus. (Yale University
Publications in Anthropology, 5)

Hillery, George A., Jr. Navajo
population: an analysis of the 1960
census. By George A. Hillery, Jr. and
Frank J. Essene. Southwestern Journal of
Anthropology, 19 (1963): 297-313.

Hillery, George A., Jr. Navajos and
Eastern Kentuckians: a comparative study
in the cultural consequences of the
demographic transition. American
Anthropologist, 68 (1966): 52-70.

Hobler, Philip M. Navajo racing circles.
By Philip M. Hobler and Audrey E.
Hobler. Plateau, 40 (1967): 45-50.

Hobson, R. Navaho acquisitive values.
Harvard University, Peabody Museum of

American Archaeology and Ethnology, Papers, 42, no. 3 (1954): 1-45.

Hocking, G. M. Some plant materials used medicinally and otherwise by the Navaho Indians in the Chaco Canyon, New Mexico. El Palacio, 63 (1956): 146-165.

Hodge, F. W. How old is Southwest Indian silverwork? El Palacio, 25 (1928): 224-232.

Hodge, F. W. The early Navajo and Apache. American Anthropologist, 8 (1895): 223-240.

Hodge, William. Navaho urban silversmiths. Anthropological Quarterly, 40 (1967): 185-200.

Hodge, William H. Navajo urban migration: an analysis from the perspective of the family. In Jack O. Waddell and O. Michael Watson, eds. The American Indian in Urban Society. Boston, Little, Brown, 1971: 346-391.

Hodge, William H. The Albuquerque Navajos. Tucson, University of Arizona Press, 1969. 76 p. maps. (Arizona, University, Anthropological Papers, 11)

Hodge, William Howard. The Albuquerque Navahos. Dissertation Abstracts, 27 (1966/1967): 3376B-3377B. UM 66-13,641.

Hoffman, F. L. The Navaho population problem. International Congress of Americanists, Proceedings, 23 (1928): 620-633.

Hoffman, Virginia. Navajo biographies. By Virginia Hoffman and Broderick H. Johnson. Rough Rock, Dine, 1970. 342 p. illus., map.

Hoffman, Virginia. Navajo Reservation. By Virginia Hoffman and Broderick H. Johnson. Chinle, Ariz., Rough Rock Demonstration School, 1970. 342 p.

Hogner, D. C. Navaho winter nights. New York, 1935. 180 p.

Hoijer, H. Cultural implications of some Navaho linguistic categories. Language, 27 (1951): 111-120.

Hoijer, H. Navaho phonology. New Mexico, University, Publications in Anthropology, 1 (1945): 1-59.

Hoijer, H. Phonetic and phonemic change in the Athapaskan languages. Language, 18 (1942): 218-220.

Hoijer, H. Pitch accent in the Apachean languages. Language, 19 (1943): 38-41.

Hoijer, H. The Apachean verb. International Journal of American Linguistics, 11 (1945): 193-203; 12 (1946): 1-13, 51-59; 14 (1948): 247-259; 15 (1949): 12-22.

Hoijer, Harry. A problem in Navaho syntax. In International Congress of Linguists, 9th. 1962, Cambridge, Mass. Proceedings. The Hague, Mouton, 1964: 601-603. (Janua Linguarum, Series Major, 12)

Hoijer, Harry. Internal reconstruction in Navaho. Word, 25 (1969): 155-159.

Hoijer, Harry. Navaho reference verbs and verb expressions made up of two verb forms. International Journal of American Linguistics, 34 (1968): 176-182.

Hoijer, Harry. Patterns of meaning in Navaho. In Mario D. Zamora, et al., eds. Themes in Culture. Quezon City, Kayumanggi, 1971: 227-237.

Hoijer, Harry. Word classes in Navaho. Lingua, 17 (1967): 88-102.

Hollister, U. S. The Navajo and his blanket. Denver, 1903. 144 p.

Hollister, Uriah S. The Navajo and his blanket. Glorieta, N.M., Rio Grande Press, 1972. 144 p. illus.

Holm, Wayne Stanley. Some aspects of Navajo orthography. Dissertation Abstracts International, 33 (1972/1973): 5706A-5707A. UM 73-8370.

Honigmann, J. J. Northern and Southern Athapaskan eschatology. American Anthropologist, n.s., 47 (1945): 467-469.

Hoover, J. W. Navajo land problems. Economic Geography, 13 (1937): 281-300.

Hoover, J. W. Navajo nomadism. Geographical Review, 21 (1931): 429-445.

Hopkins, Richard C. Kit Carson and the Navajo Expedition. Montana, the Magazine of Western History, 18, no. 2 (1968): 52-61.

Hough, W. Apache and Navaho fire-making. American Anthropologist, n.s., 3 (1901): 585-586.

Howell, Robert J. A comparison of test scores for the 16-17 year age group of Navaho Indians with standardized norms for the Wechsler Adult Intelligence Scale (Arizona and New Mexico). By Robert J. Howell, Lavon Evans, and Lester N. Downing. Journal of Social Psychology, 47 (1958): 355-359.

Howren, Robert. A formalization of the Athabaskan 'D-effect'. International Journal of American Linguistics, 37 (1971): 96-113.

Hoyt, Elizabeth E. Integration of culture: a review of concepts. [With comment by David F. Aberle.] Current Anthropology, 2 (1961): 407-426.

Hrdlička, A. Catalogue of human crania in the United States National Museum collections. United States National Museum, Proceedings, 78, no. 2 (1931): 1-95.

Hrdlička, A. Physical and physiological observations on the Navaho. American Anthropologist, n.s., 2 (1900): 339-345.

Hudson, Charles. Isometric advantages of the cradle board: a hypothesis. American Anthropologist, 68 (1966): 470-474.

Hulsizer, A. Region and culture in the curriculum of the Navaho and the Dakota. Federalsburg, 1940. 344 p.

Hung, Beverly Y. P. On the phonemic status of Navaho stress. Anthropological Linguistics, 1, no. 9 (1959): 20-23.

Hurt, W. R. Eighteenth century Navaho hogans from Canyon de Chelly National Monument. American Antiquity, 8 (1942): 89-104.

Hymes, Dell H. Lexicostatistics so far. Current Anthropology, 1 (1960): 3-34.

Indian Arts and Crafts Board. Navajo Indian rugs. Washington, D.C., 1956. 7 p.

Indian Arts and Crafts Board. Silver jewelry of the Navajo and Pueblo Indians. Washington, D.C., 1956. 7 p.

Inman, D. Don't fence me in. New York, 1955. 167 p.

Ives, J. C. Report upon the Colorado River of the West. Washington, D.C., 1861. 131 p.

Jacobson, Doranne. Navajo Enemy Way exchanges. El Palacio, 71, no. 1 (1964): 7-19.

Jaffe, Burton F. Cleft palate, cleft lip, and cleft uvula in Navajo Indians: incidence and otorhinolaryngologic problems. By Burton F. Jaffe and G. Bruce De Blanc. Cleft Palate Journal, 7 (1970): 300-305.

James, G. W. Indian blankets and their makers. Chicago, 1914. 213 p.

James, G. W. The Indians of the Painted Desert region. Boston, 1903. 268 p.

James, M. A note on Navajo pottery-making. El Palacio, 43 (1937): 13-15, 85-86.

Jayagopal, Rajabather. Problem solving abilities and psychomotor skills of Navajo Indians, Spanish Americans and Anglos in junior high school. Dissertation Abstracts International, 31 (1970/1971): 5035A. UM 71-9307.

Jeancon, J. A. and F. H. Douglas. Navaho spinning, dyeing, and weaving. Denver Art Museum, Indian Leaflet Series, 3 (1930): 1-4.

Jeancon, J. A. and F. H. Douglas. The Navaho Indians. Denver Art Museum, Indian Leaflet Series, 21 (1931): 1-4.

Jelinek, Arthur J. Environment and aboriginal population seen through the historical record. In A Prehistoric Sequence in the Middle Pecos Valley, New Mexico. Ann Arbor, University of Michigan, 1967: 18-40. (Michigan, University, Museum of Anthropology, Anthropological Papers, 31)

Jessor, Richard. The tri-ethnic study and the problem of culture. By Richard Jessor and Kettil Bruun. Quarterly Journal of Studies on Alcohol, 31 (1970): 272-277.

Jessor, Richard, et al. Society, personality, and deviant behavior; a study of a tri-ethnic community. New York, Holt, Rinehart and Winston, 1968. 11, 500 p.

Jett, Stephen C. An analysis of Navajo place-names. Names, 18 (1970): 175-184.

Jett, Stephen C. Navajo wildlands; "as long as the rivers shall run". Edited by Kenneth Brower. San Francisco, Sierra Club, 1967. 160 p. illus., map.

Jett, Stephen C. Tourism in the Navajo country: resources and planning. Window Rock, Navajo Tribal Museum, 1967. 184 p. maps.

Jett, Stephen Clinton. Tourism in the Navajo Country: resources and planning. Dissertation Abstracts, 26 (1965/1966): 980. UM 65-4136.

Jewell, D. P. A case of a "psychotic" Navaho Indian male. Human Organization, 11, no. 1 (1952): 32-36.

John, Vera P. Learning at Rough Rock. Human Organization, 31 (1972): 447-449.

Johnson, Broderick H. Navaho education at Rough Rock. Rough Rock, Rough Rock Demonstration School, 1968. 212 p. illus.

Johnson, Charlotte I. Navaho corn grinding songs. Ethnomusicology, 8 (1964): 101-120.

Johnston, B. E. A Navaho good Samaritan. Masterkey, 28 (1954): 138-140.

Johnston, Bernice E. Navaho education-- the first thirty years. Masterkey, 33 (1959): 4-12.

Johnston, Bernice E. Two ways in the desert; a study of modern Navajo-Anglo relations. Pasadena, Socio-Technical Publications, 1972. 12, 334 p. illus.

Johnston, Denis Foster. An analysis of sources of information on the population of the Navaho. Washington, D.C., Government Printing Office, 1966. 5, 220 p. maps. (U.S., Bureau of American Ethnology, Bulletin, 197)

Johnston, Denis Foster. An analysis of sources of information on the population of the Navajo. Dissertation Abstracts, 22 (1961/1962): 1738-1739. UM 61-3713.

Johnston, Francis E., et al. Alloalbuminemia in Southwestern U.S. Indians: polymorphism of albumin Naskapi and albumin Mexico. Human Biology, 41 (1969): 263-270.

Johnston, Philip. Indian jargon won our battles. Masterkey, 38 (1964): 130-137.

Jones, C. R. Spindle-spinning Navajo style. Plateau, 18 (1946): 43-51.

Jones, D. W. Forty years among the Indians. Salt Lake City, 1890. 400 p.

Jones, Oakah L., Jr. The origins of the Navajo Indian police 1872-1873. Arizona and the West, 8 (1966): 225-238.

Jones, Paul. Reclamation and the Indian. Utah Historical Quarterly, 27 (1959): 50-56.

Jones, T. J., H. B. Allen, C. T. Loram, and E. Deloria. The Navajo Indian problem. New York, 1939. 127 p.

Jones, V. H. A new and unusual Navajo dye (Endothia singularis). Plateau, 21 (1948): 17-24.

Jordan, Scott W., et al. Carcinoma of the cervix in Southwestern American Indian women. Cancer, 29 (1972): 1235-1241.

Judd, B. Ira. Tuba City, Mormon settlement. Journal of Arizona History, 10 (1969): 37-42.

Judd, Neil M. Five Navaho amulets. El Palacio, 71, no. 2 (1964): 21-22.

Kahlenberg, Mary H. The Navajo blanket. By Mary H. Kahlenberg and Anthony Berlant. New York, Praeger, 1972. 112 p. illus.

Kane, Robert L. Federal health care (with reservations). By Robert L. and Rosalie A. Kane. New York, Springer, 1972. 180 p. illus., maps.

Kaplan, B. A study of Rorschach responses in four cultures. Harvard University, Peabody Museum of American Archaeology and Ethnology, Papers, 42, no. 2 (1954): 1-54.

Kaplan, Bert. The social meaning of Navaho psychopathology and psychotherapy. By Bert Kaplan and Dale Johnson. In Ari Kiev, ed. Magic, Faith, and Healing. New York, Free Press, 1964: 203-229.

Kate, H. F. C. ten. Reizen en onderzoekingen in Noord-Amerika, 232-242, 267-270. Leiden, 1885.

Kayser, David W. A Navajo Julia Child. El Palacio, 77, no. 2 (1971): 37-40.

Keith, Anne B. The Navajo girls' puberty ceremony: function and meaning for the adolescent. El Palacio, 71, no. 1 (1964): 27-36.

Keller, Gordon N. Bicultural social work and anthropology. Social Casework, 53 (1972): 455-465.

Kelley, Roger E., et al. Navaho figurines called dolls. Santa Fe, Museum of Navaho Ceremonial Art, 1972. 75 p. illus.

Kelly, C. Chief Hoskaninni. Utah Historical Quarterly, 21 (1953): 219-226.

Kelly, Lawrence C. Navajo roundup; selected correspondence of Kit Carson's expedition against the Navajo, 1863-1865. Boulder, Pruett, 1970. 192 p. illus., maps.

Kelly, Lawrence C. The Navaho Indians: land and oil. New Mexico Historical Review, 38 (1963): 1-28.

Kelly, Lawrence C. The Navajo Indians and Federal Indian policy, 1900-1935. Tucson, University of Arizona Press, 1968. 10, 221 p. maps.

Kelly, Lawrence C. Where was Fort Canby?
New Mexico Historical Review, 42 (1967):
49-62.

Kelly, Lawrence Charles. The Navajos and
federal policy, 1913-1935. Dissertation
Abstracts, 22 (1961/1962): 2773. UM 61-
5272.

Kelly, Roger E. American Indians in small
cities: a survey of urban acculturation
in two northern Arizona communities. By
Roger E. Kelly and John O. Cramer.
Flagstaff, Northern Arizona University,
Department of Rehabilitation, 1966.
90 p. illus.

Kelly, Roger E. An old Hopi "tihu".
Plateau, 40 (1967): 62-67.

Kelly, Roger E. Disabled Navajo Indians
and rehabilitation--an anthropological
overview. Flagstaff, Northern Arizona
University, 1967. 68 p. (Navajo
Rehabilitation Project, Report, TR-2)
ERIC ED012669.

Kelly, William H. Methods and resources
for the construction and maintenance of
a Navajo population register. Tucson,
University of Arizona, Bureau of Ethnic
Research, 1964. 8, 39 p.

Kemrer, M. F. Navajo warfare and economy,
1750-1868. By M. F. Kemrer and D. A.
Graybill. Western Canadian Journal of
Anthropology, 2, no. 1 (1970): 204-211.

Kennedy, Donald Alexander. Explorations
in the cross-cultural study of mental
disorders. Dissertation Abstracts, 20
(1959/1960): 23-24. UM 59-2468.

Kennedy, John G. Psychological and social
explanations of witchcraft. Man, n.s., 2
(1967): 216-225.

Kennedy, Mary J. Tales of a trader's
wife; life on the Navajo Indian
Reservation, 1913-1938. Albuquerque,
1965. 61 p. illus.

Kent, Kate Peck. Archaeological clues to
early historic Navajo and Pueblo
weaving. Plateau, 39 (1966): 46-70.

Kent, Kate Peck. The story of Navaho
weaving. Phoenix, Heard Museum of
Anthropology and Primitive Arts, 1961.
48 p. illus., maps.

Keur, D. L. A chapter in Navaho-Pueblo
relations. American Antiquity, 10
(1944): 75-86.

Keur, D. L. Big Bead Mesa. Society for
American Archaeology, Memoirs, 1 (1941):
1-90.

Keur, D. L. New light on Navaho origins.
New York Academy of Sciences,
Transactions, n.s., 2 (1940): 182-192.

Kimball, S. T. Future problems in Navajo
administration. Human Organization, 9,
no. 2 (1950): 21-24.

Kimball, S. T. and J. H. Provinse. Navajo
social organization and land use
planning. Human Organization, 1, no. 4
(1942): 18-25.

King, J. Where the two came to their
father. Ed. by M. Oakes and J. Campbell.
Bollingen Series, 1 (1943): 1-88.

King, Jeff. Where the two came to their
father; a Navaho war ceremonial given by
Jeff King. 2d. ed. Princeton, Princeton
University Press, 1969. 55 p. illus.

Kirk, R. F. Southwestern Indian jewelry.
Archaeological Institute of America,
School of American Research, Santa Fe,
Papers, ser. 2, 38 (1945): 1-24.

Kirk, R. F. Southwestern Indian jewelry.
El Palacio, 52 (1945): 21-32, 41-50.

Kirsch, Hans Christian. Die Spur der
Navahos. Recklinghausen, Bitter, 1969.
146 p. illus., map.

Klah, H. Navaho creation myth. Navajo
Religion Series, 1 (1942): 1-237.

Kluckhohn, C. A Navaho personal document
with a brief Paretian analysis.
Southwestern Journal of Anthropology, 1
(1945): 260-283.

Kluckhohn, C. Hopi and Navajo. New Mexico
Quarterly, 3 (1933): 56-64.

Kluckhohn, C. Myths and rituals: a
general theory. Harvard Theological
Review, 35 (1942): 45-79.

*Kluckhohn, C. Navaho witchcraft. Harvard
University, Peabody Museum of American
Archaeology and Ethnology, Papers, 22,
no. 2 (1944): 1-149.

Kluckhohn, C. Navaho women's knowledge of
their song ceremonials. El Palacio, 45
(1938): 87-92.

Kluckhohn, C. Notes on the Navajo Eagle
Way. New Mexico Anthropologist, 5
(1941): 6-14.

Kluckhohn, C. Participation in
ceremonials in a Navaho community.
American Anthropologist, n.s., 40
(1938): 359-369.

Kluckhohn, C. Personality formation among the Navaho Indians. Sociometry, 9 (1946): 128-132.

Kluckhohn, C. Some aspects of Navaho infancy and early childhood. Psychoanalysis and the Social Sciences, 1 (1947): 37-86.

Kluckhohn, C. Some Navaho value terms in behavioral context. Language, 32 (1956): 140-145.

Kluckhohn, C. Some personal and social aspects of Navaho ceremonial practice. Harvard Theological Review, 32 (1939): 57-82.

Kluckhohn, C. The dance of Hasjelti. El Palacio, 15 (1923): 187-192.

Kluckhohn, C. The great chants of the Navajo. Theatre Arts Monthly, 17 (1933): 639-645.

Kluckhohn, C. The Navahos in the machine age. Technology Review, 44, no. 4 (1942): 2-6.

Kluckhohn, C. The philosophy of the Navaho Indians. In F. S. C. Northrop, ed. Ideological Differences and World Order. New Haven, 1949: 356-384.

Kluckhohn, C. What modern parents can learn from the Navajos. American Indian, 4, no. 2 (1947): 11-13.

*Kluckhohn, C. and D. C. Leighton. The Navaho. Cambridge, 1946. 258 p.

Kluckhohn, C. and J. C. Rosenzweig. Two Navaho children over a five-year period. American Journal of Orthopsychiatry, 19 (1949): 266-278.

Kluckhohn, C. and L. Wyman. An introduction to Navaho chant practice. American Anthropological Association, Memoirs, 53 (1940): 1-204.

Kluckhohn, C. and W. Morgan. Some notes on Navaho dreams. In G. B. Wilbur and W. Muensterberger, eds. Psychoanalysis and Culture. New York, 1951: 120-131.

Kluckhohn, Clyde. A Navaho politician. In Richard Kluckhohn, ed. Culture and Behavior. New York, Free Press, 1962: 182-209.

Kluckhohn, Clyde. By their speech shall ye know them. By Clyde Kluckhohn and Dorothea Leighton. In Jesse D. Jennings and E. Adamson Hoebel, eds. Readings in Anthropology. 3d ed. New York, McGraw-Hill, 1972: 305-312.

Kluckhohn, Clyde. Expressive activities. In Evon Z. Vogt and Ethel M. Albert, eds. The People of Rimrock. Cambridge, Harvard University Press, 1966: 269-298.

Kluckhohn, Clyde. Group tensions: analysis of a case history. In Richard Kluckhohn, ed. Culture and Behavior. New York, Free Press, 1962: 301-322.

Kluckhohn, Clyde. Navaho categories. In Stanley Diamond, ed. Culture in History. New York, Columbia University Press, 1960: 65-98.

Kluckhohn, Clyde. Navaho categories. In Stanley Diamond, ed. Primitive Views of the World. New York, Columbia University Press, 1964: 95-128.

Kluckhohn, Clyde. Navaho material culture. By Clyde Kluckhohn, W. W. Hill, and Lucy Wales Kluckhohn. Cambridge, Belknap Press of Harvard University Press, 1971. 14, 488 p. illus., map.

Kluckhohn, Clyde. Navaho morals. In Richard Kluckhohn, ed. Culture and Behavior. New York, Free Press, 1962: 168-176.

Kluckhohn, Clyde. Navaho witchcraft. Boston, Beacon Press, 1962. 22, 254 p.

Kluckhohn, Clyde. Navaho women's knowledge of their song ceremonials. In Richard Kluckhohn, ed. Culture and Behavior. New York, Free Press, 1962: 92-96.

Kluckhohn, Clyde. Notes on Navaho Eagle Way. In Richard Kluckhohn, ed. Culture and Behavior. New York, Free Press, 1962: 122-133.

Kluckhohn, Clyde. Notes on some anthropological aspects of communication. American Anthropologist, 63 (1961): 895-910.

Kluckhohn, Clyde. Personality formation among the Navaho Indians. In Richard Kluckhohn, ed. Culture and Behavior. New York, Free Press, 1962: 177-181.

Kluckhohn, Clyde. Religious world of the Navaho. By Clyde Kluckhohn and Dorothea C. Leighton. In Walter R. Goldschmidt, ed. Exploring the Ways of Mankind. New York, Holt, 1960: 508-520.

Kluckhohn, Clyde. Some notes on Navaho dreams. In Richard Kluckhohn, ed. Culture and Behavior. New York, Free Press, 1962: 350-363.

Kluckhohn, Clyde. Some social and personal aspects of Navaho ceremonial patterns. In Richard Kluckhohn, ed.

Culture and Behavior. New York, Free Press, 1962: 97-122.

Kluckhohn, Clyde. The language of the Navaho Indians. By Clyde Kuckhohn and Dorothea Leighton. In Philip K. Bock, ed. Culture Shock. New York, Knopf, 1970: 29-44.

*Kluckhohn, Clyde. The Navaho. Rev. ed. By Clyde Kluckhohn and Dorothea Leighton. Garden City, N.Y., Natural History Press, 1962. 355 p. illus.

Kluckhohn, Clyde. The Navaho view of life. By Clyde Kluckhohn and Dorothea C. Leighton. In Clarence Crane Brinton, ed. The Fate of Man. New York, George Braziller, 1961: 37-44.

Kluckhohn, Clyde. The Ramah Navaho. Washington, D.C., Government Printing Office, 1966. 327-377 p. (U.S., Bureau of American Ethnology, Anthropological Papers, 79. U.S., Bureau of American Ethnology, Bulletin, 196)

Kluckhohn, Clyde. Two Navaho children over a five-year period. In Richard Kluckhohn, ed. Culture and Behavior. New York, Free Press, 1962: 150-167.

Kluckhohn, Florence R., et al. Variations in value orientations. Evanston, Row, Peterson, 1961. 437 p. illus.

Kluckhohn, Florence Rockwood. A method for eliciting value orientations. Anthropological Linguistics, 2, no. 2 (1960): 1-23.

Knowlton, Clark S., ed. Indian and Spanish American adjustments to arid and semiarid environments. Lubbock, Texas Technological College, 1964. 97 p. ERIC ED024478.

Koenig, Seymour H. Sky, sand, and spirits; Navaho and Pueblo Indian art and culture. Yonkers, N.Y., Hudson River Museum, 1972. 90 p. illus.

Kositchek, Robert J. Biochemical studies in full-blooded Navajo Indians: II. Lipids and lipoproteins. By Robert J. Kositchek, Moses Wurm, and Reuben Straus. Circulation, 22 (1960): 773; 23 (1961): 219-224.

Kroeber, A. L. A Southwestern personality type. Southwestern Journal of Anthropology, 3 (1947): 108-113.

Kroeber, A. L. Recent ethnic spreads. California, University, Publications in American Archaeology and Ethnology, 47 (1959): 259-281.

Krohn, Alan. Changes in mastery style with age: a study of Navajo dreams. By Alan Krohn and David Gutmann. Psychiatry, 34 (1971): 289-300.

Krug, J. A. Report on the Navaho. Washington, D.C., 1948. 49 p.

Kunitz, S. J. Alcoholic cirrhosis among the Navaho. By S. J. Kunitz, J. E. Levy, and M. Everett. Quarterly Journal of Studies on Alcohol, 30 (1969): 672-685, 810-811.

Kunitz, S. J., et al. The epidemiology of alcoholic cirrhosis in two Southwestern Indian tribes. Quarterly Journal of Studies on Alcohol, 32 (1971): 706-720, 865.

Kunitz, Stephen J. A census of Flagstaff Navajos. By Stephen J. Kunitz, Jerrold E. Levy, Paul Bellet, and Thomas Collins. Plateau, 41 (1969): 156-163.

Kunitz, Stephen J. A one year follow-up of Navajo migrants to Flagstaff, Arizona. By Stephen J. Kunitz, Jerrold E. Levy, and Charles L. Odoroff. Plateau, 42 (1970): 92-106.

Kunitz, Stephen J. Navajo voting patterns. By Stephen J. Kunitz and Jerrold E. Levy. Plateau, 43 (1970): 1-8.

Kunitz, Stephen Joshua. Navajo drinking patterns. Dissertation Abstracts International, 31 (1970/1971): 3666A. UM 70-26,174.

Kunstadter, Peter. Southern Athabaskan herding patterns and contrasting social institutions. In Anthony Leeds and Andrew P. Vayda, eds. Man, Culture, and Animals. Washington, D.C., 1965: 67-86. (American Association for the Advancement of Science, Publication, 78)

Kurtz, Ronald J. Headmen and war chanters: role theory and the early Canyoncito Navajo. Ethnohistory, 16 (1969): 83-111.

Kurtz, Ronald Joseph. Role change and cultural change: the Canyoncito Navaho case. Dissertation Abstracts, 24 (1963/1964): 3051. UM 64-1451.

Kutnewsky, F. and C. Holbrook. Navajo rugs. Compressed Air Magazine, 47 (1942): 6658-6662.

La Farge, O. Laughing Boy. Boston, 1929. 302 p.

La Farge, O. The Navajos. Natural History, 57 (1948): 360-367.

Ladd, John. The structure of a moral code; a philosophical analysis of ethical discourse applied to the ethics of the Navaho Indians. Cambridge, Harvard University Press, 1957. 15, 474 p.

Lamphere, Louise. Ceremonial co-operation and networks: a reanalysis of the Navajo outfit. Man, n.s., 5 (1970): 38-59.

Lamphere, Louise. Symbolic elements in Navajo ritual. Southwestern Journal of Anthropology, 25 (1969): 279-305.

Landar, H. J. Four Navaho summer tales. Journal of American Folklore, 72 (1959): 161-164, 248-251, 298-309.

Landar, Herbert. Syntactic patterns in Navaho and Huichol. International Journal of American Linguistics, 33 (1967): 121-127.

Landar, Herbert J. A note on accepted and rejected arrangements of Navaho words. International Journal of American Linguistics, 26 (1960): 351-354.

Landar, Herbert J. A note on preferred arrangements of Navaho words. International Journal of American Linguistics, 27 (1961): 175-177.

Landar, Herbert J. Class co-occurrence in Navaho gender. International Journal of American Linguistics, 31 (1965): 326-331.

Landar, Herbert J. Fluctuation of forms in Navaho kinship terminology. American Anthropologist, 64 (1962): 985-1000.

Landar, Herbert J. Navaho color categories. By Herbert J. Landar, Susan M. Ervin, and Arnold E. Horowitz. Language, 36 (1960): 368-382.

Landar, Herbert J. Navaho syntax. Baltimore, Linguistic Society of America, 1963. 54 p.

Landar, Herbert J. Seven Navaho verbs of eating. International Journal of American Linguistics, 30 (1964): 94-96.

Landar, Herbert J. Ten'a classificatory verbs. International Journal of American Linguistics, 33 (1967): 263-268.

Landar, Herbert J. The language of pain in Navaho culture. In Dell H. Hymes and William E. Bittle, eds. Studies in Southwestern Ethnolinguistics. The Hague, Mouton, 1967: 117-144. (Studies in General Anthropology, 3)

Landar, Herbert J. The loss of Athapaskan words for fish in the Southwest.

International Journal of American Linguistics, 26 (1960): 75-77.

Landar, Herbert J. The Navaho intonational system. Anthropological Linguistics, 1, no. 9 (1959): 11-19.

Landar, Herbert J. Theme of incest in Navaho folklore. In Samir K. Ghosh, ed. Man, Language and Society; Contributions to the Sociology of Language. The Hague, Mouton, 1972: 118-133. (Janua Linguarum, Series Minor, 109)

Landar, Herbert J. Two Athapaskan verbs of "being". In John W. M. Verhaar, ed. The Verb 'Be' and Its Synonyms. Part 1. Dordrecht, Reidel, 1967: 40-74. (Foundations of Language, Supplementary Series, 1)

Landgraf, J. L. Land use in the Ramah Navaho area, New Mexico. New York Academy of Sciences, Transactions, ser. 2, 13 (1950): 77-84.

*Landgraf, J. L. Land-use in the Ramah area of New Mexico. Harvard University, Peabody Museum of American Archaeology and Ethnology, Papers, 42, no. 1 (1954): 1-105.

Lane, William Carr. William Carr Lane, diary. Edited by Wm. G. B. Carson. New Mexico Historical Review, 39 (1964): 181-234, 274-332.

Langley, D. Land of beginning again. Arizona Highways, 30, no. 6 (1954): 26-29, 34-39.

Lawler, Donald J., et al. Trachoma among the Navajo Indians. Archives of Ophthalmology, 83 (1970): 187-190.

Lee, Melvin. Application of a modified riboflavin load test to a field test of riboflavin nutritional status in Navajo Indians. By Melvin Lee and Richard H. Davis. Archivos Latinoamericanos de Nutrición, 17 (1967): 207-214.

Left Handed. Son of Old Man Hat; a Navaho autobiography. Recorded by Walter Dyk. Lincoln, University of Nebraska Press, 1967. 14, 378 p.

Leighton, A. H. and D. C. Leighton. A Navaho builds a house. Natural History, 47 (1941): 172-173.

Leighton, A. H. and D. C. Leighton. A Navaho makes a blanket. Natural History, 47 (1941): 274.

Leighton, A. H. and D. C. Leighton. A Navaho makes soap. Natural History, 48 (1941): 19.

Leighton, A. H. and D. C. Leighton. A
   Navaho takes a "Turkish bath". Natural
   History, 48 (1941): 20-21.

Leighton, A. H. and D. C. Leighton.
   Elements of psychotherapy in Navaho
   religion. Psychiatry, 4 (1941): 515-523.

*Leighton, A. H. and D. C. Leighton.
   Gregorio, the hand-trembler. Harvard
   University, Peabody Museum of American
   Archaeology and Ethnology, Papers, 40,
   no. 1 (1949): 1-177.

Leighton, A. H. and D. C. Leighton. Some
   types of uneasiness and fear in a Navaho
   Indian community. American
   Anthropologist, n.s., 44 (1942): 194-
   209.

Leighton, A. H. and D. C. Leighton. The
   Navaho door. Cambridge, 1944. 149 p.

Leighton, Alexander H. The Navaho door;
   an introduction to Navaho life. By
   Alexander H. Leighton and Dorothea C.
   Leighton. New York, Russell and
   Russell, 1967. 18, 149 p. illus.,
   maps.

*Leighton, D. C. and C. Kluckhohn.
   Children of the people. Cambridge,
   1947. 277 p.

*Leighton, Dorothea C. Children of the
   people; the Navaho individual and his
   development. By Dorothea Leighton and
   Clyde Kluckhohn. New York, Octagon
   Books, 1969. 11, 277 p. illus., maps.

Leighton, Dorothea C. The therapeutic
   process in cross-cultural perspective--a
   symposium. Fragments from a Navaho
   ceremonial. American Journal of
   Psychiatry, 124 (1968): 1176-1178.

Leighton, Elizabeth Roby. The nature of
   cultural factors affecting the success
   or failure of Navajo college students.
   Dissertation Abstracts, 26 (1965/1966):
   1282. UM 64-10,465.

Lemon, Frank R. Health problems of the
   Navajos in Monument Valley, Utah. U.S.,
   Public Health Service, Public Health
   Reports, 75 (1960): 1055-1061.

Letherman, J. Sketch of the Navajo tribe
   of Indians. Smithsonian Institution,
   Annual Report of the Board of Regents
   (1855): 283-297.

Levy, Jerrold E. Community organization
   of the Western Navaho. American
   Anthropologist, 64 (1962): 781-801.

Levy, Jerrold E. Indian reservations,
   anomie, and social pathologies. By
   Jerrold E. Levy and Stephen J. Kunitz.

Southwestern Journal of Anthropology, 27
   (1971): 97-128.

Levy, Jerrold E. Navajo criminal
   homicide. By Jerrold E. Levy, Stephen J.
   Kunitz, and Michael Everett.
   Southwestern Journal of Anthropology, 25
   (1969): 124-152.

Levy, Jerrold E. Navajo suicide. Human
   Organization, 24 (1965): 308-318.

Levy, Jerrold E. Navajo suicide. In
   Deward E. Walker, Jr., ed. The Emergent
   Native Americans. Boston, Little,
   Brown, 1972: 594-613.

Levy, Jerrold E. The fate of Navajo
   twins. American Anthropologist, 66
   (1964): 883-887.

Li, Fang-kuei. Some problems in
   comparative Athapaskan. Canadian Journal
   of Linguistics, 10 (1964/1965): 129-134.

Liebler, H. Baxter. Boil my heart for me.
   New York, Exposition Press, 1969.
   194 p.

Liebler, H. Baxter. The social and
   cultural patterns of the Navajo Indians.
   Utah Historical Quarterly, 30 (1962):
   298-325.

Lincoln, J. S. The dream in primitive
   cultures. London, 1935. 359 p.

Link, M. S. The pollen path. Stanford,
   1956. 211 p.

Link, Martin A., ed. Navajo: a century of
   progress, 1868-1968. Window Rock,
   Navajo Tribe, 1968. 107 p. illus.

*Lipps, O. H. The Navajos. Cedar Rapids,
   1909. 136 p.

Littell, Norman Mather. Reflections of a
   tribal attorney. Washington, D.C.,
   1957. 36 p.

Lockett, C. Hogans vs. houses. In For the
   Dean. Essays in Anthropology in Honor of
   Byron Cummings. Tucson, 1952: 137-142.

Lockett, C. Midwives and childbirth among
   the Navajo. Plateau, 12 (1939): 15-17.

Loeb, E. M. A note on two far-travelled
   kachinas. Journal of American Folklore,
   56 (1943): 192-199.

Loh, Jules. Lords of the earth; a history
   of the Navajo Indians. New York,
   Crowell-Collier, 1971. 164 p. illus.

Lomax, Alan. Special features of the sung
   communication. In June Helm, ed. Essays
   on the Verbal and Visual Arts. Seattle,

University of Washington Press, 1967: 109-127. (American Ethnological Society, Proceedings of the Annual Spring Meeting, 1966)

Looney, Ralph. The Navajos. National Geographic, 142 (1972): 740-781.

Luckert, Karl W. Traditional Navajo theories of disease and healing. Arizona Medicine, 29 (1972): 570-573.

Luebben, R. A. The Navajo dilemma. American Indian, 8, no. 2 (1958/1959): 6-16.

Luebben, Ralph A. Anglo law and Navaho behavior. Kiva, 29, no. 3 (1963/1964): 60-75.

Luebben, Ralph A. Navajo status and leadership in a modern mining situation. Plateau, 35 (1962): 1-14.

Luebben, Ralph A. Prejudice and discrimination against Navahos in a mining community. Kiva, 30, no. 1 (1964/1965): 1-17.

Luomala, K. Navaho life of yesterday and today. Berkeley, 1938. 115 p.

Malcolm, R. Archaeological remains, supposedly Navaho. American Antiquity, 5 (1939): 4-20.

Malouf, C. and A. A. Malouf. The effects of Spanish slavery on the Indians of the Intermountain West. Southwestern Journal of Anthropology, 1 (1945): 378-391.

Marino, C. C. The Seboyetanos and the Navahos. New Mexico Historical Review, 29 (1954): 8-27.

Marinsek, Edward A., et al. The effect of cultural differences in the education of Pueblo, [Apache, and Navajo] Indians [and Spanish Americans]. Albuquerque, University of New Mexico, College of Education, 1958-1960. 4 v.

Martin, Harry W. Correlates of adjustment among American Indians in an urban environment. Human Organization, 23 (1964): 290-295.

Maruyama, Magoroh. The Navaho philosophy: an esthetic ethic of mutality. Mental Hygiene, 51 (1967): 242-249.

Mason, O. T. Aboriginal skin-dressing. United States National Museum, Reports (1889): 574-580.

Matis, John A. Odontognathic discrimination of United States Indian and Eskimo groups. By John A. Matis and

Thomas J. Zwemer. Journal of Dental Research, 50 (1971): 1245-1248.

Matthews, W. A Navajo initiation. Land of Sunshine, 15 (1901): 353-356.

Matthews, W. A part of the Navajos' mythology. American Antiquarian and Oriental Journal, 5 (1883): 207-224.

Matthews, W. A study in butts and tips. American Anthropologist, 5 (1892): 345-350.

Matthews, W. A two-faced Navaho blanket. American Anthropologist, n.s., 2 (1900): 638-642.

Matthews, W. A vigil of the gods. American Anthropologist, 9 (1896): 50-57.

Matthews, W. Ichthyophobia. Journal of American Folklore, 11 (1898): 105-112.

Matthews, W. Marriage prohibitions on the father's side among Navajos. Journal of American Folklore, 4 (1891): 78-79.

Matthews, W. Mythic dry-paintings of the Navajos. American Naturalist, 19 (1885): 931-939.

Matthews, W. Myths of gestation and parturition. American Anthropologist, n.s., 4 (1902): 737-742.

Matthews, W. Navaho legends. American Folk-Lore Society, Memoirs, 5 (1897): 1-300.

Matthews, W. Navaho myths, prayers and songs. Ed. by P. E. Goddard. California, University, Publications in American Archaeology and Ethnology, 5 (1907): 21-63.

Matthews, W. Navaho Night Chant. Journal of American Folklore, 14 (1901): 12-19.

Matthews, W. Navaho. U.S. Bureau of American Ethnology, Bulletin, 30, vol. 2 (1910): 41-45.

Matthews, W. Navaho dye stuffs. Smithsonian Institution, Annual Report of the Board of Regents (1891): 613-615.

Matthews, W. Navajo gambling songs. American Anthropologist, 2 (1889): 1-19.

Matthews, W. Navajo names for plants. American Naturalist, 20 (1886): 767-777.

Matthews, W. Navajo silversmiths. U.S. Bureau of American Ethnology, Annual Reports, 2 (1883): 167-179.

Matthews, W.   Navajo weavers. U.S. Bureau
of American Ethnology, Annual Reports, 3
(1884): 371-391.

Matthews, W.   Noqoilpi, the gambler: a
Navajo myth. Journal of American
Folklore, 2 (1889): 89-94.

Matthews, W.   Serpent worship among the
Navajos. Land of Sunshine, 9 (1898):
228-235.

Matthews, W.   Some deities and demons of
the Navajos. American Naturalist, 20
(1886): 841-850.

Matthews, W.   Some illustrations of the
connection between myth and ceremony.
International Congress of Anthropology,
Memoirs (1893): 246-251.

Matthews, W.   Some sacred objects of the
Navajo rites. International Folk-Lore
Association, Archives, 1 (1893): 227-
247.

Matthews, W.   Songs of sequence of the
Navajos. Journal of American Folklore, 7
(1894): 185-194.

Matthews, W.   Songs of the Navajos. Land
of Sunshine, 5 (1896): 197-201.

Matthews, W.   The basket drum. American
Anthropologist, 7 (1894): 202-208.

Matthews, W.   The gentile system of the
Navajo Indians. Journal of American
Folklore, 3 (1890): 89-110.

Matthews, W.   The Mountain Chant. U.S.
Bureau of American Ethnology, Annual
Reports, 5 (1887): 379-467.

Matthews, W.   The Night Chant. American
Museum of Natural History, Memoirs, 6
(1902): 1-332.

Matthews, W.   The origin of the Utes, a
Navajo myth. American Antiquarian and
Oriental Journal, 7 (1885): 271-274.

Matthews, W.   The prayer of a Navajo
shaman. American Anthropologist, 1
(1888): 149-170.

Matthews, W.   The study of ceremony.
Journal of American Folklore, 10 (1897):
259-263.

Matthews, W.   The study of ethics among
the lower races. Journal of American
Folklore, 12 (1899): 1-9.

Matthews, W.   The treatment of ailing
gods. Journal of American Folklore, 14
(1901): 20-23.

Matthews, Washington.   The mountain chant,
a Navajo ceremony. Glorieta, Rio Grande
Press, 1970.   379-564 p. illus., map.

Maxwell, Gilbert S.   Navajo rugs: past,
present and future. With Eugene L.
Conrotto.   Palm Desert, Calif., Desert-
Southwest Publications, 1963.   72 p.
illus., map.

McAllester, D. P.   Enemy Way music.
Harvard University, Peabody Museum of
American Archaeology and Ethnology,
Papers, 41, no. 3 (1954): 1-106.

McAllester, D. P., ed.   The myth and
prayers of the Great Star Chant and the
myth of the Coyote Chant. Navajo
Religion Series, 4 (1956): 1-190.

McCombe, L., et al.   Navaho means people.
Cambridge, 1951.   159 p.

McCracken, Robert Dale.   Urban migration
and the changing structure of Navajo
social relations. Dissertation
Abstracts, 29 (1968/1969): 1246B.   UM
68-14,216.

McCullough, C. W.   Modiste to Miss Navajo.
Arizona Highways, 31, no. 7 (1955): 8-
17.

McDermott, W., et al.   Introducing modern
medicine in a Navajo community. Science,
131 (1960): 197-205, 280-287.

McDermott, Walsh.   Health care experiment
at Many Farms. By Walsh McDermott, Kurt
W. Deuschle, and Clifford R. Barnett.
Science, 175 (1972): 23-31.

McGregor, J. C.   Zwei gegensätzliche
Indianer-Stämme in Arizona. Natur und
Volk, 68 (1938): 535-544.

McKibbin, D. B.   Revolt of the Navaho,
1913. New Mexico Historical Review, 29
(1954): 259-289.

McNitt, Frank.   Navajo campaigns and the
occupation of New Mexico, 1847-1848. New
Mexico Historical Review, 43 (1968):
173-194.

McNitt, Frank.   Navajo wars; military
campaigns, slave raids, and reprisals.
Albuquerque, University of New Mexico
Press, 1972.   12, 477 p. illus.

McPhee, J. C.   Indians in non-Indian
communities.   Window Rock, 1953.   68 p.

Melartin, Liisa.   Albumin polymorphism
(albumin Naskapi) in Eskimos and
Navajos. By Liisa Melartin, Baruch S.
Blumberg, and John R. Martin. Nature,
218 (1968): 787-789.

Mera, H. P.   Banded-background blankets.
Santa Fe, Laboratory of Anthropology,
Bulletin, General Series, 7 (1939): 1-
13.

Mera, H. P.   Cloth-strip blankets of the
Navaho. Santa Fe, Laboratory of
Anthropology, Bulletin, General Series,
16 (1945): 1-14.

Mera, H. P.   Navaho textile arts.   Santa
Fe, 1947.   102 p.

Mera, H. P.   Navaho twilled weaving. Santa
Fe, Laboratory of Anthropology,
Bulletin, General Series, 14 (1943): 1-
12.

Mera, H. P.   Navaho woven dresses. Santa
Fe, Laboratory of Anthropology,
Bulletin, General Series, 15 (1944): 1-
13.

Mera, H. P.   Navajo blankets of the
"classic" period. Santa Fe, Laboratory
of Anthropology, Bulletin, General
Series, 3 (1938): 1-4.

Mera, H. P.   The Chinlee rug. Santa Fe,
Laboratory of Anthropology, Bulletin,
General Series, 13 (1942): 1-15.

Mera, H. P.   The serrate designs of Navajo
blanketry. Santa Fe, Laboratory of
Anthropology, Bulletin, General Series,
11 (1940): 1-15.

Mera, H. P.   The zoning treatment in
Navajo blanket design. Santa Fe,
Laboratory of Anthropology, Bulletin,
General Series, 12 (1940): 1-13.

Mera, H. P.   Wedge-weave blankets. Santa
Fe, Laboratory of Anthropology,
Bulletin, General Series, 9 (1939): 1-
13.

Michener, Bryan P.   Validation of a test
to measure need-achievement motivation
among American Indian high school
students. Final report. Bethesda, Md.,
National Institute of Mental Health,
1969.   95 p.   ERIC ED034623.

Mico, Paul R.   A task for Amerindian
school health education. Journal of
School Health, 32 (1962): 316-320.

Mico, Paul R.   Navajo perception of Anglo
medicine. Berkeley, University of
California, School of Public Health,
1962.   56 p.   ERIC ED036383.

Mico, Paul R.   Some implications of the
Navaho Health Education Project for
Indian education. Journal of American
Indian Education, 2, no. 2 (1962/1963):
17-26.

Miller, Mary R.   The language and language
beliefs of Indian children.
Anthropological Linguistics, 12 (1970):
51-61.

Miller, Sheldon I.   Suicide attempt
patterns among the Navajo Indians. By
Sheldon I. Miller and Lawrence S.
Schoenfeld. International Journal of
Social Psychiatry, 17 (1971): 189-193.

Mills, G.   Navaho art and culture.
Colorado Springs, 1959.   273 p.

Mills, Loren F.   Epidemic in a Navajo
school. Menninger Clinic, Bulletin, 26
(1962): 189-194.

Mindeleff, C.   Navaho houses. U.S. Bureau
of American Ethnology, Annual Reports,
17, vol. 2 (1898): 475-517.

Mirkowich, N.   A note on Navajo place-
names. American Anthropologist, n.s., 43
(1941): 313-314.

Mitchell, Daniel Holmes.   An Indian
trader's plea for justice, 1906. Edited
by Clifford E. Trafzer. New Mexico
Historical Review, 47 (1972): 239-256.

Mitchell, Emerson Blackhorse.   Miracle
hill; the story of a Navaho boy. By
Emerson Blackhorse Mitchell and T. D.
Allen.   Norman, University of Oklahoma
Press, 1967.   17, 230 p.

Mitchell, F. G.   Dine bizad: a handbook
for beginners in the study of the Navaho
language.   Los Angeles, 1910.   127 p.

Mitchell, F. G.   Dineh bizan: Navajo, his
language.   New York, 1944.   128 p.

Mitchell, Frank.   The first horse-song of
Frank Mitchell (blue). Alcheringa, 1
(1970): 64-65.

Mitchell, Frank.   The thirteenth horse-
song of Frank Mitchell (white).
Alcheringa, 2 (1971): 94-95.

Mollhausen, B.   Reisen in die
Felsengebirge Nord-Amerikas, Vol. 2:
227-249.   Leipzig, 1861.

Monongye, Preston.   The new Indian jewelry
art of the Southwest. Arizona Highways,
48, no. 6 (1972): 6-11, 46-47.

Moon, Sheila.   A magic dwells; a poetic
and psychological study of the Navaho
emergence myth.   Middletown, Conn.,
Wesleyan University Press, 1970.   206 p.

Moore, John Leslie.   A study of incentives
and attitudes in the motivation of
Navajo Indian children in Bureau of
Indian Affairs elementary schools for

the development of hypothetical motivational techniques. Dissertation Abstracts International, 32 (1971/1972): 3868A.   UM 72-3816.

Morgan, Dale L.   Utah before the Mormons. Utah Historical Quarterly, 36 (1968): 4-23.

Morgan, W.   Human-wolves among the Navaho. Yale University Publications in Anthropology, 11 (1936): 1-43.

Morgan, W.   Navaho dreams. American Anthropologist, n.s., 34 (1932): 390-405.

Morgan, W.   Navaho treatment of sickness. American Anthropologist, n.s., 33 (1931): 390-402.

Morgan, W.   The organization of a story and a tale. Journal of American Folklore, 58 (1945): 169-194.

Morgan, W. and R. W. Young.   Coyote tales. Washington, D. C., 1949.   53 p.

Morgan, William.   Human-wolves among the Navaho.   New Haven, Human Relations Area Files Press, 1970.   43 p.   (Yale University Publications in Anthropology, 11)

Mori, John.   Hopi silversmithing. By John Mori and Joyce Mori. Masterkey, 44 (1970): 124-142.

Moskowitz, I. and J. Collier.   Patterns and ceremonials of the Indians of the Southwest, 31-49, 163-192. New York, 1949.

Muggia, Albert L.   Diseases among the Navajo Indians. Rocky Mountain Medical Journal, 68, no. 11 (1971): 39-49.

Muggia, Albert L.   Navajo arthritis--an unusual, acute, self-limited disease. By Albert L. Muggia, David A. Bennahum, and Ralph C. Williams, Jr. Arthritis and Rheumatism, 14 (1971): 348-355.

Murbarger, N.   Sacred sheep of the Navajos. Arizona Highways, 26 (August 1950): 11-15.

Murphy, Lawrence R.   Reconstruction in New Mexico. New Mexico Historical Review, 43 (1968): 99-115.

Nagata, Shuichi.   The reservation community and the urban community: Hopi Indians of Moenkopi. In Jack O. Waddell and O. Michael Watson, eds. The American Indian in Urban Society. Boston, Little, Brown, 1971: 114-159.

Nakai, Raymond.   Inaugural address. In Lester Thonssen, ed. Representative American Speeches: 1963/1964. New York, H. W. Wilson, 1964: 49-57.

Nakai, Raymond.   Will we meet the challenge? Journal of American Indian Education, 4, no. 1 (1964/1965): 10-16.

Napier, Arch.   The Navajo in the machine age: human resources are important too. By Arch Napier and Tom T. Sasaki. New Mexico Business, 11 (July 1958): 2-5.

Navajo Indians.   Navajo tribal code. Oxford, N.H., Equity Publishing, 1962. 2 v.   illus.

Navajo School of Indian Basketry, Los Angeles.   Indian basket weaving.   New York, Dover Publications, 1971.   103 p. illus.

Navajo Tribe, Navajo Parks and Recreation Department.   Welcome to the land of the Navajo. Compiled and edited by J. Lee Correll and Editha L. Watson.   Window Rock, 1969.   121 p.   illus.

Neumann, D. L.   Modern developments in Indian jewelry. El Palacio, 57 (1950): 173-180.

Neumann, D. L.   Navaho "channel" turquoise and silver. El Palacio, 61 (1954): 410-412.

Neumann, D. L.   Navaho silversmithing survives. El Palacio, 50 (1943): 6-8.

Neumann, D. L.   Navajo silver dies. El Palacio, 35 (1933): 71-75.

Neumann, D. L.   Navajo silverwork. El Palacio, 32 (1932): 102-108.

Neumann, D. L.   The future of Navaho silversmithing. El Palacio, 53 (1946): 6-8.

New, Lloyd.   Institute of American Indian Arts. Arizona Highways, 48, no. 1 (1972): 5, 12-15, 44-45.

New Mexico, University.   The Navajo orientation program, held at the University of New Mexico, June 20-July 15, 1960.   Albuquerque, University of New Mexico Press, 1960.   5, 130 l.

Newcomb, F. J.   How the Navajo adopt rites. El Palacio, 46 (1939): 25-27.

Newcomb, F. J.   Navajo omens and taboos. Santa Fe, 1940.   79 p.

Newcomb, F. J.   Navajo symbols of the sun. New Mexico Quarterly, 6 (1936): 305-307.

Newcomb, F. J. Origin legend of the Navajo Eagle Chant. Journal of American Folklore, 53 (1940): 50-77.

Newcomb, F. J. The Navajo Listening Rite. El Palacio, 45 (1938): 46-49.

Newcomb, F. J. and G. A. Reichard. Sandpaintings of the Navajo Shooting Chant. New York, 1937. 87 p.

Newcomb, F. J., et al. A study of Navajo symbolism. Harvard University, Peabody Museum of American Archaeology and Ethnology, Papers, 32, no. 3 (1956): 1-108.

Newcomb, Franc J. Hosteen Klah, Navaho medicine man and sand painter. Norman, University of Oklahoma Press, 1964. 33, 227 p. illus., maps.

Newcomb, Franc J. Navaho folk tales. Santa Fe, Museum of Navaho Ceremonial Art, 1967. 19, 203 p. illus.

Newcomb, Franc J. Navaho neighbors. Norman, University of Oklahoma Press, 1966. 9, 236 p. illus.

Newell, W. W. Navaho legends. Journal of American Folklore, 9 (1896): 211-218.

Nigg, C. A study of the blood groups among the American Indians. Journal of Immunology, 11 (1926): 319-322.

Nixon, Bert Wootton. Navajo parental attitudes and the effect of bilingual education on student self-concept in San Juan School District 1969-70. Dissertation Abstracts International, 32 (1971/1972): 1195A. UM 71-24,300.

Nölle, W. Die Navajo und Tewa heute. Tribus, 6 (1957): 102-108.

Norman, R. D. and K. L. Midkiff. Navaho children on Raven Progressive Matrices and Goodenough Draw-a-Man Tests. Southwestern Journal of Anthropology, 11 (1955): 129-136.

Oakes, M. Where the two came to their father. New York, 1943.

*O'Bryan, A. The Diné. U.S. Bureau of American Ethnology, Bulletin, 163 (1956): 1-194.

Oglesby, Catharine. Modern primitive arts of Mexico, Guatemala, and the Southwest. Freeport, N.Y., Books for Libraries Press, 1969. 226 p. illus.

Ohannessian, Sirarpi. The study of the problems of teaching English to American Indians, report and recommendations. Washington, D.C., Center for Applied Linguistics, 1967. 46 p. ERIC ED014727.

Olsen, Robert W., Jr. Conflict in the Arizona Strip: the first skirmish of the 1865-1869 Mormon-Navaho War. Pacific Coast Archaeological Society, Quarterly, 2, no. 1 (1966): 53-60.

Olsen, Robert W., Jr. Winsor Castle: Mormon frontier fort at Pipe Spring. Utah Historical Quarterly, 34 (1966): 218-226.

Opler, M. E. Examples of ceremonial interchanges among Southwestern tribes. Masterkey, 16 (1942): 77-80.

Opler, M. E. Navaho shamanistic practice among the Jicarilla Apache. New Mexico Anthropologist, 6/7 (1943): 13-18.

Opler, M. E. The kinship systems of the Southern Athabaskan-speaking tribes. American Anthropologist, n.s., 38 (1936): 620-633.

Opler, Morris E. Remuneration to supernaturals and man in Apachean ceremonialism. Ethnology, 7 (1968): 356-393.

Ostermann, L. Navajo houses. Franciscan Missions of the Southwest, 5 (1917): 20-30.

Ostermann, L. Navajo names. Franciscan Missions of the Southwest, 6 (1918): 11-15.

Ostermann, L. Origin, characteristics, and costume of the Navajo Indians. Franciscan Missions of the Southwest, 5 (1917): 1-11.

Ostermann, L. Silversmithing among the Navajos. Franciscan Missions of the Southwest, 7 (1919): 18-24.

Ostermann, L. The Navajo Indian blanket. Franciscan Missions of the Southwest, 6 (1918): 1-11.

Ostermann, L. The Navajo Indians. Anthropos, 3 (1908): 857-869.

Ostermann, L. The Navajo noun. International Congress of Americanists, Proceedings, 15, vol. 2 (1907): 243-254.

Overholt, M. E. Pictures in sand. Art and Archaeology, 34 (1933): 262-265.

Packard, Robert C. Demographic discrimination of American Indian and Alaskan Eskimo groups by means of Ejork analysis. By Robert C. Packard and Thomas J. Zwemer. Journal of Dental Research, 50 (1971): 364-370.

Page, G. B.   Navaho house types.
Flagstaff, Ariz., Museum of Northern
Arizona, Museum Notes, 9 (1937): 47-49.

Page, G. B.   The Navajo sweat house. New
Mexico Anthropologist, 2 (1937): 19-21.

Page, Irvine H.   Plasma lipids and
proteins and their relationship to
coronary disease among Navajo Indians.
By Irvine H. Page, Lena A. Lewis, and
Jarvey Gilbert. Circulation, 13 (1956):
675-679.

Painter, S. L.   Hemophilia (AHG
deficiency) and factor VII (stable
factor) deficiency in the American
Indian. Report of four cases. By S. L.
Painter and Rosamond Ellett. Rocky
Mountain Medical Journal, 57, no. 1
(1960): 65-68.

Palmer, F. L.   The configuration pattern
of Navajo culture. El Palacio, 41
(1936): 19-24.

Parfitt, G. J.   A survey of the oral
health of Navajo Indian children.
Archives of Oral Biology, 1 (1959/1960):
193-205.

Parker, Daniel Webster.   An analysis of
the social studies program in selected
elementary schools of the Bureau of
Indian Affairs on the Navajo Indian
Reservation. Dissertation Abstracts
International, 33 (1972/1973): 2242A.
UM 72-30,512.

Parman, Donald L.   Federal programs on the
Navajo Reservation, 1933-1942. American
Philosophical Society, Yearbook (1972):
508-509.

Parman, Donald L.   J. C. Morgan: Navajo
apostle of assimilation. Prologue, 4,
no. 2 (1972): 83-98.

Parman, Donald Lee.   The Indian Civilian
Conservation Corps. Dissertation
Abstracts, 27 (1966/1967): 3819A-3820A.
UM 67-3978.

Parsons, E. C.   Navaho folk tales. Journal
of American Folklore, 36 (1923): 368-
375.

Parsons, E. C.   Note on a Navajo war
dance. American Anthropologist, n.s., 21
(1919): 465-467.

Parsons, E. C.   Note on the Night Chant at
Tuwelchedu. American Anthropologist,
n.s., 23 (1921): 240-243.

Patzman, Stephen N.   Henry Chee Dodge: a
modern chief of the Navajos. Arizoniana,
5, no. 1 (1964): 35-41.

Pauker, Guy Jean.   Political structure. In
Evon Z. Vogt and Ethel M. Albert, eds.
The People of Rimrock. Cambridge,
Harvard University Press, 1966: 191-226.

Paxton, S. Gabe, Jr.   A study of the
composite self-concept of the
Southwestern Indian adolescent; an
inservice action research project of
Sherman Institute. Washington, D.C.,
Bureau of Indian Affairs, 1966. 32 p.
ERIC ED052878.

Pearson, Keith Laurence.   Processes of
political development in a Navajo
community. Dissertation Abstracts
International, 30 (1969/1970): 476B-
477B.   UM 69-13,369.

Peet, S. D.   The suastika and fire-worship
in America. American Antiquarian and
Oriental Journal, 26 (1904): 185-192.

Pepper, G. H.   Ah-jih-lee-hah-neh, a
Navaho legend. Journal of American
Folklore, 21 (1908): 178-183.

Pepper, G. H.   Die Deckenweberei der
Navajo-Indianer. Globus, 82 (1902): 133-
140.

Pepper, G. H.   Native Navajo dyes.
Papoose, 1, no. 3 (1903): 1-11.

Pepper, G. H.   The making of a Navajo
blanket. Everybody's Magazine, 6 (1902):
33-43.

Pepper, G. H.   The Navaho Indians.
Southern Workman, 29 (1900): 639-644.

Perceval, Don Louis.   A Navajo sketch
book. With a descriptive text by Clay
Lockett. Flagstaff, Northland Press,
1962. 98 p. illus.

Perchonock, Norma.   Navaho systems of
classification: some implications for
ethnoscience. By Norma Perchonock and
Oswald Werner. Ethnology, 8 (1969): 229-
242.

Petrakis, Nicholas L.   Cerumen in American
Indians: genetic implications of sticky
and dry types. By Nicholas L. Petrakis,
Kathryn T. Molohon, and David J. Tepper.
Science, 158 (1967): 1192-1193.

Pfister, O.   Instinctive psychoanalysis
among the Navajos. Journal of Nervous
and Mental Disease, 76 (1932): 234-254.

Pfister, O.   Instinktive Psychoanalyse
unter den Navajo Indianern. Imago, 18
(1932): 81-109.

Phelps-Stokes Fund.   The Navaho Indian
problem. New York, 1939. 127 p.

Pike, Kenneth L. Progressive neutralization in dimensions of Navaho stem matrices. By Kenneth L. Pike and Alton L. Becker. International Journal of American Linguistics, 30 (1964): 144-154.

Pillsbury, D. Tribal meeting of the Navajo. Desert, 15 (October 1952): 13-16.

Platero, Dillon, et al. Skirmish at Rough Rock. School Review, 79 (1970/1971): 57-108.

Pogue, J. E. The aboriginal use of turquoise in North America. American Anthropologist, n.s., 14 (1912): 437-466.

Pollock, F. A. Cultural significance of the Navajo problem. Texas Journal of Science, 2 (1950): 28-34.

Porvaznik, John. Surgical problems of the Navajo and Hopi Indians. American Journal of Surgery, 123 (1972): 545-548.

Porvaznik, John. Traditional Navajo medicine. GP, 36, no. 4 (1967): 179-182.

Posinsky, Sollie H. Navaho infancy and childhood. Psychiatric Quarterly, 37 (1963): 306-321.

Pospisil, F. Etnologické materiálie z jihozápadu U.S.A. Brno, 1932. 256 p.

Potter, Carole A. The Dean Kirk Ketoh Collection. Plateau, 36 (1964): 115-119.

Potts, Alfred M., 2d. Developing curriculum for Indian children. By Alfred M. Potts, 2d. and Mamie Sizemore. Alamosa, Colo., Adams State College, Center for Cultural Studies, 1964. 106 l. ERIC ED012188.

Pousma, R. H. He-who-always-wins. Grand Rapids, 1934. 147 p.

Pousma, R. H. Venereal disease among the Navahos. Southwestern Medicine, 13 (1929): 503-505.

Prosnitz, Leonard R. Diabetes mellitus among Navajo and Hopi Indians: the lack of vascular complications. By Leonard R. Prosnitz and Gerald L. Mandell. American Journal of the Medical Sciences, 253 (1967): 700-705.

Rabin, David L., et al. Untreated congenital hip disease: study of the epidemiology, natural history, and social aspects of the disease in a Navajo population. American Journal of Public Health, 55, no. 2, suppl. (1965): 1-44.

Rapoport, R. N. Changing Navaho religious values. Harvard University, Peabody Museum of American Archaeology and Ethnology, Papers, 41, no. 2 (1954): 1-152.

Rapoport, Robert N. History of the Galilean mission to the Rimrock Navaho. In Deward E. Walker, Jr., ed. The Emergent Native Americans. Boston, Little, Brown, 1972: 397-423.

Rasch, Philip J. Feuding at Farmington. New Mexico Historical Review, 40 (1965): 214-232.

Reagan, A. B. A Navaho fire dance. American Anthropologist, n.s., 36 (1934): 434-437.

Reagan, A. B. Navaho sports. Primitive Man, 5 (1932): 68-71.

Reagan, A. B. The influenza and the Navajo. Indiana Academy of Science, Proceedings, 29 (1919): 243-247.

Reagan, A. B. Utilization of the Navajo country. Iowa Academy of Science, Proceedings, 41 (1934): 215-237.

Reboussin, Roland. Achievement motivation in Navaho and white students. By Roland Reboussin and Joel W. Goldstein. American Anthropologist, 68 (1966): 740-744.

Reed, E. K. Information on the Navaho in 1706. American Anthropologist, n.s., 43 (1941): 485-487.

Reed, E. K. Navajo independence and acculturation. American Anthropologist, n.s., 43 (1941): 681-682.

Reed, E. K. Navajo monolingualism. American Anthropologist, n.s., 46 (1944): 147-149.

Reeve, F. D. A Navaho struggle for land. New Mexico Historical Review, 21 (1946): 1-21.

Reeve, F. D. Early Navaho geography. New Mexico Historical Review, 31 (1956): 290-309.

Reeve, F. D. Navaho-Spanish wars: 1680-1720. New Mexico Historical Review, 33 (1958): 205-231.

Reeve, F. D. Seventeenth century Navaho-Spanish relations. New Mexico Historical Review, 32 (1957): 36-52.

Reeve, F. D. The government and the Navaho. New Mexico Historical Review, 14 (1939): 82-114.

Reeve, F. D. The government and the
Navaho, 1883-1888. New Mexico Historical
Review, 18 (1943): 17-51.

Reeve, Frank D. Navaho foreign affairs,
1795-1846. Edited by Eleanor B. Adams
and John L. Kessell. New Mexico
Historical Review, 46 (1971): 101-132,
223-251.

Reeve, Frank D. Navaho-Spanish diplomacy,
1770-1790. New Mexico Historical Review,
35 (1960): 200-235.

Reeve, Frank D. The Navaho-Spanish peace:
1720's-1770's. New Mexico Historical
Review, 34 (1959): 9-40.

Reichard, G. A. A few instances of
cultural resistance in Southwest North
America. International Congress of
Americanists, Proceedings, 22, no. 2
(1926): 289-296.

Reichard, G. A. Attitudes toward
avoidance. In Essays in Anthropology
Presented to A. L. Kroeber. Berkeley,
1936: 265-272.

Reichard, G. A. Color in Navajo weaving.
Arizona Historical Review, 7 (1936): 19-
30.

Reichard, G. A. Dezba, woman of the
desert. New York, 1939. 161 p.

Reichard, G. A. Distinctive features of
Navaho religion. Southwestern Journal of
Anthropology, 1 (1945): 199-220.

Reichard, G. A. Good characters in myth.
Journal of American Folklore, 56 (1943):
141-143.

Reichard, G. A. Human nature as conceived
by the Navajo Indians. Review of
Religion, 6 (1943): 353-360.

Reichard, G. A. Individualism and
mythological style. Journal of American
Folklore, 57 (1944): 16-25.

Reichard, G. A. Linguistic diversity
among the Navaho Indians. International
Journal of American Linguistics, 11
(1945): 156-168.

Reichard, G. A. Navaho grammar. American
Ethnological Society, Publications, 21
(1951): 1-407.

*Reichard, G. A. Navaho religion. New
York, 1950. 2 v.

Reichard, G. A. Navajo classification of
natural objects. Plateau, 21 (1948): 7-
12.

Reichard, G. A. Navajo medicine man. New
York, 1939. 83 p.

Reichard, G. A. Navajo shepherd and
weaver. New York, 1936. 222 p.

Reichard, G. A. Prayer: the compulsive
word. American Ethnological Society,
Monographs, 7 (1944): 1-97.

Reichard, G. A. Significance of
aspiration in Navaho. International
Journal of American Linguistics, 14
(1948): 15-20.

*Reichard, G. A. Social life of the Navajo
Indians. Columbia University
Contributions to Anthropology, 7 (1928):
1-239.

Reichard, G. A. Spider Woman. New York,
1934. 287 p.

Reichard, G. A. The character of the
Navaho verb stem. Word, 5 (1949): 55-76.

Reichard, G. A. The Navaho and
Christianity. American Anthropologist,
n.s., 51 (1949): 66-71.

Reichard, G. A. The story of the Navajo
Hail Chant. New York, 1944. 155 p.

Reichard, G. A. The translation of two
Navaho chant words. American
Anthropologist, n.s., 44 (1942): 421-
424.

Reichard, G. A. and A. D. Bittany.
Agentive and causative elements in
Navajo. New York, 1940. 22 p.

Reichard, Gladys A. Dezba: woman of the
desert. Glorieta, N.M., Rio Grande
Press, 1971. 26, 161 p. illus.

*Reichard, Gladys A. Navaho religion, a
study of symbolism. 2d ed. New York,
Bollingen Foundation, 1963. 47, 804 p.
illus. (Bollingen Series, 18)

Reichard, Gladys A. Navajo shepherd and
weaver. Glorieta, Rio Grande Press,
1968. 18, 222 p. illus., map.

*Reichard, Gladys A. Social life of the
Navajo Indians, with some attention to
minor ceremonies. New York, AMS Press,
1969. 7, 239 p. illus.

Reichard, Gladys A. Spider woman; a story
of Navajo weavers and chanters.
Glorieta, Rio Grande Press, 1968. 10,
287 p. illus., map.

Reno, Philip. Manpower planning for
Navajo employment: training for jobs in
a surplus-labor area. New Mexico
Business, 23, no. 6 (1970): 8-16.

Reno, Philip. Vocational education needs and opportunities for Indians; a review of the Navajo situation and a summary of its implications for Four Corners regional planning. Farmington, N.M., Four Corners Regional Commission, 1969. 34 p. tables. ERIC ED052874.

Reno, Thomas R. A demonstration in Navaho education. Journal of American Indian Education, 6, no. 3 (1966/1967): 1-5.

Ressler, John Quenton. Moenkopi: sequent occupance, landscape change, and the view of the environment in an oasis on the western Navajo Reservation, Arizona. Dissertation Abstracts International, 31 (1970/1971): 6059B-6060B. UM 71-10,777.

Reynolds, Terry Ray. Time, resources, and authority in a Navaho community. By Terry Ray Reynolds, Louise Lamphere, and Cecil E. Cook, Jr. American Anthropologist, 69 (1967): 188-199.

Rice, Josiah M. A cannoneer in Navajo country; journal of Private Josiah M. Rice, 1851. Edited by Richard H. Dillon. Denver, Published for the Denver Public Library by the Old West Publishing, 1970. 123 p. illus., map.

Richards, Cara E. Cooperation between anthropologist and medical personnel. Human Organization, 19 (1960/1961): 64-67.

Richards, Cara E. Modern residence patterns among the Navajo. El Palacio, 70 (1963): 25-33.

Riley, C. L. A survey of Navajo archaeology. Colorado, University, Studies, Series in Anthropology, 4 (1954): 45-60.

Rimoin, David L. Diabetes mellitus among the Navajo. II. Plasma glucose and insulin responses. By David L. Rimoin and John H. Saiki. Archives of Internal Medicine, 122 (1968): 6-9.

Rimoin, David L. Ethnic variability in glucose tolerance and insulin secretion. Archives of Internal Medicine, 124 (1969): 695-700.

*Roberts, J. M. Three Navaho households. Harvard University, Peabody Museum of American Archaeology and Ethnology, Papers, 40, no. 3 (1951): 1-101.

Robinson, J. S. A journal of the Santa Fe expedition under Col. Doniphan. Ed. by C. L. Cannon. Princeton, 1932. 96 p.

Roessel, Robert A., Jr. An overview of the Rough Rock Demonstration School. Journal of American Indian Education, 7, no. 3 (1967/1968): 2-14.

Roessel, Robert A., Jr. Cases and concepts in community development; a case study approach to community development among Southwestern Indians. Tempe, Arizona State University, Indian Education Center, 1963. 227 l.

Roessel, Robert A., Jr., ed. Coyote stories of the Navaho people. Edited by Robert A. Roessel, Jr. and Dillon Platero. Chinle, Ariz., Rough Rock Demonstration School, 1968. 144 p.

Roessel, Robert A., Jr., et al. Indian communities in action. Tempe, Arizona State University, Bureau of Publications, 1967. 223 p. illus.

Roessel, Ruth. Navajo studies at Navajo Community College. Many Farms, Ariz., Navajo Community College Press, 1971. 13, 129 p. illus.

Roessel, Ruth, comp. Papers on Navajo culture and life. Many Farms, Ariz., Navajo Community College Press, 1970. 2, 193 p. illus., map.

Rollins, W. E. Passing of the spirit dance. El Palacio, 7 (1919): 187-191.

Rollins, W. E. The spirit of the dead. El Palacio, 12 (1922): 71-73.

Rothenberg, Jerome. A note to accompany "The first horse-song of Frank Mitchell". Alcheringa, 1 (1970): 63.

Rush, E. M. Indian legends. El Palacio, 32 (1932): 137-154.

Sabatino, David A. Perceptual, language, and academic achievement of English, Spanish, and Navajo speaking children referred for special classes. By David A. Sabatino, David L. Hayden, and Kent Kelling. Journal of School Psychology, 10 (1972): 39-46.

Saiki, John H. Diabetes mellitus among the Navajo. I. Clinical features. By John H. Saiki and David L. Rimoin. Archives of Internal Medicine, 122 (1968): 1-5.

Salsbury, C. G. Disease incidence among the Navajoes. Southwestern Medicine, 21 (1937): 230-233.

Sampliner, James E. Biliary surgery in the Southwestern American Indian. By James E. Sampliner and Daniel J. O'Connell. Archives of Surgery, 96 (1968): 1-3.

Sanchez, G. I. "The people". Lawrence, 1948. 90 p.

Sapir, E. A Navaho sand painting blanket. American Anthropologist, n.s., 37 (1935): 609-616.

Sapir, E. Glottalized continuants in Navaho, Nootka, and Kwakiutl. Language, 14 (1938): 248-274.

Sapir, E. Internal linguistic evidence suggestive of the northern origin of the Navaho. American Anthropologist, n.s., 38 (1936): 224-235.

Sapir, E. Two Navaho puns. Language, 8 (1932): 217-219.

Sapir, E. and A. G. Sandoval. A note on Navaho pottery. American Anthropologist, n.s., 32 (1930): 575-576.

Sapir, E. and H. Hoijer. Navaho texts. Iowa City, 1942. 543 p.

Sapir, Edward. The phonology and morphology of the Navaho language. By Edward Sapir and Harry Hoijer. Berkeley, University of California Press, 1967. 10, 124 p. (California, University, Publications in Linguistics, 50)

Sasaki, T. T. Sociocultural problems in introducing new technology on a Navaho irrigation project. Rural Sociology, 21 (1956): 307-310.

Sasaki, T. T. and J. Adair. New land to farm. In Edward H. Spicer, ed. Human Problems in Technological Change. New York, 1952: 97-112.

Sasaki, Tom T. Fruitland, New Mexico: a Navaho community in transition. Ithaca, Cornell University Press, 1960. 17, 217 p. illus., map.

Sasaki, Tom T. Sources of income among Many Farms--Rough Rock Navajo and Jicarilla Apache: some comparisons and comments. By Tom T. Sasaki and Harry W. Basehart. Human Organization, 20 (1961/1962): 187-190.

Savard, Robert J. Effects of disulfiram therapy on relationships within the Navaho drinking group. Quarterly Journal of Studies on Alcohol, 29 (1968): 909-916.

Savard, Robert Joseph. Cultural stress and alcoholism: a study of their relationship among Navaho alcoholic men. Dissertation Abstracts, 29 (1968/1969): 2807A. UM 69-1532.

Saville, Muriel Renee. Navajo morphophonemics. Dissertation Abstracts, 29 (1968/1969): 3600A. UM 69-6208.

Schaafsma, Polly. Early Navaho rock paintings and carvings. Santa Fe, Museum of Navaho Ceremonial Art, 1966. 32 p. illus., map.

Schaafsma, Polly. Rock art in the Navajo reservoir district. Santa Fe, Museum of New Mexico Press, 1963. 74 p. illus., maps. (Museum of New Mexico, Papers in Anthropology, 7)

Schaafsma, Polly. Rock art of the Navajo Reservoir. El Palacio, 69 (1962): 193-212.

Schevill, M. E. Beautiful on the earth. Tucson, 1947. 155 p.

Schevill, M. E. The Navajo screen. Kiva, 11 (1945): 3-5.

Schoenfeld, Lawrence S. We like us: the attitudes of the mental health staff toward other agencies on the Navajo Reservation. By Lawrence S. Schoenfeld, R. Jeannine Lyerly, and Sheldon I. Miller. Mental Hygiene, 55 (1971): 171-173.

Scholder, Veda. Along Navajo trails. By Violet May Cummings. Washington, D.C., Review and Herald Publishing Association, 1964. 189 p. illus.

Schroeder, Albert H. Navajo and Apache relationships west of the Rio Grande. El Palacio, 70, no. 3 (1963): 5-23.

Schwartz, Douglas W. A historical analysis and synthesis of Grand Canyon archaeology. American Antiquity, 31 (1965/1966): 469-484.

Scott, Don. Progressive supranuclear palsy in a Navajo. Rocky Mountain Medical Journal, 67, no. 9 (1970): 35-37.

Sears, P. M. Tuberculosis and the Navahos. Colorado Quarterly, 4 (1955): 195-204.

Senter, D. and F. Hawley. Hopi and Navajo child burials. American Anthropologist, n.s., 39 (1937): 131-134.

Service, E. R. The Navaho of the American Southwest. In Elman R. Service. A Profile of Primitive Culture. New York, 1958: 157-181.

Shepardson, Mary. Change and persistence in an isolated Navajo community. By Mary Shepardson and Blodwen Hammond. American Anthropologist, 66 (1964): 1029-1050.

Shepardson, Mary. Navajo inheritance patterns: random or regular? By Mary Shepardson and Blodwen Hammond. Ethnology, 5 (1966): 87-96.

Shepardson, Mary. Navajo ways in government; a study in political process. Menasha, 1963. 11, 132 p. map. (American Anthropological Association, Memoir, 96)

Shepardson, Mary. Problems of the Navajo tribal courts in transition. Human Organization, 24 (1965): 250-253.

*Shepardson, Mary. The Navajo Mountain community; social organization and kinship terminology. By Mary Shepardson and Blodwen Hammond. Berkeley, University of California Press, 1970. 9, 278 p. illus., map.

Shepardson, Mary. Value theory in the prediction of political behavior: the Navajo case. American Anthropologist, 64 (1962): 742-750.

Shinkle, James D. Fort Sumner and the Bosque Redondo Indian Reservation. Roswell, Hall-Poorbaugh Press, 1965. 9, 85 p. illus.

Shipley, Alice M. I taught "related subjects" to the special Navahos. Journal of American Indian Education, 3, no. 2 (1963/1964): 19-21.

Shiya, T. S., ed. Navaho saga. St. Michaels, 1949. 56 p.

Shufeldt, R. W. A Navajo artist and his notions of mechanical drawing. Smithsonian Institution, Annual Report of the Board of Regents (1886): 240-244.

Shufeldt, R. W. A Navajo skull. Journal of Anatomy and Physiology, 20 (1886): 426-429.

Shufeldt, R. W. A skull of a Navajo child. Journal of Anatomy and Physiology, 21 (1886): 66-71.

Shufeldt, R. W. Arrow-release among the Navajos. American Naturalist, 21 (1887): 784-786.

Shufeldt, R. W. Head-flattening as seen among the Navajo Indians. Popular Science Monthly, 39 (1891): 535-539.

Shufeldt, R. W. Mortuary customs of the Navajo Indians. American Naturalist, 25 (1891): 303-306.

Shufeldt, R. W. The drawings of a Navajo artist. Magazine of American History, 22 (1889): 462-468.

Shufeldt, R. W. The evolution of house-building among the Navajo Indians. United States National Museum, Proceedings, 15 (1892): 279-282.

Shufeldt, R. W. The Navajo belt-weaver. United States National Museum, Proceedings, 14 (1891): 391-395.

Shufeldt, R. W. The Navajo tanner. United States National Museum, Proceedings, 11 (1888): 59-66.

Sievers, Maurice L. A study of achlorhydria among Southwestern American Indians. American Journal of Gastroenterology, 45 (1966): 99-108.

Sievers, Maurice L. Serum cholesterol levels in Southwestern American Indians. Journal of Chronic Diseases, 21 (1968): 107-115.

Simpson, James Hervey. Navaho expedition; journal of a military reconnaissance from Santa Fe, New Mexico, to the Navaho country made in 1849. Edited by Frank McNitt. Norman, University of Oklahoma Press, 1964. 79, 296 p. illus.

Sleight, F. W. The Navajo sacred mountain of the east--a controversy. El Palacio, 58 (1951): 379-397.

Smith, Anne Marie. New Mexico Indians; economic, educational, and social problems. Santa Fe, Museum of New Mexico, 1966. 165 p. (Museum of New Mexico, Research Records, RR-1) ERIC ED019172.

Smith, D. M. Indian tribes of the Southwest, 56-79. Stanford, 1933.

Smith, Robert Lincoln. Cardiovascular-renal and diabetes deaths among Navajos. U.S., Public Health Service, Public Health Reports, 72 (1957): 33-38.

Snyder, Peter Z. The social environment of the urban Indian. In Jack O. Waddell and O. Michael Watson, eds. The American Indian in Urban Society. Boston, Little, Brown, 1971: 206-243.

Snyder, Peter Zane. The social assimilation and adjustment of Navaho Indian migrants to Denver, Colorado. Dissertation Abstracts, 29 (1968/1969): 854B. UM 68-12,427.

Son of Bead Chant Singer. Song of the talking god: a Navajo transposition. Translated by Harry Hoijer. Alcheringa, 1 (1970): 47-49.

Specific Development Consultants. Land of the Navajo. Sherman Oaks, Calif., 1963. illus.

Spencer, K.   Mythology and values. American Folk-Lore Society, Memoirs, 48 (1957): 1-248.

Spencer, K.   Reflections of social life in the Navaho origin myth. New Mexico, University, Publications in Anthropology, 3 (1947): 1-140.

Spencer, Virginia E.   Navajo dwellings of rural Black Creek Valley, Arizona-New Mexico. By Virginia E. Spencer and Stephen C. Jett. Plateau, 43 (1971): 159-175.

Spicer, E. H. and J. Collier.   Sheepmen and technicians. In Edward H. Spicer, ed. Human Problems in Technological Change. New York, 1952: 185-208.

Spicer, Edward H.   European expansion and the enclavement of Southwestern Indians. Arizona and the West, 1 (1959): 132-145.

Spiegelberg, A. F.   Navajo blankets. Out West, 20 (1904): 447-449.

Spiegelberg, A. F.   The Navajo blanket. Old Santa Fe, 2 (1915): 323-337.

Spuhler, J. N. and C. Kluckhohn. Inbreeding coefficients of the Ramah Navaho population. Human Biology, 25 (1953): 295-317.

Stafford, Kenneth.   Problem solving by Navajo children in relation to knowledge of English. Journal of American Indian Education, 4, no. 2 (1964/1965): 23-25.

Stafford, Kenneth R.   Problem solving as a function of language. Language and Speech, 11 (1968): 104-112.

Stafford, Kenneth R.   Types of bilingualism and performance of Navaho children in school. Phase I. Final report. By Kenneth R. Stafford and Don Milam. Tempe, Arizona State University, Department of Educational Psychology, 1970. 13 p. ERIC ED044702.

Stanley, Richard.   Book review of The Phonology and Morphology of the Navaho Language, by Edward Sapir and Harry Hoijer. Language, 45 (1969): 927-939.

Steggerda, M.   Form discrimination test as given to Navajo, Negro and White school children. Human Biology, 13 (1941): 239-246.

Steggerda, M.   Physical measurements on Negro, Navajo, and White girls of college age. American Journal of Physical Anthropology, 26 (1940): 417-430.

Steggerda, M.   The McAdory Art Test applied to Navaho Indian children. Journal of Comparative Psychology, 22 (1936): 283-285.

Steggerda, M. and E. Macomber.   Mental and social characteristics of Maya and Navajo Indians. Journal of Social Psychology, 10 (1939): 51-59.

Steggerda, M. and R. B. Eckardt.   Navaho foods and their preparation. American Dietetic Association, Journal, 17 (1941): 217-225.

Steggerda, M. and T. J. Hill.   Eruption time of teeth among White, Negro, and Indian. American Journal of Orthodontics and Oral Surgery, 28 (1942): 361-370.

Steggerda, M. and T. J. Hill.   Incidence of dental caries among Maya and Navajo Indians. Journal of Dental Research, 15 (1936): 233-242.

Stegner, Wallace E.   Navajo rodeo. In his The Sound of Mountain Water. Garden City, Doubleday, 1969: 94-101.

Stephen, A. M.   Navajo origin legend. Journal of American Folklore, 43 (1932): 88-104.

Stephen, A. M.   The Navajo. American Anthropologist, 6 (1893): 345-362.

Stephen, A. M.   The Navajo shoemaker. United States National Museum, Proceedings, 11 (1888): 131-136.

Stephen, A. M.   When John the Jeweler was sick. In E. C. Parsons, ed. American Indian Life. New York, 1925: 153-156.

Stephen, Alexander M.   The Navajo. In Frederica de Laguna, ed. Selected Papers from the American Anthropologist 1888-1920. Evanston, Row, Peterson, 1960: 457-475.

Stephens, E. L. Steve.   West of the Pecos. New Mexico Historical Review, 35 (1960): 81-108, 236-256, 309-326; 36 (1961): 159-174.

Stevens, A.   Once they were nomads. Survey Graphic, 30 (1941): 60-67.

Stevenson, J.   Ceremonial of Hasjelti Dailjis and mythical sand painting of the Navajo Indians. U.S. Bureau of American Ethnology, Annual Reports, 8 (1891): 235-285.

Stewart, O. C.   The Navaho wedding basket. Flagstaff, Ariz., Museum of Northern Arizona, Museum Notes, 10 (1938): 25-28.

Stirling, Betty. Mission to the Navajo.
Mountain View, Calif., Pacific Press
Pub. Association, 1961. 147 p. illus.

Stocker, J. Indian country. Arizona
Highways, 31, no. 7 (1955): 18-29.

Straus, Reuben. Biochemical studies in
full-blooded Navajo Indians. By Reuben
Straus, Jarvey Gilbert, and Moses Wurm.
Circulation, 19 (1959): 420-423.

Streeper, R. B., et al. An
electrocardiographic and autopsy study
of coronary heart disease in the Navajo.
Diseases of the Chest, 38 (1960): 305-
312.

Streib, G. F. An attempt to unionize a
semi-literate Navaho group. Human
Organization, 11, no. 1 (1952): 23-31.

Stucki, Larry R. The case against
population control: the probable
creation of the first American Indian
state. Human Organization, 30 (1971):
393-399.

Suci, George J. A comparison of semantic
structures in American Southwest culture
groups. Journal of Abnormal and Social
Psychology, 61 (1960): 25-30.

Sullivan, B. S. The unvanishing Navajos.
Philadelphia, 1938. 141 p.

Supplee, Charles, et al. Canyon de
Chelly: the story behind the scenery.
Las Vegas, KC Publications, 1971.
32 p. illus.

Swanson, Guy E. Rules of descent: studies
in the sociology of parentage. Ann
Arbor, University of Michigan, 1969. 5,
108 p. (Michigan, University, Museum of
Anthropology, Anthropological Papers,
39)

Tanner, C. L. Navajo silver craft.
Arizona Highways, 30, no. 8 (1954): 16-
33.

Tanner, C. L. and C. R. Steen. A Navajo
burial of about 1850. Panhandle-Plains
Historical Review, 28 (1955): 110-118.

Teeter, Karl V. Consonant harmony in
Wiyot (with a note on Cree).
International Journal of American
Linguistics, 25 (1959): 41-43.

Terrell, John U. The Navajos; the past
and present of a great people. New
York, Weybright and Talley, 1970. 8,
310 p. maps.

Thiel, Richard Henry. An analysis of
social-cultural factors and performance
of primary grade children. Dissertation

Abstracts, 29 (1968/1969): 4394A. UM
69-9043.

Thompson, L. Attitudes and acculturation.
American Anthropologist, n.s., 50
(1948): 200-215.

Thomsen, Ulf. Navaho-indianerne; den
største indianerstamme i U.S.A.
København, Gyldendal, 1957. 28 p.
illus.

Topper, Martin David. The daily life of a
traditional Navajo household: an
ethnographic study in human daily
activities. Dissertation Abstracts
International, 33 (1972/1973): 4633B.
UM 73-10,303.

Tozzer, A. M. A Navajo sand picture of
the rain gods and its attendant
ceremony. International Congress of
Americanists, Proceedings, 13 (1902):
147-156.

Tozzer, A. M. A note on star-lore among
the Navajos. Journal of American
Folklore, 21 (1908): 28-32.

Tozzer, A. M. Notes on religious
ceremonials of the Navaho. In Putnam
Anniversary Volume. New York, 1909:
299-343.

Tremblay, M. A., et al. Navaho housing in
transition. América Indígena, 14 (1954):
182-219.

Tschopik, H. Navaho basketry. American
Anthropologist, n.s., 42 (1940): 444-
462.

Tschopik, H. Navaho pottery making.
Harvard University, Peabody Museum of
American Archaeology and Ethnology,
Papers, 17 (1941): 1-85.

Tschopik, H. Taboo as a possible factor
involved in the obsolescence of Navaho
pottery and basketry. American
Anthropologist, n.s., 40 (1938): 257-
262.

Tunley, Roul. Smooth path at Rough Rock.
American Education, 7, no. 2 (1971): 15-
20.

Tweedie, M. Jean. Notes on the history
and adaptation of the Apache tribes.
American Anthropologist, 70 (1968):
1132-1142.

Uchendu, Victor Chikezie. Seasonal
agricultural labor among the Navaho
Indians: a study in socio-economic
transition. Dissertation Abstracts, 27
(1966/1967): 1706B. UM 66-14,081.

Underhill, R. M. Acculturation among the
Navaho Indians. International Congress
of Americanists, Proceedings, 31, vol. 1
(1855): 11-13.

Underhill, R. M. Here come the Navaho.
Indian Life and Customs Pamphlets, 8
(1953): 1-285.

Underhill, R. M. Men of the mountain.
Arizona Quarterly, 6 (1950): 147-157.

Underhill, Ruth M. The Navajos. Rev. ed.
Norman, University of Oklahoma Press,
1967. 16, 292 p. illus., maps.

U.S., Bureau of Indian Affairs.
Curriculum needs of Navajo pupils.
Window Rock, Ariz., 1969. 51 p. ERIC
ED033773.

U.S., Bureau of Indian Affairs. Doorway
toward the light; the story of the
special Navajo education program. By L.
Madison Coombs. Washington, D.C., 1962.
10, 174 p. illus. ERIC ED024491.

U.S., Bureau of Indian Affairs. The
Navajo. Washington, D.C., 1963. 3,
18 p. illus., maps.

U.S. Bureau of Indian Affairs. You asked
about the Navajo. Lawrence, 1957.
42 p.

U.S., Commissioner of Indian Affairs.
Navajo Bordertown Dormitory Program.
Report to the Senate Appropriations
Committee by the Commissioner of Indian
Affairs. Washington, D.C., U.S. Bureau
of Indian Affairs, 1965. 74 p. ERIC
ED024490.

U.S., Congress, House, Committee on
Interior and Insular Affairs,
Subcommittee on Indian Affairs.
Partition of Navajo and Hopi 1882
reservation. Hearings, Ninety-second
Congress, second session, on H.R. 1128,
H.R. 4753, and H.R. 4754 . . . April 17
and 18, 1972. Washington, D.C.,
Government Printing Office, 1972. 6,
284 p. illus.

U.S., Congress, Senate, Committee on
Interior and Insular Affairs,
Subcommittee on Indian Affairs.
Authorize partition of surface rights of
Navaho-Hopi Indian land. Hearings . . .
on H.R. 11128 . . . September 14 and 15,
1972. Washington, D.C., Government
Printing Office, 1972. 6, 266 p.
illus.

U.S., Congress, Senate, Committee on
Interior and Insular Affairs,
Subcommittee on Water and Power
Resources. Navajo Indian irrigation

project. Washington, D.C., Government
Printing Office, 1969. 3, 34 p.

U.S. Department of the Interior.
Statistical summary; human dependency
survey, Navajo Reservation and Grazing
District. Window Rock, 1941.

U.S., General Accounting Office.
Assessment of the Teacher Corps program
at Northern Arizona University and
participating schools on the Navajo and
Hopi Indian Reservations. Washington,
D.C., 1971. 4, 38 p. illus., map.

U.S., General Accounting Office.
Deficiencies in the administration of
the Navajo Indian Reservation road
construction program. . . . Washington,
D.C., 1964. 2, 71 l.

U.S., General Accounting Office. Need for
effective guidance of Navajo Tribe of
Indians in management of tribal funds.
Washington, D.C., 1966. 2, 49 p.

U.S. Indian Service. You asked about the
Navaho! Lawrence, 1949. 69 p.

U.S., Treaties, etc., 1865-1869 (Johnson).
Treaty between the United States of
America and the Navajo Tribe of Indians.
Flagstaff, K. C. Publications, 1968.
26 p.

Utley, Robert M. The reservation trader
in Navajo history. El Palacio, 68
(1961): 5-27.

Utley, Robert M., ed. Captain John Pope's
plan of 1853 for the frontier defense of
New Mexico. Arizona and the West, 5
(1963): 149-163.

Valkenburgh, R. F. van. A short history
of the Navajo people. Window Rock,
1938. 56 p.

Valkenburgh, R. F. van. A striking Navaho
pictograph. Masterkey, 12 (1938): 153-
157.

Valkenburgh, R. F. van. Christmas legend
of the Navajo. Desert Magazine, 6
(1942): 19-23.

Valkenburgh, R. F. van. Dinebikeyah.
Window Rock, 1940. 175 p.

Valkenburgh, R. F. van. Navajo common
law. Flagstaff, Ariz., Museum of
Northern Arizona, Museum Notes, 9
(1936): 17-22, 51-54; 10 (1938): 39-45.

Valkenburgh, R. F. van. Navajo
Naat'a'ani. Kiva, 13 (1948): 14-23.

Valkenburgh, R. F. van and F. O. Walker. Old placenames in the Navaho country. Masterkey, 19 (1945): 89-94.

Valkenburgh, R. F. van and S. Begay. Sacred places and shrines of the Navajo. Flagstaff, Ariz., Museum of Northern Arizona, Museum Notes, 11 (1938): 29-34; 13 (1940): 6-10.

Van Duzen, Jean, et al. Protein and calorie malnutrition among preschool Navajo Indian children. American Journal of Clinical Nutrition, 22 (1969): 1362-1370.

Van Duzen, Jean L. Medical practice on the Navajo Reservation. American Medical Women's Association, Journal, 19 (1964): 558-560.

Vann, D. V. Meals for Navajos. Smoke Signals, 3, no. 2 (1951): 5-6.

Various. Navajo-U.S. Treaty of June 1, 1868; the complete text. Indian Historian, 1, no. 2 (1967/1968): 35-38.

*Vestal, P. A. Ethnobotany of the Ramah Navaho. Harvard University, Peabody Museum of American Archaeology and Ethnology, Papers, 40, no. 4 (1952): 1-104.

Vestal, P. A. Uncultivated food plants used by the Ramah Navaho. American Journal of Botany, 31, no. 8 (1944): 65.

Vincentia, Sister. Our students learn from the Indians. Nursing Outlook, 9 (1961): 356-358.

Vivian, G. Two Navaho baskets. El Palacio, 64 (1957): 145-155.

Vlahcevic, Z. R., et al. Relation of bile acid pool size to the formation of lithogenic bile in female Indians of the Southwest. Gastroenterology, 62 (1972): 73-83.

Vleet, T. S. van. Legendary evolution of the Navajo Indians. American Naturalist, 27 (1893): 69-79.

Voegelin, Carl F. Languages of the world: Ibero-Caucasian and Pidgin-Creole. Fascicle one. By C. F. Voegelin and F. M. Voegelin. Anthropological Linguistics, 6, no. 8 (1964): 1-71.

Voegelin, Carl F. The autonomy of linguistics and the dependence of cognitive culture. By C. F. and F. M. Voegelin. In Jesse Sawyer, ed. Studies in American Indian Languages. Berkeley and Los Angeles, University of California Press, 1971: 303-317.

(California, University, Publications in Linguistics, 65)

Vogt, E. Z. Between two worlds. American Indian, 5, no. 1 (1949): 13-21.

*Vogt, E. Z. Navaho veterans. Harvard University, Peabody Museum of American Archaeology and Ethnology, Papers, 41, no. 1 (1951): 1-243.

Vogt, E. Z. The automobile in contemporary Navaho culture. International Congress of the Anthropological and Ethnological Sciences, Acts, 5 (1960): 359-363.

Vogt, Evon Z. A study of values. By Evon Z. Vogt and John M. Roberts. Scientific American, 195, no. 1 (1956): 25-31.

Vogt, Evon Z. On the concepts of structure and process in cultural anthropology. American Anthropologist, 62 (1960): 18-33.

Vogt, Evon Zartman. Ecology and economy. In Evon Z. Vogt and Ethel M. Albert, eds. The People of Rimrock. Cambridge, Harvard University Press, 1966: 160-190.

Vogt, Evon Zartman. Intercultural relations. In Evon Z. Vogt and Ethel M. Albert, eds. The People of Rimrock. Cambridge, Harvard University Press, 1966: 46-82.

Wagner, Sallie. Christmas at Wide Ruins. El Palacio, 77, no. 2 (1971): 33-35.

Wake, C. S. A Navaho origin legend. American Antiquarian and Oriental Journal, 26 (1904): 265-271.

Walker, John G. The Navajo reconnaissance; a military exploration of the Navajo country in 1859. By J. G. Walker and O. L. Shepherd. Edited by L. R. Bailey. Los Angeles, Westernlore Press, 1964. 9, 111 p. illus., maps.

Wall, L. and W. Morgan. Navaho-English dictionary. Phoenix, 1958. 65 p.

Wallach, Edward E. Patient acceptance of oral contraceptives. I. The American Indian. By Edward E. Wallach, Alan E. Beer, and Celso-Ramon Garcia. American Journal of Obstetrics and Gynecology, 97 (1967): 984-991.

Wallis, Ethel Emily. God speaks Navajo. New York, Harper and Row, 1968. 10, 146 p. illus., map.

Walton, E. L. Dawn boy: Blackfoot and Navaho songs. New York, 1926. 82 p.

Walton, E. L. Navaho poetry. Texas Review, 7 (1922): 198-210.

Walton, E. L. Navaho verse rhythms. Poetry, 24 (1924): 40-44.

Walton, E. L. Navajo song patterning. Journal of American Folklore, 43 (1930): 105-118.

Walton, E. L. and T. T. Waterman. American Indian poetry. American Anthropologist, n.s., 27 (1925): 25-52.

Ward, Albert E. A multicomponent site with a Desert Culture affinity, near Window Rock, Arizona. Plateau, 43 (1971): 120-131.

Ward, Albert E. A Navajo anthropomorphic figurine. Plateau, 42 (1970): 146-149.

Ward, Albert E. Investigation of two hogans at Toonerville, Arizona. Plateau, 40 (1968): 136-142.

Warner, Michael J. Protestant missionary activity among the Navajo, 1890-1912. New Mexico Historical Review, 45 (1970): 209-232.

Waters, F. Masked gods. Albuquerque, 1950. 438 p.

Waters, F. Navajo Yei-bet-chai. Yale Review, 28 (1939): 558-571.

Waters, F. The Navajo missions. New Mexico Quarterly Review, 20 (1950): 5-20.

Waters, Frank. Pumpkin Seed Point. Chicago, Sage Books, Swallow Press, 1969. 175 p.

Watkins, F. E. Navaho Indians. Masterkey, 16 (1942): 109-118, 149-156, 210-214; 17 (1943): 20-24, 77-81, 136-140, 168-172.

Watkins, F. E. The Navaho. Southwest Museum Leaflets, 16 (1943): 1-45.

Watkins, F. E. Two rare Navaho masks. Masterkey, 10 (1936): 188-189.

Watson, Editha L. Navajo sacred places. Window Rock, Navajo Tribal Museum, 1964. 28 p. illus. (Navajoland Publications, 5)

Wauneka, Annie D. Helping a people to understand. American Journal of Nursing, 62, no. 7 (1962): 88-90.

Weber, A. Navajos on the warpath. Franciscan Missions of the Southwest, 7 (1918): 1-18.

Weber, A. On Navajo myths and superstitions. Franciscan Missions of the Southwest, 4 (1916): 38-46.

Weppner, Robert S. An empirical test of the assimilation of a migrant group into an urban milieu. Anthropological Quarterly, 45 (1972): 262-273.

Weppner, Robert S. Socioeconomic barriers to assimilation of Navajo migrants. Human Organization, 31 (1972): 303-314.

Weppner, Robert S. Urban economic opportunities: the example of Denver. In Jack O. Waddell and O. Michael Watkins, eds. The American Indian in Urban Society. Boston, Little, Brown, 1971: 244-273.

Weppner, Robert Stephens. The economic absorption of Navajo Indian migrants in Denver, Colorado. Dissertation Abstracts, 29 (1968/1969): 3175B-3176E. UM 69-4343.

Werner, Oscar. A typological comparison of four Trader Navaho speakers. Dissertation Abstracts, 25 (1964/1965): 752-753. UM 64-5507.

Werner, Oswald. A lexemic typology of Navaho anatomical terms I: the foot. By Oswald Werner and Kenneth Y. Begishe. International Journal of American Linguistics, 36 (1970): 247-265.

Werner, Oswald. Problems of Navaho lexicography. In Dell H. Hymes and William E. Bittle, eds. Studies in Southwestern Ethnolinguistics. The Hague, Mouton, 1967: 145-164. (Studies in General Anthropology, 3)

Werner, Oswald. Semantics of Navaho medical terms: I. International Journal of American Linguistics, 31 (1965): 1-17.

Wetherill, L. W. Navaho stories. Kiva, 12 (1947): 25-28, 36-39.

Wetherill, L. W. Some Navajo recipes. Kiva, 12 (1946): 5-6, 39-40.

Wetherill, L. W. and B. Cummings. A Navaho folk tale of Pueblo Bonito. Art and Archaeology, 14 (1922): 132-136.

Wheelwright, M. C. Atsah and Yohe. Museum of Navaho Ceremonial Art, Bulletin, 3 (1945): 1-16.

Wheelwright, M. C. Emergence myth according to the Hanelth-nayhe or Upward-reaching Rite. Navajo Religion Series, 3 (1949): 1-186.

Wheelwright, M. C. Hail Chant and Water Chant. Navajo Religion Series, 2 (1946): 1-237.

Wheelwright, M. C. Notes on some Navajo coyote myths. New Mexico Folklore Record, 4 (1949/1950): 17-19.

Wheelwright, M. C. The myth and prayers of the Great Star Chant. Santa Fe, 1956. 198 p.

Wheelwright, M. C. Tleji or Yehbechai myth. House of Navajo Religion, Bulletin, 1 (1938): 1-13.

Whilden, Charles E. Letters from a Santa Fe Army clerk, 1855-1856. Edited by John Hammond Moore. New Mexico Historical Review, 40 (1965): 141-164.

Whitman, W. Navaho tales. Boston, 1925. 217 p.

Whittemore, M. Participation in Navajo weaving. Plateau, 13 (1941): 49-52.

Wilhelm, Timothy. The Navajo: a brief ethnographic history. Na'páo, 1, no. 2 (1968): 83-91.

Wilken, Robert L. Anselm Weber, O.F.M., missionary to the Navaho 1898-1921. Milwaukee, Bruce, 1955. 14, 255 p.

Williams, Aubrey W., Jr. Navajo political process. Washington, D.C., Smithsonian Institution Press, 1970. 9, 75 p. illus., maps. (Smithsonian Contributions to Anthropology, 9)

Williams, Aubrey Willis, Jr. The function of the chapter house system in the contemporary Navajo political structure. Dissertation Abstracts, 25 (1964/1965): 4908. UM 64-10,453.

Willink, Elizabeth Wilhelmina. A comparison of two methods of teaching English to Navajo children. Dissertation Abstracts, 29 (1968/1969): 1058A. UM 68-14,910.

Wilson, E. Red, black, blond, and olive, 1-68. New York, 1956.

Wilson, E. F. The Navajo Indians. Our Forest Children, 3 (1890): 115-117.

Wilson, John P. Military campaigns in the Navajo country, northwestern New Mexico, 1800-1846. Santa Fe, Museum of New Mexico Press, 1967. 7, 38 p. illus., map. (Museum of New Mexico, Research Records, 5)

Witherspoon, Gary. A new look at Navajo social organization. American Anthropologist, 72 (1970): 55-65.

Witherspoon, Gary J. Navajo categories of objects at rest. American Anthropologist, 73 (1971): 110-127.

Woehlke, W. W. The economic rehabilitation of the Navajos. National Conference of Social Work, Proceedings (1934): 548-556.

Woerner, D. Education among the Navajo. New York, 1941. 227 p.

Wolf, Charles B. Kwashiorkor on the Navajo Indian Reservation. Detroit, Henry Ford Hospital, Medical Bulletin, 9 (1961): 566-571.

Wolman, Carol. Group therapy in two languages, English and Navajo. American Journal of Psychotherapy, 24 (1970): 677-685.

Woodward, A. A brief history of Navajo silversmithing. Flagstaff, Ariz., Museum of Northern Arizona, Bulletin, 14 (1938): 1-78.

Woodward, A. Navajo silver comes of age. Los Angeles County Museum, Museum Associates, Quarterly, 10, no. 1 (1953): 9-14.

Woodward, Arthur. Navajo silver; a brief history of Navajo silversmithing. Flagstaff, Northland Press, 1971. 12, 103 p. illus.

Woolf, Charles M. Albinism among Indians in Arizona and New Mexico. American Journal of Human Genetics, 17 (1965): 23-35.

Worcester, D. E. The Navaho during the Spanish regime in New Mexico. New Mexico Historical Review, 26 (1951): 101-118.

Worth, Sol. Navajo filmmakers. By Sol Worth and John Adair. American Anthropologist, 72 (1970): 9-34.

Worth, Sol. Through Navajo eyes. By Sol Worth and John Adair. Bloomington, Indiana University Press, 1972. 14, 286 p. illus.

Wright, Bessie L., ed. Diary of a member of the first mule pack train to leave Fort Smith for California in 1849. Panhandle-Plains Historical Review, 42 (1969): 61-119.

Wyman, L. C. Navaho diagnosticians. American Anthropologist, n.s., 38 (1936): 236-246.

Wyman, L. C. Navaho Indian painting. Boston, 1959. 28 p.

Wyman, L. C.   Notes on obsolete Navaho
   ceremonies. Plateau, 23 (1951): 44-48.

Wyman, L. C.   Origin legends of Navaho
   divinatory rites. Journal of American
   Folklore, 49 (1936): 134-142.

Wyman, L. C.   Psychotherapy of the Navaho.
   Tomorrow, 4, no. 3 (1956): 77-84.

Wyman, L. C.   The Female Shooting Life
   Chant. American Anthropologist, n.s., 38
   (1936): 634-653.

Wyman, L. C.   The sandpaintings of the
   Kayenta Navaho. New Mexico, University,
   Publications in Anthropology, (1952): 1-
   120.

Wyman, L. C. and B. Thorne.   Notes on
   Navaho suicide. American Anthropologist,
   n.s., 47 (1945): 278-288.

Wyman, L. C. and C. Amsden.   A patchwork
   cloak. Masterkey, 8 (1934): 133-137.

Wyman, L. C. and C. Kluckhohn.   Navaho
   classification of their song
   ceremonials. American Anthropological
   Association, Memoirs, 50 (1938): 1-38.

Wyman, L. C. and F. L. Bailey.   Idea and
   action patterns in Navaho Flintway.
   Southwestern Journal of Anthropology, 1
   (1945): 359-377.

Wyman, L. C. and F. L. Bailey.   Native
   Navaho methods for the control of insect
   pests. Plateau, 24 (1952): 97-103.

Wyman, L. C. and F. L. Bailey.   Navaho
   girl's puberty rite. New Mexico
   Anthropologist, 6/7 (1943): 3-12.

Wyman, L. C. and F. L. Bailey.   Navaho
   Striped Windway, an Injury-Way Chant.
   Southwestern Journal of Anthropology, 2
   (1946): 213-238.

Wyman, L. C. and F. L. Bailey.   Navaho
   Upward Reaching Way. New Mexico,
   University, Bulletin, Anthropological
   Series, 4, no. 2 (1943): 1-47.

Wyman, L. C. and F. L. Bailey.   Two
   examples of Navaho physiotherapy.
   American Anthropologist, n.s., 46
   (1944): 329-337.

Wyman, L. C. and S. K. Harris.   Navajo
   Indian medical ethnobotany. New Mexico,
   University, Bulletin, Anthropological
   Series, 3, no. 5 (1941): 1-76.

*Wyman, L. C. and S. K. Harris.   The
   ethnobotany of the Kayenta Navaho. New
   Mexico, University, Publications in
   Biology, 5 (1951): 1-66.

Wyman, L. C., et al.   Beautyway: a Navaho
   ceremonial. New York, 1957. 301 p.

Wyman, Leland C.   A Navajo medicine bundle
   for Shootingway. Plateau, 44 (1972):
   131-149.

Wyman, Leland C.   Big Lefthanded, pioneer
   Navajo artist. Plateau, 40 (1967): 1-13.

Wyman, Leland C.   Blessingway. Tucson,
   University of Arizona Press, 1970. 28,
   660 p. illus.

Wyman, Leland C.   Drypaintings used in
   divination by the Navajo. By Leland C.
   Wyman and Franc Johnson Newcomb.
   Plateau, 36 (1963): 18-24.

Wyman, Leland C.   Navaho Indian
   ethnoentomology. By Leland C. Wyman and
   Flora L. Bailey. Albuquerque,
   University of New Mexico Press, 1964.
   158 p. illus., map. (New Mexico,
   University, Publications in
   Anthropology, 12)

Wyman, Leland C.   Navaho sandpainting.
   Colorado Springs, Taylor Museum of
   Colorado Springs, 1960. 88 p. illus.

Wyman, Leland C.   Navajo ceremonial
   equipment in the Museum of Northern
   Arizona. Plateau, 45 (1972/1973): 17-30.

Wyman, Leland C.   Sandpaintings of
   Beautyway. By Leland C. Wyman and Franc
   Johnson Newcomb. Plateau, 35 (1962): 37-
   52.

Wyman, Leland C.   Sandpaintings of the
   Navaho Shootingway and the Walcott
   Collection. Washington, D.C.,
   Smithsonian Institution Press, 1970.
   12, 102 p. illus. (Smithsonian
   Contributions to Anthropology, 13)

Wyman, Leland C.   Snakeskins and hoops.
   Plateau, 39 (1966): 4-25.

Wyman, Leland C.   Ten sandpaintings from
   Male Shootingway. Plateau, 45 (1972):
   55-67.

Wyman, Leland C.   The Red Antway of the
   Navaho. Santa Fe, Museum of Navajo
   Ceremonial Art, 1965. 276 p. illus.

Wyman, Leland C.   The windways of the
   Navaho. Colorado Springs, Taylor Museum
   of the Colorado Springs Fine Arts
   Center, 1962. 327 p. illus., map.

Yazzie, Ethelou, ed. Navajo history.
   Many Farms, Ariz., Navajo Community
   College Press, 1971.

Yealth, S. The making of Navajo blankets.
   El Palacio, 40 (1936): 7-9, 43-44.

Yost, B. W. Bread upon the sands.
Caldwell, 1958. 245 p.

Young, R. W. and J. P. Harrington.
Earliest Navaho and Quechua. Acta
Americana, 2 (1944): 315-319.

Young, R. W. and W. Morgan. A vocabulary
of colloquial Navaho. Phoenix, 1951.
461 p.

Young, R. W. and W. Morgan. The A B C of
Navaho. Phoenix, 1944.

Young, R. W. and W. Morgan. The Navaho
language. Phoenix, 1943. 470 p.

Young, R. W., ed. The Navajo Yearbook,
Report No. 6, Fiscal Year 1957. Window
Rock, 1957. 353 p.

Young, Rodney Wilson. Semantics as a
determiner of linguistic comprehension
across language and cultural boundaries.
Dissertation Abstracts International, 32
(1971/1972): 5216A. UM 72-8378.

Young, S. Navajo dyes. Phoenix, 1939.

Young, S. and N. Bryan. Navaho native
dyes. Indian Handcrafts, 2 (1940): 1-75.

Youniss, James. The role of language and
experience on the use of logical
symbols. By James Youniss and Hans G.
Furth. British Journal of Psychology, 58
(1967): 435-443.

Zbinden, Ernst A. Nördliche und südliche
Elemente im Kulturheroenmythus der
Südathapasken. Anthropos, 55 (1960):
689-733.

Zelditch, M. Statistical marriage
preferences of the Ramah Navaho.
American Anthropologist, 61 (1959): 470-
491.

15-22 Nevome

Alegre, F. J. Historia de la Compañia de
Jesús en Nueva España. México, 1841.
3 v.

Anonymous. Rudo ensayo. American Catholic
Historical Society of Philadelphia,
Records, 5, no. 2 (1894): 188-192.

Bannon, John Francis. The mission
frontier in Sonora, 1620-1687. Edited by
James A. Reynolds. New York, United
States Catholic Historical Society,
1955. 4, 160 p. (United States
Catholic Historical Society, Monograph
Series, 26)

Bascom, Burton William, Jr. Proto-Tepiman
(Tepehuan-Piman). Dissertation
Abstracts, 27 (1966/1967): 192A-193A.
UM 66-5811.

Beals, R. L. The comparative ethnology of
northern Mexico. Ibero-Americana, 2
(1932): 93-225.

Brugge, David M. A Sonoran grooved-stone
tool. Katunob, 4, no. 1 (1963): 11.

Brugge, David M. History, huki, and
warfare--some random data on the Lower
Pima. Kiva, 26, no. 4 (1960/1961): 6-16.

Brugge, David M. Progress report on field
work among the Pima Bajo of northern
Mexico. Katunob, 1, no. 4 (1960): 15-18.

Dobyns, Henry F. The 1797 population of
the Presidio of Tucson. Journal of
Arizona History, 13 (1972): 205-209.

Dunnigan, Timothy. Subsistence and
reciprocity patterns among the Mountain
Pimas of Sonora, Mexico. Dissertation
Abstracts International, 31 (1970/1971):
29B. UM 70-11,976.

Escalante H., Roberto. Brief note on the
Pimas of Sonora. Translated by David M.
Brugge. Katunob, 3, no. 3 (1962): 20-21.

Escalante H., Roberto. El Pima Bajo.
México, Instituto Nacional de
Antropología e Historia, Anales, 14
(1961): 349-352.

Farman, Luis. Clamor de los Pimas.
Katunob, 5, no. 2/3 (1965): 7-8.

Hinton, Thomas B. Remnant tribes of
Sonora: Opata, Pima, Papago, and Seri.
In Evon Z. Vogt, volume editor. Handbook
of Middle American Indians. Vol. 8.
Austin, University of Texas Press, 1969:
879-888.

Hodge, F. W. Nevome. U.S. Bureau of
American Ethnology, Bulletin, 30, vol. 2
(1910): 62-63.

Mason, J. A. and D. M. Brugge. Notes on
the Lower Pima. In Miscellanea Paul
Rivet Octogenario Dicata. Vol. 1.
México, 1958: 277-297.

*Nolasco Armas, Margarita. Los Pimas Bajos
de la Sierra Madre Occidental (Yécoras y
Nébomes Altos). México, Instituto
Nacional de Antropología e Historia,
Anales, Época 7, 1 (1967/1968): 185-244.

Pérez de Ribas, Andrés. Historia de los
triunfos de nuestra santa fe entre
gentes las más bárbaras y fieras del
nuevo orbe. Madrid, A. de Paredes,
1645. 20, 763 p.

Pérez de Ribas, Andrés. My life among the savage nations of New Spain. Translated by Tomás Antonio Robertson. Los Angeles, Ward Ritchie Press, 1968. 16, 256 p. illus., maps.

Ressler, John Q. Indian and Spanish water-control on New Spain's northwest frontier. Journal of the West, 7 (1968): 10-17.

Sauer, C. The distribution of aboriginal tribes and languages in northwestern Mexico. Ibero-Americana, 5 (1934): 34-41.

Smith, Thomas Buckingham, tr. Grammar of the Pima or Nevome, a language of Sonora, from a manuscript of the 18th century. London, 1862. 97 p.

Thomas, Cyrus. Indian languages of Mexico and Central America and their geographical distribution. By Cyrus Thomas assisted by John R. Swanton. Washington, D.C., Government Printing Office, 1911. 7, 108 p. map. (U.S., Bureau of American Ethnology, Bulletin, 44)

15-23 Opata

Anonymous. Rudo ensayo. American Catholic Historical Society of Philadelphia, Records, 5, no. 2 (1894): 166-188.

Basauri, Carlos. Familia "Pimana": Opatas. In his La Poblacion Indigena de Mexico. Tomo 1. Mexico, Secretaria de Educacion Publica, 1940: 209-222.

Beals, R. L. The comparative ethnology of northern Mexico. Ibero-Americana, 2 (1932): 93-225.

Brugge, David M. History, huki, and warfare--some random data on the Lower Pima. Kiva, 26, no. 4 (1960/1961): 6-16.

Cabeza de Vaca, Alvar Núñez. Adventures in the unknown interior of America. New York, Collier, 1961. 152 p. (Collier Books, AS117)

Dávila Garibi, José Ignacio Paulino. Algunas observaciones acerca de la lengua ópata o tegüima. México, Editorial Cultura, 1950. 46 p.

Escalante H., Roberto. Material lingüístico del oriente de Sonora, Tonichi y Ponida. México, Instituto Nacional de Antropología e Historia, Anales, 16 (1963): 149-177.

Ezell, Paul H. The Hispanic acculturation of the Gila River Pimas. Menasha,

American Anthropological Association, 1961. 5, 171 p. illus., maps. (American Anthropological Association, Memoir, 90)

Featherman, A. Social history of the races of mankind, Vol. 3: 42-49. Boston, 1890.

Forbes, J. D. Historical survey of the Indians of Sonora, 1821-1910. Ethnohistory, 4 (1957): 335-368.

Griffen, William B. A case of Opata witchcraft. Kiva, 29, no. 1 (1963/1964): 1-13.

Griffith, James A. Mochicahui Judio masks: a type of Mayo Fariseo mask from northern Sinaloa, Mexico. Kiva, 32, no. 4 (1966/1967): 143-149.

Hamy, E. T. Algunas observaciones sobre la distribución geográfica de los Opatas, de los Tarahumares y de los Pimas. Museo de Arqueología, Historia y Etnografía, Anales, época 4a, 5 (1922): 93-98.

Hinton, Thomas B. Remnant tribes of Sonora: Opata, Pima, Papago, and Seri. In Evon Z. Vogt, volume editor. Handbook of Middle American Indians. Vol. 8. Austin, University of Texas Press, 1969: 879-888.

Hodge, F. W. Opata. U.S. Bureau of American Ethnology, Bulletin, 30, vol. 2 (1910): 138-139.

Hrdlička, A. Notes on the Indians of Sonora. American Anthropologist, n.s., 6 (1904): 71-84.

Ives, Ronald L., tr. and ed. The Sonoran census of 1730. American Catholic Historical Society of Philadelphia, Records, 59 (1948): 319-339.

*Johnson, J. B. The Opata. New Mexico, University, Publications in Anthropology, 6 (1950): 1-50.

Kroeber, A. L. Uto-Aztecan languages of Mexico. Ibero-Americana, 8 (1934): 1-27.

Lombardo, Natal. Arte de la lengua teguima llamada vulgarmente opata. México, 1702. 472 p.

Lumholtz, Carl. Explorations in the Sierra Madre. Scribner's Magazine, 10 (1891): 531-598.

Passin, Herbert. Some relationships in Northwest Mexican kinship systems. El México Antiguo, 6, no. 7/8 (July 1944): 205-218.

Pérez de Ribas, Andrés. My life among the savage nations of New Spain. Translated by Tomás Antonio Robertson. Los Angeles, Ward Ritchie Press, 1968. 16, 256 p. illus., maps.

Pimentel, D. F. Lenguas indígenas de México. México, 1862.

Pimentel, F. Vocabulario manual de la lengua opata. Sociedad Mexicana de Geografía y Estadística, Boletín, 10 (1863): 288-313.

Polzer, Charles W., ed. The Franciscan entrada into Sonora 1645-1652: a Jesuit chronicle. Arizona and the West, 14 (1972): 253-278.

Radin, P. Mexican kinship terms. California, University, Publications in American Archaeology and Ethnology, 31 (1931): 1-14.

Reyes, V. Terminaison du pluriel dans les langues mexicano-opata. International Congress of Americanists, Proceedings, 8 (1892): 548-549.

Sauer, C. The distribution of aboriginal tribes and languages in northwestern Mexico. Ibero-Americana, 5 (1934): 46-51.

Schroeder, A. H. The Cipias and Ypotlapiguas. Arizona Quarterly, 12 (1956): 101-110.

Smith, Thomas Buckingham, tr. A grammatical sketch of the Heve language; translated from an unpublished Spanish manuscript. New York, Cramoisy Press, 1862. 26 p. (Shea's Library of American Linguistics, 3)

Stevens, Robert Conway. Mexico's forgotten frontier: a history of Sonora, 1821-1846. Dissertation Abstracts, 24 (1963/1964): 3719-3720. UM 64-2142.

Terrell, John U. Pueblo of the Hearts. Palm-Desert, Calif., Best-West Publications, 1966. 103 p. illus., maps.

Thomas, Cyrus. Indian languages of Mexico and Central America and their geographical distribution. By Cyrus Thomas assisted by John R. Swanton. Washington, D.C., Government Printing Office, 1911. 7, 108 p. map. (U.S., Bureau of American Ethnology, Bulletin, 44)

Whiting, A. F. The Tumacacori census of 1796. Kiva, 29, no. 1 (1953): 1-12.

Zingg, Robert M. A reconstruction of Uto-Aztekan history. New York, G. E.
Stechert, 1939. 4, 274 p. (Denver, University, Contributions to Ethnography, 2)

15-24   Papago

Aamodt, Agnes Marie. Enculturation process and the Papago child: an inquiry into the acquisition of perspectives on health and healing. Dissertation Abstracts International, 32 (1971/1972): 6173B. 72-15,061.

Adams, Morton S. Health of Papago Indian children. U.S., Public Health Service, Public Health Reports, 85 (1970): 1047-1061.

Adams, Morton S. Health of the American Indian Papago children. By M. S. Adams and J. D. Niswander. Pediatric Research, 4 (1970): 474.

Allen, Terry, ed. The whispering wind; poetry by young American Indians. Garden City, Doubleday, 1972. 16, 128 p.

Alvarez, Albert. Some Papago puns. International Journal of American Linguistics, 31 (1965): 106-107.

Alvarez, Albert. Toward a manual of Papago grammar: some phonological terms. By Albert Alvarez and Kenneth Hale. International Journal of American Linguistics, 36 (1970): 83-97.

Anonymous. History of the Papago Indians. El Palacio, 14 (1923): 96-99.

Anonymous. Papago tribal judge from the United States travels to study Interamerican Indianist activities. Anuario Indigenista, 23 (1963): 94-95.

Anonymous. The fiesta of St. Francis Xavier. Kiva, 16, nos. 1/2 (1950): 1-32.

Arriquibar, Pedro Antonio de. Fray Pedro de Arriquibar's census of Tucson, 1820. Edited by Karen Sikes Collins. Journal of Arizona History, 11 (1970): 14-22.

Ayres, J. E. An early historic burial from the village of Bac. Kiva, 36, no. 1 (1970/1971): 44-48.

Bahr, Donald M. Who were the Hohokam? The evidence from Pima-Papago myths. Ethnohistory, 18 (1971): 245-266.

Basauri, Carlos. Familia "Pimana": Papagos. In his La Poblacion Indigena de Mexico. Tomo 1. Mexico, Secretaria de Educacion Publica, 1940: 195-208.

Beals, R. L. Material culture of the Pima, Papago, and Western Apache. Berkeley, 1934. 44 p.

Beals, Ralph L. The comparative ethnology of northern Mexico before 1750. Berkeley, University of California Press, 1932. 6, 93-225 p. maps. (Ibero-Americana, 2)

Becker, D. M. Music of the Papago. Smoke Signals, 6, no. 5 (1954): 2-4.

Bender, Marvin L. Chance CVC correspondences in unrelated languages. Language, 45 (1969): 519-531.

Bliss, W. L. In the wake of the wheel. In Edward H. Spicer, ed. Human Problems in Technological Change. New York, 1952: 23-34.

Bowen, R. Saguaro harvest in Papagoland. Desert Magazine, 2, no. 8 (1939): 3-5.

Brennan, Jose Lewis. Jose Lewis Brennan's account of Papago "customs and other references". Edited by Bernard L. Fontana. Ethnohistory, 6 (1959): 226-237.

Brown, K. S. Population studies on Southwestern Indian tribes: III. Serum protein variations of Zuni and Papago Indians. By K. S. Brown and R. S. Johnson. Human Heredity, 20 (1970): 281-286.

Bruhn, Jan G. Carnegiea gigantea: the saguaro and its uses. Economic Botany, 25 (1972): 320-329.

Cardenal, Ernesto, tr. Poesía de los indios de Norteamérica. América Indígena, 21 (1961): 355-362.

Casagrande, Joseph B. Semantic relationships in Papago folk-definitions. By Joseph B. Casagrande and Kenneth L. Hale. In Dell H. Hymes and William E. Bittle, eds. Studies in Southwestern Ethnolinguistics. The Hague, Mouton, 1967: 165-193. (Studies in General Anthropology, 3)

Castetter, E. F. and R. Underhill. The ethnobiology of the Papago Indians. New Mexico, University, Bulletin, Biological Series, 4, no. 3 (1935): 3-84.

*Castetter, E. F. and W. H. Bell. Pima and Papago Indian agriculture. Inter-American Studies, 1 (1942): 1-245.

Cazeneuve, L. Les Indiens de la région de Tucson. Ethnographie, 51 (1956): 37-45.

Chesky, J. The Wiikita. Kiva, 8 (1943): 3-5.

Childs, T. Sketch of the "Sand Indians". Kiva, 19, nos. 2/4 (1954): 27-39.

Clark, Geoffrey A. A cache of Papago miniature pottery from Kitt Peak, South-central Arizona. Kiva, 32, no. 4 (1966/1967): 128-142.

Corrigan, Francis Vincent. A comparison of self-concepts of American-Indian students from public or federal school backgrounds. Dissertation Abstracts International, 31 (1970/1971): 2679A-2680A. UM 70-24,959.

Coulter, Pearl Parvin. Parallel experience: an interview technique. By Pearl Parvin Coulter and Margaret J. Brower. American Journal of Nursing, 69 (1969): 1028-1030.

Curtis, E. S. The North American Indian, Vol. 2: 27-43. Cambridge, 1908.

Davis, E. H. The Papago ceremony of Vikita. Indian Notes and Monographs, 3 (1920): 155-177.

Densmore, F. Communication with the dead as practised by the American Indians. Man, 50 (1950): 40-41.

Densmore, F. Papago music. U.S. Bureau of American Ethnology, Bulletin, 90 (1929): 1-230.

Densmore, Frances. Papago music. New York, Da Capo Press, 1972. 20, 229 p. illus.

Dobyns, H. F. Blunders with bolsas. Human Organization, 10, no. 3 (1951): 25-32.

Dobyns, H. F. Experiment in conservation. In Edward H. Spicer, ed. Human Problems in Technological Change. New York, 1952: 209-224.

Dobyns, H. F. Papagos in the cotton fields. Tucson, 1950. 140 p.

Dobyns, H. F. Thirsty Indians. Human Organization, 11, no. 4 (1952): 33-36.

Dobyns, Henry F. Indian extinction in the middle Santa Cruz River Valley, Arizona. New Mexico Historical Review, 38 (1963): 163-181.

Dolan, Darrow, ed. The Plomo Papers. Ethnohistory, 19 (1972): 305-322.

Dolores, J. Papago nicknames. In Essays in Anthropology Presented to A. L. Kroeber. Berkeley, 1936: 45-47.

Dolores, J. Papago nominal stems. California, University, Publications in

American Archaeology and Ethnology, 20 (1923): 19-31.

Dolores, J. Papago verb stems. California, University, Publications in American Archaeology and Ethnology, 10 (1913): 241-263.

Drucker, Philip. Culture element distributions: XVII Yuman-Piman. Berkeley, 1941. 91-230 p. illus., map. (California, University, Publications, Anthropological Records, 6, no. 3)

Ellinwood, Sybil. Calabasas. Arizoniana, 5, no. 4 (1964): 27-41.

Ellis, Everett L. To take a scalp. Annals of Wyoming, 31 (1959): 140-143.

Ezell, Paul H. The Hispanic acculturation of the Gila River Pimas. Menasha, American Anthropological Association, 1961. 5, 171 p. illus., maps. (American Anthropological Association, Memoir, 90)

Ezell, Paul H. The Maricopas: an identification from documentary sources. Tucson, University of Arizona Press, 1963. 29 p. (Arizona, University, Anthropological Papers, 6)

Fay, George E., ed. Charters, constitutions and by-laws of the Indian tribes of North America. Part IV: The Southwest (Navajo-Zuni). Greeley, 1967. 5, 120 l. maps. (University of Northern Colorado, Museum of Anthropology, Occasional Publications in Anthropology, Ethnology Series, 5) ERIC ED046554.

Federal Writers' Project. The Papago. Arizona State Teachers College, Bulletin, 20, no. 3 (1939): 1-16.

Feldman, Kerry D. Deviation, demography, and development: differences between Papago Indian communities. Human Organization, 31 (1972): 137-147.

Fontana, B. L., ed. Jose Lewis Brennan's account of Papago "customs and other references". Ethnohistory, 6 (1959): 226-237.

Fontana, Bernard L. Johnny Ward's ranch: a study in historic archaeology. By Bernard L. Fontana and J. Cameron Greenleaf. Kiva, 28, nos. 1/2 (1962/1963): 1-115.

Fontana, Bernard L., et al. Papago Indian pottery. Seattle, University of Washington Press, 1962. 163 p. illus.

Fontana, Bernard L., et al. Techniques of pottery manufacture of the Papago

Indians. In Philip K. Bock, ed. Culture Shock. New York, Knopf, 1970: 179-193.

Fontana, Bernard Lee. Assimilative change: a Papago Indian case study. Dissertation Abstracts, 21 (1960/1961): 1330. UM 60-6156.

Gabel, H. E. A comparative racial study of the Papago. New Mexico, University, Publications in Anthropology, 4 (1949): 1-96.

Gabel, N. E. The physical status of the Papago. In For the Dean. Essays in Anthropology in Honor of Byron Cummings. Tucson, 1950: 189-200.

Gaillard, U. S. A. The Papago of Arizona and Sonora. American Anthropologist, 7 (1894): 293-296.

Gifford, E. W. Apache-Pueblo. Anthropological Records, 6 (1940): 1-207.

Gifford, E. W. Clans and moieties in southern California. California, University, Publications in American Archaeology and Ethnology, 14 (1918): 174-176.

Goldman, Stanford M. Radiculomyopathy in a Southwestern Indian due to skeletal fluorosis. By Stanford M. Goldman, Maurice L. Sievers, and David W. Templin. Arizona Medicine, 28 (1971): 675-677.

Goldman, Stanford M., et al. Roentgen manifestations of diseases in Southwestern Indians. Radiology, 103 (1972): 303-306.

Greene, R. A. The composition and uses of the fruit of the giant cactus. Journal of Chemical Education, 13 (1936): 309-312.

Griffith, James S. Magdalena revisited: the growth of a fiesta. Kiva, 33, no. 2 (1967/1968): 82-86.

Hackenberg, Beverly Heckart. Social mobility in a tribal society: the case of Papago Indian veterans. Human Organization, 31 (1972): 201-209.

Hackenberg, Robert A. An anthropological study of demographic transition; the Papago information system. Milbank Memorial Fund Quarterly, 44 (1966): 470-494.

Hackenberg, Robert A. Economic alternatives in arid lands: a case study of the Pima and Papago Indians. Ethnology, 1 (1962): 186-196.

Hackenberg, Robert A. Reluctant
emigrants: the role of migration in
Papago Indian adaptation. By Robert A.
Hackenberg and C. Roderick Wilson. Human
Organization, 31 (1972): 171-186.

Hackenberg, Robert A. Restricted
interdependence: the adaptive pattern of
Papago Indian society. Human
Organization, 31 (1972): 112-125.

Hackenberg, Robert A. The costs of
cultural change: accidental injury and
modernization among the Papago Indians.
By Robert A. Hackenberg and Mary M.
Gallagher. Human Organization, 31
(1972): 211-226.

Hackenberg, Robert A. The parameters of
an ethnic group: a method for studying
the total tribe. American
Anthropologist, 69 (1967): 478-492.

Hale, Kenneth. On Papago laryngeals. In
Earl H. Swanson, Jr., ed. Languages and
Cultures of Western North America.
Pocatello, Idaho State University Press,
1970: 54-60.

Hale, Kenneth. On the use of informants
in field-work. Canadian Journal of
Linguistics, 10 (1964/1965): 108-119.

Hale, Kenneth. Papago /čim/*.
International Journal of American
Linguistics, 35 (1969): 203-212.

Hale, Kenneth. Some preliminary
observations on Papago morphophonemics.
International Journal of American
Linguistics, 31 (1965): 295-305.

Hale, Kenneth Locke. A Papago grammar.
Dissertation Abstracts, 20 (1959/1960):
1773-1774. UM 59-4009.

Hanna, Bertram L. The biological
relationships among Indian groups of the
Southwest: analysis of morphological
traits. American Journal of Physical
Anthropology, n.s., 20 (1962): 499-508.

Hanna, Joel M. Responses of native and
migrant desert residents to arid heat.
American Journal of Physical
Anthropology, n.s., 32 (1970): 187-195.

Hayden, J. and C. R. Steen. The Vikita
ceremony of the Papago. Southwestern
Monuments Monthly Reports (April 1937):
263-283.

Hayden, Julian D. A summary prehistory
and history of the Sierra Pinacate,
Sonora. American Antiquity, 32 (1967):
335-344.

Henderson, E. Well of sacrifice. Arizona
Highways, 29 (February 1953): 2-3.

Herbert, C. W. Saguaro harvest in the
land of the Papagos. Desert Magazine,
18, no. 11 (1955): 14-17.

Hill, G. Papago legends from Santa Rosa.
Southwestern Lore, 6 (1940): 34-37.

Hinton, Thomas B. Remnant tribes of
Sonora: Opata, Pima, Papago, and Seri.
In Evon Z. Vogt, volume editor. Handbook
of Middle American Indians. Vol. 8.
Austin, University of Texas Press, 1969:
879-888.

Hodge, F. W. Papago. U.S. Bureau of
American Ethnology, Bulletin, 30, vol. 2
(1910): 200-201.

Holtsnider, Karl. Papago, the desert
people. Oakland, Franciscan Missions,
1955. 44 p.

Hoover, J. W. Generic descent of the
Papago villages. American
Anthropologist, n.s., 37 (1935): 257-
264.

Hoover, J. W. The Indian country of
southern Arizona. Geographical Review,
19 (1929): 38-60.

Hrdlička, A. Notes on the Indians of
Sonora. American Anthropologist, n.s., 6
(1904): 51-89.

Ives, R. L. Papago. International Journal
of American Linguistics, 11 (1945): 119.

Ives, R. L. Some Papago migrations in the
Sonoyta Valley. Masterkey, 10 (1936):
161-167.

Ives, R. L. The monster of Quitovac.
Masterkey, 15 (1941): 195-199.

Ives, Ronald L. Kino's exploration of the
Pinacate region. Journal of Arizona
History, 7 (1966): 59-75.

Ives, Ronald L. Population of the
Pinacate region, 1678-1706. Kiva, 31,
no. 1 (1965/1966): 37-45.

Ives, Ronald L. The problem of the
Sonoran littoral cultures. Kiva, 28,
no. 3 (1962/1963): 28-38.

Johnson, Barbara. The Wind Ceremony: a
Papago sand-painting. El Palacio, 67
(1960): 28-31.

Johnston, Betty Kendall. Gold stars and
red apples? Childhood Education, 41
(1965/1966): 466-468.

Jones, A. W. Additional information about
the Vikita. Southwestern Monuments
Monthly Reports (May 1937): 338-341.

Jones, C. F.   Demographic patterns in the Papago Indian village of Chuichu, Arizona. Human Biology, 25 (1953): 191-202.

Jones, Delmos J.   A description of settlement pattern and population movement on the Papago Reservation. Kiva, 27, no. 4 (1961/1962): 1-9.

Jones, Richard D.   The Wi'igita of Achi and Quitobac. Kiva, 36, no. 4 (1970/1971): 1-29.

Jones, Richard Donald.   An analysis of Papago communities 1900-1920. Dissertation Abstracts International, 30 (1969/1970): 1470B-1471B.   UM 69-8529.

*Joseph, A., R. Spicer, and J. Chesky.   The desert people.   Chicago, 1949.   288 p.

Kate, H. F. C. ten.   Indiens d'Amérique du Nord. Anthropologie (Paris), 28 (1917): 369-401.

Kate, H. F. C. ten.   Somatological observations on Indians of the Southwest. Journal of American Ethnology and Archaeology, 3 (1892): 117-144.

Kearns, Bessie Jean Ruley.   Childrearing practices among selected culturally deprived minorities. Journal of Genetic Psychology, 116 (1970): 149-155.

Kelly, Marsha C.   Las fiestas como reflejo del orden social: el caso de San Xavier del Bac. América Indígena, 31 (1971): 141-161.

Kelly, William H.   A study of southern Arizona school-age Indian children, 1966-1967.   Tucson, University of Arizona, Bureau of Ethnic Research, 1967.   3, 38 p.   ERIC ED024485.

Kelly, William H.   The Papago Indians of Arizona: a population and economic study.   Tucson, University of Arizona, Bureau of Ethnic Research, 1963.   10, 129 p.   maps.

Keneally, Henry J., Jr.   The inter and intra agency communication process used in a community development program. Adult Leadership, 14 (1965/1966): 294-296, 317-320.

Kessell, John L.   Father Ramón and the big debt, Tumacácori, 1821-1823. New Mexico Historical Review, 44 (1969): 53-72.

Kissell, M. L.   Basketry of the Papago and Pima. American Museum of Natural History, Anthropological Papers, 17 (1916): 115-264.

Kissell, Mary L.   Basketry of the Papago and Pima Indians.   Glorieta, N.M., Rio Grande Press, 1972.   117-264 p.   illus.

Kraus, B. S.   Carabelli's anomaly of the maxillary molar teeth. American Journal of Human Genetics, 3 (1951): 348-355.

Kraus, B. S.   Occurrence of the Carabelli trait in Southwest ethnic groups. American Journal of Physical Anthropology, n.s., 17 (1959): 117-123.

Kraus, B. S. and B. M. Jones.   Indian health in Arizona. Arizona, University, Bureau of Ethnic Research, Reports, 2 (1954): 1-164.

Kroeber, H. R.   Papago coyote tales. Journal of American Folklore, 22 (1909): 339-342.

Kroeber, H. R.   Traditions of the Papago Indians. Journal of American Folklore, 25 (1912): 95-105.

Kurath, W.   A brief introduction to Papago. Arizona, University, Social Science Bulletin, 13 (1945): 1-42.

Lamb, Neven Patterson.   Papago population biology: a study of microevolution. Dissertation Abstracts International, 30 (1969/1970): 3960B.   UM 70-5242.

León-Portilla, Miguel.   Panorama de la población indígena de México. América Indígena, 19 (1959): 43-73.

Lloyd, E.   The Papago feast of St. Francis. Southwestern Monuments Monthly Reports (1940): 389-392.

Lombardi, Thomas P.   Psycholinguistic abilities of Papago Indian school children. Exceptional Children, 36 (1969/1970): 485-493.

Lombardi, Thomas Philip.   Psycholinguistic abilities of Papago Indian children. Dissertation Abstracts International, 30 (1969/1970): 1891A.   UM 69-18,331.

Lumholtz, C.   New trails in Mexico. London, 1912.   411 p.

Lumholtz, Karl S.   New trails in Mexico. Glorieta, N.M., Rio Grande Press, 1971. 26, 25, 411 p.   illus.

Mackett, Robert.   Community background reports: Papago Reservation, Sells, Arizona. By Robert Mackett and John H. Chilcott.   Chicago, University of Chicago, 1970.   11 p.   (National Study of American Indian Education, Series I, 17, Final Report)   ERIC ED042552.

MacRoberts, Michael H. Taste sensitivity to phenylthiocarbamide (P.T.C.) among the Papago Indians of Arizona. Human Biology, 36 (1964): 28-31.

Manuel, Cipriano. Patience and other values. Journal of American Indian Education, 4, no. 2 (1964/1965): 1-4.

Marsh, Dick E. Two contemporary Papago recipes of indigenous plants and the American Southwest botanical implication. Kiva, 34, no. 4 (1968/1969): 242-245.

Mason, J. A. The Papago harvest festival. American Anthropologist, n.s., 22 (1920): 13-25.

Mason, J. A. The Papago migration legend. Journal of American Folklore, 34 (1921): 254-268.

Mathiot, Madeleine. A study of method in language-and-culture research. Final report. Los Angeles, Calif., Author, 1966. 414 p. ERIC ED011053.

Mathiot, Madeleine. An approach to the cognitive study of language. Bloomington, Indiana University, 1968. 15, 224 p. (Indiana, University, Research Center in Anthropology, Folklore, and Linguistics, Publication, 45)

Mathiot, Madeleine. An approach to the study of language-and-culture relations. Dissertation Abstracts, 27 (1966/1967): 3765B. UM 67-1258.

Mathiot, Madeleine. Noun classes and folk taxonomy in Papago. American Anthropologist, 64 (1962): 340-350.

Mathiot, Madeleine. The cognitive significance of the category of nominal number in Papago. In Dell H. Hymes and William E. Bittle, eds. Studies in Southwestern Ethnolinguistics. The Hague, Mouton, 1967: 197-237. (Studies in General Anthropology, 3)

Mathiot, Madeleine. The place of the dictionary in linguistic description. Language, 43 (1967): 703-724.

Matis, John A. Odontognathic discrimination of United States Indian and Eskimo groups. By John A. Matis and Thomas J. Zwemer. Journal of Dental Research, 50 (1971): 1245-1248.

Matson, D. S. Papago recordings. Arizona Quarterly, 9 (1953): 45-54.

Matson, G. Albin. Distribution of hereditary factors in the blood of Indians of the Gila River, Arizona. By

G. Albin Matson, Thomas A. Burch, Herbert F. Polesky, Jane Swanson, H. Eldon Sutton, and Abner Robinson. American Journal of Physical Anthropology, n.s., 29 (1968): 311-337.

McGee, W J. Piratical acculturation. In Paul Bohannan and Fred Plog, eds. Beyond the Frontier. Garden City, Natural History Press, 1967: 135-142.

McGee, W J. The beginning of agriculture. American Anthropologist, 8 (1895): 350-375.

McGinty, Doris Madeline. An analysis of the effectiveness of the secondary home economics program in meeting needs of young married Papago Indian homemakers. Dissertation Abstracts, 25 (1964/1965): 5900. UM 65-193.

Miller, Wick R. Uto-Aztecan cognate sets. Berkeley and Los Angeles, University of California Press, 1967. 5, 83 p. map. (California, University, Publications in Linguistics, 48)

Morris, Donald H. Maxillary premolar variation among the Papago Indians. Journal of Dental Research, 46 (1967): 736-738.

Morris, Donald H. Morphological analysis and age in the permanent dentitions of young American Indians. American Journal of Physical Anthropology, n.s., 25 (1966): 91-96.

Morris, Donald Harvey. The anthropological utility of dental morphology. Dissertation Abstracts, 26 (1965/1966): 4169. UM 65-13,866.

Neff, M. L. Pima and Papago legends. Journal of American Folklore, 25 (1912): 51-65.

Niswander, Jerry D., et al. Population studies on Southwestern Indian trbies: I. History, culture and genetics of the Papago. American Journal of Human Genetics, 22 (1970): 7-23.

Nolasco Armas, Margarita. Los Papagos, habitantes del desierto. México, Instituto Nacional de Antropología e Historia, Anales, 17 (1964): 375-448.

Nolasco Armas, Margarita. Problemas indígenas en los zonas áridas de México. By Margarita Nolasco, Cecilia Ramírez Cardoso, and Sergio Vivanco. Anuario Indigenista, 28 (1968): 202-213.

Norman, Rosamond. A look at the Papago "Vikita". Masterkey, 34 (1960): 98-101.

O'Neale, L. M. and J. Dolores. Notes on Papago color designations. American Anthropologist, 45 (1943): 387-397.

Packard, Robert C. Demographic discrimination of American Indian and Alaskan Eskimo groups by means of Bjork analysis. By Robert C. Packard and Thomas J. Zwemer. Journal of Dental Research, 50 (1971): 364-370.

Padfield, Harland. The Pima-Papago educational population; a census and analysis. By Harland Padfield, Peter Hemingway, and Philip Greenfeld. Journal of American Indian Education, 6, no. 1 (1966/1967): 1-24.

Padfield, Harland. Work and income patterns in a transitional population: the Papago of Arizona. By Harland Padfield and John van Willigen. Human Organization, 28 (1969): 208-216.

Parsons, Elsie Clews. Pueblo Indian religion. Vol. 2. Chicago, University of Chicago Press, 1939. 551-1275 p.

Patrick, Ralph. Papago Indian modernization: a community scale for health research. By Ralph Patrick and H. A. Tyroler. Human Organization, 31 (1972): 127-136.

Paxton, S. Gabe, Jr. A study of the composite self-concept of the Southwestern Indian adolescent; an inservice action research project of Sherman Institute. Washington, D.C., Bureau of Indian Affairs, 1966. 32 p. ERIC ED052878.

Perschl, Nicholas. Reminiscences of a Franciscan in Papagueria. Edited by Bernard L. Fontana. Kiva, 24, no. 3 (1958/1959): 1-9.

Phoenix Indian School. The new trail: a book of creative writing by Indian students. Phoenix, 1941. 158 p.

Pilcher, William W. Some comments on the folk taxonomy of the Papago. American Anthropologist, 69 (1967): 204-208.

Poe, Charlsie. Angel to the Papagos. San Antonio, Naylor, 1964. 11, 159 p. illus.

Portney, Gerald L. Epidemiology of trachoma in the San Xavier Papago Indians. By Gerald L. Portney and Susan B. Portney. Archives of Ophthalmology, 86 (1971): 260-262.

Ramos, Antonio. Father Eixarch and the visitation at Tumacácori, May 12, 1775. Edited by John L. Kessell. Kiva, 30, no. 3 (1964/1965): 77-86.

Reid, Jeanne M., et al. Nutrient intake of Pima Indian women: relationships to diabetes mellitus and gallbladder disease. American Journal of Clinical Nutrition, 24 (1971): 1281-1289.

Ressler, John Q. Indian and Spanish water-control on New Spain's northwest frontier. Journal of the West, 7 (1968): 10-17.

Rosenbaum, Louis J. Dexamethasone testing in Southwestern Indians. By Louis J. Rosenbaum, Ellen Alton, and Bernard Becker. Investigative Ophthalmology, 9 (1970): 325-330.

Ross, W. The present-day dietary habits of the Papago Indians. University of Arizona Record (1945): 1-25.

Ruley, Bessie Jean. Child-rearing practices among selected culturally deprived minorities. Dissertation Abstracts, 27 (1966/1967): 1208B. UM 66-9084.

Sabre. Tour in Arizona: footprints of an Army officer. Edited by Henry Winfred Splitter. Journal of the West, 1 (1962): 74-97.

Sanders, J. L. Quantitative guidelines for communicable disease control programs. Biometrics, 27 (1971): 883-893.

Sauer, C. The distribution of aboriginal tribes and languages in northwestern Mexico. Ibero-Americana, 5 (1934): 53-54.

Saxton, Dean, comp. Dictionary: Papago and Pima to English, O'odham-Mil-gahn; English to Papago and Pima, Mil-gahn-O'odham. Compiled by Dean and Lucille Saxton. Tucson, University of Arizona Press, 1969. 191 p.

Schroeder, Albert H. An archaeological survey of the Painted Rocks Resevoir, Western Arizona. Kiva, 27, no. 1 (1961/1962): 1-28.

Schroeder, Albert H. Comment on Johnson's "The Trincheras culture of northern Sonora". American Antiquity, 30 (1964/1965): 104-106.

Schweitzer, J. and R. K. Thomas. Fiesta of St. Francis at San Francis Quito, Sonora. Kiva, 18, nos. 1/2 (1952): 1-7.

Sedelmayr, Jacobo. Jacobo Sedelmayr missionary frontiersman explorer in Arizona and Sonora. Four original manuscript narratives 1744-1751. Translated and annotated by Peter Masten Dunne. [n.p.] Arizona Pioneers'

Historical Society, 1955. 4, 82, 7 p. map.

Segundo, T. A. From the tribe of the Papago Indians. Boletín Indigenista, 14 (March 1954): 27-30.

Serven, James E. The gun: an instrument of destiny in Arizona. Arizoniana, 5, no. 3 (1964): 14-28.

Short, Glenn Butler. Mating propinquity, inbreeding and biological fitness as measured by differential fertility and offspring vitality from Papago breeding unions. Dissertation Abstracts International, 34 (1973/1974): 967B. UM 73-18,593.

Shreve, M. Modern Papago basketry. Kiva, 8 (1943): 10-16.

Sievers, Maurice L. A study of achlorhydria among Southwestern American Indians. American Journal of Gastroenterology, 45 (1966): 99-108.

Sievers, Maurice L. Serum cholesterol levels in Southwestern American Indians. Journal of Chronic Diseases, 21 (1968): 107-115.

Simpson, James R. Uses of cultural anthropology in economic analysis: a Papago Indian case. Human Organization, 29 (1970): 162-168.

Smith, David G. Modernization, population dispersion, and Papago genetic integrity. Human Organization, 31 (1972): 187-199.

Smith, David Glenn. The genetic demography of a partially subdivided population in historical and ecological perspective: the Papago of southern Arizona. Dissertation Abstracts International, 34 (1973/1974): 1352B. UM 73-23,298.

Smith, W. N. The Papago game of "Gince Goot". Masterkey, 19 (1945): 194-197.

Spicer, E. The Papago Indians. Kiva, 6 (1941): 21-24.

Spier, L. Cultural relations of the Gila River and Lower Colorado tribes. Yale University Publications in Anthropology, 3 (1936): 1-22.

Spier, Leslie. Cultural relations of the Gila River and Lower Colorado tribes. New Haven, Human Relations Area Files Press, 1970. 22 p. (Yale University Publications in Anthropology, 3)

Stewart, Kenneth M. Southern Papago salt pilgrimages. Masterkey, 39 (1965): 84-91.

Stillwell, Margaret P. Two reports from Head Start. By Margaret P. Stillwell and R. V. Allen. Teachers College Record, 67 (1965/1966): 443-447.

Stocker, J. Tom Segundo. American Indian, 6, no. 2 (1951): 18-24.

Stone, M. Bean people of the cactus forest. Desert Magazine, 6, no. 11 (1943): 5-10.

Stricklen, E. G. Notes on eight Papago songs. California, University, Publications in American Archaeology and Ethnology, 20 (1923): 361-366.

Stull, Donald D. Victims of modernization: accident rates and Papago Indian adjustment. Human Organization, 31 (1972): 227-240.

Swadesh, M. Papago stop series. Word, 11 (1955): 191-193.

Tanner, Clara Lee. Papago burden baskets in the Arizona State Museum. Kiva, 30, no. 3 (1964/1965): 57-76.

Taylor, Benjamin J. Indian manpower resources in the Southwest: a pilot study. By Benjamin J. Taylor and Dennis J. O'Connor. Tempe, Arizona State University, 1969. 26, 374 p.

Taylor, Benjamin J. Papago Reservation manpower resources; Indian manpower resources in the Southwest. A pilot study. By Benjamin J. Taylor and Dennis J. O'Connor. Tempe, Arizona State University, College of Business Administration, 1969. 42 p. ERIC ED043445.

Thackeray, F. A. Sand food of the Papagos. Desert Magazine, 16, no. 4 (1953): 22-24.

Thackeray, F. A. and A. R. Leding. The giant cactus of Arizona. Journal of Heredity, 20 (1929): 401-414.

Thackeray, F. A. and M. F. Gilman. A rare parasitic food plant of the Southwest. Smithsonian Institution, Annual Report of the Board of Regents (1930): 409-416.

Thompson, Laura. Exploring American Indian communities in depth. In Peggy Golde, ed. Women in the Field. Chicago, Aldine, 1970: 45-64.

Tyroler, H. A. Epidemiologic studies of Papago Indian mortality. By H. A.

Tyroler and Ralph Patrick. Human Organization, 31 (1972): 163-170.

Uhlmann, Julie M. The impact of modernization on Papago Indian fertility. Human Organization, 31 (1972): 149-161.

Underhill, R. M. A Papago calendar record. New Mexico, University, Bulletin, Anthropological Series, 2, no. 5 (1938): 3-66.

Underhill, R. M. Hawk over whirlpools. New York, 1940. 255 p.

Underhill, R. M. Note on Easter devils at Kawori'k on the Papago Reservation. American Anthropologist, n.s., 36 (1934): 515-516.

*Underhill, R. M. Papago Indian religion. New York, 1946. 359 p.

Underhill, R. M. People of the crimson evening. Lawrence, 1951.

Underhill, R. M. Singing for power: the song magic of the Papago Indians. Berkeley, 1938. 158 p.

*Underhill, R. M. Social organization of the Papago Indians. Columbia University Contributions to Anthropology, 30 (1939): 1-280.

Underhill, R. M. The autobiography of a Papago woman. American Anthropological Association, Memoirs, 46 (1936): 1-64.

Underhill, R. M. The Papago Indians of Arizona and their relatives the Pima. Indian Life and Customs Pamphlets, 3 (1940): 1-68.

*Underhill, Ruth M. Papago Indian religion. New York, AMS Press, 1969. 6, 359 p.

*Underhill, Ruth M. Social organization of the Papago Indians. New York, AMS Press, 1969. 9, 280 p.

Underhill, Ruth M. The Papago Indians of Arizona and their relatives the Pima. Edited by Willard W. Beatty. Washington, D.C., U.S. Bureau of Indian Affairs, 1965. 71 p.

Vater, M. Ethnographische Gegenstände aus Arizona und Mexico. Berliner Gesellschaft für Anthropologie, Ethnologie und Urgeschichte, Verhandlungen (1892): 89-94.

Vavich, M. G., et al. Nutritional status of Papago Indian children. Journal of Nutrition, 54 (1956): 375-383.

Vivian, R. Gwinn. An archaeological survey of the Lower Gila River, Arizona. Kiva, 30, no. 4 (1964/1965): 95-146.

Voegelin, Carl F. Methods for typologizing directly and by distinctive features (in reference to Uto-Aztecan and Kiowa-Tanoan vowel systems). Lingua, 11 (1962): 469-487.

Voegelin, Carl F. Our knowledge of semantics and how it is obtained (with reference to Hopi /'as/ and Papago /čim/). By C. F. Voegelin and F. M. Voegelin. International Journal of American Linguistics, 36 (1970): 241-246.

Voegelin, Carl F. The autonomy of linguistics and the dependence of cognitive culture. By C. F. and F. M. Voegelin. In Jesse Sawyer, ed. Studies in American Indian Languages. Berkeley and Los Angeles, University of California Press, 1971: 303-317. (California, University, Publications in Linguistics, 65)

Waddell, Jack O. Papago Indians at work. Tucson, University of Arizona Press, 1969. 11, 159 p. illus. (Arizona, University, Anthropological Papers, 12)

Waddell, Jack O. Resurgent patronage and lagging bureaucracy in a Papago off-reservation community. Human Organization, 29 (1970): 37-42.

Waddell, Jack O'Brien. Adaptation of Papago workers to off-reservation occupations. Dissertation Abstracts, 27 (1966/1967): 2232B. UM 66-15,246.

Whited, S. Pima Agency. In United States, Department of the Interior, Census Office, Eleventh Census, Report on Indians Taxed and Indians not Taxed. Washington, D.C., 1890: 137-146.

Whiting, A. F. The Tumacacori census of 1796. Kiva, 29, no. 1 (1953): 1-12.

Williams, Thomas Rhys. The structure of the socialization process in Papago Indian society. Social Forces, 36 (1958): 251-256.

Williams, Thomas Rhys. The structure of the socialization process in Papago Indian society. In John Middleton, ed. From Child to Adult. Garden City, Natural History Press, 1970: 163-172.

Willigen, John Gilbert van. The role of the community level worker in Papago Indian development. Dissertation Abstracts International, 32 (1971/1972): 51B. UM 71-16,507.

Wilson, C. R. Folk and scientific models: a Papago case. Western Canadian Journal of Anthropology, 3, no. 2 (1972): 20-44.

Wilson, Charles Roderick. Migration, change, and variation: a Papago case study. Dissertation Abstracts International, 33 (1972/1973): 3439B. UM 73-1842.

Woodbury, Richard B. The changing patterns of Papago land use. By Richard B. Woodbury and Nathalie F. S. Woodbury. In Congreso Internacional de Americanistas, 35th. 1962, Mexico. Actas y Memorias. Tomo 2. Mexico, 1964: 181-186.

Woodruff, J. Indian oasis, 223-320. Caldwell, 1939.

Workman, P. L. Population studies on Southwestern Indian tribes. II. Local genetic differentiation in the Papago. By P. L. Workman and J. D. Niswander. American Journal of Human Genetics, 22 (1970): 24-49.

Wright, H. B. Long ago told: legends of the Papago Indians. New York, 1929. 290 p.

Zastrow, Leona. Papago pottery. Arts and Activities, 69 (March 1971): 25-28.

Zillatus, Mary G. Public health nursing in Papagoland. Nursing Outlook, 10 (1962): 792-794.

Zingg, Robert M. A reconstruction of Uto-Aztekan history. New York, G. E. Stechert, 1939. 4, 274 p. (Denver, University, Contributions to Ethnography, 2)

15-25   Pima

Allen, Robert J. The story of Superstition Mountain and the Lost Dutchman Gold Mine. New York, Pocket Books, 1971. 212 p.

Almada, Francisco R. Geografía humana de Chihuahua. Sociedad Mexicana de Geografía y Estadística, Boletín, 57 (1942): 227-300.

Anza, Juan Bautista de. Anza, Indian fighter; the spring campaign of 1766. Edited by John L. Kessell. Journal of Arizona History, 9 (1968): 155-163.

Bahr, Donald M. Who were the Hohokam? The evidence from Pima-Papago myths. Ethnohistory, 18 (1971): 245-266.

Bannon, John Francis. The mission frontier in Sonora, 1620-1687. Edited by James A. Reynolds. New York, United States Catholic Historical Society, 1955. 4, 160 p. (United States Catholic Historical Society, Monograph Series, 26)

Bartlett, J. R. Personal narrative of explorations and incidents in Texas, New Mexico, California, Sonora, and Chihuahua, Vol. 2: 222-238. New York, 1854.

Bartlett, John R. A letter from John R. Bartlett at Camp Yuma, 1852. Edited by Odie B. Faulk. Journal of Arizona History, 6 (1965): 204-213.

Basauri, Carlos. Familia "Pimana": Pimas. In his La Poblacion Indigena de Mexico. Tomo 1. Mexico, Secretaria de Educacion Publica, 1940: 222-242.

Bascom, Burton William, Jr. Proto-Tepiman (Tepehuan-Piman). Dissertation Abstracts, 27 (1966/1967): 192A-193A. UM 66-5811.

Beals, R. L. Material culture of the Pima, Papago, and Western Apache. Berkeley, 1934. 44 p.

Bennett, Peter H. Diabetes mellitus in American (Pima) Indians. By Peter H. Bennett, Thomas A. Burch, and Max Miller. Lancet, 2 (1971): 125-128.

Boas, F. Zur Anthropologie der nordamerikanischen Indianer. Berliner Gesellschaft für Anthropologie, Ethnologie und Urgeschichte, Verhandlungen (1895): 367-411.

Bolton, H. E., ed. Kino's historical memoir of Pimeria Alta. Cleveland, 1919. 2 v.

Breazeale, J. F. The Pima and his basket. Tucson, 1925.

Brown, Christine. Pima Central School and Blackwater School, Sacaton, Arizona. By Christine Brown and Robert J. Havighurst. Chicago, University of Chicago, 1970. 6 p. (National Study of American Indian Education, Series I, 22, Final Report) ERIC ED044211.

Brown, H. A Pima-Maricopa ceremony. American Anthropologist, n.s., 8 (1906): 688-690.

Burch, Thomas A. Epidemiological studies on rheumatic diseases. Military Medicine, 131 (1966): 507-511.

Buschmann, J. C. E. Die Pima-Sprache und die Sprache der Koloschen. Berlin,

Königliche Akademie der Wissenschaften, Abhandlungen (1856): 321-432.

Cabeza de Vaca, Alvar Núñez. Adventures in the unknown interior of America. New York, Collier, 1961. 152 p. (Collier Books, AS117)

Cain, Harvey T. Pima Indian basketry. Phoenix, Printed by McGrew Printing and Lithographing, 1962. 40 p. illus.

Castetter, E. F. Pima ethnobotany. New Mexico Quarterly Review, 20 (1950): 373-375.

*Castetter, E. F. and W. H. Bell. Pima and Papago Indian agriculture. Inter-American Studies, 1 (1942): 1-245.

Chilcott, John H., comp. Handbook for Pima and Maricopa Indian teacher aides. Tuscon, Ariz., University of Arizona, Bureau of Educational Research and Service, 1970. 20 p. ERIC ED044221.

Comess, L. J., et al. Congenital anomalies and diabetes in the Pima Indians of Arizona. Diabetes, 18 (1969): 471-477.

Comess, Leonard J. Clinical gallbladder disease in Pima Indians, its high prevalence in contrast to Framingham, Massachusetts. By Leonard J. Comess, Peter H. Bennett, and Thomas A. Burch. New England Journal of Medicine, 277 (1967): 894-898.

Cormack, Charles William. Social structure and economic production on an Arizona Indian reservation. Dissertation Abstracts, 29 (1968/1969): 3591B-3592B. UM 69-5412.

Corrigan, Francis Vincent. A comparison of self-concepts of American-Indian students from public or federal school backgrounds. Dissertation Abstracts International, 31 (1970/1971): 2679A-2680A. UM 70-24,959.

Curtin, L. S. M. By the prophet of the earth. Santa Fe, 1949. 158 p.

Curtis, E. S. The North American Indian, Vol. 2: 3-24, 39-45. Cambridge, 1908.

Curtis, N., ed. The Indians' book, 313-320. New York, 1907.

De Hoyos, Genevieve. Mobility orientation and mobility skills of youth in an institutionally dislocated group: the Pima Indian. Dissertation Abstracts, 28 (1967/1968): 4715A. UM 68-7247.

Demeke, Howard J., comp. In-service education series and consultant

services. Final report. Tempe, Arizona State University, College of Education, Bureau of Educational Research and Services, 1967. 47 p. ERIC ED046591.

*DiPeso, C. C. The Sobaipuri Indians of the Upper San Pedro River Valley, Southeastern Arizona. Amerind Foundation, Publications, 12 (1953): 1-285.

*DiPeso, C. C. The Upper Pima of San Cayetano del Tumacacori. Amerind Foundation, Publications, 7 (1956): 1-613.

Dobyns, H. F., et al. Thematic changes in Yuman warfare. In V. F. Ray, ed. Cultural Stability and Cultural Change. Seattle, 1957: 46-71.

Dobyns, Henry F. Indian extinction in the middle Santa Cruz River Valley, Arizona. New Mexico Historical Review, 38 (1963): 163-181.

Dobyns, Henry F. The 1797 population of the Presidio of Tucson. Journal of Arizona History, 13 (1972): 205-209.

Douglas, F. H. A Pima wood bowl. Denver Art Museum, Material Culture Notes, 11 (1939): 43-46.

Douglas, F. H. Pima Indian close coiled basketry. Denver Art Museum, Indian Leaflet Series, 5 (1930): 1-4.

Douglas, F. H., et al. Five Pima pots. Denver Art Museum, Material Culture Notes, 18 (1953): 1-8.

Drucker, Philip. Culture element distributions: XVII Yuman-Piman. Berkeley, 1941. 91-230 p. illus., map. (California, University, Publications, Anthropological Records, 6, no. 3)

Ellinwood, Sybil. Calabasas. Arizoniana, 5, no. 4 (1964): 27-41.

Ellis, Everett L. To take a scalp. Annals of Wyoming, 31 (1959): 140-143.

Ewing, C. R. Investigations into the causes of the Pima uprising of 1751. Mid-America, 23 (1941): 139-151.

Ewing, C. R. The Pima uprising of 1751. In Greater America: Essays in Honor of Herbert Eugene Bolton. Berkeley, 1945: 259-280.

Ezell, P. H. The conditions of Hispanic-Piman contacts on the Gila River. América Indígena, 17 (1957): 163-191.

Ezell, P. H.   The Hispanic acculturation
of the Gila River Pimas. Ethnohistory, 3
(1956): 189-190.

Ezell, Paul H.   Is there a Hohokam-Pima
culture continuum? American Antiquity,
29 (1963/1964): 61-66.

Ezell, Paul H.   The Hispanic acculturation
of the Gila River Pimas. Menasha,
American Anthropological Association,
1961. 5, 171 p. illus., maps.
(American Anthropological Association,
Memoir, 90)

Ezell, Paul H.   The Maricopas: an
identification from documentary sources.
Tucson, University of Arizona Press,
1963. 29 p. (Arizona, University,
Anthropological Papers, 6)

Fay, George E., ed.   Charters,
constitutions and by-laws of the Indian
tribes of North America. Part IV: The
Southwest (Navajo-Zuni). Greeley, 1967.
5, 120 l. maps. (University of
Northern Colorado, Museum of
Anthropology, Occasional Publications in
Anthropology, Ethnology Series, 5) ERIC
ED046554.

Fontana, Bernard L.   Johnny Ward's ranch:
a study in historic archaeology. By
Bernard L. Fontana and J. Cameron
Greenleaf. Kiva, 28, nos. 1/2
(1962/1963): 1-115.

Forbes, J. D.   Historical survey of the
Indians of Sonora, 1821-1910.
Ethnohistory, 4 (1957): 335-368.

Foster, Stanley O.   Trachoma in an
American Indian village. U.S., Public
Health Service, Public Health Reports,
80 (1965): 829-832.

Fullerton, Bill J., comp.   Instructional
centers for Pima culture. Final report:
academic year 1968-69. Compiled by Bill
J. Fullerton and John E. Bell.   Tempe,
Arizona State University, Bureau of
Education Research and Services, 1969.
66 p.   ERIC ED046608.

Gardner, Ruth Cogswell Anderson.   The
relationship of self esteem and
variables associated with reading for
fourth grade Pima Indian children.
Dissertation Abstracts International, 33
(1972/1973): 1512A.   UM 72-25,509.

Gates, John Morgan.   General George
Crook's first Apache campaign; (the use
of mobile, self-contained units against
the Apache in the Military Department of
Arizona, 1871-1873). Journal of the
West, 6 (1967): 310-320.

Genuth, S. M., et al.   Hyperinsulinism in
obese diabetic Pima Indians. Metabolism:
Clinical and Experimental, 16 (1967):
1010-1015.

Gofton, J. P., et al.   Sacro-iliitis in
eight populations. Annals of the
Rheumatic Diseases, 25 (1966): 528-533.

Gough, W. W., et al.   Evaluation of
glucose in the Pima Indians by
longitudinal studies. Diabetes, 19,
suppl. 1 (1970): 388.

Greene, R. A.   The composition and uses of
the fruit of the giant cactus. Journal
of Chemical Education, 13 (1936): 309-
312.

Griffin, William B.   Seventeenth century
Seri. Kiva, 27, no. 2 (1961/1962): 12-
21.

Grossmann, F. E.   The Pima Indians of
Arizona. Smithsonian Institution, Annual
Report of the Board of Regents (1871):
407-419.

Grossmann, F. E.   Three Pima fables. Kiva,
24 (1958): 24.

Hackenberg, Robert A.   Economic
alternatives in arid lands: a case study
of the Pima and Papago Indians.
Ethnology, 1 (1962): 186-196.

Hackenberg, Robert Allan.   Indian
administration and social change.
Dissertation Abstracts, 22 (1961/1962):
2547.   UM 62-173.

Hall, S. M.   The story of a Pima record
rod. Out West, 26 (1907): 413-423.

Halseth, O. S.   Archeology in the making.
Masterkey, 7 (1933): 37-41.

Hamy, E. T.   Algunas observaciones sobre
la distribución geográfica de los
Opatas, de los Tarahumares y de los
Pimas. Museo de Arqueología, Historia y
Etnografía, Anales, época 4a, 5 (1922):
93-98.

Hanna, B. L., et al.   A preliminary study
of the population history of the Pima
Indians. American Journal of Human
Genetics, 5 (1953): 377-388.

Hanna, Bertram L.   The biological
relationships among Indian groups of the
Southwest: analysis of morphological
traits. American Journal of Physical
Anthropology, n.s., 20 (1962): 499-508.

Hastings, James Rodney.   People of reason
and others: the colonization of Sonora
to 1767. Arizona and the West, 3 (1961):
321-340.

Hayden, Carl T. A history of the Pima Indians and the San Carlos irrigation project. Compiled in 1924 by Carl Hayden. Washington, D.C., Government Printing Office, 1965. 94 p. (U.S., 89th Congress, 1st Session, Senate, Document, 11)

Hayden, J. D. Notes on Pima pottery making. Kiva, 24, no. 3 (1959): 10-16.

Hayden, Julian D. Notes on Pima pottery making. Kiva, 24, no. 3 (1958/1959): 10-16.

Hertzog, Keith P. Shortened fifth medial phalanges. American Journal of Physical Anthropology, n.s., 27 (1967): 113-117.

Herzog, G. A comparison of Pueblo and Pima musical styles. Journal of American Folklore, 49 (1936): 283-417.

Herzog, G. Culture change and language. In Essays in Memory of Edward Sapir. Menasha, 1941: 66-74.

Herzog, G. Note on Pima moieties. American Anthropologist, n.s., 38 (1936): 520-521.

Hesse, Frank G. A dietary study of the Pima Indian. American Journal of Clinical Nutrition, 7 (1959): 532-537.

Hesse, Frank G. Incidence of cholecystitis and other diseases among the Pima Indians of southern Arizona. American Medical Association, Journal, 170 (1959): 1789-1790.

Hill, W. W. Note on the Pima berdache. American Anthropologist, n.s., 40 (1938): 338-340.

Hill, W. W. Notes on Pima land law and tenure. American Anthropologist, n.s., 38 (1936): 586-589.

Hodge, F. W. Pima. U.S. Bureau of American Ethnology, Bulletin, 30, pt. 2 (1910): 251-253.

Hodge, F. W. Sobaipuri. U.S. Bureau of American Ethnology, Bulletin, 30, pt. 2 (1910): 608.

Hrdlička, A. Notes on the Pima of Arizona. American Anthropologist, n.s., 8 (1906): 39-46.

Hufford, Kenneth. Travelers on the Gila Trail, 1824-1850. Journal of Arizona History, 7 (1966): 1-8; 8 (1967): 30-44.

Ives, R. L., ed. Sedelmayr's Relación of 1746. U.S. Bureau of American Ethnology, Bulletin, 123 (1939): 97-117.

Ives, Ronald L. Kino's exploration of the Pinacate region. Journal of Arizona History, 7 (1966): 59-75.

Jones, J. Historic record errs; Indians forced to fight for rights. Indian Historian, 3, no. 1 (1970): 41-42, 65.

Kate, H. F. C. ten. Indiens d'Amérique du Nord. Anthropologie (Paris), 28 (1917): 369-401.

Kate, H. F. C. ten. Reizen en onderzoekingen in Noord-Amerika, 152-160. Leiden, 1885.

Kate, H. F. C. ten. Somatological observations on Indians of the Southwest. Journal of American Ethnology and Archaeology, 3 (1892): 117-144.

Kayser, David W. Take a smooth pebble, add hard work: that's Maricopa pottery. El Palacio, 77, no. 1 (1970): 25-32.

Kelly, William H. A study of southern Arizona school-age Indian children, 1966-1967. Tucson, University of Arizona, Bureau of Ethnic Research, 1967. 3, 38 p. ERIC ED024485.

Kessell, John L. Father Ramón and the big debt, Tumacácori, 1821-1823. New Mexico Historical Review, 44 (1969): 53-72.

Kessell, John L. Mission of sorrows: Jesuit Guevavi and the Pimas, 1691-1767. Tucson, University of Arizona Press, 1970. 16, 224 p. illus., map.

Kessell, John L., ed. San José de Tumacácori-1773; a Franciscan reports from Arizona. Arizona and the West, 6 (1964): 303-312.

Kino, Eusebio F. Kino's biography of Francisco Javier Saeta, S.J. Rome, Jesuit Historical Institute, 1971. 15, 363 p. illus. (Sources and Studies for the History of the Americas, 9)

Kino, Eusebio Francisco. Correspondencia del P. Kino con los generales de la Compañía de Jesús 1682-1707. Prólogo y notas de Ernest J. Burrus, S.J. México, Editorial Jus, 1961. 95 p. illus., maps. (Testimonio Historica, 5)

Kino, Eusebio Francisco. Kino reports to headquarters; correspondence . . . from New Spain with Rome. Original Spanish text of fourteen unpublished letters and reports. With English translation and notes by Ernest J. Burrus, S.J. Rome, Institutum Historicum Societatis Jesu, 1954. 135 p.

Kissell, M. L. Basketry of the Papago and Pima. American Museum of Natural

History, Anthropological Papers, 17 (1916): 115-264.

Kissell, Mary L.   Basketry of the Papago and Pima Indians. Glorieta, N.M., Rio Grande Press, 1972.   117-264 p.   illus.

Knowlton, Clark S., ed.   Indian and Spanish American adjustments to arid and semiarid environments. Lubbock, Texas Technological College, 1964.   97 p. ERIC ED024478.

Kraus, B. S. and B. M. Jones.   Indian health in Arizona. Arizona, University, Bureau of Ethnic Research, Reports, 2 (1954): 1-164.

Kroeber, A. L.   Uto-Aztecan languages of Mexico. Ibero-Americana, 8 (1934): 1-27.

Kroeber, H. R.   Pima tales. American Anthropologist, n.s., 10 (1910): 231-235.

Levine, Stephen B., et al. Asymptomatic parotid enlargement in Pima Indians: relationship to age, obesity, and diabetes mellitus. Annals of Internal Medicine, 73 (1970): 571-573.

Lloyd, J. W.   Aw-aw-tam nights. Westfield, 1911.

Lumholtz, C.   New trails in Mexico. London, 1912.   411 p.

Matis, John A.   Odontognathic discrimination of United States Indian and Eskimo groups. By John A. Matis and Thomas J. Zwemer. Journal of Dental Research, 50 (1971): 1245-1248.

Matson, G. Albin.   Distribution of hereditary factors in the blood of Indians of the Gila River, Arizona. By G. Albin Matson, Thomas A. Burch, Herbert F. Polesky, Jane Swanson, H. Eldon Sutton, and Abner Robinson. American Journal of Physical Anthropology, n.s., 29 (1968): 311-337.

Merrill, W. Earl.   One hundred steps down Mesa's past. Mesa, Ariz., Lofgreen Printing, 1970.   244 p.

Miller, Mary R.   The language and language beliefs of Indian children. Anthropological Linguistics, 12 (1970): 51-61.

Neff, M. L.   Pima and Papago legends. Journal of American Folklore, 25 (1912): 51-65.

Niswander, Jerry D., et al. Population studies on Southwestern Indian trbies: I. History, culture and genetics of the

Papago. American Journal of Human Genetics, 22 (1970): 7-23.

O'Brien, William M.   Genetics of hyperuricaemia in Blackfeet and Pima Indians. By William M. O'Brien, Thomas A. Burch, and Joseph J. Bunim. Annals of the Rheumatic Diseases, 25 (1966): 117-119.

O'Brien, William M., et al.   A genetic study of rheumatoid arthritis and rheumatoid factor in Blackfeet and Pima Indians. Arthritis and Rheumatism, 10 (1967): 163-179.

Ocaranza, F.   Parva crónica de la Sierra Madre y las Pimerías. Instituto Panamericano de Geografía e Historia, Publicacion, 64 (1942): 4-156.

Ortega, José de.   Apostolicos afanes de la Compañia de Jesús. By José de Ortega and Juan Antonio Baltasar. México, Editorial Lagac, 1944.   24, 445 p.

Packard, Robert C.   Demographic discrimination of American Indian and Alaskan Eskimo groups by means of Bjork analysis. By Robert C. Packard and Thomas J. Zwemer. Journal of Dental Research, 50 (1971): 364-370.

Padfield, Harland.   The Pima-Papago educational population; a census and analysis. By Harland Padfield, Peter Hemingway, and Philip Greenfeld. Journal of American Indian Education, 6, no. 1 (1966/1967): 1-24.

Park, Joseph F.   Spanish Indian policy in northern Mexico, 1765-1810. Arizona and the West, 4 (1962): 325-344.

Parks, John H.   Diabetes among the Pima Indians of Arizona. By John H. Parks and Eleanor Waskow. Arizona Medicine, 18 (1961): 99-106.

Parsons, E. C.   Notes on the Pima. American Anthropologist, n.s., 30 (1928): 445-464.

Parsons, Elsie Clews.   Pueblo Indian religion. Vol. 2. Chicago, University of Chicago Press, 1939.   551-1275 p.

Paxton, S. Gabe, Jr.   A study of the composite self-concept of the Southwestern Indian adolescent; an inservice action research project of Sherman Institute. Washington, D.C., Bureau of Indian Affairs, 1966.   32 p. ERIC ED052878.

Phoenix Indian School.   The new trail: a book of creative writing by Indian students. Phoenix, 1941.   158 p.

Polesky, Herbert F. Serum albumin polymorphism in Indians of the Southwestern United States. By Herbert F. Polesky, Dwight A. Rokala, and Thomas A. Burch. Nature, 220 (1968): 175-176.

Polzer, Charles W., ed. The Franciscan entrada into Sonora 1645-1652: a Jesuit chronicle. Arizona and the West, 14 (1972): 253-278.

Potter, Rosario H. Yap, et al. Genetic studies of tooth size factors in Pima Indian families. American Journal of Human Genetics, 20 (1968): 89-100.

Prestwich, Sheldon G. The influence of two counseling methods on the physical and verbal aggression of pre-school Indian children. Dissertation Abstracts International, 30 (1969/1970): 2341A-2342A. UM 69-20,791.

Ramos, Antonio. Father Eixarch and the visitation at Tumacácori, May 12, 1775. Edited by John L. Kessell. Kiva, 30, no. 3 (1964/1965): 77-86.

Ramos, Antonio. Mission San Jose de Tumacacori and San Xavier del Bac in 1774. Edited by Louis Baldonado. Kiva, 24, no. 4 (1958/1959): 21-24.

Reid, Jeanne M., et al. Nutrient intake of Pima Indian women: relationships to diabetes mellitus and gallbladder disease. American Journal of Clinical Nutrition, 24 (1971): 1281-1289.

Roberts, Shirley J. Minority-group poverty in Phoenix; a socio-economic survey. Journal of Arizona History, 14 (1973): 347-362.

Robinson, B. Akimoel Awatam. Arizona Highways, 31, no. 7 (1955): 30-39.

Rushforth, Norman B., et al. Diabetes in the Pima Indians: evidence of bimodality in glucose tolerance distributions. Diabetes, 20 (1971): 756-765.

Russell, F. A Pima constitution. Journal of American Folklore, 15 (1903): 222-228.

Russell, F. Pima annals. American Anthropologist, n.s., 5 (1903): 76-80.

*Russell, F. The Pima Indians. U.S. Bureau of American Ethnology, Annual Reports, 26 (1908): 3-390.

Sabre. Tour in Arizona: footprints of an Army officer. Edited by Henry Winfred Splitter. Journal of the West, 1 (1962): 74-97.

Sampliner, Richard E., et al. Gallbladder disease in Pima Indians: demonstration of high prevalence and early onset by cholecystography. New England Journal of Medicine, 283 (1970): 1358-1364.

Sanford, George Bliss. "Thou art the man"; an address on the Indian question in 1892 by Colonel George Bliss Sanford. Edited by E. R. Hagemann. Journal of Arizona History, 9 (1968): 30-38.

Sauer, C. Distribution of aboriginal tribes and languages in northwestern Mexico. Ibero-Americana, 5 (1934): 52-54.

Saxton, Dean, comp. Dictionary: Papago and Pima to English, O'odham-Mil-gahn; English to Papago and Pima, Mil-gahn-O'odham. Compiled by Dean and Lucille Saxton. Tucson, University of Arizona Press, 1969. 191 p.

Schroeder, A. H. The Cipias and Ypotlapiguas. Arizona Quarterly, 12 (1956): 101-110.

Schroeder, Albert H. Comment on Johnson's "The Trincheras culture of northern Sonora". American Antiquity, 30 (1964/1965): 104-106.

Sedelmayr, Jacobo. Jacobo Sedelmayr missionary frontiersman explorer in Arizona and Sonora. Four original manuscript narratives 1744-1751. Translated and annotated by Peter Masten Dunne. [n.p.] Arizona Pioneers' Historical Society, 1955. 4, 82, 7 p. map.

Shaw, Anna M. Pima Indian legends. Tempe, Arizona State University, Indian Education Center, 1963. 116 l. illus.

Shaw, Anna M. Pima Indian legends. Tucson, University of Arizona Press, 1968. 15, 111 p. illus.

Sievers, Maurice L. A study of achlorhydria among Southwestern American Indians. American Journal of Gastroenterology, 45 (1966): 99-108.

Sievers, Maurice L. Serum cholesterol levels in Southwestern American Indians. Journal of Chronic Diseases, 21 (1968): 107-115.

Simpson, R. D. Those who have gone still live. Masterkey, 20 (1946): 73-80.

Smith, D. M. Indian tribes of the Southwest, 103-108. Stanford, 1933.

Spicer, Edward H. Apuntes sobre el tipo de religión de los Yuto-Aztecas Centrales. In Congreso Internacional de

Americanistas, 35th. 1962, Mexico. Actas y Memorias. Tomo 2. Mexico, 1964: 27-38.

Spicer, Edward H. European expansion and the enclavement of Southwestern Indians. Arizona and the West, 1 (1959): 132-145.

Spier, L. Cultural relations of the Gila River and Lower Colorado tribes. Yale University Publications in Anthropology, 3 (1936): 1-22.

Steen, C. R. Notes on some 19th century Pima burials. Kiva, 12 (1946): 6-10.

Steen, C. R. Some notes on the use of tobacco and cane pipes by the Pimas of the Gila Valley. American Anthropologist, n.s., 45 (1943): 641-642.

Steinberg, A. G., et al. Preliminary report on the genetics of diabetes among the Pima Indians. In Rafael A. Camerini-Davalos and Harold S. Cole. Early Diabetes. New York, Academic Press, 1970: 11-21.

Stevens, Robert Conway. Mexico's forgotten frontier: a history of Sonora, 1821-1846. Dissertation Abstracts, 24 (1963/1964): 3719-3720. UM 64-2142.

Tanner, Clara Lee. Papago burden baskets in the Arizona State Museum. Kiva, 30, no. 3 (1964/1965): 57-76.

Thomas, Cyrus. Indian languages of Mexico and Central America and their geographical distribution. By Cyrus Thomas assisted by John R. Swanton. Washington, D.C., Government Printing Office, 1911. 7, 108 p. map. (U.S., Bureau of American Ethnology, Bulletin, 44)

Underhill, R. M. The Papago Indians of Arizona and their relatives the Pima. Indian Life and Customs Pamphlets, 3 (1940): 1-68.

Underhill, Ruth M. The Papago Indians of Arizona and their relatives the Pima. Edited by Willard W. Beatty. Washington, D.C., U.S. Bureau of Indian Affairs, 1965. 71 p.

Van Valkenburgh, Sallie. The Casa Grande of Arizona as a landmark on the desert, a governmental reservation, and a National Monument. Kiva, 27, no. 3 (1961/1962): 1-31.

Walton, E. L. and T. T. Waterman. American Indian poetry. American Anthropologist, n.s., 27 (1925): 25-52.

Ware, Naomi. Survival and change in Pima Indian music. Ethnomusicology, 14 (1970): 100-113.

Whited, S. Pima Agency. In United States, Department of the Interior, Census Office, Eleventh Census, Report on Indians Taxed and Indians not Taxed. Washington, D.C., 1890: 137-146.

Whiting, A. F. The Tumacacori census of 1796. Kiva, 29, no. 1 (1953): 1-12.

Whittemore, I. T. Among the Pimas. Albany, 1893. 136 p.

Woo, Nancy. Tone in Northern Tepehuan. International Journal of American Linguistics, 36 (1970): 18-30.

Woodward, A. Historical notes on the Pima. Masterkey, 23 (1949): 144-147.

Wyllys, R. K. Padre Luis Velarde's Relacion of Pimeria Alta. New Mexico Historical Review, 6 (1931): 111-157.

Zingg, Robert M. A reconstruction of Uto-Aztekan history. New York, G. E. Stechert, 1939. 4, 274 p. (Denver, University, Contributions to Ethnography, 2)

15-26 Piro

Bandelier, A. F. Final report of investigations among the Indians of the Southwestern United States. Archaeological Institute of America, Papers, American Series, 3 (1890): 1-323; 4 (1892): 1-591.

Bartlett, J. R. The language of the Piro. American Anthropologist, n.s., 11 (1909): 426-433.

Fewkes, J. W. The Pueblo settlements near El Paso. American Anthropologist, n.s., 4 (1902): 72-75.

Hale, Kenneth. Toward a reconstruction of Kiowa-Tanoan phonology. International Journal of American Linguistics, 33 (1967): 112-120.

Hammond, G. P. and A. Rey, eds. Expedition into New Mexico made by Antonio de Espejo, 74-77. Los Angeles, 1929.

Harrington, J. P. Notes on the Piro language. American Anthropologist, n.s., 11 (1909): 563-594.

Hodge, F. W. Piros. U.S. Bureau of American Ethnology, Bulletin, 30, vol. 2 (1910): 261-262.

Leap, William L. Who were the Piro?
Anthropological Linguistics, 13 (1971):
321-330.

Schroeder, Albert H. The language of the
Saline Pueblos; Piro or Tiwa? New Mexico
Historical Review, 39 (1964): 235-249.

15-27   Queres

Davis, Irvine. Bibliography of Keresan
linguistic sources. International
Journal of American Linguistics, 29
(1963): 36-42.

Fraser, James H. Indian mission printing
in New Mexico: a bibliography. New
Mexico Historical Review, 43 (1968):
311-318.

Aberle, S. B. D. Maternal mortality among
the Pueblos. American Journal of
Physical Anthropology, 18 (1934): 431-
457.

Anonymous. Santo Domingo and San Felipe.
El Palacio, 24 (1928): 427-439.

Anonymous. The green corn ceremony. El
Palacio, 27 (1929): 48-50.

Bandelier, A. F. The delight makers. New
York, 1890. 490 p.

Benedict, R. Tales of the Cochiti
Indians. U.S. Bureau of American
Ethnology, Bulletin, 98 (1931): 1-256.

Bloom, L. B., ed. Bourke on the
Southwest. New Mexico Historical Review,
13 (1938): 192-238.

Boas, F. Abstract characteristics of
Keresan folktales. International
Congress of Americanists, Proceedings,
20, vol. 1 (1928): 223-224.

Bourke, J. G. The snake-dance of the
Moquis of Arizona, 10-53. London, 1884.

Bunzel, R. The emergence. Journal of
American Folklore, 41 (1928): 288-290.

Chapman, K. M. Pottery decorations of
Santo Domingo and Cochiti Pueblos. El
Palacio, 16 (1924): 87-93.

Chapman, K. M. The pottery of Santo
Domingo Pueblo. Santa Fe, Laboratory of
Anthropology, Memoirs, 1 (1936): 1-192.

Chavez, Angelico. The holy man of Zia.
New Mexico Historical Review, 40 (1965):
308-317.

Cochiti Dam Archaeological Salvage
Project. The Cochiti Dam:
archaeological salvage project.
Assembled by Charles H. Lange. Santa
Fe, Museum of New Mexico Press, 1968.
(Museum of New Mexico, Research Records,
6)

Concha, Fernando de la. Colonel Don
Fernando de la Concha diary, 1788.
Edited by Adlai Feather. New Mexico
Historical Review, 34 (1959): 285-304.

Curtin, L. S. M. Preparation of sacred
corn meal in the Rio Grande pueblos.
Masterkey, 41 (1967): 124-130; 42
(1968): 10-16.

*Curtis, E. S. The North American Indian,
Vol. 16: 65-249. Norwood, 1926.

Davis, Irvine. The language of Santa Ana
Pueblo. Washington, D.C., Government
Printing Office, 1964. 53-190 p.
(U.S., Bureau of American Ethnology,
Anthropological Papers, 69. U.S., Bureau
of American Ethnology, Bulletin, 191)

Davis, Irvine Elwin. Grammatical
structure of Santa Ana Keresan.
Dissertation Abstracts, 21 (1960/1961):
1706. UM 60-4938.

DeHuff, E. W. More Pueblo tales. El
Palacio, 11 (1921): 140-144.

DeHuff, E. W. Taytay's memories, 3-5, 10-
11, 129-130, 135-138, 217-223. New
York, 1924.

DeHuff, E. W. Taytay's tales, 92-94, 149-
158, 172-182. New York, 1922.

Densmore, F. Music of Acoma, Isleta,
Cochiti and Zuñi Pueblos. U.S. Bureau of
American Ethnology, Bulletin, 165
(1957): 1-129.

Densmore, F. Music of Santo Domingo
Pueblo. Southwest Museum Papers, 12
(1938): 1-186.

Densmore, Frances. Music of Acoma,
Isleta, Cochiti, and Zuñi Pueblos. New
York, Da Capo Press, 1972. 12, 117 p.
illus.

Devereux, Don. The re-location of a
Pueblo Emergence Shrine. El Palacio, 73,
no. 4 (1966): 21-26.

Douglas, F. H. Weaving of the Keres
Pueblos. Denver Art Museum, Indian
Leaflet Series, 91 (1939): 162-164.

Downing, George L. Native pottery of the
Southwest. Natural History, 78, no. 6
(1969): 34-39.

Dozier, E. P. A comparison of Eastern Keresan and Tewa kinship systems. International Congress of the Anthropological and Ethnological Sciences, Acts, 5 (1960): 430-436.

Dozier, Edward P. The Pueblo Indians of the Southwest. Current Anthropology, 5 (1964): 79-97.

*Dumarest, N. Notes on Cochiti. American Anthropological Association, Memoirs, 6 (1919): 137-237.

Ellis, Florence Hawley. A reconstruction of basic Jemez pattern of social organization, with comparisons to other Tanoan social structures. Albuquerque, University of New Mexico Press, 1964. 69 p. (New Mexico, University, Publications in Anthropology, 11)

Ellis, Florence Hawley. Pueblo boundaries and their markers. Plateau, 38 (1966): 97-106.

Ellis, Florence Hawley. The immediate history of Zia Pueblo as derived from excavation in refuse deposits. American Antiquity, 31 (1965/1966): 806-811.

Euler, R. C. Environmental adaptation at Sia Pueblo. Human Organization, 12, no. 4 (1954): 27-32.

Evans, B. and M. G. Evans. American Indian dance steps. New York, 1931. 122 p.

Fergusson, E. Dancing gods, 40-49, 56-60. New York, 1931.

Fewkes, J. W. A comparison of Sia and Tusayan snake ceremonials. American Anthropologist, 8 (1895): 118-141.

Fox, J. Robin. Multilingualism in two communities. By Robin Fox. Man, n.s., 3 (1968): 457-464.

Fox, J. Robin. The Keresan bridge: a problem in Pueblo ethnology. By Robin Fox. London, Athlone Press, 1967. 12, 216 p. maps. (London School of Economics, Monographs on Social Anthropology, 35)

Fox, J. Robin. Therapeutic rituals and social structure in Cochiti Pueblo. Human Relations, 13 (1960): 291-303.

Fox, J. Robin. Witchcraft and clanship in Cochiti therapy. In Ari Kiev, ed. Magic, Faith, and Healing. New York, Free Press, 1964: 174-200.

Fox, J. Robin. Witchcraft and clanship in Cochiti therapy. In John Middleton, ed. Magic, Witchcraft, and Curing. Garden City, Natural History Press, 1967: 255-284.

Gatschet, A. S. Classification into seven linguistic stocks of Western Indian dialects. In Report upon United States Geographical Surveys West of the One Hundredth Meridian. Vol. 7. Washington, D.C., 1879: 403-485.

Gatschet, A. S. Zwölf Sprachen aus dem Sudwesten Nordamerikas. Weimar, 1876. 150 p.

Gifford, E. W. Apache-Pueblo. Anthropological Records, 4 (1940): 1-207.

*Goldfrank, E. S. The social and ceremonial organization of Cochiti. American Anthropological Association, Memoirs, 33 (1927): 1-129.

Halseth, O. S. Report of economic and social survey of the Keres Pueblo of Zia. El Palacio, 16 (1924): 67-75.

Halseth, Odd S., et al. The Laguna santero. El Palacio, 77, no. 3 (1971): 19-22.

Hammond, G. P. and A. Rey, eds. Expedition into New Mexico made by Antonio de Espejo, 82-85. Los Angeles, 1929.

Harlow, Francis H. Tewa Indian ceremonial pottery. El Palacio, 72, no. 4 (1965): 13-23.

Hartley, M. The scientific esthetic of the Redman. Art and Archaeology, 13 (1922): 113-119.

Hawley, F. An examination of problems basic to acculturation in the Rio Grande Pueblos. American Anthropologist, n.s., 50 (1948): 612-624.

Hawley, F. Keresan patterns of kinship and social organization. American Anthropologist, n.s., 52 (1950): 499-512.

Hawley, F. and D. Fenter. Group-designed behavior patterns in two acculturating groups. Southwestern Journal of Anthropology, 2 (1946): 133-151.

Hawley, F., M. Pijoan, and C. A. Elkin. An inquiry into food economy and body economy in Zia Pueblo. American Anthropologist, n.s., 45 (1943): 547-556.

Hewett, E. L. From barter to world trade. El Palacio, 49 (1942): 219-224.

Hewett, E. L.   The corn ceremony at Santo Domingo. El Palacio, 5 (1918): 69-76.

Hodge, F. W.   Cochiti. U.S. Bureau of American Ethnology, Bulletin, 30, vol. 1 (1907): 317-318.

Hodge, F. W.   Pueblo snake ceremonials. American Anthropologist, 9 (1896): 133-136.

Hodge, F. W.   San Felipe. U.S. Bureau of American Ethnology, Bulletin, 30, vol. 2 (1910): 432-433.

Hodge, F. W.   Santa Ana. U.S. Bureau of American Ethnology, Bulletin, 30, vol. 2 (1910): 454.

Hodge, F. W.   Santo Domingo. U.S. Bureau of American Ethnology, Bulletin, 30, vol. 2 (1910): 462.

Hodge, F. W.   Sia. U.S. Bureau of American Ethnology, Bulletin, 30, vol. 2 (1910): 562-563.

Hoebel, E. A.   Keresan witchcraft. American Anthropologist, 54 (1952): 586-589.

Hoebel, E. A.   Underground kiva passages. American Antiquity, 19 (1953): 76.

Hoebel, E. Adamson.   The character of Keresan Pueblo law. American Philosophical Society, Proceedings, 112 (1968): 127-130.

Huebener, G.   The green corn dance at Santo Domingo. El Palacio, 45 (1938): 1-17.

Humphrey, N. B.   The mock battle greeting. Journal of American Folklore, 54 (1941): 186-190.

Hurt, L. R.   Notes on the Santa Ana Indians. El Palacio, 48 (1941): 131-142.

James, H. L.   Ácoma: the people of the white rock.   Glorieta, Rio Grande Press, 1970.   96 p.   illus., map.

Keech, R. A.   Green corn ceremony at the Pueblo of Zia. El Palacio, 36 (1934): 145-149.

Kupferer, Harriet J.   Material changes in a conservative Pueblo. El Palacio, 69 (1962): 248-251.

Lange, C. H.   An animal dance at Santo Domingo Pueblo, January 26, 1940. El Palacio, 61 (1954): 151-155.

Lange, C. H.   Culture change as revealed in Cochiti Pueblo hunting customs. Texas Journal of Science, 5 (1953): 178-184.

Lange, C. H.   King's Day ceremonies at a Rio Grande Pueblo, Jan. 6, 1940. El Palacio, 58 (1951): 398-406.

Lange, C. H.   San Juan's Day at Cochiti Pueblo, New Mexico, 1894 and 1947. El Palacio, 59 (1952): 175-182.

Lange, C. H.   The feast day dance at Zia Pueblo. Texas Journal of Science, 4 (1952): 19-26.

Lange, C. H.   The Keresan component of Southwestern Pueblo culture. Southwestern Journal of Anthropology, 14 (1958): 34-50.

Lange, C. H.   The role of economics in Cochiti Pueblo social change. American Anthropologist, 55 (1953): 674-694.

Lange, C. H. and W. C. Bailey. Significant factors in the comparison of explicitly heterogeneous cultures. Texas Journal of Science, 7 (1955): 256-274.

*Lange, Charles H.   Cochiti: a New Mexico pueblo, past and present.   Austin, University of Texas Press, 1960.   24, 618 p.   illus., maps.

McHarg, J. B.   The lions of Cochiti. El Palacio, 20 (1926): 99-104.

Miller, Julius J.   The anthropology of Keres identity. Dissertation Abstracts International, 33 (1972/1973): 1361B. UM 72-27,578.

Miller, Wick R.   Proto-Keresan phonology. By Wick R. Miller and Irvine Davis. International Journal of American Linguistics, 29 (1963): 310-330.

Miller, Wick R.   Spanish loanwords in Acoma. International Journal of American Linguistics, 25 (1959): 147-153; 26 (1960): 41-49.

Parsons, E. C.   Early relations between Hopi and Keres. American Anthropologist, n.s., 38 (1936): 554-560.

Parsons, E. C.   Fiesta at Sant' Ana. Scientific Monthly, 16 (1923): 178-183.

Parsons, E. C.   Notes on Isleta, Santa Ana, and Acoma. American Anthropologist, n.s., 22 (1920): 56-69.

Parsons, E. C.   Notes on San Felipe and Santo Domingo. American Anthropologist, n.s., 25 (1923): 485-494.

Parsons, E. C.   Pueblo Indian religion. Chicago, 1939.   2 v.

Parsons, E. C.   The kinship nomenclature of the Pueblo Indians. American

Anthropologist, n.s., 34 (1932): 377-389.

Polese, Richard L. The Zia sun symbol; variations on a theme. El Palacio, 75, no. 2 (1968): 30-34.

Prince, L. B. The stone lions of Cochiti. Records of the Past, 3 (1904): 151-160.

Reagan, A. B. Additional notes on the Jemez-Zia region. El Palacio, 12 (1922): 120-121.

Reagan, A. B. The Zia Indians. Southern Workman, 45 (1916): 25-29.

Reagan, A. B. The Zia Mesa and ruins. Science, 30 (1909): 713-714.

Robb, John Donald. Rhythmic patterns of the Santo Domingo Corn Dance. Ethnomusicology, 8 (1964): 154-160.

Schaafsma, Curt. Funeral bowls from a Spanish-contact Composanto. El Palacio, 75, no. 2 (1968): 40-43.

Simmons, Marc. New Mexico's smallpox epidemic of 1780-1781. New Mexico Historical Review, 41 (1966): 319-326.

Smith, D. M. Indian tribes of the Southwest, 88-94. Stanford, 1933.

Spencer, R. F. Spanish loanwords in Keresan. Southwestern Journal of Anthropology, 3 (1947): 130-146.

Spencer, R. F. The phonemes of Keresan. International Journal of American Linguistics, 12 (1946): 229-236.

Starr, F. A study of a census of the Pueblo of Cochiti. Davenport Academy of Sciences, Proceedings, 7 (1899): 33-45.

Starr, F. Shrines near Cochiti. American Antiquarian and Oriental Journal, 22 (1900): 219-223.

Stephens, E. L. Steve. West of the Pecos. New Mexico Historical Review, 35 (1960): 81-108, 236-256, 309-326; 36 (1961): 159-174.

Stevenson, J. Illustrated catalogue of the collections obtained from the Indians of New Mexico and Arizona. U.S. Bureau of American Ethnology, Annual Reports, 2 (1883): 405-409, 450-460.

Stevenson, M. C. The Sia. U.S. Bureau of American Ethnology, Annual Reports, 11 (1894): 9-157.

Trager, George L. The Tanoan settlement of the Rio Grande area: a possible chronology. In Dell H. Hymes and William

E. Bittle, eds. Studies in Southwestern Ethnolinguistics. The Hague, Mouton, 1967: 335-350. (Studies in General Anthropology, 3)

Underhill, R. M. First penthouse dwellers of America, 85-107. New York, 1938.

Voegelin, Carl F. Methods for typologizing directly and by distinctive features (in reference to Uto-Aztecan and Kiowa-Tanoan vowel systems). Lingua, 11 (1962): 469-487.

White, L. A. A comparative study of Keresen medicine societies. International Congress of Americanists, Proceedings, 23 (1928): 604-619.

White, L. A. Keresan Indian color terms. Michigan Academy of Science, Arts and Letters, Papers, 28 (1942): 559-563.

White, L. A. Miscellaneous notes on the Keresan Pueblos. Michigan Academy of Science, Arts and Letters, Papers, 32 (1946): 365-376.

White, L. A. Notes on the ethnobotany of the Keres. Michigan Academy of Science, Arts and Letters, Papers, 30 (1944): 557-568.

White, L. A. Notes on the ethnozoology of the Keresan Pueblo Indians. Michigan Academy of Science, Arts and Letters, Papers, 31 (1945): 223-246.

White, L. A. "Rohona" in Pueblo culture. Michigan Academy of Science, Arts and Letters, Papers, 29 (1943): 439-443.

*White, L. A. The Pueblo of San Felipe. American Anthropological Association, Memoirs, 38 (1932): 1-69.

*White, L. A. The Pueblo of Santa Ana. American Anthropological Association, Memoirs, 60 (1942): 1-360.

*White, L. A. The Pueblo of Santo Domingo. American Anthropological Association, Memoirs, 43 (1935): 1-210.

*White, Leslie A. The pueblo of Sia, New Mexico. Washington, D.C., Government Printing Office, 1962. 12, 358 p. illus., map. (U.S., Bureau of American Ethnology, Bulletin, 184)

White, Leslie A. The world view of the Keresan Pueblo Indians. In Stanley Diamond, ed. Primitive Views of the World. New York, Columbia University Press, 1964: 83-94.

Whitener, H. C., tr. Jesus Christo niya tawa-mani. Albuquerque, 1935. 72 p.

Wilson, E. H. Enemy Bear. Masterkey, 22 (1948): 80-85.

Wittick, Ben. Ben Wittick views the Pueblos. Edited by Carol Scott Alley. El Palacio, 73, no. 2 (1966): 4-9.

Zbinden, Ernst A. Nördliche und südliche Elemente im Kulturheroenmythus der Südathapasken. Anthropos, 55 (1960): 689-733.

15-28   Tano

Hale, Kenneth. Toward a reconstruction of Kiowa-Tanoan phonology. International Journal of American Linguistics, 33 (1967): 112-120.

Harrington, J. P. The language of the Tano Indians. International Congress of Americanists, Proceedings, 17, vol. 2 (1910): 321-329.

Hodge, F. W. Tano. U.S. Bureau of American Ethnology, Bulletin, 30, vol. 2 (1910): 686-687.

Nelson, N. C. Archeology of the Tano District. International Congress of Americanists, Proceedings, 19 (1915): 114-119.

Nelson, N. C. Chronology of the Tano ruins. American Anthropologist, n.s., 18 (1916): 159-180.

Reed, E. K. Test excavations at San Marcos Pueblo. El Palacio, 61 (1954): 323-343.

Riley, C. L. Early Spanish reports of the Galisteo Basin. El Palacio, 58 (1951): 237-243.

Whorf, B. L. and G. L. Trager. The relationship of Uto-Aztecan and Tanoan. American Anthropologist, n.s., 39 (1937): 609-624.

15-29   Taos

Aberle, S. B. D. Maternal mortality among the Pueblos. American Journal of Physical Anthropology, 18 (1934): 431-457.

Aiello, Constantine, ed. Oo-cónah art; Taos Indian for 'child,' by the Taos Pueblo Indian School's 7th-8th grade pupils of '67-68. Taos, Taos Pueblo Governor's Office, 1970. 40 p. illus.

Anderson, A. J. O. Taos uprising legends. El Palacio, 53 (1946): 331-337.

Angulo, J. de. Taos kinship terminology. American Anthropologist, n.s., 27 (1925): 482-483.

Arriquibar, Pedro Antonio de. Fray Pedro de Arriquibar's census of Tucson, 1820. Edited by Karen Sikes Collins. Journal of Arizona History, 11 (1970): 14-22.

Austin, M. and A. E. Adams. Taos Pueblo. San Francisco, 1931. 20 p.

Bailey, F. M. Some plays and dances of the Taos Indians. Natural History, 24 (1924): 85-95.

Beals, Alan R. Divisiveness and social conflict; an anthropological approach. By Alan R. Beals and Bernard J. Siegel. Stanford, Stanford University Press, 1966. 10, 185 p.

Bloom, L. B., ed. Bourke on the Southwest. New Mexico Historical Review, 11 (1936): 217-282; 12 (1937): 41-77.

Blumenschein, Helen G. Historic roads and trails to Taos. El Palacio, 75, no. 1 (1968): 9-19.

Boas, F. Zur Anthropologie der nordamerikanischen Indianer. Berliner Gesellschaft für Anthropologie, Ethnologie und Urgeschichte, Verhandlungen (1895): 367-411.

Bodine, John J. A tri-ethnic trap: the Spanish Americans in Taos. In June Helm, ed. Spanish-Speaking People in the United States. Seattle, University of Washington Press, 1968: 145-153. (American Ethnological Society, Proceedings of the Annual Spring Meeting, 1968)

Bodine, John J. Taos names: a clue to linguistic acculturation. Anthropological Linguistics, 10, no. 5 (1968): 23-27.

Bodine, John James. Attitudes and institutions of Taos, New Mexico: variables for value system expression. Dissertation Abstracts, 28 (1967/1968): 2699B-2700B. UM 67-17,901.

Brown, Donald N. The development of Taos dance. Ethnomusicology, 5 (1961): 33-41.

Brown, Donald Nelson. Taos dance classification. El Palacio, 67 (1960): 203-209.

Cassidy, I. S. New Mexico place names-- Taos. El Palacio, 61 (1954): 296-299.

Cassidy, I. S. Taos. Western Folklore, 8 (1949): 60-62.

Cobb, John C.   Trachoma among Southwestern Indians. By John C. Cobb and Chandler R. Dawson. American Medical Association, Journal, 175 (1961): 405-406.

Collins, J. J.   Law functions and judicial process at a New Mexican pueblo. International Journal of Comparative Sociology, 9 (1968): 129-131.

Collins, John James.   A descriptive introduction to the Taos peyote ceremony. Ethnology, 7 (1968): 427-449.

Collins, John James.   Peyotism at Taos Pueblo and the problem of ceremonial description. Dissertation Abstracts International, 30 (1969/1970): 2514B. UM 69-20,591.

Concha, Fernando de la.   Colonel Don Fernando de la Concha diary, 1788. Edited by Adlai Feather. New Mexico Historical Review, 34 (1959): 285-304.

Curtin, L. S. M.   Preparation of sacred corn meal in the Rio Grande pueblos. Masterkey, 41 (1967): 124-130; 42 (1968): 10-16.

Curtis, E. S.   The North American Indian, Vol. 16: 27-63.   Norwood, 1926.

DeHuff, E. W.   Infidelity. El Palacio, 31 (1931): 200-201.

DeHuff, E. W.   More Pueblo tales. El Palacio, 11 (1921): 140-144.

DeHuff, E. W.   Myths told by the Pueblos. El Palacio, 11 (1921): 86-92.

DeHuff, E. W.   Taytay's memories, 34-39, 45-48, 91-122, 147-157, 161-174, 207-212. New York, 1924.

DeHuff, E. W.   Taytay's tales, 51-54, 61-64, 112-115, 159-161, 168-169, 183-190. New York, 1922.

DeHuff, E. W.   The bear and the deer. El Palacio, 31 (1931): 2-4.

DeHuff, E. W.   The fate of yellow corn and blue corn. El Palacio, 16 (1924): 53-55.

DeHuff, E. W.   The greedy fox. El Palacio, 31 (1931): 20-22.

DeHuff, E. W.   The red winged hawk. El Palacio, 16 (1924): 51-53.

DeHuff, E. W.   The witches' feast is interrupted. El Palacio, 45 (1938): 69-73.

DeHuff, E. W.   The yellow house people. El Palacio, 30 (1931): 269-274.

Douglas, F. H.   Weaving of the Tiwa Pueblos and Jemez. Denver Art Museum, Indian Leaflet Series, 91 (1939): 162-164.

Downing, George L.   Native pottery of the Southwest. Natural History, 78, no. 6 (1969): 34-39.

Dustin, C. Burton.   Peyotism and New Mexico. Farmington, N.M., 1960. 51 p. illus.

Ellis, Florence Hawley.   A reconstruction of basic Jemez pattern of social organization, with comparisons to other Tanoan social structures. Albuquerque, University of New Mexico Press, 1964. 69 p. (New Mexico, University, Publications in Anthropology, 11)

Ellis, Florence Hawley.   Ceramic stratigraphy and tribal history at Taos Pueblo. By Florence Hawley Ellis and J. J. Brody. American Antiquity, 29 (1963/1964): 316-327.

Fenton, William N.   Factionalism at Taos Pueblo, New Mexico. Washington, D.C., Government Printing Office, 1957.   297-344 p. illus. (U.S., Bureau of American Ethnology, Anthropological Papers, 56. U.S., Bureau of American Ethnology, Bulletin, 164)

Fergusson, E.   Dancing gods, 36-40. New York, 1931.

Gatschet, A. S.   Classification into seven linguistic stocks of Western Indian dialects. In Report upon United States Geographical Surveys West of the One Hundredth Meridian. Vol. 7. Washington, D.C., 1879: 403-485.

Gatschet, A. S.   Migration of the Taos Indians. American Anthropologist, 5 (1892): 191-192.

Gatschet, A. S.   Zwölf Sprachen aus dem Südwesten Nordamerikas. Weimar, 1876. 150 p.

Goldman, Stanford M., et al.   Roentgen manifestations of diseases in Southwestern Indians. Radiology, 103 (1972): 303-306.

Grant, B. C.   Taos Indians. Taos, 1925. 127 p.

Grant, B. C.   Taos today. Taos, 1925. 47 p.

Grant, Blanche Chloe.   When old trails were new; the story of Taos. Chicago, Rio Grande Press, 1963. 8, 344 p.

Hale, Kenneth. Toward a reconstruction of kiowa-Tanoan phonology. International Journal of American Linguistics, 33 (1967): 112-120.

Hall, R. A. A note on Taos k'owena, "Horse". International Journal of American Linguistics, 13 (1947): 117-118.

Harrington, J. P. Ambiguity in the Taos personal pronoun. In Holmes Anniversary Volume. Washington, D.C., 1916: 142-156.

Harrington, J. P. An introductory paper on the Tiwa language. American Anthropologist, n.s., 12 (1910): 11-46.

Harrington, J. P. and H. H. Roberts. Picuris children's stories. U.S. Bureau of American Ethnology, Annual Reports, 43 (1928): 289-447.

Hodge, F. W. Ceremonial shields of Taos. Indian Notes, 3 (1926): 95-99.

Hodge, F. W. Old cradle from Taos. Museum of the American Indian, Heye Foundation, Contributions, 5 (1928): 231-235.

Hodge, F. W. Taos. U.S. Bureau of American Ethnology, Bulletin, 30, vol. 2 (1910): 688-691.

Hodge, F. W. Tigua. U.S. Bureau of American Ethnology, Bulletin, 30, vol. 2 (1910): 747-749.

Hogue, A. Picturesque games and ceremonials of Indians. El Palacio, 26 (1929): 177-183.

Jeançon, J. A. Archaeological investigations in Taos Valley. Smithsonian Miscellaneous Collections, 81, no. 12 (1930): 1-29.

Jeançon, J. A. Taos notes. El Palacio, 28 (1930): 3-11.

Jenkins, Myra Ellen. Taos Pueblo and its neighbors; 1540-1847. New Mexico Historical Review, 41 (1966): 85-114.

Jones, H. The fiesta of San Geronimo at Taos. El Palacio, 31 (1931): 300-302.

Jones, William M. Origin of the place-name Taos. Anthropological Linguistics, 2, no. 3 (1960): 2-4.

Kelley, D. M. Impairment of the religious liberty of the Taos Pueblo Indians by the United States government. Journal of Church and State, 9 (1967): 161-164.

Kessell, John L. The making of a martyr: the young Francisco Garcés. New Mexico Historical Review, 45 (1970): 181-196.

Lasswell, H. D. Collective autism as a consequence of culture contact: notes on religious training and the peyote cult at Taos. Zeitschrift für Sozialforschung, 4 (1935): 232-247.

Leap, William L. Tiwa noun class semology: a historical view. Anthropological Linguistics, 12 (1970): 38-45.

Leap, William Lester. The language of Isleta, New Mexico. Dissertation Abstracts International, 31 (1970/1971): 5772B-5773B. UM 71-8763.

Ledbetter, Elizabeth. The Taos Pueblo; a case of selective acculturation. Indian Historian, 2, no. 2 (1969): 24, 28.

Luhan, M. D. Taos and its artists. New York, 1947. 168 p.

Maughan, Scott Jarvis. Francisco Garcés and New Spain's northwestern frontier, 1768-1781. Dissertation Abstracts, 29 (1968/1969): 2647A-2648A. UM 69-3508.

Miller, M. L. Preliminary study of the Pueblo of Taos. Chicago, 1898.

Monahan, Forrest D., Jr. The Kiowas and New Mexico, 1800-1845. Journal of the West, 8 (1969): 67-75.

Murphy, Lawrence R. The Beaubien and Miranda land grant; 1841-1846. New Mexico Historical Review, 42 (1967): 27-47.

New, Lloyd. Institute of American Indian Arts. Arizona Highways, 48, no. 1 (1972): 5, 12-15, 44-45.

Pancoast, C. L. Last dance of the Picuris. Natural History, 18 (1918): 308-311.

Parsons, E. C. Picuris. American Anthropologist, n.s., 41 (1939): 206-222.

Parsons, E. C. Pueblo Indian religion. Chicago, 1939. 2 v.

*Parsons, E. C. Taos Pueblo. General Series in Anthropology, 2 (1936): 1-120.

Parsons, E. C. Taos tales. American Folk-Lore Society, Memoirs, 34 (1940): 1-185.

Parsons, E. C. The kinship nomenclature of the Pueblo Indians. American Anthropologist, n.s., 34 (1932): 377-389.

Parsons, Elsie Clews. Taos Pueblo. New York, Johnson Reprint, 1970. 121 p. illus., map.

Pike, Albert. Albert Pike's journeys in the prairie, 1831-1832. Edited by J. Evetts Haley. Panhandle-Plains Historical Review, 41 (1968): 1-84.

Pilling, Arnold R. Some questions on Taos dancing. Ethomusicology, 6 (1962): 88-92.

Reno, Philip. Rebellion in New Mexico--1837. New Mexico Historical Review, 40 (1965): 197-213.

Reno, Philip. Taos pueblo. Denver, Sage Books, 1963. 36 p. illus.

Reno, Philip. Tourism possibilities for the Taos Indians. New Mexico Business, 19, no. 2 (1966): 1-26.

Ressler, John Q. Indian and Spanish water-control on New Spain's northwest frontier. Journal of the West, 7 (1968): 10-17.

Roach, Dennis., ed. Taos Pueblo: a study of architecture of arid and semi-arid lands. Coedited by Dennis Roach and James West. Lubbock, Texas Tech Chapter, Student Chapter of the American Institute of Architects, 1967. 22 p. illus.

Siegel, B. J. High anxiety levels and cultural integration. Social Forces, 34 (1955): 42-48.

Siegel, B. J. Some observations of the Pueblo pattern at Taos. American Anthropologist, n.s., 51 (1949): 562-577.

Siegel, B. J. Suggested factors of culture change at Taos Pueblo. International Congress of Americanists, Proceedings, 29, vol. 2 (1952): 133-140.

Siegel, B. J. and A. R. Beals. Pervasive factionalism. American Anthropologist, 62 (1960): 394-417.

Siegel, Bernard J. Pervasive factionalism. By Bernard J. Siegel and Alan R. Beals. American Anthropologist, 62 (1960): 394-417.

Siegel, Bernard J. Social disorganization in Picuris Pueblo. International Journal of Comparative Sociology, 6 (1965): 199-206.

Siegel, Bernard J. Some structure implications for change in Pueblo and Spanish New Mexico. In Verne F. Ray, ed. Intermediate Societies, Social Mobility,

and Communication. Seattle, American Ethnological Society, 1959: 37-44. (American Ethnological Society, Proceedings of the Annual Spring Meeting, 1959)

Smith, D. M. Indian tribes of the Southwest, 112-124. Stanford, 1933.

Smith, M. Estellie. Aspects of social control among the Taos Indians. Dissertation Abstracts, 28 (1967/1968): 3143B. UM 67-10,161.

Smith, M. Estellie. Notes on an ethnolinguistic study of governing. In M. Estellie Smith, ed. Studies in Linguistics in Honor of George L. Trager. The Hague, Mouton, 1972: 487-501. (Janua Linguarum, Series Maior, 52)

Speirs, Randall H. Number in Tewa. In M. Estellie Smith, ed. Studies in Linguistics in Honor of George L. Trager. The Hague, Mouton, 1972: 479-486. (Janua Linguarum, Series Maior, 52)

Spier, Leslie. Cultural relations of the Gila River and Lower Colorado tribes. New Haven, Human Relations Area Files Press, 1970. 22 p. (Yale University Publications in Anthropology, 3)

Trager, Felicia Harben. Picurís Pueblo, New Mexico: an ethnolinguistic "salvage" study. Dissertation Abstracts, 29 (1968/1969): 458B. UM 68-11,548.

Trager, Felicia Harben. Retention and loss in Picuris kinship terms. In M. Estellie Smith, ed. Studies in Linguistics in Honor of George L. Trager. The Hague, Mouton, 1972: 475-478. (Janua Linguarum, Series Maior, 52)

Trager, Felicia Harben. Some aspects of 'time' at Picuris Pueblo (with an addendum on the Nootka). Anthropological Linguistics, 13 (1971): 331-338.

Trager, Felicia Harben. The phonology of Picuris. International Journal of American Linguistics, 37 (1971): 29-33.

Trager, G. L. A status symbol and personality at Taos Pueblo. Southwestern Journal of Anthropology, 4 (1948): 249-304.

Trager, G. L. An outline of Taos grammar. Viking Fund Publications in Anthropology, 6 (1946): 184-221.

Trager, G. L. Days of the week in the language of Taos Pueblo. Language, 15 (1939): 51-55.

Trager, G. L. Spanish and English loanwords in Taos. International Journal of American Linguistics, 10 (1944): 144-158.

Trager, G. L. Taos. International Journal of American Linguistics, 14 (1948): 155-160; 20 (1954): 173-180.

Trager, G. L. The kinship and status terms of the Tiwa languages. American Anthropologist, n.s., 45 (1943): 557-571.

Trager, George L. Semology, metalinguistics, and translation. In William M. Austin, ed. Papers in Linguistics in Honor of Léon Dostert. The Hague, Mouton, 1967: 149-154. (Janua Linguarum, Series Maior, 25)

Trager, George L. Taos and Picuris--how long separated? International Journal of American Linguistics, 35 (1969): 180-182.

Trager, George L. Taos III: paralanguage. Anthropological Linguistics, 2, no. 2 (1960): 24-30.

Trager, George L. Taos IV: morphemics, syntax, semology in nouns and in pronomial reference. International Journal of American Linguistics, 27 (1961): 211-222.

Trager, George L. The cardinal directions at Taos and Picuris. By George L. Trager and Felicia Harben Trager. Anthropological Linguistics, 12 (1970): 31-37.

Trager, George L. The name of Taos, New Mexico. Anthropological Linguistics, 2, no. 3 (1960): 5-6.

Trager, George L. The typology of paralanguage. Anthropological Linguistics, 3, no. 1 (1961): 17-21.

Underhill, R. M. First penthouse dwellers of America, 131-154. New York, 1938.

U.S., Congress, Senate, Committee on Interior and Insular Affairs, Subcommittee on Indian Affairs. Taos Indians, Blue Lake. Hearings, Ninetieth Congress, second session, on H.R. 3306 . . . S. 1624 . . . and S. 1625 . . . September 19 and 20, 1968. Washington, D.C., Government Printing Office, 1968. 5, 245 p.

Wetherington, Ronald K. Excavations at Pot Creek Pueblo. Taos, Fort Burgwin Research Center, 1968. 104 p. illus., maps.

Whatley, John T. The saga of Taos: Blue Lake. Indian Historian, 2, no. 3 (1969): 22-28.

Wright, Bessie L., ed. Diary of a member of the first mule pack train to leave Fort Smith for California in 1849. Panhandle-Plains Historical Review, 42 (1969): 61-119.

Yarrow, H. C. The Pueblo of Taos. In Report upon United States Geographical Surveys West of the One Hundredth Meridian. Vol. 7. Washington, D.C., 1879: 327-330.

15-30   Tarahumara

Aghemo, Piero. Maximal aerobic power in primitive Indians. By Piero Aghemo, Fileno Piñera Limas, and Giovanni Sassi. Internationale Zeitschrift für Angewandte Physiologie Einschliesslich Arbeitsphysiologie, 29 (1971): 337-342.

Aghemo, Piero, et al. Massima potenza muscolare in un gruppo di Indiani del Messico. Società Italiana di Biologia Sperimentale, Bollettino, 45 (1968): 458-459.

Aguilera Dorantes, Mario. Guachochi: un centro para muchachas tarahumaras. In A William Cameron Townsend. México, 1961: 209-226.

Alcocer, José Antonio. Bosquejo de la historia del Colegio de Nuestra Señora de Guadalupe y sus misiones. Introducción, bibliografía, acotaciones e ilustraciones del R.P. Fr. Rafael Cervantes. México, Editorial Porrua, 1958. 300 p. illus.

Almada, F. R. Apuntes históricos sobre la región de Chinipas. Chihuahua, 1937.

Almada, F. R. La rebelión de Tomochi. Chihuahua, 1938.

Almada, Francisco R. Geografía humana de Chihuahua. Sociedad Mexicana de Geografía y Estadística, Boletín, 57 (1942): 227-300.

Alvar Loría, Q. B. P. Estudios sobre algunas caracteristicas hematologicas hereditarias en la población mexicana. III. Deficiencia en la glucosa 6-fosfato deshidrogenasa eritrocítica en 7 grupos indígenas y algunos mestizos. Gaceta Médica de México, 93 (1963): 299-303.

Anonymous. José Cañas pinta a los Indios Tarahumaras. YAN, 2 (1953): 89-91.

Anonymous. La raza tarahumara. México, Departamento del Trabajo, 1936. 195 p.

Anonymous. Problemas de la Tarahumara. Katunob, 1, no. 3 (1960): 41-44.

Ariss, Robert M. The Tarahumar Indians of the Barranca de Cobre region of Chihuahua, Mexico. Los Angeles, County Museum of History, Science, and Art, Quarterly, 11, no. 1 (1954): 1-7.

Arpee, Levon Harris. Los indios tarahumaras de Chihuahua, México. Mexico, Museo Nacional de Arqueología, Historia y Etnografía, Anales, época 5, 2 (1935): 461-477.

Artaud, A. Au pays des Tarahumaras. Paris, 1945. 40 p.

Audubon, J. W. Western journal: 1849-1850: p. 114. Cleveland, 1906.

Balke, Bruno. Anthropological and physiological observations on Tarahumara endurance runners. By Bruno Balke and Clyde Snow. American Journal of Physical Anthropology, n.s., 23 (1965): 293-301.

Basauri, C. Creencias y prácticas de los Tarahumaras. Mexican Folkways, 3 (1927): 218-234.

Basauri, C. La resistencia de los Tarahumaras. Mexican Folkways, 2 (1926): 40-44.

*Basauri, C. Monografía de los Tarahumaras. México, 1929. 85 p.

Basauri, Carlos. Familia "Pimana": Tarahumaras. In his La Poblacion Indigena de México. Tomo 1. Mexico, Secretaria de Educacion Publica, 1940: 299-352.

Beals, Ralph L. Kinship terminology and social structure. Kroeber Anthropological Society Papers, 25 (1961): 129-148.

Beals, Ralph L. The comparative ethnology of northern Mexico before 1750. Berkeley, University of California Press, 1932. 6, 93-225 p. maps. (Ibero-Americana, 2)

Benítez, Fernando. Viaje a la Tarahumara. México, Ediciones Era, 1960. 86 p. illus.

*Bennett, Wendell C. The Tarahumara; an Indian tribe of northern Mexico. By Wendell C. Bennett and Robert M. Zingg. Chicago, University of Chicago Press, 1935. 19, 412 p. illus.

Brambila, D. Gramatica Raramuri. México, 1953.

Brambila, David. Hojas de un diario. México, Buena Prensa, 1958. 159 p.

Brambila, David. Psicología y educación del Tarahumar. América Indígena, 19 (1959): 199-208.

Brandt, G. M. The Tarahumaras. Natural History, 57 (1948): 392-399.

Brugge, David M. History, huki, and warfare--some random data on the Lower Pima. Kiva, 26, no. 4 (1960/1961): 6-16.

Buschmann, J. C. Grammatik der Sonorischen Sprache. Berlin, Königliche Akademie der Wissenschaften, Abhandlungen, 47 (1863): 369-454; 51 (1867): 23-216; 53, no. 1 (1869): 67-266.

Cabeza de Vaca, F. Apuntes sobre la vida tarahumaras. México, 1943. 49 p.

Carlson, P. and E. Carlson. Primers I-III. Glendale, 1955-1956.

Caso, Alfonso. Discurso del Dr. Alfonso Caso, Director del I.N.I., ante un grupo de tarahumaras. Boletín Indigenista, 19 (1959): 36, 38, 40.

Caso, Alfonso. Speech of Dr. Alfonso Caso, Director of the N.I.I., before a group of Tarahumara Indians. Boletín Indigenista, 19 (1959): 37, 39, 41.

Cassel, Jonathon F. Tarahumara Indians. San Antonio, Naylor, 1969. 12, 160 p. illus.

Ceballos Novelo, Roque J. Tarahumaras, Coras y Huicholes, su situación económica y social. In Homenaje al Doctor Alfonso Caso. Mexico, Imprenta Nuevo Mundo, 1951: 101-111.

Champion, Jean René. A study in culture persistence: the Tarahumaras of northwestern Mexico. Dissertation Abstracts, 24 (1963/1964): 463. UM 63-6107.

Clegg, Reed S. Tarahumara Indians. Rocky Mountain Medical Journal, 69, no. 1 (1972): 57-58.

Cross, John L. Tarahumara. Utah Archaeology, 10, no. 2 (1964): 1-3.

Dávila Garibi, J. I. Es el coca un indioma Tara-Cahita? In Homenaje al Doctor Alfonso Caso. México, 1951: 143-152.

Davis, William Robert. The Spanish borderlands of Texas and Chihuahua. Texana, 9 (1971): 142-155.

Diecker, Jimmy C. Culture change in the Tarahumara. Papers in Anthropology, 10 (1969): 41-52.

Dunne, P. M. Early Jesuit missions in Tarahumara. Berkeley, 1948. 276 p.

Dunne, Peter Masten. El gran apostol de Sisoguichi. Traducción del P. Gerardo Decorme. México, Buena Prensa, 1952. 48 p.

Dunne, Peter Masten. Las antiguas misiones de la Tarahumara. Traducción de Manuel Ocampo. México, Editorial Jus, 1958. 2 v. (354 p.).

Escalante H., Roberto. Fonemica del Guarijio. México, Instituto Nacional de Antropología e Historia, Anales, 18 (1965): 53-67.

Ewton, Ralph W., Jr., ed. Studies in language and linguistics, 1969-1970. Edited by Ralph W. Ewton, Jr. and Jacob Ornstein. El Paso, University of Texas at El Paso, Texas Western Press, 1970. 232 p. ERIC ED038653.

Fenochio, Adolfo. Noticia sobre la manera de preparar el veneno que usan los indios "ceris" en sus flechas. Sociedad Mexicana de Geografía y Estadística, Boletín, época 3, 1 (1873): 157-158.

Ferguson, H. N. America's stone age neighbors, the Tarahumaras. Desert Magazine, 27, no. 7 (1964): 28-30.

Ferrero, H. J. Pequeña gramática y diccionario de la lengua tarahumara. México, 1920.

Fried, J. Picture testing. American Anthropologist, 56 (1954): 95-97.

Fried, J. The relation of ideal norms to actual behavior in Tarahumara society. Southwestern Journal of Anthropology, 9 (1953): 286-295.

Fried, Jacob. The Tarahumara. In Evon Z. Vogt, volume editor. Handbook of Middle American Indians. Vol. 8. Austin, University of Texas Press, 1969: 846-870.

Gajdusek, D. C. The Sierra Tarahumara. Geographical Review, 43 (1953): 15-38.

Gandola, Isabel. El peyote; estudio sobre el uso del peyote, entre las tribus Huicholes, Coras, Tepehuanes y Tarahumaras. México, Editorial Orión, 1965. 66 p. illus., map.

García Manzanedo, Héctor. Notas sobre la medicina tradicional en una zona de la Sierra Tarahumara. América Indígena, 23 (1963): 61-70.

*Gentry, Howard Scott. The Warihio Indians of Sonora-Chihuahua: an ethnographic survey. Washington, D.C., Government Printing Office, 1963. 61-144 p. illus., maps. (U.S., Bureau of American Ethnology, Anthropological Papers, 65. U.S., Bureau of American Ethnology, Bulletin, 186)

Gómez Gonzalez, F. Los Tarahumares. América Indígena, 13 (1953): 109-117.

González, Luis. Cincuenta años misioneros en la Tarahumara. Nuestra Vida, 17 (1954): 50-67.

Green, Judith Strupp. Archaeological Chihuahuan textiles and modern Tarahumara weaving. Ethnos, 36 (1971): 115-130.

Griffen, William B. Culture change and shifting populations in central northern Mexico. Tucson, 1969. 12, 196 p. maps. (Arizona, University, Anthropological Papers, 13)

Groom, Dale. Cardiovascular observations on Tarahumara Indian runners--the modern Spartans. American Heart Journal, 81 (1971): 304-314.

Groth, Rodolfo. Gold, Indianer, Mennoniten; Schicksale in der nordwestlichen Sierra Madre von Mexiko. Lübeck, Vertrieb: Lübecker Nachrichten, 1960. 160 p. illus.

Hamy, E. T. Algunas observaciones sobre la distribución geográfica de los Opatas, de los Tarahumares y de los Pimas. Museo de Arqueologia, Historia y Etnografia, Anales, época 4a, 5 (1922): 93-98.

Hartman, C. V. Indianer i nordvestra Mexiko. Ymer, 15 (1895): 272-288.

Hartman, C. V. The Indians of North-Western Mexico. International Congress of Americanists, Proceedings, 10 (1894): 115-135.

Hilton, K. Cartilla Tarahumara. México, 1946.

Hilton, K. Cuentos Tarahumares. México, 1948.

Hilton, K. Palabras y frases de las lenguas tarahumara y guarijio. Instituto Nacional de Antropología e Historia, Anales, 2 (1941/1946): 307-313.

Hilton, K. and M. Hilton. Alphabet book.
Glendale, 1948.

Hilton, K. and M. Hilton. Storybook.
Glendale, 1948.

Hilton, K. and M. Hilton. Tarahumara
stories. Glendale, 1950.

Hilton, K. and M. Hilton. Tarahumara
text. Glendale, 1947.

Hilton, Kenneth S. Palabras y frases de
las lenguas tarahumara y guarijio.
México, Instituto Nacional de
Antropología e Historia, Anales, 2
(1941/1946): 307-313.

Hilton, Kenneth S. Relatos Tarahumaras.
Tlalocan, 6, no. 1 (1969): 76-88.

Hilton, Kenneth Simon, et al. Tarahumar y
español. México, Instituto Lingüístico
de Verano, 1959. 16, 216 p. illus.

Hodge, F. W. Tarahumare. U.S. Bureau of
American Ethnology, Bulletin, 30, vol. 2
(1910): 692-693.

Hrdlička, A. and C. Lumholtz. A trephined
skull. American Association for the
Advancement of Science, Proceedings, 46
(1897): 432-433.

Jenkinson, Michael. The glory of the
long-distance runner. Natural History,
81, no. 1 (1972): 54-65.

Kelley, Gordon P. Linguistic observations
for the spider concept in Mesoamerica.
Katunob, 8, no. 1 (Aug. 1972): 31-33.

*Kennedy, John G. Inápuchi, una comunidad
tarahumara gentil. México, 1970. 13,
257 p. illus. (Instituto Indigenista
Interamericano, Ediciones Especiales,
58)

Kennedy, John G. La carrera de bola
tarahumara y su significación. América
Indígena, 29 (1969): 17-42.

Kennedy, John G. Tarahumara joking
relationships: some theoretical
implications. In Congreso Internacional
de Americanistas, 36th. 1964, España.
Actas y Memorias. Tomo 3. Sevilla,
1966: 179-186.

Kennedy, John G. Tesguino complex: the
role of beer in Tarahumara culture.
American Anthropologist, 65 (1963): 620-
640.

Kino, Eusebio Francisco. Correspondencia
del P. Kino con los generales de la
Compañía de Jesús 1682-1707. Prólogo y
notas de Ernest J. Burrus, S.J. México,

Editorial Jus, 1961. 95 p. illus.,
maps. (Testimonio Historica, 5)

Kino, Eusebio Francisco. Kino reports to
headquarters; correspondence . . . from
New Spain with Rome. Original Spanish
text of fourteen unpublished letters and
reports. With English translation and
notes by Ernest J. Burrus, S.J. Rome,
Institutum Historicum Societatis Jesu,
1954. 135 p.

Kroeber, A. L. Uto-Aztecan languages of
Mexico. Ibero-Americana, 8 (1934): 1-27.

La Barre, Weston. The peyote cult. New
Haven, Yale University, Department of
Anthropology, 1938. 188 p. illus.
(Yale University Publications in
Anthropology, 19)

Leche, S. Dermatoglyphics and functional
lateral dominance in Mexican Indians.
Middle American Research Series, 5,
no. 2 (1933): 27-42.

León-Portilla, Miguel. Panorama de la
población indígena de México. América
Indígena, 19 (1959): 43-73.

Lionnet, André. Les diverses
transcriptions du Tarahumar et son
système phonologique. Linguistique, 1
(1966): 125-134.

Lionnet, André. Los intensivos en
Tarahumar. México, Instituto Nacional de
Antropología e Historia, Anales, 19
(1966): 135-146.

Lisker, Rubén. Estudios sobre algunas
caracteristicas hematologicas
hereditarias en la población mexicana.
II. Hemoglobinas anormales en 7 grupos
indígenas y algunos mestizos. Gaceta
Médica de México, 93 (1963): 289-297.

Lisker, Rubén. Frecuencia de algunas
características hereditarias en la
población indígena de México. By Rubén
Lisker, Alvar Loría and Héctor
Rodríguez. In Congreso Internacional de
Americanistas, 35th. 1962, Mexico. Actas
y Memorias. Tomo 3. Mexico, 1964: 109-
113.

Lochon, H. En 2 CV chez les primitifs.
Lyon, 1956. 224 p.

Lopez, Raul A. Tarahumara ritual
aesthetic manifestations. Kiva, 37
(1972): 207-223.

Lumholtz, C. Among the Tarahumaris.
Scribner's Magazine, 16 (1894): 31-48.

Lumholtz, C. Cave-dwellers of the Sierra
Madre. International Congress of
Anthropology, Memoirs (1893): 100-112.

Lumholtz, C. Tarahumara runners. American Anthropologist, o.s., 8 (1895): 92.

Lumholtz, C. Tarahumari dances and plant-worship. Scribner's Magazine, 16 (1894): 438-456.

Lumholtz, C. Tarahumari life and customs. Scribner's Magazine, 16 (1894): 296-311.

Lumholtz, Carl. Explorations au Mexique de 1894 a 1897. Société des Américanistes (Paris), Journal, 2 (1899): 179-184.

Lumholtz, Carl. My life of exploration. Natural History, 21 (1921): 225-243.

Lumholtz, Carl. The American cave-dwellers: the Tarahumaris of the Sierra Madre. American Geographical Society, Bulletin, 26 (1894): 299-325.

*Lumholtz, Carl. Unknown Mexico. New York, Charles Scribner's Sons, 1902. 2 v.

Mason, J. Alden. The Tepehuan, and other aborigines of the Mexican Sierra Madre Occidental. América Indígena, 8 (1948): 289-300.

Merrifield, William R. Number names in four languages of Mexico. In H. Brandt Corsius, ed. Grammars for Number Names. Dordrecht, Reidel, 1968: 91-102. (Foundations of Language, Supplement Series, 7)

Mestre, Aristides. Etnografía de América. Noticia sobre los indios tarahumaras de México. Havana, Universidad, Facultud de Letras y Ciencias, Revista, 2 (1906): 339-364.

Miller, Wick R. Uto-Aztecan cognate sets. Berkeley and Los Angeles, University of California Press, 1967. 5, 83 p. map. (California, University, Publications in Linguistics, 48)

Muñoz, Maurilio. Los Tarahumaras. Acción Indigenista, 165 (1967): 1-4.

Muñoz, Maurilio. Plan para mejorar a los Tarahumaras. Katunob, 4, no. 1 (1963): 12.

Nelson, Elmer R. Hola mi amigo. Lore, 3 (1953): 66-73.

Nelson, Elmer R. The Tarahumara. Lore, 3 (1953): 110-118.

Neumann, Joseph. Révoltes des Indien Tarahumara (1626-1724). Translated and edited by Luis Gonzalez R. Paris, 1971. 64, 191 p. illus., map. (Paris, Université, Institut des Hautes Études de l'Amérique Latine, Travaux et Mémoires, 24)

Nida, E. A. The Tarahumara language. Investigaciones Lingüísticas, 4 (1937): 140-144.

Nolasco Armas, Margarita. Seris, yaquis y tarahumaras. México, 1968. 30 p. illus. (México, Museo Nacional de Antropología, Servicios Educativos, Colección Breve, 6)

Nolasco Armas, Margarita. Un cuento. Tlatoani, Época 2, 16 (1962): 32-34.

Ccampo, Manuel. Album conmemorativo de la Misión de la Tarahumara en el quincuagesimo aniversario de su fundación. México, Buena Prensa, 1951. 111 p.

Ocampo, Manuel. Historia de la Misión de la Tarahumara (1900-1950). México, Editorial "Buena Prensa", 1950. 23, 350 p.

Paredes, A. Biosocial adaptation and correlates of acculturation in the Tarahumara ecosystem. By A. Paredes, R. L. Berger, and C. C. Snow. International Journal of Social Psychiatry, 16 (1970): 163-174.

Parsons, Elsie Clews. Pueblo Indian religion. Vol. 2. Chicago, University of Chicago Press, 1939. 551-1275 p.

Passin, H. Sorcery as a phase of Tarahumara economic relations. Man, 42 (1942): 11-15.

Passin, H. Tarahumara prevarication: a problem in field method. American Anthropologist, n.s., 44 (1942): 235-247.

Passin, H. The place of kinship in Tarahumara social organization. Acta Americana, 1 (1943): 344-359, 469-495.

Passin, Herbert. Some relationships in Northwest Mexican kinship systems. El México Antiguo, 6, no. 7/8 (July 1944): 205-218.

Pemex Travel Club. Mexico's music: its past and present. Katunob, 4, no. 4 (1963): 30-52.

Peña, M. T. de la. Ensayo económico y social sobre el pueblo tarahumar. Investigación Económica, 4 (1944): 363-400.

Peña, Moisés T. de la. Extranjeros y tarahumares en Chihuahua. In Miguel Othón de Mendizábal. Obras Completas. Tomo 1. México, 1946: 223-277.

*Pennington, Campbell W.   The Tarahumar of
   Mexico: their environment and material
   culture.   Salt Lake City, University of
   Utah Press, 1963.   267 p.   illus., maps.

Pérez de Ribas, Andrés.   Historia de los
   triunfos de nuestra santa fe entre
   gentes las más bárbaras y fieras del
   nuevo orbe.   Madrid, A. de Paredes,
   1645.   20, 763 p.

Pérez de Ribas, Andrés.   My life among the
   savage nations of New Spain. Translated
   by Tomás Antonio Robertson.   Los
   Angeles, Ward Ritchie Press, 1968.   16,
   256 p.   illus., maps.

Plancarte, F. M.   El problema indígena
   tarahumara. Instituto Nacional
   Indigenista, Memorias, 5 (1954): 1-40.

Radin, P.   Mexican kinship terms.
   California, University, Publications in
   American Archaeology and Ethnology, 31
   (1931): 1-14.

Ramos, Roberto, ed.   Historia de la
   tercera rebelión tarahumara.   Chihuahua,
   Sociedad Chihuahuense de Estudios
   Históricos, 1950.   56 p.

Reuter, Walter.   En la Tarahumara.
   Tlatoani, ser. 2, 8/9 (1954): 4-11.

Robles U., Carlos.   Problemas que se
   presentan en la expresión de los
   conceptos filosófico-religiosos del
   Cristianismo en las lenguas indígenas de
   América. In Congreso Internacional de
   Americanistas, 35th. 1962, Mexico. Actas
   y Memorias. Tomo 2.   Mexico, 1964: 615-
   634.

Sauer, C.   The distribution of aboriginal
   tribes and languages in northwestern
   Mexico. Ibero-Americana, 5 (1934): 58.

Schmutz, Richard.   Jesuit missionary
   methods in northwestern Mexico. Journal
   of the West, 8 (1969): 76-89.

Smith, Ralph A.   Apache plunder trails
   southward, 1831-1840. New Mexico
   Historical Review, 37 (1962): 20-42.

Smith, Ralph A.   The scalp hunt in
   Chihuahua--1849. New Mexico Historical
   Review, 40 (1965): 116-140.

Snyder, Richard G.   Trait analysis of the
   dentition of the Tarahumara Indians and
   Mestizos of the Sierra Madre Occidental,
   Mexico. By Richard G. Snyder, Albert A.
   Dahlberg, Clyde C. Snow, and Thelma
   Dahlberg. American Journal of Physical
   Anthropology, n.s., 31 (1969): 65-76.

Soustelle, Georgette.   Essai comparatif
   sur cinq populations autochtones du

Mexique. Ethnographie, Nouvelle Série,
   62/63 (1968/1969): 142-155.

Spicer, Edward H.   Apuntes sobre el tipo
   de religión de los Yuto-Aztecas
   Centrales. In Congreso Internacional de
   Americanistas, 35th. 1962, Mexico. Actas
   y Memorias. Tomo 2.   Mexico, 1964: 27-
   38.

Spicer, Edward H.   European expansion and
   the enclavement of Southwestern Indians.
   Arizona and the West, 1 (1959): 132-145.

Spoehr, J.   A visit to the Tarahumaras.
   Cranbrook Institute of Science, News
   Letter, 21 (1951): 2-8.

Telleches, Miguel.   Compendio gramatical
   para la inteligencia del idioma
   tarahumar. México, 1826.

Thomas, Cyrus.   Indian languages of Mexico
   and Central America and their
   geographical distribution. By Cyrus
   Thomas assisted by John R. Swanton.
   Washington, D.C., Government Printing
   Office, 1911.   7, 108 p.   map.   (U.S.,
   Bureau of American Ethnology, Bulletin,
   44)

Thord-Gray, I.   Tarahumara-English,
   English-Tarahumara dictionary and an
   introduction to Tarahumara grammar.
   Coral Gables, 1955.   1,170 p.

Toor, Frances.   A treasury of Mexican
   folkways.   New York, Crown, 1947.   32,
   566 p.   illus.

Vega, J.   La raza tarahumara y el medio
   geográfico en que vive. Sociedad
   Mexicana de Geografía y Estadística,
   Boletín, 58 (1943): 103-121.

Zingg, R. M.   Christmasing with the
   Tarahumaras. Texas Folk-Lore Society,
   Publications, 14 (1939): 207-224.

Zingg, R. M.   Juguetes y juegos de los
   niños tarahumaras. Mexican Folkways, 7
   (1932): 107-110.

Zingg, R. M.   The genuine and spurious
   values in Tarahumara culture. American
   Anthropologist, n.s., 44 (1942): 78-92.

Zingg, R. M.   The Southwestern affiliation
   of Tarahumara culture. Southwestern
   Lore, 4 (1938): 6-9.

Zingg, Robert M.   A reconstruction of Uto-
   Aztekan history.   New York, G. E.
   Stechert, 1939.   4, 274 p.   (Denver,
   University, Contributions to
   Ethnography, 2)

15-31 Tewa

Fraser, James H. Indian mission printing in New Mexico: a bibliography. New Mexico Historical Review, 43 (1968): 311-318.

Aberle, S. B. D. Child mortality among Pueblo Indians. American Journal of Physical Anthropology, 16 (1932): 339-351.

Aberle, S. B. D. Maternal mortality among the Pueblos. American Journal of Physical Anthropology, 18 (1934): 431-457.

Aberle, S. B. D., et al. The vital history of San Juan Pueblo. Human Biology, 12, no. 2 (1940): 141-187.

Aitken, B. A Tewa craftsman. El Palacio, 17 (1924): 91-97.

Aitken, B. A trance experience. Plateau, 28 (1956): 67-70.

Alvarado Cata, R. Two stories from San Juan Pueblo. Western Folklore, 15 (1956): 106-109.

Anonymous. The animal dance at San Ildefonso. El Palacio, 24 (1928): 119-122.

Arnold, C. The dance at Nambe. El Palacio, 24 (1928): 26-28.

Bandelier, A. F. Po-sé. New Mexico Historical Review, 1 (1926): 335-349.

Bandelier, A. F. The delight makers. New York, 1890. 490 p.

Bayliss, C. K. A Tewa sun myth. Journal of American Folklore, 22 (1909): 333-335.

Bloom, L. B., ed. Bourke on the Southwest. New Mexico Historical Review, 11 (1936): 217-282; 12 (1937): 41-77.

Bodine, John J. Taos names: a clue to linguistic acculturation. Anthropological Linguistics, 10, no. 5 (1968): 23-27.

Brant, C. S. Preliminary data on Tesuque Pueblo. Michigan Academy of Science, Arts and Letters, Papers, 34 (1948): 253-259.

Bunzel, R. L. The Pueblo potter. Columbia University Contributions to Anthropology, 8 (1929): 1-134.

Bunzel, Ruth L. The Pueblo potter. New York, AMS Press, 1969. 134 p. illus.

Burton, H. K. The re-establishment of the Indians in their pueblo life. Columbia University, Teachers' College, Contributions to Education, 672 (1936): 1-102.

Chapman, K. M. Sun basket dance at Santa Clara. El Palacio, 18 (1925): 45-47.

Chapman, Kenneth M. The pottery of San Ildefonso Pueblo. Supplementary text by Francis H. Harlow. Albuquerque, University of New Mexico Press, 1970. 16, 260 p. illus. (School of American Research, Monograph Series, 28)

Clemmer, Richard O. Resistance and the revitalization of anthropologists: a new perspective on cultural change and resistance. In Dell Hymes, ed. Reinventing Anthropology. New York, Panthem Books, 1973: 213-247.

Curtin, L. S. M. Preparation of sacred corn meal in the Rio Grande pueblos. Masterkey, 41 (1967): 124-130; 42 (1968): 10-16.

Curtin, L. S. M. Spanish and Indian witchcraft in New Mexico. Masterkey, 45 (1971): 89-101.

Curtis, N., ed. The Indians' book, 447-457. New York, 1907.

DeHuff, E. W. More Pueblo tales. El Palacio, 11 (1921): 140-144.

DeHuff, E. W. Myths told by the Pueblos. El Palacio, 11 (1921): 86-92.

DeHuff, E. W. Pueblo myths and legends. El Palacio, 11 (1921): 98-99.

DeHuff, E. W. Taytay's memories, 6-9, 12-19, 41-44, 49-54, 123-128, 139-146, 198-206. New York, 1924.

DeHuff, E. W. Taytay's tales, 3-17, 22-24, 55-60, 65-87, 122-124, 172-182. New York, 1922.

DeHuff, E. W. The venomous snake girl. El Palacio, 31 (1931): 73-74.

Devereux, Don. The re-location of a Pueblo Emergence Shrine. El Palacio, 73, no. 4 (1966): 21-26.

Douglas, F. H. Weaving in the Tewa Pueblos. Denver Art Museum, Indian Leaflet Series, 90 (1939): 158-160.

Douglass, W. B. A world-quarter shrine of the Tewa Indians. Records of the Past, 11 (1912): 159-172.

Douglass, W. B.   Notes on the shrines of the Tewa and other Pueblo Indians. International Congress of Americanists, Proceedings, 19 (1915): 344-378.

Downing, George L.   Native pottery of the Southwest. Natural History, 78, no. 6 (1969): 34-39.

Dozier, E. P.   A comparison of Eastern Keresan and Tewa kinship systems. International Congress of the Anthropological and Ethnological Sciences, Acts, 5 (1960): 430-436.

Dozier, E. P.   Kinship and linguistic change among the Arizona Tewa. International Journal of American Linguistics, 11 (1955): 242-251.

Dozier, E. P.   Tewa II. International Journal of American Linguistics, 19 (1953): 118-127.

*Dozier, E. P.   The Hopi-Tewa of Arizona. California, University, Publications in American Archaeology and Ethnology, 44 (1954): 259-376.

Dozier, E. P.   Two examples of linguistic acculturation. Language, 32 (1956): 146-157.

Dozier, Edward P.   Cultural matrix of singing and chanting in Tewa pueblos. International Journal of American Linguistics, 24 (1958): 268-272.

Dozier, Edward P.   Factionalism at Santa Clara Pueblo. Ethnology, 5 (1966): 172-185.

Dozier, Edward P.   Hano, a Tewa community in Arizona. New York, Holt, Rinehart and Winston, 1966. 8, 104 p. illus., map.

Dozier, Edward P.   Pueblo Indian response to culture contact. In M. Estellie Smith, ed. Studies in Linguistics in Honor of George L. Trager. The Hague, Mouton, 1972: 457-467. (Janua Linguarum, Series Maior, 52)

Dozier, Edward P.   The Hopi and the Tewa. Scientific American, 196, no. 6 (1957): 126-130, 132, 134, 136.

Dunn, D.   Awa Tsireh. El Palacio, 63 (1956): 108-115.

*Eggan, F.   Social organization of the Western Pueblos, 139-175. Chicago, 1950.

Ellis, Florence Hawley.   A reconstruction of basic Jemez pattern of social organization, with comparisons to other Tanoan social structures. Albuquerque,

University of New Mexico Press, 1964. 69 p. (New Mexico, University, Publications in Anthropology, 11)

Ellis, Florence Hawley.   Archaeological history of Nambe Pueblo, 14th century to present. American Antiquity, 30 (1964/1965): 34-42.

Evans, B. and M. G. Evans.   American Indian dance steps. New York, 1931. 122 p.

Fay, G. E.   Some notes on the cow dance, Santa Clara Pueblo. El Palacio, 59 (1952): 186-188.

Fergusson, E.   Dancing gods, 53-55, 60-61. New York, 1931.

Fewkes, J. W.   The kinship of a Tanoan-speaking community in Tusayan. American Anthropologist, 7 (1894): 162-167.

Fewkes, J. W.   The winter solstice altars at Hano Pueblo. American Anthropologist, n.s., 1 (1899): 251-276.

Fewkes, J. W.   Tusayan migration traditions. U.S. Bureau of American Ethnology, Annual Reports, 19, vol. 2 (1900): 573-633.

Ford, Richard I.   Barter, gift, or violence: an analysis of Tewa intertribal exchange. In Edwin N. Wilmsen, ed. Social Exchange and Interaction.   Ann Arbor, University of Michigan, 1972: 24-45. (Michigan, University, Musuem of Anthropology, Anthropological Papers, 46)

Ford, Richard Irving.   An ecological analysis involving the population of San Juan Pueblo, New Mexico. Dissertation Abstracts International, 30 (1969/1970): 35B-36B.   UM 69-12,096.

Freire-Marreco, B.   Tewa relationship terms from the pueblo of Hano. American Anthropologist, n.s., 16 (1914): 269-287.

Garcia, Antonio.   Ritual preludes to Tewa Indian dances. By Antonio Garcia and Carlos Garcia. Ethnomusicology, 12 (1968): 239-244.

Garcia, Antonio.   Tanoan gestures of invocation. By Antonio Garcia, Juanito and Gregorita Trujillo. Ethnomusicology, 10 (1966): 206-207.

Gatschet, A. S.   Classification into seven linguistic stocks of Western Indian dialects. In Report upon United States Geographical Surveys West of the One Hundredth Meridian. Vol. 7. Washington, D.C., 1879: 403-485.

Gatschet, A. S. Zwölf Sprachen aus dem Südwesten Nordamerikas. Weimar, 1876. 150 p.

Gifford, E. W. Apache-Pueblo. Anthropological Records, 4 (1940): 1-207.

Guthe, C. E. Pueblo pottery making. New Haven, 1925. 88 p.

Hale, Kenneth. Toward a reconstruction of Kiowa-Tanoan phonology. International Journal of American Linguistics, 33 (1967): 112-120.

Harlow, Francis H. Tewa Indian ceremonial pottery. El Palacio, 72, no. 4 (1965): 13-23.

Harrington, J. P. A brief description of the Tewa language. American Anthropologist, n.s., 12 (1910): 497-504.

Harrington, J. P. Meanings of old Tewa Indian placenames. El Palacio, 7 (1919): 78-83.

Harrington, J. P. Tewa relationship terms. American Anthropologist, n.s., 14 (1912): 472-498.

Harrington, J. P. The ethnogeography of the Tewa Indians. U.S. Bureau of American Ethnology, Annual Reports, 29 (1916): 29-618.

Harrington, J. P. The Tewa Indian game of "canute". American Anthropologist, n.s., 14 (1912): 243-286.

Harrington, J. P. Three Tewa texts. International Journal of American Linguistics, 13 (1947): 112-116.

Hawley, F. An examination of problems basic to acculturation in the Rio Grande Pueblos. American Anthropologist, n.s., 50 (1948): 612-624.

Henderson, J. and J. P. Harrington. Ethnozoology of the Tewa Indians. U.S. Bureau of American Ethnology, Bulletin, 56 (1914): 1-76.

Hodge, F. W. San Ildefonso. U.S. Bureau of American Ethnology, Bulletin, 30, vol. 2 (1910): 440-441.

Hodge, F. W. Santa Clara. U.S. Bureau of American Ethnology, Bulletin, 30, vol. 2 (1910): 456-457.

Hodge, F. W. Tesuque. U.S. Bureau of American Ethnology, Bulletin, 30, vol. 2 (1910): 735.

Hodge, F. W. Tewa. U.S. Bureau of American Ethnology, Bulletin, 30, vol. 2 (1910): 737-738.

Hodge, F. W. War god idols of San Juan. El Palacio, 23 (1927): 588-589.

Hoijer, H. and E. P. Dozier. The phonemes of Tewa, Santa Clara dialect. International Journal of American Linguistics, 15 (1949): 139-144.

Hough, W. Stone-working at Tewa. American Anthropologist, 10 (1897): 191.

James, A. Tewa firelight tales. New York, 1927. 248 p.

Jeancon, J. A. A rectangular ceremonial room. Colorado Magazine, 3 (1926): 133-137.

Jeancon, J. A. Santa Clara and San Juan pottery. Denver Art Museum, Indian Leaflet Series, 35 (1931): 1-4.

Jenkins, Myra Ellen. Spanish land grants in the Tewa area. New Mexico Historical Review, 47 (1972): 113-134.

Jones, William M. Origin of the place-name Taos. Anthropological Linguistics, 2, no. 3 (1960): 2-4.

Keech, R. A. The blue corn dance. National Archaeological News, 1, no. 9 (1937): 26-28.

Kurath, G. P. Plaza circuits of Tewa Indian dancers. El Palacio, 65 (1958): 16-26.

Kurath, Gertrude P. Music and dance of the Tewa pueblos. By Gertrude P. Kurath, with the aid of Antonio Garcia. Santa Fe, 1970. 309 p. illus. (Museum of New Mexico, Research Records, 8)

Kurath, Gertrude P. Tewa choreographic music. Studies in Ethnomusicology, 2 (1965): 4-19.

Lane, William Carr. William Carr Lane, diary. Edited by Wm. G. B. Carson. New Mexico Historical Review, 39 (1964): 181-234, 274-332.

Laski, V. P. The raingod ceremony of the Tewa. Masterkey, 31 (1957): 76-84.

Laski, Vera. Seeking life. Philadelphia, 1958. 10, 176 p. maps. (American Folklore Society, Memoirs, 50)

Leap, William L. Who were the Piro? Anthropological Linguistics, 13 (1971): 321-330.

Lewis, O. L. Fiesta at Nambé Pueblo. El Palacio, 60 (1953): 409-413.

Loeb, E. M. A note on two far-travelled kachinas. Journal of American Folklore, 56 (1943): 192-199.

Lummis, C. F. Pueblo Indian folk-stories. New York, 1910. 257 p.

Marriott, A. Greener fields. New York, 1953. 274 p.

*Marriott, A. Maria the potter of San Ildefonso. Norman, 1948. 294 p.

Morgan, L. H. Systems of consanguinity and affinity. Smithsonian Contributions to Knowledge, 17 (1871): 291-382.

Nölle, W. Die Navajo und Tewa heute. Tribus, 6 (1957): 102-108.

Ortiz, Alfonso. Dual organization as an operational concept in the Pueblo Southwest. Ethnology, 4 (1965): 389-396.

Ortiz, Alfonso. Project Head Start in an Indian community. Chicago, University of Chicago, 1965. 70 p. (U.S., Office of Economic Opportunity, 539) ERIC ED014329.

Parsons, E. C. Cérémonial Tewa au Nouveau Méxique et en Arizona. Société des Américanistes, Journal, n.s., 18 (1926): 9-15.

Parsons, E. C. Pueblo Indian religion. Chicago, 1939. 2 v.

Parsons, E. C. Tewa kin, clan, and moiety. American Anthropologist, n.s., 26 (1924): 333-339.

Parsons, E. C. Tewa mothers and children. Man, 24 (1924): 148-151.

Parsons, E. C. Tewa tales. American Folk-Lore Society, Memoirs, 19 (1926): 1-304.

Parsons, E. C. The ceremonial calendar of the Tewa of Arizona. American Anthropologist, n.s., 28 (1926): 209-229.

Parsons, E. C. The kinship nomenclature of the Pueblo Indians. American Anthropologist, n.s., 34 (1932): 377-389.

*Parsons, E. C. The social organization of the Tewa of New Mexico. American Anthropological Association, Memoirs, 36 (1929): 1-309.

Parsons, E. C. Witchcraft among the Pueblos. Man, 27 (1927): 106-112, 125-128.

Poley, H. S. An American wedding. El Palacio, 8 (1920): 74-75.

Reed, E. K. The origins of Hano Pueblo. El Palacio, 50 (1943): 73-76.

Reed, E. K. The Southern Tewa Pueblos in the historic period. El Palacio, 50 (1943): 254-266, 276-288.

Reed, E. K. The Tewa Indians of the Hopi country. Plateau, 25 (1952): 11-18.

Renaud, E. B. Kokopelli. Southwestern Lore, 14 (1948): 25-40.

Robbins, W. W., J. P. Harrington, and B. Freire-Marreco. Ethnobotany of the Tewa Indians. U.S. Bureau of American Ethnology, Bulletin, 55 (1916): 1-118.

Rosenblatt, Paul C. Wealth transfer and restrictions on sexual behavior during betrothal. By Paul C. Rosenblatt, Stephen S. Fugita, and Kenneth V. McDowell. Ethnology, 8 (1969): 319-328.

Schroeder, Gail D. San Juan pottery: methods and incentives. El Palacio, 71, no. 1 (1964): 45-51.

Smith, D. M. Indian tribes of the Southwest, 80-88. Stanford, 1933.

Smith, M. Estellie. Notes on an ethnolinguistic study of governing. In M. Estellie Smith, ed. Studies in Linguistics in Honor of George L. Trager. The Hague, Mouton, 1972: 487-501. (Janua Linguarum, Series Maior, 52)

Speirs, Randall H. Number in Tewa. In M. Estellie Smith, ed. Studies in Linguistics in Honor of George L. Trager. The Hague, Mouton, 1972: 479-486. (Janua Linguarum, Series Maior, 52)

Speirs, Randall Hannaford. Some aspects of the structure of Rio Grande Tewa. Dissertation Abstracts, 27 (1966/1967): 762A-763A. UM 66-7987.

Spinden, H. J. Home songs of the Tewa Indians. American Museum Journal, 15 (1915): 73-78.

Spinden, H. J. Songs of the Tewa. New York, 1933. 125 p.

Spinden, H. J. The making of pottery at San Ildefonso. American Museum Journal, 11 (1911): 192-196.

Stanislawski, Michael B. The ethno-archaeology of Hopi pottery making. Plateau, 42 (1969): 27-33.

Stanislawski, Michael B. The ethno-archaeology of Hopi pottery-making. In Jesse D. Jennings and E. Adamson Hoebel, eds. Readings in Anthropology. 3d ed. New York, McGraw-Hill, 1972: 80-84.

Stevenson, J. Illustrated catalogue of the collections obtained from the Indians of New Mexico and Arizona. U.S. Bureau of American Ethnology, Annual Reports, 2 (1883): 409-417, 429-464.

Stevenson, M. C. Strange rites of the Tewa Indians. Smithsonian Miscellaneous Collections, 63, no. 8 (1914): 73-83.

Stevenson, M. C. Studies of the Tewa Indians of the Rio Grande Valley. Smithsonian Miscellaneous Collections, 60, no. 30 (1913): 35-41.

Stevenson, M. C. The sun and the ice people among the Tewa Indians. Smithsonian Miscellaneous Collections, 65, no. 6 (1916): 73-78.

Swanson, Guy E. Rules of descent: studies in the sociology of parentage. Ann Arbor, University of Michigan, 1969. 5, 108 p. (Michigan, University, Museum of Anthropology, Anthropological Papers, 39)

Trager, George L. The Tanoan settlement of the Rio Grande area: a possible chronology. In Dell H. Hymes and William E. Bittle, eds. Studies in Southwestern Ethnolinguistics. The Hague, Mouton, 1967: 335-350. (Studies in General Anthropology, 3)

Underhill, R. M. First penthouse dwellers of America, 109-130. New York, 1938.

Velarde, Pablita. Old Father, the story teller. Globe, Ariz., D. S. King, 1960. 66 p. illus.

Voegelin, Carl F. Methods for typologizing directly and by distinctive features (in reference to Uto-Aztecan and Kiowa-Tanoan vowel systems). Lingua, 11 (1962): 469-487.

Wadia, Maneck S. Some aspects of Pueblo native religion. Indiana Academy of Science, Proceedings, 69 (1959): 83-85.

*Whitman, W. The Pueblo Indians of San Ildefonso. Columbia University Contributions to Anthropology, 34 (1947): 1-164.

Whitman, W. The San Ildefonso of New Mexico. In R. Linton, ed. Acculturation in Seven American Indian Tribes. New York, 1940: 390-462.

*Whitman, William. The Pueblo Indians of San Ildefonso; a changing culture. New York, AMS Press, 1969. 7, 164 p.

Wilson, O. The survival of an ancient art. Art and Archaeology, 9 (1920): 24-31.

Witt, Shirley Hill. Migration into San Juan Indian Pueblo, 1726-1968. Dissertation Abstracts International, 31 (1970/1971): 1034B-1035B. UM 70-17,249.

Woolf, Charles M. Albinism among Indians in Arizona and New Mexico. American Journal of Human Genetics, 17 (1965): 23-35.

Yegerlehner, John. Arizona Tewa. International Journal of American Linguistics, 25 (1959): 1-7, 75-80.

Yegerlehner, John. Structure of Arizona Tewa words, spoken and sung. International Journal of American Linguistics, 24 (1958): 264-267.

Zbinden, Ernst A. Nördliche und südliche Elemente im Kulturheroenmythus der Südathapasken. Anthropos, 55 (1960): 689-733.

15-32 Walapai

Anonymous. Walapai. U.S. Bureau of American Ethnology, Bulletin, 30, vol. 2 (1910): 899-900.

Brodhead, Michael J. Elliot Coues and the Apaches. Journal of Arizona History, 14 (1973): 87-94.

Curtis, E. S. The North American Indian, Vol. 2: 89-93. Cambridge, 1908.

Dobyns, Henry F. A brief history of the Northeastern Pai. By Henry F. Dobyns and Robert C. Euler. Plateau, 32 (1960): 49-57.

Dobyns, Henry F. A Mohave potter's experiment. Kiva, 24, no. 3 (1958/1959): 16-17.

Dobyns, Henry F. The ghost dance of 1889 among the Pai Indians of northwestern Arizona. By Henry F. Dobyns and Robert C. Euler. Prescott, Prescott College Press, 1967. 12, 67 p. illus., map.

Dobyns, Henry F. Wauba Yuma's people; the comparative socio-political structure of the Pai Indians of Arizona. By Henry F. Dobyns and Robert C. Euler. Prescott, Prescott College Press, 1970. 98 p.

Dozier, Edward P. The Pueblo Indians of the Southwest. Current Anthropology, 5 (1964): 79-97.

Drucker, Philip. Culture element distributions: XVII Yuman-Piman. Berkeley, 1941. 91-230 p. illus., map. (California, University, Publications, Anthropological Records, 6, no. 3)

Euler, Robert C. Ethnic group land rights in the modern state: three case studies. By Robert C. Euler and Henry F. Dobyns. Human Organization, 20 (1961/1962): 203-207.

Euler, Robert Clark. Walapai culture history. Dissertation Abstracts, 19 (1958/1959): 2428. UM 58-3513.

Ewing, Henry P. The origin of the Pai tribes. Edited by Henry F. Dobyns and Robert C. Euler. Kiva, 26, no. 3 (1961): 8-23.

Ewing, Henry P. The Pai tribes. Edited by Robert C. Euler and Henry F. Dobyns. Ethnohistory, 7 (1960): 61-80.

Fay, George E., ed. Charters, constitutions and by-laws of the Indian tribes of North America. Part III: The Southwest (Apache-Mohave). Greeley, 1967. 6, 118 l. maps. (University of Northern Colorado, Museum of Anthropology, Occasional Publications in Anthropology, Ethnology Series, 4) ERIC ED046553.

Gatschet, A. S. Classification into seven linguistic stocks of Western Indian dialects. In Report upon United States Geographical Surveys West of the One Hundredth Meridian. Vol. 7. Washington, D.C., 1879: 403-485.

Gatschet, A. S. Der Yuma-Sprachstamm. Zeitschrift für Ethnologie, 9 (1887): 377-378, 390-406.

Hoffman, W. J. Miscellaneous ethnographic observations. United States Geological and Geographical Survey of the Territories, Annual Reports, 10 (1876): 461-478.

Iliff, F. G. People of the blue water. New York, 1954. 271 p.

James, G. W. The Indians of the Painted Desert region. Boston, 1903. 268 p.

Joel, Judith. Classification of the Yuman languages. In William Bright, ed. Studies in Californian Linguistics. Berkeley and Los Angeles, University of California Press, 1964: 99-105. (California, University, Publications in Linguistics, 34)

Kroeber, A. L. A Southwestern personality type. Southwestern Journal of Anthropology, 3 (1947): 108-113.

Kroeber, A. L. Ad hoc reassurance dreams. California, University, Publications in American Archaeology and Ethnology, 47 (1957): 205-208.

*Kroeber, A. L., ed. Walapai ethnography. American Anthropological Association, Memoirs, 42 (1935): 1-293.

Law, Howard W. A reconstructed proto-culture derived from some Yuman vocabularies. Anthropological Linguistics, 3, no. 4 (1961): 45-57.

Manners, R. A. Tribe and tribal boundaries: the Walapai. Ethnohistory, 4 (1957): 1-26.

Matson, Richard Ghia. Adaptation and environment in the Cerbat Mountains, Arizona. Dissertation Abstracts International, 32 (1971/1972): 6797B. UM 72-17,916.

Miller, David H. The Ives expedition revisited: overland into Grand Canyon. Journal of Arizona History, 13 (1972): 177-196.

Moriarty, James Robert, III. The environmental variations of the Yuman culture area of Southern California. Anthropological Journal of Canada, 6, no. 2 (1968): 2-20; 6, no. 3 (1968): 9-23.

Nag, Moni. Factors affecting human fertility in nonindustrial societies: a cross-cultural study. New Haven, Human Relations Area Files Press, 1968. 227 p. (Yale University Publications in Anthropology, 66)

Nag, Moni. Factors affecting human fertility in nonindustrial societies: a cross-cultural study. New Haven, Yale University, Department of Anthropology, 1962. 227 p. (Yale University Publications in Anthropology, 66)

Parker, Rupert. Support asked, Hualapai Dam. Indian Historian, 1, no. 2 (1967/1968): 15-16.

Potter, Carole A. The Dean Kirk Ketoh Collection. Plateau, 36 (1964): 115-119.

Redden, James E. Walapai. International Journal of American Linguistics, 32 (1966): 1-16, 141-163.

Redden, James Erskine. Walapai phonology and morphology. Dissertation Abstracts, 26 (1965/1966): 4649. UM 66-1487.

Reilly, P. T. The disappearing Havasupai corn-planting ceremony. Masterkey, 44 (1970): 30-34.

Riggs, John L. William H. Hardy: merchant of the Upper Colorado. Edited by Kenneth Hufford. Journal of Arizona History, 6 (1965): 177-187.

Romney, A. Kimball. Internal reconstruction of Yuman kinship terminology. In Dell H. Hymes and William E. Bittle, eds. Studies in Southwestern Ethnolinguistics. The Hague, Mouton, 1967: 379-386. (Studies in General Anthropology, 3)

Smith, Charline G. Selé, a major vegetal component of the aboriginal Hualapai diet. Plateau, 45 (1973): 102-110.

Smith, Charline Galloway. Culture and diabetes among the Upland Yuman Indians. Dissertation Abstracts International, 31 (1970/1971): 3821B. UM 71-1045.

Wares, Alan Campbell. A comparative study of Yuman consonantism. Dissertation Abstracts, 26 (1964/1965): 2200. UM 65-10,774.

Wares, Alan Campbell. A comparative study of Yuman consonantism. The Hague, Mouton, 1968. 100 p. map. (Janua Linguarum, Series Practica, 57)

Winter, Werner. Stories and songs of the Walapai. Plateau, 35, (1962/1963): 114-122.

Winter, Werner. Yuman languages II: Wolf's Son--a Walapai text. International Journal of American Linguistics, 32 (1966): 17-40.

Writers' Program of Work Projects Administration. The Havasupai and the Hualapai. Arizona State Teachers College, Bulletin, 21, no. 5 (1940): 1-36.

15-33 Yavapai

Barnett, Franklin. Viola Jimulla: the Indian chieftess; a biography. Yuma, Printed by Southwest Printers, 1968. 8, 43 p. illus.

Bloom, L. B., ed. Bourke on the Southwest. New Mexico Historical Review, 9 (1934): 159-183.

Bret Harte, John. The San Carlos Indian Reservation, 1872-1886: an administrative history. Dissertation Abstracts International, 33 (1972/1973): 5080A. UM 73-7802.

Breternitz, David A. Orme Ranch Cave, NA 6656. Plateau, 33 (1960): 25-39.

Brugge, David M. A linguistic approach to demographic problems: the Tonto-Yavapai boundary. Ethnohistory, 12 (1965): 355-372.

Coffeen, William R. The effects of the Central Arizona Project on the Fort McDowell Indian community. Ethnohistory, 19 (1972): 345-377.

Conrad, David E. The Whipple expedition in Arizona 1853-1854. Arizona and the West, 11 (1969): 147-178.

Corbusier, W. F. The Apache-Yumas and Apache-Mohaves. American Antiquarian and Oriental Journal, 8 (1886): 276-284, 325-338.

Curtis, E. S. The North American Indian, Vol. 2: 103-107. Norwood, 1908.

Curtis, N., ed. The Indians' book, 329-338. New York, 1907.

Dobyns, H. F., et al. Thematic changes in Yuman warfare. In V. F. Ray, ed. Cultural Stability and Cultural Change. Seattle, 1957: 46-71.

Dobyns, Henry F. The ghost dance of 1889 among the Pai Indians of northwestern Arizona. By Henry F. Dobyns and Robert C. Euler. Prescott, Prescott College Press, 1967. 12, 67 p. illus., map.

Drucker, Philip. Culture element distributions: XVII Yuman-Piman. Berkeley, 1941. 91-230 p. illus., map. (California, University, Publications, Anthropological Records, 6, no. 3)

Ewing, Henry P. The Pai tribes. Edited by Robert C. Euler and Henry F. Dobyns. Ethnohistory, 7 (1960): 61-80.

Fay, George E., ed. Charters, constitutions and by-laws of the Indian tribes of North America. Part IV: The Southwest (Navajo-Zuni). Greeley, 1967. 5, 120 l. maps. (University of Northern Colorado, Museum of Anthropology, Occasional Publications in Anthropology, Ethnology Series, 5) ERIC ED046554.

Fay, George E., ed. Charters, constitutions and by-laws of the Indian tribes of North America. Part III: The Southwest (Apache-Mohave). Greeley, 1967. 6, 118 l. maps. (University of Northern Colorado, Museum of Anthropology, Occasional Publications in Anthropology, Ethnology Series, 4) ERIC ED046553.

Gatschet, A. S. Classification into seven linguistic stocks of Western Indian dialects. In Report upon United States Geographical Surveys West of the One Hundredth Meridian. Vol. 7. Washington, D.C., 1879: 403-485.

Gatschet, A. S. Der Yuma-Sprachstamm. Zeitschrift für Ethnologie, 9 (1887): 373-375, 390-406, 408-412.

Gatschet, A. S. Tulkepaia. U.S. Bureau of American Ethnology, Bulletin, 30, vol. 2 (1910): 836.

*Gifford, E. W. Northeastern and Western Yavapai. California, University, Publications in American Archaeology and Ethnology, 34 (1936): 247-354.

Gifford, E. W. Northeastern and Western Yavapai myths. Journal of American Folklore, 46 (1933): 347-415.

*Gifford, E. W. The Southeastern Yavapai. California, University, Publications in American Archaeology and Ethnology, 29 (1932): 177-252.

Gould, M. K. Two legends of the Mohave-Apache. Journal of American Folklore, 34 (1921): 319-320.

Henshaw, H. W. Yavapai. U.S. Bureau of American Ethnology, Bulletin, 30, vol. 2 (1910): 944-945.

Hoffman, W. J. Miscellaneous ethnographic observations. United States Geological and Geographical Survey of the Territories, Annual Reports, 10 (1876): 461-477.

James, G. W. Palomas Apaches and their baskets. Sunset Magazine, 11 (1903): 146-153.

Joel, Judith. Classification of the Yuman languages. In William Bright, ed. Studies in Californian Linguistics. Berkeley and Los Angeles, University of California Press, 1964: 99-105. (California, University, Publications in Linguistics, 34)

Kendall, Martha Burnett. Selected problems in Yavapai syntax. Dissertation Abstracts International, 33 (1972/1973): 4631B. UM 73-9764.

Kroeber, Clifton B., ed. The route of James O. Pattie on the Colorado in 1826. A reappraisal by A. L. Kroeber. [With comments by R. C. Euler and A. H. Schroeder]. Arizona and the West, 6 (1964): 119-136.

Law, Howard W. A reconstructed proto-culture derived from some Yuman vocabularies. Anthropological Linguistics, 3, no. 4 (1961): 45-57.

Mierau, Eric. Concerning Yavapai-Apache bilingualism. International Journal of American Linguistics, 29 (1963): 1-3.

Morris, Clyde P. A brief economic history of the Camp and Middle Verde reservations. Plateau, 44 (1971): 43-51.

Morris, Clyde P. Yavapai-Apache family organization in a reservation context. Plateau, 44 (1972): 105-110.

Ocampo, Manuel. Historia de la Misión de la Tarahumara, 1900-1965. 2d ed. México, Editorial Jus, 1966. 446 p. illus., map.

Riggs, John L. William H. Hardy: merchant of the Upper Colorado. Edited by Kenneth Hufford. Journal of Arizona History, 6 (1965): 177-187.

Romney, A. Kimball. Internal reconstruction of Yuman kinship terminology. In Dell H. Hymes and William E. Bittle, eds. Studies in Southwestern Ethnolinguistics. The Hague, Mouton, 1967: 379-386. (Studies in General Anthropology, 3)

Schroeder, A. H. A brief history of the Yavapai of the Middle Verde Valley. Plateau, 24 (1952): 111-118.

Schroeder, Albert H. Fray Marcos de Niza, Coronado and the Yavapai. New Mexico Historical Review, 30 (1955): 265-296; 31 (1956): 24-37.

Smith, Charline Galloway. Culture and diabetes among the Upland Yuman Indians. Dissertation Abstracts International, 31 (1970/1971): 3821B. UM 71-1045.

Vivian, R. Gwinn. An archaeological survey of the Lower Gila River, Arizona. Kiva, 30, no. 4 (1964/1965): 95-146.

Wares, Alan Campbell. A comparative study of Yuman consonantism. The Hague, Mouton, 1968. 100 p. map. (Janua Linguarum, Series Practica, 57)

Wares, Alan Campbell. A comparative study of Yuman consonantism. Dissertation Abstracts, 26 (1964/1965): 2200. UM 65-10,774.

15-34   Yuma

Anonymous. Yuma. U.S. Bureau of American Ethnology, Bulletin, 30, vol. 2 (1910): 1010-1011.

Aschmann, Homer. Historical sources for a contact ethnography of Baja California. California Historical Society Quarterly, 44 (1965): 99-121.

Bartlett, J. H. Personal narrative of explorations and incidents in Texas, New Mexico, California, Sonora, and Chihuahua, Vol. 2: 177-181. New York, 1854.

Bartlett, John R. A letter from John R. Bartlett at Camp Yuma, 1852. Edited by Odie B. Faulk. Journal of Arizona History, 6 (1965): 204-213.

Bee, Robert L. "Self-help" at Fort Yuma: a critique. Human Organization, 29 (1970): 155-161.

Bee, Robert Lawrence. Sociocultural change and persistence in the Yuma Indian Reservation community. Dissertation Abstracts, 28 (1967/1968): 3140B. UM 68-566.

Buschmann, J. C. E. Die Spuren der aztekischen Sprache im nördlichen Mexico und höheren amerikanischen Norden. Berlin, Königliche Akademie der Wissenschaften, Abhandlungen, Supplement-Band, 2 (1854): 267-276.

Cardenal, Ernesto, tr. Poesía de los indios de Norteamérica. América Indígena, 21 (1961): 355-362.

*Castetter, E. F. and W. H. Bell. Yuman Indian agriculture. Albuquerque, 1951. 288 p.

Chaput, Donald. Babes in arms. Journal of Arizona History, 13 (1972): 197-204.

Conrad, David E. The Whipple expedition in Arizona 1853-1854. Arizona and the West, 11 (1969): 147-178.

Curtis, E. S. The North American Indian, Vol. 2: 63-79. Cambridge, 1908.

Curtis, N. The Indians' book, 339-341. New York, 1907.

Curtis, Natalie. Creation myth of the Cochans (Yuma Indians). Craftsman, 16 (1909): 559-567.

Davis, Edward H. Yuma Koorook ceremony. Edited by Helen C. Smith. Pacific Coast Archaeological Society, Quarterly, 4, no. 1 (1968): 39-45.

Densmore, F. Communication with the dead as practised by the American Indians. Man, 50 (1950): 40-41.

Densmore, F. Yuman and Yaqui music. U.S. Bureau of American Ethnology, Bulletin, 110 (1932): 1-216.

Densmore, Frances. Yuman and Yaqui music. New York, Da Capo Press, 1972. 18, 216 p. illus.

Dixon, R. B. and A. L. Kroeber. The native languages of California. American Anthropologist, n.s., 15 (1913): 647-655.

Dobyns, H. F., et al. Thematic changes in Yuman warfare. In Verne F. Ray, ed. Cultural Stability and Cultural Change. Seattle, 1957: 46-71.

Dobyns, Henry F. A brief history of the Northeastern Pai. By Henry F. Dobyns and Robert C. Euler. Plateau, 32 (1960): 49-57.

Douglas, F. H., et al. Ten Yuma pots. Denver Art Museum, Material Culture Notes, 19 (1953): 1-10.

Driver, H. E. Estimation of intensity of land use from ethnobiology. Ethnohistory, 4 (1957): 174-197.

Drucker, P. Southern California. Anthropological Records, 1 (1937): 1-52.

Emerson, Lee. Petroglyphs of ancient man; a Quechan man speaks. Indian Historian, 4, no. 1 (1971): 4-8.

Erskine, M. H. A cattle drive from Texas to California: the diary of M. H. Erskine, 1854. Edited by Walter S. Sanderlin. Southwestern Historical Quarterly, 67 (1963/1964): 397-412.

Ezell, Paul H. The Hispanic acculturation of the Gila River Pimas. Menasha, American Anthropological Association, 1961. 5, 171 p. illus., maps. (American Anthropological Association, Memoir, 90)

Ezell, Paul H. The Maricopas: an identification from documentary sources. Tucson, University of Arizona Press, 1963. 29 p. (Arizona, University, Anthropological Papers, 6)

Fages, Pedro. From Pitic to San Gabriel in 1782: the journal of Don Pedro Fages. Edited by Ronald L. Ives. Journal of Arizona History, 9 (1968): 222-244.

Fay, George E., ed. Charters, constitutions and by-laws of the Indian tribes of North America. Part VII: The Indian tribes of California. Greeley, 1970. 12, 109 l. map. (University of Northern Colorado, Museum of Anthropology, Occasional Publications in

Anthropology, Ethnology Series, 8) ERIC ED046557.

Ferrebee, W. E. Yuma Indians. In United States, Department of the Interior, Census Office, Eleventh Census, Report on Indians Taxed and Indians not Taxed. Washington, D.C., 1890: 219-222.

*Forde, C. D. Ethnography of the Yuma Indians. California, University, Publications in American Archaeology and Ethnology, 28 (1931): 83-278.

Frisch, Jack A. Componential analysis and semantic reconstruction: the Proto Central Yuman kinship system. By Jack A. Frisch and Noel W. Schutz, Jr. Ethnology, 6 (1967): 272-293.

Gatschet, A. S. Classification into seven linguistic stocks of Western Indian dialects. In Report upon United States Geographical Surveys West of the One Hundredth Meridian. Vol. 7. Washington, D.C., 1879: 403-485.

Gatschet, A. S. Der Yuma-Sprachstamm. Zeitschrift für Ethnologie, 9 (1887): 381-382, 391-407.

Gatschet, A. S. The Waikuru, Seri and Yuma languages. Science, n.s., 12 (1900): 556-558.

Gifford, E. W. Californian kinship terminologies. California, University, Publications in American Archaeology and Ethnology, 18 (1922): 62-65.

Gifford, E. W. Clans and moieties in southern California. California, University, Publications in American Archaeology and Ethnology, 14 (1918): 156-167.

Gifford, E. W. Yuma dreams and omens. Journal of American Folklore, 39 (1926): 58-69.

Haine, J. J. F. A Belgian in the gold rush: California Indians. A memoir by J. J. F. Haine. Translated, with an introduction by Jan Albert Goris. California Historical Society Quarterly, 38 (1959): 141-155.

Halpern, A. M. Yuma. International Journal of American Linguistics, 12 (1946): 25-33, 147-151, 204-212; 13 (1947): 18-30, 92-107, 147-166.

Halpern, A. M. Yuma kinship terms. American Anthropologist, n.s., 44 (1942): 425-441.

Halpern, A. M. Yuma. Viking Fund Publications in Anthropology, 6 (1946): 249-288.

Hanna, Bertram L. The biological relationships among Indian groups of the Southwest: analysis of morphological traits. American Journal of Physical Anthropology, n.s., 20 (1962): 499-508.

Harrington, J. P. A Yuma account of origins. Journal of American Folklore, 21 (1908): 324-348.

Hendricks, W. O. On an attempt to expel some Yuma Indians from Baja California. Pacific Coast Archaeological Society, Quarterly, 4, no. 1 (1968): 55-66; 6, no. 1 (1970): 47-57.

Herzog, G. The Yuman musical style. Journal of American Folklore, 41 (1928): 183-231.

Hicks, Frederic Noble. Ecological aspects of aboriginal culture in the western Yuman area. Dissertation Abstracts, 24 (1963/1964): 1333-1334. UM 63-6591.

Ives, J. C. Report upon the Colorado River of the West. Washington, D.C., 1861. 131 p.

Ives, Ronald L. Kino's exploration of the Pinacate region. Journal of Arizona History, 7 (1966): 59-75.

Ives, Ronald L., ed. Retracing the route of the Fages expedition of 1781. Arizona and the West, 8 (1966): 49-70, 157-170.

Joel, Judith. Classification of the Yuman languages. In William Bright, ed. Studies in Californian Linguistics. Berkeley and Los Angeles, University of California Press, 1964: 99-105. (California, University, Publications in Linguistics, 34)

Johnston, Francis J. San Gorgonio Pass: forgotten route of the Californios? Journal of the West, 8 (1969): 125-136.

Kate, H. F. C. ten. Reizen en onderzoekingen in Noord-Amerika, 105-115. Leiden, 1885.

Kessell, John L. The making of a martyr: the young Francisco Garcés. New Mexico Historical Review, 45 (1970): 181-196.

Kroeber, A. L. Handbook of the Indians of California. U.S. Bureau of American Ethnology, Bulletin, 78 (1925): 781-795.

Langdon, Margaret. Sound symbolism in Yuman languages. In Jesse Sawyer, ed. Studies in American Indian Languages. Berkeley and Los Angeles, University of California Press, 1971: 149-173. (California, University, Publications in Linguistics, 65)

Law, Howard W. A reconstructed proto-culture derived from some Yuman vocabularies. Anthropological Linguistics, 3, no. 4 (1961): 45-57.

Lee, Robert L. Changes in Yuma social organization. Ethnology, 2 (1963): 207-277.

Lincoln, J. S. The dream in primitive cultures. London, 1935. 359 p.

Mallery, G. Account of Yuma ceremonies. Smithsonian Miscellaneous Collections, 34, no. 2 (1885): 143-144.

Maughan, Scott Jarvis. Francisco Garcés and New Spain's northwestern frontier, 1768-1781. Dissertation Abstracts, 29 (1968/1969): 2647A-2648A. UM 69-3508.

McCall, George Archibald. Camp Yuma--1852. Edited by Robert W. Frazer. Southern California Quarterly, 52 (1970): 170-184.

Miller, David H. The Ives expedition revisited: overland into Grand Canyon. Journal of Arizona History, 13 (1972): 177-196.

Moriarty, James Robert, III. The environmental variations of the Yuman culture area of Southern California. Anthropological Journal of Canada, 6, no. 2 (1968): 2-20; 6, no. 3 (1968): 9-23.

Nicholson, H. S. Four songs from a Yuma version of Los Pastores. Arizona, University, General Bulletin, 9 (1945): 25-28.

North, A. W. The native tribes of Lower California. American Anthropologist, n.s., 10 (1908): 236-250.

Peet, S. D. The worship of the rain-god. American Antiquarian and Oriental Journal, 16 (1894): 341-356.

Phoenix Indian School. The new trail: a book of creative writing by Indian students. Phoenix, 1941. 158 p.

Putnam, G. R. A Yuma cremation. American Anthropologist, 8 (1895): 264-267.

Ramos, Antonio. Father Eixarch and the visitation at Tumacácori, May 12, 1775. Edited by John L. Kessell. Kiva, 30, no. 3 (1964/1965): 77-86.

Ridington (Wrightington), Juana Machado Alipaz de. Times gone by in Alta California; recollections of Senora Dona Juana Machado Alipaz de Ridington (Wrightington), Bancroft Library, 1878. Translated and annotated by Raymond S.

Brandes. Southern California Quarterly, 41 (1959): 195-240.

Rogers, M. J. An outline of Yuman prehistory. Southwestern Journal of Anthropology, 1 (1945): 167-198.

Rogers, M. J. Yuman pottery making. San Diego Museum, Papers, 2, no. 7 (1936): 1-44.

Roheim, G. Psycho-analysis of primitive cultural types. International Journal of Psycho-analysis, 13 (1932): 175-198.

Romer, Margaret. Aboard ship on dry land. Journal of the West, 8 (1969): 606-612.

Romney, A. Kimball. Internal reconstruction of Yuman kinship terminology. In Dell H. Hymes and William E. Bittle, eds. Studies in Southwestern Ethnolinguistics. The Hague, Mouton, 1967: 379-386. (Studies in General Anthropology, 3)

Schroeder, Albert H. An archaeological survey of the Painted Rocks Resevoir, Western Arizona. Kiva, 27, no. 1 (1961/1962): 1-28.

Sedelmayr, Jacobo. Jacobo Sedelmayr missionary frontiersman explorer in Arizona and Sonora. Four original manuscript narratives 1744-1751. Translated and annotated by Peter Masten Dunne. [n.p.] Arizona Pioneers' Historical Society, 1955. 4, 82, 7 p. map.

Smith, Melvin T. Colorado River exploration and the Mormon War. Utah Historical Quarterly, 38 (1970): 207-223.

Spicer, Edward H. European expansion and the enclavement of Southwestern Indians. Arizona and the West, 1 (1959): 132-145.

Spier, L. Cultural relations of the Gila River and Lower Colorado tribes. Yale University Publications in Anthropology, 3 (1936): 1-22.

Stewart, Kenneth M. Chemehuevi culture changes. Plateau, 40 (1967): 14-21.

Stout, Joe A., Jr. Joseph C. Morehead and manifest destiny: a filibuster in Sonora, 1851. Pacific Historian, 15, no. 1 (1971): 62-71.

Trippel, E. J. The Yuma Indians. Overland Monthly, ser. 2, 13 (1889): 561-584; 14 (1889): 1-11.

Vivian, R. Gwinn. An archaeological survey of the Lower Gila River, Arizona. Kiva, 30, no. 4 (1964/1965): 95-146.

Wallace, William J. Indian use of California's rocks and minerals. Journal of the West, 10 (1971): 35-52.

Wares, Alan Campbell. A comparative study of Yuman consonantism. The Hague, Mouton, 1968. 100 p. map. (Janua Linguarum, Series Practica, 57)

Wares, Alan Campbell. A comparative study of Yuman consonantism. Dissertation Abstracts, 26 (1964/1965): 2200. UM 65-10,774.

Whiting, A. F. The Tumacacori census of 1796. Kiva, 29, no. 1 (1953): 1-12.

Wood, C. W. Yuma Reservation. In United States, Department of the Interior, Census Office, Eleventh Census, Report on Indians Taxed and Indians not Taxed. Washington, D.C., 1890: 216-219.

Yates, Richard. Locating the Colorado River Mission San Pedro y San Pablo de Bicuñer. Journal of Arizona History, 13 (1972): 123-130.

15-35   Zuni

Fraser, James H. Indian mission printing in New Mexico: a bibliography. New Mexico Historical Review, 43 (1968): 311-318.

Aberle, S. B. D. Maternal mortality among the Pueblos. American Journal of Physical Anthropology, 18 (1934): 431-457.

Adair, J. and E. Vogt. Navaho and Zuni veterans: a study of contrasting modes of culture change. American Anthropologist, n.s., 51 (1949): 547-561.

Adair, John. Problems of a Pueblo ex-G.I. In Philip K. Bock, ed. Culture Shock. New York, Knopf, 1970: 246-258.

Albert, E. and J. Cazeneuve. La philosophie des Indiens Zunis. Revue de Psychologie des Peuples, 11 (1956): 112-123.

Anonymous. The Pueblo of Zuni. El Palacio, 47 (1940): 162-163.

Anonymous. Turkeys at Hawikuh, New Mexico. Masterkey, 26 (1952): 13-14.

Bandelier, A. F. An outline of the documentary history of the Zuni tribe. Journal of American Ethnology and Archaeology, 3 (1892): 1-115.

Bandelier, A. F. Po-sé. New Mexico Historical Review, 1 (1926): 335-349.

Barrow, Mark V. Relapsing polychondritis in a Zuni Indian. By Mark V. Barrow and Errett E. Hummel, Jr. Archives of Internal Medicine, 127 (1971): 950-952.

Bartlett, F. The creation of the Zunis. Old Santa Fe, 2 (1915): 79-87.

Bell, C. C., Jr., et al. Relationship of bile acid pool size to the formation of lithogenous bile in male Indians of the Southwest. Surgery, Gynecology and Obstetrics, 134 (1972): 473-478.

Bellah, Robert N. Religious sytems. In Evon Z. Vogt and Ethel M. Albert, eds. The People of Rimrock. Cambridge, Harvard University Press, 1966: 227-264.

Benedict, R. Patterns of culture, 57-129. Boston, 1934.

Benedict, R. They dance for rain in Zuni. In M. Mead, ed. An Anthropologist at Work. Boston, 1959: 222-225.

Benedict, Ruth F. Zuni mythology. New York, AMS Press, 1969. 2 v.

Bloom, L. B., ed. Bourke on the Southwest. New Mexico Historical Review, 11 (1936): 77-122, 188-207.

Boas, F. Tales of Spanish provenience from Zuni. Journal of American Folklore, 35 (1922): 62-98.

Boas, F. Zur Anthropologie der nordamerikanischen Indianer. Berliner Gesellschaft für Anthropologie, Ethnologie und Urgeschichte, Verhandlungen (1895): 367-411.

Bohrer, V. L. Chinchweed (Pectes papposa), a Zuñi herb. El Palacio, 64 (1957): 365.

Bohrer, Vorsila L. Zuni agriculture. By Vorsila L. Bohrer, Lawrence Kaplan and Thomas W. Whitaker. El Palacio, 67 (1960): 181-202.

Bourke, J. G. Sacred hunts of the American Indians. International Congress of Americanists, Proceedings, 8 (1890): 357-368.

Bourke, J. G. The urine dance of the Zunis. American Association for the Advancement of Science, Proceedings, 34 (1885): 400-404.

Brandes, Raymond Stewart. Frank Hamilton Cushing: pioneer Americanist. Dissertation Abstracts, 26 (1965/1966): 2156-2157. UM 65-9951.

Brown, K. S. Population studies on Southwestern Indian tribes: III. Serum protein variations of Zuni and Papago Indians. By K. S. Brown and R. S. Johnson. Human Heredity, 20 (1970): 281-286.

Buchler, Ira R. Measuring the development of kinship terminologies: scalogram and transformational accounts of Crow-type systems. American Anthropologist, 66 (1964): 765-788.

Bunzel, R. L. Introduction to Zuni ceremonialism. U.S. Bureau of American Ethnology, Annual Reports, 47 (1930): 467-544.

Bunzel, R. L. The Pueblo potter. Columbia University Contributions to Anthropology, 8 (1929): 1-134.

Bunzel, R. L. Zuni. In F. Boas, ed. Handbook of American Indian Languages. Vol. 4. Washington, D.C., 1935: 389-415.

Bunzel, R. L. Zuni katcinas. U.S. Bureau of American Ethnology, Annual Reports, 47 (1930): 837-1086.

Bunzel, R. L. Zuni origin myths. U.S. Bureau of American Ethnology, Annual Reports, 47 (1930): 545-609.

Bunzel, R. L. Zuni ritual poetry. U.S. Bureau of American Ethnology, Annual Reports, 47 (1930): 611-835.

Bunzel, R. L. Zuni texts. American Ethnological Society, Publications, 15 (1933): 1-285.

Bunzel, Ruth L. Primitive artist at work. In Walter R. Goldschmidt, ed. Exploring the Ways of Mankind. New York, Holt, 1960: 596-602.

Bunzel, Ruth L. The Pueblo potter. New York, AMS Press, 1969. 134 p. illus.

Cabrero, L. Las sociedades de medicina de los Indios Zuñi. Noticiario Indigenista Español, 19/20 (1957): 1-2.

Cardenal, Ernesto, tr. Poesía de los indios de Norteamérica. América Indígena, 21 (1961): 355-362.

Carlson, Roy L. Eighteenth century Navajo fortresses of the Gobernador District. Boulder, University of Colorado Press, 1965. 2, 116 p. (Colorado, University, Studies, Series in Anthropology, 10)

Cazeneuve, J. Les dieux dansent à Cibola. Paris, 1957. 273 p.

Cazeneuve, J. Les Zuñis dans l'oevre de Lévy-Bruhl. Revue Philosophique, 967 (1957): 530-538.

Cazeneuve, J. Some observations on the Zuñi Shalakho. El Palacio, 62 (1955): 347-356.

Chapman, K. M. Bird forms in Zuñi pottery decoration. El Palacio, 58 (1951): 316-324.

Chapman, K. M. Bird forms in Zuni pottery decoration. El Palacio, 24 (1928): 23-25.

Chapman, K. M. The Shalako ceremony at Zuni. El Palacio, 23 (1927): 622-627.

Chauvenet, B. A Zuni Shalako. El Palacio, 27 (1929): 299-306.

Christinger, Raymond. L'origine des katchinas. Société Suisse des Américanistes, Bulletin, 26 (1963): 10-18.

Colby, Benjamin N. A study of thematic apperception tests with the General Inquirer system. El Palacio, 71, no. 4 (1964): 29-36.

Colby, Benjamin N. The analysis of culture content and the patterning of narrative concern in texts. American Anthropologist, 68 (1966): 374-388.

Collier, John. American Indian ceremonial dances: Navajo, Pueblo, Apache, Zuni. New York, Bounty Books, 1972. 192 p. illus.

Collier, John. On the gleaming way. Denver, Sage Books, 1962. 163 p. illus.

Collins, G. N. Pueblo Indian maize breeding. Journal of Heredity, 5 (1914): 255-268.

Colton, Harold S. Principal Hopi trails. Plateau, 36 (1964): 91-94.

Conrad, David E. The Whipple expedition in Arizona 1853-1854. Arizona and the West, 11 (1969): 147-178.

Corruccini, Robert S. The biological relationships of some prehistoric and historic Pueblo populations. American Journal of Physical Anthropology, 37 (1972/1973): 373-388.

Coze, P. Twenty-four hours of magic. Arizona Highways, 30, no. 11 (1954): 10-27, 34-35.

Crimmins, M. L. The rattlesnake in the art and life of the American Indian.

Texas Archeological and Paleontological Society, Bulletin, 17 (1946): 28-41.

Culin, S. Zuni pictures. In E. C. Parsons, ed. American Indian Life. New York, 1925: 175-178.

Curtis, E. S. The North American Indian, Vol. 17: 85-181. Norwood, 1926.

Curtis, N., ed. The Indians' book, 429-444. New York, 1907.

Curtis, W. E. Children of the sun. Chicago, 1883. 154 p.

Cushing, F. H. A case of primitive surgery. Science, 5 (1897): 977-981.

Cushing, F. H. A study of Pueblo pottery as illustrative of Zuni culture-growth. U.S. Bureau of American Ethnology, Annual Reports, 4 (1886): 467-521.

Cushing, F. H. A Zuni folk-tale of the underworld. Journal of American Folklore, 5 (1892): 49-56.

Cushing, F. H. Katalog einer Sammlung von Idolen, Fetishen und priesterlichen Ausrüstungsgegenständen der Zuni- oder Ashiwi-Indianer. Königliches Museum für Völkerkunde, Veröffentlichungen, 4 (1895): 1-12.

Cushing, F. H. Manual concepts: a study of the influence of hand-usage on culture-growth. American Anthropologist, 5 (1892): 289-317.

Cushing, F. H. My adventures in Zuni. Century Magazine, 25 (1882): 191-207, 500-511; 26 (1883): 28-47.

Cushing, F. H. Outlines of Zuni creation myths. U.S. Bureau of American Ethnology, Annual Reports, 13 (1896): 321-447.

Cushing, F. H. Preliminary notes on the origin, working hypothesis and primary researches of the Hemenway Southwestern Archaeological Expedition. International Congress of Americanists, Proceedings, 7 (1888): 151-194.

Cushing, F. H. Primitive copper working-- a study. American Anthropologist, 7 (1894): 93-117.

Cushing, F. H. The Zuni social, mythic, and religious systems. Popular Science Monthly, 21 (1882): 186-192.

*Cushing, F. H. Zuni breadstuffs. Indian Notes and Monographs, 8 (1920): 7-642.

Cushing, F. H. Zuni fetishes. U.S. Bureau of American Ethnology, Annual Reports, 2 (1883): 9-45.

Cushing, F. H. Zuni folk tales. New York, 1901. 474 p.

Cushing, Frank H. My adventures in Zuñi. Palmer Lake, Colo., Filter Press, 1967. 8, 49 p. illus.

Cushing, Frank H. Zuñi fetishes. Flagstaff, K. C. Publications, 1966. 43 p. illus.

DeHuff, E. W. Taytay's memories, 20-24. New York, 1924.

Denman, Leslie V. N. Pai ya tu ma, god of all dance and his customs of the flute, Zuni Pueblo, 1932. San Francisco, Grabhorn Press, 1955. 35 p. illus.

Densmore, F. Music of Acoma, Isleta, Cochiti and Zuñi Pueblos. U.S. Bureau of American Ethnology, Bulletin, 165 (1957): 1-129.

Densmore, Frances. Music of Acoma, Isleta, Cochiti, and Zuñi Pueblos. New York, Da Capo Press, 1972. 12, 117 p. illus.

Deumann, David L. Navajo silversmithing. El Palacio, 77, no. 2 (1971): 13-32.

Donaldson, T. Moqui Indians of Arizona and Pueblo Indians of New Mexico. U.S. Census Office, Eleventh Census, Extra Bulletin (1893): 1-136.

Douglas, F. H. Main types of Pueblo cotton textiles. Denver Art Museum, Indian Leaflet Series, 92/93 (1940): 166-172.

Douglas, F. H. Main types of Pueblo woolen textiles. Denver Art Museum, Indian Leaflet Series, 94/95 (1940): 174-180.

Douglas, F. H. Weaving at Zuni Pueblo. Denver Art Museum, Indian Leaflet Series, 96/97 (1940): 182-187.

Dozier, Edward P. Pueblo Indian response to culture contact. In M. Estellie Smith, ed. Studies in Linguistics in Honor of George L. Trager. The Hague, Mouton, 1972: 457-467. (Janua Linguarum, Series Maior, 52)

Duggan, E. V. Health work among the Zuni Indians. Public Health Nurse, 20 (1928): 20-22.

Dutton, Bertha P. Friendly people: the Zuñi Indians. Santa Fe, Museum of New Mexico Press, 1963. 28 p.

Dutton, Bertha P. Indian artistry in wood and other media. El Palacio, 64 (1957): 3-28.

Edmonson, Munro S. Kinship systems. In Evon Z. Vogt and Ethel M. Albert, eds. The People of Rimrock. Cambridge, Harvard University Press, 1966: 126-159.

*Eggan, F. Social organization of the Western Pueblos, 176-222. Chicago, 1950.

Ellis, Florence Hawley. A reconstruction of basic Jemez pattern of social organization, with comparisons to other Tanoan social structures. Albuquerque, University of New Mexico Press, 1964. 69 p. (New Mexico, University, Publications in Anthropology, 11)

English, Lydia E. By wagon from Kansas to Arizona in 1875--the travel diary of Lydia E. English. Edited by Joseph W. Snell. Kansas Historical Quarterly, 36 (1970): 369-389.

Espinosa, A. M. All-Souls' Day at Zuni, Acoma, and Laguna. Journal of American Folklore, 31 (1918): 550-552.

Fay, George E., ed. Treaties, land cessions, and other U.S. Congressional documents relative to American Indian tribes. Zuni Indian Pueblo, New Mexico. Part I: U.S. Congressional documents, 1877-1967. Greeley, 1971. 9, 157 l. illus., maps. (University of Northern Colorado, Museum of Anthropology, Occasional Publications in Anthropology, Ethnology Series, 20)

Fergusson, E. Dancing gods, 67-113. New York, 1931.

Fewkes, J. W. A few summer ceremonials at Zuni Pueblo. Journal of American Ethnology and Archaeology, 1 (1891): 1-61.

Fewkes, J. W. A study of summer ceremonials at Zuni and Moqui Pueblos. Essex Institute (Salem), Bulletin, 22 (1890): 89-113.

Fewkes, J. W. Ancient Zuni pottery. In Putnam Anniversary Volume. New York, 1909: 43-83.

Fewkes, J. W. Reconnaissance of ruins in or near the Zuni Reservation. Journal of American Ethnology and Archaeology, 1 (1891): 93-132.

Fleming, H. C. Medical observations on the Zuni Indians. Museum of the American Indian, Heye Foundation, Contributions, 7, no. 2 (1924): 39-48.

Gatschet, A. S. Zwölf Sprachen aus dem Südwesten Nordamerikas. Weimar, 1876. 150 p.

Gifford, E. W. Apache-Pueblo. Anthropological Records, 4 (1940): 1-207.

Gilman, B. I. Zuni melodies. Journal of American Ethnology and Archaeology, 1 (1891): 63-91.

Goldfrank, E. Linguistic note to Zuni ethnography. Word, 2 (1946): 191-196.

Goldfrank, E. Socialization, personality, and the structure of Pueblo society. American Anthropologist, n.s., 47 (1945): 516-539. ·

Goldman, I. The Zuni Indians of New Mexico. In M. Mead, ed. Cooperation and Competition among Primitive Peoples. New York, 1937: 313-353.

Gonzales, Clara. The Shalakos are coming. El Palacio, 73, no. 3 (1966): 5-17.

Gore, J. H. Regulative system of the Zuñis. Smithsonian Miscellaneous Collections, 25 (1882): 86-88.

Graham, S. The Shalaco dance. El Palacio, 15 (1923): 139-140.

Granberry, Julian. Zuni syntax. Dissertation Abstracts, 28 (1967/1968): 1770B-1771B. UM 67-13,346.

Greenwood, N. H. Sol Barth: a Jewish settler on the Arizona frontier. Journal of Arizona History, 14 (1973): 363-378.

Gronewold, Sylvia. Did Frank Hamilton Cushing go native? In Solon T. Kimball and James B. Watson, eds. Crossing Cultural Boundaries. San Francisco, Chandler, 1972: 33-50.

Hammond, G. P. and A. Rey, eds. Expedition into New Mexico made by Antonio de Espejo, 89-93. Los Angeles, 1929.

Handy, E. L. Zuni tales. Journal of American Folklore, 31 (1918): 451-471.

Herrala, Elizabeth Ann. The incidence of dental caries of pre-historic and historic Indian groups. Indiana Academy of Science, Proceedings, 71 (1961): 57-60.

Hill, G. Turquoise and the Zuni Indian. Kiva, 12 (1947): 42-51.

Hodge, F. W. A square kiva at Hawikuh. In D. D. Brand and F. E. Harvey, eds. So

Live the Works of Men. Albuquerque,
1939: 195-214.

Hodge, F. W. A Zuni foot race. American
Anthropologist, 3 (1890): 227-231.

Hodge, F. W. Circular kivas near Hawikuh.
Museum of the American Indian, Heye
Foundation, Contributions, 7, no. 1
(1923): 1-37.

Hodge, F. W. Excavations at Hawikuh.
Smithsonian Institution, Explorations
and Field-Work (1918): 61-72.

Hodge, F. W. Excavations at the Zuni
Pueblo of Hawikuh. Art and Archaeology,
7 (1918): 367-379.

Hodge, F. W. Hawikuh bonework. Indian
Notes and Monographs, 3, no. 3 (1920):
65-151.

Hodge, F. W. History of Hawikuh.
Frederick Webb Hodge Anniversary
Publication Fund, Southwest Museum,
Publications, 1 (1937): 1-155.

Hodge, F. W. Pottery of Hawikuh. Indian
Notes, 1 (1924): 8-15.

Hodge, F. W. Recent excavations at
Hawikuh. El Palacio, 12 (1922): 3-11.

Hodge, F. W. Snake pens at Hawikuh.
Indian Notes, 1 (1924): 111-120.

Hodge, F. W. The age of the Zuni Pueblo
of Kechipauan. Indian Notes and
Monographs, 3 (1920): 43-60.

Hodge, F. W. The first discovered city of
Cibola. American Anthropologist, 8
(1895): 142-152.

Hodge, F. W. Zuni. U.S. Bureau of
American Ethnology, Bulletin, 30, vol. 2
(1910): 1015-1020.

Hodge, Frederick W. The excavation of
Hawikuh by Frederick Webb Hodge. By
Watson Smith, Richard B. Woodbury, and
Nathalie F. S. Woodbury. New York,
1966. 13, 366 p. illus. (Museum of
the American Indian, Heye Foundation,
Contributions, 20)

Hodge, G. M. The kachinas are coming.
Los Angeles, 1937. 129 p.

Holland, Francis Ross, Jr. Hawikuh and
the Seven Cities of Cibola; historical
background study. Washington, D.C.,
Office of Archeology and Historic
Preservation, 1969. 6, 69 l. illus.,
map.

Hough, W. Sacred springs in the
Southwest. Records of the Past, 5
(1906): 163-170.

Houston, Susan H. A survey of
psycholinguistics. The Hague, Mouton,
1972. 299 p. illus. (Janua Linguarum,
Series Minor, 98)

Hufford, Kenneth. Travelers on the Gila
Trail, 1824-1850. Journal of Arizona
History, 7 (1966): 1-8; 8 (1967): 30-44.

Humphrey, N. B. The mock battle greeting.
Journal of American Folklore, 54 (1941):
186-190.

Johansen, J. Prytz. Maori og Zuni; to
naturfolk og deres religion. København,
Gyldendal, 1962. 331 p. illus., maps.

Jones, H. Mythology comes to life at
Zuni. El Palacio, 32 (1932): 57-66.

Jones, H. Zuni Shalako ceremony. El
Palacio, 30 (1931): 1-10.

Judd, N. M. When Jemez medicine men came
to Zuni. Journal of American Folklore,
60 (1947): 182-184.

Kaplan, B. A study of Rorschach responses
in four cultures. Harvard University,
Peabody Museum of American Archaeology
and Ethnology, Papers, 42, no. 2 (1954):
1-54.

Kaplan, Bert. Psychological themes in
Zuni mythology and Zuni TAT's. In Warner
Muensterberger and Sidney Axelrad, eds.
The Psychoanalytic Study of Society.
Vol. 2. New York, International
Universities Press, 1962: 255-262.

Kate, H. F. C. ten. A Zuni folk-tale.
Journal of American Folklore, 30 (1917):
496-499.

Kate, H. F. C. ten. Reizen en
onderzoekingen in Noord-Amerika, 273-
306. Leiden, 1885.

Kate, H. F. C. ten. Somatological
observations on Indians of the
Southwest. Journal of American Ethnology
and Archaeology, 3 (1892): 117-144.

Kate, H. F. C. ten. Zuni fetishes.
Internationales Archiv für Ethnographie,
3 (1890): 118-136.

Keech, R. A. A Zuni Indian vocabulary.
National Archaeological News, 1, no. 4
(1937): 2-3; 1, no. 5 (1937): 2-3; 1,
no. 6 (1937): 2-3; 1, no. 7 (1937): 12-
13; 1, no. 8 (1937): 11-12.

Keech, R. A. Pagans praying. Clarendon,
1940. 94 p.

Keech, R. A. The kick-stick race at Zuni. El Palacio, 37 (1934): 61-64.

Kirk, R. F. Buffalo hunting fetish jar. El Palacio, 57 (1950): 131-142.

Kirk, R. F. Introduction to Zuni fetishism. El Palacio, 50 (1943): 117-129, 146-159, 183-198, 206-219, 235-245.

Kirk, R. F. Southwestern Indian jewelry. Archaeological Institute of America, School of American Research, Santa Fe, Papers, ser. 2, 38 (1945): 1-24.

Kirk, R. F. Southwestern Indian jewelry. El Palacio, 52 (1945): 21-32, 41-50.

Kirk, R. F. War rituals at Zuni. New Mexico, 23, no. 8 (1945): 14-15, 46-47.

Kirk, R. F. Zuni fetish worship. Masterkey, 17 (1943): 129-135.

Klett, F. The cachina: a dance at the Pueblo of Zuni. In Report upon United States Geographical Surveys West of the One Hundredth Meridian. Vol. 7. Washington, D.C., 1879: 332-336.

Klett, F. The Zuni Indians of New Mexico. Popular Science Monthly, 5 (1874): 580-591.

Kluckhohn, Clyde. Expressive activities. In Evon Z. Vogt and Ethel M. Albert, eds. The People of Rimrock. Cambridge, Harvard University Press, 1966: 269-298.

Kluckhohn, Clyde. The Navaho view of life. By Clyde Kluckhohn and Dorothea C. Leighton. In Clarence Crane Brinton, ed. The Fate of Man. New York, George Braziller, 1961: 37-44.

Kluckhohn, Florence R., et al. Variations in value orientations. Evanston, Row, Peterson, 1961. 437 p. illus.

Kluckhohn, Florence Rockwood. A method for eliciting value orientations. Anthropological Linguistics, 2, no. 2 (1960): 1-23.

Kroeber, A. L. The oldest town in America and its people. American Museum Journal, 16 (1916): 81-85.

Kroeber, A. L. The speech of a Zuni child. American Anthropologist, n.s., 18 (1916): 529-534.

Kroeber, A. L. Thoughts on Zuni religion. In Holmes Anniversary Volume. Washington, D.C., 1916: 269-277.

Kroeber, A. L. Zuni culture sequences. National Academy of Sciences, Proceedings, 2 (1916): 42-45.

Kroeber, A. L. Zuni. In J. Hastings, ed. Encyclopaedia of Religion and Ethics. Vol. 10. New York, 1919: 868-873.

Kroeber, A. L. Zuni kin and clan. American Museum of Natural History, Anthropological Papers, 18 (1917): 39-206.

Kroeber, A. L. Zuni potsherds. American Museum of Natural History, Anthropological Papers, 18 (1916): 1-37.

Kuipers, Cornelius. Zuni also prays: month-by-month observations among the people. [n.p.] Christian Reformed Board of Missions, 1946. 10, 157 p. illus.

Landar, Herbert J. The loss of Athapaskan words for fish in the Southwest. International Journal of American Linguistics, 26 (1960): 75-77.

Lasersohn, William. Acute diarrheal diseases in a Zuni community. U.S., Public Health Service, Public Health Reports, 80 (1965): 457-461.

Lawrence, D. D. Sleep and dawn ritual of the Zuñi Indians. International Congress of Americanists, Proceedings, 30 (1955): 149-150.

Leigh, R. W. Dental pathology of Indian tribes. American Journal of Physical Anthropology, 8 (1925): 179-199.

*Leighton, Dorothea C. People of the Middle Place; a study of the Zuni Indians. By Dorothea C. Leighton and John Adair. New Haven, Human Relations Area Files Press, 1966. 16, 171 p. illus., maps.

Lemos, P. J. Zuni, the strangest art center in America. School Arts Magazine, 27 (1928): 489-500.

Lenneberg, E. H. and J. M. Roberts. The language of experience. International Journal of American Linguistics, Memoirs, 13 (1956): 1-33.

Lévi-Strauss, Claude. The sorcerer and his magic. In John Middleton, ed. Magic, Witchcraft, and Curing. Garden City, Natural History Press, 1967: 23-41.

Li, A. C. Zuni. American Anthropologist, n.s., 39 (1937): 62-76.

Loeb, E. M. A note on two far-travelled kachinas. Journal of American Folklore, 56 (1943): 192-199.

McFeat, Tom F. S. Some social and spatial aspects of innovation at Zuni. Anthropologica, n.s., 2 (1960): 18-47.

Michaels, David.   A note on some
exceptions in Zuni phonology.
International Journal of American
Linguistics, 37 (1971): 189-192.

Mohindra, I.   Corneal astigmatism
pedigrees and heredity. American Journal
of Optometry, 46 (1967): 781.

Neumann, D. L.   Modern developments in
Indian jewelry. El Palacio, 57 (1950):
173-180.

Neumann, D. L.   Recent lapidary
development at Zuñi. El Palacio, 58
(1951): 215-217.

Newman, S.   A practical Zuni orthography.
Harvard University, Peabody Museum of
American Archaeology and Ethnology,
Papers, 43, no. 1 (1954): 163-170.

Newman, S.   Vocabulary levels: Zuñi sacred
and slang usage. Southwestern Journal of
Anthropology, 11 (1955): 345-354.

Newman, S.   Zuni dictionary. International
Journal of American Linguistics,
Memoirs, 6 (1958): 1-122.

Newman, Stanley.   Comparison of Zuni and
California Penutian. International
Journal of American Linguistics, 30
(1964): 1-13.

Newman, Stanley.   Zuni equivalents of
English 'to be'. In John W. M. Verhaar,
ed. The Verb 'Be' and Its Synonyms. Part
2.   Dordrecht, Reidel, 1968: 60-70.
(Foundations of Language, Supplementary
Series, 6)

Newman, Stanley.   Zuni grammar.
Albuquerque, 1965.   77 p.   (New Mexico,
University, Publications in
Anthropology, 14)

Newman, Stanley.   Zuni grammar:
alternative solutions versus weakness.
International Journal of American
Linguistics, 33 (1967): 187-192.

Nusbaum, A.   The seven cities of Cibola.
New York, 1926.   167 p.

Oswalt, Wendell H.   Other peoples, other
customs; world ethnography and its
history.   New York, Holt, Rinehart and
Winston, 1972.   15, 430 p.   illus.,
maps.

Owens, J.   Some games of the Zuñi. Popular
Science Monthly, 39 (1891): 39-50.

Paine, Robert.   In search of friendship:
an exploratory analysis in 'middle-
class' culture. Man, n.s., 4 (1969):
505-524.

Pandey, Triloki Nath.   Anthropologists at
Zuni. American Philosophical Society,
Proceedings, 116 (1972): 321-337.

Pandey, Triloki Nath.   Tribal council
elections in a Southwestern pueblo.
Ethnology, 7 (1968): 71-85.

Parsons, E. C.   A few Zuni death beliefs
and practices. American Anthropologist,
n.s., 18 (1916): 245-256.

Parsons, E. C.   A note on Zuñi deer
hunting. Southwestern Journal of
Anthropology, 12 (1956): 325-326.

Parsons, E. C.   A Zuni detective. Man, 16
(1916): 168-170.

Parsons, E. C.   All-Souls' Day at Zuni,
Acoma, and Laguna. Journal of American
Folklore, 30 (1917): 495-496.

Parsons, E. C.   Census of the Shi'wannakwe
Society of Zuni. American
Anthropologist, n.s., 21 (1919): 333-
334.

Parsons, E. C.   Ceremonial dances at Zuni.
El Palacio, 13 (1922): 119-122.

Parsons, E. C.   Ceremonial friendship at
Zuni. American Anthropologist, n.s., 19
(1917): 1-8.

Parsons, E. C.   Hopi and Zuni
ceremonialism. American Anthropological
Association, Memoirs, 39 (1933): 1-108.

Parsons, E. C.   Increase by magic: a Zuni
pattern. American Anthropologist, n.s.,
21 (1919): 279-286.

Parsons, E. C.   Mothers and children at
Zuni. Man, 19 (1919): 168-173.

Parsons, E. C.   Nativity myth at Laguna
and Zuni. Journal of American Folklore,
31 (1918): 256-263.

Parsons, E. C.   Notes on Zuni. American
Anthropological Association, Memoirs, 4
(1917): 151-327.

Parsons, E. C.   Pueblo Indian religion.
Chicago, 1939.   2 v.

Parsons, E. C.   Pueblo-Indian folk-tales,
probably of Spanish provenience. Journal
of American Folklore, 31 (1918): 216-
255.

Parsons, E. C.   Reasoning from analogy at
Zuni. Scientific Monthly, 4 (1917): 365-
369.

Parsons, E. C.   Spring days in Zuni.
Scientific Monthly, 36 (1933): 49-54.

Parsons, E. C. Teshlatiwa at Zuni. Journal of Philosophy, Psychology and Scientific Method, 16 (1919): 272-273.

Parsons, E. C. The favorite number of the Zuni. Scientific Monthly, 3 (1916): 596-601.

Parsons, E. C. The kinship nomenclature of the Pueblo Indians. American Anthropologist, n.s., 34 (1932): 377-389.

Parsons, E. C. The last Zuni transvestite. American Anthropologist, n.s., 41 (1939): 338-340.

Parsons, E. C. The origin myth of Zuni. Journal of American Folklore, 36 (1923): 135-162.

Parsons, E. C. The scalp ceremonial of Zuni. American Anthropological Association, Memoirs, 31 (1924): 1-42.

Parsons, E. C. The Zuni adoshle and suuke. American Anthropologist, n.s., 18 (1916): 338-347.

Parsons, E. C. The Zuni lamana. American Anthropologist, n.s., 18 (1916): 521-528.

Parsons, E. C. The Zuni mo'lawia. Journal of American Folklore, 29 (1916): 392-399.

Parsons, E. C. Waiyautitsa of Zuni. In his American Indian Life. New York, 1925: 157-173.

Parsons, E. C. Waiyautitsa of Zuni. Scientific Monthly, 9 (1933): 443-457.

Parsons, E. C. War god shrines of Laguna and Zuni. American Anthropologist, n.s., 20 (1918): 381-405.

Parsons, E. C. Winter and summer dance series in Zuni. California, University, Publications in American Archaeology and Ethnology, 17 (1922): 171-216.

Parsons, E. C. Witchcraft among the Pueblos. Man, 27 (1927): 106-112, 125-128.

Parsons, E. C. Zuni conception and pregnancy beliefs. International Congress of Americanists, Proceedings, 19 (1915): 378-383.

Parsons, E. C. Zuni death beliefs and practices. American Anthropologist, n.s., 18 (1916): 246.

Parsons, E. C. Zuni inoculative magic. Science, n.s., 44 (1916): 469-470.

Parsons, E. C. Zuni names and naming practices. Journal of American Folklore, 36 (1923): 171-176.

Parsons, E. C. Zuni tales. Journal of American Folklore, 43 (1930): 1-58.

Parsons, E. C. and F. Boas. Spanish tales from Laguna and Zuni. Journal of American Folklore, 33 (1920): 47-72.

Pauker, Guy Jean. Political structure. In Evon Z. Vogt and Ethel M. Albert, eds. The People of Rimrock. Cambridge, Harvard University Press, 1966: 191-226.

Peet, S. D. The cross in America. American Antiquarian and Oriental Journal, 10 (1888): 292-315.

Peet, S. D. The worship of the rain god. American Antiquarian and Oriental Journal, 16 (1894): 341-356.

Peynetsa, Andrew. Finding the middle of the earth. Alcheringa, 1 (1970): 67-80.

Peynetsa, Andrew. When the old timers went deer hunting. Alcheringa, 3 (1971): 76-81.

Proper, David R. The Zuni visitation to Salem. Essex Institute Historical Collections, 104 (1968): 80-85.

Reed, E. K. Painted pottery and Zuñi history. Southwestern Journal of Anthropology, 11 (1955): 178-193.

Reeve, F. D. Albert Franklin Beuta. New Mexico Historical Review, 27 (1952): 200-255.

Renaud, E. B. Kokopelli. Southwestern Lore, 14 (1948): 25-40.

Rinaldo, John B. Notes on the origins of historic Zuni culture. Kiva, 29, no. 4 (1963/1964): 86-98.

Risser, A. Seven Zuni folk tales. El Palacio, 48 (1941): 215-226.

Roberts, F. H. H. The village of the great kivas on the Zuni Reservation. U.S. Bureau of American Ethnology, Bulletin, 111 (1932): 1-197.

Roberts, H. H. Chakwena songs of Zuni and Laguna. Journal of American Folklore, 36 (1923): 177-184.

*Roberts, J. M. Zuni daily life. Nebraska, University, Laboratory of Anthropology, Notebook, 3, no. 2 (1956): 1-143.

Roberts, John M. Dyadic elicitation in Zuni. By John M. Roberts and Malcolm J.

Arth. El Palacio, 73, no. 2 (1966): 27-41.

Roberts, John M. Kinsmen and friends in Zuni culture: a terminological note. El Palacio, 72, no. 2 (1965): 38-43.

*Roberts, John M. Zuni daily life. New Haven, Human Relations Area Files Press, 1965. 10, 137 p. illus.

Robinson, E. L. Troubles at Zuni in 1702-03. Masterkey, 18 (1944): 110-116.

Roessel, Ruth, comp. Papers on Navajo culture and life. Many Farms, Ariz., Navajo Community College Press, 1970. 2, 193 p. illus., map.

Sampliner, James E. Biliary surgery in the Southwestern American Indian. By James E. Sampliner and Daniel J. O'Connell. Archives of Surgery, 96 (1968): 1-3.

Sanchez, Walter. Pelt Kid and his grandmother. Alcheringa, 2 (1971): 19-30.

Schlater, K. An Easterner visits the Shalako. El Palacio, 54 (1947): 35-42.

Schmiedehaus, W. Las 7 ciudades doradas de Cibola. Sociedad Chihuahuense de Estudios Históricos, Boletín, 7 (1952): 571-585.

Schneider, D. M. and J. M. Roberts. Zuni kin terms. Nebraska, University, Laboratory of Anthropology, Notebook, 3, no. 1 (1956): 1-29.

Schneider, David M. Zuni kin terms. By David M. Schneider and John M. Roberts. New Haven, Human Relations Area Files Press, 1965. 6, 23 p. illus.

Seltzer, C. C. Racial prehistory in the Southwest and the Hawikuh Zunis. Harvard University, Peabody Museum of American Archaeology and Ethnology, Papers, 23 (1944): 1-37.

Shufeldt, R. W. Examples of unusual Zunian pottery. Records of the Past, 9 (1910): 208-213.

Simmons, Marc. New Mexico's smallpox epidemic of 1780-1781. New Mexico Historical Review, 41 (1966): 319-326.

Simpson, R. de E. An ancient custom in modern Zuni. Masterkey, 22 (1948): 102-104.

Smith, Alfred G. The Dionysian innovation. American Anthropologist, 66 (1964): 251-265.

Smith, D. M. Indian tribes of the Southwest, 125-144. Stanford, 1933.

Smith, W. and J. M. Roberts. Some aspects of Zuni law and legal procedure. Plateau, 27 (1954): 1-5.

*Smith, W., et al. Zuni law. Harvard University, Peabody Museum of American Archaeology and Ethnology, Papers, 43, no. 1 (1954): 1-185.

Spier, L. An outline for a chronology of Zuni ruins. American Museum of Natural History, Anthropological Papers, 18 (1917): 207-331.

Spier, L. Zuni chronology. National Academy of Sciences, Proceedings, 3 (1917): 280-283.

Spier, L. Zuni weaving technique. American Anthropologist, n.s., 26 (1924): 64-85.

Stacey, R. Some Zuni ceremonies and melodies. Music-Lovers' Calendar, 2 (1907): 54-61.

Stephens, E. L. Steve. West of the Pecos. New Mexico Historical Review, 35 (1960): 81-108, 236-256, 309-326; 36 (1961): 159-174.

Stevenson, J. Illustrated catalogue of the collections obtained from the Pueblos of Zuni, New Mexico, and Wolpi, Arizona. U.S. Bureau of American Ethnology, Annual Reports, 3 (1884): 511-586.

Stevenson, J. Illustrated catalogue of the collections obtained from the Indians of New Mexico and Arizona. U.S. Bureau of American Ethnology, Annual Reports, 2 (1883): 307-374.

Stevenson, M. C. Ethnobotany of the Zuni Indians. U.S. Bureau of American Ethnology, Annual Reports, 30 (1915): 31-102.

Stevenson, M. C. The religious life of the Zuni child. U.S. Bureau of American Ethnology, Annual Reports, 5 (1887): 533-555.

*Stevenson, M. C. The Zuni Indians. U.S. Bureau of American Ethnology, Annual Reports, 23 (1904): 13-608.

Stevenson, M. C. Zuni ancestral gods and masks. American Anthropologist, 11 (1898): 33-40.

Stevenson, M. C. Zuni games. American Anthropologist, n.s., 5 (1903): 468-493.

*Stevenson, Matilda C. The Zuñi Indians. New York, Johnson Reprint, 1970. 634 p. illus.

*Stevenson, Matilda C. The Zuñi Indians. Glorieta, N.M., Rio Grande Press, 1970. 634 p. illus.

Suci, George J. A comparison of semantic structures in American Southwest culture groups. Journal of Abnormal and Social Psychology, 61 (1960): 25-30.

Swadesh, M. Terminos de parentesco communes entre Tarasco y Zuñi. Instituto de Historia, Cuadernos, Serie Antropologica, 3 (1957): 1-39.

Swadesh, Morris. Términos de parentesco comunes entre tarasco y zuñi. México, 1957. 39 p. (México, Universidad Autónoma, Instituto de Historia, Publicación, 40)

Swanson, Guy E. Rules of descent: studies in the sociology of parentage. Ann Arbor, University of Michigan, 1969. 5, 108 p. (Michigan, University, Museum of Anthropology, Anthropological Papers, 39)

Tedlock, Dennis. Finding the center; narrative poetry of the Zuni Indians. New York, Dial Press, 1972. 35, 298 p. illus.

Tedlock, Dennis. Notes to "Finding the middle of the earth". Alcheringa, 1 (1970): 66.

Tedlock, Dennis. Pelt Kid: a humorous Zuni tale. Human Mosaic, 1, no. 1 (1966): 55-65.

Tedlock, Dennis. The boy and the deer: a Zuni tale. Kiva, 33, no. 2 (1967/1968): 67-79.

Tedlock, Dennis. The problem of k in Zuni phonemics. International Journal of American Linguistics, 35 (1969): 67-71.

Tedlock, Dennis Ernest. The ethnography of tale-telling at Zuni. Dissertation Abstracts, 29 (1968/1969): 1546B-1547B. UM 68-15,272.

Trager, George L. The Tanoan settlement of the Rio Grande area: a possible chronology. In Dell H. Hymes and William E. Bittle, eds. Studies in Southwestern Ethnolinguistics. The Hague, Mouton, 1967: 335-350. (Studies in General Anthropology, 3)

Trowbridge, L. J. Zuni. El Palacio, 22 (1927): 8-16.

Troyer, C. The Zuni Indians and their music. Philadelphia, 1913. 44 p.

Underhill, R. M. First penthouse dwellers of America, 57-84. New York, 1938.

Vlahcevic, Z. R., et al. Relation of bile acid pool size to the formation of lithogenic bile in female Indians of the Southwest. Gastroenterology, 62 (1972): 73-83.

Voegelin, Carl F. Methods for typologizing directly and by distinctive features (in reference to Uto-Aztecan and Kiowa-Tanoan vowel systems). Lingua, 11 (1962): 469-487.

Vogt, Evon Z. A study of values. By Evon Z. Vogt and John M. Roberts. Scientific American, 195, no. 1 (1956): 25-31.

Vogt, Evon Zartman. Ecology and economy. In Evon Z. Vogt and Ethel M. Albert, eds. The People of Rimrock. Cambridge, Harvard University Press, 1966: 160-190.

Vogt, Evon Zartman. Intercultural relations. In Evon Z. Vogt and Ethel M. Albert, eds. The People of Rimrock. Cambridge, Harvard University Press, 1966: 46-82.

Walker, Willard. Inflectional class and taxonomic structure in Zuni. With a note by Stanley Newman. International Journal of American Linguistics, 32 (1966): 217-227.

Walker, Willard. Toward the sound pattern of Zuni. International Journal of American Linguistics, 38 (1972): 240-259.

Walker, Willard Brewer. Reference, taxonomy, and inflection in Zuni. Dissertation Abstracts, 25 (1964/1965): 4138. UM 64-13,791.

Wengerd, Stephanie K. The role and use of color in the Zuni culture. Plateau, 44 (1972): 113-124.

Whiteside, Frank Reed. Frank Reed Whiteside, 1866-1929; the Zuni and the Indian country. Phoenix, 1971. 32 p. illus.

Wilson, E. Red, black, blond, and olive, 1-68. New York, 1956.

Woodbury, R. B. The antecedents of Zuni culture. New York Academy of Sciences, Transactions, ser. 2, 17 (1956): 557-563.

Woodbury, R. B. and N. F. S. Woodbury. Zuni prehistory and El Morro National

Monument. Southwestern Lore, 21 (1956):
56-60.

Woodward, A. A modern Zuni pilgrimage.
Masterkey, 6 (1932): 44-51.

Woolf, Charles M. Albinism among Indians
in Arizona and New Mexico. American
Journal of Human Genetics, 17 (1965):
23-35.

Yarrow, H. C. Medical facts relating to
the Zuni Indians of New Mexico. Rocky
Mountain Medical Review, 1 (1880/1881):
193-194.

*Zuni People. The Zunis; self-portrayals.
Translated by Alvina Quam. Albuquerque,
University of New Mexico Press, 1972.
12, 245 p. illus.

                15-36   Acaxee

Beals, Ralph L. The Acaxee, a mountain
tribe of Durango and Sinaloa. Berkeley,
University of California Press, 1933.
3, 36 p. (Ibero-Americana, 6)

Beals, Ralph L. The comparative ethnology
of northern Mexico before 1750.
Berkeley, University of California
Press, 1932. 6, 93-225 p. maps.
(Ibero-Americana, 2)

Pérez de Ribas, Andrés. Historia de los
triunfos de nuestra santa fe entre
gentes las más bárbaras y fieras del
nuevo orbe. Madrid, A. de Paredes,
1645. 20, 763 p.

Pérez de Ribas, Andrés. My life among the
savage nations of New Spain. Translated
by Tomás Antonio Robertson. Los
Angeles, Ward Ritchie Press, 1968. 16,
256 p. illus., maps.

Rouaix, Pastor. Manual de historia de
Durango. By Pastor Rouaix, Gerard
Decorme, and Atanasio G. Saravia.
México, Editado por el Gobierno del
Estado de Durango, 1952. 10, 403 p.

Sauer, Carl O. The distribution of
aboriginal tribes and languages in
northwestern Mexico. Berkeley,
University of California Press, 1934.
6, 94 p. map. (Ibero-Americana, 5)

Thomas, Cyrus. Indian languages of Mexico
and Central America and their
geographical distribution. By Cyrus
Thomas assisted by John R. Swanton.
Washington, D.C., Government Printing
Office, 1911. 7, 108 p. map. (U.S.,
Bureau of American Ethnology, Bulletin,
44)

Zubillaga, Félix. Los Indios Acaxes. In
Congreso Internacional de Americanistas,
36th. 1964, España. Actas y Memorias.
Tomo 3. Sevilla, 1966: 627-634.

                15-37   Cazcan

Beals, Ralph L. The comparative ethnology
of northern Mexico before 1750.
Berkeley, University of California
Press, 1932. 6, 93-225 p. maps.
(Ibero-Americana, 2)

Dávila Garibi, J. Ignacio Paulino.
Cazcanes y tochos. Revista Mexicana de
Estudios Antropológicos, 4 (1940): 203-
224.

Dávila Garibi, José Ignacio. Algunas
afinidades entre las lenguas coca y
cahita. El México Antiguo, 6 (1942): 47-
60.

Dávila Garibi, José Ignacio. Recopilación
de datos acerca del idioma coca y de su
posible influencia en el lenguaje
folklórico de Jalisco. Investigaciones
Lingüísticas, 3 (1935): 248-302.

Dávila Garibi, José Ignacio Paulino. El
problema de la clasificación de la
lengua coca. México, Librería Editorial
San Ignacio, 1943. 34 p.

Dávila Garibi, José Ignacio Paulino. Los
cazcanes. México, Editorial Cultura,
1950. 40 p.

Sauer, Carl O. The distribution of
aboriginal tribes and languages in
northwestern Mexico. Berkeley,
University of California Press, 1934.
6, 94 p. map. (Ibero-Americana, 5)

Thomas, Cyrus. Indian languages of Mexico
and Central America and their
geographical distribution. By Cyrus
Thomas assisted by John R. Swanton.
Washington, D.C., Government Printing
Office, 1911. 7, 108 p. map. (U.S.,
Bureau of American Ethnology, Bulletin,
44)

                15-38   Tepehuan

Almada, Francisco R. Geografía humana de
Chihuahua. Sociedad Mexicana de
Geografía y Estadística, Boletín, 57
(1942): 227-300.

Basauri, Carlos. Familia "Nahuatlana":
Tepecanos (Tepehuacan Mexicano). In his
La Población Indígena de Mexico. Tomo 3.
Mexico, Secretaria de Educacion Publica,
1940: 73-91.

Basauri, Carlos. Familia "Pimana": Tepehuanes. In his La Poblacion Indigena de Mexico. Tomo 1. Mexico, Secretaria de Educacion Publica, 1940: 353-363.

Bascom, Burt. Tonomechanics of Northern Tepehuan. Phonetica, 4, no. 2/3 (1959): 71-88.

Bascom, Burton William, Jr. Proto-Tepiman (Tepehuan-Piman). Dissertation Abstracts, 27 (1966/1967): 192A-193A. UM 66-5811.

Beals, Ralph L. The comparative ethnology of northern Mexico before 1750. Berkeley, University of California Press, 1932. 6, 93-225 p. maps. (Ibero-Americana, 2)

Boilés, Charles L. Tepehua thought-song: a case of semantic signalling. Ethnomusicology, 11 (1967): 267-292.

Boilès, Charles L. Tepehua thought-songs. College Music Symposium, 7 (1967): 107-108.

Bower, Bethel. Panela making by the Tepehua Indians. Boletín Indigenista, 7 (1947): 374-378.

Bower, Bethel. Stems and affixes in Tepehua numerals. International Journal of American Linguistics, 14 (1948): 20-21.

Bower, Bethel. Tepehua sentences. By Bethel Bower and Barbara Erickson. Anthropological Linguistics, 9, no. 9 (1967): 25-37.

Brugge, David M. History, huki, and warfare--some random data on the Lower Pima. Kiva, 26, no. 4 (1960/1961): 6-16.

Cardoso, Joaquín. Sangre en los Tepehuanes! . . . México, Editorial "Buena Prensa", 1948. 243 p.

Cerda Silva, Roberto de la. Los tepehuanes. Revista Mexicana de Sociología, 5 (1943): 541-567.

Cowan, George M. El idioma silbido entre los Mazatecos de Oaxaca y los Tepehuas de Hidalgo, México. Tlatoani, 1, no. 3/4 (1952): 31-33.

Diguet, Léon. Le "peyote" et son usage rituel chez les Indiens du Nayarit. Société des Américanistes (Paris), Journal, n.s., 4 (1907): 21-29.

Espinosa, Aurelio M. Comparative notes on New-Mexican and Mexican Spanish folktales. Journal of American Folk-Lore, 27 (1914): 211-231.

Fehlinger, Hans. Die Tepecano-Indianer. Globus, 85 (1904): 292-293.

Gámiz, Everardo. Monografía de la nación tepehuana que habita en la región sur del estado de Durango. México, Ediciones Gámiz, 1948. 150 p. illus., maps.

Gandola, Isabel. El peyote; estudio sobre el uso del peyote, entre las tribus Huicholes, Coras, Tepehuanes y Tarahumaras. México, Editorial Crión, 1965. 66 p. illus., map.

Gessain, Robert. Les Indiens Tepehuas de Huehuetla. Revista Mexicana de Estudios Antropológicos, 13 (1953): 187-211.

Griffen, William B. Culture change and shifting populations in central northern Mexico. Tucson, 1969. 12, 196 p. maps. (Arizona, University, Anthropological Papers, 13)

Griffen, William B. Procesos de extinción y continuidad social y cultural en el norte de México durante la Colonia. América Indígena, 30 (1970): 689-724.

Hasler, Juan A. La posición dialectológica del Tepehua. In Antonio Pompa y Pompa, ed. Summa Anthropologica en Homenaje a Roberto J. Weitlaner. México, 1966: 533-540.

Hewitt, Harry Paxton. The historical development of Nueva Vizcaya's defenses to 1646. Dissertation Abstracts International, 32 (1971/1972): 2013A. UM 71-25,011.

Hobgood, John. The prayer of a Tepehuán witch doctor. Tlalocan, 4, no. 3 (1963): 255-258.

Hrdlička, Aleš. The region of the ancient "Chichimecs", with notes on the Tepecanos and the ruin of La Quemada. American Anthropologist, n.s., 5 (1903): 385-440.

Kroeber, Alfred L. Uto-Aztecan languages of Mexico. Berkeley, University of California Press, 1934. 3, 27 p. map. (Ibero-Americana, 8)

León-Portilla, Miguel. Panorama de la población indígena de México. América Indígena, 19 (1959): 43-73.

López, Atanasio. Los indios coras, tepehuanes, cheles y guainamotas (Méjico). Archivo Ibero-Americana, 34 (1931): 341-370.

Lumholtz, Carl. Explorations au Mexique de 1894 a 1897. Société des

Américanistes (Paris), Journal, 2
(1899): 179-184.

Lumholtz, Carl. Explorations in the
Sierra Madre. Scribner's Magazine, 10
(1891): 531-598.

Lumholtz, Carl. My life of exploration.
Natural History, 21 (1921): 225-243.

Lumholtz, Carl. Unknown Mexico. New
York, Charles Scribner's Sons, 1902.
2 v.

Mason, J. Alden. Folk-tales of the
Tepecanos. Journal of American Folk-
Lore, 27 (1914): 148-210.

Mason, J. Alden. Notes and observations
on the Tepehuan. América Indígena, 12
(1952): 33-53.

Mason, J. Alden. Prácticas goéticas entre
los tepecanos. Ethnos (México), 1
(1920): 86-88.

Mason, J. Alden. Researches among the
Tepehuán Indians. Archaeological Society
of New Jersey, Newsletter, 18 (1948):
17-18.

Mason, J. Alden. Tepecano, a Piman
language of western Mexico. New York,
1917. 309-416 p. (New York Academy of
Sciences, Annals, 25)

Mason, J. Alden. Tepecano prayers.
International Journal of American
Linguistics, 1 (1918): 91-153.

Mason, J. Alden. The fiesta of the pinole
at Azqueltán. Pennsylvania, University,
University Museum, Museum Journal, 3
(1912): 44-50.

Mason, J. Alden. The Tepehuan, and other
aborigines of the Mexican Sierra Madre
Occidental. América Indígena, 8 (1948):
289-300.

Mason, J. Alden. The Tepehuan of northern
Mexico. Hamburg, Museum für Völkerkunde,
Mitteilungen, 25 (1959): 91-96.

Mason, J. Alden. The Tephuán Indians of
Azqueltán. In International Congress of
Americanists, 18th. 1912, London.
Proceedings. London, 1912: 344-351.

Mendizábal, Miguel Othón de. La evolución
del noroeste de México. In his Obras
Completas. Tomo 3. México, 1946: 7-86.

Miller, Wick R. Uto-Aztecan cognate sets.
Berkeley and Los Angeles, University of
California Press, 1967. 5, 83 p. map.
(California, University, Publications in
Linguistics, 48)

Ochoa Zazueta, Jesús Angel. Apostillas de
los Tepehuanes. México, Editorial Nueva
Hispanidad, 1967. 126 p.

Passin, Herbert. Some relationships in
Northwest Mexican kinship systems. El
México Antiguo, 6, no. 7/8 (July 1944):
205-218.

Pemex Travel Club. Mexico's music: its
past and present. Katunob, 4, no. 4
(1963): 30-52.

Pennington, Campbell W. Medicinal plants
utilized by the Tepehuán of southern
Chihuahua. América Indígena, 23 (1963):
31-47.

*Pennington, Campbell W. The Tepehuan of
Chihuahua; their material culture. Salt
Lake City, University of Utah Press,
1969. 413 p. illus., maps.

Pike, Kenneth L. Instrumental
collaboration on a Tepehuan (Uto-
Aztekan) pitch problem. By Kenneth L.
Pike, Ralph P. Barrett, and Burt Bascom.
Phonetica, 3 (1959): 1-22.

Pride, Kitty. Numerals in Chatino.
Anthropological Linguistics, 3, no. 2
(1961): 1-10(b).

Riley, Carroll L. The prehistoric
Tepehuan of northern Mexico. By Carroll
L. Riley and Howard D. Winters. In John
A. Graham, ed. Ancient Mesoamerica;
Selected Readings. Palo Alto, Calif.,
1966: 264-272.

Riley, Carroll L. The prehistoric
Tepehuan of Northern Mexico. By Carroll
L. Riley and Howard D. Winters.
Southwestern Journal of Anthropology, 19
(1963): 177-185.

Riley, Carroll L. The Southern Tepehuan
and Tepecano. In Evon Z. Vogt, volume
editor. Handbook of Middle American
Indians. Vol. 8. Austin, University of
Texas Press, 1969: 814-821.

Rouaix, Pastor. Manual de historia de
Durango. By Pastor Rouaix, Gerard
Decorme, and Atanasio G. Saravia.
México, Editado por el Gobierno del
Estado de Durango, 1952. 10, 403 p.

Service, Elman R. The Northern Tepehuan.
In Evon Z. Vogt, volume editor. Handbook
of Middle American Indians. Vol. 8.
Austin, University of Texas Press, 1969:
822-829.

Soustelle, Georgette. Essai comparatif
sur cinq populations autochtones du
Mexique. Ethnographie, Nouvelle Série,
62/63 (1968/1969): 142-155.

Thomas, Cyrus. Indian languages of Mexico and Central America and their geographical distribution. By Cyrus Thomas assisted by John R. Swanton. Washington, D.C., Government Printing Office, 1911. 7, 108 p. map. (U.S., Bureau of American Ethnology, Bulletin, 44)

Williams García, Roberto. Algunos rezos tepehuas. Revista Mexicana de Estudios Antropológicos, 21 (1967): 287-315.

*Williams García, Roberto. Los Tepehuas. Xalapa, Méx., Universidad Veracruzana, Instituto de Antropología, 1963. 308 p. illus., maps.

Williams García, Roberto. Mitos tepehuas. México, Secretaría de Educación Pública, 1972. 156 p. illus.

Woo, Nancy. Tone in Northern Tepehuan. International Journal of American Linguistics, 36 (1970): 18-30.

Zingg, Robert M. A reconstruction of Uto-Aztekan history. New York, G. E. Stechert, 1939. 4, 274 p. (Denver, University, Contributions to Ethnography, 2)

15-39 Totorame

Beals, Ralph L. The comparative ethnology of northern Mexico before 1750. Berkeley, University of California Press, 1932. 6, 93-225 p. maps. (Ibero-Americana, 2)

Sauer, Carl O. The distribution of aboriginal tribes and languages in northwestern Mexico. Berkeley, University of California Press, 1934. 6, 94 p. map. (Ibero-Americana, 5)

15-40 Zacatec

Ahumada, Pedro de. 1562 rebelión de los zacatecas y guachichiles. México, Vargas Rea, 1952. 46 p.

Barragán, Estela V. Conociendo a Coahuila; los Laguneros o Irritilas, su cultura y sus restos. By Estela V. Barragán, Carlos Cárdenas Villarreal, and Candelaria Valdes. Saltillo, Universidad de Coahuila, Escuela Preparatoria Nocturna, 1960. 113 p. illus.

Beals, Ralph L. The comparative ethnology of northern Mexico before 1750. Berkeley, University of California Press, 1932. 6, 93-225 p. maps. (Ibero-Americana, 2)

Eckhart, George B. Spanish missions of Texas, 1680-1800. Kiva, 32, no. 3 (1966/1967): 73-95.

Griffen, William B. Culture change and shifting populations in central northern Mexico. Tucson, 1969. 12, 196 p. maps. (Arizona, University, Anthropological Papers, 13)

Griffen, William B. Procesos de extinción y continuidad social y cultural en el norte de México durante la Colonia. América Indígena, 30 (1970): 689-724.

McGee, W J. Primitive rope-making in Mexico. American Anthropologist, 10 (1897): 114-119.

Powell, Philip W., comp. War and peace on the North Mexican frontier: a documentary record. Vol. 1. Madrid, Ediciones Jose Porrua Turanzas, 1971. 27, 276 p. illus. (Colección Chimalistac de Libros y Documentos acerca de la Nueva España, 32)

Quirarte, C. E. Estudio sobre el lenguaje usado en Nochistlan, Zac. Investigaciones Lingüísticas, 1 (1933): 78-102, 164-200.

Simmons, Marc. Tlascalans in the Spanish borderlands. New Mexico Historical Review, 39 (1964): 101-110.

Swadesh, Mauricio. Las lenguas indígenas del noreste de México. Anales de Antropología, 5 (1968): 75-86.

Thomas, Cyrus. Indian languages of Mexico and Central America and their geographical distribution. By Cyrus Thomas assisted by John R. Swanton. Washington, D.C., Government Printing Office, 1911. 7, 108 p. map. (U.S., Bureau of American Ethnology, Bulletin, 44)

15-41 Chichimec

Angulo, Jaime de. The Chichimec language (Central Mexico). International Journal of American Linguistics, 7 (1932/1933): 152-194.

Barlow, Robert H. El derrumbe de Huexotzinco. Cuadernos Americanos, 7, no. 3 (1948): 147-160.

Bartholomew, Doris. Some revisions of Proto-Otomi consonants. International Journal of American Linguistics, 26 (1960): 317-329.

Carrasco Pizana, Pedro. Los caciques chichimecas de Tulancingo. Estudios de Cultura Nahuatl, 4 (1963): 85-91.

Charency, H. de. Sur les idiômes de la famille Chichimèque. In Internationaler Amerikanisten-Kongress, 14th. 1904, Stuttgart. Stuttgart, 1906: 159-191.

Codex Chimalpopocatl. Historia Chichimeca. México, Vargas Rea, 1950. 54 p. (Colección Amatlacuilotl, 8)

Dávila Aguirre, J. de Jesús. Chichimécatlí; origen, cultura, lucha y extinción de los gallardos, bárbaros del Norte. Saltillo, Universidad de Coahuila y el Ateneo Guente, 1967. 127 p. illus., maps.

Di Peso, Charles C. Casas Grandes, a fallen trading center of the Gran Chichimeca. Masterkey, 42 (1968): 20-37.

Dibble, Charles E. Los chichimecas de Xólotl. Revista Mexicana de Estudios Antropológicos, 14 (1954/1955): 285-288.

*Driver, Harold E. Ethnography and acculturation of the Chichimeca-Jonaz of Northeast Mexico. By Harold E. Driver and Wilhelmine Driver. Bloomington, 1963. 265 p. illus., maps. (Indiana, University, Research Center in Anthropology, Folklore, and Linguistics, Publications, 26)

González Casanova, Pablo. Un vocabulario chichimeca. In International Congress of Americanists, 23d. 1928, New York. Proceedings. New York, 1930: 918-925.

Greenleaf, Richard E. The little war of Guadalajara--1587-1590. New Mexico Historical Review, 43 (1968): 119-135.

Hrdlička, Aleš. The region of the ancient "Chichimecs", with notes on the Tepecanos and the ruin of La Quemada. American Anthropologist, n.s., 5 (1903): 385-440.

Ixtlilxochitl, Fernando de Alva. Obras históricas. México, Oficina Tipografía de la Secretaría de Fomento, 1891-1892. 2 v.

Kirchhoff, Paul. Civilizing the Chichimecs; a chapter in the culture history of ancient Mexico. In John A. Graham, ed. Ancient Mesoamerica; Selected Readings. Palo Alto, Calif., 1966: 273-278.

Lastra de Suárez, Yolanda. Dos fiestas chichimecas. Anales de Antropología, 8 (1971): 203-212.

Lastra, Yolanda. El Conejo y el Coyote en Chichimeco. Tlalocan, 6, no. 2 (1970): 115-118.

Lastra, Yolanda. Notas sobre algunos aspectos sintácticos del Chichimeco-Jonaz. Anales de Antropología, 6 (1969): 109-114.

Longacre, Robert E. Progress in Otomanguean reconstruction. In International Congress of Linguists, 9th. 1962, Cambridge, Mass. Proceedings. The Hague, Mouton, 1964: 1016-1025. (Janua Linguarum, Series Maior, 12)

Manrique Castañeda, Leonardo. La organización social de Jiliapan. México, Instituto Nacional de Antropología e Historia, Anales, 13 (1960): 93-111.

Meade, Joaquín. Panorama indiano de San Luis Potosí en la época prehispánica. Sociedad Mexicana de Geografía y Estadística, Boletín, 60 (1945): 621-642.

Noguera, Eduardo. Culturas de la etapa chichimeca. In Jorge A. Vivó, ed. México Prehispánico. México, 1946: 215-221.

Pérez de Ribas, Andrés. Historia de los triunfos de nuestra santa fe entre gentes las más bárbaras y fieras del nuevo orbe. Madrid, A. de Paredes, 1645. 20, 763 p.

Pérez de Ribas, Andrés. My life among the savage nations of New Spain. Translated by Tomás Antonio Robertson. Los Angeles, Ward Ritchie Press, 1968. 16, 256 p. illus., maps.

Powell, Philip W., comp. War and peace on the North Mexican frontier: a documentary record. Vol. 1. Madrid, Ediciones Jose Porrua Turanzas, 1971. 27, 276 p. illus. (Colección Chimalistac de Libros y Documentos acerca de la Nueva España, 32)

Rensch, Calvin Ross. Comparative Otomanguean phonology. Dissertation Abstracts, 27 (1966/1967): 1807A. UM 66-10,661.

Romero Castillo, Moisés. Los fonemas del Chichimeco-Jonaz. México, Instituto Nacional de Antropología e Historia, Anales, 11 (1957/1958): 289-299.

Romero Castillo, Moisés. Vocabulario chichimeco-jonas. In Antonio Pompa y Pompa, ed. Summa Anthropologica en Homenaje a Roberto J. Weitlaner. México, 1966: 501-532.

Simmons, Marc. Tlascalans in the Spanish borderlands. New Mexico Historical Review, 39 (1964): 101-110.

Swadesh, Morris. The Oto-Manguean hypothesis and Macro Mixtecan. International Journal of American Linguistics, 26 (1960): 79-111.

Thomas, Cyrus. Indian languages of Mexico and Central America and their geographical distribution. By Cyrus Thomas assisted by John R. Swanton. Washington, D.C., Government Printing Office, 1911. 7, 108 p. map. (U.S., Bureau of American Ethnology, Bulletin, 44)

Toor, Frances. A treasury of Mexican folkways. New York, Crown, 1947. 32, 566 p. illus.

Wake, C. Staniland. The Chichimecs. American Antiquarian, 13 (1891): 229-233.

15-42   Pame

Bartholomew, Doris. Some revisions of Proto-Otomi consonants. International Journal of American Linguistics, 26 (1960): 317-329.

Basauri, Carlos. Familia "Otomiana": Chichimecas Pames. In his La Poblacion Indigena de Mexico. Tomo 3. Mexico, Secretaria de Educacion Publica, 1940: 363-385.

Beals, Ralph L. The comparative ethnology of northern Mexico before 1750. Berkeley, University of California Press, 1932. 6, 93-225 p. maps. (Ibero-Americana, 2)

Eguilaz de Prado, Isabel. Los indios del nordeste de Méjico en el siglo XVIII. Sevilla, 1965. 128 p. (Sevilla, Universidad, Seminario de Antropología Americana, Publicaciones, 7)

Gibson, Lorna F. Four Pame texts. By Lorna F. Gibson, Donald Olson, and Anne Olson. Tlalocan, 4 (1963): 125-143.

Gibson, Lorna F. The man who abandoned his wife. A Pame story. Tlalocan, 5, no. 2 (1966): 169-177.

León-Portilla, Miguel. Panorama de la población indígena de México. América Indígena, 19 (1959): 43-73.

Longacre, Robert E. Progress in Otomanguean reconstruction. In International Congress of Linguists, 9th. 1962, Cambridge, Mass. Proceedings.

The Hague, Mouton, 1964: 1016-1025. (Janua Linguarum, Series Maior, 12)

Manrique Castañeda, Leonardo. Dos gramáticas pames del siglo XVIII. México, Instituto Nacional de Antropología e Historia, Anales, 11 (1957/1958): 283-287.

Manrique Castaneda, Leonardo. Type linguistic descriptions: Jiliapan Pame. In Robert Wauchope, ed. Handbook of Middle American Indians. Vol. 5. Austin, University of Texas Press, 1967: 331-348.

Maza, Antonio de la. La Nación Pame. Sociedad Mexicana de Geografía y Estadística, Boletín, 63 (1947): 493-576.

Maza, Antonio de la. La pamería a través de los tiempos. Revista Mexicana de Estudios Antropológicos, 13 (1953): 269-280.

Olson, Donald. Spanish loan words in Pame. International Journal of American Linguistics, 29 (1963): 219-221.

Pride, Kitty. Numerals in Chatino. Anthropological Linguistics, 3, no. 2 (1961): 1-10(b).

Rensch, Calvin Ross. Comparative Otomanguean phonology. Dissertation Abstracts, 27 (1966/1967): 1807A. UM 66-10,661.

Swadesh, Morris. The Oto-Manguean hypothesis and Macro Mixtecan. International Journal of American Linguistics, 26 (1960): 79-111.

Thomas, Cyrus. Indian languages of Mexico and Central America and their geographical distribution. By Cyrus Thomas assisted by John R. Swanton. Washington, D.C., Government Printing Office, 1911. 7, 108 p. map. (U.S., Bureau of American Ethnology, Bulletin, 44)

15-43   Cora

Alcocer, José Antonio. Bosquejo de la historia del Colegio de Nuestra Señora de Guadalupe y sus misiones. Introducción, bibliografía, acotaciones e ilustraciones del R.P. Fr. Rafael Cervantes. México, Editorial Porrua, 1958. 300 p. illus.

Aldana E., Guillermo. Mesa del Nayar's strange holy week. National Geographic Magazine, 139 (1971): 780-795.

Anonymous. Creation of a new Indianist
   Coordinating Center in the Cora-Huichol
   region. Boletín Indigenista, 20 (1960):
   225, 227.

Basauri, Carlos. Familia "Nahuatlana":
   Coras. In his La Poblacion Indigena de
   Mexico. Tomo 3. Mexico, Secretaria de
   Educacion Publica, 1940: 3-39.

Beals, Ralph L. Kinship terminology and
   social structure. Kroeber
   Anthropological Society Papers, 25
   (1961): 129-148.

Beals, Ralph L. The comparative ethnology
   of northern Mexico before 1750.
   Berkeley, University of California
   Press, 1932. 6, 93-225 p. maps.
   (Ibero-Americana, 2)

Benítez, Fernando. Los indios de México.
   México, Ediciones Era, 1970. 280,
   273 p. illus.

Burnham, Harold B. Four looms. Toronto,
   University, Royal Ontario Museum,
   Division of Art and Archaeology, Annual
   (1962): 77-84.

Ceballos Novelo, Roque J. Tarahumaras,
   Coras y Huicholes, su situación
   económica y social. In Homenaje al
   Doctor Alfonso Caso. Mexico, Imprenta
   Nuevo Mundo, 1951: 101-111.

Cerda Silva, Roberto de la. Los Coras.
   Revista Mexicana de Sociología, 5, no. 2
   (1943): 89-117.

Cordova, Maria S. Studies on several
   genetic hematological traits of the
   Mexican population. XII. Distribution of
   blood group antigens in twelve Indian
   tribes. By Maria S. Cordova, Rubén
   Lisker, and Alvar Loria. American
   Journal of Physical Anthropology, n.s.,
   26 (1967): 55-65.

Dahlgren de Jordán, Barbo. Semejanzas y
   diferencias entre Coras y Huicholes en
   el proceso de sincretismo. In Congreso
   Internacional de Americanistas, 35th.
   1962, Mexico. Actas y Memorias. Tomo 2.
   Mexico, 1964: 565-574.

Díaz Flores, Raymundo. Textos in idioma
   cora. México, 1945. 24 p. (Escuela
   Nacional de Antropología, Publicación,
   3)

Diguet, Léon. Contribution à l'étude
   ethnographique des races primitives du
   Mexique. La Sierra de Nayarit et ses
   indigènes. Nouvelles Archives des
   Missions Scientifiques et Littéraires, 9
   (1899): 571-630.

Diguet, Léon. Le "peyote" et son usage
   rituel chez les Indiens du Nayarit.
   Société des Américanistes (Paris),
   Journal, n.s., 4 (1907): 21-29.

Diguet, Léon. Relation sommaire d'un
   voyage au versant occidental de Mexique.
   Paris, Muséum d'Histoire Naturelle,
   Bulletin, 4 (1898): 345-352.

Fisher, Glen. Directed culture change in
   Nayarit, Mexico. New Orleans, Tulane
   University of Louisiana, 1953. 67-
   173 p. illus., maps. (Middle American
   Research Institute, Publication, 17)

Flores de San Pedro, Juan. Autos hechos
   por el capitán don Juan Flores de San
   Pedro, sobre la reducción, conversión y
   conquista de los gentiles de la
   Provincia del Nayarit en 1722.
   Guadalajara, Librería Font, 1964.
   121 p.

Gandola, Isabel. El peyote; estudio sobre
   el uso del peyote, entre las tribus
   Huicholes, Coras, Tepehuanes y
   Tarahumaras. México, Editorial Orión,
   1965. 66 p. illus., map.

Gómez, Aniceto M. Estudios gramaticales
   de la lengua cora que se habla en el
   territorio de Tepic. Con una
   introducción biobibliográfica por José
   Cornejo Franco. Investigaciones
   Lingüísticas, 3 (1935): 79-142.

González Dávila, Amado. Geografía de
   Nayarit. México, El Nacional, 1943.
   214 p. illus.

González, G. Coras: religion y ritos.
   Acción Indigenista, 187/188 (1969): 1-4.

González, G. Coras: situacion y
   poblacion. Acción Indigenista, 185/186
   (1968): 1-4.

Grimes, Joseph E. Metodologia para el
   analisis de sistemas de prefijos en
   Huichol y Cora. In Congreso
   Internacional de Americanistas, 36th.
   1964, España. Actas y Memorias. Tomo 2.
   Sevilla, 1966: 217-220.

Grimes, Joseph E. The Huichol and Cora.
   By Joseph E. Grimes and Thomas B.
   Hinton. In Evon Z. Vogt, volume editor.
   Handbook of Middle American Indians.
   Vol. 8. Austin, University of Texas
   Press, 1969: 792-813.

Hepner, H. E. The Cora Indians of Mexico.
   Southern Workman, 34 (1905): 92-99.

Hinton, Thomas B. An analysis of
   religious syncretism among the Cora of
   Nayarit. In Internationale
   Amerikanistenkongress, 38th. 1968,

Stuttgart-München. Verhandlungen. Band 3. München, Klaus Renner, 1971: 275-279.

Hrdlička, Aleš. A Cora cradle. American Anthropologist, n.s., 7 (1905): 361.

Hrdlička, Aleš. Cora dances. American Anthropologist, n.s., 6 (1904): 744-745.

Hrdlička, Aleš. Jay feathers in Cora ceremony. American Anthropologist, n.s., 7 (1905): 730.

Ibarra, Alfredo, Jr. Entre los indios coras de Nayarit. Sociedad Folklórica de México, Anuario, 4 (1943): 49-60.

Kelley, Gordon P. Linguistic observations for the spider concept in Mesoamerica. Katunob, 8, no. 1 (Aug. 1972): 31-33.

Kroeber, Alfred L. Uto-Aztecan languages of Mexico. Berkeley, University of California Press, 1934. 3, 27 p. map. (Ibero-Americana, 8)

León-Portilla, Miguel. Panorama de la población indígena de México. América Indígena, 19 (1959): 43-73.

Lisker, Rubén. Studies on several genetic hematological traits of the Mexican population. XIV. Serum polymorphisms in several Indian tribes. By Rubén Lisker, Graciela Zárate and Elizabeth Rodríguez. American Journal of Physical Anthropology, n.s., 27 (1967): 27-31.

Lisker, Rubén. Studies on several genetic hematological traits of Mexicans. XI. Red cell acid phophatase and phophoglucomutase in three Indian groups. By Rubén Lisker and Eloise R. Giblett. American Journal of Human Genetics, 19 (1967): 174-177.

López, Atanasio. Los indios coras, tepehuanes, cheles y guainamotas (Méjico). Archivo Ibero-Americana, 34 (1931): 341-370.

Lumholtz, Carl. Explorations au Mexique de 1894 a 1897. Société des Américanistes (Paris), Journal, 2 (1899): 179-184.

Lumholtz, Carl. My life of exploration. Natural History, 21 (1921): 225-243.

Lumholtz, Carl. Unknown Mexico. New York, Charles Scribner's Sons, 1902. 2 v.

Malkin, Borys. Cora ethnozoology, herpetological knowledge; a bio-ecological and cross cultural approach. Anthropological Quarterly, 31 (1958): 73-90.

Mason, J. Alden. The Tepehuan, and other aborigines of the Mexican Sierra Madre Occidental. América Indígena, 8 (1948): 289-300.

McMahon, Ambrose. Phonemes and phonemic units of Cora (Mexico). International Journal of American Linguistics, 33 (1967): 128-134.

McMahon, Ambrosio. Cora y español. By Ambrosio McMahon and María Aitón de McMahon. México, Instituto Lingüístico de Verano, 1959. 20, 193 p. illus. (Serie de Vocabularios Indígenas, 2)

Mendizábal, Miguel Othón de. La evolución del noroeste de México. In his Obras Completas. Tomo 3. México, 1946: 7-86.

Menéndez, Miguel Angel. La música y las danzas entre Coras y Huicholes. Revista Musical Mexicana, 1, no. 1 (1942): 17-19.

Miller, Wick R. Uto-Aztecan cognate sets. Berkeley and Los Angeles, University of California Press, 1967. 5, 83 p. map. (California, University, Publications in Linguistics, 48)

Monzón, Arturo. Restos de clanes exogámicos entre los Cora de Nayarit. Escuela Nacional de Antropología, Publicación, 4 (1945): 12-16.

Nahmad Sittón, Salomon. La acción indigenista en comunidades dispersas y en habitat de montaña. Anuario Indigenista, 28 (1968): 33-43.

Ortega, José de. Apostolicos afanes de la Compañía de Jesús. By José de Ortega and Juan Antonio Baltasar. México, Editorial Layac, 1944. 24, 445 p.

Parkinson, Juan F. Geografía del estado de Nayarit. Mexico, Ediciones de El Nacional, 1951. 93 p. illus., map.

Parsons, Elsie Clews. Pueblo Indian religion. Vol. 2. Chicago, University of Chicago Press, 1939. 551-1275 p.

Passin, Herbert. Some relationships in Northwest Mexican kinship systems. El México Antiguo, 6, no. 7/8 (July 1944): 205-218.

Pemex Travel Club. Mexico's music: its past and present. Katunob, 4, no. 4 (1963): 30-52.

Preuss, Konrad T. Das Fest des Erwachens (Weinfest) bei den Cora-Indianern. In Internationale Amerikanisten-Kongress, 16th. 1908, Wien. Verhandlungen. Vienna, 1908: 489-512.

Preuss, Konrad T.   Das Verbum in der Sprache der Cora-Indianer. In International Congress of Americanists, 18th. 1912, London. Proceedings. London, 1912: 105-106.

Preuss, Konrad T.   Der Mitotetanz der Coraindianer. Globus, 90 (1906): 69-72.

Preuss, Konrad T.   Die Eingeborenen Amerikas. Tübingen, J. C. B. Mohr (Paul Siebeck), 1926. 3, 61 p. (Religionsgeschichtliches Lesebuch, 2)

Preuss, Konrad T.   Die Flutsage der Cora-Indianer und verwandte Stämme. Deutsche Gesellschaft für Anthropologie, Ethnologie und Urgeschichte, Korrespondenz-Blatt, 41, no. 9/12 (1910): 82-83.

Preuss, Konrad T.   Die geistige Kultur der Naturvölker. Leipzig, B. G. Teubner, 1914. 4, 112 p. illus. (Aus Natur und Geisteswelt, 452)

Preuss, Konrad T.   Die magische Denkweise der Cora-Indianer (Jalisco, Mexico). In International Congress of Americanists, 18th. 1912, London. Proceedings. London, 1912: 129-134.

*Preuss, Konrad T.   Die Nayarit-Expedition. . . . Bd. 1. Die Religion der Cora-Indianern in Texten nebst Wörterbuch. Leipzig, B. G. Teubner, 1912. 108, 396 p. illus., map.

Preuss, Konrad T.   Die Opferblutschale der alten Mexikaner erläutet nach den Angaben der Cora-Indianer. Zeitschrift für Ethnologie, 43 (1911): 293-306.

Preuss, Konrad T.   Die religiösen Gesänge und Mythen einiger Stämme der mexikanischen Sierra Madre. Archiv für Religionswissenschaft, 11 (1908): 369-398.

Preuss, Konrad T.   Ethnographische Ergebnisse einer Reise in die mexikanische Sierra Madre. Zeitschrift für Ethnologie, 40 (1908): 582-604.

Preuss, Konrad T.   Glauben und Mystik im Schatten des höchsten Wesens. Leipzig, C. L. Hirschfeld, 1926. 62 p.

Preuss, Konrad T.   Grammatik der Cora-Sprache. International Journal of American Linguistics, 7 (1932/1933): 1-84.

Preuss, Konrad T.   Reise zu den Stämmen der westlichen Sierra Madre in Mexico. Berlin, Gesellschaft für Erdkunde, Zeitschrift (1908): 147-167.

Preuss, Konrad T.   Reisebericht des Hrn. K. Th. Preuss aus San Isidro vom 30. Juni 1906. Zeitschrift für Ethnologie, 38 (1906): 955-967.

Preuss, Konrad T.   Schreibt an den Vorsitzenden aus San Isidro in Mexiko vom 10. Februar 1907. Zeitschrift für Ethnologie, 39 (1907): 404-405.

Preuss, Konrad T.   Un viaje a la Sierra Madre Occidental de México. Sociedad Mexicana de Geografía y Estadística, Boletín, 4 (1909): 187-214.

Preuss, Konrad T.   Weiteres über die religiösen Gebräuche der Coraindianer, insbesondere über die Phallophoren des Osterfestes. Globus, 90 (1906): 165-169.

Preuss, Konrad T.   Wörterbuch Deutsch-Cora. International Journal of American Linguistics, 8, no. 2 (1934): 81-102.

Soustelle, Georgette.   Essai comparatif sur cinq populations autochtones du Mexique. Ethnographie, Nouvelle Série, 62/63 (1968/1969): 142-155.

Soustelle, Jacques.   Un vocabulaire cora. Société des Américanistes (Paris), Journal, n.s., 30 (1938): 141-145.

Spicer, Edward H.   Apuntes sobre el tipo de religión de los Yuto-Aztecas Centrales. In Congreso Internacional de Americanistas, 35th. 1962, Mexico. Actas y Memorias. Tomo 2. Mexico, 1964: 27-38.

Steinberg, Arthur G.   Studies on several genetic hematologic traits of Mexicans. XV. The Gm allotypes of some Indian tribes. By Arthur G. Steinberg, M. Soledad Cordova, and Rubén Lisker. American Journal of Human Genetics, 19 (1967): 747-756.

Thomas, Cyrus.   Indian languages of Mexico and Central America and their geographical distribution. By Cyrus Thomas assisted by John R. Swanton. Washington, D.C., Government Printing Office, 1911. 7, 108 p. map. (U.S., Bureau of American Ethnology, Bulletin, 44)

Toor, Frances.   A treasury of Mexican folkways. New York, Crown, 1947. 32, 566 p. illus.

Uribe Romo, Emilio.   El medio aborigen nayarita. Revista Mexicana de Sociología, 12, no. 2 (1950): 211-225.

Uribe Romo, Emilio.   El Nayarit; del descubrimiento a la conquista a las postrimerías del Virreinato. Sociedad

Mexicana de Geografía y Estadística, Boletín, 62 (1946): 463-482.

Velázquez Rodríguez, Hector. Problemas de las tribus Cora y Huichol de Nayarit, en relación con la reforma agraria. México, 1962. 140 p.

Vogt, Evon Z. Some aspects of Cora-Huichol acculturation. América Indígena, 15 (1955): 249-263.

Weitlaner, Roberto J. Parentesco y compadrazgo coras. Escuela Nacional de Antropología, Publicación, 4 (1945): 3-11.

Zaborowski, S. Photographies d'Indiens Huichols y Coras. Société d'Anthropologie de Paris, Bulletins et Mémoires, 5 série, 2 (1901): 612-613.

Zingg, Robert M. A reconstruction of Uto-Aztekan history. New York, G. E. Stechert, 1939. 4, 274 p. (Denver, University, Contributions to Ethnography, 2)

                    15-44 Huichol

Anguiano, Marina. Mawarirra u ofrecimiento a los dioses (celebración social-religiosa). By Marina Anguiano, Yolanda Sasson, and André Breton. México, Instituto Nacional de Antropología e Historia, Boletín, 35 (1969): 22-28.

Anonymous. Creation of a new Indianist Coordinating Center in the Cora-Huichol region. Boletín Indigenista, 20 (1960): 225, 227.

Anonymous. Los Huicholes. Acción Indigenista, 20 (1955): 1-4.

Basauri, Carlos. Familia "Nahuatlana": Huicholes. In his La Poblacion Indigena de Mexico. Tomo 3. Mexico, Secretaria de Educacion Publica, 1940: 41-71.

Beals, Ralph L. Kinship terminology and social structure. Kroeber Anthropological Society Papers, 25 (1961): 129-148.

Beals, Ralph L. Review of "The Huichols: primitive artists" by Robert M. Zingg. American Anthropologist, n.s., 43 (1941): 99-102.

Beals, Ralph L. The comparative ethnology of northern Mexico before 1750. Berkeley, University of California Press, 1932. 6, 93-225 p. maps. (Ibero-Americana, 2)

Beasley, Walter L. The Huichol Indians of Mexico. Scientific American, 98, no. 3 (Jan. 18, 1908): 44-46.

Benítez, Fernando. En la tierra mágica del peyote. México, Ediciones Era, 1968. 285 p. illus.

Benítez, Fernando. Los indios de México. México, Ediciones Era, 1970. 280, 273 p. illus.

Benzi, M. Visions des Huichols sous l'effet du peyotl. Hygiène Mentale, 58 (1969): 61-87.

Benzi, Marino. Le mythe de l'ancêtre des Huichol, Huatakáme (contribution à l'étude de la mythologie Huichol). Société des Américanistes (Paris), Journal, n.s., 60 (1971): 177-190.

Benzi, Marino. Les derniers adorateurs du peyotl; croyances, coutumes et mythes des Indiens huichol. Paris, Gallimard, 1972. 446 p. illus.

Bradt, George McClellan. Huichol pilgrim. Natural History, 58 (1949): 456-459, 475.

Bruman, Henry J. The Asiatic origin of the Huichol still. Geographical Review, 34 (1944): 418-427.

Ceballos Novelo, Roque J. Tarahumaras, Coras y Huicholes, su situación económica y social. In Homenaje al Doctor Alfonso Caso. Mexico, Imprenta Nuevo Mundo, 1951: 101-111.

Cordova, Maria S. Studies on several genetic hematological traits of the Mexican population. XII. Distribution of blood group antigens in twelve Indian tribes. By Maria S. Cordova, Rubén Lisker, and Alvar Loria. American Journal of Physical Anthropology, n.s., 26 (1967): 55-65.

Dahlgren de Jordán, Barbo. Semejanzas y diferencias entre Coras y Huicholes en el proceso de sincretismo. In Congreso Internacional de Americanistas, 35th. 1962, Mexico. Actas y Memorias. Tomo 2. Mexico, 1964: 565-574.

Diguet, Léon. Contribution à l'étude ethnographique des races primitives du Mexique. La Sierra de Nayarit et ses indigènes. Nouvelles Archives des Missions Scientifiques et Littéraires, 9 (1899): 571-630.

Diguet, Léon. Idiome huichol. Contribution à l'étude des langues mexicaines. Société des Américanistes (Paris), Journal, n.s., 8 (1911): 23-54.

Diguet, Léon. Le "peyote" et son usage
  rituel chez les Indiens du Nayarit.
  Société des Américanistes (Paris),
  Journal, n.s., 4 (1907): 21-29.

Diguet, Léon. Relation sommaire d'un
  voyage au versant occidental de Mexique.
  Paris, Muséum d'Histoire Naturelle,
  Bulletin, 4 (1898): 345-352.

Duncan, Gra'delle. New art from ancient
  "ojos". New Mexico Magazine, 39,
  no. 11/12 (1961): 39-41.

Dutton, Bertha P. Happy people: the
  Huichol Indians. Santa Fe, 1962.
  56 p. illus.

Ely, Evelyn. Ojos de Dios. El Palacio,
  77, no. 3 (1971): 2-14.

*Fabila, Alfonso. Los huicholes de
  Jalisco. México, Instituto Nacional
  Indigenista, 1959. 134 p. illus.

Fabila, Alfonso. Los huicholes de
  Jalisco. Acción Indigenista, 71 (1959):
  2-3.

Fergusson, Erna. Fiesta in Mexico. New
  York, Knopf, 1934. 267 p. illus.

Fisher, Glen. Directed culture change in
  Nayarit, Mexico. New Orleans, Tulane
  University of Louisiana, 1953. 67-
  173 p. illus., maps. (Middle American
  Research Institute, Publication, 17)

Furst, Peter T. Ariocarpus retusus, the
  "false peyote" of Huichol tradition.
  Economic Botany, 25 (1972): 182-187.

Furst, Peter T. Huichols of western
  Mexico. Katunob, 6, no. 4 (1967): 18-19.

Furst, Peter T. The parching of the
  maize; an essay on the survival of
  Huichol ritual. Wien, Stiglmayr, 1968.
  42 p. illus. (Acta Ethnologica et
  Linguistica, 14)

Gandola, Isabel. El peyote; estudio sobre
  el uso del peyote, entre las tribus
  Huicholes, Coras, Tepehuanes y
  Tarahumaras. México, Editorial Orión,
  1965. 66 p. illus., map.

González Dávila, Amado. Geografía de
  Nayarit. México, El Nacional, 1943.
  214 p. illus.

Gorrell, Rebecca. Huichol material
  culture at Ranchito Cabeza Azul. By
  Rebecca Gorrell and Thomas Alexander.
  Kiva, 37 (1972): 169-184.

Grimes, Barbara F. Notes on Huichol
  kinship terminology. By Barbara F.

Grimes and Joseph E. Grimes. El México
  Antiguo, 9 (1959): 561-576.

Grimes, Joseph E. Huichol economics.
  América Indígena, 21 (1961): 281-306.

Grimes, Joseph E. Huichol grammar. The
  Hague, Mouton, 1964. 105 p. (Janua
  Linguarum, Series Practica, 11)

Grimes, Joseph E. Huichol syntax. The
  Hague, Mouton, 1964. 105 p. (Janua
  Linguarum, Series Practica, 11)

Grimes, Joseph E. Huichol tone and
  intonation. International Journal of
  American Linguistics, 25 (1959): 221-
  232.

Grimes, Joseph E. Individualism and the
  Huichol church. By Joseph E. Grimes and
  Barbara F. Grimes. Practical
  Anthropology, 1 (1954): 127-134.

Grimes, Joseph E. Individualism and the
  Huichol church. In William A. Smalley,
  ed. Readings in Missionary Anthropology.
  Tarrytown, N.Y., Practical Anthropology,
  1967: 199-203.

Grimes, Joseph E. Metodologia para el
  analisis de sistemas de prefijos en
  Huichol y Cora. In Congreso
  Internacional de Americanistas, 36th.
  1964, España. Actas y Memorias. Tomo 2.
  Sevilla, 1966: 217-220.

Grimes, Joseph E. Positional analysis.
  Language, 43 (1967): 437-444.

Grimes, Joseph E. Semantic distinctions
  in Huichol (Uto-Aztecan) kinship. By
  Joseph E. Grimes and Barbara F. Grimes.
  American Anthropologist, 64 (1962): 104-
  114.

Grimes, Joseph E. Some inter-sentence
  relationships in Huichol. In Antonio
  Pompa y Pompa, ed. Summa Anthropologica
  en Homenaje a Roberto J. Weitlaner.
  México, 1966: 465-470.

Grimes, Joseph E. Spanish-Nahuatl-Huichol
  monetary terms. International Journal of
  American Linguistics, 26 (1960): 162-
  165.

Grimes, Joseph E. Style in Huichol
  structure. Language, 31 (1955): 31-35.

Grimes, Joseph E. The Huichol and Cora.
  By Joseph E. Grimes and Thomas B.
  Hinton. In Evon Z. Vogt, volume editor.
  Handbook of Middle American Indians.
  Vol. 8. Austin, University of Texas
  Press, 1969: 792-813.

Grimes, Joseph Evans. Huichol syntax.
Dissertation Abstracts, 21 (1960/1961):
2286-2287. UM 61-20.

Gutiérrez Lopez, Gregorio. El mundo de
los huicholes; ensayo. México, B.
Costa-Amic, 1968. 136 p. illus.

Hamp, Eric P. Stylistically modified
allophones in Huichol. Language, 33
(1957): 139-142.

Hamy, E.-T. Contribution à
l'anthropologie du Nayarit. Paris,
Muséum d'Histoire Naturelle, Bulletin, 3
(1897): 190-193.

Hepner, H. E. The Huichol Indians of
Mexico. Southern Workman, 33 (1904):
280-286.

Kamffer, Raúl. Plumed arrows of the
Huicholes of western Mexico. Américas,
9, no. 6 (1957): 12-16.

Kamffer, Raúl. Plumed arrows of the
Huicholes of western Mexico. Americas,
9, no. 6 (1957): 12-16.

Kelley, Gordon P. Linguistic observations
for the spider concept in Mesoamerica.
Katunob, 8, no. 1 (Aug. 1972): 31-33.

Klineberg, Otto. Notes on the Huichol.
American Anthropologist, n.s., 36
(1934): 446-460.

Kroeber, Alfred L. Uto-Aztecan languages
of Mexico. Berkeley, University of
California Press, 1934. 3, 27 p. map.
(Ibero-Americana, 8)

La Barre, Weston. The peyote cult. New
Haven, Yale University, Department of
Anthropology, 1938. 188 p. illus.
(Yale University Publications in
Anthropology, 19)

Landar, Herbert. Syntactic patterns in
Navaho and Huichol. International
Journal of American Linguistics, 33
(1967): 121-127.

Leonard, Phyllis G. The plundered plumes.
Pacific Discovery, 25, no. 1 (1972): 15-
22.

León-Portilla, Miguel. Panorama de la
población indígena de México. América
Indígena, 19 (1959): 43-73.

Lisker, Rubén. Studies on several genetic
hematological traits of the Mexican
population. XIV. Serum polymorphisms in
several Indian tribes. By Rubén Lisker,
Graciela Zárate and Elizabeth Rodríguez.
American Journal of Physical
Anthropology, n.s., 27 (1967): 27-31.

Lisker, Rubén. Studies on several genetic
hematological traits of Mexicans. XI.
Red cell acid phophatase and
phophoglucomutase in three Indian
groups. By Rubén Lisker and Eloise R.
Giblett. American Journal of Human
Genetics, 19 (1967): 174-177.

Lumholtz, Carl. Decorative art of the
Huichol Indians. New York, 1904. 279-
327 p. illus. (American Museum of
Natural History, Memoirs, 3)

Lumholtz, Carl. Explorations au Mexique
de 1894 a 1897. Société des
Américanistes (Paris), Journal, 2
(1899): 179-184.

Lumholtz, Carl. My life of exploration.
Natural History, 21 (1921): 225-243.

Lumholtz, Carl. Symbolism of the Huichol
Indians. New York, 1900. 1-228 p.
illus., maps. (American Museum of
Natural History, Memoirs, 3)

Lumholtz, Carl. The Huichol Indians of
Mexico. American Geographical Society,
Bulletin, 35 (1903): 79-93.

Lumholtz, Carl. The Huichol Indians of
Mexico. American Museum of Natural
History, Bulletin, 10 (1898): 1-14.

Lumholtz, Carl. The meaning of the head-
plume Tawia'kami used by the Huichol
Indians. In Berthold Laufer, ed. Boas
Anniversary Volume. New York, G. E.
Stechert, 1906: 316-319.

Lumholtz, Carl. Unknown Mexico. New
York, Charles Scribner's Sons, 1902.
2 v.

Maritzer, Lois S. A study of possible
relationship between the Huichol and
Chalchihuites cultures. Southwestern
Lore, 23 (1958): 51-63.

Maritzer, Lois S. A study of possible
relationship between the Huichol and
Chalchihuites cultures. Katunob, 6,
no. 1 (1967): 5-16.

Mason, J. Alden. The Tepehuan, and other
aborigines of the Mexican Sierra Madre
Occidental. América Indígena, 8 (1948):
289-300.

Mata Torres, Ramón. Los Huicholes.
Guadalajara, Ediciones de la Casa de la
Cultura, Jalisciense, 1970. 86 p.
illus.

McIntosh, John B. Cosmogonía huichol.
Tlalocan, 3, no. 1 (1949): 14-22.

McIntosh, John B. Huichol phonemes. International Journal of American Linguistics, 11 (1945): 31-35.

McIntosh, John B. Niuqui 'Iquisicayari, vixárica niuquiyári, teivári niuquiyári hepaïsita. Vocabulario huichol-castellano, castellano-huichol. By Juan B. McIntosh and José Grimes. Mexico, Instituto Lingüístico de Verano, 1954. 4, 113 p.

Mendizábal, Miguel Othón de. La evolución del noroeste de México. In his Obras Completas. Tomo 3. México, 1946: 7-86.

Menéndez, Miguel Angel. La música y las danzas entre Coras y Huicholes. Revista Musical Mexicana, 1, no. 1 (1942): 17-19.

Miller, Wick R. Uto-Aztecan cognate sets. Berkeley and Los Angeles, University of California Press, 1967. 5, 83 p. map. (California, University, Publications in Linguistics, 48)

Myerhoff, Barbara G. The deer-maize-peyote symbol complex among the Huichol Indians of Mexico. Anthropological Quarterly, 43 (1970): 64-78.

Myerhoff, Barbara Gay. The deer-maize-peyote complex among the Huichol Indians of Mexico. Dissertation Abstracts International, 30 (1969/1970): 475B-476B. UM 69-11,899.

Nahmad Sittón, Salomón. La acción indigenista en comunidades dispersas y en habitat de montaña. Anuario Indigenista, 28 (1968): 33-43.

Nahmad Sittón, Salomón, et al. El peyote y los huicholes. México, Secretaría de Educación Publica, 1972. 196 p. illus.

Parkinson, Juan F. Geografía del estado de Nayarit. Mexico, Ediciones de El Nacional, 1951. 93 p. illus., map.

Parsons, Elsie Clews. Pueblo Indian religion. Vol. 2. Chicago, University of Chicago Press, 1939. 551-1275 p.

Pemex Travel Club. Mexico's music: its past and present. Katunob, 4, no. 4 (1963): 30-52.

Preuss, Konrad T. Au sujet du caractère des mythes et des chants huichols, que j'ai recueillis. Tucumán, Universidad Nacional, Instituto de Etnología, Revista, 2 (1931): 445-457.

Preuss, Konrad T. Der Charakter der von mir aufgenommenen Mythen und Gesänge der Huichol-Indianer. In International Congress of Americanists, 24th. 1930,

Hamburg. Verhandlungen. Hamburg, 1934. 217-218.

Preuss, Konrad T. Die Eingeborenen Amerikas. Tübingen, J. C. B. Mohr (Paul Siebeck), 1926. 3, 61 p. (Religionsgeschichtliches Lesebuch, 2)

Preuss, Konrad T. Die geistige Kultur der Naturvölker. Leipzig, B. G. Teubner, 1914. 4, 112 p. illus. (Aus Natur und Geisteswelt, 452)

Preuss, Konrad T. Die Hochzeit des Maises und andere Geschichten der Huichol-Indianer. Globus, 91 (1907): 185-192.

Preuss, Konrad T. Die religiösen Gesänge und Mythen einiger Stämme der mexikanischen Sierra Madre. Archiv für Religionswissenschaft, 11 (1908): 369-398.

Preuss, Konrad T. Ethnographische Ergebnisse einer Reise in die mexikanische Sierra Madre. Zeitschrift für Ethnologie, 40 (1908): 582-604.

Preuss, Konrad T. Glauben und Mystik im Schatten des höchsten Wesens. Leipzig, C. L. Hirschfeld, 1926. 62 p.

Preuss, Konrad T. Parallelen zwischen den alten Mexikanern und den heutigen Huicholindianern. Globus, 80 (1901): 314-315.

Preuss, Konrad T. Reise zu den Stämmen der westlichen Sierra Madre in Mexico. Berlin, Gesellschaft für Erdkunde, Zeitschrift (1908): 147-167.

Preuss, Konrad T. Ritte durch das Land der Huichol-Indianer in der mexikanischen Sierra Madre. Globus, 92 (1907): 155-161, 167-171.

Preuss, Konrad T. Un viaje a la Sierra Madre Occidental de México. Sociedad Mexicana de Geografía y Estadística, Boletín, 4 (1909): 187-214.

Price, P. David. Two types of taxonomy: a Huichol ethnobotanical example. Anthropological Linguistics, 9, no. 7 (1967): 1-28.

Pride, Kitty. Numerals in Chatino. Anthropological Linguistics, 3, no. 2 (1961): 1-10(b).

Rash, Albert. Ein Besuch bei den Huichol-Indianer. Erdball, 2 (1927): 453-455.

Reed, Karen Barbara. El INI y los huicholes. México, INI, 1972. 176 p. illus.

Robles, Francisco de P. Ensayo catequístico en Castellano y en Huichol. By Francisco de P. Robles and Manuel Velasco. Zacatecas, Imprenta del Asilo del Sgdo. C. de Jesús, 1906. 5, 84 p.

Rosell, Lauro E. Casamiento de Huicholes. Mapa, 10, no. 114 (1943): 12-13.

Sauer, Carl O. The distribution of aboriginal tribes and languages in northwestern Mexico. Berkeley, University of California Press, 1934. 6, 94 p. map. (Ibero-Americana, 5)

Seler, Eduard. Die Huichol-Indianer des Staates Jalisco in Mexico. Anthropologische Gesellschaft in Wien, Mitteilungen, 31 (1901): 138-163.

Seler, Eduard. Die Huichol-Indianer des Staates Jalisco in Mexico. In his Gesammelte Abhaudlungen zur amerikanischen Sprach- und Alterthumskunde. Band 3. Berlin, Behrend, 1908: 355-391.

Simoni-Abbat, Mireille. Collections huichol. Paris, Musée National d'Histoire Naturelle, 1963. 117 p. illus., maps. (Paris, Musée de l'Homme, Catalogues, Serie H: Amérique, 1)

Simoni-Abbat, Mireille. Un tambour huichol. Objets et Mondes, 2 (1962): 241-248.

Soustelle, Georgette. Essai comparatif sur cinq populations autochtones du Mexique. Ethnographie, Nouvelle Série, 62/63 (1968/1969): 142-155.

Spicer, Edward H. Apuntes sobre el tipo de religión de los Yuto-Aztecas Centrales. In Congreso Internacional de Americanistas, 35th. 1962, Mexico. Actas y Memorias. Tomo 2. Mexico, 1964: 27-38.

Spoehr, Alexander. New Huichol Indian exhibit. Field Museum News, 12, no. 8 (1941): 3.

Thomas, Cyrus. Indian languages of Mexico and Central America and their geographical distribution. By Cyrus Thomas assisted by John R. Swanton. Washington, D.C., Government Printing Office, 1911. 7, 108 p. map. (U.S., Bureau of American Ethnology, Bulletin, 44)

Toor, Frances. A treasury of Mexican folkways. New York, Crown, 1947. 32, 566 p. illus.

Uribe Romo, Emilio. El medio aborigen nayarita. Revista Mexicana de Sociología, 12, no. 2 (1950): 211-225.

Velázquez Rodríguez, Hector. Problemas de las tribus Cora y Huichol de Nayarit, en relación con la reforma agraria. México, 1962. 140 p.

Vogt, Evon Z. Some aspects of Cora-Huichol acculturation. América Indígena, 15 (1955): 249-263.

Weigand, Phil C. Huichol ceremonial reuse of a fluted point. American Antiquity, 35 (1970): 365-367.

Weigand, Phil C. Modern Huichol ceramics. Carbondale, 1969. 5, 47 l. illus. (Mesoamerican Studies, 3)

Zaborowski, S. Photographies d'Indiens Huichols y Coras. Société d'Anthropologie de Paris, Bulletins et Mémoires, 5 série, 2 (1901): 612-613.

Zingg, Robert M. A reconstruction of Uto-Aztekan history. New York, G. E. Stechert, 1939. 4, 274 p. (Denver, University, Contributions to Ethnography, 2)

*Zingg, Robert M. The Huichols: primitive artists. New York, G. E. Stechert, 1938. 64, 826 p. illus., map. (Denver, University, Contributions to Ethnography, 1)

Ethnonymy

Plains and Southwest Ethnonymy

An ethnonymy is a list of names of ethnic groups, together with alternate names and variant spellings. The ethnonymy on the following pages was prepared by the compilers of this bibliography to assist them in making decisions as to where to assign individual books, journal articles, etc. within the bibliography. Thus, it was designed primarily as a classificatory device for purposes unique to this bibliography. The basic ethnonymy was prepared before the compilation of this edition was begun, using as a base list the "Index of Tribal Names" compiled by Professor Murdock and published in the 1960 edition. The present compilers consulted a number of basic reference tools and added a large number of names of ethnic groups, reservations and reserves, and headings such as Pan-Indianism to this basic list. New names were also added as they were encountered in the literature. The resulting ethnonymy is comparatively extensive, but in reality contains a relatively small percentage of the total possible number of names found in the literature. However, the present list was generally sufficient for our needs in compiling this bibliography. We have supplied citations to a small number of reference works below which contain further listings and descriptions. The synonymy in Hodge (1907-1910) is particularly notable for the large number of variant names and spellings it gives, and should be the first source to be consulted for information on any name which is not in the present ethnonymy.

As noted in the General Introduction, there are now 269 individual ethnic group bibliographies in this work. In addition, there are bibliographies for each of the fifteen culture areas distinguished, as well as bibliographies for North America as a whole, Pan-Indianism, Urban Indians, Canadian Indians, United States government relations with the Native Peoples, and Canadian government relations with the Native Peoples. Adding these together gives a grand total of 290 individual bibliographies, i.e. there are 290 possible places in which bibliographic citations on a particular ethnic group might be found. The ethnonymy acts as a locator device for finding the particular bibliography which might have the citations needed by the user. The names in the ethnonymy are keyed to individual bibliographies by a four-digit code. The first two digits in the code refer to the culture area in which the group is located. The third and fourth digits in the code refer to the particular bibliography within the culture area to which citations on that particular ethnic group have been assigned. The two sets of digits have been separated by a hyphen for ease in reading. As an example, in the ethnonymy we may find the name and code "Navaho 15-21." This indicates that any bibliographic references to the Navaho which have been processed have been assigned to individual bibliography 15-21. This means that all bibliographic citations to the Navaho have been assigned to the twenty-first bibliography within culture area number 15, which on inspection turns out to be the Navajo bibliography within the Southwest culture area. Note that in this case, "Navaho" is a variant spelling of the name "Navajo." The latter name is the one used to denote this particular bibliography. Similarly, the name and code "Back River Eskimo 01-09" means that bibliographic citations on this group have been placed in the ninth bibliography within culture area number 1, which is the Netsilik Eskimo bibliography within the Arctic Coast area. Note that locating the name of an ethnic group in the ethnonymy does not necessarily mean that bibliographic references on that particular ethnic group will actually be found in the bibliography. The presence of a name in the ethnonymy simply means that if the compilers found a bibliographic reference on the Back River Eskimo, for example, they would include it in bibliography 01-09. If no references on the Back River Eskimo were located, none would be in bibliography 01-09.

The following ethnonymy contains the names and numerical codes for this volume only, that is, only those names and numerical codes applying to ethnic groups living in the Plains, the Gulf coast, and the Southwest will be found here. The first two digits of each numerical code will be one of three combinations: 09-, 14-, or 15-. These two-digit numbers refer to the Plains, Gulf, and Southwest bibliographies respectively. The third and fourth digits of the numerical codes refer to the individual bibliographies within each of the three major divisions of this volume. Thus, 09-02 refers to the Arikara bibliography, 14-05 refers to the Tonkawa bibliography, and 15-23 refers to the Opata bibliography.

The reference works which were found most useful in compiling the ethnonymy are listed below:

Canada, Department of Indian Affairs and Northern Development, Indian Affairs Branch. Linguistic and cultural affiliations of Canadian Indian bands. Ottawa, 1967.

Hodge, Frederick Webb, ed. Handbook of American Indians north of Mexico. Washington, D.C., Government Printing Office, 1907-1910. 2 pts. (U.S., Bureau of American Ethnology, Bulletin, 30). (SuDocs no. SI2.3:30) [reprint editions available]

Swanton, John R. The Indian tribes of North America. Washington, D.C., Government Printing Office, 1952. (U.S., Bureau of American Ethnology, Bulletin, 145) (SuDocs no. SI2.3:145) [reprint edition available]

U.S., Department of Commerce. Federal and State Indian reservations and Indian trust areas. Washington, D.C., 1974. (SuDocs no. C1.8/3:In2)

The following is a schedule of the code numbers of the individual bibliographies which will be found in each of the five volumes of the complete bibliography.

Volume 1, General North America, contains bibliographies for code numbers 01-00, 02-00, 03-00, 04-00, 05-00, 06-00, 07-00, 08-00, 09-00, 10-00, 11-00, 12-00, 13-00, 14-00, 15-00, 16-00, 16-01, 16-02, 16-03, 16-04, and 16-05.

Volume 2, Arctic and Subarctic, contains bibliographies for all code numbers beginning with 01-, 02-, and 11-.

Volume 3, Far West and Pacific Coast, contains bibliographies for *all* code numbers beginning with 03-, 04-, 05-, 06-, 07-, and 08-.

Volume 4, Eastern North America, contains bibliographies for *all* code numbers beginning with 10-, 12-, and 13-.

Volume 5, Plains and Southwest, contains bibliographies for *all* code numbers beginning with 09-, 14-, and 15-.

A

Aa'tam 15-25
Aays 09-05
Abasopalme 15-06
Absaroke 09-08
Acaraho 09-08
Acaxee 15-36
Achire 15-08
Acoma 15-01
Acoma Reservation 15-01
Acomita 15-01
Adai 09-05 '
Agatas 14-02
Aguastayas 14-02
Ahomamama 15-40
Ahome 15-08
Ahome 15-02
Ahuchan 15-06
Aiaha 15-04
Aibine 15-36
Aix 09-05
Ak Chin Reservation 15-24
Akansa 09-22
Akokisa 14-01
Alamama 15-40
Alamo Reservation 15-21
Alasapa 14-02
Alazapa 14-02
Albuquerque Navajo 15-21
Alexis Stoney 09-03
Aliche 09-05
Amahami 09-10
Amojave 15-20
Anachiguaies 14-04
Anadarko 09-05
Andacaminos 14-02
Annas 14-02
Apache 15-00
Apache, Apache Peaks 15-07
Apache, Bald Mountain 15-07
Apache, Canyon Creek 15-07
Apache, Carrizo 15-07
Apache, Coppermine 15-04
Apache, Eastern 15-00
Apache, Fort Sill 15-04
Apache, Fossil Creek 15-07
Apache, Kiowa 09-14
Apache, Mogollon 15-04
Apache, Mormon Lake 15-07
Apache, Oak Creek 15-07
Apache Peaks Apache 15-07
Apache, Prairie 09-14
Apache, San Carlos 15-07
Apache, Sierra Blanca 15-07
Apache, Warm Spring 15-04
Apache, Western 15-07
Apache, White Mountain 15-07
Apaches de Nabaju 15-21
Apaches-Mohaves 15-33
Apache-Yuma 15-33
Apatsiltlizihihi 15-14
Apayxam 14-02
Apostatas 14-04
Apsaroke 09-08
Aqathinena 09-01
Aqiu 15-13

Aracanaes 14-04
Aranama 14-02
Arapaho 09-01
Arapaho, Northern 09-01
Arapaho, Oklahoma 09-01
Arapaho, Southern 09-01
Areneños 15-24
Aretines 14-04
Arikara 09-02
Arikara, Fort Berthold 09-02
Arikara, Leavenworth Site 09-02
Arivaipa 15-07
Arkansa 09-22
Arkansas Band 09-18
Arkokisa 14-01
Asan 14-02
Ascani 09-25
Ashiwi 15-35
Asinai 09-05
Assinay 09-05
Assiniboin 09-03
Assiniboin, Fort Belknap 09-03
Assiniboin, Fort Peck 09-03
Assiniboine, Carry the Kettle 09-03
Assiniboine, Paul 09-03
Assiniboine, Whitebear 09-03
Atajal 14-02
Atakapa 14-01
Atastagonies 14-02
Athabaskans, Southern 15-00
Atsina 09-09
Awahu 09-02
Awatobi 15-11
Awatovi 15-11
Ayancuaras 14-02
Aycalme 15-06

B

Baachinena 09-01
Baanticiinenan 09-01
Baasanwuunenan 09-01
Bachilmi 15-06
Baciroa 15-02
Bad Pipes 09-01
Badies 14-01
Baimena 15-02
Bald Mountain Apache 15-07
Bamoa 15-02
Baopapa 15-06
Barrio Libre 15-02
Batucari 15-02
Bavispes 15-23
Beadeyes 14-01
Bearspaw Stony 09-03
Besawunena 09-01
Bidai 09-05
Bidai 14-01
Birdtail Sioux 09-27
Black Lodges 09-08
Black Pawnee 09-25
Blackfeet Reservation 09-04

Blackfoot 09-04
Blackfoot, Northern 09-04
Blackfoot [Sioux] 09-24
Blood 09-04
Boboles 14-02
Bocalos 14-02
Borrado 14-02
Borrados 14-04
Brulé 09-24
Brulé, Lower 09-24
Brulé, Upper 09-24

C

Caataaras 14-02
Cabezas 14-02
Cabia 14-02
Cacafes 14-02
Cacalotes 14-04
Cacalotito 15-06
Cacaxtes 14-02
Cachopostales 14-02
Caddo 09-05
Caddoquis 09-05
Cadimas 14-04
Cahinnio 09-05
Cahita 15-02
Cajuenche 15-05
Camai 14-02
Camaleones 14-04
Camp Verde Reservation 15-00
Canadian Dakota 09-24
Canadian Peigan 09-04
Canadian Santee 09-23
Canaynes 14-04
Canoncito Reservation 15-21
Cantunas 14-02
Canyon Creek Apache 15-07
Capiché 09-05
Caramariguanes 14-04
Caramiguaies 14-04
Caribayes 14-04
Carrizo Apache 15-07
Carrizos 14-02
Carry the Kettle 09-00
Carry the Kettle Assiniboine 09-03
Carry the Kettle Sioux 09-27
Casas Chiquitas 14-02
Casastles 14-02
Cava 14-05
Cavisera 15-40
Cawina 15-05
Cazazhita 09-24
Cazcan 15-37
Ceni 09-05
Cenis 09-05
Cetguanes 15-34
Chaguantapam 14-02
Chagustapa 14-02
Chapamaco 14-02
Chaui 09-20
Chaye 09-05
Chemoco 14-02
Cheokhba 09-24

Cherechos   15-27
Chewaerae   09-19
Cheyenne   09-06
Cheyenne, Northern   09-06
Cheyenne River Reservation
  09-24
Cheyenne, Southern   09-06
Chichimec   15-41
Chinarra   15-06
Chinipa   15-03
Chiniquay Stony   09-03
Chiricahua   15-04
Chirumas   15-34
Chiwere   09-27
Chizo   15-06
Chouman   15-15
Choyapin   14-02
Choye   09-05
Chuapas   14-02
Cibecue   15-07
Cibola   15-35
Cimataguo   14-02
Cinaloa   15-02
Cinalou   15-02
Cipias   15-23
Cluetau   14-02
Coahuiltec   14-02
Coahuilteco   14-02
Coana   15-05
Coano   15-43
Coapite   14-03
Coaque   14-03
Coca   15-37
Cochiti   15-27
Cochiti Reservation   15-27
Coco   14-03
Cocomacaque   15-22
Cocomaricopa   15-18
Cocomeioje   14-02
Coconino   15-10
Cocopa   15-05
Cocopa, Mountain   15-05
Cocopa, River   15-05
Cocopah Reservation   15-05
Cold Lake Reserve   09-00
Colorado River Reservation
  15-00
Comanche   09-07
Comanche, Oklahoma   09-07
Comanito   15-02
Comecamotes   14-04
Comecrudo   14-02
Comecrudo   14-04
Comepescados   14-02
Comopori   15-08
Concho   15-06
Conejo   15-06
Congewichacha   09-24
Conicari   15-02
Contotores   14-02
Coppermine Apache   15-04
Cora   15-43
Cotanam   14-02
Coyamit   15-06
Coyotero   15-07
Crow   09-08
Crow Creek Reservation   09-
  26
Crow, Mountain   09-08

Crow Reservation   09-08
Crow, River   09-08
Cruzados   15-33
Cuchan   15-34
Cuercos Quemados   14-04
Cupdan   14-02
Cutganes   15-05
Cutheads   09-26

                    D

Dachizhozhin   15-14
Dakota   09-27
Dakota, Canadian   09-24
Dakota, Eastern   09-23
Dakota, Western   09-24
Daparabopo   15-40
Deadose   14-01
Denver Navajo   15-21
Detsanayuka   09-07
Dhegiha   09-27
Dine   15-21
Ditsakana   09-07
Doustioni   09-05
Dzitsistas   09-06

                    E

Eastern Apache   15-00
Eastern Dakota   09-23
Eastern Siouans   09-27
Emet   14-05
Enyaevapai   15-33
E-pa   15-32
Erarapio   09-08
Ervipiame   14-05
Escaba   14-02
Espopolames   14-02
Eudeve   15-23
Eyeish   09-05

                    F

Fall Indians   09-09
Faraon   15-19
Flandreau Indians   09-23
Flandreau Reservation   09-23
Forks-of-the-River Men   09-
  01
Fort Apache Reservation   15-
  07
Fort Belknap Assiniboin   09-
  03
Fort Belknap Gros Ventre
  09-09
Fort Belknap Reservation
  09-00
Fort Berthold Arikara   09-02
Fort Berthold Hidatsa   09-10
Fort Berthold Mandan   09-15
Fort Berthold Reservation
  09-00

Fort McDowell Reservation
  15-33
Fort Mojave Reservation   15-
  20
Fort Peck Assiniboin   09-03
Fort Peck Reservation   09-00
Fort Peck Sioux   09-26
Fort Sill Apache   15-04
Fort Totten Reservation   09-
  27
Fort Totten School Sioux
  09-27
Fort Yuma Reservation   15-34
Fossil Creek Apache   15-07

                    G

Gabilan   14-02
Gawunena   09-01
Geies   14-02
Gila   15-04
Gila Bend Reservation   15-24
Gila River Indian Community
  15-00
Gila River Reservation   15-
  00
Gileño   15-04
Golkashin   15-14
Gorretas   15-17
Grand Pawnee   09-20
Greasy Faces   09-01
Great Osage   09-18
Gros Ventre   09-09
Gros Ventre, Fort Belknap
  09-09
Gros Ventres of the Missouri
  09-10
Gros Ventres of the Plains
  09-09
Guachichil   15-40
Guachichile   15-40
Guadalupe   15-02
Guage-johe   09-07
Gualiba   15-32
Guamares   15-41
Guamichicorama   15-06
Guanipas   14-02
Guasapar   15-30
Guasave   15-08
Guasco   09-05
Guazapar   15-30
Guazave   15-08
Gueiquesales   14-02
Guelasiguicme   15-06
Guerjuatida   14-02
Guhlkainde   15-19
Guiaquita   15-06
Guichol   15-44
Guinigua   14-02
Guisar   15-44
Guisoles   14-02
Guisolotes   14-04
Gulf   14-00

Loup   09-20
Lower Brulé   09-24
Lower Brule Reservation   09-24
Lower Mississippi Indians   14-00
Lower Pima   15-22
Lower Sioux Reservation   09-23
Lower Yanktonnai   09-26

M

Macapao   14-02
Macocoma   14-02
Macoyahui   15-02
Magayuteshni   09-23
Maha   09-17
Maiconera   15-40
Malinchenos   14-04
Mallopeme   14-02
Mamite   15-06
Mamncheños   14-02
Mamuqui   14-02
Manam   14-02
Mandan   09-15
Mandan, Fort Berthold   09-15
Manico   14-02
Manos Colorados   14-02
Manos de Perro   14-02
Manos Prietas   14-02
Manso   15-17
Mantanne   09-15
Maquems   14-02
Maraquites   14-02
Maricopa   15-18
Maricopa, Salt River   15-18
Mariguanes   14-04
Masikota   09-06
Matavakopai   15-32
Mathaupapaya   15-33
Matsaki   15-35
Matucar   14-02
Matuime   14-02
Maubedan   14-02
Mauyga   14-02
Mayeye   14-05
Mayo   15-02
Mazapes   14-02
Mazatzal   15-07
Mdewakanton   09-23
Menenquen   14-02
Mescal   14-02
Mescale   14-02
Mescalero   15-19
Mescalero Reservation   15-19
Mesquite   15-06
Mesquites   14-02
Métis, Red River   09-30
Metutakanke   09-15
Mevira   15-40
Mexican Southwest   15-00
Milijaes   14-02
Mimbreño   15-04
Minesepere   09-08
Miniconjou   09-24
Minisha   09-23

Minitari   09-10
Minneconjou   09-24
Minnetaree   09-10
Minnetarees of the Plains   09-09
Minnetarees of the Prairies   09-10
Miopacoa   15-40
Mishongnovi   15-11
Missouri   09-16
Mocorito   15-39
Moenkapi   15-11
Moenkopi   15-11
Mogollon Apache   15-04
Mohave   15-20
Mohave-Apache   15-33
Moiseyu   09-06
Mojave   15-20
Moki   15-11
Moose Woods Reserve   09-27
Moqui   15-11
Morbanas   14-02
Mormon Lake Apache   15-07
Mosnala   15-06
Mosquito-Grizzly Bear's Head   09-03
Motsai   09-07
Mountain Cocopa   15-05
Mountain Crow   09-08
Mulatos   14-02
Muruam   14-02
Muvinabore   09-07

N

Nabedache   09-05
Nabiti   09-05
Nacachau   09-05
Nacanish   09-05
Nacao   09-05
Nacogdoche   09-05
Nacono   09-05
Naizhan   15-16
Nakanawan   09-05
Nakanusts   09-02
Nakarik   09-02
Nakasa   09-05
Nakasé   09-05
Nakasinena   09-01
Nakota   09-26
Nambe   15-31
Nambe Reservation   15-31
Namidish   09-05
Nanatsoho   09-05
Nanwacinahaanan   09-01
Naolanes   14-04
Narices   14-02
Nasoni   09-05
Nasoni, Upper   09-05
Nataché   09-05
Nataina   15-19
Natao   14-02
Natchés   09-05
Natchitoches   09-05
Natchitoches, Upper   09-05
Nation of the Willows   15-10
Nauniem   09-07

Navaho   15-21
Navaho, Ramah   15-21
Navajo   15-21
Navajo, Albuquerque   15-21
Navajo, Denver   15-21
Navajo, Ramah   15-21
Navajo Reservation   15-21
Nawathinehena   09-01
Nawunena   09-01
Nayarit   15-43
Nayariti   15-43
Nazas   14-02
Nebome   15-22
Nebraska Iowa   09-11
Nebraska Ponca   09-21
Nebraska Santee   09-23
Nechani   09-05
Neches   09-05
Necpacha   14-02
Nemene   09-07
Nevome   15-22
New Oraibi   15-11
Newastarton   09-23
Nimenim   09-07
Nio   15-02
Nisapst   09-02
Niutachi   09-16
Nokoni   09-07
Nonapho   14-05
Northeastern Yavapai   15-33
Northern Arapaho   09-01
Northern Blackfoot   09-04
Northern Cheyenne   09-06
Northern Cheyenne Reservation   09-06
Northern Pame   15-42
Northern Tepehuan   15-38
Numakaki   09-15
Nutria   15-35
Nyavkopai   15-32

O

Oak Creek Apache   15-07
Oak Lake   09-27
Oak River Sioux   09-27
Obayos   14-02
Obone   15-06
Obozi   14-02
Ocana   14-02
Ocatameneton   09-23
Ochan   15-06
Ocho   15-40
Ocoroni   15-02
Octotatas   09-19
Odoesmades   14-02
Oglala   09-24
Ohaguames   14-02
Ohanhanska   09-23
Oivimana   09-06
Ojo Caliente   15-35
Oklahoma Arapaho   09-01
Oklahoma Comanche   09-07
Oklahoma Indians   09-28
Oklahoma Iowa   09-11
Oklahoma Kansa   09-12
Oklahoma Kiowa   09-13

Oklahoma Kiowa-Apache 09-14
Oklahoma Osage 09-18
Oklahoma Oto 09-19
Oklahoma Pawnee 09-20
Oklahoma Ponca 09-21
Oklahoma Quapaw 09-22
Oklahoma Tonkawa 14-05
Old Oraibi 15-11
Olobayaguame 15-06
Olojasme 15-06
Omaha 09-17
Omaha Reservation 09-17
Omisis 09-06
Oohenonpa 09-24
Opata 15-23
Opelousa 14-01
Oposine 15-06
Oqtoguna 09-06
Oquero 15-02
Oraibi 15-11
Oraibi, New 15-11
Oraibi, Old 15-11
Orejon 14-02
Orejone 14-02
Osage 09-18
Osage, Great 09-18
Osage, Little 09-18
Osage, Oklahoma 09-18
Osage Reservation 09-18
Oto 09-19
Oto, Oklahoma 09-19
Oto-Missouria 09-19
Ouachita 09-05
Oydican 14-02

                P

Paac 14-02
Paachiqui 14-02
Pabaksa 09-26
Pabor 14-02
Pacaruja 14-02
Pachal 14-02
Pachalaque 14-02
Pachaloco 14-02
Pachaquen 14-02
Pachaug 14-02
Pachera 15-30
Pacpul 14-02
Pacuaches 14-02
Pacuachiam 14-02
Padani 09-20
Padani 09-02
Padouca 09-07
Paduca 09-07
Pagatsu 09-07
Paguan 14-02
Paguanan 14-02
Pahodja 09-11
Pajalat 14-02
Pajarito 14-02
Pakawa 14-02
Pamaque 14-02
Pamaya 14-02
Pame 15-42
Pame, Northern 15-42
Pame, Southern 15-42

Pamoranos 14-02
Pampopa 14-02
Panana 09-20
Panguayes 14-04
Pani 09-20
Panimaha 09-02
Panis Noirs 09-25
Panis Piqués 09-25
Paoga 15-40
Papago 15-24
Papago Reservation 15-24
Papago, Sand 15-24
Papanac 14-02
Papudo 15-36
Paquache 14-02
Parantones 14-02
Parchaque 14-02
Parchinas 14-02
Parkeenaum 09-07
Pasalves 14-02
Pascua 15-02
Pasitas 14-04
Pasnacanes 14-02
Pasqual 14-02
Pastaloca 14-02
Pastancoyas 14-02
Pasteal 14-02
Patague 14-02
Patan 14-02
Patanium 14-02
Pataquilla 14-03
Patou 14-02
Patzau 14-02
Paul 09-00
Paul Assiniboine 09-03
Pausane 14-02
Pausaqui 14-02
Pausay 14-02
Pawnee 09-20
Pawnee, Black 09-25
Pawnee, Grand 09-20
Pawnee, Oklahoma 09-20
Pawnee, Republican 09-20
Pawnee, Skidi 09-20
Pawnee, Speckled 09-25
Payaya 14-02
Payson Community 15-00
Payuguan 14-02
Peana 14-02
Pecos 15-13
Peigan 09-04
Pelones 14-02
Penande 09-07
Penateka 09-07
Pescado 14-02
Pescado 15-35
Peshlaptechela 09-24
Pharaoh 15-19
Piato 15-24
Picks 09-25
Picuris 15-29
Picuris Reservation 15-29
Piedras Blancas 14-02
Piegan 09-04
Pihuique 14-02
Pilabo 15-26
Pima 15-25
Pima Alto 15-25
Pima Bajo 15-22

Pima, Lower 15-22
Pima, Upper 15-25
Pinacate 15-24
Pinaleño 15-07
Pinanaca 14-02
Pine Ridge Reservation 09-
  27
Pine Ridge Sioux 09-27
Pineshow 09-23
Piniquu 14-02
Pintos 14-02
Pipatsje 15-18
Piro 15-26
Pisones 14-04
Pita 14-02
Pitahauerat 09-20
Pitahay 14-02
Plains 09-00
Plains Indians 09-00
Plateau Yumans 15-00
Pohoi 09-07
Pojoaque 15-31
Pojoaque Reservation 15-31
Pojuaque 15-31
Polacca 15-31
Polacme 15-06
Pomuluma 14-02
Ponca 09-21
Ponca, Nebraska 09-21
Ponca, Oklahoma 09-21
Ponca Reservation [Nebraska]
  09-21
Posalme 15-06
Potam 15-02
Prairie Apache 09-14
Prairie Island Reservation
  09-23
Prietos 14-02
Prior Lake Reservation 09-
  23
Psaupsau 14-02
Psinchaton 09-24
Psinoumanitons 09-23
Pueblito 15-01
Pueblo Indians 15-00
Pueblos, Western Keresan
  15-01
Putaay 14-02

                Q

Qahatika 15-25
Quahatika 15-25
Quanataguo 14-02
Quapaw 09-22
Quapaw, Oklahoma 09-22
Quasmigdo 14-01
Quechan 15-34
Quems 14-02
Quepanos 14-02
Queres 15-27
Quesal 14-02
Quicama 15-05
Quichais 09-25
Quide 14-02
Quidehais 09-25
Quigyuma 15-05

Quilotes 14-03
Quinicuane 14-02
Quinicuanes 14-04
Quinigua 14-02
Quioborique 14-02
Quisabas 14-02
Quitacas 14-02
Quivi 14-02
Quivira 09-25
Quokim 15-05

R

Ralamuri 15-30
Ramah Navaho 15-21
Ramah Navajo 15-21
Ramah Reservation 15-21
Raramuri 15-33
Red River Métis 09-30
Ree 09-02
Republican Pawnee 09-20
Ricaree 09-02
Ricari 09-02
Riggs Institute 09-23
River Cocopa 15-05
River Crow 09-08
River Yumans 15-00
Rocky Boy's Reservation 09-00
Rosebud Reservation 09-27
Rosebud Sioux 09-27
Ruptari 09-15

S

Sabaibo 15-36
Sainoscos 14-04
Saitinde 15-14
Salapaque 14-02
Salinas 14-02
Salt River Maricopa 15-18
Salt River Reservation 15-00
Samampac 14-02
Sampanal 14-02
San Carlos Apache 15-07
San Carlos Reservation 15-07
San Felipe 15-27
San Felipe Reservation 15-27
San Ildefonso 15-31
San Ildefonso Reservation 15-31
San Juan 15-31
San Juan Reservation 15-31
San Xavier Papago Reservation 15-24
Sana 14-05
Sand Papago 15-24
Sandia 15-12
Sandia Reservation 15-12
Sanipao 14-02
Sanish 09-02
Sans Arc 09-24

Santa Ana 15-27
Santa Ana Reservation 15-27
Santa Clara 15-31
Santa Clara Reservation 15-31
Santee 09-23
Santee, Canadian 09-23
Santee, Nebraska 09-23
Santee Reservation 09-23
Santo Domingo 15-27
Santo Domingo Reservation 15-27
Saracuam 14-02
Sasabaithi 09-01
Scirihauk 09-02
Secmoco 14-02
Sells Reservation 15-24
Semat 09-14
Semonan 14-02
Senecu 15-26
Senecu del Sur 15-12
Senisos 14-02
Serranos 14-04
Shakopee Mdewakanton Sioux Community 09-23
Shipaulovi 15-11
Shongopovi 15-11
Shrub Indians 14-01
Shuman 15-15
Sia 15-27
Siaguan 14-02
Siansi 14-02
Sibayones 14-04
Sicangu 09-24
Sichomovi 15-11
Sierra Blanca Apache 15-07
Sihasapa 09-24
Sijame 14-05
Siksika 09-04
Sillanguayas 14-02
Simaomo 14-05
Sinaloa 15-02
Sinicu 14-02
Siouans 09-27
Siouans, Eastern 09-27
Sioux, Birdtail 09-27
Sioux, Carry the Kettle 09-27
Sioux, Fort Totten School 09-27
Sioux, Long Plain 09-27
Sioux, Oak River 09-27
Sioux, Pine Ridge 09-27
Sioux, Rosebud 09-27
Sioux, Standing Rock 09-27
Sioux Wahpaton 09-23
Sisseton 09-23
Sisseton Reservation 09-23
Sitconski 09-03
Sitsime 15-01
Siupam 14-02
Skidi Pawnee 09-20
Skiri 09-20
Soba 15-24
Sobaibo 15-36
Sobaipuri 15-25
Socorro 15-26
Socorro del Sur 15-26
Sonaque 14-02

Sonayan 14-02
Sotolvekopai 15-32
Souchitioni 09-05
Southeastern Yavapai 15-33
Southern Arapaho 09-01
Southern Athabaskans 15-00
Southern Cheyenne 09-06
Southern Pame 15-42
Southern Tepehuan 15-38
Southwest 15-00
Southwest, Mexican 15-00
Southwestern Indians 15-00
Soyopas 15-20
Speckled Pawnee 09-25
Spring Creek Indians 14-01
Standing Buffalo Reserve 09-27
Standing Rock Reservation 09-27
Standing Rock Sioux 09-27
Starrahhe 09-02
Stoney 09-03
Stoney, Alexis 09-03
Stonies 09-03
Stony, Bearspaw 09-03
Stony, Chiniquay 09-03
Stony, Wesley 09-03
Suahuaches 14-02
Suanas 14-02
Sucayi 15-06
Sulujame 14-02
Suma 15-15
Supai 15-10
Sutaio 09-06

T

Tacame 14-02
Tagualilos 14-04
Tahue 15-39
Tahuunde 15-19
Taimamares 14-02
Takini 09-26
Talonapin 09-24
Taltalkuwa 15-32
Tamaulipeco 14-04
Tamcan 14-02
Tamique 14-02
Tamos 15-13
Tamualipec 14-04
Tanima 09-07
Tano 15-28
Tanpacuazes 14-02
Taos 15-29
Taos Reservation 15-29
Taovayas 09-25
Tapage 09-20
Tarahumara 15-30
Tarahumare 15-30
Tarequano 14-02
Tashunkeota 09-24
Tatamaste 15-06
Tawakoni 09-25
Tawehash 09-25
Teana 14-02
Tebaca 15-36
Tecahuistes 14-02

Tecame 14-02
Tecaya 15-36
Tecual 15-43
Tecualm 15-43
Tecuexe 15-37
Tehueco 15-02
Tehuexe 15-37
Teja 09-05
Tejanos 14-02
Tejones 14-02
Temori 15-30
Tenahwit 09-07
Tenawa 09-07
Teneinamar 14-02
Tenicapeme 14-02
Tenu 14-05
Tepachuaches 14-02
Tepahue 15-02
Tepecano 15-38
Tepehua 15-38
Tepehuan 15-38
Tepehuan, Northern 15-38
Tepehuan, Southern 15-38
Tepehuane 15-38
Tepemaca 14-02
Tepemacas 14-04
Tepkinägo 09-13
Terocodame 14-02
Tesuque 15-31
Tesuque Reservation 15-31
Tet 14-02
Tetanauoica 14-02
Tetecores 14-02
Teton 09-24
Tetzino 14-05
Tewa 15-31
Tigua Reservation 15-12
Tigua, Ysleta 15-12
Tilijaes 14-02
Tilijayo 14-02
Tinapihuayas 14-02
Tinde 15-14
Tiopane 14-03
Tiopines 14-02
Tishin 14-05
Tiwa 09-25
Tlalliguamayas 15-05
Toboso 15-16
Tocas 14-02
Tocone 15-06
Tohaha 14-05
Toho 14-05
Tolkepaya 15-33
Tonkawa 14-05
Tonkawa, Oklahoma 14-05
Tonoochtam 15-24
Tonto 15-07
Tonzaumacagua 14-02
Topacolme 15-06
Tortugas 14-02
Totorame 15-39
Touchouasintons 09-24
Towa 15-13
Tripas Blancas 14-02
Tsihlinainde 15-19
Tsininatak 09-02
Tuancas 14-02
Tular 15-03
Tubare 15-03

Tuetinini 15-19
Tukatak 09-02
Tukstanu 09-02
Tulkepaia 15-33
Tumamar 14-02
Tumpzi 14-02
Tups 14-03
Tusanes 14-02
Tusayan 15-11
Tusolivi 14-05
Tusonid 14-02
Tuteneiboica 14-02
Tuwa 15-13
Tuwanhudan 09-03
Two Kettle 09-24

U

Ujuiap 14-05
Unojita 14-02
Upper Brulé 09-24
Upper Nasoni 09-05
Upper Natchitoches 09-05
Upper Pima 15-25
Upper Sioux Reservation 09-23
Upper Yanktonnai 09-26
Upper Yatasi 09-05
Uracha 14-02
Ure 15-22
Usilique 15-44
Utaca 14-02

V

Vacoregue 15-08
Varohio 15-30
Vasapalles 15-40
Venado 14-02
Vende Flechas 14-02
Viayam 14-02
Vidays 14-01
Viddaquimamar 14-02

W

Waaih 09-07
Waco 09-25
Waglukhe 09-24
Wahpekute 09-23
Wahpeton 09-23
Walapai 15-32
Walatoa 15-13
Walkamepa 15-33
Walpi 15-11
Wanxueiçi 09-01
Waquithi 09-01
Warihka 09-02
Warm Spring Apache 15-04
Warohio 15-30
Wazhazha 09-24
Wazhazhe 09-18
Wazikute 09-26

Wesley Stony 09-03
Western Apache 15-07
Western Dakota 09-24
Western Keresan Pueblos 15-01
Western Yavapai 15-33
White Mountain Apache 15-07
White Mountain Apache Reservation 15-07
Whitebear 09-00
Whitebear Assiniboine 09-03
Wichita 09-25
Wiciyela 09-26
Widyu 09-07
Wikedjasapa 15-33
Wind River Reservation 09-00
Witauk 09-02
Wolf 09-20
Wood Mountain Reserve 09-27
Wutapiu 09-06

X

Xarame 14-02
Xiabu 14-02
Xila 15-04
Xixime 15-36
Xiximole 15-06

Y

Yabipai Lipan 15-16
Yabipais Nabajay 15-21
Yacchicaua 15-06
Yacdossa 14-02
Yaculsari 15-06
Yampah 09-07
Yampaos 15-33
Yamparika 09-07
Yanabopo 15-40
Yankton 09-26
Yankton Reservation 09-26
Yanktonnai 09-26
Yanktonnai, Lower 09-26
Yanktonnai, Upper 09-26
Yaochane 15-06
Yapa 09-07
Yaqui 15-02
Yatasi 09-05
Yatasi, Upper 09-05
Yavapai 15-33
Yavapai, Northeastern 15-33
Yavapai Reservation 15-33
Yavapai, Southeastern 15-33
Yavapai, Western 15-33
Yavepe 15-33
Ybdacax 14-02
Yecora 15-22
Yeguacat 15-06
Yemé 14-02
Yman 14-02
Ymic 14-02
Yojuane 14-05
Yoricas 14-02

General Ethnic Map of Native North America

1 TSETSAUT
2 BELLABELLA
3 BELLACOOLA
4 CHILCOTIN
5 LILLOOET
6 COWICHAN
7 KLALLAM
8 QUILEUTE
9 QUINAULT
10 TWANA
11 SNUQUALMI
12 THOMPSON
13 NICOLA
14 SANPOIL
15 SPOKAN
16 KALISPEL
17 COEUR D'ALENE
18 WALLAWALLA
19 CAYUSE
20 UMATILLA
21 TENINO
22 MOLALA
23 WISHRAM
24 KLIKITAT
25 CHEHALIS
26 KWALHIOQUA
27 CHINOOK
28 TLATSKANAI
29 TILLAMOOK
30 ALSEA
31 SIUSLAW
32 COOS
33 CHASTACOSTA
34 TOLOWA
35 TAKELMA
36 KLAMATH
37 ACHOMAWI
38 YANA
39 SHASTA
40 KAROK
41 CHIMARIKO
42 HUPA
43 YUROK
44 WIYOT
45 WAILAKI
46 YUKI
47 WINTUN
48 POMO
49 WAPPO
50 OLAMENTKE
51 COSTANO
52 SALINA
53 TUBATULABAL
54 KAWAIISU
55 CHUMASH
56 GABRIELINO
57 LUISENO
58 CAHUILLA
59 KAMIA
60 COCOPA
61 YUMA
62 MARICOPA
63 HALCHIDHOMA
64 MOHAVE
65 HAVASUPAI
66 HOPI
67 ZUNI
68 MANSO
69 ACOMA
70 ISLETA
71 QUERES
72 TANO
73 TEWA
74 JEMEZ
75 TAOS
76 KIOWA APACHE
77 HIDATSA
78 MISSOURI
79 WINNEBAGO
80 SOUTHAMPTON ESKIMO
81 PENNACOOK
82 MASSACHUSET
83 MOHEGAN
84 METOAC
85 NANTICORE
86 POWHATAN
87 TUSCARORA
88 PAMLICO
89 CUSABO
90 APALACHEE
91 ALABAMA
92 CHAKCHIUMA
93 TUNICA
94 BILOXI
95 ACOLAPISSA
96 HUMA
97 CHITIMACHA
98 KARANKAWA
99 TARAHUMARA
100 CHINIPA
101 GUASAVE
102 HUICHOL
103 TAMAULIPECO
104 JANAMBRE
105 HUAXTEC
106 TOTONAC
107 CHINANTEC
108 ZAPOTEC
109 TEQUISTLATECO
110 HUAVE
111 CHIAPANEC